Restaurant Guide 2007

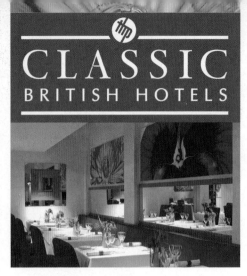

This 14th edition published 2006
Reprinted January 2007

Please contact
Advertisement Sales: advertisingsales@theaa.com
Editorial Department: lifestyleguides@theaa.com

Front cover photograph courtesy of
L'Enclume, Cartmel, Cumbria (Page 87)
Photographs in the gazetteer provided by the establishments.
Typeset/Repro: Keenes, Andover
Printed by Trento Srl, Italy.
Restaurant descriptions have been contributed by the following team of writers: Cathy Fitzgerald, David Hancock, Julia Hynard, Denise Laing, Philip Moss, Melissa Riley-Jones, Allen Stidwill, Derryck Strachan, Mark Taylor and Kate Trew

Published by AA Publishing, a trading name of Automobile Association Developments Limited, whose registered office is Fanum House, Basing View, Basingstoke, Hampshire RG21 4EA.
Registered number 1878835.
A CIP catalogue for this book is available from the British Library.
ISBN-10: 0-7495-4921-1
ISBN-13: 978-0-7495-4921-3
A03267

Contents

How to Use the Guide 4
How the AA Assesses for Rosette Awards 6
AA Accommodation Ratings Explained 7
AA Restaurants of the Year 8
Chefs' Chef 2006-07 11
The AA Wine Award 14
Food Trends - Buying British 16
The Top Ten Per Cent 18
England 28
London 231
Scotland 530
Wales 610
Northern Ireland 649
Republic of Ireland 655
Late Entries 679
Maps 684

How to Use the Guide

Sample entry

1

2 AMERSHAM MAP 06 SU99 24

3 ⚘⚘ **Harveys Restaurant** 23

4 22

5 ***Modern British***  V NOTABLE WINE LIST **NEW** 21

Friendly local restaurant with simple stylish cooking

☎ 0117 900 900 1 York Road, Montpellier, BS6 5Q8

e-mail: bookings@harveysrestaurant.com 20

web: www.harveysrestaurant.com

Dark, atmospheric and the ultimate in no-nonsense eating. Generally crowded and lively, you wait in the bar (no booking) until a table becomes available in the tiny dining area. The food is earthy and satisfying (plenty of game and good fish) and the blackboard wine list is inspired. The handful of well-spaced tables are increasingly in 19 demand and the atmosphere is relaxed, although there is enough enterprise in the cooking to ensure that there will be the occasional expression of delight.

Notable Wine List: The best of Italian wines with a large selection of sparkling varieties.

6 

7 **Chef:** Daniel Smith **Owners:** Allied Partners **Times:** 12-12/7-10, Closed
8 Sun, L Sat, 1 wk Feb, 2 wks Aug, BHs **Prices:** Fixed D £15, Starter £3.50- 18
£5, Main £6.50-£12.50, Dessert £4.50-£6, Coffee £2.50 Service added but
optional **Wine:** 10 Bottles over £20, 5 Bottles under £20, 8 by the glass 17
9 (£5-£7) **Notes:** Vegetarian menu **Seats:** 60, Pr/dining room 40 16
10 **Smoking:** N/Sm area; No pipes, Air con **Children:** Portions **Rooms:** 9
11 (9 en suite) RR **Directions:** City centre off Unity St at bottom of Park St, 15
12 opposite Harvey Square **Parking:** NCP Park Street 14

Brasserie Royale 13

☎ 01256 786787 24 The High Street

Bright and frequently bustling bistro with cheerful staff and a blackboard menu.

1 The map reference is for the atlas section at the back of the guide. The map page number is followed by the National Grid Reference. To find a location, read the first figure horizontally and the second figure vertically within the lettered square. For Central London and Greater London, there is an 8-page map section starting on page 236.

2 Restaurants are listed in country and county order, then by town and then alphabetically within the town. There is an index by restaurant at the back of the book and a similar one for the Central & Greater London sections on pages 232-235 with plan references.

3 Restaurant name.

4 ⚘ The AA Rosette Award
Main entries have been awarded one or more Rosettes, up to a maximum of five. See page 6 for an explanation of how they are graded.

5 The food style of the restaurant is in bold italics, followed by a short summary statement.

6 Restaurants awarded AA Rosettes are invited to enhance their entry with up to two photographs.

7 The names of the chef(s) and owner(s) are as up-to-date as possible at the time of going to press, but changes in personnel often occur, and may affect both the style and quality of the restaurant.

8 Prices are for fixed lunch and dinner (where available) along with à la carte dishes, coffee and mineral water.
Service charge information (see also opposite).
Note: Prices quoted are a guide only, and are subject to change without notice.

9 Additional information: e.g. availability of vegetarian dishes.

10 Establishments that do not allow smoking in the dining room but may allow it elsewhere.

11 If the establishment is in either of the AA's accommodation schemes, the number of rooms and the rating are shown.
See page 7 for further details.

12 Directions are given wherever they have been supplied by the establishment.

13 Neighbourhood restaurants. These are not AA inspected but are well worth trying.

14 Parking details.

15 Children's portions, age restrictions etc.

16 Number of seats in the restaurant, followed by private dining room (Pr/dining room).

17 Number of wines under and over £20, and the selection by the glass.

toptable.co.uk New Online Restaurant Booking Service

An exciting development this year is our new relationship with toptable, Europe's largest online booking service. During 2006 they will seat over 1.6 million diners. Readers of the AA Restaurant Guide will be able to take advantage of their experience and expertise with free online booking and hundreds of great offers. As you read through the Guide you'll see that some establishments feature the 'mouse' symbol which indicates that they are bookable online.

All you have to do is log onto the AA website, www.theAA.com, and follow the links through to the restaurant pages. Enter the restaurant name, and, if it's bookable online, you'll see the BOOK NOW! button. Click on this and you'll be able to make bookings 24 hours a day, as well as using the unique features, including 360° images, to give you a real feel for the style of the place.

Register to use the service you'll receive the very latest special offers by email.

Neighbourhood Restaurants

We've also included some new neighbourhood restaurants in this year's Guide which are bookable online. They have the mouse symbol too, and you can find them in the same way as above or use the website address quoted in their entry.

As we went to press, this service was in the final stages of planning and should be online by the time of publication.

Please note - it is possible that during the currency of the Guide more restaurants will sign up for the online booking service, and also that some, due to change of hands or other reasons, may withdraw.

18 Daily opening and closing times, the days of the week it is closed and seasonal closures. Note that opening times are liable to change without notice. It is wise to telephone in advance to avoid disappointment.

19 Description of the restaurant and the food that it serves.

20 E-mail address and website.

21 **NEW** Indicates that an entry is new to the guide this year.

22 NOTABLE WINE LIST Indicates notable wine list. Wine information is included in the entry.

23 **V** Indicates a vegetarian menu. Restaurants with some vegetarian dishes available are indicated under Notes.

24 toptable. New Online Booking Service. For explanation, see right.

All establishments take major credit cards, except where we have specified otherwise.

All information is correct at the time of print but may change without notice. Details of opening times and prices may be omitted from an entry when the establishment has not supplied us with up-to-date information. This is indicated where the establishment name is shown in *italics*.

Service Charge

We asked restaurants the following questions about service charge: (Their responses appear under **Prices** in each entry.)

- Is service included in the meal price, with no further charge added or expected?
- Is service optional – charge not automatically added to bill?
- Is service charge compulsory, and what percentage?
- Is there a service charge for larger groups, minimum number in group, and what percentage?

Many establishments automatically add service charge to the bill but tell the customer it is optional.

Smoking Regulations

A law banning smoking in public places in Scotland came into force in March 2006. This covers all Scottish establishments in this Guide. Similar laws covering England and Wales are expected to come into effect in 2007. If the freedom to smoke or to be in a non-smoking atmosphere is important to you, we recommend that you check when you book.

Facilities for Disabled Guests

The final stage (Part III) of the Disability Discrimination Act (access to Goods and Services) came into force in October 2004. This means that service providers may have to consider making permanent physical adjustments to their premises. For further information, see the government website www.disability.gov.uk/dda.

The establishments in this Guide should all be aware of their responsibilities under the Act. We recommend that you always telephone in advance. Guide dogs for the blind and assist dogs should be accepted in a restaurant, but please check beforehand.

Website Addresses

Website addresses are included where they have been supplied and specified by the respective establishment. Such websites are not under the control of The Automobile Association Developments Limited and as such The Automobile Association Developments Limited has no control over them and will not accept any responsibility or liability in respect of any and all matters whatsoever relating to such websites including access, content, material and functionality. By including the addresses of third-party websites the AA does not intend to solicit business or offer any security to any person in any country, directly or indirectly.

How the AA Assesses for Rosette Awards

The AA's Rosette award scheme was the first nationwide scheme for assessing the quality of food served by restaurants and hotels. The Rosette scheme is an award, not a classification, and although there is necessarily an element of subjectivity when it comes to assessing taste, we aim for a consistent approach throughout the UK. Our awards are made solely on the basis of a meal visit or visits by one or more of our hotel and restaurant Inspectors, who have an unrivalled breadth and depth of experience in assessing quality. They award Rosettes annually on a rising scale of one to five.

So what makes a restaurant worthy of a Rosette Award?

For our Inspectors, the top and bottom line is the food. The taste of a dish is what counts for them, and whether it successfully delivers to the diner what the menu promises. A restaurant is only as good as its worst meal. Although presentation and competent service should be appropriate to the style of the restaurant and the quality of the food, they cannot affect the Rosette assessment as such, either up or down. The summaries below attempt to explain what our Inspectors look for, but are intended only as guidelines. The AA is constantly reviewing its award criteria, and competition usually results in an all-round improvement in standards, so it becomes increasingly difficult for restaurants to reach award level. For more detailed Rosette criteria, please see www.theAA.com.

One Rosette

- Excellent restaurants, stand out in their local area
- Food prepared with care, understanding and skill
- Good quality ingredients

Around 50% of restaurants have one Rosette.

Two Rosettes

- The best local restaurants
- Higher standards
- Better consistency
- Greater precision apparent in the cooking
- Obvious attention to the quality and selection of ingredients

About 40% of restaurants have two Rosettes.

Three Rosettes

- Outstanding restaurants demanding recognition well beyond local area
- Selection and sympathetic treatment of highest quality ingredients
- Timing, seasoning and judgement of flavour combinations consistent
- Excellent intelligent service and a well-chosen wine list

Around 10% of restaurants have three Rosettes.

Four Rosettes

Dishes demonstrate:

- intense ambition
- a passion for excellence
- superb technical skills
- remarkable consistency
- appreciation of culinary traditions combined with desire for exploration and improvement.
- Cooking demands national recognition

Around twenty-seven restaurants have four Rosettes.

Five Rosettes

- Cooking stands comparison with the best in the world
- Highly individual
- Breathtaking culinary skills
- Setting the standards to which others aspire
- Knowledgeable and distinctive wine list

Around five restaurants have five Rosettes.

Accommodation Ratings

Where AA Star or Diamond ratings appear under 'Rooms' in the Guide, the establishment has been inspected under nationally recognised Classification schemes. These ratings ensure that your accommodation meets the AA's highest standards of cleanliness with emphasis on professionalism, proper booking procedures and a prompt and efficient service.

New Quality Standards

2006 is a transitional time for the AA hotel and guest accommodation ratings. In collaboration with VisitBritain, VisitScotland and the Wales Tourist Board, the AA has developed new common Quality Standards for rating accommodation. Both hotels and guest accommodation will be rated with Stars from 2006, and a descriptive 'designator' will be used to define the style of the establishment. The designators have been abbreviated in the Restaurant Guide. You will find that if an establishment has a rating for accommodation it will appear under Rooms: in the entry.

Abbreviations are as follows:

HL	Hotel
TH	Townhouse
SH	Small Hotel
CHH	Country House Hotel
GA	Guest Accommodation
RR	Restaurant with Rooms
GH	Guest House
INN	Inn
B&B	Bed & Breakfast
FH	Farmhouse

★ Hotel Star Classification

There are a number of minimum entry requirements which must be fulfilled before a hotel can be rated by the AA. The Hotel Star ratings are affected by quality, facilities and the provision of services. Stars are awarded on a rising scale, from simpler, more informal places at one star to the very finest five star hotels. Inspector's Choice hotels are the very best in their Star rating and are indicated by Red Stars.

♦ Guest Accommodation – Diamond Classification

Until January 2006 Diamond ratings were awarded to Guest Accommodation establishments. At the time we went to press some guest accommodation establishments had not yet been inspected under the new standards and will still have a Diamond rating. The criteria focussed on guest care and quality rather than provision of services. Diamonds were awarded on a rising scale of one to five. The best places in the three, four and five Diamond ratings are indicated by Red Diamonds.

If you would like to know more about how the AA inspects accommodation, or more about the new Quality Standards and what to expect at each rating level please visit www.theAA.com

AA Restaurants of the Year

for England, London, Scotland and Wales

Potential Restaurants of the Year are nominated by our team of full-time Inspectors based on their routine visits. In selecting a Restaurant of the Year, we look for somewhere that is exceptional in its chosen area of the market. Whilst the Rosette awards are based on the quality of the food alone, Restaurants of the Year takes into account all aspects of the experience.

Winner for **England**

Restaurant Sat Bains with Rooms, Nottingham Page 385

Tucked away down a quiet lane, this delightful, sympathetically converted Victorian farmhouse sits in idyllic seclusion on the banks of the Trent, only minutes from the bustling city. Smartly refurbished in fairly minimalist style, with exposed beams, flagstone floors and expressionist modern art, this fashionable and restrained backdrop is the perfect setting for flamboyant and innovative modern cooking.

Delivering a breathtaking array of textures and bright, fresh flavours that raid the senses it never fails to impress. Such is the calibre of this bold, imaginative cooking that the tasting dégustation or surprise menus are almost a requisite. The tasting menu and set five-course seasonal menu represent superb value.

Winner for **London**

Galvin - Bistrot de Luxe, W1 Page 315

The Galvin name above this little gem, located mid-way down Baker Street, gives a clue to its impeccable pedigree. Inside, with its black leather banquettes, classic bentwood chairs, panelled darkwood walls and distressed mirrors, the atmosphere is intimate and modern, yet timeless.

Created by two of London's most renowned chefs, brothers Chris and Jeff Galvin, this sophisticated Parisan-style bistro is home to highly accomplished cooking with an unmistakable Gallic accent. The chefs' distinct styles complement each other perfectly. Top-notch ingredients and superb flavours provoke pleasure across the spectrum, including a three-course set menu reported to be one of the best value menus in London.

Winner for
Scotland

Sangsters, Elie, Fife Page 563

Bruce Sangster returned to his native Fife three years ago to take over this small restaurant in a picturesque coastal village. A former Victorian house and shop, the restaurant is simply decorated and comfortably furnished with local prints and watercolours of coastal scenes, creating a peaceful and relaxed atmosphere.

The skilful modern British cooking is precise, with meticulous attention to detail and perfect timing,producing intelligently simple dishes from good-quality seasonal ingredients, including fish and seafood from the East Coast and local meat and game. Tried-and-tested favourites are enhanced by impeccable saucing, allowing bold flavours to dominate with just the right amount of restraint.

Winner for
Wales

The Drawing Room, Builth Wells, Powys Page 639

Set amidst wonderful scenery in the heart of Wales, this stylish restaurant with rooms is set in a graceful Georgian country residence that has been tastefully renovated throughout and refurbished to the highest standards. Influenced by the proprietors' passion for rural France, the refined dining room is decorated in subtle shades, with Mary Loxton French prints adorning the walls, accompanied by candlelit tables, good linen and high-backed chairs.

The seasonally-changing menu is also French-influenced - classical with a modern twist, focusing on fresh, quality ingredients that are locally sourced where possible, to deliver clean, unfussy flavours. Guests are invited to view proceedings in the open-plan kitchen.

AA Chefs' Chef 2006-07

This is the annual poll of all the chefs in The Restaurant Guide. Around 1,800 of the country's top chefs vote to recognise the achievements of one of their peers from a shortlist chosen by the AA's team of Inspectors.

'My aim is to continue to improve year-on-year and grow with the people in my business.'

'I think the diversity of establishments and of people has made running my business much easier.'

This year's winner is Andrew Fairlie, Chef-Patron of Andrew Fairlie @ Gleneagles (see page 594). Scottish Chef of the Year no fewer than three times,

Andrew's dedication and attention to detail have gained the restaurant numerous awards including four AA Rosettes since it opened in 2001. His cuisine is unashamedly French but with a Scottish twist, using many fresh ingredients from the famous Rungis market outside Paris, as well as from local suppliers.

Andrew grew up in Perth, near Gleneagles. At the age of 20 he became the youngest chef ever to have won the Roux Scholarship, which sent him to France in 1985. Andrew received much of his training in France under several three-star Michelin chefs, including celebrated chef Michel Guérard in the South of France, the creator of 'Cuisine Minceur.' Guérard recognised Andrew's talent and recommended him to the two-Michelin star chef at the Hotel de Crillon in Paris, where he received intensive training in French technique.

From there Andrew went on to become executive chef on the luxury train the *Royal Scotsman*, before becoming senior sous-chef at London's Ritz Hotel. His diverse experience also includes small family restaurants, Eurodisney and safari camps. In 1994 Andrew returned to his native Scotland to open One Devonshire Gardens in Glasgow, where he was awarded his first Michelin star. He was awarded four AA Rosettes in 2003 and his second Michelin star came in January 2006.

Personally overseeing his kitchen every evening, Andrew has a reputation for running a highly disciplined team. His exemplary signature dishes are masterpieces of culinary creation - the cooking style complex and bold, either seeking adventure through the contrast and balance of conflicting flavours, or undertaking an examination of similar flavours that are contrasted laterally through texture, density and temperature. His personality is also reflected in the service, which is pin-sharp, ensuring diners want for nothing.

Previous Winners

Germain Schwab
Winteringham Fields (Former chef), Lincolnshire p229

Raymond Blanc
Le Manoir aux Quat' Saisons, Great Milton, Oxfordshire p391

Shaun Hill

Heston Blumenthal
The Fat Duck, Bray, Berkshire p30

Jean-Christophe Novelli
A Touch of Novelli at The White Horse, Harpenden, Hertfordshire p202

Gordon Ramsay
Restaurant Gordon Ramsay, London SW3 p293

Rick Stein
The Seafood Restaurant, Padstow, Cornwall p72

Marco Pierre White

Kevin Viner

The AA Wine Award

Wine List Trends

Having reviewed well over 1,000 wine lists, it's clear that hotels and restaurants of every kind are much more likely, these days, to make a real effort with their wine lists. It's not just the presentation and layout of lists that have improved, but also the choice of wines they feature, with many lists including wines from smaller producers. We did notice a disappointing number of split vintages, however, which is a real shame. Split vintages (i.e. wines listed as '2000/2001') really should not occur - a restaurant knows if it has just one case left of the 2000, and the list should reflect this and be updated once those bottles are all sold. Despite this, the judges were impressed with the general presentation and information provided on lists, which are certainly becoming more informative, with many featuring opening sections on particular countries, discussions of the strengths of particular grape varieties, and often in-depth tasting notes for specific wines.

There has been some controversy in the last couple of years about Stelvin closures (screwtops) replacing the traditional cork. These are certainly becoming more commonplace on lists and have no bearing on the quality of the wine. There is also an increasing trend to offer more flexibility to diners with wines by the glass, with many now available in different sizes as well. Some restaurants, such as Maze in London, are offering a 'flight of wines' - perhaps three smaller glasses offering a selection of wines based on a particular grape variety or drinking style - for example three 'robust, fruity reds' or three Pinot Noirs.

New World wines continue to be the most popular choices, as they have been for the last five or six years, but it's noticeable that French wines are enjoying something of a renaissance. This is partly due to fashion, and also evidence of more competitive pricing on French wine - one of the reasons people stopped drinking it was because it was perceived as overly expensive. An increasing number of smaller, less well-known producers and vineyards are now being sourced, adding further interest and diversity.

Matching food with wine is a growing feature of many menus. As well as the frequently seen tasting menu (where a chef puts together a menu of signature dishes, perhaps six or seven small courses, often designed to be taken by a whole table of guests and including wines for each course), some restaurants also suggest particular wines as specific pairings with certain dishes. Examples of this (from last year's winner The Harrow at Little Bedwyn in Wiltshire) might be fillet of Northumberland roe venison, bashed neeps, wild mushrooms, black pudding and Vina Tondonia Tinto Reserva 1996, or ragout of langoustines and Moss Wood Chardonnay 2001.

Wine Editor

Winning selection of wines

Canapés
Lustau, Solera Gran Reserva, Emperatriz Eugena, very rare Oloroso £45

Sashimi of razor fish with lime
Picpoul de Pinet, Domaine Coustiller, Coleaux du Languedoc 2002 £18.50

Seared foie gras, scallop and black pudding, Pedro Ximenez reduction
Ruppertsberger Reiterpfao Gewürztraminer Spatlese-Pfalz-Weingut Reichsrat Von Buhl 1997 £50

Fillet of line-caught turbot, pea mash, wild mushrooms
Monthelie Les Duresses, Domaine des Comtes Lafon 2002 £41

Epoisses served on toasted raisin and hazelnut bread
Savannieres Le Vieux Clos, Nicholas Joly 2003 £33

Cardamom, pistachio and lime brûlée
Tokay Pinot Gris, Vendage Tardive, Hugel 1990 £35

Freshly brewed coffee and petits fours
Taittinger Nocturne NV £11 per glass

menu devised by Roger Jones

Wine tastings and dinners arranged by restaurants are increasingly popular, allowing the interested diner to learn more about wine-making processes, grape varieties and drinking styles, and to meet wine suppliers and wine makers. The following restaurants are well-known for their tastings and dinners, but many other restaurants also regularly arrange them and publicise them locally and on their own websites:

The Greyhound, London
The Harrow at Little Bedwyn, Wiltshire
The Devonshire Arms, Bolton Abbey, North Yorkshire
Killiekrankie House, Killiekrankie, Perth & Kinross
Lainston House, Winchester, Hampshire

The AA would like to thank Roger Jones from The Harrow at Little Bedwyn for his help in this year's judging.
The AA Wine Awards are sponsored by T&W Wines Ltd
5 Station Way, Brandon, Suffolk IP27 0BH
Tel: 01842 814414 e-mail: contact@tw-wines.com
web: www.tw-wines.com

Winner for

England & Overall Winner

The Devonshire Arms Country House Hotel & Spa, Bolton Abbey, North Yorkshire Page 493

Set in the Yorkshire Dales, this 17th-century country-house hotel offers some highly accomplished cooking in the fine-dining Burlington Restaurant. Immaculately set tables, polished wood, silver and crystal, and superb flower arrangements conspire to create an atmosphere of tranquil luxury. Featuring a choice of over 80 house wines, the comprehensive wine list continues to develop every year supported by a professional wine team and on-going significant investment in wines. Judges' comments on the winning list included 'a truly outstanding list', 'top-class producers and amazing verticals' (consecutive vintages of the same wine) and 'a wine lover's dream whilst offering great value'.

Winner for

Scotland

The Seafood Restaurant, St Andrews, Fife Page 569

Perched on the clifftop overlooking the sea and St Andrews' famous golf course, this stunning glass-walled restaurant enjoys a panoramic view across the bay to the distant horizon. The stylish interior combines high-quality place settings with fashionable seating and simple décor; the restaurant also has an open-plan kitchen that allows tantalising aromas to drift through. The wine list offers a beautiful selection of wines, chosen with much care and with a solid mix of classic Old World wines and some notable New World choices that offer value for money. An interesting selection of wines by the glass, good half-bottle listing and a rare cellar list are additional features.

Winner for

Wales

Tyddyn Llan, Llandrillo, Denbighshire Page 625

This stylish restaurant with rooms, run by proprietors Bryan and Susan Webb, is situated in a quiet corner of North Wales in an elegant Georgian house. The regularly-changing wine list shows much effort and enthusiasm for quality wines, all well-chosen to complement Bryan's assured cooking. Categorised by drinking style, over 200 wines are featured, with a good selection available by the glass. Each wine has an informative tasting note and includes some really interesting selections such as wines from the Caymus vineyards in California. Fair pricing and half-bottle and magnum listings are other impressive features. A good range of aperitifs and digestifs, as well as some excellent Cognacs and Armagnacs, Calvados and whiskies, completes the experience.

Food Trends - Buying British

by Mark Taylor

Four years ago, the 2003 edition of *The Restaurant Guide* introduced a new symbol to highlight restaurants that placed an emphasis on making the most of local ingredients. The AA's philosophy on restaurant food has always recognised that good cooking is only achievable with the very best ingredients and the first step in offering good food is the sourcing of high-quality fresh produce.

The three editions of the Guide that followed saw a rapid increase in establishments with a small green tractor next to their name to signify Best Use of Local Produce. In fact, such is the prevalence of restaurants and pubs now sourcing their ingredients from local producers that we have taken the decision to drop the Best Use of Local Produce symbol.

Buying British

There are now so many establishments in *The Restaurant Guide* utilising Britain's bounty of wonderful produce that the green tractor symbol would have to appear beside almost every entry. It seems the country's chefs have finally woken up to the fact that Britain has a staggering array of fantastic producers, growers and artisans with products that are more than a match for those in France, Italy and Spain. Whereas five years ago, many chefs were wary of buying their fresh produce from this country - preferring to have it flown in from all over the world - they are now seeking out suppliers literally on their doorstep.

After years of using imported, out-of-season fruit and vegetables, chefs are finally cooking in tune with the seasons.

Thanks to the efforts of celebrity chefs and food writers, twinned with the rise in farmers' markets and independent specialist food shops, more and more consumers are expecting and demanding the food on their plate to be fresh, seasonal and local. It is now common to pick up a menu and find the names of producers and farmers listed, as well as the breed of animal. After the food scares of the past decade, customers have never been more interested to know exactly where their food comes from. Whereas it used to be acceptable to simply list 'pork' and 'fresh vegetables' on a menu, the discerning customer now expects to see Gloucester Old Spot pork from a named farm, and details of the vegetable grower and where they were grown. A number of chefs, especially in gastro-pubs, go as far as printing a separate list of their suppliers within the menu so that customers are well-informed and have complete assurance of traceability.

Award-winning food writer and celebrated chef Mark Hix is an ambassador for British produce and cooking. As Chef Director of Le Caprice, The Ivy and J. Sheekey, he is passionate

Grazing Concept

One of the big trends in restaurants in the past year has been the increase in the number of places offering 'grazing menus'. Until recently, this has been very much a London trend thanks to top-end restaurants like Maze, Amaya, 1880 at The Bentley Kempinski Hotel and Le Cercle (the winner of AA Restaurant of The Year for London in 2006). However, the concept of grazing menus - six, eight or more tapas-sized versions of dishes from the à la carte menu - is starting to filter out into the regions. It ties in with the increase in establishments opening all day, as well as more places offering improved alfresco options - something that will inevitably grow with the introduction of the smoking ban.

Modern Indian Cuisine

One trend that has yet to really catch on outside London is the new wave of Indian restaurants. Whereas London has places like the highly regarded Rasoi Restaurant, regional restaurants have been slow to follow suit with a modern take on traditional Indian food. Although many of the old flock wallpaper tandoori houses are slowly being given 'Changing Rooms'-style makeovers in large cities, very few of them are modernising the menus. But it must only be a matter of time before we see this changing.

about getting seasonal, local produce on the menu. His book, *British Regional Food*, celebrates regional fare from the British Isles and he welcomes the huge increase of local produce being used by chefs in this country. "We've seen a fantastic turnaround in the quality of ingredients that we produce in this country which has helped us to gain confidence in our culinary heritage once again."

Farmers rejoice

Chefs are increasingly prepared to buy British produce and cook seasonally. It's difficult to pin-point the specific driving force behind the change in attitude to British produce. I am sure it's something that has been bubbling away for years, but after significant agricultural disasters such as the BSE crisis, consumers were forced to question what they were eating and as a result demanded better quality produce and more detailed provenance.

Struggling farmers had to diversify and looked to Europe for examples. Now we have farmers growing fantastic crops, they have revived heritage breeds of stock and produce cheese that easily rivals that of our European neighbours and beyond. As Mark Hix says, "The growth in farmers' markets and farm shops has meant that consumers are much more aware of what should be available to them. We have an abundance of great ingredients that is being produced with love and care - who wouldn't want to cook with this?"

Gastro-pubs

One trend that has certainly continued apace all over the country is the rise and rise of the gastro-pub. More and more restaurant chefs are escaping the cities to run food-driven country pubs. For some it is as much a lifestyle change as anything, but the migration of quality chefs to local village pubs can only be a good thing for the consumer and for the survival of the pubs themselves.

That said, the boundaries between gastro-pub and restaurant are increasingly fuzzy. The very best examples of gastro-pubs tend to be those places that retain the traditional pub element and simply add good food into the mix. This means keeping a bar for locals to enjoy well-kept pints of real ale - preferably from a local brewery - as well as having an area for destination diners.

Too many so-called gastro-pubs are being turned into exclusive restaurants with linen tablecloths and prices that exceed those of city restaurants. There are too many pubs charging £16 to £20 for a main course, which goes against the grain of what the gastro-pub movement represented in the first place. It excludes locals who simply want to pop into their local pub for a pint and a well-made shepherd's pie and still have change from £10. It's not just pricing which is in danger of tarnishing the image of gastro-pubs, but also the growing trend of serving complicated food with unnecessary garnishes.

The whole reason the gastro-pub was a breath of fresh air in the early 1990s was because it signified a return to simplicity, with three or four elements to a dish and not a chervil garnish in sight. With so many chefs using such high-quality local produce, the ingredients should be good enough to speak for themselves.

London restaurants such as Galvin, St John and Racine have proved that simple, bistro-style dishes and unpretentious presentation are what people want. Places like St John and gastro-pubs such as The Anchor and Hope have also proved that shared dishes are a growing trend. People like the idea of walking into a restaurant and ordering a large pot of cassoulet or a leg of lamb, to share with four, six or eight people as it represents simple home cooking. It's a menu trend which is already spreading into the regions and it looks like the next twelve months will see more restaurant and pub chefs offering shared dishes on their menus.

The Top Ten Per Cent

Each year all the restaurants in the AA Restaurant Guide are awarded a specially commissioned plate that marks their achievement in gaining one or more AA Rosettes. The plates represent a partnership between the AA and Villeroy & Boch two quality brands working together to recognise high standards in restaurant cooking.

Restaurants awarded three, four or five AA Rosettes represent the Top Ten Per Cent of the restaurants in this Guide. The pages that follow list those establishments that have attained this special status

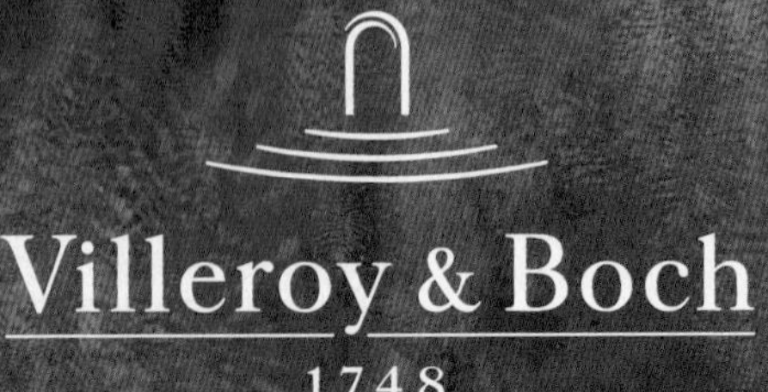

Villeroy & Boch in the restaurant

Villeroy & Boch is Europe's best selling tableware brand and, with its renowned tiles and bathrooms division, the company is also the world's leading ceramics manufacturer. At prestigious restaurants and hotels around the globe, Villeroy & Boch is the first choice of discerning chefs and restaurant managers, who choose Villeroy & Boch china, glassware and cutlery for its stunning design and uncompromising quality.

Villeroy & Boch in your home

Villeroy & Boch is no stranger to the domestic dining table either! Since 1748, brides and grooms have chosen the brand as much for the reputation and status of the name as for the quality and diversity of the designs. But the appeal of Villeroy & Boch is not limited to wedding lists. China cutlery and glass bearing the Villeroy & Boch name is simply chosen by people who want the best!

Villeroy & Boch in the future

Villeroy & Boch is leading the way in creative shaped design and is continuing to develop new products for its immensely popular New Wave tableware range.
Launching this year is 'New Wave Premium' and 'New Wave Premium Gold', two elegant bone china tableware collections continuing the New Wave theme. 'New Wave Premium Gold' is an opulent collection with accents of gold adding a decadent look to the table.
Villeroy & Boch also launches three new bold and colourful New Wave Caffè designs 'Fashionista', 'Chocolate Drops' and 'Jungle', ideal for the breakfast table or as gifts.

Villeroy & Boch for every occasion and every home

Formal or relaxed, patterned or plain, cutlery, glass and china from Villeroy & Boch suits every occasion and every budget. It will give lasting pleasure time and again, and is available from quality stores throughout the UK. Call 0208 875 6060 or visit www.villeroy-boch.com for more information.

Top Ten Per Cent

LONDON

Mandarin Oriental Hyde Park, Foliage,
66 Knightsbridge, SW1
020 7235 2000

Pétrus
The Berkeley, Wilton Place, Knightsbridge, SW1
020 7235 1200

Restaurant Gordon Ramsay
68 Royal Hospital Road, SW3
020 7352 4441

ENGLAND

BERKSHIRE

The Fat Duck
High Street, BRAY, SL6 2AQ
01628 580333

OXFORDSHIRE

Le Manoir aux Quat' Saisons
GREAT MILTON, OX44 7PD
01844 278881

LONDON

The Capital
Basil Street, SW3
020 7589 5171

Tom Aikens
43 Elystan Street, SW3
020 7584 2003

Aubergine
11 Park Walk, SW10
020 7352 3449

Locanda Locatelli
8 Seymour Street, W1
020 7935 9088

Pied à Terre
34 Charlotte Street, W1
020 7636 1178

Sketch
9 Conduit Street, W1
0870 777 4488

LONDON, GREATER

Chapter One
Farnborough Common, Locksbottom, BROMLEY, BR6 8NF
01689 85484

ENGLAND

BERKSHIRE

Waterside Inn
Ferry Road, BRAY, SL6 2AT
01628 620691

The Vineyard at Stockcross
Stockcross, NEWBURY, RG20 8JU
01635 528770

CAMBRIDGESHIRE

Midsummer House Restaurant
Midsummer Common, CAMBRIDGE, CB4 1HA
01223 369299

CUMBRIA

L'Enclume
Cavendish Street, CARTMEL, LA11 6PZ
01539 536362

DERBYSHIRE

Fischer's Baslow Hall
Calver Road, BASLOW, DE45 1RR
01246 583259

DEVON

Gidleigh Park
CHAGFORD, TQ13 8HH
01647 432367

GLOUCESTERSHIRE

Le Champignon Sauvage Restaurant
24 Suffolk Road, CHELTENHAM, GL50 2AQ
01242 573449

GREATER MANCHESTER

Juniper
21 The Downs, ALTRINCHAM, WA14 2QD
0161 929 4008

LINCOLNSHIRE

Winteringham Fields
WINTERINGHAM, DN15 9PF
01724 733096

NOTTINGHAMSHIRE

Restaurant Sat Bains with Rooms
Lenton Lane, NOTTINGHAM, NG7 2SA
0115 986 6566

RUTLAND

Hambleton Hall
Hambleton, OAKHAM, LE15 8TH
01572 756991

SHROPSHIRE

Hibiscus
17 Corve Street, LUDLOW, SY8 1DA
01584 872325

YORKSHIRE, NORTH

The Devonshire Arms Country House Hotel & Spa
BOLTON ABBEY, BD23 6AJ
01756 710441

JERSEY

Bohemia
The Club Hotel & Spa, Green Street,
ST HELIER, JE2 4UH
01534 732471

SCOTLAND

CITY OF EDINBURGH

Restaurant Martin Wishart
55 The Shore, Leith, EDINBURGH, EH6 6RA
0131 553 3557

HIGHLAND

The Boath House
Auldearn, NAIRN, IV12 5TE
01667 454896

PERTH & KINROSS

Andrew Fairlie @ Gleneagles
AUCHTERARDER, PH3 1NF
01764 694267

WALES

CEREDIGION

Ynyshir Hall
EGLWYSFACH, Machynlleth, SY20 8TA
01654 781209

NORTHERN IRELAND

Co BELFAST

Restaurant Michael Deane
34-40 Howard Street, BELFAST, BT1 6PF
028 9033 1134

REPUBLIC OF IRELAND

DUBLIN

Restaurant Patrick Guilbaud
Merrion Hotel, 21 Upper Merrion Street
01 6764192

LONDON

E14

Ubon by Nobu
34 Westferry Circus, Canary Wharf
0207 719 7800

EC1

Club Gascon
57 West Smithfield
020 7796 0600

N7

Morgan M
489 Liverpool Road, ISLINGTON
020 7609 3560

SE3

Chapter Two
43-45 Montpelier Vale,
Blackheath Village
020 8333 2666

SW1

Mju at Millennium
Knightsbridge, 17 Sloane Street
020 7201 6330

Nahm
The Halkin Hotel, Halkin Street
020 7333 1234

One-O-One
Sheraton Park Tower, 101 Knightsbridge
020 7290 7101

Zafferano
15 Lowndes Street
020 7235 5800

SW3

Rasoi Restaurant
10 Lincoln Street
020 7225 1881

SW7

The Bentley Kempinski Hotel
27-33 Harrington Gardens
020 7244 5555

SW17

Chez Bruce
2 Bellevue Road, Wandsworth Common
020 8672 0114

W1

Angela Hartnett at The Connaught
Carlos Place
020 7592 1222

The Berkeley Square
7 Davies Street, Berkeley Square
020 7629 6993

L'Escargot - The Picasso Room
48 Greek Street
020 7439 7474

Le Gavroche Restaurant
43 Upper Brook Street
020 7408 0881

Gordon Ramsay at Claridge's
Brook Street
020 7499 0099

The Greenhouse
27a Hay's Mews,
020 7499 3331

Hakkasan
No 8 Hanway Place
020 7927 7000

Lindsay House Restaurant
21 Romilly Street
020 7439 0450

Maze
London Marriott Grosvenor Hotel,
Grosvenor Square
020 7107 0000

Nobu
19 Old Park Lane
020 7447 4747

The Square
6-10 Bruton Street
020 7495 7100

Umu
14-16 Bruton Place
020 7499 8881

W4

La Trompette
5-7 Devonshire Road, CHISWICK
020 8747 1836

W6

The River Café
Thames Wharf, Rainville Road
020 7386 4200

Royal Garden Hotel, Tenth Floor Restaurant
2-24 Kensington High Street
020 7361 1910

W11

The Ledbury
127 Ledbury Road, NOTTING HILL
020 7792 9090

Notting Hill Brasserie
92 Kensington Park Road, NOTTING HILL GATE
020 7229 4481

WC2

Jaan
Swissôtel,The Howard, Temple Place
020 7836 3555

Origin
The Hospital, 24 Endell Street
020 7170 9200

Savoy Grill
The Savoy Hotel, Strand
020 7836 4343

LONDON, GREATER

The Glasshouse
14 Station Road, KEW TW9 3PZ
020 8940 6777

ENGLAND

BERKSHIRE

Fredrick's Hotel, Restaurant & Spa
Shoppenhangers Road, MAIDENHEAD, SL6 2PZ
01628 581000

L'Ortolan
Church Lane, SHINFIELD, RG2 9BY
01189 888 500

BUCKINGHAMSHIRE

Hartwell House Hotel, Restaurant & Spa
Oxford Road, AYLESBURY, HP17 8NL
01296 747444

Danesfield House Hotel & Spa
Henley Road, MARLOW, SL7 2EY
01628 891010

The Hand & Flowers
126 West Street, MARLOW, SL7 2BP
01628 482277

Macdonald Compleat Angler
Marlow Bridge, MARLOW, SL7 1RG
0870 4008100

Waldo's Restaurant Cliveden
Cliveden Estate, TAPLOW, SL6 0JF
01628 668561

CHESHIRE

The Arkle
Chester Grosvenor & Grosvenor Spa
Eastgate, CHESTER, CH1 1LT
01244 324024

Co DURHAM

Seaham Hall Hotel
Lord Byron's Walk, SEAHAM, SR7 7AG
0191 516 1400

CORNWALL & ISLES OF SCILLY

St Ervan Manor
PADSTOW, PL27 2TA
01841 540 255

The Seafood Restaurant
Riverside, PADSTOW, PL28 8BY
01841 532700

Driftwood
Rosevine, PORTSCATHO, TR2 5EW
01872 580644

St Martin's on the Isle
Lower Town, ST MARTIN'S, TR25 0QW
01720 422092

Hotel Tresanton
ST MAWES, TR2 5DR
01326 270055

Terrace Restaurant at Talland Bay
TALLAND BAY, PL13 2JB
01503 272667

CUMBRIA

Rampsbeck Country House Hotel
WATERMILLOCK, CA11 0LP
017684 86442

Gilpin Lodge Country House Hotel & Restaurant
Crook Road, WINDERMERE, LA23 3NE
015394 88818

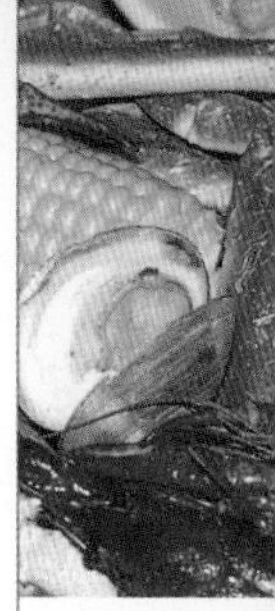

Holbeck Ghyll Country House Hotel
Holbeck Lane, WINDERMERE, LA23 1LU
015394 32375

The Samling
Ambleside Road, WINDERMERE, LA23 1LR
015394 31922

DERBYSHIRE

The Old Vicarage
Ridgeway Moor, RIDGEWAY, S12 3XW
0114 247 5814

DEVON

22 Mill Street
22 Mill Street, CHAGFORD, TQ13 8AW
01647 432244

The New Angel
2 South Embankment, DARTMOUTH, TQ6 9BH
01803 839425

The Horn of Plenty
GULWORTHY, PL19 8JD
01822 832528

Lewtrenchard Manor
LEWDON, EX20 4PN
01566 783222

Hotel Endsleigh
Milton Abbot, TAVISTOCK, PL19 0PQ
01822 870000

Corbyn Head Hotel & Orchid Restaurant
TORQUAY, TQ2 6RH
01803 296366

The Elephant Bar & Restaurant
3 & 4 Beacon Terrace, TORQUAY TQ1 2BH
01803 200044

DORSET

Summer Lodge Country House Hotel Restaurant & Spa
EVERSHOT, DT2 0JR
01935 482000

Stock Hill Country House Hotel
Stock Hill, GILLINGHAM, SP8 5NR
01747 823626

GLOUCESTERSHIRE

Buckland Manor
BUCKLAND, WR12 7LY
01386 852626

Cotswold House
CHIPPING CAMPDEN, GL55 6AN
01386 840330

Lords of the Manor
UPPER SLAUGHTER, Cheltenham, GL54 2JD
01451 820243

5 North Street
5 North Street, WINCHCOMBE GL54 5LH
01242 604566

HAMPSHIRE

Le Poussin at Whitley Ridge Country House Hotel
Beaulieu Road, BROCKENHURST, SO42 7QL
01590 622354

36 On The Quay
47 South Street, EMSWORTH, PO10 7EG
01243 375592

Westover Hall Hotel
Park Lane, Milford-On-Sea,
LYMINGTON, SO41 0PT
01590 643044

Chewton Glen Hotel
Christchurch Road, NEW MILTON, BH25 6QS
01425 275341

JSW
1 Heath Road, PETERSFIELD, GU31 4JE
01730 262030

Lainston House
Sparsholt, WINCHESTER, SO21 2LT
01962 863588

HEREFORDSHIRE

Castle House Hotel
Castle Street, HEREFORD, HR1 2NW
01432 356321

HERTFORDSHIRE

The Grove
Chandlers Cross, RICKMANSWORTH, WD3 4TG
01923 294222

ISLE OF WIGHT

George Hotel
Quay Street, YARMOUTH, PO41 0PE
01983 760331

KENT

Apicius
23 Stone Street, CRANBROOK, TN17 3HF
01580 714660

Read's Restaurant
Macknade Manor, FAVERSHAM, ME13 8XE
01795 535344

Thackeray's
TUNBRIDGE WELLS, TN1 1EA
01892 511921

LANCASHIRE

Northcote Manor
Northcote Road, LANGHO, BB6 8BE
01254 240555

The Longridge Restaurant
104-106 Higher Road, LONGRIDGE, PR3 3SY
01772 784969

LINCOLNSHIRE

Harry's Place
17 High Street, Great Gonerby, GRANTHAM,
NG31 8JS
01476 561780

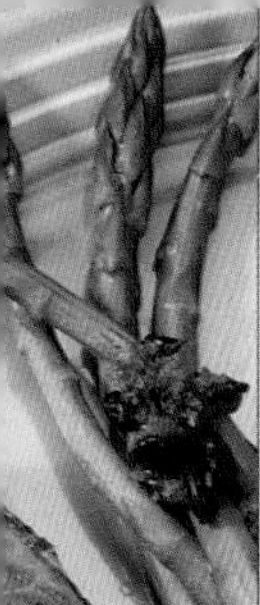

MERSEYSIDE

Fraiche
11 Rose Mount, Oxton Village, BIRKENHEAD, CH43 5SG
0151 652 2914

NORFOLK

Morston Hall
Morston, Holt, BLAKENEY, NR25 7AA
01263 741041

NORTHAMPTONSHIRE

Fawsley Hall Hotel
Fawsley, DAVENTRY, NN11 3BA
01327 892000

SHROPSHIRE

Mr Underhills
Dinham Weir, LUDLOW, SY8 IEH
01584 874431

Overton Grange Country House & Restaurant
Old Hereford Road, LUDLOW, SY8 4AD
01584 873500

Old Vicarage Hotel and Restaurant
WORFIELD, WV15 5JZ
01746 716497

SOMERSET

Bath Priory Hotel and Restaurant
Weston Road, BATH, BA1 2XT
01225 331922

The Royal Crescent Hotel - Pimpernels
16 Royal Crescent, BATH, BA1 2LS
01225 823333

Andrews on the Weir
Porlock Weir, PORLOCK, TA24 8PB
01643 863300

Little Barwick House Ltd
Barwick Village, YEOVIL, BA22 9TD
01935 423902

SUFFOLK

Hintlesham Hall
HINTLESHAM, IP8 3NS
01473 652334

SURREY

Pennyhill Park Hotel & The Spa
London Road, BAGSHOT, GU19 5EU
01276 471774

Drake's Restaurant
The Clock House, High Street, RIPLEY, GU23 6AQ
01483 224777

SUSSEX, WEST

Ockenden Manor
Ockenden Lane, CUCKFIELD, RH17 5LD
01444 416111

Gravetye Manor Hotel
EAST GRINSTEAD, RH19 4LJ
01342 810567

The Camellia Restaurant at South Lodge Hotel
Brighton Road, LOWER BEEDING, RH13 6PS
01403 891711

WARWICKSHIRE

Mallory Court Hotel
Harbury Lane, Bishop's Tachbrook, ROYAL LEAMINGTON SPA, CV33 9QB
01926 330214

WEST MIDLANDS

Simpsons
20 Highfield Road, Edgbaston, BIRMINGHAM, B15 3DU
0121 454 3434

WILTSHIRE

The Bybrook Restaurant at Manor House
CASTLE COMBE, SN14 7HR
01249 782206

Lucknam Park
COLERNE, SN14 8AZ
01225 742777

The Harrow at Little Bedwyn
LITTLE BEDWYN, SN8 3JP
01672 870871

Whatley Manor
Easton Grey, MALMESBURY, SN16 0RB
01666 822888

YORKSHIRE, NORTH

Swinton Park
MASHAM, Ripon, HGA 4JN
01765 680900

Yorke Arms
RAMSGILL, HG3 5RL
01423 755243

Middlethorpe Hall Hotel Restaurant & Spa
Bishopthorpe Road, Middlethorpe, YORK, YO23 2GB
01904 641241

YORKSHIRE, WEST

Box Tree
35-37 Church Street, ILKLEY, LS29 9DR
01943 608484

Anthony's Restaurant
19 Boat Lane, LEEDS, LS1 5DA
0113 245 5922

JERSEY

Ocean Restaurant at the Atlantic Hotel
Le Mont de la Pulente, ST BRELADE, JE3 8HE
01534 744101

Longueville Manor
ST SAVIOUR, JE2 7WF
01534 725501

SCOTLAND

ABERDEENSHIRE

Darroch Learg Hotel
Braemar Road, BALLATER, AB35 5UX
013397 55443

ANGUS

Castleton House Hotel
Castleton of Eassie, GLAMIS, DD8 1SJ
01307 840340

ARGYLL & BUTE

Isle of Eriska
ERISKA, Isle of Harns PA37 1SD
01631 720371

Airds Hotel
PORT APPIN, PA38 4DF
01631 730236

DUMFRIES & GALLOWAY

Knockinaam Lodge
PORTPATRICK, DG9 9AD
01776 810471

EAST LOTHIAN

Greywalls Hotel
Muirfield, GULLANE, EH31 2EG
01620 842144

EDINBURGH

Norton House Hotel
Ingliston, EDINBURGH, EH28 8LX
0131 333 1275

Number One, The Balmoral Hotel
Princes Street, EDINBURGH, EH2 2EQ
0131 557 6727

FIFE

Cellar Restaurant
24 East Green, ANSTRUTHER, KY10 3AA
01333 310378

The Road Hole Grill
The Old Course Hotel, ST ANDREWS, KY16 9SP
01334 474371

The Seafood Restaurant
The Scores, ST ANDREWS, KY16 9AS
01334 479475

HIGHLAND

The Three Chimneys
COLBOST, Isle of Skye IV55 8ZT
01470 511258

Inverlochy Castle Hotel
Torlundy, FORT WILLIAM, PH33 6SN
01397 702177

Glenmoriston Town House Hotel
Ness Bank, INVERNESS, IV2 4SF
01463 223777

The Cross at Kingussie
Tweed Mill Brae,
Ardbroilach Road, KINGUSSIE, PH21 ILB
01540 661166

PERTH & KINROSS

Kinnaird
Kinnaird Estate, DUNKELD, PH8 0LB
01796 482440

SOUTH AYRSHIRE

Glenapp Castle
BALLANTRAE, KA26 0NZ
01465 831212

Lochgreen House
Monktonhill Road, Southwood
TROON, KA10 7EN
01292 313343

STIRLING

Roman Camp Country House Hotel
CALLANDER, FK17 8BG
01877 330003

WEST DUNBARTONSHIRE

De Vere Cameron House
BALLOCH, G83 8QZ
01389 755565

WALES

CONWY

Tan-y-Foel Country House
Capel Garmon, BETWS-Y-COED, LL26 0RE
01690 710507

The Old Rectory Country House
Llanrwst Road, Llansanffraid Glan Conwy,
CONWY, LL28 5LF
01492 580611

Bodysgallen Hall and Spa
LLANDUDNO, LL30 1RS
01492 584466

POWYS

Carlton House
Dolycoed Road, LLANWRTYD WELLS, LD5 4RA
01591 610248

REPUBLIC OF IRELAND

Co CORK

Longueville House
MALLOW
022 47156/47306

Sheen Falls Lodge
KENMARE
064 41600

Co KILDARE

The K Club
STRAFFAN
01 6017200

Co TIPPERARY

Nuremore Hotel
CARRICKMACROSS
042 966 1438

England

England

BEDFORDSHIRE

BEDFORD MAP 12 TL04

Knife & Cleaver

Modern Seafood

Modern cooking in historic inn

01234 740387 The Grove, Houghton Conquest MK45 3LA
e-mail: info@knifeandcleaver.com
web: www.knifeandcleaver.com

Situated in the heart of the village, this 17th-century inn has links to John Bunyan. The dark oak-panelling in the lounge bar was acquired from nearby Houghton House, which was the model for House Beautiful in *The Pilgrim's Progress*. The light and airy conservatory restaurant has a buzzy atmosphere and is the place to enjoy simple British dishes with an emphasis on seasonality and local ingredients. Seafood and fish are a strength so expect warm smoked trout and mackerel tart, grilled sea bass fillets with crab and sweetcorn fritters and lobster velouté.

Chef: Chris Bishopp **Owners:** Mrs P & Mr D Loom **Times:** 12-2.30/7-9.30, Closed 26-30 Dec, BHs-dinner only, Closed L Sat, D Sun **Prices:** Fixed L £12.95, Fixed D £22.50, Starter £4.95-£7.95, Main £11.25-£24.50, Dessert £4.95, Coffee £1.85, Min/Water £3, Service optional, Group min 10 service 10% **Wine:** 33 bottles over £20, 29 bottles under £20, 20 by the glass (£2-£5.40) **Notes:** Sun L 3 courses £15.95, Vegetarian available, Smart Casual **Seats:** 65, Pr/dining room 12 **Smoking:** N/Sm in restaurant, Air con **Children:** Menu, Portions **Rooms:** 9 (9 en suite) ◆◆◆◆ **Directions:** M1 junct 12-13 just off A6, 5m S of Bedford. Follow brown tourist signs from A6. Opposite church in village **Parking:** 35

Villa Rosa

01234 269259 Ram Yard MK40 1AL
Bustling, family-run Italian.

MILTON ERNEST MAP 11 TL05

The Strawberry Tree

Traditional British

Innovative cuisine using carefully sourced produce in a lovely thatched cottage

01234 823633 3 Radwell Rd MK44 1RY
e-mail: strawberrytree_restaurant@yahoo.co.uk

A 17th-century thatched cottage which was originally divided into three, with a sweet shop at the front, laundry in the middle and cottage at the back. Run as a tea shop for ten years, the restaurant was

continued

then developed and refurbished, retaining original features like the bread oven, flag stone floors and inglenook fireplaces. Here you can enjoy carefully sourced local produce like Lincoln Red beef, Suffolk lamb and organic vegetables and herbs. Try a starter of celery and celeriac soup with a lasagne of wild mushrooms, followed by breast of local pheasant with smoked bacon, roast parsnips, pumpkin, bread sauce and cep mushroom sauce. Dessert might feature white chocolate and lime parfait with mascarpone sorbet and passionfruit.

Chef: Jason & Andrew Bona **Owners:** John & Wendy Bona **Times:** 12-1.45/7-9, Closed 2 wks Jan & Sep, Sun-Tue, Closed L Sat **Prices:** Fixed D £32.50, Starter £6-£9, Main £14-£18, Dessert £7.50, Coffee £3.50, Service optional, Group min 6 service 12.5% **Wine:** 19 bottles over £20, 11 bottles under £20, 2 by the glass **Seats:** 22, Pr/dining room 8 **Smoking:** N/Sm in restaurant **Children:** Portions **Directions:** M1 junct 13, 4m N of Bedford on A6 **Parking:** 8

WOBURN MAP 11 SP93

The Inn at Woburn

British, Mediterranean

Seamless blend of old and modern in lovely market town

01525 292292/290441 George St MK17 9PX
e-mail: enquiries@theinnatwoburn.com
web: www.theinnatwoburn.com

The original inn and courtyard-style extension are full of character with sage-green paintwork and old stock brickwork set off by old fashioned street lamps. The restaurant is named Olivier's after the chef and offers an interesting carte, a few specials and some vegetarian options. Typical main courses might include braised collar of pork garnished with crispy strip of belly pork or grilled venison cutlets with braised red cabbage, fondant potatoes and a port and fresh fig sauce. If it's wine by the glass you'd prefer, the restaurant has a choice of 24.

Times: 12-2.30/6-10.15 **Rooms:** 57 (57 en suite) ★★★ HL
Directions: 5 mins from M1 junct 13. Follow signs to Woburn. Inn in town centre at x-rds. Parking to rear via Parm St

Paris House Restaurant

French

Classical French cooking in an English park

☎ 01525 290692 Woburn Park MK17 9QP
e-mail: gailbaker@parishouse.co.uk
web: www.parishouse.co.uk

Deer roam the park outside this black and white timber house on the Woburn estate, in stark contrast to its earlier existence. It was built in 1878 for the Paris Exhibition, then dismantled and rebuilt in its current peaceful, scenic location by the 9th Duke of Bedford. Chef-patron Peter Chandler rules the roost, greeting customers with his friendly presence, and delivering the goods in classical French style. Well up to expectations are starters like confit of crispy duck in orange sauce, followed by fillet of beef in red wine sauce with classic desserts typified by hot raspberry soufflé. The pricey carte and short menu du jour, the latter cheaper on weekdays, are topped by a gastronomic menu.

Chef: Peter Chandler **Owners:** Mr P Chandler **Times:** 12-2/7-9.45, Closed 26 Dec, 1-17 Jan, Mon, Closed D Sun **Prices:** Fixed L £22, Fixed D £55, Coffee £4, Min/Water £3.75, Service optional **Wine:** 50 bottles over £20, 12 bottles under £20, 7 by the glass (£4.70-£9) **Notes:** ALC £55 (all incl), Tasting menu £60 (not Sun), Vegetarian menu **Seats:** 48, Pr/dining room 16 **Smoking:** N/Sm in restaurant **Children:** Menu, Portions **Directions:** M1 junct 13. From Woburn take A4012 Hockliffe, 1.75m out of Woburn village on left **Parking:** 24

Two Rosettes

The best local restaurants, which aim for and achieve higher standards, better consistency and where a greater precision is apparent in the cooking. There will be obvious attention to the selection of quality ingredients.

BERKSHIRE

ASCOT MAP 06 SU96

Macdonald Berystede Hotel & Spa

British, International

Elegant dining room offering classical, seasonal cuisine

☎ 01344 623311 Bagshot Rd, Sunninghill SL5 9JH
e-mail: general.berystede@macdonald-hotels.co.uk
web: www.berystede.com

This impressive, extended Victorian mansion - now a smart hotel boasting a state-of-the-art spa and leisure facilities - is but a short canter from Ascot racecourse. Its large, elegant Hyperion Restaurant (aptly named after a famous racecourse) comes laid out in crisp white linen, with friendly, attentive service and large windows that overlook the roof terrace (perfect for fair-weather alfresco dining), spa and manicured grounds. The kitchen's approach is along modern lines, underpinned by a classical base, using quality seasonal ingredients; think tournedos of cod served with creamed leeks, sweet potato chips and a béarnaise sauce.

Times: 12.30-2/7-9.45, Closed L Sat **Rooms:** 125 (125 en suite) ★★★★ HL **Directions:** Join A30 from M3 junct 3, A322 then left onto B3020 to Ascot or M25 - junct 13, follow signs for Bagshot. At Sunningdale turn right onto A330

BRACKNELL MAP 05 SU86

Coppid Beech

Modern British

Enjoyable dining in Alpine-style hotel

☎ 01344 303333 John Nike Way RG12 8TF
e-mail: welcome@coppid-beech-hotel.co.uk
web: www.coppidbeech.com

Of striking Swiss chalet design, this large and very popular hotel stands next to a dry-ski slope and also boasts a health club, ice rink and the 'Apres' night club. There's also a choice of restaurants: the basement Bier Keller with its brasserie-style menu and the fine-dining Rowans. The latter is a bright, modern, air-conditioned room with a timber ceiling and crystal chandeliers. The extensive carte offers a diverse contemporary style of cooking, blending modern British with European influences. Typical choices may include mussel soup with potato gnocchi to start, followed by roasted rump, braised leg and kidney of lamb with rösti, confit shallot and buttered spinach, and Valrhona chocolate tart with mandarin sorbet.

Chef: Paul Zolik **Owners:** Nike Group Hotels Ltd **Times:** 12-2.15/7-10.30 **Prices:** Fixed L £17.95, Fixed D £24.95, Starter £3.95-£10.25, Main £14.95-£26.95, Dessert £5.95-£6.95, Min/Water £3, Service optional **Wine:** 64 bottles over £20, 31 bottles under £20, 16 by the glass (£3.75-£7.95) **Notes:** Coffee incl, Fixed L is 3 course buffet, Civ Wed 300 **Seats:** 120, Pr/dining room 20 **Smoking:** N/Sm in restaurant, Air con **Children:** Menu, Portions **Rooms:** 205 (205 en suite) ★★★★ HL **Directions:** From M4 junct 10 follow A329(M) (Bracknell/Wokingham) to 1st exit. At rdbt take 1st exit to Binfield (B3408); hotel 200yds on right **Parking:** 350

Sultan Balti House

☎ 01344 303330 7 Great Hollands Square,
Great Hollands RG12 8UX

Step from a shopping arcade into a verdant Indian orange grove. Wide menu specialises in Balti, and dishes exhibit freshness and quality.

The Fat Duck

BRAY MAP 06 SU97

Modern European

NOTABLE WINE LIST

The epitome of contemporary dining experiences

☎ 01628 580333 High St SL6 2AQ
web: www.fatduck.co.uk

Somehow, the well-groomed, Thames-side village of Bray has become home to British gastronomy. First with the Roux brothers at the Waterside Inn (see entry) bringing French classicalism to Britain (and training a whole generation of big name chefs), and now Heston Blumenthal's Fat Duck, leading the way in innovative gastronomy. Two small cottages on the main village road seems an unassuming and unlikely international destination for the molecular gastronomy movement and home to one of the world's best chefs, but The Fat Duck oozes understated quality and chic. Oak beams and low ceilings are complemented by modern art and glass screens, which combine effortlessly with the Tudor building. Comfortable chairs and white napery are backed by impeccable service (a feature of The Fat Duck experience), which is professional, enthusiastic and friendly; with staff eager to share their knowledge without a hint of condescension.
Blumenthal is a chef par excellence as well as a true culinary pioneer, and a leading exponent of the scientific approach to cuisine. Whilst there's nothing bizarre about the ingredients he uses, it's this combination of flavours that sometimes raises eyebrows or catches the headlines; witness a dessert of nitro-scrambled egg and bacon ice cream with parsnip cereal. But it's not just the exciting combinations that are a hallmark of this stunning experience, it's Heston's absolute precision and clarity of flavour and balance that sets him apart. For the full-on show, look to the tasting menu with its eight courses and various head-turning tasters and inter-courses, though there is also a good-value lunch option and carte, which might deliver a saddle of venison with celeriac, marron glacé, sauce poivrade, civet of venison with pearl barley and red wine, and venison and frankincense tea. Wow! An extensive wine list rounds off the package in style. So just sit back and enjoy the journey with a culinary alchemist at the helm.
Notable Wine List: Stunning award-winning wine list full of the finest quality including an impressive sherry list.

Chef: Heston Blumenthal
Owners: Fat Duck Ltd
Times: 12-1.45/7-9.45, Closed 2 wks at Xmas, Mon, Closed D Sun
Prices: Set ALC £90, Service added but optional 12.5%
Wine: 900 bottles over £20, 48 by the glass (£4.25-£35)
Notes: Set tasting menu £110, Vegetarian available
Seats: 46
Smoking: N/Sm in restaurant, Air con
Children: Portions
Directions: M4 junct 8/9 (Maidenhead) take A308 towards Windsor, turn left into Bray. Restaurant in centre of village on right
Parking: Two village car parks

Hinds Head Hotel

Traditional British

Fine British pub food, destination dining

☎ 01628 626151 High St SL6 2AB
e-mail: info@hindsheadhotel.co.uk
web: www.hindsheadhotel.co.uk

The Hinds Head wants to be a local village pub, but as part of Heston Blumenthal's stable it will always invite interest from much further afield as gastronomes beat a path to its 15th-century door seeking inspiration. A fascinating place with uncertain origins, perhaps a former hunting lodge or guest house for the local Abbot, the inn was no stranger to celebrity in the past with guests including Prince Philip on his stag night. The main dining area on the ground floor offers a light restaurant and additional alcove seating, there is private dining upstairs. The menu is quite different to that at the Fat Duck so make no mistake, this is pub food with traditional British dishes like Lancashire Hotpot or Gloucester Old Spot pork chop with pease pudding. Heston Blumenthal is, however, working on reintroducing historic British dishes here so look out for some very old favourites.

Chef: Dominic Chapman **Owners:** Heston Blumenthal **Times:** 12-2.30/6.30-9.30, Closed 25-26 Dec, Closed D Sun **Prices:** Starter £5.50-£9.50, Main £12-£18.50, Dessert £4.95-£5, Coffee £2.50 **Notes:** Vegetarian available **Seats:** 90, Pr/dining room 22 **Smoking:** N/Sm in restaurant, Air con **Children:** Portions **Directions:** M4 junct 8/9, at rdbt take exit to Maidenhead Central, next rdbt take exit Bray & Windsor, after 0.5m take B3028 to Bray **Parking:** Car park across road

Monkey Island Hotel

Modern British

Fine dining in idyllic island setting

☎ 01628 623400 Old Mill Ln SL6 2EE
e-mail: salesco@monkeyisland.co.uk
web: www.monkeyisland.co.uk

This unique island hotel was once a fishing lodge used by monks, and it extended over hundreds of years to form an idyllic retreat. Accessed only by bridge, boat or helicopter, to dine here is an experience before you've even set foot in the restaurant. The Pavilion dining room is situated at the head of the island and has wonderful upstream views. In summer, business lunches and afternoon teas are served on the outside terrace. A team of chefs prepare contemporary international cuisine with main courses like ribeye of beef served with horseradish rösti, braised wilted spinach and essence of port.

Chef: Graham Turner **Owners:** Metropolitan Hotels International **Times:** 12.30-2.30/7-10 **Prices:** Fixed L £21.50, Fixed D £35, Starter £6-£11, Main £17-£30, Dessert £6-£8, Coffee £3.75, Min/Water £3.50, Service added but optional 10% **Wine:** 50 bottles over £20, 10 bottles under £20, 8 by the glass (£3.50-£6.50) **Notes:** Vegetarian available, Dress Restrictions, Smart casual, no trainers, Civ Wed 120 **Seats:** 80, Pr/dining room 120 **Smoking:** N/Sm in restaurant **Children:** Menu, Portions **Rooms:** 26 (26 en suite) ★★★★ **Directions:** M4 junct 8/9, A308 towards Windsor, before flyover turn left towards Bray Village, then follow signs **Parking:** 100

The Riverside Brasserie

French

Brasserie dining beside Thames-side marina

☎ 01628 780553 Bray Marina SL6 2EB
e-mail: grrydws@aol.com
web: www.riversidebrasserie.co.uk

Housed in a simple, café-like building in Bray marina, this contemporary, no-frills riverside eatery functions as a pit-stop for boats on the Thames, and draws the summer crowds for leisurely alfresco lunches on the waterside decked terrace. Expect wooden floors, an open-to-view kitchen, a relaxed atmosphere, and unpretentious yet accomplished brasserie fare. Using top-notch ingredients, clean, well-presented dishes mix classics such as braised belly pork with celeriac remoulade or rib-eye steak with triple-cooked chips and bone marrow sauce, with more innovative, Mediterranean-inspired ideas, for example spaghetti with cockles, and confit of sea bream on crushed potatoes with fennel purée. Classic puddings include chocolate tart and apple crumble.

Chef: Garrey Dylan Dawson **Owners:** Garrey Dylan Dawson, Lee Dixon, Alfie Hitchcock, Bob Angus **Times:** 12-3/6.30-10, Closed Winter **Prices:** Starter £5.50-£12, Main £11.50-£16, Dessert £5.50-£7, Coffee £2.50, Min/Water £2.50, Service added but optional 12.5% **Wine:** 20 bottles over £20, 3 bottles under £20, 6 by the glass (£4-£8) **Notes:** Vegetarian available **Seats:** 60 **Smoking:** No pipes, No cigars **Children:** Menu, Portions **Directions:** Off A308, signed Bray Marina **Parking:** 30

Waterside Inn

see page 32

CHIEVELEY MAP 05 SU47

The Crab at Chieveley

Modern British, French V

Award-winning seafood restaurant

☎ 01635 247550 Wantage Rd RG20 8UE
e-mail: info@crabatchieveley.com
web: www.crabatchieveley.com

This one-time pub has been tastefully transformed into a well-appointed hotel, with a cosy bar and two dining areas: a formal room with red and chocolate coloured leather seating, and a more relaxed space with polished wooden tables. A former winner of the AA award for best seafood, it specialises in dishes such as roast John Dory with seared ceps, creamed spinach and shallot jus, or oven-baked cod with smoked bacon, tarragon cream and rösti potatoes. A deceptively

continued

Waterside Inn

BRAY MAP 06 SU97

French NOTABLE WINE LIST

A gastronomic Thames-side legend delivering classic French cuisine

☎ 01628 620691 Ferry Rd SL6 2AT
e-mail: reservations@waterside-inn.co.uk
web: www.waterside-inn.co.uk

The celebrated Waterside and the Roux family - a name synonymous with fine food - have been offering their special blend of classic-French-cuisine-meets-quintessential-English setting at Bray since 1972. The Roux personnel may have changed, with son Alain having assumed the mantle of chef-patron from his father Michel in 2001, but standards at the Waterside never falter. Service here is impeccable and as good as it comes, traditional maybe, slick, polished and professional, but unstuffy, friendly and genuine, and the valet parking adds just another touch of pampering. The lovely timbered building on the water's edge sports a classic, elegant dining room, and, while most tables have a view of the river, the tiered terrace at the back is a magical setting to sip champagne and nibble canapés on a warm summer day watching Thames life go by. Inside the colour scheme is green and gold, with hand-painted frescos of flowers and lots of mirrors giving an illusion of space. Plate glass windows offer diners those views over the Thames, while tables come clothed in heavy white linen set off by fresh orchids, and vases of fresh lilies further complement the room's garden theme.

Like the service, the food still remains rooted in classical French, so expect impeccable ingredients, luxury, high skill and clear flavours to be delivered on a repertoire of fixed-price lunch, five-course menu Exceptionelle and a lengthy and appealing carte. Think a saddle of milk lamb stuffed with morels and served with baby vegetables and a minted hollandaise sauce, and perhaps a superb chocolate and raspberry tart teamed with a raspberry sorbet to finish. The extensive and equally classy wine list stays as patriotically Gallic as the food, while peripherals like breads, amuse-bouche, pre-desserts and petits fours all hold form through to the end. This delightful corner of Bray will be forever France.

Notable Wine List: Classic French list brimming full of the finest domains and the finest years.

Chef: Michel Roux, Alain Roux
Owners: Michel Roux & Alain Roux
Times: 12-2/7-10, Closed 26 Dec for 5 wks, Mon, Closed L Tue, D Tue ex Jun-Aug
Prices: Fixed L £40-£56, Fixed D £89.50, Starter £24.50-£38.70, Main £38.50-£47.50, Dessert £19-£30, Service added but optional 12.5%
Wine: 790 bottles over £20, 10 by the glass (£7.50-£15)
Notes: Fixed price L 3 courses, Fixed price D 5 courses, Vegetarian available, No jeans/trainers, Civ Wed 70
Seats: 75, Pr/dining room 8
Smoking: N/Sm in restaurant
Children: Min 12 yrs, Menu
Directions: M4 junct 8/9, A308(Windsor) then B3028 to Bray. Restaurant clearly signed
Parking: 20

CHIEVELEY *continued* MAP 05 SU47

simple style hides the abundance of skill to be found in the kitchen, but don't be fooled - this is top-notch cooking conjured from the freshest of ingredients.

The Crab at Chieveley

Chef: David Horridge **Owners:** David and Jackie Barnard **Times:** 12/11 **Prices:** Fixed L fr £16.50, Fixed D fr £19.50, Starter £5.50-£9.50, Main £10.50-£32, Dessert £6-£7, Coffee £2, Min/Water £3, Service optional, Group min 6 service 10% **Wine:** 14 bottles under £20, 12 by the glass (£3-£8.50) **Notes:** Fixed D before 7pm, Vegetarian menu, Civ Wed 30 **Seats:** 120, Pr/dining room 30 **Smoking:** N/Sm in restaurant, Air con **Children:** Menu, Portions **Rooms:** 10 (10 en suite) ★★★★ RR **Directions:** M4 junct 13 to Chieveley, School Rd to B4494, turn right to Wantage **Parking:** 80

COOKHAM MAP 06 SU88

Malik's

Traditional Indian

Genuine Indian cooking in very English setting

☎ 01628 520085 High St SL6 9SF
web: www.maliks.co.uk

continued

An ivy-clad former coaching inn in a village on the River Thames may be an unlikely setting for an Indian restaurant, but this place is a firm favourite with locals and reservations are strongly recommended. The lengthy menu contains traditional favourites such as chicken bhuna, but the Bengali chef offers a comprehensive selection of seafood and vegetarian dishes. From mild to highly spiced, each one is executed with care with dishes like badami murgh (skewered grilled chicken breast with peanut sauce) and lamb jhalpiazi showing a certain lightness of touch. Desserts of pear simmered in a cinnamon syrup are complemented by more familiar Indian ice creams.

Chef: Malik Ahmed, Shapon Miah **Owners:** Malik Ahmed **Times:** 12-2.30/6-11.00, Closed 25-26 Dec, Closed L Eid festival **Prices:** Fixed D fr £25, Starter £3.95-£7.95, Main £7.25-£15.95, Dessert £3.50-£6.95, Coffee £2.50, Min/Water £3.95, Service optional **Wine:** 31 bottles over £20, 7 bottles under £20, 2 by the glass (£3.95-£4.95) **Notes:** Sun L buffet £9.95, Vegetarian available, Smart dress **Seats:** 70, Pr/dining room 30 **Smoking:** N/Sm area, No pipes, No cigars **Children:** Portions **Directions:** M4 junct 7, take A4 towards Maidenhead, 2m **Parking:** 26

COOKHAM DEAN MAP 05 SU88

The Inn on The Green

Modern European

Modern classics at a boutique hotel

☎ 01628 482638 The Old Cricket Common SL6 9NZ
e-mail: reception@theinnonthegreen.com
web: www.theinnonthegreen.com

Inconspicuously nestled in a rural Berkshire village, this fashionable little hotel has a sophisticated décor that combines a touch of the boudoir with the intimacy of a club. Deep red velvet sofas beckon beside leather armchairs, while the restaurant is comprised of three individually styled dining areas: an airy conservatory leading on to a courtyard, the wood-panelled Stublie Room, and the Lamp Room, a modern creation with exposed brickwork and a magnificent chandelier. Expect imaginative modern French classics with international influences from a kitchen that doesn't disappoint: Japanese-style sea bass with miso broth and spring onions perhaps, or smoked rump of lamb with boulangère potatoes, dried tomato and shallot jus.

Chef: Garry Hollihead **Owners:** Andy Taylor, Mark Fuller & Garry Hollihead **Times:** 1-4/7-10, Closed Mon, Closed L Tue-Sat, D Sun **Prices:** Fixed D £19.95, Starter £6-£15, Main £12-£22, Dessert £6, Coffee £3, Min/Water £3.50, Service added but optional 12.5% **Wine:** 43 bottles over £20, 9 bottles under £20, 9 by the glass (£3.75-£6) **Notes:** Fixed D Tues-Fri, Sun L 2 courses £19.95, 3 courses £23.50, Civ Wed 100 **Seats:** 60, Pr/dining room 35 **Smoking:** N/Sm in restaurant, Air con **Children:** Portions **Rooms:** 9 (9 en suite) ★★★★ RR **Directions:** From Marlow or Maidenhead follow Cookham Dean signs. In Cookham Dean turn into Hills Lane; into National Trust road by War Memorial **Parking:** 50

HURLEY MAP 05 SU88

Black Boys Inn

British, French **NEW**

Welcoming family-run inn offering French cooking using quality British produce

☎ 01628 824212 Henley Rd SL6 5NQ
e-mail: info@blackboysinn.co.uk
web: www.blackboysinn.co.uk

continued

HURLEY *continued* MAP 05 SU88

Sympathetically restored, this 16th-century pub retains original features such as a huge wood-burning stove, wooden beams and a polished wood floor. The décor has a light modern feel with farmhouse-style tables. Service is friendly and professional. Cooking is French using classic techniques, with good flavours drawing the best from carefully sourced produce. A selection from the menu may include fresh Salcombe crab, pink ginger and pink grapefruit gelée to start, followed by petit sale of duck leg, paysanne lentils and potato purée, or roasted rack of Buckinghamshire pork flavoured with mountain herbs.

Chef: Simon Bonwick **Owners:** Adrian & Helen Bannister **Times:** 12-2/6.30-9, Closed 2 wks Xmas, 2 wks Aug, BHs, Closed D Sun **Prices:** Starter £5.50-£8.50, Main £11.50-£14.95, Dessert fr £5.50, Coffee £2, Min/Water £3, Service optional **Wine:** 36 bottles over £20, 15 bottles under £20, 36 by the glass (£3.25-£8.25) **Seats:** 45, Pr/dining room 12 **Smoking:** N/Sm in restaurant **Children:** Min 12 yrs **Rooms:** 8 (8 en suite) ★★★★ RR **Directions:** M40 junct 4, A404 towards Henley, then A4130. Restaurant 3m from Henley-on-Thames **Parking:** 30

HURST MAP 05 SU77

⚘⚘ Castle Brasserie

Modern European

Fine dining in an ancient building

☎ 0118 934 0034 Church Hill RG10 0SJ
e-mail: info@castlerestaurant.co.uk
web: www.castlerestaurant.co.uk

Step back in time as you stand outside this 500-year-old building opposite the church. Inside, an upstairs gallery room overlooks beautiful countryside and the décor has been brought up to date with a modern, minimalist feel. The cooking style is similarly modern with European dishes based on fine produce. Try a starter like home-smoked venison with foie gras and green bean salad. For a main course, you might choose rump of lamb with a range of accompaniments like buttered spinach, potato gnocchi, garlic fritters, aubergine crisps and sauce Niçoise. Dessert might be a simple chocolate fondant.

Chef: Mark Speirs **Owners:** Amanda Hill **Times:** 12-2.30/7-10, Closed 26-30 Dec, Mon, Closed D Sun **Prices:** Fixed L fr £12.95, Starter £5.25-£8.95, Main £13.95-£22, Dessert £4.95-£6.25, Coffee £2, Min/Water £3, Group min 6 service 10% **Wine:** 12 bottles over £20, 22 bottles under £20, 6 by the glass (£3.50-£3.75) **Notes:** Sun L 2 courses £12.95, 3 courses £15.95 **Seats:** 80, Pr/dining room 40 **Smoking:** N/Sm in restaurant **Children:** Menu, Portions **Directions:** M4 junct 10, A329(M) towards Reading (E). Take first exit to Winnersh/Wokingham. Continue for 1m, at Sainsburys turn left into Robin Hood Lane. Continue for 1.5m and go straight when approaching sharp left bend towards St Nicholas Church **Parking:** 43

LAMBOURN MAP 05 SU37

⚘⚘ The Hare Restaurant @ The Hare & Hounds

Modern European

Interesting menus in stylishly converted pub

☎ 01488 71386 RG17 7SD
e-mail: cuisine@theharerestaurant.co.uk
web: www.theharerestaurant.co.uk

A smartly painted former pub located at an isolated crossroads just outside the horse racing village of Lambourn. Rambling dining rooms sport a bright, modern and stylish décor, with slate floors, exposed beams, rustic wooden tables, and squashy leather sofas by the log fire. This is a relaxing and informal setting in which to sample some ambitious cooking that combines British with modern European influences. Short menus are well balanced, using top-notch ingredients and interesting combinations to produce adventurous dishes, perhaps scallops with nage of clams and ginger, confit ginger and fennel purée, confit pork belly with osso buco ravioli and saffron gnocchi, and chocolate fondant with yogurt and pistachio ice cream and chocolate sorbet. The lunch menu is great value.

Chef: Tristan Lee Mason **Owners:** Paul Whitford, Helen Windridge **Times:** 12-2/7-9.30, Closed Xmas-30 Dec, 1 Jan, 9-20 Jan, Mon, Closed D Sun **Prices:** Fixed L £17, Starter £8-£12, Main £17-£25, Dessert £8-£10, Coffee £3, Min/Water £3.50, Service optional, Group min 10 service 10% **Wine:** 60 bottles over £20, 9 bottles under £20, 7 by the glass (£3.75-£5) **Notes:** Tasting menu £55-60, Vegetarian available **Seats:** 50, Pr/dining room 24 **Smoking:** N/Sm in restaurant **Directions:** M4 junct 14, A338 towards Wantage, left onto B4000 towards Lambourne, restaurant 3m on left **Parking:** 30

MAIDENHEAD MAP 06 SU88

⚘⚘⚘ Fredrick's Hotel, Restaurant & Spa

see page 35

⚘ The Royal Oak

International

Village gastro-pub with celebrity connections

☎ 01628 620541 Paley St, Littlefield Green SL6 3JN
e-mail: royaloakmail@aol.com
web: www.theroyaloakpaleystreet.com

Low oak beams, polished wood floors and blazing log fires set the relaxing and convivial scene at this whitewashed village pub south of Maidenhead. Added touches include daily newspapers to peruse, good piped jazz and a gallery of framed pictures from the landlord's father's (Michael Parkinson) star-studded career. Expect pub food at its best - honest, bold and simple cooking based on quality seasonal produce. French inspired dishes include salmon with chargrilled vegetables and hollandaise, and fillet steak with foie gras and roasted shallots. Good value set menu and bar meals at lunchtime.

Chef: Daniel Royneau **Owners:** Nick Parkinson **Times:** 11-3/6-12, Closed 27 Dec-1 Jan, Closed D Sun **Prices:** Fixed L £16.50, Fixed D £35, Starter £4.75-£12, Main £9.50-£21, Dessert £5.50, Coffee £2.50, Min/Water £3.50, Service optional, Group min 10 service 10% **Wine:** 80 bottles over £20, 10 bottles under £20, 6 by the glass (£3.20-£4.50) **Notes:** Sun L 2 courses

continued

Fredrick's Hotel, Restaurant & Spa

MAIDENHEAD MAP 06 SU88

British, French

Country-style retreat with polished German hospitality

☎ 01628 581000 Shoppenhangers Rd SL6 2PZ
e-mail: eat@fredricks-hotel.co.uk
web: www.fredricks-hotel.co.uk

A calm oasis only minutes from the M4, Fredrick's - owned by the Lösel family - is an immaculate, luxury hotel with formal fine dining, classically based cuisine and highly professional service. Its traditionally styled, elegant dining room is decked out with pristine table settings, and comes richly decorated in blues and golds to a backdrop of striking artwork - including oils and sculptures from the Lösel's personal collection - and views over terrace, patio and well-tended gardens. Take aperitifs in the club-style bar, replete with leather tub chairs and bar stalls, while in summer the patio's the place for fair-weather dining or cocktails beneath the shadow of colonial-style parasols.
The highly accomplished food is rooted in the French classics with modern interpretations and the occasional German influence, the menus dotted with luxury ingredients and graced by high-quality produce. The daily-changing, fixed-price jour and seasonal carte - bolstered by a handful of Fredrick's Classics like tournedos au poivre - might take in roast monkfish with oysters, leeks and truffle, or quince soufflé and plum ice cream. A swanky new spa and luxurious rooms offer the perfect excuse to make a day and night of it.

Chef: Brian Cutler
Owners: F W Lösel
Times: 12-2.30/7-10, Closed 25 Dec, 1 Jan, Closed L Sat
Prices: Fixed L £21.50, Fixed D £39.50, Starter £13.50-£16.50, Main £24.50-£28.50, Dessert £10.50, Coffee £4.50, Min/Water £4.50, Service optional
Wine: All bottles over £20, 5 by the glass (£5.20)
Notes: Fixed L 4 courses, Sun L 3 courses & coffee £32.50, Vegetarian available, Dress Restrictions, Smart casual, Civ Wed 120
Seats: 60, Pr/dining room 130
Smoking: N/Sm in restaurant, Air con
Children: Portions
Rooms: 34 (34 en suite) ★★★★ HL
Directions: From M4 junct 8/9 take A404(M), then turning (junct 9A) for Cox Green/White Waltham. Left on to Shoppenhangers Rd, restaurant 400 mtrs on right
Parking: 90

England

MAIDENHEAD *continued* MAP 06 SU88

£17.50, 3 courses £21.50, Vegetarian available **Seats:** 45 **Smoking:** N/Sm in restaurant **Children:** Portions **Directions:** M4 junct 8/9. Take A308 towards Maidenhead Central. Take A330 to Ascot, continue for 2m, then right onto B3024 to Twyford. The Royal Oak is second pub on left **Parking:** 50

MARSH BENHAM MAP 05 SU46

Red House

British, French

Anglo-French dining in countryside restaurant

☎ 01635 582017 RG20 8LY
web: www.theredhousepub.com

This well-presented thatched, 18th-century country dining pub started life long ago as a bakery. There's a smoking bar and an L-shaped, non-smoking dining room with delightful countryside views. Bookcases line the dining room and tables are well spaced; the formal look balanced by friendly and efficient service. Expect generous modern European menus of unpretentious dishes with clear flavours with the occasional French and international accent. Starters of pheasant and ceps lasagne, main courses of pan-fried monkfish with caramelised chicory and desserts of Bakewell tart and clotted cream exemplify this kitchen's rock-solid style.

Chef: Yves Girard **Owners:** Tricrane Ltd **Times:** 11.30-2.30/7-9.30, Closed Xmas, New Year, Closed D Sun **Prices:** Fixed L £13.95, Coffee £2, Service added but optional 10%, Group min 6 service 10% **Notes:** Vegetarian available **Seats:** 60, Pr/dining room 30 **Smoking:** N/Sm in restaurant **Children:** Menu, Portions **Directions:** 400yds off A4, 3m from Newbury, 5m from Hungerford **Parking:** 60

NEWBURY MAP 05 SU46

Donnington Valley Hotel

Traditional NOTABLE WINE LIST

Modern dining in impressive golfing hotel

☎ 01635 551199 Old Oxford Rd, Donnington RG14 3AG
e-mail: general@donningtonvalley.co.uk
web: www.donningtonvalley.co.uk

A smart, modern golfing hotel, with extensive conference facilities and lovely grounds. The Wine Press Restaurant is an impressive contemporary dining area with a raised gallery around the outside looking down on to the central restaurant area. The wine theme extends to a well-balanced list with a large number of wines offered by the glass. When it comes to the food, the emphasis is firmly on fresh produce, locally-sourced and simply prepared. Both traditional and modern dishes are offered on a varied menu, with a good choice of shellfish, fish, meat and vegetarian dishes. Try a starter like foie gras, ham hock terrine and wild mushroom pickle, followed perhaps by a main course of veal cutlet, shallot, wild mushroom, parmesan tart and Savoy cabbage.

Notable Wine List: An extensive and award winning wine list offering over 300 wines with a great Californian selection.

Donnington Valley Hotel

Chef: Kelvin Johnson **Owners:** Sir Peter Michael **Times:** 12-2/7-10 **Prices:** Fixed L fr £19, Fixed D fr £26, Starter £7-£11, Main £12-£24, Dessert £7-£8, Coffee £3, Min/Water £3.25, Service optional **Wine:** 270 bottles over £20, 30 bottles under £20, 30 by the glass (£3.25-£9.50) **Notes:** Vegetarian available, Smart casual, Civ Wed 85 **Seats:** 120, Pr/dining room 130 **Smoking:** N/Sm in restaurant **Children:** Menu, Portions **Rooms:** 58 (58 en suite) ★★★★ HL **Directions:** M4 junct 13, A34 towards Newbury. Take immediate left signed Donnington Hotels. At rdbt take right, at 3rd rdbt take left, follow road for 2m, hotel on right **Parking:** 100

Regency Park Hotel

Modern British

Imaginative cuisine with eye-catching views

☎ 01635 871555 Bowling Green Rd, Thatcham RG18 3RP
e-mail: info@regencyparkhotel.co.uk
web: www.regencyparkhotel.co.uk

Large windows, crisp linen and attractive polished wood floors give a sense of class to the airy, modern Watermark Restaurant that overlooks the delightful waterfall gardens. Staff are friendly and attentive making diners perfectly at ease in this serene setting. The food is well executed, with some daring combinations, on this modern British menu with brasserie classics. Try poached quail egg with girolles and choron sauce parmesan and chive muffin to start, for example, followed by baked red mullet with rocket and onion relish. The chocolate plate makes a grand finale and includes a pannacotta, mousse and torte.

continued

Chef: Paul Green **Owners:** Pedersen Caterers **Times:** 12.30-2/7-10, Closed L Sat **Prices:** Fixed L £20-£25, Fixed D £25-£30, Starter £5.50-£9, Main £12.50-£20, Dessert £6.50-£9.50, Coffee £3, Min/Water £3.05, Service optional **Wine:** 48 bottles over £20, 12 by the glass (£3.15-£5.50) **Notes:** Sun L from £19.50, Vegetarian available, Civ Wed 100 **Seats:** 100, Pr/dining room 140 **Smoking:** N/Sm in restaurant **Children:** Menu, Portions **Rooms:** 109 (109 en suite) ★★★★ **Directions:** M4 junct 13, follow A339 to Newbury for 2m, then take the A4 (Reading), the hotel is signed **Parking:** 210

The Vineyard at Stockcross

see page 38

READING MAP 05 SU77

Forburys Restaurant

French New NEW

Contemporary restaurant in a new area around Forbury Park

☎ 0118 957 4044/0118 956 9191 1 Forbury Square, The Forbury RG1 3BB
e-mail: forburys@btconnect.com
web: www.forburys.com

Designed by the same architect responsible for Canary Wharf, the building has floor-to-ceiling windows which afford great views on to a piazza and an area cordoned off for outside dining. Great jars of the restaurant's wares line a shelf set against the glass. The colour scheme within is sand and cream with brown leather seating and oak floors; the walls relieved by blown-up big name wine labels. There's space enough, too, for a contemporary-style bar in stainless steel and brown leather. Cooking is French influenced and some dishes have a rustic touch, such as a wonderfully tender dish of pig's trotter with caramelised calves' sweetbreads, morels, cream mash and Madeira jus.

Chef: Jose Cau **Owners:** Xavier Le-Bellego **Times:** 12-2.15/6-10, Closed 26-28 Dec, 1-2 Jan, Closed D Sun **Prices:** Fixed L £15-£18, Fixed D £18-£23, Starter £7-£11, Main £12.50-£22.50, Dessert £5.50-£7.95, Coffee £2, Min/Water £3.50, Service optional, Group min 4 service 12.5% **Wine:** 130 bottles over £20, 11 bottles under £20, 9 by the glass (£3.85-£10.50) **Notes:** Market menu available Mon-Sat L, Mon-Fri D, Vegetarian available **Seats:** 70, Pr/dining room 16 **Smoking:** N/Sm in restaurant, Air con **Children:** Min 8 yrs, Portions **Directions:** M4 junct 11, 3m to town centre, opposite Forbury Gardens **Parking:** 40

Millennium Madejski Hotel Reading

French

Contemporary food in striking, modern stadium complex

☎ 0118 925 3500 Madejski Stadium RG2 0FL
e-mail: sales.reading@mill-cop.com
web: www.millennium-hotels.com

Part of the Madejski Stadium complex that houses Reading Football Club and London Irish Rugby Club, the Cilantro is a stylish, modern restaurant serving contemporary French dishes. The buzzy atmosphere is made more enjoyable by the friendly and efficient service. Have an aperitif in the Atrium bar before trying starters of warm aubergine and goat's cheese fondant or red mullet fillet with pistachio and date crumble. Main courses might include wild mushroom cannelloni with celeriac and chive purée or John Dory poached in milk and cardamom. Crunchy peanut parfait, pear Tatin or chocolate fondant with Guinness ice cream brings the meal to a close. Menu gourmand and vegetarian menu gourmand also available.

continued

Millennium Madejski Hotel

Chef: John O'Reilly **Owners:** Madejski Hotel Co **Times:** 7-10, Closed 25 Dec, 1 Jan, BHs, Sun, Closed L all week **Prices:** Fixed D fr £45, Coffee £3.50, Min/Water £3.85, Service optional **Wine:** 60 bottles over £20, 34 bottles under £20, 13 by the glass (£3.50-£8.95) **Notes:** Tasting menu £49.50, Vegetarian available, Dress Restrictions, Smart casual **Seats:** 55, Pr/dining room 12 **Smoking:** N/Sm in restaurant, Air con **Children:** Min 12 yrs, Portions **Rooms:** 140 (140 en suite) ★★★★ **Directions:** 1m N from M4 junct 11. 2m S from Reading town centre **Parking:** 100

Loch Fyne Restaurant

☎ 0118 918 5850 The Maltings, Bear Wharf, Fobney St RG1 6BT

Quality seafood chain.

LSQ2 Bar and Brasserie

☎ 0118 987 3702 Lime Square, 220 South Oak Way, Green Park RG2 6UP

Modern British fare in business park location.

Pepe Sale

☎ 0118 959 7700 3 Queens Walk RG1 7QF

Buzzing Italian/Sardinian.

SHINFIELD MAP 05 SU76

L'Ortolan

see page 39

England

The Vineyard at Stockcross

NEWBURY MAP 05 SU46

Modern French

Superb blend of innovation and tradition in the kitchen and setting

☎ 01635 528770 Stockcross RG20 8JU
e-mail: general@the-vineyard.co.uk
web: www.the-vineyard.co.uk

Chef: John Campbell
Owners: Sir Peter Michael
Times: 12-2/7-9.45
Prices: Fixed L £22-£50, Fixed D £35-£60, Coffee £4.25, Min/Water £3.75, Service optional
Wine: 1900 bottles over £20, 60 bottles under £20, 20 by the glass
Notes: Tasting menu £75, Vegetarian available, Civ Wed 60
Seats: 70, Pr/dining room 60
Smoking: N/Sm in restaurant, Air con
Children: Menu, Portions
Rooms: 49 (49 en suite)
★★★★★
Directions: M4 junct 13 join A34 Newbury by-pass southbound, take 3rd exit signed Hungerford/Bath road interchange. Take 2nd exit at 1st and 2nd rdbt signed Stockcross, 0.6 mile on right
Parking: 100

A dramatic steel grapevine balustrade wraps its way around the bright, stylish, split-level dining room at The Vineyard, a nod to the contemporary hotel's name. Oddly, there's actually no vineyard here at Stockcross, it takes its name and inspiration from proprietor Sir Peter Michael's winery in California. But, there are two dazzling wine lists; one magnificent tome devoted appropriately to California, the other volume takes on the rest of the world. However, this little slice of California in the Berkshire countryside is nothing if not individual, mixing the contemporary with a dash of country-house décor, and, its ultimate jewel in the crown, the platform for renowned chef John Campbell's inspired modern cuisine.

Opulence reigns at this plush modern venue, though it's not over the top, with calming colours and a pleasing sense of space. Art and sculpture are another important facet of The Vineyard experience, as demonstrated by the contemporary 'Fire and Water' sculpture outside, which makes a dramatic statement, especially at night, with its flaming torches set on a large pond. Public areas provide the backcloth for a fine art collection, and there are two comfortable lounges for aperitifs or coffee. Service is expectedly slick and professional but with a friendly touch, while dining tables are attractively set in homage to John Campbell's poised, contemporary and striking cooking.

Campbell's style is based on the state-of-the-art scientific approach, delivering an exciting blend of flavours, textures and top-notch ingredients. So expect innovative and visually striking dishes to thrill the palate and senses; think roast saddle of lamb teamed with a risotto of peas and single-bean chocolate and, to close, perhaps a brûlée of strawberry with black olives and Pedro Ximenez jelly.

England

L'Ortolan

SHINFIELD MAP 05 SU76

French, British

Serious fine dining in stylish listed building

☎ 01189 888 500 Church Ln RG2 9BY
e-mail: info@lortolan.com
web: www.lortolan.com

This red-brick, 17th-century former vicarage will be familiar to many foodies from its previous incarnations, receiving past acclaim under the likes of Nico Ladenis and more recently John Burton-Race. Today's highly talented incumbent, Alan Murchison, is a worthy successor, having in fact worked with Burton-Race and also the likes of Raymond Blanc in the past. His modern French-focused cuisine - underpinned by classical foundations - now drawing its own plaudits. L'Ortolan's interior under Murchison is an altogether modern, design-focused affair, cool and sophisticated, stylish and uncluttered, the long dining room enhanced by a conservatory and small bar, while two first-floor private dining rooms complement the package further, alongside confident, professional and friendly service.

The kitchen focuses on high-quality seasonal produce, delivering via excellent-value lunch jour, plus an appealing carte and seven-course gourmand offering. Clean, refined flavours, interesting combinations, polished presentation and high skill feature in sometimes complex dishes; think sea bass served with confit fennel, roasted scallops and a red wine sauce, and pistachio and chocolate soufflé with a chocolate sorbet finish. Peripherals like excellent breads and amuse-bouche deliver with style, too.

Chef: Alan Murchison
Times: 11.45-2/7-10, Closed Xmas & New Year, Mon/Sun
Prices: Fixed L fr £49, Fixed D fr £55, Starter fr £15, Main fr £30, Dessert fr £10, Service added but optional
Notes: Vegetarian available, Civ Wed 50
Seats: 64, Pr/dining room 20
Smoking: N/Sm in restaurant
Children: Menu, Portions
Directions: From M4 junct 11 take A33 towards Basingstoke. At 1st rdbt turn left, after garage turn left, 1m turn right at Six Bells pub. Restaurant 1st left (follow English Tourist Board Signs)
Parking: 45

England

SLOUGH *continued* MAP 06 SU97

The Pinewood Hotel

Modern European NEW

Simple but appealing dining in newly completed, modern hotel

☎ 01753 824848 Uxbridge Rd, George Green SL3 6AP
e-mail: info@pinewoodhotel.co.uk
web: www.bespokehotels.com

This recently completed small luxury hotel is just outside Slough. Striking design is backed up with good levels of comfort and modern facilities. The Eden Brasserie specialises in European dishes cooked on a wood-burning oven and stove. Start with Portobello mushrooms stuffed with dolcelatte and sun-dried tomato or scallops wrapped in pancetta before a main course roast lamb rump with celeriac mash and red wine jus or the delicious beef fillet with red berry jus and rösti. Finish with orange and chocolate torte.

Times: 12.00-3.00/6.00-10.00 **Rooms:** 49 (49 en suite) ★★★ HL **Directions:** Telephone for directions

SONNING MAP 05 SU77

The French Horn

Traditional French V NOTABLE WINE LIST

Classical dining on the Thames

☎ 0118 969 2204 RG4 6TN
e-mail: info@thefrenchhorn.co.uk
web: www.thefrenchhorn.co.uk

Nestled on the banks of a sleepy stretch of the Thames, this restaurant has a long-standing reputation for quality cuisine. Take a drink in the cosy bar where a spit-roast duck turns above the fire promising good things to come, and then move through to the elegant dining room where you'll find tables set with quality ware, many with views of the river. A classical menu suits the formal setting; start with foie gras terrine with marinated baby figs perhaps, and then tuck into lobster thermidor, Chateaubriand or lamb with mint sauce and redcurrant jelly.
Notable Wine List: A classic wine list with many fine growers.

Chef: G Company **Owners:** Emmanuel Family **Times:** 12-1.45/7-9.15, Closed 26-30 Dec **Prices:** Fixed L £24, Fixed D £40, Starter fr £11, Main £25.50-£37, Dessert £11, Coffee £4.50, Min/Water £3.70, Service included **Wine:** 550 bottles over £20, 5 bottles under £20, 8 by the glass (£6-£16.50) **Notes:** Vegetarian menu, Dress Restrictions, No shorts **Seats:** 70, Pr/dining room 24 **Smoking:** No pipes, No cigars **Children:** Portions **Rooms:** 21 (21 en suite) ★★★ HL **Directions:** A4 into Sonning. Follow B478 through village over bridge, hotel on right, car park on left **Parking:** 40

STREATLEY MAP 05 SU58

The Swan at Streatley

British, International

Thames-side fine-dining hotel restaurant

☎ 01491 878800 High St RG8 9HR
e-mail: sales@swan-at-streatley.co.uk
web: www.swanatstreatley.co.uk

This 17th-century inn was one of the original inns established to service the ferry crossings before the Goring bridge was built; it also has a literary claim to fame as it was here that Jerome K. Jerome wrote *Three Men in a Boat*. These days it still enjoys the beautiful Thameside location and the Cygnetures restaurant offers a relaxed venue to dine in while enjoying the spectacular river views. The menu draws on modern British, European and international cooking and is complemented by a well-chosen wine list. Try a starter like cappuccino of wild mushrooms with white truffle oil, followed by a main course of roast monkfish with herb tagliatelle, English oysters, Hendred vineyard wine and parsley oil.

Owners: John Nike Group **Times:** 12.30-2/7-10 **Prices:** Fixed L £15-£18, Fixed D £28-£32.50, Starter £6.50-£9.50, Main £19.95-£25, Dessert £6.50-£13.50, Coffee £3.50, Min/Water £3.50, Service optional **Wine:** 50 bottles over £20, 20 bottles under £20, 11 by the glass (£3.50-£10.50) **Notes:** Sun L 3 courses £18, Vegetarian available, Dress Restrictions, Smart casual, Civ Wed 150 **Seats:** 70, Pr/dining room 130 **Smoking:** N/Sm in restaurant **Children:** Menu, Portions **Rooms:** 46 (46 en suite) ★★★★ **Directions:** Follow A329 from Pangbourne, on entering Streatley turn right at lights. Hotel on left before bridge **Parking:** 120

WINDSOR MAP 06 SU97

Macdonald Castle Hotel

International

Fine dining in centrally located hotel with castle views

☎ 0870 4008300 High St SL4 1LJ
e-mail: castle@macdonald-hotels.co.uk
web: www.macdonaldhotels.co.uk/castle

This former coaching inn, dating from the 16th century, is prominently situated opposite Sir Christopher Wren's Guildhall, with fine views of Windsor Castle. The hotel is popular for functions and weddings from small dinners up to formal evening balls. The elegant restaurant has been newly refurbished in contemporary style in shades of aubergine and soft beige and offers comprehensive modern international cuisine. These make good use of the finest seasonal produce, sourced from a range of suppliers countrywide. Cooking is thoughtful and innovative with a variety of classical dishes and modern interpretations, complemented by an extensive wine list. Expect dishes such as marbled foie gras terrine with quince millefeuille, and monkfish tail on herbed saffron rice and creamy curried mussel bouillabaisse.

Times: 12-2.30/6.30-9.45 **Rooms:** 108 (108 en suite) ★★★ **Directions:** M25 junct 13 take A308 towards Windsor Town Centre then onto B470 to High St. M4 junct 6 towards A332, at rdbt first exit into Clarence Rd, left at lights to High St

Sir Christopher Wren's House Hotel & Spa

French, Mediterranean

Relaxed fine dining with unbeatable views

☎ 01753 861354 Thames St SL4 1PX
e-mail: reservations@wrensgroup.com
web: www.sirchristopherwren.co.uk

Wren himself may well have approved of the Thames-side views from Strok's Restaurant - overlooking Eton Bridge - at his one-time home; watch the sun set behind the riverbank trees from the champagne terrace. Soft downlights, flickering candles, modern and contemporary with a hint of traditional elegance is the style. The European menu with Mediterranean twists takes a modern approach from classical influences. Quality ingredients meet skilful, balanced dishes with understated presentation on a carte of one-priced starters, mains and desserts, save a few supplements, while a six-course tasting and fixed-

continued

price lunch and pre-theatre menu completes an upbeat package. Rabbit leg with roasted foie gras, sweet grapes and a truffle cigar is a fine example of the fare.

Sir Christopher Wren's House Hotel & Spa

Chef: Stephen Boucher **Owners:** The Wrens Hotel Group **Times:** 12.30-2.30/6.30-10 **Prices:** Fixed L £18.50-£21.50, Fixed D £25-£28.50, Starter £8.50-£11.50, Main £17.50-£29.50, Dessert £6.50-£10, Coffee £3.20, Min/Water £3.50, Service added but optional 12.5% **Wine:** 50 bottles over £20, 11 bottles under £20, 7 by the glass (£4.50-£7.50) **Notes:** Tasting menu 6 courses £39.50, Sun L £24.95, Vegetarian available, Dress Restrictions, Smart casual preferred, Civ Wed 90 **Seats:** 60, Pr/dining room 90 **Smoking:** N/Sm in restaurant, Air con **Children:** Menu, Portions **Rooms:** 90 (90 en suite) ★★★★ **Directions:** Telephone for directions **Parking:** 14

Thai Square

☎ 01753 868900 29 Thames St SL4 1PR
web: www.theaa.com/restaurants/113891.html

In a prime position opposite the famous castle, and with décor that combines the best of modern European and Thai design with traditional Thai artefacts. Warm, charming service.

YATTENDON MAP 05 SU57

Royal Oak Hotel

Modern European

Top-notch cuisine and a setting to suit all occasions

☎ 01635 201325 The Square RG18 0UG
e-mail: info@royaloakyattendon.com
web: www.royaloakyattendon.com

Nestled in a pretty Berkshire village within easy reach of the M4, this 16th-century inn delivers the same tempting menu in a choice of settings, boasting a relaxed brasserie, a formal restaurant and a walled garden for alfresco dining in summer. Rooted in traditional English cooking, its accomplished mains are simple but innovative creations which make the most of local produce - poached fillet of cod in lettuce with champagne sauce, bubble-and-squeak and asparagus perhaps, or roast supreme of duck with black pudding, sauté potatoes, caramelised apple and a parsley and cider sauce - while indulgent desserts might include chocolate crème brûlée with mint sorbet, or roast figs and brown sugar parfait with port wine syrup.

Chef: Anton Barbarovie **Owners:** William Boyle **Times:** 12-2.15/7-10, Closed 1 Jan **Prices:** Fixed L £12, Starter £6-£7, Main £12.75-£16.75, Dessert £5.95-£7.25, Coffee £2, Min/Water £2.95, Service added but optional 10% **Wine:** 41 bottles over £20, 18 bottles under £20, 6 by the glass (£3.70-£6.50) **Notes:** Sun L 2 courses £19.50, 3 courses £23.50, Dress Restrictions, Smart casual preferred **Seats:** 60, Pr/dining room 10 **Smoking:** N/Sm in restaurant **Children:** Portions **Rooms:** 5 (5 en suite) ★★ HL **Directions:** M4 junct 12, follow signs to Pangbourne, left to Yattendon, or M4 junct 13 follow signs to Hermitage, after Post Office turn right to Yattendon **Parking:** 25

BRISTOL

BRISTOL MAP 04 ST57

Arno's Manor Hotel

British, Mediterranean

Atmospheric hotel dining

☎ 0117 971 1461 470 Bath Rd, Arno's Vale BS4 3HQ
e-mail: arnos.manor@forestdale.com
web: www.forestdale.com

This historic 18th-century hotel was once the home of a wealthy merchant. The chapel has been transformed into a comfortable lounge and the refurbished restaurant is housed in an atmospheric conservatory-style area, created by placing a glass-domed roof over an internal courtyard. The menu is lengthy and features popular favourites alongside modern British fare. You might find starters like duck confit salad with beetroot dressing, and main courses like venison with Brussels sprout purée with port and pancetta sauce.

Times: 7-10 **Rooms:** 73 (73 en suite) ★★★ HL

Bells Diner

Modern European

Inventive European cuisine in rustic surroundings

☎ 0117 924 0357 1-3 York Rd, Montpellier BS6 5QB
e-mail: info@bellsdiner.com
web: www.bellsdiner.com

Now celebrating thirty years as Bells Diner, the former grocery shop at the heart of one of Bristol's oldest districts continues to serve a loyal clientele. The intimate, rustic restaurant retains some of the original shop fittings and shaker-style décor. Inventive European cooking remains the central focus with classic flavour combinations using modern and traditional techniques. Investment in new equipment reflects the owner's commitment to developing and evolving the menu to the highest standard. Typical dishes might include a starter of quail jelly consommé, tea smoked quail breast, pea shoots and peanuts. For a main course try rump of lamb with sweet potato, beetroot, onion soubise and liquorice. Surprising desserts include coconut delice with vindaloo ice cream and poppadom tuile.

Chef: Christopher Wicks **Owners:** Christopher Wicks **Times:** 12-2.30/7-10.30, Closed 24-30 Dec, Sun, Closed L Mon & Sat **Prices:** Starter £6.50-£9.50, Main £14.50-£18.50, Dessert £6.50-£12.50, Coffee £1.60, Min/Water £3, Service added but optional 10% **Wine:** 113 bottles over £20, 17 bottles under £20, 13 by the glass (£3.50-£7.50) **Notes:** 8 course tasting menu £45, Dress Restrictions **Seats:** 60 **Smoking:** N/Sm in restaurant **Children:** Portions **Directions:** Telephone for further details **Parking:** On street

BRISTOL *continued* MAP 04 ST57

City Café

European

Simple modern cuisine in a great central location

☎ 0117 925 1001 City Inn Bristol, Temple Way BS1 6BF
e-mail: bristol.reservations@cityinn.com
web: www.cityinn.com

This popular central hotel has a bustling café and lovely terrace for alfresco dining in summer. The menu is arranged in three sections with a formal à la carte option offering dishes like market fish of the day or grilled fillet of Welsh beef with chunky chips, tomato compote and balsamic jus. The simple fixed price kitchen menu and vegetarian garden menu offer similar dishes, such as twice baked spinach and Welsh cheese soufflé to start, or a main course like Welsh Black beef and ale stew or aubergine and confit tomato lasagne. City Café cuisine offers Sunday brunch from 1-2.30 every week.

Times: 12-2.30/6-10.30 **Rooms:** 167 (167 en suite) ★★★ HL

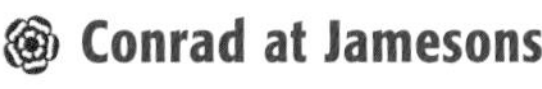

Conrad at Jamesons

Modern British

Busy modern bistro with good choice of menus

☎ 0117 927 6565 Upper Maudlin St BS2 8BJ
e-mail: info@conradatjamesons.co.uk
web: www.conradatjamesons.co.uk

Close to the city centre, Conrad's is a modern, friendly and relaxed bistro-style operation with a vibrant atmosphere. High ceilings, full-length windows, white-clothed tables and a range of four distinct seating areas - providing space for groups as well as intimate couples - prove a feature of this popular, split-level restaurant. The cooking follows the modern approach via a variety of menus options, with fish fresh brought in daily from the Cornish ports. Think pan-fried swordfish steak with lime and coriander cream, or perhaps a fillet of Aberdeen Angus beef served with spinach, potato galette, foie gras and a Périgord jus.

Chef: C Lynton-Jenkins & P Salmon **Owners:** Conrad & Simon Lynton-Jenkins **Times:** noon/mdnt **Prices:** Fixed L £10.20-£17.95, Fixed D £15.95-£24.95, Starter £6.75-£8.95, Main £14.50-£18.95, Dessert £5.25-£5.95, Coffee £1.95, Min/Water £2.95, Service optional, Group min 10 service 10% **Wine:** 25 bottles over £20, 19 bottles under £20, 15 by the glass (£3.75-£6.75) **Notes:** Sun L & Express L available, Vegetarian available **Seats:** 95, Pr/dining room 25 **Smoking:** N/Sm area, No pipes, No cigars **Children:** Portions **Directions:** Opposite childrens hospital and BRI **Parking:** NCP & on street

Culinaria

Traditional Mediterranean

Simple, popular concept, Mediterranean cuisine to eat in or takeaway

☎ 0117 973 7999 1 Chandos Rd, Redland BS6 6PG
web: www.culinariabristol.co.uk

Culinaria is a great concept combining the popularity of restaurant dining with the takeaway option of enjoying a meal in your own home. The traditional bistro restaurant serves simple, beautifully executed dishes in a contemporary setting, while in another room the deli and takeaway serve a growing customer base, offering chilled and frozen dishes to warm at home. Mediterranean-style cooking sees classics like Provençal fish soup to start. Main courses range from pan-fried scallops with sun-dried tomato risotto to grilled fillet of halibut with roasted fennel and red pepper sauce. The menus change weekly and are updated on the restaurant website so it's easy to see what's on offer either to eat in or take away.

Chef: Stephen Markwick **Owners:** Stephen & Judy Markwick **Times:** 12-2/6.30-9.30, Closed Xmas, New Year, BHs, Sun-Tue, Closed L Wed-Thur **Prices:** Starter £5.95-£7.50, Main £11.50-£14.50, Dessert £5.95-£6.25, Coffee £1.65, Min/Water £2.85, Service optional **Wine:** 13 bottles over £20, 22 bottles under £20, 4 by the glass (£2.75-£3.50) **Notes:** Vegetarian available **Seats:** 30 **Smoking:** N/Sm in restaurant **Children:** Portions **Parking:** On street

Glass Boat Restaurant

British, European

Accurate cooking in a unique riverside setting

☎ 0117 929 0704 Welsh Back BS1 4SB
e-mail: bookings@glassboat.co.uk
web: www.glassboat.co.uk

The name sums it up; a glass-topped barge - anchored in the city centre's historic docks close to the famous Bristol Bridge - proves a popular draw for lunch or romantic candlelit dinner to the backdrop of waterfront life. Original wooden floors, simple table settings and nicely worn fixtures offer further character. The crowd-pleasing, modern-focused menu comes awash with the flavour of the Mediterranean, the cooking honest and appealing, and service friendly and efficient. The menu may include roast breast of duck on creamed polenta with crispy leek and red wine sauce, or roasted monkfish Bourguignon style.

Chef: Matthew Woods **Owners:** Arne Ringer **Times:** 12-2.30/6.30-11, Closed 24-26 Dec, 1 Jan, Sun, Closed L Sat **Prices:** Fixed L £10.95-£21, Fixed D £22.50-£24.95, Starter £4.50-£8.25, Main £13.50-£19.95, Dessert £5.75-£6.50, Coffee £1.85, Min/Water £2.95, Service added but optional 10% **Wine:** 94 bottles over £20, 43 bottles under £20, 8 by the glass (£3-£4.60) **Notes:** Vegetarian available, Civ Wed 100 **Seats:** 120, Pr/dining room 40 **Smoking:** N/Sm in restaurant, Air con **Directions:** Moored below Bristol Bridge in the old centre of Bristol **Parking:** NCP

continued

Hotel du Vin & Bistro

French, European NOTABLE WINE LIST

Relaxed and friendly French bistro style

☎ 0117 925 5577 The Sugar House, Narrow Lewins Mead BS1 2NU
e-mail: info@bristol.hotelduvin.com
web: www.hotelduvin.com

This city-centre hotel is housed in a Grade II listed converted 18th-century sugar refinery. The bistro-style restaurant has a pleasant, lively feel and is very popular so be sure to book ahead. The menu includes a good selection of vegetarian options and a 'simple classics' selection offering favourites like calves' liver and baby onions and moules marinière. All the dishes show attention to detail and good quality ingredients. Typical mains might include poached smoked haddock with sun blushed tomato and basil risotto. Naturally, the extensive wine list is a highlight.
Notable Wine List: A key hallmark of all Hotels du Vin is the extensive wine list, packed full of interest and high quality wines.

Chef: Marcus Lang **Owners:** Hotel du Vin Ltd **Times:** 12-2/6-10 **Prices:** Fixed L £15, Starter £6.50-£7.50, Main £12.50-£14.50, Dessert £6.75, Coffee £2.75, Min/Water £3, Service optional, Group min 12 service 10% **Wine:** 600 bottles over £20, 50 bottles under £20, 10 by the glass (£3.50-£6.80) **Notes:** Sun L 3 courses £22.50, Vegetarian available **Seats:** 85, Pr/dining room 72 **Smoking:** N/Sm in restaurant, Air con **Children:** Menu, Portions **Rooms:** 40 (40 en suite) ★★★★ TH **Directions:** From M4 junct 19, M32 into Bristol. With Bentalls on left take right lane at next lights. Turn right onto opposite side of carriageway. Hotel 200yds in side road **Parking:** 20

riverstation

Modern European

Riverside location for excellent European cooking

☎ 0117 914 4434 The Grove BS1 4RB
e-mail: relax@riverstation.co.uk
web: www.riverstation.co.uk

On the water's edge, this chic restaurant is decked out in contemporary style with lots of glass, wood and steel. Downstairs there is a popular café/deli serving light meals and hot and cold snacks, while upstairs the airy restaurant caters to a smarter business crowd. In summer you can watch the busy river from a balcony table outside. The modern European menu offers good quality fresh food, simply prepared. Flavours are beautifully combined in dishes like crab and ginger ravioli with tomato and saffron salsa, while desserts such as blackcurrant and port jelly with macaroons are well worth leaving room for.

Chef: Peter Taylor, Ross Wills **Owners:** J Payne, P Taylor **Times:** 12-2.30/6-10.30, Closed Xmas, 1 Jan **Prices:** Fixed L fr £12, Starter £6-£10.50, Main £12-£18, Dessert £4.50-£6.50, Coffee £1.70, Min/Water £2, Service optional, Group min 8 service 10% **Wine:** 50 bottles over £20, 16 bottles under £20, 10 by the glass (£3.50-£9.50) **Notes:** Sun L 2 course £15.50, 3 course £18.75 **Seats:** 120 **Smoking:** N/Sm in restaurant **Children:** Portions **Directions:** On the dock side in central Bristol **Parking:** Pay & display, meter parking opposite

Michael Caines at The Bristol Marriott Royal

BRISTOL MAP 04 ST57

Modern French

Stylish dining on a grand scale

Rosettes not confirmed at time of going to press

☎ 0117 925 5100 College Green BS1 5TA
e-mail: bristol.royal@marriotthotels.co.uk
web: www.marriott.co.uk

Right in the city centre, next to the Cathedral, this stunning hotel has an array of impressive facilities including a leisure club, spa, informal Terrace and the more formal Michael Caines restaurant, adjacent to the champagne bar in the grand Palm Court of the hotel. Opulent surroundings are created amongst Greek statues, old paintings, gold upholstered seats and amazing architecture that combines Bath stone pillars with arches, balconies and a stained-glass ceiling. Professional staff offer a warm welcome, creating a relaxed environment despite the grandeur of the setting.
Head Chef Ian Matfin produces consistently high quality dishes with the finest ingredients handled with much care and respect. Dishes are kept simple with the emphasis on clarity of flavour and texture, allowing the main ingredients to shine through. Produce is carefully sourced using local suppliers where possible. Menu options vary throughout the week and include a tasting menu, set lunches, pre-theatre dinners on Saturdays and a full carte. High-quality canapés include parsnip shavings and mini fillet of beef. Starters like a classic wild mushroom risotto with fresh parmesan are accurately cooked and full of flavour. Main courses offer the likes of roast breast of guinea fowl, melting in the mouth, with a selection of baby vegetables and a light white wine sauce. A Chef's special dessert entitled 'Memories of childhood' is a very imaginative collection of four mini desserts in individual glasses.

As we went to print, there were changes to the restaurant concept.

Chef: Ian Matfin **Times:** 12-2.30/7-10, Closed Sun, Mon, BHs **Prices:** Fixed L fr £17.50, Starter £7-£13.50, Main £12-£25, Dessert £6-£12, Coffee £3.95 **Notes:** Vegetarian available, Dress Restrictions, Smart casual **Seats:** 60, Pr/dining room 12 **Smoking:** N/Sm in restaurant **Children:** Min 12 yrs **Rooms:** 242 (242 en suite) ★★★★ HL **Directions:** Next to cathedral by College Green **Parking:** 200

BRISTOL *continued* MAP 04 ST57

The Boars Head

☎ 01454 632278 The Main Rd, Aust BS35 4AX

Cosy candlelit pub with delightful ambience serving very good fresh fish dishes and excellent Sunday lunch.

Howards Restaurant

☎ 0117 926 2921 1a - 2a Avon Crescent, Hotwells BS1 6XQ

Lively restaurant, with an easy flair, offering a well-priced bistro menu.

BUCKINGHAMSHIRE

AMERSHAM MAP 06 SU99

®® The Artichoke

Modern French V

Smart high street restaurant with refined cooking

☎ 01494 726611 9 Market Square, Old Amersham HP7 0DF
e-mail: info@theartichokerestaurant.co.uk
web: www.theartichokerestaurant.co.uk

Situated in an attractive market square, this unfussy, cottage-style restaurant occupies a charming 16th-century, Grade II listed building. The stylish interior is all muted natural colours and good-quality Italian leather furniture. It has a warm, comfortable ambience. A tiny courtyard offers alfresco dining in summer. Service is formal and well briefed. Modern French dishes using high-quality local and seasonal ingredients are notable for innovative combinations and good saucing. An amuse-bouche of cucumber and mascarpone is followed by ravioli of confit quail, toasted hazelnut, parsley and sage beurre noisette and a main course of veal fillet, herb gnocchi, sweetbreads and black truffle sauce. Coffee and chocolate tart with lavender ice cream to finish.

Chef: Laurie Gear **Owners:** Laurie & Jacquline Gear **Times:** 12-2/6.45-10, Closed 1 wk Xmas, 2 wks Aug BH, 1 wk Apr, Sun, Mon **Prices:** Fixed L £18.50, Fixed D £32.50, Starter £8-£11, Main £12-£18, Dessert £6.50, Coffee £3.50, Min/Water £3, Service added but optional 12.5% **Wine:** 42 bottles over £20, 16 bottles under £20, 6 by the glass (£5-£7) **Notes:** Tasting menu 7 courses £49, Vegetarian menu, Smart casual **Seats:** 25 **Smoking:** N/Sm in restaurant **Children:** Portions **Directions:** M40 junct 2. 1m from Amersham New Town **Parking:** On street, nearby car park

® The Plough

Modern European NEW

Modern gastro-pub with classic dishes

☎ 01494 721001 Winchcombe Hill HP7 0PA

The whitewashed stone frontage hides an interior that mixes contemporary décor with older architectural features. There is a comfortable bar with cream leather chairs, while the split-level dining area has neutral walls, small flagstone floors and bright artwork. The tables are well spaced with high-back chairs and good quality settings, and service is relaxed and attentive. The cooking style is brasserie style with classic dishes given modern presentation. Start with the ham hock terrine with apple purée. Follow with the crispy-skinned roast chicken served with baby onion jus, potato purée and pancetta. Finish with a rhubarb tart with vanilla ice cream.

Times: 12-2.30/6.30-9.30, Closed D Sun **Prices:** Food prices not confirmed for 2007. Please telephone for details **Directions:** Telephone for directions

AYLESBURY MAP 11 SP81

®®® Hartwell House Hotel Restaurant & Spa

see page 45

BLETCHLEY MAP 11 SP83

® The Crooked Billet

Modern British NOTABLE WINE LIST

Popular village pub serious about its food

☎ 01908 373936 2 Westbrook End, Newton Longville MK17 0DF
e-mail: john@thebillet.co.uk
web: www.thebillet.co.uk

A thatched village pub with a separate restaurant, originally built around 1665 as a farmhouse, and the oak beams and wooden floors remain. Informal dining takes place in the pub area at lunchtime when the menu offers a range of sandwiches, salads and pastas plus some traditional pub dishes. The dinner menu offers a weightier selection, prepared from seasonal ingredients; the produce arrives fresh each morning from local and national suppliers. The cheeseboard is particularly noteworthy with choices from Longman Dairy and individual UK cheesemakers. All this is complemented by a very fine wine list and an enormous selection of wines by the glass.

Notable Wine List: An award-winning wine list which starts with a wine and food recommendation section followed by high quality selections in each wine area.

Chef: Emma Gilchrist **Owners:** John & Emma Gilchrist **Times:** 12.30-2.30/7-10.30, Closed 25-26 Dec, Closed L Mon-Sat, D Sun **Prices:** Starter £4-£11, Main £8-£25, Dessert £4-£10, Coffee £1.95, Min/Water £1.95, Service optional **Wine:** 300 bottles over £20, 30 bottles under £20, 300 by the glass (£2.95-£200) **Notes:** Tasting Menu 8 courses £50-£60, with wine £70-£80, Vegetarian available **Seats:** 50 **Smoking:** N/Sm in restaurant

continued

Hartwell House Hotel, Restaurant & Spa

AYLESBURY MAP 11 SP81

Modern European NOTABLE WINE LIST

An imposing setting for a special occasion or treat

☎ 01296 747444 Oxford Rd HP17 8NL
e-mail: info@hartwell-house.com
web: www.hartwell-house.com

This stateliest of stately homes played home to the exiled king of France Louis XVIII for many years in the early 19th century, but these days its magnificent public rooms and landscaped grounds are open to all. A dramatic Gothic hall and staircase with carved Jacobean figures set the scene, followed by a series of elegant day-rooms decorated with oak panelling, fine paintings and antiques.
The restaurant is a graceful, high-ceilinged affair and makes an understated backdrop for the talented kitchen's elaborate creations; expect thoughtful and imaginative cuisine with a classical foundation, distinguished by technical genius and quality ingredients. Pan-fried sea scallops are a typical starter, served with caramelised baby onions, a shallot purée and smoked bacon froth, while mains might include pan-roasted loin of wild venison with a chestnut mousse, celeriac fondant and braised red cabbage, or monkfish in pancetta on a provençale of tomato and fine beans. Take a stroll around the garden if there's time - as well as serpentine walks, a picturesque lake and 18th-century statues, they contain a luxurious spa with a buttery for light meals and snacks.
Notable Wine List: A traditional wine list with a comprehensive offering from all the major wine producing areas.

Chef: Daniel Richardson **Owners:** Historic House Hotels **Times:** 12.30-1.45/7.30-9.45 **Prices:** Fixed L £22, Fixed D £46, Min/Water £3.80, Service included **Wine:** 293 bottles over £20, 9 bottles under £20, 13 by the glass (£4.75-£7.50) **Notes:** Coffee incl, Tasting menu £65, Sun L £31, Vegetarian available, Dress Restrictions, Smart casual-no jeans, tracksuits or trainers, Civ Wed 60 **Seats:** 56, Pr/dining room 30 **Smoking:** N/Sm in restaurant **Children:** Min 6 yrs, Portions **Rooms:** 46 (46 en suite) ★★★★ HL **Directions:** 2m SW of Aylesbury on A418 (Oxford road) **Parking:** 50

Children: Portions **Directions:** M1 junct 14 follow A421 towards Buckingham. Turn left at Bottledump rdbt to Newton Longville. Restaurant on right as you enter the village **Parking:** 30

BUCKINGHAM MAP 11 SP63

Villiers Hotel Restaurant & Bar

Modern British

Stylish restaurant serving interesting modern cuisine

☎ 01280 822444 3 Castle St MK18 1BS
e-mail: buckingham@villiershotels.com
web: www.villiershotels.com/buckinghamshire

Originally a coaching inn, the hotel is steeped in history and has been tastefully modernised over the years. A completely new look sees the restaurant achieving a modern, brasserie style and feel. Simple modern cooking to match provides some classics, alongside some new and interesting combinations. Starters include a simple cream of cauliflower soup and more luxurious choices, like marbled terrine of foie gras with pear compôte and toasted brioche. Main courses might feature fillet of sea bass with oriental pak choi, creamed potatoes and red wine sauce, or a vegetarian alternative like a filo basket with tomato casserole and goat's cheese glazed with balsamic dressing. Try an unusual dessert like dark chocolate mousse with Turkish delight and orange blossom milkshake.

continued

Villiers Hotel Restaurant & Bar

Chef: Paul Stopps **Owners:** Oxfordshire Hotels Ltd **Times:** 12-2.30/6-9.30 **Prices:** Starter £3.50-£7.95, Main £9.95-£21, Dessert £4.95-£6.95, Coffee £1.50, Min/Water £2.50, Service optional **Wine:** 25 bottles over £20, 25 bottles under £20, 8 by the glass (£2.85-£3.95) **Notes:** Civ Wed 150 **Seats:** 55, Pr/dining room 150 **Smoking:** N/Sm in restaurant, Air con **Rooms:** 46 (46 en suite) ★★★★ HL **Directions:** Town centre - Castle Street is to the right of Town Hall near main square **Parking:** 46

DINTON MAP 05 SP71

La Chouette

Belgian NOTABLE WINE LIST

Charming, quirky Belgian restaurant

☎ 01296 747422 Westlington Green HP17 8UW

Set on the green in the delightful village of Dinton, this former pub is now a characterful, rustic-style Belgian restaurant. Original 16th-century features have been retained, including stone walls, wooden beams and a large inglenook fireplace. An interesting menu offers charming comments and humorous touches, like a 'surprise' dessert and a salad of Belgian grey shrimps, described as 'bloody good'. The fixed-price and tasting menus offer a range of traditional dishes using produce like wild pigeon, partridge, pheasant, wild duck with wild mushroom ('not bad, not bad') and Scottish red deer.

Notable Wine List: A wine list showing much knowledge and dedication throughout focusing purely on France with an impressive Rhone section.

Chef: Frederic Desmette **Owners:** M F Desmette **Times:** 12-2/7-9, Closed Sun, Closed L Sat **Prices:** Fixed L fr £13.50, Fixed D £29.80, Starter £9-£16, Main £13.50-£17, Dessert £4.85-£7, Coffee £2, Min/Water £4.50, Service added but optional 12.5% **Wine:** 300 bottles over £20, 3 bottles under £20, 2 by the glass (£3) **Notes:** Fixed L 3 courses, Fixed D 4 courses, 5 courses £36.50, Vegetarian available **Seats:** 35 **Smoking:** N/Sm in restaurant **Children:** Portions **Directions:** On A418 at Dinton **Parking:** 20

GREAT MISSENDEN MAP 06 SP80

Annie Bailey's

Modern European

Ever-popular rural restaurant

☎ 01494 865625 Chesham Rd, Hyde End HP16 0QT
e-mail: david@anniebaileys.com
web: www.anniebaileys.com

Named after a local landlady from over 150 years ago, this is an informal and friendly place to seek out for a relaxing meal. A change of location and owners over the years has done little to diminish its popularity. Diners can expect a range of modern cuisine with some Mediterranean influences. Starters might include seared king scallops with pancetta and truffle vinaigrette, followed by herb-crusted cushion of lamb, sauté potatoes and baby vegetables. Be sure to leave enough room for the crunchie cheesecake.

Chef: Malcolm Nolan **Owners:** Open All Hours (UK) Ltd **Times:** 12-2.30/7-9.30, Closed D Sun **Prices:** Fixed L fr £12.50, Fixed D fr £16.50, Starter £4.50-£7.50, Main £8.95-£18.95, Dessert £4.50-£6, Coffee £2, Min/Water £2.50, Service optional **Wine:** 6 bottles over £20, 20 bottles under £20, 12 by the glass (£2.75-£7.50) **Notes:** Vegetarian available **Seats:** 65 **Smoking:** N/Sm in restaurant **Children:** Portions **Directions:** Off A413 at Great Missenden. On B485 towards Chesham **Parking:** 40

HADDENHAM MAP 05 SP70

Green Dragon

British

Quality food in a village inn atmosphere

☎ 01844 291403 8 Churchway HP17 8AA
e-mail: paul@eatatthedragon.co.uk
web: www.eatatthedragon.co.uk

The picturesque location of this 17th-century pub, close to the church and duck pond, has attracted several TV film crews. Although it is a gastro business, customers who just want a drink are welcome and the village beer is certainly worth sampling. Lunchtime options range from sandwiches to full meals, plus the popular Sunday lunch, and there's a simple dinner menu available on Tuesday and Thursday priced for two courses. Dishes from the full carte range from calves' liver and bacon to dry-aged prime fillet steak on the bone with traditional garnishes. Produce is generally locally sourced, apart from fresh fish from Devon, served within a day of being caught.

Times: 12-2/6.30-9.30, Closed 25 Dec & 1 Jan, Closed D Sun **Directions:** From M40 take A329 towards Thame, then A418. Turn 1st right after entering Haddenham

IVINGHOE MAP 11 SP91

The King's Head

Modern British V

Charming inn with bags of character

☎ 01296 668388 LU7 9EB
e-mail: info@kingsheadivinghoe.co.uk
web: www.kingsheadivinghoe.co.uk

This 17th century, ivy-clad inn is a former posting house and oozes olde worlde charm. The exposed beams, whitewashed walls and

continued

antiques add to the traditional feel, with open fireplaces in the cosy bar areas providing a comforting glow in winter months. The menu takes classic dishes and gives them a modern twist, with a refreshing simplicity to both the menu descriptions and to the food itself. Try terrine of guinea fowl with green bean salad and walnut and apricot toast to start, and a main of leg of lamb slow cooked in claret for seven hours.

The King's Head

Chef: Jonathan O'Keeffe **Owners:** G.A.P.J Ltd **Times:** 12-2.30/7-9.30, Closed 27-30 Dec, Closed D Sun **Prices:** Fixed L £19.50, Starter £7.50-£12.50, Main £18.50-£22.50, Dessert £6.95, Coffee £3.95, Min/Water £3.95, Service added but optional 12.5% **Wine:** 78 bottles over £20, 8 bottles under £20, 4 by the glass (£4-£5.50) **Notes:** Fixed L 3 courses, Vegetarian menu, Dress Restrictions, No jeans, trainers or shorts **Seats:** 55, Pr/dining room 40 **Smoking:** N/Sm in restaurant, Air con **Children:** Portions **Directions:** From M25 junct 20 take A41 past Tring. Turn right on to B488 (Ivinghoe), hotel at junction with B489 **Parking:** 20

LONG CRENDON MAP 05 SP60

The Angel Restaurant

Modern European, Pacific Rim

Gastro-pub with a friendly atmosphere

☎ 01844 208268 47 Bicester Rd HP18 9EE
e-mail: angelrestaurant@aol.com
web: www.angelrestaurant.co.uk

A 17th-century coaching inn turned gastro-pub; with original wattle and daub wall, exposed beams and fireplaces. Formal table service is managed by professional, attentive staff. The British menu has Mediterranean and Pacific Rim influences and includes imaginative dishes using local produce. Fish is a real feature with daily specials chalked up on the blackboard to take advantage of the latest catch. Try the likes of pan-seared fillet of sea trout on hot green vegetable salad with lobster vinaigrette. The wine list offers an extensive selection and a good choice of wines by the glass.

Chef: Trevor Bosch, Donald Joyce **Owners:** Trevor Bosch, Annie Bosch **Times:** 12-2.30/7-9.30, Closed D Sun **Prices:** Fixed L £20-£35, Starter £2.95-£6.95, Main £14-£24, Dessert £5, Coffee £2.95, Min/Water £3, Service optional **Notes:** Vegetarian available **Seats:** 75, Pr/dining room 14 **Smoking:** N/Sm area, Air con **Children:** Portions **Directions:** Beside B4011, 2m NW of Thame **Parking:** 30

MARLOW MAP 05 SU88

Danesfield House Hotel & Spa

see page 48

The Hand & Flowers

MARLOW MAP 05 SU88

Modern British NEW

Unpretentious gastro-pub offering first-rate cooking

☎ 01628 482277 SL7 2BP
web: www.thehandandflowers.co.uk

This white-washed pub on the outskirts of town may give a rather unassuming first impression, but the savvy know this place is a class act, with chef-patron Tom Kerridge at the stove (ex Adlard's in Norwich and Monsieur Max at Hampton) it has fine pedigree. Low beams and natural stone walls help retain that country-pub feel, with a few pieces of modern art thrown in to add a contemporary twist. Plain, solid-wood furniture (no cloths), subdued lighting and relaxed, friendly service from an enthusiastic young team (led by wife Beth), all help maintain the warm, cosy unstuffy atmosphere.

Tom's cooking is intelligently simple and elegant, with flavour and high skill top of his agenda. The style is modern-focused Anglo-French, with fresh, top-quality produce of the utmost importance, while presentation is equally simple and true to each dish. Expect the likes of tenderloin of Suffolk pork served with Toulouse sausage, Savoy cabbage and artichoke and truffle macaroni, with perhaps a glazed nutmeg tart with banana ice cream heading-up desserts. At lunchtimes a three-dish bar menu is also offered, while there's a patio for summer alfresco dining.

Chef: Tom Kerridge **Owners:** Tom & Beth Kerridge **Times:** 12-2.30/7-9.30, Closed 25-26 Dec, Closed D Sun **Prices:** Starter £4.50-£12, Main £15-£22, Dessert £6.50, Coffee £2, Min/Water £3, Service optional, Group min 6 service 10% **Wine:** 31 bottles over £20, 23 bottles under £20, 13 by the glass (£4-£4.75) **Seats:** 50 **Smoking:** N/Sm in restaurant
Children: Portions **Directions:** M40 junct 4/M4 junct 8/9 follow A404 to Marlow **Parking:** 30

England

Danesfield House Hotel & Spa

MARLOW MAP 05 SU88

Modern French

Stunning cuisine in fairytale surroundings

☎ 01628 891010 Henley Rd SL7 2EY
e-mail: sales@danesfieldhouse.co.uk
web: www.danesfieldhouse.co.uk

Overlooking the Thames in a fantastic location, Danesfield House is the third house to enjoy the magnificent view here since 1664, the present house was built in 1899 as a family home. Constructed of white stone with castellated towers, tall chimneys and raised terraces, it has all the hallmarks of a fairytale castle. The Oak Room Restaurant was redesigned with a light airy feel in 2005 by Anouska Hempel. The bleached wood panelling, soft shades of fawn and latte and top-notch napery give a luxurious yet relaxing impression as you enter. Nothing prepares you, however, for the dazzling culinary display.

The chef brings with him considerable experience as former Head Chef at Aikens (see entry) and his technical skill shines through. Cooking is exquisite, complex in style with modern French influences and very much in the mould of Tom Aikens. Stunning presentation and great use of different textures, skills and flavours ensure a real treat for the taste buds. Superb seasonality and luxury ingredients pepper the menu like jewels in a crown. A wonderful dish that exemplifies these techniques is the truffle risotto with white chocolate and roasted scallops. Beautifully presented, it seems a shame to bite into the perfectly seared scallop, but it bursts in the mouth and adds flavour to the creamy, loose rice, with the underlying richness of the chocolate and top-quality truffle. Once you've eaten here, you'll certainly want to repeat the experience.

Chef: Aiden Byrne
Owners: Danesfield House Hotel Ltd
Times: 12-2/7-10
Prices: Fixed L fr £20, Fixed D fr £49, Coffee £4.25, Service added but optional 12.5%
Notes: Tasting menu 8 courses £70, Vegetarian available, Dress Restrictions, Smart casual, jacket & tie, Civ Wed 100
Seats: 45, Pr/dining room 100
Smoking: N/Sm in restaurant
Children: Min 4 yrs, Menu, Portions
Rooms: 87 (87 en suite) ★★★★ HL
Directions: M4 junct 8/9 to Marlow. 2m from Marlow on A4155
Parking: 100

England

Macdonald Compleat Angler

MARLOW MAP 05 SU88

International

Assured cooking in formal restaurant overlooking the Thames

☎ 0870 400 8100 Marlow Bridge SL7 1RG
e-mail: general.compleatangler@macdonald-hotels.co.uk
web: www.macdonald-hotels.co.uk/compleatangler-hotel.co.uk

Chef: Dean Timpson
Owners: Macdonald Hotels
Times: 12.30-2/7-10
Prices: Food prices not confirmed for 2007. Please telephone for details
Wine: 100 bottles over £20, 4 bottles under £20, 8 by the glass (£4.25-£6.75)
Notes: Vegetarian available, Dress Restrictions, Smart casual, no jeans or trainers, Civ Wed 100
Seats: 80, Pr/dining room 110
Smoking: N/Sm in restaurant
Children: Menu, Portions
Rooms: 64 (64 en suite) ★★★★ HL
Directions: From M4 junct8/9, A404 to rdbt, take Bisham exit, 1m to Marlow Bridge, hotel on right
Parking: 60

Named after Izaak Walton's famous book on angling and aptly enjoying an enviable position on the banks of the River Thames, this well-established, elegant Georgian hotel overlooks the rushing waters at Marlow weir. Whether enjoying a cosy fireside drink in the 350-year-old cocktail bar in winter, perhaps a champagne picnic aboard one of the hotel's private boats, or aperitifs outside on the terrace on warm summer days, the location's perfect. The formal Riverside restaurant offers those Thames-side views, too, through windows dotted with the occasional pane of stained glass, while high-backed chairs and crisp white linen provide the dining comforts. A warm approach from friendly staff makes for a relaxed atmosphere, enhanced by a roaring fire in winter and flickering candlelight at night. The accomplished kitchen's approach is via imaginative fixed-price menus - though dotted with the odd supplement here and there. Dish construction is kept intelligently simple, the modern approach based around classical themes, featuring bags of technical skill and focusing on high-quality ingredients, clean flavours and attractive presentation. For mains, why not try loin of rabbit on a bed of celeriac with mash potato, or line-caught sea bass with chestnut crème caramel and baby spinach, while an assiette of chocolate might catch the eye at dessert. The hotel's Alfresco brasserie, located in a charming conservatory, offers a more informal dining option.

MARLOW *continued* MAP 05 SU88

The Hand & Flowers

see page 47

Macdonald Compleat Angler

see page 49

The Vanilla Pod

British, French V

Cottage restaurant offering imaginative modern cuisine

☎ 01628 898101 31 West St SL7 2LS
e-mail: info@thevanillapod.co.uk
web: www.thevanillapod.co.uk

The former home of TS Eliot, poet and critic, this cosy cottage is located in the town centre, with the dining room at the rear overlooking a small courtyard. Contemporary design complements the rustic room with its bright Mediterranean décor, beamed walls and ceiling. The atmosphere is intimate and welcoming, with polite, professional and knowledgeable service. Modern cooking combines British style and French influences, with a deft touch and well judged ingredients, in dishes of seared scallops with a purée of Tahitian vanilla poached pear, braised short rib of beef in port with parsley shallots and mousseline potato, and pistachio centred chocolate fondant.

Chef: Michael Macdonald **Owners:** Michael & Stephanie Macdonald **Times:** 12-2.30/7-11, Closed 23 Dec-3 Jan, 22 Aug-6 Sep, Sun-Mon **Prices:** Fixed L £17.50, Fixed D £40, Coffee £2.50, Min/Water £3, Service optional **Wine:** 41 bottles over £20, 5 bottles under £20, 4 by the glass (£3.50) **Notes:** Tasting menu 7 courses £45, Vegetarian menu, Smart casual **Seats:** 34, Pr/dining room 8 **Smoking:** N/Sm in restaurant **Directions:** From M4 junct 8/9 or M40 junct 4 take A404, A4155 to Marlow. From Henley take A4155 **Parking:** On West Street

Villa D'Este

☎ 01628 474798 2 Chapel St SL7 1DD

Popular local Italian restaurant serving familiar favourites and attracting loyal clientele.

TAPLOW MAP 06 SU98

Taplow House Hotel

British, French

Skilful modern British cooking at a luxurious hotel

☎ 01628 670056 Berry Hill SL6 0DA
e-mail: reception@taplow.wrensgroup.com
web: www.taplowhouse.com

This Georgian mansion combines period charm with country-house comfort, and sits amid leafy gardens not far from the M4. There's a champagne terrace for summer drinks, or a whisky bar for those who'd rather sup a malt by the fire, and an elegant restaurant offering pretty views from well-spaced tables. Tried and tested combinations form the mainstay of the modern British menu, although the odd innovation creeps in; starters might include ham hock terrine with a fried quail egg, tomato fondue and chips, while a typical main features beef served with oxtail faggot, shallot marmalade and red wine sauce. The seven-course tasting menu is also worth a flutter.

continued

Chef: Neil Dore **Owners:** Wren's Hotels **Times:** 12-2/7-9.30, Closed L Sat **Prices:** Fixed L £18.95, Starter £7.50-£11.95, Main £18.95-£22.95, Dessert £5.95, Coffee £3, Min/Water £3.50, Service included **Wine:** 58 bottles over £20, 26 bottles under £20, 10 by the glass (£3.50-£5.25) **Notes:** Fixed L 3 courses, Sun L 3 courses £18.95, Vegetarian available, Dress Restrictions, Smart casual, Civ Wed 90 **Seats:** 40, Pr/dining room 90 **Smoking:** N/Sm in restaurant, Air con **Children:** Portions **Rooms:** 32 (32 en suite) ★★★ HL **Directions:** From Maidenhead follow A4 towards Slough, over Thames, 3m turn right at lights into Berry Hill, or M4 junct 7 towards Maidenhead, at lights follow signs to Berry Hill **Parking:** 100

The Terrace Dining Room, Cliveden

French

Classical fine dining in historic surroundings

☎ 01628 668561 Cliveden Estate SL6 0JF
e-mail: reservations@clivedenhouse.co.uk
web: www.clivedenhouse.co.uk

One of England's finest country houses, Cliveden was the former home of Lady Nancy Astor, who entertained the likes of Winston Churchill, Charlie Chaplin and George Bernard Shaw at the house. The stunning south-facing Terrace Dining Room radiates with sunlight and looks out over the parterre and the River Thames. Fine works of art and elegant décor make it an impressive place to dine. Modern interpretations of classic French dishes make use of the finest British seasonal produce. Starters might include ballotine of duck and duck liver foie gras with a tian of ceps, artichokes and courgettes. For a main course perhaps fillet of Devon lamb, wrapped in a 'brique pasta' semolina infused with Bourbon vanilla and jus scented with lemon thyme.

Chef: Daniel Galmiche **Owners:** von Essen Hotels **Times:** 12-2.30/7-9.30 **Prices:** Fixed L £29.50, Fixed D £53, Coffee £4.20, Min/Water £4.50, Service optional **Wine:** 650 bottles over £20, 12 by the glass (£9-£30) **Notes:** Fixed L 3 courses, Sun L 3 courses £43.50, Vegetarian available, Dress Restrictions, Jacket & tie, Civ Wed 120 **Seats:** 80, Pr/dining room 60 **Smoking:** N/Sm in restaurant **Children:** Menu, Portions **Rooms:** 39 (39 en suite) ★★★★★ CHH **Directions:** M40 junct 2 onto A355, right into Burnham Rd/Littleworth Rd. Follow signs for Wooburn/Taplow, then for Cliveden **Parking:** 60

Waldo's Restaurant, Cliveden

see page 51

Waldo's Restaurant, Cliveden

TAPLOW MAP 06 SU98

French V NOTABLE WINE LIST

Enjoyable classical cuisine in sumptuous surroundings

☎ 01628 668561 Cliveden Estate SL6 0JF
e-mail: reservations@clivedenhouse.co.uk
web: www.clivedenhouse.co.uk

Stately homes do not come any statelier than this. Some glitter may have faded since Nancy Astor threw her parties here, but the façade of this imposing property remains impressive. Inside, the grand salons overlooking the formal parterre are simply spectacular. Waldo's Restaurant - named after the sculptor of the Fountain of Love in Cliveden's driveway - is quite unstuffy despite its grand setting. Photos of the Astor years, society portraits and charcoal sketches add a whiff of past scandals.

Formal table service delivers classical dishes with the occasional modern twist. Menus here follow the seasons and there is extensive use of carefully sourced, quality ingredients. Start with the rich quail ballotine with truffle and foie gras and pickled cherries. Main courses might be tender, corn-fed Anjou farmed pigeon with sautéed potatoes, or pink, flavour-filled loin of Devon lamb roasted with rosemary. Finish with the warm pineapple beignet infused with lemongrass, coconut and Malibu sorbet.

Notable Wine List: An extensive wine list brimming with the great classics.

Chef: Daniel Galmiche
Owners: von Essen Hotels
Times: 7-9.30, Closed Sun & Mon, Closed L all week
Prices: Fixed D fr £65, Coffee £4.20, Min/Water £4.50, Service optional
Wine: 650 bottles over £20, 12 by the glass (£9-£30)
Notes: Vegetarian menu, Dress Restrictions, Jacket & tie, Civ Wed 120
Seats: 28, Pr/dining room 12
Smoking: N/Sm in restaurant, Air con
Children: Min 12 yrs
Rooms: 39 (39 en suite) ★★★★★ CHH
Directions: M40 junct 2 onto A355, right into Burnham Rd/Littleworth Rd. Follow signs for Wooburn/Taplow, then for Cliveden
Parking: 60

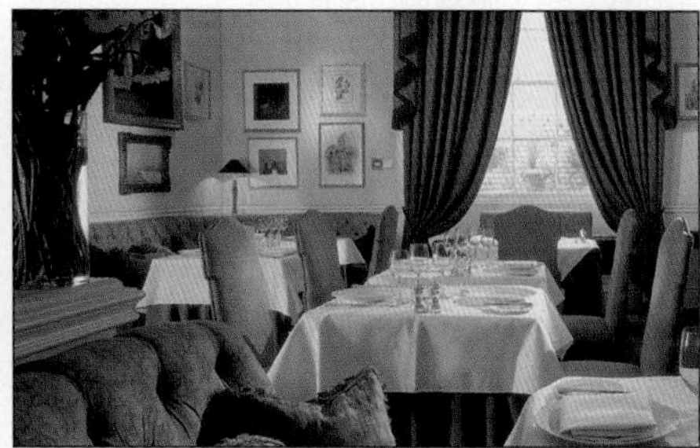

England

WOOBURN COMMON MAP 06 SU98

Chequers Inn

Modern European

Cosy inn with simple style

☎ 01628 529575 Kiln Ln HP10 0JQ
e-mail: info@chequers-inn.com
web: www.chequers-inn.com

Oak-beamed and flagstone-floored, this 17th-century inn is a snug haven with deep sofas, quiet corners and an open fire in winter. An extensive menu of pub grub is available in the bar, or you can opt for classier fare in the conservatory, a pleasant room away from the hustle and bustle that's decked with greenery and an eclectic mix of memorabilia. Superb ingredients are the headline; they're handled simply by a confident kitchen and arrive at the table in straightforward dishes such as pot-roast corn-fed chicken with a Toulouse sausage cassoulet.

Chef: Darren Ingrham **Owners:** PJ Roehrig **Times:** 12-2.30/7-9.30 **Prices:** Fixed L £13.95, Starter £5.75-£9.75, Main £14.95-£21.95, Dessert £5.75, Coffee £2.75, Min/Water £3.95, Service optional **Wine:** 40 bottles over £20, 20 bottles under £20, 15 by the glass **Notes:** Sun L £26.95, Vegetarian available **Seats:** 60, Pr/dining room 60 **Smoking:** No pipes, No cigars **Children:** Portions **Rooms:** 17 (17 en suite) ★★ **Directions:** Telephone for directions **Parking:** 50

CAMBRIDGESHIRE

BRAMPTON MAP 12 TL27

The Grange Hotel

Modern European

Modern cuisine in impressive, historic building

☎ 01480 459516 115 High St PE28 4RA
e-mail: info@grangehotelbrampton.co.uk
web: www.grangehotelbrampton.co.uk

A historic building on the village high street, which has in its time been the HQ of the American Eighth Airforce and a girls' school. Overlooking the garden, the restaurant is light and airy with comfortable seating and classic décor. A modern menu, supplemented by blackboard specials, is served throughout the bar and restaurant by relaxed, friendly staff. Local food is sourced carefully so you'll find sausages, bacon, pork and venison from the Denham estate. Typical dishes include terrine of guinea fowl with roasted chicory to start, followed by noisettes of lamb with fondant potato, roasted yam, mushroom purée and a basil sauce, or seared tuna with caramelised fennel, roast cherry tomatoes and crushed potatoes.

continued

Chef: Nick Steiger **Owners:** Susanna & Nick Steiger **Times:** 12-2/6.30-9.30, Closed BHs, Sun **Prices:** Starter £2.50-£6.50, Main £6.50-£18.50, Dessert £4.50-£7, Coffee £2, Min/Water £2.50, Service optional **Wine:** 33 bottles over £20, 42 bottles under £20, 12 by the glass (£2.30-£4.75) **Notes:** Vegetarian available, Dress Restrictions, No shorts or bare feet, Civ Wed 40 **Seats:** 32, Pr/dining room 16 **Smoking:** N/Sm in restaurant **Children:** Portions **Rooms:** 7 (7 en suite) ★★ **Directions:** 0.5m E from A1/A14 junct 21 on B1514. Close to Brampton racecourse, 1.5m W from Huntingdon **Parking:** 25

CAMBOURNE MAP 12 TL35

The Cambridge Belfry

French NEW

Modern restaurant with classical French dishes

☎ 01954 714995 Back St CB3 6BW
e-mail: cambridge@marstonhotels.com
web: www.marstonhotels.com

A newly-built hotel with great views over the lake and business park. The Bridge restaurant is contemporary in style with sleek lines, polished tile floor and deep red accent colours. A mixture of business and leisure guests use the restaurant, cocktail bar and brasserie, where simpler dishes are served. The Belfry signature menu offers mainly classical French dishes with starters like assiette of duck and foie gras with celeriac remoulade and truffle dressing. Main courses include fillet of beef with ragout of snails, confit garlic and shallots and port wine jus.

Times: 12.30-2.30/7.30-9 **Prices:** Food prices not confirmed for 2007. Please telephone for details **Rooms:** 120 (120 en suite) ★★★★ **Directions:** Telephone for directions

CAMBRIDGE MAP 12 TL45

Cambridge Quy Mill Hotel

Modern British

Listed property with a modern take on traditional fare

☎ 01223 293383 Newmarket Rd, Stow Cum Quy CB5 9AG
e-mail: cambridgequy@bestwestern.co.uk

The hotel is a conversion of a former watermill and miller's house. The restaurant occupies the dining room, kitchen and buttery of the old house, and the private dining room features a waterwheel behind glass. All the menus (chef's recommendations, specials, light bites and desserts) are available in the restaurant, bars, conservatory and terrace. Traditional dishes are presented in a modern context: duck liver, port and orange parfait with fig and apple chutney; and roast rack of lamb with Mediterranean tian, cocotte potatoes and Niçoise jus.

Chef: Nick Claxton-Webb **Owners:** David Munro **Times:** 12-2.30/7-9.45, Closed 27-31 Dec, Closed D 24-26 Dec **Prices:** Starter £5.25-£7.95, Main £10.95-£22, Dessert £5.25-£6.95, Coffee £2.75, Min/Water £3.75, Service optional, Group min 8 service 10% **Wine:** 10 bottles over £20, 20 bottles under £20, 13 by the glass (£3.25-£5.25) **Notes:** Vegetarian available, Dress Restrictions, Smart dress/smart casual - no shorts (men), Civ Wed 80 **Seats:** 48, Pr/dining room 80 **Smoking:** N/Sm area, No pipes, No cigars **Children:** Menu, Portions **Rooms:** 41 (41 en suite) ★★★ HL **Directions:** Turn off A14 at junction 35 E of Cambridge onto B1102 for 50yds, hotel entrance opposite church **Parking:** 90

Graffiti at Hotel Felix

Modern Mediterranean NOTABLE WINE LIST

Enjoyable brasserie dining in stylish hotel

☎ 01223 277977 Whitehouse Ln CB3 0LX
e-mail: help@hotelfelix.co.uk
web: www.hotelfelix.co.uk

Originally built for a local surgeon, this beautifully refurbished Victorian mansion is set in three acres of landscaped gardens. It retains many original features and the décor throughout is simple and contemporary in style. The Graffiti restaurant is a stylish dining venue, decked out with raspberry-coloured chairs and modern art. Expect a brasserie-style menu comprising mainly Mediterranean inspired dishes and a smattering of British dishes given a modern twist. Choices range from simple classics like a frothy pea and mint soup or a risotto of crab with lemongrass, to more complex and innovative dishes such as roast venison loin with celeriac purée, bitter chocolate beignet and espresso syrup.
Notable Wine List: A delightful, small and well selected list with a modern layout and concise tasting notes.

Chef: Ian Morgan **Owners:** Jeremy Cassel **Times:** 12-2/6.30-10.30 **Prices:** Fixed L £12.50, Starter £5.95-£10.25, Main £13.95-£23.95, Dessert £6.50-£6.75, Coffee £2.50, Min/Water £3.75, Service optional, Group min 10 service 10% **Wine:** 32 bottles over £20, 18 bottles under £20, 14 by the glass (£3.95-£6.50) **Notes:** Vegetarian available, Civ Wed 75 **Seats:** 45, Pr/dining room 60 **Smoking:** N/Sm in restaurant **Children:** Portions **Rooms:** 52 (52 en suite) ★★★★ **Directions:** M11 junct 12. From A1 N take A14 turning onto A1307. At City of Cambridge sign turn left into Whitehouse Lane **Parking:** 90

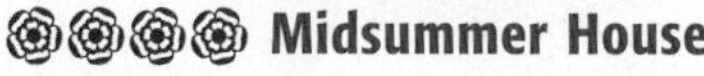

Midsummer House

see page 54

22 Chesterton Road

Modern European

Accomplished cooking and intimate dining

☎ 01223 351880 22 Chesterton Rd CB4 3AX
e-mail: davidcarter@restaurant22.co.uk
web: www.restaurant22.co.uk

A relaxed, candlelit Victorian dining room with tables cosily close together and the atmosphere of a private house, which is precisely what it once was. Academics, families and business people are equally comfortable here. The European set menu is short but versatile, with an optional fish and cheese course. A sound mastery of techniques and an emphasis on quality, fresh local ingredients ensure that the finished results meet with approval. Start with roast butternut squash soup, continue with sautéed calves' liver with roast beetroot, red wine and shallot jus, and finish with a trio of sweet fruit fritters with apricot ice cream.

Chef: Martin Cullum/Seb Mansfield **Owners:** Mr D Carter **Times:** 7-9.45, Closed 25 Dec & New Year, Sun-Mon, Closed L all week **Prices:** Fixed D £31.45, Coffee £2.50, Min/Water £3, Service optional **Wine:** 4 by the glass (£3.75-£3.95) **Notes:** Vegetarian available **Seats:** 26, Pr/dining room 12 **Smoking:** N/Sm in restaurant, Air con **Children:** Min 10 yrs, Portions **Directions:** Telephone for directions **Parking:** On street

Anatolies

☎ 01223 312412 Bridge St CB2 1UJ

This Turkish restaurant is set in the basement of the building and has a charcoal grill and even live belly dancing entertainment.

Loch Fyne Restaurant & Oyster Bar

☎ 01223 362433 The Little Rose,
37 Trumpington St CB2 1QY

Quality seafood chain.

The Venue

☎ 01223 367333 1st Floor,
Cambridge Art Theatre Building CB2 3PJ

A modern, leather and chrome style restaurant with contemporary fusion cooking and live piano music.

DUXFORD MAP 12 TL44

Duxford Lodge Hotel

British, French

A sedate setting for imaginative cuisine

☎ 01223 836444 Ickleton Rd CB2 4RT
e-mail: admin@duxfordlodgehotel.co.uk
web: www.duxfordlodgehotel.co.uk

Just a few minutes' drive from the Imperial War Museum at Duxford, this attractive red-brick hotel was formerly an RAF barracks, and numbers Winston Churchill, Douglas Bader and Bing Crosby among past visitors. Pictures of brightly coloured parrots liven up its restaurant, a genteel affair with large windows on to the garden, fine china and neatly clothed tables, and there's also a cosy lounge bar for after-dinner drinks. The classically trained chef knows his stuff and likes to impress; expect intriguing combinations that work well on the plate, such as rosemary-roasted loin of Limousin veal with white pudding sausage, apple rösti, and roast garlic sauce.

continued on page 55

Midsummer House

CAMBRIDGE MAP 12 TL45

Modern French, Mediterranean NOTABLE WINE LIST

Seriously sophisticated, inspired cooking from a high-flyer

☎ 01223 369299 Midsummer Common CB4 1HA
e-mail: reservations@midsummerhouse.co.uk
web: www.midsummerhouse.co.uk

On the appealingly named Midsummer Common beside the River Cam, this delightful, high-flying restaurant is housed in a handsome Victorian villa. Its airy, elegant, conservatory-style dining room is stylishly decked out with white walls, Indian slate floors and large, well-spaced tables dressed in crisp white linen. The atrium-style glass roof, windows and large mirrors deliver a feeling of light and space, while cream leather chairs follow the natural colour theme, with the room appropriately opening on to a pretty, secluded walled garden of fragrant herbs cultivated for the kitchen. Upstairs there's a private dining room, and a sophisticated bar and terrace for alfresco drinks with views over the river. Predominantly French service is polished and attentive, the team as enthusiastic about Daniel Clifford's innovative cooking as the chef himself. Clifford's quest for culinary perfection has taken the restaurant to another level over the past few years; his is cooking at its best, modern-focused but underpinned by classical French technique. Superb-quality ingredients, advanced technique and technical prowess add wow-factor to the carte and tasting menu but allow flavours to shine, while unexpected texture contrasts and combinations hit the spot. Take confit fillet of cod paired with langoustine and cauliflower purée, sautéed langoustine and Jerusalem artichokes, perhaps followed by a wonderful organic lemon tart, lemon jelly, lemon sorbet, lemon meringue and syrup. Peripherals such as superb, freshly baked breads, home-made chocolates, foams and shooters are all top-drawer.

Notable Wine List: An extensive wine list featuring some of the finest wines from around the world.

Chef: Daniel Clifford
Owners: Midsummer House Ltd
Times: 12-2/7-9, Closed 16-26 Apr, 20 Aug-6 Sep, Sun-Mon, Closed L Tues-Thurs
Prices: Fixed L £20-£24, Coffee £5, Min/Water £4.50, Service optional, Group min 7 service 12.5%
Wine: 650 bottles over £20, 17 by the glass (£5-£14)
Notes: Tasting menu £70, ALC £50
Seats: 50, Pr/dining room 20
Smoking: N/Sm in restaurant
Children: Menu, Portions
Directions: Park in Pretoria Rd, then walk across footbridge. Restaurant on left
Parking: On street

DUXFORD *continued* MAP 12 TL44

Duxford Lodge Hotel

Chef: Jason Burridge **Owners:** Mr Hemant Amin **Times:** 12-2.30/7-9.30, Closed 26-30 Dec **Prices:** Fixed L fr £10.99, Fixed D fr £27.50, Starter £8.50-£11.95, Main £16.95-£22.95, Dessert £7.95-£8.50, Coffee £2.50, Min/Water £2.50, Service optional **Wine:** 24 bottles over £20, 23 bottles under £20, 7 by the glass (£3-£3.50) **Notes:** Vegetarian available, Dress Restrictions, Smart dress/smart casual, Civ Wed 50 **Seats:** 45, Pr/dining room 30 **Smoking:** N/Sm in restaurant, Air con **Children:** Portions **Rooms:** 15 (15 en suite) ★★★ HL **Directions:** M11 junct 10, take A505 E, then 1st right at rdbt to Duxford; take right fork at T-junction, entrance 70 yds on left **Parking:** 30

ELY MAP 12 TL58

The Anchor Inn

Modern British

Tranquil venue with timeless charm serving local produce

☎ 01353 778537 Sutton Gault, Sutton CB6 2BD
e-mail: AnchorInnSG@aol.com
web: www.anchor-inn-restaurant.co.uk

Built around 1650 in the shelter of the bank of the New Bedford River, or the 100-ft drain as it is also called, the inn originally provided lodgings for the men conscripted to dig the new rivers. The menu offers a mixture of traditional English cooking with influences from Europe and the wider world using seasonal, fresh local produce. Thus dishes might encompass rillettes of Bottisham smoked eel with Melba toast, or roasted duck breast on puréed sweet potato with pak choi and a sesame and honey sauce.

Chef: Adam Pickup **Owners:** Robin & Heather Moore **Times:** 12-3.30/7-11, Closed 26 Dec **Prices:** Fixed L £10.95, Starter £4.95-£8.50, Main £8.50-£22, Dessert £4.50-£7.25, Coffee £2.35, Min/Water £3.20, Service optional, Group min 10 service 10% **Wine:** 26 bottles over £20, 27 bottles under £20, 9 by the glass (£3.20-£5.95) **Notes:** Sun L 3 courses £21.50, Vegetarian available **Seats:** 70 **Smoking:** N/Sm in restaurant **Children:** Menu, Portions **Rooms:** 2 (2 en suite) ◆◆◆◆ **Directions:** Signed off B1381 in Sutton village, 7m W of Ely via A142 **Parking:** 16

HUNTINGDON MAP 12 TL27

Old Bridge Hotel

Modern British NOTABLE WINE LIST

Hotel with uncompromising standards and a choice of dining venues

☎ 01480 424300 PE29 3TQ
e-mail: oldbridge@huntsbridge.co.uk
web: www.huntsbridge.com

A highly regarded townhouse hotel guarding the old bridge into Huntingdon. The emphasis here is on food and wine, combined with traditional values of hospitality and service. The Terrace is the main restaurant - an airy room with an informal atmosphere - open every day for full meals, good-value lunches and snacks. The Dining Room, serving the full carte, is open for dinner on Friday and Saturday and is used for private dining the rest of the week. The style of food is rustic French meets classic modern British, as in confit sea trout with fennel purée, chive oil and caviar, followed perhaps by braised oxtail with pearl barley, baby carrots, beans and bacon, offered from a constantly changing menu.

Notable Wine List: A really interesting and good value wine list offering around 300 bins with a notable range of wines by the glass and sherry listing.

Chef: Chris Tabbit **Owners:** J Hoskins **Times:** 12-2.30/6.30-9.30 **Prices:** Fixed L £13.50, Starter £5.95-£8.95, Main £13.50-£23, Dessert £5.95-£7.95, Coffee £2.50, Min/Water £3, Service optional **Wine:** 250 bottles over £20, 40 bottles under £20, 16 by the glass (£3.50-£9.50) **Notes:** Vegetarian available, Civ Wed 80 **Seats:** 100, Pr/dining room 40 **Smoking:** N/Sm in restaurant, Air con **Children:** Menu, Portions **Rooms:** 24 (24 en suite) ★★★ HL **Directions:** Off A1 near junction with A1/M1 link and A604/M11 **Parking:** 60

KEYSTON MAP 11 TL07

Pheasant Inn

Modern British NOTABLE WINE LIST

Gastronomic delights in a charming village inn

☎ 01832 710241 Village Loop Rd PE28 0RE
e-mail: pheasant.keyston@btopenworld.com
web: www.huntsbridge.com

Part of the Huntsbridge group of restaurants, the Pheasant is a beautiful thatched inn in a sleepy farming village. Old farming

continued

England

KEYSTON *continued* MAP 11 TL07

equipment is displayed as a decorative feature. Wooden polished tables and pine settles give a rustic feel, although still comfortable and spacious. Monthly-changing menus have individually priced dishes, supplemented by blackboard specials. Smaller portions and a separate children's menu are also available. Modern British and French cooking shows imagination and technical expertise, with starters like deep-fried calves' brain with crème fraîche and chilli jam, or quail Thai salad with nahm jimg; followed by a main course like crisp cod with braised lentils, chorizo and salsa verde.

Notable Wine List: An expertly chosen wine list full of interest and quality, personal tasting notes and great value for money.

Chef: Jay Scrimshaw **Owners:** John Hoskins **Times:** 12-2/6.30-9.30 **Prices:** Starter £4.95-£8.95, Main £12.50-£22, Dessert £4.75-£6.95, Coffee £2.50, Min/Water £2.95, Service optional, Group min 10 service 10% **Wine:** 100 bottles over £20, 40 bottles under £20, 16 by the glass (£3.50-£9.50) **Notes:** Vegetarian available **Seats:** 100, Pr/dining room 30 **Smoking:** N/Sm in restaurant **Children:** Menu, Portions **Directions:** 0.5m off A14, clearly signed, 10m W of Huntingdon **Parking:** 40

MADINGLEY MAP 12 TL36

Three Horseshoes Restaurant

Italian, Mediterranean 

Modern Italian dining in village setting

☎ 01954 210221 High St CB3 8AB
e-mail: 3hs@btconnect.co.uk
web: www.huntsbridge.com

With a garden stretching down to the village cricket pitch, this thatched gastro-pub may have a quintessentially English location, but step inside and it has a decidedly relaxed, continental feel with table service. The Italian-influenced menus are written daily and choices may include mozzarella di bufala with balsamic pickled vegetables, basil, marjoram, garlic and new season's olive oil, chargrilled marinated Cornish leg of lamb with celeriac purée, fried fennel, trevise and green olive sauce or caramelised lemon tart with crème fraîche. Wash these down with a bottle from the well-chosen list.

Notable Wine List: A wine list full of interest and passion, from John Hoskins MW.

Chef: Richard Stokes **Owners:** Huntsbridge **Times:** 12-2/6.30-9.30, Closed 31 Dec-1 Jan, Closed D Sun **Prices:** Starter £5.95-£8.50, Main £9.50-£22.95, Dessert £5.50-£7.95, Coffee £1.80, Min/Water £3, Service optional, Group min 10 service 10% **Wine:** 74 bottles over £20, 44 bottles under £20, 16 by the glass (£3.50-£6.75) **Notes:** Vegetarian available **Seats:** 65 **Smoking:** N/Sm in restaurant **Children:** Portions **Directions:** M11 junct 13, turn left, then next right and continue to end of road, and at mini-rdbt turn right **Parking:** 50

MELBOURN MAP 12 TL34

Pink Geranium

International

Secluded fine dining in an English country cottage setting

☎ 01763 260215 Station Rd SG8 6DX
e-mail: lawrence@pinkgeranium.co.uk
web: www.pinkgeranium.co.uk

This pink-washed, 16th-century thatched cottage has comfortable sofas, open fires and low beams in the lounge and high-backed leather chairs and clothed tables in the dining room. Aperitifs in the garden on summer evenings give a continental feel to dining here. Dishes are rooted in the French tradition but skilfully involve seasonal local produce. Great care is taken to maintain strong, clear flavours in starters such as potted pheasant with port and cranberry with a bacon and parsley salad. Main courses of lamb rump are spiced up with lamb samosa, comforting mushy peas, delicate sweetbreads and a celeriac and caper jus. Finish with the hot Valrhona chocolate and caramel fondant.

Times: 12-2/7-late, Closed BHs, Mon, Closed D Sun **Directions:** On A10 between Royston & Cambridge. In village centre, opposite church

Sheene Mill

Modern International

Pretty setting for relaxed dining

☎ 01763 261393 Station Rd SG8 6DX
e-mail: info@sheenemill.co.uk
web: www.sheenemill.co.uk

This cheerfully decorated, smart dining room is situated in a former mill house overlooking a pretty stream, complete with ducks. Anna Ryder Richardson and David Emanuel designed the delightful bedrooms. Dishes are carefully prepared in the modern European idiom - with some Asian influences. There's extensive use of seasonal, fresh and organic produce. Friendly staff keep diners supplied with starters of seared blue fin tuna with Thai carrot cake and sweet chilli sauce and main courses of red snapper with stir-fry noodles and soy butter, or a more traditional Welsh lamb rump with dauphinoise potatoes. To finish, there's melon, vodka and orange jelly with pistachio ice cream, or rhubarb Pavlova sundae.

Chef: Mr S Saunders & Mr C Lawrence **Owners:** Mr & Mrs S Saunders **Times:** 12-2.30/7-9.30, Closed 26 Dec, 1 Jan, Closed D Sun **Prices:** Fixed L £18, Fixed D £35, Coffee £2.50, Min/Water £2.85, Service added but optional 10% **Wine:** 90 bottles over £20, 18 bottles under £20, 10 by the glass (£4.50-£10) **Notes:** Sun L 3 courses £25, Vegetarian available, Dress Restrictions, Smart casual, Civ Wed 125 **Seats:** 110 **Smoking:** N/Sm in restaurant, Air con **Children:** Portions **Directions:** Take 2nd exit from A10 Melbourn by-pass signed Melbourn. Sheene Mill is 300yds down Station Rd on right **Parking:** 50

England

PETERBOROUGH MAP 12 TL19

Best Western Orton Hall Hotel

Modern British

Historic old building serving modern cuisine

☎ 01733 391111 Orton Longueville PE2 7DN
e-mail: reception@ortonhall.co.uk
web: www.bw-ortonhall.co.uk

Next to the parish church, this impressive, tastefully restored, 17th-century country house is set in 20 acres of parkland on the outskirts of town and retains many of its original features. Think oak panelling and beautiful stained glass for its formal Huntly restaurant, for instance, where you can expect a warm, calm and friendly atmosphere. The kitchen's approach is rooted in the present day though, its well-balanced, fixed-price repertoire delivering accomplished dishes, like confit duck leg with Savoy cabbage and bacon, or roasted lamb rump with black pudding, crushed new potatoes, red cabbage and redcurrant sauce.

Chef: Kevin Wood **Owners:** Abacus Hotels **Times:** 12.30-2/7-9.30, Closed 25 Dec, Closed L Mon-Sat **Prices:** Fixed L fr £15.95, Fixed D fr £27, Starter £5.50-£7.50, Main £16-£21, Dessert fr £5.50, Min/Water £3.60, Service optional **Wine:** 25 bottles over £20, 36 bottles under £20, 6 by the glass (£2.90) **Notes:** Coffee included, Civ Wed 90 **Seats:** 34, Pr/dining room 40 **Smoking:** N/Sm in restaurant **Rooms:** 65 (65 en suite) ★★★ HL **Directions:** Telephone for directions **Parking:** 200

Gaston Café Bar & Restaurant

☎ 01733 3 344170 44 Broadway PE1 1RS
An open-plan, modern informal dining room. Watch the pizzas being made.

Loch Fyne Restaurant & Oyster Bar

☎ 01832 280298 The Old Dairy, Elton PE8 6SH
Quality seafood chain.

ST IVES MAP 12 TL37

Olivers Lodge Hotel

Indian, International

Interesting range of dishes in a light, airy restaurant

☎ 01480 463252 Needingworth Rd PE27 5JP
e-mail: reception@oliverslodge.co.uk
web: www.oliverslodge.co.uk

The conservatory restaurant here is built out into a secluded garden at the rear of the hotel. Light and spacious, it is comfortably furnished

continued

and tables are set with crisp linen. Service is friendly and attentive. The large carte menu offers an impressive range of British, French and Asian dishes including authentic Thai, Indonesian and Indian options; there is also an extensive bar menu. You could start with home-made Asian tapas, followed by Indonesian fried rice featuring shrimp, chicken and basmati rice with chilli and spices, served with chicken satay and satay sauce.

Chef: Vinay Mani **Owners:** Shiren Patel **Times:** 12-2.30/6.30-9.30 **Prices:** Fixed L £12.25-£18.50, Starter £3.75-£4.25, Main £8.50-£14.95, Dessert £3.75-£4.25, Coffee £1.65, Min/Water £3.50, Service optional **Wine:** 5 bottles over £20, 29 bottles under £20, 10 by the glass (£3.50-£4.25) **Notes:** Sun L £14.95, Vegetarian available, Smart dress, Civ Wed 120 **Seats:** 20, Pr/dining room 20 **Smoking:** N/Sm in restaurant **Children:** Menu, Portions **Rooms:** 17 (17 en suite) ★★★ **Directions:** Telephone for directions **Parking:** 30

SIX MILE BOTTOM MAP 12 TL55

Swynford Paddocks

British, Mediterranean V

Historic country-house hotel with reliable cooking

☎ 01638 570234 CB8 0UE
e-mail: info@swynfordpaddocks.com
web: www.swynfordpaddocks.com

Set in 64 acres of parkland, this impressive country-house hotel has associations with both the races (at nearby Newmarket) and Lord Byron, who lends his name to the fine-dining restaurant here. The sumptuous restaurant, with its jade walls and canvases featuring words from the great poet, is a bay-fronted dining room overlooking the impeccable front lawn, with smartly uniformed staff who are both friendly and professional. The food is modern British with a traditional feel and Mediterranean influences, with an emphasis on satisfying, flavoursome fare rather than adventurous experiments - mixed salad of proscuitto ham, marinated olives and baby figs to start, for example, followed by honey-glazed duck breast with pancetta mash or roast shank of lamb with dauphinoise potato and rosemary jus.

Chef: Patrick Collins **Owners:** Paul & Lucie Smith **Times:** 12-2/7-10, Closed Sat (if sole occupancy wedding) **Prices:** Fixed L £12.95-£14.95, Fixed D fr £29.50, Starter £5.50-£8.95, Main £13-£25, Dessert £5-£7.50, Coffee £2.75, Min/Water £2.95, Service optional **Wine:** 33 bottles over £20, 26 bottles under £20, 10 by the glass (£3.75-£6.50) **Notes:** Vegetarian menu, Dress Restrictions, No jeans/trainers at dinner, Civ Wed 100 **Seats:** 25, Pr/dining room 40 **Smoking:** N/Sm in restaurant **Children:** Portions **Rooms:** 15 (15 en suite) ★★★ **Directions:** M11 junct 9, take A11 towards Newmarket, then onto A1304 to Newmarket, hotel is 0.75m on left **Parking:** 100

STILTON MAP 12 TL18

Bell Inn Hotel

Modern British

Charming inn with bags of character

☎ 01733 241066 Great North Rd PE7 3RA
e-mail: reception@thebellstilton.co.uk
web: www.thebellstilton.co.uk

Set in a delightful village on the outskirts of Peterborough, this wonderfully agreeable inn is steeped in history and possessed of numerous original features. The imaginative and consistent food is served in the atmospheric village bar and elegant, beamed first-floor restaurant, as well as the smart new bistro - you can also eat outside if weather permits. With quality produce at its core, the menu is generally well executed and precisely flavoured, and might include such delights as seared king scallops with beetroot risotto and samphire, or red wine-poached cod fillet with a bittersweet caper jelly.

Chef: Robin Devonshire **Owners:** Mr L A McGivern **Times:** 12-2/7-9.30, Closed 25 Dec, Closed L Sat, D Sun **Prices:** Fixed L fr £10.95, Fixed D £25.95, Starter £3.95-£6.95, Main £9.95-£14.95, Dessert £4.25, Coffee £1.35, Min/Water £2.50, Service included **Wine:** 20 bottles over £20, 40 bottles under £20, 7 by the glass (£3.30) **Notes:** Vegetarian available, Civ Wed 90 **Seats:** 60, Pr/dining room 20 **Smoking:** N/Sm in restaurant, Air con **Children:** Min 5 yrs **Rooms:** 22 (22 en suite) ★★★ **Directions:** 1m N A1(M) junct 16 follow signs to Stilton. Hotel on High Street in centre of village **Parking:** 30

WANSFORD MAP 12 TL09

Bentley's Restaurant

Modern British, French NEW

Stylish restaurant offering imaginative cooking

☎ 01780 782223 The Haycock Hotel PE8 6JA
e-mail: sales@thehaycock.co.uk
web: www.thehaycock.co.uk

This charming 17th-century coaching inn parades a wealth of character and is set amid attractive landscaped grounds in the heart of this peaceful village. The stylish, intimate Bentley's restaurant comes decked out with well-spaced round tables, upholstered chairs, crisp white linen and plush drapes, while the accompanying service from smartly uniformed staff is well informed and professional. The kitchen has pedigree and displays highly accomplished technical skills, the modern British cuisine reflecting influences from both America and Spain. Imaginative dishes might include a starter of langoustines with griddled pineapple, green lentil dahl and green tea foam, followed perhaps by line-caught sea bass with a crayfish nage and kaffir lime leaves, and a dessert of chocolate delice with parsnip ice cream.

continued

Bentley's Restaurant

Chef: Nigel Godwin **Owners:** Philip & Judith Carter **Times:** 12-2.30/7-10, Closed 1st week Jan, Sun, Mon, Closed D 25 & 31 Dec **Prices:** Fixed L fr £15.95, Starter £6.95-£10.95, Main fr £38, Dessert £5.95-£7.50, Coffee £3.95, Min/Water £3.50, Service optional **Wine:** 110 bottles over £20, 31 bottles under £20, 14 by the glass (£3.40-£5) **Notes:** Tasting menu L 5 courses £27.95, D 8 courses £45, Vegetarian available, Dress Restrictions, Smart casual, Civ Wed 150 **Seats:** 30, Pr/dining room 12 **Smoking:** N/Sm in restaurant **Children:** Menu, Portions **Rooms:** 48 (48 en suite) ★★★ HL **Directions:** In village centre accessible from A1/A47 intersection **Parking:** 200

see advert opposite

CHESHIRE

ALDERLEY EDGE MAP 16 SJ87

Alderley Edge Hotel

Modern British V

Imaginative cuisine in country-house conservatory

☎ 01625 583033 Macclesfield Rd SK9 7BJ
e-mail: sales@alderlyedgehotel.com
web: www.alderleyedgehotel.com

Built as a textile merchant's house, the hotel has been modernised and extended but retains its classic design. Comfort and quality are reflected in the airy split-level conservatory restaurant with its warm colour scheme, high-backed leather chairs and well-appointed tables. Good use of fine ingredients and an imaginative menu mean you are in for a treat when dining here. You could try the broth of smoked haddock, Jersey Royals and young leeks with chive purée to start, or an interesting Brixham crab omelette with cucumber and roasted pimento salsa and langoustine foam. Main courses are along the lines of baked rump of lamb scented with lemon and sea salt with rosemary butter, or baked fillet of sea bass with wilted wild garlic and a cassoulet of broad beans and peas. The selection of cheeses is excellent and the whole package is complemented by a truly extensive wine list.

Chef: Chris Holland **Owners:** J W Lees (Brewers) Ltd **Times:** 12-2/7-10, Closed 1 Jan, Closed L 31 Dec, D 25-26 Dec **Prices:** Fixed L £17.95, Fixed D

continued

£29.50, Starter £6.20-£10.50, Main £22.95-£25.25, Dessert £5.95, Coffee £2.50, Min/Water £2.90, Service optional **Wine:** 220 bottles over £20, 45 bottles under £20, 12 by the glass (£2.75-£6.95) **Notes:** Fixed L 3 courses, Vegetarian menu, Dress Restrictions, Smart casual, Civ Wed 100 **Seats:** 65, Pr/dining room 100 **Smoking:** N/Sm in restaurant, Air con **Children:** Portions **Rooms:** 52 (52 en suite) ★★★ HL **Directions:** A538 to Alderley Edge, then B5087 Macclesfield Rd **Parking:** 82

ALSAGER MAP 15 SJ75

Manor House Hotel

Traditional British, French V NEW

Traditional dishes using choice ingredients

☎ 01270 884000 Audley Rd ST7 2QQ
e-mail: mhres@compasshotels.co.uk
web: www.compasshotels.co.uk

Based around an old farmhouse, this modern hotel retains some of its original character and features. Ostler's restaurant is in the converted 17th-century coaching inn, with original oak beams and fireplace. Fixed-price three-course lunches and two or three courses at dinner are supplemented by a carte. British and French dishes are lovingly created using good locally sourced produce. The likes of quail terrine and saddle of venison are complemented by innovative combinations like roulade of pork fillet with Staffordshire black pudding, cheese and red onion tartlet and apple and cider reduction.

Chef: Ian Turner **Owners:** Compass Hotels Ltd **Times:** 12-2/7.15-9.30, Closed 27-30 Dec, Closed L Sat, D Sun **Prices:** Food prices not confirmed for 2007. Please telephone for details **Wine:** 17 bottles over £20, 26 bottles under £20, 4 by the glass (£2.10-£3.95) **Notes:** Vegetarian menu, Civ Wed 200 **Seats:** 90, Pr/dining room 28 **Smoking:** N/Sm in restaurant

continued

Children: Menu, Portions **Rooms:** 57 (57 en suite) ★★★ HL **Directions:** M6 J16, follow A500 towards Stoke on Trent. Leave A500 on 1st slip road, turn left & follow road for 3m. Hotel on left **Parking:** 150

BURWARDSLEY MAP 15 SJ55

The Pheasant Inn

Traditional British

Sandstone inn with cosy bar, restaurant and rooms

☎ 01829 770434 Higher Burwardsley CH3 9PF
e-mail: info@thepheasantinn.co.uk
web: www.thepheasantinn.co.uk

This 300-year-old sandstone, half-timbered, former farmhouse is set in beautiful rural surroundings. There's a stone-flagged conservatory and flower-filled courtyard, ideal for summer. The owners aim to provide the best food, with friendly service in a relaxed environment. Try a starter like tempura tiger prawns on crisp endive with a sweet chilli dip. Main courses might include the likes of pan-fried fillet of beef medallions on rösti potato with a baby onion and smoked bacon red wine sauce, while dessert keeps to traditional favourites like sticky toffee pudding with toffee sauce and vanilla ice cream.

Chef: Mark Johnston, Jeff Griffiths **Owners:** Sue and Harold Nelson **Times:** 12/10, Closed D Mon (no food 3-6pm) **Prices:** Starter £3.95-£8.25, Main £7.45-£16.95, Dessert £3.95-£4.95, Coffee £1.85, Min/Water £3.50 **Wine:** 18 bottles over £20, 14 bottles under £20, 8 by the glass (£3.40-£6.50) **Notes:** Vegetarian available **Seats:** 100, Pr/dining room 20 **Smoking:** N/Sm in restaurant **Children:** Menu, Portions **Rooms:** 10 (10 en suite) ★★ HL **Directions:** A41 from Chester towards Whitchurch. After 6m turn left for Tattenhall. In village signs for Burwardsley. Top of hill left at PO **Parking:** 70

The Arkle

CHESTER MAP 15 SJ46

Modern French

Gorgeous hotel restaurant with magnificent modern French cooking

☎ 01244 324024 Chester Grosvenor & Spa, Eastgate CH1 1LT
e-mail: hotel@chestergrosvenor.co.uk
web: www.chestergrosvenor.co.uk

Named after the famous steeplechase horse owned by the late Anne, Duchess of Westminster, you might expect there to be a racing theme to this smart contemporary restaurant located in one of the area's swishest hotels and you wouldn't be disappointed. Yet the equine influence is subtle and understated with prints of the eponymous steed and a colour scheme that takes its lead from the black and gold racing colours of the owner with an elegant art deco feel. Stylish modern furniture completes the picture.
The cuisine is based on classical French with a modern twist - it's a description that, though accurate, doesn't do justice to the sophistication of chef Simon Radley's seasonally inspired cooking and the assurance and imagination with which every dish is delivered. There's a tongue-in-cheek modesty to the menu too - a starter described as 'ravioli' turns out to be fine celeriac sheets filled with foie gras, poached with Banyuls pickled onions while a main course of 'turbot' is the most divine braised turbot pavé with langoustine paella, spiced chorizo and smoked pimento.

Chef: Simon Radley
Owners: Grosvenor - Duke of Westminster
Times: 7-9.30, Closed 1st 3 wks Jan, 1 wk Aug, Sun, Mon, Closed L all week
Prices: Fixed D £55, Coffee £4, Min/Water £4, Service added but optional 12.5%, Group service 12.5%
Wine: 613 bottles over £20, 10 bottles under £20, 25 by the glass (£6.50-£20)
Notes: Fixed D 5 courses £65, Vegetarian available, Dress Restrictions, Jacket in The Arkle, no jeans or trainers, Civ Wed 120
Seats: 45
Smoking: N/Sm in restaurant, Air con
Children: Min 12 yrs
Rooms: 80 (80 en suite) ★★★★★
Directions: Chester city centre adjacent to the Eastgate Clock and Roman walls
Parking: 600

CHESTER MAP 15 SJ46

La Brasserie at the Chester Grosvenor & Spa

Modern International

Enjoyable brasserie dining in Chester's ancient heart

☎ 01244 324024 Eastgate CH1 1LT
e-mail: hotel@chestergrosvenor.co.uk
web: www.chestergrosvenor.co.uk

This art deco-style brasserie provides a good alternative to the more formal Arkle restaurant in this well-known hotel. Leather banquettes, a richly hand-painted skylight, lots of mirrors and marble tabletops are redolent of fin-de-siècle Paris. The same menu for lunch and dinner includes confidently cooked brasserie classics including starters of glazed oyster croustade with spinach and parmesan followed by whole lemon sole, then lemon tart with raspberries and mint. There are also unexpected but welcome items such as Mulligatawny soup and tuna burgers. Good-quality home-baked breads accompany.

Chef: Simon Radley **Owners:** Grosvenor - Duke of Westminster **Times:** 12/10.30, Closed 25-26 Dec **Prices:** Starter £5.50-£16, Main £11.95-£19.95, Dessert £4.25-£4.95, Coffee £3.50, Min/Water £3.75, Service optional, Group min 8 service 12.5% **Wine:** 35 bottles over £20, 19 bottles under £20, 14 by the glass (£3.95-£13.95) **Notes:** Vegetarian available, Dress Restrictions, Smart casual, Civ Wed 120 **Seats:** 80 **Smoking:** N/Sm in restaurant, Air con **Children:** Menu, Portions **Directions:** 2m from M53, located in city centre **Parking:** 600

Mollington Hotel & Spa Chester

Modern, Traditional

Stylish modern hotel restaurant serving classic dishes

☎ 01244 851471 Parkgate Rd CH1 6NN
e-mail: info@mollingtonhotel.co.uk
web: www.mollingtonhotel.co.uk

A manor house stood here in 1066, later replaced by a handsome Victorian mansion built in 1853. In 1964 the house became a hotel and it has been extended over the years so that it now provides extensive modern spa, conference and leisure facilities. The Garden Room restaurant offers lunch and a fixed-price dinner menu with seven choices per course. Typical dishes might include a starter of home-made black pudding on crushed new potatoes with devilled haricot bean sauce, or a main course of monkfish tail, wrapped in Parma ham and served with crushed new potatoes, braised red cabbage and courgette chips.

Chef: Ian Fellowes **Owners:** Hand Picked Hotels **Times:** 7-10, Closed Xmas, 31 Dec, Closed L all week, D Sun **Prices:** Fixed D £27.50, Starter £4.75-£7, Main £16-£22.50, Dessert £4-£7.50, Coffee £2.50, Min/Water £2.95, Service optional **Wine:** 31 bottles over £20, 12 bottles under £20, 11 by the glass (£3.50-£7.50) **Notes:** Civ Wed 150 **Seats:** 65, Pr/dining room 150 **Smoking:** N/Sm in restaurant, Air con **Children:** Menu, Portions **Rooms:** 63 (63 en suite) ★★★★ **Directions:** Please telephone for directions **Parking:** 250

Rowton Hall Country House Hotel

Modern, Traditional

Magnificent Georgian country-house hotel with fine dining

☎ 01244 335262 Whitchurch Rd, Rowton CH3 6AD
e-mail: rowtonhall@rowtonhall.co.uk
web: www.rowtonhallhotel.co.uk

Originally built in 1779, this long-established country-house hotel stands on the site of a major battle in the English Civil War. The battlefield has since been replaced by beautifully landscaped, award-winning gardens and contemporary spa facilities. Inside, the main hall retains many period features including an impressive Robert Adams fireplace and a self-supporting hand-carved staircase, while the Langdale restaurant is adorned with attractive oak panelling. The traditional English feel of the menu is bolstered by a strong French bias - try shellfish bisque with a crab and scallop gateau to start, followed by a main of slow-roasted duck and mint pomme purée.

Chef: Matthew Hulmes **Owners:** Mr Wiggington **Times:** 12-2/7-9.30 **Prices:** Fixed L £13, Fixed D £19.95, Starter £6-£9.50, Main £15.50-£20, Dessert £6-£8.50, Coffee £3, Min/Water £3.50, Service optional **Wine:** 102 bottles over £20, 32 bottles under £20 **Notes:** Fixed L 3 courses, Sun D £15.50, Dress Restrictions, Smart casual, Civ Wed 120 **Seats:** 56, Pr/dining room 120 **Smoking:** N/Sm in restaurant, Air con **Children:** Menu, Portions **Rooms:** 38 (38 en suite) ★★★★ HL **Directions:** M56 junct 12 take A56 to Chester. At rdbt turn left on A41 to Whitchurch. Approx 1m and follow signs for hotel **Parking:** 90

CREWE MAP 15 SJ75

Crewe Hall

British

Fine dining in the sumptuous setting of a Jacobean manor

☎ 01270 253333 Weston Rd CW1 6UZ
e-mail: reservationsch@marstonhotels.com
web: www.marstonhotels.com

The stateliest of homes, Crewe Hall stands in 500 acres of mature grounds and was once owned by the Queen. It dates from the 17th century, but the interior was destroyed by fire in 1866 and replaced in elaborate Victorian style with stained glass, oak panelling and marble fireplaces. A more recent addition is the west wing, including a brasserie with a unique revolving bar. However, the fine-dining option is the Ranulph restaurant, an elegant room located in the historic hall. The menu offers modern dishes with some classical influences.

Times: 12-2/7-9.30, Closed L Sat, D Sun **Rooms:** 65 (65 en suite) ★★★★ **Directions:** From M6 junct 16 take A500 towards Crewe. At 1st rdbt take last exit, at next rdbt take 1st exit, then right into drive after 0.5m

England

CREWE *continued* MAP 15 SJ75

Hunters Lodge Hotel

British, European

Seasonal menus in an 18th-century former farmhouse

☎ 01270 583440 Sydney Rd, Sydney CW1 5LU
e-mail: info@hunterslodge.co.uk
web: www.hunterslodge.co.uk

Set in 16 acres of south Cheshire countryside, this 18th-century property started out as a farmhouse, and now boasts comfortable accommodation and a popular bar with an extensive menu for relaxed eating. The more serious dining takes place in the spacious beamed restaurant, where the ever-changing menus reflect both British and European trends. Interesting choices include a mosaic of ham hock and foie gras, then carved loin of venison with crushed parsnips, bubble-and-squeak and sauce bordelaise followed by a memorable trio of desserts - Baileys brûlée, sticky toffee pudding and caramel ice cream. Good home-made breads and petits fours are an added bonus.

Chef: David Wall **Owners:** Mr A Panayi **Times:** 12-2/7-9.30, Closed BHs, Closed D Sun **Prices:** Fixed L £26.25-£29.50, Fixed D £29.50-£33.50, Starter £7.95-£8.95, Main £18.75-£22.50, Dessert £7.75-£9.50, Coffee £3.50, Min/Water £2.95 **Wine:** 22 bottles over £20, 21 bottles under £20, 6 by the glass (£3-£4.95) **Notes:** Civ Wed 130 **Seats:** 60, Pr/dining room 30 **Smoking:** N/Sm in restaurant **Children:** Menu, Portions **Rooms:** 57 (57 en suite) ★★★ HL **Directions:** 1m from station, follow signs to Leighton Hospital **Parking:** 200

NANTWICH MAP 15 SJ65

Rookery Hall

Modern British

Classic cooking in a grand château setting

☎ 01270 610016 Main Rd, Worleston CW5 6DQ
e-mail: rookeryhall@handpicked.co.uk
web: www.handpicked.co.uk

Dine with the resident ghosts at this magnificent mansion, built in 1816 and set in 38 acres of gardens and parkland. The mahogany panelled dining room has a spectacular ceiling, roaring fires, attractive paintings and highly polished tables, and makes for a romantic setting by candlelight. Intimate private dining rooms are also available. Classic British food with international influences is carefully prepared using prime ingredients. Complex and originally themed dishes offer interesting flavour combinations, such as Cheshire ham with pressed leeks, poached egg and truffle hollandaise, or rump of Aberdeen Angus beef with sautéed potatoes, slowly braised beef, Madeira jus and béarnaise. Service is smooth, efficient and unobtrusive.

Chef: Craig Malone **Owners:** Hand Picked Hotels/Julia Hands **Times:** 12-2/7-9.30, Closed L Sat **Prices:** Fixed L £15.95, Fixed D £29.50, Starter £7.95-£12.95, Main £16.50-£24.50, Dessert £6.95-£8.50, Coffee £3.50, Min/Water £3.75, Service optional **Wine:** 130 bottles over £20, 6 bottles under £20, 8 by the glass (£4.50-£8) **Notes:** Vegetarian available, Dress Restrictions, Smart casual, no jeans or trainers, Civ Wed 66 **Seats:** 50, Pr/dining room 60 **Smoking:** N/Sm in restaurant **Children:** Menu, Portions **Rooms:** 46 (46 en suite) ★★★★ HL **Directions:** On B5074 N of Nantwich, 1.5m on right towards Worleston **Parking:** 100

PRESTBURY MAP 16 SJ87

White House Restaurant

Modern European

Chic modern restaurant with a good track record

☎ 01625 829376 SK10 4DG
e-mail: info@thewhitehouse.uk.com
web: www.thewhitehouse.uk.com

Housed in a 17th-century farmhouse, this chic restaurant is modishly littered with modern paintings and sculptures, and etched glass screens, and is a popular dinner destination for affluent locals. A straightforward menu is available in the bar, while the dining room offers more challenging fare; it's all served up courtesy of a long-serving chef who knows his stuff and consistently delivers quality contemporary cuisine. Starters might include meli-melo of mushrooms (wild mushroom mousse, strudel and fricassee), or a warm goat's cheese terrine with caramelised red onion coulis, while mains range from hearty dishes - venison with braised red cabbage - to lighter choices such as tempura organic salmon with tangy lime mayo and French fries.

Chef: R Wakeham & D Davallou **Owners:** Ryland & Judith Wakeham **Times:** 12-2/7-10, Closed 25 Dec, Closed L Mon, D Sun **Prices:** Fixed L £16.95-£18.95, Fixed D £19.95, Starter £4.25-£9.50, Main £11.95-£19.50, Dessert £4.95-£7.50, Coffee £2.75, Min/Water £3, Service optional **Wine:** 38 bottles over £20, 24 bottles under £20, 10 by the glass (£3.95-£5) **Notes:** Fixed L 3 courses, Vegetarian available **Seats:** 70, Pr/dining room 40 **Smoking:** No pipes, No cigars **Children:** Portions **Directions:** Village centre on A538 N of Macclesfield **Parking:** 11

PUDDINGTON MAP 15 SJ37

Macdonald Craxton Wood

European

Stylish hotel for fine dining

☎ 0151 347 4000 Parkgate Rd, Ledsham, Nr Chester CH66 9PB
e-mail: info@craxton.macdonald-hotels.co.uk
web: www.macdonaldhotels.co.uk

This smart hotel offers excellent leisure facilities and an impressive conservatory, lounge and bar. The Garden Room restaurant is divided into three areas giving more privacy to diners, while the conservatory adds a bright and airy dimension. The menu continues to offer a varied choice of carefully prepared dishes using excellent produce. Starters might feature venison terrine laced with Madeira, sliced onto Jersey Royal salad, bound in herb jelly. Main courses include the likes of grilled fillet of sea bass with fennel and orange salad and rosemary butter sauce.

Times: 12.30-2/7-9.30, Closed L Sat **Rooms:** 72 (72 en suite) ★★★★ HL **Directions:** From end of M56 W take A5117 Queensferry, right at 1st rdbt onto A540 (Hoylake). Hotel 200yds after next traffic lights

SANDIWAY MAP 15 SJ67

Nunsmere Hall Country House Hotel

Modern British NEW

Traditional fine dining in elegant surroundings

☎ 01606 889100 Tarporley Rd CW8 2ES
e-mail: reservations@nunsmere.co.uk
web: www.nunsmere.co.uk

Dating back to 1900, this grand country-house hotel with 60-acre lake and extensive grounds was originally owned by the Brocklebank family, renowned for the Cunard - Brocklebank shipping line. The Crystal restaurant offers an elegant and intimate dining experience, overlooking the south facing terrace and sunken garden. Modern British and European-style cooking is accomplished and makes use of quality ingredients. A seven-course tasting menu is available for a whole table to sample, or try individual dishes like ravioli of blue cheese and roast walnut with wilted baby spinach and smoked oil essence or pheasant breast stuffed with oatmeal and bacon, with turnip dauphinoise, braised red cabbage and thyme jus.

Chef: Gordon Campbell **Owners:** Mr & Mrs M S McHardy **Times:** 12-2/7-10 **Prices:** Fixed L £22.50, Starter £8-£14, Main £15.25-£27, Dessert £8.50-£10.25, Coffee £5.25, Min/Water £3.50, Service optional **Wine:** 111 bottles over £20, 18 bottles under £20, 18 by the glass (£4-£14.25) **Notes:** Tasting menu £55, Vegetarian available, Dress Restrictions, No jeans, trainers or shorts, Civ Wed 100 **Seats:** 60, Pr/dining room 45 **Smoking:** N/Sm in restaurant **Children:** Min 12 yrs, Portions **Rooms:** 36 (36 en suite) ★★★★ HL **Directions:** From M6 junct 19 take A56 for 9 miles. Turn left onto A49 towards Tarporley. Hotel is 1m on left **Parking:** 80

WILMSLOW MAP 16 SJ88

Stanneylands Hotel

Modern British

Country-house hotel with an engaging cooking style

☎ 01625 525225 Stanneylands Rd SK9 4EY
e-mail: enquiries@stanneylandshotel.co.uk
web: www.stanneylandshotel.co.uk

A sympathetic refurbishment has given this traditional country-house hotel a tasteful facelift, though the elegant panelled restaurant has kept its timeless appeal. Beautifully clothed and set tables and soft lighting make this a sought after venue both locally and with visiting guests. The modern lounges invite relaxation over a drink or coffee. A set menu in the evening and a choice of menus at lunchtime showcase the modern and classical cooking in all its creative glory. Baked goat's cheese with roasted beetroot tartare and watercress pesto makes an interesting starter that might be followed by roast chicken supreme served with parmesan polenta, bacon, Savoy cabbage and thyme jus.

Owners: Mr L Walshe **Times:** 12.30-2.30/7-9.30, Closed D Sun **Prices:** Fixed L fr £13.50, Fixed D £27.50, Starter £6.85-£9.85, Main £16.95-£24.95, Dessert £6, Coffee £2.50, Min/Water £3.75, Service optional **Wine:** 53 bottles over £20, 21 bottles under £20, 6 by the glass (£3.75-£5.50) **Notes:** Fixed D 4 courses, Vegetarian available, Dress Restrictions, Smart casual, Civ Wed 100 **Seats:** 60, Pr/dining room 120 **Smoking:** N/Sm in restaurant **Children:** Portions **Rooms:** 31 (31 en suite) ★★★★ HL **Directions:** From M56 junct 5 follow signs for Cheadle. At lights turn right, through Styal, left at Handforth sign, follow into Stanneylands Rd **Parking:** 110

CORNWALL & ISLES OF SCILLY

England

BODMIN MAP 02 SX06

Trehellas House Hotel & Restaurant

Traditional British

Romantic restaurant offering Cornish produce

☎ 01208 72700 Washaway PL30 3AD
e-mail: enquiries@trehellashouse.co.uk
web: www.trehellashouse.co.uk

Formerly used as a court house by travelling magistrates, this 18th-century former coaching inn has a lovely candlelit restaurant with exposed beams and overlooking an attractive courtyard. Here you will find formal table service and cuisine based on classic meat and fish dishes using market produce and fine Cornish ingredients. Try Looe scallops sautéed with white wine, garlic and cream to start, followed by pan-fried venison liver with dry cured bacon, balsamic caramelised onions and beetroot jus. For a warming dessert, look no further than whisky rice pudding with warm syruped dried fruits.

Chef: Garth Borrowdale **Owners:** Alan & Chris Street **Times:** 7-8.30, Closed Xmas & New Year, Sun (non-res), Closed L all week **Prices:** Starter £3.50-£7.50, Main £14.50-£22, Dessert £3.50-£7.50, Coffee £2.40, Min/Water £3.25, Service optional, Group min 10 service 10% **Wine:** 7 bottles over £20, 24 bottles under £20, 4 by the glass (£3.50-£5) **Notes:** Vegetarian available **Seats:** 40 **Smoking:** N/Sm in restaurant **Children:** Portions **Rooms:** 11 (11 en suite) ★★ **Directions:** 4m from Bodmin on A389 to Wadebridge, adjacent to Pencarrow **Parking:** 25

BOSCASTLE MAP 02 SX09

The Bottreaux Restaurant

Modern British

Local produce in a modernised 200-year-old building

☎ 01840 250231 PL35 0BG
e-mail: info@boscastlecornwall.co.uk
web: www.boscastlecornwall.co.uk

Named after the founders of the village, this hotel and restaurant combines a17th-century stables (now the bar), with a former village store (now the restaurant), and the hotel rooms above, which have been a guest house since the house was first built. The restaurant specialises in fish and seafood dishes in a comfortable setting with modern leather chairs, wooden flooring and simple white-clothed tables. Local Cornish produce is at the heart of the imaginative menu. You might try a starter of pan-seared Mevagissey scallops with saffron risotto, followed by rosemary-roasted rump of Michaelstow lamb, served with garden mint jelly glaze and herb dumplings. Desserts are truly wicked with temptations such as dark chocolate torte with Delabole clotted cream and white chocolate crème anglaise.

Chef: Alan Cooper **Owners:** Alan & Carlotta Cooper **Times:** 6.30-11, Closed 2 weeks in low season, Mon, Closed L all week **Prices:** Fixed D £25, Coffee £2, Min/Water £2.75, Service optional **Wine:** 10 bottles over £20, 20 bottles under £20, 6 by the glass (£3.50-£4) **Seats:** 24 **Smoking:** N/Sm in restaurant **Children:** Min 10 yrs **Rooms:** 9 (9 en suite) ★★ SHL **Directions:** From A30, take A39 towards North Cornwall, and follow signs to Boscastle/Tintagel **Parking:** 9

England

BOSCASTLE *continued* MAP 02 SX09

The Wellington Hotel

British NEW

Imaginative cooking in quaint Cornish village

☎ 01840 250202 The Harbour PL35 0AQ
e-mail: info@boscastle-wellington.com
web: www.boscastle-wellington.com

Following the devastation of the Boscastle floods in 2004, the Roberts family has brought this old lady of a hotel back from ruin. The stylish Waterloo restaurant, with a little help from the BBC's 'Changing Rooms' team, provides the perfect setting for son Scottie's imaginative cooking. Dishes such as smoked Boscastle mackerel salad, seared tronçon of Cornish monkfish on creamed leeks, and ravioli of celeriac and Davidstowe cheddar, make good use of local produce, with fish figuring strongly alongside Michaelstowe fillet steak. Service is friendly and relaxed without losing any efficiency. Booking is essential as the restaurant has a fairly limited number of tables. Bar meals are also available.

Chef: Scott Roberts **Owners:** Paul Roberts **Times:** 7-9 **Prices:** Food prices not confirmed for 2007. Please telephone for details **Rooms:** 15 (15 en suite) ★★ HL **Directions:** Telephone for directions

CALLINGTON MAP 03 SX36

Langmans Restaurant

Modern British V

Accomplished cuisine in friendly and relaxed town restaurant

☎ 01579 384933 3 Church St PL17 7RE
e-mail: dine@langmansrestaurant.co.uk
web: www.langmansrestaurant.co.uk

Tucked away off the main street, this Grade II listed former bakery has a friendly, relaxed atmosphere and is comfortably furnished with modern, stylish leather sofas in the bar and crisply-clothed, candlelit tables in the dining room. All staff are well-trained and well-briefed on the menu and wine list. The skilful kitchen makes everything from best quality local, seasonal and - where possible - organic produce. Start with the sea bass with fennel and saffron risotto and fennel foam followed by the Cornish beef fillet with red wine and shallot sauce, rösti and buttered spinach. To finish, there's walnut tart or prune and Armagnac ice cream.

Chef: Anton Buttery **Owners:** Anton & Gail Buttery **Times:** 7.30-12, Closed 25 Dec, Sun-Wed, Closed L all week **Prices:** Fixed D £29.95, Coffee £2.50, Min/Water £2.75, Service optional **Wine:** 28 bottles over £20, 55 bottles under £20, 6 by the glass (£3.50-£4.50) **Notes:** Fixed D 6 courses, Tasting menu available, Vegetarian menu, Dress Restrictions, Smart casual preferred **Seats:** 20 **Smoking:** N/Sm in restaurant **Children:** Min 12 yrs **Directions:** From the direction of Plymouth into Callington town centre, left at lights and right into Church St **Parking:** Town centre car park

CONSTANTINE BAY MAP 02 SW87

Treglos Hotel

British

Seaside hotel with bay views and fish on the menu

☎ 01841 520727 PL28 8JH
e-mail: stay@tregloshotel.com
web: www.tregloshotel.com

Set on the spectacular north Cornwall coast, the hotel has wonderful views over Constantine Bay. It has been in the Barlow family for over 30 years and maintains a tradition of high standards. Dinner is served in a spacious restaurant with a conservatory extension, and seafood is a speciality along with vegetables from the garden. Dishes might include fish and shellfish soup, local Dover sole and lobster. Alternatives are roast duckling or Thai vegetable curry. Finish with West Country cheeses and Cornish wafer biscuits, or toffee apple pudding with clotted cream.

Times: 12.15-2.15/7.30-9.15, Closed mid Nov-Mar **Rooms:** 42 (42 en suite) ★★★★ HL **Directions:** Take B3276 (Constantine Bay). At village stores turn right, hotel 50yds on left

FALMOUTH MAP 02 SW83

The Flying Fish Restaurant

Modern, Traditional

Relaxed dining by the sea

☎ 01326 312707 St Michael's Hotel and Spa, Gyllyngvase Beach, Seafront TR11 4NB
e-mail: info@stmichaelshotel.co.uk
web: www.stmichaels.co.uk

Stylish hotel with a nautical theme reflected in the giant sails at the entrance. Reception is formed as a yacht with broadwalk decking, seaside cobbles and gentle seashore sound effects. The Flying Fish Bar & Grill is a fun place to eat, overlooking the sea with its own commodious sun terrace, serving coffee, lunch, snacks, dinner and drinks. A children's menu is available and grownups can eat fresh local fish and seafood landed daily, salads, grills and daily specials. Favourite dishes are home-made crab cakes and chargrilled steaks.

Chef: Simon Morley **Owners:** Nigel & Julie Carpenter **Times:** 12-2/7-9 **Prices:** Starter £3.50-£8.50, Main £7.95-£28.50, Dessert £3.95-£7.50, Coffee £1.50, Min/Water £2.75, Service optional **Wine:** 17 bottles over £20, 19 bottles under £20, 8 by the glass (£2.60-£4.90) **Notes:** Vegetarian available, Dress Restrictions, Smart casual **Seats:** 90, Pr/dining room 30 **Smoking:** N/Sm in restaurant **Children:** Menu, Portions **Rooms:** 62 (62 en suite) ★★★ **Directions:** Please telephone for directions

Harbourside Restaurant

Modern British

Contemporary-style restaurant with great harbour views

☎ 01326 312440 Greenbank Hotel, Harbourside TR11 2SR
e-mail: sales@greenbank-hotel.com
web: www.greenbank-hotel.com

A lovely old hotel at the side of the harbour, once the base for package ship captains, where guests can now arrive by boat at the private pier if they choose. The restaurant makes the most of the spectacular waterside views, and the maritime theme is sustained inside. Accomplished cooking is the order of the day here, with the carte offering interest at each course; open wild mushroom lasagne with tarragon and Cornish goat's cheese, whole grilled Dover sole with herbs, tomato and caper butter, and classic lemon tart with orange jelly and citrus sorbet to finish.

Chef: Colin Hankins **Owners:** Greenbank Hotel (Falmouth) Ltd **Times:** 12-2/7-9.30, Closed L Sat **Prices:** Fixed L fr £10.50, Fixed D £24.50, Coffee £1.75, Min/Water £3.50, Service optional **Wine:** 25 bottles over £20, 43 bottles under £20, 12 by the glass (£3.10-£3.85) **Notes:** Coffee incl, Sun L £14.50, Vegetarian available, Dress Restrictions, Smart casual, Civ Wed 90 **Seats:** 60, Pr/dining room 16 **Smoking:** N/Sm in restaurant **Children:** Portions **Rooms:** 60 (60 en suite) ★★★ HL **Directions:** Approaching Falmouth from Penryn, take left along North Parade. Follow sign to Falmouth Marina and Greenbank Hotel **Parking:** 60

The Terrace Restaurant

Modern International

Modern hotel dining with sea views

☎ 01326 313042 The Royal Duchy Hotel, Cliff Rd TR11 4NX
e-mail: info@royalduchy.co.uk
web: www.brend-hotels.co.uk

Looking out over the sea towards Pendennis Castle, the Royal Duchy is a well-maintained, spacious and hospitable hotel. The dining room has comfortable furnishings and traditional table settings with glamorous touches like the chandeliers and grand piano. The cuisine focuses on top-quality local and seasonal ingredients using lots of fresh local seafood. Strong combinations and clarity of flavours demonstrate a passion for food and accurate cooking. International dishes feature starters like cured wild salmon, langoustine and scallop terrine with watercress salad. Main courses might include roast loin of venison with spiced red cabbage, kohlrabi fondant and bitter chocolate. A range of sandwiches, focaccias, omelettes and jackets are also on offer in the Terrace Restaurant.

The Terrace Restaurant

Chef: Dez Turland, Bob Hunt **Owners:** Brend Hotel Group **Times:** 12.30-2/7-9, Closed L Mon-Sat **Prices:** Fixed L £14.95, Fixed D £31, Coffee £2.25, Min/Water £2.95, Service optional **Wine:** 65 bottles over £20, 60 bottles under £20, 12 by the glass (£2.80-£6.50) **Notes:** Fixed L 3 courses, Fixed D 4 courses, Gourmet menu available, Vegetarian available, Dress Restrictions, Jacket & tie, Civ Wed 150 **Seats:** 100, Pr/dining room 24 **Smoking:** No pipes, Air con **Children:** Menu, Portions **Rooms:** 43 (43 en suite) ★★★★ HL **Directions:** At Pendennis Castle end of Promenade **Parking:** 40

FOWEY MAP 02 SX15

Fowey Hall

Modern British

Family-friendly hotel serving local produce

☎ 01726 833866 Hanson Dr PL23 1ET
e-mail: info@foweyhall.com
web: www.luxuryfamilyhotels.com

Built by the Lord Mayor of London in 1899, this stunning building has exceptional views. Hansons restaurant is light and airy, looking out across the Fowey estuary. Candlelit in the evening, it has a romantic atmosphere. The chef creates modern country-house style dishes using the best of local ingredients. You can see the mussel beds in the river from the restaurant and these - as well as local lobster, fish and shellfish - are the mainstays of a daily-changing menu. Try a starter

continued

FOWEY *continued* MAP 02 SX15

like tartlet of Fowey River mussels and baby leeks, with poached hen's egg and a light curry dressing. Main courses include the assiette of local game with a Jerusalem artichoke purée, wilted greens and cassis reduction. Soufflé of the day or star anise and vanilla pannacotta with braised local rhubarb make grand finales.

Chef: Glynn Wellington **Owners:** Andrew Davis **Times:** 12-2.15/7-10 **Prices:** Fixed D £32.50, Starter £5-£6.95, Main £9.25-£11.95, Dessert £5.25, Coffee £2, Min/Water £3.50, Service optional **Wine:** 58 bottles over £20, 18 bottles under £20, 4 by the glass (£4.50-£5.50) **Notes:** ALC L only, Vegetarian available, Civ Wed 50 **Seats:** 60, Pr/dining room 20 **Smoking:** N/Sm in restaurant **Children:** Menu, Portions **Rooms:** 24 (24 en suite) ★★★ HL **Directions:** Into town centre, pass school on right, 400yds turn right onto Hanson Drive **Parking:** 35

Fowey Hotel

Modern European

Super views and elegant dining

☎ 01726 832551 The Esplanade PL23 1HX
e-mail: info@thefoweyhotel.co.uk
web: www.richardsonhotels.co.uk

Perched above the cliffs at the harbour entrance with spectacular views, this hotel has Victorian origins, and many of the rooms are decorated in keeping with its grand architecture. Plush drapes and rich wall coverings adorn the restaurant, and with its glorious outlook, the window tables are at a premium. Attentive staff bring the daily changing set menu with some supplements, where an accomplished set of dishes is in keeping with the kitchen's growing reputation. A commitment to local produce inevitably means plenty of fish, pan-seared fillet of John Dory with smoked haddock brandard, petit ratatouille and pea velouté perhaps, but meat and poultry dishes like honey-glazed breast of duck with dauphinoise potatoes, buttered savoy, parsnip purée and artichokes are also worthy of praise.

Chef: Mark Griffiths **Owners:** Keith Richardson **Times:** 12-3/6.30-9 **Prices:** Fixed D £37, Coffee £1.95, Min/Water £3.50, Service optional **Wine:** 16 bottles over £20, 28 bottles under £20, 6 by the glass (£2.75-£5) **Notes:** Fixed D 5 courses, Sun L 3 courses £15, Vegetarian available, Dress Restrictions, No torn denim, trainers or shorts **Seats:** 60 **Smoking:** N/Sm in restaurant **Children:** Menu, Portions **Rooms:** 37 (37 en suite) ★★★ HL **Directions:** From A390 take B3269 for approx 5m, follow signs for Fowey continue along Pavillion Rd for 0.75m, 2nd right **Parking:** 13

Marina Hotel

Modern British

Ambitious cuisine on the water's edge

☎ 01726 833315 Esplanade PL23 1HY
e-mail: marina.hotel@dial.pipex.com
web: www.themarinahotel.co.uk

Perched within toe-dipping distance of the River Fowey, this boutique hotel provides guests to its Waterside restaurant with binoculars for watching the passing wildlife and marina traffic. Picture windows make the most of the setting, while blue-and-white striped curtains create a nautical feel - it's all very chic and tasteful, just like the food, which arrives in arrangements artistic enough to divert attention from the view. Dishes are carefully assembled from high-quality Cornish produce, with the best of the morning's catch delivered straight to the kitchen door; your choice of mains might include steamed lemon sole with parsley tagliatelle and champagne cappuccino, or roast rump of Cornish lamb with creamed potato and caramelised sweetbreads.

Times: 12-2/7-9.30 **Rooms:** 13 (13 en suite) ★★ HL **Directions:** Please telephone for directions

The Old Quay House Hotel

Modern European NEW

Fresh local produce served in a stylish waterfront location

☎ 01726 833302 28 Fore St PL23 1AQ
e-mail: info@theoldquayhouse.com
web: www.theoldquayhouse.com

Beautifully restored boutique hotel in an idyllic waterfront location. The terrace on the old quay itself juts out into the harbour and you can dine or take drinks here, or eat inside the stylish restaurant dining room. Here the walls are decorated with local artwork and unusual plaques. Accomplished cuisine sees influences from France, Italy and Britain. The emphasis is firmly on good use of fresh produce including Cornish specialities like Fowey River mussels, local megrim sole and local chicken. The starter of roast local scallops with leek purée, cauliflower fritters and saffron cream is a particular high point. Well worth the drive through Fowey's steep and winding streets.

Chef: Ben Bass & Peter Bublik **Owners:** Jane & Roy Carson **Times:** 12.30-2.30/7-9, Closed L Mon to Fri (Oct to May) **Prices:** Fixed L £16-£18, Starter £6-£10, Main £12.50-£18, Dessert £6, Coffee £2.50, Min/Water £2.75, Service optional, Group min 6 **Wine:** 16 bottles over £20, 13 bottles under £20, 4 by the glass (£4.50) **Notes:** Vegetarian available **Seats:** 38 **Smoking:** N/Sm in restaurant **Children:** Min 12 yrs **Rooms:** 12 (12 en suite) ★★★★★ RR

Food for Thought

☎ 01726 832221 The Quay PL23 1AT

Modern European menu in smart eatery.

HELSTON MAP 02 SW62

New Yard Restaurant

Modern British V

Something for everyone at this stately restaurant

☎ 01326 221595 Trelowarren, Mawgan TR12 6AF
e-mail: info@trelowarren.com
web: www.trelowarren.com

A revitalised stable yard on the Trelowarren estate near the Lizard

continued

peninsula, the backdrop for this well-appointed restaurant is the stunning medieval manor house. The current owner, Sir Ferrers Vyvyan, has personally selected the wine for this French-inspired restaurant. Local ingredients are firmly in place - saffron cake and Cornish heavy cake are worth a go if you happen by for afternoon tea, while dinner offers more exciting fare - oysters and scallops in a cream vermouth and leek sauce for example, followed by roasted monkfish with sweet buttered cabbage and a creamed parsley and foie gras sauce. Enjoy the long drive through the estate.

Chef: Greg Laskey **Owners:** Sir Ferrers Vyvyan **Times:** 12-2.15/7-9.30, Closed 1 wk Feb, 1 wk Nov, Mon, Closed D Sun **Prices:** Starter £5-£10, Main £11.50-£17.50, Dessert £5.50-£6.95, Service optional **Wine:** 23 bottles over £20, 34 bottles under £20, 7 by the glass (£3.75) **Notes:** Sun L 3 courses £14.95, music nights 3 courses £25, Vegetarian available **Seats:** 45 **Smoking:** N/Sm area **Children:** Portions **Directions:** 5m from Helston **Parking:** 20

LISKEARD MAP 02 SX26

Well House Hotel

Rosettes not confirmed at time of going to press

Modern British

Culinary hideaway in a tranquil valley

☎ 01579 342001 St Keyne PL14 4RN
e-mail: enquiries@wellhouse.co.uk
web: www.wellhouse.co.uk

This enchanting hotel is hidden away along a leafy lane in a tranquil Cornish valley, just 30 minutes from the Eden Project. A late Victorian country house, it sits in pretty grounds alongside an all-weather tennis court, swimming pool and croquet lawn, and is the perfect venue for a gourmet getaway. Crisp cloths, sparkling cutlery and quality glassware adorn the tables in the restaurant, a spacious room with a muted modern colour scheme and large bay windows that offer views to the garden beyond. The cooking is assured - the menu changes daily and features a well-balanced selection of modern British dishes which are distinguished by carefully sourced local ingredients and a mature simplicity that sees nothing unnecessary find its way to the plate. Starters might include confit of duck, buttered spinach and star anise jus, while mains are straightforward creations uncluttered by superfluous flavours, prosciutto wrapped monkfish with leeks carbonara.
There was a change of hands taking place at the time of going to press.

Chef: Glenn Gatland **Owners:** Mr N Wainford, Mrs Ione Nurdin **Times:** 12.30-1.30/7-8.30, Closed 1 wk Jan **Prices:** Fixed L fr £18.50, Fixed D fr £32.50, Service optional **Wine:** 86 bottles over £20, 52 bottles under £20, 5 by the glass (£2.75) **Notes:** Vegetarian available, Dress Restrictions, Smart casual **Seats:** 36 **Smoking:** N/Sm in restaurant **Children:** Min 8 yrs D, Portions **Rooms:** 9 (9 en suite) ★★ **Directions:** From Liskeard take B3254 to St Keyne 3m. In village take left fork at church signed St Keyne. Hotel 0.5m on left **Parking:** 30

MARAZION MAP 02 SW53

Mount Haven Hotel

Modern British

Local produce in light, stylish surroundings

☎ 01736 710249 Turnpike Rd TR17 0DQ
e-mail: reception@mounthaven.co.uk
web: www.mounthaven.co.uk

White walls, tables and crockery and pale-coloured chairs emphasise the lightness of this idyllically located hotel restaurant. There is a

continued

beautiful terrace with stunning views for pre-dinner drinks. Fresh fish dominates the main courses, unsurprisingly given the location and, like the meat dishes, is refreshingly uncomplicated. The best of local and seasonal produce is used whenever possible. Menu choices may include starters like twice-baked leek and asparagus soufflé with Chardonnay beurre blanc, or seared Falmouth Bay scallops with a smoked salmon risotto, followed by honey-glazed breast of Barbary duck with black pepper bubble-and-squeak and Calvados sauce, or Cornish pollack with saffron-buttered cabbage and new potatoes.

Mount Haven Hotel

Chef: Julie Manley **Owners:** Orange & Mike Trevillion **Times:** 12-2.30/6.45-8.45, Closed last wk Dec-end Jan **Prices:** Starter £4.95-£7.95, Main £13.95-£17.95, Dessert £4.95-£6.50, Coffee £2.50, Min/Water £2.75, Service optional **Wine:** 8 bottles over £20, 43 bottles under £20, 6 by the glass (£3-£3.75) **Notes:** Sun L 2 courses £ 12.50, 3 courses £15, Dress Restrictions, Smart casual **Seats:** 50 **Smoking:** N/Sm in restaurant **Children:** Portions **Rooms:** 18 (18 en suite) ★★ **Directions:** From centre of Marazion, up hill E, hotel 400yds on right **Parking:** 30

MAWGAN PORTH

Bedruthan Steps Hotel

Modern British

Atlantic views and full-flavoured food with visual impact

☎ 01637 860555 TR8 4BU
e-mail: office@bedruthan.com
web: www.bedruthan.com

Smartly refurbished family hotel in a glorious setting overlooking a fine beach and the clear Atlantic waters, between Newquay and Padstow. Enjoy alfresco summer drinks on grassed terraces before dining in the spacious and comfortable Indigo Bay restaurant. Cool and contemporary, with white linen, candles and orchids, it's the place to watch the setting sun while savouring some accomplished cooking. Adventurous menus use fresh local produce and dishes are well presented, perhaps taking in seared fillet of sea bass with tagine of mussels, fennel and saffron, and venison with juniper and truffle jus.

Times: 12-2/7.30-9.30, Closed Xmas **Rooms:** 99 (99 en suite) ★★★★

see advert on page 67

MAWNAN SMITH MAP 02 SW72

Budock Vean - The Hotel on the River

Traditional British [V]

Cornish produce in smart hotel surroundings

☎ 01326 252100 & 250230 TR11 5LG
e-mail: relax@budockvean.co.uk
web: www.budockvean.co.uk

The high-ceilinged restaurant with its beams and minstrels' gallery has local musicians playing each evening. Popular for special occasions, the restaurant offers quality Cornish ingredients, formal table service and friendly service. Local produce is clearly identified on the menu with imaginatively prepared and presented dishes like best end of Cornish lamb with a garlic and mint mash, red onion marmalade and rosemary jus or tenderloin of Bodmin Moor venison with potato rösti, wilted greens and a port and sage sauce. If you've any room left you can retire to the lounge for coffee with Cornish fudge and petits fours.

Chef: Darren Kelly **Owners:** Barlow family **Times:** 12.30-2.30/7.30-9, Closed 3 wks Jan, Closed L Mon-Sat **Prices:** Fixed L fr £17.50, Fixed D fr £31, Starter £7.75-£18.25, Main £13-£32.75, Coffee £2.50, Min/Water £3, Service optional **Wine:** 47 bottles over £20, 35 bottles under £20, 4 by the glass (£3.15-£3.75) **Notes:** Fixed L 3 courses, Fixed D 4 courses, Vegetarian menu, Dress Restrictions, Jacket & tie, Civ Wed 60 **Seats:** 100, Pr/dining room 40 **Smoking:** N/Sm in restaurant, Air con **Children:** Min 7 yrs, Menu, Portions **Rooms:** 57 (57 en suite) ★★★★ CHH **Directions:** Telephone for directions **Parking:** 100

Meudon Hotel

British, International

Accomplished cooking at a friendly Cornish hotel

☎ 01326 250541 TR11 5HT
e-mail: wecare@meudon.co.uk
web: www.meudon.co.uk

Run by the same family for five generations, this sedate Cornish hotel sits amid sub-tropical gardens running down to a private beach at Falmouth Bay. Conservatory windows allow diners in the spacious restaurant to enjoy the view while sampling cuisine conjured from the finest local produce. Fish is delivered fresh off the boat from nearby Newlyn, while West Country cheeses are also well represented. Starters might include warm seared scallops with sweet chilli jam, while mains range from breast of local wild pheasant served with a venison sausage, wild mushrooms and Drambuie jus, to fillet of local line-caught sea bass with a tarragon and sun-dried tomato hollandaise.

Chef: Alan Webb **Owners:** Mr. Pilgrim **Times:** 12.30-2.00/7.30-9, Closed Jan **Prices:** Food prices not confirmed for 2007. Please telephone for details **Notes:** Dress Restrictions, Jacket & tie required **Seats:** 60 **Smoking:** N/Sm in restaurant **Children:** Menu, Portions **Rooms:** 29 (29 en suite) ★★★ CHH **Parking:** 30

Trelawne Hotel

Modern British [V]

Modern British cooking in popular hotel with magnificent views

☎ 01326 250226 TR11 5HS
e-mail: info@trelawnehotel.co.uk
web: www.trelawnehotel.co.uk

This small family-run hotel is surrounded by attractive lawns and gardens and enjoys superb coastal views. It's also close to the Eden Project and Trebah Gardens. An informal atmosphere prevails in the restaurant, which boasts good linen, crockery and glassware. Quality

continued

local produce is used in imaginative dishes, with fish and meat being well sourced from the area. Seared Cornish scallops with saffron sauce acknowledges the culinary heritage of the region, as do roast Cornish chicken with tomato and basil sauce and bread-and-butter pudding with vanilla Cornish egg custard.

Chef: Martin Jones/Oliver Wyatt **Owners:** G P Gibbons **Times:** 7-9, Closed 17 Dec-10 Feb, Closed L all week **Prices:** Fixed D fr £24.90, Min/Water £2.50, Service optional **Wine:** 12 bottles over £20, 84 bottles under £20, 6 by the glass (£3.50-£4.25) **Notes:** Coffee incl, Vegetarian menu, Dress Restrictions, Smart casual **Seats:** 30 **Smoking:** N/Sm in restaurant **Children:** Min 10 yrs, Menu, Portions **Rooms:** 14 (14 en suite) ★★★ HL **Directions:** From Truro take A39 towards Falmouth. Right at Hillhead rdbt, take exit signed Maenporth. After 3m, past Maenporth Beach, hotel at top of hill **Parking:** 20

MOUSEHOLE MAP 02 SW42

The Cornish Range Restaurant with Rooms

European, Seafood

Atmospheric restaurant with great seafood

☎ 01736 731488 6 Chapel St TR19 6BD
e-mail: info@cornishrange.co.uk
web: www.cornishrange.co.uk

A former pilchard processing factory, this vibrant restaurant with rooms has a long standing association with the sea and, as you would expect, fish and seafood play a prominent part on the menu with the freshest produce landed locally at Newlyn and delivered daily. Interiors are decorated with earthy tones with sturdy chairs and tables, soft lighting, flowers and local contemporary artwork giving a rustic, almost Mediterranean feel to the dining room. Flavours from around the world make their way onto this straightforward menu that delivers consistent, interesting dishes with some unusual elements. A typical meal might consist of potted Newlyn crab with dill mayonnaise and melted gruyère to start and a main course of roasted wing of ray with sauté of fennel and saffron broth.

continued

Times: 6-9.30, Closed L all week, D Sun-Tue (Nov-Mar) **Rooms:** 3 (3 en suite) ★★★★ RR **Directions:** Mousehole is 3m S from Penzance, via Newlyn

Old Coastguard Hotel

Modern British, Seafood

Popular summer alfresco destination with stunning sea views

☎ 01736 731222 The Parade TR19 6PR
e-mail: bookings@oldcoastguardhotel.co.uk
web: www.oldcoastguardhotel.co.uk

As the name might suggest this commanding hotel and restaurant overlooks the sea - what the name doesn't reveal is how splendid those sea views are and just how quaint and absorbingly lovely the location is, situated in what Dylan Thomas described as 'the most beautiful village in England'. Simple, effective décor inside provides a suitably unobtrusive backdrop to the food; fish - most from nearby Newlyn - features heavily on a menu that might include dishes such as shellfish and anise bisque or wild sea bass fillet with orange glazed fennel and Muscat cream sauce.

Chef: K Terry, A Gilbert, M Pearce **Owners:** A W Treloar **Times:** 12-2.30/6-10, Closed 25 Dec (reservations only), Closed D 31 Dec (reservations only) **Prices:** D £23-£32.50, Starter £5.50-£7.50, Main £14-£19.50, Dessert £4-£5.50, Coffee £1.50, Min/Water £3.20, Service optional **Wine:** 36 bottles over £20, 15 bottles under £20, 8 by the glass (£2.50-£6) **Notes:** D is ALC, Vegetarian available, Dress Restrictions, Smart casual preferred **Seats:** 80 **Smoking:** N/Sm in restaurant **Children:** Menu, Portions **Rooms:** 21 (21 en suite) ★★ HL **Directions:** A30 to Penzance. From Penzance take coast road through Newlyn to Mousehole. Inn 1st large building on left on entering village, after car park **Parking:** 15

see advert on page 71

NEWQUAY MAP 02 SW86

Corisande Manor Hotel

Traditional British

Friendly atmosphere and good home cooking

☎ 01637 872042 Riverside Av, Pentire TR7 1PL
e-mail: relax@corisande.com
web: www.corisande.com

Originally built by a German in 1895, the hotel looks like a small schloss on the Rhine, but it's actually a country-house hotel right on the sea in Cornwall. Personally run by the owners for ten years, the atmosphere is relaxed and friendly. Fresh home-made meals are cooked by your hosts, with the daily-changing menu offering a choice of different meat or fish main courses. A typical dinner might start with game soup, then grapefruit soufflé, followed by marinated lamb steak and for dessert a lemon syllabub.

continued

NEWQUAY *continued* MAP 02 SW86

Chef: Chris Grant **Owners:** Mr & Mrs D Grant **Times:** 8, Closed Nov-Mar, Closed L all week **Prices:** Fixed D £25-£28, Min/Water £2, Service included **Wine:** 300 bottles over £20, 40 bottles under £20, 3 by the glass (£2.50-£3.50) **Notes:** Coffee incl, Fixed D 4 courses **Seats:** 20 **Smoking:** N/Sm in restaurant **Children:** Portions **Rooms:** 12 (12 en suite) ♦♦♦♦♦ **Directions:** Main road to Pentire headland, left at Newquay Nursing Home on to Pentire Crescent, then right onto Riverside Ave **Parking:** 10

Finn's

Modern British

Modern, lively surf-style café with a harbour-side location

☎ 01637 874062 & 854367 The Old Boat House, South Quay Hill TR7 1HR
e-mail: info@finnscafe.com
web: www.finnscafe.com

This harbour-side restaurant benefits from a harbour beach where small boats ride at anchor or unload their catch. Much of Finn's fresh fish is bought from here and you might see a fisherman tucked away in the trendy crowd at the bar. Lively music is a feature here with live bands and funky upbeat sounds creating a great atmosphere for the outdoor barbecue. Cocktails feature on the drinks menu while the food naturally makes good use of fresh fish and shellfish, especially the crab claw salad or roasted harbour lobster. Sit outside in summer or enjoy the bright décor inside on cooler days.

Times: 10.00-3.00/6.30-11.00, Closed Xmas **Directions:** Newquay town centre, by harbour off Fore St

Headland Hotel

French, British

Elegant dining with wonderful sea views

☎ 01637 872211 Fistral Beach TR7 1EW
e-mail: office@headlandhotel.co.uk
web: www.headlandhotel.co.uk

Away from the hustle and bustle of the town, this imposing Victorian hotel enjoys a stunning location on a rocky headland with the sea on three sides. Views can be savoured from most of the windows, the best from the ornate restaurant, which overlooks Fistral Beach and is the place to dine watching the setting sun. Sound cooking using quality ingredients is the strength from a confident kitchen. The fixed-price dinner menu may offer saffron risotto with roast asparagus to start, followed by Cornish lobster with herb butter, and summer pudding with clotted cream.

Chef: Chris Wyburn-Ridsdale **Owners:** John & Carolyn Armstrong **Times:** 12.30-2/7-9.45, Closed 25-26 Dec, Closed L Mon-Sat **Prices:** Fixed D £30, Service included **Notes:** Sun L available, Fixed D 4 courses, Dress Restrictions, Smart casual, Civ Wed 200 **Seats:** 250, Pr/dining room 40 **Smoking:** N/Sm in restaurant **Children:** Min 3 yrs, Portions **Rooms:** 104 (104 en suite) ★★★★ HL **Directions:** A30 onto A392 towards Newquay, follow signs to Fistral Beach, hotel is adjacent **Parking:** 200

PADSTOW MAP 02 SW97

Margot's

British

Friendly family-run bistro serving good fresh food

☎ 01841 533441 11 Duke St PL28 8AB
e-mail: enquiries@margots.co.uk
web: www.margots.co.uk

Cheerful little shop-fronted bistro with a genial chef-proprietor combining serving and cooking, a formula that is both efficient and popular. There are just nine tables and the walls are hung with paintings by local artists, most of them for sale. The menu changes constantly according to the supplies of produce available, including fresh fish from the harbour. Cooking is accurate and straightforward, with dishes such as seared scallops with bacon and balsamic dressing, grilled fillet of wild sea bass with lemon oil and new potatoes, and sticky toffee pudding.

Times: 12.30-2/7-9, Closed Nov, Jan, Sun-Mon **Directions:** Telephone for directions

The Metropole

Modern British

Victorian grandeur in this famously foodie village

☎ 01841 532486 Station Rd PL28 8DB
e-mail: info@the-metropole.co.uk
web: www.richardsonhotels.co.uk

The Metropole is a grand Victorian property with fabulous views of the harbour and Camel estuary. It was a favourite haunt of the Prince of Wales in the 1930s and public rooms retain the sophistication of a bygone era. Local produce forms the basis of the seasonal menus, and cooking is modern aiming for simple, strong flavours: crispy haddock in Doom Bar batter and home-made chips with caviar tartare; grilled local sea bass with crayfish and pea risotto and langoustine jus. Light meals and afternoon tea are served in the Met Café Bar.

Chef: Jon Guest **Owners:** Richardson Hotels Ltd **Times:** 6.30-9.00, Closed L Mon-Sat **Prices:** Fixed D £29.95-£35.95, Coffee £1.95, Min/Water £3.50, Service added but optional 12.5% **Wine:** 16 bottles over £20, 29 bottles under £20, 7 by the glass (£3.50-£5.95) **Notes:** Sun L £14.95, Vegetarian available, Dress Restrictions, No jeans, shorts, swimwear, trainers **Seats:** 70 **Smoking:** N/Sm in restaurant **Children:** Menu, Portions **Rooms:** 50 (50 en suite) ★★★ HL **Directions:** M5/A30 pass Launceston, follow signs for Wadebridge and N Cornwall. Then take A39 and follow signs for Padstow **Parking:** 40

St Ervan Manor

see below

St Petroc's Bistro

French

Rick Stein's bustling seafood bistro

☎ 01841 532700 4 New St PL28 8EA
e-mail: reservations@rickstein.com
web: www.rickstein.com

The fifth oldest building in Padstow built by a friend of Sir Walter Raleigh. Clean white walls adorned with modern paintings set the scene in the dining room, with an open fire in winter. In summer, sit outside under a huge canopy with excellent heating. There's a sitting room and reading room, ideal for after-dinner coffee. The emphasis is on fish and dishes featured in Rick Stein's television series. Success depends on the freshness of the ingredients rather than on complicated combinations: mackerel escabeche, whole sea bass with beurre blanc and crème brûlée.

Chef: Alistair Clive, David Sharland **Owners:** R & J Stein **Times:** 12-2/7-10, Closed 24-26 Dec, 1 May **Prices:** Starter £6.50-£7.50, Main £13.95-£17.95, Dessert £6, Coffee £2.75, Min/Water £2.30, Service optional **Wine:** 16 bottles over £20, 17 bottles under £20, 11 by the glass (£3.55-£6.50) **Seats:** 54 **Smoking:** N/Sm in restaurant, Air con **Children:** Menu, Portions **Rooms:** 10 (10 en suite) ★★ SHL **Directions:** Follow one-way around harbour, 1st left, situated on right **Parking:** 10

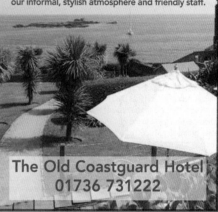

St Ervan Manor

PADSTOW MAP 02 SW97

Modern British

An essential visit for any gourmet tour of Cornwall

☎ 01841 540255 The Old Rectory, St Ervan PL27 7TA
e-mail: info@stervanmanor.co.uk
web: www.stervanmanor.co.uk

This elegant Grade II listed stone manor house has five acres of grounds and a kitchen garden. Sympathetic decoration retains lots of original features and gives a relaxing informality to rooms and public areas. Unshowy dining rooms do little to detract from the food's star-billing. Modern British dishes based on seasonal, local produce - some of which comes from the Manor's own vegetable garden and orchard - populate this six-course menu. Superb canapés such as a cube of seared mackerel with pickled veg or a cube of feta on a mini pizza get things off to a great start. Simple presentation, good clear flavours and a general air of confidence characterise dishes like celeriac soup with rosemary oil - full of crunchy chunks and intense flavours. Perfectly cooked scallops with curried butternut squash purée and seeds also impress. A dessert of toffee cream and green apple balances tartness with sweetness, or perhaps try the bitter chocolate malt and espresso with a lovely molten core.

Chef: Nathan Outlaw **Owners:** Allan & Lorraine Clarke **Times:** 7-9, Closed 19 Dec-19 Jan, Mon, Tue, Closed L all week **Prices:** Fixed D £45-£65, Coffee £3, Min/Water £2.50, Service optional **Wine:** 80 bottles over £20, 16 bottles under £20, 13 by the glass (£3.50-£9) **Notes:** Tasting menu 6 courses, Vegetarian available, Dress Restrictions, Smart casual, jacket & tie **Seats:** 20, Pr/dining room 12 **Smoking:** N/Sm in restaurant **Children:** Min 14 yrs **Rooms:** 6 (5 en suite) ★★★★★ RR **Directions:** From A39 take B3274 signed Padstow. 2.5 m turn left & follow brown signs to St Ervan Manor **Parking:** 16

England

The Seafood Restaurant

PADSTOW MAP 02 SW97

International Seafood

Rick Stein's famous restaurant

☎ 01841 532700 Riverside PL28 8BY
e-mail: reservations@rickstein.com
web: www.rickstein.com

Rick Stein says on the menu that he has never seen his restaurant as a gastronomic temple, but perhaps this statement ought to be reviewed, given that so many pay homage to the cooking made popular by his many TV series. At the door, crowds huddle to read the menu displayed outside this his flagship Padstow enterprise, an empire which now runs to the St Petroc's Hotel and bistro, a café, deli, pâtisserie, fish 'n' chip shop and seafood cookery school. The small frontage here belies its tardis-like interior, with a spacious front conservatory for aperitifs overlooking estuary and fishing boats. Otherwise, it's straight to the light-and-airy dining room's linen-clothed tables and white walls decked out with large, colourful paintings, which, in turn, contrast against the black uniforms of the well-orchestrated, attentive staff. Superbly fresh and intelligently simply prepared, well-conceived fish cookery from an accomplished team is the admirable style, with an ethos for using the finest local produce. The approach, via a daily-changing carte and six-course tasting option, comes dotted with luxury items, a crowd-pleasing blend of classic (roast tronçon of turbot with hollandaise) and modern (Loch Duart salmon recheado - pan-fried with chilli masala and served with fragrant potato curry), all backed by a notable wine list.

Chef: S Delourme, David Sharland **Owners:** R & J Stein **Times:** 12-2/7-10, Closed 24-26 Dec, 1 May **Prices:** Starter £8.50-£21.50, Main £17.50-£45, Dessert £8.50, Coffee £3.20, Min/Water £2.25, Service optional **Wine:** 200 bottles over £20, 11 bottles under £20, 13 by the glass (£3.55-£6.50) **Notes:** Tasting menu 6 courses £65 and coffee **Seats:** 104 **Smoking:** Air con **Children:** Min 3 yrs+, Menu, Portions **Rooms:** 33 (33 en suite) RR **Directions:** Follow signs for town centre. Restaurant on riverside **Parking:** Directly opposite restaurant (pay & display)

PADSTOW *continued* MAP 02 SW97

Rick Stein's Café

☎ 01841 532700 10 Middle St PL28 8AP

Fish in the Stein style, mostly deliciously simple sometimes bold and striking. No lunch bookings taken, so arrive early.

Stein's Fish & Chip Shop

☎ 01841 532700 South Quay

Traditional fish and chips on the quayside where you can watch the fish being landed.

PENZANCE MAP 02 SW43

The Abbey Restaurant

Modern International

Skilful cooking in modern setting with harbour views

☎ 01736 330680 Abbey St TR18 4AR
e-mail: kinga@theabbeyonline.com
web: www.theabbeyonline.com

This restaurant's bar and lounge has a comfortable, relaxing atmosphere with the occasional reminder of its past as a Sixties nightclub such as the bright red walls and tub seating. The upstairs dining room is more refined with white walls, sculpture and good views of the harbour and St Michael's Mount. Simple, effective, seasonal dishes with international flair are the norm here. Top quality produce is sourced from specialist suppliers and carefully prepared to produce starters of crab saffron and tomato tart with lemon and dill mayonnaise or potted duck with pumpkin and tomato chutney. Follow with roast woodcock bourguignon. For dessert, there's chocolate soufflé and chocolate sorbet.

Chef: Ben Tunnicliffe **Owners:** B & K Tunnicliffe **Times:** 12-1.30/6.30-10.30, Closed Winter closure (annual holiday), Mon (Jun-Sep) Mon-Tue (Mar-May, Sep-Oct), Closed L Tue-Thu, D Mon **Prices:** Fixed L £18, Starter £5.50-£9.50, Main £17-£23, Dessert £5.50-£6.50, Coffee £2, Min/Water £3.20, Service optional **Wine:** 30 bottles over £20, 50 bottles under £20, 14 by the glass (£3.95-£4.25) **Seats:** 26 **Smoking:** N/Sm in restaurant, Air con **Children:** Portions **Directions:** In centre of Penzance turn into Chapel Street opposite Lloyds TSB Bank, 500 yds & turn left at Admiral Benon public house, onto Abbey St **Parking:** On street

The Bay Restaurant

Modern European, International

Contemporary hotel restaurant with fabulous views

☎ 01736 366890 Mount Prospect Hotel, Britons Hill TR18 3AE
e-mail: table@bay-penzance.co.uk
web: www.bay-penzance.co.uk

With stunning views over Penzance harbour, this tastefully restored Edwardian house is an utterly marvellous place for a leisurely dinner. Take a walk through the well-tended, terraced gardens before heading to the spacious, airy dining room with its floor-to-ceiling windows affording grand views of the eponymous bay. Granite tables, polished wooden floors and local artwork on clean white walls make for a pleasant backdrop to the simple, accurate cookery here. The chef has a proven track record, most recently at The Pickled Fish, and has created a seasonally inspired menu utilising the freshest Cornish

continued

produce imaginable - particularly fish and seafood. Dishes might include smoked haddock chowder with paprika croutons or roast duck breast with pink grapefruit reduction.

Chef: Ben Reeve, Katie Semmens **Owners:** Yvonne & Stephen Hill **Times:** 11-2/6.15-11, Closed L Oct-Apr **Prices:** Starter £4.75-£7.95, Main £12.95-£17.75, Dessert £5.50, Coffee £1.75, Min/Water £2.75, Service optional, Group min 8 service 10% **Wine:** 13 bottles over £20, 24 bottles under £20, 5 by the glass (£3.25-£4.50) **Notes:** Vegetarian available, Dress Restrictions, Smart casual, no shorts **Seats:** 60, Pr/dining room 12 **Smoking:** N/Sm in restaurant, Air con **Children:** Menu, Portions **Rooms:** 24 (24 en suite) ★★★ HL **Directions:** Approaching Penzance from A30, at 'Tesco' rdbt take first exit towards town centre. Britons Hill is third turning on right **Parking:** 13

Harris's Restaurant

English, French

Simple freshly cooked food in a family-run restaurant

☎ 01736 364408 46 New St TR18 2LZ
e-mail: contact@harrissrestaurant.co.uk
web: www.harrissrestaurant.co.uk

This address has been the site of a food business since 1860 and the current restaurant has been in the Harris family for over 30 years. The restaurant is on two floors, connected by a spiral staircase. Downstairs, there is a very impressive pressed metal ceiling. Fresh local produce features on a British and French influenced menu, featuring starters like grilled scallops on salad leaves with a fresh herb dressing. Mains might include grilled fillet steak with a béarnaise sauce. Delectable desserts range from treacle tart to a little pot of chocolate.

Chef: Roger Harris **Owners:** Roger & Anne Harris **Times:** 12-2/7-9.30, Closed 3 wks winter, 25-26 Dec, 1 Jan, Sun, Closed L Mon **Prices:** Food prices not confirmed for 2007. Please telephone for details **Wine:** 25 bottles over £20, 30 bottles under £20, 6 by the glass (£3.50-£4.50) **Seats:** 40, Pr/dining room 20 **Smoking:** N/Sm in restaurant **Children:** Min 5 yrs **Directions:** Located down narrow cobbled street opposite Lloyds TSB **Parking:** On street, local car park

The Navy Inn

Modern British

Penzance local with an ambitious kitchen

☎ 01736 333232 Lower Queen St TR18 4DE
e-mail: keir@navyinn.co.uk

Just a short walk from Penzance promenade with its stunning views, this friendly pub has a brightly coloured exterior to match its name and a reputation for great food. It's decked out in shabby-chic style with wooden floors, open fires, and an array of marine artefacts. Working with the best of local ingredients, the Navy's accomplished kitchen conjures an eclectic mix of dishes. Ranging from typical pub grub (fisherman's pie, sausage and mash) to more ambitious fare, such as honey-roast duck with a lime marmalade glace or braised trio of local fish in a mild Thai sauce.

Chef: Keir Meikle **Owners:** Keir Meikle **Times:** 12-10, Closed D 25 Dec **Prices:** Starter £3.50-£6.50, Main £7.50-£15.95, Dessert £3.95, Coffee £1.50, Min/Water £2.50, Service optional **Wine:** 5 bottles over £20, 14 bottles under £20, 8 by the glass (£2-£4.50) **Notes:** Sun L £7.95, Vegetarian available **Seats:** 54 **Smoking:** N/Sm area **Children:** Menu, Portions **Directions:** In town centre, follow Chapel St for 50yds turn right into Queen St and follow to the bottom of road **Parking:** Free parking on promenade

The Summerhouse

Mediterranean

Mediterranean style and Cornish produce

☎ 01736 363744 Cornwall Ter TR18 4HL
e-mail: reception@summerhouse-cornwall.com
web: www.summerhouse-cornwall.com

Once home to one of Cornwall's leading artists, this listed Regency house is now a delightful restaurant with stylish rooms. The philosophy is simple, great food, beautiful surroundings and an informal, happy atmosphere. The restaurant has a Mediterranean theme and spills out into a walled garden full of terracotta pots and palm trees. The chef-patron Ciro Zaino spent years managing some of London's famous hotels but he has found true inspiration in Cornwall's fine larder, providing a daily-changing menu of fresh choices including lots of local fish and seafood. Try a starter of rigatoni al basilica, followed by a main course of baccala Livornese - Newlyn cod cooked traditional Italian style with tomatoes and black olives. For dessert, treat yourself to lavender ice cream with spiced figs.

Chef: Ciro Zaino **Owners:** Ciro & Linda Zaino **Times:** 7-9.30, Closed Nov-Feb, Mon-Wed, Closed L all week **Prices:** Fixed D £28.50, Coffee £2.50, Min/Water £3.50, Service added 10% **Wine:** 30 bottles over £20, 10 bottles under £20, 4 by the glass (£3.50-£5) **Seats:** 22 **Smoking:** N/Sm

continued

England

PENZANCE *continued* MAP 02 SW43

in restaurant **Children:** Min 8 yrs **Rooms:** 5 (5 en suite) ◆◆◆◆◆ **Directions:** Into Penzance on A30. Along harbour past open air bathing pool & the Promenade to Queens Hotel. Turn right immediately after hotel & restaurant 30mtrs on left **Parking:** 5

PORTSCATHO MAP 02 SW83

Driftwood

see below

Rosevine Hotel - Didiers Restaurant

European V

Old-fashioned flair on the Cornish coast

☎ 01872 580206 TR2 5EW
e-mail: info@rosevine.co.uk
web: www.rosevine.co.uk

Set on the Cornish coast, this comfortable family-run hotel sits in pretty gardens overlooking the sea. Its airy restaurant is decked out in heavy fabrics and shades of gold and cream, and there's a grand piano for entertainment in the evenings. Expect traditional European dishes with an occasional twist. The concise menu offers four choices at each course and changes daily; a beef main shows the style, served with a girolle and red onion purée, fondant potatoes and wild mushroom velouté. Local seafood is a speciality.

continued

Chef: Didier Bienaime, Tom Rhodes **Owners:** The Makepeace Family **Times:** 12-3/7.15-9.30, Closed Jan **Prices:** Fixed L £20-£26, Fixed D £38, Min/Water £3.50, Service optional **Wine:** 40 bottles over £20, 6 bottles under £20, 20 by the glass (£4.50-£10) **Notes:** Coffee incl, Fixed L 3 courses, fixed D 4 courses, Vegetarian menu, Dress Restrictions, Smart casual **Seats:** 50 **Smoking:** N/Sm in restaurant **Children:** Menu, Portions **Rooms:** 17 (17 en suite) ★★★ CHH **Directions:** Off A3078, hotel signed on right, 2m after Ruan High Lanes **Parking:** 40

ROCK MAP 02 SW97

The St Enodoc Hotel Restaurant

Mediterranean, European

Contemporary cooking in bright modern hotel

☎ 01208 863394 The St Enodoc Hotel PL27 6LA
e-mail: enodochotel@aol.com
web: www.enodoc-hotel.co.uk

A striking location above the Camel estuary, stunning views across to Padstow, and a fresh, contemporary décor draw discerning guests to this chic hotel on Cornwall's rugged north coast. Housed in a conservatory-style extension, with big windows and an eclectic collection of local art, the split-level bar and restaurant opens out on to a panoramic terrace - perfect for pre-dinner drinks. Local seasonal produce, notably fresh fish, highlight the changing daily menu. Begin with smoked haddock and bacon chowder, move on to chargrilled swordfish with sweet potato, mussel and coconut curry, and finish with lemon pannacotta.

continued

Driftwood

PORTSCATHO MAP 02 SW83

Modern French

Unique, relaxing location for exquisite cuisine

☎ 01872 580644 Rosevine TR2 5EW
e-mail: info@driftwoodhotel.co.uk
web: www.driftwood.co.uk

Perched on the side of a cliff overlooking the English Channel and the Atlantic beyond, this hotel is aptly named. Many of the charming decorative features are made from driftwood or other sea themed items. Contemporary New England style décor in neutral colours creates a calming environment where you instantly feel relaxed. The smart dining room is bright and airy, decorated in shades of white, with lots of windows to take in views of the bay.

Simple cuisine with classical French and modern European influences makes use of the finest seasonal produce available, particularly fresh fish and shellfish from local waters. Locally reared meat, organic vegetables and salad contribute to a veritable feast of top-notch ingredients. Dived scallops are a popular starter, served with lasagne of potato brandade and leek velouté. An imaginative main course comprises noisettes of pig's trotters with pork belly, Jerusalem artichoke and morels. If you prefer to stick with seafood you can order in advance and have wonderfully fresh lobster and fruit de mer platters to share; alternatively a tasting menu for the whole table can be ordered in advance. Beautifully prepared desserts might include caramelised lemon tart with lemon curd ice cream and raspberry coulis to round off what will surely be a memorable meal.

Chef: Rury Duncan **Owners:** Robinsons **Times:** 7-9.30, Closed Xmas, Jan, Closed L all week **Prices:** Fixed D £38, Coffee £2.50, Min/Water £2.50, Service optional **Wine:** 36 bottles over £20, 12 bottles under £20, 7 by the glass (£3.75-£5) **Notes:** Tasting menu available summer only **Seats:** 36 **Smoking:** N/Sm in restaurant **Rooms:** 15 (15 en suite) ★★★ HL **Directions:** 5m from St Mawes off the A3078, signposted Rosevine **Parking:** 30

The St Enodoc Hotel Restaurant

Chef: Rupert Brown **Owners:** Linedegree Ltd **Times:** 12.30-2.30/7-10, Closed 2 mths (late Dec, Jan, early Feb) **Prices:** Starter £4.25-£6.95, Main £11.75-£19.95, Dessert £4.25-£5.95, Service added but optional 10% **Wine:** 39 bottles over £20, 14 bottles under £20, 9 by the glass (£3.75-£5) **Notes:** Sun L fr £22.50, Fixed L seasonal, Vegetarian available, Dress Restrictions, Smart casual **Seats:** 55, Pr/dining room 30 **Smoking:** N/Sm in restaurant, Air con **Children:** Menu, Portions **Parking:** 60

ST AUSTELL MAP 02 SX05

Carlyon Bay Hotel

British [V]

Sweeping sea views and a fine dining restaurant

☎ 01726 812304 Sea Rd, Carlyon Bay PL25 3RD
e-mail: info@carlyonbay.co.uk
web: www.carlyonbay.com

An imposing art-deco style hotel, purpose-built in 1929 in a fantastic cliff-top location. The restaurant has sea views from an elegant dining room and a choice of daily changing fixed-price menu or carte. Modern British cuisine is inspired here by the Cornish coast and local produce, with starters like Cornish crab and lobster timbale with lobster fumet on the menu. Main courses might feature local spring lamb with wild thyme and potatoes, while desserts could include the likes of gooseberry pannacotta with gooseberry compote and sloe berry consommé. Formal table service is delivered by friendly, professional staff.

Chef: Paul Leakey **Owners:** PR Brend Hoteliers Ltd. **Times:** 12.30-2/7-9.30 **Prices:** Fixed L £14.50-£16.50, Fixed D fr £32, Starter £5.10-£7.50, Main £13.50-£16.50, Dessert fr £6.95, Coffee £2.50, Min/Water £4, Service optional **Wine:** 103 bottles over £20, 83 bottles under £20, 16 by the glass (£3.70-£13.25) **Notes:** Fixed D 4 courses, Sun L £16.50, Vegetarian menu, Dress Restrictions, Smart dress, no jeans/T-shirts, Civ Wed 120 **Seats:** 120, Pr/dining room 60 **Smoking:** N/Sm in restaurant, Air con **Children:** Menu, Portions **Rooms:** 87 (87 en suite) ★★★★ HL **Directions:** A390 towards St Austell; from town follow Charlestown then Carlyon Bay/Crinnis. Hotel at end of Sea Rd near Cornwall Coliseum. Hotel at end of Sea Rd

Revival

Modern International

Fresh, exciting cooking in historic Charlestown Harbour

☎ 01726 879053 Charlestown Harbour PL25 3NJ
web: www.cornwall-revival.co.uk

Contemporary style blends with interesting old features at this white-painted building (a former sail and rope store) set alongside the port.

continued

A terrace offers a great place for fair-weather aperitifs, while inside, burgundy chairs, white tablecloths and attentive service deliver the comforts. Clear flavours, quality ingredients and a confident kitchen impress, alongside a deserved reputation for fresh fish and seafood. Lunch is a lighter affair, while dinner cranks up a gear with an appealing repertoire awash with the fruits of the sea, though meat-lovers aren't forgotten, with fine produce from the abundant West Country larder. Typical mains include Kilhallon Cornish fillet of beef with pomme fondant, wild mushrooms and red wine jus, and spiced monkfish with a crab cake and red pepper sauce.

Chef: Grady Boone **Owners:** Ashley Waller, Angela Husband **Times:** 10-2.45/6.30-10, Closed Mon, Closed D Sun **Prices:** Starter £2.95-£7.95, Main £9.95-£18.95, Dessert £5.65, Coffee £1.30, Min/Water £3, Service optional **Wine:** 31 bottles over £20, 21 bottles under £20, 7 by the glass (£3.50-£5.45) **Notes:** ALC minimum prices for lunch, Vegetarian available, Dress Restrictions, Smart casual **Seats:** 40 **Smoking:** N/Sm in restaurant **Children:** Portions **Directions:** Follow signs for Charlestown from St Austell bypass, restaurant on right **Parking:** Pay & display nearby

---

ST IVES MAP 02 SW54

Alba Restaurant

Modern European [V]

Sea views and fresh local produce

☎ 01736 797222 Old Lifeboat House, Wharf Rd TR26 1LF
e-mail: julia.stevens@tiscali.co.uk
web: www.alba-restaurant.co.uk

Formerly a lifeboat house, the restaurant is on the water's edge with large picture windows making the most of the views. Bright modern art adorns the neutral walls in a clean, contemporary interior. The cooking style here is straightforward with modern European dishes showcasing local produce, fish and vegetables. The choice of dishes is enormous, the set menu is available at lunch and at dinner before 7.30pm. The lunch menu offers an extensive choice including fresh fish, seafood, pasta and burgers. At dinner you'll find imaginative dishes like open ravioli of crab and spinach with a basil nage to start, followed perhaps by cassoulet of monkfish with chorizo, smoked pancetta, beans and tomatoes.

Chef: Grant Nethercott **Owners:** Harbour Kitchen Co Ltd **Times:** 11.30-2/5-9.45, Closed 25-26 Dec **Prices:** Fixed L fr £13, Fixed D fr £16, Starter £4.95-£7.95, Main £13.95-£19.95, Dessert £4.95-£6.95, Coffee £2.75, Min/Water £2.95, Service optional, Group min 6 service 10% **Wine:** 26 bottles over £20, 35 bottles under £20, 32 by the glass (£3.25-£9) **Notes:** Fixed price menus only available L and 5-7pm, Vegetarian menu **Seats:** 60 **Smoking:** N/Sm in restaurant, Air con **Children:** Menu, Portions **Directions:** First building onto St Ives harbour front, opposite the new Lifeboat House

England

ST IVES *continued* MAP 02 SW54

Carbis Bay Hotel

European, International

Traditional beachside hotel with enjoyable dining

☎ 01736 795311 Carbis Bay Hotel, Carbis Bay TR26 2NP
e-mail: carisbayhotel@btconnect.com
web: www.carbisbayhotel.co.uk

This comfortable 1890s hotel stands back from its beach on the golden sands of Carbis Bay. The conservatory has excellent views and there's a smartly presented bar and lounge. The spacious restaurant offers a modern British menu with dishes based on the best of local produce. Let the formal but friendly staff help you to starters of pheasant terrine with pistachio and apple dressing followed by a plaice paupiette with julienned vegetables with a comforting white sauce. Or you might prefer the local lobster. Finish with raspberry crème brûlée served with a delicious chocolate cookie.

Chef: Alan Haag **Owners:** Mr M W Baker **Times:** 12.00-3/6-8.30, Closed 3 wks Jan **Prices:** Fixed L £11.95-£14.95, Fixed D £25-£40, Starter £5-£11, Main £10-£15, Dessert £5-£8, Coffee £2.25, Min/Water £3, Service optional **Wine:** 9 bottles over £20, 25 bottles under £20, 2 by the glass (£3.10-£3.85) **Notes:** Vegetarian available, Dress Restrictions, Smart casual, Civ Wed 150 **Seats:** 150, Pr/dining room 40 **Smoking:** N/Sm in restaurant **Children:** Menu, Portions **Rooms:** 40 (40 en suite) ★★★ HL **Directions:** A3074 to Carbis Bay, turn right along Porthrepta Rd to the sea **Parking:** 100

Garrack Hotel & Restaurant

Modern British

Relaxed, traditional hotel dining with great fish choices

☎ 01736 796199 Burthallan Ln, Higher Ayr TR26 3AA
e-mail: aarest@garrack.com
web: www.garrack.com

Overlooking the town and harbour of St Ives, the Garrack is a well-established hotel with a cosy bar, comfortable lounge and L-shaped traditional, country-house style restaurant with splendid views towards Godrevy lighthouse and Porthmeor beach. A wide range of dishes feature on a fixed price and carte modern British menu. This includes a seafood special, fruits de mer and fresh lobster priced by live weight per kilo. Meat-eaters are not forgotten with roast loin of St Just lamb with prune and chorizo compôte, red onion tartlet and rosemary jus being an excellent main course choice.

Chef: Phil Thomas **Owners:** Kilby family **Times:** 7-9, Closed L all week **Prices:** Fixed D £22, Starter £6.25-£7.25, Main £11.90-£17.50, Dessert £4-£4.50, Min/Water £1.35, Service optional **Wine:** 14 bottles over £20, 66

continued

bottles under £20, 5 by the glass (£1.80-£4.50) **Notes:** Vegetarian available, Dress Restrictions, Smart casual **Seats:** 40 **Smoking:** N/Sm in restaurant **Children:** Menu, Portions **Rooms:** 18 (18 en suite) ★★★ HL **Directions:** From Tate Gallery & Porthmeor Beach car park follow road uphill to top. Burthallan Lane & Garrack Rd signs on right **Parking:** 36

Porthminster Beach Restaurant

Mediterranean, Pacific Rim

Contemporary cooking by the sea

☎ 01736 795352 Porthminster TR26 2EB
e-mail: pminster@btconnect.com
web: www.porthminstercafe.co.uk

A former 1930s tea room, this beachside restaurant has a distinctly Mediterranean feel, particularly with its sunny, alfresco patio. Local artwork adorns the plain walls and locally-caught fish and shellfish dominate menus which display some very assured cooking in dishes such as smoked haddock chowder with mussels and truffled quail egg, pan-fried line-caught local sea bass with smoked eel and sticky toffee pudding with banana ice cream. Dishes such as spicy braised lamb tagine with coddled egg or twice-cooked Barbary duck with seared foie gras show that the kitchen looks beyond the sea for inspiration.

Times: 12-3.30/6, Closed from end Autumn half term to 1 Apr **Directions:** On Porthminster Beach, beneath the St Ives Railway Station

The Wave Restaurant

Mediterranean, Asian

Modern cuisine close to picturesque beaches

☎ 01736 796661 17 St Andrews St TR26 1AH
web: www.wave-restaurant.co.uk

Tucked away in a quiet street a pebble's throw from St Ives harbour, this modern, stylish restaurant has a Mediterranean feel to it. With two separate dining areas, clean lines and lots of local artwork add to the intimacy of the place, which is friendly and owner-run. The Mediterranean feel extends to the food, which also has Asian influences. Although the menu changes regularly, you could start with hand-dived local scallops with prosciutto, goat's cheese and coriander pesto, and follow it with Cornish beef fillet with sweet potato cake, caramelised red onions and oven-dried tomatoes.

Chef: S M Pellow **Owners:** Mr&Mrs Cowling, Mr&Mrs Pellow **Times:** 12-2/6.30-9.30, Closed End Nov-Beg Mar, Sun **Prices:** Fixed D £12.50, Starter £3.95-£7.95, Main £12.50-£17.95, Dessert £4.95, Coffee £1.75, Min/Water £3.25, Service optional **Wine:** 4 bottles over £20, 25 bottles under £20, 7 by the glass (£3.50-£4.25) **Notes:** Fixed D 2 courses, Dress Restrictions, Smart casual, no swim wear or bare chests **Seats:** 50 **Smoking:** N/Sm in restaurant **Children:** Menu, Portions **Directions:** Located just outside the town centre, 100yds from the Parish Church **Parking:** Station car park

England

Onshore

☎ 01736 796000 Wharf Rd TR26
Quality, wood-baked pizza.

Russets

☎ 01736 794700 18a Fore St TR26 1AB
web: www.theaa.com/restaurants/113901.html
The focus of this Cornish favourite is high quality seafood. There are classic dishes, newer inventions and diverse global influences.

ST MAWES MAP 02 SW83

Hotel Tresanton

see below

Idle Rocks Hotel

Modern French V

Innovative cooking at the water's edge

☎ 01326 270771 Harbour Side TR2 5AN
e-mail: reception@idlerocks.co.uk
web: www.idlerocks.co.uk

Set smack on the waterside, Idle Rocks enjoys fantastic views over the bay and harbour. It's aptly named, split-level Water's Edge restaurant echoes the surroundings, decked out in shades of blue, gold and sand with lightwood floor and picture windows that allow all diners a view.

continued

And, summer dining on the terrace is just perfect. The talented kitchen takes a modern approach - underpinned by classic technique - and features top-notch local produce and clean flavours on its appealing, daily-changing menus. Take John Dory with marinated vegetables, roasted scallops and a tomato and basil vinaigrette, or warm Valrhona chocolate coulant with bitter chocolate ice cream and poached orange syrup. Breads, amuse-bouche, pre-dessert and petits fours all hit top form, too.

Idle Rocks Hotel

Chef: Damian Broom **Owners:** E K Richardson **Times:** 12-3/6.30-9 **Prices:** Fixed D £39.99, Starter £6.50-£9, Main £12-£15, Dessert £4.50-£6.50, Coffee £2.30, Min/Water £3.69, Service optional **Wine:** 50 bottles over £20, 48 bottles under £20, 30 by the glass (£4.68-£5.79) **Notes:** Fixed D 5 courses incl coffee, Vegetarian menu, Dress Restrictions, Smart casual, no jeans **Seats:** 70 **Smoking:** N/Sm in restaurant **Children:** Portions **Rooms:** 33 (33 en suite) ★★★ HL **Directions:** From St Austell take A390 towards Truro, turn left onto B3287 signed Tregony, through Tregony, left at T-junct onto A3078, hotel is on left on waterfront **Parking:** 5

Hotel Tresanton

ST MAWES MAP 02 SW83

British, Mediterranean

Reinventing seaside dining

☎ 01326 270055 Lower Castle Rd TR2 5DR
e-mail: info@tresanton.com
web: www.tresanton.com

Perched just above the water, fashionable Tresanton is an idyllic place to dine or stay - with its magical views over the bay to the Roseland Peninsula and St Anthony's Lighthouse, it is hard not to be seduced. But add Olga Polizzi's much-admired stylish, urban-retro design (she's sister of Sir Rocco Forte), and you have a stunning original gem. The dining room comes appropriately surrounded by glass to make the best of those views and has a terrace on two sides. Like the hotel, it's design-led and very stylish with a calm, cool Mediterranean air and fine mosaic floor and nautical themes. An impeccable team of staff, both in appearance and skill, fit the bill perfectly.
The accomplished kitchen's approach majors on cracking, high-quality ingredients - sourced locally wherever possible - simply cooked with integrity to maximise freshness and flavour, with the fruits of the sea an obvious strength. Take a fillet of hake for example, teamed with mash potato, purple sprouting broccoli, pancetta and broad beans, while dessert might feature a strawberry sable with Chantilly cream and strawberry coulis. And aperitifs on the terrace on a warm summer's day just can't be beat.

Chef: Paul Wadham **Owners:** Olga Polizzi **Times:** 12.30-2.30/7-9.30 **Notes:** Vegetarian available, Civ Wed 50 **Seats:** 50, Pr/dining room 40 **Smoking:** No pipes, No cigars **Children:** Min 6 yrs D, Menu **Directions:** On the waterfront in town centre **Parking:** 30

England

ST MAWES *continued* MAP 02 SW83

Rising Sun Hotel

Traditional British

Smart harbourside hotel dining

☎ 01326 270233 TR2 5DJ
e-mail: info@risingsunstmawes.co.uk
web: www.risingsunstmawes.com

Occupying a splendid position overlooking the quaint harbour and the Fal estuary, this stylish small hotel is a popular venue in pretty St Mawes. Gig-rowers and locals fill the lively bar, while the refined restaurant and conservatory brasserie, which take full advantage of the views, are frequented by tourists and the yachting fraternity. An imaginative fixed-price menu features the harvest of the local catch, as well as fresh Cornish produce. Examples are hot smoked salmon kedgeree, grilled sea bass fillets with sesame dressing, and pink coriander duck served with red wine sauce and winter fruit compôte.

Chef: Ann Long **Owners:** Mr R J Milan **Times:** 12-2/7-9, Closed L Mon-Sat **Prices:** Fixed L £11-£15, Fixed D £33.50, Coffee £1.40, Min/Water £3, Service optional **Wine:** 11 bottles over £20, 33 bottles under £20, 11 by the glass (£3) **Notes:** Vegetarian available **Seats:** 50 **Smoking:** N/Sm in restaurant **Children:** Min 6 yrs, Portions **Rooms:** 8 (8 en suite) ★★ HL **Directions:** On harbour front **Parking:** 8

ST MERRYN MAP 02 SW87

Ripley's

British, French

Unpretentious eatery serving seriously tasty food

☎ 01841 520179 PL28 8NQ

Set in a quaint Cornish village just outside Padstow, this popular restaurant has a relaxed rustic feel. Simple contemporary décor highlights features like stone flag flooring, lightwood furniture and unstained oak beams. The dining area at the rear is small and intimate, light wooden furniture and darkwood flooring continue the natural contemporary style. Friendly, unfussy service is a real attraction, as is the straightforward, beautifully prepared food, making the most of traditional ingredients. Try a starter like braised oxtail with herb and mustard dumplings and crisp shallots. Main courses might feature 35-day dry-aged rump steak bordelaise with bone marrow butter. Desserts include warm pecan nut tart with clotted cream ice cream, complemented by a good choice of dessert wines, port and digestifs.

Times: 12-2/7-9.30, Closed 2 wks Xmas, BHs, Sun-Mon, Closed L Limited lunch opening, phone for details

---

SCILLY, ISLES OF
BRYHER MAP 02 SV81

Hell Bay

Modern International

Stunning location, stunning seafood

☎ 01720 422947 TR23 0PR
e-mail: contactus@hellbay.co.uk
web: www.hellbay.co.uk

Located on the smallest of the Scilly Isles, and perfect for a relaxing break, this hotel overlooks the constantly changing Atlantic seascape. Subtle lighting creates a warm atmosphere in the evenings, and the cream walls are a perfect foil for the oil paintings. The freshest of island and Cornish produce appears on the menu, from the top-quality seafood (tian of Bryher crab with a lime yogurt dressing, and whole grilled lemon sole with hollandaise glaze), to the likes of honey roast rack of lamb, Moroccan couscous and red wine jus, followed by chilli orange vodka cake with home-made berry ice cream. The daily-changing set menu is a guide only, and guests are invited to suggest their own preferences.

Chef: Graham Shone **Owners:** Tresco Estate **Times:** 12-3/6.30-9.30, Closed Jan-Feb **Prices:** Fixed L £9-£25, Fixed D £20-£25, Starter £5-£10, Main £10-£15, Dessert £4-£8, Coffee £2.50, Min/Water £2, Service optional **Wine:** 37 bottles over £20, 36 bottles under £20, 11 by the glass (£3.50-£4.75) **Notes:** Vegetarian available, No jeans, T-shirts in eve, Civ Wed 60 **Seats:** 75, Pr/dining room 20 **Smoking:** N/Sm in restaurant **Children:** Menu, Portions **Rooms:** 25 (25 en suite) ★★★ **Directions:** Helicopter from Penzance to Tresco, St Mary's. Plane from Southampton, Bristol, Exeter, Newquay or Land's End

---

ST MARTIN'S MAP 02 SV91

St Martin's on the Isle

see page 79

TRESCO MAP 02 SV81

Island Hotel

Modern British

Island living, seafood a speciality

☎ 01720 422883 TR24 0PU
e-mail: islandhotel@tresco.co.uk
web: www.tresco.co.uk/holidays/island_hotel.asp

This uniquely private island hotel offers a memorable seaside location. The restaurant has been refurbished in contemporary style, creating an elegant backdrop for displays of original art. Diners can make the most of dramatic sea views from the restaurant. Modern British cuisine is the order of the day, drawing inspiration from international sources and from local ingredients, particularly seafood. This is exemplified in dishes like a starter of Tresco and Bryher seafood mousse with spring onion and crab vermouth. For mains, you could stick with fish and try poached fillet of brill in red wine with creamed mash and wild mushrooms. Desserts feature tempting options like black cherry and almond tartlet with Cornish clotted cream.

Chef: Peter Marshall **Owners:** Robert Dorrien-Smith **Times:** 12-2.30/7-9, Closed 5 Nov-1 Mar, Closed L all week **Prices:** Fixed L £12.50-£26.50, Fixed D £38, Coffee £3.25, Min/Water £2, Service optional **Wine:** 89 bottles over £20, 9 bottles under £20, 18 by the glass (£4-£9.50) **Notes:** Dress Restrictions, Smart casual, no jeans or T-shirts **Seats:** 150, Pr/dining room 25 **Smoking:** N/Sm in restaurant **Children:** Menu, Portions **Rooms:** 48 (48 en suite) ★★★ **Directions:** 20 minutes from Penzance by helicopter **Parking:** No cars on island

New Inn

Modern British

Traditional coaching inn with a contemporary restaurant

☎ 01720 422844 TR24 0QQ
e-mail: newinn@tresco.co.uk
web: www.tresco.co.uk/holidays/new_inn.asp

Steeped in history, The New Inn is owned by the same estate that

continued on page 80

St Martin's on the Isle

SCILLY, ISLES OF - ST MARTIN'S MAP 02 SV91

British, Mediterranean V

Accomplished cooking in idyllic island paradise

☎ 01720 422092 Lower Town TR25 0QW
e-mail: stay@stmartinshotel.co.uk
web: www.stmartinshotel.co.uk

This attractive waterfront hotel, complete with its own sandy beach, enjoys an idyllic position overlooking the islands of Tean and Tresco. The elegant, award-winning restaurant has a split-level lounge where guests can relax and enjoy the stunning views. Tables are well spaced and table appointments are stylish and simple with seasonal flower displays.
An accomplished kitchen team provides cuisine to match the impressive location with daily-changing menus utilising the abundance of local produce, particularly fish and seafood, where freshness and quality is notable. Expect elaborate, but well-defined flavours in tian of crab with avocado and gazpacho sauce, one of many dishes that allows each ingredient to shine through. The same bold flavour combinations are to be found in roast rump of lamb with potato purée, wild mushroom fricassée and rosemary jus, as well as savarin of raspberries with raspberry ripple ice cream. A cheese board dominated by artisan West Country cheeses is equally as impressive. The vegetarian menu has plenty of interesting choices.

Chef: John Mijatovic
Owners: Peter Sykes
Times: 12.30-2/7-10, Closed Nov-Feb, Closed L Mon-Sun
Prices: Fixed D fr £39.50, Coffee £2, Min/Water £2, Service included
Wine: 50 bottles over £20, 25 bottles under £20, 12 by the glass (£2.50-£4.95)
Notes: Vegetarian menu, No jeans, T-shirts or shorts, Civ Wed 100
Seats: 60
Smoking: N/Sm in restaurant
Children: Min 9 yrs, Menu, Portions
Rooms: 30 (30 en suite) ★★★
Directions: By helicopter or boat from Penzance to St Mary's - flights from Bristol, Exeter, Southampton, Newquay or Land's End. Then 20 min launch transfer to St Martin's

SCILLY, ISLES OF - TRESCO *continued* MAP 02 SV81

owns the other three main hotels on Tresco and the island itself, which is the only privately owned land in the Scillies. There's stacks of old world character here in the bar and lounges - although the restaurant has a modern 'New England' style - light and airy, with stained wood floors, panelled walls and brightly coloured table settings. International with a leaning toward France, the food is also quite contemporary with local produce - especially seafood - featured prominently and dishes boasting simple flavours cooked well. You could try pan-fried scallops with Puy lentils and a pear coulis to start, followed by grilled John Dory with a mixed seafood risotto and fennel cream.

Chef: Stephanie Clark **Owners:** Mr R Dorien-Smith **Times:** 7-9, Closed L all week **Prices:** Fixed D fr £35, Min/Water £3, Service optional **Wine:** 11 bottles over £20, 24 bottles under £20, 10 by the glass (£2.30-£6) **Notes:** Fixed D 4 courses, coffee incl, Vegetarian available **Seats:** 40 **Smoking:** N/Sm in restaurant **Children:** Menu, Portions **Rooms:** 16 (16 en suite) ★★ **Directions:** 250yds from harbour (private island, contact hotel for details)

SUMMERCOURT MAP 02 SW85

Viners Bar & Restaurant

Rosettes not confirmed at time of going to press

British

Destination dining for real food-lovers

☎ 01872 510544 Carvynick TR8 5AF

Dating back to 1669, this impressive granite manor house has found a new lease of life as the setting for celebrity chef Kevin Viner's special blend of gastro-dining. The interior offers a tasteful combination of original features and contemporary style, leaving space to showcase Kevin's many accolades, photographs and trophies. The upstairs restaurant offers a smart, formal atmosphere, softened by fresh flowers and church candles. This sets the scene for surprisingly simple but immensely successful cooking that has diners coming back for more as often as they can. Delivered in hearty portions with stylish presentation, expect plenty of fresh Cornish fish, plus shoulder of lamb, filled chicken breast and chargrilled steak.

Times: 12.30-3.00/6.30-9.30, Closed D Sun

TALLAND BAY MAP 02 SX25

✿✿✿ Terrace Restaurant at Talland Bay Hotel

see below

TRURO MAP 02 SW84

✿✿ Alverton Manor

British V

Contemporary Cornish cooking in converted convent

☎ 01872 276633 Tregolls Rd TR1 1ZQ
e-mail: reception@alvertonmanor.co.uk
web: www.connexions.co.uk

Set in six acres of well-tended gardens, this Grade II listed former

continued

Terrace Restaurant at Talland Bay Hotel

TALLAND BAY MAP 02 SX25

Modern British

Wonderful location and refined cuisine

☎ 01503 272667 PL13 2JB
e-mail: reception@tallandbayhotel.co.uk
web: www.tallandbayhotel.co.uk

Spectacular sea views and direct access to the coastal path from the end of the garden are just some of the attractions at this friendly, family-run hotel. The traditional wood-panelled dining room makes the most of views of the sea and garden, but even these won't distract diners once they see the menu. A new chef here demonstrates modern British cooking with pleasing simplicity, relying on top quality ingredients, well-judged seasoning and serious attention to the clarity of flavours. Presentation is refreshingly neat and unfussy, focusing on the main ingredients. Seasonal highlights are reflected in a carefully chosen menu, making the most of local produce like freshly landed fish, crab and scallops from nearby fishing villages. If that has whet your appetite, you won't be able to resist a well-balanced starter of Cornish crab lasagne with tomato fondue, mixed herbs and shellfish bisque. Main courses offer interesting combinations like fillet of beef with wild mushroom ravioli, fine beans, parsnip purée and black pepper emulsion. Sound technical skills are demonstrated in every course and you will be hard pressed to decide on a dessert, a simple option might be white chocolate mousse with champagne jelly and fresh berries. Service is professional and formal but the atmosphere is relaxed.

Chef: Shane Hughes **Owners:** Mr & Mrs G Granville **Times:** 12.30-2/7-9, Closed L Mon-Sat (Oct-mid Apr) **Prices:** Fixed D £32.50, Coffee £3.75, Min/Water £2.50, Service optional **Wine:** 60 bottles over £20, 16 bottles under £20, 7 by the glass (£3.50-£4.75) **Notes:** Tasting menu & Sun L available, Dress Restrictions, Smart casual minimum **Seats:** 40 **Smoking:** N/Sm in restaurant **Rooms:** 23 (23 en suite) ★★★ CHH **Directions:** Signed from x-rds on A387 between Looe and Polperro **Parking:** 20

convent has been converted into a modern hotel with an elegant dining room. Gothic windows, ornate wooden staircases and large windows make the most of its elevated, city centre position. Service is thoughtful and attentive. Modern British and European dishes are cooked using local produce - organic where possible. Start with smoked foie gras with cherry purée and Gewürztraminer jelly or pressed guinea fowl with prunes before a main course of Cornish lamb - carved from the trolley - and glazed vegetables with rosemary. A generous dessert menu offers rhubarb and apple pie with rhubarb and custard ice cream.

Alverton Manor

Chef: Keith Brooksbank **Owners:** Mr M Sagin **Times:** 11.45-1.45/7-9.15, Closed L Sat **Prices:** Fixed L £14.50, Fixed D £31.50, Coffee £2.50, Min/Water £3, Service optional **Wine:** 80 bottles over £20, 40 bottles under £20, 15 by the glass (£3.50-£7.95) **Notes:** Fixed D 4 courses, Vegetarian menu, Civ Wed 80 **Seats:** 30, Pr/dining room 80 **Smoking:** N/Sm in restaurant **Children:** Min 12 yrs, Menu, Portions **Rooms:** 32 (32 en suite) ★★★ HL **Directions:** From Truro bypass take A39 to St Austell. Just past the church on left **Parking:** 80

®® Probus Lamplighter Restaurant

Modern British

Truro favourite with a sound reputation

☎ 01726 882453 Fore St, Probus TR2 4JL
e-mail: maireadvogel@aol.com
web: www.lamplighter-probus.co.uk

This veteran establishment has fed locals and tourists alike since the 1950s, and has a reputation for top-notch cooking. It's a warm and cosy venue with log fires, comfy sofas, and two candlelit dining areas decked out in white and blue. Modern British dishes predominate; expect good quality local ingredients brought together in combinations designed to tempt and intrigue. Venison terrine is a typical starter, served with home-made elderberry chutney and brioche, while mains might include Cornish rack of lamb with dauphinoise potatoes and merlot and rosemary jus, or wild fillet of sea bass with vanilla, chervil, tomato and warm butter dressing.

Chef: Robert Vogel **Owners:** Robert & Mairead Vogel **Times:** 7-10, Closed Sun-Mon, Closed L all week **Prices:** Fixed D £28.90, Coffee £2.50, Min/Water £4.50 **Wine:** 15 bottles over £20, 16 bottles under £20, 6 by the glass (£3.75-£7) **Notes:** Dress Restrictions, Smart casual **Seats:** 32, Pr/dining room 8 **Smoking:** N/Sm in restaurant **Children:** Portions **Directions:** 5m from Truro on A390 towards St Austell **Parking:** On street & car park

TYWARDREATH MAP 02 SX05

® Trenython Manor

British, International

Imaginative cuisine in Palladian setting

☎ 01726 814797 Castle Dore Rd PL24 2TS
e-mail: enquiries@trenython.co.uk
web: www.trenython.co.uk

Dating from the 1800s, there is something distinctly different about Trenython, a classic English manor house designed by an Italian architect. The impressive dining room with carved oak panelling looks out across the gardens, towards St Austell Bay. Modern eclectic cooking is the order of the day with a menu rich in its diversity. Starters could include seared scallops with cabbage and bacon, truffle oil and balsamic. Main courses range from oven-roasted cod with spring onion mash and warm tomato salsa, to glazed breast of duck with linguini noodles, stir-fry vegetables and five peppercorn jus.

Chef: Alan Ward **Owners:** Club La Costa **Times:** 12-2.30/7-9.30, Closed L Mon-Sat **Prices:** Starter £6.95-£9.50, Main £12.50-£21.50, Dessert £6.95-£7.95, Coffee £2, Min/Water £2.95, Service optional **Wine:** 16 bottles over £20, 21 bottles under £20, 3 by the glass (£2.75-£3.50) **Notes:** Civ Wed 85 **Seats:** 60, Pr/dining room 30 **Smoking:** N/Sm in restaurant **Children:** Menu, Portions **Rooms:** 24 (24 en suite) ★★★ CHH **Directions:** From Exeter join A30 towards Cornwall, then B3269 to Lostwithiel. Take A390 St Austell/Fowey, follow Fowey signs for approx 4m. The hotel is then signed **Parking:** 50

VERYAN MAP 02 SW93

® *Nare Hotel*

Traditional British

Traditional dining in seaside hotel with great views

☎ 01872 501279 Carne Beach TR2 5PF
e-mail: office@narehotel.co.uk
web: www.narehotel.co.uk

On the Roseland peninsula, the Nare has an enviable position overlooking the mile-long Carne Beach. Fronted by terraces and lawns, the lounges, bar and restaurants offer comfort and wonderful views across Gerrans Bay. The staff are friendly and the service in the main dining room is formal, so expect hors d'oeuvre and flambé trolleys. Traditional dishes are given a modern twist and specialities include Portloe lobster and crab, fresh locally-landed fish and top-notch local produce. The nautically-themed Quarterdeck restaurant offers a more contemporary, less formal dining experience.

Times: 12.30-2.30/7.30, Closed L Mon-Sat **Rooms:** 38 (38 en suite) ★★★★ CHH **Directions:** Through village passing New Inn on left, continue 1 mile to the sea

---

WATERGATE BAY MAP 02 SW86

® The Brasserie

Modern British NEW

Dine in comfort with superb views after a day on the beach

☎ 01637 860543 Watergate Bay Hotel, The Hotel and Extreme Academy TR8 4AA
e-mail: life@watergatebay.co.uk
web: www.watergatebay.co.uk

You can enjoy fantastic beach and sea views from the spacious

continued

WATERGATE BAY *continued* MAP 02 SW86

decking of the bar and lounge of this modern, stylish hotel or from the Brasserie restaurant. The beach is home to the 'Extreme Academy' hosting sports competitions and lessons in watersports like kite surfing, traction surfing, and just plain old surfing. The imaginative modern British menu changes every week and makes good use of local and seasonal produce, particularly seafood, in dishes such as pan-roasted scallops with cauliflower pannacotta and balsamic caramel starter or cannelloni of crab and basil with langoustine sauce.

Chef: Tom Bradbury **Owners:** Watergate Bay Hotel Ltd **Times:** 7-10, Closed L all week **Prices:** Fixed D £24.95-£40, Min/Water £2.50, Service optional **Wine:** 19 bottles over £20, 25 bottles under £20, 10 by the glass (£2.75-£6.25) **Notes:** Coffee incl, Children accepted for bookings 7-7.30pm, Civ Wed 110 **Seats:** 140, Pr/dining room 16 **Smoking:** N/Sm in restaurant, Air con **Children:** Menu, Portions **Rooms:** 71 (71 en suite) ★★★ HL **Directions:** 2nd right off A30 after The Victoria Inn onto A3059 straight across rdbt following airport signs. Turn right after 1.5m at B3276 T-junct, turn left to bay **Parking:** 70

CUMBRIA

ALSTON MAP 18 NY74

Lovelady Shield House

British, European

Country-house cuisine in beautiful surroundings

☎ 01434 381203 CA9 3LF
e-mail: enquiries@lovelady.co.uk
web: www.lovelady.co.uk

A family-run country-house hotel set in three acres of grounds close to Alston. The dining room is elegant but informal, with stylish décor, antiques and paintings. The menu offers a mix of modern European and classical French dishes, complemented by an excellent wine list. The bar also has an impressive display of fine malts and brandies so you can relax after dinner with a drink in one of the reception rooms. Typical main courses might include roast breast of Gressingham duckling served with a sweet potato and swede galette, bacon and kumquat jus.

Times: 12-2/7-8.30, Closed L Mon-Sat **Rooms:** 10 (10 en suite) ★★★ HL **Directions:** 2m E of Alston, signed off A689 at junct with B6294

AMBLESIDE MAP 18 NY30

Drunken Duck Inn

British

Great local produce in a fantastic Lakeland setting

☎ 015394 36347 Barngates LA22 0NG
e-mail: info@drunkenduckinn.co.uk
web: www.drunkenduckinn.co.uk

More than an inn, the 'Duck' as it is known is really an institution with a reputation for great food, ales and comfortable rooms. The restaurant is relaxed and informal with two traditional areas and one more modern. The emphasis is on top-quality locally sourced produce with all suppliers listed. Barngates Brewery at the Duck brews up to six beers using its own water supply from the nearby fells. In the restaurant, modern and traditional British cuisine sees starters like grilled crumpet with Kelthwaite gold brie with Cumbrian air-dried ham. For a main course try chargrilled Galloway beef fillet with slow roast tomato and wild rocket muffin. Don't miss the cheese menu.

Chef: Nick Foster **Owners:** Stephanie Barton **Times:** 12-2.30/6-9, Closed 25 Dec **Prices:** Starter £6.25-£7.95, Main £13.95-£24.95, Dessert £5.95-£6.95, Coffee £1.75, Min/Water £2.50, Service optional **Wine:** 27 bottles over £20, 21 bottles under £20, 10 by the glass (£2.95-£5.95) **Seats:** 60 **Smoking:** N/Sm in restaurant **Children:** Portions **Rooms:** 11 (11 en suite) ★★★★★ INN **Directions:** Take A592 from Kendal, follow signs for Hawkshead(from Ambleside), in 2.5m sign for inn on right, 1m up hill **Parking:** 40

Regent Hotel

British

Long-established hotel with a contemporary flavour

☎ 015394 32254 Waterhead Bay LA22 0ES
e-mail: info@regentlakes.co.uk
web: www.regentlakes.co.uk

A family-run hotel located at Waterhead Bay on the shores of Lake Windermere, the Regent is well known locally for its award-winning display of summer flowers. The contemporary restaurant overlooks a pretty Italianate courtyard, and the walls are hung with modern art. Cumbrian produce is well represented on the brasserie-style menu, offering up-beat dishes such as grilled skewer of warm mackerel with home-made piccalilli, and slow-braised shank of Lakeland lamb with dauphinoise potatoes and creamed minted peas. Children are made welcome and a children's menu is available from 5.30pm.

Times: 12-2/6.30-8, Closed Xmas wk **Rooms:** 30 (30 en suite) ★★★ **Directions:** 1m S of Ambleside at Waterhead Bay

Rothay Manor

Traditional British

Fine dining in the Lakes

☎ 015394 33605 Rothay Bridge LA22 0EH
e-mail: hotel@rothaymanor.co.uk
web: www.rothaymanor.co.uk

Built as a summer residence for a prosperous Liverpool merchant in 1825, this listed manor sits in pretty gardens just a short walk from the centre of Ambleside. Furnished in sedate style with antiques and floral displays, it's a friendly, family-run concern offering a tempting modern British menu in elegant and airy surroundings. Dishes consistently impress and are notable for quality ingredients and clear flavours; your choice might include roast rack of Cumbrian fell-bred lamb with pea and mint purée, or sea bass with an asparagus, tomato and basil salsa.

Chef: Jane Binns **Owners:** Nigel and Stephen Nixon **Times:** 12.30-1.45/7.15-9, Closed 3-27 Jan **Prices:** Fixed L £8-£14.50, Fixed D £35, Starter £3.50-£4.50, Main £7-£10, Dessert £4, Coffee £2, Min/Water £2.70, Service optional **Wine:** 82 bottles over £20, 63 bottles under £20, 8 by the glass (£3.50) **Notes:** ALC L only, Mon-Sat, Sun L 3 courses avail, Dress Restrictions, Smart casual **Seats:** 65, Pr/dining room 34 **Smoking:** N/Sm in restaurant, Air con **Children:** Min 7 yrs D, Menu, Portions **Rooms:** 19 (19 en suite) ★★★ HL **Directions:** From Ambleside, follow signs for Coniston (A593). Establishment is 0.25 mile SW from the centre of Ambleside opposite the rugby club **Parking:** 35

APPLEBY-IN-WESTMORLAND MAP 18 NY62

Appleby Manor Country House Hotel

Modern British V

Modern cuisine in relaxed country-house hotel

☎ 017683 51571 Roman Rd CA16 6JB
e-mail: reception@applebymanor.co.uk
web: www.applebymanor.co.uk

Two very different styles distinguish the separate parts of this restaurant, one featuring wood panelling and original fireplace, and the other a light and airy conservatory. Both share views over the manor house gardens and the surrounding fells, and there's a welcoming atmosphere throughout. The impressively presented food comes in interesting combinations of modern and traditional British cooking marked by French influences. Daily specials pad out the carte, which might feature braised daube of Cumbrian Galloway beef with wild mushroom dauphinoise and butternut squash fondant, or whole roasted monkfish tail wrapped in air-dried ham and spinach, with a lemon and rosemary risotto. Don't miss the impressive cheese trolley.

Chef: Chris Thompson **Owners:** Dunbobbin family **Times:** 12-2/7-9, Closed 24-26 Dec **Prices:** Starter £4.95-£8.95, Main £12.95-£17.95, Dessert £5.95, Coffee £3.25, Service included **Wine:** 10 bottles over £20, 74 bottles under £20, 6 by the glass (£3.45-£5) **Notes:** Vegetarian menu, Smart casual **Seats:** 96, Pr/dining room 20 **Smoking:** N/Sm in restaurant **Children:** Menu, Portions **Rooms:** 30 (30 en suite) ★★★ HL **Directions:** M6 junct 40 take A66 for Scotch Corner for 12m, take turn for Appleby. Manor 1.5m on right **Parking:** 60

BARROW-IN-FURNESS MAP 18 SD26

Clarence House Country Hotel & Restaurant

Modern British, International

Enjoyable dining in comfortable conservatory surroundings

☎ 01229 462508 Skelgate LA15 8BQ
e-mail: info@clarencehouse-hotel.co.uk
web: www.clarencehouse-hotel.co.uk

Good, friendly family-style service in this well-presented conservatory restaurant with its fine views over the surrounding countryside. The gardens of this brightly decorated Victorian house are worthy of note, as are the individually styled bedrooms. There's a good mixture of straightforward local dishes as well as British and European items on the menu. French onion soup, Welsh mussels and Scottish cock-a-leekie jostle for the diner's attention with Stavely lamb, Cumbrian beef and North West coastal fish. Good use is made of local and seasonal ingredients and service is helpful and efficient.

continued

England

BARROW-IN-FURNESS *continued* MAP 18 SD26

Chef: Mr Alan Forsyth **Owners:** Mrs Pauline Barber **Times:** 12-2/7-9, Closed 25-26 Dec, Closed D Sun **Prices:** Fixed L £12.95, Fixed D £29.95, Starter £4.95-£8.95, Main £14.95-£22.95, Dessert £6.50-£8.95, Coffee £1.95, Min/Water £3, Service included **Wine:** 26 bottles over £20, 28 bottles under £20, 6 by the glass (£2.90-£5.90) **Notes:** Fixed D 5 courses, Sun L £15.95, Vegetarian available, Dress Restrictions, Smart dress, Civ Wed 100 **Seats:** 100, Pr/dining room 14 **Smoking:** N/Sm in restaurant **Children:** Portions **Rooms:** 19 (19 en suite) ★★★ HL **Directions:** Telephone for directions

BASSENTHWAITE MAP 18 NY23

Lake View Restaurant at Armathwaite Hall

Traditional British V

Classic cuisine in a genteel setting

☎ 017687 76551 Armathwaite Hall CA12 4RE
e-mail: reservations@armathwaite-hall.com
web: www.armathwaite-hall.com

Hidden away in 400 acres of peaceful deer park, this imposing 17th-century mansion is a haven of civilised living. Antiques and ornate wood panelling set a genteel tone, while roaring log fires keep things cosy, and for those who drag themselves away from the hearth, there's also an extensive range of leisure facilities to sample. The restaurant is a grand affair overlooking nearby Bassenthwaite Lake, and offers a concise menu that mixes classic dishes such as fillet of beef bourguignon or flambé loin pork, with more adventurous creations such as medallions of venison with an onion and blueberry tarte Tatin and star anise sauce.

Chef: Kevin Dowling **Owners:** Graves Family **Times:** 12.30-1.45/7.30-9.15 **Prices:** Fixed L fr £20.95, Fixed D fr £40.95, Min/Water £3, Service optional **Wine:** 46 bottles over £20, 34 bottles under £20 **Notes:** Fixed L 4 courses, Fixed D 6 courses, Vegetarian menu, Dress Restrictions, Smart casual, no jeans/T-shirts/trainers, Civ Wed 80 **Seats:** 80, Pr/dining room 25 **Smoking:** N/Sm in restaurant **Children:** Portions **Rooms:** 43 (43 en suite) ★★★★ HL **Directions:** From M6 junct 40/A66 to Keswick then A591 towards Carlisle. Continue for 7m and turn left at Castle Inn **Parking:** 100

The Pheasant

Traditional

Good honest food in traditional inn

☎ 017687 76234 CA13 9YE
e-mail: info@the-pheasant.co.uk
web: www.the-pheasant.co.uk

continued

Dating back to the 16th century, this large former coaching inn close to Bassenthwaite Lake boasts many traditional features, with log fires, oak-panelled rooms and polished parquet floors. Privately owned by the same family for the past seven years, it has a relaxed atmosphere and the restaurant benefits from a sound menu of modern British dishes conjured from high quality ingredients. Expect assured cooking in seared king scallops with lime and peanut risotto, and roasted rack of Lakeland lamb with mini shepherd's pie, creamed leeks and rosemary and garlic mash.

Chef: Malcolm Ennis **Owners:** Trustees of Lord Inglewood **Times:** 12-2/7-9, Closed 25 Dec **Prices:** Fixed D fr £29.95, Starter £4.25-£11.25, Main £13.75-£22.50, Dessert fr £5.95, Coffee £2.10, Min/Water £2.25, Service optional, Group min 8 service 10% **Wine:** 43 bottles over £20, 20 bottles under £20, 12 by the glass (£3.25-£7.95) **Notes:** ALC L only, Vegetarian available, Dress Restrictions, Smart casual, no jeans, T-shirts, trainers **Seats:** 45, Pr/dining room 12 **Smoking:** N/Sm in restaurant **Children:** Min 8 yrs D **Rooms:** 15 (15 en suite) ★★★ HL **Directions:** M6 junct 40, take A66 (Keswick and North Lakes). Continue past Keswick and head for Cockermouth. Signed from A66 **Parking:** 40

BORROWDALE MAP 18 NY21

Borrowdale Gates Country House Hotel

British, French V

Ambitious cuisine in a peaceful Cumbrian setting

☎ 017687 77204 CA12 5UQ
e-mail: hotel@borrowdale-gates.com
web: www.borrowdale-gates.com

Nestled quietly in the Borrowdale Valley, this friendly hotel boasts stunning views of the rugged fells from its elegant restaurant. Dishes are modern in style with a country-house feel, and an ambitious kitchen creates an excellent balance of flavours in dishes such as Holker Estate woodcock with fondant potato, Puy lentils and game jus for example, or slow-roast lamb with rosemary jus and horseradish dumplings. An

continued

8-course Menu Gourmand complements the carte selection, and there's also a concise vegetarian range. Book ahead for a window table.

Chef: Mr Michael Wilkinson **Owners:** Mr Roland Ayling **Times:** 12.15-1.30/7-8.45 **Prices:** Fixed L £12.50-£22.50, Fixed D £32.50-£34.50, Starter £6.25-£10.50, Main £16.50-£22.50, Dessert £6.75-£10.75, Coffee £3.25, Min/Water £3.25, Service optional **Wine:** 68 bottles over £20, 18 bottles under £20, 6 by the glass (£4.50-£6) **Notes:** Fixed D 5 courses, Tasting menu £45, Sun L £19.50, Vegetarian menu, Dress Restrictions, Shirt & tie preferred, no jeans or trainers **Seats:** 55 **Smoking:** N/Sm in restaurant **Children:** Min 7 yrs, Portions **Rooms:** 29 (29 en suite) ★★★ HL **Directions:** B5289 from Keswick, after 4m turn right over bridge to Grange. Hotel 400yds on right **Parking:** 30

֍ Hazel Bank Country House

British, European

Victorian house with sweeping views and good honest food

☎ 017687 77248 Rosthwaite CA12 5XB
e-mail: enquiries@hazelbankhotel.co.uk
web: www.hazelbankhotel.co.uk

Set in the heart of Lakeland, with magnificent views of Borrowdale and fine fell walking across nearby Langdale Pikes, this traditional Victorian residence stands in four acres of well-tended lawns and woodland. Expect high levels of comfort, attentive service and a house party-style atmosphere. Set four-course dinners are cooked with imagination and skill, offering good honest food and the best local ingredients available. Simple, traditional British dishes with European influences may include hot smoked salmon with mango and avocado salsa, chicken wrapped in Cumbrian bacon with tomato sauce, and chocolate and orange cheesecake.

Chef: Brenda Davies **Owners:** Glen & Brenda Davies **Times:** 7, Closed 25-26 Dec, Closed L Mon-Sun **Prices:** Fixed D £32.50, Service optional **Wine:** 6 bottles over £20, 46 bottles under £20, 5 by the glass (£4.90) **Notes:** Fixed D 4 courses, Dress Restrictions, Smart casual, no shorts or jeans **Seats:** 22 **Smoking:** N/Sm in restaurant **Children:** Min 12 yrs **Rooms:** 8 (8 en suite) ★★★★★ GH **Directions:** From M6 junct 40, leave the A66 and take the B5289 to Borrowdale. Just before Rosthwaite turn left over hump-back bridge **Parking:** 12

֍ Leathes Head Hotel

Modern British

Solid cooking in restaurant with fabulous views

☎ 017687 77247 CA12 5UY
e-mail: enq@leatheshead.co.uk
web: www.leatheshead.co.uk

Located within well-tended gardens in the picturesque Borrowdale Valley - the most beautiful valley in England, according to many - this family-run hotel offers a haven of calm and tranquillity. Once an Edwardian gentleman's residence, there are three comfortable lounge areas and an elegant restaurant offering stunning views. Well sourced ingredients are handled with respect in unpretentious dishes with strong flavour marriages: slow-baked terrine of rabbit, Waberthwaite ham, venison and guinea fowl could be followed by pan-fried beef fillet served on fresh oxtail confit and rich beer pan jus. Finish with traditional Cumberland Rum Nicky.

Chef: David Jackson **Owners:** Roy & Janice Smith **Times:** 7.30-8.15, Closed mid Nov-mid Feb **Prices:** Fixed D £29.95-£34.95, Min/Water £2.95, Service optional **Wine:** 12 bottles over £20, 60 bottles under £20, 10 by the glass (£3.30-£4) **Notes:** Coffee incl, Fixed D 4 courses **Seats:** 24 **Smoking:** N/Sm in restaurant **Children:** Min 9 yrs **Rooms:** 12 (12 en suite) ★★★ CHH **Directions:** 3.75m S of Keswick on B5289, set back on the left **Parking:** 15

BRAITHWAITE MAP 18 NY22

֍ The Cottage in the Wood

British, European

Good food and service in tranquil setting

☎ 017687 78409 Whinlatter Pass CA12 5TW
e-mail: info@thecottageinthewood.co.uk
web: www.thecottageinthewood.co.uk

This former 17th-century coaching inn enjoys a wonderful forest setting with views down the valley to the Skiddaw mountain range. Diners at this charming cottage-style hotel can enjoy a fixed three-course menu based upon seasonal and local produce. The modern British cooking has European/Mediterranean influences on the daily-changing menu. Expect quality favourites like terrine of Gloucester Old Spot pork with pruneaux d'Agen, or roasted Galloway beef with wild mushroom casserole, caramelised shallots and celeriac rosti.

Chef: Liam Berney **Owners:** Liam & Kath Berney **Times:** 7-9.30, Closed Jan, Mon, Closed L all week **Prices:** Fixed D £22.50, Min/Water £2.50, Service included **Wine:** 15 bottles over £20, 15 bottles under £20, 6 by the glass (£3.25-£4.40) **Notes:** Coffee incl, Vegetarian available **Seats:** 26 **Smoking:** N/Sm in restaurant **Children:** Min 7yrs, Portions **Rooms:** 10 (10 en suite) ★★ HL **Directions:** M6 junct 40. take A66 signed Keswick, 1m after Keswick take B5292 signed Braithwaite, hotel 2m from Braithwaite **Parking:** 10

BRAMPTON MAP 21 NY56

֍֍ Farlam Hall Hotel

Modern British

The epitome of modern English country-house style

☎ 016977 46234 Hallbankgate CA8 2NG
e-mail: farlam@relaischateaux.com
web: www.farlamhall.co.uk

A beautiful Victorian country house with earlier origins dating back to the 'manor' of Farlam around 1428. Landscaped Victorian gardens include an ornamental lake and stream. The interior fine furnishings and fabrics recall an earlier age when the house was used for a large family, frequently entertaining guests. The dining room with huge bay windows has lovely garden views and makes a fine setting to use the traditional English china, crystal glasses and silver cutlery. English country-house cooking can be enjoyed here with a simple dinner menu featuring starters like cream of parsnip and ginger soup. Main

continued

BRAMPTON *continued* MAP 21 NY56

courses make use of fine produce in dishes like medallion of local beef fillet, griddled and presented on horseradish mashed potato with crisp fried onions and a red wine sauce.

Farlam Hall Hotel

Chef: Barry Quinion **Owners:** Quinion & Stevenson families **Times:** 8-8.30, Closed 25-30 Dec, Closed L all week **Prices:** Fixed D £37-£39, Min/Water £2.50, Service optional **Wine:** 36 bottles over £20, 10 bottles under £20, 5 by the glass (£4.95-£5.50) **Notes:** Coffee incl, Fixed D 4 courses, Vegetarian available, Smart dress preferred, no jeans **Seats:** 40, Pr/dining room 20 **Smoking:** N/Sm in restaurant **Children:** Min 5 yrs, Portions **Rooms:** 12 (12 en suite) ★★★ **Directions:** On A689, 2.5m SE of Brampton (not in Farlam Village) **Parking:** 25

CARTMEL MAP 18 SD37

Aynsome Manor Hotel

British

Country-house hotel with traditional cuisine

☎ 01539 536653 LA11 6HH
e-mail: info@aynsomemanorhotel.co.uk
web: www.aynsomemanorhotel.co.uk

Originally built in 1512, there's an old-fashioned sense of refinement at this beautifully situated country house. A dress code of jacket and tie is required for gentlemen diners, tables are set with a well-rehearsed formality and soup is served in tureens. That said, the cosy dining room enjoys a jolly, house party atmosphere when the house is full with residents - at other times there's never any sense of stuffiness. The food likewise follows traditional lines - chicken liver parfait with cranberry and port compôte for example, or roast leg of Cumbrian lamb with redcurrant and wine jus.

Chef: Gordon Topp **Owners:** P A Varley **Times:** 1/7-8.30, Closed 2-28 Jan, Closed L Mon-Sat, D Sun (ex residents) **Prices:** Fixed L £14.75-£14.95, Fixed D £22-£23, Coffee £2, Min/Water £2.25, Service optional **Wine:** 35 bottles over £20, 50 bottles under £20, 8 by the glass (£2.50-£2.60) **Notes:** Fixed L 3 courses, Dress Restrictions, Jacket & Tie preferred **Seats:** 28 **Smoking:** N/Sm in restaurant **Children:** Min 5 yrs, Menu, Portions **Rooms:** 12 (12 en suite) ★★ HL **Directions:** Leave A590 signed Cartmel. Hotel is 0.5m N of Cartmel village on right, opposite Pig & Whistle pub **Parking:** 20

L'Enclume

see page 87

CASTLE CARROCK MAP 18 NY55

The Weary at Castle Carrock

Modern British NEW

Refurbished country inn with contemporary charm and cuisine

☎ 01228 670230 CA8 9LU
e-mail: relax@theweary.com
web: www.theweary.com

The frontage of this 18th-century inn gives no indication of the transformed, stylish interior. The restaurant is split into two sections - an elegant dining room and a bar/lounge with sofas and tub chairs. Subtle lighting, rich colours and an understated décor create an effective backdrop for the original modern art and fine artefacts collected by the owners. The cooking is simple and straightforward, based on the plentiful quality local produce and with a touch of Asian flavouring to spice up the modern, seasonal British menu. Fish and vegetarian choices are good, along with a range of fresh game in season, and the list might include Barbary duck breast with plum charlotte and fruity cassis sauce.

Chef: Ian Whiteman **Owners:** Ian & Gill Boyd **Times:** 12-2/6-9, Closed Mon **Prices:** Starter £3.95-£7.50, Main £10.95-£17.95, Dessert £3.25-£7.95, Coffee £1.95, Min/Water £3.50, Service optional **Wine:** 40 bottles over £20, 15 bottles under £20, 11 by the glass (£3.95-£5.95) **Notes:** Vegetarian available **Seats:** 85, Pr/dining room 14 **Smoking:** N/Sm in restaurant **Children:** Menu, Portions **Rooms:** 5 (5 en suite) ★★★★ RR **Directions:** M6 junct 43 onto A69 towards Hexham for 2m, at x-rds take right filter lane and turn right, onto B6413 for 4m to Castle Carrock **Parking:** 8

COCKERMOUTH MAP 18 NY13

The Trout Hotel

Traditional International

Traditional dishes in a lovely setting

☎ 01900 823591 Crown St CA13 0EJ
e-mail: enquiries@trouthotel.co.uk
web: www.trouthotel.co.uk

Situated next to Wordsworth's House by the River Derwent, the original part of the hotel dates back to 1670 and although altered over the years it retains many period features. The hotel restaurant is traditional in décor and has a friendly, relaxed atmosphere. Cooking sees a combination of classic, local and international cuisine reflecting demand for lighter sauces and use of local produce. This is seen in starters using smoked Cumbrian sausage, and main dishes like Cumbrian fell-bred fillet of beef. The Terrace Bar is open for lunch, serving informal pub food in a relaxed setting.

Chef: Alex Hartley **Owners:** Mr N Mills **Times:** 12-2/7-9.30, Closed L Mon-Sat **Prices:** Fixed L £14.95-£19.95, Fixed D fr £28.95, Coffee £2.40, Min/Water £3, Service optional **Wine:** 13 bottles over £20, 24 bottles under £20, 11 by the glass (£3-£5.35) **Notes:** Fixed L 3 courses, Vegetarian available, Civ Wed 60 **Seats:** 60, Pr/dining room 20 **Smoking:** N/Sm in restaurant **Children:** Menu, Portions **Rooms:** 43 (43 en suite) ★★★ HL **Directions:** M6 junct 40, follow A66 to Cockermouth, Hotel situated next to Wordsworth House **Parking:** Nearby car park

Quince & Medlar

☎ 01900 823579 13 Castlegate CA13 9EU

Imaginative and very good value vegetarian cooking in the centre of town.

L'Enclume

CARTMEL MAP 18 SD37

Modern NOTABLE WINE LIST

Exhilarating, innovative cuisine to stir a quiet Lakeland village

☎ 015395 36362 Cavendish St LA11 6PZ
e-mail: info@lenclume.co.uk
web: www.lenclume.co.uk

A former village blacksmiths dating back to the 13th century and set in the southern Lakeland seems an unlikely location for one of the most avant-garde restaurants in the country, home to Simon Rogan's bold and inventive cooking. Now a smart restaurant with rooms, this northern star is decorated in slick, understated fashion, while retaining original features and a relaxed atmosphere. Exposed ceiling beams, flagstone floor and uneven whitewashed walls are married with dramatic modern artwork, clothed tables and simple but striking flower arrangements. A small conservatory at the back is the place for aperitifs, while gazing up at the priory and out over the riverside garden. Simon's cuisine has a modern French base, but a highly individual and unorthodox voice; this is bold, precise, sophisticated and complex contemporary cuisine, yet shows restraint. The unique trademarks here are Simon's 'Taste and Texture' menus; three fixed-price, set offerings that range from the eight-course Introduction, through to 14-course Intermediate. These incorporate many unusual herbs and plants that are a signature of his cooking. Stunning flavours, temperatures and textures arrive in well-judged sequence and leave the senses stimulated but not overwhelmed. Innovative and unusual combinations flow with rhythm and balance, while technique and presentation skills ooze artistry. Think beef fillet with passion cannelloni, hazelnut Pavlova and fennel coulis, and an upside down coconut soufflé, meli-melo dessert. There's a 3-course carte too and a value lunch menu. The front-of-house team reflects the quality of the dining experience, highly professional, necessarily well informed, but friendly, too.

Notable Wine List: A well chosen and balanced list offering an interesting range of quality wines.

Chef: Simon Rogan
Owners: Simon Rogan, Penny Tapsell
Times: 12-1.45/7-9.30, Closed 1st 2 wks Jan, Mon & Tue, Closed D Sun
Prices: Fixed L £25, Starter £15.50-£16, Main £23-£27, Dessert £10, Coffee £5, Min/Water £3, Service optional
Wine: 166 bottles over £20, 3 bottles under £20, 8 by the glass (£3.10-£8)
Notes: Tasting menu 8 courses £55, 14 courses £80, 20 courses £100, Vegetarian available
Seats: 35
Smoking: N/Sm in restaurant
Children: Min 10 yrs
Directions: 10m from M6 junct 36 follow signs for A590 W, turn left for Cartmel before Newby Bridge
Parking: 7

CROSTHWAITE MAP 18 SD49

The Punchbowl Inn at Crosthwaite

Modern British NEW

Historic, elegantly refurbished inn with refined cooking

☎ 01539 568327 Lyth Valley LA8 8HR
e-mail: info@the-punchbowl.co.uk
web: www.the-punchbowl.co.uk

Stunningly set beside the ancient village church, this historic inn, (sibling to The Drunken Duck Inn, Ambleside, see entry) has been sympathetically but stylishly remodelled, yet retains bags of character. Witness oak beams, open fireplaces and an elegant restaurant that takes on a minimalist formula, enhanced by artwork, leather chairs, white linen and polished-wood floors. Service is professional and well informed, while the kitchen shows pedigree, too, its accomplished modern approach utilizing well-sourced, local ingredients on an appealing repertoire. Goats' cheese tart Tatin, caramelised onions and roasted fig dressing, fillet of Galloway beef with shin tortellini, pickled walnut and sarsparilla jus, and damson gin and vanilla pannacotta with poached plums and candied vanilla pods show the style.

Chef: Matthew Waddington **Owners:** Paul Spencer, Steph Barton, Richard Rose, Amanda Robinson **Times:** 12-2/6.30-9 **Prices:** Starter £6.95-£10.50, Main £16.95-£24.50, Dessert £6.95-£8.50, Coffee £1.80, Min/Water £2.50, Service optional, Group min 10 service 10% **Wine:** 35 bottles over £20, 22 bottles under £20, 15 by the glass (£3.25-£5.90) **Notes:** Vegetarian available **Seats:** 30 **Smoking:** N/Sm in restaurant **Children:** Portions **Rooms:** 9 (9 en suite) ◆◆◆◆◆ **Directions:** 6m from Kendal **Parking:** 40

GRANGE-OVER-SANDS MAP 18 SD47

Clare House

British, French

Satisfying country-house cooking in relaxing surroundings

☎ 015395 33026 & 34253 Park Rd LA11 7HQ
e-mail: info@clarehousehotel.co.uk
web: www.clarehousehotel.co.uk

This family-run hotel with well-tended gardens overlooks Morecambe Bay. The dining room has elegant, high ceilings, open fireplaces, polished mahogany furniture and traditional settings. Efficient service and the friendly manner keep regulars coming back every year. Simple, effective traditional and modern dishes populate the menu. Starters include roasted mushroom soup and sourdough bread with a possible main course of roast pork loin, fondant potatoes, fennel baked in cream and parmesan. A tarte Tatin of Granny Smith apples with sauce Anglaise finishes the meal. Dinner is at 6.45pm prompt.

Chef: Andrew Read, Mark Johnston **Owners:** Mr & Mrs D S Read **Times:** 6.45-7.15, Closed Dec-Apr, Closed L Mon-Sun **Prices:** Fixed D £28, Coffee £1.60, Min/Water 75p, Service included **Wine:** 4 bottles over £20, 35 bottles under £20 **Notes:** Fixed D 4 courses, Vegetarian available **Seats:** 32 **Smoking:** N/Sm in restaurant **Children:** Menu, Portions **Rooms:** 19 (18 en suite) ★ **Directions:** From M6 take A590 then B5277 to Grange-over-Sands Park Road follows the shore line. Hotel on left next to swimming pool **Parking:** 16

GRASMERE MAP 18 NY30

Grasmere Hotel

Traditional European V

Traditional country-house hotel with fine food

☎ 015394 35277 Broadgate LA22 9TA
e-mail: enquiries@grasmerehotel.co.uk
web: www.grasmerehotel.co.uk

A former Victorian gentleman's residence, this traditionally decorated mansion house retains many original features including attractive wood panelling in the lounge areas and a stunning acanthus chandelier in the dining room. Service is an intriguing part of the experience with guests congregating in the lounge for drinks, before being called through to eat en masse. Cooking is very much in the country house vein with a daily-changing menu and local produce featured throughout. Start with peppered mackerel pâté and follow with Hawkshead trout baked in white wine with lemon and parsley butter.

Chef: Mr P Hetherington **Owners:** Stuart & Janet Cardwell **Times:** 7, Closed Jan-early Feb, Closed L all week **Prices:** Fixed D fr £29.50, Coffee £1.50, Min/Water £3, Service optional **Wine:** 11 bottles over £20, 43 bottles under £20, 8 by the glass (£3-£4) **Notes:** Fixed D 4 courses, Vegetarian menu, Dress Restrictions, No jeans or shorts **Seats:** 30 **Smoking:** N/Sm in restaurant **Children:** Min 10 yrs, Portions **Rooms:** 13 (13 en suite) ★★ HL **Directions:** Off A591 close to village centre **Parking:** 13

❀❀ Rothay Garden Hotel & Restaurant

Modern International

Delightful hotel with fine dining

☎ 015394 35334 Broadgate LA22 9RJ
e-mail: stay@rothay-garden.com
web: www.rothay-garden.com

Set amidst large riverside gardens on the outskirts of Grasmere village, this splendid Lakeland hotel offers fine dining in an airy and elegant conservatory with well spaced tables, which are candlelit at night. Professional, but relaxed service pervades and the seasonal menu blends modern and traditional dishes with some innovative flavour combinations - seared scallops and 'haddie' sausage is paired with celeriac and horseradish remoulade and a mild curry cream, roast pork fillet is wrapped in Parma ham and spinach and served with sage jus, apple onion jam and goat's cheese charlotte. Finish with baba bread-and-butter pudding with Baileys sauce and Horlicks ice cream.

Chef: Andrew Burton **Owners:** Chris Carss **Times:** 12-1.45/7.30-9, Closed L 24, 25, 31 Dec, 1 Jan **Prices:** Fixed D £29.95-£32, Min/Water £2.95, Service optional **Wine:** 78 bottles over £20, 55 bottles under £20, 75 by the glass (£4.70-£7.50) **Notes:** Coffee incl, Fixed D 4 courses, Vegetarian available. Dress Restrictions, Smart casual, no jeans or T-shirts **Seats:** 60 **Smoking:** N/Sm in restaurant **Children:** Min 5 yrs **Rooms:** 25 (25 en suite) ★★★ **Directions:** From N M6 junct 40, A66 to Keswick, then S on A591 to Grasmere. From S M6 junct 36 take A591 through Windermere/Ambleside to Grasmere. At N end of village adjacent to park **Parking:** 35

❀ White Moss House

Modern British [V]

Idyllic haven offering a Cumbrian feast

☎ 015394 35295 Rydal Water LA22 9SE
e-mail: sue@whitemoss.com
web: www.whitemoss.com

Poet William Wordsworth so loved White Moss House, which dates from 1730, that he bought it for his son and the family who lived here until the 1930s. A traditional Lakeland slate building, this family-run hotel is furnished in country-house style, with deep sofas, comfortable armchairs and open fires. The no-choice (apart from pudding) dinner menu showcases traditional Cumbrian dishes and utilises the very best local ingredients: rack of Herdwick organic lamb with herb crust or free-range maize-fed Vale of Lune guinea fowl braised in dry cider, finishing with a traditional English dessert such as huntsman's pudding with malmsey sauce.

Chef: Peter Dixon **Owners:** Peter & Sue Dixon **Times:** 8, Closed Dec-Jan, Sun, Closed L all week **Prices:** Fixed D £39.50, Min/Water £2.75, Service optional **Wine:** 107 bottles over £20, 61 bottles under £20, 7 by the glass (£4.65-£6.95) **Notes:** Fixed D 5 courses incl coffee, Vegetarian menu **Seats:** 18 **Smoking:** N/Sm in restaurant **Children:** Portions **Rooms:** 7 (7 en suite) ★★ HL **Directions:** On A591 between Grasmere and Ambleside opposite Rydal Water **Parking:** 10

❀❀ Wordsworth Hotel

Modern British

Impressive culinary display in the heart of Lakeland

☎ 015394 35592 LA22 9SW
e-mail: enquiry@thewordsworthhotel.co.uk
web: www.thewordsworthhotel.co.uk

Situated in the centre of the village in its own peaceful grounds against a backdrop of towering fells, next to the churchyard where Wordsworth is buried, this very traditional hotel offers a pleasant haven from the constant tourist rush around the Lakes. Classically based, the fixed-price menu in the Prelude restaurant continues to impress through the use of quality local produce and some interesting and unusual ingredients. Dishes are cooked with care and flair, resulting in good flavours and textures, and presentation is first class. You might start with ravioli of black pudding, caramelised apples and mustard and then move on to seared red mullet with langoustine ravioli and chive butter or assiette of Old Spot pork.

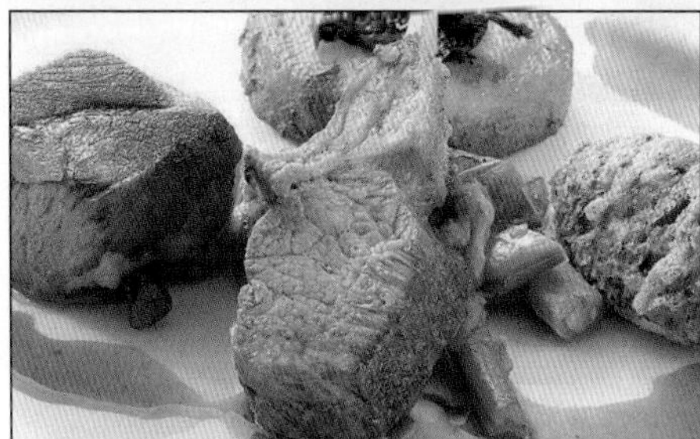

Chef: Leigh Myers **Owners:** Mr Gifford **Times:** 12.30-2/7-9.30 **Prices:** Fixed L fr £12, Fixed D fr £39.50, Coffee £2.95, Min/Water £3.75, Service optional **Wine:** 161 bottles over £20, 48 bottles under £20, 14 by the glass (£3.75-£7.50) **Notes:** Fixed D 4 courses, Vegetarian available, Dress Restrictions, Smart casual, jacket preferred, Civ Wed 110 **Seats:** 65, Pr/dining room 26 **Smoking:** N/Sm in restaurant, Air con **Children:** Min 8 yrs, Menu, Portions **Rooms:** 37 (37 en suite) ★★★★ HL **Directions:** From Ambleside follow A591 N to Grasmere. Hotel in town centre next to church **Parking:** 50

HAWKSHEAD MAP 18 SD39

Queen's Head Hotel

British, Mediterranean

Old-world inn serving honest fare

☎ 015394 36271 Main St LA22 0NS
e-mail: enquiries@queensheadhotel.co.uk
web: www.queensheadhotel.co.uk

Popular, archetypal, 16th-century coaching inn at the heart of the village, with a warm, friendly atmosphere and wealth of original features. Think flagstone floors, wood-panelled bar, log fire and low, oak-beamed ceilings. Uncomplicated, generous and robust modern cooking is the style. The lengthy, crowd-pleasing carte employs quality, locally sourced produce and comes bolstered by daily blackboard specials. Eat in the pretty dining room or bar. Start your meal with Scottish mussels, cream and white wine sauce, followed by venison medallions, root vegetable mash, juniper and red wine glaze.

Times: 12-2.30/6.15-9.15 **Rooms:** 14 (12 en suite) ★★ HL
Directions: Village centre

West Vale Country House

Traditional French

Fine dining in classic country house

☎ 01539 442817 Far Sawrey LA22 0LQ
e-mail: enquiries@westvalecountryhouse.co.uk
web: www.westvalecountryhouse.co.uk

This charming, small retreat nestles in the heart of the Lake District National Park on the edge of the beautiful village of Far Sawrey, with delightful views across the vale to Grizedale Forest. Elegant style and a warm ambience combine with textbook service and hospitality, while the restaurant continues the theme and comforts, with well-spaced tables, white linen and quality china and glassware. The country-house cooking, with its modern approach, fits the surroundings and features

continued

the best of local produce and clear flavours on the daily-changing menu. Take a Graythwaite venison steak with garlic potato crush drizzled with port and cranberry jus, and a dark chocolate and brandy torte finale.

Chef: Glynn Pennington **Owners:** Dee & Glynn Pennington **Times:** 6.30-8, Closed 25 Dec, Mon, Closed L all week **Prices:** Fixed D £34-£37.25, Coffee £3.25, Min/Water £2.95, Service optional **Wine:** 14 bottles over £20, 14 bottles under £20, 2 by the glass (£3.75-£4.60) **Notes:** Fixed D 4 courses, Smart casual **Seats:** 16 **Smoking:** N/Sm in restaurant **Children:** Min 12 yrs, Menu, Portions **Rooms:** 7 (7 en suite) ◆◆◆◆◆ **Directions:** Please telephone for directions **Parking:** 10

HOWTOWN MAP 18 NY41

Sharrow Bay Country House Hotel

British, International NOTABLE WINE LIST

Elegant lakeside country-house dining with stunning views

☎ 017684 86301 Sharrow Bay CA10 2LZ
e-mail: info@sharrowbay.co.uk
web: www.sharrowbay.co.uk

Popularly described as the 'original country-house hotel', Sharrow Bay's Italianate façade - set smack on the shores of Ullswater - brings a touch of the Italian Lakes to Cumbria. Décor is opulent and in typical English country-house mode, brimful of antiques, soft furnishings and fresh flowers. Take a stroll in the extensive grounds, or enjoy the views from a table in the elegant restaurant, where the classic country-house cooking continues the theme. Tip-top local produce is delivered in highly accomplished dishes that blend traditional and modern ideas; take tournedos of Scottish fillet steak with braised ox cheek, roasted tomato, root vegetables and a Burgundy sauce, and perhaps a trio of chocolate desserts finale.

Notable Wine List: Award-winning wine list with a comprehensive offering from all the major wine producing areas of the world.

continued

Chef: Juan Martin, Colin Akrigg **Owners:** Sharrow Bay Hotels Ltd **Times:** 1/8 **Prices:** Fixed L fr £25, Fixed D fr £52.50, Coffee £2.50, Min/Water £2.75, Service optional **Wine:** 650 bottles over £20, 30 bottles under £20, 20 by the glass (£4.50-£8.75) **Notes:** Fixed L 3 courses, Fixed D 5 courses, Dress Restrictions, Smart casual, Civ Wed 35 **Seats:** 55, Pr/dining room 40 **Smoking:** N/Sm in restaurant, Air con **Children:** Min 13 yrs **Rooms:** 22 (24 en suite) ★★★ **Directions:** M6 junct 40. From Pooley Bridge fork right by church towards Howtown. At x-rds turn right and follow lakeside road for 2m **Parking:** 30

KENDAL MAP 18 SD59

The Castle Green Hotel in Kendal

Modern European

Modern restaurant with the kitchen on view

☎ 01539 734000 Castle Green Ln LA9 6BH
e-mail: reception@castlegreen.co.uk
web: www.castlegreen.co.uk

This popular hotel offers a relaxed stay in a typical Lakeland setting overlooking fells and castle ruins. The very smart modern dining room has been decorated in muted shades that provide a perfect foil for the dramatic scenery outside the large plate glass windows. The ambitious cooking is showcased on the modern European menu, where nursery favourites (apple crumble with apple fritters and caramel ice cream) can be found alongside globally-inspired dishes: perhaps roasted scallops, beetroot, pea shoots and dill cream, or tuna loin with coconut rice, coriander and pickled vegetables. You can watch the chef at work through a window into the new state-of-the-art theatre kitchen.

Chef: Justin Woods **Owners:** James & Catherine Alexander **Times:** 12-2/6-10 **Prices:** Fixed D £24.95, Coffee £2.25, Min/Water £3.50, Service included **Wine:** 23 bottles over £20, 36 bottles under £20, 12 by the glass (£3.55-£7.70) **Notes:** Vegetarian available, Dress Restrictions, Smart casual, Civ Wed 100 **Seats:** 80 **Smoking:** N/Sm in restaurant, Air con **Children:** Menu, Portions **Rooms:** 100 (100 en suite) ★★★ HL **Directions:** From Kendal High St, take A684 towards Sedbergh, hotel is last on left leaving Kendal **Parking:** 200

KESWICK MAP 18 NY22

Dale Head Hall Lakeside Hotel

Modern British

Immaculate lakeside hotel under new family ownership

☎ 017687 72478 Lake Thirlmere CA12 4TN
e-mail: onthelakeside@daleheadhall.co.uk
web: www.daleheadhall.co.uk

Historic lakeside residence dating from the 16th century and set in attractive grounds. Inviting public areas include a choice of lounges, an atmospheric restaurant with exposed stone and low beams, and a smaller alternative dining room looking towards the lake. The daily menu offers a choice of two dishes at each of four courses, such as warm spiced breast of pigeon on confit artichoke with lentil and sherry dressing, followed by soup or sorbet, then perhaps poached fillet of baby halibut with spinach purée and celery, bacon and oregano sauce. Finish with dessert (iced lavender and honey terrine with poached rhubarb) or a selection of four cheeses.

Chef: Fred Salvini, Jose Lopez **Owners:** Mr & Mrs A Lowe **Times:** 7.30-8, Closed Jan **Prices:** Food prices not confirmed for 2007. Please telephone for details **Wine:** 55 bottles over £20, 17 bottles under £20, 8 by the glass (£4) **Notes:** Vegetarian available, Dress Restrictions, No jeans or casual wear **Seats:** 28, Pr/dining room 12 **Smoking:** N/Sm in restaurant **Children:** Min 10yrs, Portions **Rooms:** 12 (12 en suite) ★★★ CHH **Directions:** 5m from Keswick on A591 **Parking:** 16

Highfield Hotel & Restaurant

British, European

Ambitious cooking in friendly Lakeland hotel

☎ 017687 72508 The Heads CA12 5ER
e-mail: info@highfieldkeswick.co.uk
web: www.highfieldkeswick.co.uk

Country house in style, this lovely Victorian hotel retains many original features - think balconies, turrets, bay windows and veranda - and comes set on the edge of town with Lakeland views and a relaxed, friendly atmosphere. The restaurant continues the theme, with original ceiling roses and cornice, while taking advantage of the views. And, while traditional may sum up the setting, the cooking takes a modern approach - classical in style but with contemporary twist. The ambitious, daily changing, dinner-only menu comes peppered with quality Cumbrian produce and dishes set to tickle the taste buds; take a trio of wild mallard, pigeon and pheasant breasts, set on a black pudding tattie pot, sweet red cabbage and green peppercorn sauce.

Chef: Gus Cleghorn **Owners:** Howard & Caroline Speck **Times:** 6.30-8.30, Closed Late Nov-Early Feb, Closed L all week **Prices:** Fixed D £32.50-£37, Coffee £1.50, Min/Water £2, Service optional **Wine:** 13 bottles over £20, 47 bottles under £20, 6 by the glass (£3.75-£4.75) **Notes:** Fixed D 4 courses, Vegetarian available, Dress Restrictions, Smart casual **Seats:** 40 **Smoking:** N/Sm in restaurant **Children:** Min 8 yrs, Portions **Rooms:** 19 (19 en suite) ★★ HL **Directions:** M6 junct 40, follow signs for Keswick, approaching Keswick, ignore first sign. Continue on A66, at Peach rdbt turn left. At next t-junct turn left, and continue to mini-rdbt and take right exit then third right onto the Heads **Parking:** 20

Lyzzick Hall Country House Hotel

Modern British NEW

Quality cooking accompanied by Lakeland views

☎ 017687 72277 Under Skiddaw CA12 4PY
e-mail: info@lyzzickhall.co.uk
web: www.lyzzickhall.co.uk

Perched in the foothills of Skiddaw overlooking Keswick, this cosy Lakeland hotel boasts beautiful views all year round. Nothing is too much trouble for its friendly staff, while the kitchen team conjure a menu of accomplished fare from the finest ingredients Cumbria has to offer. Dishes are modern British in style, and feature the odd nod to sunny climes and Spain in particular - you might start with mussels in

continued

England

KESWICK *continued* MAP 18 NY22

white wine, garlic and herbs with chorizo sausage perhaps, and then move on to chargrilled medallions of beef fillet with asparagus spears and béarnaise sauce, or braised lamb shank with potato mash, rosemary and thyme sauce.

Chef: Chris Cooper **Owners:** Mr & Mrs Fernandez **Times:** 12-2/7-9, Closed Jan **Prices:** Fixed L £12-£14, Fixed D £25-£27, Coffee £1.50, Service optional **Wine:** 40 bottles over £20, 110 bottles under £20, 4 by the glass (£2.95) **Notes:** Fixed D 4 courses, Sun L £16 - booking essential, Dress Restrictions, Smart casual **Seats:** 75 **Smoking:** N/Sm in restaurant **Children:** Menu, Portions **Rooms:** 31 (31 en suite) ★★ HL **Directions:** Leave Keswick towards Carlisle, at main rdbt take 2nd exit signed A591 Carlisle, Lyzzick Hall 1.5m on right **Parking:** 60

Swinside Lodge

British, European

Charming country house with indulgent food and service

☎ 017687 72948 Grange Rd, Newlands CA12 5UE
e-mail: info@swinsidelodge-hotel.co.uk
web: www.swinsidelodge-hotel.co.uk

Just five minutes' stroll from the shores of Derwentwater, this Georgian Lakeland house is a hidden gem and a real home-from-home, with its attentive, relaxed and friendly service that leaves you feeling like old friends. The décor is very much country-house elegance, its small, romantic dining room replete in reds, with interesting artwork, fresh flowers, candlelight and clothed tables. The kitchen's output is via set, four-course, daily-changing, dinner-only menus (though there's an optional choice at dessert). Quality produce combines with clear, clean flavoured, well-presented dishes and combinations that really work. Consistency and skill are evident throughout, as in roast breast of pheasant with chestnut stuffing, kumquat chutney, rosemary and red wine sauce.

Chef: Clive Imber **Owners:** Eric & Irene Fell **Times:** 7-10.30, Closed 25 Dec, Closed L Mon-Sun **Prices:** Fixed D £35, Service optional **Wine:** 12 bottles over £20, 17 bottles under £20, 4 by the glass (£3) **Notes:** Fixed D 4 courses, Vegetarian available **Seats:** 18 **Smoking:** N/Sm in restaurant **Children:** Min 12 yrs, Portions **Rooms:** 8 (7 en suite) ★★ HL **Directions:** M1 junct 40 take A66 to Cockermouth, ignore exits to Keswick, next left to Portinscale. Follow country road for 2m (do not leave this road). Hotel on right **Parking:** 12

Underscar Manor

British, French

Formal fine dining in a beautiful country house

☎ 017687 75000 Applethwaite CA12 4PH
web: www.underscar.co.uk

continued

A friendly Italianate country-house hotel set on a flank of Skiddaw with picture postcard views of Keswick, Derwentwater and the surrounding fells. The lavish restaurant is traditionally furnished in keeping with the character and style of the building. There is an evening dress code with jackets required for men, and formal service. The classic setting is matched by some ambitious classic cooking and impressive presentation. An extensive menu offers starters like goat's cheese soufflé with spiced cauliflower fritters. Main courses might feature medallions of roast pork, garnished with ham knuckle and foie gras terrine, Calvados sauce and pease pudding or a medley of fish poached in white wine.

Times: 12-1/7-8.30 **Directions:** Exit M6 at junct 36 on to Keswick, follow for 17 miles (don't turn off in to Keswick). At rdbt take 3rd exit and turn immediately right at sign for Underscar Manor

Morrel's

☎ 017687 72666 34 Lake Rd CA12 5DQ
Non-smoking restaurant, handy for the theatre.

KIRKBY LONSDALE MAP 18 SD67

The Whoop Hall

Modern, Traditional

Modern restaurant offering traditional dishes

☎ 015242 71284 Burrow with Burrow LA6 2HP
e-mail: info@whoophall.co.uk
web: www.whoophall.co.uk

Originally a 17th-century coaching inn, Whoop Hall is now a fully-fledged hotel. Here Connor's restaurant is a bright room on two floors, a galleried area above. The lightwood furniture and stone-tiled floor give a modern feel. A light bites menu offers a choice of fillings for sandwiches, baguettes, jackets or tortillas, alongside salads, chips and pasta. The main menu offers traditional dishes like prawn cocktail with Marie rose sauce to start, followed by local Cumberland sausage with creamy mash and onion gravy.

Chef: R Lockyer **Owners:** Jo & Kim Boleta **Times:** 12-6/6-10 **Prices:** Starter £2.95-£5.50, Main £7.95-£14.95, Dessert £2.95-£5.50, Coffee £1.50, Min/Water £3.50 **Wine:** 6 bottles over £20, 35 bottles under £20, 4 by the glass (£2.90-£3.90) **Notes:** Vegetarian available, Civ Wed 150 **Seats:** 70, Pr/dining room 25 **Smoking:** N/Sm in restaurant **Children:** Menu, Portions **Rooms:** 24 (23 en suite) ★★ HL **Directions:** Please telephone for directions **Parking:** 100

NEAR SAWREY MAP 18 SD39

Sawrey House Country Hotel

British

Skilful country-house cooking with views of Lakeland fells

☎ 015394 36387 LA22 0LF
e-mail: enquiries@sawreyhouse.com
web: www.sawrey-house.com

The house, built in 1830, is located next to Beatrix Potter's home, Hilltop Farm. The dining room has a traditional feel and looks out over Esthwaite Water and the surrounding fells. Guests are entertained throughout the evening by music from the piano. The modern British cooking uses local and home-grown produce where possible, and the proprietor infuses his own oils for the kitchen. Well presented and straightforward dishes include warm goat's cheese with salad leaves, walnuts, grapes and wild garlic oil, and tender lamb with garlic and mint potatoes and a Madeira jus.

continued

Chef: William Steele **Owners:** Mr & Mrs C Whiteside **Times:** 7.30-8, Closed Jan, Closed L all week **Prices:** Fixed D £35-£45, Coffee £3.50, Min/Water £3.95, Service included **Wine:** 32 bottles over £20, 8 bottles under £20 **Notes:** Fixed D 4 courses, Vegetarian available, Dress Restrictions, Smart casual **Seats:** 30 **Smoking:** N/Sm in restaurant, Air con **Children:** Min 10 yrs **Rooms:** 12 (12 en suite) ◆◆◆◆◆ **Directions:** From Ambleside A593 S left at Clappersgate onto B5286 towards Hawkshead then take B5285 towards Sawrey/Ferry. Hotel 1.5m on right **Parking:** 25

NETHER WASDALE MAP 18 NY10

Low Wood Hall Hotel

European

Fresh modern dishes in Victorian country-house style

☎ 019467 26100 CA20 1ET
e-mail: enquiries@lowwoodhall.co.uk
web: www.lowwoodhall.co.uk

This Victorian hotel is tucked away in a remote valley with beautiful landscaped gardens, surrounded by 5 acres of woodland. The conservatory restaurant offers glorious views and looks very romantic when candlelit at night. Built in the 1860s for a local brewer, Thomas Dalzell and his family, the house retains many features from the Victorian era, including gasoliers in the lounges, tiled and pine stripped floors and marble fireplaces. The chef serves up modern classic dishes using fresh local ingredients including herbs from the kitchen garden. The menu changes daily to reflect seasonal availability and produce from local suppliers.

Times: 7-9, Closed L all wk **Rooms:** 12 (11 en suite) ★★ HL **Directions:** Exit A595 at Gosforth & bear left for Wasdale, after 3m turn right for Nether Wasdale

NEWBY BRIDGE MAP 18 SD38

Lakeside Hotel

British, European

Fine dining in picturesque Lakeland shore setting

☎ 015395 30001 Lakeside, Lake Windermere LA12 8AT
e-mail: sales@lakesidehotel.co.uk
web: www.lakesidehotel.co.uk

Set on the peaceful southern shore of Lake Windermere, next to the steamer dock, this is an impressive, family-run hotel where guests can expect high standards of service. Dinner is served in the elegant, oak-panelled restaurant, with its fresh flowers, floor-length tablecloths and sparkling glassware, but more informal meals can be enjoyed in the contemporary brasserie. Cooking is accomplished, with traditional British and European dishes prepared and presented with flair and expertise. Classical dishes are given a modern twist. Typically, choose crab and tomato risotto with chilli cappuccino, poached fillet of brill with an open lasagne of brown shrimps with asparagus and tomato, and trio of Belgian chocolate. Service is professional and highly skilled.

continued

Times: 12.30-2.30/6.45-9.30 **Rooms:** 76 (76 en suite) ★★★★ HL **Directions:** M6 junct 36 follow A590 to Newby Bridge, straight over rdbt, right over bridge, Hotel within 1m

Swan Hotel

Traditional

Moor up for some comfort cooking

☎ 015395 31681 LA12 8NB
e-mail: enquiries@swanhotel.com
web: www.swanhotel.com

Set beside the river Leven at the southern end of Lake Windermere, this 17th-century coaching inn boasts a choice of eateries. Revells restaurant is the main draw, a traditional dining room with smartly turned out waiting staff and panoramic views. Mains are hearty, comforting creations such as chargrilled fillet of Scottish beef with Meaux mustard mash and beetroot gravy, or a baked open winter vegetable pie with neeps, tatties and roast shallots in cheddar cream sauce, while desserts include old favourites (citrus sponge pudding) and classier fare such as baked toffee and pecan tart with pistachio ice cream.

Chef: Andrew Turner **Owners:** Roland Bardsley Ltd **Times:** 12-2/7-9.30, Closed L Mon-Sat **Prices:** Fixed D £32.50, Coffee £2.20, Min/Water £3.55, Service optional **Wine:** 44 bottles over £20, 37 bottles under £20, 9 by the glass (£3.45-£6.05) **Notes:** Sun L 3 courses £15.75, Dress Restrictions, No jeans, Civ Wed 140 **Seats:** 70, Pr/dining room 120 **Smoking:** N/Sm in restaurant, Air con **Children:** Menu, Portions **Rooms:** 55 (55 en suite) ★★★★ HL **Directions:** A59, at Newby Bridge take right over 5 arch bridge, hotel is immediately opposite **Parking:** 80

PENRITH MAP 18 NY53

Edenhall Country Hotel

Modern British

Formal dining in a friendly village hotel - don't forget your tackle

☎ 01768 881454 Edenhall CA11 8SX
e-mail: reception@edenhallhotel.co.uk
web: www.edenhallhotel.co.uk

Originally a bolt-hole for fishermen taking advantage of the nearby River Eden, this comfortable retreat is set in picturesque grounds and has become just as popular with walkers enjoying the Lakeland countryside. The large dining room is blessed with huge windows overlooking the garden and surrounding countryside; the local area is an inspiration too for the menu, which showcases the best of local Cumbrian produce in a cosmopolitan array of dishes. You could start with twice-baked smoked salmon and stilton soufflé and then move on to roast rump of Lakeland lamb with a minted jus.

Chef: Colin Sim **Owners:** Clare Simmons/Tony Simpson **Times:** 6.30-9.30, Closed L all week (bar meals only) **Prices:** Starter £3.95-£5.95, Main £8.95-£14.95, Dessert £4.95, Coffee £1.75, Min/Water £3, Service optional **Wine:** 3 bottles over £20, 22 bottles under £20, 4 by the glass (£3-£3.55) **Notes:** Sun L 3 courses £14.95, Civ Wed 60 **Seats:** 60, Pr/dining room 25 **Smoking:** N/Sm in restaurant **Children:** Menu, Portions **Rooms:** 25 (25 en suite) ★★ HL **Directions:** M6 junct 40, take A66 towards Scotch Corner. At rdbt follow signs to Alston (A686). Edenhall is 3m on right **Parking:** 60

England

SEASCALE MAP 18 NY00

۞ Cumbrian Lodge

International

Homely restaurant with wonderful speciality dishes

☎ 019467 27309 Gosforth Rd CA20 1JG
e-mail: cumbrianlodge@btconnect.com
web: www.cumbrianlodge.com

This congenial village restaurant was built in 1874 and housed the same family until 1999. As a restaurant with rooms, Cumbrian Lodge now has a modern, minimalist feel to the décor with modern art on the walls and crisp linen on the tables. The bistro-style menu features an eclectic mix of familiar favourites with an international bent - French onion soup, for example, or Maryland crab cake - there are some interesting specialities too - regulars rave about Geschnetzeltes Schweinefleisch (thinly sliced pork fillet sautéed in butter, wine and cream) served with a heavenly rösti potato.

Chef: R Hickson & A Carnall **Owners:** David J Morgan **Times:** 12-2/6.30-9.30, Closed Xmas, New Year, BHs, Sun, Closed L Mon & Sat **Prices:** Starter £4.50-£6.95, Main £9.95-£18.95, Dessert £3.95, Coffee £1.90, Min/Water £1.50, Service optional **Wine:** 12 bottles over £20, 18 bottles under £20, 10 by the glass (£3.75-£4.95) **Notes:** Vegetarian available **Seats:** 32 **Smoking:** N/Sm in restaurant **Rooms:** 6 (6 en suite) ◆◆◆◆ **Directions:** From A595 onto B5344, hotel on left after 2m **Parking:** 17

TEBAY MAP 18 NY60

۞ Westmorland Hotel & Bretherdale Restaurant

Modern NEW

Friendly modern hotel overlooking rugged moorland

☎ 015396 24351 Orton CA10 3SB
e-mail: reservations@westmorlandhotel.com
web: www.westmorlandhotel.com

There are picture-postcard views of the fells just half a mile from the M6 at this modern hotel. The split-level Bretherdale restaurant affords nearly every table a scenic outlook and outside a cascading water feature runs from the restaurant and past reception to the public areas. Imaginative modern cooking includes a great dish of seared diver-caught king scallops with salmon keta, quail eggs and braised couscous. There are close ties here with the local farming community with an award-winning farm shop as part of the complex.

Chef: Graham Evans **Times:** 6.30-9, Closed 1 Jan **Prices:** Starter £4.50-£5.95, Main £10.95-£19, Dessert fr £4.50, Coffee £2.25, Min/Water £3.10, Service optional **Wine:** 4 bottles over £20, 31 bottles under £20, 8 by the glass (£4.60) **Notes:** Dress Restrictions, Smart casual, no jeans or T-shirts, Civ Wed 100 **Seats:** 100, Pr/dining room 40 **Smoking:** N/Sm in restaurant, Air con **Children:** Menu, Portions **Rooms:** 50 (50 en suite) ★★★ HL **Directions:** Accessed from the Westmorland Motorway Services between J38 & J39 of M6 **Parking:** 60

TEMPLE SOWERBY MAP 18 NY62

۞۞ Temple Sowerby House Hotel & Restaurant

Modern British

Intimate setting for ambitious cooking

☎ 017683 61578 CA10 1RZ
e-mail: stay@templesowerby.com
web: www.templesowerby.com

This high-quality, country-house style hotel, set in the heart of the Eden Valley, dates back to the 16th century when it was the village's principal house. Its delightful, oak-beamed restaurant comes complete with open fire, smartly presented tables, candlelight and attentive service. The menu delivers an ambitious kaleidoscope of adventurous dishes that showcase innovative technique, bold combinations and fresh, quality local produce. Take a roasted rack of Cumbrian lamb with a tagliatelle salsa verde, poached new turnips and jus rôti, or pan-fried fillet of sea bass with baby château potatoes, ratatouille and rocket pesto to promote an agony of choice. And, there's a delightful walled garden for summer drinks, too.

Chef: Ashley Whittaker **Owners:** Paul & Julie Evans **Times:** 7-9, Closed 8 days Xmas, Closed L all week **Prices:** Starter £5.25-£8, Main £15.85-£20, Dessert £5.25-£8, Coffee £2.85, Min/Water £2.80, Service optional **Wine:** 29 bottles over £20, 13 bottles under £20, 6 by the glass (£3.10-£5) **Notes:** Vegetarian available, Dress Restrictions, Smart casual preferred, Civ Wed 40 **Seats:** 24, Pr/dining room 24 **Smoking:** N/Sm in restaurant **Rooms:** 12 (12 en suite) ★★★ HL **Directions:** On A66, 7m E of Penrith in village centre **Parking:** 20

WATERMILLOCK MAP 18 NY42

۞ *Macdonald Leeming House*

British, French

A taste of Cumbria in sumptuous country house with a view

☎ 0870 4008131 CA11 0JJ
e-mail: leeminghouse@macdonald-hotels.co.uk
web: www.macdonald-hotels.co.uk

Set in a stunning location, in 20 acres of landscaped grounds on the shores of Ullswater, Macdonald Leeming House dates from the 1800s and retains many original features. Beautiful views enhance the ornate but informal surroundings in the Regency-style restaurant. Classical dishes are given a modern, lighter twist, which reveals imagination and flair, and a willingness to experiment with the best seasonal

continued

England

produce that Cumbria has to offer. Dishes may include seared scallops with cauliflower purée, breast of Goosnargh duck with creamy cabbage, duck confit and vanilla jus, and steamed lemon and ginger sponge with vanilla custard.

Times: 12-2/6.30-9 **Rooms:** 41 (41 en suite) ★★★★ HL
Directions: A592 towards Ullswater, at T-junct turn right, hotel 3m on left

Rampsbeck Country House Hotel

see below

WINDERMERE MAP 18 SD49

Beech Hill Hotel

British, French

Modern cuisine and stunning lake views

☎ 015394 42137 Newby Bridge Rd LA23 3LR
e-mail: reservations@beechhillhotel.co.uk
web: www.beechhillhotel.co.uk

The great views over Lake Windermere and wonderful summer sunsets are not the only draws at this hotel dining room. The rich furnishings, smart interior designs and oak panelling make an elegant statement that is also hard to resist. After drinks on the terrace or in the lounge, guests need no prompting to order from the popular Simple Taste of the Lakes or five-course Gourmet menu. The cooking takes account of Cumbrian produce in peak condition, with several dimensions to each dish: Barbary duck three ways - confit, sausage and foie gras, might be followed by hot-pot, roast rack and grilled kidney of Swaledale lamb with spinach, crushed new potatoes and salsa verde.

Chef: Christopher Davies **Owners:** Mr & Mrs E K Richardson **Times:** 7-9, Closed L all week **Prices:** Fixed D £24.95, Coffee £1.25, Min/Water £3.50, Service optional **Wine:** 29 bottles over £20, 33 bottles under £20, 4 by the glass (£3.60) **Notes:** Vegetarian available, Dress Restrictions, Smart casual, no denim or trainers, Civ Wed 130 **Seats:** 130, Pr/dining room 90 **Smoking:** N/Sm in restaurant **Children:** Menu, Portions **Rooms:** 59 (59 en suite) ★★★ HL **Directions:** M6 junct 36, take A591 to Windermere, left onto A592 to Newby Bridge, hotel 4m on right **Parking:** 60

Burn How Garden House Hotel

Modern British V

Formal dining overlooking pretty gardens

☎ 015394 46226 Back Belsfield Rd, Bowness LA23 3HH
e-mail: info@burnhow.co.uk
web: www.burnhow.co.uk

Within walking distance of both the lakeside and the town centre, this delightful Victorian hotel is set in its own leafy grounds and has a relaxed country-house feel. Enjoyable, creative dinners can be enjoyed in the stylish dining room, which has interesting art on the walls and peaceful garden views. Using locally sourced ingredients, both the carte and daily specials menu offer traditional favourites, such as Cumberland sausage with red onion jus, alongside more elaborate dishes, perhaps Cumbrian beef fillet with red wine and thyme reduction. Service is friendly and attentive.

continued

Rampsbeck Country House Hotel

WATERMILLOCK MAP 18 NY42

Modern British, French

Innovative modern cooking in lakeside hotel

☎ 017684 86442 CA11 0LP
e-mail: enquiries@rampsbeck.fsnet.co.uk
web: www.rampsbeck.fsnet.co.uk

This idyllic 18th-century country house is set in 18 acres of parkland overlooking Lake Ullswater, with attractive gardens, hedges and paths running down to the shore. It boasts many original features - including carved fireplaces - and comes furnished with period and antique pieces. There are three delightful and comfortable lounges plus a small traditional bar (that opens out on to a terrace on warm summer days), as well as the attractive, candlelit restaurant with its large windows that make the best of those views. Tables are well spaced and service nicely traditional, though appropriately friendly and attentive, while the cooking proves a real highlight. The kitchen's innovative, modern approach uses fresh, top-quality produce in thoughtful, well-judged combinations. Expect clean flavours and interesting textures in complex dishes, like pan-fried calves' liver teamed with a rösti potato, curried creamed Savoy cabbage, glazed baby carrots and a caraway seed flavoured jus, or perhaps steamed fillet of sea bass teamed with noodles, a brochette of langoustines and

pimento sauce, while a hot Muscat grape soufflé accompanied by spiced pear ice cream might feature at dessert.

Chef: Andrew McGeorge **Owners:** Mr & Mrs T Gibb **Times:** 12-1.15/7-8.30, Closed 5 Jan-9 Feb, L booking only **Prices:** Fixed L £28, Fixed D £39.50-£45, Coffee £2.50, Min/Water £3.50, Service optional **Wine:** 34 bottles over £20, 60 bottles under £20, 6 by the glass (£2.50)
Notes: Coffee incl, Dress Restrictions, Smart casual, no jeans or shorts, Civ Wed 45 **Seats:** 40, Pr/dining room 15 **Smoking:** N/Sm in restaurant
Children: Min 7 yrs, Portions **Rooms:** 19 (19 en suite) ★★★ HL
Directions: M6 junct 40, A592 to Ullswater, T-junct turn right at lake's edge. Hotel 1.25m **Parking:** 30

WINDERMERE *continued* MAP 18 SD49

Chef: Jane Kimani **Owners:** Michael Robinson **Times:** 6.30-8.30, Closed Xmas, Closed L all week **Prices:** Food prices not confirmed for 2007. Please telephone for details **Wine:** 25 bottles over £20, 35 bottles under £20, 6 by the glass (£3.50-£5.50) **Notes:** Vegetarian menu **Seats:** 40 **Smoking:** N/Sm in restaurant **Children:** Min 5 yrs, Menu, Portions **Rooms:** 28 (28 en suite) ★★★ HL **Directions:** 7m from M6. Follow A590 to A591 (Windermere to Bowness) **Parking:** 28

Fayrer Garden Hotel

Modern British

Country-house dining overlooking Lake Windermere

☎ 015394 88195 Lyth Valley Rd, Bowness on Windermere LA23 3JP
e-mail: lakescene@fayrergarden.com
web: www.fayrergarden.com

This former Edwardian gentleman's residence is set in five acres of beautiful gardens and has spectacular views of the Lake. The interior is decorated in the country-house style, and the Terrace restaurant has crisp linen on the tables and formal settings. Generously priced, five-course, daily-changing menus use local, seasonal ingredients that keep locals and visitors returning. Try the Lakeland venison terrine with date and pear chutney and brioche, or a tart of red onion and Thornby Moor stumpy goat's cheese to start. The rack of Kentmere lamb is accompanied by a tian of shepherd's pie, while the supreme of local chicken with wild mushrooms and butter bean cassoulet is full of flavour. Finish with a classic chocolate tart perhaps.

Chef: Edward Wilkinson **Owners:** Mr & Mrs Wildsmith **Times:** 7-8.30, Closed 1st 2wks Jan, Closed L all week **Prices:** Fixed D £25-£35, Min/Water £1.50, Service optional **Wine:** 51 bottles over £20, 52 bottles under £20, 8 by the glass (£3-£4) **Notes:** Fixed D 4 courses, coffee incl, Dress Restrictions, Smart casual, no jeans or T-shirts, Civ Wed 60 **Seats:** 60, Pr/dining room 20 **Smoking:** N/Sm in restaurant, Air con **Children:** Min 5 yrs, Portions **Rooms:** 29 (29 en suite) ★★★ HL **Directions:** M6 junct 36, onto A591. Past Kendal, at rdbt turn left onto B5284 (signposted Crook Bowness & Ferry) and continue for 8m, then turn left onto A5074 for 400yds **Parking:** 40

Gilpin Lodge Country House Hotel & Restaurant

see page 97

Holbeck Ghyll Country House Hotel

see page 98

Jambo

Modern British

Welcoming restaurant serving quality food at reasonable prices

☎ 015394 43429 7 Victoria St LA23 1AE
e-mail: kevatjambo@aol.com
web: www.jamborestaurant.co.uk

Small, cosy restaurant in Windermere, renowned for its friendly atmosphere and attentive service. Free-range meat and organic produce are used where possible, and vegetarian, vegan and food-intolerant customers are willingly catered for with notice. The menu changes monthly taking account of the seasons, with spring flavours coming through in Cumbrian lamb (roasted and carved onto parmesan mash with slow roasted bell peppers and caramelised shallots) and a trio of rhubarb desserts. There's a daily fresh fish option and a selection of British cheeses served with home-made bread.

Chef: Kevin & Andrea Wyper **Owners:** Kevin & Andrea Wyper **Times:** 6.30-10.30, Closed 1st 2 wks in Jan, Thurs, Closed L all week **Prices:** Starter £5-£6.95, Main £14.50-£17.50, Dessert £4.50-£5.95, Coffee £3.25, Min/Water £3, Service optional **Wine:** 9 bottles over £20, 35 bottles under £20, 8 by the glass (£2.95-£3.75) **Seats:** 28 **Smoking:** N/Sm in restaurant **Children:** Min 12 yrs **Directions:** M6 junct 36, towards Windermere A591, turn left into village. Restaurant 100yds on left, past the tourist info **Parking:** On Victoria Street

Jerichos

Modern British

Warm and intimate restaurant serving creative food

☎ 015394 42522 Birch Street LA23 1EG
e-mail: enquiries@jerichos.co.uk
web: www.jerichos.co.uk

Friendly and unpretentious with a great atmosphere, Jerichos is a modern restaurant off the main street in the centre of town. There are two dining areas, one available for private parties. Modern British cooking, with an emphasis on simplicity and flavour, includes some Mediterranean influences: roast provençale vegetables with Parma ham, macerated olives, red pepper vinaigrette and home-made walnut bread, followed by pan-seared strip loin of local venison with creamed celeriac and potato, juniper and orange glazed cabbage and red wine sauce. An effort is made to marry wine with food.

Chef: Chris Blaydes, Tim Dalzell **Owners:** Mr & Mrs C Blaydes **Times:** 6.45-10, Closed 2 wk end Nov-1st wk Dec, Xmas, 1 Jan, Mon, Sun (Jan-Mar), Closed L Tue-Sun **Prices:** Starter £3.95-£8.50, Main £14.50-£19.50, Dessert £5.95-£7.50, Coffee £2.50, Min/Water £2.50, Service optional **Wine:** 28 bottles over £20, 37 bottles under £20, 9 by the glass (£3.35-£8.50) **Seats:** 36, Pr/dining room 24 **Smoking:** N/Sm in restaurant **Children:** Min 12 yrs **Directions:** M6 junct 36, then A591

Langdale Chase Hotel

European

Dining with a view in stunning lakeside setting

☎ 015394 32201 Langdale Chase LA23 1LW
e-mail: sales@langdalechase.co.uk
web: www.langdalechase.co.uk

A fine late-Victorian mansion with plenty to please the discerning guest in the heart of the Lake District - a lakeside setting, splendid

continued on page 99

England

🏵🏵🏵 Gilpin Lodge Country House Hotel & Restaurant

WINDERMERE MAP 18 SD49

International V

A culinary paradise in the Lakes

☎ 015394 88818 Crook Rd LA23 3NE
e-mail: hotel@gilpinlodge.co.uk
web: www.gilpinlodge.co.uk

An oasis of luxury in the Lake District, this family-run hotel has won accolades from all quarters for its attentive hospitality and vibrant food. Surrounded by acres of woodland, moor and award-winning garden, it sits in leafy tranquillity just a short drive from Windermere. Each of the 14 bedrooms is immaculately decorated in chic contemporary style, while dinner - the highlight of any stay - is served in four intimate dining rooms, at tables elegantly dressed with fresh flowers, gleaming silver and crisp white linen.
And the food? Bold, imaginative, and technically daring, yet firmly rooted in classical cuisine. Gilpin Lodge consistently impresses, handling the best and freshest of local ingredients with deft simplicity to ensure intense flavours on the plate. Expect an imaginative selection of dishes; pan-fried foie gras with Umbrian lentils, wild mushrooms and smoked bacon to start perhaps, followed by breast of Barbary duck with fig purée, and a creamed épice sauce.

Chef: Chris Meredith
Owners: John & Christine Cunliffe
Times: 12-2/6.45-9
Prices: Fixed L £20, Fixed D £45, Starter £4-£7, Main £8-£13, Dessert £5, Coffee £2, Min/Water £3, Service optional
Wine: 151 bottles over £20, 22 bottles under £20, 9 by the glass (£4.50-£5.25)
Notes: ALC L only, Fixed D 4 courses, Vegetarian menu, Dress Restrictions, Smart casual
Seats: 60, Pr/dining room 20
Smoking: N/Sm in restaurant
Children: Min 7 yrs
Rooms: 20 (20 en suite) ★★★★
Directions: M6 junct 36 & A590, then B5284 for 5m
Parking: 40

Holbeck Ghyll Country House Hotel

WINDERMERE MAP 18 SD49

Modern British

Classical cuisine in former hunting lodge

☎ 015394 32375 Holbeck Ln LA23 1LU
e-mail: stay@holbeckghyll.com
web: www.holbeckghyll.com

Breathtaking views over Lake Windermere and the Langdale Fells are among the much-prized assets at this sumptuous hotel, set in pretty gardens on a hillside above the Lake. It comes appropriately decorated in luxurious country-house style with deep sofas and antiques, while a brace of elegant, classical-style dining rooms (one oak-panelled, the other with French doors leading on to the terrace) take full advantage of the scenery. The professionalism and attentiveness of the staff are exemplary, though aptly unstuffy, while the terrace provides opportunities for alfresco drinks, lunches or early evening meals on warm summer days.

The kitchen's modern approach is underpinned by a classical theme and rides in harmony with the surroundings, delivering a repertoire of fixed-price, compact menus (bolstered by a weekend gourmet option) that aren't short on appeal or imagination. An intelligent simplicity allows the high-quality produce to shine in well-presented, clear-flavoured dishes; think roasted brill served with potato, apple, braised gem lettuce and cider foam, while elaborate desserts might be headed-up by an assiette of strawberry and vanilla. An extensive wine list, with a good range of half bottles, and a fine selection of cheeses complete a class act.

Chef: David McLaughlin
Owners: David & Patricia Nicholson
Times: 12.30-2/7-9.30
Prices: Fixed L £22.50-£30, Fixed D £47.50-£57.50, Coffee £3.75, Min/Water £4.75, Service optional
Wine: 250 bottles over £20, 2 bottles under £20, 8 by the glass (£4.75-£6)
Notes: Fixed D 4 courses, Tasting menu £75, Vegetarian available, Dress Restrictions, Smart casual, no jeans or T-shirts, Civ Wed 65
Seats: 50, Pr/dining room 20
Smoking: N/Sm in restaurant
Children: Min 8 yrs, Portions
Rooms: 20 (20 en suite) ★★★★ CHH
Directions: 3m N of Windermere on A591. Past Brockhole Visitor Centre. Turn right into Holbeck Lane. Hotel is 0.5m on left
Parking: 25

WINDERMERE *continued* MAP 18 SD49

gardens and grounds, stunning mountain views and oak-panelled public areas with carved fireplaces. Picture windows in the pillared dining room take full advantage of the panorama, and terraced gardens lead down to the shores of Lake Windermere. An interesting, daily fixed-price menu is offered at lunch and dinner and may include vegetable and pearl barley broth and roast saddle of venison with port and chocolate sauce. Good-value wines by the glass.

Times: 12-2/7-9 **Rooms:** 27 (27 en suite) ★★★ HL **Directions:** 2m S of Ambleside & 3m N of Windermere

֍ Lindeth Fell Country House Hotel

Modern British

A tranquil haven in the Lakes

☎ 015394 43286 & 44287 Lyth Valley Rd, Bowness-on-Windermere LA23 3JP
e-mail: kennedy@lindethfell.co.uk
web: www.lindethfell.co.uk

This Lakeland hideaway perches on the wooded slopes above Windermere and boasts stunning views from two well-placed dining rooms. A former gentleman's residence, it's done out in sedate style and sits in pretty gardens full of rhododendrons and azaleas. A concise menu offers three or four choices for each course and changes daily. Modern British fare predominates, with mains along the lines of pan-fried guinea fowl with a damson and gin sauce, fillet of red bream with lemon and dill butter or pear and stilton flan with a tomato coulis.

Chef: Philip Taylor **Owners:** Pat & Diana Kennedy **Times:** 12.30-1.45/7.30-9.00, Closed 3 wks in Jan **Prices:** Food prices not confirmed for 2007. Please telephone for details **Wine:** 41 bottles over £20, 47 bottles under £20, 4 by the glass (£3.25-£3.50) **Notes:** Vegetarian available, Dress Restrictions, Smart casual preferred **Seats:** 50, Pr/dining room 30 **Smoking:** N/Sm in restaurant **Children:** Min 7 yrs D, Menu, Portions **Rooms:** 14 (14 en suite) ★★ **Directions:** 1m S of Bowness-on-Windermere on A5074 **Parking:** 20

֍ Lindeth Howe Country House Hotel

Modern British

Hearty fare in the former home of a famous author

☎ 015394 45759 Lindeth Dr, Longtail Hill LA23 3JF
e-mail: hotel@lindeth-howe.co.uk
web: www.lindeth-howe.co.uk

continued

Lindeth Howe Country House Hotel

The former family home of Beatrix Potter is now a charming country-house hotel set on a hill overlooking the valley, Lake Windermere and distant fells. The bright, conservatory-style restaurant overlooks the secluded gardens and provides an elegant setting in which to enjoy some unpretentious British cooking. Work up an appetite with a walk across the fells to do justice to the daily-changing four-course dinner menu. Dishes are generously served and typified by halibut and salmon terrine, roast lamb with redcurrant and red wine jus, and then an assiette of strawberry and vanilla for dessert.

Chef: Graham Gelder **Owners:** Lakeinvest Ltd **Times:** 12-2.30/7-9 **Prices:** Fixed D £35-£42, Coffee £2.50, Min/Water £2.75, Service optional **Wine:** 35 bottles over £20, 35 bottles under £20, 8 by the glass (£3.75-£4.95) **Notes:** Fixed D 4 courses, Vegetarian available, Dress Restrictions, Smart casual, no jeans or T-shirts **Seats:** 70, Pr/dining room 20 **Smoking:** N/Sm in restaurant **Children:** Min 7 yrs, Menu, Portions **Rooms:** 36 (36 en suite) ★★★ **Directions:** 1m S of Bowness onto B5284, signed Kendal and Lancaster. Hotel 2nd driveway on right **Parking:** 50

֍֍ Linthwaite House Hotel

Modern British

Accomplished cooking and stunning views

☎ 015394 88600 Crook Rd LA23 3JA
e-mail: stay@linthwaite.com
web: www.linthwaite.com

Built in 1901, this elegant Edwardian country house sits in 14 acres of gardens and woods in the heart of the Lake District and has enviable views looking over Lake Windermere to the fells beyond, with a new conservatory ensuring that guests can enjoy the scenery whatever the weather. The décor is a refined combination of period chic with a clean, modern colour scheme and plenty of natural light. Using the best of local produce, the chef clearly has high aspirations for the food with a menu full of ambitious dishes that hit their target with clean flavours and technical precision very much in evidence. Start with a

continued

England

England

WINDERMERE *continued* MAP 18 SD49

near perfect Flookburgh shrimp and tomato risotto with nutmeg, and continue with line-caught sea bass and scallop with basil foam.

Chef: Simon Bolsover **Owners:** Mike Bevans **Times:** 12.30-2/7-9.30 **Prices:** Fixed L £10-£13.95, Fixed D £46, Coffee £3.50, Min/Water £3.50, Service optional **Wine:** 114 bottles over £20, 6 bottles under £20, 13 by the glass (£3.40-£9.40) **Notes:** Fixed D 4 courses, Vegetarian available, Dress Restrictions, Smart casual, Civ Wed 52 **Seats:** 60, Pr/dining room 16 **Smoking:** N/Sm in restaurant **Children:** Min 7yrs D, Menu, Portions **Rooms:** 27 (27 en suite) ★★★ CHH **Directions:** Take 1st left off A591 at rdbt NW of Kendal (B5284). Follow for 6m, hotel is 1m after Windermere Golf Club on left **Parking:** 30

Miller Howe Hotel

Rosettes not confirmed at time of going to press

Modern British NOTABLE WINE LIST

Fantastic location with a well-earned reputation for fine dining

☎ 015394 42536 Rayrigg Rd LA23 1EY
e-mail: lakeview@millerhowe.com
web: www.millerhowe.com

This magnificent Edwardian country-house hotel has outstanding views over Lake Windermere and Langdale Pikes. The interiors have a traditional feel with many period features, although the dining room itself with its honey colours, gilded ceilings, tiled floors and wrought ironwork manages to evoke a sense of the Mediterranean. The food is described as modern English with a twist, but there are influences from all over Europe incorporated in sophisticated and accomplished

continued

dishes. The menu gourmand is an enjoyable way of sampling all the delights on offer and might include roasted Périgord quail to start, with an intermediate course of spiced mussel, saffron and anise soup and a main of roasted loin of Roughfell lamb.

Notable Wine List: Extensive and eclectic wine list with informative tasting notes throughout.

There was a change of chef as we went to press.

Miller Howe Hotel

Owners: Charles Garside **Times:** 12.30-1.45/6.45-8.45 **Prices:** Fixed L £19, Fixed D £35, Starter £9.50, Main fr £18.50, Dessert fr £7, Coffee £3, Min/Water £4, Service added but optional 10% **Wine:** 200 bottles over £20, 6 bottles under £20, 8 by the glass (£4-£8) **Notes:** Gourmet D 6 courses £42.50, Sun L 3 courses £25, Vegetarian available, Dress Restrictions, Smart casual, Civ Wed 64 **Seats:** 64, Pr/dining room 30 **Smoking:** N/Sm in restaurant, Air con **Children:** Portions **Rooms:** 15 (15 en suite) ★★★ **Directions:** M6 junct 36. Follow the A591 bypass for Kendal. Enter Windermere, continue to mini rdbt, take left onto A592. Miller Howe is 1/4m on right **Parking:** 40

❀❀❀

The Samling

WINDERMERE MAP 18 SD49

Modern British V

Impressive dining in Lakeland hillside retreat

☎ 015394 31922 Ambleside Rd LA23 1LR
e-mail: info@thesamling.com
web: www.thesamling.com

This 18th-century house with its lovely grounds sits high above Lake Windermere. The bedrooms and two small dining areas make it ideal for crowd-haters who like being spoilt by unstuffy, helpful staff. Despite its Wordsworth connections - the poet used to pay his rent here - nostalgia is eschewed in favour of a more fashionable emphasis on comfort and relaxation. This unashamedly modern approach extends to food as well. Local seasonal ingredients provide the basis for simply presented, creative cooking in modern British style. There are technical skills aplenty in this kitchen. Good clear flavours characterise appetisers and starters such as the moist slow-cooked Old Spot pork belly with crackling accompanied by plump langoustines and celeriac purée. Main courses might include a carefully cooked brill fillet served with creamed potatoes - woodland mushrooms and chicken jus reinforced with onions and lardons delivering depth of flavour. Finish with the refreshing grapefruit terrine with zingy passionfruit sorbet.

Chef: Nigel Mendham **Owners:** Tom Maxfield **Times:** 12.30-2/7-10, Closed L Mon-Sun (ex bookings) **Prices:** Fixed L £48, Fixed D £48, Coffee £3.50, Min/Water £3.50, Service included **Wine:** 80 bottles over £20, 12 by the glass **Notes:** Fixed L 3 courses, Vegetarian menu, Civ Wed 20 **Seats:** 22 **Smoking:** N/Sm in restaurant **Children:** Min 12 yrs, Menu, Portions **Rooms:** 11 (11 en suite) ★★★ HL **Directions:** On A591 towards Ambleside. 1st on right after Low Wood Hotel. 2m from Windermere **Parking:** 15

The Samling

see page 100

Storrs Hall Hotel

Modern British

Accomplished, imaginative cuisine in luxurious country surroundings

☎ 015394 47111 Storrs Park LA23 3LG
e-mail: storrshall@elhmail.co.uk
web: www.elh.co.uk/hotels/storrshall

This imposing Georgian mansion is set in 17 acres of landscaped grounds on the shores of Lake Windermere. There are numerous comfortable lounges and a smart bar in which to enjoy pre-dinner drinks and canapés, all furnished with fine art and antiques of the period. Ask for a window table as the spacious dining room affords wonderful views over the lake. The food is bold and imaginative, using quality seasonal ingredients throughout with dishes like salt cod and split pea tortellini with white onion and garlic espuma, or rack of Cumbrian lamb with tarragon and trompette noir combining flavours with real flair. Dishes like Fairground Favourites (a dessert plate of bubblegum jelly, popcorn, lemonade sorbet and strawberry candyfloss) inject a real sense of fun, too.

Chef: Craig Sherrington **Owners:** English Lakes Hotels **Times:** 12/7 **Prices:** Fixed L £19.75, Fixed D £39.50, Min/Water £3.95, Service included **Wine:** 142 bottles over £20, 18 bottles under £20, 6 by the glass (£3.95-£4.50) **Notes:** Fixed L 3 courses, Fixed D 4 courses, Vegetarian available, Dress Restrictions, Smart casual, Civ Wed 64 **Seats:** 64, Pr/dining room 40 **Smoking:** N/Sm in restaurant **Children:** Min 12 yrs, Portions **Rooms:** 29 (29 en suite) ★★★ HL **Directions:** On A592, 2 miles S of Bowness on the Newby Bridge Road **Parking:** 50

WORKINGTON MAP 18 NY02

Washington Central Hotel

Modern European

Relaxing, upmarket dining with renowned hospitality

☎ 01900 65772 Washington St CA14 3AY
e-mail: kawildwchotel@aol.com
web: www.washingtoncentralhotelworkington.com

This modern, town-centre hotel is a popular base for tourists exploring the Lake District. Hospitality is a key factor in both the hotel's and restaurant's enduring appeal - with solid cooking skills making for consistent and enjoyable food. Modern European in style, there's a bias toward classic combinations rather than risky innovation, although there are creative touches throughout. A typical appetiser would be Lakeland game terrine with celeriac remoulade, while mains might include a tian of sea bass filled with prawn mousse, with a chive butter. For special occasions, ask to dine in the clock tower.

Washington Central Hotel

Chef: Michael Buckley, Lee Poland **Owners:** William Dobie **Times:** 12-2/7-9.30, Closed 25 Dec, Closed L BHs **Prices:** Fixed L £20, Fixed D £25, Starter £4.50-£6.95, Main £17.50, Dessert £4.95, Coffee £2, Min/Water £3.95, Service optional **Wine:** 10 bottles over £20, 40 bottles under £20, 10 by the glass (£2.75-£3.95) **Notes:** Fixed L 4 courses, Vegetarian available, Dress Restrictions, No jeans or trainers, Civ Wed 350 **Seats:** 45, Pr/dining room 40 **Smoking:** N/Sm in restaurant **Children:** Menu, Portions **Rooms:** 46 (46 en suite) ★★★ HL **Directions:** M6 junct 40, follow A66 to Workington **Parking:** 10

DERBYSHIRE

ASHBOURNE MAP 10 SK14

Bramhall's

Modern British

Imaginative cooking in a relaxed bistro setting

☎ 01335 346158 6 Buxton Rd DE6 1EX
e-mail: info@bramhalls.co.uk
web: www.bramhalls.co.uk

An authentic bistro with bags of charm, this establishment occupies two converted cottages in the heart of historic Ashbourne. It's a hub of local gastronomy with a sound reputation for imaginative cooking at pocket-friendly prices, and offers an eclectic menu with its roots in old-fashioned country cuisine. The cooking is bright and simple - the ingredients are market-fresh, and brought together in simple combinations that wow, such as salmon with lemon thyme risotto, asparagus, and black bean and corn salsa. If you like ice cream ask what home-made flavours are on offer.

continued

England

ASHBOURNE *continued* MAP 10 SK14

Chef: Timothy Bramhall **Owners:** Timothy Bramhall, Tracey Bramhall **Times:** 12-2.30/6.30-9.30, Closed 25-26 Dec, 1 Jan, Closed D Sun (Dec-Apr) **Prices:** Fixed L £10.95, Starter £3.75-£6.95, Main £10.95-£15.95, Dessert £3.95-£5.25, Coffee £1.95, Min/Water £2.75, Service included **Wine:** 15 bottles over £20, 20 bottles under £20, 7 by the glass (£3-£4.25) **Seats:** 60 **Smoking:** N/Sm area, No pipes **Children:** Menu, Portions **Rooms:** 10 (8 en suite) ◆◆◆◆ **Directions:** From Ashbourne Market Square take Buxton road N. Restaurant 30yds on left **Parking:** 5

Callow Hall

British, European

Dining in country-house luxury

☎ 01335 300900 Mappleton Rd DE6 2AA
e-mail: reservations@callowhall.co.uk
web: www.callowhall.co.uk

Callow Hall stands at the end of a tree-lined drive in 44 acres of woods and garden overlooking the Bentley Brook and the Dove Valley. Period features abound throughout the creeper-clad early Victorian mansion, most notably in the 'William Morris' dining room with its warm red décor. The kitchen relies heavily on local produce and fresh fish when preparing the traditional British menus. The result is honest, full-flavoured dishes such as smoked haddock fishcake with home-smoked organic salmon, tender beef fillet with tomato fondue, olive purée, mozzarella glaze and a lovely basil-scented red wine sauce, and a light vanilla soufflé served with rhubarb to finish. Excellent traditional Sunday lunches.

Chef: David & Anthony Spencer **Owners:** David, Dorothy, Anthony & Emma Spencer **Times:** 12.30-1.30/7.30-9, Closed 25-26 Dec, Closed L Mon-Sat, D Sun (ex residents) **Prices:** Fixed L £25, Fixed D £42, Starter £7-£10.25, Main £17.25-£20.75, Dessert £7.50, Coffee £3.50, Min/Water £3.25, Service optional **Wine:** 113 bottles over £20, 46 bottles under £20, 7 by the glass (£5-£7) **Notes:** Fixed L 3 courses, Fixed D 4 courses, incl coffee, Vegetarian available, Dress Restrictions, Smart casual **Seats:** 70, Pr/dining room 40 **Smoking:** N/Sm in restaurant **Children:** Portions **Rooms:** 16 (16 en suite) ★★★ CHH **Directions:** A515 through Ashbourne in Buxton direction, left at Bowling Green Pub, 1st right Mappleton Rd **Parking:** 30

Dining Room

Modern British

Imaginative modern cuisine in intimate surroundings

☎ 01335 300666 33 St John St DE6 1GP
web: www.thediningroomashbourne.co.uk

This 16th-century building is full of character, with the original cast-iron range still in place and low-beamed ceilings. The restaurant is chic with neutral tones serving up modern British cuisine using locally-sourced, organic seasonal produce. The carte starts with a choice of appetisers like a mini burger, followed by a starter like Pete's smoked organic salmon with Thornham oyster. A refreshing sorbet makes way for a main course like blackened fish of the day, served with new farm asparagus spears, roasted sweet potato and sweetcorn pancake. Desserts need to be ordered with the other courses, and might include chocolate brownie with white chocolate ice cream. There is also an impressive tasting menu and an award-winning cheese board.

Chef: Peter Dale **Owners:** Peter & Laura Dale **Times:** 12-1.30/7-8.30, Closed 2 wks 26 Dec, 1 wk Sep, 1 wk Mar, BH Mon, Sun-Mon **Prices:** Fixed L fr £22, Starter fr £10, Main fr £20, Dessert fr £6, Coffee £2.20, Min/Water £3.50, Service optional **Wine:** 34 bottles over £20, 10 bottles under £20, 2 by the glass (£4.25) **Notes:** Fixed L 3 courses, Tasting menu £40 pre-booked only **Seats:** 16 **Smoking:** N/Sm in restaurant **Children:** Min 12 yrs, Portions **Directions:** On A52 Derby to Leek road **Parking:** Opposite restaurant (evening)

ASHFORD-IN-THE-WATER MAP 16 SK16

Riverside House Hotel

British, French

Fine dining in opulent surroundings on the Wye

☎ 01629 814275 Fennel St DE45 1QF
e-mail: riversidehouse@enta.net
web: www.riversidehousehotel.co.uk

Gracious Georgian country house set in its own grounds on the banks of the River Wye in the lovely Peak District village of Ashford-in-the-Water. The property is full of character and guests can dine in luxurious comfort surrounded by beautiful artwork and rich furnishings. An imaginative choice of dishes includes a starter of spiced Scottish salmon served with watercress salad and a sesame biscuit. A main course of pan-roasted fillet of Derbyshire beef comes with Macaire potatoes, creamed leeks and shallots. For dessert, a house speciality is

continued

Valhrona chocolate and raspberry tian accompanied by a raspberry sorbet. Lighter food is also served in the Conservatory restaurant.

Times: 12-2.30/7-9.30 **Rooms:** 15 (15 en suite) ★★★ **Directions:** M1 junct 29 take A619 and continue to Bakewell. 2m from the centre of Bakewell on A6 towards Buxton. In Ashford village located on Fennel St

---

BAKEWELL MAP 16 SK26

The Prospect

Modern British

Comfortable, town-centre restaurant with good atmosphere

☎ 01629 810077 Unit 6, Theme Court, Bridge St DE45 1DS
e-mail: thepropect@btinternet.com

Once a furniture shop, The Prospect is now a buzzing town-centre restaurant with nearby parking. Old polished oak panelling mixes well with polished tabletops and modern settings. There are plans to double this space and add a wine bar. Modern British dishes make good use of local produce, especially vegetables. Starters include a memorable salmon and crab fishcake with zingy avocado salsa and basil crème fraîche. Try the slow-roasted pork belly with local black pudding mash and red onion marmalade for mains, and finish with the crème brûlée.

Times: 12-2.30/6.30-12, Closed 25-26 Dec, 1 Jan, Easter Sun & Mon, Mon, Closed D Sun, Tue **Directions:** From A6 (Matlock to Buxton road), follow signs for Baslow. Theme Court is opposite Castle Pub

Renaissance Restaurant

French, European

Beautifully appointed French restaurant in the town centre

☎ 01629 812687 Bath St DE45 1BX
web: www.renaissance-restaurant.com

Stone-built townhouse in the centre of Bakewell offering three eating styles: the full menu, priced for three courses with some supplements; a good-value set menu from Tuesday to Thursday evening; and a lunchtime Bistro serving traditional French dishes with a European twist. Classics from the main menu include double-baked frogs' legs soufflé with watercress sauce, and fisherman's casserole with Chablis sauce under home-made puff pastry. The speciality dessert is Eric's Renaissance chocolate and caramel gâteau on white chocolate sauce. A private dining room is provided and outside catering is available.

Chef: E Piedaniel, J Gibbard **Owners:** E Piedaniel **Times:** 12-2/7-10, Closed Xmas & New Year, 2wks Jan, 2wks Aug, Mon, Closed D Sun **Prices:** Fixed L £28.95, Fixed D £28.95, Coffee £2.10, Min/Water £2.90, Service included **Wine:** 29 bottles over £20, 19 bottles under £20, 3 by the glass (£2.50-£3.95) **Notes:** Sun L £18.95 **Seats:** 50, Pr/dining room 25 **Smoking:** N/Sm in restaurant **Children:** Portions **Directions:** From Bakewell rdbt in town centre take A6 Buxton exit. 1st right into Bath St (one-way) **Parking:** Town centre

Rutland Arms Hotel

International

Enjoyable dining in welcoming, traditional hotel

☎ 01629 812812 The Square DE45 1BT
e-mail: rutland@bakewell.demon.co.uk
web: www.bakewell.demon.co.uk

This imposing 19th-century stone-built hotel - in whose kitchens the Bakewell pudding was invented - is a local landmark at the heart of

continued

town. Its Four Seasons restaurant is classically traditional in style, with polished granite fireplace, lofty ceilings, chandeliers and several clocks that never seem to chime at the same time, evoking an endearing air of a bygone era. By contrast, the accomplished cooking is up-to-date, showcasing local Peak District fare - pan-fried breast of duck with Savoy cabbage and orange and cranberry jus, and, of course, there's that traditional Bakewell pudding to follow.

Rutland Arms Hotel

Chef: Brian Lee **Owners:** David Donegan **Times:** 12-2/7-9 **Prices:** Fixed L £13.95, Fixed D £28.50, Coffee £1.80, Min/Water £3, Service optional **Wine:** 7 bottles over £20, 29 bottles under £20, 6 by the glass (£3.25-£4.25) **Notes:** Sun L 2 courses £10.95, 3 courses £14.50, Vegetarian available, Dress Restrictions, Smart casual **Seats:** 80, Pr/dining room 32 **Smoking:** N/Sm in restaurant **Children:** Menu, Portions **Rooms:** 35 (35 en suite) ★★★ HL **Directions:** On A6 in Bakewell centre opposite war memorial. Parking opposite side entrance **Parking:** 30

BASLOW MAP 16 SK27

Cavendish Hotel

Modern International

Luxurious surroundings for sumptuous cooking

☎ 01246 582311 Church Ln DE45 1SP
e-mail: info@cavendish-hotel.net
web: www.cavendish-hotel.net

On the site of a hostelry dating back countless years, this hotel on the edge of the Chatsworth Estate has a smart, contemporary-style restaurant with classical influences. The bright walls and seating are complemented by original artwork and rich table settings with candles. There is a real sense of luxury here and service is excellent, combining friendliness and helpful advice. The cooking style balances technique and flavour well and presentation is minimalist with some precise garnishing and restrained artistry. Take your time and enjoy dishes such as sautéed pigeon breast with Derbyshire black pudding, and fillet steak lasagne, buttered spinach and tomato confit, rounded off by a hot steamed praline pudding. The wine list offers a good choice, clearly listed by drinking style.

Chef: Chris Allison, Ben Handley **Owners:** Eric Marsh **Times:** 12.30-2.30/6.30-10 **Prices:** Fixed L £29.50, Fixed D fr £36, Coffee £2.50, Min/Water £2.75, Service added 5% **Wine:** 34 bottles over £20, 16 bottles under £20, 4 by the glass (£3.95) **Notes:** Traditional Sun menu, Vegetarian available, Dress Restrictions, No trainers, T-shirts, Civ Wed 50 **Seats:** 50, Pr/dining room 16 **Smoking:** N/Sm in restaurant **Children:** Portions **Rooms:** 24 (24 en suite) ★★★ HL **Directions:** M1 junct 29 follow signs for Chesterfield. From Chesterfield take A619 to Bakewell, Chatsworth & Baslow **Parking:** 40

Fischer's Baslow Hall

see page 104

Fischer's Baslow Hall

BASLOW MAP 16 SK27

Modern European

Sophisticated cuisine in memorable setting

☎ 01246 583259 Calver Rd DE45 1RR
e-mail: m.s@fischers-baslowhall.co.uk
web: www.fischers-baslowhall.co.uk

A chestnut tree-lined drive leading up to this fine Grade II listed manor house - built at the turn of the 20th century and set in five acres of marvellous gardens bordering the Chatsworth Estate - seems an appropriately fitting curtain-raiser to some outstanding cooking. Baslow is full of charm at every turn, an intimate hotel personally run by its dedicated owners Max and Susan Fischer, and there's plenty of cosseting at hand, with the likes of log fires and comfortable sofas adding to the welcoming approach. A lavish use of fabrics, antiques and pictures all add to the appeal, and, while service is polished and formal, it's suitably friendly, too. The dining room has an elegant classical edge, complemented by fine china, cutlery and glassware, and proves the real focus of the house. Max Fischer is a dedicated chef-patron and has developed a strong brigade of disciplined chefs led by head chef Rupert Rowley. Their approach - via a fixed-price medley of carte, jour and tasting menu - is modern European, but underpinned by classical French technique.

This is serious cooking; precision, high skill, accuracy, clear flavours and the very best of local produce (aided by the Hall's own kitchen garden) deliver in consistent style on the plate. Think roast Scottish langoustine tails, caramelised salsify and Jerusalem artichoke purée, followed by oxtail braised in red wine, salt cod brandade ravioli and winter vegetables, with perhaps rhubarb and champagne jelly with rhubarb Madeleine to finish. Peripherals like breads, canapés, amuse bouche, pre-desserts and petits fours are a delight, too, while the superbly maintained gardens - Max's other love - with their hidden corners and potager, offer the perfect pre- or post-meal stroll to complete the Baslow Hall experience.

Chef: Max Fischer/Rupert Rowley
Owners: Mr & Mrs M Fischer
Times: 12-2/7-10, Closed 25 -26 Dec, Closed L Mon, D Sun (ex residents)
Prices: Fixed L £20-£25, Fixed D £35, Min/Water £3.75, Service optional
Wine: 125 bottles over £20, 4 bottles under £20, 5 by the glass (£4.25-£5.50)
Notes: Tasting menu £60, Dress Restrictions, No jeans, sweatshirts or trainers, Civ Wed 40
Seats: 40, Pr/dining room 20
Smoking: N/Sm in restaurant
Children: Min 12 yrs, Portions
Rooms: 11 (11 en suite) ★★★
Directions: From Baslow on A623 towards Calver. Hotel on right
Parking: 40

BREADSALL MAP 11 SK33

Marriott Breadsall Priory

European

Historic property with popular fine dining

☎ 01332 832235 Moor Rd DE7 6DL
web: www.marriott.co.uk

Just a few miles from the Peak District, this Grade II listed building was originally founded in 1260 and is surrounded by beautifully landscaped grounds with huge mature trees and a charming ornamental lake. It's the oldest property in the Marriott group and offers modern health and spa facilities, which sit comfortably alongside the historic features of the property. The restaurant itself is set amid the exposed beams and archways of the old wine cellar and oozes character. It's a popular venue with a crowd-pleasing menu that delivers classically-based cooking with dashes of innovation, using the best local, seasonal produce to hand. Try a lobster bisque laced with Cognac crème fraîche to start and then continue with Chatsworth Farm herb-crusted rack of lamb with sweet potato.

Times: 1-3/7-10.15, Closed L Mon-Sat (conference only) **Rooms:** 112 (112 en suite) ★★★★ HL **Directions:** M1 junct 28 take A38 towards Derby. Signposted from rdbt. Approx 4m from Derby city centre

---

BUXTON MAP 16 SK07

Best Western Lee Wood Hotel

Modern International

Family-run hotel with elegant conservatory dining

☎ 01298 23002 The Park SK17 6TQ
e-mail: leewoodhotel@btinternet.com
web: www.leewoodhotel.co.uk

This fine hotel was created in 1860 from three separate houses built in 1832. It is the oldest established hotel in Buxton and has been owned by two generations of the Millican family since 1958. Lunch and dinner are served in the conservatory-style Garden Restaurant overlooking a mature shrubbery. A wide choice of dishes from around the globe is prepared from fresh, often local produce, cooked with imagination and style. Typical dishes include roast monkfish tail wrapped in pak choi and pancetta with pear and apple risotto and cinnamon jus, and herb-crusted loin of lamb with roasted Mediterranean vegetables, stir-fried duck liver and rosemary and tapenade jus. Private dining and theatre suppers by arrangement.

Chef: Darren Clarke **Owners:** Mr J C Millican **Times:** 12-2.15/7.15-9.30 **Prices:** Fixed L £12.50-£17.50, Fixed D £22-£27.50, Starter £4.75-£8.25, Main £10.95-£19.95, Dessert £4.50-£7.25, Coffee £2.40, Min/Water £2.25, Service added but optional 10% **Wine:** 15 bottles over £20, 20 bottles under £20, 8 by the glass (£3.75-£5.25) **Notes:** Vegetarian available, Dress Restrictions, Smart casual preferred, Civ Wed 120 **Seats:** 80, Pr/dining room 120 **Smoking:** N/Sm in restaurant **Children:** Portions **Rooms:** 40 (40 en suite) ★★★ **Directions:** M1 junct 24, A50 towards Ashbourne, A515 to Buxton. From Buxton town centre follow A5004 Long Hill to Whaley Bridge. Hotel approx 200mtrs beyond University of Derby Campus **Parking:** 50

CHESTERFIELD MAP 16 SK37

Old Post Restaurant

Modern British, French

Converted shop with bold cuisine

☎ 01246 279479 43 Holywell St S41 7SH
e-mail: theoldpostrestaurant@btopenworld.com

Close to the town's landmark church with its crooked spire, this intimate, split-level restaurant is housed in two character buildings dating from the 15th and 18th centuries. Formerly a butcher's, grocer's, Victorian laundry and later a post office, the new incarnation is proving popular with local diners for ambitious modern European cooking. Everything is made on the premises, with the adventurous kitchen producing dishes with bold flavours and beguiling presentations. Follow asparagus and pea risotto topped with grilled goat's cheese, with fillet of halibut braised in lobster butter and round off with brandy snap basket filled with ginger cheesecake mousse.

Chef: Hugh Cocker **Owners:** Hugh & Mary Cocker **Times:** 12-2/7-9.30, Closed 1 wk Jan, 1wk Apr, Mon, Closed L Sat, D Sun **Prices:** Fixed L £11.25, Fixed D £25.50, Starter £5.50-£7.25, Main £15.95-£21.50, Dessert £5.75-£6.50, Coffee £2.25, Min/Water £3.50, Service optional **Wine:** 5 bottles over £20, 24 bottles under £20, 4 by the glass (£3.50) **Notes:** Fixed D 4 courses, Sun L £17.50-£20.75, Vegetarian available **Seats:** 24 **Smoking:** N/Sm in restaurant **Directions:** M1 junct 29, follow signs for town centre and central parking. Pass Crooked Spire on left and use Holywell Cross Car Park. Restaurant opposite **Parking:** Car park opposite

---

DARLEY ABBEY MAP 11 SK33

Darleys Restaurant

Modern European V

Accomplished cuisine delivered in a former cotton mill

☎ 01332 364987 Darley Abbey Mill DE22 1DZ
e-mail: info@darleys.com
web: www.darleys.com

continued

DARLEY ABBEY *continued* MAP 11 SK33

Sophisticated, contemporary-styled restaurant housed in a former cotton mill right at the River Derwent's edge, with a decked terrace overlooking a weir. Once the canteen for the workers, it now sports a sleek, modern look with neutral tones of leather, suede and silk and, as befits the décor and the relaxed, informal service, the sensibly short menus are modern in style. Slick, well-presented dishes show intelligent handling of tip-top ingredients as seen in a fine starter of brown shrimp risotto with a well-made bouillabaisse sauce, a crispy confit duck leg main course of exceptional flavour, served with a rich Toulouse sausage and bean casserole, and a creamy cinder toffee parfait for dessert.

Chef: Jonathan Hobson **Owners:** Jonathan & Kathryn Hobson **Times:** 12-2/7-10, Closed BHs, Closed D Sun **Prices:** Fixed L fr £13.95, Starter £6.90-£8.50, Main £16.50-£18.90, Dessert fr £5.90, Coffee £2.20, Min/Water £3.50, Service optional **Wine:** 41 bottles over £20, 65 bottles under £20, 16 by the glass (£3.50-£5.50) **Notes:** Sun L £15.95-£17.95, Vegetarian menu **Seats:** 70 **Smoking:** N/Sm in restaurant, Air con **Children:** Portions **Directions:** A6 N from Derby (Duffield Rd). After 1m turn right into Mileash Lane, down to Old Lane, turn right and follow road over bridge. Restaurant on right **Parking:** 12

ETWALL MAP 10 SK23

The Blenheim House

Modern British NEW

Modern cooking in lovely location

☎ 01283 732254 56-58 Main St DE65 6LP
e-mail: info@theblenheimhouse.com
web: www.theblenheimhouse.com

In a lovely village setting, parts of this house date back to the 1700s and feature traditional wooden flooring and beams. There is a large bar area where bar meals are also served. The comfortable restaurant features quality table settings. Modern cooking with classical roots is the basis for a menu featuring good local produce. Try a starter like scallops with crispy belly pork, followed perhaps by beef with wild mushroom and red wine sauce and light fondant potato. Classic desserts include the likes of lemon tart and pecan pie.

Chef: Ian Cooper **Owners:** Peter Simpson **Times:** 12-2.30/6-9.30 **Prices:** Food prices not confirmed for 2007. Please telephone for details **Rooms:** 9 (9 en suite) ★★ HL **Directions:** Telephone for directions

---

FROGGATT MAP 16 SK27

The Chequers Inn

Modern European

A popular inn for those in need of fresh air and gratifying food

☎ 01433 630231 S32 3ZJ
e-mail: info@chequers-froggatt.com
web: www.chequers-froggatt.com

This inn has its origins in the 16th century and, while there are modern touches throughout, the building still retains its historic charm. Near to Chatsworth House, it's a great place to explore the surrounding Peak District. There's a printed menu with regularly changing blackboard specials - food tends toward British favourites done with aplomb and featuring local ingredients heavily: local pork sausage and Scarborough Fair mash, for example, or minted Barnsley chop with roast plums and redcurrant jus. Those interested in food history should try the Bakewell pudding - it was invented nearby and there's usually a great version on the menu here.

Chef: Marcus Jefford **Owners:** Jonathan & Joanne Tindall **Times:** 12-2/6-9.30, Closed 25 Dec **Prices:** Starter £3.95-£6.50, Main £7.75-£15.95, Dessert £4.95, Coffee £1.65, Min/Water £3.50, Service optional **Wine:** 11 bottles over £20, 28 bottles under £20, 10 by the glass (£2.80-£4.60) **Notes:** Vegetarian available **Seats:** 90 **Smoking:** N/Sm in restaurant **Rooms:** 5 (5 en suite) ◆◆◆◆ **Directions:** On the A625 in Froggatt, 0.75m from Calver **Parking:** 50

HATHERSAGE MAP 16 SK28

The George at Hathersage

Modern European V

Modern comforts and sophisticated cooking at historic inn

☎ 01433 650436 Main Rd S32 1BB
e-mail: info@george-hotel.net
web: www.george-hotel.net

This grey-stone former coaching inn has a rich history extending back some 400 years - reputedly frequented by Charlotte Brontë while writing *Jane Eyre* - and is set at the heart of the picturesque small town. Today, it's a relaxing mix of old and new, with a character-packed, beamed bar-lounge, while the restaurant is light and airy in modern minimalist vogue, with cool beige and browns, bold artwork and spacious tables. The cooking follows modern thinking, too, with accomplished, imaginative dishes delivered with consistent accuracy and with emphasis on quality, fresh local produce and flavour. Take roast best end of Castlegate lamb filled with Parma ham and herbs, or plum strudel with cinnamon ice cream.

Chef: Ben Handley **Owners:** Eric Marsh **Times:** 12-2.30/7-10 **Prices:** Fixed L £12.95, Fixed D £15.95, Starter £5.75-£7.50, Main £12-£21.50, Dessert £5.75-£7, Coffee £3.25, Min/Water £2.95, Service included **Wine:** 14 bottles over £20, 15 bottles under £20, 8 by the glass (£3.95-£5.35) **Notes:** Traditional L menu Sun, Vegetarian menu, Civ Wed 45 **Seats:** 45, Pr/dining room 80 **Smoking:** N/Sm in restaurant **Children:** Portions **Rooms:** 21 (21 en suite) ★★★ HL **Directions:** In village centre on junction of A625/B6001 **Parking:** 45

The Plough Inn

Modern

Destination dining in great location

☎ 01433 650319 Leadmill Bridge S32 1BA
e-mail: sales@theploughinn-hathersage.co.uk
web: www.theploughinn-hathersage.co.uk

Built on the site of a former corn mill, lead smelting house and farm, this 17th-century inn is idyllically located and has gone through many changes since it was built. Now a popular and busy pub with the emphasis on gastro, the food is the big draw here, with a European menu that mixes the modern with the traditional, using local produce when possible. Simple combinations can be found in flavoursome dishes like smoked haddock with potato salad, poached egg and sweet mustard dressing, sauté liver and bacon with spring onion mash or chocolate pudding.

Chef: Robert Navarro **Owners:** Robert & Cynthia Emery **Times:** 11.30-2.30/6.30-9.30, Closed 25 Dec **Prices:** Fixed L £12.95-£15.95, Fixed D £18.95-£22.50, Starter £5.95-£7.25, Dessert £4.25-£5.50, Coffee £1.40, Min/Water £3, Service optional **Wine:** 10 bottles over £20, 28 bottles under £20, 16 by the glass (£3.50-£6.75) **Notes:** Set Sun L £18.95-22.50, Vegetarian available, Dress Restrictions, Smart casual **Seats:** 40, Pr/dining

continued

room 24 **Smoking:** N/Sm in restaurant, Air con **Children:** Portions **Rooms:** 5 (5 en suite) ◆◆◆◆ **Directions:** 1m from Hathersage village on B6001, 12m from Sheffield city centre via A625 **Parking:** 40

HIGHAM MAP 16 SK35

Santo's Higham Farm Hotel

International **NEW**

Modern Italian cuisine in romantic setting

☎ 01773 833812 Main Rd DE55 6EH
e-mail: reception@santoshighamfarm.demon.co.uk
web: www.santoshighamfarm.co.uk

Located within a sympathetically renovated 15th-century former farmhouse overlooking the Amber Valley, this Italian-influenced restaurant has quality crockery, polished glassware and crisp linen. A strong emphasis on locally sourced produce permeates the modern menu, with fresh, simple flavours to be found in ravioli of Jerusalem artichoke, lemon sole fillets with asparagus and hollandaise sauce and a dessert of apple and rhubarb pie. A French and Italian-biased wine list boasts some good bargains and impressive champagnes.

Chef: Raymond Moody **Owners:** Santo Cusimano **Times:** 12-2/7-9.30, Closed L Mon-Sat, D Sun **Prices:** Fixed L fr £13, Fixed D £23-£27, Starter £4.50-£9, Main £15-£24, Dessert £4.50-£7.50, Coffee £1.80, Min/Water £4.50, Service added but optional 5% **Wine:** 26 bottles over £20, 24 bottles under £20, 3 by the glass (£1.85-£2.75) **Notes:** Vegetarian available, Dress Restrictions, Smart casual, Civ Wed 70 **Seats:** 50, Pr/dining room 34 **Smoking:** N/Sm in restaurant **Children:** Portions **Rooms:** 28 (28 en suite) ★★★ HL **Directions:** M1 junct 28, A38 towards Derby, then A61 to Higham, left onto B6013 **Parking:** 100

MARSTON MONTGOMERY MAP 10 SK13

The Crown Inn

British, European

Modern brasserie in traditional village setting

☎ 01889 590541 Riggs Ln DE6 2FF
e-mail: info@thecrowninn-derbyshire.co.uk
web: www.thecrowninn-derbyshire.co.uk

Georgian farmhouse features combine with contemporary furnishings and décor at this modern brasserie. Local painters' works hung on earthy coloured walls complement sumptuous leather sofas and armchairs. Dishes range from traditional to modern British in style with some oriental influences. Starters might include pressed ham hock and black pudding terrine, or wok-steamed mussels in red Thai cream. For mains, expect the likes of roasted lamb shank with braised red cabbage or chorizo, red onion and spinach pasta. Be sure to leave room for imaginative puddings like white chocolate and griottine crème brûlée. Menus are competitively priced and service is attentive.

Chef: Leighton Bradbury **Owners:** Janice & Craig Southway **Times:** 12-2.30/7-9.30, Closed 25 Dec, 1 Jan, Closed D Sun **Prices:** Fixed L fr £11.95, Starter £3.95-£6.95, Main £10.95-£15.95, Dessert £3.95-£4.95, Coffee £1.95, Min/Water £2.50, Service optional **Wine:** 8 bottles over £20, 25 bottles under £20, 7 by the glass (£3-£4.25) **Notes:** Vegetarian available **Seats:** 40 **Smoking:** N/Sm in restaurant **Children:** Menu, Portions **Rooms:** 7 (7 en suite) ★★★★ INN **Directions:** From Ashbourne take A515 towards Lichfield, after 5m turn right at Cubley x-rds then follow signs to Marston Montgomery for 1m, take left into Marston Montgomery. The Crown Inn is in centre of village **Parking:** 16

MATLOCK MAP 16 SK35

Riber Hall

Traditional French V

NOTABLE WINE LIST

Impressive cooking in a manor house setting

☎ 01629 582795 DE4 5JU
e-mail: info@riber-hall.co.uk
web: www.riber-hall.co.uk

More like a country retreat than a hotel, this charming Elizabethan manor enjoys an idyllic setting in lovely grounds in the foothills of the Pennines. Period furniture, open fires and cosy lounges offer comfortable grandeur and true country-house atmosphere, while the traditional-styled restaurant follows the theme and a pretty walled garden offers views across Matlock. The kitchen's well-executed, modern-focused repertoire of fixed-price dinner and simpler, individually-priced lunch dishes might deliver the likes of a fillet of sea bream served with truffled sweet potato mash, baby ratatouille and a saffron nage, and to finish, perhaps a Grand Marnier and lemongrass crème brûlée with espresso ice cream and biscotti.

Notable Wine List: A beautifully presented wine list with some informative notes on both grape varieties and each of the carefullly chosen wines including its cepage.

continued

continued

MATLOCK *continued* MAP 16 SK35

Chef: Michael Kulczak **Owners:** Alex Biggin **Times:** 12-1.30/7-9.30, Closed 25 Dec **Prices:** Fixed D fr £40, Starter £3.50-£7.95, Main £9.50-£13.50, Dessert £3.95-£5.25, Coffee £3.85, Min/Water £2.85, Service optional **Wine:** 120 bottles over £20, 11 bottles under £20, 5 by the glass (£4.60-£5.20) **Notes:** ALC L only, Vegetarian menu, Dress Restrictions, Jacket & tie requested, Civ Wed 70 **Seats:** 60, Pr/dining room 30 **Smoking:** N/Sm in restaurant **Children:** Portions **Rooms:** 14 (14 en suite) ★★★ CHH **Directions:** Off A615 at Tansley, 1m up Alders Lane & Carr Lane **Parking:** 50

MELBOURNE MAP 11 SK32

® *The Bay Tree*

Modern British

Imaginative cuisine in contemporary village setting

☎ 01332 863358 4 Potter St DE73 8HW
e-mail: enquiries@baytreerestaurant.co.uk
web: www.baytreerestaurant.co.uk

Expect robust modern brasserie-style cuisine at this smart, but unpretentious village-centre eatery. The 17th-century building has been extended to create a new bar. The spacious, informal dining room is smartly decorated in warm yellow with timber floors and modern artwork on the walls. Dishes have a rustic style and attention is given to presentation, depth of flavour and use of good-quality produce. Dishes include smoked haddock and vodka risotto, calves' liver, sausage and mash with onion gravy, and a creamy and peppery beef stroganoff. Try the champagne breakfast.

Times: 10.30-3/6.30-10.30 **Directions:** Telephone for directions

---

MORLEY MAP 11 SK34

® The Morley Hayes Hotel - Dovecote Restaurant

Modern British NEW

Converted dovecote in modern golfing destination serving creative cooking

☎ 01332 780480 Main Rd DE7 6DG
e-mail: enquiries@morleyhayes.com
web: www.morleyhayes.com

Taking its name from the converted dovecote which it occupies, this brightly lit restaurant oozes character from its vaulted ceiling and exposed beams to the original brickwork walls. Smart napery and rich furnishings bring their own touch of class. After a pre-dinner drink in the piano bar, guests have a choice of menus to peruse: one leans towards the luxurious, while the other is more simply conceived and cooked. Ravioli of guinea fowl might be followed by local spring lamb with French beans, baby carrots and shallot purée.

Chef: Nigel Stuart **Owners:** Robert & Andrew Allsop/Morley Hayes Leisure Ltd **Times:** 12-2/7-9.30, Closed L Sat **Prices:** Fixed L £9.95-£13.45, Fixed D £14.45-£30.95, Starter £4.75-£6.25, Main £14.25-£18.45, Dessert £4.75-£6.25, Coffee £2, Min/Water £2.50, Service optional **Wine:** 19 bottles over £20, 44 bottles under £20, 7 by the glass (£2.70-£3.55) **Notes:** Sun L 3 courses £18.25, Vegetarian available, Dress Restrictions, Smart casual **Seats:** 100, Pr/dining room 24 **Smoking:** N/Sm in restaurant, Air con **Children:** Menu, Portions **Rooms:** 32 (32 en suite) ★★★★ **Directions:** Please telephone for directions **Parking:** 250

RIDGEWAY MAP 16 SK48

®®® The Old Vicarage

see opposite

ROWSLEY MAP 16 SK26

®® East Lodge Hotel

Modern British

Country-house hotel dining in romantic setting

☎ 01629 734474 DE4 2EF
e-mail: info@eastlodge.com
web: www.eastlodge.com

Relax in modern country-house style at this comfortable hotel set in 10 acres of beautiful grounds. Peruse the menu in the smart conservatory lounge area before entering the refurbished modern country-look restaurant overlooking the grounds. Choose from an appealing range of unpretentious dishes served by attentive staff. Cooking focuses on big flavours and generous portions. Quality ingredients are crafted into traditional dishes with modern twists and interesting accompaniments, such as seared cod with vanilla scented potato purée, wilted spinach, fresh asparagus and sauce vièrge, or pan-seared duck breast, confit duck leg, bubble-and-squeak potato cake, celeriac purée, roasted figs and thyme and port jus. Vegetarians are well catered for on the regularly changing menus and there is a great selection of local cheeses.

Chef: Marcus Hall **Owners:** Elyzian Hospitality Ltd **Times:** 12-2/7-9.30 **Prices:** Fixed L fr £14.50, Fixed D £29.95-£34.95, Coffee £2.50, Min/Water £2.75, Service optional **Wine:** 36 bottles over £20, 37 bottles under £20, 12 by the glass (£3.95-£10.50) **Notes:** Sun L £23.95, Vegetarian available, Dress Restrictions, Smart casual, no jeans or trainers, Civ Wed 66 **Seats:** 50, Pr/dining room 36 **Smoking:** N/Sm in restaurant, Air con **Children:** Min 12 yrs, Menu, Portions **Rooms:** 14 (14 en suite) ★★★ HL **Directions:** On A6, 5m from Matlock & 3m from Bakewell, at junct with B6012 **Parking:** 40

The Old Vicarage

RIDGEWAY MAP 16 SK48

Modern British

Memorable dining in striking house and gardens

☎ 0114 247 5814 Ridgeway Moor S12 3XW
e-mail: eat@theoldvicarage.co.uk
web: www.theoldvicarage.co.uk

A sweeping gravel drive and backdrop of lush, rolling lawns and hidden copses of mature yew trees and cedars of the Lebanon give this grand, stone-built Victorian house and one-time vicarage a timeless sense of grace. The welcome is equally warm and friendly, the décor pleasingly unfussy country-house, while cosy lounges and open fires beckon to sip aperitifs and nibble canapés, and on warm summer days the terrace comes into play for outdoor dining. The main dining room comes in soft pastel shades with modern watercolours bringing the room to life. Bright and sunny in summer and warm and cosy in winter with log fires and candlelight, it's decked out with parquet flooring and crisp white linen tablecloths.
The conservatory dining area opens out on to the terrace and lovely views, while the kitchen's modern focus is admirably inspired by top-quality, seasonal produce from local and specialist suppliers. Expect some unusual blends of flavours, but the precision cooking is not tied to fashion or gimmicks. Sound combinations, accomplished skills and clear flavours abound in signature dishes like roasted loin of veal served on a potato gratin with roasted garlic, buttered veal sweetbreads, cauliflower and sprouts in almond oil with toasted almonds, or perhaps pan-fried fillet of Whitby cod on saffron noodles with mussel and tarragon broth and Sévruga caviar.

Chef: T Bramley, N Smith
Owners: Tessa Bramley
Times: 12.30/6.30, Closed 25-26 Dec, 1 Jan, 10 days Xmas/New Year, 2 wks Aug & BHs, Sun & Mon, Closed L Sat
Prices: Fixed L £30, Fixed D £50, Coffee £2, Min/Water £3, Service optional
Wine: 460 bottles over £20, 24 bottles under £20, 24 by the glass (£4.50-£20)
Notes: Tasting menu £60, Civ Wed 50
Seats: 46, Pr/dining room 24
Smoking: N/Sm in restaurant
Children: Portions
Directions: Please telephone for directions
Parking: 30

ROWSLEY *continued* MAP 16 SK26

Peacock Hotel

Modern V

Fine dining in wonderful riverside setting

☎ 01629 733518 Bakewell Rd, Rowsley DE4 2EB
e-mail: reception@thepeacockatrowsley.com
web: www.thepeacockatrowsley.com

Now owned once again by the estate of Haddon Hall, this stylish small hotel (once the dower house) has undergone a contemporary makeover - a clever and stylish fusion of ancient manor with ultra-modern boutique-hotel styling. The mix is appealing to the eye, with cool interiors enriched with original features and period furnishings. The dining room follows the theme, backed by well-drilled, hospitable service and garden views. Highly accomplished, clear-flavoured dishes come dressed to thrill and testify to the kitchen's ambition and technical skill. The enticing repertoire takes a modern approach and decisions on what to choose are often difficult to make; perhaps Dorset crab with vegetables à la Greque or an exceptional confit of belly pork with cabbage, mash and cider jus.

Chef: Mathew Rushton **Owners:** Rutland Hotels **Times:** 12-2/7-9 **Prices:** Fixed L £21.50-£25, Starter £5.95-£9.95, Main £19.50-£27, Dessert £5.95-£7.95, Coffee £3.50, Min/Water £3.75, Service optional **Wine:** 25 bottles over £20, 8 bottles under £20, 13 by the glass (£3.25-£7.50) **Notes:** Fixed L 3 courses, Vegetarian menu, Smart casual, Civ Wed 20 **Seats:** 40, Pr/dining room 20 **Smoking:** N/Sm in restaurant **Children:** Min 10 yrs, Menu, Portions **Rooms:** 16 (16 en suite) ★★★ HL **Directions:** M1 junct 29 (Chesterfield), 20 mins to Rowsley **Parking:** 25

THORPE MAP 16 SK15

Izaak Walton Hotel

Traditional British

Fisherman's paradise serving modern cuisine

☎ 01335 350555 Dovedale DE6 2AY
e-mail: reception@izaakwaltonhotel.com
web: www.izaakwaltonhotel.com

A converted 17th-century farmhouse, named after the famous author of *The Compleat Angler*; with its own two-mile stretch of the River Dove for excellent fishing. The restaurant is traditionally decorated and offers outstanding views of Thorpe Cloud in the Peak District National Park. Modern cooking is exemplified in dishes like loin of Derbyshire lamb with pancetta, fondant potato and wilted spinach. Desserts might include iced raspberry parfait served with Turkish delight syrup. The bar features fishing memorabilia and pictures, and bar meals are served here.

continued

Chef: Dean Sweeting **Owners:** Mr & Mrs J W Day **Times:** 12-2.30/7-9.30 **Prices:** Fixed L £20.50, Fixed D £28, Service optional **Wine:** 50 bottles over £20, 30 bottles under £20, 8 by the glass **Notes:** Fixed L 3 courses, Fixed D 4 courses, Civ Wed 80 **Seats:** 120, Pr/dining room 15 **Smoking:** N/Sm in restaurant **Children:** Menu, Portions **Rooms:** 34 (34 en suite) ★★★ HL **Directions:** Telephone for directions **Parking:** 80

DEVON

ASHBURTON MAP 03 SX77

Agaric

Modern British

Interesting dishes in a chic shop-fronted restaurant

☎ 01364 654478 30 North St TQ13 7QD
e-mail: eat@agaricrestaurant.co.uk
web: www.agaricrestaurant.co.uk

This bustling and increasingly popular village, full of antique shops, is the setting for this restaurant located in a 300-year-old listed building, complete with large fireplace, granite walls and a beautiful courtyard garden. There is a wood-fired bread oven where, in summer, bread and pizzas are cooked and fish and meat are home smoked. Much of the salads and herbs are home grown and wild produce, such as samphire, mushrooms and laver, is picked locally. Imaginative dishes include smoked salmon with spinach and beetroot pancakes, and roast pork tenderloin with black pudding and home-cured ham served with a caramelised apple and local cider sauce.

Chef: Nick Coiley **Owners:** Mr N Coiley & Mrs S Coiley **Times:** 12-2.30/7-9.30, Closed 2 wks Aug, Xmas, 1wk Jan, Mon-Tue, Closed L Sat, D Sun **Prices:** Fixed L £10.95-£14.95, Starter £4.95-£8.95, Main £12.95-£17.50, Dessert £5.95-£6.95, Coffee £1.80, Min/Water £3, Service optional **Wine:** 14 bottles over £20, 10 bottles under £20, 2 by the glass (£3.65) **Seats:** 30 **Smoking:** N/Sm in restaurant **Children:** Portions **Directions:** Opposite town hall. Ashburton off A38 between Exeter & Plymouth **Parking:** Car park opposite

Holne Chase Hotel

Traditional British

Peaceful country retreat offering fine dining

☎ 01364 631471 Two Bridges Rd TQ13 7NS
e-mail: info@holne-chase.co.uk
web: www.holne-chase.co.uk

An original Domesday manor, Holne Chase was used as a hunting lodge for Buckfast Abbey for many years until it became a hotel in 1934. The restaurant offers diners fantastic views over the lawn and terrace. In winter log fires burn and candlelight casts a warm glow

continued

over the soft décor. Seasonally influenced menus make full use of local produce including fish from Brixham and Looe, local game and home-grown vegetables from the Victorian walled kitchen garden. Typically, you could start dinner with lightly baked peppered goat's cheese with caramelised Williams pear and toasted pine nuts. This might be followed by softly roasted belly of Holwell pork served on curly kale with miniature châteaux potatoes.

Chef: Joe Barrett **Owners:** Sebastian & P Hughes West Country Hotels Ltd **Times:** 12-2/7-8.45, Closed L Mon **Prices:** Fixed L £10-£15, Fixed D £35.50, Starter £5.25-£8.50, Main £8.50-£14.50, Dessert £5.25, Coffee £2.50, Service optional **Wine:** 30 bottles over £20, 20 bottles under £20, 5 by the glass (£4-£6.50) **Notes:** Dress Restrictions, Smart casual, Civ Wed 60 **Seats:** 80, Pr/dining room 12 **Smoking:** N/Sm in restaurant **Children:** Min 12 yrs D, Menu, Portions **Rooms:** 17 (18 en suite) ★★★ CHH **Directions:** Travelling N & E, take 2nd Ashburton turn off A38. 2m to Holne Bridge, hotel is 0.25m on right. From Plymouth take 1st Ashburton turn **Parking:** 40

ASHWATER MAP 03 SX39

Blagdon Manor Hotel & Restaurant

British, Mediterranean

Confident cooking in delightful Devon retreat

☎ 01409 211224 EX21 5DF
e-mail: stay@blagdon.com
web: www.blagdon.com

A delightful country-house hotel on the Devon/Cornwall border, the manor has existed in some form since Saxon times, although the present building dates back to the 16th century. The restaurant is housed between the candlelit dining room of the house and a conservatory extension, both of which are stylish and comfortable. Accomplished cooking is complemented by the use of high-quality fish, meat, game and vegetables from local suppliers. Classic meets traditional British cooking in a risotto of air-dried ham, sun-dried tomatoes and olives with roasted scallops and a fillet of Ruby Red Devon beef and smoked bacon with beetroot, and oxtail jus.

Chef: Stephen Morey **Owners:** Stephen & Liz Morey **Times:** 12-2/7-9, Closed 2 wks Oct, 2 wks Jan, Mon (ex residents), Closed L Tue, D Sun (ex residents) **Prices:** Fixed L £17, Fixed D £35, Coffee £2.95, Min/Water £2.50, Service optional **Wine:** 16 bottles over £20, 14 bottles under £20, 5 by the glass (£3.25-£3.75) **Notes:** Sun L £23.50, Dress Restrictions, Smart casual **Seats:** 24, Pr/dining room 16 **Smoking:** N/Sm in restaurant **Children:** Min 12 yrs **Rooms:** 7 (7 en suite) ★★★ HL **Directions:** From A388 towards Holsworthy, 2m N of Chapman's Well take 2nd right towards Ashwater. Next right by Blagdon Lodge. Hotel 2nd on right **Parking:** 12

AXMINSTER MAP 04 SY29

Fairwater Head Country House Hotel

Modern European

Pleasantly understated country-house dining

☎ 01297 678349 Hawkchurch EX13 5TX
e-mail: info@fairwaterheadhotel.co.uk
web: www.fairwaterheadhotel.co.uk

Edwardian country house with unassuming public rooms: a couple of cosy sitting areas and lounges, a hall with a log fire and more seating, and the restaurant, which is more contemporary in style. Views are wonderful, and sufficient space is available to provide intimate dining areas. A pianist plays quite beautifully on busier evenings and candlelight contributes to the atmosphere. Food is well pitched, introducing some innovation and interest into what could be construed as quite traditional cooking; crab risotto, aromatic steamed cod, chargrilled rib-eye steaks and a date and toffee pudding show the style.

Chef: Andre Moore, Anthony Muir **Owners:** Christian & Sarah Leydet **Times:** 12-2/7-9, Closed Jan, Closed L Sun **Prices:** Fixed L £9.50-£12.50, Fixed D £27.50-£36.50, Coffee £2.50, Min/Water £4, Service optional, Group min 15 service 10% **Wine:** 35 bottles over £20, 27 bottles under £20, 8 by the glass (£3.10-£3.75) **Notes:** Vegetarian available **Seats:** 50, Pr/dining room 18 **Smoking:** N/Sm in restaurant **Children:** Portions **Rooms:** 21 (21 en suite) ★★★ HL **Directions:** Turn off B3165 Crewkerne to Lyme Regis road, hotel signed from Hawkchurch **Parking:** 40

BARNSTAPLE MAP 03 SS53

Halmpstone Manor

British

Fine-dining in idyllic country-house hotel oozing history

☎ 01271 830321 Bishop's Tawton EX32 0EA
e-mail: jane@halmpstonemanor.co.uk
web: www.halmpstonemanor.co.uk

With panoramic views of Dartmoor, this elegant country house offers a relaxing and tranquil place to stay in one of the most beautiful parts of England. The house itself has a history stretching back several hundred years with parts of the 12th and 13th centuries still in evidence - it was even mentioned in the Domesday Book. The service is superb and it seems nothing is too much trouble for the guests here; the restaurant itself blends low-key formality with unassuming and friendly staff. The creative, daily-changing menu takes full advantage of the wide range of produce available in the area and regularly incorporates whatever happens to be in season at the time. Try twice-baked soufflé of Cornish village cheese with a balsamic dressing to start, then best end of local lamb with a herb and brioche crust and a port wine sauce.

Times: 7-9, Closed Xmas, N Yr, Feb (Closed non-res), Closed L Mon-Sun (ex by arrangement) **Rooms:** 5 (5 en suite) ◆◆◆◆◆ **Directions:** From Barnstaple take A377 to Bishop's Tawton. At end of village turn L for Cobbaton; sign on right after 2m

BIDEFORD MAP 03 SS42

Yeoldon Country House Hotel

British

Modern cooking in traditional country-house setting

☎ 01237 474400 Durrant Ln, Northam EX39 2RL
e-mail: yeoldonhouse@aol.com
web: www.yeoldonhousehotel.co.uk

In a tranquil location offering superb views over the River Torridge, this character Victorian country house is set in attractive grounds. The ground-floor Soyer's Restaurant (named after Victorian chef Alexis Soyer) has an air of casual elegance, making the most of the views thanks to large windows. There's an intelligent simplicity to the cooking style, the accomplished kitchen delivering well-executed, honest, unpretentious British dishes using fresh, local produce. From the daily-changing menu, look out for main dishes such as venison, red wine and garlic sausage on crushed saffron potatoes, or pan-fried supreme of maize-fed chicken with a mushroom and tarragon jus.

Chef: Brian Steele **Owners:** Brian & Jennifer Steele **Times:** 7-8, Closed Xmas, Sun, Closed L all week **Prices:** Fixed D £27.50, Starter £6, Main £17.50, Dessert £6, Coffee £2.50, Min/Water £3.50, Service included **Wine:** 9 bottles over £20, 28 bottles under £20, 3 by the glass (£3.25) **Seats:** 30 **Smoking:** N/Sm in restaurant **Children:** Portions **Rooms:** 10 (10 en suite) ★★ HL **Directions:** A361 to Bideford. Go over Torridge Bridge and at rdbt turn right. Take 3rd right into Durrant Lane. Hotel 0.25m **Parking:** 30

BRANSCOMBE MAP 04 SY18

The Masons Arms

British

Popular 17th-century village inn with bags of character and a wonderful beach nearby

☎ 01297 680300 EX12 3DJ
e-mail: reception@masonsarms.co.uk
web: www.masonsarms.co.uk

Set in a pretty chocolate-box village near one of Devon's loveliest beaches, The Masons Arms is a real destination gastro-pub with oodles of olde worlde charm but an unaffectedly modern approach to food. The décor is enjoyably rustic but uncluttered. In the summer the extensive outdoor seating, busy bar and two restaurant areas are usually packed with happy diners enjoying imaginative dishes such as tuna carpaccio, slow-roast pork belly with buttered cabbage and bacon, or vanilla and lemon pannacotta with honey roasted figs. There are open fires in winter with regular spit roasts.

Chef: R Reddaway, S Garland **Owners:** Mr & Mrs C Slaney **Times:** 12-2/7-9, Closed L all week **Prices:** Fixed D £25, Coffee £1.50, Min/Water £3, Service optional **Wine:** 17 bottles over £20, 37 bottles under £20, 15 by the glass (£2.50-£3.20) **Notes:** Vegetarian available, Dress Restrictions, No shorts or jeans **Seats:** 70, Pr/dining room 20 **Smoking:** N/Sm in restaurant, Air con **Children:** Min 14 yrs **Rooms:** 22 (20 en suite) ★★ HL **Parking:** 45

BROADHEMBURY MAP 03 ST10

Drewe Arms

Modern, Seafood

Classic seafood dining pub

☎ 01404 841267 EX14 0NF

Grade II listed inn, dating from 1228, with an abundance of appealing features, including a large garden and an attractive thatched village setting. Inside there are oak beams, open fires and a welcoming atmosphere. The food is 98 per cent fresh fish and seafood, and a recommended selection from the three-course dining menu is crab thermidor, John Dory with anchovy and capers, and almond cake with rhubarb compôte. Open sandwiches and light meals are also served, like the intriguing gang plank, a combination of bread, salad, prawns, gravad lax, beef and brie.

Chef: Andrew Burge **Owners:** Andrew Burge **Times:** 12-2/7-9, Closed D Sun **Prices:** Starter £5-£6.75, Main £10-£30, Dessert £5-£5.50, Coffee £2, Min/Water £3, Service optional, Group min 10 **Wine:** 20 bottles over £20, 10 bottles under £20, 8 by the glass (£3-£5.50) **Seats:** 50, Pr/dining room 20 **Smoking:** N/Sm in restaurant **Children:** Portions **Directions:** M5 junct 28, take A373 Cullompton to Honiton. Follow signs for 5.2m **Parking:** 40

BURRINGTON MAP 03 SS61

Northcote Manor

Modern British V

Accomplished cooking in historic country house

☎ 01769 560501 EX37 9LZ
e-mail: rest@northcotemanor.co.uk
web: www.northcotemanor.co.uk

An idyllic setting, impressive grounds and the warmth and natural friendliness of the staff make this lovely gabled manor house a delightful place to stay. Built in 1716, the house has a long and varied history, dating back to its origins as a Benedictine monastery, and bright murals depicting the colourful history adorn the comfortable, newly refurbished dining room. Good sourcing of local produce, notably game from nearby shoots, highlights the daily fixed-price dinner menus. Dishes are well executed and show good combinations of natural flavours through careful cooking. Typically, tuck into king prawns with herb risotto and light truffle cream, followed by venison saddle with Madeira sauce.

Chef: Richie Herkes **Owners:** J Pierre Mifsud **Times:** 12-2/7-9 **Prices:** Fixed L £18.50, Fixed D £38, Starter £9.50, Main £21, Dessert £7.50, Coffee £3, Min/Water £3.50, Service optional **Wine:** 73 bottles over £20, 19 bottles under £20, 8 by the glass (£4.65-£7.50) **Notes:** L Mon-Fri £15, Vegetarian menu, Dress Restrictions, Smart casual preferred, Civ Wed 80 **Seats:** 34, Pr/dining room 14 **Smoking:** N/Sm in restaurant **Children:** Portions **Rooms:** 11 (11 en suite) ★★★ CHH **Directions:** M5 junct 27 towards Barnstaple. Left at rdbt to South Molton. Do not enter Burrington village. Follow A377. Right at T-junct to Barnstaple. Entrance after 3m, opp Portsmouth Arms railway station and pub **Parking:** 30

Gidleigh Park

CHAGFORD MAP 03 SX78

Modern European NOTABLE WINE LIST

The epitome of modern country-house fine dining

☎ 01647 432367 TQ13 8HH
e-mail: gidleighpark@gidleigh.co.uk
web: www.gidleigh.com

The tricky journey out to this black-and-white mock-Tudor Dartmoor retreat is so worth the effort - magically set in manicured gardens traversed by the tumbling River Teign, it's nothing short of idyllic! A road sign halfway along the twisting, 1.5 mile single-track lane from Chagford reminds you to 'have heart, you're nearly there', but when you do finally arrive, you'll realise you've landed somewhere very special. Longstanding owners Paul and Kay Henderson may have moved on, but with Gidleigh now in the hands of Andrew Brownsword, you can be confident things continue in assured style, with longtime super-hostess, Catherine Endicott and culinary icon Michael Caines still at the helm at this relaxed and peaceful, luxury country-house hotel. A pre- or post-meal stroll in the 45 acres of grounds is a requisite, sauntering among delightful terraced gardens and beech woods, on manicured lawns and beside the riverbank, while the views from the newly refurbished interior and the terrace over the peerless Dartmoor setting are unforgettable. Michael Caines' modern, classically-inspired seasonal cuisine showcases fresh, tip-top quality local ingredients with plentiful of luxury and intricate presentation, the approach via fixed-price lunch, dinner and eight-course tasting option. Think local beef fillet topped with shallot and horseradish confit, served with celeriac purée and a red wine sauce, with a hot apple tart and crème anglaise to finish. The cheeseboard is amazing, the wine list superb, while peripherals like canapés, breads, amuse-bouche and petits fours all hit top form, too. At the time of going to press Gidleigh Park was in the midst of a complete refurbishment.

Notable Wine List: A well renowned wine list with a particularly strong American listing.

Chef: Michael Caines
Owners: The Bath Priory Ltd
Times: 12.30-2/7-9
Prices: Fixed L £27-£33, Fixed D £70, Coffee £5, Min/Water £1.50, Service optional
Notes: Fixed D 4 courses, Tasting menu 8 courses £80, Vegetarian available, Dress Restrictions, No jeans, trainers or T-shirts
Seats: 35, Pr/dining room 22
Smoking: N/Sm in restaurant
Children: Min 7 yrs, Portions
Rooms: 15 (15 en suite) ★★★
Directions: From Chagford Sq turn right at Lloyds Bank into Mill St, after 150yds right fork, across x-rds into Holy St. Restaurant 1.5m
Parking: 20

CHAGFORD *continued* MAP 03 SX78

Mill End

Modern British, French V

A watermill with terrific food in a quiet Dartmoor location

01647 432282 TQ13 8JN
e-mail: info@millendhotel.com
web: www.millendhotel.com

Mill End is an 18th-century watermill - complete with a working wheel that churns away pleasantly just outside the dining room. A refurbishment has given it an understated elegance without losing any of the period charm of the building. Service is a key factor to the experience with staff treating all their guests like returning friends. The cooking here is both confident and innovative, with a rich vein of creativity running through all the dishes on this fairly short but consistent menu. A typical starter might be baked Crottin goat's cheese with walnut and caper compôte, while a main course could be beef Wellington with roast butternut squash purée.

Chef: Barnaby Mason **Owners:** Keith Green **Times:** 12-2/7-9, Closed L (by appoint. only), open Sun L **Prices:** Fixed L £20, Fixed D £38, Coffee £2.50, Min/Water £3, Service optional, Group min 8 service 10% **Wine:** 93 bottles over £20, 27 bottles under £20, 6 by the glass (£4.50-£5) **Notes:** Fixed L 3 courses £20, fixed D 4 courses £38, Vegetarian menu, Dress Restrictions, No jeans, trainers **Seats:** 42 **Smoking:** N/Sm in restaurant **Children:** Min 12 yrs **Rooms:** 15 (15 en suite) ★★ HL **Directions:** From A30 turn on to A382. Establishment on right before Chagford turning **Parking:** 20

22 Mill Street

see below

COLYFORD MAP 04 SY29

Swallows Eaves

British

Classical cuisine in a welcoming traditional environment

01297 553184 Swan Hill Rd EX24 6QJ
e-mail: swallows_eaves@hotmail.com
web: www.lymeregis.com/swallowseaveshotel

A short distance from the coast, this Edwardian hotel restaurant is very much of the old school with a genuinely warm welcome and a comfortable feel to the décor - lots of homely touches like china ornaments, oil paintings and prints and, outside, lovingly tended gardens. The small, French-inspired menu likewise has a traditional

continued on page 116

22 Mill Street

CHAGFORD MAP 03 SX78

Modern European

Laid-back neighbourhood restaurant in quaint moor setting

01647 432244 22 Mill St TQ13 8AW

Located in the pretty Dartmoor town of Chagford, this unassuming restaurant has a shop front façade and a simply decorated interior that immediately puts guests at ease. Rich earthy colours, stone floors and striking original artwork provide a backdrop for this highly regarded chef-proprietor's culinary offerings.

The cooking is as unpretentious as the service - the chef takes on front-of-house duties himself, which makes for an engaging eating experience. The menu focuses on intensity of flavour and quality of produce, with modest but attractive presentation; a lot of effort clearly goes in to balancing all the elements at work in each dish and in the menu as a whole - the results certainly have that wow factor.

Typical is the superb starter of crab ravioli with red peppers and shellfish velouté, followed by calves' sweetbreads and liver with oxtail, and Madeira tortellini. Diners should not miss pudding - the chef clearly enjoys creating special dessert plates and they are undoubtedly a highlight. Try the marinated cherries with champagne sabayon and vanilla ice cream - popped under the grill to give it an extra dimension. The breads alone are worth a trip here - especially the addictive buttermilk bread.

Chef: D Walker, R Lapin **Owners:** Duncan Walker **Times:** 12.30-1.45/7.30-9, Closed 2 wks Jan, 10 days Jun, Sun-Mon, Closed L Tue **Prices:** Fixed L fr £22, Fixed D £37, Coffee £2.75, Min/Water £2.75, Service included **Wine:** 42 bottles over £20, 14 bottles under £20, 4 by the glass (£4.40-£4.60) **Seats:** 22 **Smoking:** N/Sm in restaurant **Directions:** Please telephone for directions **Parking:** On street

The New Angel

DARTMOUTH MAP 03 SX85

British, French

Revitalised harbour-side eatery from one of England's master chefs

☎ 01803 839425 2 South Embankment TQ6 9BH
e-mail: reservations@thenewangel.co.uk
web: www.thenewangel.co.uk

The TV serialisation of John Burton-Race's exploits in setting up this place (and his 'French Leave' series) have helped draw the crowds to this wonderful, half-timbered Tudor building on the waterfront. It's incredibly busy peak season, a testament to its success and the quality of the cuisine, while menus outside attract throngs of interest from passers-by. There are two floors, both simply but stylishly decorated and both with fabulous views over the busy river Dart estuary and harbour. Pale grey floorboards, darkwood tables, comfortable wicker chairs and antique chandeliers set a relaxed modern edge. The lively ground-floor room has an open kitchen with all the theatre of the chefs on show, which bumps up the atmosphere and volume, while upstairs provides a quieter, more intimate option. Service is relaxed and friendly but appropriately professional.
Burton-Race's kitchen shows polished skill, with great respect paid to the simple treatment of the very best and freshest local Devon produce, for example grilled Dartmouth lobster with herb butter or roast breast of Crediton duck with Dittisham plums and cocotte potatoes. The cooking's modern approach is French-orientated with daily specials supporting the repertoire and reacting to availability, and there's no obligation to have more than one course, a further nod to the restaurant's philosophy for easy and relaxed dining.

Chef: J Burton-Race & N Mariage
Owners: Kim & John Burton-Race
Times: 12-2.30/6.30-10, Closed Jan, Mon, Closed D Sun
Prices: Starter £7.50-£12, Main £15-£29, Dessert £8.50, Coffee £2.75, Min/Water £3, Service optional, Group min 8 service 10%
Wine: 100 bottles over £20, 23 bottles under £20, 14 by the glass (£2-£8.90)
Notes: Vegetarian available
Seats: 70, Pr/dining room 50
Smoking: N/Sm area, Air con
Children: Menu, Portions
Directions: Dartmouth centre, on the water's edge
Parking: Mayor's Avenue, centre of Dartmouth

COLYFORD *continued* MAP 04 SY29

feel with dishes like salad of chicken livers to start, for example, or warm cherry clafoutis with vanilla ice cream for dessert executed with panache and good-quality ingredients allowed to take centre stage.

Chef: Jane Beck **Owners:** Mr & Mrs J Beck **Times:** 7-8, Closed Nov-Feb, Closed L Mon-Sun **Prices:** Food prices not confirmed for 2007. Please telephone for details **Wine:** 2 bottles over £20, 24 bottles under £20, 11 by the glass (£3.50) **Notes:** Vegetarian available **Seats:** 16 **Smoking:** N/Sm in restaurant **Children:** Min 14 yrs **Rooms:** 8 (8 en suite) ★★ HL **Directions:** In village centre on A3052 opposite village shop **Parking:** 10

DARTMOUTH MAP 03 SX85

The New Angel

see page 115

EXETER MAP 03 SX99

Alias Hotel Barcelona

Mediterranean

Bright, lively restaurant with a relaxed atmosphere

☎ 01392 281000 Magdalen St EX2 4HY
e-mail: barcelona@aliashotels.com
web: www.aliasbarcelona.com

Set in a converted Victorian eye hospital just outside Exeter city centre, Hotel Barcelona is part of the Alias group of boutique hotels. Located in a modern marquee-style conservatory, Café Paradiso is a buzzing, stylish restaurant with a distinct lack of pretension, very much in keeping with the trendy feel of the hotel. Good use is made of the wood-fired oven - pizzas and oven-baked dishes are among the most popular here - while an eclectic selection of bistro-style dishes, largely Mediterranean in inspiration (seared tuna with peperonata for example), make up the rest of this appetising menu.

continued

Chef: Chris Archambault **Owners:** Alias Hotels plc **Times:** 12-2/7-10, Closed 25 Dec (evening), Closed D Residents only **Prices:** Fixed L £22-£30, Fixed D £22-£30, Starter £2.95-£6.95, Main £7.50-£18.95, Dessert £4.95-£5.95, Coffee £2.50, Min/Water £2.50, Service optional, Group min 10 service 10% **Wine:** 21 bottles over £20, 31 bottles under £20, 13 by the glass (£3.50-£4.80) **Notes:** Fixed L 3 courses, Vegetarian available **Seats:** 72, Pr/dining room 22 **Smoking:** N/Sm in restaurant, Air con **Children:** Menu, Portions **Rooms:** 46 (46 en suite) ★★★★ TH **Directions:** From M5 junct 30 take A379 to Exeter. At Countess Wear rdbt take 3rd exit to city centre and follow Topsham Rd for 2m. At main jnct follow into right lane into Magdalen St. Hotel on right **Parking:** 45

Barton Cross Hotel

British, French

Small country hotel with an intimate dining room

☎ 01392 841245 Huxham, Stoke Canon EX5 4EJ
e-mail: bartonxhuxham@aol.com

The hotel is a conversion of a 17th-century thatched longhouse in a pretty rural setting just five miles from Exeter. Deep cob walls and low beams make for a rustic atmosphere. The restaurant is an impressive room with a huge inglenook fireplace and a minstrels' gallery, and looks fabulous by candlelight. Seasonal menus are supplemented by occasional specials, and around six dishes are offered per course with a soup or sorbet as an intermediary. Ingredients are well sourced, including good fresh fish, and the dishes are imaginative and enjoyable.

Times: 6.30-11, Closed Sun, Closed L Mon **Rooms:** 9 (9 en suite) ★★★ HL **Directions:** 0.5 mile off A396 at Stoke Canon, 3m N of Exeter

Carved Angel

Modern International

Imaginative bistro cooking opposite Exeter cathedral

☎ 01392 210303 21A Cathedral Yard EX1 1HB
e-mail: enquiries@thecarvedangel.com

A period building with a shop window frontage houses this ground floor and basement modern bistro opposite the cathedral. During the day it's also a coffee shop serving breakfasts, snacks and pastries. The lunchtime carte with blackboard specials is extended and formalised in the evening, but the mixture of influences and modern international cooking styles is the same. Look out for herb-coated Vulscombe goat's cheese with pear, walnut and rocket salad, followed by chargrilled sirloin steak with wild mushroom gratin, or risotto of ratatouille with parmesan and pesto sauce. Service is relaxed and friendly.
At the time of going to press we learned there was a change of hands taking place.

Chef: Jeremy Woollven **Owners:** Peter Gorton & Paul Roston **Times:** 12-3/7-10, Closed 25-26 Dec, 1 Jan, Closed D Sun **Prices:** Starter £4.95-£6.50, Main £8.95-£12.95, Dessert £4.50-£4.95, Coffee £1.40, Min/Water £3.25, Service optional, Group min 10 service 10% **Notes:** Vegetarian available **Seats:** 50, Pr/dining room 25 **Smoking:** N/Sm in restaurant, Air con **Children:** Menu, Portions **Directions:** Opposite Exeter Cathedral, just off the High St **Parking:** City centre

Galley Fish & Seafood Restaurant with Rooms

Seafood V

Contemporary seafood in rustic seafood restaurant

☎ 0845 602 6862 41 Fore St, Topsham EX3 0HU
e-mail: fish@galleyrestaurant.co.uk
web: www.galleyrestaurant.co.uk

This isn't your traditional seafood restaurant, although the historic brick and beam building provides a traditional location. The informal welcome is part of the philosophy here, embracing Zen styling and 'balancing the Yin and Yang' in some exotic dishes. Fresh local fish and seafood is transformed on the premises into innovative, healthy dishes. Thai, Indian and Caribbean influences feature on a menu including the likes of grilled fillets of sea bass on crushed potatoes with pesto liquor, wrapped in a banana leaf. The chef puts his heart and soul into the food and the lively descriptions of dishes, so kick back and relax while your fish is freshly cooked.

Chef: P Da-Costa Greaves, F Roseler **Owners:** Mark Wright/Paul Da-Costa Greaves **Times:** 12-1.30/7-9.30, Closed Sun **Prices:** Fixed L £28.50-£34.50, Starter £4.95-£9.95, Main £19.95, Dessert £7.95, Coffee £2.95, Min/Water £3.80, Service optional, Group min 7 service 10% **Wine:** 6 bottles over £20, 16 bottles under £20, 6 by the glass (£4.50-£6.95)

continued

Notes: Vegetarian menu **Seats:** 48 **Smoking:** N/Sm in restaurant **Children:** Min 12 yrs **Rooms:** 4 (4 en suite) ◆◆◆◆◆ **Directions:** M5 junct 30, follow signs for Topsham. Come through High St see Globe Hotel on left, continue for 250yds **Parking:** 3

Lord Haldon Hotel

Modern European

Stylish country-house dining near Exeter

☎ 01392 832483 Dunchideock EX6 7YF
e-mail: enquiries@lordhaldonhotel.co.uk
web: www.lordhaldonhotel.co.uk

Former country seat of the Lords of Haldon hidden away amidst rural tranquillity four miles from Exeter. A popular dining venue for locals and guests, the historic country house affords glorious views over the Exe. The elegant Courtyard Restaurant makes full use of the views of the 'Capability' Brown landscape. Cooking combines classics with European influences, the daily changing menus featuring skilfully conceived and executed dishes using locally-sourced produce. A typical meal may take in scallops wrapped in pancetta with an orange and caviar emulsion to start, followed by caramelised pork belly with Cognac and apple reduction, and a passionfruit parfait with Chantilly cream finale. Knowledgeable service from uniformed staff.

Chef: Darren Knockton **Owners:** Pullman Premier Leisure **Times:** 12-2.30/7.15-9.30, Closed L Mon-Sat **Prices:** Fixed D £35, Coffee £1.70, Min/Water £2.50, Service optional **Wine:** 3 bottles over £20, 40 bottles under £20, 7 by the glass (£3.50) **Notes:** Sun L 2 courses £12, 3 courses £15, Vegetarian available, Dress Restrictions, Smart casual, Civ Wed 120 **Seats:** 60, Pr/dining room 25 **Smoking:** N/Sm in restaurant **Children:** Menu, Portions **Rooms:** 23 (23 en suite) ★★★ HL **Directions:** From M5 junct 31 or A30 follow signs to Ide, continue through village for 2.5m, left after red phone box , 0.5m, pass under stone bridge, left **Parking:** 120

Michael Caines at Abode Exeter

Modern European

Classy modern cooking in the heart of Exeter

☎ 01392 223638 Cathedral Yard EX1 1HD
e-mail: tablesexeter@michaelcaines.com
web: www.michaelcaines.com

A recent refurbishment has turned this Exeter veteran into the first of a chain of boutique hotels set to roll out in historic towns and key city centres across the UK. Fashionable art decks the walls in the bright modern dining room, setting the scene for some tempting contemporary cooking. A saddle of venison shows the style, served

continued

EXETER *continued* MAP 03 SX99

with spiced red cabbage, roasted figs and chestnut gnocchi, or you might plump for roasted Gressingham duckling with pan-fried foie gras and a millefeuille of turnip and apple. Temptation comes in the form of a seven-course tasting menu which features similarly luxurious fare, plus treats such as hot chocolate cappuccino, or warm pigeon salad with walnuts and quince.

Michael Caines at Abode Exeter

Chef: Simon Dow **Owners:** Michael Caines & Andrew Brownsword **Times:** 12-2.30/7-10, Closed Sun, Closed D Xmas **Prices:** Fixed L £12.50, Starter £7.50-£13.95, Main £18.50-£23.50, Dessert £8.50, Coffee £2.25, Min/Water £3.25, Service optional, Group min 10 service 12.5% **Wine:** 80 bottles over £20, 14 bottles under £20, 8 by the glass (£2.90-£3.95) **Notes:** Tasting menu £58, Vegetarian available, Dress Restrictions, Smart casual, Civ Wed 50 **Seats:** 70, Pr/dining room 80 **Smoking:** N/Sm in restaurant, Air con **Children:** Menu, Portions **Rooms:** 53 (53 en suite) ★★★ HL **Directions:** Town centre, opposite Cathedral **Parking:** 7

֍֍ The Puffing Billy

Modern European

Contemporary gastro-pub serving good local produce

☎ 01392 877888 Station Rd, Exton EX3 0PR
e-mail: food@thepuffingbilly.com
web: www.thepuffingbilly.com

A modern makeover has given this gastro-pub a chic, contemporary feel, with polished wood tables and open viewing access to the kitchen. Photographs of local culinary suppliers are a feature and reflect the good relationship between restaurant and producers. With a reputation for modern, spacious and relaxed dining, the restaurant is home to modern dishes with French influences to suit most tastes. The likes of artichoke salad, aged balsamic with marinated aubergine, crispy sea bass with a warm potato salad or a dish of duck breast with sweet potato fondant and roasted pear make excellent choices. Follow any of these with bitter chocolate tart and salted peanut ice cream perhaps.

continued

Chef: Spencer Jones **Owners:** Palace Family **Times:** noon-2.30/6.30-9.30, Closed Xmas & New Year 2 wks **Prices:** Starter £4.50-£8.50, Main £9.50-£18.50, Dessert £4.50-£5.50, Coffee £1.75, Min/Water £2.95, Service optional **Wine:** 10 bottles over £20, 20 bottles under £20, 10 by the glass (£3.50-£5.50) **Notes:** Sun L available, Vegetarian available **Seats:** 75 **Smoking:** N/Sm in restaurant, Air con **Children:** Menu, Portions **Directions:** 3m from M5 junct 30 take A376 signed Exmouth, pass through Ebford and follow signs for The Puffing Billy **Parking:** 30

֍֍ St Olaves Hotel & The Treasury Restaurant

British, European

City-centre dining with a country-house feel

☎ 01392 217736 Mary Arches St EX4 3AZ
e-mail: info@olaves.co.uk
web: www.olaves.co.uk

Tucked away in a secluded courtyard in the city centre, passers-by could easily miss this charming oasis of calm. Situated in a Georgian townhouse with an impressive curved staircase as its centrepiece, St Olaves adheres to a traditional approach to formal eating with a smartly set-up dining room full of period detail (there is a separate bistro for more informal eating). Although in the heart of the city, there's a country-house feel to the place - and to the cooking. Starters might include a parsnip and apple soup with parsnip crisps, while a typical main course would be grilled fillets of John Dory on pan-fried leeks with saffron and tomato River Exe mussels.

Chef: Simeon Baber **Owners:** Carole A Livingston **Times:** 12-2.30/7-9.30, Closed 3 days between Xmas and New Year **Prices:** Fixed L fr £14.95, Fixed D £31.95, Coffee £2, Min/Water £3, Service optional **Wine:** 23 bottles over £20, 21 bottles under £20, 8 by the glass (£2.45-£3.95) **Notes:** Vegetarian available, Dress Restrictions, Smart Casual, Civ Wed 100 **Seats:** 50, Pr/dining room **Smoking:** N/Sm in restaurant **Children:** Portions **Rooms:** 15 (15 en suite) ★★★ **Directions:** M5 junct 30. Follow signs to city centre, then 'Mary Arches car park'; hotel entrance directly opp car park **Parking:** 15

England

The Horn of Plenty

GULWORTHY MAP 03 SX47

British, International

Country-house setting with focus on fine cuisine

☎ 01822 832528 PL19 8JD
e-mail: enquiries@thehornofplenty.co.uk
web: www.thehornofplenty.co.uk

This archetypal country-house hotel was originally built in 1870 for the Mine Captain of the Great Devon Consol. Creeper-clad, it is well established in 5 acres of wonderful gardens with mature trees, walled gardens and wild orchards. The light, airy restaurant is simply decorated and all eyes are drawn to the windows, where magnificent views can be enjoyed across the Tamar Valley. The mood is romantic at night, when the room is lit by table lanterns.

In the kitchen, a well-established team led by Peter Gorton produce modern British cuisine with international influences, drawing on fine seasonal ingredients. Clever combinations produce complementary flavours and textures; sample a starter like warm crisp belly pork salad for example, served with apple, foie gras and a white bean, truffle dressing. A simple but perfectly executed main course choice would be grilled turbot with baby leeks and a wild mushroom ravioli. Sound technical skills are demonstrated in desserts like an individual apple and Calvados tartlet with maple ice cream and cranberry confit. The wine list is equally well constructed, offering an extensive selection plus a good range of ports and digestifs.

Chef: Peter Gorton
Owners: Mr & Mrs P Roston, Peter Gorton
Times: 12-4/7-12, Closed 24-26 Dec, Closed L Mon
Prices: Fixed L £25, Fixed D £42, Coffee £2.75, Min/Water £3.50, Service included, Group min 10 service 10%
Wine: 115 bottles over £20, 20 bottles under £20, 11 by the glass (£3.75-£7.50)
Notes: Fixed L 3 courses, Dress Restrictions, Smart casual, Civ Wed 150
Seats: 60, Pr/dining room 20
Smoking: N/Sm in restaurant
Children: Menu, Portions
Rooms: 10 (10 en suite) ★★★
Directions: 3m from Tavistock on A390. Turn right at Gulworthy cross, follow signpost
Parking: 20

GULWORTHY *continued* MAP 03 SX47

The Horn of Plenty

see page 119

HAYTOR VALE MAP 03 SX77

Rock Inn

Classic

Beautifully located country inn serving traditional British food

☎ 01364 661305 TQ13 9XP
e-mail: reservations@rockinn.co.uk
web: www.rock-inn.co.uk

Old world country inn with beams and flagstone floors, dating from the 1750s and set below the Haytor Rocks just inside the Dartmoor National Park. It is a family-run establishment, very traditional in style, with classic fare such as River Teign mussels in white wine and garlic, and Devon lamb noisettes on wilted spinach with dauphinoise potatoes and Madeira jus. Dishes are based on best-quality local ingredients, with vegetables, fish, poultry and meat delivered fresh daily. Devon cheeses are a special feature and wines include the county's own Dart Valley Reserve from the Sharpham Vineyard.

Chef: Sue Beaumont Graves **Owners:** Mr C Graves **Times:** 12-2.15/6.30-9, Closed 25-26 Dec **Prices:** Fixed D £27.40-£28.95, Starter £4.55-£9, Main £12.95-£15.95, Dessert £5.25, Service optional **Wine:** 29 bottles over £20, 36 bottles under £20, 11 by the glass (£2.05-£7.15) **Notes:** Vegetarian available, Dress Restrictions, No jeans **Seats:** 75 **Smoking:** N/Sm in restaurant **Children:** Menu, Portions **Rooms:** 9 (9 en suite) ★★ HL **Directions:** From A38 at Drum Bridges, join the A382 to Bovey Tracey. After 2m join B3387 towards Haytor and continue for 3.5m, follow brown signs **Parking:** 25

HOLBETON MAP 03 SX65

The Dartmoor Union Inn

International

Stylish restaurant in a village setting

☎ 01752 830288 Fore St PL8 1NE
e-mail: sue.constantine@dartmoorunion.co.uk

There's plenty of style at this lively establishment. The interior is all clean lines with lots of wood and a log fire surrounded by deep sofas and comfortable seating. The long bar has shelves at the back displaying a large selection of wines, and the small restaurant area has

continued

The Dartmoor Union Inn

separate tables and good quality high-backed leather chairs. Bar snacks are served in addition to a comprehensive carte and daily specials. Modern dishes include confit chicken and leek terrine; home-baked fish pie on buttered spinach or oriental pork belly with apple wontons; and a trio' of chocolate desserts.

Times: 12-2.30/5.30-11

HONITON MAP 04 ST10

Combe House Hotel and Restaurant, Gittisham

Modern British V NOTABLE WINE LIST

Fine dining experience in stunning Elizabethan mansion

☎ 01404 540400 Gittisham EX14 3AD
e-mail: stay@thishotel.com
web: www.thishotel.com

A romantic Elizabethan mansion set amid lush Devon countryside at the end of a winding mile-long drive. It's a grand setting and the hotel is hugely atmospheric, furnished and decorated in keeping with the age and style of this magnificent building - ornate ceilings, ancestral portraits, fine antiques, fresh flowers and blazing log fires throughout panelled public rooms. Dining is equally impressive, with a skilled kitchen using the best of local, seasonal and home-grown produce to underpin contemporary British dishes with French influences. Cooking is deceptively simple allowing clear flavours to shine through, as seen in roasted lamb rump with couscous and a well balanced black olive jus, and pan-fried brill with crab ravioli. Excellent vegetarian and tasting menus available.

Notable Wine List: A well-balanced wine list which offers much interest and quality, including an excellent Chablis section.

Chef: Philip Leach **Owners:** Ken & Ruth Hunt **Times:** 12-2/7-9.30, Closed 2 wks end Jan **Prices:** Fixed L fr £20, Fixed D fr £39.50, Coffee £3.50, Service optional **Wine:** 189 bottles over £20, 16 bottles under £20, 6 by

continued

the glass (£3.60-£8.50) **Notes:** Tasting menu £49 Sun-Thurs, Sun L 3 courses £29.50, Vegetarian menu, Dress Restrictions, Smart casual, Civ Wed 100 **Seats:** 60, Pr/dining room 48 **Smoking:** N/Sm in restaurant **Children:** Menu, Portions **Rooms:** 15 (15 en suite) ★★★ HL **Directions:** M5 junct 28/29, A373 to Honiton. Right in High Street and follow signs for Sidmouth A375, then brown tourist signs for Combe **Parking:** 35

HORNS CROSS MAP 03 SS32

The Hoops Inn & Country Hotel

Modern British

Gastro-pub fare at an ancient inn

☎ 01237 451222 EX39 5DL
e-mail: sales@hoopsinn.co.uk
web: www.hoopsinn.co.uk

Over 700 years old, this Devon longhouse makes a pretty dinner destination with its thatched roof, whitewashed walls and oak-panelled restaurant. Open fires keep things cosy in winter, and there's a courtyard for alfresco dining in the warmer months. The menu offers a tempting range of dishes from old favourites to classier fare, so whether you're in the mood for shepherd's pie and sticky toffee pudding, or Exmoor venison with cherry sauce, you should find something to suit. Expect honest cooking created from best quality local ingredients.

Chef: M Somerville & Jo Winter **Owners:** Gerry & Dee Goodwin **Times:** 12-3.30/6-10.30 **Prices:** Fixed L £10-£25, Fixed D fr £25, Starter £3.95-£8.90, Main £6.95-£18.95, Dessert £4.95, Coffee £1.50, Min/Water £2.50, Service optional **Wine:** 20 by the glass **Notes:** Vegetarian available, Dress Restrictions, Smart casual **Seats:** 90, Pr/dining room 16 **Smoking:** N/Sm in restaurant **Children:** Menu, Portions **Rooms:** 13 (13 en suite) ★★★ **Directions:** Follow A39 from Bideford towards Clovelly/Bude, through Fairy Cross and Horns Cross, restaurant on the right **Parking:** 100

ILFRACOMBE MAP 03 SS54

The Quay

Modern British NEW

Exciting food in an 'upturned boat'

☎ 01271 868090 11 The Quay EX34 9EQ
e-mail: info@11thequay.com
web: www.11thequay.com

Owned by Damien Hirst and adorned with his art, you wouldn't expect a traditional restaurant and you won't be disappointed, it's a first floor dining room in the shape of a fish, but with the appearance of an upturned boat! The white-painted boards, clothed tables, banquette seating and chairs are all pretty straightforward however, as is the traditional British cooking, with a modern emphasis. The Taste Menu also comes with the option of selected wines so you really don't have to worry about making any choices. If you prefer to get a bit more involved, choose the likes of seared skate wing with roasted vine tomatoes and caper butter sauce from the Dining Menu.

Chef: Lawrence Hill-Whickham **Owners:** Simon Bousquet Browne **Times:** 10 until late **Prices:** Food prices not confirmed for 2007. Please telephone for details **Notes:** Tasting menu £42.50

ILSINGTON MAP 03 SX77

The Ilsington Country House Hotel

Traditional French

Traditional dining in Dartmoor country-house hotel

☎ 01364 661452 Ilsington Village TQ13 9RR
e-mail: hotel@ilsington.co.uk
web: www.ilsington.co.uk

This family-owned country-house hotel enjoys a secluded, elevated position on the edge of Dartmoor. The newly built restaurant has been specifically designed to capture the impressive views across the moor and the Haytor Rocks. The walls are hung with moor views by local painters. The kitchen takes care in its sourcing of top quality ingredients and skilful preparation produces mostly French dishes full of flavour. Try the starter of mini fillet of salmon with a Niçoise salad and tomato dressing or a main course of West Country pork tenderloin with caramelised pear, celeriac raita and cinnamon sauce. Desserts include an egg custard tart served with braised plums.

Chef: Mike O'Donnell **Owners:** Tim & Maura Hassell **Times:** 12-2/6.30-9 **Prices:** Fixed L £15.95, Fixed D £28.95, Coffee £2.25, Min/Water £3.10, Service included **Wine:** 25 bottles over £20, 36 bottles under £20, 6 by the glass (£2.75) **Notes:** Fixed L 3 courses, Sun L 3 courses £15.95, Dress Restrictions, Shirt with a collar (smart casual) **Seats:** 75, Pr/dining room 75 **Smoking:** N/Sm in restaurant, Air con **Children:** Portions **Rooms:** 25 (25 en suite) ★★★ HL **Directions:** A38 to Plymouth, exit at Bovey Tracey turn, then 3rd exit from rdbt to Ilsington, then 1st right and hotel 5m after Post Office **Parking:** 60

INSTOW MAP 03 SS43

Decks Restaurant

Modern British

Hearty modern cooking at a renowned Devon restaurant

☎ 01271 860671 Hatton Croft House, Marine Pde EX39 4JJ
e-mail: decks@instow.net
web: www.decksrestaurant.co.uk

Many eateries share Decks' nautical theme, but few pull it off with quite such style and verve. A full-length mast runs through both floors of the beach-side restaurant, while ships' wheels partition the eating area. Eat alfresco or at a window table to make the most of the stunning estuary views, and expect hearty, contemporary cuisine: fillet of West Country beef on rösti potato with watercress, confit garlic and red wine jus perhaps, or sea bass fillet with Savoy cabbage, roast potatoes and marjoram butter sauce. Lighter fare is available at lunchtime, plus a short menu for children.

Chef: Lee Timmins **Owners:** Lee Timmins **Times:** 12-2.30/7-9.30, Closed 25-26 Dec, 1 Jan, Sun-Mon **Prices:** Fixed D £19.50-£21.50, Starter £6.50-£7.25, Main £16.50-£17.50, Dessert £5.75-£6.50, Coffee £1.80, Min/Water £2.50, Service optional **Wine:** 23 bottles over £20, 25 bottles under £20, 9 by the glass (£3.10-£3.55) **Seats:** 50 **Smoking:** N/Sm area, Air con **Children:** Menu, Portions **Directions:** From Barnstaple follow A38 to Bideford. Following signs for Instow, restaurant situated at far end of sea front **Parking:** On street; beach car park

---

KINGSBRIDGE MAP 03 SX74

Buckland-Tout-Saints

British, French

Quality cooking in a Queen Anne country house

☎ 01548 853055 Goveton TQ7 2DS
e-mail: buckland@tout-saints.co.uk
web: www.tout-saints.co.uk

The hotel is a conversion of a manor house dating back some 300 years, set in extensive gardens surrounded by beautiful countryside. Wood panelling, antiques and open fires are features of the restfully luxurious interior, and a large function room opening on to the terrace makes it a popular choice for weddings. The restaurant has quality table appointments and comfortable high-backed suede chairs and offers the best of the county's abundant produce from a concise seasonal menu. Fresh local fish, Devon lamb and beef appear, with dishes such as baked cod with rösti potatoes and saffron butter sauce, and pan-fried fillet steak with fondant potatoes and wild mushroom casserole.

continued

Buckland-Tout-Saints

Times: 12-1.30/7-9, Closed 3 wks end Jan **Rooms:** 16 (16 en suite) ★★★ **Directions:** 3m NE of Kingsbridge off A381. Through hamlet to Goveton, 500 yds past church

---

KNOWSTONE MAP 03 SS82

The Mason's Arms Inn

Modern, Classical NEW

Honest food in stunning and relaxed setting

☎ 01398 341231 EX36 4RY
e-mail: dodsonmasonsarms@aol.com
web: www.masonsarmsdevon.co.uk

This 13th-century thatched village inn has been welcoming people for generations. The beamed bar has a very low doorway with steps towards the restaurant and a modern rear extension overlooking the Exmoor countryside. Since the arrival of the new owners, the food has created a real stir with its modern take on British and French classics. Try a starter like pan-fried scallops, apple and hazelnut salad with cider nage, or for mains a duo of local game, stuffed cabbage and root vegetables. Desserts are also worth a mention - the warm fig tart with sweet onion jam is irresistible. This place is deservedly busy so book well in advance, especially for weekends.

continued

Chef: Mark Dodson **Owners:** Mark & Sarah Dodson **Times:** 12-2/7-9, Closed First two wks Jan, Mon, Closed D Sun **Prices:** Starter £8.50-£12, Main £12.50-£16.50, Dessert £6.50-£7, Coffee £3, Min/Water £3, Service optional **Wine:** 19 bottles over £20, 8 bottles under £20, 7 by the glass (£3-£3.50) **Notes:** Vegetarian available **Seats:** 24 **Smoking:** N/Sm in restaurant **Children:** Portions **Directions:** Signed from A361, turn right once in Knowstone. **Parking:** 10

LEWDOWN MAP 03 SX48

Lewtrenchard Manor

see below

LIFTON MAP 03 SX38

Arundell Arms

Modern British V

Luxurious coaching inn focusing on local produce

☎ 01566 784666 PL16 0AA
e-mail: reservations@arundellarms.com
web: www.arundellarms.com

Delightfully located old coaching inn near the River Tamar on the edge of Dartmoor. The 18th-century inn has been lovingly renovated to create stylish rooms, including a well-lit restaurant with a tasteful yellow and cream décor. Fresh flowers bring additional appeal to the tables. The cooking is a celebration of seasonal local produce, with major suppliers being individually identified on the menu. A six-course tasting menu offers excellent value for money, while the main menu

continued

brings a modern slant to the likes of roasted rack of lamb, here with a walnut and hazelnut crust, compôte of rhubarb, and a saffron and white wine sauce. Interesting cheeses from award-winning supplier.

Arundell Arms

Chef: Steven Pidgeon **Owners:** Anne Voss-Bark **Times:** 12.30-2.30/7.30-10, Closed 24 Dec, Closed D 25-26 Dec **Prices:** Fixed L £21, Fixed D £36, Coffee £2.50, Min/Water £2.50, Service optional **Wine:** 40 bottles over £20, 34 bottles under £20, 7 by the glass (£3.75-£4.75) **Notes:** Fixed L 5 courses, ALC 2 courses £36, 3 courses £40, Vegetarian menu, Smart casual, Civ Wed 80 **Seats:** 70, Pr/dining room 24 **Smoking:** N/Sm in restaurant **Children:** Menu, Portions **Rooms:** 21 (21 en suite) ★★★ HL **Directions:** Just off A30 in village of Lifton, 3m E of Launceston **Parking:** 70

Lewtrenchard Manor

LEWDOWN MAP 03 SX48

Modern British, Eclectic

Fine food in Jacobean splendour in a secret valley

☎ 01566 783222 EX20 4PN
e-mail: info@lewtrenchard.co.uk
web: www.lewtrenchard.co.uk

A magnificent Jacobean manor house, Lewtrenchard is surrounded by idyllic gardens and peaceful parkland, in a quiet valley on the fringe of Dartmoor. The interior oozes understated charm, complete with oak panelling, ornate ceilings, stained-glass windows, large fireplaces, period furnishings and family portraits. The candlelit, panelled dining room continues the theme - it's an intimate affair overlooking the pretty colonnaded courtyard, bedecked with flowers in summer and providing the perfect setting for dining alfresco. The kitchen's modern approach focuses on top-quality fresh local produce and seasonality; Devonshire game, fish from Looe and herbs and vegetables from Lewtrenchard's own walled garden. Deceptively and intelligently simple dishes conceal a flair and confidence to allow clear, clean flavours to shine, as in a fillet of venison with quince purée, mushroom duxelle and red cabbage, or perhaps slow-cooked organic salmon with a scallop and mussel nage, spinach and tomato fondue. Service is formal, but with a friendly yet professional approach.

Lewtrenchard Manor

Chef: Jason Hornbuckle **Owners:** von Essen Hotels **Times:** 12-1.30/7-9, Closed L Mon **Prices:** Fixed L £12, Fixed D fr £37.50, Coffee £2.50, Min/Water £3, Service optional **Wine:** 175 bottles over £20, 62 bottles under £20, 6 by the glass (£3.50-£4.25) **Notes:** Fixed D 4 courses, Vegetarian available, Dress Restrictions, L smart casual, D no jeans or T-shirts, Civ Wed 100 **Seats:** 45, Pr/dining room 16 **Smoking:** N/Sm in restaurant **Children:** Min 8 yrs, Portions **Rooms:** 14 (14 en suite) ★★★ **Directions:** Take A30 signed Okehampton from M5 junct 31. Continue for 25m and exit at Sourton Cross. Follow signs to Lewdown, then Lewtrenchard **Parking:** 40

England

LIFTON *continued* MAP 03 SX38

Tinhay Mill Guest House and Restaurant

British, French

Cottage-style restaurant for food of uncompromising quality

☎ 01566 784201 Tinhay PL16 0AJ
e-mail: tinhay.mill@talk21.com
web: www.tinhaymillrestaurant.co.uk

Chef-proprietor Margaret Wilson was a champion of local produce long before it became the popular practice; she has 30 years' experience and is the author of three cookbooks. Her food is traditionally based, simple and effective, as in rillette of salmon flavoured with Cornish smoked bacon and capers, served with a vibrant salad. Saucing is good, with an excellent port, brandy and citrus sauce accompanying roast breast of duckling. The restaurant, originally two mill cottages, also has a traditional feel, with thick whitewashed walls, low beams, fires and ticking clocks.

Chef: Margaret Wilson **Owners:** Mr P & Mrs M Wilson **Times:** 7-9.30, Closed 2 wks Nov, 2 wks Apr, Sun & Mon (ex residents), Closed L all week **Prices:** Fixed D £27.50, Starter £4.50-£8.50, Main £12.95-£19.50, Dessert £4.50-£7.50, Coffee £2.25, Min/Water £1.60, Service optional **Wine:** 12 bottles over £20, 17 bottles under £20, 4 by the glass (£3.20-£4) **Notes:** Vegetarian available, Dress Restrictions, No jeans or trainers **Seats:** 24, Pr/dining room 24 **Smoking:** N/Sm in restaurant **Children:** Min 12 yrs **Rooms:** 3 (3 en suite) ★★★★ GA **Directions:** From M5 take A30 towards Okehampton/Launceston. Lifton off A30 on left. Follow brown tourist signs. Restaurant at bottom of village near river **Parking:** 20

LYDFORD MAP 03 SX58

Dartmoor Inn

Modern British

Stylish, rural gastro-pub

☎ 01822 820221 EX20 4AY
e-mail: info@dartmoorinn.co.uk
web: www.dartmoorinn.com

This smart, contemporary country inn successfully balances modern style with old-fashioned charm. There's a tiny bar, but the real action takes place in a series of small dining rooms laid out with well-spaced tables and upholstered chairs. A modern colour scheme and striking flowers bring things up to date, while log fires and patchworks add a cosy, rustic note. The cooking adopts the modern vogue, with good sourcing of quality local ingredients - names of suppliers come chalked on a blackboard. Skill and accuracy combine with interesting combinations and imaginative presentation in dishes of refreshing simplicity, such as pan-fried scallops, courgettes, chilli and ginger relish or fillet of duck and raspberry vinegar reduction sauce.

Chef: Philip Burgess & Andrew Honey **Owners:** Karen & Phillip Burgess **Times:** 12-2.15/6.30-9.30, Closed BHs, Mon, Closed D Sun **Prices:** Fixed L £16.95, Fixed D £16.95, Starter £4.95-£6.75, Main £13.75-£21, Dessert £5.95, Coffee £1.85, Min/Water £2.50, Service optional **Wine:** 23 bottles over £20, 12 bottles under £20, 6 by the glass (£3.25-£4.10) **Notes:** Vegetarian available **Seats:** 65, Pr/dining room 20 **Smoking:** N/Sm in restaurant **Children:** Min 5 yrs, Menu, Portions **Directions:** On A386, Tavistock to Okehampton road **Parking:** 35

LYNMOUTH MAP 03 SS74

Rising Sun Hotel

British, French

Former smugglers' inn with literary connections

☎ 01598 753223 Harbourside EX35 6EG
e-mail: risingsunlynmouth@easynet.co.uk
web: www.risingsunlynmouth.co.uk

Classic thatched inn dating from the 14th century in a fine location overlooking the harbour and Lynmouth Bay. Once the haunt of smugglers, the inn has a fascinating history; R D Blackmore wrote *Lorna Doone* here, and Shelley purportedly chose the place as his honeymoon tryst. The building is full of character, outside and in, and has recently been refurbished. The oak-panelled dining room is candlelit at night. Quality local produce, cooked with care, appears in dishes of cold-smoked warm scallops with watercress risotto and Italian liqueur dressing, and Exmoor venison, English confit fondant, with sweet red onion purée and blackberry and game fume demi-glace.

Times: 7-9, Closed L all week **Rooms:** 16 (16 en suite) ★★ HL **Directions:** M5 junct 23 (Minehead). Take A39 to Lynmouth. Opposite the harbour

🏵 Tors Hotel

Modern British NEW

Enjoyable dining in relaxed surroundings

☎ 01598 753236 EX35 6NA
e-mail: torshotel@torslynmouth.co.uk
web: www.torslynmouth.co.uk

The hotel is set high up on a hill amid 5 acres of woodland, and has superb views of the harbour and out to sea. The smartly-decorated restaurant is spacious and welcoming with plenty of natural light. Ingredients are local and fresh and the modern British dishes are not overworked and have good clean flavours - particularly a neatly presented starter of pan-fried pigeon supreme with braised red cabbage and rosemary jus. Drinks and afternoon tea are served on the terrace, where you can relax and enjoy the outlook.

Chef: Steve Bachelor **Owners:** Mrs Braunton **Times:** 7-9 **Prices:** Food prices not confirmed for 2007. Please telephone for details **Rooms:** 31 (31 en suite) ★★★ HL

LYNTON MAP 03 SS74

🏵🏵 Lynton Cottage Hotel

Modern British

Stunning views and carefully cooked food

☎ 01598 752342 North Walk EX35 6ED
e-mail: enquiries@lynton-cottage.co.uk
web: www.lynton-cottage.co.uk

With the sea pounding 500 ft below this country-house hotel, perched as it is on the hillside, the view is understandably one to marvel at. The intimate Sanford's Restaurant makes the best of the magnificent outlook, and well-spaced tables encourage relaxation. The short carte is well balanced between fish and meat, with local, organic and seasonal produce making their own positive statement. Tasteful modern presentations are a feast for the eyes. Start with warm Somerset goat's cheese and roasted beetroot, or pan-fried foie gras with mustard leaves and orange relish, then move on to pan-fried monkfish, mussel vinaigrette and smoked pancetta, or Gressingham duck breast, wild mushrooms, apricots and sage.

Chef: Allan Earl **Owners:** Allan Earl, Heather Biancardi **Times:** 12-2.30/7-9.30, Closed Dec & Jan **Prices:** Fixed D £26, Coffee £2, Min/Water £2.05, Service optional **Wine:** 9 bottles over £20, 30 bottles under £20, 4 by the glass (£3.20-£3.95) **Notes:** Vegetarian available, Smart casual **Seats:** 40 **Smoking:** N/Sm in restaurant **Children:** Portions **Rooms:** 16 (16 en suite) ★★★ HL **Directions:** M5 junct 27, follow A361 towards Barnstaple. Follow signs to Lynton A39. In Lynton turn right at church. Hotel on right **Parking:** 18

MARTINHOE MAP 03 SS64

🏵 The Old Rectory

Traditional

Honest country cooking in a peaceful setting

☎ 01598 763368 EX31 4QT
e-mail: info@oldrectoryhotel.co.uk
web: www.oldrectoryhotel.co.uk

Located in Exmoor National Park and set in well-tended gardens with a gently babbling stream, next-door to a tiny church, the Old Rectory is a picture of English country charm, and a haven of total peace and quiet. The spacious dining room and friendly informal service immediately put guests at ease. The small set menu offers up good, hearty fare with a minimum of fussiness, all cooked impeccably and showcasing local ingredients - Exmoor Blue and walnut tartlet, for example, or green vegetable casserole with buttered trout. The cheese course and local hand-made chocolates are not to be missed.

Chef: Stewart Willis **Owners:** Christopher Legg & Stewart Willis **Times:** 7.30-8.30, Closed Nov-Feb, Sun-Thu (Mar), Closed L all week **Prices:** Fixed D £33, Coffee £2.50, Min/Water £3, Service optional **Wine:** 8 bottles over £20, 22 bottles under £20, 4 by the glass (£3.40-£3.75) **Notes:** Fixed D 4 courses, Vegetarian available **Seats:** 18 **Smoking:** N/Sm in restaurant **Children:** Min 14 yrs **Rooms:** 9 (9 en suite) ★★ **Directions:** M5 junct 27/A361, right onto A399 Blackmoor Gate, right onto A39 Parracombe. At Martinhoe Cross, take unclass road to Martinhoe **Parking:** 9

NEWTON ABBOT MAP 03 SX87

🏵 *Sampsons Hotel & Restaurant*

British

Fresh local produce in charming farmhouse hotel

☎ 01626 354913 Preston TQ12 3PP
e-mail: info@sampsonsfarm.com
web: www.sampsonsfarm.com

An attractive, thatched medieval farmhouse in a quiet location. The restaurant features fresh local produce from South Devon suppliers and accomplished cooking. There is a daily-changing blackboard menu and an evening carte. Pre-dinner drinks can be taken in the charming beamed sitting room by a log fire, before going through to one of two dining rooms. Typical main courses include breast of wild duck on a bed of roasted beetroot with a blackcurrant jus, served with a medley of fresh seasonal vegetables.

Times: 12-2/7-9, Closed 25-26 Dec **Rooms:** 11 (8 en suite) ◆◆◆◆ **Directions:** M5/A380/B3195 signed Kingsteington. Pass Ten Tors Inn on left & take 2nd rd signed B3193 to Chudleigh. At rdbt 3rd exit, left after 1m

---

NEWTON POPPLEFORD MAP 03 SY08

🏵🏵 Moores Restaurant & Rooms

Modern British NEW

Stylish village restaurant serving imaginative dishes

☎ 01395 568100 6 Greenbank, High St EX10 0EB
e-mail: mooresrestaurant@aol.com
web: www.mooresrestaurant.co.uk

Formerly two cottages, one of which doubled as a grocer's store, this attractive building now houses an elegant restaurant. The dining room

continued

NEWTON POPPLEFORD *continued* MAP 03 SY08

is classically furnished in neutral colours, with two wide windows overlooking the village. Fresh ingredients are the key to the simple but flavoursome cooking here. Traditional British dishes are given a twist with the likes of grilled fillet of John Dory with seared diver scallop, pistou of summer vegetables and chive fish cream, or roast breast of local pheasant with organic Creedy duck and creamed potatoes. Service is friendly but professional, waiting staff are happy to advise on the menu or wine list. Book early and get a window seat.

Chef: Jonathan Moore **Owners:** Jonathan & Kate Moore **Times:** 12-2.30/7-10, Closed 25 & 26 Dec, first 2 wks in Jan, Mon, Closed D Sun **Prices:** Fixed L £9.50-£12.50, Fixed D £19.50-£24.50, Coffee £2.50, Min/Water £3, Service optional **Wine:** 20 bottles over £20, 12 bottles under £20, 5 by the glass (£3.75-£4) **Notes:** Sun L £9.50, Vegetarian available **Seats:** 32, Pr/dining room 12 **Smoking:** N/Sm in restaurant **Children:** Portions **Rooms:** 3 (1 en suite) ◆◆◆ **Directions:** Located on A3052, close to M5 junct 30 **Parking:** 2

PARKHAM MAP 03 SS32

Penhaven Country Hotel

Modern British V

Country-house style cooking in an orangery restaurant

☎ 01237 451711 Rectory Ln EX39 5PL
e-mail: reception@penhaven.co.uk
web: www.penhaven.co.uk

This Victorian house on the edge of the village is set in lovely gardens with views to Exmoor in the distance. The restaurant is found in a beautiful orangery with well-spaced tables. Country-house style cooking features local produce and a particularly good choice of vegetarian dishes. Starters include sautéed mushrooms with garlic, shallots, sherry, tarragon and crème fraîche on toasted brioche, or a lovely home-made roasted butternut squash soup with parsley purée. Main courses might include marinated shoulder of lamb with red wine and vegetables. There is a good choice of home-made desserts.

Chef: Richard Copp **Owners:** Mr & Mrs Wade **Times:** 12.15-1.30/7.15-9.00, Closed L Mon-Sat **Prices:** Fixed L £13.95, Fixed D £21.95, Starter £4.50-£8, Main £16-£19, Dessert £5, Coffee £1.60, Min/Water £2, Service optional **Wine:** 10 bottles over £20, 25 bottles under £20, 3 by the glass (£2.80) **Notes:** Fixed L 3 courses, Vegetarian menu, Dress Restrictions, Smart casual, no jeans **Seats:** 45 **Smoking:** N/Sm in restaurant **Children:** Min 10 yrs **Rooms:** 12 (12 en suite) ★★★ CHH **Directions:** From Bideford A39 to Horns Cross, left opposite pub, follow signs to Parkham; turn 2nd left with church on right **Parking:** 50

PLYMOUTH MAP 03 SX45

Artillery Tower Restaurant

British

Accomplished cooking in historic and unusual setting at Plymouth's waterside

☎ 01752 257610 Firestone Bay PL1 3QR
web: www.artillerytower.co.uk

This round 16th-century grey stone tower looks out across Plymouth Sound towards Drakes Island. A stone spiral staircase leads down to a further dining area and up to a 'top deck' on the roof where relaxed

continued

diners can enjoy a pre-dinner drink in summer. The seasonal British menu with French influences reflects a desire to use fresh local produce, naming the source wherever possible. Accurate cooking can be enjoyed in dishes such as shoulder of lamb layered with potatoes and herbs, roast monkfish with Greek salad and salsa verde or rib of beef with shallots and thyme gravy.

Chef: Peter Constable **Owners:** Peter Constable **Times:** 12-2.15/7-9.30, Closed Xmas & New Year, Sun-Mon, Closed L Sat **Prices:** Fixed L £13, Starter £4.90-£10.75, Main £13.50-£25.50, Dessert £5-£5.50, Coffee £2.50, Min/Water £3 **Wine:** 15 bottles over £20, 10 bottles under £20, 6 by the glass **Notes:** Vegetarian available **Seats:** 40, Pr/dining room 16 **Children:** Portions **Directions:** 1m from city centre and train station **Parking:** 20

Duke of Cornwall Hotel

British, European

Contemporary dishes in elegant hotel surroundings

☎ 01752 275850 Millbay Rd PL1 3LG
e-mail: info@thedukeofcornwallhotel.com
web: www.thedukeofcornwallhotel.com

A grand hotel, much refurbished, with a stunning restaurant. A huge domed ceiling and enormous chandelier attract the eye and there are also some impressive paintings of marine scenes. Service is friendly, attentive and efficient, with some staff here on a foreign exchange scheme through the local catering college. Cooking is some of the best in Plymouth, with attractively presented dishes like seared red mullet with tagliatelle of courgette, tapenade and saffron oil, chargrilled sirloin steak with sauce béarnaise, and a well textured cherry and almond clafoutis.

Chef: Darren Kester **Owners:** L Smith, W Combstock, J Morcom **Times:** 7-10, Closed 26-31 Dec, Closed L all week **Prices:** Starter £4.50-£7.50, Main £9.95-£18.50, Dessert £4.50-£6.95, Coffee £2.50, Min/Water £2.50 **Wine:** 50% bottles over £20, 50% bottles under £20 **Notes:** Vegetarian available, Civ Wed 300 **Seats:** 80, Pr/dining room 30 **Smoking:** N/Sm in restaurant **Children:** Portions **Rooms:** 71 (71 en suite) ★★★ HL **Directions:** City centre, follow signs 'Pavilions', hotel road is opposite **Parking:** 40

Langdon Court Hotel

British, European

Wonderful produce and creative cuisine

☎ 01752 862358 Down Thomas PL9 0DY
e-mail: enquiries@langdoncourt.com
web: www.langdoncourt.com

A magnificent Grade II listed Tudor manor, set in 7 acres of lush countryside with direct access to the beach and coastal footpaths. A simple menu is on offer in the bar, while the restaurant serves up fine cooking producing lots of interesting flavours and making good use of spices. Fresh local seafood is a speciality; you will also find organically reared meat, game and local produce. Try Thai-style fishcakes with a sweet-and-sour sauce, or rack of Loddiswell lamb with red onions, shallots and a honey and ginger glaze.

Times: 12-2.30/6.30-9.30, Closed 25-26 Dec **Rooms:** 18 (18 en suite) ★★ **Directions:** From A379 at Elburton, follow brown tourist signs

Tanners Restaurant

Modern British V

Modern cuisine in medieval West Country setting

☎ 01752 252001 Prysten House, Finewell St PL1 2AE
e-mail: tannerbros@aol.com
web: www.tannersrestaurant.co.uk

Housed in Plymouth's oldest building, this restaurant offers modern fare in an impressive 15th-century setting complete with flagstones, beams, vaults and an ancient well. The Pilgrim Fathers may have eaten their last meal in England in the courtyard here, but it's unlikely it would have included dishes cooked with such flair. Expect the likes of maple-glazed slow-cooked pork belly with apple and black pudding salad as a starter, followed by turbot wrapped in Parma ham with wild mushrooms and beef juices for mains. Desserts might include a mulled pear with vanilla sabayon and cinnamon ice cream. This is a popular venue thanks to consistent standards and the owners' TV appearances. Booking is advisable especially at weekends.

Chef: Christopher & James Tanner **Owners:** Christopher & James Tanner **Times:** 12-2.30/7-9.30, Closed 25, 31 Dec, 1st wk Jan, Sun & Mon **Prices:** Fixed L £13.50, Fixed D £30, Coffee £2.60, Min/Water £2.95, Service optional **Wine:** 24 bottles over £20, 27 bottles under £20, 6 by the glass (£3.50) **Notes:** Fixed D 5 courses £35, Vegetarian menu, Dress Restrictions, Smart casual preferred **Seats:** 45, Pr/dining room 26 **Smoking:** N/Sm in restaurant **Children:** Portions **Directions:** Town centre. Behind St Andrews Church on Royal Parade **Parking:** On street, Car parks

---

ROCKBEARE MAP 03 SY09

The Jack In The Green

Modern British V

An informal setting for some serious cooking

☎ 01404 822240 EX5 2EE
e-mail: info@jackinthegreen.uk.com
web: www.jackinthegreen.uk.com

A popular dining pub with a great atmosphere, the restaurant at The Jack In the Green Inn is contemporary and relaxed, happily accommodating all comers, whether in jeans or suits. Fresh local produce is used wherever possible and menus change every six weeks to make best use of seasonal fare. Dishes are traditional using French principles of cooking, as in a starter of mutton and caper faggot with sautéed sweetbreads and kidney with honey mustard jus, and a main course of roast pork loin with celeriac purée, morel mushrooms and roast pink fir potatoes. There's an impressive choice of bar meals, and private rooms are available for celebrating special occasions.

continued

The Jack In The Green

Chef: Matthew Mason, Craig Sampson **Owners:** Paul Parnell **Times:** 11-2/5.30-9.30, Closed 25 Dec-6 Jan **Prices:** Starter £4.25-£8.50, Main £12.50-£19.50, Dessert £5.25-£5.95, Coffee £1.50, Min/Water £3.25 **Wine:** 21 bottles over £20, 63 bottles under £20, 12 by the glass (£2.85-£3.50) **Notes:** Sun L 2 courses £18.75, 3 courses £23.95, Vegetarian menu, Dress Restrictions, Smart casual **Seats:** 60, Pr/dining room 80 **Smoking:** N/Sm in restaurant, Air con **Children:** Menu, Portions **Directions:** 3m E of M5 junct 29 on old A30 **Parking:** 140

ROUSDON MAP 04 SY29

Dower House Hotel

Modern British

Imaginative cuisine in country house on the Dorset/Devon border

☎ 01297 21047 Rousdon DT7 3RB
e-mail: info@dhhotel.com
web: www.dhhotel.com

The Dower House is a late Victorian country property located 3 miles west of Lyme Regis on the main road to Seaton, set back in its own grounds. There's an attractive contemporary-style bar and two eating options: the traditional fine-dining restaurant, Peeks, or the more light-hearted Bistro 3. Cooking offers an impressive level of creative flair and innovation, using local produce to good effect in dishes such as crab and mussels with carrot Sauternes and chervil, and free-range pork tenderloin with Savoy cabbage, black pudding, apple and walnut. Vegetarian dishes are available from the longer bistro menu. Relaxed and friendly service is an important element of the experience.

Times: 12-2/6.30-9 **Rooms:** 10 (10 en suite) ★★ HL **Directions:** 3m W of Lyme Regis on A3052 coast road

SALCOMBE MAP 03 SX73

®® Restaurant 42

Modern French

Classy cooking in idyllic setting

☎ 01548 843408 Fore St TQ8 8JG
e-mail: jane@restaurant42.co.uk
web: www.restaurant42.co.uk

Salcombe has to be one of England's most picturesque seaside towns and any restaurant situated here - with the additional blessing of great views over the Dart estuary - already has much in its favour. With its stylishly appointed dining room that resounds with the atmospheric chatter that always confirms satisfied diners, Restaurant 42 takes its name from Douglas Adams' memorable '42 - The Answer to Life, the Universe and Everything...' and capitalises on its splendid location by offering diners sensible, serious food with ingenious touches. Try carpaccio of beetroot with goat's cheese mousseline to start, then a main of pork fillet with faux foie gras, prunes, grain mustard spätzle, Madeira jus and crispy sage.

Chef: Elliot Moss **Owners:** Jane & Neil Storkey **Times:** 7-12, Closed 6 weeks Jan, Sun, (Mon Sep-Apr) **Prices:** Starter £7.20-£9.80, Main £16.20-£20, Dessert £7.50, Coffee £3.50, Min/Water £3.95, Service optional **Wine:** 38 bottles over £20, 6 bottles under £20, 11 by the glass (£4.18-£5.80) **Notes:** Wine tasting dinners, Vegetarian available **Seats:** 42 **Smoking:** N/Sm in restaurant **Directions:** 15m from A38 Exeter to Plymouth **Parking:** Whitestrands Car Park

®® Soar Mill Cove Hotel

Modern European V

Stunning coastal views and superb local ingredients

☎ 01548 561566 Soar Mill Cove, Marlborough TQ7 3DS
e-mail: info@soarmillcove.co.uk
web: www.soarmillcove.co.uk

continued

The elegant restaurant and lounge take full advantage of the spectacular sea views from the hotel's enviable position above the lovely tranquil cove, and make the approach along a series of narrow, winding roads well worth the effort. Service is friendly and attentive. The cooking is ingredient-led, with an emphasis on quality produce from the abundant West Country larder. The accomplished kitchen's approach is via a fixed-price menu and tasting option that, considering the location, not surprisingly displays a penchant for fish. Look out for Soar Bay chowder or carpaccio of pineapple with lime sorbet followed by lobster saffron served with queen scallops or grilled fillet of West Country beef with celeriac purée and roasted shallot and Madeira sauce.

Chef: I Macdonald **Owners:** Mr & Mrs K Makepeace & family **Times:** 12-3/7.15-10, Closed Jan **Prices:** Fixed D £39, Starter £8-£10, Main £10-£15, Dessert £6-£8, Min/Water £3, Service optional **Wine:** 40 bottles over £20, 6 bottles under £20, 4 by the glass (£4-£6) **Notes:** Coffee incl, Fixed D 4 courses, Tasting menu £50, Vegetarian menu, Dress Restrictions, Smart casual **Seats:** 60 **Smoking:** N/Sm in restaurant **Children:** Min 8 yrs D, Menu, Portions **Rooms:** 22 (22 en suite) ★★★★ HL **Directions:** A381 to Salcombe, through village follow signs to sea **Parking:** 25

® Tides Reach Hotel

Modern British

Holiday hotel dining in splendid beach location

☎ 01548 843466 South Sands TQ8 8LJ
e-mail: enquire@tidesreach.com
web: www.tidesreach.com

Snugly situated in the valley immediately behind South Sands beach, with beautiful views over Salcombe estuary, this personally-run, traditional holiday hotel has a modern yet somehow timeless feel throughout elegant public areas. Competition for the well-presented window tables is brisk in the conservatory-style Garden Room restaurant. Cooking breathes a contemporary feel into a traditional British menu, which specialises in fresh local fish and seafood. Daily fixed-price menus may list smoked haddock and watercress risotto to start, followed by pan-fried fillet of brill with shellfish velouté, with red wine poached pear trifle for dessert.

Chef: Finn Ibsen **Owners:** Edwards Family **Times:** 7-9, Closed Dec-Jan, Closed L all week **Prices:** Fixed D £35, Min/Water £3.25, Service included **Wine:** 53 bottles over £20, 18 bottles under £20, 7 by the glass (£4.10-£5.50) **Notes:** Coffee incl, Fixed D 4 courses, Dress Restrictions, Smart casual, no jeans or T-shirts **Seats:** 80 **Smoking:** N/Sm in restaurant **Children:** Min 8 yrs **Rooms:** 35 (35 en suite) ★★★ **Directions:** Take cliff road towards sea and Bolt Head **Parking:** 80

SIDMOUTH MAP 03 SY18

®® Riviera Hotel

Traditional British

Fine Regency hotel dining with sea views

☎ 01395 515201 The Esplanade EX10 8AY
e-mail: enquiries@hotelriviera.co.uk
web: www.hotelriviera.co.uk

This smart, bow-windowed Regency building at the centre of the Esplanade is true to its name - a classic English Riviera hotel with fine views over Lyme Bay. The chintzy-styled restaurant epitomises traditional standards, comfort and elegance, with windows offering sea views and a terrace perfect for alfresco summer dining. The kitchen's intelligent combination of innovative and more traditional dishes admirably plays to the gallery, with fixed-priced menus bolstered by

continued

carte and dedicated vegetarian options. Expect roast rack of lamb with baby butter spinach, boulangère potatoes, ratatouille and rosemary jus, perhaps followed up by profiteroles and chocolate sauce or 'sweets from the trolley'.

Riviera Hotel

Chef: Matthew Weaver **Owners:** Peter Wharton **Times:** 12.30-2/7-9 **Prices:** Fixed L £23, Fixed D £35, Starter £8.50-£12, Main £20.50-£28, Dessert £6-£6.95, Coffee £2.50, Min/Water £3.70 **Wine:** 43 bottles over £20, 35 bottles under £20, 4 by the glass (£3.75-£4.75) **Notes:** Fixed L 5 courses, Fixed D 6 courses, Vegetarian available, Dress Restrictions, Smart casual **Seats:** 85, Pr/dining room 65 **Smoking:** N/Sm in restaurant, Air con **Children:** Menu, Portions **Rooms:** 26 (26 en suite) ★★★★ HL **Directions:** From M5 junct 30 take A3052 to Sidmouth. Situated in centre of Esplanade **Parking:** 26

The Salty Monk

Modern British

Talented and stylish cooking in an old ecclesiastical building

☎ 01395 513174 Church St, Sidford EX10 9QP
e-mail: saltymonk@btconnect.com
web: www.saltymonk.co.uk

Originally a salt house used by Benedictine monks, this roadside building dates from the 16th century and is kept in immaculate condition. The lounge and bar are full of original character, while the L-shaped restaurant at the rear has a more contemporary feel; light and airy with views over the award-winning garden. Tables are well spaced and West Country artists' work adorns the walls. Good use is made of local produce, especially fresh fish such as brochette of scallops and local weaver with black linguini. Alternatives include loin of Gloucester Old Spot woodland-reared pork, served with a pattie of minced pork and Bramley apple and an apple and Calvados glaze with celery mash.

Chef: Annette & Andy Witheridge **Owners:** Annette & Andy Witheridge **Times:** 12-1.30/7-9, Closed 2 wks Jan, 2 wks Nov, Closed L Mon-Wed

continued

Prices: Fixed D £32-£38, Starter £4.75-£8, Main £9.75-£18, Dessert £5.50, Coffee £2.75, Service optional **Wine:** 24 bottles over £20, 37 bottles under £20, 6 by the glass (£3.85) **Notes:** Fixed D 4 courses, Vegetarian available, Dress Restrictions, Smart casual **Seats:** 55, Pr/dining room 14 **Smoking:** N/Sm in restaurant **Children:** Portions **Rooms:** 5 (5 en suite) ◆◆◆◆◆ **Directions:** From M5 junct 30 take A3052 to Sidmouth, or from Honiton take A375 to Sidmouth, left at lights in Sidford, 200yds on right **Parking:** 18

Victoria Hotel

Traditional

Victorian splendour, friendly service and appetising dishes

☎ 01395 512651 The Esplanade EX10 8RY
e-mail: info@victoriahotel.co.uk
web: www.victoriahotel.co.uk

The Victoria is a smart hotel in an elevated position at the end of the promenade, set in well tended gardens overlooking the bay. The interior retains its period character and the restaurant is a large room with high ceilings and ornate plaster moulding. The décor is restful and dividers with plantings break up the well spaced tables. The menu offers traditional-style dishes with modern influences - grilled salmon fillet with mustard sauce, roast loin of pork with apple sauce, Exmoor venison casserole or grilled lobster with lemon butter, prawns and saffron rice - notable for quality, freshness and flavour.

Times: 1-2/7-9 **Rooms:** 61 (61 en suite) ★★★★ HL **Directions:** At the western end of The Esplanade

---

SOUTH BRENT MAP 03 SX66

Glazebrook House Hotel & Restaurant

Modern British

Straightforward cooking in an elegant setting

☎ 01364 73322 TQ10 9JE
e-mail: enquiries@glazebrookhouse.com
web: www.glazebrookhouse.com

The hotel is an 18th-century former gentleman's residence, set in 4 acres of gardens next to the Dartmoor National Park. Beautifully maintained and classic in style, it is the most relaxing of places to eat, with a log fire you won't want to move away from in winter. The restaurant comprises two rooms, the larger and more atmospheric of which tends to be used for bigger parties. Local produce is selected for quality, and dishes are cooked to order and quite simply presented, relying on the accuracy of the cooking, as in seared scallops with orange and cardamom dressing, or beef fillet medallions with stilton and port butter glaze.

Chef: David Merriman **Owners:** Mr & Mrs Davey **Times:** 7-9, Closed 1 wk Jan, 1 wk Aug, Sun, Closed L all week **Prices:** Fixed D fr £19.50, Starter £4.50-£6.50, Main £16.50-£20.50, Dessert £4.50, Coffee £1.95, Min/Water £2, Service optional **Wine:** 7 bottles over £20, 30 bottles under £20, 9 by the glass (£3) **Notes:** Vegetarian available, Civ Wed 80 **Seats:** 60, Pr/dining room 12 **Smoking:** N/Sm in restaurant **Children:** Portions **Rooms:** 10 (10 en suite) ★★ HL **Directions:** From A38, between Ivybridge and Buckfastleigh, follow 'Hotel' signs to South Brent **Parking:** 30

England

STOKE GABRIEL MAP 03 SX85

Gabriel Court Hotel

***Modern British* NEW**

Relaxed, modern dining in gracious surroundings

☎ 01803 782206 Stoke Hill TQ9 6SF
e-mail: reservations@gabrielcourthotel.co.uk
web: www.gabrielcourthotel.co.uk

In a peaceful setting, the hotel stands in terraced Elizabethan gardens with clipped hedges and yew arches. The Churchward Restaurant has a modern feel with red walls, shutters framing the wide windows, wooden flooring and spacious table settings. The modern style of cooking here draws the best from traditional fresh ingredients in dishes like garden herb risotto and caramelised breast of local duck. Fresh fruit and vegetables are sourced from the hotel gardens; other local suppliers are listed from local game shoots through to suppliers of eggs, milk and even mineral water. The Sunday lunch menu with service starting at 1pm exemplifies the restaurant's philosophy that 'to dine well is to dine leisurely' so why not settle in for the afternoon.

Times: 12-2/7-9 **Rooms:** 16 (16 en suite) ★★★ **Directions:** A385 for 0.5m, turn left towards Stoke Gabriel at the Parkers Arms

TAVISTOCK MAP 03 SX47

Hotel Endsleigh

see below

THURLESTONE MAP 03 SX64

Thurlestone Hotel

Modern Mediterranean V

Simple enjoyable food in long-established seaside hotel

☎ 01548 560382 TQ7 3NN
e-mail: enquiries@thurlestone.co.uk
web: www.thurlestone.co.uk

In the same family ownership since 1896, this seaside hotel doesn't rest on its laurels, with an extensive selection of leisure facilities added over the years, including indoor and outdoor pools, a beauty salon and golf course. The elegant restaurant benefits from floor-to-ceiling windows overlooking the bay. The menu changes daily and always acknowledges its seaside location with plenty of local fish and seafood taking starring roles in dishes like grilled sardines with fresh lemon and black olive tapenade or whole grilled Brixham lemon sole with wilted baby spinach and chive beurre blanc.

Chef: David Bunn **Owners:** Grose family **Times:** 12.30-2.30/7.30-9, Closed L Mon-Sat **Prices:** Fixed L £18.50, Fixed D £35-£60, Starter £4.50-£10, Main £7-£21, Dessert £3.95-£7.50, Coffee £2.60, Min/Water £3.50, Service optional **Wine:** 10 by the glass (£2.70-£8.90) **Notes:** Fixed L 3 courses, Vegetarian menu, Dress Restrictions, Jacket, Civ Wed 150 **Seats:** 150, Pr/dining room 150 **Smoking:** N/Sm in restaurant, Air con **Children:** Menu, Portions **Rooms:** 64 (64 en suite) ★★★★ **Directions:** At Buckfastleigh on A38, take A384 into Totnes and then A381 (Kingsbridge). Continue for 10m then turn right at mini rdbt onto A379 towards Churchstow, turn left at rdbt onto B3197, then turn right into lane signed Thurlestone **Parking:** 120

Hotel Endsleigh

TAVISTOCK MAP 03 SX47

***British* NEW**

Memorable setting, stunning surroundings, accomplished cooking

☎ 01822 870000 Milton Abbot PL19 0PQ
e-mail: mail@hotelendsleigh.com
web: www.hotelendsleigh.com

This former shooting lodge, built in 1812 for the Duke of Bedford, is perched on a hillside in 108 acres of beautifully kept gardens and woodlands along a lovely stretch of the Tamar River - the location is quite stunning. Recently transformed into a boutique-style hotel by Olga Polizzi (see entry for Hotel Tresanton, St Mawes), it is a grand, design-led place with many facets; some could be likened to French, some to traditional English and others really cottagey and quaint. Uniformed staff are professional, though with a friendly air, while the dining room itself splits into two, and on fine sunny days the terrace overlooking the valley offers alfresco opportunities.
The accomplished kitchen shows pedigree, too, with Shay Cooper (ex Talland Bay Hotel, Talland Bay) at the helm, and focuses on high-quality local ingredients, the accurate cooking running on clean lines without too many unnecessary complexities. Its modern approach delivers accuracy and clear flavours - take a lunch offering of slow-cooked blade of beef served with parsley mash, young spinach, confit beetroot and a red wine sauce, while a caramel-poached pear with champagne mousse and crème fraîche ice cream might head-up desserts.

Chef: Shay Cooper **Owners:** Olga Polizzi **Times:** 12.30-2.30/7-10 **Prices:** Fixed L £21-£27, Fixed D £38 **Directions:** Follow Tavistock signs for B3362, continue through Milton Abbot. At brow of hill next to school turn right. Past garden centre, next right for hotel

England

❀❀❀ Corbyn Head Hotel & Orchid Restaurant

TORQUAY MAP 03 SX96

British, French V

Superb views combine with superlative cooking

☎ 01803 296366 Sea Front TQ2 6RH
e-mail: dine@orchidrestaurant.net
web: www.orchidrestaurant.net

The Orchid is the separate, first-floor, fine-dining restaurant at this white-painted resort hotel, which occupies a prime position overlooking Torbay. Smartly refurbished in chic minimalist lines, the Orchid's fresh décor (dotted with pictures of the namesake plant) comes dressed with well-spaced, smartly clothed tables and comfortable chairs that offer stunning views across the bay - around half are window tables, so try for one when booking. Service here is appropriately professional and mainly French.

The cooking style fits the surroundings perfectly; modern, refreshingly simple, clean and sharp. There's a confidence that impresses about the food, the imaginative but intelligently uncluttered style comes carefully presented using the best of local produce, the majority organic. Think roast sea bass with tiger prawn beignet, caramelised fennel and rock oyster cream, followed by a vanilla cheesecake with rhubarb and rhubarb sorbet to impress, while ancillaries like canapés, bread and petits fours (the blueberry muffin is not to be missed) hold top form through to the end.

Chef: Daniel Kay / Marc Evans
Owners: Rew Hotels Ltd
Times: 12.30-2.30/7-9.30, Closed 2 wks Jan, 2 wks Nov, 1wk Apr, Sun-Mon, Closed L Tue
Prices: Fixed L £19.95, Fixed D £34.95, Coffee £2.50, Min/Water £3.50, Service optional
Wine: 44 bottles over £20, 67 bottles under £20, 11 by the glass (£3.95-£5.50)
Notes: Vegetarian menu, Dress Restrictions, Formal dress/smart casual, no trainers
Seats: 26
Smoking: N/Sm in restaurant, Air con
Children: Min 6 yrs, Portions
Rooms: 44 (44 en suite) ★★★ HL
Directions: Follow signs to Torquay seafront, turn right, hotel on right on the edge of Cockington Valley, on seafront
Parking: 50

England

TORQUAY *continued* MAP 03 SX96

❀❀❀ Corbyn Head Hotel & Orchid Restaurant

see page 131

❀❀❀ The Elephant Bar & Restaurant see below

❀ Grand Hotel

Traditional British, International

A truly grand hotel with something for everyone

☎ 01803 296677 Sea Front TQ2 6NT
e-mail: info@grandtorquay.co.uk
web: www.richardsonhotels.co.uk

An imposing entrance and well-tended grounds make a striking first impression on visitors to this coastal hotel, whether they be traditional seaside holidaymakers or business people. The recently refurbished Gainsborough Restaurant is spacious and smart, and most tables have good views across Torbay. The cooking is an enjoyable mix of traditional and more contemporary dishes, epitomised by a starter of tian of Brixham crab meat with mango and chilli crème fraîche, and a pan-fried beef fillet with crispy pancetta, turned mushrooms, baby spinach, saffron creamed potato and wild mushroom sauce. The West Country cheese platter makes a pleasant finale. Serving staff make their own attentive and friendly contribution.

Chef: Wayne Maddern **Owners:** Richardson Hotels **Times:** 12.30-2/7-9.30, Closed L Mon-Sat **Prices:** Fixed D £25, Min/Water £3.50, Service included **Wine:** 31 bottles over £20, 47 bottles under £20, 9 by the glass (£4.95-£6.65) **Notes:** Coffee incl, Dress Restrictions, Smart casual, no jeans or trainers, Civ Wed 300 **Seats:** 180, Pr/dining room 200 **Smoking:** N/Sm in restaurant **Children:** Menu, Portions **Rooms:** 117 (117 en suite) ★★★★ HL **Directions:** A380 to Torquay seafront, hotel immediately on right **Parking:** 20

continued

❀❀❀

The Elephant Bar & Restaurant

TORQUAY MAP 03 SX96

Modern British

Contemporary restaurant with fresh vibrant food

☎ 01803 200044 3&4 Beacon Ter TQ1 2BH
e-mail: elephant@orestone.co.uk
web: www.elephantrestaurant.co.uk

Located in two stylishly converted Georgian houses overlooking the bustling harbour, the Elephant is a smart, contemporary restaurant that continues to impress. Expect an upbeat atmosphere, a stylish décor featuring carved elephants, potted palms, smartly clothed tables and blue leather chairs in the restaurant, and relaxing deep sofas and big windows in the upstairs bar.

At the stove is a chef with a strong culinary pedigree, whose growing reputation for precise, confident and accomplished cooking will see this establishment aspire to greater things. Quality West Country ingredients and vibrant flavours shine through well-constructed dishes, perhaps venison loin with braised red cabbage, celeriac, salsify and wild mushroom parmentier or pork with a langoustine and squid risotto followed by bitter chocolate terrine and salted butter ice cream or lemon crème brûlée.

Chef: Simon Hulstone **Owners:** Peter Morgan **Times:** 11.30-2.30/6.30-10, Closed Sun (Wed in Feb-Mar) **Prices:** Fixed L fr £12.50, Fixed D fr £18.50, Starter £3.95-£8.95, Main £12.50-£21, Dessert £3-£4, Coffee £1.50, Min/Water £1.75, Service optional, Group min 8 service 10% **Wine:** 20 bottles over £20, 16 bottles under £20, 10 by the glass (£3.50-£5.50) **Seats:** 65, Pr/dining room 25 **Smoking:** N/Sm in restaurant, Air con **Children:** Portions **Directions:** Follow signs for Living Coast, restaurant opposite **Parking:** Opposite restaurant

❀❀ Orestone Manor Hotel & Restaurant

Modern V

Modern cooking in a colonial atmosphere

☎ 01803 328098 Rock House Lane, Maidencombe TQ1 4SX
e-mail: enquiries@orestonemanor.com
web: www.orestonemanor.com

This colonial-style manor house is located away from Torquay town centre in wooded seclusion with views of the coast and Lyme Bay. An elephant motif recurs throughout, and there are lots of high-backed wicker chairs in the restaurant. Full advantage is taken of wonderful local produce, including Exmoor lamb and venison, dayboat fish from Brixham, Start Bay and Dartmouth shellfish, free-range pork and poultry, and organic fruits and vegetables from the kitchen garden. Led by Darron Bunn, the kitchen delivers exemplary dishes such as tian of Dartmouth crab and avocado with tomato vinaigrette, and fillet of aged prime South Devon beef with braised celeriac, pan-fried foie gras and port jus.

Chef: Darren Bunn **Owners:** Rose & Mark Ashton **Times:** 12-2.30/7-9 **Prices:** Fixed L £14.75, Starter £7.50-£13.95, Main £17.50-£24.95, Dessert £7.50, Coffee £1.80, Min/Water £2.25, Service added but optional 10%, Group min 8 service 10% **Wine:** 150 bottles over £20, 12 bottles under £20, 12 by the glass (£3.75-£5.50) **Notes:** Sun L £19.50, Vegetarian menu, Dress Restrictions, No jeans, Civ Wed 75 **Seats:** 65, Pr/dining room 18 **Smoking:** N/Sm in restaurant **Children:** Min 7 yrs, Menu, Portions **Rooms:** 12 (12 en suite) ★★★ **Directions:** From Teignmouth take A379, through Shaldon towards Torquay. 3m take sharp left into Rockhouse Lane. Hotel signed **Parking:** 40

Hanburys

☎ 01803 314616 Princes St, Babbacombe TQ1 3LW
Popular fish restaurant.

No 7 Fish Bistro

☎ 01803 295055 Beacon Ter, Inner Harbour TQ1 2BH
Deliciously simple treatment of local fish in family-run bistro near the harbour.

TOTNES MAP 03 SX86

❀ Effings

Modern International

Simple modern cooking at a friendly delicatessen

☎ 01803 863435 50 Fore St TQ9 5RP
e-mail: info@effings.co.uk
web: www.effings.co.uk

continued

Delightful little deli, where food is served all day at a few wooden tables at the back of the shop. Start the day with continental breakfast and move on to tart of the day or Effings' own ice cream. Snacks range through Spanish tapas, Italian antipasti, a selection of air-cured hams, or the shop's own pâtés and terrines. From the blackboard lunch menu you might choose poached Brixham skate with crispy vegetables and tomato, caper and parsley butter sauce, or pan-fried local black pudding and hogs pudding with potato purée, caramelised apple and cider sauce.

Chef: Karl Rasmussen **Owners:** Michael Kann, Jacqueline Williams **Times:** 9.30-5, Closed BHs, Sun, Closed D Mon-Sat **Prices:** Starter £5.25-£6.95, Main £8.95-£16.95, Dessert £5.25, Coffee £1.25, Min/Water £2.50, Service optional **Wine:** 3 bottles over £20, 8 bottles under £20, 2 by the glass (£3.75) **Notes:** Vegetarian available **Seats:** 14 **Smoking:** N/Sm in restaurant, Air con **Children:** Portions **Directions:** From A38 (Exeter to Plymouth) follow signs for Totnes, then for town centre and car parks. Restaurant located approx 100mtrs below Eastgate Arch **Parking:** On street

---

TWO BRIDGES MAP 03 SX67

❀ Prince Hall Hotel

Traditional, International

Country hotel in Dartmoor serving essentially traditional food

☎ 01822 890403 PL20 6SA
e-mail: info@princehall.co.uk
web: www.princehall.co.uk

Once owned by the Astor family, the hotel was built as a private residence for the youngest ever high court judge, aged 32, some 200 years ago. The restaurant, stylish but not pretentious, has exposed granite walls hung with modern paintings and offers stunning moor and river views. Dishes are based on local produce, and though at heart traditional they do reflect modern and international influences, with the likes of wholemeal blinis and smoked salmon with chive crème fraîche, and West Country venison with Jerusalem artichoke and woodland mushroom jus.

Chef: Marc Slater, Anne Grove **Owners:** John & Anne Grove **Times:** 7-8.30, Closed Jan-early Feb, Closed L Mon-Sun **Prices:** Starter £4.95-£7.50, Main £16.95-£21.50, Dessert £4.95-£7.25, Coffee £2.75, Min/Water £3, Service optional, Group min 8 service 10% **Wine:** 20 bottles over £20, 40 bottles under £20, 4 by the glass (£3.80-£4.25) **Notes:** Vegetarian available, Dress Restrictions, Smart casual preferred **Seats:** 24 **Smoking:** N/Sm in restaurant **Children:** Min 10 yrs **Rooms:** 8 (8 en suite) ★★ HL **Directions:** Located on B3357 (Ashburton to Tavistock road), 1m E of Two Bridges junct with B3212 **Parking:** 12

WOODBURY MAP 03 SY08

Woodbury Park Hotel & Golf Country Club

British

Modern hotel with good food and lavish leisure facilities

☎ 01395 233382 Woodbury Castle EX5 1JJ
e-mail: enquiries@woodburypark.co.uk
web: www.woodburypark.co.uk

Owned by Grand Prix champion Nigel Mansell and set in 500 acres of grounds, this hotel has good leisure facilities including golf and The World of Racing Museum. The Atrium Restaurant is modern in style and has a warm and welcoming feel with staff striking the right balance between formality and friendliness. The menus comprise simple, well-cooked modern British dishes with the occasional Mediterranean accent. Expect starters of smoked pigeon salad with crisp pancetta and Jerez vinaigrette. Main courses might include roast Aylesbury duck breast with rösti millefeuille and red onion marmalade. Finish with spiced chilli pineapple and caramel ice cream.

Chef: Marion Dorricott **Owners:** Rosanne Mansell **Times:** 12-2.30/6-9.30, Closed L Mon-Sat **Prices:** Fixed L £24.95-£26.50, Fixed D £29.95-£35, Starter £6.95-£8.50, Main £15.50-£21, Dessert £6.95-£7.50, Coffee £2.50, Min/Water £2.50, Service optional **Wine:** 16 bottles over £20, 27 bottles under £20, 6 by the glass (£2.35) **Notes:** Vegetarian available, Dress Restrictions, Smart casual, no jeans or T-shirts, Civ Wed 150 **Seats:** 100, Pr/dining room 180 **Smoking:** N/Sm in restaurant, Air con **Children:** Menu, Portions **Rooms:** 57 (57 en suite) ★★★★ HL **Directions:** M5 junct 30, take A376 towards Sidmouth, then A3052 towards Sidmouth, turn right opposite Halfway Inn onto B3180 towards Budleigh Salterton to Woodbury Common, hotel signed on right **Parking:** 400

WOOLACOMBE MAP 03 SS44

Watersmeet Hotel

European

Edwardian property in a stunning seaside location

☎ 01271 870333 Mortehoe EX34 7EB
e-mail: info@watersmeethotel.co.uk
web: www.watersmeethotel.co.uk

Located right at the water's edge, this privately owned hotel has wonderful sea views across Woolacombe Bay to Lundy Island. The restaurant is tiered with most tables achieving a sea view and, although they are a little close together, the atmosphere is relaxed and pleasant. The daily menu draws on quality local produce, notably fresh fish, with dishes such as seared scallops with fresh herb risotto and lobster sauce to start, then a choice of soup or sorbet, followed by perhaps a trio of monkfish, sea trout and cod with wilted spinach and a tomato and horseradish relish.

Times: 12-2/7-8.30, Closed L all week **Rooms:** 25 (25 en suite) ★★★ HL **Directions:** M5 junct 27. Follow A361 to Woolacombe, right at beach car park, 300yds on right

---

YEALMPTON MAP 03 SX55

Rose & Crown

Modern British, Pacific Rim NEW

Good value village gastro-pub

☎ 01752 880223 Market St PL8 2EB
e-mail: info@theroseandcrown.co.uk
web: www.theroseandcrown.co.uk

Part of owner John Steven's burgeoning empire of gastro-pubs which include the Dartmoor Union at Holbeton, this village local has been transformed. Large sofas and a log fire in the large open-plan bar help to create a comfortable feel to this stylish place, which attracts locals and destination diners alike. A Pacific Rim influence to the locally sourced menu means that diners can expect flavour combinations such as confit duck leg with chilli mango salsa, pan-fried haddock with baby gem hearts and Jerusalem artichoke velouté, finishing with glazed lemon tart and milk ice cream.

Chef: Dan Gillard **Owners:** Wykeham Inns Ltd **Times:** 12-2/6.30-9.30 **Prices:** Food prices not confirmed for 2007. **Seats:** 38 **Children:** Min 12yrs **Directions:** Please telephone for directions

The Seafood Restaurant

Seafood NEW

Quality dining in contemporary setting

☎ 01752 880502 Market St PL8 2EB
e-mail: info@theroseandcrown.co.uk

Sister establishment to the gastro-pub next door, this contemporary seafood restaurant's white-walled dining room has well spaced tables with crisp linen and an open kitchen giving diners a feeling of involvement. Lobster pots outside and marine photographs within complement the seaside theme of the menus, which display accomplished, confident cooking in vibrant dishes like Lyme Bay diver-caught scallops with sweet potato, mushroom hash and coriander oil, red mullet with plum tomato galette or line-caught local sea bass with sautéed tiger prawns and sauce vièrge. Desserts such as banana parfait with passionfruit jelly, lemongrass foam and passionfruit sorbet or grand assiette of chocolate make a fitting finale.

Chef: Craig Stevens **Owners:** Wykeham Inns Ltd **Times:** 12-2/6.30-9.30, Closed Mon, D Sun **Prices:** Food prices not confirmed for 2007. Please telephone for details **Seats:** 40 **Children:** Min 12yrs **Directions:** Please telephone for directions

---

YELVERTON MAP 03 SX56

Moorland Links Hotel

Modern British NEW

Classic cooking in hotel with views

☎ 01822 852245 PL20 6DA
e-mail: moorland.links@forestdale.com
web: www.forestdale.com

Set in 9 acres of well-tended grounds in Dartmoor National Park, this

continued

veteran hotel has spectacular views from many of the rooms across moorland and the Tamar Valley, making it an ideal retreat. The bedrooms are well-equipped and comfortably furnished, with some benefiting from open balconies. Popular for weddings, the hotel's restaurant is formal, but relaxed and friendly. The classic décor of the room is matched with traditional British cuisine with French influences in simple dishes such as coquilles St Jacques or poached egg Benedict to start, with main courses such as steak, stilton and tarragon filo parcels with Dijon cream sauce.

Chef: Steven Holmes **Owners:** Forestdale Hotels Ltd **Times:** 12.30-2/7.30-10 **Prices:** Fixed L £8.25, Starter £3-£6, Main £12-£18, Dessert £3.50-£4, Coffee £1.95, Min/Water £3.25 **Wine:** 4 bottles over £20, 38 bottles under £20, 6 by the glass (£3.35-£3.60) **Notes:** Sun L £13.95, Civ Wed 150 **Seats:** 90, Pr/dining room 150 **Smoking:** N/Sm in restaurant **Children:** Menu, Portions **Rooms:** 45 (45 en suite) ★★★ HL **Directions:** Please telephone for directions **Parking:** 100

DORSET

BEAMINSTER MAP 04 ST40

Bridge House Hotel

Traditional British V

Good food, locally sourced, in Beaminster's oldest building

☎ 01308 862200 3 Prout Bridge DT8 3AY
e-mail: enquiries@bridge-house.co.uk
web: www.bridge-house.co.uk

A lovely period property with immense character, dating from the 13th century and with plenty of original features like mullioned windows, inglenook fireplaces and even a priest's hole. There is nothing covert about the restaurant, a striking panelled room with a small conservatory to one side. An enthusiastic team of chefs makes good use of local produce on an exciting modern menu. A short carte and slightly longer set menu offer a versatile choice that might include a heart-warming sweet potato, orange and coriander soup, a sophisticated duo of Gressingham duck breast and confit leg with star anise and plums, or a lighter poached salmon fillet with sorrel sauce. Home-made rolls, petits fours and coffee are all excellent.

Chef: Mrs Linda Paget **Owners:** Mark and Joanna Donovan **Times:** 12-2/7-9, Closed 30-31 Dec, Closed L Mon-Wed **Prices:** Fixed D £14.85-£18.95, Starter £7.95-£9.50, Main £23-£24.50, Dessert £7.50-£7.75, Coffee £2.85, Min/Water £2.80, Service optional, Group min 10 service 10% **Wine:** 24 bottles over £20, 31 bottles under £20, 10 by the glass (£3.20-£3.80) **Notes:** Vegetarian menu, Civ Wed 50 **Seats:** 36, Pr/dining room 30 **Smoking:** N/Sm in restaurant **Children:** Portions **Rooms:** 14 (14 en suite) ★★★ HL **Directions:** From A303 take A356 towards Dorchester. Turn right onto A3066, 200mtrs down hill from town centre **Parking:** 20

BLANDFORD FORUM MAP 04 ST80

Castleman Hotel

Modern British

Pleasant country hotel with good-value food

☎ 01258 830096 Chettle DT11 8DB
e-mail: enquiry@castlemanhotel.co.uk
web: www.castlemanhotel.co.uk

The former dower house to the Chettle Estate dates back 400 years and oozes atmosphere, from the Regency-style drawing room and ornate plasterwork ceilings in the dining room to Jacobean fireplaces and a fine galleried hall. It prides itself on its restaurant, a long airy dining room with soft yellow walls and crisp table linen, where the British-based menu makes good use of local seasonal produce. The robust, dinner-party style menu may list mushroom and rosemary soup, cassoulet of partridge with flageolet beans, sausage and shallots, and bread-and-butter pudding.

Chef: Barbara Garnsworthy, R Morris **Owners:** Edward Bourke **Times:** 12/7, Closed Feb, 25, 26 & 31 Dec, Closed L Mon-Sat **Prices:** Fixed L £20, Starter £3.50-£6, Main £9-£16.50, Dessert £4, Coffee £1.50, Min/Water £1.50, Service optional **Wine:** 25% bottles over £20, 75% bottles under £20, 4 by the glass (£2.75) **Notes:** Fixed L 3 courses **Seats:** 40 **Smoking:** N/Sm in restaurant **Children:** Portions **Directions:** 1m from A354. Hotel is signed in village **Parking:** 20

BOURNEMOUTH MAP 05 SZ09

Bistro on the Beach

Modern British

Popular, thoroughly unpretentious seaside café-bistro

☎ 01202 431473 Solent Promenade, Southbourne Coast Rd, Southbourne BH6 4BE
e-mail: bistroonthebeach@yahoo.co.uk
web: www.bistroonthebeach.co.uk

continued

BOURNEMOUTH *continued* MAP 05 SZ09

The name says it all, sat smack on the seafront promenade with superb sea views through floor-to-ceiling windows and aqua-coloured walls that bring the seaside theme indoors. Unpretentious, relaxed and informal, this is strictly no-frills dining; by day a beachfront café, by night, cranking up a gear as a casual bistro. The food is fresh and vibrant, presentation careful but unfussy, the evening carte awash with the fruits of the sea and some meatier options. Expect dishes such as poached halibut with saffron and new potato broth or free-range chicken supreme with goat's cheese, tempura vegetables and sweet-and-sour sauce. Friendly, attentive service.

Chef: Ian Hewitt **Owners:** Sheila Ryan **Times:** 6.30-12, Closed Sun & Mon, Closed L all week **Prices:** Fixed D fr £19.95, Starter £4.50-£7.50, Main £11.95-£18.95, Dessert £4.50-£6.25, Coffee £1.30, Min/Water £2.75, Service optional, Group min 6 service 10% **Notes:** Dress Restrictions, Smart casual **Seats:** 67 **Smoking:** N/Sm in restaurant, Air con **Children:** Menu, Portions **Directions:** From Bournemouth take coast road to East Cliff, at lights right, then right again. Join overcliff. 1m to mini rdbt, take 2nd turn. 400yds to car park **Parking:** Public car park nearby, on street

Chine Hotel

Modern British

Seaside hotel with views from spacious restaurant

☎ 01202 396234 Boscombe Spa Rd BH5 1AX
e-mail: reservations@chinehotel.co.uk
web: www.fjbhotels.co.uk

In a fine position overlooking Poole Bay, this popular Victorian hotel stands in peaceful gardens with private access to the seafront and beach. The restaurant has a warm atmosphere and huge picture windows make the most of the view - across the gardens to the sea. Set dinners are well balanced, make good use of quality ingredients, and offer an eclectic choice of dishes such as Thai spinach soup with coriander, sea bass with mango salsa, and beef medallions with onion confit and Burgundy sauce. Finish with chocolate fondant with orange sorbet perhaps.

continued

Chef: Jesse Uzzell **Owners:** Brownsea Haven Properties Ltd **Times:** 12.30-2/7-9, Closed L Sat **Prices:** Fixed D £25.95-£36.45, Coffee £1.80, Min/Water £3, Service optional **Wine:** 6 by the glass (£3.60-£6.50) **Notes:** Vegetarian available, Dress Restrictions, No jeans, T-shirts or trainers at D, Civ Wed 130 **Seats:** 160, Pr/dining room 130 **Smoking:** N/Sm in restaurant **Children:** Menu, Portions **Rooms:** 87 (87 en suite) ★★★ **Directions:** From M27, A31 and A338 follow signs to Boscombe Pier, Boscombe Spa Rd is off Christchurch Rd near Boscombe Gardens **Parking:** 67

Langtry Restaurant

Modern Traditional V

Contemporary cuisine in an Edwardian setting

☎ 01202 553887 Langtry Manor, 26 Derby Rd, East Cliff BH1 3QB
e-mail: lillie@langtrymanor.com
web: www.langtrymanor.com

A splendid Edwardian manor built by Edward VII in 1877 for Lillie Langtry as a 'lovenest' for their illicit affair. The restaurant is in keeping with the house's origins with rich décor, elegant tableware and a balcony where musicians can play and Edwardian banquets are held. A fixed-price menu give lots of choice and interest, featuring some local and seasonal produce such as pavé of venison, roasted beetroot, shallots and rich chocolate jus. A filo basket of forest mushrooms and shallots with a spinach and Madeira sauce can be found on the separate vegetarian menu.

Chef: Matthew Clements **Owners:** Mrs P Hamilton-Howard **Times:** 12-2/7-9, Closed 1st 2 wks Jan, Closed L all week **Prices:** Fixed D fr £29, Min/Water £3.95, Service optional **Wine:** 26 bottles over £20, 33 bottles under £20, 6 by the glass (£3.75-£4.50) **Notes:** Fixed D 4 courses, Edwardian Banquet Sat night £35, Vegetarian menu, Dress Restrictions, Civ Wed 100 **Seats:** 60, Pr/dining room 16 **Smoking:** N/Sm in restaurant **Children:** Menu, Portions **Rooms:** 20 (20 en suite) ★★★ HL **Directions:** On the East Cliff, at corner of Derby & Knyveton Roads **Parking:** 20

'Oscars' at the De Vere Royal Bath Hotel

Modern British

City-centre hotel restaurant with a fine reputation

☎ 01202 555555 Bath Rd BH1 2EW
e-mail: royal.bath@devere-hotels.com
web: www.devereonline.co.uk

Oscar Wilde once stayed at this historic Victorian hotel with views overlooking the bay in Bournemouth and has lent his name to the restaurant; attentive staff add to the formal yet friendly atmosphere

continued

that pervades the stylishly retro-themed dining rooms. The menu consists largely of modern British dishes with French influences using good quality ingredients including plenty of locally sourced produce. Start with a pressed rillette of pork with plum and chilli chutney and an onion seed tuile and then - perhaps after a refreshing pink gin and grapefruit sorbet - progress onto roast cod fillet with bean risotto and white wine and thyme cream.

Chef: Andrew Crowley **Owners:** De Vere Hotels **Times:** 12.30-2/7.30-9.30, Closed Mon, Closed D Sun **Prices:** Fixed L fr £16.50, Starter £8-£12.50, Main £20-£32, Dessert fr £7, Coffee £3.50, Min/Water £3.50, Service optional **Wine:** 60 bottles over £20, 15 bottles under £20, 8 by the glass (£4-£6) **Notes:** Vegetarian available, Dress Restrictions, Strictly no denim or sportswear, Civ Wed 200 **Seats:** 40 **Smoking:** N/Sm in restaurant, Air con **Children:** Min 16 yrs, Portions **Rooms:** 140 (140 en suite) ★★★★ HL **Directions:** Follow signs for Bournemouth Pier and beaches **Parking:** 95

West Beach

British, Seafood

Buzzy, modern, relaxed beachfront restaurant

☎ 01202 587785 Pier Approach BH2 5AA
web: www.west-beach.co.uk

On the prom overlooking pier and beach, this upbeat, contemporary, relaxed brasserie has uninterrupted sea views through floor-to-ceiling windows, which open in summer. A bar, open kitchen (with chefs on show) and pale wood create a bright, airy, modern vibe, and a decked terrace offers alfresco dining. The kitchen keeps things intelligently simple, with the freshness of ingredients taking pride of place on a suitably modern menu appropriately focusing on seafood. The menu might include lobster, crevette and cucumber salad with pistachio yogurt dressing, followed by shallow-fried fillets of gurnard, sea bass and John Dory with wilted baby spinach, sautéed new potatoes and roasted cherry tomatoes.

Chef: Greg & Phil Etheridge **Owners:** Andrew Price **Times:** 12-6/6-10, Closed 25 Dec, Closed D 26 Dec-1 Jan **Prices:** Starter £4.50-£10, Main fr £7.50, Dessert £3.50-£6, Coffee £2, Min/Water £3, Service optional, Group min 10 service 10% **Wine:** 33 bottles over £20, 11 bottles under £20, 11 by the glass (£3.75-£7) **Notes:** Fixed pre-theatre D 2 courses £12, 6-7.30pm, Vegetarian available, Dress Restrictions, No bare feet or bikinis **Seats:** 90 **Smoking:** N/Sm area, Air con **Children:** Menu, Portions **Directions:** 100yds W of the pier **Parking:** Restaurant parking evening only; NCP 2 mins

BRIDPORT MAP 04 SY49

Riverside Restaurant

Seafood

Seaside location for celebrated 1970s architecture and local seafood

☎ 01308 422011 West Bay DT6 4EZ
e-mail: artwatfish@hotmail.com
web: thefishrestaurant-westbay.co.uk

The restaurant was designed in the late 1970s by the well-known architect Piers Gough, and has been widely acclaimed for its use of natural materials. The business has been in the same family for over 40 years, and for the last 25 the emphasis has been on fish and shellfish, mostly from local waters. Meat and vegetarian items are also listed, with extensive use made of local produce. Signature dishes are linguine of local crab with lemon and coriander, brill and sorrel sauce with crispy spinach, and to finish warm Valhrona chocolate cake with praline semi-fredo.

Chef: N Larcombe, G Marsh, G Blogg **Owners:** Mr & Mrs A Watson **Times:** 12-2.30/6.30-9.00, Closed 26 Nov-mid Feb/Valentines Day, Mon (ex BHs), Closed D Sun **Prices:** Fixed L £16, Starter £5.50-£10.50, Main fr £12.50, Dessert £4.25-£6.50, Coffee £2, Min/Water £2.90, Service optional, Group min 6 service 10% **Wine:** 16 bottles over £20, 50 bottles under £20, 9 by the glass (£2.75-£4.75) **Notes:** Vegetarian available **Seats:** 70, Pr/dining room 20 **Smoking:** N/Sm in restaurant **Children:** Menu, Portions **Directions:** A35 Bridport ring road, turn to West Bay at Crown rdbt **Parking:** Public car park

CHRISTCHURCH MAP 05 SZ19

The Avonmouth

Modern British

Hotel restaurant offering innovative cuisine

☎ 01202 483434 95 Mudeford BH23 3NT
e-mail: info@theavonmouth.co.uk
web: www.theavonmouth.co.uk

Built in the 1830s as a gentleman's residence, this elegant hotel offers lovely views of Mudeford Quay and Christchurch harbour. The Quay

continued

CHRISTCHURCH *continued* MAP 05 SZ19

restaurant is tastefully decorated in muted shades of green and blue. Local produce features on an interesting menu with dishes like melon jelly with Dorset air-dried ham and rocket salad to start. Main courses might include fillet of sea bream served with cauliflower purée and wok stir-fried vegetables. Desserts offer some unusual combinations like dark Belgian chocolate torte with a fresh kiwi fruit sauce.

The Avonmouth

Chef: Nigel Popperwell **Owners:** Christchurch Hotels Ltd **Times:** 12-2/7-9.30 **Prices:** Starter £6-£9, Main £14-£18, Dessert £6-£8, Coffee £2.50, Min/Water £2.95, Service optional **Wine:** 30 bottles over £20, 18 bottles under £20, 7 by the glass (£3.25-£5.50) **Notes:** Vegetarian available, Dress Restrictions, Smart casual, Civ Wed 60 **Seats:** 85, Pr/dining room 14 **Smoking:** N/Sm in restaurant **Children:** Menu, Portions **Rooms:** 40 (40 en suite) ★★★ HL **Directions:** 1m from A35, outside Christchurch **Parking:** 70

The Lord Bute Hotel & Restaurant

British, European NEW

A fine-dining destination in the local area

☎ 01425 278884 170 - 181 Lymington Rd, Highcliffe-on-Sea BH23 4JS
e-mail: mail@lordbute.co.uk
web: www.lordbute.co.uk

The historic setting for this hotel and restaurant is in grounds just behind the original entrance lodges of Highcliffe Castle. A favourite destination for discerning locals and visitors, it is also popular for weddings and conferences. The entrance hall displays pictures of former resident Lord Bute as well as famous visitors to the castle. Diners can relax in the orangery or patio area for pre-dinner drinks before taking a seat in the elegantly furnished restaurant. French brasserie-style food is on offer here, making good use of quality produce, sourced locally where possible. Expect mains such as tea-smoked goose breast with summer berry and rosemary glaze and fresh berries, or fillet of Romsey lamb filled with garlic, thyme, spinach and asparagus. Service is professional and efficient with knowledgeable, friendly staff.

Chef: Kevin & Laura Brown **Owners:** S Box & G Payne **Times:** 12-2/7-9.30, Closed Mon, Closed L Sat, D Sun **Prices:** Fixed L £16.95, Fixed D £29.95, Starter £4.25-£7.25, Main £16.50-£21.95, Dessert £5.95, Coffee £2.25, Min/Water £3.50, Service optional **Wine:** 28 bottles over £20, 32 bottles under £20, 6 by the glass (£3.50-£5.50) **Notes:** Sun L 4 courses £19.95, Vegetarian available, Dress Restrictions, Smart casual, no jeans or T-shirts **Seats:** 95 **Smoking:** N/Sm in restaurant, Air con **Children:** Portions **Rooms:** 12 (12 en suite) ◆◆◆◆◆ **Directions:** Follow A337 to Lymington, opposite St Mark's churchyard in Highcliffe **Parking:** 50

Splinters Restaurant

International

Family-run restaurant in listed building

☎ 01202 483454 12 Church St BH23 1BW
e-mail: eating@splinters.uk.com
web: www.splinters.uk.com

In a row of quaint buildings on the cobble street leading to the old priory, of which this is perhaps the prettiest. Inside it oozes character with its winding corridor, old wooden staircase, well-trodden wooden floor and various nooks and crannies. The main area is the bar lounge from which five private dining areas lead. You can choose a snack, salad or soup like curried parsnip and apple soup with black pepper crème fraîche, or go for a risotto, a pasta dish or something more involved from the modern international menu. Expect main dishes such as roast English rump of lamb on pea-minted mash with redcurrant port wine sauce, or pan-fried sea bass with new potatoes, roasted vine tomatoes, asparagus and basil dressing. The cooking, like the service and setting, is consistently appealing.

Chef: Paul Putt **Owners:** Paul and Agnes Putt **Times:** 11-2/7-10, Closed 26 Dec, 1 Jan, Sun-Mon **Prices:** Fixed L fr £9.95, Fixed D £24.95-£36.50, Coffee £2.95, Min/Water £2.95, Service included, Group min 8 service 10% **Wine:** 60 bottles over £20, 40 bottles under £20, 4 by the glass (£3.40-£3.70) **Notes:** ALC 2 courses £29.50, 3 courses £36.50, Vegetarian available **Seats:** 42, Pr/dining room 26 **Smoking:** N/Sm in restaurant **Children:** Portions **Directions:** Directly in front of Priory gates

Waterford Lodge Hotel

British

Informal restaurant with knowledgeable staff

☎ 01425 272948 87 Bure Ln, Friars Cliff, Mudeford BH23 4DN
e-mail: waterford@bestwestern.co.uk
web: www.waterfordlodge.com

It used to be the lodge to Highcliffe Castle, but this old building has been extended and modernised to become a hotel popular with business and holiday users. The intimate restaurant is relaxed and friendly, and overlooks the pretty gardens complete with fish pond. The carefully prepared food is brought by attentive staff who make everyone feel at home. Modern creations like millefeuille of oak-smoked salmon and crisp wafer potatoes might appear on the fixed-price menus, with perhaps slow-braised haunch of New Forest venison cooked with juniper, red wine and thyme, and dark chocolate torte with Kirsch-soaked cherries, coffee sauce and hazelnut crisp.

Chef: Jason Fuller **Owners:** Michael & Vicki Harrison **Times:** 12-1.30/7-9 **Prices:** Fixed L £12.50, Fixed D £27.50-£29, Coffee £1.75, Min/Water £2.90,

continued

Service optional **Wine:** 18 bottles over £20, 27 bottles under £20, 4 by the glass (£3-£5) **Notes:** Vegetarian available, Dress Restrictions, No jeans, trainers or T-shirts **Seats:** 40, Pr/dining room 70 **Smoking:** N/Sm in restaurant **Children:** Min 7 yrs, Menu, Portions **Rooms:** 18 (18 en suite) ★★★ HL **Directions:** A35 through Lyndhurst to Christchurch. Turn left onto A337. Follow signs on rdbt to Hotel **Parking:** 36

The Ship in Distress

☎ 01202 485123 68 Stanpit BH23 3NA

Offers a varied and imaginative selection of fresh fish dishes.

CORFE CASTLE MAP 04 SY98

Mortons House Hotel

British, European

Notable dining in Elizabethan surroundings

☎ 01929 480988 East St BH20 5EE
e-mail: stay@mortonshouse.co.uk
web: www.mortonshouse.co.uk

With the ruins of Corfe Castle as a backdrop and set in delightful gardens and grounds, this impressive Tudor house was built in an 'E' shape to honour Queen Elizabeth I. Beautifully updated and stylishly furnished, it retains a timeless feel. The serene oak-panelled dining room may have formal table settings, but service is friendly and knowledgeable. Classical in style, the British and international cooking is skilful and accomplished, with well-executed dishes utilising produce of high quality and as local as possible. With a complementary amuse-bouche served at the table, roast squab pigeon, boulangère potatoes and braised salsify with red wine and shallot sauce are fine examples of the fare.

Chef: Derek Woods **Owners:** Mr & Mrs Hageman, Mr & Mrs Clayton **Times:** 12-2/7-9.30 **Prices:** Fixed L £19.50-£30, Starter £5-£10, Main £15-£28, Dessert £4.50-£8.50, Coffee £2.50, Min/Water £2.80, Service optional, Group min 20 service 10% **Wine:** 42 bottles over £20, 10 bottles under £20, 6 by the glass (£3.40-£3.80) **Notes:** Fixed L 3 courses, Vegetarian available, Dress Restrictions, Smart casual preferred, no denim or shorts, Civ Wed 60 **Seats:** 60, Pr/dining room 22 **Smoking:** N/Sm in restaurant **Children:** Min 5 yrs, Portions **Rooms:** 19 (19 en suite) ★★★ **Directions:** In centre of village on A351 **Parking:** 45

CORFE MULLEN MAP 04 SY99

The Coventry Arms

Modern British NEW

Local delicacies in popular country pub

☎ 01258 857284 Mill St BH21 3RH

A converted 15th-century watermill makes the most of its location with a beer garden overlooking the river. The interior is full of nooks and crannies, large brick fireplaces, flagstones and fishing paraphernalia. The emphasis is firmly on locally caught produce from trout to a variety of game when in season. Venison, pigeon and pheasant are all sourced from local estates and trout is rod-caught by the proprietor. Samples from the modern British menu include Dorset fish broth, fillet of local venison on saffron fondant with port jus, or seared fillets of John Dory, Dorset crab and ginger risotto with shellfish cream.

Chef: Ian Gibbs **Owners:** John Hugo & David Armstrong Reed **Times:** 12-2.30/6-9.30 **Prices:** Starter £4.50-£8.50, Main £9-£18, Dessert £4.50-£5.50, Coffee £1.75, Min/Water £2.50, Service included **Wine:** 12 bottles over £20, 15 bottles under £20, 12 by the glass (£3-£6) **Notes:** Sun L 2 courses £11.50, Vegetarian available **Seats:** 70 **Smoking:** N/Sm in restaurant **Children:** Menu, Portions **Directions:** A31 2m from Wimborne **Parking:** 50

CRANBORNE MAP 05 SU01

La Fosse at Cranborne

Modern British

Long-established friendly village restaurant

☎ 01725 517604 London House, The Square BH21 5PR
e-mail: mac@la-fosse.com
web: www.la-fosse.com

This large Victorian house was developed from a 16th-century farmhouse, as evidenced by some low ceilings, beams and an inglenook fireplace. The building has been a butcher's, a haberdasher's, a hairdresser's and a garage in its time, but for over 20 years has been owned and run by chef Mac La Fosse and his wife Sue. The food is modern British with ethnic touches and classical French undertones: perhaps slow-roasted rare breeds pork with five spice and grain mustard mash, followed by Sue's extra special summer pudding with home-made blueberry ice cream.

continued

CRANBORNE *continued* MAP 05 SU01

La Fosse at Cranborne

Chef: Mac La Fosse **Owners:** MJ & S La Fosse **Times:** 12-2/7-9.30, Closed Mon-Tue, Closed D Sun **Prices:** Fixed L £7.50-£12.95, Fixed D £17.45-£24.50, Min/Water £1.75, Service optional **Wine:** 18 bottles over £20, 45 bottles under £20, 10 by the glass (£3.50) **Notes:** Vegetarian available, Dress Restrictions, Smart casual, no shorts or T-shirts **Seats:** 30 **Smoking:** N/Sm in restaurant **Children:** Portions **Rooms:** 3 (3 en suite) ♦♦♦♦ **Directions:** M3, M27 W to A31 to Ringwood. Turn left to B3081 to Verwood, then Cranborne (5 m) **Parking:** In square

---

DORCHESTER MAP 04 SY69

Sienna

Modern British

Small but beautifully formed restaurant with real class

☎ 01305 250022 36 High West St DT1 1UP
e-mail: browns@siennarestaurant.co.uk
web: www.siennarestaurant.co.uk

Located at the top of the high street with an unassuming shop front, this high-achieving restaurant is a tiny gem of Dorchester dining. With only 15 covers, there's a lovely intimacy and such a bijou scale means booking is essential. The décor is suitably unobtrusive with modern art on the walls, a restful colour scheme and unclothed wooden tables. Run by a husband-and-wife team, service is personal, graceful and unhurried while the food is mature, accurate and well conceived, eschewing needless elaboration. Try a warm salad of chorizo, pancetta and sautéed potatoes with piquillo pepper dressing, followed by a roast leg of chicken with tarragon cream sauce. Pastry is exquisite too.

Chef: Russell Brown **Owners:** Russell & Elena Brown **Times:** 12-2/7-9.30, Closed 2 wks Feb/Mar, 2 wks Sep/Oct, Sun-Mon **Prices:** Fixed L £15.50, Fixed D fr £32, Coffee £2.50, Min/Water £2.50, Service optional **Wine:** 20 bottles over £20, 15 bottles under £20, 6 by the glass (£3.65-£5.70) **Seats:** 15 **Smoking:** N/Sm in restaurant, Air con **Children:** Min 10 yrs **Directions:** Near top of town rdbt in Dorchester **Parking:** Top of town car park, on street

One Rosette

Excellent local restaurants serving food prepared with care, understanding and skill, using good quality ingredients. These restaurants stand out in their local area.

Yalbury Cottage

Modern British

A quintessentially English country cottage with an idyllic, tranquil feel

☎ 01305 262382 Lower Bockhampton DT2 8PZ
e-mail: yalburyemails@aol.com
web: www.yalburycottage.com

This small hamlet was the inspiration for the village of Mellstock in Thomas Hardy's *Under the Greenwood Tree*. The 300-year-old thatched cottage (in its time home to both the keeper of the water meadow and a local shepherd) that houses the restaurant is steeped in tradition, replete with inglenook fireplaces, oak beams and exposed stonework - yet it's in no sense old-fashioned. The food itself puts an inventive twist on all things Great and British, with a soupçon of France and Italy thrown in for good measure. Thus you might expect to start with a smoked chicken Caesar salad followed by slow-roasted Dorset Horn lamb, and finish with buttermilk and citrus pannacotta.

Chef: Ben Streak **Owners:** Fiddemont Hotels Ltd **Times:** 7-9, Closed 2 wks Jan, Closed L all week **Prices:** Fixed D £32, Coffee £1.75, Min/Water £3, Group min 10 service 10% **Wine:** 11 bottles over £20, 17 bottles under £20, 3 by the glass (£3.60) **Seats:** 24 **Smoking:** N/Sm in restaurant **Children:** Portions **Rooms:** 8 (8 en suite) ♦♦♦♦♦ **Directions:** 2m E of Dorchester, off A35 **Parking:** 15

EVERSHOT MAP 04 ST50

The Acorn Inn

British, Mediterranean

Village inn of literary legend and local fare

☎ 01935 83228 DT2 0JW
e-mail: stay@acorn-inn.co.uk
web: www.acorn-inn.co.uk

Called The Sow and Acorn from *Tess of the D'Urbervilles* by Thomas Hardy, this 16th-century stone-built inn has a lovely village setting in the heart of Thomas Hardy country. Historic features include beams, flagstone floors, oak panelling and open fires. A good choice of food ranges from a popular bar menu to more formal fare in the cosy restaurant. Local produce figures strongly with dishes of pan-fried fillet of brill with white wine, feta and olive sauce, and slow-braised shank of Dorset lamb on parsnip and celeriac purée with a port wine reduction.

Times: 12-2/6.45-9.30 **Rooms:** 10 (10 en suite) ♦♦♦♦
Directions: 2m off A37, between Dorchester and Yeovil. In village centre

Summer Lodge Country House Hotel

EVERSHOT MAP 04 ST50

International NOTABLE WINE LIST

Idyllic, intimate retreat meets refined cooking

☎ 01935 482000 DT2 0JR
e-mail: summer@relaischateaux.com
web: www.summerlodgehotel.com

Nestling in a fold of the Dorset Downs in lovely grounds, this former dower house turned intimate, quintessential country-house hotel (designed in part by local architect and celebrated chronicler, Thomas Hardy no less), is a true hideaway, blessed with a picture-postcard village setting. There's an air of luxury and high quality about the interior, decked out in classic, chintzy country-house style. Service is predictably on the formal side (with cheese trolley, dessert wine trolley and roast trolleys for Sunday lunch), but appropriately friendly too, while the sommelier brings serious expertise to the classy wine list. The spacious, split-level dining room follows the theme, and is elegant and classically traditional with fabric-covered walls, fine table appointments and views over the gardens through full-length windows, while the rose- and honeysuckle-covered gazebo offers an enchanting alfresco summer option. The accomplished kitchen's modern focus, underpinned by a classical theme, suits the surroundings to a tee, focusing on prime local produce, its refined treatment displaying high skill, clean, clear flavours and modern presentation. Mains might include the signature roast loin of Dorset lamb and braised shoulder 'shepherd's pie' served with Savoy cabbage and a rosemary jus, while a hot passionfruit soufflé with a lychee sorbet and hot passionfruit sauce might rock your boat at dessert.

Notable Wine List: Award-winning, extensive wine list offering a comprehensive range of wines from around the world under the expert eye of cellarmaster Eric Zwiebel.

Chef: Steven Titman **Owners:** Beatrice Tollmans **Times:** 12-2.30/7-9.30 **Prices:** Fixed L £22, Fixed D £37.50, Main £48, Coffee £4, Min/Water £4, Service included, Group min 12 service 12.5% **Wine:** 804 bottles over £20, 12 bottles under £20, 8 by the glass (£5-£15) **Notes:** Set ALC 3 courses, Vegetarian available, Dress Restrictions, No shorts, T-shirts or sandals, jackets pref, Civ Wed 30 **Seats:** 48, Pr/dining room 12 **Smoking:** N/Sm in restaurant, Air con **Children:** Min 7 yrs D, Menu, Portions **Rooms:** 24 (24 en suite) ★★★★ **Directions:** 1.5m off A37 between Yeovil and Dorchester **Parking:** 60

FARNHAM MAP 04 ST91

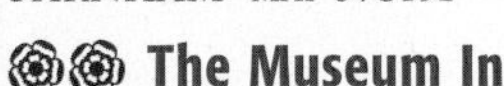

The Museum Inn

Modern, European

Modern British food in pretty setting

☎ 01725 516261 DT11 8DE
e-mail: enquiries@museuminn.co.uk
web: www.museuminn.co.uk

This historic part-thatched country pub was built in the 17th century to offer accommodation for the nearby museum. It has been sympathetically refurbished to create a traditional inn, separate restaurant (The Shed) and en suite accommodation. Local produce, organic where possible, is carefully sourced to find meat from traceable stock, free-range poultry and eggs, fish delivered daily from the South Coast and game from neighbouring estates. This attention to detail means dishes can be kept simple yet have impressive flavour. The menu ranges from tasty starters of French onion and thyme soup to mains of slow-roasted belly pork with cider apple sauce, colcannon potato and red wine jus or baby beetroot risotto, crème fraîche and parmesan crisps.

Chef: Daniel Turner **Owners:** Mark Stephenson, Vicky Elliot **Times:** 12-2/7-9.30, Closed 25 & 31 Dec **Prices:** Starter £5.50-£9, Main £12.50-£18.50, Dessert £4.50-£5.50, Coffee £2, Min/Water £3, Service optional **Wine:** 54 bottles over £20, 46 bottles under £20, 11 by the glass (£3-£6.50) **Seats:** 80, Pr/dining room 30 **Smoking:** N/Sm in restaurant **Children:** Min 10 yrs, Portions **Directions:** 12m S of Salisbury, 7m N of Blandford Forum on A354 **Parking:** 20

FONTMELL MAGNA MAP 04 ST81

The Crown Inn

British

Honest food in a cosy village inn

☎ 01747 811441 SP1 0PA
e-mail: crowninnfm@hotmail.com
web: www.crowninn.me.uk

Once part of the defunct Flowers Brewery of Fontmell, this traditional Georgian-style country inn has a farmhouse feel to it, with a cosy bar and a popular restaurant area with linen table cloths and heavy cutlery. The menus should appeal to all tastes and much of the simply prepared dishes feature local produce, including fish from Poole Bay and Lyme Bay and dairy products from the Blackmore Vale. Twice-baked Dorset Blue Vinney soufflé makes for a suitably regional dish, as does pan-fried Dorset lamb's liver with bacon and onion gravy.

Chef: Robin Davies **Owners:** Mrs & Mr AJ Neilson **Times:** 12-2.45/6.45-9, Closed 25 Dec **Prices:** Fixed L fr £9.95, Fixed D fr £12.95, Starter £4.75-£9.95, Main £8.95-£19.95, Dessert £4.75-£9.95, Coffee £1.85, Min/Water £2.95, Service optional **Wine:** 30 bottles over £20, 12 bottles under £20, 6 by the glass (£3.25-£4.25) **Notes:** Sun L 1 course £11.50, 2 courses £14.95, 3 courses £19.95, Vegetarian available **Seats:** 35 **Smoking:** N/Sm in restaurant, Air con **Children:** Min 9 yrs, Portions **Rooms:** 5 (3 en suite) ◆◆◆ **Directions:** On A350 towards Blandford S, pass through Cann & Compton Abbas villages - restaurant on x-rds centre of Fontmell Magna on right **Parking:** 17

GILLINGHAM MAP 04 ST82

®®® Stock Hill Country House Hotel & Restaurant

see below

LYME REGIS MAP 04 SY39

® Alexandra Hotel

British, International V

Attractively presented food in an elegant setting

☎ 01297 442010 Pound St DT7 3HZ
e-mail: enquiries@hotelalexandra.co.uk
web: www.hotelalexandra.co.uk

The plethora of model sailing ships, and marine and local pictures around this Grade II listed hotel leave you in no doubt that this elegant restaurant is by the sea, even if you miss the amazing view over Lyme Bay. The good value menu also leans towards the sea, though you'll find meaty choices amongst the seafood. A typical meal may start with blackened tiger prawns or Teriyaki duck breast with mango and coriander risotto, and continue with paupiette of plaice with spinach mousse, seared calves' liver with roasted garlic mash, or seafood lasagne.

Chef: David Percival **Owners:** Kathryn Richards **Times:** 12-2/7-9, Closed last Sun before Xmas-end Jan **Prices:** Fixed L fr £16.95, Fixed D fr £25.50, Min/Water £3, Service optional **Wine:** 36 bottles over £20, 32 bottles under £20, 6 by the glass (£2.50-£4.50) **Notes:** Coffee incl, Fixed L 3 courses, Fixed D 4 courses, Vegetarian menu, Dress Restrictions, Smart casual **Seats:** 60, Pr/dining room 24 **Smoking:** N/Sm in restaurant, Air con **Children:** Min 10 yrs, Menu, Portions **Rooms:** 26 (26 en suite) ★★★ HL **Directions:** From Bridport, follow A35 to Lyme Regis, through Chideock, Marcombe Lake, past Charmouth, take left at Charmouth rdbt, follow road for 2m **Parking:** 26

continued

Alexandra Hotel

®®®

Stock Hill Country House Hotel & Restaurant

GILLINGHAM MAP 04 ST82

British, European V

Classic cuisine with an Austrian twist in elegant country house

☎ 01747 823626 Stock Hill SP8 5NR
e-mail: reception@stockhillhouse.co.uk
web: www.stockhillhouse.co.uk

Set at the end of a beech-lined drive, this elegant, lovingly restored Victorian country house is set in 11 acres of attractive gardens. Luxurious décor in the period style with fine antique furnishings, rich fabrics, oil paintings and deep sofas grace public rooms, while the elegant dining room continues the theme with views over the manicured lawns from comfortable chairs and white-clothed tables. Service is friendly but efficient and sets the scene for chef-patron Peter Hauser's fine classical cuisine with its Austrian accent. Quality, fresh seasonal ingredients parade on Stock Hill's daily-changing menus, with meat sourced locally and fish fresh from Brixham, while herbs, fruit and vegetables come direct from the hotel's wall potager. Highly skilled technique, flair, balanced combinations and full-on flavours deliver on the repertoire, where the Austrian flag denotes specialities, such as supreme of chicken, dipped in egg and parmesan and shallow-fried, served with parsley new potatoes and a warm beetroot salad, and for dessert, perhaps a bitter chocolate, crystallised ginger and Grand Marnier mousse.

Chef: Peter Hauser, Lorna Connor **Owners:** Peter & Nita Hauser **Times:** 12.30-1.45/7.30-8.45, Closed L Sat & Mon **Prices:** Fixed L £26-£28, Fixed D £36-£38, Min/Water £3.60 **Wine:** 83 bottles over £20, 7 bottles under £20, 7 by the glass (£3.40-£5.40) **Notes:** Fixed L 3 courses, Fixed D 4 courses, Vegetarian menu, Dress Restrictions, No jeans or T-shirts **Seats:** 24, Pr/dining room 12 **Smoking:** N/Sm in restaurant **Children:** Min 7 yrs, Portions **Rooms:** 9 (9 en suite) ★★★ **Directions:** 3m E on B3081, off A303 **Parking:** 20

LYME REGIS *continued* MAP 04 SY39

Mariners Hotel

International

Good value food in hotel with sea views

☎ 01297 442753 Silver St DT7 3HS
e-mail: marinershotel@btopenworld.com
web: hotellymeregis.co.uk

Located in the heart of the town, this small, friendly hotel has plenty of period character and charm. A conversion from a 17th-century coaching inn, the hotel was immortalised by Beatrix Potter in her *Tale of Little Pig Robinson*. From the garden there are views of Lyme Bay and the surrounding countryside. Locally caught fish is a highlight on the menu: pan-fried monkfish is coated in Cajun spices and served with home-made spiced mango chutney, whilst whole grilled Dover sole may be served with lime and ginger butter.

Chef: Nick Larby **Owners:** Nick & Claire Larby **Times:** 12-2/7-9, Closed 27 Dec-28 Jan, Closed L Mon-Sat, D Sun **Prices:** Fixed D £21.50-£22.50, Coffee £1.50, Min/Water £3, Service optional **Wine:** 5 bottles over £20, 23 bottles under £20, 3 by the glass (£2.50-£5) **Seats:** 40 **Smoking:** N/Sm in restaurant **Children:** Min 10 yrs **Rooms:** 12 (12 en suite) ★★ HL **Directions:** Please telephone for directions **Parking:** 20

Rumours

British, French NEW

Friendly, family-run restaurant with emphasis on fresh local fish

☎ 01297 444740 14-15 Monmouth St DT7 3PX
e-mail: rumoursrestaurant@whsmithnet.co.uk
web: www.lyme-regis-charmouth.co.uk/rumours.

Located on a quiet side street in the old part of town and just a few minutes from the sea, Rumours is a very friendly, relaxed husband-and-wife affair; Lynda behind the stove. The repertoire is awash with the fruits of the sea, Lyme Bay-caught where possible. Local scallops seared with crispy Parma ham, on a rocket salad with lemon and honey dressing, and grilled Dover sole with tarragon butter might feature on the blackboard specials. There are plenty of non-fish options on the regular menu, too, and all the desserts are home-made. Intelligently simple presentation lets the quality fresh produce shine.

Chef: Lynda Skelton **Owners:** Lynda and Ron Skelton **Times:** 7-10, Closed Dec-Feb, Sun & Wed (open Sun Bank Hols), Closed L All week **Prices:** Starter £4.25-£7.50, Main £9.95-£19.95, Dessert £4.50-£4.95, Coffee £1.50, Service optional **Wine:** 1 bottle over £20, 21 bottles under £20, 3 by the glass (£2.95) **Notes:** Vegetarian available **Seats:** 26 **Smoking:** N/Sm in restaurant **Children:** Min 14 yrs **Directions:** Please telephone for directions **Parking:** On street 25 yds

MAIDEN NEWTON MAP 04 SY59

Le Petit Canard

Modern British

Pretty village restaurant, delicious dining

☎ 01300 320536 Dorchester Rd DT2 0BE
e-mail: craigs@le-petit-canard.co.uk
web: www.le-petit-canard.co.uk

Pretty, 350-year-old building in a conservation area contains a small but charming dining room with exposed brickwork and old beams highlighted by sensitive décor and lighting. Service is professional and attentive with a good knowledge of ingredients and the wine list.

continued

Menus are modern British in style with mainly French and some Asian influences evident in starters of goat's cheese and caramelised onion tartlet and the tenderloin of pork with a chilli-tamarind glaze. Try the local venison with red wine and redcurrant sauce before finishing with black pepper ice cream and mango sorbet.

Le Petit Canard

Chef: Gerry Craig **Owners:** Mr & Mrs G Craig **Times:** 12-2/7-9, Closed Mon, Closed L all week (ex 1st & 3rd Sun in month), D Sun **Prices:** Fixed D £29-£32, Coffee £2.50, Min/Water £3, Service optional **Wine:** 15 bottles over £20, 14 bottles under £20, 6 by the glass (£3.75-£4.75) **Notes:** Sun L 3 courses £9.50, Vegetarian available, Dress Restrictions, Smart casual preferred **Seats:** 28 **Smoking:** N/Sm in restaurant **Children:** Min 12 yrs **Directions:** In centre of Maiden Newton, 8m W of Dorchester **Parking:** On street/village car park

POOLE MAP 04 SZ09

Harbour Heights Hotel

Modern British, International

Contemporary bistro commanding the best views across Poole Harbour

☎ 01202 707272 73 Haven Rd, Sandbanks BH13 7LW
e-mail: enquiries@harbourheights.net
web: www.fjbhotels.co.uk

continued

England

POOLE *continued* MAP 04 SZ09

The name gives a clue to this modern, stylish seaside hotel's plum drawcard; a contemporary 'Harbar' bistro with floor-to-ceiling picture windows and a sun terrace (for alfresco summer dining) that offers panoramic views across Poole Harbour. It's a smart, open-planned affair of lounge, bar and restaurant, the latter decked out with modern polished-wood tables and matching chairs with brown leather upholstery. Service is relaxed, efficient and friendly, while the kitchen's modern brasserie approach suits the surroundings, with skilfully prepared, well-presented and conceived dishes that utilise quality local ingredients. Think wild Portland sea bass with vanilla butter vinaigrette, dandelion and linguine, and perhaps a warm chocolate fondant finish, served with pistachio ice cream.

Chef: Glen Elie **Owners:** FJB Hotels **Times:** 12-2.30/7-9.30 **Prices:** Fixed L fr £17.50, Fixed D fr £28.25, Starter £5.85-£15.20, Main £13-£19.90, Dessert £5.85, Coffee £2.25, Min/Water £3.50, Service optional **Wine:** 348 bottles over £20, 9 bottles under £20, 11 by the glass (£3.75-£8.60) **Notes:** Vegetarian available, Dress Restrictions, Smart casual, Civ Wed 120 **Seats:** 90, Pr/dining room 120 **Smoking:** N/Sm in restaurant, Air con **Children:** Menu, Portions **Rooms:** 38 (38 en suite) ★★★★ HL **Directions:** From A338 follow signs to Sandbanks, restaurant on left past Canford Cliffs **Parking:** 80

Haven Hotel

Modern British V

Fine dining with stunning sea views

☎ 01202 707333 Banks Rd, Sandbanks BH13 7QL
e-mail: reservations@havenhotel.co.uk
web: www.havenhotel.co.uk

With unrivalled views over the entrance to Poole Harbour, La Roche has an interesting claim to fame as the location of many of Marconi's first experiments in radio. The restaurant has a relaxed atmosphere with chic modern décor and formal table service. The menu offers locally sourced seasonal produce in British dishes with an emphasis on seafood. Fish specials often include fresh lobster or catch of the day. Starters might include salad of locally caught crab with mango, snow pea and orange cardamom dressing. For a substantial main course, try 21-day matured Twelve Green Acres organic beef, served with creamed leeks, truffle croquette and red wine jus, with Valrhona chocolate pudding with gingerbread ice cream and chocolate wafers to finish.

continued

Chef: Carl France **Owners:** Mr J Butterworth **Times:** 12-2/7-9, Closed Xmas, Mon (winter), Closed D Sun (winter) **Prices:** Starter £5.50-£9.50, Main £11.50-£17.95, Dessert £6.50-£7.50, Coffee £1.95, Min/Water £3.50, Service optional **Wine:** 46 bottles over £20, 21 bottles under £20, 8 by the glass (£3.25-£8.50) **Notes:** Vegetarian menu, Dress Restrictions, No shorts or beach wear, Civ Wed 180 **Seats:** 59, Pr/dining room 160 **Smoking:** N/Sm in restaurant, Air con **Children:** Menu, Portions **Rooms:** 78 (78 en suite) ★★★★ HL **Directions:** Follow signs to Sandbanks Peninsula; hotel next to Swanage ferry departure point **Parking:** 90

Mansion House Hotel

Modern British

Modern cooking in an exclusive townhouse setting

☎ 01202 685666 Thames St BH15 1JN
e-mail: enquiries@themansionhouse.co.uk
web: www.themansionhouse.co.uk

This elegant Georgian townhouse is peacefully located in a cobbled mews, just a pebble's skim from Poole's vibrant quayside. Its smart restaurant has a clubby feel, with cherrywood-panelled walls, oil paintings and quality tableware. Expect straightforward modern British cooking with an emphasis on first-rate local ingredients, including fish from the nearby quay, meat, pheasant, pigeon and partridge from Dorset, and West Country cheeses. Home-cured beef is a typical starter, served with beetroot chutney and horseradish cream, while mains range from Dover sole with herb butter to more complex dishes such as baked haddock wrapped in pancake with sunblushed tomatoes, flageolet beans and pancetta, or beef with aubergine purée, caramelized endive, and a Madeira and garlic sauce.

Chef: Gerry Godden & Darren Rockett **Owners:** Jackie & Gerry Godden **Times:** 12-2/7-9.30, Closed L Sat, D Sun (ex BHs) **Prices:** Fixed L £15.50-£17.50, Fixed D £27.50-£29.50, Coffee £2, Min/Water £2.80, Service optional **Wine:** 86 bottles over £20, 42 bottles under £20, 10 by the glass (£3.25-£5.50) **Notes:** Sun L available, Vegetarian available, Dress Restrictions, Smart casual, Civ Wed 35 **Seats:** 85, Pr/dining room 36 **Smoking:** N/Sm in restaurant, Air con **Children:** Menu, Portions **Rooms:** 32 (32 en suite) ★★★ HL **Directions:** A350 into town centre follow signs to Channel Ferry/Poole Quay, left at bridge, 1st left is Thames St **Parking:** 46

❀ Sandbanks Hotel

European

Beachside, conservatory-style brasserie with exciting menu

☎ 01202 707377 15 Banks Rd, Sandbanks BH13 7PS
e-mail: reservations@sandbankshotel.co.uk
web: www.fjbhotels.co.uk

This waterfront hotel's aptly named Sands Brasserie, with its minimalist-styled, glass-walled dining room and fair-weather terrace overlooking the beach, comes awash with stunning views across Poole Bay. Unsurprising perhaps, the modern-focused carte has a suitably sunny, Mediterranean tilt, too. The freshest local ingredients are delivered in assured, well-presented and clear-flavoured dishes. Start with hand-made blue crab lasagne, shellfish bisque and Avruga caviar or Somerset belly pork beignet with Japanese panko breadcrumbs and fine green bean salad, followed by chargrilled salmon, watercress risotto and smoked mussels.

Chef: Stephan Jouan **Owners:** Mr J Butterworth **Times:** 12-3/6-10, Closed D Sun-Tue **Prices:** Fixed L fr £14.50, Fixed D fr £19.50, Starter £6.50-£9.50, Main £13.50-£19, Dessert £6.50-£6.90, Coffee £2.35, Min/Water £3.50, Service optional **Wine:** 62 bottles over £20, 21 bottles under £20, 6 by the glass (£3.90-£5.25) **Notes:** Vegetarian available, Dress Restrictions, No jeans, smart casual, Civ Wed 40 **Seats:** 65, Pr/dining room 40 **Smoking:** N/Sm in restaurant, Air con **Children:** Menu, Portions **Rooms:** 110 (110 en suite) ★★★★ HL **Directions:** From Poole or Bournemouth, follow signs to Sandbanks Peninsula. Hotel on left **Parking:** 130

PORTLAND MAP 04 SY67

❀ The Bluefish Restaurant

Modern European

Relaxed dining in simple surroundings

☎ 01305 822991 15-17a Chiswell DT5 1AN
e-mail: thebluefish@tesco.net
web: www.thebluefishcafe.co.uk

This 400-year-old Portland stone building houses a rustic yet stylish restaurant. You can eat outside when it's fine, or sit in one of the two interconnecting dining rooms under starry little lights. Lunch is very relaxed, with a bit more formality injected at dinner. Despite the name you'll find meat and vegetarian choices on the modern European menu. Starters include confit belly of pork and tiger prawn with creamed artichoke purée with honey and soy, followed by braised shoulder of venison and celeriac purée.

The Bluefish Restaurant

Chef: Luciano Da Silva **Owners:** Jo & Luciano Da Silva **Times:** 12-3/6.30-10, Closed L Times seasonal, D Times seasonal **Prices:** Starter £4.50-£9.50, Main £10.50-£15.50, Dessert £4.50, Coffee £1.10, Min/Water £2.50, Group min 8 service 10% **Wine:** Nearly all bottles under £20, 6 by the glass (£2.75-£5.50) **Notes:** Vegetarian available, Smart casual **Seats:** 35 **Smoking:** N/Sm in restaurant **Children:** Portions **Directions:** Take A354 by Chesil Bank, off Victoria Square in Portland, over rdbt towards Chesil Beach **Parking:** 72-hr free car park, on street

SHAFTESBURY MAP 04 ST82

❀❀ La Fleur de Lys Restaurant with Rooms

Modern European

Smart restaurant with rooms to suit all tastes

☎ 01747 853717 Bleke St SP7 8AW
e-mail: info@fleurdelys.co.uk
web: www.lafleurdelys.co.uk

Located just a few minutes' walk from the famous Gold Hill, this light and airy restaurant with rooms has undergone major refurbishment, and combines efficient service within a relaxed and friendly atmosphere. The elegant, L-shaped dining room, with conservatory extension, comes decked out in beige carpet, white cloths and Queen Anne-style upholstered chairs. A comfortable lounge for pre-dinner drinks rounds off the package. The kitchen's approach is modern focused, underpinned by a classical French theme. Straightforward, accomplished dishes, with some interesting combinations, utilise

continued

SHAFTESBURY *continued* MAP 04 ST82

quality, seasonal ingredients and confident delivery and presentation. Expect dishes such as saddle of local roe venison with figs and Armagnac or lobster ravioli, scallops, lemon and caviar sauce.

Chef: D Shepherd & M Preston **Owners:** D Shepherd, M Preston & M Griffin **Times:** 12-2.30/7-10.30, Closed 3 wks Jan, Closed L Mon & Tue, D Sun **Prices:** Fixed L £24, Fixed D £29, Starter £6-£12, Main £20-£25, Dessert £6-£10, Coffee £3, Min/Water £3, Service optional **Wine:** 150 bottles over £20, 30 bottles under £20, 10 by the glass (£3.50-£7.50) **Notes:** Dress Restrictions, Smart casual, no T-shirts or dirty clothes **Seats:** 45, Pr/dining room 12 **Smoking:** N/Sm in restaurant **Children:** Portions **Rooms:** 7 (7 en suite) ★★★★ RR **Directions:** Junct A350/A30 **Parking:** 10

❀ Royal Chase Hotel

Modern British

Imaginative cooking in friendly, formal surroundings

☎ 01747 853355 Royal Chase Roundabout SP7 8DB
e-mail: royalchasehotel@btinternet.com
web: www.theroyalchasehotel.co.uk

Once a monastery and now said to be haunted by a monk, this hotel has an intimate dining room with friendly and formal service. The modern British cooking uses ingredients from local suppliers whenever possible in imaginatively presented dishes. Typical dishes are local smoked trout and halibut terrine, with fennel and aïoli brioche, marinated rack of pork smoked with lemon and ginger, warm Rosary goat's cheese, tomato and red onion tart, with steamed lemon and lime pudding accompanied by tangy lemon curd sauce to finish.

Chef: Stuart Robbins **Owners:** Travel West Inns **Times:** 12-2/7-9.30 **Prices:** Fixed L £10.95, Starter £3.75-£5.50, Main £11.95-£17.95, Dessert £4.50-£6.25, Coffee £2, Min/Water £3.60 **Wine:** 9 bottles over £20, 39 bottles under £20, 4 by the glass (£3-£4.40) **Notes:** Sun L starter £3.95, main £7.95, dessert £3.95, Vegetarian available, Civ Wed 78 **Seats:** 65, Pr/dining room 120 **Smoking:** N/Sm in restaurant **Children:** Menu, Portions **Rooms:** 33 (33 en suite) ★★★ HL **Directions:** On rdbt at A350 & A30 junction (avoid town centre) **Parking:** 100

see advert opposite

❀❀ Wayfarers Restaurant

Modern European

Contemporary inn with intriguing tastes

☎ 01747 852821 Sherborne Causeway SP7 9PX
e-mail: mark.newtonwayfarers@tesco.net
web: www.wayfarersdorset.co.uk

With its stone walls, beamed ceiling and inglenook fireplace, this 18th-century cottage makes a cosy setting for a contemporary restaurant. The walls are hung with the chef's modern art, bringing individuality to the atmosphere of the restaurant. French and Mediterranean flavours predominate at the Wayfarers, where the ambitious kitchen likes to tease guests with unexpected combinations. With presentation always enticing, expect dishes like seared king scallops on parsnip with lightly curried parsnip fondant and parsnip crisps, followed by slow-roast pork belly in Chinese spice with saddle of venison in tea and spices.

Chef: Mark Newton **Owners:** Clare & Mark Newton **Times:** 12-1.30/7-9 Closed 3 wks after 25 Dec, 2 wks June/Jul, Mon, closed L Sat and Tue, closed D Sun **Prices:** Fixed L fr £23, Fixed D fr £23 **Notes:** Sun L 4 courses £24, Vegetarian available, Dress Restrictions, Smart casual, no sportswear **Seats:** 34 **Smoking:** N/Sm in restaurant **Children:** Min 8yrs **Rooms:** 1 (1 en suite) ◆◆◆◆ **Directions:** 2m W of Shaftesbury on A30 to Sherborne and Yeovil **Parking:** 30

SHERBORNE MAP 04 ST61

❀❀ *Eastbury Hotel*

British, European

Handsome Georgian property serving modern British cuisine

☎ 01935 813131 Long St DT9 3BY
e-mail: enquiries@theeastburyhotel.com
web: www.theeastburyhotel.co.uk

The Eastbury is an elegant townhouse, five minutes walk from the historic abbey, with extensive gardens and secure parking to the rear. It offers a choice of lounges in which to enjoy a drink and mull over the menu before entering the restaurant, a split-level conservatory, with great character and appeal, overlooking the walled garden. Good sized tables are well spaced and the chairs comfortably upholstered. There is also a terrace for summer dining. The style of cooking suits a varied clientele, attracting residents and non-residents alike. Dorset produce stars in dishes of seared scallops with red pepper coulis and breast of guinea fowl with prune stuffing and Armagnac sauce.

Times: 12-2/7-9.30 **Rooms:** 21 (21 en suite) ★★★ **Directions:** 5m E of Yeovil, follow brown signs for The Eastbury Hotel

❀❀ The Green

Modern European

Modern cooking in a popular West Country location

☎ 01935 813821 3 The Green DT9 3HY
web: www.thegreensherborne.co.uk

The smart green painted woodwork makes this attractive old stone Grade II listed property easy to spot. Inside, the character of the old building remains in the exposed beams. The period ground floor restaurant is complemented by private dining on the first floor. Relaxed, friendly service makes this a great choice for an enjoyable meal. Cooking is modern European in style with simple but stylish

continued

presentation from a talented team. You might try an adventurous starter like pink roasted pigeon breast, savoury Puy lentils, parsnip crisps and tarragon dressing followed by Cornish brill with mussels, saffron, artichokes and thyme.

Chef: Michael Rust **Owners:** Michael & Judith Rust **Times:** 12-2/7-9, Closed 2 wks Jan,1 wk Jun,1 wk Sept,BHs,Xmas, Sun-Mon **Prices:** Fixed L £14.45-£22.45, Fixed D £28.95, Coffee £1.70, Min/Water £2.40, Service optional **Wine:** 21 bottles over £20, 25 bottles under £20, 19 by the glass (£3.65-£5.55) **Seats:** 40, Pr/dining room 25 **Smoking:** N/Sm in restaurant **Parking:** on street, car park

---

TARRANT MONKTON MAP 04 ST90

The Langton Arms

Modern European NEW

Refurbished country inn serving modern food

☎ 01258 830225 DT11 8RX
e-mail: info@thelangtonarms.co.uk
web: www.thelangtonarms.co.uk

Colourful hanging baskets in summer mark out this refurbished, traditional, 17th-century thatched inn tucked away in a sleepy Dorset village. The relaxed Stables Restaurant has a small lounge with an intimate inner dining room and light and airy conservatory overlooking the beautiful countryside, both displaying a local artist's paintings on the walls. The European cooking with modern twists takes on a straightforward, unfussy approach, making sound use of quality local ingredients, especially Dorset Down rare breed beef, lamb, pork, chicken and game. Expect mains like chargrilled venison steak with sweet potatoes and slow gin and rosemary sauce.

Chef: Francis Baumer **Owners:** Barbara & James Cossins **Times:** 12-2.30/7-12 (Last Orders 9), Closed Mon & Tue, Closed L Wed to Sat, D Sun **Prices:** Fixed L £16.95-£27.95, Fixed D £19.95-£30.95, Coffee £2.25, Min/Water £2.60, Service optional **Wine:** 12 bottles over £20, 17 bottles under £20, 7 by the glass (£2.95-£4.25) **Notes:** Vegetarian available, Civ Wed 50 **Seats:** 40, Pr/dining room 24 **Smoking:** N/Sm in restaurant **Children:** Menu, Portions **Rooms:** 6 (6 en suite) ◆◆◆◆ **Parking:** 100

WAREHAM

Kemps Hotel

Modern British

Quiet country house with simple, effective cuisine

☎ 01929 462563 East Stoke BH20 6AL
e-mail: kemps@hollybushhotels.co.uk
web: www.kempshotel.com

This former Victorian rectory has well-kept grounds and overlooks the Purbeck Hills and the Frome Valley. There's a formal, yet friendly atmosphere to the cosy, low-lit dining room while the conservatory is a lovely spot for lunch as it overlooks the gardens; service is professional and unobtrusive. The cooking is simple, unpretentious and enjoyable with clear, unfussy menus delivering every dish exactly as promised. A typical meal might consist of braised pigeon with lentils, followed by grilled sea bass fillets with sautéed wild mushrooms, then saffron poached pear with chocolate sauce.

Chef: Anton Goodwin **Owners:** Holly Bush Hotels **Times:** 12-2/7-9.30, Closed L Sat **Prices:** Fixed L fr £15, Fixed D fr £26, Coffee £2.25, Min/Water £2.75, Service optional **Wine:** 12 bottles over £20, 18 bottles under £20, 4 by the glass (£4-£5.50) **Notes:** Smart casual **Seats:** 66, Pr/dining room 100 **Smoking:** N/Sm in restaurant **Children:** Min L only, Portions **Rooms:** 14 (14 en suite) ★★ CHH **Directions:** On A352 midway between Wareham and Wool **Parking:** 50

WEYMOUTH MAP 04 SY67

Glenburn Hotel

European, Pacific Rim

Friendly, relaxed seaside hotel dining

☎ 01305 832353 42 Preston Rd DT3 6PZ
e-mail: info@glenburnhotel.com
web: www.glenburnhotel.com

A comfortable family-run hotel close to the seafront, with ample parking and attractive gardens. The restaurant has a relaxed, modern feel and good views. The menu offers daily specials and is European in style, typically featuring local produce in a variety of salad, pasta, fish, steak and chicken dishes. Vegetarians are particularly well catered for with a special menu if booked in advance. Try a main course like whole baked Dorset mackerel stuffed with fresh herbs on lemon couscous.

Times: 6.30-9.30, Closed Xmas-31 Dec, Sun (ex residents), Closed L Mon-Sun (ex functions) **Rooms:** 13 (13 en suite) ★★ HL **Directions:** 1m from town centre on A353. From town follow beach road by sea wall, hotel 500yds on right

Moonfleet Manor

Modern British

Top-notch cooking in an enchanting hideaway

☎ 01305 786948 Fleet DT3 4ED
e-mail: info@moonfleetmanor.com
web: www.moonfleetmanor.com

Popular with young families, this enchanting Georgian house is tucked

continued

WEYMOUTH *continued* MAP 04 SY67

away in the village of Fleet, overlooking Chesil Bay and the sea. Its airy restaurant is a relaxed and informal venue staffed by a friendly and attentive waiting team, who deliver tempting dishes of acclaimed modern British cuisine. Tease your taste buds with a starter of pan-fried squab pigeon with a fine bean and foie gras salad, before tucking into loin of venison with buttered spinach, rösti potatoes and poached blackberries, and desserts such as hot Grand Marnier soufflé with vanilla anglaise and berry compôte.

Chef: Tony Smith **Owners:** Mr A Davies (von Essen) **Times:** 12.30-2.00/7-9.30 **Prices:** Fixed D £30-£32.50, Coffee £1.75, Min/Water £3, Group min 10 service 10% **Wine:** 60 bottles over £20, 10 bottles under £20, 4 by the glass (£3.75-£7.50) **Notes:** Vegetarian available, Dress Restrictions, Smart casual preferred **Seats:** 80, Pr/dining room 12 **Smoking:** N/Sm in restaurant **Children:** Portions **Rooms:** 36 (36 en suite) ★★★ HL **Directions:** A354 from Dorchester, right into Weymouth at Manor Rdbt, right at next rdbt, left at next rdbt, up hill (B3157) then left, 2m towards sea **Parking:** 60

Perry's Restaurant

Modern British

Satisfying food in a pleasant harbourside location

☎ 01305 785799 4 Trinity Rd,
The Old Harbour DT4 8TJ
e-mail: enquiries@perrysrestaurant.co.uk
web: www.perrysrestaurant.co.uk

A former merchant's house facing the harbour (ask for a table with a harbour view if you can), this unpretentious eatery has been serving up food to Weymouth diners for over 15 years with the kind of consistency most restaurateurs can only dream of. Fish, as you would hope, is prominent on this attractive-sounding menu, but local pork, beef and cheeses all play their part. You might start with a robust chicken liver pâté, continue with gusto on to a hearty plate of beef fillet with green peppercorn sauce and, if you still have room, a warm treacle tart with marmalade ice cream.

Chef: Andy Pike **Owners:** A, V & R Hodder **Times:** 12-2/7-9.30, Closed 25-27 Dec,1 Jan, Sun & Mon (winter), Closed L Mon & Sat **Prices:** Starter £4.95-£7.95, Main £10.95-£17.95, Dessert £4.95, Coffee £1.70, Min/Water £2.75, Service optional **Wine:** 16 bottles over £20, 32 bottles under £20, 2 by the glass (£2.50) **Notes:** Vegetarian available **Seats:** 60, Pr/dining room 30 **Smoking:** N/Sm in restaurant **Children:** Portions **Directions:** On western side of old harbour - follow signs for Brewers Quay **Parking:** On street or Brewers Quay car park (200yds)

WIMBORNE MINSTER MAP 05 SZ09

Les Bouviers Restaurant & Hotel

Modern French V

Well established restaurant outside town

☎ 01202 889555 Arrowsmith Rd,
Canford Magna BH21 3BD
e-mail: info@lesbouviers.co.uk
web: www.lesbouviers.co.uk

Smart and welcoming, Les Bouviers is set in tranquil grounds, complete with lake and stream. The modern, country-house style dining room offers a regularly changing set menu and formal à la carte extended by a 7-course surprise menu and a Menu Gourmand. Expect dishes such as assiette of duck starter, followed by wild loin of venison, rosemary and chorizo sausage, and hot chocolate and tarragon soufflé to finish. Alfresco dining is available in warmer weather.

Chef: James Coward **Owners:** James & Kate Coward **Times:** 12-2.15/7-10 **Prices:** Fixed L fr £16.95, Fixed D fr £29.95, Main £35-£40, Coffee £3.25, Min/Water £3.50, Service optional, Group min 8 service 10% **Wine:** 153 bottles over £20, 172 bottles under £20, 18 by the glass (£3.50-£12.75) **Notes:** Fixed D 4 courses, ALC prices min 2 courses, max 3 courses, Vegetarian menu, Dress Restrictions, No jeans or shorts, Civ Wed 100 **Seats:** 50, Pr/dining room 150 **Smoking:** N/Sm area, Air con **Children:** Menu, Portions **Directions:** 1.5m S of Wimborne on A349, turn left on A341, turn right after 1m into Arrowsmith Rd **Parking:** 40

England

CO DURHAM

BEAMISH MAP 19 NZ25

Beamish Park Hotel

Modern International

International bistro dining in jazzy, modern surroundings

☎ 01207 230666 Beamish Burn Rd NE16 5EG
e-mail: reception@beamish-park-hotel.co.uk
web: www.beamish-park-hotel.co.uk

Situated in beautiful countryside, this stylish, split-level modern hotel restaurant courts controversy with its jazzy décor, daring furry curtains and jazz figurines. Colours, though, are subtle Mediterranean and the conservatory has good views and background music at a proper level. Service is relaxed and helpful. You can take coffee on a small terrace adjoining the dining room. Dishes here are modern British in style with occasional French and Asian influences and based on local seasonal produce. Try the lamb and lime leaf kebab with peanut and lime dressing before a main course of juicy Craster smoked mackerel on roasted garlic pommes purée. Finish with white chocolate and raspberry crème brûlée.

Chef: Christopher Walker **Owners:** William Walker **Times:** 12-2.30/7-10.30 **Prices:** Fixed D £12.95, Starter £3.50-£6.25, Main £9.50-£18, Dessert £4.75-£4.95, Coffee £1.60, Min/Water £3.75, Service optional **Wine:** 7 bottles over £20, 18 bottles under £20, 7 by the glass (£2.60-£3.30) **Notes:** Vegetarian available, Dress Restrictions, Smart casual preferred **Seats:** 70, Pr/dining room 80 **Smoking:** N/Sm area, Air con **Children:** Portions **Rooms:** 47 (47 en suite) ★★★ HL **Directions:** A1(M) turn off onto A692, continue for 2m into Sunniside. At traffic lights take A6076 signposted Beamish Museum & Tanfield Museum. Hotel is situated behind Causey Arch Inn **Parking:** 100

DARLINGTON MAP 19 NZ21

Hall Garth Hotel

Modern British

16th-century manor with short modern menu

☎ 01325 300400 Coatham Mundeville DL1 3LU
e-mail: hallgerth@corushotels.com
web: www.corushotels.com

A 16th-century manor house just off the A1(M), now a hotel offering golf, leisure and conference facilities. Expect civilised country-house style lounges warmed by log fires, a relaxed atmosphere enhanced by soft music, and good views over the grounds from Hugo's, an intimate candlelit restaurant. Cooking is traditional and straightforward using good ingredients. The short menu focuses on British fare, perhaps taking in rillette of pork with apple chutney, seared salmon with white wine and prawn cream sauce, and sticky toffee pudding. Service is friendly from a mostly young team.

Times: 7-9.30 **Rooms:** 51 (51 en suite) ★★★ HL **Directions:** A1(M) junct 59 (A167) (Darlington), top of hill turn left signed Brafferton, hotel 200yds on right

Headlam Hall

Modern British

Interesting modern dishes served in a Jacobean hall

☎ 01325 730238 Headlam, Gainford DL2 3HA
e-mail: admin@headlamhall.co.uk
web: www.headlamhall.co.uk

A grand 17th-century mansion, Headlam Hall is set in beautiful walled gardens and its own nine-hole golf course surrounded by rolling countryside. The restaurant is divided into four areas, with distinctive and contrasting styles, from the airy patio room to the splendour of the panelled dining room. A menu of modern dishes is based on locally supplied fresh ingredients wherever possible, and includes spaghetti with crab, chilli and garlic, caramelised pork fillet with potato and apple rösti and roast garlic jus, and rich chocolate tart with red berry ice cream.

Chef: Austen Shaw **Owners:** JH Robinson **Times:** 12-2.30/7-9.30, Closed 25-26 Dec **Prices:** Fixed L £12.50-£17.50, Starter £5-£8, Main £12-£18, Dessert £5-£8, Coffee £2, Min/Water £2.50, Service included **Wine:** 40 bottles over £20, 20 bottles under £20, 6 by the glass (£3.25-£8.50) **Notes:** Fixed L 3 courses, Dress Restrictions, No sportswear or shorts, Civ Wed 150 **Seats:** 70, Pr/dining room 30 **Smoking:** N/Sm in restaurant **Children:** Menu, Portions **Rooms:** 34 (34 en suite) ★★★ HL **Directions:** 8m W of Darlington off A67 **Parking:** 70

DURHAM MAP 19 NZ24

Bistro 21

British, European

Stylish bistro offering popular cuisine

☎ 0191 384 4354 Aykley Heads House, Aykley Heads DH1 5TS

Part of a small group of local restaurants and owned by Terry Laybourne, this is a popular modern bistro-style restaurant offering some of the owner's famous signature dishes. Originally an 18th-century farmhouse, many original features remain, such as the wooden and stone floors and inner courtyard. A modern business park has sprung up around it, providing a ready supply of clientele happy to fill the seats at lunch or dinner. Consistent and accurate

continued

England

DURHAM *continued* MAP 19 NZ24

cooking produces great flavour in dishes like slow-cooked shoulder of pork with braised cabbage, black pudding mash and crispy crackling.

Times: 12-2/7-10.25, Closed 25 Dec, 1Jan, BHs, Sun **Directions:** Off B6532 from Durham centre, pass County Hall on right and Dryburn Hospital on left. Turn right at double rdbt into Aykley Heads

ROMALDKIRK MAP 19 NY92

Rose & Crown Hotel

Modern British

Cosy country inn in a quintessential English setting

☎ 01833 650213 DL12 9EB
e-mail: hotel@rose-and-crown.co.uk
web: www.rose-and-crown.co.uk

Secreted away in a picture-postcard Teesdale village, this sophisticated but informal and relaxed, 18th-century coaching inn sits on the village green opposite the old stocks and water pump and next to the Saxon church, and oozes charm and character. Eat in the bar with its crackling fire, carriage lamps and old settle and prints, or the traditionally styled oak-panelled restaurant replete with starched white linen and evening candlelight. The kitchen appropriately showcases well-executed, clear-flavoured classic British fare with modern and regional influences; think roast breast of Lunesdale duckling with a sage and onion pudding, compôte of fruit and port and orange sauce, and, to finish, perhaps a sticky walnut tart with Amaretto ice cream.

continued

Rose & Crown Hotel

Chef: Chris Davy, Andrew Lee **Owners:** Mr & Mrs C Davy **Times:** 12-1.30/7.30-9, Closed Xmas, Closed L Mon-Sat **Prices:** Fixed L £16.75-£18.50, Fixed D £26-£28.75, Coffee £1.75, Min/Water £3, Service optional **Wine:** 22 bottles over £20, 26 bottles under £20, 8 by the glass (£3.05-£4.55) **Notes:** Fixed L 3 courses, Fixed D 4 courses, Vegetarian available **Seats:** 24 **Smoking:** N/Sm in restaurant **Children:** Min 6 yrs, Portions **Rooms:** 12 (12 en suite) ★★ HL **Directions:** 6m NW of Barnard Castle on B6277 **Parking:** 24

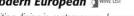

Seaham Hall Hotel - The White Room Restaurant

SEAHAM MAP 19 NZ44

Modern European NOTABLE WINE LIST

Exciting dining in contemporary, luxury spa hotel

☎ 0191 516 1400 Lord Byron's Walk SR7 7AG
e-mail: reservations@seaham-hall.com
web: www.seaham-hall.com

In 1815 Lord Byron married Annabella Milbanke here, and stayed on for their honeymoon, no doubt, benefiting from the bracing North Sea coastal ozone. This imposing, listed hotel with its 19th-century façade, stylish, modern interiors and lavish spa facilities continues to attract visitors from far and wide. The contemporary theme continues in the dining room with wooden floors, neutral colours and quality furnishings creating a calm and comfortable ambience. Fully draped tables have expensive settings, and service is formal and discreet. Adventurous and skilfully executed combinations characterise unashamedly modern dishes that make full use of best quality ingredients. In between the numerous appetisers, amuses and extras, fit a starter of perfectly pan-fried veal sweetbreads with bee pollen, maple syrup, morels and crisp Parma ham or a main course of well-timed sea bass, spinach, parsley root purée, ceps and salsify. More exotica to finish with the kalamansi (lemon/grapefruit cross) soufflé, passionfruit sour and coconut sorbet.

Notable Wine List: A well-presented and chosen wine list with quality wine selections in all areas.

Chef: Stephen Smith **Owners:** Tom & Jocelyn Maxfield **Times:** 12-2.30/7-10 **Prices:** Fixed L £17.50, Starter £8-£16, Main £20-£34, Dessert £6-£11, Coffee £3.50, Min/Water £3.50, Service optional **Wine:** 100% bottles over £20, 6 by the glass (£5-£6.50) **Notes:** Menu Gourmand £65, Sun L £27.50, Afternoon Treats £17.50, Vegetarian available, Civ Wed 112 **Seats:** 55, Pr/dining room 20 **Smoking:** N/Sm in restaurant, Air con **Children:** Portions **Rooms:** 19 (19 en suite) ★★★★★ HL **Directions:** A19 at 1st exit signed B1404 Seaham and follow signs to Seaham Hall **Parking:** 150

ESSEX

BRENTWOOD MAP 06 TQ59

Marygreen Manor

French

Exciting dining in baronial setting

☎ 01277 225252 London Rd CM14 4NR
e-mail: info@marygreenmanor.co.uk
web: www.marygreenmanor.co.uk

Located in this striking 16th-century manor house, the dining room is the original baronial hall decorated in grand style complete with barley-twist columns and crests of arms. Clothed tables with formal settings and helpful staff create a pleasant dining ambience. Dishes on the carte and tasting menu are mostly French-inspired and based on seasonal produce. To start, try the roasted veal sweetbread flamed in cognac and served with braised chicory. Main courses include pan-fried John Dory with minted peas, girolles and sweet-and-sour verjuice. Finish with warm chocolate mousse and cherry sorbet.

Chef: Paul Peters **Owners:** Mr S Bhattessa **Times:** 12.30-2.30/7.15-10.15, Closed D Sun **Prices:** Fixed L £19.50, Fixed D £40, Coffee £3, Min/Water £3.50, Service included **Wine:** 114 bottles over £20, 24 bottles under £20, 7 by the glass (£4-£7.20) **Notes:** Tasting menu £49, Sun L £22.50, ALC 3 courses £40, Dress Restrictions, No jeans or trainers, Civ Wed 60 **Seats:** 80, Pr/dining room 85 **Smoking:** N/Sm in restaurant, Air con **Children:** Portions **Rooms:** 44 (44 en suite) ★★★★ **Directions:** 1m from Brentwood town centre, 0.5m from M25 junct 28 **Parking:** 100

CHELMSFORD MAP 06 TL70

New Street Brasserie

Modern, International

Brasserie dining in modern town-centre hotel

☎ 01245 268179 Atlantic Hotel, New St CM1 1PP
e-mail: info@atlantichotel.co.uk
web: www.newstreetbrasserie.com

Stylish modern seating and designer wall coverings and panels strike a contemporary note at the brasserie of this purpose-built, modern hotel. White-linen dressed tables and professional, yet relaxed service from uniformed staff fit the bill, too, while the hotel's funky open-plan public areas include a lounge bar. The cooking follows the modern approach with a relaxed brasserie style, delivering accomplished dishes using good quality produce. As in grilled scallops, roasted hazelnut and coriander butter, followed by lemon and sage roasted pork, with white chocolate and passionfruit cheesecake with coconut sorbet to finish.

continued

Chef: Jon Tindle **Owners:** Shahrohh Bagherzadeh **Times:** 12-3/6-10.30, Closed 27-30 Dec, Closed L Sat-Sun **Prices:** Fixed L £14.75-£18.95, Fixed D £18.95-£25, Starter £5.50-£10, Main £12-£25, Dessert £4.50-£7.50, Coffee £1.95, Min/Water £3.50, Service optional, Group min 10 service 10% **Wine:** 45 bottles over £20, 21 bottles under £20, 11 by the glass (£3.50-£8.50) **Notes:** Vegetarian available **Seats:** 100, Pr/dining room 35 **Smoking:** N/Sm in restaurant, Air con **Children:** Portions **Rooms:** 59 (59 en suite) ★★★ HL **Directions:** 5-minute walk from High Street **Parking:** 70

Russells

Modern British, French

Innovative cuisine in a converted barn

☎ 01245 478484 Bell St, Great Baddow CM2 7JF
e-mail: russellsrestaurant@hotmail.com
web: www.russellsrest.co.uk

Built in 1372 as a barn, the Grade II listed conversion now offers a lounge, bar area and restaurant divided into four areas. The décor is traditional and very smart with formal service. You will find modern English and French cuisine here with interesting twists. Starters might feature fresh large king scallops wrapped in Parma ham, griddled and served on a bed of rocket, with fresh orange-scented truffle oil. Main courses include a duo of prime English lamb, rack and fillet, with rosemary rösti, Puy lentils with quince, pea purée and a light port jus.

Chef: Barry Warren-Watson **Owners:** Mr B J Warren-Watson **Times:** 12-2.30/7-11.30, Closed 2 wks from 2 Jan, Mon, Closed L Sat, D Sun **Prices:** Fixed L £10-£20, Fixed D £15-£25, Starter £5.50-£11.95, Main £12.95-£21.95, Dessert £4.50-£6.50, Coffee £2.25, Min/Water £3.50, Service optional, Group min 10 service 15% **Wine:** 40 bottles over £20, 30 bottles under £20, 7 by the glass (£2.95-£4.95) **Notes:** Vegetarian available, Dress Restrictions, No jeans **Seats:** 70, Pr/dining room 36 **Smoking:** N/Sm in restaurant, Air con **Children:** Portions **Directions:** Please telephone for directions **Parking:** 40

COGGESHALL MAP 07 TL82

Baumann's Brasserie

British, French

Serious food in a light-hearted atmosphere

☎ 01376 561453 4-6 Stoneham St CO6 1TT
e-mail: food@baumannsbrasserie.co.uk
web: www.baumannsbrasserie.co.uk

Busy brasserie occupying a historic hall house in the heart of town. Clothed tables and an array of antique chairs are set against stripped floors and whitewashed walls hung with colourful paintings. The menu is gutsy, interesting, fresh and fun, offering an eclectic mix of well-

continued

England

COGGESHALL *continued* MAP 07 TL82

executed dishes. Expect the likes of bang bang chicken in a bag, toad in the hole or blanquette of veal with woodland mushroom and tarragon rice, followed by white peach and poppyseed parfait with pineapple salsa. Check out 'The Billingsgate Best' for daily fresh fish, and the light lunch for great value. Jazz nights feature.

Baumann's Brasserie

Chef: Mark Baumann, C Jeanneau **Owners:** Baumanns Brasserie Ltd **Times:** 12-2/7-9.30, Closed 2 wks Jan, Mon-Tue **Prices:** Fixed L £12.95, Fixed D £21, Starter £5.50-£8.50, Main £16.50-£19.50, Dessert £6.50, Coffee £1.40, Min/Water £2.75, Service optional **Wine:** 21 bottles over £20, 26 bottles under £20, 11 by the glass (£2.95-£6.95) **Notes:** Sun L £21 (incl coffee, petits fours), Vegetarian available **Seats:** 80 **Smoking:** N/Sm in restaurant **Children:** Portions **Directions:** A12 from Chelmsford, turn off at Kelvedon into Coggleshall, restaurant is in centre opposite The Clock Tower **Parking:** Opposite

---

COLCHESTER MAP 13 TL92

The Rose & Crown Hotel

Rosettes not confirmed at time of going to press

Casual contemporary dining in a traditional Tudor building

☎ 01206 866677 East St CO1 2TZ
e-mail: info@rose-and-crown.com
web: www.rose-and-crown.com

This 15th-century posting inn - said to be the oldest hotel in the oldest recorded town in England - retains much of its original character. Furniture has a contemporary look, which works well in the historic setting.
At the time of going to press we learned that the restaurant and type of cuisine had changed.

Times: 12-2/7-9.45, Closed 27-30 Dec, Closed D Sun **Prices:** Food prices not confirmed for 2007 **Notes:** Civ Wed 150 **Seats:** 80, Pr/dining room 50 **Smoking:** N/Sm in restaurant **Rooms:** 38 (38 en suite) ★★★ HL **Directions:** From A12 take exit to Colchester North onto the A1232 **Parking:** 90

DEDHAM MAP 13 TM03

🏵🏵 Le Talbooth Restaurant

British NOTABLE WINE LIST

Traditional quality in a picture postcard setting

☎ 01206 323150 CO7 6HP
e-mail: talbooth@milsomhotels.com
web: www.milsomhotels.com

A riverside setting, immaculate lawns, a picturesque bridge, leaded windows and a timber frame - no wonder Constable painted this magnificent property. Inside it boasts very old beams, leather chairs, striking artwork and smart table settings, and you'd need a powerful imagination to picture it as the weaver's cottage and toll booth it once was. There is a terrace for all weather alfresco dining, complete with sail canopy and heaters. The food matches the setting, with its big emphasis on superior ingredients, local whenever possible, revealed on a balanced carte with modern undertones. You might choose duck breast rillette and duck spring roll to start, and go on to sea bass with lobster sauce, and vanilla soufflé and pistachio ice cream. The stunning service enhances the whole experience.
Notable Wine List: A classic, traditional wine list with interesting South African wines.

Chef: Terry Barber, Ian Rhodes **Owners:** Paul Milsom **Times:** 12-2/7-9, Closed D Sun (Oct-Apr) **Prices:** Fixed L £21, Starter £5.50-£12, Main £16.50-£28, Dessert £5.75-£8.25, Coffee £3.55, Min/Water £3.75, Service added 10% **Wine:** 200 bottles over £20, 34 bottles under £20, 10 by the glass (£4) **Notes:** Sun L 3 courses £30, Vegetarian available, Dress Restrictions, Smart casual, no jeans, Civ Wed 50 **Seats:** 75, Pr/dining room 34 **Smoking:** N/Sm in restaurant **Children:** Portions **Rooms:** 10 (10 en suite) ★★★ **Directions:** 6m from Colchester: follow signs from A12 to Stratford St Mary, restaurant on left before village **Parking:** 50

England

⚘ milsoms

International

Fun and informal dining experience in the Dedham Vale

☎ 01206 322795 Stratford Rd CO7 6HN
e-mail: milsoms@milsomhotels.com
web: www.milsomhotels.com

This split-level bar/restaurant has a relaxed contemporary look achieved with natural fabrics, stone, wood and leather. There is a no-booking policy and guests write up their own orders on the notepads provided. There's no dress code and no predominant age group and the customers love it. The chef's travels have brought a variety of influences to bear on the menu, which features Asian, Greek and British favourites. These include potted salt beef with pickles and relish, gourmet burger with foie gras and Roquefort cheese, and baklava with Greek yogurt.

Chef: Stas Anastasiades **Owners:** Paul Milsom **Times:** 12-2.15/6-9.30 **Prices:** Starter £4-£6.75, Main £8.50-£18.50, Dessert £5.50, Coffee £2, Min/Water £4, Service optional **Wine:** 52 bottles over £20, 16 bottles under £20, 12 by the glass (£3.20-£7.75) **Notes:** Sun L 2 courses £19, 3 courses £25, Vegetarian available **Seats:** 80, Pr/dining room 16 **Smoking:** N/Sm area, Air con **Children:** Menu, Portions **Rooms:** 15 (15 en suite) ★★★ HL **Directions:** 7m N of Colchester, just off A12 **Parking:** 60

EARLS COLNE MAP 13 TL82

⚘⚘ de Vere Arms

Traditional, Modern V

Balanced cooking amongst interesting artworks

☎ 01787 223353 53 High St CO6 2PB
e-mail: dining@deverearms.com
web: www.deverearms.com

Funky artwork and ornaments make a contemporary statement at this former village inn, now an appealing small hotel with a beautiful restaurant. The reception area is bright with modern murals and the work of local and international artists, while the dining room features old beams and open brickwork. Accomplished cooking keeps the standards high, and local produce is handled with skill and innovation. A separate vegetarian menu is offered along with a short carte and shorter set menu; pan-fried fillet of turbot, tempura of curried cauliflower with roasted scallop, and roast loin of venison with thyme and juniper sauce are among the repertoire.

Chef: Chris Standhaven **Owners:** Michael & Melissa Deckers **Times:** 12-2/7-9.30, Closed 1st wk Jan, Closed L Sat **Prices:** Fixed L fr £15, Fixed D £23, Coffee £3.25, Min/Water £3.75, Service included **Wine:** 47 bottles over £20, 60 bottles under £20, 15 by the glass **Notes:** ALC set price £35, Vegetarian menu, Dress Restrictions, Smart casual **Seats:** 52 **Smoking:** N/Sm in restaurant **Children:** Portions **Rooms:** 9 (9 en suite) ★★★ HL **Directions:** B1024 towards Earls Colne, left at mini-rdbt onto High St, hotel on right **Parking:** 15

FELSTED MAP 06 TL62

Reeves Restaurant

Modern British

Seasonal produce in charming setting

☎ 01371 820996 Rumbles Cottage, Braintree Rd CM6 3DJ
e-mail: reevesrestaurant@tiscali.co.uk
web: www.reeves-restaurant.co.uk

Housed in a 16th-century cottage, this intimate oak-beamed restaurant is full of character with large windows, starched linen and plenty of fresh flowers. The cosy lounge is a lovely place for after-dinner drinks. Fixed-price and carte menus offer a range of interesting dishes. Starters might feature home-smoked chicken with caramelised oranges, raspberry and hazelnut dressing. Main courses include the likes of cannon of lamb in a cured bacon and rosemary farce, wrapped in puff pastry served with crushed potatoes and a green peppercorn sauce.

Times: 12-2/7, Closed Mon-Wed **Directions:** A120 E from Braintree, B1417 to Felsted

---

GREAT CHESTERFORD MAP 12 TL54

The Crown House

British

Refreshing cooking in a historic coaching inn

☎ 01799 530515 CB10 1NY
e-mail: stayatthecrownhouse@onetel.net
web: www.thecrownhousehotel.com

Sympathetically restored Georgian coaching inn with a peaceful village location close to the M11. Much of the original character has been retained and public rooms include an attractive lounge bar, oak-panelled restaurant and airy conservatory. Terrace dining is an option

continued

The Crown House

in the summer months, between the main house and the walled garden. Cooking is fairly simple in style offering nicely presented dishes with decent flavours - fishcakes with sweet chilli sauce, roast duck breast with sweet and sour compôte and orange and brandy jus, and chocolate roulade with chocolate sauce.

Times: 12-2/7-9.15 **Rooms:** 22 (22 en suite) ★★★ HL

GREAT DUNMOW MAP 06 TL62

Starr Restaurant

Modern British

Skilful English cooking with a French accent

☎ 01371 874321 Market Place CM6 1AX
e-mail: starrrestaurant@btinternet.com
web: www.the-starr.co.uk

This charming timber-framed 15th-century coaching inn overlooks the market place of this Essex village. Smart décor, good food and service has built up a loyal local following. The elegant, beamed restaurant and conservatory make an excellent venue for some serious dining helped by friendly, well-informed staff. Short, hand-written menus change daily depending on availability of top-quality ingredients from

continued

near and far. A skilful kitchen team produces modern British dishes with classic touches that might include starters of confit Loch Duart salmon, well-timed seared scallops and smoked haddock brandade. Your main course might be succulent Dornach lamb rump surrounded by a Niçoise garnish. Finish with a rich Armagnac baba with prune and roasted almond ice cream.

Chef: Mark Pearson **Owners:** Terence & Louise George **Times:** 12-1.30/7-9.30, Closed 27 Dec-3 Jan, Closed D Sun **Prices:** Fixed L £17.50-£27.50, Fixed D £42.50, Min/Water £3.50, Service added but optional 10% **Wine:** 6 by the glass (£4.75-£5.50) **Notes:** Mon-Fri 7 courses £57.50, Vegetarian available, Dress Restrictions, No jeans, trainers or shorts **Seats:** 70, Pr/dining room 36 **Smoking:** N/Sm in restaurant **Children:** Portions **Rooms:** 8 (8 en suite) ★★★ HL **Directions:** M11 junct 8, A120 7m E towards Colchester. In town centre **Parking:** 16

GREAT YELDHAM MAP 13 TL73

White Hart

British, European

Historic inn with an extensive menu

☎ 01787 237250 CO9 4HJ
e-mail: reservations@whitehartyeldham.co.uk
web: www.whitehartyeldham.com

This ancient inn has just celebrated its 500th birthday and boasts a number of historic curiosities, from a tiny prison that was used to hold highwaymen, to a private dining room that served as a communications centre in World War II. Heavily timbered, it stands on the banks of the River Colne in landscaped grounds and offers an extensive selection of crowd-pleasers (calves' liver and bacon with herb rösti and balsamic jus), alongside more adventurous fare, such as grilled marinated barramundi fillet served on sugar snap peas with a crayfish and chive beurre blanc. Lighter brasserie menu also available.

Chef: Stuart Barber/Kevin White **Owners:** Matthew Mason **Times:** 12-3/6-9.30, Closed D 25-26 Dec **Prices:** Fixed L £10-£12.95, Fixed D £16.95-£18.95, Starter £4.95-£10.95, Main £10-£21.95, Dessert £4.95-£5.50, Coffee £1.60, Min/Water £2.95, Service optional, Group min 7 service 10% **Wine:** 47 bottles over £20, 28 bottles under £20, 7 by the glass (£3.50-£4.15) **Notes:** Civ Wed 75 **Seats:** 60, Pr/dining room 36 **Smoking:** N/Sm in restaurant **Children:** Menu, Portions **Directions:** On A1017, between Halstead and Haverhill **Parking:** 40

HARWICH MAP 13 TM23

The Pier at Harwich

British, European

Modish seafood restaurant in quayside hotel

☎ 01255 241212 The Quay CO12 3HH
e-mail: pier@milsomhotels.com
web: www.milsomhotels.co.uk

Perfect for seafood lovers, The Pier comes situated smack on the quay overlooking the ports of Harwich and Felixstowe. Converted into a small contemporary hotel, its first-floor Harbourside Restaurant is a stylish affair, replete with chrome cocktail bar and leather armchairs, open-plan dining space decked out with neatly-clothed, well-spaced tables, fantastic clear-weather views and relaxed but professional service. The lengthy menu (offering a good choice of dishes that can be taken as starter or mains) unsurprisingly comes awash with the fruits of the ocean, its wide selection of fish and shellfish featuring fresh, locally caught and locally smoked produce. Expect grilled Harwich lobster or the chef's speciality - Zarzuela de pescado - a ragout of fish and shellfish.

The Pier at Harwich

Chef: Chris Oakley **Owners:** Mr P Milsom **Times:** 12-2/6.30-9.30, Closed 25 Dec evening **Prices:** Fixed L fr £19, Starter £6.95-£15, Main £14.50-£27.50, Dessert £6.95, Coffee £2.95, Min/Water £3.50, Service added 10% **Wine:** 40 bottles over £20, 45 bottles under £20, 6 by the glass **Notes:** Sun L £25, Vegetarian available, Dress Restrictions, Smart casual, Civ Wed 50 **Seats:** 80, Pr/dining room 16 **Smoking:** N/Sm in restaurant, Air con **Children:** Menu, Portions **Rooms:** 14 (14 en suite) ★★★ HL **Directions:** A12 to Colchester then A120 to Harwich harbour front **Parking:** 20

INGATESTONE MAP 06 TQ69

The Woolpack

Modern European NEW

Innovative fare in stylish setting combining traditional and modern elements

☎ 01277 352189 Mill Green Rd CM4 0HS
e-mail: info@thewoolpack-fryerning.co.uk
web: www.thewoolpack-fryerning.co.uk

An inn has been on this site for around 800 years, although the current building was constructed in the 19th century. More recently still, the inn has been extensively renovated and updated with clean modern lines. Solid oak flooring, striking beams, ivory-coloured wall panelling and luxurious leather chairs and banquettes give a stylish feel. Cooking is accomplished and versatile, drawing clear flavours from excellent produce. The modern European cuisine includes starters like quail four ways (poached quails' egg, roasted breast, deep-fried crumbed leg and quail rilette), followed by slow roasted belly pork on a bed of spinach with apple sauce or fillet of dorade, Scottish langoustines with Sauternes sauce.

continued

INGATESTONE *continued* MAP 06 TQ69

Chef: Dean Bouvet **Owners:** John & Lisa Hood **Times:** 12-4/7-12.30 am, Closed 2 wks in Aug, 2 wks after Xmas, Mon, Closed L Tue & Sat, D Sun **Prices:** Food prices not confirmed for 2007. Please telephone for details **Wine:** 25 bottles over £20, 10 bottles under £20, 6 by the glass (£3.50-£5.75) **Notes:** Vegetarian available, Dress Restrictions, Smart casual, no headgear **Seats:** 45 **Smoking:** N/Sm in restaurant, Air con **Children:** Min 12 yrs **Directions:** M25 junct A12, between Brentwood & Chelmsford **Parking:** 20

MANNINGTREE MAP 13 TM13

The Mistley Thorn

Modern International NEW

Delightful inn serving quality, locally sourced produce

☎ 01206 392821 High St, Mistley CO11 1HE
e-mail: info@mistleythorn.co.uk
web: www.mistleythorn.co.uk

A setting beside the River Stour is part of the appeal of this bustling Georgian inn, built on what was once the site of some of Matthew Hopkins' infamous witchfinding trials. Inside the bistro-style restaurant is light and airy with terracotta-tiled floors, high quality furnishings, exposed beams and tongue and groove walls. With a simple approach to cooking, the abundant local, seasonal produce ensures good clean flavours on the plate. Sample dishes include roast breast of Sutton Hoo chicken in mustard cider sauce, Cioppino, 'Cal-Ital' seafood stew in tomato saffron broth, or chargrilled marinated Norfolk venison saddle with warm cranberry chutney. Cookery workshops available.

Chef: Sherri Singleton **Owners:** Sherri Singleton, David McKay **Times:** 12-2.30/6.30-9.30, Closed 25 Dec **Prices:** Food prices not confirmed for 2007. Please telephone for details **Wine:** 14 bottles over £20, 19 bottles under £20, 11 by the glass (£2.85-£5.65) **Notes:** Vegetarian available **Seats:** 75, Pr/dining room 28 **Smoking:** N/Sm in restaurant **Children:** Menu, Portions **Directions:** From A12 take A137 for Manningtree and Mistley **Parking:** 7

SOUTHEND-ON-SEA MAP 07 TQ88

Fleur de Provence

French

Modern French cooking in resort restaurant

☎ 01702 352987 52-54 Alexander St SS1 1BJ
e-mail: mancel@fleurdeprovence.co.uk
web: www.fleurdeprovence.co.uk

A stone's throw from Southend-on-Sea city centre, the frosted glass high street frontage of this French restaurant may not promise much at first glance, but inside it's a very different story. Stylish, intimate and cosy, the restaurant has soft colours and lighting to create a genuinely romantic setting. Modern meets classical in the menu, with a crown of red mullet fillet baked on puff pastry with onion purée and vinaigrette Niçoise, followed by a grilled sirloin of veal served with prunes, pommes Anna and a fricassée of vegetables with truffle oil.

Chef: Marcel Bouchenga **Owners:** Marcel Bouchenga **Times:** 12-2/7-10, Closed 1st 2 wks Jan, BHs, Sun, Closed L Sat **Prices:** Fixed L £15, Fixed D fr £15, Starter £7.95-£11.95, Main £17.95-£18.95, Dessert £6.95-£7.95, Coffee £2.50, Min/Water £3.50, Service optional, Group min 6 service 10% **Wine:** 59 bottles over £20, 16 bottles under £20, 8 by the glass (£3.25-£3.95) **Notes:** Fixed L 3 courses, Vegetarian available, Dress Restrictions, Smart casual **Seats:** 45, Pr/dining room 20 **Smoking:** N/Sm area, No pipes, Air con **Children:** Portions **Parking:** Street parking, public car parks

STOCK MAP 06 TQ69

Bear Restaurant & Bar

Modern International

Innovative cuisine in historic surroundings

☎ 01277 829100 The Square CM4 9LH
e-mail: info@thebearinn.biz
web: www.thebearinn.biz

This historic 16th-century coaching inn is found in the village square. The informal bar and bistro-style dining area offer alternatives to the fine dining restaurant. Here you will find modern international cuisine and innovative dishes. The extensive choice of menus includes a mid-week carte, Sunday lunch and a six- or seven-course tasting menu. Typical dishes might include a starter of open ravioli of asparagus with baby leeks and wild mushrooms, or a main course of saddle of lamb with thyme-scented white beans, fondant potato, basil oil and red wine jus. For dessert you could try banoffee bread and butter pudding served with a banana smoothie.

Chef: Phil Utz, Scott Hiskett **Owners:** Lee & Kathryn Anderson-Frogley **Times:** 12-3/5-12.30, Closed 25-26 Dec, Closed L Mon **Prices:** Fixed L £25, Fixed D £25, Starter £4.95-£10.95, Main £12.95-£23.95, Dessert £5.95-£10.95, Coffee £2.50, Min/Water £3.50, Service optional **Wine:** 62 bottles over £20, 18 bottles under £20, 16 by the glass (£3.45-£6.65) **Notes:** Fixed L & D 3-5 courses, Tasting menu £60, Sun L available, Vegetarian available **Seats:** 90, Pr/dining room 26 **Smoking:** N/Sm in restaurant **Children:** Portions **Directions:** M25 junct 28, onto A12, turn off for Billericay, into village, restaurant just off High St **Parking:** 30

TOLLESHUNT KNIGHTS MAP 07 TL91

Five Lakes Resort

Modern British

Fine dining restaurant in a resort hotel

☎ 01621 868888 Colchester Rd CM9 8HX
e-mail: enquiries@fivelakes.co.uk
web: www.fivelakes.co.uk

This well-equipped resort hotel sits in 320 acres of open countryside where guests can use the extensive country club and other health and leisure facilities. The split-level Camelot restaurant, themed around the romantic myth of King Arthur, is serenaded by live piano music from the lobby. Close attention to detail keeps the modern British and European food to a high standard, with a short Indulgence Menu offering what it promises in two or three courses, and a longer carte finishing with a good choice of cheeses. Seared scallop and tiger prawns in a light nage of saffron and lemon thyme, to the robust braised venison and oyster pie with winter vegetables show the spread on a seasonal offering.

continued

Five Lakes Resort

Chef: David Newstead **Owners:** Mr A Bejerano **Times:** 7-10, Closed 26, 31 Dec, 1 Jan, Mon & Sun **Prices:** Fixed D £27, Starter £5.25-£7.50, Main £11.25-£22.50, Dessert £5.50-£8.95, Coffee £1.90, Min/Water £3.75, Service optional **Wine:** 65 bottles over £20, 22 bottles under £20, 11 by the glass (£3.75-£5.75) **Notes:** Dress Restrictions, Smart casual, No trainers/T-shirts/ jeans, Civ Wed 300 **Seats:** 80 **Smoking:** N/Sm in restaurant, Air con **Children:** Menu, Portions **Rooms:** 194 (194 en suite) ★★★★ HL **Directions:** M25 junct 28, then on A12. At Kelvedon take B1024 then B1023 to Tolleshunt Knights, clearly marked by brown tourist signs **Parking:** 550

GLOUCESTERSHIRE

ALMONDSBURY MAP 04 ST68

Aztec Hotel

Modern British

Relaxed, brasserie-style dining in modern business hotel

☎ 01454 201090 Aztec West Business Park BS32 4TS
e-mail: aztec@shirehotels.co.uk
web: www.shirehotels.co.uk

This stylish, modern hotel - located to the north of Bristol - is built in the Nordic style, its timber beams, vaulted ceilings and log fires blending with contemporary artwork and stone-flagged floors. The Quarterjacks Restaurant looks out across a terrace - perfect for alfresco summer dining - and gardens at the rear, and oozes a relaxed, informal brasserie vibe. The kitchen offers simply prepared dishes from high-quality ingredients - honey-roasted belly of Gloucestershire pork with Bramley apple sauce, mash and crackling. A bar menu offers lighter options.

Chef: Mike Riordan **Owners:** Shire Hotels **Times:** 12.30-2/7-10, Closed 26 Dec, Closed L Sat & Sun **Prices:** Fixed L £16.25, Starter £6-£9.50, Main £15.95-£23.50, Dessert £6.95-£7.50, Coffee £3.50, Min/Water £2.95, Service optional **Wine:** 25 bottles over £20, 10 bottles under £20, 12 by the glass (£4.50-£10.50) **Notes:** Vegetarian available **Seats:** 80, Pr/dining room 40 **Smoking:** N/Sm in restaurant **Children:** Menu, Portions **Rooms:** 128 (128 en suite) ★★★★ **Directions:** Telephone for directions **Parking:** 200

ARLINGHAM MAP 04 SO71

The Old Passage Inn

European, Seafood

Seafood restaurant with river and forest views

☎ 01452 740547 Passage Rd GL2 7JR
e-mail: oldpassage@ukonline.co.uk
web: www.fishattheoldpassageinn.co.uk

The Old Passage is a charming early 19th-century inn on the banks of the tidal River Severn. The large dining room has a fresh and airy look

continued

in mint and cream, and in summer there is a garden terrace for meals outside with river views. For private parties there is a second intimate dining room. The food is almost exclusively fish and shellfish, with two seawater tanks to store the latter. Dishes are imaginatively presented: dayboat scallop thermidor with a creamy sherry and mustard sauce topped with parmesan cheese, and seared fillet of sea bass with celeriac purée, roasted salsify, wild mushrooms and a duo of white and red wine sauces.

Chef: P Le Mesurieur, Raoul Moore **Owners:** The Moore Family **Times:** 12-2/6.30-9, Closed 24-30 Dec, Mon, Closed D Sun **Prices:** Starter £4.90-£15, Main £11.90-£35, Dessert £4.50-£5.50, Service optional **Wine:** 66 bottles over £20, 26 bottles under £20, 8 by the glass (£3.20-£4) **Seats:** 60, Pr/dining room 14 **Smoking:** N/Sm in restaurant, Air con **Children:** Portions **Rooms:** 3 (3 en suite) ◆◆◆◆ **Directions:** Telephone for directions **Parking:** 40

BARNSLEY MAP 05 SP00

The Village Pub

British, Italian

An inn for all seasons

☎ 01285 740421 GL7 5EF
e-mail: info@thevillagepub.co.uk
web: www.thevillagepub.co.uk

As the name might suggest, you can still expect a warm welcome, flagstones and floorboards, beams and open winter fires at this revamped, weathered-stone Cotswold inn. But this is no average village pub. Here five interconnecting dining areas radiate round a central bar, decked out with eclectic wooden furniture and contemporary décor. There's a garden patio for summer eating too. Modern thinking shows its hand in the cooking, with dishes having a strong reliance on quality local produce such as Barnsley chop with fresh greens and dauphinoise that appears on the daily-changing menu.

Chef: Pierro Bio **Owners:** Tim Haigh & Rupert Penered **Times:** 11-3/7-11 **Prices:** Main £10.50-£16, Dessert fr £6, Coffee £1.75, Min/Water £2.40, Service optional **Wine:** 28 bottles over £20, 23 bottles under £20, 12 by the glass (£3-£6.50) **Seats:** 100, Pr/dining room 16 **Smoking:** N/Sm in restaurant **Children:** Portions **Directions:** 4m from Cirencester **Parking:** 40

BIBURY MAP 05 SP10

Bibury Court

British, European

Comfortable and relaxing formal dining in Tudor manor

☎ 01285 740337 & 740324 GL7 5NT
e-mail: info@biburycourt.com
web: www.biburycourt.com

Grand country mansion tucked away behind a beautiful Cotswold village in a picture-postcard spot with 6 acres of grounds on the River Coln. Dating back to 1633, it offers an oasis of calm in gracious rooms that ooze historic charm and character, with traditional wood-panelled rooms, log fires, comfy sofas and antique furniture, but the atmosphere is warm, relaxed and informal. For such a grand and elegant setting the cooking is refreshingly unfussy, unpretentious and understated. A confident kitchen uses fine, seasonal ingredients to create quality, modern dishes, for example spaghetti of lobster, basil and tomato, assiette of rabbit with sweetcorn purée, and roast halibut with sautéed ceps and potato rösti.

continued on page 159

England

Buckland Manor

BUCKLAND MAP 10 SP03

British, European NOTABLE WINE LIST

Contemporary cooking in medieval manor

☎ 01386 852626 WR12 7LY
e-mail: enquire@bucklandmanor.com
web: www.bucklandmanor.com

There's quite the feeling of quintessential Englishness and stepping back in history about this grand, 13th-century mellow-stone Cotswold manor house. Inside has more a feeling of traditional country home than luxury country-house hotel, with roaring open fires, stone floors, tapestries and comfortable sitting rooms, while the atmosphere is one of calm and tranquility, with only the odd chime from the next-door church clock or the scrunch of gravel in the car park to disturb. The equally traditional restaurant (jacket and tie for dinner and Sunday lunch please gentlemen) has unusual white-painted wood panelling, portraits, blue velvet curtains and a quiet atmosphere, buoyed by flickering evening candlelight and backed by skilled, attentive and friendly service. A stroll in the immaculate 10-acre grounds is a pre- or post-meal requisite, while the food is certainly worthy of a special occasion.
The accomplished modern British approach is fused with French and Mediterranean influences and showcases fresh, quality local produce - including herbs from the hotel's own garden - in interesting dish combinations. Take roasted fillet of line-caught sea bass teamed with truffled boulangère potato, langoustines and a cauliflower foam, while a warm chocolate and hazelnut soufflé, served with milk ice cream, might head up desserts. And do save room for tasters, inter-courses and petits fours.
Notable Wine List: A classic and well chosen list with a comprehensive offering across all major wine areas including a notable Bordeaux selection.

Chef: Adrian Jarrad
Owners: von Essen
Times: 12.30-1.45/7.30-9
Prices: Fixed L £19.50, Starter £7.95-£11.50, Main £22.50-£29.50, Dessert £8.75-£10.95, Coffee £3.75, Min/Water £3.95, Service optional
Wine: 536 bottles over £20, 23 bottles under £20, 17 by the glass (£5.50-£13.25)
Notes: Sun L £25.50, Vegetarian available, Dress Restrictions, Jacket & tie
Seats: 40
Smoking: N/Sm in restaurant
Children: Min 8 yrs
Rooms: 13 (13 en suite) ★★★ HL
Directions: 2m SW of Broadway. Take B4632 signed Cheltenham, then take turn for Buckland. Hotel through village on right
Parking: 30

BIBURY *continued* MAP 05 SP10

Chef: Antony Ely **Owners:** Robert Johnston & Sam Pearman **Times:** 12-2/7-9 **Prices:** Fixed L £12.50, Fixed D £35, Starter £3.20-£7.50, Main £8.95-£16.50, Dessert £4.50-£5.95, Coffee £2.25, Min/Water £3, Service optional, Group min 6 service 10% **Wine:** 79 bottles over £20, 30 bottles under £20, 14 by the glass (£3.75-£5) **Notes:** Tasting menu 6 courses £45 on request, Civ Wed 32 **Seats:** 65, Pr/dining room 30 **Smoking:** N/Sm in restaurant **Children:** Menu, Portions **Rooms:** 18 (18 en suite) ★★★ CHH **Directions:** On B4425 between Cirencester & Burford; hotel behind church **Parking:** 100

BUCKLAND MAP 10 SP03

Buckland Manor

see opposite

CHARINGWORTH

Charingworth Manor

European NEW

Modern cuisine in an ancient manor

☎ 01386 593555 GL55 6NS
e-mail: charingworthmanor@englishrosehotels.co.uk
web: www.englishrosehotels.co.uk/hotels/charingworth/index.html

The ancient manor of Charingworth lies in beautiful Cotswold countryside within a 54-acre estate. The present building dates back to the early 14th century, with beams showing original medieval decoration. The restaurant has beamed ceilings and warm décor with tables divided into separate areas. Service is informal and relaxed, although there is a dress code of smart trousers with shirt and tie or jacket for men. Food is modern British in style with clear flavours. Menus were under development with a new chef at the stove as we went to press, however typical dishes might include a starter of chicken, chorizo and bacon terrine. Expect mains like marinated and pan-roasted rump of Welsh lamb, while desserts include white chocolate crème brûlée with crisp glaze, fresh raspberries and marbled chocolate disk.

Times: 12.30-2/6.30-9.30, Closed L Mon-Sat **Rooms:** 26 (26 en suite) ★★★ CHH **Directions:** From A429 Fosse Way, take B4035 towards Chipping Campden. Hotel 3m on R.

CHELTENHAM MAP 10 SO92

Café Paradiso at Alias Hotel Kandinsky

Modern Mediterranean

Funky townhouse with a cool vibe and warm Mediterranean menu

☎ 01242 527788 Bayshill Rd, Montpellier GL50 3AS
e-mail: kandinsky@aliashotels.com
web: www.aliashotels.com

Regency villa with a quirky decorative style that is welcoming and bright, with a touch of mid-20th century furniture, art and paraphernalia (expect the odd puppet and discarded top hat). The overall effect is pretty cool, especially when you throw in the

continued

soundtrack. Staffing is contemporary with an informally dressed young team, but there is nothing casual about the service. An interesting menu for a refreshingly different hotel is offered in the Café Paradiso, including authentic pizzas from the wood-fired oven. If time is short, try the Pronto Paradiso option.

Café Paradiso at Alias Hotel Kandinsky

Chef: Adam Murray **Owners:** Alias Hotels **Times:** 12-2/6.30-10 **Prices:** Fixed L fr £13.95, Starter £4.50-£7.95, Main £7.50-£15.95, Dessert £3.50-£5.50, Coffee £2.50, Min/Water £3.50, Service optional **Wine:** 23 bottles over £20, 37 bottles under £20, 15 by the glass (£3.50-£4.80) **Notes:** Vegetarian available **Seats:** 40, Pr/dining room 24 **Smoking:** N/Sm in restaurant **Children:** Menu, Portions **Rooms:** 48 (48 en suite) ★★★★ TH **Directions:** From M5 junct 11 follow A40 towards town centre. Right at rdbt, 2nd exit at next rdbt into Bayshill Rd **Parking:** 25

Le Champignon Sauvage

see page 160

George Hotel - Monty's Seafood

Modern International

Confident seafood cooking in stylish, contemporary setting

☎ 01242 235751 St Georges Rd GL50 3DZ
e-mail: hotel@stayatthegeorge.co.uk
web: www.montysseafood.co.uk

Though this long-established hotel set in a Regency terrace wears a traditional face, its interior has been stylishly remodelled. Monty's Seafood restaurant is the fine-dining arm - contemporary, stylish and upbeat, with clothed tables and attentive but relaxed service and atmosphere. The lively Monty's Brasserie continues the modern vibe, while in the basement below, there's a buzzy designer cocktail bar. The confident, innovative, elegant modern cooking fits the bill, and reflects skilled treatment of quality ingredients; take fillets of sea bass with braised pak choi and a caviar velouté. The brasserie has a separate menu.

continued on page 161

Le Champignon Sauvage

CHELTENHAM MAP 10 SO92

French

Serious French cooking, attentive service and modern, stylish environment

☎ 01242 573449 24 Suffolk Rd GL50 2AQ
e-mail: mail@lechampignonsauvage.co.uk
web: www.lechampignonsauvage.com

Recently expanded and refurbished, this culinary big hitter has a long-standing, much-deserved reputation for culinary excellence. With chef-patron David Everitt-Matthias' innovative and polished skills combining with some surprisingly reasonable prices, it's set to continue as a national favourite with regulars, foodies and professionals alike, all beating a path to its doors for memorable dining and inspiration.
Unassumingly tucked away in a terrace of shops on a busy main road in the quieter Montpellier district of town, this smart French restaurant provides few clues from outside of its premier-league status and enduring charm. Inside however, the new spaciousness is immediately apparent to all but first-timers, though there's an instant warmth and vitality here that can be appreciated by all. Bright and spacious, it makes the most of its shop-front windows, and there's a small lounge area with comfortable leather chairs. Decorated with lovely white ash panelling, its light blue walls are hung with striking modern art. Carpet and darkwood upholstered chairs continue the blue theme alongside simply but elegantly dressed tables, while service, headed-up by wife Helen, is friendly, attentive and knowledgeable.
There's no shortage of flair and imagination from David's new kitchen and increased brigade either, technical skill seems to abound here, the highly accomplished style delivering some classic combinations alongside more contemporary flashes, and always pleases. A peerless reputation for hard work and dedication to his craft, David's matching and balancing of flavours is exemplary, combined with the use of some interesting ingredients. Think poached, roasted belly of Gloucestershire Old Spot pork, perhaps served with pumpkin purée and razor clams, or there may be a fillet of zander paired with a risotto of Herefordshire snails and ground elder and chicken juices. Peripherals like breads, amuse-bouche, pre-desserts and petits fours are equally impressive. This is inspirational cooking from start to finish!

Chef: David Everitt-Matthias
Owners: Mr & Mrs D Everitt-Matthias
Times: 12.30-1.30/7.30-9, Closed 10 days Xmas, 3 wks Jun, Sun-Mon
Prices: Fixed L £22-£38, Fixed D £27-£47, Coffee £3.50, Min/Water £2.50, Service optional
Wine: 93 bottles over £20, 43 bottles under £20, 6 by the glass (£2.75-£3.75)
Seats: 40
Smoking: N/Sm in restaurant
Directions: S of the town centre, on A40, near Cheltenham College
Parking: Public car park (Bath Rd)

CHELTENHAM *continued* MAP 10 SO92

Chef: Kevin Harris & Rob Owen **Owners:** Jeremy Shaw **Times:** 6.30-10, Closed Xmas, Sun-Mon, Closed L all week **Prices:** Starter £6.50-£8.50, Main £14-£19.50, Dessert fr £5.50, Coffee £1.75, Min/Water £3, Group min 8 service 10% **Wine:** 30 bottles over £20, 20 bottles under £20, 8 by the glass (£3.15-£6.35) **Notes:** Sun L 2 courses £15, 3 courses £18 **Seats:** 26, Pr/dining room 26 **Smoking:** N/Sm in restaurant, Air con **Children:** Menu **Rooms:** 38 (38 en suite) ★★★ HL **Parking:** 30

The Greenway

Rosettes not confirmed at time of going to press

Modern British

Modern cooking in an Elizabethan manor

☎ 01242 862352 Shurdington GL51 4UG
e-mail: info@thegreenway.co.uk
web: www.the-greenway.co.uk

Classic country house in style - albeit on the outskirts of Cheltenham rather than in the depths of the countryside - this mellow Elizabethan manor house offers plenty of period features and a timeless quality of understated relaxed charm and elegance. Think deep sofas and crackling fire in the cosy lounge and a bright, elegant conservatory restaurant furnished in appropriate style, with clothed tables and all the reassuring touches, and views over the sunken garden. At the time of going to press, a change of chef occurred at the kitchens of the Greenway. Marc Hardiman has a proven track record, recently being in charge of proceedings at Charlton House in Shepton Mallet (see entry). Marc brings with him a wealth of experience with the aim of mirroring the success previously enjoyed by the hotel. The finest local produce can be expected to feature on menus and dishes following classical principles coupled with modern innovative twists.

Chef: Marc Hardiman **Owners:** von Essen Hotels **Times:** 12-2.30/7-10 **Prices:** Fixed L £15.50, Fixed D £32.50-£45, Coffee £3, Min/Water £3.50, Service optional **Wine:** 180 bottles over £20, 6 by the glass (£6) **Notes:** ALC 3 courses £45,Tasting menu from £32.50, Vegetarian available, Dress Restrictions, Smart casual, no jeans, T-shirts or trainers, Civ Wed 45 **Seats:** 50, Pr/dining room 30 **Smoking:** N/Sm in restaurant **Children:** Portions **Rooms:** 21 (21 en suite) ★★★ HL **Directions:** 3m S of Cheltenham on A46 (Stroud), pass through the village of Shurdington **Parking:** 50

 Lumière

Modern NOTABLE WINE LIST

Bold modern cooking at a chic haunt in Cheltenham

☎ 01242 222200 Clarence Pde GL50 3PA
e-mail: dinner@lumiere.cc
web: www.lumiere.cc

Run by a husband and wife team, this chic little restaurant has a pared-down modern décor. Contemporary art hangs on plain walls, while tables are well-spaced and simply dressed with white linen and quality china. The cooking is clean and bold to match; a short modern menu features an eclectic mix of dishes, ranging from straightforward to more complex combinations of quality ingredients. Foie gras wrapped in seared Parma ham is a typical starter, while mains might include chargrilled springbok fillet with sweet onion mash and a red wine sauce, or baked halibut with smoked salmon salsa and red pepper rice. A pecan torte with caramel mascarpone and Jack Daniels ice cream might tempt too.

Notable Wine List: A small, well balanced list which shows much passion and enthusiasm for quality wines.

Chef: Geoff Chapman **Owners:** Lin & Geoff Chapman **Times:** 7-8.30, Closed 2 wks Jan, 2 wks summer, Sun-Mon, Closed L all week, D 25 Dec **Prices:** Fixed D fr £36, Coffee £1.50, Min/Water £1.50, Service optional **Wine:** 3 bottles under £20, 4 by the glass (£3.50-£6) **Seats:** 30 **Smoking:** N/Sm in restaurant, Air con **Children:** Min 8 yrs **Directions:** Town centre, near bus station **Parking:** On street, nearby car parks

Parkers

Modern British

Brasserie food in contemporary surroundings in period building

☎ 01242 518898 The Hotel on the Park, 38 Evesham Rd GL52 2AH
e-mail: stay@hotelonthepark.co.uk
web: www.hotelonthepark.com

This Grade II listed building dating from 1830 has been given a modern lease of life as a contemporary brasserie. The polished oak floors, American black walnut tables and stylish cutlery make this a place to be seen. Carefully cooked seasonal produce features on a menu offering some old favourites as well as more modern dishes. Try the likes of pan-fried scallops with a cauliflower and coconut purée and Keta caviar to start. Main courses might include a more traditional rack of lamb, or perhaps roasted cod fillet with bubble and squeak, poached egg, parmesan and hollandaise. Tempting desserts on offer might be lemon delicious with vanilla ice cream, or bitter chocolate tart with mint sorbet.

Chef: Wayne Sullivan **Owners:** Joanne Gregory **Times:** 12-2/6.30-9.30, Closed D 25 Dec **Prices:** Fixed L £13.50, Starter £5.95-£8.95, Main £14.95-£19.95, Dessert £5.95-£8.50, Coffee £2.50, Min/Water £3.25, Service optional, Group min 8 service 10% **Wine:** 15 bottles over £20, 10 bottles under £20, 4 by the glass (£3.25-£4.50) **Notes:** Dress Restrictions, Smart casual **Seats:** 42 **Smoking:** N/Sm in restaurant **Children:** Min 12 yrs **Rooms:** 12 (12 en suite) ★★★ SHL **Directions:** 4m from M5 junct 10. 0.75m from Cheltenham racecourse **Parking:** 8

Mayflower

☎ 01242 522426 32-34 Clarence St GL50 3NX

Chinese with an extensive menu that includes plenty of the familiar as well as more unusual dishes.

England

England

CHIPPING CAMPDEN MAP 10 SP13

Cotswold House

see below

The Kings

Traditional British, European

Flavour-packed food in busy Cotswold inn

☎ 01386 840256 The Square GL55 6AW
e-mail: info@kingscampden.co.uk
web: www.kingscampden.co.uk

Located in the heart of historic Chipping Campden, this Grade II listed town house hotel is popular with visitors and locals. There's a friendly atmosphere in the brasserie-style restaurant and relaxing bar. Simply constructed British food with European influences is made with good quality ingredients in dishes like fresh fig and Parma ham salad with balsamic reduction, roast breast of Magret duck, thyme crushed potatoes, braised red cabbage and red wine jus, or pan-fried delice of organic salmon with wilted Chinese leaf and caramel soy. Alfresco dining available in warmer weather.

Chef: Ellery Powell **Owners:** Vanessa Rees **Times:** 12-2.30/6.30-9.30 **Prices:** Starter £4.50-£6.95, Main £10.50-£18.50, Dessert £5, Coffee £2.25, Min/Water £3.70, Service optional **Wine:** 25 bottles over £20, 25 bottles under £20, 10 by the glass (£3.50-£7.50) **Notes:** Sun roast available **Seats:** 50, Pr/dining room 20 **Smoking:** N/Sm in restaurant **Children:** Menu, Portions **Rooms:** 14 (14 en suite) ◆◆◆◆ **Directions:** 10m from Stratford **Parking:** 8

Three Ways House

Modern British

Cotswold home of the famous Pudding Club

☎ 01386 438429 Mickleton GL55 6SB
e-mail: threeways@puddingclub.com
web: www.puddingclub.com

A Cotswold country house offering traditional comforts, though the restaurant is more contemporary in style, with a light and simple décor, and plenty of fresh flowers. This is the home of the famous Pudding Club, founded over 20 years ago to promote the great British dessert, where you will find pudding-themed rooms. The menu offers contemporary to traditional British fare, with some oriental flavours used with great success. Baked guinea fowl breast with sauté pak choi, or a medley of fish with prawn and chive cream sauce might be followed by one of those scrumptious custard-enhanced English puddings.

continued

Cotswold House

CHIPPING CAMPDEN MAP 10 SP13

British, French V NOTABLE WINE LIST

Vibrant and stylish cooking and interior design

☎ 01386 840330 The Square GL55 6AN
e-mail: reception@cotswoldhouse.com
web: www.cotswoldhouse.com

Surprises are certainly in store beyond the front door of this otherwise archetypal, mellow Cotswold-stone former Regency wool merchant's house at the heart of this delightful town. An amazing staircase and bold, design-led decorative style cuts an unexpectedly stylish, contemporary edge inside; the artwork and design as exciting as the food on the plate. But this is contemporary elegance without pomposity, the service professional but nicely relaxed. Juliana's restaurant continues the theme, while the kitchen's appropriately modern approach comes underpinned by a classical theme on intelligently compact, enticing, fixed-price menus that bring high skill, flair and clean, clear flavours to top-notch produce. Think Cornish brill served with carrot and cucumber choucroute, crab tortellini and Gewürztraminer, or perhaps Gressingham duck with honey glaze, confit leg and baby beetroots, and, heading up dessert, maybe an espresso and toffee mousse served with pecan crust, banana bonbon and ice cream. An extensive wine list, decent range of cheeses and ancillaries like excellent breads, canapés and petits fours all hold form through to the end, while bedrooms offer the same pampering, with a beguiling blend of style, quality and comfort at this much-talked-about hotel.

Notable Wine List: A well laid out wine list featuring good producers and some very informative tasting notes.

Chef: Jamie Forman **Owners:** Christa & Ian Taylor **Times:** 12-2.30/7-10, Closed L Mon-Sat **Prices:** Fixed D £45, Min/Water £3.50, Service optional, Group min 8 service 10% **Wine:** 70 bottles over £20, 10 by the glass (£4.95-£8.95) **Notes:** Coffee incl, Sun L 3 courses £27.50, Vegetarian menu, Smart casual, Civ Wed 80 **Seats:** 40, Pr/dining room 96 **Smoking:** N/Sm in restaurant, Air con **Children:** Portions **Rooms:** 29 (29 en suite) ★★★★ HL **Directions:** 1m N of A44 between Moreton-in-Marsh & Broadway on B4081 **Parking:** 25

Chef: Mark Rowlandson **Owners:** Simon Coombe & Peter Henderson **Times:** 12-2.30/7-9.30, Closed L Mon-Sat **Prices:** Fixed L £17-£18, Fixed D £31-£38, Coffee £2.50, Min/Water £3, Service optional **Wine:** 20 bottles over £20, 22 bottles under £20, 10 by the glass (£2.85-£4.75) **Notes:** Vegetarian available, Civ Wed 80 **Seats:** 80, Pr/dining room 70 **Smoking:** N/Sm in restaurant, Air con **Children:** Menu, Portions **Rooms:** 48 (48 en suite) ★★★ HL **Directions:** On B4632, in village centre **Parking:** 37

CIRENCESTER MAP 05 SP00

Hare & Hounds

Modern, International **NEW**

Satisfying food in a charming Cotswold inn

☎ 01285 720288 Fosse-Cross GL54 4NN
e-mail: stay@thehareandhoundsinn.com
web: www.hareandhoundsinn.com

This typical Cotswold inn, parts of which date back to the 14th century, is bursting with character with open fires, stone and wood floors and cosy, candlelit nooks and crannies for intimate dining. The mix of traditional and international cooking is certainly drawing much praise and there is clearly a big effort to incorporate local produce. You could expect a starter of twice-baked North Cerney goat's cheese soufflé, or cream of smoked haddock and butternut squash soup followed by pork fillet on stilton dauphinoise with cider and sage sauce. The dessert list is heavy on robust favourites such as sticky toffee pudding or coconut and banana cheesecake.

Chef: G Ragosa, M Howe & P Cowel **Owners:** Geraldo Ragosa & Angela Howe **Times:** 12-3/6-10 **Prices:** Fixed L £10.95-£20.95, Fixed D £17-£27.95, Starter £4.95-£7.50, Main £8.95-£18.95, Dessert £4.50-£5.50, Coffee £1.50, Min/Water £3.75, Group min 10 service 10% **Wine:** 6 bottles over £20, 9 bottles under £20, 10 by the glass (£3.75-£4.50) **Notes:** Sun L £9.95, Vegetarian available **Seats:** 97, Pr/dining room 18 **Smoking:** N/Sm area **Children:** Menu, Portions **Rooms:** 10 (10 en suite) ◆◆◆◆ **Directions:** On A429 Stow rd 6m from Cirencester **Parking:** 80

CLEARWELL MAP 04 SO50

Tudor Farmhouse Hotel

Traditional British

Hearty fare at this romantic period farm

☎ 01594 833046 GL16 8JS
e-mail: info@tudorfarmhousehotel.co.uk
web: www.tudorfarmhousehotel.co.uk

Situated within walking distance of Clearwell Castle in the heart of the Forest of Dean, Tudor Farmhouse is an ideal place to stay to explore the area. The architectural style is heavily hinted at in the name: this 13th-century, Grade II listed converted farm has the requisite oak beams, exposed stone and, more unusually, wooden spiral staircases. With a growing reputation in the area, the cooking is certainly accomplished and demonstrates clear technical ability. Seasonality and local ingredients are duly celebrated in modern British dishes such as loin of Lydney Farm venison with candied pears and sloe gin sauce or wild mushroom, broccoli and single Gloucester tartlet. Portions are generous and fully flavoured.

Chef: Peter Teague **Owners:** Owen & Eirwen Evans **Times:** 12-5.30/7-9, Closed 24-27 Dec **Prices:** Fixed L £10-£13, Starter £3.95-£6.50, Main £12.95-£17.50, Dessert £5.25, Coffee £2.25, Min/Water £2.50, Service optional **Wine:** 7 bottles over £20, 29 bottles under £20, 7 by the glass (£4-£4.65) **Notes:** Vegetarian available **Seats:** 30, Pr/dining room 22 **Smoking:** N/Sm in restaurant **Children:** Menu, Portions **Rooms:** 22 (22 en suite) ★★★ HL **Directions:** Leave Monmouth to Chepstow road at Redbrook, follow signs Clearwell, turn left at village cross. Hotel on left **Parking:** 24

COLN ST ALDWYNS MAP 05 SP10

The New Inn At Coln

British, French

Traditional Cotswold charm with enjoyable modern British cuisine

☎ 01285 750651 GL7 5AN
e-mail: stay@new-inn.co.uk
web: www.new-inn.co.uk

Despite its name, the New Inn has been in existence as a coaching inn since the 16th century. The sense of history is deeply ingrained in the exposed beams, worn flagged floors and Cotswold stone walls - and yet, the dining room itself feels very contemporary with yellow pastel walls and subtle lighting. A definite destination restaurant for the surrounding towns and villages, the food here is conspicuously modern and there can be no doubt about the technical abilities of the kitchen. On this delicious-sounding menu you might be tempted by crab and smoked salmon tian with anchovy aïoli caviar, followed by lamb noisette and Moroccan couscous with olive and shallot ragout.

Chef: Matthew Haines **Owners:** Mr & Mrs R Kimmet **Times:** 12-2/7-9 **Prices:** Fixed D £38, Coffee £2.95, Min/Water £3.75, Group min 5 service 10% **Wine:** 35 bottles over £20, 7 bottles under £20, 7 by the glass (£3.50-£3.95) **Notes:** Set price Sun L available, Vegetarian available **Seats:** 32, Pr/dining room 20 **Smoking:** N/Sm in restaurant **Children:** Min 10 yrs **Rooms:** 14 (14 en suite) ★★ HL **Directions:** 8m E of Cirencester, between Bibury and Fairford. **Parking:** 22

CORSE LAWN MAP 10 SO83

Corse Lawn House Hotel

Modern British V NOTABLE WINE LIST

Attractive Queen Anne house with dining of long-standing reputation

☎ 01452 780771 GL19 4LZ
e-mail: enquiries@corselawn.com
web: www.corselawn.com

This Grade II listed Queen Anne house was once a coaching inn and still retains the only existing coach wash in England. The hotel has been home to the Hine family since 1978 and continues to maintain high standards of service and impressive cuisine. Both modern and classic French and English culinary influences blend seamlessly on an

continued

England

CORSE LAWN *continued* MAP 10 SO83

extensive menu that features plenty of fish and game (when in season); cooking is precise and unfussy - and done with obvious care and affection for each dish. Chargrilled squid with rocket salad and chilli oil would be a good example of the starters on offer, while truffled guinea fowl breast with wild mushrooms and Madeira sauce is a representative main course.

Notable Wine List: The wine list offers a fine selection with lots of top producers.

Chef: Baba Hine, Andrew Poole **Owners:** Hine Family **Times:** 12-2/7-9.30, Closed 24-26 Dec **Prices:** Fixed L £19.50, Fixed D £29.50, Starter £4.95-£9.95, Main £14.95-£19.95, Dessert £5.95-£6.95, Coffee £2.75, Min/Water £2.40, Service optional **Wine:** 300 bottles over £20, 30 bottles under £20, 8 by the glass (£3.40-£5.20) **Notes:** Vegetarian menu, Dress Restrictions, Smart casual, no jeans or T-shirts, Civ Wed 80 **Seats:** 50, Pr/dining room 28 **Smoking:** N/Sm in restaurant **Children:** Portions **Rooms:** 19 (19 en suite) ★★★ HL **Directions:** 5m SW of Tewkesbury on B4211, in village centre **Parking:** 60

FRAMPTON MANSELL MAP 04 SO90

White Horse

Modern British

Colourful foodie pub

☎ 01285 760960 Cirencester Rd GL6 8HZ
e-mail: emmawhitehorse@aol.com
web: www.cotswoldwhitehorse.com

This unassuming roadside pub on the A419 has a remodelled interior and relaxed, dining-pub vibe. Pastel-coloured walls, seagrass carpeting, high-backed chairs and colourful artwork create that restaurant edge, while a large bow window overlooks the garden with its alfresco dining opportunities. The modern British menu makes sound use of local suppliers and comes sprinkled with a few luxury items, perhaps rock oysters from Cornwall and whole lobster live from the pub's tank. Plenty of cream saucing in dishes like guinea fowl breast with pak choi and red wine cream sauce, plus crowd-pleasing desserts with favourites like summer pudding on offer.

Chef: Howard Matthews **Owners:** Emma & Shaun Davis **Times:** 11-3/6-11, Closed 24-26 Dec, 1 Jan, Closed D Sun **Prices:** Starter £3.95-£8.95, Main £10.95-£15.95, Dessert £4.95, Coffee £1.75, Min/Water £2.50, Service optional **Wine:** 27 bottles over £20, 22 bottles under £20, 8 by the glass (£3.50-£5.75) **Notes:** Sun L from £10.50, Vegetarian available **Seats:** 45 **Smoking:** N/Sm in restaurant **Children:** Portions **Directions:** 6m from Cirencester on the A419 towards Stroud **Parking:** 30

GLOUCESTER MAP 10 SO81

Carringtons Restaurant

Traditional European NEW

Traditional service and cuisine in this charming hotel

☎ 01452 617412 Hatton Court Hotel, Upton Hill, Upton St Leonards GL4 8DE
e-mail: res@hatton-court.co.uk
web: www.hatton-court.co.uk

Delightful views over the surrounding countryside and the thoughtful arrangement of outdoor seating make this a wonderful place to enjoy in summer. Part of the Hatton collection of hotels, there's an emphasis on traditional style and service - one of the most popular attractions is the waiting staff flambéing at the table. That style of traditional European cuisine is continued throughout the attractive à la carte menu, though dishes like scallops with pea purée and cauliflower tempura or Cornish crab tagalinni with basil pesto betray touches of Mediterranean and even fusion cooking. Select your wines from the restaurant's unique wine shop.

continued

Chef: Uffe Broberg **Owners:** Hatton Hotels **Times:** 12-2/7-10 **Prices:** Fixed L £12.95, Fixed D £26.25, Starter £6.25-£7.95, Main £13.95-£22.95, Dessert £6.50, Coffee £2.50, Min/Water £2.75, Service optional **Wine:** 20 bottles over £20, 16 bottles under £20, 8 by the glass (£3.95-£8.50) **Notes:** Sun L £13.95, Vegetarian available, Dress Restrictions, Smart casual, Civ Wed 75 **Seats:** 100, Pr/dining room 50 **Smoking:** N/Sm in restaurant, Air con **Children:** Portions **Rooms:** 45 (45 en suite) ★★★ HL **Directions:** On B4017 between Gloucester and Painswick **Parking:** 70

LOWER SLAUGHTER MAP 10 SP12

Lower Slaughter Manor

British, French V

Historic manor house offering traditional country-house dining

☎ 01451 820456 GL54 2HP
e-mail: info@lowerslaughter.co.uk
web: www.lowerslaughter.co.uk

History dates a manor house to this site in 1004 AD with nuns using the manor as a convent in the 15th century. It was rebuilt as a house in the 17th century by Valentine Strong, whose son was employed as principal constructor for St Paul's Cathedral by Sir Christopher Wren. The restaurant is entered through what was the chapel used by the nuns; nowadays you will find a traditionally decorated country-house restaurant with formal table service. Refined cuisine is on offer with starters like warm goat's cheese bavarois with sweet onion and dressed rocket. Main courses make use of wonderful produce in dishes like glazed rump of Welsh lamb with fondant potato, buttered baby gem lettuce, braised faggot and red wine jus.

Chef: David Kelman **Owners:** von Essen Collection **Times:** 12-2.30/7-9.30 **Prices:** Fixed L £15-£19.95, Fixed D £45-£75, Coffee £2.50, Min/Water £3.75, Service optional **Wine:** 100 bottles over £20, 20 bottles under £20 **Notes:** Fixed D 4 courses, Vegetarian menu, Dress Restrictions, Smart, no jeans or trainers, Civ Wed 60 **Seats:** 34, Pr/dining room 20 **Smoking:** N/Sm in restaurant **Children:** Min 12 yrs, Portions **Rooms:** 16 (16 en suite) ★★★ **Directions:** Off A429, signposted The Slaughters. 0.5m into village on right **Parking:** 30

Washbourne Court Hotel

Modern European

Fine-dining in Cotswold country-house hotel on River Eye

☎ 01451 822143 GL54 2HS
e-mail: info@washbournecourt.co.uk
web: www.washbournecourt.co.uk

Four acres of pristine riverbank garden, French windows opening on to a terrace and a beautiful Cotswold village setting are just some of the delights on offer at this old stone-built hotel, once a school. Beamed ceilings, log fires and flagstone floors reinforce its 17th-century character, while an elegant dining room, replete with chandeliers and gold wall lights, provides a relaxed but fairly formal atmosphere. The modern cooking draws on quality seasonal ingredients, displaying clear flavours and some interesting combinations. Take confit of duck and foie gras starter, followed by fillet of beef with celeriac, wild mushrooms and Madeira sauce, and finish with a trio of lemon. The garden terrace proves an added bonus for summer drinks and light lunches.

Chef: Matt Pashley **Owners:** von Essen Hotels **Times:** 12.30-3/7-9, Closed L Mon-Sat **Prices:** Fixed D £40, Coffee £2.50, Min/Water £3.75, Service optional, Group min 10 service 10% **Wine:** 100% bottles over £20, 6 by the glass (£4.90-£4.95) **Notes:** Dress Restrictions, Smart casual, Civ Wed 60 **Seats:** 60, Pr/dining room 16 **Smoking:** N/Sm in restaurant **Children:** Min 8 yrs, Menu, Portions **Rooms:** 28 (28 en suite) ★★★ HL **Directions:** Off A429, village centre by river **Parking:** 40

MORETON-IN-MARSH MAP 10 SP23

Mulberry Restaurant

British, French

Contemporary dining in ancient Cotswold manor house

☎ 01608 650501 Manor House Hotel, High St GL56 0LJ
e-mail: bookings@cotswold-inns-hotels.co.uk
web: www.cotswold-inns-hotel.co.uk

continued

The Cotswold stone frontage of this 16th-century manor house hides a melange of ancient and modern decoration. Ancient beams and fireplaces are still evident but the dining room has been given a modern makeover with vibrant red chair covers and modern flower paintings. Service is of a high standard throughout. The simple dishes tend to be most satisfying, showing off top quality ingredients. The lack of fussiness in presentation is laudable in modern British dishes with French influences like the confit beetroot pressé, apple jelly, baby squid with Cerney goat's cheese and kitchen skills evident in main courses like roast John Dory with oxtail bourguignon. Finish with confit ginger rice pudding, avocado ice cream, froth of coconut and bee pollen.

Chef: A Troughton **Owners:** Michael & Pamela Horton **Times:** 12-2.30/7-9.30 **Prices:** Fixed L fr £12.50, Fixed D £32.50, Coffee £2.20, Min/Water £4, Service optional **Wine:** 56 bottles over £20, 27 bottles under £20, 8 by the glass (£3.75-£6) **Notes:** Vegetarian available, Dress Restrictions, Smart casual, no jeans, shorts or trainers, Civ Wed 120 **Seats:** 76, Pr/dining room 120 **Smoking:** N/Sm in restaurant **Children:** Min 8 yrs, Portions **Rooms:** 38 (38 en suite) ★★★ HL **Directions:** Off A429 at south end of town **Parking:** 32

NAILSWORTH MAP 04 ST89

Egypt Mill Hotel

British

Pleasant waterside inn with rewarding food

☎ 01453 833449 GL6 0AE
e-mail: reception@egyptmill.com
web: www.egyptmill.com

A former corn mill with its origins in the 16th century, this attractive hotel is situated on the edge of the River Frome in a pretty Cotswold village and still has the original millstones and working waterwheels. The cellar bar and atmospheric restaurant have both been refurbished sensitively with comfortable, up-to-date décor and quirky objets d'art. The lengthy menu ranges from simple, familiar classics to rather bolder, more complex dishes. Try home-smoked chicken salad to start, then a main course of roast venison with chocolate and raspberry jus. Desserts should not be overlooked.

Times: 12-2/6.30-9.30 **Rooms:** 27 (27 en suite) ★★ HL **Directions:** Centre of Nailsworth, on A46

England

NAILSWORTH *continued* MAP 04 ST89

The Mad Hatters Restaurant

British, French

Enjoyable dining in a modern rustic setting

☎ 01453 832615 3 Cossack Square GL6 0DB
e-mail: mafindlay@waitrose.com

This old Cotswold farmhouse has big bay windows looking on to a picturesque square. The interior is a riot of stained glass in oak frames, paintings from good local artists and locally handcrafted furniture. Staff are both friendly and well informed about the menu. Hand-written menus comprise mainly French with some Arab, Asian and Mediterranean influences. Start with the well-made fish soup before a main course of local roebuck tournedos with green peppercorn and brandy sauce. Finish with soft pistachio meringue with seasonal fruit and cream.

Chef: Michael Findlay **Owners:** Michael Findlay & Carolyn Findlay **Times:** 12.30-2/7.30-9, Closed end Jan-early Feb,1st wk Jun,1st 2wk Aug, Mon-Tue, Closed D Sun-Tue **Prices:** Fixed L £17-£19, Fixed D £28.50-£30, Starter £5.50-£7.50, Main £17.50-£21, Dessert £5.50, Coffee £2, Min/Water £2.50, Service optional **Wine:** 6 bottles over £20, 19 bottles under £20, 3 by the glass (£3.50-£4.50) **Notes:** Sun L 3 courses £18, Vegetarian available **Seats:** 45 **Smoking:** N/Sm in restaurant **Rooms:** 3 (1 en suite) ◆◆◆◆ **Directions:** M5 junct 13. A419 to Stroud and then A46 to Nailsworth. Take a right at rdbt and then an immediate left, restaurant is located opposite Britannia Pub **Parking:** NCP, parking on street

NEWENT MAP 10 SO72

Three Choirs Vineyards

Modern British

Tuscan-style vineyard views and summer terrace dining

☎ 01531 890223 GL18 1LS
e-mail: ts@threechoirs.com
web: www.threechoirs.com

The full output from the 70-acre vineyard is available at this thriving restaurant with rooms, which provides a wonderfully different (and convenient) place to stay for wine lovers. Spacious, high-quality bedrooms have their own private patio and, like the modern Vineyard Restaurant, with its leather-backed chairs and large picture windows, look out across acres of rolling vineyards. Well-executed up-to-date British dishes are given a modern twist (mainly Mediterranean), resulting in uncomplicated and simple food that relies on accuracy of flavours and well-sourced, quality ingredients. Typical choices include rib-eye of Herefordshire beef with béarnaise and shallot marmalade, seared fillet of sea bass, buttered celeriac and pea and horseradish emulsion, and iced honey parfait with chocolate honeycomb biscuit.

Chef: Darren Leonard **Owners:** Three Choirs Vineyards Ltd **Times:** 12-2/7-9 **Prices:** Starter £4.50-£8.95, Main £10.50-£18.50, Dessert £4.95-£5.50, Min/Water £2.50, Service optional, Group min 10 service 10% **Wine:** 15 bottles over £20, 40 bottles under £20, 14 by the glass (£3-£8) **Notes:** Smart casual, Civ Wed 20 **Seats:** 50, Pr/dining room 20 **Smoking:** N/Sm in restaurant **Children:** Menu, Portions **Rooms:** 8 (8 en suite) ★★★★ RR **Directions:** 2m N of Newent on B4215, follow brown tourist signs **Parking:** 50

NORTHLEACH MAP 10 SP11

The Puesdown Inn

Modern British

Local produce cooked with flair

☎ 01451 860262 Compton Abdale GL54 4DN
e-mail: inn4food@btopenworld.com
web: www.puesdown.cotswoldinns.com

This traditional Cotswold coaching inn, said to date back to 1236, has been lovingly refurbished by its hands-on owners. The warm colours, cosy sofas and log fires create a welcoming atmosphere. Outside, the garden behind the inn provides spacious tables and deckchairs while patio parasols and heaters make for comfortable alfresco dining. The daily changing menu reflects market and seasonal variations, with produce carefully sourced from local producers. Chef-proprietor John Armstrong had a classical training at The Savoy and is passionate about attention to detail. Typical dishes might include a starter of ravioli of sea scallop with purple potato and Jerusalem artichoke foam. A main course choice might be trio of pork with cider fondant, caramelised apples and green apple jus.

Chef: John Armstrong **Owners:** John & Maggie Armstrong **Times:** 12-3/7-11 **Prices:** Fixed L £14.75-£16.50, Fixed D £27.50, Starter £4-£8, Main £13.50-£20, Dessert £4.95, Coffee £1.70, Min/Water £2.20, Service optional **Wine:** 13 bottles over £20, 23 bottles under £20, 13 by the glass (£2.85-£7.75) **Notes:** Sun L 3 courses £17.75 & Jazz D £19.95, Vegetarian available **Seats:** 45, Pr/dining room 26 **Smoking:** N/Sm in restaurant **Children:** Portions **Rooms:** 3 (3 en suite) ◆◆◆◆ **Directions:** On A40 (Cheltenham-Oxford), 7m from Cheltenham, 3m from Northleach **Parking:** 80

PAINSWICK MAP 04 SO80

Painswick Hotel

Modern European

Grandeur and tranquillity in equal measure at this Cotswold favourite

☎ 01452 812160 Kemps Ln GL6 6YB
e-mail: reservations@painswickhotel.com
web: www.painswickhotel.com

Situated in an enchanting village (known as 'Queen Of The Cotswolds'), this former rectory with Palladian features is built in the yellow limestone typical of the region. The oak-panelled restaurant (with the bar now located in the chapel) is decorated in a traditional, formal style. With a commitment to using local produce, the menu is steadfastly modern European in style with an interesting selection of dishes that are largely contemporary takes on classic themes - foie gras and chicken terrine with fig and apple jam and toasted brioche to start, for example, or pavé of brill poached in red wine as a main. There's a good selection of local cheeses too.

Chef: Mark Redwood **Owners:** Max & Jane Sabatini, Robert & Pauline Young **Times:** 12-2/7-9.15 **Prices:** Fixed L fr £25, Fixed D fr £35, Starter £6.50-£12, Main £19.25-£24, Dessert £7-£8, Service included **Wine:** 101 bottles over £20, 11 bottles under £20, 7 by the glass (£4.75-£5.25) **Notes:** Fixed L 3 courses, Fixed D 4 courses, Vegetarian available, Dress Restrictions, No jeans or T-shirts, Civ Wed 66 **Seats:** 36, Pr/dining room 16 **Smoking:** N/Sm in restaurant **Children:** Portions **Rooms:** 19 (19 en suite) ★★★ HL **Directions:** From A46 turn by church in Painswick, right at The March Hare. Hotel 200yds on right **Parking:** 22

PAXFORD MAP 10 SP13

Churchill Arms

Modern British

Confident cooking in charming Cotswold pub

☎ 01386 594000 GL55 6XH
e-mail: mail@thechurchillarms.com
web: www.thechurchillarms.com

This archetypal, mellow Cotswold stone pub with inglenook, beams and huge flagstones is endearingly rustic and unpretentious. Sympathetically refurbished in pastel shades and oak flooring, with mix-and-match wood furniture that delivers character and informality. Blackboards for wines and food, home-made chutney for sale and an attractive rear garden add further charm. Clean-cut dishes and presentation deliver a thoroughly modern approach. Attractive, light, confident, straightforward modern British cooking with some European influences, incorporating quality local produce, graces sensibly compact chalkboard menus. Expect the likes of organic salmon with creamed celeriac, tomato and thyme or loin of lamb with butternut caponata.

Chef: D Toon & S Brooke-Little **Owners:** Sonya & Leo Brooke-Little **Times:** 12-2/7-9, Closed 25 Dec **Prices:** Starter £4-£8.50, Main £7.50-£16, Dessert £3.50-£5, Coffee £1.75, Min/Water £2, Service optional **Wine:** 10 bottles over £20, 19 bottles under £20, 10 by the glass (£3-£5.50) **Seats:** 60 **Smoking:** N/Sm area, Air con **Children:** Portions **Directions:** Situated 2m E of Chipping Campden **Parking:** On street

STOW-ON-THE-WOLD MAP 11 SP12

The Conservatory Restaurant

British, French

Venerable Cotswold hotel with punchy cooking

☎ 01451 830344 Grapevine Hotel, Sheep St GL54 1AU
e-mail: enquiries@vines.co.uk
web: www.vines.co.uk

A typically beautiful Cotswold-stone building, this long-established watering and lodging venue has its roots in the 17th century. The conservatory restaurant lies close to the eponymous 100-year-old vine, providing a canopy for romantic, candlelit dining in the evenings; a youthful team ensures service is unstuffy and there's just enough formality to make it special. Good flavours abound on this competently cooked, ambitious menu - try confit belly pork with parsnip purée. A second restaurant, La Vigna, serves lighter Mediterranean-style dishes.

Times: 12-2.30/7-9.30 **Rooms:** 22 (22 en suite) ★★★ HL **Directions:** Take A436 towards Chipping Norton; 150yds on right facing green

Fosse Manor

Modern British

Modern British cuisine in country-house setting

☎ 01451 830354 GL54 1JX
e-mail: enquiries@fossemanor.co.uk
web: www.fossemanor.co.uk

A stylish and comfortable country-house hotel, with an elegant combination of contemporary and traditional décor. Choose from the informal bistro-style dining area, or the more formal dining room, with wooden flooring and high-backed leather chairs. Modern British cuisine is very much rooted in classical techniques here, using lots of interesting ingredients. Try a starter of marinated tuna loin for example, served with wasabi, soy, pickled cucumber and chilli jam. You could choose a fresh fish main course, like pan-fried fillet of sea bass served with saffron creamed potato, broad beans and chive cream sauce. Delicious desserts include spiced berry jelly with mascarpone and fine biscuit. The wine list offers a nice selection of dessert wines and port.

Chef: Simon Walford **Owners:** Fosse Manor Hotel Ltd **Times:** 12.30-2/7-9 **Prices:** Fixed L £14.50, Fixed D £29, Coffee £2, Min/Water £3.50, Service optional **Wine:** 96 bottles over £20, 14 bottles under £20, 10 by the glass (£3.75-£5.60) **Notes:** Vegetarian available, Dress Restrictions, Smart casual, Civ Wed 40 **Seats:** 40 **Smoking:** N/Sm in restaurant **Children:** Portions **Rooms:** 20 (20 en suite) ★★★ HL **Directions:** From Stow-on-the-Wold take A429 S for 1m **Parking:** 40

England

STOW-ON-THE-WOLD *continued* MAP 11 SP12

The Kings Arms

Modern British

Bustling, atmospheric 500-year-old coaching inn

☎ 01451 830364 Market Square GL54 1AF
web: www.kingsarmsstowonthewold.co.uk

This tall mellow-stone building oozes a blend of character and modernity. Dining is spread over two floors, with a bustling bar downstairs and first floor restaurant. Floorboards, exposed stone and beams rub shoulders with modern lighting, while wines, displayed on shelves with price tags round their necks, replace the conventional list upstairs. Confident modern cooking in generous portions with robust flavours and a straightforward approach is the style. Fresh Cornish fish parades alongside local specialities like Gloucestershire Old Spot pork. The menu is bolstered by blackboard specials like pork tenderloin fillet with a mustard and basil crust, truffle mash and veal jus.

Times: 12-3/7-10 **Directions:** Telephone for details

947AD at the Royalist

Modern European

Assured cooking in historic hostelry

☎ 01451 830670 Digbeth St GL54 1BN
e-mail: info@theroyalisthotel.co.uk
web: www.theroyalisthotel.co.uk

Officially designated as the oldest inn in Britain, this delightful Jacobean building dates from 947AD and oozes great charm and character. History is around every corner, with such curiosities as 1,000-year-old timbers, a leper hole and, in the contemporary-styled restaurant, a grand fireplace featuring markings of a witch. Cooking is accomplished and bang up-to-date, with well-judged flavour combinations and good use of fresh ingredients. A set dinner may take in goat's cheese soufflé with garlic and chive cream, tournedos of beef with oxtail ravioli or herb-crusted cod with saffron cream, and warm chocolate fondant. Desserts are a highlight and it's best to book ahead, especially at weekends.

Chef: Eugene McClusky & Mathew Dare **Owners:** Alan Corlett **Times:** 12-2.30/7-9.30, Closed Sun-Mon **Prices:** Fixed L £10-£28.50, Fixed D £34.50, Coffee £1.50, Min/Water £3, Service added 10% **Wine:** 7 bottles over £20, 13 bottles under £20, 8 by the glass (£3.25-£5.50) **Notes:** Vegetarian available, Dress Restrictions, Smart dress/smart casual **Seats:** 30, Pr/dining room 30 **Smoking:** N/Sm in restaurant **Children:** Portions **Rooms:** 8 (8 en suite) ★★★ HL **Directions:** Please telephone for directions **Parking:** 8

Wyck Hill House Hotel

Modern British

Sample local flavours in 18th-century Cotswold setting

☎ 01451 831936 Burford Rd GL54 1HY
e-mail: enquiries@wyckhillhouse.com
web: www.wyckhillhouse.com

The interior of this Cotswold mansion house has been given a cool, contemporary makeover with comfortable furniture, log fires and lots of oak surfaces. The dining room is more traditional with its oak panelling and wonderful views. Formal but friendly service is attentive but never intrusive. Dishes are in the modern British style with occasional French accents and ingredients are seasonal and local. Deft handling produces dishes that are full of flavour like the starter of pheasant, chestnut and fig tian with port and plum chutney and the main course of guinea fowl breast with grilled pancetta and roasted vegetables. To finish, try the trio of seasonal desserts.

Chef: Mathew Dare **Owners:** Niche Hotels **Times:** 12.30-2/7-9.30 **Prices:** Fixed L £14.50-£16.25, Fixed D £36.50-£41.45, Coffee £2.95, Min/Water £2.95, Service optional **Wine:** 30 bottles over £20, 4 bottles under £20, 4 by the glass (£3.95-£4.45) **Notes:** Sun L £18.50, Vegetarian available, Dress Restrictions, No denim or trainers, Civ Wed 80 **Seats:** 60, Pr/dining room 80 **Smoking:** N/Sm in restaurant, Air con **Children:** Menu, Portions **Rooms:** 32 (32 en suite) ★★★★ HL **Directions:** A429 for Cirencester, pass through 2 sets of traffic lights in Stow-on-the-Wold, at 3rd set of lights bear left signed Burford, then A424 signed Stow-on-the-Wold, hotel 7m on left **Parking:** 120

STROUD MAP 04 SO80

The Bear of Rodborough

Traditional British

A welcoming inn offering traditional British cuisine

☎ 01453 878522 Rodborough Common GL5 5DE
e-mail: info@bearofrodborough.info
web: www.cotswold-inns-hotels.co.uk

This historic hostelry is set in 300 acres of National Trust land and enjoys lovely views. A stone archway separates the brightly decorated dining areas, softened by luxurious drapes and paintings of the local area. The British cuisine is inspired by local produce and good ingredients. Typical starters might include warm Cerney goat's cheese bruschetta with olive tapenade, while main courses include traditional favourites like fillet of beef with a horseradish crust. There is a grill menu and extensive bar menu offering sandwiches, selected starters and mains, pasta dishes and salads.

Chef: Terry Woolcock **Owners:** Cotswold Inns & Hotels Ltd **Times:** 12-2.30/7-9.30, Closed L Mon & Sat **Prices:** Fixed L £12.95, Fixed D £28.95,

continued

Coffee £2.15, Min/Water £3.95, Service optional **Wine:** 37 bottles over £20, 24 bottles under £20, 8 by the glass (£3.65-£5.20) **Notes:** Vegetarian available, Civ Wed 70 **Seats:** 70, Pr/dining room 50 **Smoking:** N/Sm in restaurant **Children:** Menu, Portions **Rooms:** 46 (46 en suite) ★★★ HL **Directions:** 2.5m S from Stroud **Parking:** 100

Burleigh Court Hotel

British, Mediterranean

Classical country-house style

☎ 01453 883804 Burleigh, Minchinhampton GL5 2PF
e-mail: info@burleighcourthotel.co.uk
web: www.burleighcourthotel.co.uk

This Grade II listed, 18th-century Cotswold-stone manor house is set in 3.5 acres of gardens. The restaurant is true to these classical country-house roots, providing a formal setting for enjoyable modern British cuisine. The freshest local produce is used and many herbs and vegetables are home grown. The menu is extensive at lunch and dinner with the likes of sautéed chicken livers and crispy pancetta to start, or duo of Cornish lamb as a main course. The Sunday lunch menu has a range of traditional options and the wine list offers a selection of wines from around the world.

Chef: Stephen Woodcock **Owners:** Louise Noble **Times:** 12-2/7-9, Closed 24-26 Dec **Prices:** Fixed L fr £16.95, Fixed D fr £28.50, Coffee £2, Min/Water £3.50 **Wine:** 55 bottles over £20, 16 bottles under £20, 6 by the glass (£3.50-£5.50) **Notes:** Vegetarian available, Dress Restrictions, Smart casual, no jeans, Civ Wed 50 **Seats:** 34, Pr/dining room 18 **Smoking:** N/Sm in restaurant **Children:** Menu, Portions **Rooms:** 18 (18 en suite) ★★★ HL **Directions:** 2.5m SE of Stroud, off A419 **Parking:** 28

TETBURY MAP 04 ST89

Calcot Manor

Modern Mediterranean

NOTABLE WINE LIST

Perfect Cotswold retreat with enjoyable dining

☎ 01666 890391 Calcot GL8 8YJ
e-mail: reception@calcotmanor.co.uk
web: www.calcotmanor.co.uk

Cistercian monks built this farmhouse in the 14th century but this establishment is very much in the 21st with its beautifully designed bedrooms, stunning health spa and outstanding facilities for children. The understated elegance of the light and airy Conservatory Restaurant makes a delightful dinner venue with its white linen-clad tables and good-quality settings. Service is both professional and friendly. Modern English dishes include touches of the Mediterranean as in starters like pumpkin ravioli, sautéed wild mushrooms, parmesan and truffle emulsion, as well as more substantial fare such as marinated beef fillet on the bone roasted in a wood oven. Dessert might be a nursery-redolent hot apple and cinnamon rice pudding with clotted cream ice cream.

Notable Wine List: The wine list offers a good selection and well chosen range of growers and vintages.

Calcot Manor

Chef: Michael Croft **Owners:** Richard Ball (MD) **Times:** 12-2/7-9.30 **Prices:** Starter £8.95-£18, Main £8.95-£20, Dessert £6.75-£7.25, Coffee £2.50, Min/Water £3.75, Service included **Wine:** 10 bottles under £20, 12 by the glass (£4.35-£10.60) **Notes:** Sun L 2 courses £21, 3 courses £25, Vegetarian available, Civ Wed 100 **Seats:** 100, Pr/dining room 100 **Smoking:** N/Sm in restaurant, Air con **Children:** Menu, Portions **Rooms:** 30 (30 en suite) ★★★★ **Directions:** M4 junct 18, take A46 towards Stroud and at x-roads with A4135 turn right and then 1st left **Parking:** 100

The Trouble House

British, French

Exquisite, innovative food with a relaxed atmosphere that favours drinkers as well as diners

☎ 01666 502206 Cirencester Rd GL8 8SG
e-mail: enquiries@troublehouse.co.uk
web: www.troublehouse.co.uk

At first glance this unassuming roadside inn looks no different from any of the other pleasant traditional pubs in the area. Step inside and it's a different matter - it's usually bustling with both drinkers and diners who flock here for this next-generation gastro-pub food. Interiors have been sensitively upgraded to a contemporary style accentuating the spaciousness and light throughout - white walls, bare wood unclothed tables and wood floors. On the menu simple, straightforward dishes (roast Old Spot pork with sweet and sour braised red cabbage) rub shoulders with more complex offerings (sea bass with fennel purée and fresh linguini, marjoram and chilli) that betray the chef's background at high-end establishments such as Le Manoir (see entry) and City Rhodes.

continued

TETBURY *continued* MAP 04 ST89

Chef: Michael Bedford **Owners:** Michael & Sarah Bedford **Times:** 12-2/7-9.30, Closed Xmas to New Year & BHs, Mon, Closed D Sun **Prices:** Starter £5-£12, Main £15-£20, Dessert £5-£9, Coffee £2, Min/Water £2.80, Service optional, Group min 8 service 10% **Wine:** 25 bottles over £20, 25 bottles under £20, 12 by the glass (£3.50-£10) **Notes:** Vegetarian available **Seats:** 50 **Smoking:** N/Sm area **Children:** Min 10 yrs D, Portions **Directions:** Telephone for directions **Parking:** 25

THORNBURY MAP 04 ST69

Thornbury Castle

British, International NOTABLE WINE LIST

Modern cuisine in a fairytale castle setting

☎ 01454 281182 Castle St BS35 1HH
e-mail: info@thornburycastle.co.uk
web: www.thornburycastle.co.uk

A grand Tudor castle that today combines atmosphere and history with modern comforts. Baronial public rooms are impressive, featuring magnificent fireplaces, high mullioned windows, tapestries, grand portraits and suits of armour. Elegant, wood-panelled dining rooms are candlelit at night and make a memorable setting for a leisurely meal. Sensibly compact and straightforward British based menus are enhanced with international influences. A competent kitchen makes good use of quality seasonal ingredients, including home-grown herbs and vegetables. Choices include the likes of noisette of pig's trotter, celeriac purée, millefeuille of duck, cherry and balsamic compôte, and banana suet pudding with dark rum ice cream. The serious wine list contains choice and quality.

Notable Wine List: A classic and well chosen list with a particularly strong Bordeaux section.

Chef: Paul Mottram **Owners:** von Essen **Times:** 12-2/7-9.30 **Prices:** Fixed L fr £25, Fixed D fr £42.50, Coffee £3.50, Min/Water £3.50, Service optional **Wine:** 300 bottles over £20, 2 bottles under £20, 7 by the glass (£5-£7.50) **Notes:** Fixed L 3 courses, Mid week Menu Rapide L 3 courses £15, Vegetarian available, Dress Restrictions, Smart casual, Civ Wed 50 **Seats:** 72, Pr/dining room 22 **Smoking:** N/Sm in restaurant **Children:** Min 12 yrs, Menu, Portions **Rooms:** 25 (25 en suite) ★★★ HL **Directions:** M5 junct 16. N on A38. Continue for 4m to lights and turn left. Following brown Historic Castle signs **Parking:** 50

UPPER SLAUGHTER MAP 10 SP12

Lords of the Manor

see opposite

WINCHCOMBE MAP 10 SP02

5 North Street

see page 172

Wesley House

British, European

Popular Cotswold restaurant noted for quality

☎ 01242 602366 High St GL54 5LJ
e-mail: enquiries@wesleyhouse.co.uk
web: www.wesleyhouse.co.uk

An oasis at the heart of bustling Winchcombe, this black and white timbered former merchant's house dates from the 15th century and has all the proper credentials to prove it. Beamed ceilings and open stone fireplaces sit comfortably with modern aspects like a glass atrium over the terrace, and effective modern lighting. Seasonal variations ring the changes on the modern British menus with Mediterranean influences, and look out for special offers at lunch. A sample menu starts with cured organic salmon with Cornish crab salad and cucumber spaghetti, or terrine of duck confit foie gras and quince, followed by steamed halibut, risotto of Cornish crab and leek, or roast Balmoral venison, parsnip tarte Tatin and chestnut jus.

Chef: Martin Dunn **Owners:** Matthew Brown **Times:** 12-2/7-9, Closed Xmas, Closed D Sun **Prices:** Fixed L fr £12.50, Starter £5.50-£8.50, Main £15.50-£19.50, Dessert £6.50, Coffee £2.75, Min/Water £3, Service optional **Wine:** 70 bottles over £20, 20 bottles under £20, 12 by the glass (£3.75-£12) **Notes:** Fixed D 2 courses, Fixed D 3 courses Sat only £35-£38, Vegetarian available, Civ Wed 60 **Seats:** 70, Pr/dining room 24 **Smoking:** N/Sm in restaurant, Air con **Children:** Portions **Rooms:** 6 (6 en suite) ★★★★ RR **Directions:** In centre of Winchcombe

Lords of the Manor

UPPER SLAUGHTER MAP 10 SP12

Modern European

Relaxed and welcoming country-house dining

☎ 01451 820243 GL54 2JD
e-mail: enquiries@lordsofthemanor.com
web: www.lordsofthemanor.com

A 17th-century former rectory of mellow Cotswold stone, this welcoming hotel - with Victorian-era additions - sits in 8 acres of gardens and parkland that deliver an idyllic, picture-postcard setting. There's a feeling of home from home, its traditional interiors decked out in true country-house style with open winter fires, deep sofas and period pieces. The smart dining room continues the theme, with cream walls, heavy tapestry drapes, comfortable high-backed chairs and tables set with eye-catching flowers, while service is friendly, attentive and informed.
The kitchen's modern approach comes underpinned by a classical theme and uses well-sourced, quality local ingredients. Attention to detail and consistency characterise the style, with plentiful skill parading alongside some innovative elements on a repertoire of crisply scripted, fixed-price menus, including lunch, carte and tasting options. Think slow-roast fillet of Scottish beef paired with parsnip risotto and trevisio, or roast loin of venison with braised chicory and pomegranate, and perhaps a warm plum tart with hazelnut parfait and golden sultanas to finish. Alfresco summer dining completes the accomplished package.

Chef: Les Rennie
Owners: Empire Ventures
Times: 12-2/7.00-9.30, Closed L Mon
Prices: Fixed L fr £19.50, Fixed D fr £40, Coffee £2.95, Min/Water £3.75, Service added but optional 10%
Wine: 150 bottles over £20, 18 bottles under £20, 14 by the glass (£4.50-£12)
Notes: Tasting menu 8 courses £59, Vegetarian available, Dress Restrictions, Smart casual, no trainers, Civ Wed 50
Seats: 55, Pr/dining room 30
Smoking: N/Sm in restaurant
Children: Min 7 yrs, Menu, Portions
Rooms: 27 (27 en suite) ★★★ HL
Directions: Follow signs towards The Slaughters 2m W of A429. Hotel on right in centre of Upper Slaughter
Parking: 40

England

5 North Street

WINCHCOMBE MAP 10 SP02

French, European

Unpretentious, stunning cooking in Cotswolds

☎ 01242 604566 5 North St GL54 5LH
e-mail: marcusashenford@yahoo.co.uk

Wooden beams, bare tables and understated, friendly service emphasise the relaxed, yet professional style at the Ashenfords' mellow-stone, bay-windowed, shop-front restaurant at the heart of the village. It's all relatively simple and pared back, the split-level dining areas cosy and intimate and oozing rustic charm.
Marcus Ashenford's cooking follows the theme, clean-cut in style and delightfully simple, but delivering wonderful flavours without pretension. Focusing on quality ingredients and high skill, combinations are interesting, seasonality is well respected and those flavours prominent. Expect a modern approach underpinned by a classical French theme, the sensibly compact, fixed-price menus bolstered by a ten-course surprise tasting option (though wife Kate, who heads-up front-of-house, will explain individual courses if preferred). From the carte, expect the likes of braised ox cheek served with creamed celeriac and horseradish, field mushrooms with baby spinach and a reduced cooking liqueur, while a presentation of pear or a warm chocolate tart with caramelised banana and banana ice cream might feature on the dessert menu. And our advice, don't go to the Cotswolds without a visit to No 5.

Chef: Marcus Ashenford **Owners:** Marcus & Kate Ashenford **Times:** 12.30-1.30/7-9, Closed 1st 2 wks Jan, 1st wk Aug, Mon, Closed L Tue, D Sun **Prices:** Fixed L fr £18.50, Fixed D £26-£36, Coffee £3, Min/Water £2.75, Service optional **Wine:** 60 bottles over £20, 8 bottles under £20, 6 by the glass (£4-£6) **Notes:** Tasting menu 10 courses £50, Vegetarian available **Seats:** 26 **Smoking:** N/Sm in restaurant **Children:** Menu, Portions **Directions:** 7m from Cheltenham **Parking:** On street, pay & display

GREATER MANCHESTER

ALTRINCHAM MAP 15 SJ78

Juniper

see page 174

HORWICH MAP 15 SD61

De Vere Whites

Modern British, French

Football fans' dream restaurant

☎ 01204 667788 De Havilland Way BL6 6SF
e-mail: whites@devere-hotels.com
web: www.devereonline.co.uk

This classy restaurant is part of the Reebok stadium, home to Bolton Wanderers. Situated on the second floor, Reflections restaurant is accessed via a wooden illuminated walkway and offers a bird's eye view of the football pitch. Booths in front of a plate glass window that overhangs the pitch offer the best seats in the house. The restaurant has its own cocktail-style bar, well-spaced tables, classic white linen and fresh flowers. Service is relatively formal with cloched dishes, reflecting the classical feel of the French-influenced menu which offers the likes of John Dory on potato rösti, with an etuve of leek and sauce lie de vin. You can dine here Wednesday to Saturday evenings, although on a match night it might be difficult to keep your eye on the ball and enjoy the fine cuisine at the same time.

continued

Chef: Paul Hoad **Owners:** Reflections - De Vere Hotels **Times:** 7-10, Closed 25 Dec, Sun, Mon & Tues, Closed L all week **Prices:** Starter £5.95-£9.95, Main £16.95-£25.50, Dessert £6-£7, Coffee £2.50, Min/Water £3.75, Service optional **Wine:** 30 bottles over £20, 6 bottles under £20, 4 by the glass **Notes:** Vegetarian available, Dress Restrictions, Smart casual, no jeans or trainers, Civ Wed 60 **Seats:** 65 **Smoking:** N/Sm in restaurant, Air con **Children:** Min 14 yrs, Portions **Rooms:** 125 (125 en suite) ★★★★ **Directions:** Off M61 junct 6 **Parking:** 2500

MANCHESTER MAP 16 SJ89

Alias Hotel Rossetti

Mediterranean

Friendly, funky retro-style café

☎ 0161 247 7744 107 Piccadilly M1 2DB
e-mail: rossetti@aliashotels.com
web: www.aliashotels.com

continued

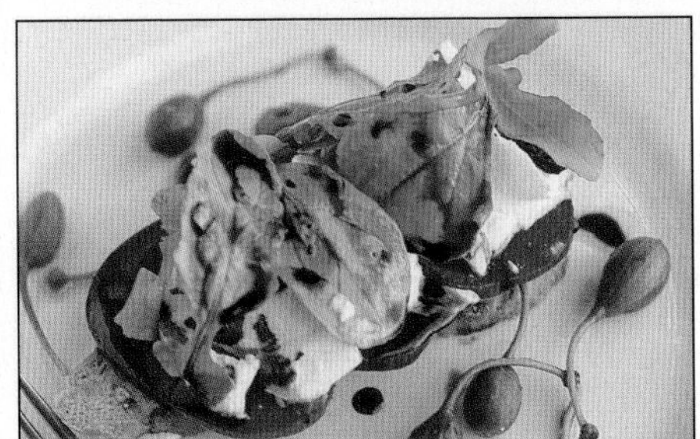

Alias Hotel Rossetti

This funky, retro-style hotel is close to Piccadilly station, major shops and business district. The Mediterranean brasserie has a modern, open plan feel with polished wooden floors, high ceilings and sculpted metal railings separating the bar from the raised restaurant area. The food is rustic with good seasonal ingredients like oysters and wild sea trout creating a true brasserie feel. Cooking is mainly Mediterranean, with dishes like antipasti, grilled scallops with confit duck in red wine sauce or baked turbot with fennel and confit lemon. Try the 'Bring me Food' concept for all the table (not Sat night), a great way to try a mix of dishes.

Chef: David Gale **Owners:** Nigel Chapman & Nicholas Dickinson **Times:** 12-5.30/5.30-10 **Prices:** Starter £3.75-£7, Main £8.50-£15.50, Dessert £3.95-£4.75, Coffee £2.20, Min/Water £3, Service optional **Wine:** 16 bottles over £20, 21 bottles under £20, 5 by the glass (£4.40-£6) **Notes:** Brunch menu on Sun, Vegetarian available **Seats:** 70, Pr/dining room 24 **Smoking:** N/Sm in restaurant **Children:** Menu, Portions **Rooms:** 61 (61 en suite) **Directions:** Located in city centre close to Piccadilly station **Parking:** Opposite hotel 25% discount

Choice Bar & Restaurant

Modern British NEW

Friendly waterside restaurant offering fine dining

☎ 0161 833 3400 Castle Quay, Castlefield M15 4NT
e-mail: book@choicebarandrestaurant.co.uk
web: www.choicebarandrestaurant.co.uk

In a leafy development overlooking the canal, the former spice mill with cream furnishings, exposed brickwork, low ceilings and candlelight has a cosy feel in the evening. For a different experience, come on Saturday night when there's live music, or at lunchtime on a fine day for alfresco dining, or visit the bar with its feature wine cellar. The menu offers modern dishes with some unusual takes on traditional and regional combinations. Take a starter of pan-fried king scallops on a Cheshire cheese scone for example, then move on to rack of Bowland lamb with rissole of lamb shank in Cheshire air-dried ham with colcannon potato and rosemary and red wine jus.

Chef: Mark Urry **Owners:** Jon Grieves **Times:** 11/11, Closed 25-31 Dec **Prices:** Fixed L fr £12.95, Fixed D fr £15.95, Starter £4.95-£7.50, Main £11.95-£18.95, Dessert £4.95, Coffee £1.50, Min/Water £3.70, Service added but optional 10% **Wine:** 15 bottles over £20, 21 bottles under £20, 33 by the glass (£3.50-£12) **Notes:** Fixed L & D available Sun-Thur, Vegetarian available **Seats:** 60 **Smoking:** N/Sm in restaurant, Air con **Children:** Portions **Directions:** A5067 & A56 x-rds, off Bridgewater viaduct **Parking:** Limited day 30 spaces evening, NCP 50yds

Copthorne Hotel Manchester

International

Stylish waterfront dining

☎ 0161 873 7321 Clippers Quay, Salford Quays M50 3SN
e-mail: roomsales.manchester@mill-cop.com
web: www.copthorne.com

This smart modern red-brick hotel enjoys an enviable location next to the quays in the redeveloped Salford Docks, close to Old Trafford and the Lowry Centre. The crescent-shaped Chandler's Restaurant makes the most of waterfront views with a new minimalist look featuring stripped pine flooring and clean lines. A couple of Lowry prints adorn the walls alongside changing artwork by a local artist. The chef serves up an interesting mix of classical dishes with modern twists and some fusion elements using oils and spices. Typical starters might include pan-fried foie gras with home-made gingerbread and olive and fig chutney. Classically-inspired mains include a cannon of lamb slow poached in red wine on mint pea velouté.

Times: 7-9.30, Closed Xmas, 1 Jan, Sun, Closed L Tue-Sat **Rooms:** 166 (166 en suite) ★★★★ HL **Directions:** From M602 follow signs to Salford Quays/Trafford Park. Hotel is 0.75m along A5063 (Trafford Rd)

The Establishment

Modern British, French V

Stylish modern cuisine in grand setting

☎ 0161 839 6300 43-45 Spring Gardens M2 2BG
e-mail: info@establishmentrestaurants.com
web: www.establishmentrestaurant.com

Centrally located, this grand building used to be a bank, and more recently a pub. It was converted to a stylish, airy restaurant in 2004 and has become a firm favourite with business types attracted to the smart, contemporary feel, as well as the great value lunch menus. Some of the impressive original features have been retained, including the double domed glass atrium and imposing marble columns. The food is deceptively simple, and there's some accomplished cooking in dishes like mosaic of rabbit, foie gras and ox cheek or roast breast of Goosenargh duck with boudin of winter truffles, foie gras and potato tart and raisin purée.

Chef: Ian Morgan **Owners:** K Lewis, T Maloy, I Morgan **Times:** 12-2.30/7-10, Closed 25 Dec & BHs, Sun, Closed L Sat **Prices:** Fixed L £18-£38.50, Fixed D £25-£48, Starter £6.50-£12.50, Main £21-£26, Dessert £7.50-£10.50, Coffee £2.50, Min/Water £2.95 **Wine:** 195 bottles over £20, 7 bottles under £20, 12 by the glass (£3.75-£6.95) **Notes:** Vegetarian menu, Dress Restrictions, Smart casual **Seats:** 85, Pr/dining room 30 **Smoking:** N/Sm in restaurant, Air con **Children:** Portions **Directions:** City centre at top of King St

England

Juniper

ALTRINCHAM MAP 15 SJ78

Modern French, Unique

Dazzling culinary fun

☎ 0161 929 4008 21 The Downs WA14 2QD
e-mail: reservations@juniper-restaurant.co.uk
web: www.juniper-restaurant.co.uk

Chef: Paul Kitching
Owners: P & D Keeling, P Kitching, K O'Brien
Times: 12-2/7-10, Closed 1 wk Feb, 2 wks summer, Sun-Mon, Closed L Tue-Thur
Prices: Fixed L £20, Fixed D £40, Coffee £3.75, Min/Water £3, Service included
Wine: 50 bottles over £20, 6 bottles under £20, 4 by the glass (£4.50)
Notes: Fixed L 3 courses, Gourmet menu 12 courses £60
Seats: 36
Smoking: N/Sm in restaurant, Air con
Directions: A556, Chester-Manchester road. Altrincham town centre

Physically, there's little to distinguish Juniper from the average mild-mannered suburban restaurant, with its classic shop-front conversion, but don't be fooled, this is the culinary playground of an expressionist chef and one of the country's most renowned and talked about restaurants. The interior, decked out on two levels, is equally discreet and unpretentious, yet cool, the dining room decorated in shades of green, with quirky artwork, subdued lighting and tables dressed in crisp white linen resplendent with highly polished glassware and cutlery. Service is equally polished and nothing less than flawless, while a swish basement bar kicks off the Juniper adventure over cocktails while perusing the flamboyant menu.
But, there's little to prepare the uninitiated for chef-patron Paul Kitching's highly individual style - reading the menu is an eye-opening experience that challenges conventional thinking. No one else comes close to his expressional and aspirational cooking style - it's a one-off, idiosyncratic, bold, improvisational and breathtaking, delivered with masterful technique. Expect exquisite, full flavours of freshness and vitality on a repertoire of predominantly fixed-price menus that include gourmet surprise offerings (ten-course lunch, twelve-course dinner) that deliver an impromptu medley unique to each table, where one simply sits back and enjoys the ride. Main menu dishes sometimes come with witty subtitles or the odd supplement, but whatever, be prepared to be wowed. Take a threesome: creamy gruyère cheese risotto with chilled Avruga caviar, onion and pimento lemon cream; baked fillet of turbot with Savoy cabbage, lemon tart, olive and onion gâteau, red barley, dried blueberries and kipper glaze; and a dessert grande assiette.

MANCHESTER *continued* MAP 16 SJ89

Greens

Modern Vegetarian V

Well-established vegetarian restaurant

☎ 0161 434 4259 43 Lapwing Ln, Didsbury M20 2NT
e-mail: greensrestaurant@tiscali.co.uk

Serving up classy vegetarian food for over ten years, Greens is something of an institution, which goes some way to explaining the permanently bustling atmosphere. Rather peculiarly for a vegetarian restaurant, the chef-owner is actually a meat-eater - a fact that can only be impacting on the food in a good way, as the menu here is a both eclectic and exciting. Try deep-fried oyster mushrooms with Chinese pancakes and plum sauce to start, for example, then continue with a main such as filo pastry strudel with leeks, mushrooms, tomatoes, ricotta and a port wine sauce.

Chef: Simon Connolly & Simon Rimmer **Owners:** Simon Connolly & Simon Rimmer **Times:** 12-2/5.30-10.30, Closed BHs, Closed L Mon-Sat **Prices:** Food prices not confirmed for 2007. Please telephone for details **Notes:** Vegetarian only **Seats:** 48 **Smoking:** N/Sm in restaurant **Children:** Menu **Directions:** Telephone for directions **Parking:** On street

Harvey Nichols 2nd Floor Restaurant

Modern European NOTABLE WINE LIST

Trendy dining for designer shoppers, overlooking Exchange Square

☎ 0161 828 8898 21 New Cathedral St M1 1AD
e-mail: secondfloor.reservations@harveynichols.com
web: www.harveynichols.com

This stylish contemporary restaurant shares the second floor of the designer department store with an interesting food hall and a more relaxed bar/brasserie. The black and white colour scheme makes a bold statement and the floor to ceiling plate glass windows offer views over the trendy Exchange Square and neighbouring Selfridges. The modern menu has classic ingredients like terrine of ham hock, parsley and sweet garlic, combined with European influences like French-style braised rabbit leg, Meaux mustard and tarragon. The wine list has global coverage and the added benefit that you can buy the wines in the food hall.
Notable Wine List: A most comprehensive wine list, full of quality in every area.

Chef: Robert Craggs **Owners:** Harvey Nichols **Times:** 10-3/6-10.30, Closed 25-26 Dec, 1 Jan, Easter Sun, Closed D Sun-Mon **Prices:** Starter £5.50-£10.50, Main £11.50-£21, Dessert £6-£7.50, Coffee £2, Min/Water £3, Service added but optional 10% **Wine:** 338 bottles over £20, 62 bottles under £20, 16 by the glass (£3.50-£7.50) **Notes:** Vegetarian available **Seats:** 50 **Smoking:** N/Sm in restaurant, Air con **Directions:** Just off Deansgate, town centre. 5 min walk from Victoria Station **Parking:** Under store, across road

Lowry Hotel, The River Restaurant

Modern European

A designer setting for contemporary European cuisine

☎ 0161 827 4000 50 Dearmans Place, Chapel Wharf, Salford M3 5LH
e-mail: enquiries@thelowryhotel.com
web: www.thelowryhotel.com

Chic hotel on the edge of the city centre with a modish restaurant to match. Overlooking the River Irwell, it's a bright and airy space decked out in brown and cream, with leather banquettes and tables dressed in crisp white linen. The accomplished kitchen delivers an extensive brasserie menu of modern European fare; kick off with warm chicken liver salad with apple and parsnip purée perhaps, before tucking into salmon with a horseradish crust, or tournedos of Aberdeen Angus with five onion sauce. Coconut pannacotta with spiced roast pineapple might follow.

Chef: Eyck Zimmer **Owners:** Sir Rocco Forte & family **Times:** 12-2.30/6-10.30 **Prices:** Fixed L £13.50, Fixed D £20.50, Starter £7-£12.50, Main £17-£34.50, Dessert £7-£10.50, Service added but optional 10% **Wine:** 122 bottles over £20, 9 bottles under £20, 18 by the glass (£4.75-£14) **Notes:** British Classics Menu 4 courses £38, Vegetarian available, Smart casual prefered, Civ Wed 120 **Seats:** 120, Pr/dining room 20 **Smoking:** N/Sm area, Air con **Children:** Menu, Portions **Rooms:** 165 (165 en suite) ★★★★★ HL **Directions:** Telephone for directions **Parking:** 100

Midland Hotel

French

Imposing Edwardian hotel for an opulent dining experience

☎ 0161 236 3333 Peter St M60 2DS
web: www.themidland.co.uk

Grade II listed property, purpose-built for the Midland Railway in 1903 to accommodate the discerning traveller. Still one of Manchester's most popular hotels, it attracts plenty of VIPs and has recently undergone a £15 million refurbishment. The restaurant is magnificent, with high ceilings, chandeliers, and a colour scheme of pale pinks and golds. Staff are superb and a long-standing crowd of regulars flock here to enjoy the excellent service as well as the food. The menu is

continued

England

MANCHESTER *continued* MAP 16 SJ89

not so classical these days; more modern British/European (accurately cooked roasted fillet of brill topped with braised oxtail and a rich morel sauce), with classical elements (Chateaubriand from the flambé trolley).

Chef: Gary Jenkins & Andre Matter **Owners:** QHotels **Times:** 7-11, Closed BHs, Sun, Closed L all week **Prices:** Fixed D £29, Starter £7.50-£14.95, Main £19.95-£32.95, Dessert £7.50, Coffee £3.95, Min/Water £3.50, Service optional **Wine:** 50 bottles over £20, 5 bottles under £20, 15 by the glass (£4.10-£6.60) **Notes:** Dress Restrictions, Smart casual, Civ Wed 500 **Seats:** 55 **Smoking:** N/Sm in restaurant, Air con **Children:** Menu, Portions **Rooms:** 303 (303 en suite) ★★★★ HL **Directions:** Telephone for directions **Parking:** Behind hotel

Le Mont @ Urbis

Modern French

Classical French cooking in futuristic surroundings

☎ 0161 605 8282
Levels 5 & 6 Cathedral Gardens M4 3BG
e-mail: info@le-mont.co.uk
web: www.urbis.org.uk

Set on two floors of the futuristic Urbis Centre, this glass-walled restaurant offers stunning views across Manchester from every table. Its minimalist modern décor is teamed with high quality tableware and double-clothed tables, traditional touches that prepare the way for a classical French menu of impeccable cuisine. Dishes seem simple, but are in fact labour-intensive works of art that make good use both of top-notch British produce and luxury ingredients such as foie gras, lobster and caviar. Mains might include loin of Bowland Forest heather-fed lamb in filo with shiitake and ginger-scented jus, or rib of Galloway beef with white wine shallot sauce and chive mash, while desserts are sophisticated concoctions such as bitter chocolate tart, with white chocolate sorbet and raisin syrup.

Owners: SMG Europe **Times:** 12-2.30/7-10.30, Closed Xmas, BHs, Mon, Sun, Closed L Sat **Prices:** Fixed L fr £17.50, Fixed D fr £26.95, Starter £6.25-£11.95, Main £15.50-£29.95, Dessert £6.75, Coffee £2.95, Min/Water £3.95, Service added but optional 10% **Wine:** 170 bottles over £20, 11 bottles under £20, 6 by the glass (£4.75-£5.25) **Notes:** Vegetarian available **Seats:** 70, Pr/dining room 40 **Smoking:** N/Sm area, Air con **Directions:** Please telephone for directions **Parking:** NCP Victoria Station

Moss Nook

Modern British, French

Classical food in formal setting

☎ 0161 437 4778 Ringway Rd, Moss Nook M22 5WD

This spacious open-plan restaurant is decorated in modern style with well-spaced tables. These are laid with crisp linen and quality tableware, befitting the formal cloche service delivered by friendly staff. Cuisine is classical French with some modern interpretations of traditional dishes, meeting the expectations of discerning customers. If you're undecided you can choose a surprise menu for the whole table and let the chef guide you through several tasting courses from canapés to petits fours. You can also choose fresh fish of the day, or a traditional main course like grilled fillet of British beef with wild mushrooms, glazed shallots and a red wine sauce.

Chef: Kevin Lofthouse **Owners:** P & D Harrison **Times:** 12-1.30/7-10, Closed 2 wks Xmas, Sun & Mon, Closed L Sat **Prices:** Fixed L £19.50, Fixed

continued

D £37, Starter £8-£14, Main £19.50-£22.50, Dessert £4.50-£7.50, Coffee £3.75, Min/Water £3, Service included **Wine:** 92 bottles over £20, 23 bottles under £20, 4 by the glass (£3.75-£4.40) **Notes:** Fixed L 5 courses, Fixed D 7 courses, Vegetarian available, Dress Restrictions, No jeans, trainers **Seats:** 65 **Smoking:** No pipes, Air con **Children:** Min 12 yrs **Directions:** 1m from airport at junction of Ringway with B5166 **Parking:** 30

Palmiro

Modern Italian NEW

Contemporary Italian dining in up-and-coming area of Manchester

☎ 0161 860 7330 197 Upper Chorlton Rd M16 0BH
e-mail: bookings@palmiro.net
web: www.palmiro.net

Behind a frosted glass frontage in a small row of shops in Manchester's Chorlton district, you'll find this atypical, modern Italian restaurant. Distressed wooden floors and beige walls hung with colourful photos of fruit and vegetables contribute to a cheerful interior. Expect simple, well-executed rustic Italian combinations based on good, fresh ingredients and some flown in from specialist shops in Italy. Begin with gnochetti and sea bass or pappardelle with rabbit perhaps, followed by main courses such as lamb with prosciutto rotolo and beans ragu. Finish with Venetian rice pudding or lemon cheesecake.

Chef: Paul Trello **Owners:** Stefano Bagnoli **Times:** 12-5/4-10.30, Closed 25-30 Dec, 1-4 Jan, Closed L Mon-Fri **Prices:** Fixed D £10, Starter £4.95-£6.25, Main £8.50-£14.55, Dessert £4.25, Coffee £1.50, Min/Water £3, Service optional, Group min 8 service 10% **Wine:** 20 bottles over £20, 41 bottles under £20, 16 by the glass (£2.95-£6.50) **Notes:** Fixed D 2 courses before 7pm, Sun L 4 course £14.95, Vegetarian available **Seats:** 80 **Smoking:** N/Sm in restaurant, Air con **Children:** Portions **Directions:** Please telephone for directions **Parking:** On street

Le Petit Blanc

Modern French

Authentic French cooking at a slick modern bistro

☎ 0161 832 1000 55 Kings St M2 4LQ
e-mail: manchester@lepetitblanc.co.uk
web: www.lepetitblanc.co.uk

Despite a minimalist modern décor, this funky brasserie is a comfortable venue and appeals to business and leisure diners alike. Staff are knowledgeable and the menu is imaginative; expect classical French dishes with a modern twist, conjured from the best and freshest of seasonal British produce. The confident kitchen avoids fuss in favour of delivering clear and vibrant flavours; you might start with hot smoked salmon with champagne choucroute and crab butter perhaps, and then tuck into mains of Barbary duck with butternut squash and Madeira dressing, lemon sole meunière, or pan-fried calves' liver with sage and shallot mousseline and pan juices. Good vegetarian selection.

Chef: Anshul Dhayani **Owners:** Raymond Blanc, Loch Fyne Restaurants **Times:** 12-3/5.30-11, Closed 25, 26 Dec, 1 Jan **Prices:** Fixed L £12, Fixed D £14.50, Starter £3.50-£7.50, Main £9.50-£18.50, Dessert £3.50-£5.50, Coffee £1.75, Min/Water £3, Group min 6 service 10% **Wine:** 15 bottles over £20, 18 bottles under £20, 16 by the glass (£3.25-£5.75) **Notes:** Vegetarian available **Seats:** 120, Pr/dining room 30 **Smoking:** N/Sm in restaurant, Air con **Children:** Menu, Portions **Directions:** King St, city centre **Parking:** NCP Deansgate

Simply Heathcotes

British 

Stylish metropolitan dining with extensive menu

☎ 0161 835 3536 Jacksons Row, Deansgate M2 5WD
e-mail: manchester@simplyheathcotes.co.uk
web: www.heathcotes.co.uk/simply/index.php

Tucked away in Manchester's old registry office, this buzzy, spacious, first-floor restaurant - accessed via a sweeping staircase - has a cool designer interior. Modern and minimalist, with high ceilings, natural surfaces, Philippe Starck bucket chairs and smiley, knowledgeable staff, its lengthy menu plays to the gallery and deals in modern brasserie staples that embrace regional British cooking. Think glazed Pendle lamb shepherd's pie with home-made brown sauce, or roast breast of Goosnargh duck with fondant potato and braised red cabbage, and classic desserts like bread-and-butter pudding with apricot compôte and clotted cream.

Chef: Eve Worsick **Owners:** Mr P Heathcote **Times:** 12-2.30/5.30-10, Closed 25-26 Dec, 1-3 Jan, BHs **Prices:** Fixed L £12.95-£17.50, Fixed D £15-£37.50, Starter £2.75-£6, Main £8.25-£20, Dessert £4-£4.95, Coffee £2.75, Min/Water £3.25, Service optional, Group service 10% **Wine:** 60 bottles over £20, 75 bottles under £20, 15 by the glass (£3.55-£4.95) **Notes:** Pre theatre menu available, Vegetarian menu, Civ Wed 60 **Seats:** 170, Pr/dining room 60 **Smoking:** N/Sm in restaurant, Air con **Children:** Menu, Portions **Directions:** M62 junct 17. Restaurant at top end of Deansgate **Parking:** On street

Tai Pan

Chinese NEW

Family-friendly community spirited restaurant with fantastic dim sum

☎ 0161 273 2798 81-97 Upper Brook St M13 9TX

Neither an anglicised takeaway emporium nor authentic Chinese experience, Tai Pan provides a blend of both styles of cooking, which sees the minority English clientele keep to their sweet and sour favourites (familiar and delicious) while the majority of Chinese customers order lip-smacking dishes of great wonderment ... if only the rest of us knew what they were! The answer is to be adventurous with the extensive menu. The food is fresh, alluring and full of flavour, so your palate can expect a vibrant and truly rare international experience. The Sunday lunch dim sum extravaganza is not to be missed.

Times: 12/11.30 **Directions:** 2 miles from city centre

Waters Reach

Mediterranean

A bustling, contemporary eatery at Man U's official hotel

☎ 0161 873 8899 Golden Tulip, Trafford Park M17 1WS
e-mail: info@goldentulipmanchester.co.uk
web: www.goldentulipmanchester.co.uk

Situated opposite Old Trafford football stadium and within easy reach of the airport and motorway network, this modern establishment is the official hotel of Manchester United FC. The interiors here are spacious and comfortable, designed to contemporary standards and with the kind of slick service you might expect from a busy city hotel. The Watersreach restaurant is fashionable and popular - and if there's a home win you can guarantee a good atmosphere. Consistent, interesting modern British food is very much the order of the day, with fresh flavours throughout - try a starter of roast scallop with parsnips and wasabi and a pickled ginger dressing then continue with a main of truffle stuffed chicken breast with wild mushroom risotto and chives.

Times: 12-2.30/6-10, Closed L Sat-Sun **Rooms:** 160 (160 en suite) ★★★ HL **Directions:** Telephone for directions.

Yang Sing Restaurant

Chinese, Cantonese

Famous Chinese restaurant and banqueting rooms

☎ 0161 236 2200 34 Princess St M1 4JY
e-mail: info@yang-sing.com
web: www.yang-sing.com

Established in Manchester's China Town in 1977, this ever popular restaurant is something of an institution. Occupying several floors, with function rooms as well, the place is packed day and night with people flocking here for parties and the renowned banquets. The décor is white with red pillars, red upholstered chairs, red carpets and napkins. Chinese artefacts, two fish tanks and a couple of oriental murals make interesting features. The dim sum is a great strength and typical dishes are salt and pepper spare ribs, and squid with prawn sauce.

Times: 12-11.30/12-10.30 **Directions:** Located in city centre on Princes St, which runs from Albert Square

Label

☎ 0161 833 1878 78 Deansgate M3 2FW
web: www.theaa.com/restaurants/113903.html
In a prime spot on Manchester's Deansgate. The British/Med menu is a happy-go-lucky mix of nibbles, sharing plates, salads, mains, sandwiches and great desserts.

MANCHESTER *continued* MAP 16 SJ89

Market Restaurant

☎ 0161 834 3743 104 High St, Northern Quarter M4 1HQ

Quirky, well-established restaurant focusing on freshly-prepared dishes and organic ingredients.

Restaurant Bar and Grill

☎ 0161 839 1999 14 John Dalton St M2 6JR

Trendy, fusion oriented bar and restaurant.

Royal Naz

☎ 0161 256 1060 16-18 Wilmslow Rd, Rusholme M14 5TQ

Pakistani and Indian dishes with top-quality spices.

Royal Orchid Thai Restaurant

☎ 0161 236 5183 36 Charlotte St M1 4FD

web: www.theaa.com/restaurants/113904.html

Excellent food and a chatty menu to guide you through the whole ordering procedure and direct you to the range of flavours of classic Thai cuisine. The food is authentic, the ambience friendly and relaxed.

Samsi

☎ 0161 279 0022 36-38 Whitworth St M1 3NR

web: www.theaa.com/restaurants/113905.html

The basement is home to Samsi Express (casual eating in a modern space) and a colourful Japanese supermarket. Upstairs, things are slightly more formal. The exciting menu lists a huge range of dishes from every corner of Japan.

Shere Khan

☎ 0161 256 2624 52 Wilmslow Rd, Rusholme M14 5TQ

Something of a local legend, justly popular and a haunt of celebrities.

Shimla Pinks Manchester

☎ 0161 831 7099 Dolefield, Crown Square M3 3HA

web: www.theaa.com/restaurants/113906.html

One of a chain of very funky, modern Indian eateries. Traditional and lesser known dishes on offer.

Stock

☎ 0161 839 6644 The Stock Exchange, 4 Norfolk St M2 1DW

web: www.theaa.com/restaurants/113907.html

Stunning location in the old Stock Exchange building. Hearty and inventive Southern Italian dishes.

Wagamama

☎ 0161 839 5916 1 The Printworks, Corporation St M4 4DG

Informal noodle bar with no booking.

Zinc Bar and Grill

☎ 0161 827 4200 The Triangle, Hanging Ditch M4 3ES

Contemporary Conran-owned eatery.

MANCHESTER AIRPORT MAP 15 SJ88

Etrop Grange Hotel

British, French

Country-house elegance handy for the airport

☎ 0161 499 0500 Thorley Ln M90 4EG
e-mail: etropgrange@corushotels.com
web: www.corushotels.com

Given its proximity to the airport, it might be surprising that the Georgian Etrop Grange still manages to attain an ambience more akin to a rural country house than a heaving international thoroughfare. The chandeliers, fine napery and refined decorating sensibilities enhance the luxurious atmosphere and attentive service completes the picture. The Coach House restaurant offers a menu consisting largely of favourites from the French classics - terrine of ham hock and duck confit to start, for instance, or herb-crusted lamb cutlets with dauphinoise as a main.

Chef: Andrew Firth **Owners:** Corus & Regal Hotels **Times:** 12-2/7-10, Closed L Sat **Prices:** Fixed D £35.95, Coffee £2.95, Min/Water £3, Service optional **Wine:** 30 bottles over £20, 8 bottles under £20, 2 by the glass (£3.50) **Notes:** Vegetarian available, Dress Restrictions, No Jeans, Civ Wed 80 **Seats:** 50, Pr/dining room 90 **Smoking:** N/Sm in restaurant **Children:** Portions **Rooms:** 64 (64 en suite) ★★★ HL **Directions:** Off M56 junct 5. Follow signs to Terminal 2, take 1st left (Thornley Ln), 200yds on right **Parking:** 80

Radisson SAS Hotel Manchester Airport

Modern International

Sophisticated restaurant overlooking the runway

☎ 0161 490 5000 Chicago Av M90 3RA
e-mail: sales.manchester.airport@radisson.com
web: www.radissonsas.com

Perfect for plane spotters, a crescent-shaped restaurant, with an *Around the World in 80 Days* theme, has plate glass windows down one side that look out onto the airport and runway. Quick access to the terminals, and smart tables with comfortable seating make this a must for travellers too. Given the setting, the creative international cuisine goes down a treat with well-heeled guests and locals, though it's only available in the evenings. On an imaginative menu you might find slow-cooked rare beef fillet with celeriac mash, curried oxtail, and red wine sauce, and baked pineapple carpaccio, mascarpone and basil pannacotta with tequila syrup.

Chef: R Faulkner-Walford **Owners:** Radisson SAS **Times:** 12-2.30/7-10.30, Closed L Sat-Sun **Prices:** Fixed D £27.50, Starter £6-£11, Main £14.50-£24, Dessert £6, Coffee £2, Min/Water £3.75, Service optional **Wine:** 36 bottles over £20, 6 bottles under £20, 7 by the glass (£4.75-£7.50) **Notes:** Vegetarian available, Civ Wed 80 **Seats:** 180 **Smoking:** N/Sm area, Air con **Children:** Menu, Portions **Rooms:** 360 (360 en suite) ★★★★ HL **Directions:** M56 junct5, follow signs for Terminal 2, take 1st exit at rdbt for railway station, hotel opposite station **Parking:** 220

OLDHAM MAP 16 SD90

White Hart Inn

British, European

Great food in a restored inn with bags of character

☎ 01457 872566 51 Stockport Rd, Lydgate OL4 4JJ
e-mail: bookings@thewhitehart.co.uk
web: www.thewhitehart.co.uk

The rugged moors above Oldham might seem an unlikely place for a destination dining venue, but this 200-year-old inn has reinvented itself with much success. The relaxed rustic brasserie with beams, brickwork and open fire is in sharp contrast to the stylish appeal of the contemporary restaurant, but the bold and imaginative cooking is the same in each. High quality seasonal ingredients are handled with a classic skill that gives more than a passing nod to modern trends. Hereford beef fillet with rag pudding, carrot purée and shallot jus or roast maize-fed chicken breast stuffed with garlic tiger prawns and tomato and leek spatzeli satisfies the eyes as well as the palate. Look out for special dining events.

Chef: John Rudden **Owners:** Mr C Brierley & J Rudden **Times:** 12-2.30/6-9.30, Closed Mon (brasserie open Mon-Sun), Closed L Tue-Sat, D Sun **Prices:** Fixed L £14.25-£15.75, Fixed D fr £17.75, Starter £4.95-£7.50, Main £13.75-£19, Dessert £4.75-£6, Coffee £1.60, Min/Water £3.25, Service optional **Wine:** 250 bottles over £20, 69 bottles under £20, 20 by the glass (£2.85-£4) **Notes:** Vegetarian available, Civ Wed 85 **Seats:** 50, Pr/dining room 38 **Smoking:** N/Sm in restaurant, Air con **Children:** Portions **Directions:** M62 junct 20, take A627 and continue to the end of bypass, then take the A669 to Saddleworth. Enter Lydgate turn right onto Stockport road, White Hart In is 50yds on left **Parking:** 75

ROCHDALE MAP 16 SD81

Nutters

Modern British V

'Not just a meal but an adventure'

☎ 01706 650167 Edenfield Rd (A680), Norden OL12 7TT
e-mail: enquiries@nuttersrestaurant.com
web: www.nuttersrestaurant.com

continued

England

ROCHDALE *continued* MAP 16 SD81

Nutters

Built in 1888 as Wolstonholme Manor, this building has superb gothic arches. Bought by Lord Shawcross, it was donated to Rochdale Council by his family in 1929 for use as a hospital. It eventually opened its doors as a restaurant in 1988 and in 1994 became Nutters Restaurant. The interior is no less impressive than the exterior, a cosy bar and relaxed but formal dining rooms overlook Ashworth Moor. Andrew Nutter is of course found in the kitchen, producing modern British cuisine using the finest of local and regional produce, sometimes in a rather quirky fashion. Try seared venison salad with hazelnut and asparagus shoots to start, then perhaps roast sea bass with diver-caught scallops and truffled mash. For dessert, feast on strawberry chocolate chip soufflé pudding.

Chef: Andrew Nutter **Owners:** Mr A Nutter, Mr R Nutter, Mrs K J Nutter **Times:** 12-2/6.30-9.30, Closed 1-2 days after Xmas and New Year, Mon **Prices:** Fixed L fr £12.95, Starter £4.80-£8.50, Main £16.50-£18.90, Dessert £3.95-£6.50, Coffee £2, Min/Water £2.80, Service optional, Group min 10 service 10% **Wine:** 103 bottles over £20, 32 bottles under £20, 8 by the glass (£3.60-£4.20) **Notes:** Gourmet menu 6 courses £34, Sun L 3 courses £22, Vegetarian menu, Dress Restrictions, Smart casual, Civ Wed 120 **Seats:** 154, Pr/dining room 30 **Smoking:** N/Sm in restaurant, Air con **Children:** Menu, Portions **Directions:** From Rochdale take A680 signed Blackburn. Nutters is situated on Edenfield Rd and is on right when leaving Norden **Parking:** 100

WIGAN

Simply Heathcotes Wrightington

Modern British V

Simple British cooking at its best

☎ 01257 478244 & 424500 Wrightington Hotel, Moss Ln, Wrightington WN6 9PB
e-mail: wrightington@heathcotes.co.uk
web: www.heathcotes.co.uk

continued

Situated in the Wrightington Hotel, this Heathcote offspring is a typically contemporary affair. Think bright, minimalist, split-level dining room with large stylistic artwork and unclothed, polished wood tables. An open-plan kitchen provides distraction, as do the views over rolling countryside, while the menu is unmistakably Heathcote, the brasserie-style concept wonderfully seasonal and sensationally regional. Cooking and presentation is refreshingly simple with flavour combinations and textures easy on the palate. Take a breast of Goosnargh chicken with grilled asparagus, sauté ratte potatoes and a herb butter broth, and a baked Yorkshire curd tart with rhubarb compôte and clotted cream.

Chef: Michael Noonan **Owners:** Heathcotes Restaurants **Times:** 12-2.30/6-10, Closed BHs, 1-2 Jan, Closed L 3 Jan **Prices:** Fixed L £12, Fixed D £20-£30, Starter £3.75-£6.50, Main £8.50-£22, Dessert £4-£6.50, Coffee £1.80, Min/Water £3.25, Service optional, Group min 8 service 10% **Wine:** 48 bottles over £20, 18 bottles under £20, 10 by the glass (£3.85-£5.25) **Notes:** Sun L 2 courses £14.50, 3 courses £17, Vegetarian menu, Dress Restrictions, Smart casual **Seats:** 72, Pr/dining room 12 **Smoking:** N/Sm in restaurant, Air con **Children:** Menu, Portions **Directions:** From M6 junct 27, at rdbt onto Crow Orchard Rd, then right onto Moss Ln, hotel on right **Parking:** 100

HAMPSHIRE

ALTON MAP 05 SU73

Alton Grange Hotel

Modern British, European

Contemporary cuisine in a family-run country hotel

☎ 01420 86565 London Rd GU34 4EG
e-mail: info@altongrange.co.uk
web: www.altongrange.co.uk

A large family home, Alton Grange has been sympathetically extended to create space for public areas incorporating a cocktail bar and lounge for drinks before and after dinner. The intimate atmosphere in Truffles restaurant is created by a host of Tiffany lamps, oriental objets d'art and lush green plants. Outside there are 8 acres of landscaped grounds with seating for meals on the fragrant sun terrace. Dishes like home-smoked Gressingham duck breast with pickled vegetables, watercress, plum and ginger sauce, draw on best quality seasonal ingredients, as does roast cannon of lamb, with braised lentils, spinach, celeriac and garlic purée. Lighter meals are served in Muffins brasserie.

Chef: David Heath **Owners:** Andrea & David Levene **Times:** 12-2.30/7-9.30, Closed 24 Dec-3 Jan, ex 31 Dec **Prices:** Starter £5.50-£7.95, Main £14-£19.95, Dessert £6-£7.50, Coffee £2.95, Min/Water £3.50, Service added but optional 10% **Wine:** 40 bottles over £20, 15 bottles under £20, 12 by the glass (£3-£6.50) **Notes:** 7 course Gourmet menu £42.50, Vegetarian available, Dress Restrictions, No shorts or jeans, Civ Wed 100 **Seats:** 45, Pr/dining room 18 **Smoking:** N/Sm in restaurant **Children:** Min 5 yrs, Portions **Rooms:** 30 (30 en suite) ★★★ HL **Directions:** 300yds from A31 on A339 **Parking:** 40

ANDOVER MAP 05 SU34

Esseborne Manor

Modern European

Contemporary cooking in timeless country-house setting

☎ 01264 736444 Hurstbourne Tarrant SP11 0ER
e-mail: esseborne@aol.com
web: www.esseborne-manor.co.UK

This attractive Victorian country house is surrounded by well-tended gardens and rolling countryside, both visible from its smart restaurant's large windows. Elegant fabric-lined walls, floor-to-ceiling curtains and an open log fire feature in the coral red dining room, while canapés are taken in the adjoining bar and coffees in the comfortable lounge. The kitchen's modern approach is reflected in a range of menus, with the carte a typically more ambitious, innovative experience (the fixed-priced Menu du Vin comes with the option of selected wines), displaying high technique, quality produce and clear flavours. Choose perhaps slow-roasted duck supreme with glazed carrots, potato gratin and an orange sauce, followed by a chocolate fondant with pistachio ice cream.

Chef: Steven Ratic **Owners:** Ian Hamilton **Times:** 12-2/7-9.30 **Prices:** Fixed L £13, Fixed D £22, Starter £5.50-£9.50, Main £14-£27, Dessert £6-£7.50, Coffee £2, Min/Water £2.50, Service optional **Wine:** 78 bottles over £20, 37 bottles under £20, 9 by the glass (£3-£4) **Notes:** Vegetarian available, Dress Restrictions, Smart dress, Civ Wed 100 **Seats:** 35, Pr/dining room 80 **Smoking:** N/Sm in restaurant **Children:** Portions **Rooms:** 20 (20 en suite) ★★★ HL **Directions:** On A343, halfway between Andover and Newbury **Parking:** 40

BARTON-ON-SEA MAP 05 SZ29

Pebble Beach

French, International

Clifftop restaurant specialising in seafood

☎ 01425 627777 Marine Dr BH25 7DZ
e-mail: mail@pebblebeach-uk.com
web: www.pebblebeach-uk.com

Full-length windows make the most of the wonderful views over The Needles, Hurst Castle and the Isle of Wight coast. Even on dull days the bright yellow walls and curtains impart a cheerful glow, and in summer a terrace is available for dining. There is an open kitchen that provides good entertainment for diners. A versatile modern international menu with French influences encompasses plenty of fresh local seafood (pot au feu of haddock, salmon and sea bass) along with some meaty options like beef bourguignon and pan-fried noisettes of Scottish venison with potato and celeriac rösti, roasted pear and spinach and blackberry jus. Breton-style fish soup, Gigas rock oysters and double-baked crab and ginger soufflé head the starter list.

Chef: Pierre Chevillard **Owners:** Mike Caddy **Times:** 11-2.30/6-10, Closed D 25 Dec & 1 Jan **Prices:** Fixed L £17-£25, Fixed D £23-£33, Starter £3.95-£10.50, Main £12.90-£17.50, Dessert £6-£15, Coffee £1.90, Min/Water £3.35, Service optional, Group min 10 service 10% **Wine:** 40 bottles over £20, 25 bottles under £20, 10 by the glass (£2.95-£5.50) **Notes:** Vegetarian available, Smart casual, no beach wear **Seats:** 70 **Smoking:** N/Sm in restaurant, Air con **Children:** Portions **Directions:** Follow A35 from Southampton on to A337 to New Milton, turn left down Barton Court Ave to cliff top **Parking:** 20

BASINGSTOKE MAP 05 SU65

Apollo Hotel

Modern British

Elegant hotel dining

☎ 01256 796700
Aldermaston Roundabout RG24 9NU
e-mail: admin@apollo-hotels.co.uk
web: www.apollohotels.com

This well-appointed hotel is popular with business and leisure guests alike, and offers a choice of two restaurants. Vespers is the fine dining option, a small but elegant room where the tables are dressed with crisp white napery, unusual glassware and fresh flowers. It's only open for dinner and serves a modern British menu of well-balanced dishes; your choice might include duck confit ravioli on pak choi with star anise jus, pork rolled with prunes in pancetta with a cider cream, or roast cod with a sage crust and parsnip purée. Book in advance.

Chef: Jo Booth **Owners:** Huggler Hotel **Times:** 12-2/7, Closed Xmas, New Year, Sun, Closed L Sat **Prices:** Starter £4.95-£6.50, Main £15.50-£19.95, Dessert £5.95-£6.50, Coffee £2.25, Min/Water £3.95, Service included **Wine:** 23 bottles over £20, 13 bottles under £20 **Notes:** Vegetarian available, Civ Wed 200 **Seats:** 28, Pr/dining room 200 **Smoking:** N/Sm in restaurant, Air con **Children:** Portions **Rooms:** 125 (125 en suite) ★★★★ HL **Directions:** From M3 junct 6 follow ring road N & signs for Aldermaston/Newbury. Follow signs for A340 (Aldermaston) & on rdbt take 5th exit onto Popley Way. Hotel entrance 1st left **Parking:** 120

Ciao Baby Cucina

☎ 01256 477299 Festival Place RG21 7BB

Honest Italian cooking in relaxed modern surroundings.

BEAULIEU MAP 05 SU30

Beaulieu Hotel

British

Classic country-house cuisine

☎ 023 8029 3344 Beaulieu Rd SO42 7YQ
e-mail: beaulieu@newforesthotels.co.uk
web: www.newforesthotels.co.uk

A lovely country-house hotel set in open heathland with stunning panoramic views of the New Forest. The cosy restaurant has cream walls with sumptuous red carpets and window dressings. Traditional country-house cooking is popular with locals and guests alike. Starters might feature oak-smoked salmon fishcakes with lemon salad and sweet chilli sauce. Main courses offer some interesting combinations like roasted duck breast with garlic mashed potato and griottine cherry jus. Irresistible desserts include warm chocolate fudge brownies with chocolate ice cream and chocolate sauce.

Times: 7-9, Closed L all week **Rooms:** 18 (18 en suite) ★★★ HL **Directions:** On B3056 between Lyndhurst & Beaulieu. Near Beaulieu Rd railway station

Montagu Arms Hotel

Traditional European

Old-world charm meets modern cuisine

☎ 01590 612324 Palace Ln SO42 7ZL
e-mail: reservations@montaguarmshotel.co.uk
web: www.montaguarmshotel.co.uk

Nestling at the heart of this famous, picturesque village, in sight of the river and palace, this traditional country-house hotel is brimful of original features. The oak-panelled Terrace Restaurant overlooks a rear courtyard with well-kept gardens, while high-backed seating, smartly dressed tables and friendly, formally turned-out staff complete the fine-dining experience. The accomplished cooking takes on a surprisingly modern, simple and unfussy approach, letting local, seasonal and organic ingredients do the talking. (Shaun Hill - ex Merchant House, Ludlow - has joined the hotel as Director of Cooking, so expect some big changes.) Rack of lamb with a pistachio crust and scented parsnip purée or roast saddle of New Forest venison with jabron potatoes and Armagnac-soaked sultanas are fine examples of the fare.

Chef: Scott Fox **Owners:** Greenclose Ltd **Times:** 12-2.30/7-9.30 **Prices:** Fixed L £22.50, Fixed D £39, Coffee £3.30, Min/Water £3, Service optional **Wine:** 104 bottles over £20, 12 bottles under £20, 42 by the glass (£4-£10) **Notes:** Vegetarian available, Dress Restrictions, Smart casual, Civ Wed 50 **Seats:** 60, Pr/dining room 34 **Smoking:** N/Sm in restaurant **Children:** Min 8 yrs, Portions **Rooms:** 23 (23 en suite) ★★★ HL **Directions:** From M27 junct 2 take A326 & B3054 for Beaulieu **Parking:** 45

BROCKENHURST MAP 05 SU30

Balmer Lawn Hotel

Modern British

Fine dining at a grand New Forest hotel

☎ 01590 623116 Lyndhurst Rd SO42 7ZB
e-mail: info@balmerlawnhotel.com
web: www.balmerlawnhotel.com

This imposing hotel in a gorgeous New Forest setting, just outside Brockenhurst, was once a hunting lodge. The restaurant is the last word in luxury, with its leather seating, rich decorations and understated contemporary style. The menu is modern British sitting comfortably beside a more traditional set of choices, enhanced by an eclectic range of ingredients and accompaniments. A very classic shellfish bisque with rouille or crab, lobster and scallop ravioli might be followed by twice cooked pork belly with ginger, creamed potatoes and tarragon jus, or fillet of Scotch beef with shallots and tarragon butter.

Chef: John Underhill **Owners:** Mr C Wilson **Times:** 12.30-2.30/6.30-9.30 **Prices:** Fixed L £13.95, Starter £4.95-£13.95, Main £12.95-£19.75, Dessert £5.50-£8.95, Coffee £1.95, Min/Water £3.50, Service optional **Wine:** 23 bottles over £20, 21 bottles under £20, 7 by the glass (£3.75-£5.75) **Notes:** Vegetarian available, Dress Restrictions, Smart casual, no jeans or trainers, Civ Wed 120 **Seats:** 90, Pr/dining room 100 **Smoking:** N/Sm in restaurant, Air con **Children:** Menu, Portions **Rooms:** 55 (55 en suite) ★★★ HL **Directions:** Take A337 towards Brockenhurst, hotel on left after 'Welcome to Brockenhurst' sign **Parking:** 100

Brookleys

Modern British NEW

Contemporary bistro in popular New Forest village

☎ 01590 624625 58 Brookley Rd SO42 7RA
e-mail: info@brookleysbistro.co.uk
web: www.brookleysbistro.co.uk

Fronted by a terrace with seating and parasols, this relaxed, contemporary restaurant - remodelled from a former shop - cuts a clean, minimalist edge. Suede tub chairs and banquettes in the small bar give way to the dining room decked out with darkwood Venetian blinds or modern wall-lighting panels, while unclothed tables are broken up by screens to create intimacy. The carte plays to the gallery, offering simple, crowd-pleasing, bistro-style dishes alongside snacks and chargrilled sandwiches, bolstered by a few daily blackboard specials. Think Thai crab soufflé with Asian condiments as a starter, followed by chargrilled calves' liver with crushed new potatoes, black pudding, bacon crisps and red wine sauce.

Chef: Gareth Bowen & Chris Howard **Owners:** Gareth Bowen & Matthew Cromie **Times:** 12-2.30/6.30-9.30, Closed Mon (in winter), Closed D Sun (in winter) **Prices:** Starter £4.50-£5.25, Main £9.95-£15.95, Dessert £4.25-£6.50, Coffee £1.95, Min/Water £2.25, Service optional **Wine:** 10 bottles over £20, 22 bottles under £20, 10 by the glass (£3.35-£5) **Notes:** Vegetarian available **Seats:** 60 **Smoking:** N/Sm in restaurant, Air con **Children:** Portions **Directions:** M27 junct 1, follow signs for Lyndhurst then signposted Brockenhurst **Parking:** 50

Carey's Manor Hotel

British, European

Great local produce in elegant manor house surroundings

☎ 08707 512305 SO42 7RH
e-mail: stay@careysmanor.com
web: www.careysmanor.com

More than just a hotel, Carey's Manor has quite a range of eating and relaxation options. Blaireau's French bistro and bar is found in the grounds, there is also a fabulous Thai style 'Sen Spa' with its own Zen Garden Restaurant. Finally the Manor Restaurant in the main hotel offers traditional hotel dining in formal surroundings. Service is attentive and professional but also friendly. The chef takes care to source quality products, as far as possible these are local, free-range and organic. The cooking style is British with French and European influences. A typical starter would be wild mushroom parfait with crispy leeks and roasted garlic cream sauce, while a main course might be loin of New Forest venison with root vegetable pressing and beetroot reduction. For dessert you could try a hot chocolate pudding with pear ice cream and toffee sauce.

Chef: Steven Sweeting **Owners:** Greenclose Ltd **Times:** 12-2/7-10, Closed L Mon-Sat **Prices:** Fixed D fr £29.50, Coffee £2.50, Min/Water £3, Service optional **Wine:** 79 bottles over £20, 23 bottles under £20, 8 by the glass (£4.10-£5.25) **Notes:** Sun L 3 courses £19.95, Vegetarian available, Dress Restrictions, No jeans, T-shirts or trainers, Civ Wed 100 **Seats:** 80, Pr/dining room 100 **Smoking:** N/Sm in restaurant **Children:** Min 7 yrs, Portions **Rooms:** 80 (80 en suite) ★★★★ HL **Directions:** M27 junct 1, follow signs for Lyndhurst and Lymington A337. Railway station 5 mins from hotel **Parking:** 100

New Park Manor Hotel & Spa

Modern British V

Honest cuisine in historic country setting

☎ 01590 623467 Lyndhurst Rd SO42 7QH
e-mail: info@newparkmanorhotel.co.uk
web: www.newparkmanorhotel.co.uk

Once the favoured hunting lodge of King Charles II, this well-presented hotel enjoys a peaceful setting in the New Forest and comes complete with its own equestrian centre, croquet lawn and spa. Comfortable and contemporary with sofas and log fires in winter, the public rooms are very comfortable. Dinner is served in an oak-panelled room adorned with oil paintings, with large windows providing good views of the parkland and forest, but it's refreshingly informal and friendly, and lighter meals are served in the Polo Bar. The British menu with Mediterranean influences is based on seasonal

continued

Le Poussin at Whitley Ridge Country House Hotel

BROCKENHURST MAP 05 SU30

Modern British, French

Fine dining, a tranquil setting and some of the best food in the New Forest

☎ 01590 622354 Beaulieu Rd SO42 7QL
e-mail: sales@lepoussin.co.uk
web: www.lepoussin.co.uk

Set in secluded grounds in the heart of the New Forest, this Georgian former hunting lodge plays host to Alex Aitken's renowned restaurant. The Aitkens haven't abandoned their original Parkhill hotel at nearby Lyndhurst though, rather using this as a staging post while Parkhill undergoes major refurbishment. But they don't stand still wherever they are, with plans to revamp the endearing fading grandeur at Whitley Ridge, with bar and restaurant changing round to create more dining space. Until then, the restaurant continues in understated style, enhanced by flower displays, evening candlelight and views over the garden. Alex has always been at the forefront of New Forest gastronomy, and continues to go from strength to strength, his modern approach underpinned by a classical theme. High quality reigns supreme, from breads to petits fours or tasting menu, with dishes displaying accomplished skill and professionalism. So expect the carte to deliver the likes of a saddle of venison and New Forest

haggis with pears, caramelised walnuts and fondant potato, or perhaps a roast tranche of halibut served with truffles, wild mushrooms and chicken-stock sauce.

Chef: Alex Aitken, Neil Duffet **Owners:** Alex & Caroline Aitken **Times:** 12.30-2/6.30-9.30 **Prices:** Fixed L fr £15, Fixed D fr £39.50, Starter £9.50-£12.50, Main £15-£25, Dessert £7.50-£10, Coffee £3.50, Min/Water £3.25, Service added but optional 10% **Wine:** 8 by the glass **Notes:** Gastronomic menu £55, Sun L 3 courses £25, Vegetarian available, Dress Restrictions, Smart casual, Civ Wed 45 **Seats:** 40, Pr/dining room 20 **Smoking:** N/Sm in restaurant **Children:** Min 10 yrs **Rooms:** 18 (18 en suite) ★★★ HL **Directions:** From Brockenhurst, 1m along Beaulieu Rd **Parking:** 30

BROCKENHURST *continued* MAP 05 SU30

produce, especially game. Expect dishes such as tempura of seafood with hot sweet and sour sauce followed by stuffed leg of rabbit with wild mushrooms and asparagus risotto.

Chef: Mark Davison **Owners:** von Essen Hotels **Times:** 12-2/7-9 **Prices:** Fixed D fr £38 **Wine:** 30 bottles over £20, 7 bottles under £20, 19 by the glass (£4.75-£10) **Notes:** Chef's menu £60, Vegetarian menu, Dress Restrictions, Smart casual, no jeans or trainers, Civ Wed 50 **Seats:** 40, Pr/dining room 12 **Smoking:** N/Sm in restaurant **Children:** Menu, Portions **Rooms:** 24 (24 en suite) ★★★ HL **Directions:** On A337, 8m S of M27 junct 1 **Parking:** 70

❀❀❀ Le Poussin at Whitley Ridge Country House Hotel

see page 183

❀❀ Rhinefield House

British, European

Enjoyable dining in magnificent surroundings

☎ 01590 622922 Rhinefield Rd SO42 7QB
e-mail: info@rhinefieldhousehotel.co.uk
web: www.rhinefieldhousehotel.co.uk

This impressive baronial-style hotel is set in 40 acres of the New Forest. The Italianate ponds and ornamental gardens are nearly as stunning as the Alhambra and Parliament inspired décor inside. The Armada Restaurant sports a huge Elizabethan-style carved fireplace which took seven years to complete. It's a great dining venue with helpful and friendly service. Modern British dishes with European and Asian influences are based on good local, seasonal ingredients. To start expect well-timed Portland scallops or duck with mango; main courses might include rack of South Downs lamb with seared kidney and artichoke purée, or poached guinea fowl with spring vegetables. To finish, there's rhubarb 'four ways' or banana soufflé with pecans.

Chef: Kevin Hartley **Owners:** Hand Picked Hotels Ltd **Times:** 12.30-2/7-9.30 **Prices:** Food prices not confirmed for 2007. Please telephone for details **Wine:** 100 bottles over £20, 6 bottles under £20 **Notes:** Tasting menu £60, Sun L £19.95, Vegetarian available, Dress Restrictions, Smart casual preferred, Civ Wed 125 **Seats:** 58, Pr/dining room 28 **Smoking:** N/Sm in restaurant **Children:** Menu, Portions **Rooms:** 34 (34 en suite) ★★★★ HL **Directions:** From M27 junct 1 take A337 to Lyndhurst, follow A35 W towards Christchurch. 3.5m from Lyndhurst, turn left into the Forest at sign for Rhinefield House. Hotel 1.5m on right **Parking:** 150

❀❀ Simply Poussin

Modern British, French

Pretty village dining destination

☎ 01590 623063 The Courtyard, Brookley Rd SO42 7RB
e-mail: simply@lepoussin.co.uk
web: www.lepoussin.co.uk

Specialising in local and wild produce, this welcoming courtyard eatery is tucked away behind Brockenhurst's high street. Once a stable block, the premises have been sympathetically converted showcasing the York stone entrance. A traditional-style conservatory provides the dining area and polite and cheerful staff the welcome.

continued

French brasserie classics populate this menu, the simpler dishes being the most effective like the starter of creamy tomato and basil velouté and the main course of eponymous poussin served on roasted vegetables with garlic and herb butter. Local interest is provided by the roasted haunch and slow-cooked shoulder of venison. Finish with the passionfruit soufflé with passionfruit sorbet.

Simply Poussin

Chef: Steven Stiles **Owners:** Mr Alex Aitken **Times:** 12-2/6.30-9.45, Closed Sun-Mon **Prices:** Fixed L £10.50, Fixed D £15.50, Starter £3.80-£6.25, Main £10.50-£15.95, Dessert £5-£7.50, Coffee £2.95, Min/Water £3, Service added but optional 10% **Wine:** 30 bottles over £20, 10 bottles under £20, 6 by the glass (£2.95-£7.50) **Notes:** Vegetarian available **Seats:** 36 **Smoking:** N/Sm in restaurant **Children:** Portions **Directions:** Village centre through an archway between two shops on the High St **Parking:** 4

BROOK MAP 05 SU21

❀ Bell Inn

Traditional British

Friendly golfing hotel near the New Forest

☎ 023 8081 2214 SO43 7HE
e-mail: bell@bramshaw.co.uk
web: www.bramshaw.co.uk

This cosy hotel, a popular golfing venue, has been run by the same family for 200 years, and combines inglenook fireplaces and ancient beams with modern facilities. The menu changes daily and offers dishes such as ham hock rillette with celeriac remoulade, followed by pan-fried calves' liver with a grain mustard sauce and deep-fried parsnips or fillet of sea bass with ginger and lime sabayon. Desserts might include an old favourite - sticky toffee pudding with butterscotch sauce and vanilla ice cream. Come hungry as portions are hearty.

Chef: Richard Jones **Owners:** Crosthwaite Eyre Family **Times:** 12-2.30/7.30-9.30 **Prices:** Fixed L £12.95-£16.95, Fixed D £25-£35, Starter £3.25-£5.75, Main £8.25-£17.50, Dessert £3.75-£5.75, Coffee £2, Min/Water £3.50, Service included **Wine:** 24 bottles over £20, 26 bottles under £20, 6 by the glass (£3.50-£4.75) **Notes:** Vegetarian available, Dress Restrictions, No jeans, T-shirts, trainers or shorts **Seats:** 50, Pr/dining room 40 **Smoking:** N/Sm in restaurant **Children:** Menu, Portions **Rooms:** 25 (25 en suite) ★★★ HL **Directions:** M27 junct 1 (Cadnam) 3rd exit onto B3079, signed Brook, follow for 1m on right **Parking:** 40

BUCKLERS HARD MAP 05 SU40

Master Builders House Hotel

Modern

Contemporary cooking in historic maritime setting

☎ 01590 616253 SO42 7XB
e-mail: res@themasterbuilders.co.uk
web: www.themasterbuilders.co.uk

An 18th-century building in a village famed for shipbuilding and once the home of the master shipbuilder, Henry Adams, who oversaw the construction of the Navy's fleet during the great age of sail. The grounds run down to the Beaulieu River, while heavy beams and maritime memorabilia abound in the popular Yachtsman's Bar. The brasserie-style Riverside Restaurant, with its wood flooring and light modern décor, enjoys tranquil river views. A light modern menu combines excellent local ingredients, innovative ideas and sound cooking skills to produce honest and uncomplicated dishes, typically a smooth chicken liver parfait with pear chutney, chicken breast with sweet potato purée and wild mushroom sauce, and a light chocolate mousse with raspberry sorbet.

Chef: Denis Rhoden **Owners:** Jeremy Willcock, John Illsley **Times:** 12-3/7-11 **Prices:** Fixed L £19.50-£27.50, Fixed D £32.50-£38, Starter £5.25-£7.50, Main £13.95-£21.95, Dessert £6.25, Coffee £2.25, Min/Water £3.50, Service included **Wine:** 30 bottles over £20, 10 bottles under £20, 10 by the glass (£3.50) **Notes:** Vegetarian available, Civ Wed 60 **Seats:** 80, Pr/dining room 40 **Smoking:** N/Sm in restaurant **Children:** Menu, Portions **Rooms:** 25 (25 en suite) ★★★ HL **Directions:** From M27 junct 2 follow signs to Beaulieu. Turn left onto B3056. 1st left. Hotel in 2m **Parking:** 60

BURLEY MAP 05 SU20

Moorhill House

Modern British

New Forest hotel dining

☎ 01425 403285 BH24 4AG
e-mail: moorhill@newforesthotels.co.uk
web: www.newforesthotels.co.uk

Built as a gentleman's residence, this grand house with extensive grounds is located deep in the New Forest on the edge of a pretty village. The hotel's Burley Restaurant overlooks the attractive gardens and opens on to a patio area. Here the fixed-price, three-course dinner menu is available to non-residents, comprising modern British dishes with some European influences. The emphasis is on local produce in dishes of spicy seafood risotto cakes, and baked pork tenderloin with fondant potato and grain mustard café crème. Sunday lunch is also served.

Times: 12-2/7-9, Closed L Mon-Sat **Rooms:** 31 (31 en suite) ★★★ HL

CADNAM MAP 05 SZ21

Bartley Lodge

Modern British

Former hunting lodge with food that hits the spot

☎ 023 8081 2248 Lyndhurst Rd SO40 2NR
e-mail: reservations@newforesthotels.co.uk
web: www.newforesthotels.co.uk

Built in 1759 as a hunting lodge for the founder of the New Forest hounds, the lodge is set in 8 acres of picturesque grounds with a host of charming period features such as the hand-crafted oak panelling, minstrels' gallery and magnificent fireplace. The Crystal restaurant has wonderful views over the garden and offers a traditionally based menu with influences from France, the Mediterranean and Asia. You might expect to start with lightly poached salmon with a tarragon hollandaise and roasted pimento salad and then indulge in a main course of crispy confit duck leg in oriental spices and a coarse mustard sauce.

Chef: John Lightfoot **Owners:** New Forest Hotels Plc **Times:** 12.30-2.30/7-9, Closed L Mon-Sat **Prices:** Fixed D £21.50, Coffee £1.75, Min/Water £3, Service optional **Wine:** 39 bottles under £20, 21 by the glass (£2.35-£3.10) **Notes:** Sun L 3 courses £12.95, Vegetarian available, Civ Wed 80 **Seats:** 60 **Smoking:** N/Sm in restaurant **Children:** Menu, Portions **Rooms:** 31 (31 en suite) ★★★ HL **Directions:** M27 junct 1, A337 and follow signs for Lyndhurst. Hotel on left **Parking:** 60

DENMEAD MAP 05 SU61

Barnard's Restaurant

British, Mediterranean

Adventurous cooking in friendly neighbourhood restaurant

☎ 023 9225 7788 Hambledon Rd PO7 6NU
e-mail: mail@barnardsrestaurant.co.uk
web: www.barnardsrestaurant.co.uk

Exposed brick walls, a warm yellow décor and floral prints enliven this small, family-run country restaurant tucked away in a row of shops in sleepy Denmead. Expect relaxed and informal service and consistent modern British cooking using fresh local produce. The dishes are well presented and clear flavours are evident in such dishes as chicken, smoked bacon and wild mushroom terrine with mustard vinaigrette, braised shank of lamb with rosemary and garlic, and duck breast with peppery pineapple compôte. Leave room for a delectable dessert.

Chef: David Barnard & Sandie Barnard **Owners:** Mr & Mrs D Barnard, Mrs S Barnard **Times:** 12-1.30/7-9.30, Closed 25-26 Dec, New Year, Sun-Mon, Closed L Sat **Prices:** Food prices not confirmed for 2007. Please telephone for details **Wine:** 6 bottles over £20, 28 bottles under £20, 6 by the glass (£3-£4.50) **Seats:** 40, Pr/dining room 34 **Smoking:** N/Sm in restaurant **Children:** Portions **Directions:** A3M junct 3, B1250 into Denmead. Opposite church **Parking:** 3

England

EAST TYTHERLEY MAP 05 SU22

The Star at Tytherley

Modern British

Typically English inn with heart-warming food

☎ 01794 340225 SO51 0LW
e-mail: info@starinn-uk.com
web: www.starinn-uk.com

This 16th-century coaching inn has a quintessentially English feel with views of the village cricket green, a pretty courtyard garden and a traditional theme to the décor. The atmosphere is cosy with warm colours, exposed beams, open log fires and an extensive library that guests are encouraged to browse at their leisure. The menu is largely based around British classics cooked with clear technical skill and some surprising and largely successful innovations adding a touch of sparkle to familiar favourites - cauliflower and smoked paprika soup for example, to start, followed by pan-fried duck breast with celeriac purée, rhubarb marmalade and star anise jus.

Chef: Justin Newitt **Owners:** Allan & Lesley Newitt **Times:** 11-2.30/6-11, Closed D Sun **Prices:** Starter £3.95-£7.50, Main £11.50-£17.50, Dessert £5-£6.50, Coffee £1.75, Min/Water £3.50, Service optional **Wine:** 20 bottles over £20, 30 bottles under £20, 8 by the glass (£3.50-£5) **Notes:** Sun L, Vegetarian available, Dress Restrictions, Smart casual **Seats:** 30, Pr/dining room 15 **Smoking:** N/Sm in restaurant **Rooms:** 3 (3 en suite) ★★★★ INN **Directions:** Romsey A3057 N, left to Awbridge, Kents Oak, through Lockerley on right **Parking:** 60

EMSWORTH MAP 05 SU70

Fat Olives

Modern British

Friendly brasserie by the sea

☎ 01243 377914 30 South St PO10 7EH
e-mail: info@fatolives.co.uk
web: www.fatolives.co.uk

You can almost smell the sea air from this cosy, traditional fisherman's cottage just up from the quayside. A bowl of the eponymous fat olives sits on every table, and the stripped floorboards and plain wooden tables strike a pleasing contemporary note. 'Fresh' is the kitchen's keyword, with the sensibly short menu making good use of the adjacent sea as well as local game and meats, and producing wonderful honest flavours. The modern British menu with Mediterranean influences may include seared tuna, griddled salsify, confit garlic and chermoula dressing, sea bass with polenta, trompettes and tomato sauce, or pork fillet with rillette, celeriac rösti and apple cream sauce.

Chef: Lawrence Murphy **Owners:** Lawrence & Julia Murphy **Times:** 12-1.45/7-9.15, Closed 2 wks Xmas-Jan, 1 wk Oct, Sun-Mon & Tue after a BH **Prices:** Fixed L £14.75, Starter £5-£7.50, Main £13-£20, Dessert £5.50-£6.25, Coffee £2, Min/Water £3, Service optional, Group min 10 service 10% **Wine:** 29 bottles over £20, 14 bottles under £20, 5 by the glass (£3-£4) **Notes:** Vegetarian available **Seats:** 28 **Smoking:** N/Sm in restaurant **Children:** Min 8 yrs **Directions:** In town centre, 1st right after Emsworth Square, 100yds towards the Quay. Restaurant on left with public car park opposite **Parking:** Opposite restaurant

Spencers Restaurant & Brasserie

Modern British

Skilled, cosmopolitan cooking in former cottages turned stylish restaurant

☎ 01243 372744 & 379017 36 North St PO10 7DG
web: www.spencersrestaurant.co.uk

This former bakery is a short walk from the town centre. The Spencers have been here since the 1980s and converted the building into a restaurant. Recently refurbished, the ground floor brasserie and first floor restaurant have been given a modern, stylish make-over. European-inspired modern British cuisine with generous portions and unusual flavour combinations can be found amongst the choices on the carte, blackboard specials and good-value lunch menu. Try the likes of fish soup to start, and medallions of monkfish sautéed with pak choy, and shiitake mushrooms in black bean sauce as a main course.

Chef: Denis Spencer **Owners:** Denis & Lesley Spencer **Times:** 12-2/6-10, Closed 25-26 Dec, BHs, Sun, Closed L Sun/Mon, D Mon (Brasserie Mon-Sat 12-2, 6-10) **Prices:** Fixed L £9.25, Starter £3.40-£5.95, Main £12.75-£16.95, Dessert £4.95, Coffee £1.40, Min/Water £2.65, Service optional **Wine:** 11 bottles over £20, 17 bottles under £20, 5 by the glass (£2.50-£3.10) **Notes:** Set price menu also avail 6-7pm **Seats:** 64, Pr/dining room 8 **Smoking:** N/Sm in restaurant, Air con **Children:** Portions **Directions:** Off A259, in town centre

36 on the Quay

see opposite

EVERSLEY MAP 05 SU76

New Mill

British, International

NOTABLE WINE LIST

Waterside dining in an old mill setting

☎ 0118 973 2277 New Mill Rd RG27 0RA
e-mail: info@thenewmill.co.uk
web: www.thenewmill.co.uk

Perched on the River Blackwater, this 400-year-old converted mill oozes character, complete with working waterwheel and machinery. Inside it's full of traditional country character, with beams, open fires, floorboards and flagstones. The formal Riverside Restaurant comes with clothed tables, round-backed chairs, carpet, vaulted timber roof and conservatory-style River Room extension, while The Grill Room option provides a more casual setting and menu. Expect the likes of halibut on a lobster mash with rich Chablis and saffron beurre blanc or saddle of New Forest venison on MacSween haggis dauphinois. **Notable Wine List:** A previous winner of the AA Wine Award, this list offers extensive tasting notes and an interesting twelve of best selection.

continued

England

36 on the Quay

EMSWORTH MAP 05 SU70

Modern French NOTABLE WINE LIST

Exciting modern food by the waterfront

☎ 01243 375592 & 372257 47 South St PO10 7EG
web: www.36onthequay.co.uk

The name says it all. Set smack on the quayside, this pristine 17th-century house comes with all the sights and sounds of the sea and lovely views over the estuary. What it doesn't tell you though, is that the 36 - under chef-patron Ramon Farthing - serves some of the best cuisine on the South Coast. Inside, the dining room has been refurbished and now sports a smart, more contemporary edge. Cream predominates, with hints of browns punctuated by brightly coloured artwork. Tables are well spaced, the service is polished and friendly. and the mood relaxed. There's a cosy bar for aperitifs and canapés, while a small terrace comes into play on sunny summer days. The kitchen's modern approach is delivered via a fixed-price repertoire that includes a value lunch, impressive carte and eleven-course tasting option. Fantastic quality ingredients, luxury, flawless execution and memorable flavours distinguish Ramon's complex cooking style, while new plates and presentation styles nicely complement the restaurant's new look. Expect the likes of poussin breasts, butter-roasted with sage and served with confited leg, truffled potatoes and a little chicken pie on an Albufera sauce, and perhaps a 36 speciality dessert, presenting the flavours of banana and caramel in five miniature offerings. An impressive wine list and four en-suite bedrooms complete the upbeat package.

Notable Wine List: The wine list offers a great selection by drinking style and also featuring a seasonal selection at the front.

Chef: Ramon Farthing **Owners:** Ramon & Karen Farthing **Times:** 12-2/7-10, Closed 23-30 Oct, 1-22 Jan, Sun, Mon **Prices:** Fixed L fr £17.95, Fixed D £42.95-£60, Coffee £3.75, Min/Water £3.50, Service optional **Wine:** 250 bottles over £20, 25 bottles under £20, 6 by the glass (£4-£4.75) **Notes:** Dress Restrictions, Smart casual, no shorts **Seats:** 45, Pr/dining room 12 **Smoking:** N/Sm in restaurant **Children:** Portions **Rooms:** 5 (5 en suite) ★★★★ RR **Parking:** 6

Chef: Colin Robson-Wright **Owners:** Judith & Nick Scade **Times:** 12-2/7-10, Closed 26-29 Dec, 1 Jan, Closed L Sat **Prices:** Fixed L £13.50, Fixed D £25, Starter £5.25-£12.50, Main £17.75-£25.50, Dessert £6.25-£9, Coffee £3.25, Min/Water £3.50, Service optional **Wine:** 200 bottles over £20, 52 bottles under £20, 13 by the glass (£2.75-£7.50) **Notes:** Sun L/D 3 courses £17.50, Vegetarian available, Dress Restrictions, Smart casual, Civ Wed 180 **Seats:** 80, Pr/dining room 40 **Smoking:** N/Sm in restaurant, Air con **Children:** Portions **Directions:** Off A327 2m S of Arborfield Cross. N of village and follow brown signs. Approach from New Mill Rd **Parking:** 40

FAREHAM MAP 05 SU50

The Richmond Restaurant

Modern French NEW

Elegant surroundings for fine French-style cuisine

☎ 01329 822622 Lysses House Hotel,
51 High St PO16 7BQ
e-mail: lysses@lysses.co.uk
web: www.lysses.co.uk

Once a private residence, built in Georgian times, the house is now an elegant hotel. The Richmond Restaurant is housed in a later addition to the main building, and offers a calm, relaxing atmosphere and soft décor in shades of green, pale pink and cream. Cooking is mainly modern French in style, using fresh ingredients cooked to order. The menu includes a range of dishes from the grill, such as meats grilled over charcoal, cooked to your liking and served with mushrooms and tomato. Starters might include roasted vegetables sandwiched with parmesan cheese and drizzled with lemon olive oil, while main courses could comprise medallions of pork fillet topped with cheddar cheese and roasted apple, served with a creamy seed mustard sauce.

continued

Chef: Clive Wright **Owners:** Dr Colin Mercer **Times:** 12-1.45/7.30-9.45, Closed 24 Dec-2 Jan, BHs, Sun, Closed L Sat **Prices:** Fixed L £13-£13.95, Fixed D £20.50-£21.50, Starter £3.95-£6.95, Main £12.50-£18.50, Dessert £5.25-£5.50, Coffee £1.95, Min/Water £2.95, Service optional **Wine:** 7 bottles over £20, 26 bottles under £20, 3 by the glass (£3.50-£5) **Notes:** Vegetarian available, Civ Wed 95 **Seats:** 60, Pr/dining room 10 **Smoking:** N/Sm in restaurant, Air con **Children:** Portions **Rooms:** 21 (21 en suite) ★★★ HL **Directions:** M27 junct 11, follow signs for Fareham. Stay in left lane to rdbt, 3rd exit into East St - road veers to right onto High St. Hotel on left opposite junction with Civic Way **Parking:** 30

Solent Hotel

Traditional, Mediterranean

Modern cuisine in revamped setting

☎ 01489 880000 Rookery Av, Whiteley PO15 7AJ
e-mail: solent@shirehotels.com
web: www.shirehotels.com

Close to the M27 and not far from the Solent, this smart, purpose-built hotel enjoys a peaceful location, set in landscaped gardens surrounded by meadowland. The Woodlands Restaurant has a fresh new feel, though it still retains its signature log fires, while the informal Nightingales Bar has a new look, too, and the extended alfresco terrace adds another dimension in summer. The kitchen delivers simple, well-executed, colourful dishes using quality local produce; dishes like harissa-spiced rump of lamb with lemon couscous and cinnamon carrots might appear on the crowd-pleasing carte.

continued

England

FAREHAM *continued* MAP 05 SU50

Chef: Peter Williams **Owners:** Shire Hotels Ltd **Times:** 12.15-2/7-9.30, Closed Xmas, New Year, Easter (residents only), Closed L Sat-Sun **Prices:** Fixed L £16.50, Fixed D £35.45-£40.95, Starter £6-£8.50, Main £12.50-£19.95, Dessert £3-£6.50, Coffee £3.50, Min/Water £3.50, Service optional **Wine:** 41 bottles over £20, 14 bottles under £20, 14 by the glass (£5.25-£9.95) **Notes:** Vegetarian available, Dress Restrictions, No jeans, T-shirts, Civ Wed 160 **Seats:** 130, Pr/dining room 40 **Smoking:** N/Sm in restaurant, Air con **Children:** Before 8.30pm, Menu, Portions **Rooms:** 111 (111 en suite) ★★★★ **Directions:** From M27 junct 9 follow signs to Solent Business Park & Whiteley. At rdbt take 1st left, then right at mini rdbt **Parking:** 200

FLEET MAP 05 SU85

The Gurkha Square

Nepalese

Subtle and delicate Nepalese specialities in unpretentious, traditional surroundings

☎ 01252 810286 & 811588 327 Fleet Rd GU51 3BU
e-mail: gurkhasquare@hotmail.com

Set in a parade of shops, this small, simple restaurant wears a highly traditional face, its white textured walls lined with wooden roof awnings are covered in authentic pictures, woodcarvings and artefacts that transport you to the Himalayan Kingdom. A red carpet, clothed tables and cane chairs further develop the theme, while service, by friendly uniformed waiters, guides you through the extensive menu of Nepalese specialities, which include some clay oven dishes. Perhaps try methi chicken (a famous dish in Nepalese households) of chargrill cooked chicken, dry-fried in ginger, garlic and dry coriander sauce.

Chef: Pradip Basnet, Indra Guruna **Owners:** Bishnu & Imansingh Ghale **Times:** 12-2.30/6-11, Closed 25-26 Dec, Nepalese festivals **Prices:** Fixed L £15, Fixed D £17.50, Starter £3.25-£9, Main £6.25-£10.90, Dessert £1.95-£3.75, Coffee £1.50, Min/Water £3.75 **Wine:** all bottles under £20 **Seats:** 44 **Smoking:** No pipes, No cigars, Air con **Directions:** Telephone for directions **Parking:** Gurkha Square public car park

FORDINGBRIDGE MAP 05 SU11

Hour Glass

Modern British

Imaginative cuisine in charming restaurant

☎ 01425 652348 Burgate SP6 1LX
e-mail: hglassrestaurant@aol.com

continued

The 16th-century rustic exterior hides a surprisingly modern, understated interior, with lovely features like a brick-built bar and huge inglenook fireplace With low beamed ceilings, open beams divide up the dining area to create an intimate country style restaurant. Menus are modern British with French influences, serving up interesting combinations using well-sourced ingredients. Try a starter like Shetland island king scallops with raisin purée and fennel and orange salad. Main courses might feature New Forest mushroom and Exmoor blue cheese suet pudding with clotted cream mash and crispy parsley carrots.

Chef: Paul Layton, Danny Morel **Owners:** Hannah & Charlotte Wiggins **Times:** 12-2/7-10, Closed 1st 2 wks Jan, BH Mon, Mon, Closed D Sun **Prices:** Starter £5-£9.95, Main £11.50-£22.50, Dessert £5.95-£6.75, Coffee £1.75, Min/Water £3, Service optional, Group min 6 service 10% **Wine:** 15 bottles over £20, 29 bottles under £20, 10 by the glass (£3.30-£4.30) **Notes:** ALC Sun L, Vegetarian available **Seats:** 45 **Smoking:** N/Sm in restaurant **Children:** Portions **Directions:** 1m from Fordingbridge on A338 towards Salisbury **Parking:** 30

HIGHCLERE MAP 05 SU45

Marco Pierre White's Yew Tree Inn

British, French NEW

Dining pub close to Highclere Castle

☎ 01635 253360 Hollington Cross, Andover Rd RG20 9SE
e-mail: gareth.mcainsh@theyewtree.net
web: www.theyewtree.net

This sympathetically remodelled, white-washed, 17th-century inn retains bags of character, its low-beamed ceilings and log fires blending harmoniously with more contemporary dining-pub spin. While the bar area has dining tables, there's a more formal restaurant laid with white linen off to one side. The classical British cooking with French influences takes on a modern brasserie approach - the menu backed by daily specials - to produce accomplished (no surprises here with Marco Pierre White as a director), well-presented, relatively simple dishes. Try salad of lobster à la Russe to start and follow with venison Pierre Koffman au chocolat amer.

Chef: Neil Thornley **Owners:** Marco Pierre White **Times:** 12-3/6-10 **Prices:** Fixed L £13.50, Starter £6.50-£13.95, Main £10.50-£27.50, Dessert £5.50, Coffee £2.50, Min/Water £3, Service included **Wine:** 52 bottles over £20, 18 bottles under £20, 23 by the glass (£5-£11.50) **Notes:** Sun L 3 courses £19.95, Sun supper 3 courses £14.50 **Seats:** 90 **Smoking:** N/Sm in restaurant **Children:** Portions **Directions:** M4 junct 13, A34 S, 4th junct on left signed Highclere/Wash Common, turn right towards Andover A343, Yew Tree Inn on right **Parking:** 40

LIPHOOK MAP 05 SU83

Nippon-Kan

Japanese V

Refined Japanese cooking in country-club location

☎ 01428 724555 Old Thorns Hotel, Golf & Country Club, Griggs Green GU30 7PE
e-mail: info@oldthorns.com
web: www.oldthorns.com

This Japanese-owned and run hotel restaurant has only five normal tables and two teppan-yaki tables so there's an air of exclusivity and intimacy that sits well with the traditional décor. Gold wallpaper, wood panelling and bare wood tables laid with chopsticks ensure a thoroughly oriental experience with courteous and professional staff on hand to explain the menu. The presentation is simple with food speaking for itself and the interactive thrills of teppan-yaki on offer for many of the dishes on the menu. There's an elegance and skill in evidence throughout, particularly in the artful sushi dishes. The set menu starts with a selection of sushi, then moves on to chicken yakitori, various tempura, sukiyaki (sliced beef in a sauce) and a more prosaic pudding of fruit and ice cream.

Chef: Mr T Suzuki **Owners:** London Kosido Ltd **Times:** 12-2/6.30-10, Closed Mon **Prices:** Fixed L £10.50-£12.50, Fixed D £25-£28, Starter £3.50-£15, Main £8-£18.50, Dessert £3-£5.50, Coffee £2, Min/Water £3.50 **Wine:** 23 bottles over £20, 9 bottles under £20, 2 by the glass (£3.50-£4.50) **Notes:** Fixed D 5 courses, Sun buffet £16.95, Vegetarian menu, Dress Restrictions, Smart casual, Civ Wed 75 **Seats:** 40 **Smoking:** N/Sm in restaurant **Children:** Portions **Rooms:** 33 (32 en suite) ★★★ HL **Directions:** Telephone for directions **Parking:** 120

LYMINGTON MAP 05 SZ39

Stanwell House

British, European

Hearty cooking in a stylish setting

☎ 01590 677123 High St SO41 9AA
e-mail: sales@stanwellhousehotel.co.uk
web: www.stanwellhousehotel.co.uk

This former Georgian coaching inn offers a carte menu in both the restaurant and the bistro. Both rooms are decorated with luxurious purple fabrics and dark stained wood; the restaurant tables have large candles creating a romantic feel, plus there's a bistro adjoining the bar. Robust cookery is attractively presented and hearty appetites are well catered for. Diners might choose a starter of seared scallops with Parma ham and chilli dressing, followed by fillet of beef, dauphinoise potatoes, oxtail and watercress. For an extra special night out go on a Tuesday when there is live jazz in the restaurant.

continued

Chef: Colin Nash **Owners:** Mrs J McIntyre **Times:** 12-2/7-9.30 **Prices:** Fixed L £10-£18, Fixed D £15-£25, Starter £4.95-£6.95, Main £12.95-£18.95, Dessert £5.95, Coffee £2.25, Min/Water £4.10, Service included **Wine:** 10 by the glass (£3.70-£8.50) **Notes:** Vegetarian available, Civ Wed 60 **Seats:** 60, Pr/dining room 40 **Smoking:** N/Sm in restaurant **Children:** Portions **Rooms:** 29 (29 en suite) ★★★ **Directions:** M27 junct 1, follow signs for Lyndhurst/Brockenhurst, A337 and Lymington. Head into the main high street for hotel **Parking:** Public car park or on street

MILFORD ON SEA MAP 05 SZ29

Rouille Restaurant

Modern British

Competent cooking with plenty of choice near the sea

☎ 01590 642340 69-71 High St SO41 0QG
e-mail: rouille2003@aol.com

A civilised spot not far from the coast, with well-dressed tables that take on a warm glow in the evening once the candles are lit. There's a small bar area where guests are greeted on arrival, and presented with the choice of daily dishes. At lunchtime you'll find a short set menu offering the likes of fillet of peppered smoked mackerel with horseradish mayonnaise, and crispy confit of duck leg. Dinner brings a wider choice that might include oven-baked rack of lamb or pepper-crusted monkfish, and the well presented desserts are always worth savouring.

Times: 7-10, Closed 2 wks Jan, Mon, Closed D Sun **Directions:** From A337 take B3058 to Milford, 150yds on L in village centre

Westover Hall

see page 190

NEW MILTON MAP 05 SZ29

Chewton Glen Hotel

see page 191

OLD BURGHCLERE MAP 05 SU45

The Dew Pond Restaurant

British

Country-house cooking with fine views

☎ 01635 278408 RG20 9LH
web: www.dewpond.co.uk

This 16th-century country-house restaurant has some fine views over rural Hampshire including the famous Watership Down, Beacon Hill and Highclere Castle. The outdoor terrace in particular is a great place for pre- or post-dinner drinks when the weather's fine. Inside there are two beautiful dining rooms with original oak beams and pleasant staff that provide unassuming service. The food is British in style taking its cue from local, seasonal produce with simple, yet flavourful dishes like a terrine of foie gras and ham hock with cider and hazelnut dressing to start, followed by saddle of roe deer in a light pastry with shallot and mushroom purée and port wine sauce.

Times: 7-9.30, Closed Xmas, 2 wks Aug, Sun-Mon **Directions:** Telephone for details

Westover Hall

MILFORD ON SEA MAP 05 SZ29

French

Magnificent Victorian mansion with stunning sea views

☎ 01590 643044 Park Ln SO41 0PT
e-mail: info@westoverhallhotel.com
web: www.westoverhallhotel.com

A Grade II listed Victorian mansion with superb sea views overlooking the Needles and the Isle of Wight, this family-run hotel is packed with magnificent stained-glass windows, oak panelling and decorative ceiling friezes. One of the owners is an artist and the walls are filled with his contemporary-style artwork and photography. Service is friendly and professional and the intimate, stylish restaurant offers a sophisticated, eclectic French menu with a backbone of classical techniques. High-quality seasonal produce from local suppliers shines through in flavoursome dishes like a starter of pan-fried langoustine, hot cauliflower pannacotta, shellfish and mussel foam, followed by a main course of poached turbot with morels and girolles. Finish with a delightful dessert of red fruit and pink champagne soup with rose sorbet or alternatively a hot chocolate coulant served with rosemary ganache and fromage blanc sorbet. Request a window seat to complete a memorable dining experience.

Chef: Jimmy Desrivières
Owners: N Musetti & S Mechem
Times: 12-1.45/7-8.45
Prices: Fixed L fr £19.50, Fixed D £38.50-£45.50, Starter £10-£13.50, Main £20-£24, Dessert £8.50, Coffee £2.50, Min/Water £3.75, Service optional
Wine: 58 bottles over £20, 11 bottles under £20, 11 by the glass (£3.50-£5)
Notes: Tasting menu £60, Vegetarian available, Civ Wed 50
Seats: 40, Pr/dining room 10
Smoking: N/Sm in restaurant
Children: Min 12 yrs, Portions
Rooms: 12 (12 en suite) ★★★ HL
Directions: From M27 junct 1 take A337 then B3058. Hotel just outside centre of Milford, towards clifftop
Parking: 60

Chewton Glen Hotel

NEW MILTON MAP 05 SZ29

Eclectic V

Fine dining in impeccable, Palladian-style country-house hotel

☎ 01425 275341 Christchurch Rd BH25 6QS
e-mail: reservations@chewtonglen.com
web: www.chewtonglen.com

Martin and Brigitte Skan's outstanding and internationally renowned landmark, country-house hotel has been at the forefront of British hotel keeping for many years and is without question a class act. From the moment you drive through the iron entrance gates you know you've arrived at a very special place indeed. Set in landscaped grounds, it's a haven of luxury and tranquility, with impeccable service that endures throughout any visit. Warming log fires, afternoon teas and traditional country-house furnishings cosset, alongside views from lounges and bar over the sweeping, picture-postcard croquet lawn. The equally renowned and stylish restaurant, also focused around garden views, has a refreshed styling and a more contemporary feel, while the chic, mainstay conservatory impresses with a tented ceiling.
Like the surroundings, plenty of luxury graces the menus, with carefully sourced, fresh, top-quality produce the key, and the kitchen's suppliers are laudably chronicled at the back of the menu. Classical dishes form the backbone, with the accomplished, refined cooking delivering clear, clean and well-balanced flavours on an appealing repertoire of fixed-priced options and five-course Menu Gourmand - bolstered by the option of a glass of wine per course from a dazzling, appropriately classically-led wine list of over 500 bins.

Chef: Luke Matthews
Owners: Martin & Brigitte Skan
Times: 12.30-1.45/7.30-9.30
Prices: Fixed L fr £22.50, Fixed D fr £59.50, Starter £10-£16.50, Main £20-£35, Dessert £8.75, Coffee £4.50, Min/Water £3.80, Service included
Wine: 480 bottles over £20, 6 bottles under £20, 20 by the glass (£6-£14)
Notes: Fixed L 3 courses, Sun L £37.50, Vegetarian menu, Dress Restrictions, Jackets preferred, no denim, Civ Wed 60
Seats: 120, Pr/dining room 120
Smoking: N/Sm in restaurant, Air con
Children: Min 5 yrs, Menu, Portions
Rooms: 58 (58 en suite) ★★★★★
Directions: Off A35 (Lyndhurst) turn right through Walkford, 4th left into Chewton Farm Rd
Parking: 150

PETERSFIELD MAP 05 SU72

JSW

see below

Langrish House

British, French

Historic setting for accomplished cooking

☎ 01730 266941 Langrish GU32 1RN
e-mail: frontdesk@langrishhouse.co.uk
web: www.langrishhouse.co.uk

Home to the same family for seven generations, this 17th-century manor house in the rolling Hampshire countryside is brimming with history: prisoners taken by Cromwell in the Battle of Chewton were made to dig the vaults. Now a peaceful country house hotel, Frederick's restaurant is an intimate dining room with garden views and a log fire in winter. A French influence in the classic British cooking means that fillet of beef may arrive with seared foie gras and oyster mushroom risotto and slow baked meringues are served with crème anglais and bitter sweet chocolate.

Chef: Duncan Wilson **Owners:** Mr & Mrs Talbot-Ponsonby **Times:** 12-2/7-9.30 **Prices:** Fixed L £15.50, Fixed D £29.95, Coffee £2.50, Service optional **Wine:** 14 bottles over £20, 15 bottles under £20, 2 by the glass (£3) **Notes:** Dress Restrictions, Smart casual, Civ Wed 60 **Seats:** 24, Pr/dining room 20 **Smoking:** N/Sm in restaurant **Children:** Min 8 yrs, Menu, Portions **Rooms:** 13 (13 en suite) ★★ HL **Directions:** From Petersfield A272 towards Winchester, turn left into Langrish & follow hotel signs **Parking:** 100

ROMSEY MAP 05 SU32

Bertie's

Modern British

Lively converted inn with French atmosphere

☎ 01794 830708 80 The Hundred SO51 8BX
e-mail: sales@berties.co.uk
web: www.berties.co.uk

This converted, one-time coaching inn continues to offer a relaxed, bistro-style experience, with its friendly and attentive front-of-house team proving a real bonus. There's a warm, cosy character to the original building, while a conservatory extension at the back adds a contemporary edge. Original artworks and mirrors decorate light walls, while polished-wood furniture and blue carpet add to the comforts. The kitchen's modern British cooking - with a nod to the Mediterranean - ideally suits the surroundings. Clear-flavoured, cleanly

continued

JSW

PETERSFIELD MAP 05 SU72

British, French V NOTABLE WINE LIST

Quality and élan are the bywords of this restaurant with exceptional wines

☎ 01730 262030 1 Heath Rd GU31 4JE

Discreetly located down a side street, JSW's eye-catching sign directs diners into the simple delights of this extremely accomplished restaurant. Thoughtful line drawings of nudes (by the chef-proprietor's sister) adorn the walls of this small, restful dining room; service here is skilled and attentive with a young, knowledgeable team on hand to recommend dishes and relay information on the outstanding wines from the chef himself. The fact that the wine cellar is bigger than the kitchen should give you some idea of the importance of the grape here - but don't forget it's chosen to accompany the dazzling food. Remarkable ingredients and superb tastes are at work throughout the menu - good examples would be roasted scallops with Jerusalem artichoke risotto, fresh foie gras and shallot tarte Tatin or suckling pig belly with spiced carrot purée. The nine-course tasting menu is thoroughly recommended.
Notable Wine List: An excellent all-round wine list, full of top quality wines.

Chef: Jake Watkins **Owners:** Jake Watkins **Times:** 12-1.30/7-9.30, Closed 2 wks Jan, 2 wks Aug, Sun-Mon **Prices:** Fixed L £23.50, Fixed D £40.50, Coffee £2.50, Min/Water £3, Service optional, Group min 10 service 10% **Wine:** 500 bottles over £20, 16 bottles under £20, 5 by the glass (£3.75-£9.50) **Notes:** Tasting menu 8 courses L £35, D £45, Vegetarian menu **Seats:** 22 **Smoking:** N/Sm in restaurant **Children:** Min 6 yrs **Directions:** A3 to Petersfield town centre, follow signs to Festival Hall car park. Restaurant 80yds from car park **Parking:** 80yds from restaurant

presented, straightforward dishes are the style; take chargrilled fillet steak with woodland mushrooms, mustard mash and red wine jus or fillets of sea bass on a mussel and vegetable chowder.

Bertie's

Chef: David Heyward **Owners:** David Birmingham **Times:** 12-2/7-10, Closed 26-30 Dec, Sun **Prices:** Fixed L £12.95, Fixed D £15.95, Starter £4.95-£7.95, Main £11.95-£18.95, Dessert £5.75, Coffee £2.50, Min/Water £2.75, Group min 6 service 10% **Wine:** 25 bottles over £20, 25 bottles under £20, 8 by the glass (£3.10-£4.75) **Notes:** Vegetarian available **Seats:** 34, Pr/dining room 36 **Smoking:** N/Sm area, No pipes **Children:** Portions **Directions:** 200yds from Broadlands' gate in town centre **Parking:** 10

The Three Tuns

☎ 01794 512639 58 Middlebridge St SO51 8HL

Smart, modern character pub serving quality food.

ROTHERWICK MAP 05 SU75

Tylney Hall

Modern European

Smart formal dining in opulent surroundings

☎ 01256 764881 RG27 9AZ
e-mail: sales@tylneyhall.com
web: www.tylneyhall.com

An imposing, 19th-century, red-brick mansion set in 66 acres of grounds, with fine Gertrude Jekyll gardens that include cascading waterfalls, ornamental lakes and woodland walks. Within, expect oak panelling, ornate ceilings, log fires, an old-fashioned style of service, and a sense of grandeur, with the glass-domed restaurant overlooking the garden. The style of cooking is modern while retaining the qualities of classical cuisine. Emphasis is on the use of the best (often luxurious) English produce, as seen in scallops with vegetable vinaigrette, and Angus beef fillet with red onion tarte Tatin.

continued

Tylney Hall

Chef: Stephen Hine **Owners:** Elite Hotels **Times:** 12.30-2/7-10 **Prices:** Fixed L fr £16, Fixed D £35-£46, Coffee £2.95, Min/Water £3.50, Service included **Wine:** 254 bottles over £20, 15 bottles under £20, 10 by the glass (£5.20-£6.25) **Notes:** Sun L £27.50, Vegetarian available, Dress Restrictions, Jacket & tie at D, Civ Wed 100 **Seats:** 80, Pr/dining room 100 **Smoking:** N/Sm in restaurant **Children:** Menu, Portions **Rooms:** 112 (112 en suite) ★★★★ HL **Directions:** M3 junct 5 take A287 (Newnham). From M4 junct 11 take B3349 (Hook), at sharp bend left (Rotherwick), left again & left in village (Newnham), 1m on right **Parking:** 150

SOUTHAMPTON MAP 05 SU41

Botleigh Grange

European

Country-house hotel offering a formal dining experience

☎ 01489 787700 Hedge End, Grange Rd SO30 2GA
e-mail: enquiries@botleighgrangehotel.co.uk
web: www.botleighgrangehotel.co.uk

Botleigh Grange is an impressive mansion set in extensive grounds with two lakes. The restaurant was added in 1992 and is spacious and well appointed, flooded with light from the domed glass ceiling and windows looking out on to the terrace and well tended garden. Access is via the oak-panelled cocktail lounge, perfect for drinks and coffee. When there's a function on, dinner may be served in a smaller dining room of similar style. The menu draws on quality local produce for dishes such as scallops with tempura and purée of cauliflower to start, followed by veal cutlet osso buco with seared sweetbreads and saffron risotto. The cooking attracts a local following as well as hotel residents.

Chef: Paul Dickinson **Owners:** David K Plumpton **Times:** 12.30-2.30/7-9.45, Closed L Sat **Prices:** Fixed L £24.95, Fixed D £24.95, Coffee £2.35, Min/Water £3.95, Service optional **Wine:** 22 bottles over £20, 26 bottles under £20, 15 by the glass (£3.50-£7.50) **Notes:** Vegetarian available, Dress Restrictions, No jeans, Civ Wed 200 **Seats:** 80, Pr/dining room 180 **Smoking:** N/Sm in restaurant **Children:** Menu, Portions **Rooms:** 56 (56 en suite) ★★★★ HL **Directions:** On A334, 1m from M27 junct 7 **Parking:** 300

England

SOUTHAMPTON *continued* MAP 05 SU41

De Vere Grand Harbour Hotel

Traditional European V

Eclectic fine dining at Southampton's premier hotel

☎ 023 8063 3033 West Quay Rd SO15 1AG
e-mail: grandharbour@devere-hotels.com
web: www.devereonline.co.uk

You can't help but feel inspired by the bold modern architecture of this soaring glass structure on Southampton's waterfront. It's the city's only five-star hotel and with fabulous leisure facilities and a choice of three dining options it certainly exerts a pull on the local affluent set. Through large windows, Allertons looks across at the old fortified walls of the town and almost has the feel of a luxury ocean liner. Gueridon dishes (which means they are cooked at the table) form an integral part of the menu - smoked salmon with capers, shallots and lemon, followed by Chateaubriand with pommes Pont-Neuf and béarnaise, with a dessert of crêpes Suzette. Elsewhere you might expect rabbit stuffed with pancetta and herbs or cassoulet with truffle potato purée.

Chef: Wayne Third **Owners:** De Vere Hotels **Times:** 12.30-1.45/7-9.45, Closed Sun, Mon **Prices:** Fixed L £19.50-£26.50, Fixed D £39.50-£54.50, Starter £6.50-£9.50, Main £24.50-£34.50, Dessert £6.50-£8, Coffee £5, Min/Water £3.50, Service included **Wine:** 42 bottles over £20, 3 bottles under £20, 6 by the glass (£6.75-£8.25) **Notes:** Vegetarian menu, Dress Restrictions, Smart - jacket & tie not required, Civ Wed 300 **Seats:** 50 **Smoking:** N/Sm in restaurant, Air con **Children:** Min 8 yrs **Rooms:** 172 (172 en suite) ★★★★★ HL **Directions:** M3 junct 13/M27 junct 3, follow Waterfront signs to West Quay Rd **Parking:** 190

Woodlands Lodge Hotel

Modern British

Forest hotel with an accent on fresh local produce

☎ 023 8029 2257 Bartley Rd, Woodlands SO40 7GN
e-mail: reception@woodlands-lodge.co.uk
web: www.woodlands-lodge.co.uk

This New Forest hotel is reputed to have been a royal hunting lodge. The restaurant, a Victorian addition with ornate plasterwork, was originally the music room, and from here there are views through the conservatory out onto the gardens and forest. Guests order their meals in the bar before taking their seats in the restaurant when the food is ready. Produce from local growers and suppliers inspires dishes of smoked venison with rocket, orange and pine nut salad, and roasted salmon fillet wrapped in prosciutto with lentils, olive mash and crème fraîche.

Chef: David Giles **Owners:** David & Jenny Norbury **Times:** 12-1.45/7-9, Closed L Mon-Sat **Prices:** Fixed L fr £14.95, Fixed D £31.50, Coffee £2.25, Min/Water £3.50, Service optional **Wine:** 15 bottles over £20, 11 bottles under £20, 5 by the glass (£3.80-£4.20) **Notes:** Fixed L 3 courses, Fixed D 4 courses, Vegetarian available, Dress Restrictions, Jacket & tie, no jeans, Civ Wed 60 **Seats:** 30, Pr/dining room 35 **Smoking:** N/Sm in restaurant **Children:** Portions **Rooms:** 16 (16 en suite) ★★★ HL **Directions:** M27 junct 1, through Cadnam towards Netley Marsh, at Bartley Cross right into Bourne Rd, over cattle grid, hotel on right **Parking:** 45

White Star Tavern & Dining Rooms

☎ 023 8082 1990 28 Oxford St SO14 3DJ

A stylish bar and restaurant, with a relaxed, informal atmosphere combined with a menu of modern British dishes.

STOCKBRIDGE MAP 05 SU33

The Greyhound

Modern British

Popular, gastro-pub on the River Test

☎ 01264 810833 High St SO20 6EY

A smart gastro-pub remodelling of an 18th-century high street inn, set in the charming market village of Stockbridge, famous as a fly-fishing centre, the Greyhound makes good use of its back garden setting on the River Test. Inside it has a relaxed, informal character but with a modern edge. Old beams and timbers, floorboards and inglenook fireplaces meet with stripped wooden tables and high-backed leather chairs. The kitchen's modern approach sits well, delivering high-quality 'city' food without pretension, based around fresh, high-quality seasonal produce. Expect the likes of pan-fried halibut served with boulangère potatoes, wild mushrooms and sauce lie de vin, and perhaps a warm chocolate fondant with roast hazelnut ice cream to finish.

Chef: Helene Schoeman **Owners:** Tim Fiducia **Times:** 12-2.30/7-9.30, Closed 25-26 Dec, 1 Jan, Closed D Sun **Prices:** Starter £5.50-£7.50, Main £11.50-£22.95, Dessert fr £6, Coffee £2, Min/Water £2.95, Service added but optional 10% **Wine:** 150 bottles over £20, 40 bottles under £20, 10 by the glass (£3-£5.50) **Notes:** Vegetarian available **Seats:** 52 **Smoking:** N/Sm area, No pipes, No cigars **Children:** Portions **Directions:** 9m NW of Winchester, 8m S of Andover **Parking:** 20

TITCHFIELD MAP 05 SU50

The Radcliffe Dining Rooms

Modern French

Fine dining in rural Hampshire

☎ 01329 845981 Whiteley Ln PO15 6RQ
e-mail: enquiries@theradcliffe.co.uk
web: www.theradcliffe.co.uk

This modern members' club/restaurant has been created from a Grade II listed Hampshire farmhouse. Oak and flagstone floors, an inglenook fireplace and exposed beams combine with more contemporary elements to create a comfortable, eclectic feel. On the ground floor the Champagne bar offers a choice of lounges, while upstairs there is the 80-seater dining room and a balcony for sunny days. Described as 'contemporary French', this is serious, accomplished cooking which makes good use of great ingredients. The cooking style is simple, unfussy and precise, with classical favourites sitting well with more innovative dishes.

Times: 12-2.30/7-11, Closed Mon, Closed D Sun **Directions:** From M27 junct 9 follow A27 towards Fareham. At rdbt for Holiday Inn turn left onto Cartwright Dr. Turn right at next rdbt onto Whiteley Ln. 200 yds on left

WHITCHURCH MAP 05 SU44

Red House Inn

Modern European

Busy roadside inn popular with locals

☎ 01256 895558 London St RG28 7LH

The Red House is actually a white-painted inn on the main road of this busy town famed for its one-time silk industry. Inside there's a bar, where informal meals are served, leading through to the restaurant,

continued

with its stripped pine flooring, polished wooden tables, exposed red brickwork and blackened beams. An honest approach is taken to food with clear menu descriptions and well defined flavours in dishes of salmon and crab fishcakes with white wine and onion sauce, Barbary duck with white courgette and wild mushrooms, and a deeply flavoured wedge of dark chocolate pie.

Times: 12-2/6.30-9.30 **Directions:** Between Andover and Basingstoke, off the A34

WICKHAM MAP 05 SU51

Old House Hotel & Restaurant

Modern International

Georgian splendour and impressive cuisine

☎ 01329 833049 The Square PO17 5JG
e-mail: oldhousehotel@aol.com
web: www.oldhousehotel.co.uk

You can't help admiring this handsome Grade II listed early Georgian townhouse in the village square. Three separate dining areas have a contemporary look and can easily be adapted for private dining. Staff are dressed smartly in black and white with long black aprons adding to the European brasserie-type feel. This fits in with the menu that features British and Continental dishes using local produce. Starters might feature Lymington crab while mains might be whole lobster thermidor or cep-crusted pork fillet with mustard seed crushed potato and honey and apple reduction. Good value lunchtime specials are also on offer with dishes like corned beef hash, egg and chips.

Chef: James Fairchild-Dickson **Owners:** Mr & Mrs P Scott **Times:** 12-2.30/7-9.30, Closed 26-30 Dec, Closed D Sun **Prices:** Starter £4.95-£6.95, Main £12.95-£19.50, Dessert £5.95-£7.95, Coffee £2.50, Min/Water £3, Group min 8 service 10% **Wine:** 40 bottles over £20, 18 bottles under £20, 10 by the glass (£4-£6) **Notes:** Sun TDH 2 courses £14.95, 3 courses £19.95, Vegetarian available, Civ Wed 70 **Seats:** 85, Pr/dining room 45 **Smoking:** N/Sm in restaurant **Children:** Portions **Rooms:** 12 (12 en suite) ★★ HL **Directions:** In centre of Wickham, 2m N of Fareham at junct of A32 & B2177 **Parking:** 12

WINCHESTER MAP 05 SU42

The Chesil Rectory

Modern French

Ancient building hosts accomplished modern fine dining

☎ 01962 851555 1 Chesil St SO23 0HU
web: www.chesilrectory.co.uk

Reputed to be Winchester's oldest house, this 15th-century building oozes ancient character and charm, situated at the foot of town beyond King Alfred's Statue and the River Itchen. Original beams and timbers, low ceilings, white walls and an inglenook fireplace create a warm, uncluttered setting for dining. While the compact, fixed-price dinner menu is bolstered by an amuse-bouche and petits fours, the accomplished kitchen's modern French output comes dotted with luxury items and is boosted by quality local produce, including superbly fresh fish. Take line-caught Solent sea bass with fleur de sel, black Périgord truffle with oyster and vanilla foam, or Pyrenees lamb rubbed with garlic, spinach and roasted ceps with baby morel sauce, for instance, and to finish, a classic Valrhona chocolate fondant with candied orange ice cream.

The Chesil Rectory

Chef: Mr R Quehan **Owners:** Mr & Mrs Carl Reeve **Times:** 12-1.30/7-9.30, Closed 2 wks Xmas-New Year, 2 wks Aug, Sun-Mon, Closed L Tue **Prices:** Fixed L fr £19, Fixed D fr £45, Coffee £2.50, Min/Water £4, Service optional, Group min 7 service 12.5% **Wine:** 94 bottles over £20, 5 bottles under £20, 8 by the glass (£4.75-£8.50) **Notes:** Tasting menu £55, Vegetarian available, Civ Wed 30 **Seats:** 42, Pr/dining room 15 **Smoking:** N/Sm area **Directions:** S from King Alfred's statue at bottom of The Broadway, cross small bridge, turn right, restaurant on left, just off mini rdbt **Parking:** 600

Hotel du Vin & Bistro

British, European NOTABLE WINE LIST

Busy bistro in popular, city-centre, boutique-chain hotel

☎ 01962 841414 14 Southgate St SO23 9EF
e-mail: info@winchester.hotelduvin.co.uk
web: www.hotelduvin.com

As its name suggests, wine is the dominant theme at this early 18th-century townhouse, which occupies a splendid city-centre location. The interior is charming, a touch of elegance mixed with an easy, relaxed style. This stylish informality is perhaps best seen in the bustling, French-style bistro and bar, where bare boards, an eclectic mix of polished tables and chairs, and wine memorabilia crowding the walls, form the backdrop for a modern, Mediterranean-influenced menu. Expect simple, light, clean-cut, well-presented classics with imaginative twists, as seen in oxtail soup with thyme dumplings, roast brill with mussel and clam broth, and rib-eye steak with béarnaise. Knowledgeable staff apply Gallic commitment, while the wine list is a delight.
Notable Wine List: A key hallmark of this group is an extensive wine list, packed full of interest and high-quality wines.

Chef: Matthew Sussex **Owners:** MWB **Times:** 12-1.45/7-9.45 **Prices:** Starter £4.50-£7.50, Main £13.50-£18.50, Dessert £2.50-£6.75, Coffee £2.75, Min/Water £3.50, Service optional, Group service 10% **Wine:** 650 bottles over £20, 50 bottles under £20, 12 by the glass (£3.50-£11.50) **Notes:** Sun L £23.50, Vegetarian available, Civ Wed 60 **Seats:** 65, Pr/dining room 48 **Smoking:** N/Sm in restaurant **Children:** Menu, Portions **Rooms:** 24 (24 en suite) ★★★★ TH **Directions:** M3 junct 11, follow signs to Winchester town centre **Parking:** 40

Lainston House Hotel

WINCHESTER MAP 05 SU42

British, International NOTABLE WINE LIST

An elegant country-house restaurant serving quality food

☎ 01962 863588 Sparsholt SO21 2LT
e-mail: enquiries@lainstonhouse.com
web: www.exclusivehotels.co.uk

A grand William and Mary country house at the end of a long winding drive, surrounded by 50 acres of beautifully kept grounds. Inside is just as majestic, with expansive lounges looking out over an impressive avenue of lime trees, and a bar made entirely from a single cedar that fell in the grounds in the 1930s. The elegant panelled restaurant is reminiscent of an English manor house dining room and is complemented by a terrace for alfresco dining or to enjoy one of the house speciality cocktails.

The cooking in these fine surroundings more than lives up to the billing, offering a classical menu with some tried and tested combinations. Perhaps start with a delicate marinated salmon and Portland crab, or confit belly pork with black pudding and foie gras parfait with Sauternes jelly. Main courses might include an excellent wild sea bass with courgette spaghetti, pan-fried turbot with vegetable salsa and a technically adept cherry tomato Tatin or glazed fillet of English beef, red pepper polenta and wild mushroom tortellini.

Notable Wine List: This well-presented wine list offers a fine selection of wines from around the world.

Chef: Andrew Mackenzie
Owners: Exclusive Hotels
Times: 12-2.30/6.30-10
Prices: Fixed L fr £19.50, Fixed D fr £37, Starter £9.60-£15.50, Main £17.50-£28.50, Dessert £9.50, Coffee £4.50, Min/Water £3.95, Service optional
Wine: 170 bottles over £20, 6 bottles under £20, 150 by the glass (£4-£150)
Notes: Tasting menu, Sun L available, Vegetarian available, Dress Restrictions, Smart casual, No jeans or trainers; Civ Wed 90
Seats: 55, Pr/dining room 18
Smoking: N/Sm in restaurant
Children: Before 7pm, Menu, Portions
Rooms: 50 (50 en suite) ★★★★ HL
Directions: Off A272, road to Stockbridge, signed
Parking: 200

England

WINCHESTER *continued* MAP 05 SU42

The Running Horse

Modern International NEW

Great produce meets eclectic dishes in bistro-styled gastro-pub

☎ 01962 880218 88 Main Rd, Littleton SO22 6QS
e-mail: runninghorse@btconnect.com
web: www.therunninghorsepubrestaurant.co.uk

Set in a small village tucked away on the western outskirts of the city, this refurbished rural gastro-pub has hit the ground with a canter, blending high-quality cuisine with local atmosphere. Think warm colours, clean lines, tiled floors, leather sofas, marble-top bar and friendly service. The enthusiastic kitchen has pedigree too, and displays a passion for sourcing fine local produce and delivering innovative flavour combinations. Portion sizes are generous, the cooking accomplished, while dinner cranks things up a gear to showcase the kitchen's true flair and imagination, with some dishes influenced by the chef's American roots. Take Cornish cod fillet with a crab chowder Manhattan-style, for instance, or perhaps English lamb rack served with dauphinoise potato, red pepper ragout and balsamic. *As we went to press there was a change of hands planned.*

Times: 11-3/5.30-11, Closed 25 Dec, Closed D Sun **Rooms:** 9 (9 en suite) ◆◆◆◆ **Directions:** 3m from Winchester city centre, 2m off A34

Loch Fyne Restaurant & Oyster Bar

☎ 01962 872930 18 Jewry St SO23 8RZ
Quality seafood chain.

HEREFORD MAP 10 SO53

Castle House

see page 198

KINGTON MAP 09 SO25

The Stagg Inn and Restaurant

Modern British

Friendly, quality-driven gastro-pub

☎ 01544 230221 Titley HR5 3RL
e-mail: reservations@thestagg.co.uk
web: www.thestagg.co.uk

Large farmhouse tables, open fires and welcoming, friendly service await at this country gastro-pub oozing a relaxed, traditional atmosphere. Staying true to its roots, its down-to-earth mood is reflected in the rustic décor, original features and small bar, while there are three dining rooms on different levels, the largest in a medieval barn. The assured kitchen's classy but unpretentious modern approach makes admirable use of top-notch, local seasonal produce. Expect a fillet of Herefordshire beef served with potato rösti, caramelised shallots and red wine sauce, or rack of Marches lamb with braised shoulder and a potato cake. An extensive range of regional cheeses bolsters the repertoire, alongside desserts like caramelised lemon tart with a Cassis sorbet.

continued

Chef: S Reynolds, G Powell, M Handley **Owners:** Steve & Nicola Reynolds **Times:** 12-3/6.30-10, Closed 1st 2 wk Nov, 25-26 Dec, 1 Jan, May Day, Mon (Tue after a BH), Closed D Sun **Prices:** Starter £3.70-£7.90, Main £12.90-£16.95, Dessert £4.90, Coffee £2.30, Min/Water £2.30, Service included **Wine:** 34 bottles over £20, 35 bottles under £20, 8 by the glass (£2.20-£2.40) **Seats:** 70, Pr/dining room 30 **Smoking:** N/Sm in restaurant **Children:** Portions **Directions:** Between Kington and Presteigne on B4335 **Parking:** 22

LEDBURY MAP 10 SO73

Feathers Hotel

Modern British

Popular and well-established inn serving modern food

☎ 01531 635266 High St HR8 1DS
e-mail: mary@feathers-ledbury.co.uk
web: www.feathers-ledbury.co.uk

Since Elizabethan times, this famous black and white coaching inn has dominated historic Ledbury's main street. Oozing charm and character, Feathers Hotel combines all the characteristics of a town-centre hostelry with the comforts of a modern hotel. Dinner is served in the elegant Quills Restaurant or the bustling Fuggles brasserie with adjoining bar. Modern British cuisine features local beef and lamb, and a range of good fresh fish and shellfish dishes. At dinner you could tuck into baked crottin goat's cheese with roasted beetroot and watercress salad starter, followed by roast rump of local lamb, ratatouille and pesto rösti potato.

Chef: Steve Rimmer **Owners:** David Elliston **Times:** 12-2/7-9.30 **Prices:** Starter £4.25-£6.95, Main £9.50-£18.95, Dessert £5.25, Coffee £1.20, Min/Water £2.50, Service added but optional 10% **Wine:** 33 bottles over £20, 62 bottles under £20, 12 by the glass (£3.20-£6) **Notes:** Vegetarian available, Civ Wed 100 **Seats:** 55, Pr/dining room 60 **Smoking:** N/Sm in restaurant, Air con **Rooms:** 19 (19 en suite) ★★★ **Directions:** M50 junct 2, Ledbury is on A449/A438/A417, hotel is on main street **Parking:** 30

Seven Ledbury

Modern British, Mediterranean NEW

Quality cuisine in modern bistro

☎ 01531 631317 11 The Homend HR8 1BN
e-mail: jasonkay@btconnect.com

An ancient black and white timber-framed building, typical of the area, houses this relaxed bistro and newcomer to the Ledbury dining scene. The tastefully refurbished interior comes as a delightful surprise, while the efficient service is everything you would expect. The menus emphasise local beef, lamb and chicken, all traceable to local farms, and include dishes such as Hereford beef fillet on creamed potato and beetroot salsa, gnocchi in Roquefort cream sauce with rocket and crumbled walnuts, or smoked haddock and saffron risotto with baby spinach and a poached egg. If you want a lighter option you can just as easily enjoy olives and bread with a bottle of wine if you choose.

Chef: Jason Kay **Owners:** Jason Kay **Times:** 11-10 **Prices:** Food prices not confirmed for 2007. Please telephone for details
Rooms: 3 (3 en suite) ★★★ RR **Directions:** Telephone for directions

Castle House

HEREFORD MAP 10 SO53

Classic with modern twist

Adventurous cooking in contemporary luxury

☎ 01432 356321 Castle St HR1 2NW
e-mail: info@castlehse.co.uk
web: www.castlehse.co.uk

Tucked away in a residential street, this ancient building is now a stylish and elegant hotel. The bar is sumptuously furnished and decorated with bold lamps, silver-framed pictures and coats of arms. The La Rive restaurant has less decoration to distract from the food and views over the old castle moat and gardens. Tables are clothed in best quality linen with good quality settings of silver and crystal. Staff are impeccably trained, well-informed and knowledgeable. Fresh, contemporary interpretations of cooking with classical roots are offered on either the main or seven-course tasting menu. Careful handling of top-quality ingredients from near and far creates starters of confit goose rillettes with orange and sage jelly and pine nut salad. Main courses may include a delicious Herefordshire beef fillet with beetroot fondant and braised beef and horseradish faggot and truffle jus. To finish there's a satisfying apple and sultana tart Tatin with vanilla ice cream and Calvados cappuccino.

Chef: Claire Nicholls
Owners: Dr & Mrs A Heijn
Times: 12.30-2.30/7.00-10.00
Prices: Food prices not confirmed for 2007. Please telephone for details
Notes: Vegetarian available, Dress Restrictions, No jeans, T-shirts or trainers
Seats: 30
Smoking: N/Sm in restaurant
Rooms: 15 (15 en suite) ★★★ HL
Directions: City centre, near cathedral
Parking: 12

LEDBURY *continued* MAP 10 SO73

The Verzon Bar, Brasserie & Hotel

British, European

Quality local produce in a modern brasserie environment

☎ 01531 670381 Hereford Rd, Trumpet HR8 2PZ
e-mail: info@theverzon.co.uk
web: www.theverzon.co.uk

This large Georgian country house - with far-reaching views of the Malvern Hills from its extensive grounds - has now been refurbished throughout. Modern and stylish interiors abound, with a selection of dining areas - from main restaurant to bar/brasserie option - sharing the same menu and relaxed but attentive service. The accomplished kitchen deals in high-quality, locally-sourced and carefully prepared ingredients; maybe Gloucestershire Old Spot pork with a cider jus and potato rösti, or perhaps Hereford beef, pan-fried rib-eye with sautéed potatoes and sauce au poivre, all treated with due care and respect. Classics bolster the repertoire, too, maybe poached salmon with a chive hollandaise, while careful balance and flavour combinations prove a strength of the intelligently uncomplicated style.

Times: 12-2/7-9.30 **Rooms:** 8 (8 en suite) ★★ HL **Directions:** M5 junct 8, M50 junct 2 (signposted Ledbury A417). Follow signs for Hereford (A438)

MUCH MARCLE MAP 10 SO63

The Scrumpy House Restaurant & Bar

Traditional British NEW

Fine-quality local produce in genuine scrumpy house

☎ 01531 660626 The Bounds HR8 2NQ
e-mail: matt@scrumpyhouse.co.uk
web: www.scrumpyhouse.co.uk

Part of the Weston's cider estate at Much Marcle but independently owned and operated by a husband and wife team, the restaurant is in a genuine scrumpy house barn with lots of cider memorabilia. A varied menu takes you through from lighter lunches to dinner with high quality local and seasonal produce. Choices from the traditional menu may include rare roast Marcle orchard reared beef with home-made horseradish and Yorkshire pudding, or Madgetts Farm duck breast with honey, soy and sesame. The huge list of home-made ice creams is extremely popular, as are the ciders, including a draft perry.

continued

Chef: Matthew & Annalisa Slocombe **Owners:** Matthew & Annalisa Slocombe **Times:** 12-3/6.30-11, Closed 1 Jan, Mon (in Jan), Closed D Sun, Mon, Tue & 2 weeks in Jan **Prices:** Fixed L fr £14.95, Fixed D £18.95-£25, Starter £3.95-£9, Main £8.95-£17, Dessert £4.95-£6.95, Coffee £1.75, Min/Water £3.60, Service optional, Group min 10 service 10% **Wine:** 11 bottles over £20, 13 bottles under £20, 6 by the glass (£3.10-£3.50) **Notes:** Vegetarian available, Dress Restrictions, Smart casual preferred **Seats:** 45 **Smoking:** N/Sm in restaurant, Air con **Children:** Portions **Directions:** On A417 between Ross-on-Wye & Ledbury. At village shop follow signs to Cider Mill **Parking:** 100

ROSS-ON-WYE MAP 10 SO52

The Bridge House

British, French

Hotel by the Wye serving top Herefordshire produce

☎ 01989 562655 Wilton HR9 6AA
e-mail: info@bridge-house-hotel.com
web: www.bridge-house-hotel.com

Once a private residence, this period property has been turned into a boutique-style hotel. It is located on the banks of the River Wye by the 12th-century bridge and the ancient remains of Wilton Castle. The partially walled garden runs right down to the water's edge, the perfect spot for drinks in the summer. The restaurant is comfortable and stylish from the gnarled solid oak floorboards to the contemporary paintings by a local artist. Quality ingredients feature in tempting combinations, such as five-spice dusted John Dory with crab tortellini and carrot and mint nage, and saffron poached pear with pink grapefruit ice cream and rice condé.

Chef: James Arbourne **Owners:** Mike & Jane Pritchard **Times:** 12-2/7-9 **Prices:** Fixed L £16.50, Starter £5.50-£9.50, Main £15-£22.50, Dessert £5.50, Coffee £3, Min/Water £3.50, Service optional **Wine:** 19 bottles over £20, 14 bottles under £20, 2 by the glass (£3.50) **Notes:** Sun L 1 course £14.95, 2 courses £19.95, 3 courses £24.95, Dress Restrictions, Smart casual **Seats:** 30, Pr/dining room 18 **Smoking:** N/Sm in restaurant **Children:** Min 14 yrs **Rooms:** 9 (9 en suite) ★★★★ RR **Directions:** A49 3rd rdbt and left into Ross. 150yds on left before river bridge **Parking:** 40

ROSS-ON-WYE *continued* MAP 10 SO52

Glewstone Court

Modern British

Local produce lovingly prepared in fine surroundings

☎ 01989 770367 Glewstone HR9 6AW
e-mail: glewstone@aol.com
web: www.glewstonecourt.com

A Georgian and late Regency house, with lots of original features, including a carved oak staircase that spirals up to a galleried and porticoed landing. The Georgian dining room is decorated in contemporary style, and houses a changing display of local artwork. Service is relaxed and friendly but with formal touches like wine service. Cuisine here is based on traditional methods using the very best that local suppliers have to offer. The menu has a wide choice including the likes of chargrilled fresh king scallops to start, and a main like tenderloin of Pontrilas pork, wrapped in Carmarthen ham and Y'Fenni cheese, served with a Weston's dry cider and grain mustard cream.

Chef: C Reeve-Tucker, P Meek, M Price **Owners:** C & W Reeve-Tucker **Times:** 12-2/7-10, Closed 25-27 Dec **Prices:** Starter £4.25-£7.95, Main £11.95-£16.95, Dessert £3.95-£5.25, Coffee £1.75, Min/Water £3, Service optional, Group min 8 service 10% **Wine:** 14 bottles over £20, 23 bottles under £20, 6 by the glass (£2.85-£3.75) **Notes:** Vegetarian available, Dress Restrictions, No baseball caps or mobile phones **Seats:** 36, Pr/dining room 36 **Smoking:** N/Sm in restaurant **Children:** Menu, Portions **Rooms:** 8 (8 en suite) ★★ CHH **Directions:** From Ross Market Place take A40/A49 (Monmouth/Hereford) over Wilton Bridge. At rdbt left onto A40 (Monmouth/S Wales), after 1m turn right for Glewstone. Hotel 0.5m on left **Parking:** 28

Harry's

Modern British

Ambitious cuisine in elegant Georgian hotel

☎ 01989 763161 Chase Hotel, Gloucester Rd HR9 5LH
e-mail: res@chasehotel.co.uk
web: www.chasehotel.co.uk

Old-world charm blends with the modern décor at this restored Georgian mansion standing in landscaped grounds only a short walk from the town centre. Harry's offers a contemporary dining experience within the more traditional environment of the hotel. Competent cooking from an ambitious kitchen fuses a modern British style with strong European influences. Expect to find ham hock terrine, ballotine of salmon and dill with beetroot purée and caviar dressing, braised venison with celeriac purée and Kirsch jus, and beef medallions with sweet onion ravioli on the extensive carte.

Chef: Jonathan Howe **Owners:** The Porter Family **Times:** 12-2/7-10, Closed 24-30 Dec **Prices:** Fixed L £10-£17, Fixed D £15-£25, Starter £4.95-£7.95, Main £11.95-£23, Dessert £5.50-£7.50, Coffee £3.25, Min/Water £3.50 **Wine:** 20 bottles over £20, 23 bottles under £20, 6 by the glass (£2.95-£3.75) **Notes:** Vegetarian available, Civ Wed 300 **Seats:** 70, Pr/dining room 60 **Smoking:** N/Sm in restaurant **Children:** Portions **Rooms:** 36 (36 en suite) ★★★ HL **Directions:** M50 junct 4 A449, A440 towards Ross-on-Wye **Parking:** 150

The Lough Pool Inn

Modern British

Popular inn of great charm serving rustic fare

☎ 01989 730236 Sellack HR9 6LX

Set in a peaceful valley just outside Ross-on-Wye, this pub is full of character, with inglenook fireplaces, beams, flagstone floors and a granite-topped bar. Food can be taken in the bar or the restaurant, which is altogether lighter in decorative style. Both offer a relaxed and informal atmosphere. Cooking is modern British using high quality, carefully sourced ingredients served in rustic dishes of generous proportions: try succulent belly of pork on crushed potatoes with caramelised apple, spring onions and sweet spiced sauce, or breast of chicken with woodland mushrooms and pea risotto, with sticky toffee pudding accompanied by butterscotch sauce to finish.

Times: 12-2.30/6.30-9.30, Closed Nov, Jan, Feb, Mon, Closed D Sun **Directions:** 2.5m N of Ross-on-Wye, on Hoarwithy Rd

֍֍ Wilton Court Hotel

European

Charming period property with good food

☎ 01989 562569 Wilton Ln HR9 6AQ
e-mail: info@wiltoncourthotel.com
web: www.wiltoncourthotel.com

There's a wonderful informality to this riverside country house hotel that's evident as much in the considerate service as in the honest, carefully cooked food. Set in a walled garden, the hotel dates back to the 16th century and features stone mullion windows, original oak beams and Lloyd Loom tables and chairs - the conservatory is a particularly pleasant place to dine. Local sources for the produce are listed on the menu, wherein you might expect dishes such as ham hock and pistachio terrine with red onion chutney, or venison loin with roast shallot mousseline and a thyme and hazelnut brandy snap.

Chef: Alistair Forster **Owners:** Roger and Helen Wynn **Times:** 12-2.30/7-9.30, Closed L Mon-Sat, D Sun **Prices:** Fixed D £25-£27.50, Starter £4.50-£7.25, Main £8.95-£18.50, Dessert £4.95-£5.25, Coffee £1.75, Min/Water £3.50, Service optional **Wine:** 6 bottles over £20, 19 bottles under £20, 6 by the glass (£2.95-£4.20) **Notes:** Sun L 2/3 courses £14.50-17.50, Vegetarian available, Dress Restrictions, Smart casual preferred **Seats:** 40, Pr/dining room 12 **Smoking:** N/Sm in restaurant **Children:** Portions **Rooms:** 10 (10 en suite) ★★★ HL **Directions:** M50 junct 4 follow signs to Ross, turn into Ross at rdbt at junct of A40 and A49. Take 1st right after 100yds, hotel opposite river **Parking:** 25

ULLINGSWICK MAP 10 SO54

֍ Three Crowns Inn

British, European

Traditional English village inn with a gastro-pub menu

☎ 01432 820279 HR1 3JQ
e-mail: info@threecrownsinn.com
web: www.threecrownsinn.com

This black and white village inn is a converted 16th-century farmhouse, which was a cider house for many years. Dark oak beams, quarry tiled floors and log fires in a brick fireplace set the scene for a mix and match collection of wooden tables and chairs, creating a warm, welcoming and relaxed atmosphere. A straightforward menu of mainly modern British dishes includes the odd classic sauce and Asian influence. Local produce features in seasonally appropriate selections, such as chicken liver and winter vegetable risotto, followed by crisp belly of Shortwood Farm pork with Three Crowns black pudding, red cabbage and mustard mash.

Chef: Brent Castle **Owners:** Brent Castle & Rachel Baker **Times:** 12-3/7-10, Closed 2 wks from 24 Dec, Mon **Prices:** Fixed L £12.95, Starter £6, Main £14.25, Dessert £4.50, Coffee £2.25, Min/Water £2.50, Service optional

continued

Wine: 14 bottles under £20, 13 by the glass (£3.75-£5.24) **Notes:** Vegetarian available **Seats:** 75, Pr/dining room 36 **Smoking:** N/Sm in restaurant **Children:** Portions **Directions:** Telephone for directions **Parking:** 30

WEOBLEY MAP 09 SO45

֍ *The Salutation Inn*

Traditional British NEW

Popular country inn serving good local produce

☎ 01544 318443 Market Pitch HR4 8SJ

This traditional village inn has plenty of character, and you can sit in the bar, lounge or restaurant and enjoy relaxed and friendly service. There's a selection of real ales and local ciders and the food choice ranges through blackboard specials, bar snacks and the main menu. More than a hint of French influence is evident in the cuisine, and the emphasis is on local produce with traditional sauces - roast fillet of sea bass with beurre blanc, or pan-fried sirloin of Hereford beef with saffron mash and wild mushroom sauce.

Times: 12-2/7-9.30, Closed 25 Dec, Closed D Sun (bar meals served all week) **Rooms:** 4 (4 en suite) ◆◆◆◆ **Directions:** On A4112, just off Leominster-Hereford road

HERTFORDSHIRE

BISHOP'S STORTFORD MAP 06 TL42

֍֍ Ibbetson's Restaurant

European

Stylish dining in imposing country-house hotel

☎ 01279 731441 Down Hall Country House Hotel, Hatfield Heath CM22 7AS
e-mail: reservations@downhall.co.uk
web: www.downhall.co.uk

continued

England

BISHOP'S STORTFORD *continued* MAP 06 TL42

Built by Sir Henry Selwin Ibbetson, this imposing Victorian structure is surrounded by 100 acres of grounds. The beautifully presented public areas and dining room are impressive, full of Victorian design excess and open fires. Seasonal availability of ingredients dictates the daily menus which comprise carefully cooked modern European dishes with exacting flavours. Start with a delicate courgette and wild mushroom roulade with Paris Brown and endive salad. Then for a main course try the well-timed confit halibut on globe artichoke, roast aubergine and sun-dried tomatoes, or for an extra bit of theatre the carved-at-your-table whole guinea fowl, boned and stuffed with shiitake mushrooms. Finish with the lemon grass crème brûlée or well-kept English cheeses.

Chef: Chris Wheeldon **Owners:** Mr Gulhati, Veladail Hotels Ltd **Times:** 12-1.45/7-9.45, Closed Sun-Mon, Closed L Sat **Prices:** Fixed L £16.50-£19.50, Fixed D £25.50-£41.75, Starter £7.75-£12.50, Main £14.85-£21.75, Dessert £6.25-£7.50, Coffee £3.25, Min/Water £3.50, Service added but optional 10% **Wine:** 82 bottles over £20, 7 bottles under £20, 9 by the glass (£4.50-£10.50) **Notes:** Vegetarian available, Dress Restrictions, No denim or trainers, Civ Wed 120 **Seats:** 36 **Smoking:** N/Sm in restaurant, Air con **Children:** Min 12 yrs **Rooms:** 99 (99 en suite) ★★★★ **Directions:** Take A414 towards Harlow. At 4th rdbt follow B183 towards Hatfield Heath, keep left and follow hotel sign **Parking:** 150

ELSTREE MAP 06 TQ19

Corus hotel Elstree

European

Tudor-style grandeur with views of the city

☎ 0870 6096151 Barnet Ln WD6 3RE
e-mail: elstree@corushotels.com
web: www.corushotels.com/elstree

Standing in a beautiful landscaped garden, itself surrounded by 10 acres of natural woodland, this Tudor-style hotel is decorated to a traditional design with good views of nearby London. The newly appointed chef at the popular Cavendish restaurant brings a strong French influence to the well-conceived menu, yet there is a liberal sprinkling of Mediterranean flavours throughout. Try a starter of smoked haddock chowder with pancetta gougère and parmesan, followed by braised monkfish tail with Parisienne potatoes, spinach and gremolata, and a dessert of white chocolate ganache with banana ice cream and passionfruit bavarois.

Chef: Nic Robic **Owners:** Corus Hotels **Times:** 12.30-2.15/7-9.30 **Prices:** Fixed L £22.50, Starter £4.95-£7.25, Main £12.95-£18.95, Dessert £5.95, Coffee £3.50, Min/Water £3.50, Service optional **Wine:** 12 bottles over £20, 20 bottles under £20, 4 by the glass (£3.75-£5.20) **Notes:** Vegetarian available, Dress Restrictions, Smart casual, Civ Wed 100 **Seats:** 60, Pr/dining room 40 **Smoking:** N/Sm in restaurant **Children:** Menu, Portions **Rooms:** 47 (47 en suite) ★★★ HL **Directions:** From A1 take A411 from Stirling Corner **Parking:** 100

HARPENDEN MAP 06 TL11

A Touch of Novelli at the White Horse

British, French NEW

Gastro-pub with a touch of glamour

☎ 01582 713428 Hatching Green AL5 2JP
e-mail: info@atouchofnovelli.com
web: www.atouchofnovelli.co.uk

Novelli's latest venture, set to be the first in a small chain of gastro-pubs. This old village inn is now decked out with sparkly chandeliers. For those wanting to order a pint, there's a modern wooden bar and small seating area. The menu is loosely based on local and seasonal produce. 'Pot au pain' is a lovely feature, freshly baked wholemeal bread served hot in a terracotta flowerpot. Garden pea and mint cappuccino with mi-cuit foie gras is a typical starter, with a main course like honey and ale glazed pork belly with celeriac crisps, chipoline onions and pomme mousseline.

Chef: Mr Wesley Smalley **Owners:** Sweet Medicine **Times:** 12.30-3/6-10, Closed 25 & 26 Dec **Prices:** Starter £4.50-£9.95, Main £9.50-£17.90, Dessert £6, Coffee £1.75, Min/Water £2.50, Service optional **Wine:** 30 bottles over £20, 20 bottles under £20, 12 by the glass (£3-£6) **Seats:** 55, Pr/dining room 12 **Smoking:** N/Sm in restaurant **Children:** Portions **Directions:** Telephone for directions **Parking:** 65

The Bean Tree

☎ 01582 460901 20a Leyton Rd AL5 2HU
web: www.theaa.com/restaurants/113910.html

A cosy converted cottage with a relaxed atmosphere. The seasonally-changing menu is French and the chef is passionate about the quality and freshness of his ingredients.

HATFIELD MAP 06 TL20

Bush Hall

British, European

Accomplished modern cooking at a popular hotel

☎ 01707 271251 Mill Green AL9 5NT
e-mail: enquiries@bush-hall.com
web: www.bush-hall.com

A popular wedding and conference venue, Bush Hall stands amid 120 acres of parkland within easy reach of the M1 and M25. Riverside terraces and a lake garden make the most of the Lea as it meanders

continued

through the grounds, while a host of outdoor activities are available for those who feel like more than a stroll. Dinner is served in a cosy room with a green and gold décor and oak panelling, and there's a comfortable lounge for aperitifs or late-night tipples. Expect an accomplished modern British menu: a game terrine starter perhaps, followed by pork with beer braised cabbage and Calvados jus, or steak and Guinness pie with horseradish rösti.

Chef: Steve Moore, Nick Reed **Owners:** Kiplings **Times:** 12-2/7-10, Closed D 25 Dec-early Jan, Closed L Sat-Sun **Prices:** Starter £4.95-£9.75, Main £9.75-£19.95, Dessert £5.95-£9.95, Coffee £2.95, Min/Water £3.50, Service added but optional 12.5% **Wine:** 92 bottles over £20, 44 bottles under £20, 8 by the glass (£3.50-£5.75) **Notes:** Vegetarian available, Dress Restrictions, Smart casual, Civ Wed 150 **Seats:** 38, Pr/dining room 22 **Smoking:** No pipes or cigars, Air con **Children:** Min 8 yrs, Portions **Rooms:** 25 (25 en suite) ★★★ HL **Directions:** From A1 (M) follow signs for A414 (Hereford/Welwyn Garden City). Take slip rd onto A1000 (signs for Hatfield Hse). Left at lights, immediately left into hotel drive **Parking:** 100

HITCHIN MAP 12 TL12

Redcoats Farmhouse Hotel

British, Mediterranean

Pleasant former farmhouse with a busy restaurant

☎ 01438 729500 Redcoats Green SG4 7JR
e-mail: sales@redcoats.co.uk
web: www.redcoats.co.uk

This delightful 14th-century farmhouse is set in 4 acres of landscaped grounds a short drive from the A1. While many of the features are original (exposed brickwork, oak beams and open fireplaces), the building has been restored over the years and now has an attractive Victorian red brick frontage. The menu at this thriving, busy restaurant consists of enduring classics cooked with precision using good quality produce throughout - expect dishes such as duck liver and orange pâté to start and grilled skate with caper and balsamic butter as a main.

Chef: Scott Liversedge **Owners:** Mr P Butterfield & Mrs J Gainsford **Times:** 12/6.30, Closed 1 wk after Xmas, BH Mons, Closed L Sat, D Sun **Prices:** Fixed L £14.75, Fixed D £25, Starter £3.75-£8.50, Main £15-£26, Dessert £5.75-£10, Coffee £1, Min/Water £2.75, Service optional, Group min 8 service 10% **Wine:** 40 bottles over £20, 30 bottles under £20, 12 by the glass (£3.25-£6.50) **Notes:** Vegetarian available, Dress Restrictions, Smart casual, No jeans or T-shirts, Civ Wed 70 **Seats:** 70, Pr/dining room 24 **Smoking:** N/Sm in restaurant **Children:** Portions **Rooms:** 14 (12 en suite) ◆◆◆◆ **Directions:** Telephone for directions **Parking:** 30

POTTERS BAR MAP 06 TL20

Ponsbourne Park Hotel

European, International NEW

Stately manor with a contemporary taste

☎ 01707 876191 & 879277 SG13 8QZ
e-mail: reservations@ponsbournepark.co.uk
web: www.ponsbournepark.co.uk

Ponsbourne makes an imposing first impression. A grand old house dating back to the 17th century, it sits amid a 200-acre estate in peaceful countryside. Inside is a restrained contemporary affair by contrast - all bold colours and clean lines - and the restaurant offers

continued

food to match, delivering a comprehensive menu of modern dishes firmly with roots in classic French cuisine. Expect the likes of rillette of rabbit wrapped in Parma ham, pan-fried fillet of cod with a pancetta, mussel and broad bean broth and chocolate fondant with pistachio ice cream.

Ponsbourne Park Hotel

Chef: Sushmito Roy **Owners:** Tesco **Times:** 12-4/6.30-11 **Prices:** Fixed L £21.95, Fixed D £29.95, Coffee £2, Min/Water £3.75, Service optional **Wine:** 7 bottles over £20, 22 bottles under £20 **Notes:** Fixed L 3 courses, Vegetarian available, Dress Restrictions, Smart casual, Civ Wed 86 **Seats:** 70, Pr/dining room 90 **Smoking:** N/Sm in restaurant, Air con **Children:** Menu, Portions **Rooms:** 51 (51 en suite) ★★★★ **Directions:** Telephone or see website for directions **Parking:** 80

See advert above

RICKMANSWORTH MAP 06 TQ09

 The Grove

see below

ROYSTON MAP 12 TL34

The Cabinet at Reed

European

Impressive food in a cosy village pub

☎ 01763 848366 High St, Reed SG8 8AH
e-mail: thecabinet@btconnect.com
web: www.thecabinetatreed.co.uk

The Cabinet (meaning small room or meeting place) is a 16th-century inn with low ceilings, original beams and an open fire, located in a little Hertfordshire village. The restaurant has been refurbished and a good choice of food is offered from both fixed-price and à la carte menus, changing with the seasons. Locally sourced dry-aged beef is a feature, perhaps to follow a starter of half a dozen oysters served on crushed ice with raspberry vinaigrette.

At the time of going to press, a change of hands was taking place.

Times: 12-2.30/7-9, Closed 25 Dec, 1 Jan, Mon, Closed D Sun
Directions: Just off A10 between Buntingford and Royston

ST ALBANS MAP 06 TL10

St Michael's Manor

Modern European

Accomplished cooking in a luxury hotel

☎ 01727 864444 Fishpool St AL3 4RY
e-mail: reservations@stmichaelsmanor.com
web: www.stmichaelsmanor.com

Set by a lake in attractive landscaped gardens, this luxurious country-house hotel has an airy dining room within an elegant conservatory. Simply decorated with fresh flowers, mirrors and sparkling glassware, it also boasts a sun terrace - perfect for a pre-dinner glass of champagne. Tables are covered in linen cloths and smart, uniformed staff provide friendly, professional service. The lengthy menus offer a broad choice of accomplished modern British dishes displaying technical skill and deceptive simplicity: Ballic salmon, horseradish cream, spring roll and citrus dressing may be followed by a rack of hay-baked lamb with dauphinoise potatoes and crème brûlée cheesecake and blackcurrant compôte.

continued

The Grove

RICKMANSWORTH MAP 06 TQ09

Modern, Traditional V

Fine dining in smart, contemporary, relaxed setting of 'London's country estate'

☎ 01923 296015 Chandler's Cross WD3 4TG
e-mail: restaurants@thegrove.co.uk
web: www.thegrove.co.uk

An 18th-century stately home transformed into a world-class, contemporary hotel, The Grove successfully combines historic character with cutting edge modern design. It stands in 300 acres of rolling grounds, replete with championship golf course, impressive formal gardens and beautiful views over Charlotte's Vale. This sophisticated and stylish hotel houses a fabulous spa, stunning suites, a relaxing bar and lounge, and three dining choices. Colette's is the fine dining operation, the two high-ceilinged dining rooms blending Georgian features with stripped wood floors, cream leather chairs and modern art.

Cooking is classically based with a great level of refinement, the ambitious menu showcasing British dishes with modern and European twists. Luxury ingredients are successfully combined using classic techniques, resulting in excellent clarity of flavours and some exciting dishes. Typically, foie gras, quince mousse and almond foam or Cornish crab with Sévruga caviar, coriander-cured tuna and lemon dressing, followed by braised turbot with lemongrass sauce and honey-roasted squid, and hot chocolate fondant with banana tarte Tatin and lemon curd ice cream.

Chef: Chris Harrod **Owners:** Ralph Trustees Ltd **Times:** 7-10.30, Closed 1-15 Jan & 6-21 Aug, Closed L all week, D Sun except BH wknds
Prices: Food prices not confirmed for 2007. Please telephone for details
Wine: 100% bottles over £20, 20 by the glass (£7-£21) **Notes:** Vegetarian menu, Civ Wed 40 **Seats:** 40 **Smoking:** N/Sm in restaurant, Air con
Children: Min 12 yrs **Rooms:** 227 (227 en suite) ★★★★★ HL
Directions: M25 junct 19, follow signs to Watford. At first large rdbt take 3rd exit. Continue on 0.5m entrance on right **Parking:** 500

St Michael's Manor

Chef: Robin Dudley **Owners:** David & Sheila Newling-Ward **Times:** 12-2.30/7-9.30, Closed L 31 Dec **Prices:** Fixed L £19.65, Starter £5.95-£12.90, Main £12.50-£20.90, Dessert £5-£10.90, Coffee £2.50, Min/Water £3.25, Service added but optional 10% **Wine:** 44 bottles over £20, 27 bottles under £20, 11 by the glass (£4.75-£7.75) **Notes:** Sun L 3 courses £28.50, Vegetarian available, Dress Restrictions, Smart casual, Civ Wed 90 **Seats:** 95, Pr/dining room 24 **Smoking:** N/Sm in restaurant **Children:** Menu, Portions **Rooms:** 30 (30 en suite) ★★★ HL **Directions:** At the Tudor Tavern in High St turn into George St. After abbey & school on left, rd continues onto Fishpool St. Hotel is 1m on left **Parking:** 75

Sopwell House

Modern European

Sophisticated dining in an elegant country-house hotel

☎ 01727 864477 Cottonmill Ln, Sopwell AL1 2HQ
e-mail: enquiries@sopwellhouse.co.uk
web: www.sopwellhouse.co.uk

The former home of Lord Mountbatten houses this modernised hotel with impressive spa, leisure and conference facilities. The stunning centrepiece of the Georgian country house is the split-level Magnolia

continued

Restaurant, with its huge magnolia tree and glass ceiling, well serviced by a professional team. Silver cloches lend a traditional feel to the British and European food, which is chosen from a constantly changing menu at lunch and dinner. Baby leeks with poached quail's eggs and Sauternes hollandaise is a typical starter that might be followed by confit of organic salmon, truffle mash and brown shrimp.

Chef: Warren Jones **Owners:** Abraham Bejerano **Times:** 12-2.30/7-10.30, Closed L Sat, Mon **Prices:** Fixed L £11, Fixed D £18-£25.95, Starter £5.75-£12.85, Main £15.95-£22.75, Dessert £5.25-£6.70, Coffee £2.95, Min/Water £3.50, Service optional **Wine:** 71 bottles over £20, 24 bottles under £20, 11 by the glass (£3.95-£9.55) **Notes:** Vegetarian available, Dress Restrictions, No jeans or trainers, Civ Wed 250 **Seats:** 100, Pr/dining room 12 **Smoking:** N/Sm in restaurant, Air con **Children:** Menu, Portions **Rooms:** 129 (129 en suite) ★★★★ **Directions:** On London rd from St Albans follow signs to Sopwell, under railway bridge, over mini-rdbt, hotel 0.25m on left **Parking:** 350

Carluccio's Caffè

☎ 01727 837681 Christopher Place AL3 5DQ
Quality Italian chain.

Sukiyaki

☎ 01727 865009 6 Spencer St AL3 5EG
Neat and authentic Japanese offering a range of good value dishes.

Wagamama

☎ 01727 865 122 Unit 6, Christopher Place AL3 5DQ
Informal noodle bar with no booking.

TRING MAP 06 SP91

Pendley Manor

Traditional British

Fine dining in a historic old manor house

☎ 01442 891891 Cow Ln HP23 5QY
e-mail: admin.pmanor@btconnect.com
web: www.pendley-manor.co.uk

Set in extensive grounds, this old manor house dates back to the Domesday Book. The Oak Room restaurant is a grand dining room with oak panelling, high ceilings, large bay windows and heavy drapes. Traditional napery and large well-spaced tables give an opulent feel. The chef favours modern English cooking with traditional dishes making good use of seasonal and local produce. Typical starters might include seared sea scallops with a spicy prawn fritter. Main courses include the likes of loin of Ashridge venison in chestnut and sage mousse with liver bon bon and cranberry jus. The menu features 'principal' dishes and 'signature' dishes (attracting a supplement) for each course.

continued

TRING *continued* MAP 06 SP91

Chef: Simon Green **Owners:** Craydawn Pendley Manor **Times:** 12.30-2.30/7-9.30 **Prices:** Fixed L fr £17.95, Fixed D fr £31, Starter £5.50-£7.95, Main £15.95-£22.50, Dessert £5.25-£6.50, Coffee £2.50, Min/Water £3.50, Service optional **Wine:** 24 bottles over £20, 23 bottles under £20, 2 by the glass (£2.95) **Notes:** Sun L £22.50, Vegetarian available, Smart casual, Civ Wed 225 **Seats:** 75, Pr/dining room 200 **Smoking:** N/Sm in restaurant **Children:** Portions **Rooms:** 74 (74 en suite) ★★★★ **Directions:** M25 junct 20. Take A41 and Tring exit, follow signs for Berkhamsted. 1st left, right after rugby club **Parking:** 250

WARE MAP 06 TL31

Marriott Hanbury Manor Hotel

French, European

Exciting dining in chain hotel restaurant

☎ 01920 487722 SG12 0SD
e-mail: gisele.clark@marriotthotels.co.uk
web: www.hanbury-manor.com

Built in 1890, this Jacobean-style mansion is surrounded by 200 acres of grounds and has wonderful views across the lake. Once the house's summer dining room, the restaurant is now decorated in opulent style with richly coloured drapery. Lit by huge chandeliers, the painted ceiling depicts the signs of the Zodiac. Crisply clothed tables are given the final touch with expensive crockery and glassware. Classic dishes are presented with modern and exotic twists. Start with the truffle sandwich and lobster burger with tuna sushi and Caesar salad. Try main courses of grilled John Dory on aubergine and orange purée, or duck flauta and cardamom yogurt. Finish with warm Austrian topfenknoedel with quince compôte perhaps.

Chef: Andreas Mahl **Owners:** Whitbread Hotels **Times:** 12-2/7.30-9.30, Closed BHs, 1-9 Jan, Mon, Closed L Sat, D Sun **Prices:** Fixed L fr £20, Fixed D fr £55, Starter fr £7.95, Main fr £25.50, Dessert fr £5.50, Min/Water £3.50, Service optional **Wine:** 300 bottles over £20 **Notes:** Vegetarian available, Dress Restrictions, Smart casual, jacket preferred for men, Civ Wed 120 **Seats:** 50, Pr/dining room 20 **Smoking:** N/Sm in restaurant **Children:** Min 12 yrs, Portions **Rooms:** 161 (161 en suite) ★★★★★ HL **Directions:** From M25 junct 25, take A10 towards Cambridge. Follow A10 for 12m. Leave A10 Wadesmill/Thundridge/Ware. Right at roundabout, hotel on left **Parking:** 200

WELWYN MAP 06 TL21

Auberge du Lac

Modern European NOTABLE WINE LIST

Exclusive restaurant in fabulous location

☎ 01707 368888 Brocket Hall AL8 7XG
e-mail: auberge@brocket-hall.co.uk
web: www.brocket-hall.co.uk

This beautifully restored, former 18th-century hunting lodge sits - not unsurprisingly - beside a tranquil lake overlooking the stately Brocket Hall, whose estate also encompasses a swish golf complex. The airy, elegant restaurant - with large windows to take in the views - is very French, as is the attentive, formal service. While there are cheese and Armagnac trolleys and fabulous flower arrangements to ponder over, the kitchen's focus is on a modern French approach, delivering well-presented dishes with some unusual combinations. Tip-top, fresh, seasonal produce and high skills shine throughout; think roast

continued

Aylesbury duck breast with orange toasted confit leg, pain d'épice, turnip dauphinoise and a citrus jus. And, if the sun is shining, try for a table on the terrace.
Notable Wine List: The wine list offers a great selection from around the world from classic old world wines to some notable New World choices.

Chef: Phil Thompson **Owners:** CCA International **Times:** 12-2.30/7-10, Closed 27 Dec-6 Jan, Mon, Closed D Sun **Prices:** Fixed L fr £29.50, Fixed D fr £45, Starter £6.50-£16, Main £21-£32, Dessert £8.50-£24, Coffee £1.95, Min/Water £3.50, Service added but optional 10% **Wine:** 650 bottles over £20, 22 by the glass (£5-£12) **Notes:** Fixed D 4 courses, Tasting menu fr £65, Sun L 5 courses £35, Vegetarian available, Dress Restrictions, Smart casual preferred, no jeans or trainers, Civ Wed 65 **Seats:** 70, Pr/dining room 24 **Smoking:** N/Sm in restaurant, Air con **Children:** Menu, Portions **Directions:** Telephone for directions or see website **Parking:** 50

WILLIAN MAP 12 TL23

The Fox

Modern International **NEW**

Relaxed gastro-pub in a peaceful village setting

☎ 01462 480233 Baldock Ln SG6 2AE
e-mail: restaurant@foxatwillian.co.uk
web: www.foxatwillian.co.uk

The sister restaurant to the widely acclaimed White Horse at Brancaster Staithe in Norfolk (see entry), this popular contemporary 'eating pub' is informal but well-presented with oak floors, cream walls, sage painted woodwork and a fashionable collection of furniture. Staff are relaxed but provide efficient service while the cooking is simple, unpretentious and effective with quality ingredients centre stage. A typical meal might consist of Brancaster oysters with lemon and shallot vinegar, chargrilled North Sea lobster with aïoli, then a sumptuous duo of chocolate-filled millefeuille with poached fruits - there's an attractive bar menu too. Very busy at weekends, so book in advance.

Chef: Frank Skinner, Harry Kodagoda **Owners:** Cliff Nye **Times:** 12-2/6.45-9.15, Closed Mon, Closed D Sun **Prices:** Starter £4.50-£7.95, Main £10.95-£17.95, Dessert £4.95, Coffee £1.50, Min/Water £2.95, Service optional, Group min 10 service 10% **Wine:** 46 bottles over £20, 33 bottles under £20, 12 by the glass (£2.80-£3.95) **Notes:** Dress Restrictions, Smart casual, no sleeveless shirts or shorts **Seats:** 70 **Smoking:** N/Sm in restaurant, Air con **Children:** Portions **Directions:** A1M junct 9 towards Letchworth, 1st left to Willian village, The Fox is 0.5m on left **Parking:** 40

KENT

ASHFORD MAP 07 TR04

Eastwell Manor

British, European

Grand country-house hotel with classical cooking

☎ 01233 213000 Eastwell Park, Boughton Lees TN25 4HR
e-mail: enquiries@eastwellmanor.co.uk
web: www.eastwellmanor.co.uk

Magnificently set in 62 acres of manicured grounds, this historic hotel exudes grandeur, with its carved wood-panelled rooms, rich fabrics and huge baronial fireplaces. The restaurant is breathtaking too - a long room replete with Italianate chairs and contemporary artwork, high ceilings and oak panelling, laid out with elegant table appointments - while the polished, formal service suits this dress-for-dinner affair. The

continued

menus reflect a modern interpretation of classical cooking, based on well-sourced fresh produce, local wherever possible. Culinary skill, refined presentation and clean, precise flavours deliver in dishes like a breast of Kentish ranger chicken with a sweetcorn and bacon risotto, or perhaps a warm chocolate fondant with vanilla ice cream.

Eastwell Manor

Chef: Neil Wiggins **Owners:** Turrloo Parrett **Times:** 12-2.30/7-10 **Prices:** Fixed L £10-£21, Fixed D £37.50, Starter £8.50-£18, Main £26.50-£65, Dessert £8.50-£12, Coffee £4.50, Min/Water £4, Service optional **Wine:** 214 bottles over £20, 20 bottles under £20, 13 by the glass (£4.50-£6) **Notes:** Vegetarian available, Dress Restrictions, Jacket and tie at D, no jeans, Civ Wed 250 **Seats:** 80, Pr/dining room 80 **Smoking:** N/Sm in restaurant **Children:** Menu, Portions **Rooms:** 62 (62 en suite) ★★★★ **Directions:** From M20 junct 9 take 1st left (Trinity Rd). Through 4 rdbts to lights. Take left filter onto A251 signed Faversham. 1.5m to sign for Boughton Aluph, then 200yds to hotel **Parking:** 120

AYLESFORD MAP 06 TQ75

Hengist Restaurant

Modern French NEW

Fine dining with design impact and culinary success

☎ 01622 719273 7 - 9 High St ME20 7AX
e-mail: the.hengist@btconnect.com
web: www.thackeraysrestaurant.co.uk

Hengist and his brother Horsa led the invasion that landed in Aylesford in AD 449 and named themselves the first kings of Kent. Here the lavish interior design is worthy of royalty, set in a building dating back to the 1560s. There is also private dining available in the dramatic Japanese Room and romantic Crystal Room. The French cuisine uses traditional rich ingredients but with modern twists and inspirational touches, and makes use of excellent local produce. Presentation is straightforward, allowing combinations like roast fillet of beef with fondant potato, pea purée and caramelised onion sauce to speak for themselves. Try a 'Perfect Hengist' champagne cocktail in the bar before dinner.

continued

Hengist Restaurant

Chef: R Phillips & Jean-Marc Zanetti **Owners:** Richard Phillips, Paul Smith & Kevin James **Times:** 12-2.30/6.30-10.30, Closed 26 Dec & 1 Jan, Mon, Closed D Sun **Prices:** Fixed L £10.95-£12.45, Fixed D £19.95-£21.45, Starter £4.95-£10.95, Main £13.75-£17.95, Dessert £5.95, Coffee £2.95, Min/Water £3.25, Service added but optional 11% **Wine:** 62 bottles over £20, 25 bottles under £20, 15 by the glass (£3.50-£9.50) **Notes:** Tasting menu £42.50, Sun L from £16.50, Vegetarian available, Dress Restrictions, Smart casual **Seats:** 70, Pr/dining room 18 **Smoking:** N/Sm in restaurant, Air con **Children:** Portions **Directions:** M20 junct 5 & 6, follow signs to Aylesford village **Parking:** Free car park nearby

BEARSTED MAP 07 TQ85

Soufflé Restaurant

Modern European

Understated, cosy and relaxed village dining

☎ 01622 737065 31 The Green ME14 4DN
web: www.soufflerestaurant.co.uk

This charming 16th-century cottage - once the village bakery - overlooks the historic village green; its cricket ground is said to be the oldest in Kent where overarm bowling was pioneered. Inside, exposed brick, low beams, timbers and an inglenook add traditional character, while high-backed, burgundy coloured chairs and white linen provide the comforts. Oriental-themed pictures and artefacts add another dimension, while the front terrace is perfect for fair-weather dining. The accomplished kitchen takes an appealing modern approach, underpinned by a classical theme; think fillet of beef with red wine and a shallot and thyme fondue and, of course, there's a namesake soufflé to head up desserts, perhaps an orange and Grand Marnier version with a bitter chocolate sorbet.

Chef: Nick Evenden **Owners:** Nick & Karen Evenden **Times:** 12-2.30/7-10, Closed Mon, Closed L Sat, D Sun **Prices:** Fixed L fr £13.50, Fixed D fr £25, Starter £7.50-£8.50, Main £16-£18, Dessert £7.50-£8.50, Coffee £2.50, Min/Water £4, Service added but optional 10% **Wine:** 30 bottles over £20, 24 bottles under £20, 6 by the glass (£3.50-£5) **Notes:** Sun L 3 courses £18.50 **Seats:** 40, Pr/dining room 23 **Smoking:** N/Sm in restaurant **Children:** Portions **Directions:** Please telephone for directions **Parking:** 15

BIDDENDEN MAP 07 TQ83

֍֍ The West House

Modern European

Assured modern cooking in picturesque village setting

☎ 01580 291341 28 High St TN27 8AH
e-mail: thewesthouse@btconnect.com
web: www.westhouserestaurant.com

At the heart of the tiny Wealden village with its charming ancient houses and shops, The West House - formerly 15th-century weavers' cottages - oozes character, charm and confidence. Think old beams and timbers, white walls and an inglenook with log-burning stove, teamed with fashionable high-backed cream leather chairs, polished-wood tables and colourful contemporary artwork. Modern floorboards and a relaxed, friendly atmosphere complete the smart but unstuffy setting. The kitchen's modern approach - underpinned by a classical theme - fits the bill, delivering accomplished, clean, clear-flavoured dishes on appealing fixed-price, daily-changing menus using local seasonal ingredients and accomplished skills. Think a fillet of brill with mussel ragout.

Times: 12-2/7-9.30, Closed 25 Dec-1 Jan, Mon, Closed L Sat, D Sun **Directions:** Junct of A2862 & A274. 14m S of Maidstone

---

BRANDS HATCH MAP 06 TQ56

֍֍ Brandshatch Place Hotel

Modern British

Georgian country house near Brands Hatch

☎ 01474 875000 Brands Hatch Rd, Fawkham DA3 8NQ
e-mail: brandshatchplace@handpicked.co.uk
web: www.handpicked.co.uk

Close to the entrance to Brands Hatch racing circuit, this red-brick Georgian manor dates back to 1806 and stands in 12 acres of tranquil gardens. Elegant public rooms, a charming country-house feel and smart leisure and spa facilities make the hotel a peaceful place to unwind after a day at the track. The dining room is tastefully decked out in cream with mirrors, objets d'art, and gleaming glassware on linen-clothed tables. Expect a good range of modern British dishes on a choice of fixed-price menus. The kitchen uses first-rate ingredients to produce rillette of hare with grape chutney, poached cod with vegetable broth, and warm chocolate fondant with pistachio ice cream.

Chef: Mark Murphy **Owners:** Hand Picked Hotels **Times:** 12-2/7-9.30, Closed L Sat **Prices:** Fixed L £19.95, Fixed D £28.50-£38.50, Service optional **Wine:** 64 bottles over £20, 2 bottles under £20, 6 by the glass (£4.50-£6.50) **Notes:** Civ Wed 110 **Seats:** 60, Pr/dining room 35 **Smoking:** N/Sm in restaurant, Air con **Children:** Menu, Portions **Rooms:** 38 (38 en suite) ★★★★ **Directions:** From M25/M20 follow signs for Brands Hatch Circuit onto A20. Follow signs to Paddock entrance, hotel is located on Brands Hatch Rd **Parking:** 100

CANTERBURY MAP 07 TR15

֍ Augustine's Restaurant

Modern European V

Fine dining in elegant Georgian setting

☎ 01227 453063 1 & 2 Longport CT1 1PE
e-mail: info@augustinesrestaurant.co.uk
web: www.augustinesrestaurant.co.uk

This double-fronted, two-storey period townhouse, with large sash windows overlooking the street, provides intimate dining in stylish surroundings. Think lightwood panelling, cream walls with colourful abstract art, marble tables and fireplace, a separate lounge, and a cosy, friendly atmosphere. The kitchen's modern European approach comes underpinned by a classical base and uses good quality produce in generous, accurately cooked dishes. Take roasted organic poussin with pomme gratin, stuffed legs, buttered Savoy cabbage and a foie gras sauce, and perhaps a hot banana Tatin teamed with a pineapple sorbet to finish. Menu gourmand available.

Chef: Darren Jory **Owners:** Nigel Willis & Lesley Stephens **Times:** 12-2/6.30-9.30, Closed Xmas, 2 wks Jan, Mon, Closed D Sun **Prices:** Fixed L fr £15, Starter £5.95-£9, Main £14-£20, Dessert fr £6, Coffee £2, Min/Water £3, Service optional **Wine:** 72 bottles over £20, 24 bottles under £20, 4 by the glass (£3.50-£3.75) **Notes:** Tasting menu £49, Vegetarian menu **Seats:** 38, Pr/dining room 18 **Smoking:** N/Sm in restaurant **Directions:** Follow signs to St Augustine's Abbey, facing entrance to Abbey turn left, restaurant is ahead **Parking:** On street

֍ The Dove Inn

French

French flavours visit deepest Kent

☎ 01227 751360 Plumpudding Ln, Dargate ME13 9HB
e-mail: nigel@thedoveinn.fsnet.co.uk

This attractive converted pub makes a great venue for enjoyable dining. The ivy-clad, brick exterior hides a plain and simple interior with wooden floors, wooden tables and bags of character. It's a popular place so booking is advisable at weekends. Menus comprise mainly British and French dishes and there's a blackboard advertising the daily specials. Start with Bayonne ham and oyster mushroom tart and follow with either fresh fish from nearby Whitstable or perhaps braised lamb shank with a tomato and basil jus flavoured with local beetroot. Finish with tarte Tatin and vanilla ice cream.

Chef: Nigel & Bridget Morris **Owners:** Nigel Morris **Times:** 12-2/7-9, Closed Mon, Closed D Sun, Tue **Prices:** Starter £4.75-£8.50, Main £14.50-£21, Dessert £5-£6, Coffee £1.50, Min/Water £3, Service optional **Wine:** 13 bottles over £20, 14 bottles under £20, 10 by the glass (£3.30-£4) **Seats:** 26 **Smoking:** N/Sm area **Children:** Portions **Directions:** 5m NW of Canterbury. Telephone for directions **Parking:** 15

֍ The White Horse Inn

Traditional British

Sophisticated dining in country inn setting

☎ 01227 832814 High St, Bridge CT4 5LA
web: www.whitehorsebridge.co.uk

This historic village inn is now an upmarket gastro-pub. The smart restaurant is one half traditionally styled, the other modern and bright with doors into the garden. The friendly staff really know their stuff. The list of local suppliers on the menu suggests a passion for quality, a passion reflected in some excellent cooking. Starters may include cold poached Hythe Bay lobster or Laughton goat's cheese ravioli, then move on to olive-crusted loin of pork, beer battered fillet of cod, or braised shank of lamb with sage and parsley mash.

At the time of going to press we learned that there was a change of hands taking place.

Owners: Charles Toomey **Times:** 12-3/7-11, Closed 25 Dec, 1 Jan **Prices:** Food prices not confirmed for 2007. Please telephone for details **Wine:** 17 bottles over £20, 43 bottles under £20, 11 by the glass (£3-£4.50)

continued

Notes: Vegetarian available **Seats:** 30 **Smoking:** N/Sm in restaurant **Children:** Menu, Portions **Directions:** 3m S of Canterbury on the Dover rd, A2 signed for Bridge **Parking:** 20

CHATHAM MAP 07 TQ76

Bridgewood Manor

British, French

Modern, purpose-built hotel with informal or fine dining

☎ 01634 201333 Bridgewood Roundabout, Walderslade Woods ME5 9AX
e-mail: bridgewoodmanor@marstonhotels.com
web: www.marstonhotels.com

There's a subtle gothic theme to the décor at this modern, purpose-built hotel on the outskirts of Rochester, with warm colours creating an inviting ambience in the dining areas. Dine in the more informal Terrace Bistro, or - if you're in a celebratory mood - choose the more formal Squires restaurant. Staff are smartly dressed, friendly and attentive while the food on this reasonably-priced modern British menu with international influences relies on classical principles and is accurately cooked and well presented. Starters might include a pan-seared red mullet with herb crostini, while a typical main would be baked fillet of cod with crushed olive potatoes and goat's cheese fondue.

Chef: Nigel Stringer **Owners:** Marston Hotels **Times:** 12.30-2.30/7-9.45, Closed 24-27 Dec (ex residents), Closed L Sat **Prices:** Fixed L £11.95, Starter £4.50-£7.50, Main £14-£19, Dessert £4.50-£7.50, Coffee £1.75, Min/Water £3.50, Service optional **Wine:** 36 bottles over £20, 21 bottles under £20, 10 by the glass (£3.80-£5.55) **Notes:** Sun L carvery £15.95,

continued

Vegetarian available, Dress Restrictions, Smart casual, no denim or trainers, Civ Wed 150 **Seats:** 120, Pr/dining room 30 **Smoking:** N/Sm in restaurant, Air con **Children:** Menu, Portions **Rooms:** 100 (100 en suite) ★★★★ HL **Directions:** From M2 junct 3 or M20 junct 6 follow A229 towards Chatham. At Bridgewood rdbt take 3rd exit (Walderslade). Hotel 50yds on left **Parking:** 170

CRANBROOK MAP 07 TQ73

Apicius

see below

The George Hotel

British, French

Beautiful restaurant serving fresh local produce

☎ 01580 713348 Stone St TN17 3HE
e-mail: reservations@thegeorgehotelkent.co.uk
web: www.thegeorgehotelkent.co.uk

Dating back to the 14th century, The George Hotel and Brasserie is a landmark building in Cranbrook. The huge 16th-century inglenook fireplace is the focal point of the contemporary décor of the restaurant. Modern English dishes with European influences are found on a straightforward menu, offering starters like pigeon and foie gras terrine, main courses such as baked cod fillet with a soft herb crust on boulangère potato and buttered green beans, or popular fare like Thai green chicken curry with sticky jasmine rice. Meat comes from a local farm and fresh fish arrives daily from Billingsgate markets.

continued

Apicius

CRANBROOK MAP 07 TQ73

Modern European

Serious cuisine in pretty town setting

☎ 01580 714666 23 Stone St TN17 3HF

Tucked away in the narrow streets of this pretty Kent town (keep an eye out for the 18th-century smock windmill rising above the rooftops), Apicius - named after the famous Roman gastronome - oozes understated class. Once used by Flemish weavers to ply their trade, the glass-fronted, timber-clad building dates from 1530 and retains rustic charm blended with modern comforts. Think low-beamed ceilings and old timbers teamed with blue high-backed chairs, lightwood floorboards and white tablecloths. It's intimate and relaxed, with cream walls hung with menus from the chef's travels. Service, led by Faith Hawkins, is personal, friendly and attentive, while the kitchen is strictly Tim Johnson's domain, his sensibly compact, good-value, fixed-price menus taking a modern approach underpinned by a classical theme.

Quality, fresh seasonal ingredients shine in clear-flavoured, refined, well-presented dishes that reflect high skill and plentiful workmanship, including some wow-factor moments. Take a starter of smoked duck breast with a foie gras velouté and confit duck leg, then perhaps slow-roasted shoulder of pork with creamed potato, Savoy cabbage and

caramelised apples or boneless braised shin of veal with pomme purée and deep-fried bone marrow to follow.

Chef: Timothy Johnson **Owners:** Timothy Johnson, Faith Hawkins **Times:** 12-2/7-9, Closed 2 wks summer, 2 wks Xmas/New Year, Mon, Closed L Mon, Tue, Sat, D Sunday & Monday **Prices:** Fixed L fr £18.50, Fixed D fr £26.50, Coffee £2.50, Min/Water £2, Service added but optional 10% **Wine:** 19 bottles over £20, 7 bottles under £20, 11 by the glass (£4-£5) **Seats:** 22 **Smoking:** N/Sm in restaurant **Children:** Min 8 yrs **Directions:** In town centre, opposite Barclays Bank, 50yds from church **Parking:** Public car park at rear premises

England

CRANBROOK *continued* MAP 07 TQ73

Chef: Ben Miell **Owners:** Mark & Sara Colley **Times:** 12-3/7-9.30, Closed D Sun-Mon **Prices:** Starter £5-£7, Main £9-£16, Dessert £6-£7, Coffee £1.80, Min/Water £4, Service optional **Wine:** 12 bottles over £20, 12 bottles under £20, 8 by the glass (£3-£4.50) **Notes:** Vegetarian available **Seats:** 40 **Smoking:** N/Sm in restaurant **Children:** Menu, Portions **Rooms:** 8 (8 en suite) ★★ HL **Directions:** A229 into Cranbrook and Stone St, on left. **Parking:** 12

DARTFORD MAP 06 TQ57

Rowhill Grange

European, International

Classy country setting for a formal conservatory restaurant

☎ 01322 615136 DA2 7QH
e-mail: admin@rowhillgrange.com
web: www.rowhillgrange.co.uk

A part-thatched 19th-century country house set amid 9 acres of grounds with a lake, woodland and walled Victorian garden. The place seems miles from anywhere but is in fact quite handy for the M25 and M20. Truffles, the conservatory restaurant, with its high-backed leather chairs, crisp linen and heavy drapes is rather romantic at night, with subdued lighting and candles, but in summer you may prefer to eat on the terrace. The brasserie offers a limited menu for a relaxed meal, but the hotel's main culinary attraction is Truffles, with a menu of fairly elaborate modern dishes. Perhaps lobster ravioli with Cognac sauce, or roast pork belly with foie gras.

Chef: Richard Cameron **Owners:** Utopia Leisure **Times:** 12-2.30/7-9.30, Closed L Sat **Prices:** Fixed L £20-£25, Fixed D £35-£42, Starter £8-£10, Main £19-£24, Dessert £8, Coffee £2.95, Min/Water £3.50, Service added but optional 12.5% **Wine:** 65 bottles over £20, 15 bottles under £20, 5 by the glass (£4.35-£6.20) **Notes:** Vegetarian available, Dress Restrictions, No shorts, T-shirts, trainers, Civ Wed 120 **Seats:** 100, Pr/dining room 150 **Smoking:** N/Sm in restaurant **Children:** Min 16 yrs D **Rooms:** 38 (38 en suite) ★★★★ **Directions:** M25 junct 3, take B2173 towards Swanley, then B258 towards Hextable. Straight on at 3 rdbts. Hotel 1.5m on left **Parking:** 200

DEAL MAP 07 TR35

Dunkerleys Hotel

Modern British

Fresh seafood on the seafront

☎ 01304 375016 19 Beach St CT14 7AH
e-mail: info@dunkerleys.co.uk
web: www.dunkerleys.co.uk

The seafront hotel opposite the pier is the location for this friendly bistro-style restaurant run by the chef-proprietor. Have a pre-dinner drink in the small bar where you can relax on a comfy sofa. Seafood is definitely the draw here, with some of the freshest produce around given simple but skilful treatment in the kitchen. The carte is complemented by a set menu, popular with guests staying over for dinner, bed and breakfast. Try the likes of scallops with bacon or perhaps roasted sea bass with creamy mash and delicate asparagus. Desserts are worth leaving room for, with delicious options like chocolate tart with kumquat syrup and lemongrass ice cream.

Times: 12-2.30/7-9.30, Closed L Mon **Rooms:** 16 (16 en suite) ★★★ HL **Directions:** Turn off A2 onto A258 to Deal - situated 100yds before Deal Pier

DOVER MAP 07 TR34

Wallett's Court

Modern British

Historic manor not far from the white cliffs

☎ 01304 852424 West Cliffe, St Margarets-at-Cliffe CT15 6EW
e-mail: dine@wallettscourt.com
web: www.wallettscourt.com

Set in pretty gardens in a peaceful location in the town outskirts, this country-house hotel is based around a lovely Jacobean manor. The cosy lounge bar has a buzzy atmosphere, while the restaurant is formally laid with white linen and high-back chairs, set to a backdrop of oak beams, inglenook fireplaces and evening candlelight. Walls are hung with original art, and there are carved pillars dating back to 1627. But there's nothing remotely historic about the cooking, the accomplished modern British repertoire - based on the chef's commitment to using quality local produce - comes fashionably dotted with global influences. Ravioli of Rye Bay scallops, then pan-fried loin of Sussex wild boar with pickled white cabbage could be followed by Valrhona chocolate and orange tart with clove pomander ice cream.

Chef: Stephen Harvey **Owners:** Gavin Oakley **Times:** 12-2/7-9, Closed 25-26 Dec, Closed L Mon **Prices:** Fixed L £17.50-£23.50, Fixed D £35-£42, Coffee £2.50, Min/Water £2.95, Service optional, Group min 8 service 10% **Wine:** 70 bottles over £20, 20 bottles under £20, 20 by the glass (£3.95-£7.95) **Notes:** Vegetarian available **Seats:** 60, Pr/dining room 40 **Smoking:** N/Sm in restaurant **Children:** Menu, Portions **Rooms:** 16 (16 en suite) ★★★ HL **Directions:** M2/A2 or M20/A20, follow signs for Deal (A258), 1st right for St Margaret's at Cliffe. Restaurant 1m on right **Parking:** 50

EDENBRIDGE MAP 06 TQ44

Haxted Mill & Riverside Brasserie

Modern French

Quality ingredients in riverside setting

☎ 01732 862914 Haxted Rd TN8 6PU
e-mail: david@haxtedmill.co.uk
web: www.haxtedmill.co.uk

A roadside working watermill with a restaurant in adjacent converted stables. Enter via the ground-floor bar, up a steep staircase to the beamed restaurant, featuring photos and angling memorabilia. Jazz plays in the background, with service professional but quite informal.

continued

A terrace overlooks the millpond, ideal for summer dining. An evolving list of dishes is offered from the carte, with Mediterranean and international influences, and an emphasis on fresh seasonal ingredients, fish, seafood and game. Try the whole fish of the day or cioppino, a lightly chillied fish casserole from San Francisco.

Haxted Mill & Riverside Brasserie

Chef: David Peek, Olivier Betremieux **Owners:** David & Linda Peek **Times:** 12-2/7-9, Closed 23 Dec-6 Jan, Mon, Closed D Sun **Prices:** Fixed L £17.95, Fixed D £22, Starter £6.95-£13.95, Main £15.95-£27, Dessert £7, Coffee £1.50, Min/Water £3.50, Service added but optional 12.5% **Wine:** 68 bottles over £20, 6 bottles under £20, 8 by the glass (£3.90-£4.20) **Notes:** Sun L £17.95, Fixed D 2 courses, Vegetarian available, Dress Restrictions, Smart casual **Seats:** 52 **Smoking:** N/Sm in restaurant **Directions:** M25 junct 6, A22 towards East Grinstead. Through Blindley Heath and after Texaco garage left at lights, 1m take 1st left after Red Barn PH. 2m to Haxted Mill **Parking:** 100

FAVERSHAM MAP 07 TR06

Read's Restaurant

see below

HYTHE MAP 07 TR13

The Hythe Imperial Hotel

British, European

Smart restaurant in elegant Victorian surroundings

☎ 01303 267441 The Mews, Prince's Pde CT21 6AQ
e-mail: hytheimperial@marstonhotels.com
web: www.marstonhotels.com

There's much to recommend this smart seaside hotel, with its elegant Victorian splendour and 50-acre golf course. Superb indoor and outdoor leisure facilities are complemented by treatment rooms, a hairdresser's and, not least, a plush restaurant with views over the Channel. The sense of luxury extends to the menu, where a starter of seared tranche of goose foie gras might precede an inventive cannon of lamb and braised shoulder with Venezuelan chocolate jus. Seasonal herbs come straight from the garden.

Times: 12.30-2/7-9.30 **Rooms:** 100 (100 en suite) ★★★★ **Directions:** M20 junct 11/A261 to Hythe signs to Folkestone, right into the Twiss Road to hotel

Read's Restaurant

FAVERSHAM MAP 07 TR06

Modern British (NOTABLE WINE LIST)

Distinctive cuisine in an elegant Georgian manor house

☎ 01795 535344 Macknade Manor, Canterbury Rd ME13 8XE
e-mail: enquiries@reads.com
web: www.reads.com

Set in 4 acres of mature gardens including a walled kitchen garden, Read's Restaurant can be found in a beautiful Georgian building built in 1778. Six individually designed bedrooms are tastefully furnished in period style, complemented by an elegant drawing room and the grand, spacious restaurant. Here you will find distinctive cooking using home-grown herbs and vegetables in dishes making good use of local game and fresh fish from nearby Whitstable and Hythe. Modern British cuisine is the order of the day with dinner a grander affair than lunch. The menu offers a wonderful choice of dishes with detailed descriptions and little gems of quotations to accompany them, like the immortal words of Miss Piggy 'Never eat more than you can lift'. With that in mind, you could try the seven-course tasting menu, or order from the carte. You might start with sautéed Rye Bay scallops with a purée of Jerusalem artichokes, smoked bacon powder and a port-wine reduction. For a main course perhaps the roasted rump of Kentish lamb on buttered flageolet beans, served with fondant potatoes and semi-dried tomato, olive oil and lamb jus. If you can't decide on a pudding then simply choose the selection of Read's desserts for a little of everything.

Notable Wine List: An extensive wine list offering some 300 bins, including an interesting opening section of best buys and informative tasting notes.

Chef: David Pitchford & Ricky Martin **Owners:** David & Rona Pitchford **Times:** 12-2.30/7-10, Closed BHs, Sun, Mon **Prices:** Fixed L fr £21, Fixed D fr £48, Coffee £2.50, Min/Water £3, Service optional **Wine:** 280 bottles over £20, 20 bottles under £20, 6 by the glass (£4) **Notes:** Fixed L 3 courses, Vegetarian available, Dress Restrictions, Smart casual, Civ Wed 60 **Seats:** 40, Pr/dining room 30 **Smoking:** N/Sm in restaurant **Children:** Portions **Directions:** From M2 junct 6 follow A251 towards Faversham. At T-junct with A2 (Canterbury road) turn right. Hotel 0.5m on right **Parking:** 30

England

LENHAM MAP 07 TQ85

Chilston Park Hotel

British, French

Stylish cooking in splendid Georgian mansion

☎ 01622 859803 Sandway ME17 2BE
e-mail: chilstonpark@handpicked.co.uk
web: www.handpicked.co.uk

An English country house with impeccable credentials, Chilston Park dates back to at least 1100. Set in beautiful parkland, the Georgian mansion houses a wonderful collection of paintings and antiques. The sunken Venetian-style restaurant has a grand fireplace and elegant crystal chandeliers. The British menu with French influences offers thoughtful wine recommendations by the glass or bottle for many of the dishes. Using the best of ingredients, accurate cooking and clarity of flavour is the key to success here with many interesting and unusual combinations to choose from. Take confit tomato, goat's cheese crust and basil pesto or roasted saddle of rabbit with black pudding, baby vegetables and watercress sauce for example; alternatively, choose something more traditional like Chateaubriand to share.

Times: 12-1.30/7-9.30, Closed L Sat **Rooms:** 53 (53 en suite) ★★★★ HL **Directions:** Telephone for directions.

SEVENOAKS MAP 06 TQ55

Brasserie St Nicholas

French NEW

Sophisticated dining in modern relaxed French brasserie

☎ 01732 456974 61 London Rd TN13 1AU
e-mail: info@brasseriestnicholas.com
web: www.brasseriestnicholas.com

Set back off a busy town centre street, it is hard to believe that this chic French brasserie was once a schoolhouse. The smart décor of pale walls, darkwood, lots of black and gold, plenty of mirrors and modern lighting sets a relaxed, inviting scene. A la carte lunch, prix fixe and dinner menus offer a wide selection of traditional French dishes with modern influences. The stylish fare is ideal for a business lunch or a special evening meal, where you might sample roasted guinea fowl breast with foie gras, confit leg and cep mousse. The kitchen bakes its own bread daily.

Chef: Francois Cantin **Owners:** Jane Armstrong & Louise O'Sullivan **Times:** 12-3/6-10.30, Closed Mon, Closed D Sun **Prices:** Fixed L £12.50-£13, Fixed D £15-£16.50, Starter £6.50-£10.50, Main £12.50-£25, Dessert £5.50-£7, Coffee £2.90, Min/Water £3, Group min 6 service 12.5% **Wine:** 27 bottles over £20, 20 bottles under £20, 9 by the glass (£3.75-£5.50) **Notes:** Sun L 2 courses £14, 3 courses £18, Vegetarian available **Seats:** 75 **Smoking:** N/Sm in restaurant, Air con **Children:** Portions **Directions:** M25 junct 5 follow signs to town centre **Parking:** Car park opposite

Greggs Restaurant

Mediterranean, European

Popular high-street restaurant with hands-on owners

☎ 01732 456373 28-30 High St TN13 1HX
web: www.greggsrestaurant.com

Set in a listed 16th-century building at the top of town - close to the entrance to the National Trust's Knole House - Greggs' triple-bay window frontage and black-and-white paintwork draws an adoring local crowd. Inside, original features blend with contemporary comforts; think darkwood beams and timbers and a painted boarded ceiling versus lightwood floors or beige carpet, cream or sage walls, black leather high-backed chairs and white tablecloths. The atmosphere's suitably relaxed and friendly, while the kitchen follows a modern line, its imaginative approach delivered with creative presentation. Take baked supreme of halibut served on braised pak choi with a crab, potato and coriander cake and lemon grass sauce, and perhaps an assiette of apple to finish.

Greggs Restaurant

Chef: Gavin Gregg, Mark Constable **Owners:** Gavin & Lucinda Gregg **Times:** 12-2.30/6.30-9.30, Closed 25-26 Dec, 1st week Jan, Mon, Closed D Sun **Prices:** Fixed L £11-£12, Fixed D £22-£27.50, Starter £6.50-£10, Main £14-£18, Dessert £5-£7, Coffee £1.50, Min/Water £3, Service added but optional 12% **Wine:** 12 bottles over £20, 8 bottles under £20, 4 by the glass (£3.75-£9) **Notes:** Sun L 3 courses £19.95, Vegetarian available **Seats:** 50, Pr/dining room 32 **Smoking:** N/Sm in restaurant, Air con **Children:** Portions **Directions:** 1m from Sevenoaks train station. 500yds from top of town centre towards Tonbridge on left **Parking:** Town centre

see advert opposite

SISSINGHURST MAP 07 TQ73

Rankins

Modern British

Bistro-style cuisine in rustic surroundings

☎ 01580 713964 The Street TN17 2JH
e-mail: rankins@btconnect.com
web: www.rankinsrestaurant.com

Constructed in 1898, the timber-framed building was a saddlers at one time, and a general store during the war. There was no running water until 1958, but it found a new lease of life as a restaurant in 1971. The atmosphere is warm and friendly and the interior has a bistro-style feel with traditional rustic décor. Cooking here is bistro style with the emphasis on taste and good raw ingredients. A typical starter would be roast red pepper mousse with caponata, olives, anchovies and basil oil. Try a main course like lamb noisettes with apricots, cumin and fresh mint.

Chef: Hugh Rankin **Owners:** Hugh & Leonora Rankin **Times:** 12.30-2/7.30-9, Closed BHs, Mon, Tue, Closed L Wed-Sat, D Sun **Prices:** Fixed L £22.50-£26.50, Fixed D £30.50-£31.50, Coffee £2.75, Min/Water £2.50, Service optional **Wine:** 11 bottles over £20, 16 bottles under £20, 2 by the glass (£4) **Notes:** Dress Restrictions, Smart casual minimum **Seats:** 25 **Smoking:** N/Sm in restaurant **Children:** Portions **Directions:** Village centre, on A262 **Parking:** On street

SITTINGBOURNE MAP 07 TQ96

Lakes Restaurant

British, French V

Elegant conservatory restaurant serving imaginative cuisine

☎ 01795 428020 Hempstead House Country Hotel, London Rd, Bapchild ME9 9PP
e-mail: lakes@hempsteadhouse.co.uk
web: www.hempsteadhouse.co.uk

Named after Robert Lake who built Hempstead House in 1850, the restaurant commemorates his life with portraits and a historical album which guests can read. Housed in an elegant conservatory extension, the restaurant offers fine dining in a relaxed atmosphere. Cooking is ambitious with interesting ideas skilfully executed on the British menu with French influences. Produce is flavoursome and good quality in dishes like roasted pigeon on Savoy cabbage and creamed bacon starter, followed by chargrilled fillet of beef, sweet potato and thyme cake and a duxelle of wild mushroom and spinach.

Chef: Marcus Guhren **Owners:** Mr & Mrs A J Holdstock **Times:** 12-2.30/7-10 **Prices:** Fixed L £10, Fixed D £24.50-£32.50, Starter £5.50-£9.50, Main £12.50-£21.50, Dessert £5.50, Coffee £2, Min/Water £3, Service optional **Wine:** 29 bottles over £20, 25 bottles under £20, 2 by the glass (£2.95-£4.50) **Notes:** Sun L £17.50, tasting menu £32.50, Vegetarian menu, Dress Restrictions, Smart casual, Civ Wed 150 **Seats:** 70, Pr/dining room 30 **Smoking:** N/Sm in restaurant **Children:** Portions **Rooms:** 27 (27 en suite) ★★★ HL **Directions:** On A2 1.5m E of Sittingbourne **Parking:** 100

TUNBRIDGE WELLS (ROYAL) MAP 06 TQ53

Hotel du Vin & Bistro

French, European NOTABLE WINE LIST

Elegant bistro in stylish townhouse

☎ 01892 526455 Crescent Rd TN1 2LY
e-mail: info@tunbridgewells.hotelduvin.com
web: www.hotelduvin.com

A contemporary boutique hotel housed in one of this spa town's architectural landmarks, an impressive, 18th-century, Grade II listed sandstone building, which once welcomed Queen Victoria as a guest in her days as a princess. Transformed into a hotel by the hugely respected Hotel du Vin chain, it has stylish bedrooms and a tastefully designed bar and bistro. The latter draws discerning diners for inspired, modern eclectic cooking, which successfully balances modern dishes and simple classics. Typically, order oxtail soup with thyme dumplings to start, move on to halibut with chorizo and harissa mash and sauce vièrge, or braised saddle of venison with juniper jus.

Notable Wine List: A key hallmark of this group is an extensive wine list, packed full of interest and high quality wines.

continued

Chef: Matt Green Armytage **Owners:** Hotel du Vin Ltd **Times:** 12-1.45/7-9.45, Closed L 31 Dec **Prices:** Starter £6.50-£9, Main £12.50-£21.50, Dessert £6.95, Coffee £2.75, Min/Water £3.50, Service optional, Group min 14 service 10% **Wine:** 400 bottles over £20, 73 bottles under £20, 19 by the glass (£3) **Notes:** Vegetarian available, Civ Wed 60 **Seats:** 80, Pr/dining room 80 **Smoking:** N/Sm in restaurant **Children:** Menu, Portions **Rooms:** 34 (34 en suite) ★★★★ **Directions:** Please telephone for directions **Parking:** 30

Right on the Green

Modern British

Pleasant bistro-style dining with a monthly-changing menu

☎ 01892 513161 15A Church Rd, Southborough TN4 0RX
e-mail: info@rightonthegreen.co.uk
web: www.rightonthegreen.co.uk

Originally an antiques warehouse, this comfortable, cosy restaurant has an intimate feel to it - especially when tables are candlelit in the evening. The décor in the main dining area is pleasantly eccentric with striking ceiling beams and large windows overlooking the green, while a central staircase spirals up to a secluded private dining room (and the kitchen) upstairs. The food puts an interesting twist on upmarket bistro-style cooking with a large selection of great-sounding dishes that are cooked with aplomb. Start with shredded ham knuckle, honey and mustard cream sauce, for example, then move on to rabbit casserole with Jerusalem artichokes. Straightforward cooking which delivers good flavours without any unnecessary complexities.

Chef: Adrian Martin **Owners:** Adrian & Erica Martin **Times:** 12-2.30/7-12, Closed 25-26 Dec, 4 Jan, Mon, Sun, Closed L Sat **Prices:** Fixed L £12.50,

continued

England

TUNBRIDGE WELLS (ROYAL) *continued*
MAP 06 TQ53

Starter £5.50-£7.50, Main £16-£18, Dessert £5-£6.50, Coffee £3, Min/Water £3, Service optional, Group min 8 service 12.5% **Wine:** 31 bottles over £20, 10 bottles under £20, 6 by the glass (£4.50-£7) **Seats:** 32, Pr/dining room 16 **Smoking:** N/Sm in restaurant **Children:** Portions **Directions:** A26 towards Tunbridge Wells next to Henry Baines antique shop and Southborough cricket green **Parking:** On street

The Spa Hotel

Modern British

Serious cuisine in fine-dining environment

☎ 01892 520331 Mount Ephraim TN4 8XJ
e-mail: info@spahotel.co.uk
web: www.spahotel.co.uk

The restaurant at this Georgian country house provides a grand, spacious setting for elegant dining. Sparkling chandeliers, freshly cut flowers and quality tableware set the scene for a memorable experience. Formal table service is the order of the day in this traditional hotel. The menu offers a broad range of modern British dishes featuring seasonal produce and traditional techniques. Try a main course like beef three ways (mini steak-and-kidney pudding on braised cabbage, slow-cooked brisket and barley dumpling on mustard mash and oxtail jus).

Chef: Steve Cole **Owners:** Goring Family **Times:** 12.30-2/7-10, Closed L Sat **Prices:** Fixed L £15-£20, Fixed D £31-£40, Coffee £3, Min/Water £3.50, Service included **Wine:** 30 bottles over £20, 20 bottles under £20, 5 by the glass (£3.50-£7.50) **Notes:** Vegetarian available, Dress Restrictions, Smart casual, no jeans or T-shirts, Civ Wed 200 **Seats:** 80, Pr/dining room 250 **Smoking:** N/Sm in restaurant **Children:** Menu, Portions **Rooms:** 69 (69 en suite) ★★★★ **Directions:** On A264 leaving Tunbridge Wells towards East Grinstead **Parking:** 140

Thackeray's

see opposite

WEST MALLING MAP 06 TQ65

The Swan

Modern British

Brasserie cooking in lively, modern setting of a transformed pub

☎ 01732 521910 35 Swan St ME19 6JU
e-mail: info@theswanwestmalling.co.uk
web: www.theswanwestmalling.co.uk

This radical conversion of a one time15th-century coaching inn brings a contemporary, brasserie-style vibe to this pretty Kent village. Think wood, granite and stainless steel softened by fashionable neutral tones, banquette seating with large scatter cushions, high-backed chairs and modern artwork and mirrors. It's lively and vibrant, with two sleek bars, dining on two levels, a smart lounge and, for warm summer days, a paved and shaded terrace for alfresco dining. An army of youthful, black-clad staff provide attentive service, while the accomplished kitchen's simple, modern, clean-cut, brasserie-inspired dishes hit all the right notes, too. Think belly of Tamworth pork served with Jerusalem artichoke and curly kale, and straightforward desserts like rhubarb crumble with clotted cream or cinnamon burnt cream with shortbread.

Chef: C Reeves **Owners:** Fishbone Ltd **Times:** 12-3.15/6-11.15, Closed 26 Dec, 1 Jan **Prices:** Fixed L £12, Fixed D £15, Starter £5-£6, Main £10-£14, Dessert £4.50-£5, Coffee £2.50, Min/Water £3.50, Service added but optional 12.5% **Wine:** 59 bottles over £20, 17 bottles under £20, 9 by the glass (£2.75-£5.50) **Notes:** Fixed L 3 courses, Dress Restrictions, Smart dress, Civ Wed 100 **Seats:** 90, Pr/dining room 20 **Smoking:** N/Sm in restaurant, Air con **Children:** Menu, Portions **Directions:** M20 junct 4 follow signs for West Malling **Parking:** Long-stay car park

WHITSTABLE MAP 07 TR16

Crab & Winkle Seafood Restaurant

Modern British

Buzzy harbour restaurant with faultless fish

☎ 01227 779377 South Quay, The Harbour CT5 1AB
web: www.crabandwinkle.co.uk

Located above a fish market on the quay overlooking the harbour, this modern restaurant has a light and airy feel with appropriately maritime art adorning the walls, polished lightwood tables and chairs and sensitive lighting throughout. The decked balcony is a great place for alfresco dining in summer, and on less clement days the views of the harbour add a certain nautical feel. Given its location it's no surprise that the menu leans toward fish and seafood, straight from the harbour and cooked simply - dishes like seared scallops with garlic mayonnaise, Whitstable Bay organic ale battered cod and chips or crab and winkle paella let the freshness of the ingredients sing out.

Chef: Ben Walton **Owners:** Andrew & Victoria Bennett **Times:** 11.30-3.30/6-9, Closed D Sun (Nov-Jan) **Prices:** Fixed L £11-£16, Fixed D £21-£28.50, Coffee £1.50, Min/Water £3, Service added but optional 12.5%, Group min 8 service 12.5% **Wine:** 10 bottles over £20, 15 bottles under £20, 7 by the glass (£3.15-£6.95) **Notes:** Vegetarian available **Seats:** 72 **Smoking:** N/Sm in restaurant, Air con **Children:** Portions **Directions:** Please telephone for directions **Parking:** Gorrel Tank Car Park

continued

Thackeray's

TUNBRIDGE WELLS (ROYAL) MAP 06 TQ53

Modern French V

Inventive, contemporary cuisine in chic surroundings

☎ 01892 511921 TN1 1EA
e-mail: reservations@thackeraysrestaurant.co.uk
web: www.thackerays-restaurant.co.uk

This handsome building dating back to 1660 - and named after erstwhile owner and celebrated novelist William Makepeace Thackeray - faces the common and comes covered in original, whitewashed Kent Peg tiles. The stylish interior harmoniously combines period architecture with modern, minimalist touches; think chocolate suede banquettes, cream tub chairs, warm neutral tones, wooden floors, glass and mirror panels and modern artwork. There's also a Japanese terrace garden for alfresco dining or aperitifs, and a choice of cool bars and themed function rooms (deep red Fish Room and African Function Room), while service is formal and attentive but delivered in a friendly and relaxed style.

The kitchen's modern approach - underpinned by a classical theme - sits perfectly with its sleek surroundings and oozes confidence and ambition. High-quality luxury ingredients, modern presentation, flair, style and high technical skill all deliver on a repertoire of value fixed-price lunch and dinner menus, plus tasting option and enticing carte. Expect the likes of a dégustation of Gloucestershire Old Spot pork cooked four ways, served with pomme purée, caramelised black pudding, apple and sage purée and spiced red wine sauce, with perhaps a raspberry soufflé - with marinated raspberries and raspberry sorbet - heading up desserts.

Chef: Richard Phillips
Owners: Richard Phillips
Times: 12-2.30/6.30-10.30, Closed Mon, Closed D Sun
Prices: Fixed L £14.95-£17.45, Fixed D £28.50-£31, Starter £9.25-£14.95, Main £18.95-£22.50, Dessert £8.95, Coffee £3.75, Min/Water £3.25, Service added but optional 12.5%
Wine: 127 bottles over £20, 7 bottles under £20, 20 by the glass (£3.75-£12.40)
Notes: Tasting menu £58, Sun L 2 courses £22.50, 3 courses £26.50, Vegetarian menu
Seats: 54, Pr/dining room 16
Smoking: N/Sm in restaurant, Air con
Children: Portions
Directions: A21/A26, towards Tunbridge Wells. On left 500yds after the Kent & Sussex Hospital
Parking: NCP, on street in evening

England

WHITSTABLE *continued* MAP 07 TR16

The Sportsman

Modern European

Superb fresh fish in unpretentious surroundings

☎ 01227 273370 Faversham Rd CT5 4BP

Relaxed and cheery gastro-pub with a stripped back colonial cum shaker style - wooden floors, half wood-clad walls, scrubbed pine tables and a couple of open fireplaces. The daily changing modern European menu offers a good choice of mainly fish, but also other local produce. Presentation is simple - almost rustic - letting the quality and freshness of the ingredients speak for themselves. A good example would be three Rye Bay scallops with black pudding and apple, steamed wild sea bass fillet with a mussel pistou, and raspberry and almond tart with unpasteurised Jersey cream.

Chef: Stephen Harris **Owners:** Stephen & Philip Harris **Times:** 12-3/6-11, Closed 25-26 Dec, Mon, Closed D Sun **Prices:** Starter £3.95-£8.95, Main £9.95-£18.95, Dessert £5.50-£5.95, Coffee £1.60, Min/Water £2.50, Service optional, Group min 6 **Wine:** 11 bottles over £20, 22 bottles under £20, 8 by the glass (£2.95-£3.60) **Notes:** Vegetarian available **Seats:** 60 **Smoking:** N/Sm area, No pipes or cigars, Air con **Children:** Portions **Directions:** 3.5m W of Whitstable **Parking:** 20

WYE MAP 07 TR04

Wife of Bath Restaurant

Modern French

Top-notch cooking at a charming restaurant

☎ 01233 812540 4 Upper Bridge St TN25 5AF
e-mail: reservations@wifeofbath.com
web: www.wifeofbath.com

This family-run restaurant has been sympathetically converted and combines cosy country-house furnishings with period timbers and flagstone floors. French windows open out on to a leafy garden from the pretty dining room where tables are simply set with white cloths and a single flower. It's a popular venue for special occasions and lures an appreciative crowd of regulars from the village and further afield with an accomplished menu of modern French and British dishes. Cauliflower and sorrel soup is a typical starter, while mains might include partridge with Savoy cabbage and bacon, or Romney Marsh lamb with dauphinoise potatoes and honey-roast carrots.

Chef: Robert Hymers **Owners:** Andrew & Nicola Fraser **Times:** 12-1.30/7-9.30, Closed 2 wks from 25 Dec, 2 wks from mid August, Sun & Mon **Prices:** Fixed L fr £15, Fixed D fr £24.50, Starter £6.50-£13.50, Main £18.50-£24.50, Dessert fr £7, Coffee £2.85, Min/Water £3, Group min 8 service 10% **Wine:** 78 bottles over £20, 8 bottles under £20, 2 by the glass (£2.50-£8) **Notes:** Vegetarian available **Seats:** 50 **Smoking:** N/Sm in restaurant **Directions:** Just off A28 Ashford to Canterbury Rd **Parking:** 18

LANCASHIRE

BLACKBURN MAP 18 SD62

Clarion Hotel & Suites Foxfields

Traditional European

Bold cooking and modern hotel dining

☎ 01254 822556 Whalley Rd, Billington BB7 9HY
e-mail: enquiries@hotels-blackburn.com
web: www.hotels-blackburn.com

Located in rolling countryside in the heart of the Ribble Valley, this modern hotel and leisure club's dining room has a traditional country-house feel and views over Pendle Hill. Service is friendly and courteous, while the kitchen's innovative ideas are balanced by more classical dishes; take leek, stilton and cherry tomato risotto, in between perhaps, grilled seared chicken fillet served with Mediterranean vegetables roasted in fresh basil, garlic, pine nuts, parmesan and olive oil, with a classic raspberry crème brûlée to finish.

Chef: John Fleet **Owners:** Choice Hotels Europe **Times:** 12-2/7-9.30, Closed L BHs (ex 25-26 Dec, 1 Jan) **Prices:** Fixed L £8.95, Fixed D £24.95-£31.95, Starter £3.95-£6.95, Main £12.95-£22.95, Dessert £3.95-£5.95, Coffee £2, Min/Water £3.50, Service included **Wine:** 8 bottles over £20, 16 bottles under £20, 12 by the glass (£3.50-£5.50) **Notes:** Vegetarian available, Civ Wed 150 **Seats:** 70, Pr/dining room 20 **Smoking:** N/Sm in restaurant, Air con **Children:** Menu, Portions **Rooms:** 44 (44 en suite) ★★★★ HL **Directions:** M6 junct 31, follow A59. Hotel is situated on A666 signed Whalley **Parking:** 200

The Millstone at Mellor

Traditional British

Cosy, traditional restaurant, a firm favourite with locals and residents

☎ 01254 813333 Church Ln, Mellor BB2 7JR
e-mail: info@millstone.co.uk
web: www.shirehotels.com

The Millstone has a traditional bar and an elegant, recently refurbished restaurant, both immaculately presented. The restaurant is wood-panelled with a beamed ceiling, grandfather clock and framed prints of countryside images. These set the scene for tables clothed in white linen adorned with fresh flowers and laid with quality glassware. A flexible approach is taken to food, with the bar and restaurant menu available in either venue. Simple, straightforward classic dishes of some imagination are offered, cooked from the best local, seasonal ingredients: pan-fried sea bass with potted Morecambe Bay shrimps and spiced parsnip purée or supreme of chicken, creamed Savoy cabbage and smoked bacon with bread sauce fritter.

Chef: Anson Bolton **Owners:** Shire Hotels Ltd **Times:** 12-2.15/6.30-9.30 **Prices:** Fixed L £20, Fixed D £27.95, Coffee £2.25, Min/Water £3.50 **Wine:** 44 bottles over £20, 28 bottles under £20, 10 by the glass (£3.50-£6.25) **Notes:** Vegetarian available, Civ Wed 60 **Seats:** 62, Pr/dining room 20 **Smoking:** N/Sm in restaurant **Children:** Menu, Portions **Rooms:** 23 (23 en suite) ★★ HL **Directions:** 4m from M6 junct 31 follow signs for Blackburn. Mellor is on right 1m after 1st set of lights **Parking:** 45

England

Northcote Manor

LANGHO MAP 18 SD73

Modern British V 

A powerhouse of regional British gastronomy

☎ 01254 240555 Northcote Rd BB6 8BE
e-mail: sales@northcotemanor.com
web: www.northcotemanor.com

A gastronomic haven, its famous kitchen twice producing the Young Chef of the Year, Northcote and chef-patron Nigel Haworth celebrated their 21st year in business in 2005. The restaurant itself is a spacious affair with contemporary styling, minimalist and softly lit with displays of eye-catching, somewhat surreal, local modern art. Light and airy with a conservatory front, it has views over Nigel's organic garden where many of the herbs, salads and vegetables are used in season. Crisp white linen, a 450-bin wine list and service with a formal air of professionalism all play their part at this foodie destination.

Nigel creates an enticing repertoire (carte, seasonal lunch, tasting and gourmet options), which have their roots firmly in Lancashire, making the most of the North West's abundant local larder and creating dishes of true terroir. The cooking is intelligently simple, with an emphasis on freshness and the quality of seasonal ingredients, and exudes high technique. Think a loin of Bowland venison matched with chocolate jelly, grilled ceps, butternut squash and spice, or perhaps a bramley apple crumble soufflé with Lancashire cheese ice cream to head up desserts.

Notable Wine List: A super wine list, full of enthusiasm and expertise.

Chef: Nigel Haworth, Lisa Allen
Owners: Nigel Haworth, Craig Bancroft
Times: 12-2/7-9.30, Closed 25 Dec, 1-2 Jan, BH Mon
Prices: Fixed L £15, Fixed D £50, Starter £9.50-£14.50, Main £19.50-£29.50, Dessert £8.50-£10.50, Coffee £2.50, Min/Water £3.75, Service optional
Wine: 290 bottles over £20, 42 bottles under £20, 8 by the glass (£4.50-£8)
Notes: Fixed D 5 courses, Vegetarian menu, Dress Restrictions, No jeans, Civ Wed 40
Seats: 80, Pr/dining room 40
Smoking: N/Sm in restaurant
Children: Menu, Portions
Rooms: 14 (14 en suite) ★★★★ RR
Directions: M6 junct 31 take A59, follow signs for Clitheroe. Left at 1st traffic light, onto Skipton/Clitheroe Rd for 9m. Left into Northcote Rd, hotel on right
Parking: 60

BLACKPOOL MAP 18 SD33

Kwizeen

European

Serious cooking in an area normally renowned for its fast food

☎ 01253 290045 47-49 Kings St FY1 3EJ
e-mail: info@kwizeen.co.uk
web: www.kwizeen.co.uk

The oriental façade of this chic modern British restaurant looks right at home amid the joke shops, pubs and nightclubs close to the famous Tower, but the exterior belies the cool, minimalist décor of the interior with its wood floors, chrome furniture and subtle lighting. The good value menu betrays eastern and Mediterranean influences - you could expect salmon fillets wrapped in Parma ham with basil pesto, followed by caramelised duck breast with Thai cherry jam. Puddings are real crowd-pleasers - chocolate fudge pudding with chocolate ice cream, for example.

Chef: Marco Calle-Calatayud **Owners:** Marco Calle-Calatayud, Antony Beswick **Times:** 12-1.45/6, Closed 21 Feb-10 Mar, last wk Aug, Sun, Closed L Sat **Prices:** Fixed L £6.50, Starter £4.85-£8.95, Main £12-£22, Dessert £4.50, Coffee £2.50, Min/Water £3, Service included **Seats:** 40 **Smoking:** No pipes or cigars **Directions:** From front of Blackpool Winter Gardens, 100yds to King St, and as road forks restaurant 30yds on left **Parking:** On street

LANCASTER MAP 18 SD46

Lancaster House Hotel

Modern, Traditional British

Modern hotel dining offering local produce

☎ 01524 844822 Green Ln, Ellel LA1 4GJ
e-mail: lancaster@elhmail.co.uk
web: www.elh.co.uk/hotels/lancaster

This modern country-house hotel enjoys a rural setting south of the city and close to the university. The Gressingham Restaurant has a split-level dining room where the three-course menu and 'Gressingham Selection' are served. The modern British cooking makes good use of interesting local ingredients and there is an informative weekly cheese menu with local choices like Westmorland smoked cheddar. Fell-bred lamb or beef feature in imaginative dishes such as fillet of Cumbrian fell-bred beef with Madeira sauce topped with chicken liver parfait, watercress purée, panaché vegetables and Anna potatoes.

Chef: Michael Weston-Cole **Owners:** English Lakes Hotels **Times:** 12.30-2/7-9.30, Closed L Sun **Prices:** Fixed L £15.95, Fixed D £24.95, Coffee £2.25, Min/Water £2.95, Service included **Wine:** 35 bottles over £20, 48 bottles under £20, 12 by the glass (£3.65-£5.95) **Notes:** ALC 2 courses £19.95, 3 courses £24.95, Dress Restrictions, Smart casual, no jeans or sportswear, Civ Wed 100 **Seats:** 82, Pr/dining room 110 **Smoking:** N/Sm in restaurant, Air con **Children:** Menu **Rooms:** 99 (99 en suite) ★★★★ HL **Directions:** 3m from Lancaster city centre. From S M6 junct 33, head towards Lancaster. Continue through Galgate village, and turn left up Green Ln just before Lancaster University **Parking:** 140

LANGHO MAP 18 SD73

Northcote Manor

see page 217

LONGRIDGE MAP 18 SD63

The Longridge Restaurant

see page 220

LYTHAM ST ANNES MAP 18 SD32

Chicory

Modern European

Generous, eclectic menus in a lively ambience

☎ 01253 737111 5 Henry St FY8 5LE
web: www.chicorygroup.co.uk

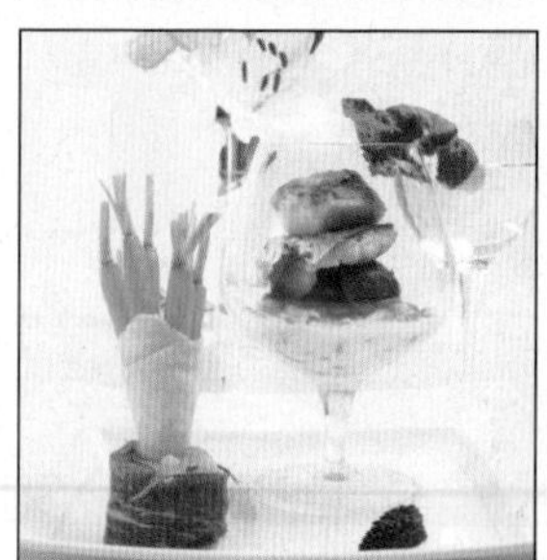

continued

A full-on mix of bold colours and music creates a lively, party atmosphere in this restaurant and its adjacent cocktail bar and café. Well-drilled staff serve dishes from a generous, eclectic menu where starters of duck and haggis faggot sit comfortably alongside mascarpone-gratinated green-lipped mussels. Main courses also range from a notably Gallic and rustic rabbit en cocotte through to a more contemporary confit of boned lamb shank wrapped in Mediterranean vegetables and Parma ham. Home-made desserts include an unmissable lemon tart with fresh fruit basket and blackcurrant coulis.

Times: 12-2/6-9.30, Closed 25 Dec, 1 Jan **Directions:** In Lytham town centre, behind Clifton Arms Hotel

❁ Greens Bistro

Modern British

Imaginative modern British cooking in an intimate atmosphere

☎ 01253 789990 3-9 St Andrews Rd South, St Annes On Sea FY8 1SX
e-mail: info@greensbistro.co.uk
web: www.greensbistro.co.uk

Hidden among the shops and residences in the heart of town, the stairs down to this romantic cellar restaurant create an immediate sense of expectation, even, perhaps, a little theatre. Inside, the subtle décor and lighting with tables discreetly hidden in nooks and crannies and smart uniformed staff all conspire to create an ideal atmosphere for a special night out. The food is Modern British and punches above its weight with great ingredients ticking the requisite local and seasonal boxes - start with salad of crayfish tails and mango salsa, then move on to Pendle lamb with fresh mint sauce, perhaps, followed by prune and Armagnac crème brûlée.

Chef: Paul Webster **Owners:** Paul Webster **Times:** 6-10, Closed 25 Dec, BHs, Sun-Mon, Closed L all week **Prices:** Food prices not confirmed for 2007. Please telephone for details **Wine:** 6 by the glass **Notes:** Vegetarian available **Seats:** 38 **Smoking:** N/Sm in restaurant **Children:** Portions **Directions:** Telephone for directions **Parking:** On street

❁ The West Beach Restaurant

Modern British [V]

Chic hotel restaurant offering fine dining

☎ 01253 739898 Clifton Arms Hotel, West Beach FY8 5QJ
e-mail: welcome@cliftonarms-lytham.com
web: www.cliftonarms-lytham.com

Some 300 years ago, the hotel was just a small inn on the Clifton family estate. These days it's an impressive, modern seafront hotel

continued

overlooking Lytham Green and the Ribble estuary. Newly refurbished, the West Beach Restaurant offers a unique setting and an intimate ambience. Enjoy candlelit dining from an imaginative menu, complemented by fine wines. Modern British cuisine is exemplified by dishes like potted Lytham shrimps on melba toast, or roast sirloin of beef with Yorkshire pudding and traditional gravy. No surprise then to find sticky toffee pudding on the menu, with a lovely butterscotch sauce, or chocolate pudding with white chocolate sorbet.

Chef: Craig Chappell **Owners:** Paul Caddy **Times:** 7-9.30, Closed L Mon-Sat **Prices:** Fixed D £25, Starter £3.50-£7, Main £9.95-£19.50, Dessert £4.50, Coffee £2.50, Min/Water £3.50, Service optional **Wine:** 55 bottles over £20, 18 bottles under £20, 9 by the glass (£3.50-£4.80) **Notes:** Sun L £17.50, Vegetarian menu, Civ Wed 100 **Seats:** 60, Pr/dining room 140 **Smoking:** N/Sm in restaurant **Children:** Portions **Rooms:** 48 (48 en suite) ★★★★ HL **Directions:** M55 junct 4, first left onto A583 (Preston), take right hand lane. At lights turn right onto Peel Rd. Turn right at T-junct into Ballam Rd. Continue onto Lytham town centre. Turn right and then left into Queen St **Parking:** 50

see advert above

PRESTON MAP 18 SD52

❁❁ The Park Restaurant Hotel

Modern British

Solid Northern cooking in elegant Edwardian setting

☎ 01772 726250 728096 209 Tulketh Rd, Ashton-on-Ribble PR2 1ES
e-mail: parkrestaurant@hotmail.com
web: www.theparkpreston.com

This imposing Edwardian mansion has bags of character. A mosaic-

continued on page 221

England

The Longridge Restaurant

LONGRIDGE MAP 18 SD63

Modern British

A chic contemporary setting for first-rate cuisine

☎ 01772 784969 104-106 Higher Rd PR3 3SY
e-mail: longridge@heathcotes.co.uk
web: www.heathcotes.co.uk/longridge.htm

This chic eatery started life as a series of working men's cottages, and moonlighted as a pub, a cyclists' café and an Indian restaurant before assuming its current incarnation as the flagship of Paul Heathcote's culinary empire. A lounge leads the way to a warren of interconnected dining areas, decorated in bold colours with suede seating and elegantly clothed tables, while upstairs discreet windows on to the kitchen let diners in on all the culinary action.

Its brigade consistently impresses, handling quality ingredients with confident simplicity to deliver an extensive bistro-style carte of straightforward modern British fare. Mains show the style: roast suckling pig is served with black pudding fritter, spring cabbage and cider butter, while herb-roasted rack of lamb arrives with rosemary-creamed polenta, tomatoes, black olives and anchovies. Treat yourself to the seven-course tasting menu to really do the place justice, or a day course at the cookery school, many of which are hosted by Heathcote himself.

Chef: Chris Bell
Owners: Paul Heathcote
Times: 12-2.30/6-10, Closed 1 Jan, Mon, Closed L Sat
Prices: Fixed L £14, Fixed D £25, Starter £4.25-£8.50, Main £12.50-£25, Dessert £5.50-£8.50, Coffee £1.80, Min/Water £3.50, Service optional, Group min 8 service 10%
Wine: 87 bottles over £20, 10 bottles under £20, 13 by the glass (£3.85-£6.25)
Notes: Fixed D 3 courses £25 incl 1/2 bottle wine, 6-7pm, Vegetarian available
Seats: 70, Pr/dining room 18
Smoking: N/Sm area, No pipes
Children: Portions
Directions: Follow signs for Golf Club & Jeffrey Hill. Higher Rd is beside White Bull Pub in Longridge
Parking: 10

PRESTON *continued* MAP 18 SD52

tiled lobby floor, stained-glass windows and high ceilings help to create a grand impression, although the small, cosy snug bar and friendly staff add a homely feel. The traditional dining room is complemented by a modern British menu with a careful use of quality local ingredients. Expect bold cooking in dishes like Lancashire hot pot with home-pickled red cabbage, carrot and swede or roast loin of lamb with Lancashire black pudding, potato purée and rosemary jus. Desserts such as roast spiced pineapple with melon sorbet and cinnamon syrup have a more international flavour.

Chef: Derek Cheetham **Owners:** Nicola & Derek Cheetham **Times:** 6.30, Closed 25-28 Dec, Sun, Closed L all week **Prices:** Starter £4.45-£8.95, Main £10.95-£18.95, Dessert £4.50-£5.95, Coffee £1.75, Min/Water £3.25, Service optional **Wine:** 30 bottles over £20, 20 bottles under £20, 12 by the glass (£3.10-£5.95) **Notes:** Vegetarian available, Dress Restrictions, Smart casual **Seats:** 36 **Smoking:** N/Sm in restaurant **Children:** Min 12 yrs **Rooms:** 14 (14 en suite) ◆◆◆◆◆ **Directions:** Telephone for directions **Parking:** 14

⊛ Pines Hotel

Modern, Traditional

Imaginative cuisine in a unique setting

☎ 01772 338551 570 Preston Rd, Clayton Le-Woods PR6 7ED
e-mail: mail@thepineshotel.co.uk
web: www.thepineshotel.co.uk

This stylish hotel sits in 4 acres of mature grounds. Haworths Bistro offers a range of menus from lunch through to dinner with something for everyone. Starters might feature twice-baked goat's cheese soufflé while main dishes might include 'fish of the day' from the blackboard, or chicken breast filled with apricot and walnut stuffing, stilton sauce, rice and stir-fried vegetables. Vegetarian dishes include the likes of parsnips roasted with honey accompanied by goat's cheese and sun-ripened tomatoes in a herb basket with tomato and basil sauce.

Chef: Richard Jarvis **Owners:** Betty Duffin **Times:** 12-2.45/6-9.45, Closed 26 Dec **Prices:** Fixed L fr £10, Fixed D fr £12.50, Starter fr £4.50, Main fr £10.50, Dessert fr £3.95, Coffee £1.50, Min/Water £2.50, Service optional **Notes:** Sun L/D 4 courses £15, Vegetarian available, Dress Restrictions, Smart casual, Civ Wed 200 **Seats:** 95, Pr/dining room 46 **Smoking:** N/Sm area, No pipes **Children:** Menu, Portions **Rooms:** 37 (37 en suite) ★★★ HL **Directions:** Telephone for directions **Parking:** 150

⊛ Winckley Square Chop House and Bar

Modern British

Classic town-centre brasserie dining

☎ 01772 252732 23 Winckley Square PR1 3JJ
e-mail: preston@heathcotes.co.uk
web: www.heathcotes.co.uk

Right in the town centre, this former convent school has been converted into one of celebrity chef, Paul Heathcote's chain of brasseries. The interior boasts an impressive bar space and eclectic décor with lots of marble and hardwood surfaces and a mixture of contemporary and antique furniture. The menu is a crowd-pleaser, mixing classic hand-made dishes like fish and chips with local produce such as roasted Goosnargh duckling with spiced griottine cherries and red wine. Puddings include a traditional bread-and-butter pudding with apricot compôte and clotted cream, or try the home-made ice creams.

Chef: Thomas Lowe **Owners:** Heathcotes Restaurants **Times:** 12-2.30/6-10, Closed 1-2 Jan, BHs, Closed L 3 Jan **Prices:** Starter £3.75-£6.50, Main £9.50-£22, Dessert £4-£6.50, Coffee £1.80, Min/Water £3.25, Service optional, Group min 8 service 10% **Wine:** 48 bottles over £20, 18 bottles under £20, 10 by the glass (£3.85-£5.50) **Notes:** Sun L 2 courses £14.50, 3 courses £17, Vegetarian available, Dress Restrictions, Smart casual **Seats:** 80 **Smoking:** N/Sm in restaurant, Air con **Children:** Menu, Portions **Directions:** City centre, on Winckley Sq, near train station **Parking:** On street

THORNTON MAP 18 SD34

⊛ Twelve Restaurant

Modern British

Modern food in a contemporary setting

☎ 01253 821212 Marsh Mill Village, Marsh Mill-in-Wyre FY5 4JZ
e-mail: info@twelve-restaurant.co.uk
web: www.twelve-restaurant.co.uk

Converted dance studio in the shadow of a beautifully restored windmill (Marsh Mill 1794). The restaurant is contemporary in design with a sculptural feel and an industrial theme: exposed brickwork, steel girders and aluminium fencing on the mezzanine floor. The focal point is a huge wall-mounted projector screen showing pictures of the food, restaurant and the local area. The menu features many traditional dishes with a modern twist, such as corned beef hash terrine with home-made brown sauce, and rump of Cumbrian fell-bred lamb with pea and mint purée.

continued

THORNTON *continued* MAP 18 SD34

Chef: Paul Moss **Owners:** Paul Moss & Caroline Upton **Times:** 12-3/6.30-12, Closed 1st 2wks Jan, Mon, Closed L Tue-Wed, Fri-Sun **Prices:** Fixed L £13.95, Fixed D £17.95-£23.50, Starter £4.95-£7.25, Main £14.50-£19.95, Dessert £4.95-£7.50, Coffee £1.60, Min/Water £2.85, Service optional **Wine:** 25 bottles over £20, 30 bottles under £20, 5 by the glass (£3.40-£5) **Notes:** Vegetarian available **Seats:** 70 **Smoking:** N/Sm in restaurant **Children:** Portions **Directions:** A585 follow signs for Marsh Mill Complex. Turn right into Victoria Rd East, entrance 0.5m on left **Parking:** 150

WHITEWELL MAP 18 SD64

The Inn at Whitewell

Modern British NEW

Historic inn with imaginative cooking in an area of outstanding natural beauty

☎ 01200 448222 Forest of Bowland, Clitheroe BB7 3AT
e-mail: reception@innatwhitewell.com
web: www.inn@whitewell.com

Within the Forest of Bowland, beside the River Hodder this period inn (parts of which date back to the 1300s) has immense charm with rustic furniture, antiques and memorabilia throughout adding to its character. The dishes on this humourously written menu are modern British in style with an obvious Mediterranean influence - chicken and pistachio ravioli with morel cream sauce for example, or loin of Bowland lamb with carrot and cumin seed purée. The appealing wine list might have something to do with the wine merchants business sharing the premises.

Chef: Jamie Cadman **Owners:** The Inn at Whitewell Ltd **Times:** 12-2/7.30-9.30 **Prices:** Starter £4-£8.50, Main £14-£23, Dessert £3.50-£4.30, Coffee £1.90, Service optional **Wine:** 70 bottles over £20, 60 bottles under £20, 14 by the glass (£2.50-£5.50) **Notes:** Vegetarian available, Civ Wed 80 **Seats:** 60, Pr/dining room 20 **Smoking:** N/Sm in restaurant **Children:** Portions **Rooms:** 17 (17 en suite) ★★★★★ INN **Directions:** Telephone for directions **Parking:** 70

WRIGHTINGTON MAP 15 SD51

The Mulberry Tree

British, French

Ambitious cooking in Lancashire village gastro-pub

☎ 01257 451400 Wrightington Bar WN6 9SE

Just 2 miles off the M6, this family-run gastro-pub in a tranquil Lancashire village setting is popular with the locals for its generously-sized, imaginative dishes in a bright, modern setting. Simple table settings and personable service make this a popular lunchtime venue with its bar and restaurant menu for more refined items. Cooking is modern British with European influences so expect starters of Brixham crab salad with guacamole and Bloody Mary dressing with lime oil or Mortreaux sausage with crushed new potatoes, soft poached egg and hollandaise and main courses of either roast Cumbrian fell lamb or lemon sole with prawns capers, anchovies and lemon butter. Finish with summer pudding with Chantilly cream.

Times: 12-2/6-9.30, Closed 26 Dec, 1 Jan **Directions:** 4m from Wigan. From M6 junct 27 towards Parbold, right after motorway exit, by BP garage into Mossy Lea Rd. On right after 2m

LEICESTERSHIRE

BUCKMINSTER MAP 11 SK82

The Tollemache Arms

Modern British NEW

Vibrant restaurant at the cutting edge of modern cooking

☎ 01476 860007 48 Main St NG33 5SA
e-mail: enquiries@thetollemachearms.com
web: www.thetollemachearms.com

This 19th-century village pub on the Tollemache estate has been given a new focus as a restaurant with rooms, though locals can still prop up the bar and chat to visitors. The grey stone roadside inn now has a smart minimalist interior furnished with leather chairs and filled with fresh flowers. Lovers of good food appreciate the skills of Mark Gough, whose classical training and love of fresh produce have made this venture an immediate hit. Try Buckminster pigeon breast with shallot Tatin and red wine sauce to start, followed by grilled sea bass with basil mash and baby chorizo sausages. The signature dessert of apple and stilton tart is thoughtfully crafted.

Chef: Mark Gough **Owners:** Mark Gough **Times:** 12-3.30/5.30-12, Closed Mon, Closed D Sun **Prices:** Fixed L £10, Fixed D £14, Starter £4.50-£10, Main £9.50-£18, Dessert £5-£7, Coffee £2.50, Min/Water £2.50, Service optional **Wine:** 24 bottles over £20, 6 bottles under £20, 8 by the glass (£2.50-£3.80) **Seats:** 50, Pr/dining room 20 **Smoking:** N/Sm in restaurant **Children:** Menu, Portions **Rooms:** 5 (5 en suite) ◆◆◆◆ **Parking:** 15

CASTLE DONINGTON MAP 11 SK42 FOR RESTAURANT DETAILS SEE NOTTINGHAM EAST MIDLANDS AIRPORT

HINCKLEY MAP 11 SP49

Sketchley Grange Hotel

British, European

Modern hotel with its finger on the culinary pulse

☎ 01455 251133 Sketchley Ln, Burbage LE10 3HU
e-mail: reservations@sketchleygrange.co.uk
web: www.sketchleygrange.co.uk

This modern hotel boasts an impressive line up of facilities including a health and leisure complex, choice of bars, and two eateries. A brasserie serves light meals, but the real draw is the Willow Restaurant, a spacious venue that overlooks pretty gardens and is candlelit by night. It's staffed by a well-trained and enthusiastic kitchen brigade, who incorporate the best of culinary fashion in their food and

continued

offer an ambitious modern menu of dishes. Duck confit is a typical starter, served with seared foie gras, poached duck egg and Cassis jus, while mains might include loin of venison with parsnip purée, fondant potato, Valhrona chocolate and orange oil. One to watch.

Sketchley Grange Hotel

Chef: Darren Curson **Owners:** Nigel Downes **Times:** 7-9.30, Closed Mon, Closed L Mon-Sat, D Sun **Prices:** Starter £7-£10, Main £15-£21, Dessert £6, Coffee £2.50, Min/Water £3.95, Service optional **Wine:** 32 bottles over £20, 36 bottles under £20, 4 by the glass (£4.50-£6.95) **Notes:** Sun L £15.95, child £7.95, Vegetarian available, Dress Restrictions, Smart casual, Civ Wed 250 **Seats:** 80, Pr/dining room 40 **Smoking:** N/Sm in restaurant, Air con **Children:** Portions **Rooms:** 52 (52 en suite) ★★★★ HL **Directions:** From M69 junct 1 take B4109 (Hinckley). Straight on 1st rdbt, left at 2nd rdbt & immediately right into Sketchley Lane. Hotel at end of lane **Parking:** 200

KEGWORTH MAP 11 SK42 FOR RESTAURANT DETAILS SEE NOTTINGHAM EAST MIDLANDS AIRPORT

LEICESTER MAP 11 SK50

Belmont House Hotel

British

Calm dining in a busy city

☎ 0116 254 4773 De Montfort St LE1 7GR
e-mail: info@belmonthotel.co.uk
web: www.belmonthotel.co.uk

An elegant hotel offering a refreshing oasis from the bustle of the city centre. Three dining areas offer a variety of eating options including lunches in Jamie's Bar and Bowies, an informal eating area for lunchtime and early evening, as an alternative to Cherry's, the main restaurant. Cooking styles vary but the restaurant offers the likes of pan-fried foie gras with toasted brioche as a starter, or roast best end of lamb with port and redcurrant sauce. The wine list is comprehensive with wines for both enthusiasts and connoisseurs.

continued

Chef: Stewart Westwater **Owners:** The Bowie Family **Times:** 12.30-2.00/7-10.00, Closed BH Mondays, Closed L Sat, D Sun **Prices:** Fixed L £11.95, Fixed D £19.85-£33.85, Starter £3.95-£7.95, Main £9.95-£19.95, Dessert fr £5.95, Coffee £2.25, Service added but optional 10% **Wine:** 40 bottles over £20, 34 bottles under £20, 11 by the glass (£3.25-£4.25) **Notes:** Dress Restrictions, Smart casual, Civ Wed 100 **Seats:** 65, Pr/dining room 30 **Smoking:** N/Sm in restaurant, Air con **Children:** Portions **Rooms:** 77 (77 en suite) ★★★ HL **Directions:** M1 junct 21/A6 S onto A6 rdbt follow signs for railway station **Parking:** 70

Entropy

Modern British

Contemporary dining in the heart of the city

☎ 0116 254 8530 3 Dover St LE1 6PW
e-mail: mail@entropylife.com
web: www.entropylife.com

Located opposite a car park, Entropy may not have the most glamorous of settings, but don't be deterred - inside is an altogether classier affair. Head upstairs to the first floor, where you'll find a contemporary décor of muted whites, polished wood and stainless steel, plus a bar for aperitifs. The food comes courtesy of a kitchen team with a solid pedigree; expect a tempting modern menu of dishes such as lemon roasted monkfish with pea risotto and pancetta, or beef with rösti, mushroom purée and red wine sauce. There are interesting options for vegetarians too.

Chef: Tom Cockerill **Owners:** Tom & Cassandra Cockerill **Times:** 12-2.30/6-10, Closed BHs, 24 Dec-4 Jan, Sun **Prices:** Fixed L fr £12.95, Fixed D fr £15.95, Starter £6.50-£10.95, Main £17.50-£23.95, Dessert £5.95-£7.95, Coffee £1.50, Min/Water £4.50, Service optional **Wine:** 9 bottles over £20, 17 bottles under £20, 7 by the glass (£3.25-£5) **Notes:** Express menu available, Vegetarian available **Seats:** 60, Pr/dining room 20 **Smoking:** N/Sm in restaurant, Air con **Directions:** Located in Leicester city centre, 2 min walk from station. From Train Station on A6 take Granby St into city centre, Dover St is second on left. Restaurant is located opposite Dover St car park **Parking:** On street, NCP

Watsons Restaurant & Bar

Modern British, Mediterranean

Top nosh in one of Leicester's most popular eateries

☎ 0116 222 7770 5-9 Upper Brown St LE1 5TE
e-mail: watsons.restaurant@virgin.net

Set in an 18th-century former cotton mill, this well-established restaurant has a strong regular clientele - booking is advisable even at lunchtime. There's a compelling contemporary feel to the décor - polished wood floors, subtle halogen lighting and generously spaced tables. Service is relaxed, friendly and professional and as for the food - classic French and Mediterranean influences run throughout the menu and there's a high level of skill and obvious attention to detail in the cooking. Try tuna sashimi with crispy oyster and salad of baby corn, mange-tout and sesame followed by sea bream with honey and orange-roasted vegetables.

Chef: Graeme Watson, Marc Billings **Owners:** Graeme Watson **Times:** 12-2.30/7-10.30, Closed BHs, 10 days at Xmas, Sun **Prices:** Fixed L fr £9.50, Fixed D £15, Starter £5-£6.95, Main £10-£17.50, Dessert £5.50, Coffee £1.95, Min/Water £3, Service added but optional 10% **Wine:** 12 bottles over £20, 20 bottles under £20, 14 by the glass (£2.95-£5.75) **Notes:** Express L menu £7.50, Vegetarian available **Seats:** 80 **Smoking:** N/Sm in restaurant, Air con **Children:** Portions **Directions:** City centre, next to Phoenix Arts Theatre

England

LEICESTER *continued* MAP 11 SK50

San Carlo

☎ 0116 251 9332 Granby St LE1 1DE

Extremely busy Italian with open kitchen and wood-burning oven.

Stones

☎ 0116 291 0004 29 Millstone Ln LE1 5JN
web: www.theaa.com/restaurants/113923.html

A good-looking, modern restaurant where you can watch the fast-paced culinary spectacle on display in the open kitchen. The menu is modern European, and there's tapas too.

MEDBOURNE MAP 11 SP89

The Horse & Trumpet

Modern British

Culinary adventures in a sleepy village

☎ 01858 565000 Old Green LE16 8DX
e-mail: info@horseandtrumpet.com
web: www.horseandtrumpet.com

This thatched farmhouse sits in a pretty village beside a bowling green, and has been converted into a tasteful restaurant with rooms. Food is served in three intimate dining areas, or alfresco in summer, and comes courtesy of an accomplished kitchen team, who deliver a creative menu of modern dishes distinguished by quality ingredients, fresh flavours, and clever combinations - all washed down with a bottle from the competitive and carefully selected wine list. Start with cured foie gras with parsnip ice cream, rhubarb and gingerbread perhaps, and then tuck into lamb with butterbean and lemon cream, honey-roast aubergine and capers, or - better still - treat yourself to the twelve-course tasting menu.

Chef: D Lennox, G Magnani, L Goodwill **Owners:** Horse & Trumpet Ltd **Times:** 12-1.45/7-9.30, Closed 1st Week Jan, Mon, Closed D Sun **Prices:** Fixed L £17, Starter £6.50-£11.50, Main £16.75-£22.50, Dessert £6.75-£10, Coffee £2, Min/Water £3, Service optional, Group min 16 service 10% **Wine:** 50 bottles over £20, 10 bottles under £20, 10 by the glass (£3.50-£6) **Notes:** Tasting menu L £30, D £50, Sun L £17.25, Vegetarian available, Dress Restrictions, Smart casual, no trainers or baseball caps **Seats:** 50, Pr/dining room 32 **Smoking:** N/Sm area **Children:** Min 12 yrs **Rooms:** 4 (4 en suite) RR **Directions:** Between Market Harborough and Uppingham on B664 **Parking:** 4

MELTON MOWBRAY MAP 11 SK71

Stapleford Park

British, French

British country cooking amid the splendour of 500 acres of Capability Brown parkland

☎ 01572 787522 Stapleford LE14 2EF
e-mail: reservations@stapleford.co.uk
web: www.staplefordpark.com

This former stately home dates back to the 14th century - it's a stunning place with 500 acres of classic Augustan-style parklands, designed by Capability Brown himself. There are two dining rooms; the main room boasts Grinling Gibbons carvings inspired by the Spanish Riding School in Vienna; while The Old Kitchen, a cosier room with an impressive vaulted ceiling, has a more medieval feel. The food has its foundations in classical technique with slick presentation; essentially it's the epitome of modern British food - try the tasting menu for a complete overview. Starters might include goat's cheese mousse with shaved fennel and tomato essence; for a main course you could have sea bass with cauliflower, langoustines and Oscietra caviar.

Chef: Wayne Vickerage **Owners:** Shuif Hussain **Times:** 12-2.30/7.30-9.30, Closed L Mon-Sat **Prices:** Fixed L £26.50, Fixed D fr £44, Starter £12-£16, Main £22.50-£29, Dessert £11.50-£12, Coffee £3.95, Min/Water £3.95, Service optional, Group service 5% **Wine:** 300 bottles over £20, 10 by the glass (£5.50-£6.50) **Notes:** 3 course L Sun only £26.50, tasting menu available, Dress Restrictions, Jacket required, no jeans, Civ Wed 200 **Seats:** 60, Pr/dining room 190 **Smoking:** N/Sm in restaurant **Children:** Min 9 yrs, Menu **Rooms:** 52 (52 en suite) ★★★★ **Directions:** Follow Melton ring road A607 (Grantham) onto B676, 4m turn right signed Stapleford **Parking:** 200

NORTH KILWORTH MAP 11 SP68

Kilworth House Hotel

Modern British V

Country-house hotel offering comfortable elegance and fine dining

☎ 01858 880058 Lutterworth Rd LE17 6JE
e-mail: info@kilworthhouse.co.uk
web: www.kilworthhouse.co.uk

This beautiful country-house hotel, set in 38 acres of parkland and gardens, makes an elegant and luxurious setting for the Gothic-style restaurant, with its ornate vaulted ceiling. The adjacent restored Victorian orangery has fine views and offers a lighter menu. Fine dining in the Wordsworth Restaurant makes the most of some excellent produce like superb local lamb. Expect mains such as duo of lamb with tomato and garlic confit, wilted spinach and fondant potato, or pan-fried halibut with crab and avocado pancakes and lobster cream sauce. The desserts, like three flavours of banana, are particularly artistic, described as 'modern interpretations, not classic imitations', they are all made to order and are well worth a short wait.

Chef: Carl Dovey **Owners:** Mr & Mrs Mackay **Times:** 12-3/7-9.30 **Prices:** Fixed L £15-£25, Fixed D fr £30, Starter £8.50-£12, Main £15.50-£25, Dessert £7.95-£8.50, Coffee £2.50, Min/Water £4, Service optional **Wine:** 75 bottles over £20, 15 bottles under £20, 8 by the glass (£4.50-£6) **Notes:** Vegetarian menu, Dress Restrictions, No jeans or trainers, Civ Wed 130 **Seats:** 70, Pr/dining room 130 **Smoking:** N/Sm in restaurant **Children:** Menu, Portions **Rooms:** 44 (44 en suite) ★★★★ HL **Directions:** Located on A4304, 4m E of M1 junct 20 towards Market Harborough **Parking:** 140

continued

NOTTINGHAM EAST MIDLANDS AIRPORT
MAP 11 SK42

Best Western Yew Lodge Hotel

Traditional

Imaginative cooking in relaxed surroundings

☎ 01509 672518 Packington Hill, Kegworth DE74 2DF
e-mail: info@yewlodgehotel.co.uk
web: www.yewlodgehotel.co.uk

A smart, conservatively decorated hotel close to Nottingham East Midlands Airport, Yew Lodge is a popular venue for conferences, weddings and, of course, for diners who come to check out the food at the Orchard Restaurant. As with the décor, you could describe the food as traditional with a modern twist, with influences coming from all over the world - though favouring French and Italian. There's plenty of creative flair shining through too - especially in dishes such as red onion tarte Tatin with gorgonzola ice cream, or roasted brill with aubergine caviar and crayfish vinaigrette.

Chef: Trevor Bearder **Owners:** Jeremy Pick **Times:** 12-2.30/6.30-10, Closed L Sat **Prices:** Fixed L £11.95, Fixed D £24.95, Starter £7.50-£9.25, Main £17.50-£23.50, Dessert £4.95, Coffee £2.50, Min/Water £2.40, Service optional **Wine:** 17 bottles over £20, 18 bottles under £20, 6 by the glass (£3.35-£4.95) **Notes:** Vegetarian available, Dress Restrictions, No jeans, Civ Wed 130 **Seats:** 80, Pr/dining room 150 **Smoking:** N/Sm in restaurant, Air con **Children:** Menu, Portions **Rooms:** 98 (98 en suite) ★★★ HL **Directions:** M1 junct 24, follow signs for Loughborough & Kegworth on A6. At bottom of hill take 1st right onto Packington Hill. Hotel 400yds on right **Parking:** 177

The Priest House on the River

Modern British

Unique location for fine dining

☎ 01332 810649 Kings Mills
Castle Donnington DE74 2RR
e-mail: priesthouse@handpicked.co.uk
web: www.handpicked.co.uk

A historic setting on the banks of the River Trent, where the Domesday Book noted the original watermills on the site of the Priest House in 1086. Nowadays modern comforts can be found throughout the hotel, which has conference rooms, a modern brasserie and a fine-dining restaurant. Here the stylish décor reflects the considerable attention to detail seen elsewhere. The menu offers a balanced selection of traditional dishes with contemporary elements, making good use of the best seasonal produce from top suppliers. Service is smooth and efficient with a genuine feeling of warmth and hospitality.

continued

Times: 12-3/7-9.30, Closed L Mon-Sat **Rooms:** 42 (42 en suite) ★★★★ HL **Directions:** Northbound: M1 junct 23A to airport. After 1.5m turn right to Castle Donington. Left at 1st lights, 2m. Southbound: M1 junct 24A onto A50. Take 1st sliproad signed Long Eaton/Castle Donington. Turn right at lights in Castle Donington

QUORN MAP 11 SK51

Quorn Country Hotel

Traditional British

Country-house dining where tradition rules

☎ 01509 415050 Charnwood House,
66 Leicester Rd LE12 8BB
e-mail: sales@quorncountryhotel.co.uk
web: www.quorncountryhotel.co.uk

A riverside setting in 4 acres of landscaped gardens and professional service are the key strengths of this pleasing 17th-century manor house hotel. The Shires Restaurant is the more formal dining option, an intimate little affair with low-beamed ceilings, candlelight and close-set tables, while the Orangery is an informal, conservatory bistro. Predominantly traditional country-house cooking with the occasional modern foray is the style, appropriately backed by silver service and a comprehensive wine list. Dishes are presented via a fixed-price option and extensive carte, and deliver accurate, accomplished cooking, with the double-roasted Gressingham duck with fruit compôte and Grand Marnier sauce being the favourite choice. To work up an appetite or work off dessert, take a stroll around the riverside gardens.

Chef: David Wilkinson **Owners:** Mr Walshe **Times:** 12-2.30/7-9.30, Closed L Sat **Prices:** Fixed D £23.50, Starter £5-£7.95, Main £16.50-£25.95, Dessert £5.50, Coffee £3, Min/Water £4.25 **Wine:** 49 bottles over £20, 17 bottles under £20, 4 by the glass (£3-£6) **Notes:** Sun L 3 courses £14.50, Vegetarian available, Civ Wed 120 **Seats:** 112, Pr/dining room 240 **Children:** Menu, Portions **Rooms:** 30 (30 en suite) ★★★★ HL **Directions:** M1junct 23/A6 towards Leicester, follow signs for Quorn **Parking:** 120

Ferrari's Trattoria

☎ 01509 412191 4 High St LE12 8DT

Family-run Italian in an old cottage in the main street.

STATHERN MAP 11 SK73

Red Lion Inn

British

Modern bistro food in a friendly village inn

☎ 01949 860868 Red Lion St LE14 4HS
e-mail: info@theredlioninn.co.uk
web: www.theredlioninn.co.uk

Set in a lovely village nestling under Belvoir Scarp, this country inn has a traditional feel without being overbearingly olde worlde. It's a comfortable British pub in the best possible sense, with furniture and fittings that show the wear of regular use and a settled atmosphere that is deeply ingrained. The food is rustic and well done, using local produce throughout; the daily-changing menu might include smoked haddock rarebit with tomato and chive salad followed by loin of venison, fondant potato and port and red wine sauce. Also on site is Red Olive Foods offering everything from takeaway jams, pickles and chutneys to hampers for a day at the races at Tolethorpe.

continued

England

STATHERN *continued* MAP 11 SK73

Chef: Phillip Lowe **Owners:** Ben Jones, Marcus Welford, Sean Hope **Times:** 12-2/7-9.30, Closed D 25 Dec & 1 Jan, Closed D Sun **Prices:** Fixed L £13, Starter £4.25-£7.50, Main £9.95-£18.50, Dessert £4.50-£6.50, Coffee £2.50, Min/Water £3, Service optional, Group min 11 service 10% **Wine:** 10 bottles over £20, 27 bottles under £20, 7 by the glass (£2.75-£3.75) **Notes:** Fixed Sun L 3 courses £17.50, Vegetarian available **Seats:** 50 **Smoking:** N/Sm in restaurant **Children:** Menu, Portions **Directions:** From A1 take A52 towards Nottingham signed Belvoir Castle, take turn to Strathern on left **Parking:** 20

LINCOLNSHIRE

CLEETHORPES MAP 17 TA30

Kingsway Hotel

Traditional British

Traditional dining by the sea

☎ 01472 601122 Kingsway DN35 0AE
e-mail: reception@kingsway-hotel.com
web: www.kingsway-hotel.com

Family-owned for four generations, there are many long-serving staff here and equally long-returning guests and locals. The traditional seaside hotel has commanding views of the Humber Estuary from the restaurant windows. Good straightforward cooking is evident with the flavour of fresh ingredients like asparagus, fish and fruit coming to the fore. The British menu with modern and international influences offers an extensive choice of dishes such as medallions of monkfish with sweet and sour sauce and crispy noodle basket, or roasted Gressingham duck with orange, brandy and thyme sauce. To start, try the chicken liver pâté with Cumberland sauce.

Chef: Guy Stevens **Owners:** Mr J Harris **Times:** 12.30-1.45/7-9, Closed 26-27 Dec **Prices:** Fixed L fr £15, Fixed D fr £23.95, Starter £5.75-£8.95, Main £13.95-£19.95, Dessert £5.50, Coffee £2, Min/Water £3, Service optional **Wine:** 31 bottles over £20, 39 bottles under £20, 5 by the glass (£3.60) **Notes:** Vegetarian available **Seats:** 85, Pr/dining room 24 **Smoking:** N/Sm in restaurant **Children:** Min 5 yrs, Portions **Rooms:** 49 (49 en suite) ★★★ HL **Directions:** At junction of A1098 and seafront **Parking:** 50

GRANTHAM MAP 11 SK93

Angel & Royal Hotel

Modern British, Traditional

Historic haunt of kings

☎ 01476 565816 High St NG31 6PN
e-mail: enquiries@angelandroyal.co.uk
web: www.angelandroyal.co.uk

Reputedly one of the oldest inns in Britain, this rare survivor dates from the 14th century and retains many original features. The historic King's Dining Room is regal and impressive, with fine plaster ceilings, huge log fire, and elaborate stone oriel windows. The new owners are keen to maintain the standard of cooking in both the modern and stylish bistro and in the main dining room, the fixed-price menu in the latter listing cured salmon with cucumber salsa, roasted pork loin with black pudding, and steamed ginger sponge with apple compôte.

Chef: Daniel Bland **Owners:** Angel & Royal Hotel Limited **Times:** 12-2/7-9.30, Closed L Mon-Sat, D Sun-Thur **Prices:** Fixed L £11-£15, Fixed D £25.95-£29.95, Starter £4.95-£7.95, Main £11.95-£17.95, Dessert £4.50-£7.50, Coffee £1.95, Min/Water £2.95, Service optional **Wine:** 21 bottles over £20,

continued

14 bottles under £20, 4 by the glass (£2.95-£3.95) **Notes:** Vegetarian available, Dress Restrictions, Smart casual **Seats:** 55, Pr/dining room 16 **Smoking:** N/Sm in restaurant, Air con **Children:** Menu, Portions **Rooms:** 29 (29 en suite) ★★★ HL **Directions:** Grantham exit off A1 and follow signs to the town centre **Parking:** 55

Harry's Place

see opposite

GRIMSBY MAP 17 TA21

Beeches Hotel

Modern French

Airy and spacious bistro-style surroundings for international cuisine

☎ 01472 278830 42 Waltham Rd, Scartho DN33 2LX
e-mail: joeramsden@freeuk.com
web: www.thebeecheshotel.com

A modern hotel in a remodelled Victorian building, with a minimalist feel to the bar and conservatory restaurant. The cool cream and brown colour scheme is highly conducive to relaxing, aided by oriental rugs on hardwood floors, and low leather sofas. The cooking is well respected locally, with an exciting menu offering some international flavours. Thai-style smoked haddock fishcakes might be followed by oven-roasted Gressingham duck break with sauce Forestière, or griddled calves' liver with caramelised apples and onions.

Chef: David Ramackers **Owners:** Ramsden Family **Times:** 12-2/7-9, Closed Xmas & New Year, Closed L Mon-Tue **Prices:** Starter £4-£6, Main £15.50-£21, Dessert £4.95-£5.50, Coffee £1.20, Min/Water £2.10, Service optional **Wine:** 18 bottles over £20, 20 bottles under £20, 2 by the glass (£2.70) **Notes:** Sun L 3 courses incl. coffee £12.95 **Seats:** 50 **Smoking:** N/Sm in restaurant **Children:** Portions **Rooms:** 18 (18 en suite) ★★★ HL **Directions:** On A1203, off A16 from Louth **Parking:** 30

LINCOLN MAP 17 SK97

Branston Hall Hotel

Modern International

Contemporary food in country-house splendour

☎ 01522 793305 Branston Park, Branston LN4 1PD
e-mail: jon@branstonhall.com
web: www.branstonhall.com

Smart and imposing country house, brimful of Victorian splendour and set in attractive grounds complete with a lake. The elegant Lakeside Restaurant comes suitably decked out with chandeliers, paintings, Italian-style chairs and plenty of original features. The ambitious carte and fixed-price menus take a distinctly modern

continued

Harry's Place

GRANTHAM MAP 11 SK93

Modern French

Tiny restaurant with exquisite food

☎ 01476 561780 17 High St, Great Gonerby NG31 8JS

With only three tables and an international reputation for fine food, you can expect a fairly serious wait for a table at Harry's Place. The restaurant itself is set in an attractive listed Georgian building, which was once a farmhouse and a wheelwrights.
The intimacy of the dining room and the fact your meal is guaranteed to have been lovingly cooked by chef-owner Harry Hallam are major factors in the restaurant's appeal. Add into this a passion for quality ingredients that borders on the obsessive and imaginative, technically impressive cooking with real panache and you have a winning formula for one of the North East's best restaurants.
With only two choices for each course, deliberating over the menu needn't be the trial faced in some restaurants - everything is exceptional. Start with sautéed foie gras enrobed in spicy sherry aspic, then continue with a main of Lincolnshire woodcock and white wine, Chartreuse and herbs then finish off with a splendid apricot soufflé.

Chef: Harry Hallam **Owners:** Harry & Caroline Hallam **Times:** 12.30-2.30/7-9.30, Closed 1 wk Xmas, BHs, Sun & Mon **Prices:** Starter £8.50-£17.50, Main £32-£35, Dessert £7, Coffee £2, Service optional **Wine:** 99% bottles over £20, 1% bottles under £20, 4 by the glass (£4.50-£5) **Notes:** Mineral water free of charge **Seats:** 10 **Smoking:** N/Sm in restaurant **Children:** Min 5 yrs, Portions **Directions:** 1.5m NW of Grantham on B1174 **Parking:** 4

approach, the kitchen not afraid to use flavours and influences from around the globe. Fine regional produce, imagination, culinary skill and careful service all come together in style. Start with carpaccio of venison with spiced figs and Perigord goat's cheese, then continue with herb-crusted beef fillet, wild mushrooms, glazed shallots and Madeira sauce.

Chef: Miles Collins **Owners:** Southsprings Ltd **Times:** 12-2/7-9.30, Closed 1 Jan **Prices:** Fixed L fr £13.95, Fixed D fr £24.50, Starter £4.75-£8.75, Main £14.50-£19.50, Dessert £4.75-£6.25, Coffee £1.50, Min/Water £3.50, Service optional **Wine:** 8 by the glass **Notes:** Menu Gourmand £37.50, Vegetarian available, Dress Restrictions, Smart casual, no jeans or T-shirts, Civ Wed 120 **Seats:** 75, Pr/dining room 28 **Smoking:** N/Sm in restaurant **Children:** Min 12 yrs, Portions **Rooms:** 50 (50 en suite) ★★★ HL **Directions:** On B1188, 3m S of Lincoln. In village, hotel drive opposite village hall **Parking:** 75

The Restaurant in the Jew's House

British, French

Modern cooking in one of Lincoln's oldest buildings

☎ 01522 524851 15 The Strait LN2 1JD

Dating from the 12th century and tucked away along a small passageway near Lincoln Castle, this stone house is one of the few surviving buildings of its type in the world. Ancient beams, fireplaces blackened with centuries of use and wide windows overlooking cobbled streets take you back to another age. The chef has a passion for interesting flavours and fresh produce accurately cooked, reflected in the modern British menu with French influences. Expect the likes of

continued

Gressingham duck magret, dark baby fig and Madeira jus, or red bream fillet en papillotte with château potatoes.

Times: 12-2.30/6-10, Closed Xmas, Mon **Directions:** At bottom of Steep Hill from cathedral

Wig & Mitre

British, International

A shrine to good eating on the old pilgrim trail

☎ 01522 535190 30/32 Steep Hill LN2 1TL
e-mail: email@wigandmitre.com
web: www.wigandmitre.com

Located at the top of the well-named Steep Hill, this old inn is open from early to late, offering comfort and good food throughout the day. From the front bar you can watch the tourists struggling up the precipitous cobbles outside, or enjoy striking views of the cathedral from the upstairs dining room. The food is an unfussy but imaginative blend of modern ideas, listed on a carte and blackboard, with the likes of baked cheese and spinach soufflé, followed by rack of lamb with garlic flageolet ragout, and for dessert a trio of white chocolate sorbet, chocolate mousse and a shot of milk chocolate. Wines by the glass and bottle are suggested for each dish.

Chef: Valerie Hope **Owners:** Hope family **Times:** 8/11 **Prices:** Fixed L £11.50-£12.50, Starter £4.50-£19.50, Main £10.50-£23.95, Dessert £4.95-£5.95, Coffee 80p, Min/Water £2.70, Service optional **Wine:** 38 bottles over £20, 31 bottles under £20, 24 by the glass (£3.20-£14.05) **Notes:** Vegetarian available **Seats:** 65, Pr/dining room 20 **Smoking:** N/Sm in restaurant **Children:** Portions **Directions:** At the top of Steep Hill, adjacent to Lincoln Cathedral and Lincoln Castle car parks **Parking:** Public car park adjacent

LINCOLN *continued* MAP 17 SK97

The Cheese Society

☎ 01522 511003 1 St Martin's Ln LN2 1HY

Wide range of cheese dishes served in modern café attached to specialist cheese outlet.

SCUNTHORPE MAP 17 SE81

Forest Pines Hotel

European, British

Modern hotel with an elegant restaurant

☎ 01652 650770 Ermine St, Broughton DN20 0AQ
e-mail: enquiries@forestpines.co.uk
web: www.forestpines.co.uk

A well-equipped leisure hotel with three eating areas, ranging from an informal clubhouse to a more formal air-conditioned restaurant. This comfortable room is as smart and modern as the rest of the hotel, with well-spaced tables and quality settings. The food is highly regarded locally, with menus based on carefully selected ingredients put together with skill and flair. Fresh fish from nearby Grimsby always features, and Scottish beef - perhaps as a rump steak served with a peppercorn sauce - is well-hung and tender. A table d'hôte and gourmet menu offer interesting choices.

Times: 12-2/7-9.45, Closed L Sat **Rooms:** 114 (114 en suite) ★★★★ **Directions:** From M180 junct 4, travel towards Scunthorpe on A18. Continue straight over rdbt, hotel is situated on left

SPALDING

Cley Hall Hotel

British, International

Overlooking the River Welland, a fine Georgian hotel

☎ 01775 725157 22 High St PE11 1TX
e-mail: cleyhall@enterprise.net
web: www.cleyhallhotel.com

Grade II listed after being rescued from near dereliction in the 1960s, this fine Georgian property has again undergone a refurbishment. The restaurant is divided in two, but forms an integral part of the ground floor area, and has a pleasant atmosphere. The straightforward use of quality ingredients results in a consistently good menu, with plenty to interest even the most jaded palates. Confit of pork wrapped in Parma ham, roast rack of lamb with stuffed vegetables, and a superb rib-eye steak with mustard butter and hand cut chips are some of the reasons for its popularity.

Times: 12-2.00/6.30-9.30, Closed D 25-26 Dec **Rooms:** 15 (15 en suite) ★★ HL **Directions:** Telephone for directions

STAMFORD MAP 11 TF00

George of Stamford Hotel

Traditional British NOTABLE WINE LIST

Coaching inn popular for its old-fashioned charm

☎ 01780 750750 71 St Martins PE9 2LB
e-mail: reservations@georgehotelofstamford.com
web: www.georgehotelofstamford.com/

The open stonework and architectural features of this splendid building stand testimony to its colourful history as a hostelry to the great and the good as they travelled the length of England. Meals are served in the oak-panelled restaurant, the Garden Room or in the ivy-clad courtyard. Cooking is careful and accurate with much traditionally based fare on offer - freshly carved roast beef, saddle of venison with celeriac purée, calves' liver with sage and lime butter, and sherry trifle. The more adventurous might choose wild sea bass with chorizo cassoulet.

Notable Wine List: The wine list offers a beautiful selection, with informative tasting notes.

Chef: Chris Pitman, Paul Reseigh **Owners:** Lawrence Hoskins **Times:** 12.30-2.30/7.30-10.30 **Prices:** Fixed L £17.50, Starter £5.50-£13.95, Main £16.95-£29, Dessert £5.55, Coffee £3.25, Min/Water £2.95, Service optional **Wine:** 94 bottles over £20, 72 bottles under £20, 14 by the glass (£4.35-£6.50) **Notes:** Vegetarian available, Dress Restrictions, Jacket & tie, Civ Wed 50 **Seats:** 90, Pr/dining room 40 **Smoking:** No pipes or cigars **Children:** Min 10 yrs **Rooms:** 47 (47 en suite) ★★★ **Directions:** From A1(Peterborough) take rdbt signed B1081. Follow road to 1st set of lights, hotel on left **Parking:** 120

Fratelli's

☎ 01780 754333 PE9 2DP

Very popular Italian serving a good selection of reliable dishes.

SUTTON ON SEA MAP 17 TF58

Grange & Links Hotel

British, French

A beautiful setting for really good fresh food

☎ 01507 441334 Sea Ln, Sandilands LN12 2RA
e-mail: grangeandlinkshotel@btconnect.com
web: www.grangeandlinkshotel.co.uk

A friendly family-run hotel in 5 acres of grounds close to the beach, with its own 18-hole links golf course. Traditional English offerings of superb fresh food, simply cooked and served are what this place is all about. Fish from Grimsby, Lincolnshire Red beef and local vegetables are examples of some of the fine produce on the menu. Try succulent, grilled on the bone, whole Grimsby Dover sole, fennel butter and caper flowers, followed by whiskey bread and butter pudding, made with Jameson's whiskey, a house speciality not to be missed.

Chef: Tina Harrison **Owners:** Ann Askew **Times:** 7-10, Closed L all week **Prices:** Starter £3.50-£6.50, Main £11-£15, Dessert £4, Coffee £2.50, Min/Water £3.50, Service optional **Wine:** 11 bottles over £20, 22 bottles under £20, 3 by the glass (£3) **Notes:** Vegetarian available, Dress Restrictions, Jacket & tie, Civ Wed 150 **Seats:** 60 **Children:** Menu, Portions **Rooms:** 23 (23 en suite) ★★★ HL **Directions:** Please telephone for directions **Parking:** 60

England

Winteringham Fields

WINTERINGHAM MAP 17 SE92

French, European

Famous haunt lives on in new hands

☎ 01724 733096 DN15 9PF
e-mail: wintfields@aol.com
web: www.winteringhamfields.com

After something like two decades, Germain and Annie Schwab sold up and left, though with new owners running Winteringham in the same fashion and highly talented Germain protégé Robert Thompson at the helm in the kitchen (he'd been heading up the kitchen brigade for a couple of years under Germain), continuity at this much-loved venue is guaranteed in a safe pair of young hands. The endearing 16th-century former manor house remains the same; original beams, log fires, sloping floors and period features. Victorian predominates here with chintz, antiques, pictures and collectables, while quality and comfort prevail alongside a warm, inviting and relaxed atmosphere. There's a choice of sitting rooms and a conservatory for aperitifs, while in summer the rose garden comes into play. The restaurant is a long, slim room with a tiled floor and country feel, decked out with flowing tablecloths, and there's plenty of showmanship with cheese and bread trolleys. Staff are French, knowledgeable and attentive but not at all stuffy, while the sommelier is very sharp - do use his skills.

Robert Thompson's cooking takes a modern French approach underpinned by a classical theme and focuses on top-quality, seasonal ingredients (including vegetables, fruit and herbs from Winteringham's own potager when available), delivering via a repertoire of lunch, carte and eleven-course tasting menu surprise. Expect refined, precision cooking, with clean, clear flavours, interesting combinations and supreme technical skill; think crispy suckling pig teamed with aubergine caviar, truffle polenta and boudin noir, while a classic vanilla crème brûlée paired with red fruit and brandy snaps might head up desserts. Ancillaries (amuse-bouche, breads, pre-desserts and petits fours) all hit top form, while the wine list is considerable and expectedly classy.

Chef: R Thompson
Owners: Colin McGurran
Times: 12-2/7-10, Closed 2 wks Xmas, 1st wk Aug, last wk Mar, Sun-Mon
Prices: Fixed L £30, Fixed D £56-£65, Starter £18-£24, Main £24-£36, Dessert £15-£20, Service optional
Wine: 300 bottles over £20, 26 by the glass (£4.10-£12.50)
Notes: Menu Surprise 7 courses £75, Vegetarian available, Dress Restrictions, Smart dress preferred
Seats: 42, Pr/dining room 10
Smoking: N/Sm in restaurant
Rooms: 10 (10 en suite) ★★★ HL
Directions: Village centre, off A1077, 4m S of Humber Bridge
Parking: 20

England

WINTERINGHAM MAP 17 SE92

Winteringham Fields

see page 229

WOOLSTHORPE MAP 11 SK83

The Chequers Inn

Modern British

Coaching inn turned gastro-pub

☎ 01476 870701 Main St NG32 1LU
e-mail: justinnabar@yahoo.co.uk
web: www.chequers-inn.net

A cosy warren of open fires, sleepy nooks, and exposed beams, this gastro-pub dates back to the 17th century and combines historic charm with contemporary informality. Set in the lee of Belvoir Castle, it has its own petanque lawn and is the perfect place to while away a summer evening. Dine in the restaurant or the bar, and take your pick from a lengthy menu that teams old favourites (sausage and mash, sirloin steak and hand-cut chips) with more modern fare, such as roast rump of lamb with sweet potato purée, redcurrant and rosemary, or baked sea bass with fondant leeks, caper and tomato butter.

Chef: Danny Cornell **Owners:** Justin & Joanne Chad **Times:** 12-3/5.30-11, Closed D 25-26 Dec **Prices:** Fixed L £9.50, Fixed D £15, Starter £4.50-£7, Main £12.50-£20, Dessert £5-£6, Coffee £1.75, Min/Water £3, Service optional **Wine:** 26 bottles over £20, 29 bottles under £20, 29 by the glass (£3-£7.50) **Notes:** Sun L 2 courses £10.95, Vegetarian available **Seats:** 70, Pr/dining room 14 **Smoking:** N/Sm in restaurant **Children:** Menu, Portions **Rooms:** 4 (4 en suite) ◆◆◆◆ **Directions:** From A1 exit A607 towards Melton Mowbray follow heritage signs for Belvoir Castle **Parking:** 35

continued

London

Index of London Restaurants

This index shows rosetted restaurants in London in alphabetical order, followed by their postal district. Page numbers precede each entry.

A

259 1 Lombard Street, Fine Dining Restaurant EC3
273 3 Monkeys Restaurant SE24
349 Admiralty Restaurant, The WC2
339 Agni W6
273 Al Duca SW1
306 Alastair Little Restaurant W1
349 Albannach WC2
306 Alloro W1
261 Almeida Restaurant N1
274 Amaya SW1
267 Anchor & Hope, The SE1
307 Angela Hartnett at The Connaught W1
339 Anglesea Arms W6
307 Archipelago W1
341 Ark, The W8
349 Asia de Cuba WC2
336 Assaggi W2
307 Athenaeum Hotel, Bullochs at 116 W1
301 Aubergine SW10
256 Aurora at Great Eastern Hotel EC2
308 Automat W1
274 Avenue, The SW1
288 Awana SW3
358 Ayudhya Thai Restaurant KINGSTON UPON THAMES

B

273 Babur SE23
341 Babylon W8
268 Baltic SE1
308 Bam-Bou W1
349 Bank Aldwych Restaurant & Bar WC2
308 Bellamy's W1
342 Belvedere W8
308 Benares W1
299 Bentley Kempinski Hotel, The SW7
309 Bentley's Oyster Bar & Grill W1
309 Berkeley Square, The W1
288 Bibendum Restaurant SW3
360 Bingham Hotel, Restaurant & Bar RICHMOND UPON THAMES
309 Blandford Street W1
253 Bleeding Heart, The EC1
289 Bluebird Dining Rooms SW3
296 Blue Elephant SW6
274 Boisdale of Belgravia SW1
256 Boisdale of Bishopsgate EC2
256 Bonds EC2
274 Boxwood Café SW1
340 Brackenbury, The W6
362 La Brasserie Ma Cuisine Bourgeoise TWICKENHAM
275 Brasserie Roux SW1
310 Brian Turner Mayfair W1
363 Brula TWICKENHAM
297 Brunello SW7
263 Bull Pub & Dining Room, The N6
310 Butlers W1
268 Butlers Wharf Chop House SE1
360 Buvette, La RICHMOND UPON THAMES

C

253 Café du Marché, Le EC1
297 Café Lazeez SW7
249 Café Spice Namasté E1
296 Cambio De Tercio SW5
310 Camerino W1
249 Canteen E1
268 Cantina del Ponte SE1
268 Cantina Vinopolis SE1
290 Capital, The SW3
275 Caprice Restaurant, Le SW1
275 Caraffini SW1
310 Cecconi's W1
276 Cercle, Le SW1
258 Chamberlains Restaurant EC3
268 Champor Champor SE1
260 Chancery, The EC4
357 Chapter One BROMLEY
271 Chapter Two SE3
342 Cheneston's (The Milestone Hotel) W8
305 Chez Bruce SW17
340 Chez Kristof W6
311 China Tang W1
350 Christopher's WC2
300 Chutney Mary Restaurant SW10
347 Cibo W14
276 Cinnamon Club, The SW1
311 Cipriani W1
342 Clarke's W8
257 Clerkenwell Dining Room EC1
253 Club Gascon EC1
311 Cocoon W1
289 Collection, The SW3

289 Colombier, Le SW3
254 Comptoir Gascon EC1
276 Convivio, Il SW1
312 Crescent Restaurant at The Montcalm Nikko London W1
312 The Cumberland - Rhodes W1

D

296 Deep SW6
303 Depot Waterfront Brasserie, The SW14
311 Deya W1
265 Dorset Square Hotel NW1
261 Drapers Arms, The N1
277 Drones of Pont Street SW1

E

345 E&O W11
277 Ebury SW1
345 Edera W11
289 Eight Over Eight SW3
343 Eleven Abingdon Road W8
312 Embassy W1
304 Enoteca Turi SW15
313 Escargot L' - The Ground Floor Restaurant W1
314 Escargot L' - The Picasso Room W1
298 Etranger, L' SW7
257 Eyre Brothers EC2

F

262 Fifteen N1
277 Fifth Floor Restaurant, The SW1
313 Fino W1
269 Fire Station SE1
257 Fishmarket EC2
300 Food Room, The SW8
251 Four Seasons Hotel Canary Wharf E14
313 Four Seasons Hotel London W1
278 Franco's SW1
315 Frankie's at Criterion Grill W1
289 Frankie's Italian Bar & Grill SW3
272 Franklins SE22
262 Frederick's Restaurant N1
362 French Table, The SURBITON
360 Friends Restaurant PINNER

G

315 Galvin - Bistrot de Luxe W1
315 Galvin at Windows W1
340 Gate, The W6
316 Gavroche Restaurant, Le W1
269 Glas SE1
359 Glasshouse, The KEW
316 Gordon Ramsay at Claridge's W1
278 Goring Hotel SW1
257 Great Eastern Dining Room EC2
317 Greenhouse Restaurant, The W1
302 Greyhound at Battersea, The SW11
315 Grill, The (Brown's Hotel) W1
318 Grill Room, The (Dorchester Hotel, The) W1
251 Gun, The E14

H

317 Hakkasan W1
362 Hawtrey's Restaurant at the Barn Hotel RUISLIP
262 House, The N1

I

350 Imperial China WC2
350 Incognico WC2
278 Inn the Park SW1
337 Island Restaurant & Bar W2
350 Ivy, The WC2

J

351 Jaan Restaurant (Swissotel London, The Howard) WC2
351 J. Sheekey WC2
347 Jurys Great Russell Street WC1
278 Just St James SW1

K

318 Kai Mayfair W1
306 Kastoori Restaurant SW17
279 Ken Lo's Memories of China SW1
343 Kensington Place W8
318 Kilo W1

L

271 Laicram Thai Restaurant SE3
249 Lanes Restaurant & Bar E1
279 Lanesborough, The SW1
318 Latium W1
343 Launceston Place Restaurant W8
346 Ledbury, The W11
318 Levant W1
306 Light House Restaurant, The SW19
321 Lindsay House Restaurant W1
322 Locanda Locatelli W1
264 Lock Dining Bar, The N17
279 Luciano SW1

M

251 London Marriott West India Quay E14

347 Lonsdale W11

361 Ma Cuisine Le Petit Bistrot RICHMOND UPON THAMES

363 Ma Cuisine Le Petit Bistrot TWICKENHAM

351 Maggiore's WC2

254 Malmaison Charterhouse Square EC1

281 Mandarin Oriental Hyde Park, Foliage SW1

291 Manicomio SW3

266 Manna NW3

348 Matsuri High Holborn WC1

321 Maze W1

257 Mehek EC2

352 Mela WC2

355 Mello BECKENHAM

320 Memories - The Langham Hotel W1

279 Mint Leaf SW1

320 Mirabelle W1

280 Mitsukoshi SW1

282 Mju at Millennium Knightsbridge SW1

339 Momo W5

352 Mon Plaisir WC2

348 Montague on the Gardens, The WC1

263 Morgan M. N7

254 Moro EC1

323 Mosaico W1

303 MVH SW13

N

283 Nahm SW1

291 Nathalie SW3

352 Neal Street Restaurant WC2

323 Nicole's W1

337 Nipa Thai Restaurant W2

324 No 6 Restaurant W1

323 Nobu W1

324 Nobu Berkeley Street W1

346 Notting Hill Brasserie W11

265 Novotel London Euston, Mirrors Restaurant & Bar NW1

291 Nozomi SW3

O

265 Odette's NW1

352 One Aldwych - Axis WC2

353 One Aldwych - Indigo WC2

283 One-O-One SW1

280 Oranger, L' SW1

324 Orrery W1

354 Orso Restaurant WC2

303 Osteria Antica Bologna SW11

300 Osteria dell'Arancio SW10

269 Oxo Tower Restaurant, The SE1

325 Ozer W1

270 Ozu SE1

P

300 Painted Heron, The SW10

272 Palmerston, The SE22

264 Parsee, The N19

325 Passione W1

325 Patterson's W1

348 Pearl Restaurant & Bar WC1

284 Pétrus SW1

326 Pied à Terre W1

251 Plateau E14

270 Pont de la Tour, Le SE1

354 Portrait Restaurant, The WC2

259 Prism Restaurant & Bar EC3

325 Providores, The W1

Q

282 Quaglino's SW1

282 Quirinale SW1

327 Quo Vadis W1

R

291 Racine SW3

302 Ransome's Dock SW11

264 Rasa N16

327 Rasa Samudra W1

327 Rasa W1 W1

292 Rasoi Restaurant SW3

262 Real Greek, The N1

327 Red Fort, The W1

304 Redmond's SW14

260 Refettorio (Crowne Plaza Hotel) EC4

361 Restaurant at The Petersham RICHMOND UPON THAMES

293 Restaurant Gordon Ramsay SW3

259 Restaurant Sauterelle C3

257 Rhodes Twenty Four EC2

285 Rib Room & Oyster Bar, The SW1

361 Richmond Gate Hotel RICHMOND UPON THAMES

328 Ritz, The W1

341 River Café, The W6

258 Rivington Bar & Grill EC2

270 Roast SE1

328 Roka W1

285 Roussillon SW1

356 Royal Chace Hotel ENFIELD

252 Royal China E14

337 Royal China W2

344 Royal Garden Hotel, Tenth Floor Restaurant W8

270 RSJ The Restaurant on the South Bank SE1
285 Rubens at the Palace, The SW1

S

267 Sabras Restaurant NW10
340 Sagar W6
285 Salloos Restaurant SW1
328 Salt Yard W1
338 Sam's Brasserie W4
286 Santini Restaurant SW1
296 Saran Rom SW6
265 Sardo Canale NW1
328 Sartoria W1
354 Savoy Grill WC2
329 Sherlock Holmes Hotel W1
329 Shogun, Millennium Hotel Mayfair W1
358 Simply Nico HEATHROW AIRPORT
267 Singapore Garden Restaurant NW6
330 Sketch (Lecture Room & Library) W1
255 Smiths of Smithfield EC1
340 Snows-on-the-Green Restaurant W6
303 Sonny's Restaurant SW13
329 Soufflé, Le InterContinental London W1
304 Spencer Arms SW15
329 Spiga W1
331 Spoon at Sanderson W1
331 Square, The W1
255 St John EC1
249 St John Bread & Wine E1
286 Stafford Hotel, The SW1
331 Sumosan Restaurant W1
298 Swag and Tails, The SW7

T

304 Talad Thai SW15
332 Taman Gang W1
332 Tamarind W1
258 Tatsuso Restaurant EC2
332 Teca W1
250 Thai Garden, The E2
343 Timo W8
294 Tom Aikens SW3
292 Toto's SW3
250 Trois Garçons, Les E1
338 Trompette, La W4
332 Trouvaille, La W1
295 Tsunami SW4
292 Tugga SW3

U

252 Ubon by Nobu E14
333 Umu W1

V

338 Vacherin, Le W4
302 Vama SW10
333 Vasco & Piero's Pavilion Restaurant W1
333 Veeraswamy Restaurant W1
304 Victoria, The SW14
334 Villandry W1
286 Volt SW1

W

250 Wapping Food E1
266 Wells Tavern, The NW3
356 West Lodge Park Hotel, Cedar Restaurant, The HADLEY WOOD
334 Westbury Hotel W1
261 White Swan Pub & Dining Room, The EC4
286 Wiltons Since 1742 SW1
265 Winter Garden, The NW1
297 Wizzy SW6
334 Wolseley, The W1
287 W'Sens by La Compagnie des Comptoirs SW1

Y

335 Yauatcha W1
297 Yi-Ban Chelsea SW6
335 YMing W1
335 Yumi Restaurant W1

Z

287 Zafferano SW1
345 Zaika W8
298 Zuma SW7

London Plan 1
0 1 2 miles
0 1 2 3 kilometres
Central London Congestion Charging Zone
Charging Zone extension (from February 2007)
Bushey Heath
Totteridge
Highwood Hill
Mill Hill
South Oxhey
Stanmore
Edgware
Northwood
Hatch End
Harrow Weald
Belmont
Burnt Oak
Queensbury
Church End
Pinner
Friends Restaurant
Wealdstone
Colindale
Eastcote Village
Kenton
Kingsbury
Hendon
West Hendon
HARROW
North Harrow
Eastcote
Preston
Golders Green
Rayners Lane
Harrow on the Hill
Ruislip
Barn Hotel
North Wembley
Neasden
Cricklewood
Ickenham
South Harrow
South Ruislip
Sudbury
Northolt Aerodrome
WEMBLEY
Willesden
North Hillingdon
Northolt
Sabras Restaurant
Willesden Green
Stonebridge
Kilburn
Alperton
Perivale
Harlesden
Kensal Green
Park Royal
Hillingdon
Hayes End
Yeading
Greenford
North Acton
Wood End
Momo
North Kensington
E&O
Notting Hill Brasserie
Notting Hill
EALING
Southall
Hanwell
East Acton
Edera
Hayes
Acton
Shepherds Bush
Chez Kristof
Simply Nico
Anglesea Arms
Snows-on-the-Green
Agni
The Brackenbury
Sam's Brasserie & Bar
La Trompette
Sagar
Norwood Green
Chiswick
Devonshire House
HAMMERSMITH
Heston Services
Heston
OSTERLEY PARK
The Gate
Harlington
The River Café
Kew
Brentford
FULHAM
Cranford
Ma Cuisine
Sonny's Restaurant
KEW GARDENS
The Glasshouse
Barnes
HEATHROW AIRPORT
The Depot
Mortlake
Waterfront Brasserie
MVH
Enoteca Turi
Isleworth
HOUNSLOW
Redmond's
Spencer Arms
Talad Thai
East Sheen
Hatton
Putney
RICHMOND
Bingham Hotel, Restaurant & Bar
La Buvette
The Victoria
Richmond Gate Hotel
Ma Cuisine
Brula
Whitton
La Brasserie
Ma Cuisine Bourgeoise
Restaurant at the Petersham
Roehampton
East Bedfont
Twickenham
Petersham
RICHMOND PARK
Feltham
Ham
Lower Feltham
WIMBLEDON COMMON
Ashford
Felthamhill
Hanworth
WIMBLEDON
Hampton Hill
Teddington
The Light House Restaurant
BUSHY PARK
Ayudhya Thai Restaurant
Hampton
Hampton Wick
Charlton
KINGSTON UPON THAMES
Norbiton
New Malden
Raynes Park
Littleton
HAMPTON COURT PARK
The French Table
Berrylands
Motspur Park
Shepperton
Queen Elizabeth II Reservoir
Island Barn Reservoir
Thames Ditton
Surbiton
Walton-on-Thames
Long Ditton
Tolworth
Old Malden
Worcester

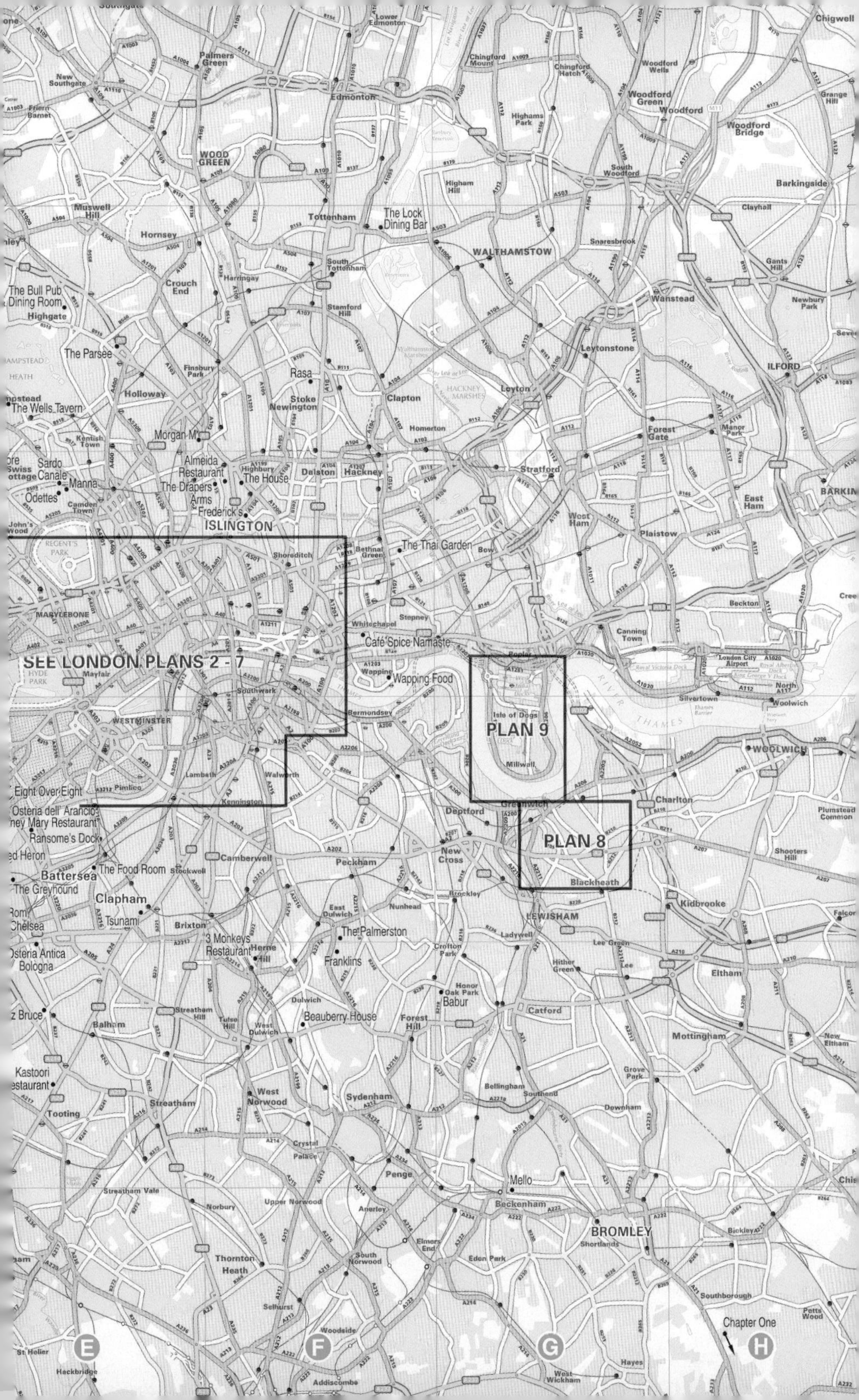

SEE LONDON PLANS 2 - 7
PLAN 9
PLAN 8
Lower Edmonton
Chingford Mount
Chingford Hatch
Chigwell
Palmers Green
New Southgate
Friern Barnet
Edmonton
Highams Park
Woodford Wells
Woodford Green
Woodford
Grange Hill
Woodford Bridge
WOOD GREEN
Higham Hill
South Woodford
Barkingside
Muswell Hill
Hornsey
Tottenham
The Lock Dining Bar
Clayhall
WALTHAMSTOW
Snaresbrook
South Tottenham
Harringay
Crouch End
Gants Hill
The Bull Pub Dining Room
Highgate
Stamford Hill
Wanstead
Newbury Park
The Parsee
Leytonstone
ILFORD
HEATH
Finsbury Park
Rasa
Holloway
Stoke Newington
Clapton
Leyton
The Wells Tavern
Kentish Town
HACKNEY MARSHES
Morgan M
Homerton
Forest Gate
Manor Park
Sardo Canale
Almeida Restaurant
Highbury
The House
Dalston
Hackney
Stratford
Manna
The Drapers Arms
Odettes
Camden Town
Frederick's
East Ham
BARKIN
ISLINGTON
West Ham
Plaistow
REGENT'S PARK
Shoreditch
Bethnal Green
The Thai Garden
Bow
MARYLEBONE
Stepney
Beckton
Whitechapel
Canning Town
Cafe Spice Namaste
Poplar
London City Airport
Royal Victoria Dock
HYDE PARK
Mayfair
Wapping
Wapping Food
RIVER THAMES
North Woolwich
Southwark
Silvertown
Isle of Dogs
WESTMINSTER
Bermondsey
Thames Barrier
Woolwich
Millwall
WOOLWICH
Lambeth
Walworth
Charlton
Eight Over Eight
Pimlico
Kennington
Osteria dell' Arancio
Deptford
Greenwich
Plumstead Common
Ransome's Dock
New Cross
Camberwell
Peckham
Shooters Hill
Battersea
The Food Room
Stockwell
The Greyhound
Blackheath
Brockley
Clapham
Nunhead
Kidbrooke
Chelsea
Tsunami
East Dulwich
LEWISHAM
Brixton
The Palmerston
Ladywell
3 Monkeys Restaurant
Herne Hill
Crofton Park
Lee Green
Osteria Antica Bologna
Franklins
Hither Green
Lee
Eltham
Dulwich
Honor Oak Park
Babur
Balham
Streatham Hill
Tulse Hill
West Dulwich
Beauberry House
Forest Hill
Catford
Mottingham
New Eltham
Kastoori Restaurant
Grove Park
West Norwood
Bellingham
Tooting
Streatham
Sydenham
Southend
Downham
Crystal Palace
Penge
Mello
Streatham Vale
Norbury
Upper Norwood
Anerley
Beckenham
BROMLEY
Bickley
Elmers End
Shortlands
Thornton Heath
South Norwood
Eden Park
Selhurst
Southborough
Petts Wood
Chapter One
Woodside
Hayes
St Helier
Hackbridge
Addiscombe
West Wickham
E
F
G
H

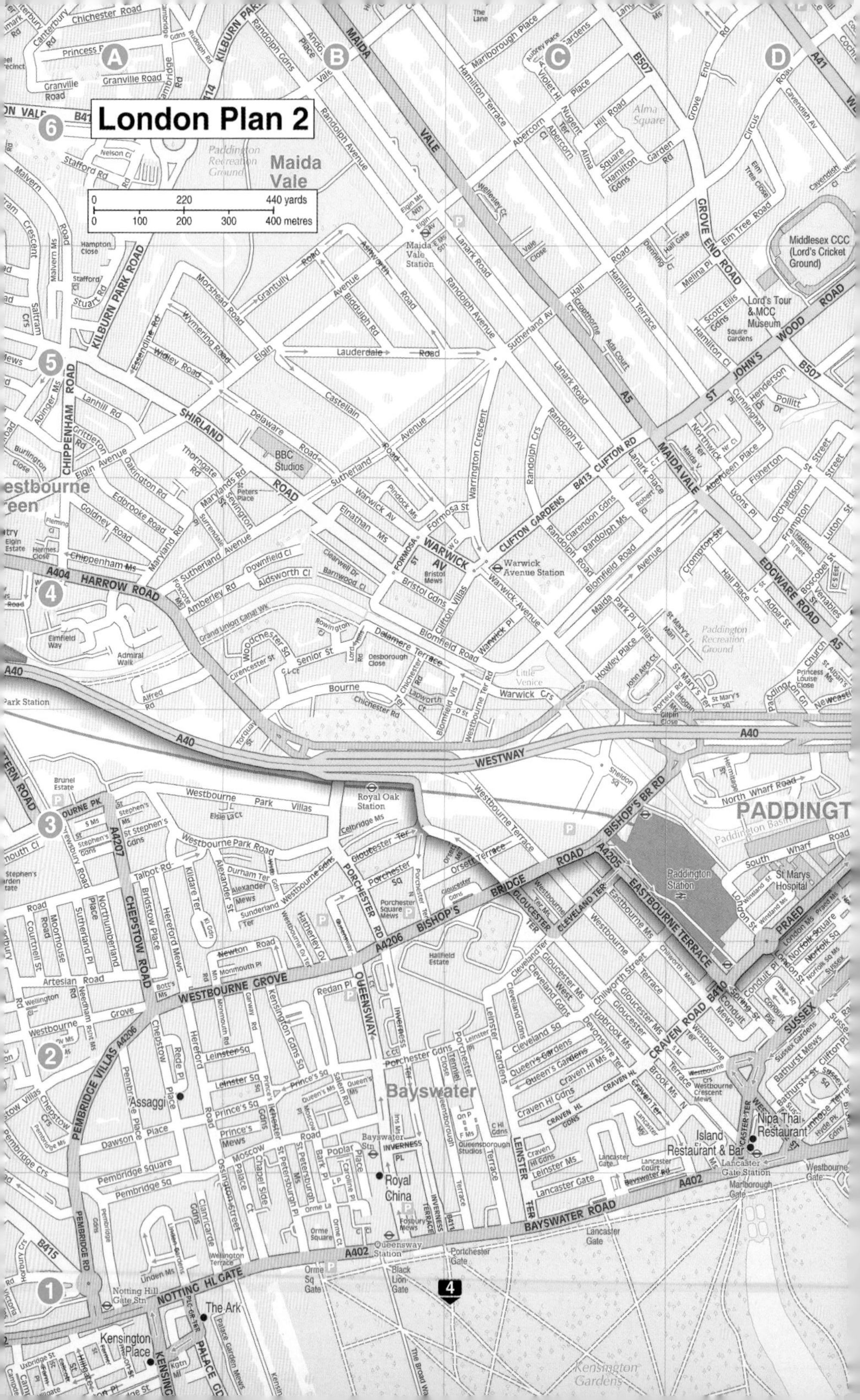

London Plan 2
0
220
440 yards
0
100
200
300
400 metres
A
B
C
D
1
2
3
4
5
6
Maida Vale
Paddington Recreation Ground
Maida Vale Station
Warwick Avenue Station
Royal Oak Station
Paddington Station
Bayswater
Bayswater Stn
Queensway Station
Lancaster Gate Station
Notting Hill Gate Stn
Middlesex CCC (Lord's Cricket Ground)
Lord's Tour & MCC Museum
BBC Studios
Little Venice
Hallfield Estate
Brunel Estate
St Marys Hospital
Paddington Basin
PADDINGT
Kensington Gardens
Assaggi
The Ark
Kensington Place
Royal China
Island Restaurant & Bar
Nipa Thai Restaurant
Westbourne Green
MAIDA VALE
KILBURN PARK ROAD
SHIRLAND ROAD
HARROW ROAD
CHIPPENHAM ROAD
ST JOHN'S WOOD ROAD
GROVE END ROAD
EDGWARE ROAD
CLIFTON GARDENS
CLIFTON RD
WARWICK AV
WESTWAY
A40
A5
A404
A4206
A4207
A4205
A402
B413
B507
B415
BISHOP'S BR RD
BISHOP'S BRIDGE ROAD
EASTBOURNE TERRACE
WESTBOURNE GROVE
PORCHESTER RD
QUEENSWAY
CHEPSTOW ROAD
PEMBRIDGE VILLAS
PEMBRIDGE RD
NOTTING HL GATE
BAYSWATER ROAD
CRAVEN ROAD
PRAED
SUSSEX
LEINSTER TER
INVERNESS TERRACE
Randolph Avenue
Sutherland Avenue
Elgin Avenue
Lauderdale Road
Warrington Crescent
Westbourne Park Road
Westbourne Park Villas
Westbourne Terrace
Porchester Gdns
Pembridge Square
Kensington Gdns Sq
Hamilton Terrace
Abercorn Pl
Blomfield Road
Delamere Terrace
Warwick Crs
North Wharf Road
South Wharf Road
London St
Sussex Gardens
Lancaster Gate
Black Lion Gate
Orme Sq Gate
Porchester Gate
Marlborough Gate
Westbourne Gate
4

E
F
G
H
Regent's Park
Regent's Park
London Central Mosque
Boating Lake
Queen Mary's Garden
Inner Circle
Outer Circle
Chester Road
York Bridge
Clarence Gate
Cumberland Gate
London Business School
Royal Academy of Music
Park Square
Regent's Park Stn
Great Portland St Stn
Madame Tussaud's & The London Planetarium
Baker Street Stn
Marylebone Station
Lisson Grove
MARYLEBONE
MARYLEBONE ROAD
PARK ROAD
PRINCE ALBERT
ALBANY STREET
PORTLAND PL
PK CR
BAKER ST
GLOUCESTER PLACE
DORSET SQ
PADDINGTON ST
YORK ST
EDGWARE ROAD A5
OLD MARYLEBONE RD
CHAPEL ST
Edgware Road Stn
WIGMORE STREET
CAVENDISH PL
OXFORD ST
Bond Street Stn
Marble Arch Station
Marble Arch
CUMBERLAND GATE
PARK LA
PARK LANE
NEW BOND STREET
PORTMAN SQUARE
ORCHARD ST
Grosvenor Square
Mayfair
Hyde Park
Speakers Corner
Stanhope Gate
North Carriage Drive
Brook Gate
Grosvenor Gate
Albion Gate
Clarendon Gate
Winter Garden (The Landmark)
Dorset Square Hotel
Sherlock Holmes Hotel
Galvin-Bistrot de Luxe
The Providores
Blandford Street
No. 6 Restaurant & Shop
Yumi Restaurant
Orrery
Memories – The Langham Hotel
Villandry
Levant
Crescent Restaurant at The Montcalm Nikko London
Locanda Locatelli
Deya (Mostyn Hotel)
The Cumberland
Rasa W1
Sketch (Room &
Taman Gang
London Marriott Grosvenor Square
Teca
Gordon Ramsay at Claridge's
Maze
Cipriani
Millennium Hotel Mayfair
Berkeley Square Café
Umu
Bellamy's
Pattersons
Le Gavroche Restaurant
Angela Hartnett at The Connaught
Benares
The Square
Sumosan
Automat
Nobu Berkeley
Kai Mayfair
Butlers
The Greenhouse
Mirabelle
China Tang & The Grill Room
Emb of USA
3
3
4
Congestion Charging Zone boundary
Congestion Zone extension boundary (from February 2007)

London Plan 3
0
220
440 yards
0
100
200
300
400 metres
A
B
C
D
Regent's Park
Somers Town
St Pancras
Bloomsbury
St Giles
Soho
China Town
Strand
Mayfair
Euston Station
St Pancras Station
King's Cross Station
King's Cross Thameslink Stn
British Library
Novotel London Euston
University Coll.Hosp
Euston Square Station
Warren Street Stn
Great Portland St Stn
University College London
Birkbeck Coll
Uni of London
British Museum
The Montague on the Gardens
Russell Square Station
National Hosp for Sick Children (Great Ormond St)
Coram's Fields Playground
Archipelago
Villandry
Salt Yard
Goodge St Station
Pied à Terre
Fino
Roka
Passione
Camerino
Rasa Samudra
Bam-Bou
Latium
Ozer
Spoon+ at Sanderson
Hakkasan
Jurys Great Russell Street
Tottenham Court Road Stn
ST GILES CIRCUS
Holborn Station
Pearl Res & B
Oxford Circus Station
Vasco & Piero's Pavilion Restaurant
Rasa W1
The Red Fort
Quo Vadis
L'Escargot
Spiga
Alastair Little
Yauatcha
La Trouvaille
Incognico
Mela
SEVEN DIALS
CAMBRIDGE CIRCUS
Mon Plaisir
Neal Street Restaurant
Royal Opera House
Covent Garden Station
Sketch (Lecture Room & Library)
Kilo
Pattersons
Lindsay House
YMing
The Ivy
Imperial China
Leicester Square Stn
Maggiore's
Orso Restaurant
Christophe
One Aldwych Axis & Indigo
Bank Aldwych Restaurant & Ba
The Westbury Hotel
Sartoria
Umu
Bellamy's
Nicole's
The Square
Embassy
Cecconi's
Sumosan
Veeraswamy Restaurant
Le Meridien Piccadilly - The Terrace
Piccadilly Circus Stn
Cocoon
J. Sheekey
Asia de Cuba
The Admiralty Restaurant
The Savoy
Benares
The Grill (Brown's)
Royal Academy of Arts
Bentley's Oyster Bar & Grill
Frankie's at Criterion
Mitsukoshi
National Gallery
National Portrait Gal
The Portrait Restaurant
Automat
Alloro
Mosaico
Nobu Berkeley
Trafalgar Square
Mint Leaf
Charing Cross Stn
Embankment Station
Victoria Embankment Gardens
Al Duca
Brasserie Roux
The Wolseley
Wiltons Since 1742
Franco's
Albannach
The Ritz
Quaglino's
W'Sens by La Compagnie
EUSTON ROAD
TOTTENHAM COURT RD
GOWER ST
OXFORD STREET (restricted)
REGENT STREET
CHARING CROSS RD
SHAFTESBURY AV
PICCADILLY
PALL MALL
STRAND
HIGH HOLBORN
NEW OXFORD ST
BLOOMSBURY WY
SOUTHAMPTON ROW
WOBURN PLACE
RUSSELL SQ
GREAT PORTLAND ST
PORTLAND PLACE
HAMPSTEAD RD
GUILFORD ST
PENTONVILLE RD
GRAY'S INN RD
NEW BOND STREET
CONDUIT ST
KINGSWAY
VICTORIA EMBANKMENT
2
5

Congestion Charging Zone boundary
E
F
G
H
6
5
4
3
2
1
7
9
5
FINSBURY
Clerkenwell
St Luke's
CITY OF
LONDON
River Thames
PENTONVILLE ROAD
A501
CITY ROAD
GOSWELL ROAD
ROSEBERY AVENUE
FARRINGDON ROAD
CLERKENWELL ROAD
OLD STREET
A5201
LEVER STREET
B502
BUNHILL ROW
CHISWELL
BEECH ST (B FLOW)
A1 ALDERSGATE ST
HOLBORN
HIGH HOLBORN
HOLBORN VIAD
NEWGATE ST
A40
FLEET ST
STRAND
VICTORIA EMB
UPPER THAMES ST
QUEEN ST PLACE
SOUTHWARK BRIDGE ROAD
NEW BRIDGE STREET
FARRINGDON STREET
A201
A3200
LONDON WALL
A1211
CHANCERY LA
HATTON GARDEN
ST JOHN ST
Moro
Mount Pleasant (Postal Sorting Office)
Clerkenwell Dining Room
Malmaison Charterhouse Square
Le Café du Marché
St John
Farringdon Station
Smiths of Smithfield
The Bleeding Heart
Comptoir Gascon
Club Gascon
Central London Mkts
St Bartholomews Hospital
The Barbican
Barbican Station
Moorfields Eye Hospital
Fifteen
Chancery Lane Stn
The Chancery
White Swan Pub & Dining Room
Lincoln's Inn
Gray's Inn
Royal Courts of Justice
Inns of Court and Chancery
City Thameslink Station
Central Criminal Court
Stock Exchange
St Paul's Station
St Paul's Cathedral
Guildhall
Mansion House Station
Bank
1 Lombard Street
Novelli in the City
Cannon Street Stn
Reffetorio
Blackfriars Station
Blackfriars Stn
Blackfriars Bridge
Millennium Bridge
Southwark Bridge
Temple Stn
Moorgate Stn
Old Station
The Oxo Tower Restaurant
Oxo Tower Wharf
The London Television Centre (LWT)
Royal National Theatre
National Film Theatre
Shakespeare's Globe Exhibition & Theatre
Tate Modern
Cantina, Vinopolis
Ludgate Circus
Holborn Circus
Postman Park
Golden Lane Estate
Finsbury Estate
St Luke's Estate
Provost Estate

London Plan 4
KENSINGTON
South Kensington
Earl's Court
West Brompton
Kensington Gardens
Round Pond
Kensington Palace
BAYSWATER ROAD
NOTTING HL GATE
KENSINGTON CHURCH ST
KENSINGTON HIGH ST
KENSINGTON ROAD
HYDE PARK GATE
KENSINGTON GORE
CROMWELL ROAD
OLD BROMPTON ROAD
FULHAM ROAD
EARL'S COURT ROAD
WARWICK ROAD
PEMBROKE ROAD
REDCLIFFE GARDENS
FINBOROUGH ROAD
GLOUCESTER ROAD
PALACE GDNS TER
PALACE GA
A402
A4204
A315
A4
A3218
A3220
A308
B405
B316
B304
B415
Royal China
Queensway Station
Notting Hill Gate Stn
The Ark
Kensington Place
Clarke's
Royal Garden Hotel
Zaika
Cheneston's Restaurant
Brunello
Babylon
High Street Kensington Stn
Kensington & Chelsea Town Hall
11 Abingdon Road
Launceston Place Restaurant
L'Etranger
Royal College of Art
Royal Albert Hall
Royal Geographical Soc
Royal College of Music
Imperial College
Science Museum
Natural History Museum
Earth Galleries
Albert Memorial
Cromwell Hospital
Gloucester Rd Stn
South Kensington Station
Earl's Court Station
Earl's Court Exhibition Centre
West Brompton Station
The Bentley Kempinski Hotel
Cafe Lazeez
Cambio De Tercio
Le Colombier
Aubergine
Bluebird Dining Room
1
2
3
4
5
6
A
B
C
D
2

Hyde Park
Knightsbridge
Mayfair
Belgravia
Brompton
The Serpentine
Green Park
Buckingham Palace
Victoria Station
Congestion Charging Zone boundary
Congestion Zone extension boundary (from February 2007)
0 220 440 yards
0 100 200 300 400 metres

London Plan 5
Nicole's
The Square
Sumosan
Embassy
Cecconi's
Le Meridien Piccadilly
Veeraswamy
Benares
Mayfair
Automat
Alloro
Mosaico
Nobu Berkeley
Academy of Arts
Bentley's Oyster Bar & Grill
Cocoon
Frankie's at Criterion
Mitsukoshi
Piccadilly Circus Stn
Asia de Cuba
Strand
The Admiralty Restaurant
The Savoy
National Portrait Gal
National Gallery
The Portrait Restaurant
Trafalgar Square
Charing Cross Stn
Embankment Station
Victoria Embankment Gardens
Mint Leaf
Al Duca
Brasserie Roux
Wiltons Since 1742
Franco's
The Wolseley
The Ritz
Quaglino's
Le Caprice
Just St James
L'Oranger
The Stafford
Luciano
The Avenue
W'Sens by La Compagnie des Comptoirs
Albannach
Admiralty Arch
Old Admiralty
Green Park Station
Horse Guards Parade
Banqueting House
Ministry of Defence
St James's
St James's Palace
Clarence House
Lancaster House
Inn the Park
Green Park
London Eye
Dali Universe
London Aquarium
Foreign & Commonwealth Office
Treasury
Churchill Museum & Cabinet War Rooms
St James's Park
Buckingham Palace
Buckingham Palace Gardens
Portcullis House
Westminster Station
Westminster Bridge
Guards' Chapel & Museum
Home Office
St James's Park Stn
New Scotland Yard
Westminster Abbey
Houses of Parliament
St Thomas' Hospital
The Royal Mews
The Rubens at the Palace
The Goring
Westminster School
Victoria Tower Gardens
The Cinnamon Club
Quirinale
Westminster Cathedral
WESTMINSTER
Victoria Station
Lambeth Bridge
Westminster Sch Playing Field
Millbank Estate
Tate Britain
Lillington Gardens Estate
Pimlico
Pimlico Station
Vauxhall Bridge
Vauxhall
Vauxhall Station
River Thames
Pimlico Gardens
Churchill Gardens
Grosvenor Bridge
PICCADILLY
PALL MALL
WHITEHALL
PARLIAMENT ST
ABINGDON STREET
MILLBANK
HORSEFERRY ROAD
MARSHAM STREET
VICTORIA STREET
BUCKINGHAM GATE
VAUXHALL BRIDGE ROAD
BELGRAVE ROAD
GROSVENOR ROAD
ALBERT EMBANKMENT
WESTMINSTER BRIDGE RD
A B C D

CITY OF LONDON
River Thames
Millennium Bridge
Blackfriars Bridge
Southwark Bridge
Waterloo Bridge
Oxo Tower Wharf
The Oxo Tower Restaurant
Shakespeare's Globe Exhibition & Theatre
Tate Modern
Bankside
The London Television Centre (LWT)
Royal National Theatre
National Film Theatre
RSJ, The Restaurant on the South Bank
IMAX Cinema
Cantina, Vinopolis
Roast
Glas
Anchor & Hope
Baltic
The Fire Station
Waterloo East Stn
Southwark Station
International Rail Terminal
Waterloo Station
Lambeth North Stn
LAMBETH
ST GEORGE'S CIRCUS
South Bank University
Imperial War Museum
Geraldine Mary Harmsworth Park
Newington
Newington Gardens
Elephant and Castle Stn
London College of Communication
The Borough
Borough Stn
Kennington Station
Surrey Cricket Club (The Oval)
Walworth
Faraday Gardens
STAMFORD ST
SOUTHWARK STREET
UNION STREET
THE CUT
BLACKFRIARS ROAD
WATERLOO ROAD
WESTMINSTER BR RD
BOROUGH ROAD
LONDON ROAD
ST GEORGE'S RD
LAMBETH ROAD
KENNINGTON ROAD
KENNINGTON LANE
KENNINGTON PARK ROAD
NEWINGTON BUTTS
NEW KENT ROAD
WALWORTH ROAD
BOROUGH HIGH ST
SOUTHWARK BRIDGE ROAD
MARSHALSEA RD
GREAT DOVER ST
A3200
A201
A23
A3
A302
A3202
A3204
A215
B300
3
6
5
4
3
2
1
E
F
G
H
Congestion Charging Zone boundary
Congestion Zone extension boundary (from February 2007)
0
220
440 yards
0
100
200
300
400 metres

London Plan 6
SPITALFIELDS
The Barbican
Guildhall
Bank of England (& Mus)
Royal Exchange
Mansion House Station
Cannon Street Stn
Liverpool Street Station
Liverpool St Stn
Broadgate
Tower 42
Rhodes Twentyfour
Lloyd's
Swiss Re Insurance Tower
Fenchurch Street Stn
Tower Gateway Stn
Tower Hill Stn
Tower of London
St Katharine Docks
Tower Bridge
HMS Belfast
Hays Galleria
Greater London Authority Headquarters (City Hall)
London Bridge
London Bridge Hospital
London Bridge Station
Guys Hospital
Southwark Cath
Southwark Bridge
Millennium Bridge
Custom House
Old Spitalfields Market Hall
Monument Stn
Borough Stn
The Borough
Tabard Garden
St Paul's Station
Mehek
Tatsuso Restaurant
Lanes Restaurant & Bar
Boisdale of Bishopsgate
Aurora & Fishmarket at Great Eastern Hotel
Canteen
St John Bread & Wine
Bonds
Prism Restaurant & Bar
Restaurant Sauterelle
1 Lombard Street
Novelli in the City
Chamberlains Restaurant
Cantina, Vinopolis
Roast
Glas
Champor Champor
Butlers Wharf Chop House
Le Pont de la Tour
Cantina del Ponte
CITY ROAD
MOORGATE
LONDON WALL
BISHOPSGATE
SHOREDITCH HIGH ST
COMMERCIAL STREET
CHISWELL ST
FINSBURY SQ
GRACECHURCH ST
KG WILLIAM ST
UPPER THAMES ST
LWR THAMES ST
TOWER HILL
MINORIES
HOUNDSDITCH
CAMOMILE ST
ALDGATE HIGH ST
WHITECHAPEL HIGH ST
MANSELL ST
SOUTHWARK BRIDGE ROAD
BOROUGH HIGH ST
TOOLEY STREET
ST THOMAS ST
DUKE ST HL
BERMONDSEY STREET
TOWER BR APPROACH
LONG LANE
GREAT DOVER STREET
MARSHALSEA RD
A1 ALDERSGATE ST
A
B
C
D
1
2
3
4
5
6
Congestion Charging Zone boundary
0 220 440 yards
0 100 200 300 400 metres

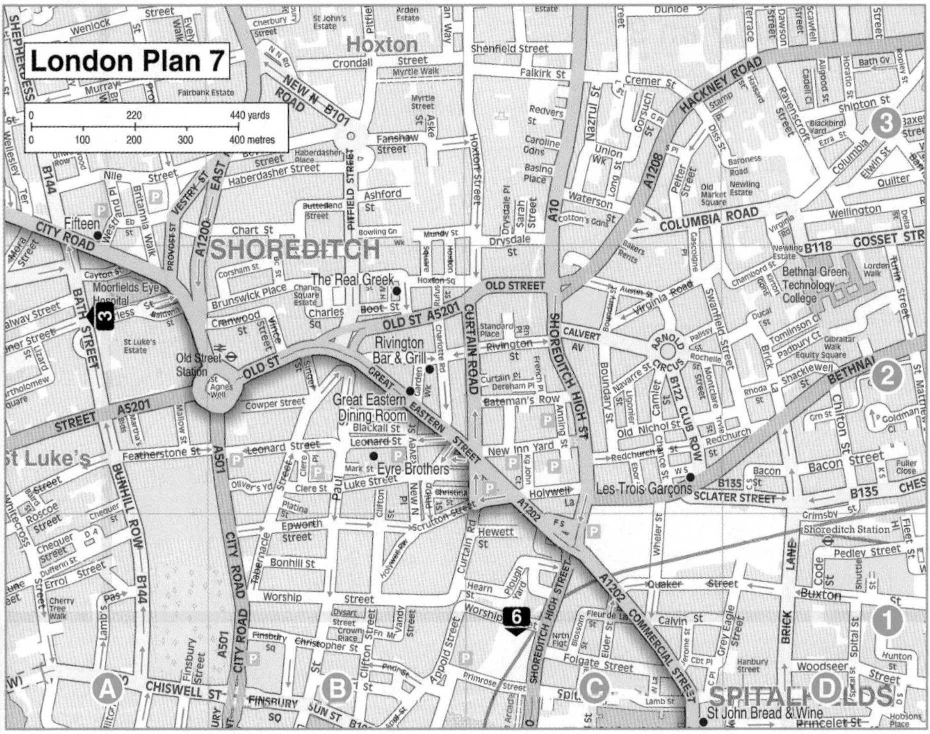

London Plan 7

0 220 440 yards
0 100 200 300 400 metres

Hoxton

SHOREDITCH

St Luke's

SPITALFIELDS

Fifteen

Moorfields Eye Hospital

Old Street Station

The Real Greek

Rivington Bar & Grill

Great Eastern Dining Room

Eyre Brothers

Les Trois Garçons

Bethnal Green Technology College

Shoreditch Station

St John Bread & Wine

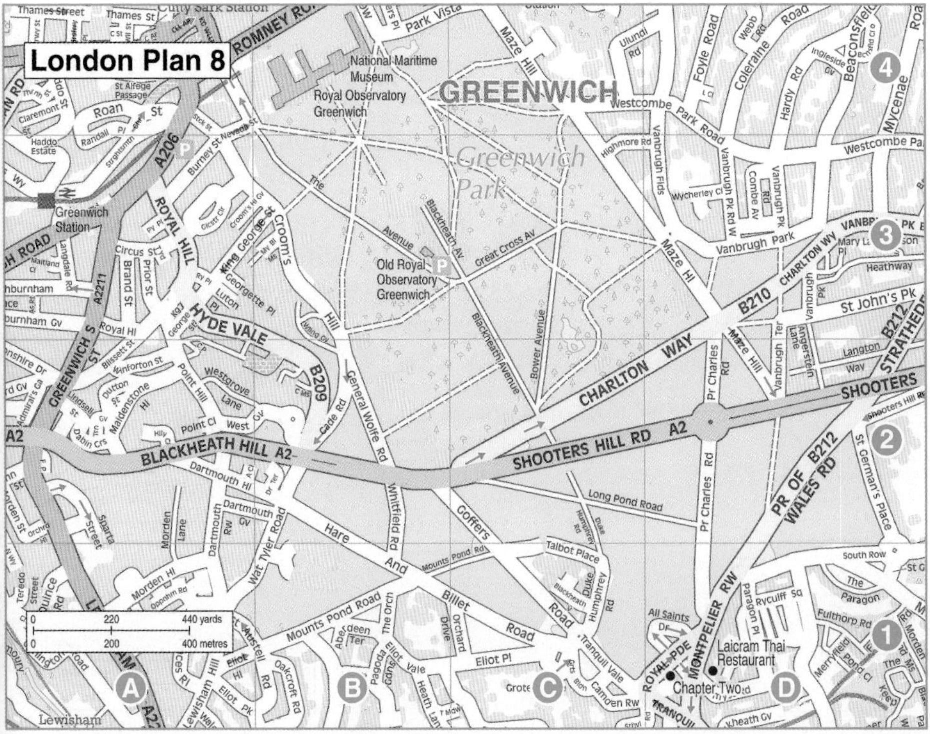

London Plan 8

GREENWICH

Greenwich Park

National Maritime Museum

Royal Observatory Greenwich

Old Royal Observatory Greenwich

Greenwich Station

Cutty Sark Station

Laicram Thai Restaurant

Chapter Two

Lewisham

0 220 440 yards
0 200 400 metres

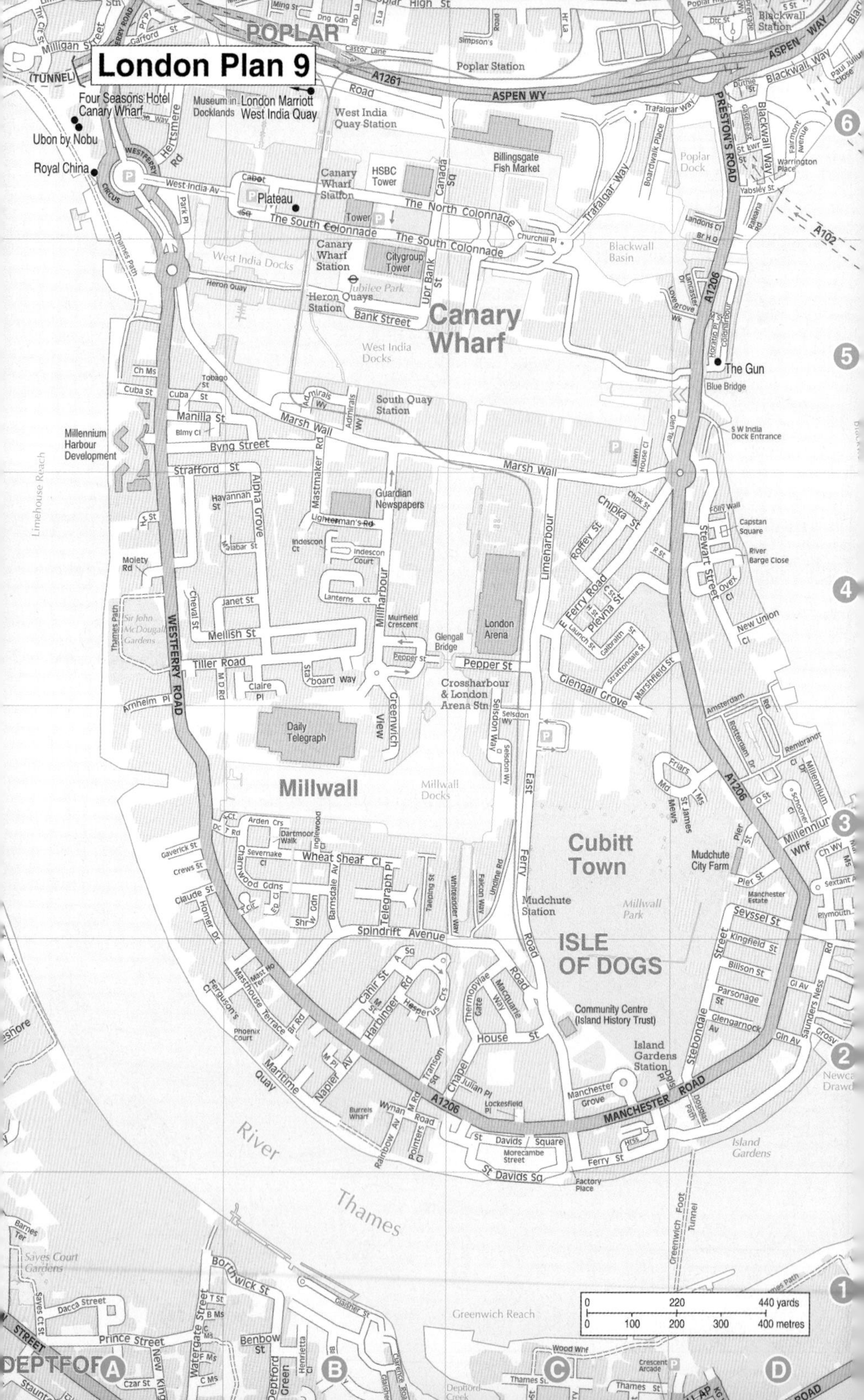

London Plan 9
POPLAR
(TUNNEL)
Milligan St
Garford St
Poplar High Street
Castor Lane
A1261
ASPEN WY
ASPEN WAY
Blackwall Station
Blackwall Way
Poplar Station
Simpson's Rd
Four Seasons Hotel Canary Wharf
Ubon by Nobu
Royal China
Museum in Docklands
London Marriott West India Quay
West India Quay Station
WESTFERRY CIRCUS
Hertsmere Rd
West India Av
Cabot Sq
Plateau
Canary Wharf Station
HSBC Tower
Tower
Canada Sq
Billingsgate Fish Market
Trafalgar Way
Boardwalk Place
Poplar Dock
PRESTON'S ROAD
The North Colonnade
The South Colonnade
Churchill Pl
Citygroup Tower
Park Pl
West India Docks
Heron Quay
Heron Quays Station
Jubilee Park
Upr Bank St
Bank Street
Canary Wharf
Blackwall Basin
A1206
A102
Yabsley St
Warrington Place
Fairmont Avenue
Landons Cl
Lancaster Dr
Lovegrove Wk
Horatio Pl
Coldharbour
The Gun
Blue Bridge
S W India Dock Entrance
Thames Path
Ch Ms
Cuba St
Tobago St
Admirals Wy
South Quay Station
Manilla St
Marsh Wall
Millennium Harbour Development
Blmy Cl
Byng Street
Strafford St
Limehouse Reach
Mastmaker Rd
Guardian Newspapers
Havannah St
Alpha Grove
Lighterman's Rd
Indescon Ct
Indescon Court
Malabar St
Moiety Rd
Limeharbour
London Arena
Chipka St
Roffey St
Folly Wall
Capstan Square
River Barge Close
Stewart Street
Overx Cl
Lanterns Ct
Millharbour
Janet St
Cheval St
Mellish St
Sir John McDougall Gardens
WESTFERRY ROAD
Muirfield Crescent
Glengall Bridge
Pepper St
Tiller Road
M D Rd
Starboard Way
Claire Pl
Arnheim Pl
Crossharbour & London Arena Stn
Selsdon Way
Selsdon Wy
Greenwich View
E Ferry Road
Plevna St
Launch St
Galbraith St
Strattondale St
Marshfield St
Glengall Grove
New Union Cl
Amsterdam Rd
Rotterdam Dr
Rembrandt Cl
Daily Telegraph
Millwall
Millwall Docks
East Ferry Road
Friars Mead
St James Mews
Millennium Dr
Schooner Cl
O St
Millennium Whf
Arden Crs
Dartmoor Walk
Inglewood Cl
Gaverick St
Severnake Cl
Wheat Sheaf Cl
Crews St
Charnwood Gdns
Claude St
Homer Dr
Barnsdale Av
Telegraph Pl
Taeping St
Whiteadder Way
Falcon Way
Undine Rd
Cubitt Town
Mudchute City Farm
Pier St
Manchester Estate
Sextant Av
Mudchute Station
Millwall Park
Seyssel St
Kingfield St
Spindrift Avenue
ISLE OF DOGS
Billson St
Parsonage St
Glengarnock Av
Saunders Ness Rd
Cahir St
Harbinger Rd
Hesperus Crs
Masthouse Terrace
Ferguson's Cl
Mast Ho Ter
Thermopylae Gate
Macquarie Way
Community Centre (Island History Trust)
Stebondale Street
Phoenix Court
Maritime Quay
Napier Av
Transom Sq
House St
Chapel
Julian Pl
Island Gardens Station
Manchester Grove
MANCHESTER ROAD
Douglas Path
Gln Av
Burrells Wharf
Wynan Rd
M Rd
Road
Lockesfield Pl
River Thames
Rainbow Av
Pointers Cl
St Davids Square
Morecambe Street
Ferry St
Island Gardens
St Davids Sq
Factory Place
Greenwich Foot Tunnel
Barnes Ter
Sayes Court Gardens
Borthwick St
Sayes Ct St
Dacca Street
Glaisher St
Greenwich Reach
Prince Street
Watergate Street
Benbow St
New King
DEPTFORD
STREET
Czar St
Henrietta Cl
Deptford Green
Clarence Road
Deptford Creek
Wood Whf
Thames St
Crescent Arcade
Thames St
ROAD
0 220 440 yards
0 100 200 300 400 metres
A
B
C
D
1
2
3
4
5
6

LONDON

Greater London Plans 1-9, pages 236-248. (Small-scale maps 6 & 7 at back of guide.) Restaurants are listed below in postal district order, commencing East, then North, South and West, with a brief indication of the area covered. Detailed plans 2-9 show the locations of restaurants with AA Rosette Awards within the Central London postal districts. If you do not know the postal district of the restaurant you want, please refer to the index preceding the street plans for the entry and map pages. The Plan reference for each restaurant also appears within its directory entry.

LONDON E1

Café Spice Namasté

Pan-Asian

Authentic Indian café dining

☎ 020 7488 9242 16 Prescot St E1 8AZ Plan 1-F4
e-mail: binay@cafespice.co.uk
web: www.cafespice.co.uk

Found in a rather unusual location, the restaurant occupies an early 19th-century Grade II listed building formerly a magistrates court. Namasté means a gracious hello, and you'll certainly be received like an old friend here. The speciality menu changes fortnightly, and this together with an extensive and well-annotated carte offers unusual dishes from all over Asia, often with European influences. The menu is helpfully coded to show the level of spice and which dishes are vegetarian or Halal, or contain nuts or gluten. Typical dishes include choris javali (Goan king prawn curry) and desserts like Parsee apricot and toffee ice cream.

Chef: Cyrus Todiwala **Owners:** Cafe Spice Ltd **Times:** 12-3/6.15-10.30, Closed Xmas, BHs, Sun, Closed L Sat **Prices:** Fixed L fr £25, Fixed D fr £30, Starter £3.25-£7.95, Main £10.50-£16.95, Dessert £3.50-£4.75, Coffee £1.50, Min/Water £2.50, Service added but optional 12.5% **Wine:** 19 bottles over £20, 16 bottles under £20, 11 by the glass (£3.95-£5.25) **Notes:** Weekly speciality menu, Vegetarian available, Dress Restrictions, Smart casual **Seats:** 120 **Smoking:** Air con **Children:** Portions **Directions:** Nearest station: Tower Gateway (DLR), Aldgate East, Tower Hill Walking distance from Tower Hill **Parking:** On street; NCP

Canteen

British NEW

All-day eatery in Spitalfields

☎ 0845 686 1122 2 Crispin Place, Spitalfields E1 6DW
Plan 6-D6
e-mail: info@canteen.co.uk
web: www.canteen.co.uk

Inside the new Spitalfield's Market development, Canteen - a contemporary, near cube of glass - serves an all-day menu. The well-designed, informal space offers booth seating around walls and, in the centre, a long shared table, while a semi-open kitchen catches the eye. It's modern and sleek, with lightwood tables and linen napkins. The same lengthy, good-value, all-day menu includes breakfast items, designated 'fast service' dishes and there's a daily roast, in-house

continued

baked pies and fish options. The produce is well sourced and food is accurately cooked in a straightforward style with clear flavours. Mealtime favourites could take in rib-eye steak with anchovy butter, or lamb and pearl barley stew, while desserts are equally homely, perhaps treacle tart with Jersey cream.

Chef: Cass Titcombe **Owners:** Patrick Clayton-Malone, Dom Lake **Times:** 11/11, Closed 25-26 Dec **Prices:** Fixed D £17-£25.50, Starter £2-£7.50, Main £7-£12.50, Dessert £5, Coffee £2, Min/Water £2, Service added but optional 12.5% **Wine:** 22 bottles over £20, 10 bottles under £20, 22 by the glass (£3.25-£10) **Notes:** Vegetarian available **Seats:** 120 **Smoking:** N/Sm in restaurant, Air con **Children:** Portions **Directions:** Nearest station: Liverpool Street Overlooking Spitalfields Market

Lanes Restaurant & Bar

Modern European

Fashionable venue meets modern European cuisine

☎ 020 7247 5050 109-117 Middlesex St E1 7JF
Plan 6-C5
e-mail: info@lanesrestaurant.co.uk
web: www.lanesrestaurant.co.uk

This stylish but informal and fashionable basement restaurant - at the foot of an office block - comes decked out with wooden floors and panelling, cream high-backed chairs and leather banquettes, and walls adorned with bright modern prints. There's a lively inviting bar with high stalls and sofas, too (perfect for aperitifs or a wind-down drink), while the accomplished modern-brasserie approach to the cooking fits the bill admirably. Expect crisp, clean dishes with plenty of flavour using quality ingredients, perhaps from the pasta options, tagliolini of courgettes and lemon butter, alternatively, maybe sea bass fillet served with a fennel fondant and lobster and saffron mash. (Light meals can also be enjoyed in the bar.)

Chef: Simon Conboy **Owners:** James Robertson & Hamish Smith **Times:** 12-3/5.30-10, Closed BHs, 25 Dec, 1 Jan, Sun, Closed L Sat **Prices:** Fixed D £21.50, Starter £6.50-£13.50, Main £9.95-£19.95, Dessert £6.50-£8.50, Coffee £2.75, Min/Water £3.50, Service added but optional 12.5% **Wine:** 55 bottles over £20, 6 bottles under £20, 14 by the glass (£3.95-£8.25) **Notes:** Vegetarian available **Seats:** 70, Pr/dining room 28 **Smoking:** Air con **Children:** Min 7 yrs L, Portions **Parking:** On street after 6.30 pm

St John Bread & Wine

British

Unpretentious restaurant, bakery and wine shop in old Clerkenwell

☎ 020 7251 0848 94-96 Commercial St E1 6LZ
Plan 6-D6
e-mail: reservations@stjohnbreadandwine.com
web: www.stjohnbreadandwine.com

Tucked behind the old Spitalfields Market, this no-frills sibling to big brother St John (see entry) is a resolutely British affair. Whitewashed walls, parquet flooring and simple wooden tables and chairs set a wholly unpretentious, utilitarian edge. The drawcard British food is flavour-driven and unfussy, using quality produce while delivering some earthy dishes using humble ingredients; take chitterlings with dandelion and bacon, or devilled kidneys and mash. Service, by staff clad in long white aprons, is attentive, friendly and informed, while wines, like the wonderful breads, are on sale to take out.

Times: 9/11, Closed 24 Dec-2 Jan, BHs, Closed D Sun

England

LONDON E1 *continued*

Les Trois Garçons

Modern French

Playful, warm and atmospheric French restaurant

☎ 020 7613 1924 1 Club Row E1 6JX Plan 7-C2
e-mail: info@lestroisgarcons.com
web: www.lestroisgarcons.com

Expect the unexpected at this former Victorian corner pub. Step inside to find a fascinating French restaurant, with a glitzy, jaw-dropping interior décor, surreally packed with all manner of objets d'art, from dangling chandeliers and handbags to a menagerie of bejewelled stuffed creatures. A lighthearted place in which to sample some rich, well-presented classic French cooking. Typically, tuck into a starter of foie gras encased in caramel with braised endive and orange emulsion, followed by pan-seared loin of wild venison with roasted red onion and coffee jus, with apple tarte Tatin with caramel sauce to finish.

Chef: Daniel Phippard **Owners:** Stefan Karlson, Hussan Abdullah, Michel Lasserre **Times:** 12-4/7-12, Closed Sun **Prices:** Fixed L £22, Fixed D £26, Starter £9-£14, Main £18-£22, Dessert £7-£8, Min/Water £3.75, Service added but optional 12.5% **Wine:** 130 bottles over £20, 6 bottles under £20, 16 by the glass (£5.50-£9) **Notes:** Vegetarian available **Seats:** 80, Pr/dining room 12 **Smoking:** Air con **Children:** Min 12 yrs **Directions:** Nearest station: Liverpool Street 10mins walk from station, at the end of Brick Ln **Parking:** On street after 7pm

Wapping Food

Modern International

Inspired cooking meets industrial heritage at the Wapping Project

☎ 020 7680 2080 Wapping Hydraulic, Power Station, Wapping Wall E1W 3ST Plan 1-F4
e-mail: info@wapping-wpt.com
web: www.thewappingproject.com

The conversion of this former East End hydraulic pumping station into a restaurant and gallery makes an intriguing setting. Old machinery, brick, tiles and iron girders are set juxtaposed with dangling chandeliers, modern minimalist furniture, flickering candles and a backing track of haunting heavenly music. The cooking more than lives up to the billing though, with a daily-changing repertoire of inspired modern international cooking, based around high-quality ingredients, imaginative combinations and skilful delivery. Expect the likes of roast sea bream with green beans, artichokes and a green olive tapenade, with attentive and informed service, and an excellent range of Australian wines.

continued

Chef: Cameron Emiroli **Owners:** Womens Playhouse Trust **Times:** 12-3/6.30-11, Closed 24 Dec-3 Jan, Closed D Sun **Prices:** Starter £5-£10, Main £12.75-£17.50, Dessert £5.50-£6, Coffee £2, Min/Water £3, Service added but optional 12.5% **Wine:** 73 bottles over £20, 9 bottles under £20, 18 by the glass (£4.50-£8) **Notes:** 3 course menu for 9+ £242.50, Vegetarian available **Seats:** 100 **Smoking:** No pipes, No cigars **Children:** Portions **Directions:** Nearest station: Wapping Turn right from tube, walk east & parallel to the river (approx 4 mins) **Parking:** 20

Café Naz

☎ 020 7247 0234 46-48 Brick Ln E1 6RF
Smart Bangladeshi with a touch of sophistication.

Lilly's

☎ 020 7702 2040 75 Wapping High St E1W 2YN
web: www.theaa.com/restaurants/113949.html
A real local crowd pleaser, this neighbourhood restaurant offers classic American brasserie-style dishes; a selection of starters, dishes from the grill, platters to share, mains from the kitchen, sandwiches and salads, and daily changing lunch specials.

One Blossom Street

☎ 020 7247 6532 1 Blossom St E1 6BX
Stylish restaurant with simple but effective Italian food and a good wine list.

LONDON E2

The Thai Garden

Thai V

Authentic vegetarian Thai restaurant

☎ 020 8981 5748 249 Globe Rd E2 0JD Plan 1-F4
e-mail: thaigarden@hotmail.com
web: www.thethaigarden.co.uk

The authentic vegetarian and seafood Thai cuisine here is the real deal, despite its unlikely setting in Bethnal Green. The unpretentious shop-front bistro gives way to a small dining room with 20 seats. The cooking is fragrant with some serious chillis, so be prepared - or go for dishes with fragrant herb flavours as a gentler option on the tongue. The menu is in Thai and English and sticks to vegetarian and seafood dishes with a wide choice and unique, flavoursome options. Try something like Gang Phed Ped Yang Jay for some interesting combinations: Thai aubergines, fried gluten (vegetarian mock duck meat), pineapples, tomatoes, grapes, bamboo shoots and sweet basil leaves, all served in red curry with coconut cream.

Chef: Napathorn Duff **Owners:** S & J Hufton **Times:** 12-2.30/6-11, Closed BHs, Closed L Sat & Sun **Prices:** Food prices not confirmed for 2007. Please telephone for details **Wine:** all bottles under £20, 2 by the glass (£2.25) **Notes:** Vegetarian menu **Seats:** 32, Pr/dining room 12 **Smoking:** N/Sm area **Children:** Portions **Directions:** Nearest station: Bethnal Green 2nd left off Roman Rd (one-way street). Near London Buddhist Centre **Parking:** on street

Hanoi Cafe

☎ 020 7729 5610 98 Kingsland Rd E2 8DP
web: www.theaa.com/restaurants/114002.html

Choose from over 100 freshly home-made Vietnamese dishes in a buzzy atmosphere.

LONDON E8

Shanghai

☎ 020 7254 2878 41 Kingsland High St E8 2JS
web: www.theaa.com/restaurants/113966.html

A former Victorian pie and mash shop with marble counter and tiled walls. Classic Chinese favourites and westernised versions.

LONDON E14

Four Seasons Hotel Canary Wharf

Italian

Sophisticated Italian at Canary Wharf

☎ 020 7510 1999 Westferry Circus, Canary Wharf E14 8RS Plan 9-A6
web: www.fourseasons.com/canarywharf

Expect Italian sophistication at Quadrato, a sleek and chic Thames-side eatery housed in this stylishly modern Docklands hotel. With superb views over the London skyline, you can tuck into a versatile range of modern Italian dishes or some classic regional specialities, all prepared with contemporary flair from first-class ingredients in the impressive theatre kitchen. Simple, flavoursome combinations include bean and cereal soup, roast cod with globe artichoke, shellfish and saffron broth, veal loin milanese, and tiramisù. The predominantly Italian staff are friendly, enthusiastic and passionate about food and wine.

Chef: Sebastiano Spriveri **Owners:** Four Seasons Hotels **Times:** 12-3/6-10.30 **Prices:** Fixed L £29, Starter £8.30-£14.50, Main £12.50-£24.50, Dessert £9, Coffee £3.90, Min/Water £4, Service optional, Group min 8 service 12.5% **Wine:** 124 bottles over £20, 29 by the glass (£5.50-£16) **Notes:** Sun brunch £25, Vegetarian available, Dress Restrictions, Smart casual preferred, Civ Wed 200 **Seats:** 90 **Smoking:** N/Sm area, No pipes, No cigars, Air con **Children:** Menu, Portions **Rooms:** 142 (142 en suite) ★★★★★ HL **Directions:** Nearest station: Canary Wharf Just off Westbury Circus rdbt **Parking:** 26

The Gun

British, French

Smart docklands gastro-pub serving modern British food

☎ 020 7515 5222 27 Coldharbour, Docklands E14 9NS Plan 9-D5
e-mail: info@thegundocklands.com
web: www.thegundocklands.com

A fabulous Thames-side location with a stunning terrace affording great views of the Millennium Dome and the river are among the attractions at this beautifully restored 18th-century dockers' pub. No longer spit-and-sawdust, expect oak timber floors, Georgian-style fireplaces, crisp linen-clothed tables in smart dining rooms, and an inviting bar. Competent modern British cooking results in versatile menus listing the likes of potted duck with pear chutney, and traditional venison stew alongside monkfish with sea urchin linguine and leek sauce. The Gun is also a great spot for Sunday brunch.

Chef: Scott Wade **Owners:** Tom & Ed Martin **Times:** 12-3/6-10.30, Closed 26 Dec **Prices:** Starter £4.50-£12.50, Main £11-£21, Dessert £4-£6, Coffee £2, Min/Water £3.80, Service added but optional 12.5% **Wine:** 80 bottles over £20, 30 bottles under £20, 22 by the glass (£3.10-£6.70) **Seats:** Pr/dining room 12 **Smoking:** N/Sm in restaurant, Air con **Children:** Portions **Directions:** Nearest station: South Quay DLR, Canary Wharf From South Quay DLR, E down Marsh Wall to mini rdbt, turn left, over bridge then take 1st right

London Marriott West India Quay

American, Seafood

Relaxed docklands dining

☎ 020 7517 2808 22 Hertsmere Rd, Canary Wharf E14 4ED Plan 9-B6
e-mail: mhrs.loncw.restaurant.supervisor@marriotthotels.com
web: www.marriott.co.uk

Housed in a spectacular skyscraper, this bright modern hotel overlooks West India Quay in the heart of Docklands. The Curve restaurant takes its name from the imposing glass sweep of the building's façade and is an upmarket choice for a relaxed bite. There's plenty to tempt - a lengthy menu features American-inspired dishes such as barbeque ribs with corn mash, plus a range of deli sandwiches and steaks. Healthy options come in the form of a 'fit for you' selection that includes the likes of Cajun seared snapper and miso black cod.

Chef: David Dent **Owners:** Marriott Hotels **Times:** 12-2.30/5-10.30 **Prices:** Fixed L £20-£30, Fixed D £20-£30, Starter £5-£8, Main £8-£20, Dessert £5, Service added but optional 12.5% **Notes:** Fixed L 3 courses, Vegetarian available **Seats:** 86, Pr/dining room 40 **Smoking:** N/Sm in restaurant, Air con **Children:** Menu, Portions **Rooms:** 301 (301 en suite) ★★★★★ HL **Directions:** Nearest station: Canary Wharf/West India Quay DLR Telephone for directions

Plateau

French

Fine-dining Conran restaurant

☎ 020 7715 7100 Canada Place, Canada Square, Canary Wharf E14 4QS Plan 9-B6
e-mail: plateau@conran-restaurants.co.uk
web: www.conran.com

The epitome of Conran style, this buzzy, modern restaurant is on the

continued

England

LONDON E14 *continued*

fourth floor of the Canada Place complex in Canary Wharf, accessed via a lift from the shopping mall (next to Waitrose). You're elevated to a stunning complex with two dining areas divided by a semi-open kitchen, each side with its own outside terrace, not to mention two bars, private dining and a cigar room. The Bar & Grill offers a simpler menu, while the Plateau restaurant offers an interesting carte based on fine produce from across the British Isles. You'll find Loch Fyne smoked salmon to start, followed perhaps by grouse with bread sauce and watercress. Simple side dishes include honey-glazed parsnips and an organic mixed leaf salad. For dessert you could try wet walnut soup with poached pear and pain d'épice, or opt for the interesting choice of unpasteurised, farmed cheeses.

Times: 12-2/6-10.15, Closed 25-26 Dec, 1 Jan, Sun, Closed L Sat **Directions:** Nearest station: Canary Wharf Facing Canary Wharf Tower

Royal China

Chinese NEW

Accomplished Chinese food with wonderful views of the river

☎ 020 7719 0888 Canary Wharf Riverside, 30 Westferry Circus E14 8RR Plan 9-A6
e-mail: info@royalchinagroup.co.uk
web: www.royalchinagroup.co.uk

An impressive glass-fronted building on the river's edge at Canary Wharf. Outdoor seating offers fantastic views, so alfresco dining is a must whenever possible. The restaurant features lots of black and gold lacquering and crisp white linen. Traditional Cantonese cooking makes

continued

the most of good ingredients. Dishes range from set meals and gourmet seafood including lobster to dim sum, cold appetisers, abalone, soup, plenty of seafood, meat dishes, vegetables and bean curd. As you would expect, there is a good selection of rice and noodles as well as desserts such as chilled mango pudding.

Chef: Man Chau **Times:** noon/11, Closed 23-25 Dec **Prices:** Fixed L £9, Fixed D £28-£36, Starter £4-£25, Main £7-£150, Dessert £4-£6, Coffee £2, Min/Water £3.50, Service added but optional 13% **Wine:** 47 bottles over £20, 8 bottles under £20, 6 by the glass (£4-£6) **Notes:** Vegetarian available **Seats:** 155, Pr/dining room 40 **Smoking:** Air con **Parking:** 2 mins away

Ubon by Nobu

see below

Carluccio's Caffè

☎ 020 7719 1749 2 Nash Court, Canary Wharf E14 5AG

Quality Italian chain.

Corney & Barrow at Canary Wharf

☎ 020 7512 0397 9 Cabot Square E14 4QF

City wine bar chain offering contemporary dishes.

Ubon by Nobu

LONDON E14

Japanese, American

Swish celebrity hangout with an impeccable dining experience

☎ 020 7719 7800 34 Westferry Circus, Canary Wharf E14 8RR Plan 9-A6
e-mail: ubon@noburestaurants.com
web: www.noburestaurants.com

One of London's most fashionable restaurants, Ubon continues the exceptional fusion of stylish design, flawless service and innovative food that has made Nobu one of the hottest names in restaurant dining in the world. This chic Docklands restaurant with an exceptional Thames-side location has a panoramic view with floor to ceiling glass walls on three sides of the dining room. For kudos it's almost unmatchable - booking is essential and while you're not guaranteed to spot any A-list celebrities, there's always the slim chance that co-owner Robert De Niro will be at an adjacent table.

As long as your wallet can take the strain, you can sample some truly cutting edge cuisine that takes classic Japanese and adds a liberal sprinkling of South American tastes and textures with oodles of contemporary panache. Indulge your palate with dishes such as yellowtail sashimi with jalapeno, Nobu's signature black cod with miso, or a chocolate bento box with green tea ice cream.

Chef: Youcef Khelil, Mark Edwards **Owners:** Nobu Matsuhisa, B S Ong
Times: 12-2.15/6-10.15, Closed Xmas, all BHs, Sun, Closed L Sat
Prices: Starter £5.50-£19.50, Main £5-£29.50, Dessert £7-£9.50, Coffee £1.75, Min/Water £4.50, Service added 15% **Wine:** 74 bottles over £20, 6 by the glass (£6-£8.50) **Notes:** Omakase menu from £50-£90, Vegetarian available **Seats:** 120 **Smoking:** N/Sm in restaurant, Air con
Directions: Nearest station: Westferry, Canary Wharf Follow signs to Canary Riverside Restaurant behind Four Seasons Hotel **Parking:** Riverside car park

LONDON E16

Yi-Ban

☎ 020 7473 6699 London Regatta Centre, Dockside Rd, Royal Albert Dock E16 2QT
web: www.theaa.com/restaurants/113982.html

A large open Chinese restaurant with great river views. Gigantic menu of traditional dishes, with an emphasis on seafood.

LONDON EC1

The Bleeding Heart

Modern French NOTABLE WINE LIST

Discreet and hospitable Hatton Garden French restaurant

☎ 020 7242 2056 19 Greville St, Bleeding Heart Yard EC1N 8SQ Plan 3-F4
e-mail: bookings@bleedingheart.co.uk
web: www.bleedingheart.co.uk

Secreted away in a Dickensian building on a cobbled courtyard (where Lady Elizabeth Hatton was found murdered in the 17th century, hence the name) and behind the tavern and beneath the bistro of the same name, this popular basement restaurant exudes character and atmosphere. Wood floors and beams lend a dark, romantic, old-world charm, while service is French and professional. The cooking speaks with a modern Gallic accent, perhaps delivering pan-fried halibut with sweet potato and paprika sauce alongside classics like Chateaubriand with sauce béarnaise and pommes frites (for two)

Notable Wine List: A carefully chosen list which features the award-winning Trinity Hill wines from New Zealand - a vineyard which the restaurant owns.

Chef: Pascal Even **Owners:** Robert & Robyn Wilson **Times:** 12-3.15/6-11, Closed Xmas & New Year (10 days), Sat-Sun **Prices:** Starter £5.95-£9.95, Main £11.95-£21.50, Dessert £5.95-£6.95, Coffee £2.25, Min/Water £3.50, Service added but optional 12.5% **Wine:** 500 bottles over £20, 14 bottles under £20, 30 by the glass (£4.50-£13.65) **Notes:** Vegetarian available **Seats:** 110, Pr/dining room 40 **Smoking:** No pipes, Air con **Children:** Min 7 yrs **Directions:** Nearest station: Farringdon Turn right out of Farringdon Station onto Cowcross St, continue down Greville St for 50mtrs. Turn left into Bleeding Heart Yard **Parking:** 20 evening only, NCP nearby

Le Café du Marché

French

Authentic French market café

☎ 020 7608 1609 Charterhouse Mews, Charterhouse Square EC1M 6AH Plan 3-G4
web: www.cafedumarche.co.uk

Hidden away in a quiet cobbled mews a stone's throw from Smithfield Market, this aptly-named brasserie is perfectly located to make the most of abundant fresh ingredients. Bare-brick walls, floorboards, exposed rafters and cane chairs with striped cushions all serve to create a charming, unpretentious interior that takes you straight back to provincial France. Attentive, Gallic staff add to the colourful, lively atmosphere. The French-language, fixed-price menu changes regularly and showcases the accomplished French cooking with dishes like navarin d'agneau printanière.

continued

Club Gascon

LONDON EC1

French NOTABLE WINE LIST

With the cuisine of Gascony as its bedrock this Smithfield stalwart has a huge following

☎ 020 7796 0600 57 West Smithfield EC1A 9DS Plan 3-G3
e-mail: info@clubgascon.com

With a location overlooking St Bart's hospital and the main entrance to Smithfield's market, this chic London restaurant is endowed with a rich sense of history in both its surroundings and the building it occupies. A favourite spot for the fabled 'long lunch' of the city, you can expect to be greeted on arrival by stunning flower arrangements created by the chef himself, then drink in the marble-clad walls and old oak flooring in this small bustling dining room. Advance booking is imperative - as is confirming the booking; service from the smart, black-tied waiting staff can be unhurried so leave plenty of time to indulge. The cuisine here has its roots in the French provincial cooking of Gascony - foie gras is a speciality with six versions of this venerable ingredient on offer. You might expect such dishes as duck foie gras with winter citrus fruits, followed by a country-style daube of Chalosse beef.

Notable Wine List: Extensive French wine list specialising in the South and South West of France.

Chef: Pascal Aussignac **Owners:** P Aussignac & V Labeyrie **Times:** 12-2/7-10, Closed Xmas, New Year, BHs, Sun, Closed L Sat **Prices:** Fixed L £35, Fixed D £39, Starter £7.50-£14, Main £12-£18.50, Dessert £7-£9, Coffee £2.25, Min/Water £3, Service added but optional 12.5% **Wine:** 180 bottles over £20, 1 bottle under £20, 9 by the glass (£5.50-£8.50) **Notes:** Fixed L 3 courses, Fixed D 5 courses, Vegetarian available **Seats:** 45 **Smoking:** N/Sm in restaurant, Air con **Children:** Portions **Directions:** Nearest station: Barbican or Farringdon Telephone for directions **Parking:** NCP opposite restaurant

LONDON EC1 *continued*

Chef: Simon Cottard **Owners:** Anna Graham-Wood **Times:** 12-2.30/6-10, Closed Xmas, New Year, Easter, BHs, Sun, Closed L Sat **Prices:** Fixed L £28.95, Fixed D £28.95, Coffee £2, Min/Water £2, Service added but optional 15% **Notes:** Fixed L 3 courses, Vegetarian available **Seats:** 120, Pr/dining room 65 **Smoking:** Air con **Children:** Portions **Directions:** Nearest station: Barbican Telephone for directions **Parking:** Next door, free after 6pm

Clerkenwell Dining Room

Modern European

Fine dining in trendy Clerkenwell

☎ 020 7253 9000 69-73 St. John St EC1 4AN Plan 3-G4
e-mail: zak@theclerkenwell.com
web: www.theclerkenwell.com

Behind the trendy dark blue and red Clerkenwell frontage you'll find a modern, split-level restaurant with a wooden floor, bar and an upper mezzanine for private hire. The table service may be efficient and formal but the atmosphere is relaxed and comfortable. The modern European menu comprises dishes based on best-quality ingredients. Technical skills and imagination combine to produce clear flavours and good combinations such as the starter of seared scallops with curry spices and pakora and main courses of nine vegetable ravolini with sage and parmesan broth or the braised short rib of beef with truffle sauce. Finish with the hot chocolate fondant and malt ice cream.

Chef: Andrew Thompson **Owners:** Zak Jones & Andrew Thompson **Times:** 12-2.30/6-10.30, Closed Xmas, Closed L Sat, D Sun **Prices:** Fixed L £14.50, Fixed D £19.50, Starter £7-£9, Main £14-£17.50, Dessert £7-£8, Coffee £2.50, Min/Water £3, Service added but optional 12.5% **Wine:** 16 bottles over £20, 7 bottles under £20, 3 by the glass (£5-£7) **Notes:** Sun L 2 courses £14.50, 3 courses £19.50 **Seats:** 80, Pr/dining room 40 **Smoking:** N/Sm area, No pipes, Air con **Children:** Portions **Directions:** Nearest station: Farringdon Please telephone for directions **Parking:** On street

Club Gascon

see page 253

Comptoir Gascon

French NEW

Classic French bistro and deli

☎ 020 7608 0851 61-63 Charterhouse St EC1M 6HJ Plan 3-F4
e-mail: comptoirgascon@btconnect.com

It's best to book ahead to get one of the limited number of tables at this popular eatery opposite Smithfield Market. Part of the Club Gascon collection, it's a small rustic, bistro-style restaurant with a deli in the same room, serving up traditional dishes from South Western France. Many items are sourced direct from France, and are available to take away from the deli. Flavoursome starters might feature roast pumpkin soup served with a slice of rustic French bread. Expect main courses like home-made mini cheese, and crab-filled ravioli with a rich crab sauce, served with crabmeat and a claw.

Chef: Laurent Sanchis **Owners:** Vincent Labeyrie, Pascal Aussignac **Times:** 12-2/7-11, Closed 25 Dec, 1 Jan, Sun, Mon **Prices:** Starter £4-£10.50, Main £7-£14, Dessert £2.50-£3.50, Coffee £1.20, Min/Water £2, Service added but optional 12.5% **Wine:** 16 bottles over £20, 6 bottles under £20, 21 by the glass (£3.50-£7) **Seats:** 32 **Smoking:** N/Sm in restaurant, Air con **Directions:** Nearest station: Farringdon, Barbican, St Paul's, Chancery Lane Telephone for directions

Malmaison Charterhouse Square

Modern British, French

Boutique hotel with accessible, easy-going brasserie

☎ 020 7012 3700 18-21 Charterhouse Square, Clerkenwell EC1M 6AH Plan 3-G4
e-mail: london@malmaison.com
web: www.malmaison.com

Set in an attractive red brick Victorian building in a cobbled courtyard just off Charterhouse Square, this upmarket boutique hotel has similar high production values to the rest of the outlets in this stylish chain. The building itself was once a nurses' residence for St Bartholomew's, now revamped with the chic Malmaison livery and housing a buzzing brasserie-style restaurant. Tables are set on two levels, some in brick-backed alcoves. The menu offers mainly French cuisine delivered with simplicity and skill, with fresh flavours throughout - a starter of smoked bacon and crème fraîche tart, for example, then pan-fried sea trout with crushed fresh peas and citrus dressing.

Times: 12-2.30/6-10.30 **Rooms:** 97 (97 en suite) ★★★

Moro

Mediterranean, North African

Exotic fare from an open kitchen in the City

☎ 020 7833 8336 34/36 Exmouth Market EC1R 4QE Plan 3-F5
e-mail: info@moro.co.uk
web: www.moro.co.uk

High ceilings and a simple understated style make the long zinc bar all the more striking at this expansive restaurant. Tapas is served all day at the bar, and food generally explores something less familiar, with the robust flavours of Spain and the exotic spices of North Africa and the Middle East. Typical of this Spanish Muslim Mediterranean genre is a starter of quail baked in flat bread with pistachio sauce. For a main try pollo al ajillo (chicken cooked with bay, garlic and fino sherry), and finish with a fragrant rosewater and cardamom ice cream. The toilets have recently been refurbished by cutting edge interior designer Precious McBane.

Chef: Samuel & Samantha Clark **Owners:** Mr & Mrs S Clark & Mark Sainsbury **Times:** 12.30-2.30/7-10.30, Closed Xmas, New Year, BHs, Sun **Prices:** Starter £5-£8.50, Main £13.50-£17.50, Dessert £5, Coffee £2, Min/Water £2.75, Group min 6 service 12.5% **Wine:** 38 bottles over £20, 15 bottles under £20, 27 by the glass (£3-£11.90) **Notes:** Sherry tasting menu Sat L, Vegetarian available **Seats:** 90, Pr/dining room 14 **Smoking:** N/Sm in restaurant, Air con **Children:** Portions **Directions:** Nearest station: Farringdon or Angel 5 mins walk from Sadler's Wells theatre, between Farringdon Road and Rosebery Ave **Parking:** NCP Farringdon Rd

St John

British

The best of British nose-to-tail cooking

☎ 020 7251 0848 26 St John St EC1M 4AY Plan 3-G4
e-mail: reservations@stjohnrestaurant.com
web: www.stjohnrestaurant.com

Close to Smithfield Market, this stark, plain restaurant is housed in a former smokehouse, and has its own bakery and a lively bar. A leaping pig illustrates the unique menu and is uncompromising, indeed almost austere, in style. Meat lovers are drawn here for the robust old British dishes, those that feature little used cuts of meat, which have been reinvented for modern day consumption. There's plenty of offal, like venison liver and beetroot, plus unusual ingredients such as lambs' tongues with green beans and anchovy and roast bone marrow and parsley salad. Cautious diners may go for the hare broth, followed by roast Middlewhite and swede, and hot chocolate pudding for dessert.

Chef: Christopher Gillard **Owners:** T Gulliver & F Henderson **Times:** 12-3/6-11, Closed Xmas, New Year, Easter BH, Sun, Closed L Sat **Prices:** Starter £5.80-£12.80, Main £12.80-£24, Dessert £5.80-£6.50, Coffee £2.25, Min/Water £3, Service optional, Group min 6 service 12.5% **Wine:** 24 bottles over £20, 6 bottles under £20, 6 by the glass (£3.90-£5) **Seats:** 100, Pr/dining room 18 **Smoking:** N/Sm area, Air con **Directions:** Nearest station: Farringdon 100yds from Smithfield Market, northside **Parking:** Meters in street

Smiths of Smithfield

Modern British

Impressive warehouse conversion in Smithfield Meat Market

☎ 020 7251 7950 (Top Floor), 67-77 Charterhouse St EC1M 6HJ Plan 3-F4
e-mail: reservations@smithsofsmithfield.co.uk
web: www.smithsofsmithfield.co.uk

There are views over the City, St Paul's Cathedral and the market itself from this Grade II listed four-floor restaurant in London's Smithfield Meat Market. The building had been empty for over 40 years before the Smiths team got to grips with it. The interior has a great sense of space and light, with sandblasted bricks, reclaimed timber and industrial steel. There is a different style for each floor - food and décor - something to suit every pocket and occasion including breakfast, weekend brunches and a drink with friends. The Top Floor offers Irish rock oysters, caviar, the best aged steaks and dishes such as roast red leg partridge with swede purée and roast shallots.

Chef: Tony Moyse, Ashley Shergold **Owners:** John Torode **Times:** 12-3.30/6.30-12, Closed 25-26 Dec, 1 Jan, Closed L Sat **Prices:** Starter fr £6.50, Main £15-£35, Dessert £4.50-£7.50, Coffee £2.50, Min/Water £2.50, Service added but optional 12.5% **Wine:** 150 bottles over £20, 4 bottles under £20, 29 by the glass (£4.25-£11) **Notes:** Vegetarian available **Seats:** 80, Pr/dining room 30 **Smoking:** Air con **Children:** Portions **Directions:** Nearest station: Farringdon, Barbican, Chancery Lane Opposite Smithfield Meat Market **Parking:** NCP: Snowhill

Alba

☎ 020 7588 1798 107 Whitecross St EC1Y 8JD
Contemporary Italian within a short walk of the Barbican. The generous carte is supplemented by daily specials.

Carluccio's Caffè

☎ 020 7329 5904 12 West Smithfield EC1A 9JR
Quality Italian chain.

Cicada

☎ 020 7608 1550 132-136 St John St, Farringdon EC1V 4JT
web: www.theaa.com/restaurants/113930.html
A trendy bar-restaurant in fashionable Clerkenwell, serving great Pan-Asian dishes from an open-plan kitchen.

Coconut Lagoon

☎ 020 7253 2546 7 Goswell Rd, Barbican EC1M 7AH
web: www.theaa.com/restaurants/113995.html

Southern Indian cuisine from Goa, Kerala, Karnataka and Andhra Pradesh. Many vegetarian options. Knowledgeable staff.

Fish Shop on St John Street

☎ 020 7837 1199 360-362 St John St EC1V 4NR
web: www.theaa.com/restaurants/113936.html
A modern, minimalist take on that old British favourite, the chippy. Try the deep fried fish of the day (in batter, egg or matzo meal) and chips, or something more adventurous. The menu consists solely of fish and shellfish fresh from Billingsgate Market, and changes daily.

The Peasant

☎ 020 7336 7726 240 St John St, Clerkenwell EC1V 4PH
web: www.theaa.com/restaurants/114055.html
One of the original gastro-pubs, the Peasant has a beautiful first floor restaurant, with soaring ceilings and huge windows looking out over Clerkenwell and the City University. Terrific vegetarian options.

Sofra - Exmouth Market

☎ 020 7833 1111 19-21 Exmouth Market EC1R 4QD
web: www.theaa.com/restaurants/113969.html
A sister restaurant to Ozer in Langham Place, offering a similar mix of modern and traditional Turkish dishes.

Strada

☎ 020 7278 0800 8-10 Exmouth Market EC1R 4QA
Superior pizza from quality ingredients cooked in wood-fired ovens.

Yo! Sushi

☎ 020 7841 0785 95 Farringdon Rd EC1R 3BT
Sushi, sashimi, noodles and more delivered by conveyor belt and priced according to colour coded plates.

England

LONDON EC2

❀❀❀ Aurora at Great Eastern Hotel see below

❀ Boisdale of Bishopsgate

Modern British

A great taste of Scotland in the heart of the city

☎ 020 7283 1763 Swedeland Court, 202 Bishopsgate EC2M 4NR Plan 7-C5
e-mail: katie@boisdale-city.co.uk
web: www.boisdale.co.uk

In the heart of the city this restaurant has a great pedigree. The ground floor has a traditional champagne and oyster bar while the McGonagall Room, restaurant and piano bar are found downstairs. The place has a clubby feel and the restaurant is popular with live jazz often played. Banquette seating and warm décor in dark reds and greens are complemented by hints of tartan. Scottish influences are also found on a menu rich in Scottish produce including wild game and 42-day matured Scottish beef. House specialities feature award-winning Lochcarnan hot-smoked salmon from the Isle of South Uist with new potato and horseradish cream salad.

Chef: Neil Churchill **Owners:** Ronald Macdonald **Times:** 11.30-3/6-12, Closed Xmas, 31 Dec, BHs, Sat & Sun **Prices:** Fixed L £17.80, Fixed D £17.80, Starter £5.50-£14.50, Main £12.15-£25.50, Dessert £5.50-£6, Coffee £2.50, Service added but optional 12.5% **Wine:** 108 bottles over £20, 16 bottles under £20, 13 by the glass (£3.50-£7.25) **Notes:** Fixed D 2 courses, Vegetarian available **Seats:** 100 **Smoking:** Air con **Directions:** Nearest station: Liverpool Street Opposite Liverpool St station

❀❀ Bonds

Modern French NOTABLE WINE LIST

A grand setting for some slick modern cooking

☎ 020 7657 8080 Threadneedles, 5 Threadneedle St EC2R 8AY Plan 6-B4
e-mail: bonds@theetongroup.com
web: www.bonds-restaurant.com

Built to imperious Victorian specifications, this grand dining room retains many features recognisable from its days as a financial institution. The client base is strictly city business folk with generous expense accounts, and the menu is succinctly scripted and studded with luxury produce. A good-value lighter lunch is offered while the carte lifts quality, technique and pricing accordingly. Try a tian of Colchester crab with smoked salmon, Oscietra caviar, crème fraîche and warm blinis, followed by roast loin of Denham Estate hare with Aragon ham, braised endive, beetroot marmalade and jus with pomegranate. Nostalgic desserts (bubble gum ice cream and a Snickers-inspired peanut butter parfait) are a novelty.

Notable Wine List: A well presented and organised wine list with good tasting notes.

Chef: Barry Tonks **Owners:** The Eton Collection **Times:** 12-2.30/6-10, Closed 2 wks Xmas, 4 days Etr & BHs, Sat, Sun **Prices:** Fixed L £20, Starter £8.50-£16.50, Main £15.50-£23.50, Dessert £6-£10, Coffee £3, Min/Water £5, Service added but optional 12.5% **Notes:** Tasting menu 5 courses £55, Vegetarian available, Dress Restrictions, Smart casual **Seats:** 80, Pr/dining room 16 **Smoking:** N/Sm in restaurant, Air con **Parking:** London Wall NCP

Rosettes not confirmed at time of going to press

Aurora at Great Eastern Hotel

LONDON EC2

Modern European

Flavourful modern cooking in a dramatic setting

☎ 020 7618 7000 Liverpool St EC2M 7QN Plan 6-C5
e-mail: restaurantres@great-eastern-hotel.co.uk
web: www.aurora-restaurant.co.uk

Set within the chic, designer city hotel adjacent to Liverpool Street Station, Aurora is a stunning, palatial Victorian dining room dominated by a majestic stained-glass dome, while ceilings reach lofty cathedral height and there are pillars and high arched windows. Billowing voiles in deep red and grey and enormous, striking funky chandeliers keep things contemporary while making the most of the original architecture. A stylish, brushed-steel bar lines one side of the room and maintains an extensive wine, spirit and cocktail list. Service is knowledgeable, slick and professional (including the sommelier). The kitchen's modern approach - underpinned by a classical theme - is delivered via an appealing range of menus that make the best of top-quality seasonal produce. And at lunch there's the addition of a daily carving trolley - of imposing dimensions - serving more traditional roasts. Bold, clear flavours, perfect timing, balanced combinations and high technical skill blossom in dishes like hay-baked leg of Pyrenean lamb teamed with a white bean stew and confit garlic, or perhaps steamed halibut served with an oxtail and morel jus and dauphinoise potatoes, while a chocolate and cinnamon soufflé might head-up desserts. A seven-course dégustation option and big-hitting wine list complete the slick city package.

We learned that there was a change of chef as we went to print

Owners: Great Eastern Hotel **Times:** 12-2.30/6.45-10, Closed Xmas, New Year, BHs, Sat-Sun **Prices:** Fixed L £23.50, Starter £9.50-£16.50, Main £16.50-£24, Dessert £7.50-£10, Coffee £4.50, Min/Water £3.85, Service added but optional 12.5% **Wine:** 700 bottles over £20, 35 bottles under £20, 25 by the glass (£4.50-£15.50) **Notes:** Tasting menu 7 courses £50, £75 with wine, Vegetarian available, Civ Wed 160 **Seats:** 100 **Smoking:** Air con **Rooms:** 267 (267 en suite) ★★★★★ **Directions:** Nearest station: Liverpool Street Telephone for directions **Parking:** NCP

Eyre Brothers

Iberian

Bustling, contemporary Shoreditch chic

☎ 020 7613 5346 70 Leonard St EC2A 4QX
Plan 7-B2
e-mail: eyrebros@btconnect.com
web: www.eyrebrothers.co.uk

This lively, urban-chic restaurant and bar proves something of a Shoreditch trendsetter, with its cool, upmarket metropolitan edge - mahogany-panelled ceiling and floors, American black walnut and leather chairs and banquettes set to a backing track of loud jazz music. Four booth-style areas break up the large dining space, while a bar runs along the back wall and offers tantalising glimpses of the kitchen that delivers its vibrant, Iberian-influenced cooking. Modern, refined rusticity is the style and it so catches the mood, with big, punchy flavours, top-notch ingredients and colour and texture variation adding further interest. Take grilled fillet of Ibérico pork, marinated with smoked paprika and garlic and served with patatas pobres to whet the appetite.

Chef: Dave Eyre, Joao Cleto **Owners:** Eyre Bros Restaurants Ltd **Times:** 12-3/6.30 11, Closed Xmas-New Year, BHs, Closed L Sat **Prices:** Starter £4.50-£10, Main £11.95-£23, Dessert £4.50-£6.50 **Wine:** 40 bottles over £20, 8 bottles under £20, 6 by the glass **Notes:** Vegetarian available **Seats:** 100 **Smoking:** N/Sm area, Air con **Parking:** On street, 2 car parks on Leonard St

Fishmarket

Traditional European

Enjoyable seafood dining in trendy city hotel

☎ 020 7618 7200 Great Eastern Hotel,
Liverpool St EC2M 7QN Plan 6-C5
e-mail: restaurantres@great-eastern-hotel.co.uk
web: www.fish-market.co.uk

This trendy eatery is located in a marble corner of the Great Eastern Hotel. There are no more than 15 closely spaced tables occupied by affluent city types served by young enthusiastic staff. A buzzy atmosphere is further enhanced by dramatic lighting and the horseshoe-shaped bar. There are good technical skills here evident in amuses and accurate saucing. Start with a rich foie gras, leek and smoked eel terrine or half a dozen Falmouth native oysters before a main course of plateau de fruits de mer or roast bream with squid fricassée. Side dishes include chips, French beans or mushy peas. Finish with a rich praline and chocolate mousseline.

Chef: Stuart Lyall **Owners:** Great Eastern Hotel **Times:** 12-2.30/6-10.30, Closed Xmas, New Year, BHs, Sat-Sun **Prices:** Fixed L £35, Fixed D £35-£45, Starter £5.85-£10.50, Main £11.50-£28, Dessert £5-£6.50, Coffee £3, Min/Water £3.50, Service added but optional 12.5% **Wine:** 219 bottles over £20, 7 bottles under £20, 9 by the glass (£4.25-£11.50) **Notes:** Vegetarian available **Seats:** 96 **Smoking:** Air con **Directions:** Nearest station: Liverpool Street Please telephone for directions **Parking:** NCP

Great Eastern Dining Room

Pan Asian

High octane Asian-style eatery

☎ 020 7613 4545 54 Great Eastern St
EC2A 3QR Plan 7-B2
e-mail: martyn@thediningrooms.com
web: www.greateasterndining.co.uk

A trendy modern bar-restaurant in a vibrant location on the northern edge of the city. It gets packed even on mid-week evenings, so don't expect much space at your table. Service is casual and relaxed with knowledgeable staff. A Pan-Asian menu based on the grazing concept makes this ideal for a group of friends wanting to explore a range of dishes. On the menu you'll find a selection of dim sum, sushi/sashimi, tempura, salads, house dishes like beef fillet toban-yaki, side orders like wok-fried vegetables and desserts along the lines of warm chocolate pudding with green tea ice cream.

Chef: Gerrard Mitchel **Owners:** Will Ricker **Times:** 12-3/6-10.30, Closed Xmas & Etr, Sun, Closed L Sat **Prices:** Starter £4-£8, Main £7-£19, Dessert £4-£6, Coffee £2, Min/Water £3, Service included, Service added but optional 12.5% **Wine:** 40 bottles over £20, 10 bottles under £20, 10 by the glass (£3-£7) **Notes:** Vegetarian available **Seats:** 70 **Smoking:** N/Sm in restaurant, Air con

Mehek

Indian

Stylish Indian dining in discreet city location

☎ 020 7588 5043 & 7588 5044 45 London Wall,
Moorgate EC2M 5TE Plan 7-B5
e-mail: info@mehek.co.uk
web: www.mehek.co.uk

This stylish, upmarket restaurant serving South Asian regional specialities is hidden away in an arcade of shops by the old London Wall. The Bollywood director-designed dining room is spacious with sumptuous furnishings and gentle light levels. The relaxed ambience is helped by diligent, well-trained staff. Dishes are drawn from across the Northern sub-continent so a meal might comprise a tandoori starter selection, Malai chops followed by a vindaloo, coconut chicken from Goa, or a more North Western Akbari lamb shank. Delicious desserts include gulab jamon.

Chef: A Matlib **Owners:** Salim B Rashid **Times:** 11.30-3/5.30-11, Closed Xmas, New Year, BHs, Sat-Sun **Prices:** Fixed L £11.50-£16.90, Fixed D £24.50-£26.50, Starter £3.20-£6.90, Main £6.90-£18, Dessert £2.95-£3.95, Coffee £1.50, Min/Water £3.90, Service added but optional 10% **Wine:** 19 bottles over £20, 11 bottles under £20, 9 by the glass (£3.20-£7.20) **Notes:** Fixed L 5 courses, Fixed D 8 courses, Vegetarian available, Dress Restrictions, Smart casual **Seats:** 120 **Smoking:** N/Sm area, Air con **Parking:** On street, NCP

Rhodes Twenty Four

Modern British

Classic Rhodes overlooking the city

☎ 020 7877 7703 Tower 42, Old Broad St
EC2N 1HQ Plan 6-C5
web: www.rhodes24.co.uk

This ear-poppingly high restaurant is found on the 24th floor of the tallest building in the Square Mile, with stunning views over London

continued

LONDON EC2 *continued*

by day or night. At the heart of the city, it positively reels with money and, as stunning destinations go, it's sure to impress the right clients, or perhaps a special date. Service is slick and formal with particular attention to wine. Cuisine is modern British with a twist, as you would expect. A clearly defined menu lists dishes by their main ingredient, then a short description tells it like it is, so you'll find a starter of globe artichoke: artichoke bottom, chopped wild mushrooms, poached egg and hollandaise sauce. Easy really, so move on to a main course of pork: slow roast belly of pork with sage, onion and apple tart and champ potatoes.

Chef: Gary Rhodes, Adam Gray **Owners:** Restaurant Associates **Times:** 12-2.30/6-9.00, Closed BHs, Xmas, Sat-Sun **Prices:** Starter £8.50-£16.50, Main £17.50-£25, Dessert £8.50, Coffee £3, Min/Water £3.50, Service added but optional **Wine:** 130 bottles over £20, 5 bottles under £20, 10 by the glass (£5.50-£9.30) **Notes:** Dress Restrictions, No ripped jeans or dirty trainers **Seats:** 75 **Smoking:** N/Sm in restaurant, Air con **Children:** Portions **Directions:** Nearest station: Bank/Liverpool Street Telephone for directions **Parking:** On street

❀ Rivington Bar & Grill

British V

Straightforward British classics in buzzy setting

☎ 020 7729 7053 28-30 Rivington St EC2A 3DZ Plan 7-B2
e-mail: shoreditch@rivingtongrill.co.uk
web: www.rivingtongrill.co.uk

A combined restaurant, bar and deli, this buzzy place is tucked away down a narrow side street in fashionable Hoxton. White walls and wooden floors make for a suitably minimalist backdrop to a parade of simple, seasonal, no-frills modern British dishes: Haslet with fried duck's egg and wild garlic, Barnsley chop with bubble and squeak and a comforting rhubarb and apple crumble. There's also a special 'things on toast' menu, ranging from home-made beans to potted Morecambe Bay shrimps, and occasional banquets of roast Lancashire suckling pig for parties of eight or more to share.

Chef: Mohammed Azzu **Owners:** Caprice-Holdings Ltd **Times:** 12-3/6.30-11, Closed Xmas & New Year, Closed L Sat **Prices:** Starter £2-£9.75, Main £10.50-£24.50, Dessert £5.50-£5.75, Coffee £1.75, Min/Water £2.50, Service added but optional 12.5% **Wine:** 40 bottles over £20, 10 bottles under £20, 8 by the glass (£3.50-£6.25) **Notes:** Sun L/D 3 courses £22.50, Vegetarian menu **Seats:** 85, Pr/dining room 25 **Smoking:** Air con **Directions:** Nearest station: Old St/Liverpool St Telephone for directions **Parking:** On street

❀ *Tatsuso Restaurant*

Japanese

Authentic City Oriental

☎ 020 7638 5863 32 Broadgate Circle EC2M 2QS Plan 6-C5

This slick, glass-fronted, atmospheric, two-tier City Japanese - on the lower level of Broadgate Circle - comes brimming with corporate suits, professional service and clean modern lines. Lightwood furniture and screens set the scene with waitresses in traditional Japanese dress. On the ground floor there's the theatre of the teppan-yaki grill to enjoy, where lobster, Dover sole and sirloin with foie gras tempt, while in the basement, a lengthy, authentic carte and sushi menu reign in a more relaxed atmosphere. You will find quality ingredients, plentiful set-menu options and City prices.

continued

Times: 11.45-2.45/6.30-10.30, Closed Xmas, New Year, BHs, Sat-Sun **Directions:** Nearest station: Liverpool Street. Ground floor of Broadgate Circle

Corney & Barrow at Broadgate Circle

☎ 020 7628 1251 19 Broadgate Circle EC2M 2QS
Wine bar offshoot from famous wine merchants.

Corney & Barrow at Citypoint

☎ 020 7382 0606 1 Ropemaker St EC2Y 9AW
Wine bar offshoot from famous wine merchants.

Corney & Barrow at Exchange Square

☎ 020 7628 4367 5 Exchange Square EC2A 2EH
Wine bar offshoot from famous wine merchants.

Corney & Barrow at Mason's Avenue

☎ 020 7726 6030 12 Mason's Av EC2V 5BT
City wine bar chain offering contemporary dishes.

Corney & Barrow at Old Broad Street

☎ 020 7638 9308 111 Old Broad St EC2N 1AP
Wine bar offshoot from famous wine merchants.

The Fox Dining Room

☎ 020 7729 5708 28 Paul St EC2A 4LB
Rustic, unfussy food in a restaurant designed to create the impression of a 1950s municipal library.

Wagamama

☎ 020 7588 2688 1a Ropemaker St EC2V 9AW
Informal noodle bar with no booking.

Wagamama

☎ 020 7256 9992 22 Old Broad St EC2N 1HQ
Informal noodle bar with no booking.

LONDON EC3

❀❀ Chamberlains Restaurant

Traditional International

Three-storey seafood restaurant in a Victorian market

☎ 020 7648 8690 23/25 Leadenhall Market EC3V 1LR Plan 6-C4
e-mail: info@chamberlains.org
web: www.chamberlains.org

Located in Leadenhall Market, complete with cobbled walkways and a glass roof, Chamberlains is a three storey seafood restaurant with an old fashioned shop frontage. There is a ground floor restaurant and bar with a staircase leading to a mezzanine level, a basement wine bar and first floor restaurant. Chamberlain & Thelwell are fish suppliers to the trade, so the quality of seafood delivered daily to their restaurant is assured. Cappuccino of lobster bisque and fresh tian of Cornish crab are typical starters, and among the main courses are Chamberlain's speciality fish and chips, and seared sea bass with spinach and pine nut rotolo and olive broth.

continued

Chef: Glen Watson **Owners:** Chamberlain & Thelwell **Times:** 12-3/5.30-9.30, Closed Xmas, New Year & BHs, Sat & Sun **Prices:** Fixed D £16.95, Starter £6.95-£16.50, Main £16.50-£29.50, Dessert £5.50-£7.50, Service included **Wine:** 25 bottles over £20, 8 bottles under £20, 6 by the glass **Notes:** Vegetarian available **Seats:** 150, Pr/dining room 65 **Smoking:** N/Sm area, Air con **Children:** Portions **Directions:** Nearest station: Bank and Monument Telephone for directions

1 Lombard Street - Fine Dining Restaurant

Modern French

Bank on luxurious dining at luxury prices

☎ 020 7929 6611 1 Lombard St EC3V 9AA
Plan 6-B4
e-mail: hb@1lombardstreet.com
web: www.1lombardstreet.com

This former City bank has combined its old, neo-classical interior with more practical, contemporary design and neutral colours to produce an intimate dining venue. Service is formal and discreet. The menu comprises modern British dishes with French influences that, in keeping with this location, are unashamedly expensive. Good flavours and precise cooking produce luxurious dishes of warm calves' sweetbread fritters with apple and celeriac remoulade, and feuilleté of smoked Finnan haddock with quail's eggs. Perhaps follow this with main courses of roast turbot on the bone with woodland mushroom and herb ragout, or mignon of veal with sage and pancetta. Desserts include an imaginative feuillantine of caramelised Granny Smiths with Guinness ice cream or bitter Ecuador chocolate pyramid and almond milk granitée.

Chef: Herbet Berger **Owners:** Jessen & Co **Times:** 12-2.30/6-10, Closed Xmas, New Year, BHs, Sat-Sun, Closed D 24 Dec **Prices:** Fixed L £34, Starter £14.50-£19.50, Main £28.50-£32.50, Dessert £9.50, Coffee £3.50, Min/Water £3.75, Service added but optional 12.5%, Group min 10 service 15% **Wine:** 186 bottles over £20, 3 bottles under £20, 13 by the glass (£4.75-£15) **Notes:** Fixed D 9 courses £45 **Seats:** 40, Pr/dining room 40 **Smoking:** N/Sm in restaurant, Air con **Directions:** Nearest station: Bank Opposite Bank of England **Parking:** NCP Cannon Street

Prism Restaurant and Bar

Modern Eclectic

Harvey Nichols quality dining in the Square Mile

☎ 020 7256 3888 147 Leadenhall St EC3V 4QT
Plan 6-C4
e-mail: prism@harveynichols.com
web: www.harveynichols.com

continued

Once the Bank of New York, this elegant City building with its alabaster pillars, marble floors and high ceilings now houses this stylish restaurant. The bar is no less striking and might even be a little intimidating if the staff were not so enthusiastic and helpful. Like its sister restaurant on the 5th floor of Harvey Nichols, the menu is somewhat eclectic bringing together top-quality ingredients from around the world in menus of well thought-out, carefully prepared dishes. Start with the langoustine and baby leek terrine, confit citrus fruit and basil salsa with crème fraîche before a main course of roast rump of veal with polenta, sweetbread and osso buco faggot. Finish with a rich chocolate mousse with griottine cherries.

Chef: Jonathan Warner **Owners:** Harvey Nichols **Times:** 11-3/6-10, Closed Xmas, New Year, BHs, Sat & Sun **Prices:** Starter £8-£12.50, Main £15-£23, Dessert £7.50, Coffee £3.50, Min/Water £3.50, Service added but optional 12.5% **Wine:** 550 bottles over £20, 3 bottles under £20, 19 by the glass (£4.10-£17.50) **Notes:** Tasting menu available D, Vegetarian available **Seats:** 120, Pr/dining room 40 **Smoking:** Air con **Children:** Portions **Directions:** Nearest station: Bank and Monument Please telephone for directions **Parking:** On street & NCP

Restaurant Sauterelle

French NEW

Stylish French cuisine inside the Royal Exchange building

☎ 020 7618 2483 The Royal Exchange
EC3V 3LR Plan 6-B4
e-mail: alessandrop@conran-restaurants.co.uk
web: www.conran.com

Set on the first-floor mezzanine of the Royal Exchange (one of the top three most important historical buildings in the City), Restaurant Sauterelle overlooks the bustling courtyard interior, where the Grand Café (also part of the Conran Group) and many world-famous jewellers and retailers ply their trade. The atmosphere is fittingly chic, while service is correspondingly efficient, welcoming and professional. The carefully prepared, straightforward but classy, classic regional French cuisine uses the freshest produce from the markets and sits well with the surroundings. Think crustacea and fish stew 'Sauterelle', or Chateaubriand steak with roast field mushrooms, tomato and watercress, and, to finish, choose between a crème brûlée or the likes of tarte au citron.

Chef: Stuart Smith **Owners:** Conran Restaurants **Times:** 12-2.30/6-10, Closed BHs, Sat & Sun **Prices:** Starter £5-£15, Main £13.50-£20, Dessert £5.50-£8, Coffee £2, Min/Water £3.85, Service added but optional 12.5% **Wine:** 60 bottles over £20, 1 bottle under £20, 6 by the glass (£5.50-£6.75) **Seats:** 66, Pr/dining room 20 **Smoking:** N/Sm in restaurant, Air con **Children:** Portions **Directions:** Nearest station: Bank In heart of business centre. Bank tube station exit 4

Corney & Barrow at Jewry Street

☎ 020 7680 8550 37A Jewry St EC3N 2EX
City wine bar chain offering contemporary dishes.

Corney & Barrow at Lloyds of London

☎ 020 7261 9201 Lloyds of London,
1 Leadenhall Place EC3M 7DX
City wine bar chain offering contemporary dishes.

Corney & Barrow at Monument

☎ 020 7929 3220 2B Eastcheap EC3M 1AB
Wine bar offshoot from famous wine merchants.

LONDON EC3 *continued*

Corney & Barrow at Royal Exchange

☎ 020 7929 3131 16 Royal Exchange EC3V 3LP
Wine bar offshoot from famous wine merchants.

Just Gladwins

☎ 020 7444 0004 Minster Court, Mark Ln, Tower Hill EC3R 7AA
web: www.theaa.com/restaurants/113944.html
A stylish basement dining room, with plenty of space between the tables. The menu is internationally inspired and the ice cream home-made.

Kasturi

☎ 020 7480 7402 57 Aldgate High St EC3N 1AL
web: www.theaa.com/restaurants/114005.html

One of a chain of Indian restaurants offering Pakhtoon cuisine - a healthier variety of Indian dishes.

Ruskin's

☎ 020 7680 1234 60 Mark Ln, Tower Hill EC3R 7NE
web: www.theaa.com/restaurants/113963.html
City bar and restaurant housed in an old rum importer's, built in 1864. A friendly, professional atmosphere, it's busy with City boys at lunchtime.

LONDON EC4

The Chancery

Modern European

Enjoyable brasserie dining in legal land

☎ 020 7831 4000 9 Cursitor St EC4A 1LL Plan 3-E3
e-mail: reservations@thechancery.co.uk
web: www.thechancery.co.uk

Tucked away between Lincoln's Inn Fields and Chancery Lane, this bijou, glass-fronted, split-level restaurant with its basement bar is surrounded by the offices and chambers of the law industry. Darkwood and leather furniture contrasts nicely with smartly dressed tables and good settings. Service is keen and French, while dishes are French with some oriental twists. The starter of confit foie gras with Earl Grey tea jelly and honey-glazed cippolini onions has strong, clear

continued

flavours, as does the perfectly cooked main course of roast breast of corn-fed chicken stuffed with merguez sausage, tabouleh and minted yogurt. Finish with an iced nougat soufflé with berry compôte and honeycomb or the excellent cheese selection.

Chef: John Newton **Owners:** Zak Jones & Andrew Thompson **Times:** 12-2.30/6-10.30, Closed Xmas, Sat-Sun **Prices:** Fixed L £14.50, Fixed D £19.50-£32, Coffee £2.50, Min/Water £3, Service added but optional 12.5% **Wine:** 12 bottles over £20, 5 bottles under £20, 3 by the glass (£4.50-£7) **Seats:** 50 **Smoking:** Air con **Children:** Portions **Directions:** Nearest station: Chancery Lane Situated between High Holborn and Fleet St **Parking:** On street

Refettorio

Traditional, Italian

Authentic Italian concept in chic surroundings

☎ 020 7438 8052 Crowne Plaza Hotel, 19 New Bridge St EC4V 6DB Plan 3-F2
e-mail: loncy.refettorio@ichotelsgroup.com
web: www.tableinthecity.com

Sleek, stylish and contemporary, Refettorio blends comfortably with the swish modernism of the Crown Plaza Hotel. The L-shaped room has a long bar, high windows hung with Venetian blinds and polished-wood floors and tables. Smart, brown leather booth-style seating provides discreet dining along one wall, while black-clad staff are suitably attentive. Authentic Italian food; excellent breads, a superb array of impeccably-sourced regional cheeses, hams and salamis, home-made pasta and an all-Italian wine list provide the impressive backdrop to an appealing menu of straightforward but accomplished and well-presented dishes. Try one of the selections of cured meats and cheeses (for sharing) that head up the menu, followed by lamb roasted with rosemary and oven-baked tomatoes.

Chef: Mattia Camorani **Owners:** Parallel/Crown Plaza **Times:** 12-2.30/6-10.30, Closed Xmas, New Year & BHs, Sun, Closed L Sat **Prices:** Starter £5.50-£9.50, Main £16-£20, Dessert £6-£7, Coffee £3.75, Min/Water £3.50, Service added but optional 12.5% **Wine:** 61 bottles over £20, 7 bottles under £20, 8 by the glass (£5.50-£6) **Notes:** Dress restrictions, Smart casual, Vegetarian available **Seats:** 70, Pr/dining room 30 **Smoking:** No pipes or cigars, Air con **Children:** Portions **Directions:** Nearest station: Blackfriars Situated on New Bridge St, opposite Blackfriars underground (exit 8) **Parking:** NCP - Queen Victoria St

The White Swan Pub & Dining Room

British, French

Busy, upmarket gastro-pub with smart dining room

☎ 020 7242 9696 108 Fetter Ln EC4A 1ES Plan 3-F3
e-mail: info@thewhiteswanlondon.com
web: www.thewhiteswanlondon.com

Beyond the bar of this tastefully restored pub, a mirror-lined staircase leads up to the bright, formal Dining Room. Decked out with white-clothed tables, its handsome wooden floors, contemporary chairs, banquettes and mirrored ceiling, cut an upmarket edge. Friendly, attentive and relaxed French service adds to the experience. The appealing, crowd-pleasing modern British and French menu combines classics alongside more esoteric ideas; think English asparagus with hollandaise and Piedmontese peppers with buffalo mozzarella versus seared foie gras with dried fruit compôte and truffle ice cream to start, with mains such as Scottish West Coast lemon sole à la meunière. Daily specials add interest.

Chef: Grant Murray **Owners:** Tom & Ed Martin **Times:** 12-3/6-10, Closed 25 Dec, 1 Jan and BHs, Sat-Sun (except private parties), Closed D Mon **Prices:** Fixed L £20, Starter £4.50-£8, Main £11-£17, Dessert £4.50-£5.50, Coffee £2.50, Min/Water £3.50, Service added but optional 12.5% **Wine:** 75 bottles over £20, 13 bottles under £20, 13 by the glass (£3.10-£6.70) **Notes:** Vegetarian available **Seats:** 44, Pr/dining room 44 **Smoking:** Air con **Children:** Portions **Directions:** Nearest station: Chancery Lane Tube Station Fetter Lane runs parallel with Chancery Lane in the City of London and it joins Fleet St with Holborn **Parking:** On Street and NCP (Hatton Garden)

Corney & Barrow at Fleet Place

☎ 020 7329 3141 3 Fleet Place EC4M 7RD
City wine bar chain offering contemporary dishes.

The Don

☎ 020 7626 2606 The Courtyard, 20 St Swithins Ln EC4 8AD
Modern European menu, in vibrant city restaurant.

Vivat Bacchus

☎ 020 7353 2648 47 Farringdon St, Holborn EC4A 4LL
web: www.theaa.com/restaurants/114014.html

Classic French and international dishes and three wine cellars to choose wine from, plus a cheese cellar.

LONDON N1

Almeida Restaurant

Traditional French

Conran eatery serving rustic French food

☎ 020 7354 4777 30 Almeida St, Islington N1 1TD Plan 1-F4
e-mail: almeida-reservations@conran-restaurants.co.uk
web: www.almeida-restaurants.co.uk

Just down from Highbury corner on the way to Islington, the Almeida is one of the cosiest eateries in the Conran empire, combining rustic French cooking with a fashionably muted décor. Take a drink in the intimate bar, and then move through to the expansive dining area, where a theatre kitchen puts all the culinary action on show - you'll find an extensive menu on offer with dishes distinguished by a pared down approach that lets top notch ingredients shine through. A few straightforward mains show the style; choose from the likes of coq au vin, grilled halibut with hollandaise, or rump of lamb with fondant potato and thyme jus.

Chef: Ian Wood **Owners:** Sir Terence Conran **Times:** 12-2.30/5.30-11, Closed 25-26 Dec, 1 Jan, Good Fri, 17 Apr **Prices:** Fixed L £14.50, Fixed D £17.50, Starter £4.50-£10.50, Main £11-£19.50, Dessert £3.50-£5.50, Coffee £3.50, Min/Water £3.50, Service added but optional 12.5% **Wine:** 270 bottles over £20, 26 bottles under £20, 30 by the glass (£2.75-£10.95) **Notes:** Vegetarian available **Seats:** 100, Pr/dining room 20 **Smoking:** N/Sm area, No pipes, Air con **Children:** Portions **Directions:** Nearest station: Angel/Islington/Highbury Turn right from station, along Upper St, past church **Parking:** Parking around building

The Drapers Arms

Modern Mediterranean

Convivial gastro-pub in trendy Islington

☎ 020 7619 0348 44 Barnsbury St N1 1ER Plan 1-F4
e-mail: info@thedrapersarms.co.uk
web: www.thedrapersarms.co.uk

Gastro-pub in a smart residential area of Islington; a lovely building with wooden floors and comfy sofas. A central door opens into the bar area with long wide spaces on either side for tables. The place is packed Sunday lunchtime with young families, older couples and groups of friends. The restaurant upstairs occupies the same large space with a fireplace at either end. Cooking is modern with influences from around the world. Think squash risotto cake with broccoli and parmesan fritters and corn cream, or Moroccan chicken with chickpea purée and tzatziki.

continued

LONDON N1 *continued*

Chef: Mark Emberton **Owners:** Paul McElhinney & Mark Emberton **Times:** 12-3/7-10.30, Closed 24-27 Dec, 1-2 Jan, Closed L Mon-Sat, D Sun **Prices:** Starter £5-£8, Main £11-£16, Dessert £5.50, Coffee £1.50, Min/Water £2.50, Service added but optional 12.5% **Wine:** 18 bottles over £20, 10 bottles under £20, 11 by the glass (£3.60-£5.20) **Notes:** Vegetarian available **Seats:** 50 **Smoking:** N/Sm in restaurant **Children:** Menu, Portions **Directions:** Nearest station: Highbury & Islington/Angel Please telephone for directions

Fifteen

Italian, Mediterranean V

Funky not-for-profit eatery

☎ 0871 330 1515 13 Westland Place N1 7LP
Plan 3-H6
web: www.fifteenrestaurant.com

It's rare to see the culinary crusader at the stove these days, but Jamie Oliver's pioneering venture into youth training is still going strong (Fifteen Foundation). Tucked away in a side street in the fashionably scruffy margins of the Square Mile, the not-for-profit eatery is a funky, unpretentious joint with a laid back trattoria on the ground floor for light meals, and a fine dining restaurant downstairs, which offers a short carte at lunchtimes, and a six-course tasting menu at night. Rooted in Italian-Mediterranean cuisine, the cooking makes the most of top-notch produce from the UK and Italy, delivering dishes such as Sicilian fish stew, or chargrilled Welsh lamb with butternut squash, sage, chestnuts, garlic and chilli.

Chef: Jamie Oliver, Andrew Parkinson **Owners:** Fifteen Foundation **Times:** 12-2.45/6.30-9.30, Closed Xmas-New Year, BHs, Closed D Sun **Prices:** Fixed L fr £22, Starter £8-£12, Main £17.50-£23.50, Dessert £6.50-£8, Coffee £2.25, Min/Water £3.25, Service added but optional 12.5% **Wine:** All bottles over £20, 8 by the glass (£5-£13) **Notes:** Tasting menu 6 courses £60, Vegetarian £50, Vegetarian menu, Dress Restrictions, Smart casual **Seats:** 68 **Smoking:** N/Sm in restaurant, Air con **Children:** Portions **Directions:** Nearest station: Old Street Exit 1 from Old St tube station, walk up City road, opposite Moorfields Eye Hospital **Parking:** On street & NCP

Frederick's Restaurant

Modern

Fashionable food in contemporary setting

☎ 020 7359 2888 Camden Passage, Islington N1 8EG Plan 1-F4
e-mail: eat@fredericks.co.uk
web: www.fredericks.co.uk

A modern glass frontage among the old shops of the antiques quarter picks out this well-established restaurant. Up front, the bar has a smart metropolitan edge, while the surprisingly spacious dining area includes an airy rear conservatory. Contemporary styling, modern art, clothed tables and efficient, youthful service create a fashionable vibe. The menu and cooking are equally modern, sprinkled with a few classics (tournedos Rossini, for instance) and offer plenty of choice. Expect roast rump of lamb with infused French beans and crushed new potatoes, and a tarte Tatin to finish, served with vanilla ice cream.

Chef: Adam Hilliard **Owners:** Louis Segal **Times:** 12-2.30/5.45-11.30, Closed Xmas, New Year, BHs, Sun (ex functions) **Prices:** Fixed L £14, Fixed D £17, Starter £7-£11.50, Main £12.50-£21, Dessert £5.50, Coffee £1.90, Min/Water £3, Service added but optional 12.5% **Wine:** 128 bottles over £20, 25 bottles under £20 **Notes:** Vegetarian available, Civ Wed 200 **Seats:** 150, Pr/dining room 30 **Smoking:** N/Sm area, Air con **Children:** Menu, Portions **Directions:** Nearest station: Angel From underground 2 mins walk to Camden Passage. Restaurant among the antique shops **Parking:** NCP Business Design Centre

The House

Traditional British, European V

Enjoyable, simple cooking in a relaxed and comfortable environment

☎ 020 7704 7410 63-69 Canonbury Rd N1 2DG
Plan 1-F4
e-mail: info@inthehouse.biz
web: www.inthehouse.biz

Behind a maroon awninged, red-brick façade lies this cosy neighbourhood restaurant which has quite a local following. Wooden floors, whitewashed walls and simple artwork give the dining room a light and airy feel during the day. In the evening, locals gather around the comfortable bar sofas and well-spaced dining tables. Simple dishes prove very satisfying in this setting. Try the sea bass sashimi with yuzu and pickled ginger to start and a main course of chargrilled rib of Buccleuch beef with gratinated mushroom and shallot crust. Finish with lemon ricotta cake.

Chef: Jeremy Hollingsworth **Owners:** Barnaby & Grace Meredith/Jeremy Hollingsworth **Times:** 12-2.30/6-10.30, Closed 24-26 Dec, Closed L Mon **Prices:** Fixed L fr £14.95, Starter £5.50-£12.50, Main £12.95-£22.50, Dessert £6, Coffee £1.70, Min/Water £3.20, Service added but optional 12.5% **Wine:** 57 bottles over £20, 18 bottles under £20, 12 by the glass (£3.25-£6.50) **Notes:** Vegetarian available **Seats:** 60 **Smoking:** N/Sm in restaurant **Children:** Menu, Portions **Directions:** Nearest station: Highbury & Islington tube Behind town hall on Upper St Islington. Between Highbury Corner and Essex Rd **Parking:** Meter parking on street

The Real Greek

Greek

Popular, bustling, earthy, authentic Hoxton Greek

☎ 020 7739 8212 15 Hoxton Market N1 6HG
Plan 7-B2
e-mail: admin@therealgreek.demon.co.uk
web: www.therealgreek.co.uk

The name sums it up; a fashionable, authentic, unpretentious Greek outfit located on the market square between two old buildings. While retaining some of this old charm, stripped-wood floors, closely packed plain wooden tables, an open kitchen and youthful, friendly service fit the bill, while the adjoining Mezedopolis (a wine and mezedes bar) cranks up the volume. The lengthy menu (in English and Greek) draws on the plentiful Greek larder, delivering simple, robust and colourful authentic dishes, packed with mezedes (appetisers) and partnered by Greek wines. A typical meal might begin with crevettes saganaki with Ismir-style meat dumplings served with trahana to follow.

Chef: Alasdair Fraser **Owners:** Theodore Kyriakou & Paloma Campbell **Times:** 12-3/5.30-10.30, Closed 23-27 Dec, BHs, Sun **Prices:** Starter £3.20-£8.95, Main £13.50-£17.50, Dessert £5.50, Coffee £1.95, Min/Water £2.80, Service added but optional 12.5% **Wine:** 16 bottles over £20, 26 bottles under £20, 10 by the glass (£12.50-£37) **Notes:** Vegetarian available **Seats:** 76, Pr/dining room 24 **Smoking:** No pipes, No cigars **Directions:** Nearest station: Old Street Situated in square behind Holiday Inn on Old St. From tube station walk down Old St past Fire Station then 1st left 1st right to the back of inn **Parking:** Meter parking available

Canal 125

☎ 020 7837 1924 125 Caledonian Rd N1 9RG
web: www.theaa.com/restaurants/113929.html
A real find, unassumingly tucked away, with three floors, including a restaurant, bar and two terraces and a Modern European menu.

Cru

☎ 020 7729 5252 2-4 Rufus St, Hoxton N1 6PE
European dishes with some global additions, served in a relaxing friendly environment.

Le Montmartre

☎ 020 7688 1497 196 Essex Rd, Islington N1 8LZ
web: www.theaa.com/restaurants/113947.html
An unfussy, atmospheric bistro serving delicious, regional French food at decent prices.

Masala Zones

☎ 020 7359 3399 80 Upper St N1 0NP
Modern Indian with a balanced approach.

Strada

☎ 020 7226 9742 105-106 Upper St N1 1QN
Superior pizza from quality ingredients cooked in wood-fired ovens.

Wagamama

☎ 020 7226 2664 The N1 Centre, Parkfield St, Islington N1
Informal noodle bar with no booking.

Zigni House

☎ 020 7226 7418 330 Essex Rd N1 3PB
web: www.theaa.com/restaurants/113983.html
A vibrant East African restaurant and bar that is a place of pilgrimage for those who love this cuisine. As well as the à la carte menu there's a superb buffet - very popular.

England

LONDON N5

Iznik

☎ 020 7354 5697 19 Highbury Park N5 1QJ
web: www.theaa.com/restaurants/113940.html
Turkish restaurant with bright walls and darkwood fittings. Authentic, freshly prepared Ottoman dishes.

LONDON N6

The Bull Pub & Dining Room

European **NEW**

Lively contemporary and traditional gastro-pub offering confident cooking

☎ 0845 456 5033 13 North Hill N6 4AB Plan 1-E5
e-mail: info@inthebull.biz
web: www.inthebull.biz

A contemporary, informal gastro-pub, sister to The House at Islington, with buzzy, ground-floor dining area and open hatch to the kitchen. Upstairs is the 'pub' with beautiful ceiling windows and cherrywood bar. There is a large terrace for alfresco dining on summer days.

continued

Morgan M

LONDON N7

Modern French NOTABLE WINE LIST

Authentic, top-notch French cooking in intimate surroundings

☎ 020 7609 3560 489 Liverpool Rd, Islington N7 8NS
Plan 1-F5
web: www.morganm.com

The small, unassuming, frosted-glass frontage seems perfectly in keeping with the restrained elegance of chef-patron Morgan Meunier's highly intimate, neighbourhood eatery. The square room comes decked out in polished-wood floors, magnolia and pale green walls, white linen cloths and simple, but elegant table appointments. Service is predictably very French, polished and attentive, while Morgan himself circulates tables at the end of service with style and good humour. His is real French cooking, technically highly adept while using superb-quality seasonal ingredients, with lots of produce brought in fresh from France and cooked with true passion. Think a ravioli of snails in Chablis, poached garlic and a red wine jus, for instance, perhaps followed by grilled Anjou squab pigeon with Puy lentils, glazed apple, pommes Anna and sauce soubise, with maybe a dark chocolate moelleux partnered by a milk sorbet and Armagnac drink heading up desserts. Morgan's intelligently compact carte comes bolstered by a six-course tasting option (including a superb vegetarian alternative), while the wine list takes an unsurprisingly, predominantly patriotically French wine list.

Notable Wine List: A well presented, predominately French wine list.

Chef: M Meunier & S Soulard **Owners:** Morgan Meunier **Times:** 12-2.30/7-10.30, Closed 24 Dec-30 Dec, Mon, Closed L Tues, Sat, D Sun **Prices:** Fixed L fr £19.50, Fixed D fr £32, Coffee £3.50, Min/Water £3.50, Service added but optional 12.5% **Wine:** 100 bottles over £20, 10 bottles under £20, 12 by the glass (£4.50-£10.50) **Notes:** Tasting menu 6 courses £34-39, Vegetarian available, Dress Restrictions, Smart casual **Seats:** 48, Pr/dining room 12 **Smoking:** N/Sm in restaurant, Air con **Children:** Portions **Parking:** On Liverpool Rd

LONDON N6 *continued*

French-influenced modern British cuisine is on offer here with the emphasis on simplicity and quality produce. The main menu is supplemented by blackboard specials and an express lunch menu. Confident cooking is demonstrated with some interesting combinations. Try roast cod with octopus and chorizo stew and sauce Romesco, or gnocchi of girolles, shallots, tomato, rocket and pesto, with warm gingerbread to finish.

Chef: Jeremy Hollingsworth **Owners:** J E Barnaby Meredith **Times:** 12-3.30/6-10.30, Closed 25 Dec, Closed L Mon **Prices:** Fixed L fr £14.95, Fixed D £20-£35.95, Starter £5.50-£10.50, Main £11.95-£16.95, Dessert £5-£6, Coffee £1.50, Min/Water £3, Service optional **Wine:** 65 bottles over £20, 19 bottles under £20, 16 by the glass (£3.25-£9.75) **Notes:** Brunch served Sat & Sun, Vegetarian available **Seats:** 100, Pr/dining room 20 **Smoking:** N/Sm area, No pipes **Children:** Portions **Directions:** Nearest station: Highgate 5 min walk from Highgate tube station **Parking:** 3

LONDON N7

Morgan M

see page 263

LONDON N8

Les Associes

☎ 020 8348 8944 172 Park Rd,
Crouch End N8 8JY
web: www.theaa.com/restaurants/113948.html

French through and through, from décor to menu and wine list. Intimate atmosphere. Some tables outside too.

LONDON N16

Rasa

Indian V

Keralan cooking in authentic surroundings

☎ 020 7249 0344 55 Stoke Newington Church St
N16 0AR Plan 1-F5
e-mail: dasrasa@hotmail.com
web: www.rasarestaurants.com

A simple family-run restaurant with two separate dining areas, decorated in Keralan style. The décor is in keeping with the authentic vegetarian cooking which is a speciality here, coming from the famous Nair community in Kerala. The restaurant name is very apt. Rasa is a Sanskrit word with many meanings, including taste and flavour. Choose from a huge variety of dishes including lots of specialities from traditional Keralan villages, Brahmin recipes and popular dishes from Southern India. Moru Kachiathu for example, is a sweet and sour dish combining sweet mangoes and green bananas, cooked in yogurt with green chillies, ginger and fresh curry leaves.

Chef: Rajan Karattil **Owners:** Mr S Sreedharan **Times:** 12-3/6-11.30, Closed 24-26 Dec, 1 Jan, Closed L Mon-Fri **Prices:** Fixed L £16, Fixed D £16, Starter £2.75-£3, Main £3.70-£5.95, Dessert £2.75-£3, Coffee £1.75, Min/Water £2.50, Service added but optional 12.5% **Wine:** 5 bottles over £20, 4 bottles under £20, 1 by the glass (£2.25) **Notes:** Fixed L 3 courses, Vegetarian menu **Seats:** 64, Pr/dining room 40 **Smoking:** N/Sm in restaurant, Air con **Directions:** Nearest station: Angel or Finsbury Park Telephone for directions **Parking:** On street

LONDON N17

The Lock Dining Bar

British, International NEW

Great value destination

☎ 020 8885 2829 Heron House, Hale Wharf,
Ferry Ln N17 9NF Plan 1-F5
e-mail: thelock06@btconnect.com
web: thelock-diningbar.com

You'll find this new restaurant in a modern building right on the lock just minutes away from the station. Don't be put off by the tube journey as it's well worth a little time to enjoy the warm hospitality and fine cooking here. Inside it's New York loft style with pine flooring and an open-plan kitchen. Modern British dishes with Italian influences focus on fresh seasonal produce. Quality is carefully controlled with bread made on the premises and all butchering and filleting also done on site. The menu changes every six weeks but you might try a starter like ham hock terrine with taleggio cheese and bruschetta. Main courses, supplemented by daily specials, might feature roast monkish with potato gnocchi and mushrooms.

Chef: Adebola Adeshina **Owners:** Adebola Adeshina, Fabrizio Russo **Times:** 12-2.30/6.30-10, Closed L Sat (except match days), D Mon, Sun **Prices:** Fixed L £10-£12, Starter £4-£8.50, Main £8-£17.95, Dessert £5, Coffee £1.50, Min/Water £3.50, Service added but optional 10% **Wine:** 28 bottles over £20, 14 bottles under £20, 10 by the glass (£3-£3.95) **Notes:** Sun L £10, 7 course tasting menu incl wine £75, Vegetarian available, Dress Restrictions, Smart casual, no hats/caps **Seats:** 60, Pr/dining room 18 **Smoking:** Air con **Children:** Menu, Portions **Directions:** Nearest station: Tottenham Hale, Black Horse Station Telephone for directions **Parking:** 20

LONDON N19

The Parsee

Indian, Parsee

Authentic Parsee cooking from quality fresh ingredients

☎ 020 7272 9091 34 Highgate Hill N19 5NL
Plan 1-E5
e-mail: dining@theparsee.co.uk
web: www.theparsee.co.uk

Parsee cuisine (a blend of Persian and Indian traditions) is offered from an extensive menu at this contemporary restaurant. Informative descriptions aid your choice, and a platter of assorted starters is a great way to experience the variety. A selection of chargrilled dishes includes Loch Fyne salmon marinated in red hot masala, but perhaps one of the favourite main courses is khari murghi nay tarelo papeto, as prepared in every Parsee home - chicken cooked with whole spices and onion in a light gravy, served with steamed rice and deep-fried chunks of potato.

Chef: Cyrus Todiwala & Chef Angelo **Owners:** The Parsee **Times:** 6-10.45, Closed Xmas, 1 Jan, BHs, Sun, Closed L all week **Prices:** Fixed D £30, Starter £3.50-£6.75, Main £9.75-£12.75, Dessert £3.50-£4.25, Coffee £1.25, Min/Water £2.75, Service added but optional 10% **Wine:** 100% bottles under £20, 8 by the glass (£3.25-£4.50) **Notes:** Vegetarian available **Seats:** 50, Pr/dining room 40 **Smoking:** N/Sm area, No pipes, Air con **Children:** Portions **Directions:** Nearest station: Archway Opposite Whittington Hospital **Parking:** On street

LONDON NW1

Dorset Square Hotel

Modern British NEW

Intimate, relaxed bar-restaurant resembling a garden potting shed

☎ 020 7723 7874 39-40 Dorset Square NW1 8QN
Plan 2-F4
e-mail: info@dorsetsquare.co.uk
web: www.dorsetsquare.co.uk

This smart, delightfully restored Regency townhouse hotel stands on the original site of Lord's cricket ground. Its popular, lower-ground-floor Potting Shed Restaurant and Bar is a split-level affair with part atrium roof and a warm, sunny feel, and, as its name suggests, develops the gardening theme with an array of terracotta pots and seed boxes across one wall. The menu is simple, accomplished and seasonal, focusing on accurate flavours. Take baked goat's cheese wrapped in filo pastry with red pepper dressing, rump of lamb with a tapenade crust and courgette Provençal, or a classic cottage pie with baby turnip, swede and peas.

Chef: Martin Halls **Owners:** LHP **Times:** 12-3/6-10.30, Closed L Sat, D Sun **Prices:** Fixed L £16.95, Fixed D £24.50, Starter £4.95-£8.95, Main £11.50-£17.95, Dessert £5.95, Coffee £2.75, Min/Water £3.50, Service added but optional 12.5% **Wine:** 23 bottles over £20, 5 bottles under £20, 10 by the glass (£4.50-£6.50) **Notes:** Dress Restrictions, Smart casual **Seats:** 45, Pr/dining room 10 **Smoking:** N/Sm area, No pipes, No cigars, Air con **Children:** Portions **Rooms:** 37 (37 en suite) ★★★★ TH
Directions: Nearest station: Baker St/Marylebone Telephone for directions
Parking: NCP Marylebone Rd

Novotel London Euston

Modern European

Sleek modern hotel restaurant with a wide-ranging carte

☎ 020 7666 9080 100-110 Euston Rd NW1 2AJ
Plan 3-C5
e-mail: h5309-fb@accor.com
web: www.novotel.com

Popular hotel in a central location with a wide range of facilities, including Mirrors restaurant and bar. Open-plan public areas give a great sense of space and have a contemporary look with lots of glass and neutral woods. The food is modern European, combining the classics with modern global influences to bring an element of excitement to the dishes. Specialities include baked oysters on creamed leeks with pommery mustard and toasted pine nuts, and Scottish premier steak with pomme sablé, sautéed baby spinach, pumpkin and ceps.

Chef: Denzil Newton **Owners:** Accor UK Business & Leisure **Times:** 12-2.30/6-10.30, Closed L Sat, Sun, BHs **Prices:** Fixed L £16.95, Fixed D £21-£35, Starter £5.25-£7.50, Main £12.50-£19.95, Dessert £5, Coffee £2.50, Min/Water £3.95, Service added but optional 10% **Wine:** 9 bottles over £20, 10 bottles under £20, 17 by the glass (£3.95-£7.50) **Seats:** 89, Pr/dining room 250 **Smoking:** No pipes, No cigars, Air con **Children:** Menu, Portions **Rooms:** 312 (312 en suite) ★★★★
Directions: Nearest station: King's Cross/Euston 5 mins walk between King's Cross and Euston Station, opposite British Library. 1m from Regent's Park **Parking:** Ibis Euston

Odette's

French, European

Intimate neighbourhood restaurant with loyal local clientele

☎ 020 7586 5486 130 Regents Park Rd NW1 8XL
Plan 1-E4

An enduringly popular Primrose Hill institution, this intimate restaurant and wine bar with its green awning and exterior paintwork continues to pull in an adoring crowd. Ornate, gilt-framed mirrors line the walls in the front, green-themed dining room, with two further dining areas at the back and downstairs in the plant-filled conservatory and small bar. Candlelit tables create an intimate atmosphere at night. The modern European carte has strong French influences and is a lengthy affair. Luxury items and some unusual combinations make for a colourful and creative menu, strong on presentation. The wine list is seriously impressive.

Times: 12.30-2.30/7-11, Closed BHs, Closed L Sat, D Sun
Directions: Nearest station: Chalk Farm. By Primrose Hill. Telephone for directions

Sardo Canale

Modern Italian

Authentic Italian cuisine in surprising setting

☎ 020 7722 2800 42 Gloucester Av NW1 8JD
Plan 1-E4
e-mail: info@sardocanale.com
web: www.sardocanale.com

This unusual restaurant is located in a new building, designed around an old tunnel and tower dating back to 1850. The original brick tunnel with cobbled stones was used by horses pulling barges in the nearby Grand Union Canal. It's certainly a novel place to find a modern Italian restaurant, serving up regional Italian cooking using fresh ingredients and authentic Sardinian recipes. Service is formal, but the atmosphere is relaxed and friendly, so take some time to peruse the extensive Italian menu, thankfully with translations. Signature dishes include spaghetti alla bottarga, a popular Sardinian pasta served with a sauce made of fresh tomatoes and aromatic sausage. There's a great Italian Sunday lunch menu too.

Chef: Roberto Sardu **Owners:** Romolo & Bianca Mudu **Times:** 12-3/6-11, Closed 25-26 Dec, BHs, Closed L Mon **Prices:** Fixed L £13, Starter £6.90-£8.90, Main £12-£17.50, Dessert £5.50-£6, Coffee £2, Min/Water £2.90, Service added but optional 12.5% **Notes:** Sun L 3 courses £23, Vegetarian available **Seats:** 100, Pr/dining room 40 **Smoking:** N/Sm area, No pipes, No cigars, Air con **Children:** Portions **Directions:** Nearest station: Chalk Farm/Camden Town Please telephone for directions **Parking:** On street

The Winter Garden

Modern British

Stunning atrium restaurant

☎ 020 7631 8000 The Landmark London, 222 Marylebone Rd NW1 6JQ Plan 2-F4
e-mail: dining@thelandmark.co.uk
web: www.landmarklondon.co.uk

One of the last great railway hotels and former headquarters of British Rail, the building is over 100 years old. The Winter Garden is a stunning open-plan restaurant situated at the base of an eight-storey atrium. At night, the restaurant turns into a more intimate affair. A selection of modern British dishes is offered on a menu featuring

continued

England

LONDON NW1 *continued*

fresh quality produce. Typical starters might include seared diver scallops while a main course of honey-roasted Gressingham duck breast would be accompanied by rosemary mash, Savoy cabbage and glazed baby onions. A tempting range of desserts might include Valrhona chocolate fondant with cardamom ice cream.

The Winter Garden

Chef: Gary Klaner **Owners:** Jatuporn Sihanatkathakul **Times:** 11.30-3/6-11.30 **Prices:** Fixed L £23.50-£24.50, Fixed D £33.95, Starter £6-£12, Main £19-£28, Dessert £8-£9, Coffee £4.50, Min/Water £4.50, Service optional **Wine:** 30 bottles over £20, 14 by the glass (£7-£9.25) **Notes:** Vegetarian available, Civ Wed 280 **Seats:** 80, Pr/dining room 360 **Smoking:** N/Sm area, Air con **Children:** Menu, Portions **Rooms:** 299 (299 en suite) ★★★★★ HL **Directions:** Nearest station: Marylebone M25 turn on to the A40 and continue 16m following signs for West End. Continue along Marlybone Rd for 300 mtrs. Restaurant on left **Parking:** 75

Belgo

☎ 020 7267 0718 72 Chalk Farm Rd NW1 8AN

Belgian style, with strong beer, good seafood (mussels of course) and staff in habits.

Wagamama

☎ 020 7428 0800 11 Jamestown Rd, Camden NW1 7BW

Informal noodle bar with no booking.

LONDON NW2

King Sitric

☎ 020 8452 4175

142-152 Cricklewood Broadway NW2 3ED

web: www.theaa.com/restaurants/114006.html

A fusion of modern Irish and international dishes in modern, art deco influenced surroundings.

Philpotts Mezzaluna

☎ 020 7794 0455 424 Finchley Rd NW2 2HY

web: www.theaa.com/restaurants/113962.html

Italian restaurant with modern interior. Clothed tables, red walls and modern art set the scene for enjoying inventive dishes.

Spice of Hampstead

☎ 020 7794 5922 448 Finchley Rd, Child's Hill NW2 2HY

web: www.theaa.com/restaurants/113972.html

Bright white walls, wooden floors and modern art at this friendly Indian restaurant.

LONDON NW3

Manna

Vegetarian V

Charming, fun and informal vegetarian restaurant

☎ 020 7722 8028 4 Erskine Rd, Primrose Hill NW3 3AJ Plan 1-E4

e-mail: yourhost@manna-veg.com

web: www.manna-veg.com

Believed to be the oldest vegetarian dinner restaurant in England, Manna was founded in the 1960s to bring a gourmet experience to vegetarians and vegans. Top quality organic ingredients are used, and the menu takes its inspiration from around the world with dishes such as Hydrabad aubergine poppadom wrap on tamarind chutney and raita, spinach and emmental timbale with griddled asparagus, potato Lyonnaise and pea purée, and pistachio and date chocolate brownie with a chilli chocolate sauce and stem ginger ice cream. Manna also offers takeaway and outside catering services.

Times: 12.30-3/6.30-11, Closed 25 Dec-1 Jan, Closed L Mon-Sat **Directions:** Nearest station: Chalk Farm Telephone for directions.

The Wells Tavern

European

Relaxed but stylish dining in a delightful former coaching inn

☎ 020 7794 3785 30 Well Walk NW3 1BX Plan 1-G5

e-mail: info@thewellshampstead.co.uk

web: www.thewellshampstead.co.uk

Popular gastro-pub located in a beautiful Georgian building with three intimate dining rooms upstairs and a spacious bar restaurant downstairs, complete with comfy sofas and an open-plan kitchen. In the bar you can snack on olives and freshly baked breads or go for a set lunch priced for one or two courses. Upstairs the carte offers carefully executed European-style cooking using seasonal ingredients. Expect dishes like foie gras terrine with sauce gribiche to start, followed by tournedos of venison with caramelised onions and celeriac purée and crème brûlée with Baileys for dessert.

Chef: Ian Sutton **Owners:** Beth Coventry **Times:** 12-3/7-10.30, Closed 1 Jan, Closed D 24-26 Dec **Prices:** Fixed L fr £13.95, Fixed D fr £28.50, Starter £4.50-£5.75, Main £9.95-£13.95, Dessert fr £3.75, Coffee £2.20, Min/Water £2.90, Service added but optional 12.5% **Wine:** 36 bottles over £20, 9 bottles under £20, 12 by the glass (£3.50-£6.25) **Notes:** Vegetarian available **Seats:** 50, Pr/dining room 12 **Smoking:** N/Sm in restaurant, Air con **Children:** Portions **Directions:** Nearest station: Hampstead Left out of station, 1st left through Flask Walk. 5 mins from Hampstead Heath **Parking:** On street pay & display

Artigiano

☎ 020 7794 4288 12a Belsize Ter NW3 4AX
web: www.etruscarestaurants.com
Mix of contemporary Italian cuisine.

Hellenic

☎ 020 7431 1001 291 Finchley Rd NW3 6ND
web: www.theaa.com/restaurants/113938.html
Home-made Greek cooking - Mezedes a speciality (ten cold starters and ten hot main dishes). Fantastic value.

Yo! Sushi

☎ 020 7431 4499 02 Centre, 255 Finchley Rd NW3 6LH
Sushi, sashimi, noodles and more delivered by conveyor belt and priced according to colour-coded plates.

LONDON NW4

The Gallery

☎ 020 8202 4000 407-411 Hendon Way NW4 3LH
web: www.theaa.com/restaurants/114012.html

Art gallery highlighting the talents of young British and French artists. English cuisine with French influences.

LONDON NW6

Singapore Garden Restaurant

Singaporean, Malaysian

Well established Oriental with a mixture of Chinese and Singaporean dishes

☎ 020 7328 5314 & 7624 8233 83-83a Fairfax Rd, West Hampstead NW6 4DY Plan 1-E4

Now refurbished and re-designed to occupy one room, this family-run affair is situated in a parade of upmarket shops close to Finchley Road tube. The Lim family have built up a loyal clientele, drawn by the animated atmosphere and by the fact that the mainly standard Chinese menu is extended by the inclusion of Singaporean and Malay specialities. So, look to these and choose from what the house excels at, namely fiery curries and decent noodle dishes. Typical dishes include starters like kuay pie tee - crispy pastry cups with bamboo shoots, chicken and prawns - followed by the likes of squid blachan, Assam fish curry, and Ayam curry - chicken cooked with coconut and Malaysian spices.

Chef: Kok Sum Toh **Owners:** Hibiscus Restaurants Ltd **Times:** 12-2.45/6-10.45, Closed 4 days at Xmas **Prices:** Fixed D £22-£37.50, Starter £5.20-

continued

£35, Main £6.50-£32.50, Dessert £4.50-£6, Coffee £2, Min/Water £3.30, Service added but optional 12.5% **Wine:** 34 bottles over £20, 4 bottles under £20, 4 by the glass (£4-£4.80) **Notes:** Fixed D 5 courses, Vegetarian available **Seats:** 100, Pr/dining room 6 **Smoking:** N/Sm in restaurant, Air con **Directions:** Nearest station: Swiss Cottage, Finchley Road Off Finchley Rd, on right before Belsize Rd rdbt **Parking:** Meters on street

Gourmet Burger Kitchen

☎ 020 7794 5455 331 West End Ln, West Hampstead NW6 1RS
New Zealand inspired burger joint using top notch beef.

LONDON NW8

Sofra - St John's Wood

☎ 020 7240 4411 11 Circus Rd NW8 6NX
web: www.theaa.com/restaurants/113971.html
Traditional Turkish restaurant with modern approach. Menu includes healthy eating choices.

LONDON NW10

Sabras Restaurant

Indian vegetarian V

Surati regional restaurant serving exclusively vegetarian Indian cooking

☎ 020 8459 0340 263 High Rd, Willesden Green NW10 2RX Plan 1-D4
web: www.sabras.co.uk

In a high street location with glass shop front looking onto the street, the interior of this restaurant is well-lit with light white and cream décor. For over 30 years it has served exclusively vegetarian cuisine from the Surati region of India, cooked with enthusiasm and skill. With a well-established reputation, the specialist cuisine draws a wide following to enjoy dishes like Ragda patish (spiced potato cake with a mild yellow pea sauce) and Makai Kaju (sweetcorn, sweet peppers and cashew nuts in a tomato sauce). If you enjoy Indian cuisine and fancy trying something a bit different this would be an excellent choice.

Chef: Mrs H Desai **Owners:** Mr H Desai **Times:** 6-10, Closed 25 & 26 Dec, BH Mon, Mon, Closed L all week **Prices:** Starter £3.50-£6.50, Main £4.25-£7.50, Dessert £3.50, Coffee £1.25, Min/Water £3, Service added but optional 10% **Wine:** 8 by the glass (£2.50) **Notes:** Vegetarian only **Seats:** 32 **Smoking:** N/Sm in restaurant **Children:** Portions **Directions:** Nearest station: Dollis Hill Telephone for directions **Parking:** On street

LONDON SE1

The Anchor & Hope

Traditional European

Lively gastro-pub with attitude

☎ 020 7928 9898 36 The Cut SE1 8LP Plan 5-F5
e-mail: anchorandhope@btconnect.com

This popular classic pub is packed as soon as the doors open and, as there's no booking, it's a case of turning up early and waiting for a table. Wooden floors and furniture, bare walls, open kitchen and a buzzy, lively, informal atmosphere all crank up the volume. A heavy curtain separates the bar from the restaurant area, though it's a

continued

England

LONDON SE1 *continued*

similarly sociable affair with close-set tables that you may have to share, while the kitchen's twice-daily-changing menus show an equally rustic simplicity with their fresh quality ingredients and uncompromising flavours. Think rabbit served with butter beans and fennel, or partridge with smoked sausage and choucroute, and perhaps a quince and almond tart heading up desserts.

Chef: Jonathon Jones, Harry Lester **Owners:** Robert Shaw, Mike Belben, Jonathon Jones, Harry Lester **Times:** 12-2.30/6-10.30, Closed BHs, 25 Dec-1 Jan, Sun, Closed L Mon **Prices:** Starter £3.60-£10, Main £9.80-£22, Dessert £3.80-£5, Coffee £1, Min/Water £2.50, Service optional **Wine:** 25 bottles over £20, 26 bottles under £20, 13 by the glass (£1.80-£3.25) **Notes:** Vegetarian available **Seats:** 58 **Smoking:** N/Sm in restaurant **Directions:** Nearest station: Southwark/Waterloo Telephone for directions

Baltic

Eastern European

Eastern European restaurant with hearty modern food

☎ 020 7928 1111 74 Blackfriars Rd SE1 8HA Plan 5-F5
e-mail: info@balticrestaurant.co.uk
web: www.balticrestaurant.co.uk

Spacious open-plan restaurant with understated modern décor, comfortable seating, soft lighting and ceiling fans. Eastern European specialities appeal to both ex-pats and customers reliving a holiday experience. The menu is comprehensive, including set meal options. There's a good choice of blinis in starter or main course proportions and favourites such as sorrel soup, smoked eel, marinated herrings and pierogi. Mains take in leczo (spiced beef, sausage and paprika goulash), stroganoff, and whole baked bream with fennel, dill and red onion salad. Finish with rhum baba or vodka cherry ice cream.

Times: 12-3.30/6-11, Closed Xmas, 1 Jan, BHs **Directions:** Nearest station: Southwark Opposite Southwark Station, 5 mins walk from Waterloo

Butlers Wharf Chop House

British

Traditional British fare beside Old Father Thames

☎ 020 7403 3403 The Butlers Wharf Building, 36e Shad Thames SE1 2YE Plan 6-D2
e-mail: bwchophouse@conran-restaurants.co.uk
web: www.conran.com

Part of London's revitalised wharf-land, this lively eatery remains a favourite in the Conran stable of restaurants. The long terrace is the place to hang out in the warmer months and commands fantastic views of Tower Bridge and the comings and goings on the Thames. Those who like traditional British fare flock here to sample the likes of roast beef and Yorkshire pudding, steak and kidney pie with oysters, and fish and chips with mushy peas. Leave room for desserts such as bread-and-butter pudding with custard or savouries such as Devils on Horseback.

Chef: Craig James **Owners:** Conran Restaurants **Times:** 12-3/6-11, Closed 1 Jan, Closed D Sun (mid Oct-May) **Prices:** Fixed L £22, Starter £6.50-£13.50, Main £14-£26, Dessert £4.75-£6.50, Coffee £2, Min/Water £3.25, Service added but optional 12.5% **Wine:** 352 bottles over £20, 11 bottles under £20, 14 by the glass (£4.50-£8.95) **Notes:** Vegetarian available **Seats:** 110 **Children:** Portions **Directions:** Nearest station: Tower Hill, London Bridge On river front, SE side of Tower Bridge **Parking:** NCP, on street, multi-storey

Cantina del Ponte

Italian

Fashionable riverside Italian

☎ 020 7403 5403 The Butlers Wharf Building, 36c Shad Thames SE1 2YE Plan 6-D2
e-mail: cantina@conran-restaurants.co.uk
web: www.conran.com/eat

Situated on Butler's Wharf quayside, this typical Conran restaurant is strong on service and dependable, gratifying food in trendy surroundings. With its Thames-side location and large mural of an Italian marketplace running the length of the restaurant, it's almost unbeatable for alfresco eating in warm summer weather and on a day-to-day basis there is more than enough on this lengthy menu of bold flavours and simple, authentic dishes to please everyone. If the pizzas from the wood-fired ovens aren't sophisticated enough then head toward starters such as a robust panzanella, followed by pan-fried John Dory with leeks, capers and olives.

Times: 12-3/6-11, Closed 24-26 Dec **Directions:** Nearest station: Tower Hill, London Bridge. SE side of Tower Bridge, on riverfront

Cantina Vinopolis

Italian

Delightful dishes to complement the wine cellar tours

☎ 020 7940 8333 1 Bankside SE1 9BU Plan 6-A3
e-mail: info@cantinavinopolis.com
web: www.cantinavinopolis.com

The wine-related attraction Vinopolis is located in the cavernous old railway vaults on Bankside by the Thames, with a large new glass entrance and cocktail lounge. The restaurant is set against a backdrop of vaulted arches with an open-plan kitchen at the far end. Produce comes fresh from Borough Market next door and is carefully prepared, accurately cooked and served in traditional style. Calves' liver with crispy bacon, spinach, confit shallot, mash and sauce diable delivers simple and true flavours. The wine list reflects Vinopolis expertise and offers great value.

Chef: Moges A Wolde **Times:** 12-3/6-10.30, Closed BHs, Closed D Sun **Prices:** Fixed L £14.50, Fixed D £17.50-£29.50, Starter £4.95-£7.95, Main £9.50-£19.50, Dessert £4.50-£6.50, Coffee £2, Min/Water £3.50, Service added but optional **Wine:** 35 bottles over £20, 16 bottles under £20, 18 by the glass (£4.95-£9.95) **Notes:** Tasting menu available, Vegetarian available, Dress Restrictions, Smart casual **Seats:** 160 **Smoking:** N/Sm in restaurant, Air con **Directions:** Nearest station: London Bridge 5 min walk from London Bridge on Bankside between Southwark Cathedral & Shakespeare's Globe Theatre

Champor Champor

Modern Malaysian

Creative modern Malaysian cooking in atmospheric, ethnic surroundings

☎ 020 7403 4600 62-64 Weston St SE1 3QJ Plan 6-B2
e-mail: mail@champor-champor.com
web: www.champor-champor.com

Forgive the side street location behind London Bridge Station as, once through the door, this intimate Malay restaurant comes brimful of atmosphere. Champor-Champor means 'mix-and-match' in Malay, and

continued

this applies to the bohemian décor as well as the food. Vivid colours, tribal artefacts and Buddhist statues mingle with modern art and the whiff of incense in the busily decorated space. The creative cooking follows the theme, with its mix of Asian cuisines grafted onto Malay roots; think warm beef fillet kerabu with steamed snake beans and yellow rice.

Chef: Adu Amran Hassan **Owners:** Charles Tyler, Adu Amran Hassan **Times:** 6.15-10.15, Closed Xmas-N Year (7 days), Etr (5 days), BHs, Closed L, Times may vary - please check **Prices:** Fixed D fr £26, Coffee £1.90, Min/Water £2.70, Service added but optional 15% **Wine:** 15 bottles over £20, 28 bottles under £20, 4 by the glass (£4-£4.50) **Notes:** Tasting menu 7 courses £39.50, Vegetarian available **Seats:** 38, Pr/dining room 8 **Smoking:** N/Sm in restaurant, Air con **Directions:** Nearest station: London Bridge Joiner St exit. Follow Saint Thomas St & 1st right into Weston St, restaurant 100yds on left **Parking:** Snowsfields multi-storey

Fire Station

Modern European

Bustling gastro-pub in a former fire station close to Waterloo station

☎ 020 7620 2226 150 Waterloo Rd SE1 8SB
Plan 5-E5
e-mail: firestation.waterloo@pathfinderpubs.co.uk
web: www.pathfinderpubs.co.uk

Converted brick-built fire station with a bar area at the front and particularly large windows - once the drive-in doors for the fire engines - and a spacious dining area with an open-plan kitchen to the rear. Rough red brick walls are adorned with fire service paraphernalia. It is an unpretentious pub setting offering speedy service of fresh, seasonal, quality food, mostly cooked to order - Fire Station fish platter, braised half pheasant, crème brûlée - to a crowd of regulars. Bar snacks are also served and there's an extensive list of easy drinking, good value wines.

Times: 12-3/5.30-11 **Directions:** Nearest station: Waterloo Adjacent to Waterloo station

Glas

Modern Swedish NEW

Scandinavian small plates in foodie heaven

☎ 020 7357 6060 3 Park St SE1 9AB Plan 6-B2
e-mail: glas.staff@glasrestaurant.com
web: www.glasrestaurant.com

Located in the trendy Borough Market area of London, Glas is one of a number of artisan food specialists in this foodie's paradise. The restaurant itself has a Scandinavian theme with 'small plate', tapas-style dining using much of the high quality produce available on their doorstep. The plain green-painted shop front opens up into a sunny yellow room with a crystal candelabra and polished aluminium furniture. Mix and match simple dishes with an abundance of fresh herbs, flavoured oils and herring from a menu divided into cold and hot sections - citrus herring for example, or pan-fried cod with mustard sauce. Desserts like Swedish cheesecake are a must.

Chef: Andreas Aberg & Mikael Kron Broberg **Owners:** Anna Mosesson **Times:** 12-3/6.30-11, Closed Xmas, New Year, 10 days Aug, Sun **Prices:** Fixed D £25, Starter £4.45-£8.95, Main £9.95, Dessert £4.45-£5.95, Service optional, Group service 12% **Wine:** 41 bottles over £20, 8 bottles under £20, 20 by the glass (£3.95-£8.25) **Notes:** Fixed L/D 5 courses £25, Vegetarian available **Seats:** 42 **Smoking:** N/Sm in restaurant, Air con **Directions:** Nearest station: London Bridge Please telephone for directions **Parking:** NCP 5 mins walk

The Oxo Tower Restaurant

Modern European V

Stylish venue with a 'top of the world' feel and innovative food

☎ 020 7803 3888 8th Floor, Oxo Tower Wharf, Barge House St SE1 9PH Plan 3-F1
e-mail: oxo.reservations@harveynichols.co.uk
web: www.harveynichols.co.uk

The long open terrace overlooking the Thames is a magnet on warm summer days, though with glass down both sides of this stylish eighth-floor restaurant the view from inside is stunning too. Echoing the design of a 1930's ocean liner, a feature is the ceiling, which is made up of double-sided louvers - white during the day, revolving to midnight blue at dusk. Attentive waiters, smart table coverings and settings complete the scene. The innovative modern European menu is agony for the indecisive, with tempting descriptions that highlight each dish's many component parts: foie gras ballontine with fig chutney and warm brioche starter, followed by slow roast venison with ricotta, wild boar speck and sauce grand veneur.

continued

LONDON SE1 *continued*

Chef: Jeremy Bloor **Owners:** Harvey Nichols & Co Ltd **Times:** 12-2.30/6-11, Closed 25-26 Dec, Closed D 24 Dec **Prices:** Fixed L £29.50, Starter £9.50-£18, Main £16.50-£26, Dessert £7.25-£8, Coffee £3, Min/Water £3.80, Service added but optional 12.5% **Wine:** 660 bottles over £20, 19 bottles under £20, 23 by the glass (£4.50-£8.50) **Notes:** Vegetarian menu **Seats:** 250 **Smoking:** N/Sm in restaurant, Air con **Children:** Menu, Portions **Directions:** Nearest station: Blackfriars/Waterloo Between Blackfriars & Waterloo Bridge **Parking:** On street

Ozu

Japanese V

Skilfully prepared Japanese dishes in sophisticated surroundings

☎ 020 7928 7766 County Hall Riverside Building, Westminster Bridge Rd SE1 7PB Plan 5-D5
e-mail: info@ozulondon.com

Located in London's County Hall, this 1950s retro-style interior with kitchens clearly visible through a glass wall serves both set and à la carte menus of traditional Japanese food. Plain white walls work well with chunky, hardwood furniture to create a calming ambience. If the set menus don't appeal, try exotic sea urchin or salmon egg sushi before a bowl of nameko jiru (miso with mushroom). Main courses of yaki tori (grilled chicken skewers) or aigamo misoyaki (grilled duck breast with white miso sauce) are carefully prepared and attractively presented. Finish with fresh fruit.

Chef: Lin Pattamabong **Owners:** Ozu (London) Ltd. **Times:** 12-3/5.30-10.30 **Prices:** Fixed L £11.50-£20.50, Fixed D £37.50-£47.50, Starter £5-£11, Main £11-£21, Dessert £3-£4.25, Coffee £2.95, Min/Water £4.25, Service added but optional 12.5% **Wine:** 20 bottles over £20, 2 bottles under £20, 5 by the glass (£4.25-£5.50) **Notes:** Vegetarian menu **Seats:** 65 **Smoking:** N/Sm area, No pipes, No cigars **Directions:** Nearest station: Waterloo/Westminster Part of County Hall, building next to London Eye **Parking:** Waterloo Station

Le Pont de la Tour

French

Conran wharfside restaurant, stylish destination dining

☎ 020 7403 8403 The Butlers Wharf Building, 36d Shad Thames SE1 2YE Plan 6-D2
web: www.conran.com

A popular waterfront wharf location with stunning views of Tower Bridge, especially at night when it is floodlit. The terrace is busy in summer as diners flock to watch the world go by on the river. Inside this elegant Conran restaurant you step into the luxury world of a cruise liner. Smart table settings, clean lines and well-dressed staff set the tone for some serious cooking. The modern French menu offers an extensive choice of dishes, drawing on traditional ingredients, like Morteau

continued

Le Pont de la Tour

sausage with Puy lentils and mustard vinaigrette to start. There's lots of fresh fish, a few vegetarian dishes, and meat options like rack of lamb with herb crust and red beetroot mash. Desserts include mouth-watering combinations like champagne jelly with lime mascarpone.

Times: 12-3/6-11, Closed 25-26 Dec, Closed L Sat **Directions:** Nearest station: Tower Hill, London Bridge SE of Tower Bridge

RSJ, The Restaurant on the South Bank

Modern British

Perfect pre-theatre dining

☎ 020 7928 4554 33 Coin St SE1 9NR Plan 5-F6
e-mail: sally.webber@rsj.uk.com
web: www.rsj.uk.com

A plain and simple first-floor restaurant, popular with media types and theatre- or concert-goers from the adjacent South Bank. Friendly staff keep everything moving efficiently with an eye on performance times. The menu changes monthly or more frequently, reflecting a passion for fresh seasonal produce. Loire Valley wines are a speciality here and there are wine events from time to time. The cuisine makes good use of fine ingredients from across the British Isles, like potted Scottish prawns with lemon and toast, or roast Cornish monkfish with spicy chorizo and coriander risotto.

Times: 12-2/5.30-11, Closed Xmas, 1 Jan, Sun, Closed L Sat **Directions:** Nearest station: Waterloo Telephone for directions

Roast

British NEW

Airy modern restaurant perched above Borough Market

☎ 020 7940 1300 The Floral Hall, Borough Market, Stoney St SE1 1TL Plan 6-B3
e-mail: info@roast-restaurant.com
web: www.roast-restaurant.com

Bustling by day and impossibly romantic by night, Borough Market is an atmospheric setting for a restaurant, and this chic first-floor eatery makes the most of it, offering views to the hubbub down below from a comfortable bar, and over to St Paul's Cathedral from its glass-fronted dining room. The menu changes daily and makes good use of quality produce in classic British dishes such as Herdwick mutton leg stew with mint jelly, roast Banham chicken with Ayrshire bacon and bread sauce, or steak and ox kidney pudding. Also open for breakfast, Monday to Saturday.

Chef: Lawrence Keogh **Owners:** Iqbal Wahhab **Times:** 12-3/5.30-11, Closed D Sun **Prices:** Fixed L fr £18, Fixed D fr £21, Starter £5-£15, Main £10-£20, Dessert £5.50, Coffee £2.50, Min/Water £2.50, Service included

continued

Wine: 106 bottles over £20, 5 bottles under £20, 10 by the glass (£5-£10) **Notes:** Seasonal tasting menu 6 courses £45, £75 with wine **Seats:** 110 **Smoking:** N/Sm in restaurant, Air con **Children:** Menu, Portions **Directions:** Nearest station: London Bridge Please telephone for directions

Georgetown

☎ 020 7357 7359 10 London Bridge St SE1 9SG
web: www.theaa.com/restaurants/113999.html

Authentic Malay plus Indian Malaysian and Chinese Malaysian dishes. Décor is colonial with wicker chairs and lots of plants.

The Loft

☎ 020 7902 0820 Mercure London City Bankside, 71-79 Southwark St, Bankside SE1 0JA
web: www.theaa.com/restaurants/113977.html
Light bright restaurant with regularly changing menu to include seasonal produce. Vegetarian options; special diets catered for.

Shakespeare's Globe Restaurant

☎ 020 7928 9444 Shakespeare's Globe, New Globe Walk, Southwark SE1 9DT
web: www.theaa.com/restaurants/113964.html
Wonderful views at this restaurant beside the Globe Theatre. Seasonal English cooking. Service is never rushed.

Yo! Sushi

☎ 020 7928 8871 County Hall, Belvedere Rd SE1 7GP
Sushi, sashimi, noodles and more delivered by conveyor belt and priced according to colour-coded plates

LONDON SE3

Chapter Two

see below

Laicram Thai Restaurant

Thai V

Authentic Thai in a cosy setting

☎ 020 8852 4710 1 Blackheath Grove, Blackheath SE3 0DD Plan 8-D1

This Thai restaurant of long-standing is in the centre of Blackheath village, enjoying a fine reputation in the area for good food and being mercifully easy on the wallet. The décor has a homely feel with understated Thai touches such as prints of the Thai royal family on the

continued

Chapter Two

LONDON SE3

Modern European

Prominent and stylish heathside restaurant with imaginative cuisine

☎ 020 8333 2666 43-45 Montpelier Vale, Blackheath Village SE3 0TJ Plan 8-D1
e-mail: richard@chaptersrestaurants.co.uk
web: www.chapterrestaurants.co.uk

Sibling to big brother Chapter One (see entry), this chic, modern glass-fronted restaurant's small ground-floor dining room is visible from the street, while a spiral staircase connects it to a larger basement space and bar. Decked out in vibrant colours (blues, reds and dark browns), lightwood floors and chrome, the clever use of mirrors adds to the feeling of lightness and space, while a combination of banquette seating and high-backed chairs bears out the modern styling. Service is equally slick, but friendly and well-informed. The kitchen's modern European approach is thoroughly imaginative, with accurate, skilful cooking displaying culinary pedigree, utilising produce of high quality and delivering fresh, clean flavours; and all this at affordable prices. Expect the likes of pressed terrine of duck foie gras and pickled rhubarb starter, followed by slow roast belly of pork with braised white cabbage and white onion purée, with

desserts such as coffee pannacotta with whisky ice cream and cinnamon doughnuts.

Chef: Trevor Tobin **Owners:** Selective Restaurants Group **Times:** 12-2.30/6.30-10.30, Closed 2-4 Jan **Prices:** Fixed L £16-£19, Fixed D £23.95-£25.95, Starter £5-£8.50, Main £11.95-£15.95, Dessert £4-£6.50, Coffee £2.20, Min/Water £3, Service added but optional 12.5% **Wine:** 50 bottles over £20, 12 bottles under £20, 12 by the glass (£3.95-£5.50) **Notes:** Vegetarian available, Dress Restrictions, Smart casual, no shorts or trainers **Seats:** 70 **Smoking:** N/Sm in restaurant, Air con **Children:** Portions **Directions:** Nearest station: Blackheath 5 mins from Blackheath Village train station **Parking:** Car park by station

LONDON SE3 *continued*

walls and typically welcoming and friendly service from the staff. The menu consists largely of mainstream Thai dishes such as prawn satay, fishcakes, phat Thai noodles, weeping tiger (grilled beef in spicy sauce) and some extremely authentic curry dishes including a deliciously rich gaeng phed ped yang (roast duck red curry).

Chef: Mrs S Dhirabutra **Owners:** Mr D Dhirabutra **Times:** 12-2.30/6-11, Closed Xmas & BHs, Mon **Prices:** Starter £3-£6.50, Main £4.90-£13.90, Dessert £3-£4.50, Coffee £2.50, Min/Water £3.50, Service added but optional 10% **Wine:** 2 bottles over £20 **Notes:** Vegetarian menu **Seats:** 50 **Smoking:** Air con **Directions:** Nearest station: Blackheath Off main shopping street, in a side road near the Post Office. Opposite station, near library

---

LONDON SE5

Mozarella e Pomodoro

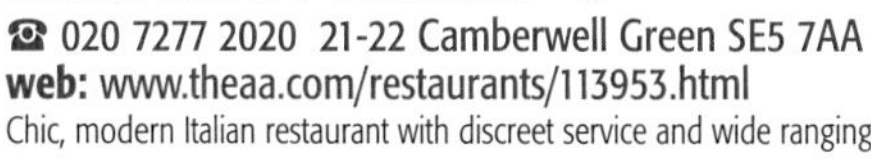

☎ 020 7277 2020 21-22 Camberwell Green SE5 7AA
web: www.theaa.com/restaurants/113953.html

Chic, modern Italian restaurant with discreet service and wide ranging menu.

LONDON SE10

North Pole Piano Restaurant

☎ 020 8853 3020 131 Greenwich High Rd, Greenwich SE10 8JA
web: www.theaa.com/restaurants/113954.html

Elegant restaurant serving European dishes. Roast Sunday lunch a good deal and live jazz Sunday evenings.

The Spread Eagle

☎ 020 8853 2333 1-2 Stockwell St, Greenwich SE10 9JN
web: www.theaa.com/restaurants/113980.html

A tavern since 1650, this is now a traditional French restaurant.

LONDON SE11

The Lobster Pot

☎ 020 7582 5556 3 Kennington Ln, Kennington SE11 4RG
web: www.theaa.com/restaurants/113975.html

Small eatery with nautical theme and French cooking - mainly seafood.

LONDON SE21

Beauberry House

Rosettes not confirmed at time of going to press

French, Japanese

Interesting mix of French and Japanese cuisine in amazing surroundings

☎ 020 8299 9788 Gallery Rd SE21 7AB Plan 1-F2
web: www.circagroupltd.co.uk

A stunning Grade II listed building, the completely renovated Beauberry House reopened in April 2006. The atmosphere is friendly and contemporary and the style of the cuisine an interesting combination of French and Japanese. Start perhaps with foie gras terrine, followed by a main course of black cod with miso, and a chocolate grill roll to finish. The Rosette rating was unconfirmed as we went to press, so please visit our website for the latest update.

continued

Chef: Jerome Tauvron **Owners:** Ibi Issolah **Times:** 12-3/7-12 **Prices:** Fixed L £14.50, Service added 12.5% **Wine:** 61 bottles over £20, 15 bottles under £20, 20 by the glass (£4.50-£11) **Notes:** Sun brunch 2 courses £18.50, 3 courses £22.50, Vegetarian available, Dress Restrictions, Smart casual **Children:** Menu, Portions **Directions:** Nearest station: West Dulwich Telephone for directions

---

LONDON SE22

Franklins

British

Best of British produce in former pub

☎ 020 8299 9598 157 Lordship Ln SE22 8HX Plan 1-F2
e-mail: info@franklinsrestaurant.com
web: www.franklinsrestaurant.com

A traditional local pub called 'The Victory' until the 1950s, this classic bistro-style restaurant now serves up the best of seasonal British produce. Carefully-sourced ingredients are as local as possible with some regional specialities like Irish rock oysters and Cornish Red chicken. The menu changes daily but typically you could start with devilled kidneys, moving on to Oxford Down lamb with aubergine and anchovy. Spotted Dick and rhubarb crumble are among the traditional desserts.

Chef: Tim Sheehan **Owners:** Tim Sheehan & Rodney Franklin **Times:** 12/12, Closed 25-26, 31 Dec, 1 Jan **Prices:** Fixed L £9, Starter £5-£8.50, Main £11-£18, Dessert £4.75, Coffee £2, Min/Water £2.50, Service optional, Group min 6 service 10% **Wine:** 20 bottles over £20, 15 bottles under £20, 9 by the glass (£3-£4) **Notes:** Fixed D £28.50 for larger parties, Vegetarian available **Seats:** 42, Pr/dining room 24 **Smoking:** N/Sm area, No pipes **Children:** Portions **Directions:** Nearest station: East Dulwich Please telephone for directions **Parking:** Bawdale Road

The Palmerston

Modern British

Smart pub serving good modern food

☎ 020 8693 1629 91 Lordship Ln, East Dulwich SE22 8EP Plan 1-F3
e-mail: thepalmerston@tiscali.co.uk
web: www.thepalmerston.co.uk

Oak-panelled walls, wooden floors, ornate chandeliers and deep red walls set the convivial scene at this stylishly refurbished old pub on the corner of trendy Lordship Lane. Original charm and character have been retained and there's a relaxed, friendly and informal atmosphere throughout the lively bar and smart dining areas. Accurate modern British cooking uses top-notch ingredients and draws an appreciative crowd. The short, innovative menu may list Middlewhite pork terrine with onion confit, braised oxtail with parsnip purée and bourguignonne sauce, and fig and almond tart.

Chef: Jamie Younger **Owners:** Jamie Younger, Paul Rigby, Reg Buckley, Remi Olajoyegbe **Times:** 12-2.30/7-midnight, Closed Xmas/New Year, Closed D Sun **Prices:** Fixed L £10, Starter £4.75-£8.50, Main £9-£14.75, Dessert £3.75-£5, Coffee £1.50, Min/Water £3, Service added but optional 10% **Wine:** 28 bottles over £20, 25 bottles under £20, 20 by the glass (£3.50-£6) **Seats:** 70 **Smoking:** N/Sm area, Air con **Directions:** Nearest station: East Dulwich 2m from Clapham, 0.5m from Dulwich Village **Parking:** On street

England

LONDON SE23

Babur

Indian

New look Indian restaurant

☎ 020 8291 2400 & 8291 4881 119 Brockley Rise, Forest Hill SE23 1JP Plan 1-G2
e-mail: mail@babur.info
web: www.babur.info

Now totally refurbished to reflect ethnic Indian traditions and culture, this friendly brasserie has been serving southeast London for 20 years and is still easily spotted by the life-size, prowling Bengal tiger on its roof. The menu is dotted with tiger heads to indicate the intensity of the chilli heat expected. One head equals hot and two means roaring hot! Start perhaps with the spicy crab cakes or the surprise dish of ostrich infused with sandlewood and fenugreek. Then hit the taste buds with the 'two-tiger' Lal maas - smoked venison in Rajasthani hot masala.

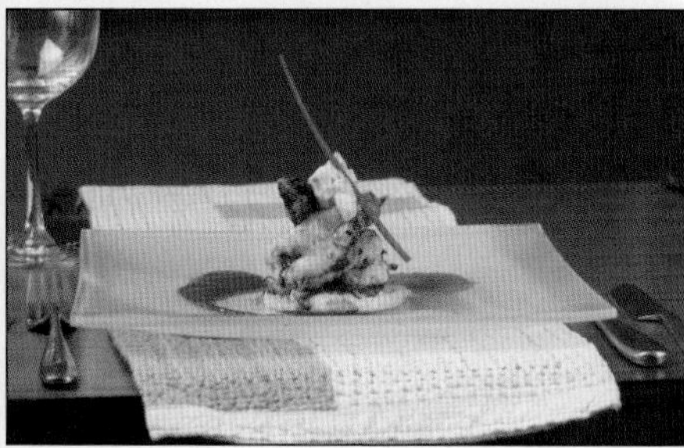

Chef: Enam Rahman & Jiwan Lal **Owners:** Babur 1998 Ltd **Times:** 12.30-2.30/6-11.30, Closed 25-26 Dec, Closed L Fri **Prices:** Starter £4.95-£6.95, Main £7.95-£16.95, Min/Water £2.95, Service optional **Wine:** 13 bottles over £20, 29 bottles under £20, 6 by the glass (£3.50-£4.50) **Notes:** Sun buffet L £10.95, Vegetarian available **Seats:** 72 **Smoking:** N/Sm in restaurant, Air con **Directions:** Nearest station: Honor Oak 5 mins walk from Honor Oak Station, where parking is available **Parking:** On street

Equal

☎ 020 8699 6674 68-70 Honor Oak Park SE23 1DY
web: www.theaa.com/restaurants/113997.html

Intimate restaurant with booth-style European dining. Monthly changing menu and live DJ music.

LONDON SE24

3 Monkeys Restaurant

Indian V

Ayurvedic-inspired vintage Indian cookery in contemporary surroundings

☎ 020 7738 5500 136-140 Herne Hill SE24 9QH Plan 1-F2
e-mail: info@3monkeysrestaurant.com
web: www.3monkeysrestaurant.com

Arranged over two levels with stripped wooden floors and white-washed walls replete with attractive modern artwork, this is certainly not your run-of-the-mill curry house. Staff are knowledgeable and happy to make recommendations to those less au fait with the cuisine of the sub-continent, while the chef-patron is Ayurvedic-trained and able to provide special 'health' menus. A typical starter would be karara kekda (soft shell crab fried in a spicy batter served with crab meat sautéed in fennel seeds) and mains could include Laurence Road ke tikkey (pot-roasted lamb tikka). Takeaways are also available.

Chef: Raminder Malhotra **Owners:** Kuldeep Singh, Raminder Malhotra **Times:** 12-2.30/6-11 **Prices:** Fixed L fr £7.95, Fixed D fr £17.95, Starter £3.45-£5.95, Main £3.95-£13.95, Dessert £2.95-£4.50, Coffee £1.95, Min/Water £2.75, Service added but optional 12.5% **Wine:** 9 bottles over £20, 18 bottles under £20, 4 by the glass (£3.25-£3.95) **Notes:** Sunday buffet £6.95, Vegetarian menu **Seats:** 90 **Smoking:** N/Sm area, Air con **Children:** Menu, Portions **Directions:** Nearest station: Herne Hill, Brixton Adjacent to Herne Hill Station

LONDON SW1

Al Duca

Italian

Enjoyable Italian cooking in a sophisticated Piccadilly setting

☎ 020 7839 3090 4-5 Duke of York St SW1Y 6LA Plan 5-B6
e-mail: info@alduca-restaurant.co.uk
web: www.alduca-restaurant.co.uk

If you're looking for authentic Italian cuisine, this smart Piccadilly eatery is a good place to start. A buzzy joint, it lures a relaxed crowd

continued

LONDON SW1 *continued*

of regulars with a tempting selection of tasty and unpretentious Mediterranean fare, which includes pasta dishes like pappardelle with rabbit ragout and artichokes, and linguine with clams, garlic and chilli oil, as well as mains such as chargrilled medallions of swordfish with Savoy cabbage and pink grapefruit sauce. Service is fast and friendly, and there's a good value pre- or post-theatre menu for those in a rush.

Chef: Aron Johnson **Owners:** Cuisine Collection **Times:** 12-2.30/6-11, Closed Christmas, New Year, BHs, Sun **Prices:** Fixed L £18.50-£23.50, Fixed D £24.50-£29.50, Coffee £2, Min/Water £3, Service added but optional 12.5% **Wine:** 100 bottles over £20, 20 bottles under £20, 13 by the glass (£4.50-£14) **Notes:** Vegetarian available, Dress Restrictions, Smart casual, no shorts **Seats:** 56 **Smoking:** No pipes, No cigars, Air con **Children:** Portions **Directions:** Nearest station: Piccadilly 5 mins walk from station towards Piccadilly. Right into St James, left into Jermyn St. Duke of York St halfway along on right **Parking:** Jermyn St, Duke St

Amaya

Modern Indian

Entertaining kitchen theatre with enticing South Asian food

☎ 020 7823 1166 Halkin Arcade, Motcomb St SW1X 8JT Plan 4-G4
e-mail: amaya@realindianfood.com
web: www.realindianfood.com

The pink sandstone panels, hardwood floors and rosewood furniture of this contemporary Indian grill are flooded with light from the glass atrium. Indian statuary and glass plates add to the vibrant ambience created by the open-plan kitchen where chefs marinate meats or labour over tandoors or sigris - charcoal grills. Dishes are mostly North Western in style but regional dishes also figure. Starters could include Goan mussels peri peri or lamb's liver and kidney keema kaleji stirfry. For main course, try the tandoori quail-bater prepared in an apricot and ginger marinade, or the grilled hamour in pandan leaf. Finish with refreshing pomegranate granita.

Chef: Karunesh Khanna **Owners:** R Mathrani, C Panjabi, N Panjabi **Times:** 12-2.30/6.30-11.15, Closed 25 Dec **Prices:** Fixed L fr £17.50, Starter £4-£25, Main £14.75-£19.75, Dessert £7.50, Coffee £2.50, Min/Water £3.95, Service added but optional 12.5% **Wine:** 75 bottles over £20, 2 bottles under £20, 29 by the glass (£4.45-£12.50) **Notes:** Fixed light L 3 courses, Tasting menus £34-£56.50 **Seats:** 90, Pr/dining room 14 **Smoking:** N/Sm in restaurant, Air con **Directions:** Nearest station: Knightsbridge Please telephone for directions **Parking:** NCP

The Avenue

British

Buzzy contemporary bar and restaurant

☎ 020 7321 2111 7-9 St James's St SW1A 1EE Plan 5-B5
e-mail: avenue@egami.co.uk
web: www.egami.co.uk

A large, buzzy restaurant with white walls hung with huge contemporary paintings, high ceilings dotted with spotlighting and an all-glass frontage decked out with a long bar and piano, create a modern, minimalist statement. Limestone floors, trendy chairs, banquettes and white-clothed tables continue the theme. The lengthy, brasserie-format menus offers straightforward but colourful, modern cooking, blending a few classics with a fashionable nod to the Mediterranean and beyond. Expect dishes such as bresaola, rocket and truffled pecorino or roast pollack, spring peas, broad beans, Dorset shrimps and marjoram.

Times: 12-3/5.45-11.30, Closed 25-26 Dec, 1 Jan, Sun **Directions:** Nearest station: Green Park Turn right past The Ritz, 2nd turning into St James's St. Telephone for further details

Boisdale of Belgravia

British, Scottish

Traditional, clubby but fun Scottish restaurant

☎ 020 7730 6922 15 Eccleston St SW1W 9LX Plan 4-H3
e-mail: info@boisdale.co.uk
web: www.boisdale.co.uk

Deep reds and greens, tartan, dark floorboards and panelled, picture-laden walls deliver a resolutely traditional Scottish experience at this buzzy, Belgravia restaurant-cum-whisky and cigar bar. Its labyrinth of dining areas and bars oozes an endearing clubby atmosphere, backed by live jazz in the evenings. White tablecloths, darkwood furniture, candlelight and a patriotic Caledonian menu further support the theme, with the kitchen's traditional approach aptly showcasing quality Scottish produce. Think Macsween haggis, Dunkeld wild smoked salmon and 28-day matured beef steaks from the glens. And there are some 150 malts and 100 cigars to choose from, too.

Chef: Colin Wint **Owners:** Mr R Macdonald **Times:** 12-2.30/7-11.15, Closed Xmas, New Year, Easter, BHs, Sun, Closed L Sat **Prices:** Fixed L £14-£17.80, Starter £7.50-£17.50, Main £16.50-£28.50, Dessert £5.50-£6.50, Service added but optional 12.5% **Wine:** 102 bottles over £20, 18 bottles under £20, 12 by the glass (£3.85-£7) **Notes:** Party menus 3 courses £36-£50, Vegetarian available **Seats:** 100, Pr/dining room 22 **Smoking:** Air con **Directions:** Nearest station: Victoria Turn left along Buckingham Palace Rd heading W, Eccleston St is 1st on right **Parking:** On street, Belgrave Sq

Boxwood Café

British, American NOTABLE WINE LIST

Upmarket brasserie in high-class hotel

☎ 020 7235 1010 The Berkeley Hotel, Wilton Place, Knightsbridge SW1X 7RL Plan 4-G4
e-mail: boxwoodcafe@gordonramsay.com
web: www.gordonramsay.com

From the Gordon Ramsay stable, this upmarket New York style café

continued

England

predictably oozes class, located on one corner of The Berkeley Hotel with its own street entrance on Knightsbridge. The elegant dining room is a stylish, split-level basement affair, with a bar and smart table settings. Natural earthy tones parade alongside golds and bronzes and lashings of darkwood and leather, while service is youthful, attentive but relaxed, and there's a vibrant metropolitan buzz. The accomplished kitchen's upmarket brasserie repertoire hits the spot, utilising high-quality seasonal ingredients with the emphasis on intelligent simplicity; think Dornoch lamb braised and roasted, served with rosemary polenta and a tomato and olive sauce.
Notable Wine List: A quality wine list catergorised by drinking styles; includes a reserve listing of some rare wines.

Chef: Stuart Gillies **Owners:** Gordon Ramsay Holdings Ltd **Times:** 12-3/6-11 **Prices:** Fixed L £21, Fixed D £55, Starter £7.50-£13.50, Main £9-£25, Dessert £6.50-£7, Coffee £4, Min/Water £4, Service added but optional 12.5% **Wine:** 150 bottles over £20, 1 bottle under £20, 10 by the glass (£5-£8.50) **Notes:** Fixed L 3 courses, Fixed D 6 courses, Vegetarian available **Seats:** 140, Pr/dining room 16 **Smoking:** N/Sm in restaurant, Air con **Children:** Menu, Portions **Directions:** Nearest station: Knightsbridge Please telephone for directions **Parking:** On street

Brasserie Roux

French

Popular brasserie serving rustic French cuisine

☎ 020 7968 2900 Sofitel St James London, 6 Waterloo Place SW1Y 4AN Plan 5-B6
e-mail: h3144-fb8@accor.com
web: www.sofitelstjames.com

With an entrance from the street and the hotel, this vibrant, elegant, high-ceilinged brasserie comes with stylish Pierre Yves Rochon design. Its main decorative theme, the cockerel, is the logo of this former banking hall's owners (Cox's & King's) and also, of course, the symbol of France. Bright red leather chairs, pale yellow walls, huge lampshades and bare-wood tables embody the modern, chic but relaxed styling, backed by friendly, knowledgeable and professional service. The traditional, wholesome, unfussy French regional cuisine fits the authentic brasserie style, offering classics that utilise quality produce with flavour at their heart - as in coq au Riesling with spätzle, Toulouse sausage with onion gravy and mash, or classic lemon tart.

Chef: Richard Tonks **Owners:** Accor UK **Times:** 12-3/5.30-11.30 **Prices:** Fixed L £24.50, Fixed D £15-£24.50, Starter £6-£13, Main £8-£17, Dessert £5.50-£6.50, Coffee £3.20, Service added but optional 12.5% **Wine:** 23 bottles under £20, 18 by the glass (£5.50-£13) **Notes:** Fixed L 3 courses, Vegetarian available, Civ Wed 150 **Seats:** 100, Pr/dining room 130 **Smoking:** N/Sm area, Air con **Children:** Menu, Portions **Rooms:** 186 (186 en suite) ★★★★★ HL **Directions:** Nearest station: Piccadilly Circus. Telephone for directions **Parking:** NCP at Piccadilly

Le Caprice Restaurant

Modern European V

Quality cooking in a restaurant that brings out the stars

☎ 020 7629 2239 Arlington House, Arlington St SW1A 1RT Plan 5-A6
web: www.le-caprice.co.uk

This classy restaurant has been a darling of the celebrity circuit for many years. The interior is predominantly black and white, with David Bailey photographs, large mirrors and comfortable seating at fairly closely set tables. There are no airs and graces here, and friendly waiting staff treat all guests with the same even handed respect. Cooking is based on excellent produce and the comprehensive European menu offers comfort eating to appeal to every taste: creamed chicken and cep soup with tarragon, confit shoulder of lamb with mashed root vegetables and rosemary, and cinnamon fritters with dark chocolate sauce. Sunday brunch is a popular option with pitchers of bloody Mary or bucks fizz. Separate vegan and vegetarian menu available.

Chef: Paul Brown **Owners:** Caprice Holdings Ltd **Times:** 12-3/5.30-12, Closed 25-26 Dec, 1 Jan, Aug BH, Closed D 24 Dec **Prices:** Starter £6.25-£15.75, Main £14.25-£26.50, Dessert £6.25-£8.50, Coffee £2.75, Service optional **Wine:** 16 by the glass (£5-£13.50) **Notes:** Vegetarian menu **Seats:** 80 **Smoking:** No pipes, Air con **Children:** Portions **Directions:** Nearest station: Green Park Arlington St runs beside The Ritz. Restaurant is at end **Parking:** On street, NCP

Caraffini

Traditional Italian

Busy, lively traditional Italian

☎ 020 7259 0235 61-63 Lower Sloane St SW1W 8DH Plan 4-G2
e-mail: info@caraffini.co.uk
web: www.caraffini.co.uk

A large white awning picks out this smart and welcoming Chelsea Italian close to Sloane Square, flush with cheery Latin service. Pastel yellow walls hung with prints and mirrors, a large leafy palm, blond-wood floorboards and blue banquettes and upholstered rattan-style chairs help cut a sunny, relaxed atmosphere. The lengthy carte, bolstered by daily specials and all-Italian wines, runs in traditional format with modern overtones; classic regional dishes with the emphasis on simplicity, freshness and flavour. Why not begin your meal with beef carpaccio, followed by pan-fried cod with Tuscan olive oil, olives, capers and chopped tomatoes.

Chef: John Patino, S Ramalhoto **Owners:** F di Rienzo & Paolo Caraffini **Times:** 12.15-2.30/6.30-11.30, Closed BHs, Xmas, Sun **Prices:** Starter

continued

LONDON SW1 *continued*

£4.50-£10.25, Main £11-£19.50, Dessert £4.25-£4.95, Coffee £1.95, Min/Water £3.35, Service optional, Group min 6 service 12.5% **Wine:** 37 bottles over £20, 13 bottles under £20, 4 by the glass (£3.95-£5.60) **Notes:** Vegetarian available **Seats:** 70 **Smoking:** No pipes, Air con **Directions:** Nearest station: Sloane Square Please telephone for directions **Parking:** Meters on street

Le Cercle

French

Discreet basement restaurant offering modern French grazing food

☎ 020 7901 9999 1 Wilbraham Place SW1X 9AE Plan 4-F3
e-mail: info@lecercle.co.uk

Close to Sloane Square, this discreet basement restaurant continues to pull in the punters. The dining areas combine a sense of refined intimacy with a surprising spaciousness, accentuated by the tall ceilings, neutral colour scheme and artful lighting, while a recently refurbished private lounge is an additional attraction. The glass-fronted wine cave and cheese room provide suitable stages to highlight two French passions celebrated here, while the menu offers a good overview of the rest of Gallic gastronomy. Dishes such as roasted squab, with spicy caramel pumpkin ravioli or braised shoulder of veal with salsify and a rosemary jus are cooked with aplomb with small but perfectly formed portions and refined presentation.

Chef: Thierry Beyris **Owners:** Vincent Labeyrie & Pascal Aussignac **Times:** 12-3/6-11, Closed Xmas & New Year, Sun, Mon **Prices:** Fixed L £15-£17.50, Starter £4.50-£35, Main £4.50-£35, Dessert £4.50-£35, Coffee £2.25, Min/Water £3.50, Service added 12.5% **Wine:** 200 bottles over £20, 12 bottles under £20, 20 by the glass (£3.50-£8.50) **Notes:** Fixed L 3 courses, Vegetarian available **Seats:** 60 **Smoking:** N/Sm in restaurant, Air con **Directions:** Nearest station: Sloane Square Just off Sloane St **Parking:** Outside after 6, NCP in Cadogan Sq

The Cinnamon Club

Indian

Sophisticated Indian dining in former library

☎ 020 7222 2555 The Old Westminster Library, Great Smith St SW1P 3BU Plan 5-C4
e-mail: info@cinnamonclub.com
web: www.cinnamonclub.com

The former Westminster library makes an unusual setting for a contemporary Indian restaurant. Polished parquet floors, darkwood, high ceilings, domed skylights and a gallery of books retain the building's heritage and old English charm. The restaurant has a clubby feel with high-backed suede chairs and crisp white tablecloths, all very simple and elegant. Traditional Indian cuisine is based around fine ingredients and well-judged spicing. Breakfast, lunch, pre- and post-theatre and carte menus offer a wide selection of dishes. Try an appetiser of Rajasthani spiced lamb escalope with garlic and chilli, followed by a main course like chargrilled red snapper fillets with Goan curry sauce and tamarind rice. A good choice of desserts features date pancake with vanilla and toasted coconut ice cream.

Times: 12-3/6-11, Closed Xmas, Easter, BHs, Sun, Closed L Sat **Directions:** Nearest station: Westminster Take exit 6, across Parliament Sq, then pass Westminister Abbey on left. Take 1st left into Great Smith St

Il Convivio

Modern Italian

Stylish Italian dining in upmarket Belgravia

☎ 020 7730 4099 143 Ebury St SW1W 9QN Plan 4-H2
e-mail: comments@etruscarestaurants.com
web: www.etruscarestaurants.com

An elegant restaurant with customers to match, this chic Belgravia haunt located in a Georgian townhouse draws a well-heeled, sophisticated crowd. Quotes from Dante's *Il Convivo* are inscribed on the red and white walls, while tables are set with modish cutlery and tableware. The cuisine is upmarket Italian with a few unconventional touches such as fresh burrata cheese with crisp aubergines, and a timbale of crab with spiced mustard fruit. The menu, in English and Italian, offers a wide-ranging choice supplemented by specials each day, such as seared diver scallops with angel hair pasta in a champagne sauce, followed by black spaghetti with lobster and spring onions perhaps, or duck breast with celeriac and parsnip purée and blackberry sauce. The impressive wine list covers all regions and features some interesting choices.

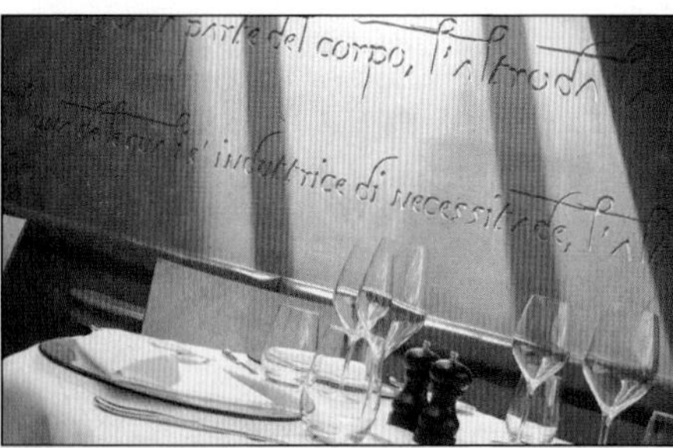

Chef: Lukas Pfaff **Owners:** Piero & Enzo Quaradeghini **Times:** 12-2.45/7-10.45, Closed Xmas, New Year, BHs, Sun **Prices:** Fixed L £15.50, Fixed D £32.50, Starter £5.50-£14.50, Main £11-£19, Dessert £5-£9, Coffee £2.50, Min/Water £3.90, Service added but optional 12.5% **Wine:** 141 bottles over £20, 10 bottles under £20, 10 by the glass (£3.90-£12.50) **Notes:** Vegetarian available, Dress Restrictions, Smart casual **Seats:** 65, Pr/dining room 14 **Smoking:** No pipes, No cigars, Air con **Directions:** Nearest station: Victoria 7 min walk from Victoria Station - corner of Ebury St and Elizabeth St. **Parking:** On street

Drones of Pont Street

French, British

Stylish restaurant for top-quality cuisine

☎ 020 7235 9555 1 Pont St SW1X 9EJ Plan 4-G3
e-mail: sales@whitestarline.org.uk
web: www.whitestarline.org.uk

This London classic from the Marco Pierre White empire is a popular choice for discerning diners. Glamorous décor, a large bar and mood lighting make it a stylish place to impress friends, clients or for a special date. The set two- or three-course lunch is great value, with a choice of three classic dishes at each course. The carte is more extensive and features hors d'oeuvre like carpaccio of beef maison. Main courses include a selection of fish and shellfish dishes like grilled lobster with sauce Charon, or roasts and grills like roast free-range poulet chasseur, served with traditional accompaniments. Classic desserts include Harvey's lemon tart, or Drones rice pudding with compôte of red fruits.

Times: 12-2.30/6-11, Closed 26 Dec-1 Jan, Closed D Sun

Ebury

British, French

Buzzing eatery with an imaginative menu

☎ 020 7730 6784 11 Pimlico Rd SW1W 8NA
Plan 4-G2
e-mail: info@theebury.co.uk
web: www.theebury.co.uk

A short walk from the hustle and bustle of Sloane Square, this popular, stylish gastro-pub attracts a bright, young crowd who enjoy seeing and being seen as much as eating the refined brasserie-style food. Downstairs has a more informal feel while the smart upstairs dining room is the place for a more leisurely lunch or dinner. The décor combines a minimal backdrop with some striking, funky features such as the magnificent chandelier. The cooking uses well-sourced ingredients in dishes inspired by classical combinations with imaginative twists - goat's cheese mousse with red onion marmalade and pomegranate syrup for example, or roast saddle of lamb with shallot purée, flageolet beans and roasting juices.

Chef: James Holah **Owners:** Tom Etridge **Times:** 12-3.30/6-10.30, Closed 24-30 Dec **Prices:** Starter £4.50-£7.50, Main £9.50-£16.95, Dessert £5.50, Coffee £2, Min/Water £2.95, Service added but optional 12.5% **Wine:** 77 bottles over £20, 90 bottles under £20, 16 by the glass (£3.50-£5.50) **Notes:** Vegetarian available **Seats:** 60 **Smoking:** No pipes, No cigars, Air con **Directions:** Nearest station: Sloane Sq/Victoria From Sloane Sq Tube left into Holbein Place, then left at intersection with Pimlico Rd. The Ebury is on right on corner of Pimlico Rd & Ranelagh Grove. From Victoria, left down Buckingham Palace Rd, then right onto Pimlico Rd **Parking:** NCP

The Fifth Floor Restaurant

Modern European NOTABLE WINE LIST

Star-studded dining at top London store

☎ 020 7235 5250 Harvey Nichols,
109-125 Knightsbridge SW1X 7RJ Plan 4-F4
e-mail: reception@harveynichols.com
web: www.harveynichols.com

This well-appointed restaurant, bar and café remains as popular as ever with the rich and glamorous. The light, bright space high above the Knightsbridge traffic is as chic as it is comfortable with its fibre-optic lighting under a glass-domed ceiling and white leather tubular chairs. Service is efficient and friendly. The menu comprises modern European dishes with an emphasis on best-quality ingredients and clear, strong flavours. Try the red mullet escabèche with pickled beetroot salad and horseradish emulsion to start before a main course of pan-fried baby squid stuffed with acacia honey-roast ham and preserved lemon. Finish with a parcel of rare English apple and vanilla rice pudding.

Notable Wine List: A comprehensive wine list offering depth in every area. Really good selection of wines by the glass as well as some wine flights focusing on regionality and grape variety.

continued

England

LONDON SW1 *continued*

Chef: Helena Puolakka **Owners:** Harvey Nichols & Co Ltd **Times:** 12-3/6-11, Closed 25-26 Dec, Easter Sun, Closed D Sun **Prices:** Fixed L £19.50, Fixed D £24.50-£39.50, Starter £7.50-£13, Main £14.50-£23, Dessert £5-£7.50, Coffee £2.50, Min/Water £3.50, Service added but optional 12.5% **Wine:** 100+ bottles over £20, 12 bottles under £20, 25 by the glass (£4-£10.20) **Notes:** Tasting menu £55, Vegetarian available **Seats:** 114 **Smoking:** N/Sm area, Air con **Children:** Menu, Portions **Directions:** Nearest station: Knightsbridge, Hyde Park Corner Entrance on Sloane St **Parking:** On street, NCP opposite

Franco's Restaurant

Italian NEW

A classy reincarnation of an Italian institution

☎ 020 7499 2211 63 Jermyn St SW1 6LX Plan 5-A6

Situated in the heart of St James' this long-established Italian has been purchased by Wiltons, the restaurant next door. A dark green awning overhangs the part-frosted windows and some popular outside tables, while inside there are two interconnecting rooms, the first with a long, well-stocked bar. The food is classically-based Italian with a few more modern twists, like slow-roasted pork belly with Jerusalem artichokes and mandarin-flavoured sauce. Highlights are home-made grissini and chocolate fondant with a lovely liquid centre and a hint of chilli.

Times: 7.30-11 **Prices:** Food prices not confirmed for 2007. Please telephone for details **Seats:** 100 **Directions:** Telephone for directions

Goring Hotel

British V

Carefully prepared food in grand hotel setting

☎ 020 7396 9000 Beeston Place SW1W 0JW Plan 4-H4
e-mail: reception@goringhotel.co.uk
web: www.goringhotel.co.uk

A sumptuous and elaborate hotel done out in the grand style as befits a traditional hotel in its central London location just behind Buckingham Palace. This family-owned hotel may be traditional in style but it's anything but stuffy with staff providing friendly and efficient service. David Linley's design has created a lighter touch to this grand Victorian dining room with two huge chandeliers as centrepieces. Menus include traditional English dishes as well as French classics. There's good use of quality fresh produce in starters of Somerset smoked eel salad, quail eggs and bacon and main courses of beef Wellington from the carving trolley or the Goring fishcake.

Chef: Derek Quelch **Owners:** Goring Family **Times:** 12.30-2.30/6-10, Closed L Sat **Prices:** Fixed L £27, Fixed D £44, Coffee £3.50, Min/Water £3.75, Service added but optional 12.5% **Wine:** 400 bottles over £20, 8 by the glass (£5.75-£16) **Notes:** Sun L £32, Vegetarian available, Civ Wed 50 **Seats:** 70, Pr/dining room 50 **Smoking:** No pipes, No cigars, Air con **Children:** Portions **Rooms:** 72 (72 en suite) ★★★★★ HL **Directions:** Nearest station: Victoria From Victoria St turn left into Grosvenor Gdns, cross Buckingham Palace Rd, 75yds turn right into Beeston Place **Parking:** 5

Inn the Park

British

All-day eatery in park setting

☎ 020 7451 9999 St James's Park SW1A 1AA
Plan 5-C5
e-mail: info@innthepark.co.uk
web: www.innthepark.co.uk

The long, grass-roofed, Scandinavian-style building blends invisibly into the rolling landscape of St James's Park. The cleverly named all-day eatery looks out across the lake to Duck Island and beyond to the London Eye. A café by day, with a counter for quick snacks, it becomes a restaurant at night offering simple, full-flavoured, brasserie-style dishes using quality produce from small suppliers. Expect Cornish fish pie, steamed sea bass with Norfolk mussels and black cabbage, and calves' liver with mustard mash and onion gravy. Super decked area for summer alfresco dining.

Chef: Simon Wadham **Owners:** Oliver Peyton **Times:** 12-3/6-10.45, Closed D Sun-Mon (winter) **Prices:** Fixed L fr £22, Fixed D £27-£32, Starter £5-£8.50, Main £12-£17.50, Dessert fr £5, Coffee £1.50, Min/Water £3, Service optional, Group min 6 service 12.5% **Wine:** 11 bottles over £20, 8 by the glass (£4-£6.20) **Notes:** Vegetarian available **Seats:** 134 **Smoking:** N/Sm in restaurant, Air con **Children:** Menu, Portions **Directions:** Nearest station: St James, Charing Cross 200 metres down The Mall towards Buckingham Palace **Parking:** On street

Just St James

Modern British

Dining in high style in old St James's

☎ 020 7976 2222 12 St James's St SW1A 1ER
Plan 5-B5
e-mail: bookings@juststjames.com
web: www.juststjames.com

The lavish, Edwardian Baroque interior with its marble columns, arched windows and corniced ceilings has been softened with a contemporary style, and provides a comfortable setting for some good modern British dining. It used to be a private bank so don't be too shocked at some of the prices - after all, this is St James's. The menu is full of luxurious elements so spoil yourself with langoustine tails with asparagus and basil bisque to start before a main course of Aberdeen Angus fillet with

continued

seared foie gras, black truffle and rosti pancakes. The warm almond galette with vanilla ice cream provides a comforting conclusion.

Chef: Peter Gladwin **Owners:** Peter Gladwin **Times:** 12-3/6-11, Closed 25-26 Dec, 1 Jan, Sun, Closed L Sat **Prices:** Fixed L fr £21.50, Fixed D £16.50-£36, Starter £6.75-£14.50, Main £13.50-£22.50, Dessert £5.50-£8.75, Coffee £2.50, Min/Water £3, Service added but optional 12.5% **Wine:** 85 bottles over £20, 13 bottles under £20, 21 by the glass (£4-£7.50) **Notes:** Pre & post theatre menu(6-7pm, 10-11pm) 3 courses £16.50, Vegetarian available **Seats:** 120, Pr/dining room 140 **Smoking:** No pipes, No cigars, Air con **Children:** Portions **Directions:** Nearest station: Green Park Turn right on Piccadilly towards Piccadilly Circus, then right into St James St. Restaurant on corner of St James St & King St **Parking:** St James Square - meters

Ken Lo's Memories of China

Chinese

Refined Chinese cooking close to Victoria

☎ 020 7730 7734 65-69 Ebury St SW1W 0NZ Plan 4-H3
e-mail: memoriesofchina@btconnect.com

A Pimlico restaurant with a refined, upmarket feel that owes much to the very stylish table settings. Quality abounds from the starched linen to the chopsticks, and the subtle Chinese decor has a contemporary edge. A lengthy carte showcases the classic Chinese food, backed up by a set menu that offers excellent value for money from the same quality produce and refined presentations. Accurate flavours reflect the skilful handling of good raw ingredients, yielding the likes of Peking quick-fried chicken with a sticky cashew sauce, and sautéed spicy salt and pepper soft shell crabs. Service is speedy and efficient.

Chef: Mr But **Owners:** London and Henley **Times:** 12-3/7-12, Closed 24-25 Dec, BHs, Closed L Sun **Prices:** Fixed L £18.50-£21.50, Fixed D £30-£48, Starter £4.80-£13.50, Main £6.50-£32.50, Dessert £4.50-£7, Coffee £2.50, Min/Water £3.50, Service added but optional 12.5%, Group min 15 service 15% **Wine:** 115 bottles over £20, 8 bottles under £20, 6 by the glass (£4-£8) **Notes:** Fixed L 3 courses, Fixed D 4 courses, Vegetarian available **Seats:** 120, Pr/dining room 26 **Smoking:** N/Sm area, No pipes, No cigars, Air con **Directions:** Nearest station: Victoria At junction of Ebury Street & Eccleston St. Near Victoria station **Parking:** On street

The Lanesborough

International

Park Lane grandee with a leafy conservatory

☎ 020 7259 5599 Hyde Park Corner SW1X 7TA Plan 4-G5
e-mail: info@lanesborough.com
web: www.lanesborough.com

One of London's most prestigious hotels, the Lanesborough sits in stately grandeur at Hyde Park corner. Sip an aperitif in the swanky cocktail bar, and then move through to the glass-roofed conservatory restaurant, where a pianist plays softly as you take a seat among exotic palms and trickling fountains, at a table set with the finest crystal and china. Quality ingredients are to the fore on the wide-ranging modern British menu and there's no shortage of skill; kick off with a salad of roast scallop, crisp squid and seaweed perhaps, followed by roasted rack of Welsh lamb with tomato marmalade and spring vegetables, or grilled Dover sole with aubergine tapenade and capers. Vegetarian dishes are a speciality.

Chef: Paul Gayler **Owners:** St Regis Hotels and Resorts **Times:** 12-2.30/6-11.30 **Prices:** Fixed L £24-£30, Fixed D £38-£48, Starter £6.50-£21,

continued

Main £17-£40, Dessert £11.50-£12.50, Coffee £5.50, Min/Water £4.75, Service added but optional 12.5% **Wine:** all bottles over £20, 8 by the glass (£6.50-£14) **Notes:** Fixed L 3 courses, Vegetarian available, Dress Restrictions, Smart casual, Civ Wed 100 **Seats:** 120, Pr/dining room 100 **Smoking:** N/Sm area, No pipes, No cigars, Air con **Children:** Menu, Portions **Rooms:** 95 (95 en suite) ★★★★★ HL **Directions:** Nearest station: Hyde Park Corner On Hyde Park corner **Parking:** 50

Luciano

Italian NEW

Classy Italian restaurant with a touch of 'Marco' magic in the heart of St James'

☎ 020 7408 1440 72-73 St James's St SW1A 1PH Plan 5-B5
e-mail: info@lucianorestaurant.co.uk
web: www.lucianorestaurant.co.uk

Marco Pierre White's latest London venture is as glamorous and classy as its St James' address. Entry to the restaurant is via a large bar with a mosaic-tiled floor and sumptuous leather seating. Columns, distressed mirrors, original artworks and darkwood and leather seating, mixed with some banquette seating, are set off by crisp white table linen. Smartly dressed staff are mainly Italian, and the Italian dominated wine list is very impressive. Cooking is classic Italian using top-quality ingredients, resulting in simple, full-flavoured dishes, such as grilled sea scallops with a salad of potato and bottarga, and roast sea bass with rosemary, garnished with fresh artichokes and anchovies.

Chef: Marco Corsica **Owners:** Marco Pierre White **Times:** Closed 25-28 Dec **Prices:** Fixed L £17.50-£17.95, Fixed D fr £22.50, Starter £6-£11.50, Main £12.50-£25, Dessert £6.50-£7.50, Coffee £2, Min/Water £3.50, Service optional **Wine:** 150 bottles over £20, 25 bottles under £20, 8 by the glass (£4.50-£14.50) **Notes:** Vegetarian available **Seats:** 130, Pr/dining room 24 **Smoking:** No cigars, Air con **Children:** Portions **Directions:** Please telephone for directions

Mandarin Oriental Hyde Park

see page 281

Mint Leaf

Indian

Trendy Indian restaurant offering authentic modern cuisine

☎ 020 7930 9020 Suffolk Place SW1Y 4HX Plan 5-C3
e-mail: reservations@mintleafrestaurant.com
web: www.mintleafrestaurant.co.uk

continued

LONDON SW1 *continued*

This restaurant was once a bank vault but wire mesh divisions and special lighting effects now reveal a delightful modern Indian restaurant, and in addition to a glamorous cocktail bar that serves snacks until midnight. Relatively simple contemporary Indian cooking uses quality produce, vibrant spicing and modern presentation. Try the likes of Hydrabadi lamb korma with onion, mint and coconut milk or a platter of mixed dishes like grilled lamb cutlets, chicken tikka with basil, grilled duck minced roll, and guinea fowl breast with fennel and onion seed.

Chef: K K Anand **Owners:** Out of Africa Investments **Times:** 12-3/5.30-11, Closed 25 & 26 Dec, 1 Jan, Closed L Sat, Sun **Prices:** Fixed L £15, Starter £6-£11, Main £11-£32, Dessert £5.50-£7.50, Coffee £2.95, Min/Water £4.50, Service added but optional 12.5% **Wine:** 140 bottles over £20, 10 bottles under £20, 12 by the glass (£4.75-£8) **Notes:** Vegetarian available, Dress Restrictions, Smart casual, no scruffy jeans or trainers, Civ Wed 450 **Seats:** 140, Pr/dining room 60 **Smoking:** No pipes, No cigars, Air con **Directions:** Nearest station: Piccadilly/Charing Cross At end of Haymarket **Parking:** NCP, on street

Mitsukoshi

Japanese

Authentic Japanese cooking in a department store restaurant

☎ 020 7930 0317 Dorland House,
14-20 Lower Regent St SW1Y 4PH Plan 3-B1
e-mail: lonrest@mitsukoshi.co.jp
web: www.mitsukoshi-restaurant.co.uk

Mitsukoshi is a long established restaurant and separate sushi bar located in the basement of its namesake Japanese department store. Excellent ingredients are used, particularly the fish, and diners can enjoy the theatre of food preparation in the sushi bar. Alternatively try shabu-shabu, quick-cooked beef prepared at the table and served with a special sauce, followed by green tea ice cream. Set meals are also listed, including a quick lunch bowl with soup and pickles. Private dining is available in a traditional Japanese-style room or a Western-style room.

Chef: Kenji Hirai **Owners:** Mitsukoshi (UK) Ltd. **Times:** 12-2/6-10, Closed 25, 26 Dec, 1 Jan, Easter **Prices:** Fixed L £10-£25, Fixed D £22-£28, Starter £3-£7, Main £8-£20, Dessert £3-£6.50, Coffee £2, Min/Water £4, Service added 15% **Wine:** 6 bottles over £20, 7 bottles under £20, 2 by the glass (£2.50) **Notes:** Vegetarian available **Seats:** 56, Pr/dining room 20 **Smoking:** N/Sm area, No pipes, No cigars, Air con **Children:** Menu, Portions

Mju at Millennium Knightsbridge

see page 282

Nahm

see page 283

One-O-One

see page 283

L'Oranger

French, Mediterranean

Classic French cuisine at one of London's most beautiful restaurants

☎ 020 7839 3774 5 St James's St SW1A 1EF
Plan 5-B5
e-mail: oranger.restaurant@fsmail.net

In keeping with its classy St James' address, L'Oranger is an impeccably elegant dinner destination. The long panelled room is adorned with flower displays and antique mirrors, with a domed glass ceiling to let in the light, and there's a pretty courtyard for alfresco dining in summer. Fish is a speciality, but the wide-ranging French menu covers all the bases, featuring a selection of classics brought back to life by the odd modern twist. Confit duck liver is a typical starter, served with celeriac and a granite of green apple, while mains might include pigeon with pommes mousseline, mushroom and black truffle jus, or grilled lobster with sauce vièrge and deep-fried basilica leaves.

Chef: Laurent Michel **Owners:** London & Henley Ltd **Times:** 12-3.30/6-11, Closed Xmas, BHs, Sun, Closed L Sat **Prices:** Fixed L £27-£32, Fixed D £40-£45, Starter £14-£26, Main £24-£29, Dessert £6-£8, Coffee £3.50, Min/Water £3.50, Service added but optional 12.5% **Notes:** Tasting menu £75, Vegetarian available, Dress Restrictions, Smart casual **Seats:** 55, Pr/dining room 30 **Smoking:** No pipes, No cigars, Air con **Children:** Portions **Directions:** Nearest station: Green Park Access by car via Pall Mall **Parking:** On street or NCP

 Pétrus

see page 284

England

Mandarin Oriental Hyde Park

LONDON SW1

Modern European NOTABLE WINE LIST

One of the capital's finest

☎ 020 7235 2000 66 Knightsbridge SW1X 7LA Plan 4-F4
e-mail: molon-reservations@mohg.com
web: www.mandarinoriental.com/london

This imposing hotel, opposite Harvey Nichols and backing onto Hyde Park, fairly bristles with class. From the liveried doorman and fluttering flags outside, it might give the impression of a grand Edwardian edifice in the old tradition, yet it's anything but. There is a fashionable bar and glass-fronted wine-store entrance to Foliage, the signature fine-dining restaurant. Chic, stylish and intimate, the restaurant's theme is all in the name, with Adam Tihany's design conceiving to 'bring the park into the restaurant'. Giant glass wall panels enclose thousands of white silk leaves that come alive with lighting and change colour to echo the seasons, while a split-level floor ensures all have a view of park life. Clean lines and luxury fabrics and furnishings add to the sophisticated modern tone, while leaves picked daily from the park are placed beneath diners' glass table plates to reinforce the foliage theme. These fine details support the dining room's reputation as one of London's finest under chef's David Nicholls' and Chris Staines' sublime cooking. Their approach is via an enticing repertoire of fixed-price menu options that take in a terrific value lunch jour, carte and tasting dinner offering. Tip-top quality, luxury ingredients grace the intricate cooking showcasing the kitchen's technical skills, with well-conceived, well-presented dishes of clean, balanced flavours that live up to the setting. Think pot-roast saddle of rabbit teamed with a Pithiviers of wild mushrooms, asparagus, Alsace bacon and vanilla cream, or dessert of tart Tatin and croustillant of banana, 'ponchu crema' and sea-salt caramel ice cream.

Notable Wine List: A beautifully presented wine list brimming full of quality selections including some great vintages within the Bordeaux section.

Chef: David Nicholls, Chris Staines
Owners: Mandarin Oriental Hyde Park Hotel
Times: 12-2.30/7-10
Prices: Fixed L £25-£47.50, Fixed D fr £50, Coffee £3.50, Min/Water £5, Service added but optional 12.5%
Wine: 590 bottles over £20, 65 bottles under £20, 20 by the glass (£5.70-£18)
Notes: Fixed L 3 courses, Tasting menu 5 courses £70, Vegetarian available, Dress Restrictions, Smart casual, Civ Wed 220
Seats: 46, Pr/dining room 250
Smoking: No pipes or cigars, Air con
Rooms: 200 (200 en suite) ★★★★★
Directions: Nearest station: Knightsbridge With Harrods on right, hotel is 0.5m on left, opposite Harvey Nichols
Parking: Valet parking

England

LONDON SW1 *continued*

Quaglino's

Modern European

Vast basement brasserie from the Conran stable

☎ 020 7930 6767 16 Bury St, St James's SW1Y 6AJ Plan 5-B6
e-mail: kateg@conran-restaurants.co.uk
web: www.conran.com

Built on the site of the original society restaurant, there's no shortage of glamour in this contemporary incarnation. A dramatic staircase sweeps down into a cavernous space supported by colourful columns, and there's a bar, live music and a room for private dining. The restaurant attracts an animated crowd, which adds to the atmosphere and sense of theatre. Simple seasonal dishes are the staple of the brasserie-style menu: crustacea, Chateaubriand with sauce béarnaise, fish and chips, and calves' liver and bacon. A fixed-price lunch and pre-theatre menu are also available.

Times: 12-3/5.30-12, Closed 24-25 Dec, 1 Jan, Closed L 26, 31 Dec, 2 Jan **Directions:** Nearest station: Green Park/Piccadilly Circus Bury St is off Jermyn St

Quirinale

Italian

High-end Italian food, a stone's throw from Parliament

☎ 020 7222 7080 North Court, 1 Great Peter St SW1P 3LL Plan 5-C3
e-mail: info@quirnale.co.uk

Designed by Irish architect David Collins, this basement restaurant is set in an attractive building on a pleasant street, light and airy by day, romantic and candle-lit for dinner. Just a few minutes from Parliament, it's popular with politicians, journalists and business people. Attractively dressed tables and central banquettes ensure discreet seating arrangements. The cooking style is distinctly Italian and dishes are a mixture of classic and modern. Pasta can be served as either starter or main, and many ingredients are specially imported from Italy. For mains take a fillet of cod with clams, tomato and cannellini beans, followed by chocolate pannacotta with caramelised bananas and coconut ice cream. An impressive selection of breads, cheeses and Italian wines completes the picture.

Times: 12-3/6-12, Closed Xmas & New Year, 2 wks Aug, Sat & Sun

Mju at Millennium Knightsbridge

LONDON SW1

French, Pacific Rim

Contemporary dining to really dress up for

☎ 020 7201 6330 17 Sloane St, Knightsbridge SW1X 9NU Plan 4-F4
e-mail: mju@mill-cop.com
web: www.millenniumhotels.com/knightsbridge

Occupying a curvaceous space on the first floor of the swish, fashionable and contemporary Millennium Hotel in the prestigious shopping area of Knightsbridge, the chic, funky Mju Restaurant and Cocktail Bar fits in perfectly. From the hotel lobby, a winding staircase leads to the spacious atrium dining room, an exclusive, suitably stylish affair, resolutely modern, almost club-like and cloaked in a hint of the orient. There's a wealth of darkwood, with rich olive green wall-coverings and deep maroon upholstery, while subtle lighting, bright artwork and cool music play their part, too, as do the enthusiastic, engaging, slick and knowledgeable staff. The cooking is equally contemporary, taking an adventurous, innovative and hugely creative modern French approach that draws on influences from Asia and the Mediterranean. The carte is somewhat outgunned by signature tasting menus inspired by seasonal themes that have become synonymous with the Mju experience, presenting dishes of unique composition, flavour, texture and balance that really work. Think lobster linguini with prawns, shellfish oil, aromatic seaweed and Asian herbs, and desserts like baked chocolate - a fondant of bitter chocolate with spiced fig ice cream, honey yogurt and berries. Definitely a restaurant of the moment.

Chef: Tom Thomsen **Owners:** Millennium & Copthorne Hotels **Times:** 12-2.30/6-10.30, Closed Sun, Closed L Sat **Prices:** Fixed D £38, Coffee £3.50, Min/Water £5, Service added but optional 12.5% **Wine:** 310 bottles over £20, 30 by the glass (£6.50-£22) **Notes:** Tasting menu £46, Vegetarian available **Seats:** 110, Pr/dining room 50 **Smoking:** N/Sm in restaurant, Air con **Children:** Portions **Rooms:** 222 (222 en suite) ★★★★ HL **Directions:** Nearest station: Knightsbridge/Victoria 200yds from Knightsbridge Stn/near Harrods **Parking:** 8

Nahm

LONDON SW1

Thai 

One of the best Thai restaurants in the world

☎ 020 7333 1234 The Halkin Hotel, Halkin St, Belgravia SW1X 7DJ Plan 4-G4
e-mail: res@nahm.como.bz
web: www.halkin.como.bz

Located in Belgravia, the Halkin is a discreet and luxurious bolthole for the well heeled. It's perhaps a surprising choice for an internationally renowned chef to set up home but it works - particularly in the evening when Nahm resounds with the cooing of diners enjoying the unforgettable flavours of what many consider the world's best Thai food. The unassuming décor allows the food to do the talking - backed up by assured and knowledgeable service. The Arharn Thai tasting menu offers the best overview of this sophisticated and very often extraordinary cuisine. Tickle the palate with a deeply flavoured ma hor appetiser, a meaty, caramel treat; then sample dishes such as deep-fried fish in three-flavoured sauce (crisp and zingy), yam pak (a lip-smackingly savoury Thai salad) or a rich, creamy panaeng curry. If the prices leave you a little breathless you can content yourself with the knowledge that it's a darn site cheaper than flying to Bangkok - you certainly won't find Thai food better than this anywhere in Europe.

Chef: David Thompson, Matthew Albert **Owners:** Halkin Hotel Ltd **Times:** 12-2.30/7-11, Closed 25 Dec & BHs, Closed L Sat-Sun **Prices:** Fixed L £26-£35, Fixed D £49.50-£75, Starter £13.50, Main £7.50-£15.50, Coffee £4, Min/Water £4.50, Service added but optional 12.5% **Wine:** 200 bottles over £20, 10 by the glass (£7.50-£9.25) **Notes:** Fixed L 3 courses, Fixed D 4 courses, Vegetarian available, Dress Restrictions, No jeans **Seats:** 78, Pr/dining room 36 **Smoking:** N/Sm in restaurant, Air con **Children:** Portions **Rooms:** 41 (41 en suite) ★★★★★ HL **Directions:** Nearest station: Hyde Park Halkin Street just off Hyde Park Corner **Parking:** NCP

One-O-One

LONDON SW1

French, seafood

First-rate seafood restaurant

☎ 020 7290 7101 Sheraton Park Tower, 101 Knightsbridge SW1X 7RN Plan 4-F4
e-mail: darren.neilan@luxurycollection.com
web: www.luxurycollection.com/parktowerlondon

The place makes its intentions clear right from the off, with its aquatic-inspired blue-and-white interior, blue swirling carpet, aquamarine leather chairs and a stainless steel sculpture of a fish, but then One-O-One is one of the country's finest seafood restaurants after all. You might almost imagine you're in a goldfish bowl, looking out through the curvaceous windows of the ground-floor dining room at the base of the modern, circular Sheraton Park Tower hotel onto bustling Knightsbridge next to Harvey Nichols. Discreet frosted glass puts paid to pedestrians ogling though, while service is slick but delightfully friendly and brings a cheerful note to proceedings, and the kitchen never misses a beat either. Brittany-born chef Pascal Proyart insists on superb quality ingredients and their freshness shines through. Classic combinations, clear, clean flavours and some innovative twists parade on the extensive carte plus tasting Menu Gormandise. There are a few meaty options, but the key driving force here is the fabulous seafood. Take a pavé of Dover sole meunière with pan-fried langoustines, celeriac mash and Nantua sauce, or perhaps fillet of John Dory and baby squid à la plancha served with a cassoulet bean purée and braised pork belly. When someone fancies fish in London, this is the place that first springs to mind.

Chef: Pascal Proyart **Owners:** Starwood Hotels & Resorts **Times:** 12-2.30/7-10.30 **Prices:** Fixed L £25, Fixed D £48, Starter £14-£19, Main £21-£28, Dessert £8, Coffee £3.95, Min/Water £4.80, Service optional **Wine:** 101 bottles over £20, 12 by the glass (£6-£13.50) **Notes:** Fixed L 3 courses, Fixed D 5 courses, Tasting menu 5 course £48, 9 course £79, Vegetarian available, Dress Restrictions, Smart casual preferred **Seats:** 70, Pr/dining room 10 **Smoking:** N/Sm in restaurant, Air con **Children:** Portions **Rooms:** 280 (280 en suite) ★★★★★ HL **Directions:** Nearest station: Knightsbridge E from station, just after Harvey Nichols **Parking:** 60

England

Pétrus

LONDON SW1

French, European V NOTABLE WINE LIST

Top-of-the-range dining in opulent Knightsbridge

☎ 020 7235 1200 The Berkeley, Wilton Place, Knightsbridge SW1X 7RL Plan 4-G4
e-mail: petrus@marcuswareing.com
web: www.marcuswareing.com

Off the foyer and at the far end of the stylish Berkeley Hotel's Caramel Room lounge-bar (the discreet name on the handles of the tinted-glass doors lets you know you've arrived), Pétrus oozes sophistication and opulence. As soon as you enter you're cosseted by slick and attentive staff, consummate professionals, though not at all stuffy. Rich, vivid and sexy, the interior is the work of design guru David Collins, the sensual claret colours and textures reflecting that of the world-renowned wine that lends the restaurant its name. Eye-catching features grab the attention - two giant abacuses complete with blown-glass beads act as a screen for the wine chillers; fantastic chandeliers, stunning French blinds, chairs of soft burgundy leather and red velvety walls all seduce. Trolleys for cheeses, liqueurs and, most importantly, the bonbons, with its wonderful selection of sweetmeats, all circle the floor in style and add a sense of theatre to the occasion. There's also a small lounge area for aperitifs and a chef's table in the kitchen for up to eight guests. It's all a bold and striking complement to the impeccable cooking that makes Pétrus a dining magnet on the international culinary map.
Marcus Wareing's modern approach is classically based, has great integrity and owes much to the insistence on the absolute best in raw ingredients. The elegant, richly detailed cuisine oozes technical wizardry, precision, balance, clear flavours and wow factor ... this is skill of the highest order. Think roasted Scottish lobster teamed with sautéed scallops, lobster and salmon ravioli and shellfish vinaigrette, while dessert might feature an almond pannacotta with vanilla poached pear and tonka bean ice cream. A serious wine list, with a good selection by glass, naturally includes offerings from that namesake château, while set-price lunch offers great value at this level.
Notable Wine List: A classic wine list full of high quality wines including, as you might expect, a fabulous range of Pétrus.

Chef: Marcus Wareing
Owners: Marcus Wareing at the Berkeley Ltd
Times: 12-2.30/6-11, Closed 1 week Xmas, Sun, Closed L Sat
Prices: Fixed L £30-£80, Fixed D £60, Coffee £5, Min/Water £4, Service added but optional 12.5%
Wine: 850 bottles over £20, 20 bottles under £20, 10 by the glass (£5-£25)
Notes: Fixed L 3 courses, Fixed D 6 courses £80, Vegetarian menu, Dress Restrictions, Smart-jacket preferred, no jeans/trainers
Seats: 70, Pr/dining room 16
Smoking: N/Sm in restaurant, Air con
Children: Portions
Rooms: 214 (214 en suite) ★★★★★ HL
Parking: NCP and on street

LONDON SW1 *continued*

The Rib Room & Oyster Bar

British NOTABLE WINE LIST

Robust British cooking in the heart of Knightsbridge

☎ 020 7858 7053 The Carlton Tower Hotel, Cadogan Place SW1X 9PY Plan 4-F4
e-mail: JCTinfo@jumeirah.com
web: www.jumeirah.com

This truly British restaurant, with its sophisticated, moody, club-like atmosphere comes richly furnished with acres of wood panelling, awesome floral displays, seductive lighting, artwork by Feliks Topolski and crisp napery. The service gently balances British etiquette with friendliness. From the open 'theatre' kitchen tantalising aromas waft, its repertoire pure British gastronomy with the best home-reared produce delivered in a simple, straightforward style that allows flavours to sing. Take classics like Aberdeen Angus rib of beef with Yorkshire pudding, roast Gressingham duck with apple and sage, or grilled Dover sole, and from the Oyster Bar, the namesake crustacea and caviar. A pianist entertains in the evenings.
Notable Wine List: A traditional wine list with a comprehensive offering from all the major wine producing areas.

Chef: Simon Young **Owners:** Carlton Tower Ltd **Times:** 12.30-2.45/7-10.45 **Prices:** Fixed L £29.50-£81, Starter £10.50-£17.30, Main £22.40-£46.90, Dessert £8, Coffee £4, Min/Water £6, Service added 12.5% **Wine:** 235 bottles over £20, 10 by the glass (£7.50-£10) **Notes:** Vegetarian available, Dress Restrictions, Smart casual, Civ Wed 400 **Seats:** 64, Pr/dining room 18 **Smoking:** N/Sm area, Air con **Children:** Menu, Portions **Rooms:** 220 (220 en suite) ★★★★★ **Directions:** Nearest station: Knightsbridge From major roads follow signs for City Centre, towards Knightsbridge/Hyde Park/Sloane Sq, then into Sloane St/Cadogan Place **Parking:** 70

Roussillon

Classical French

Discreet French restaurant focused on the seasons

☎ 020 7730 5550 16 St Barnabas St SW1W 8PB Plan 4-G2
e-mail: michael@roussillon.co.uk
web: www.roussillon.co.uk

There is no doubting the serious aspirations of this Pimlico restaurant with its large curved bay window: a formal and professional French team complete with sommelier matches the fine dining menus and sophisticated modern ambience. The generously sized, spacious tables are ideal for business lunches or evening get-togethers. A short lunch menu, boosted by a carte and several specialist menus, present classical French dishes based on luxury seasonal ingredients. The cooking is accurate and very imaginative, and there's a rustic style to the presentation. Typical dishes include smoked eels and scrambled eggs, Appleton Old Spot pork in 3 ways, open ravioli of lobster, and grilled calves' sweetbread with sautéed purple artichoke.

Times: 12-2.30/6.30-11, Closed 24 Dec-5 Jan, Sun **Directions:** Nearest station: Sloane Square Telephone for directions

The Rubens at the Palace

International

Quintessentially British hotel overlooking Buckingham Palace

☎ 020 7834 6600 39 Buckingham Palace Rd SW1W 0PS Plan 5-A4
e-mail: bookrb@rchmail.com
web: www.redcarnationhotels.com

Just opposite Buckingham Palace, this tourist favourite was the headquarters of the commander in chief of the Polish forces in World War II. The library restaurant has the intimate feel of a Gentleman's club, with rich, embroidered fabrics and large comfortable armchairs. There's an unobtrusive formality to the service, with traditional flourishes, such as smoked salmon being carved at the table. Simple presentation, good-sized portions and quality ingredients are evident throughout the menu, epitomised by dishes such as seared scallops with spicy cauliflower purée or pot-roasted pheasant with fondant potato and juniper berries.

Chef: Daniel Collins **Owners:** Red Carnation Hotels **Times:** 7-10.30, Closed Xmas week, Closed L all week **Prices:** Fixed D £35, Starter £6-£11, Main £16.50-£39.50, Dessert £6.50-£7.50, Coffee £3.95, Min/Water £3.95, Service added but optional 12.5% **Wine:** 30 bottles over £20, 7 bottles under £20, 6 by the glass (£3.95-£8.50) **Notes:** Vegetarian available, Dress Restrictions, No shorts or track suits **Seats:** 30, Pr/dining room 50 **Smoking:** N/Sm in restaurant, Air con **Children:** Menu **Rooms:** 172 (172 en suite) ★★★★ HL **Directions:** Nearest station: Victoria From station head towards Buckingham Palace **Parking:** NCP at Victoria Coach Station

Salloos Restaurant

Pakistani

Romantic mews restaurant with Mughlai menu

☎ 020 7235 4444 62-64 Kinnerton St SW1X 8ER Plan 4-G4

The mews-house frontage adds to the appeal of this glamorous South Asian restaurant. The interior has a distinct touch of luxury to its décor whilst remaining contemporary in style. Service is friendly with formal touches. Mughlai dishes make up the menu, with some unusual items making a welcome appearance amongst the parathas and kebabs, such as the refreshing almond soup appetiser. Main dish specialities include juicy tandoori lamb chops, a Khyber-style chicken karahi and a haleem akbari - shredded lamb in wheatgerm, lentils and spices. Finish with pistachio kulfi.

Chef: Abdul Aziz **Owners:** Mr & Mrs M Salahuddin **Times:** 12-3/7-11.45, Closed Xmas, Sun **Prices:** Starter £4.50-£8.50, Main £9.50-£16.50, Dessert £5.50, Coffee £3, Min/Water £3.50, Service added but optional 12.5% **Wine:** 2 by the glass (£3.50) **Notes:** Vegetarian available **Seats:** 65 **Smoking:** No pipes, No cigars, Air con **Children:** Min 6 yrs **Directions:** Nearest station: Knightsbridge Kinnerton St is opposite Berkeley Hotel on Wilton Place **Parking:** Meters & car park Kinnerton St

LONDON SW1 *continued*

 Santini

Italian

Sophisticated, family-run Italian restaurant

☎ 020 7730 4094 & 7730 8745 29 Ebury St SW1W 0NZ Plan 4-H3
e-mail: info@santini-restaurant.com
web: www.santini-restaurant.com

A long-established, refined Belgravia Italian restaurant with alfresco terrace dining in summer. Inside, large windows, slatted blinds, light marble floors, pastel walls and suede banquettes and tub-style chairs cut an elegant, modern edge. The carte offers a typically lengthy choice of authentic, regional Italian dishes with a strong Venetian accent and an emphasis on simplicity, flavour and quality seasonal ingredients. Expect starters such as the freshest home-made ravioli with ricotta and spinach or carciofo Santini, followed by grilled calves' liver, baby spinach and crisp pancetta, then traditional Roman apple fritters. Attentive, professional service and good Italian wines hit the mark too.

Chef: Luca Lamari **Owners:** Mr G Santin **Times:** 12.30-2.30/6-11.30, Closed Xmas, 1 Jan, Easter Sun, Closed L Sat & Sun **Prices:** Fixed L £16.50, Starter £8.50-£17.50, Main £14.50-£27.50, Dessert £6.50-£7.50, Coffee £2.75, Min/Water £3.50, Service added but optional 12.5% **Wine:** 80 bottles over £20, 2 bottles under £20, 10 by the glass (£3.75-£17.50) **Notes:** Vegetarian available, Dress Restrictions, Smart casual **Seats:** 65, Pr/dining room 30 **Smoking:** No pipes, Air con **Children:** Portions **Directions:** Nearest station: Victoria Take Lower Belgrave St off Buckingham Palace Rd. Restaurant on 1st corner on left opposite Grosvenor Hotel
Parking: Meters (no charge after 6.30pm)

The Stafford Hotel

British, French

Romantic hotel dining in an exclusive location

☎ 020 7493 0111 16-18 St James's Place SW1A 1NJ Plan 5-A5
e-mail: info@thestaffordhotel.com
web: www.shirehotels.com

Clubby hotel close to the hub of the city but uniquely secluded in St James. Public areas are comfortable with an understated opulence. The world famous American bar, known for mixing a mean martini, displays an eccentric collection of caps and ties and signed celebrity photographs. The restaurant is on two levels and serves a range of modern and classical dishes. A simpler menu is offered at lunchtime with a daily special from the trolley Sunday to Friday, generally a roast, with fish on Friday. From the dinner menu there is a choice from the stoves (Dover sole meunière) and from the classics (chargrilled calves' liver and bacon).

continued

Times: 12.30-2.30/6-10.30, Closed L Sat **Rooms:** 81 (81 en suite) ★★★★ HL **Directions:** Nearest station: Green Park 5 mins St James' Palace

 Volt

Modern Mediterranean NEW

Funky modern restaurant with Mediterranean-influenced cuisine

☎ 020 7235 9696 17 Hobart Place SW1W 0HH Plan 4-H4
e-mail: info@voltlounge.com
web: www.voltlounge.com

There's a club-like feel to this funky south-of-the-river restaurant, and an eclectic range of styles. The curved walls of the main restaurant are inset with purple light strips, and seating is arranged around a central bar. Three other areas, called Cognac, Crystal and Diamond, can be closed off for private dining. A laid-back Italian team brings the modern menu, with its emphasis on daily seasonal produce sourced from the London and Paris markets. The clean, vibrant flavours of veal fillet with seared diver-caught scallops with warm asparagus, pomegranate and saffron vinaigrette might kick off a meal, with pan-fried wild sea bass with artichoke sauce making an accomplished main course. Great choice of cocktails and the home-made breads served with olive and balsamic oils are very moreish.

Chef: Santino Busciglio **Owners:** Bou Antoun **Times:** 12-3/5.30-11.00, Closed Xmas, last 2 wks Aug, Sun, Closed L Sat **Prices:** Fixed L fr £17, Fixed D fr £15, Starter £7-£11, Main £15-£24, Dessert £6, Coffee £2.50, Min/Water £4, Service optional **Wine:** 99 bottles over £20, 8 bottles under £20, 8 by the glass (£4-£7) **Notes:** Fixed D 2 courses, Tasting menu 5 courses £35, Vegetarian available, Dress Restrictions, Smart casual
Seats: 120, Pr/dining room 30 **Smoking:** Air con **Children:** Portions
Directions: Nearest station: Victoria Behind Buckingham Palace
Parking: On street

Wiltons Since 1742

British

One of London's finest fish and game restaurants

☎ 020 7629 9955 55 Jermyn St SW1Y 6LX Plan 5-A6
e-mail: wiltons@wiltons.co.uk
web: www.wiltons.co.uk

This endearing, old-established conservative gem is something of a St James's institution and belongs to a dying breed. Dating back to 1742 and somewhat in the tradition of a gentleman's club (with jacket and tie still obligatory), service, from charming staff smartly clad in waistcoats and long white aprons, is surprisingly unstuffy. The restaurant's size is deceptive, a series of interconnecting rooms spread out beyond the small bar, offering a mix of secluded booths, darkwood panelling, crisply-clothed tables and walls adorned with game and sporting memorabilia. The menu follows suit - resolutely traditional with dishes intelligently simply prepared to allow the freshest of ingredients to shine. Expect classics like grilled scallops with crab thermidor, roast rack of lamb with herb crust and thyme jus, and bread-and-butter pudding.

Chef: Jerome Ponchelle **Owners:** The Hambro Family **Times:** 12-2.30/6-10.45, Closed Xmas-New Year, BHs, Sat, Sun **Prices:** Starter £9-£23, Main £19-£41, Dessert £7.50, Coffee £3.50, Service added but optional 12.5%
Wine: 300 bottles over £20, 10 by the glass (£7-£17) **Notes:** Tasting menu 4 courses available Fri £50, Vegetarian available, Dress Restrictions, Jackets, Mon-Fri **Seats:** 100, Pr/dining room 18 **Smoking:** No pipes, Air con
Directions: Nearest station: Green Park/Piccadilly At the junct of Bury St and Jermyn St, opposite Turnbull & Asser **Parking:** NCP Arlington St

W'Sens by La Compagnie des Comptoirs

Modern French

Chic Waterloo dining choice

☎ 020 7484 1355 12 Waterloo Place, St James SW1Y 4AU Plan 5-B6
e-mail: reservation@wsens.co.uk
web: www.wsens.co.uk

Inside this Grade II listed building you'll find a long retro-lit marble bar designed by an ex student of Philippe Starck. This is one of the highlights of the warm, contemporary chic design, featuring a mix of fireplaces, black leather tables and a library. The menu offers French and Mediterranean style cooking with influences from North Africa and Asia. This is in keeping with the group's other properties in the South of France, Cap d'Agde and Mauritius. Look out for starters like tempura of tiger prawns with sweetcorn purée and mains like roasted fillet of turbot served with Vénére risotto and emulsion of citrus butter.

Chef: Clement Bonano **Owners:** Jacques & Laurent Pourcel & Olivier Chateau **Times:** 12-2.30/6.30-11, Closed 2 wks before Xmas, Sun, Closed L Sat **Prices:** Fixed L £18.50, Fixed D £23.50, Starter £9-£17, Main £11-£35, Dessert £5-£7.50, Coffee £1.95, Min/Water £3.50, Service added but optional 12.5% **Wine:** 100 bottles over £20, 10 bottles under £20, 10 by the glass (£4.25-£8.75) **Notes:** Vegetarian available **Seats:** 120, Pr/dining room 60 **Smoking:** N/Sm area, Air con **Children:** Portions **Directions:** Nearest station: Piccadilly Telephone for directions **Parking:** On street

Zafferano

see below

Aura Kitchen and Bar

☎ 020 7499 9999 48-49 St James St SW1A 1JT
web: www.theaa.com/restaurants/113984.html

Pan-Asian menu under Caviar House in St James's. Silent movies flicker over the bar and there's live DJ music.

The Contented Vine

☎ 020 7834 0044 17 Sussex St SW1V 4RR
web: www.theaa.com/restaurants/113973.html
Chefs are on view at this popular brasserie. English/European menu of freshly prepared dishes.

Zafferano

LONDON SW1

Italian

Chic and popular Knightsbridge Italian

☎ 020 7235 5800 15 Lowndes St SW1X 9EY Plan 4-F4
e-mail: info@zafferanorestaurant.com
web: www.zafferanorestaurant.com

Drawing an adoring crowd, this stylish, deservedly popular Italian may look somewhat understated from the outside, but when judged by the difficulty in securing a table, it's clear that this is somewhere special. The suave, upmarket refurbishment and expansion - which includes a chic cocktail bar-lounge and new private dining room with a view of the walk-in wine cellar - hasn't detracted from the relaxed, friendly vibe and vibrant see-and-be-seen atmosphere. Darkwood, glass, exposed brick and tiled floors deliver a sophisticated modern edge, punctuated by flower displays, crisp white linen, elegant chairs and banquettes and oodles of friendly, professional service. Andrew Needham's drawcard cooking makes certain this Italian is packed for all the right reasons. Intelligently simple, accomplished dishes allow the freshest, top-notch seasonal ingredients to shine. Flawless execution, clear flavours and clean, colourful presentation feature on the appealing fixed-price menus (and separate list of supplemented specials), while a well-constructed, patriotic Italian wine list and fabulous bread selection rounds things off in style. Expect to be seduced by the likes of pan-fried scallops with leeks and black truffle sauce, perhaps chargrilled lamb with artichokes and Taggiasche olives, or a chocolate fondant dessert served with gianduia ice cream.

Chef: Andrew Needham **Owners:** A-Z Restaurants **Times:** 12-2.30/7-11, Closed 1 wk Xmas & New Year, BHs **Prices:** Fixed L £25.50, Fixed D £39.50, Coffee £2.50, Min/Water £3.50, Service added but optional 13.5%, Group min 8 service 15% **Wine:** 312 bottles over £20, 9 bottles under £20, 6 by the glass (£3.50-£6.50) **Notes:** Dress Restrictions, Smart casual **Seats:** 54 **Smoking:** N/Sm in restaurant, Air con **Children:** No Children **Directions:** Nearest station: Knightsbridge Located off Sloane St, behind Carlton Tower Hotel **Parking:** NCP behind Restaurant

LONDON SW1 *continued*

The Footstool

☎ 020 7222 2779 St John's, Smith Square SW1P 3HA
web: www.theaa.com/restaurants/113974.html
Modern, atmospheric restaurant in St John's crypt with modern European menu. Open at concert times.

Greens Restaurant and Oyster Bar

☎ 020 7930 4566 36 Duke St, St James' SW1Y 6DF
web: www.theaa.com/restaurants/113937.html
Clubby atmosphere and an emphasis on fish, which is perfectly cooked. Classic nursery puddings round things off.

Harvard Bar & Grill

☎ 020 7868 6249 101 Buckingham Palace Rd, Victoria SW1W 0SJ
Within walking distance of many famous landmarks. Open early morning to late in the evening

Quilon

☎ 020 7821 1899 41 Buckingham Gate, St James' SW1E 6AF
web: www.theaa.com/restaurants/114008.html

New generation lighter Indian cuisine on eclectic menu.

Wagamama

☎ 020 7321 2755 8 Norris St SW1Y 4RJ
Informal noodle bar with no booking.

Yo! Sushi

☎ 020 7235 5000 5th Floor, Harvey Nichols Food Hall, 109-125 Knightsbridge SW1X 7RJ
Sushi, sashimi, noodles and more delivered by conveyor belt and priced according to colour-coded plates.

LONDON SW3

Awana

Malaysian 

Authentic Malaysian restaurant

☎ 020 7584 8880 85 Sloane Av SW3 3DX
Plan 4-E2

The name means 'in the clouds' in Malay and this restaurant is the newest venture of Eddie Lim, owner of The Mango Tree in Victoria. The dining room is inspired by traditional Malaysian teak houses, with lush silk panels and delicate glass screens highlighting the darkwood interior. Modern style is given to authentic Malaysian cuisine featuring satay dishes, skewered dishes, starters, soups, curry, grills and stirfrys. Typical dishes include assorted seafood from the Satay Bar like skewered fresh prawns, scallops and squid with a home-made spicy peanut sauce, or slow-cooked rib of beef with curry, coconut milk and Awana blended herbs. Why not try a dessert cocktail. Takeaway menu also available.

Times: 11-3/6-11 **Prices:** Food prices not confirmed for 2007. Please telephone for detail **Seats:** 110

Bibendum

European

Classic and contemporary dishes with Conran style

☎ 020 7581 5817 Michelin House, 81 Fulham Rd SW3 6RD Plan 4-E3
e-mail: manager@bibendum.co.uk
web: www.bibendum.co.uk

Light, airy and elegant restaurant occupying the first floor of the art deco Michelin building, with its fabulous stained glass windows portraying Bibendum, the Michelin man, in various poses. It is accessed via the ground floor oyster bar, which serves all manner of crustacea, and the complex also includes a coffee bar and gift shop selling Michelin man monogrammed products. French and British brasserie dishes are brought up to date, Bibendum-style, with fresh ingredients and accurate execution - terrine of foie gras with Armagnac jelly, John Dory with linguine and pimento, olive and parsley dressing, and hot chocolate fondant with pistachio cream. There's a great atmosphere, too, perfect for celebrity spotting.

Times: 12-2.30/7-11.30, Closed Dec 25-26, 1 Jan, Closed D Dec 24

Bluebird Dining Rooms

British

British dining at its best in the most elegant surroundings

☎ 020 7559 1129 350 King's Rd SW3 5UU Plan 4-D1
e-mail: info@bluebirdclub.co.uk
web: www.conran.com

The Bluebird Dining Rooms, under the direction of Tom Conran, are located over the food shop of the same name and next to (and not to be confused with) the Bluebird Restaurant, with a separate entrance on Beaufort Street. Designed to capture the glamour of the 1920s and 30s, the restaurant is large, sleek and stylish with a small pewter bar serving classic cocktails, a glass atrium roof, shellfish tank and papier-mâché rhino. Top class ingredients are selected with care and the menu is structured to accommodate the classics: game in season, puddings and pies, lobsters, oysters and crabs. Expect mains such as slow roast crackled organic white belly of pork with roast potatoes and apple compôte. Service is polished and prices are in line with the chic atmosphere.

Times: 6-10.30, Closed Xmas, Easter Fri & Mon, Closed L Mon-Sat, D Sun

The Capital

see page 290

The Collection

International

Buzzy, vibrant and fashion conscious bar restaurant

☎ 020 7225 1212 264 Brompton Rd SW3 2AS
Plan 4-E3
e-mail: office@thecollection.co.uk
web: www.the-collection.co.uk

Strut your stuff across the long, neon-lit catwalk entrance to this huge, trendy, one-time fashion warehouse, now bustling ground-floor bar and mezzanine restaurant. Loud music and a vibrant atmosphere crank up the volume, exposed brick and metal add an urban edge, while attentive staff come clad in black and tables white-clothed. The crowd-pleasing, appealing, modern-focused menus (including a great-value Early Dinner option) look to the global larder for inspiration. Expect wild halibut wontons with sweet-and-sour dipping sauce to parade alongside classics like chargrilled rib-eye and béarnaise sauce.

Times: 5-12.30, Closed 25-26 Dec, 1 Jan, BHs, Closed L Lunch Xmas period **Directions:** Nearest station: South Kensington Pelham Street to traffic lights and turn left

Le Colombier

Traditional French

Stylish dining in the heart of Chelsea

☎ 020 7351 1155 145 Dovehouse St SW3 6LB
Plan 4-D2
e-mail: lecolombier1998@aol.com

Popular with the Chelsea ladies-who-lunch, this traditional French brasserie benefits from a lightness of touch in décor, service and menus. Creams and blue walls lead on to a glass-covered terrace for dining throughout the year. Well-prepared, brasserie classics jostle for the diner's attention. Start with either native oysters or the fish soup served with rouille, gruyère and croûtons and follow with a main course of Dover sole meunière or chicken breast with tarragon sauce. Finish with a rum baba or crêpes Suzette.

continued

Chef: Chris McLean **Owners:** Didier Garnier **Times:** 12-3/6.30-10.30 **Prices:** Fixed L £16-£19, Starter £5.30-£12.50, Main £13.50-£19.90, Dessert £5.80, Coffee £1.80, Min/Water £3, Service optional **Wine:** 130 bottles over £20, 16 bottles under £20, 8 by the glass (£3.90-£9.75) **Notes:** Dress Restrictions, Smart casual **Seats:** 70, Pr/dining room 30 **Smoking:** N/Sm in restaurant **Children:** Min 10 yrs **Directions:** Nearest station: South Kensington Please telephone for directions **Parking:** Metered parking

Eight Over Eight

Pan-Asian

Pan-Asian cooking with real attitude

☎ 020 7349 9934 392 King's Rd SW3 5UZ
Plan 1-E3
e-mail: richard@eightovereight.nu
web: www.eightovereight.nu

The bright red Eight Over Eight logo (it means 'lucky forever' in China) stands out over the pale grey walls of this corner bar/restaurant, divided inside by Japanese-style mock ironwork. The contemporary brown-and-beige look is spare and stylish, with beautiful low-hanging oriental lampshades. The menu takes in the standard Pan-Asian cooking styles of sushi/sashimi, curries, dim sum, salads, tempura and specials, but there is nothing bland about the cooking. Flavours are electric, with gentle spices, sharp citruses, and sweet fruits bringing chicken, lobster, tofu etc into sharp focus.

Chef: Richard Francis **Owners:** Will Ricker **Times:** 12-3/6-11, Closed 24-29 Dec, Closed L Sun **Prices:** Fixed L £15, Fixed D £35-£59, Starter £3-£11, Main £7-£21.50, Dessert £5.50-£6.50, Coffee £2.50, Min/Water £3, Service added but optional 12.5% **Wine:** 68 bottles over £20, 7 bottles under £20, 12 by the glass (£3.30-£12.70) **Notes:** Fixed D private dining room, Vegetarian available **Seats:** 95, Pr/dining room 12 **Smoking:** N/Sm in restaurant, Air con **Directions:** Nearest station: Sloane Sq Telephone for directions

Frankie's Italian Bar & Grill

Italian

Glitzy basement restaurant serving simple Italian food

☎ 020 7590 9999 3 Yeoman's Row, Brompton Rd
SW3 2AL Plan 4-E3
e-mail: infofrankies@btconnect.com
web: www.frankiesitalianbarandgrill.com

Tucked away in a Knightsbridge side street, the ground-level entrance hardly prepares you for the shimmering basement interior. A collaboration between Marco Pierre White and jockey Frankie Dettori, the glitzy décor oozes Marco class, from mirror-lined walls and huge revolving disco balls to good-sized tables, leather seating and attentive, informed staff. A chequered mosaic-style floor and small bar complete a sparkling line up, served up to a 1950s backing track and buzzy atmosphere. No fuss, quality Italian food, accurately cooked, on a simple repertoire of antipasti, insalate, pasta, pizza and grills hits just the right note.

Chef: Callum Watson **Owners:** Marco Pierre White & Frankie Dettori **Times:** 12-3/6-11, Closed 26 Dec, Closed D 25 Dec **Prices:** Fixed L £11.75-£18.50, Starter £5.50-£9.50, Main £9.50-£18.50, Dessert £5.50, Coffee £2.50, Min/Water £4, Service added but optional 12.5% **Wine:** 28 bottles over £20, 7 bottles under £20, 9 by the glass (£3.75-£8.75) **Notes:** Vegetarian available **Seats:** 170 **Smoking:** Air con **Children:** Menu, Portions **Directions:** Nearest station: South Kensington/Knightsbridge Near The Oratory on Brompton Rd, close to Harrods **Parking:** South Kensington/Knightsbridge

England

The Capital

LONDON SW3

French  NOTABLE WINE LIST

Inspired cooking and impeccable service at Knightsbridge landmark

☎ 020 7589 5171 Basil St, Knightsbridge SW3 1AT Plan 4-F4
e-mail: reservations@capitalhotel.co.uk
web: www.capitalhotel.co.uk

Secreted away in the heart of Knightsbridge, just around the corner from Harrods and Harvey Nichols, this discreet, luxury boutique hotel thoroughly lives up to its name. From the welcoming foyer winter fire to the hotel's understated elegance, The Capital is bound to impress. Its stylish, new-look restaurant is a sophisticated, light and airy affair, delivering a suave but understated look inspired by the 1940s, while the adjoining cocktail bar has a Harry's Bar vibe. Lightwood panelling is partnered by cool, pale blue velvet upholstered chairs, drapes and blinds in the intimate dining room, while contemporary styled chandeliers hang from high ceilings. Artwork by Dalí and sculpture by Henry Moore further enhance the elegance and chic, but add crisp white napery, highly professional table service, a serious wine list and inspired cooking from a formidably talented kitchen, and you have premier-league status. Chef Eric Chavot's cuisine comes close to perfection, sophisticated and utilising the finest-quality ingredients and plenty of luxury. Though his roots are firmly entrenched in the French classical style, there's nothing staid or strait-laced here, instead a wonderful light, modern approach that comes dotted with some surprise elements. Refinement, balance and high skill reign supreme, with flavours clear and pronounced. Take roasted veal cutlet with a balsamic jus and mushroom fricassée, or perhaps pot-roasted lobster with foie gras boudin and white coco beans, while a caramel and dark chocolate millefeuille might head-up desserts. Superbly made in-house breads, amuse-bouche, pre-dessert and petits fours hold style through to the end, while an excellent-value lunch bolsters the enticing carte and Menu Dégustation.

Notable Wine List: An excellent, serious wine list with high quality and depth in every area; Burgundy and Bordeaux listings impress in particular.

Chef: Eric Chavot
Owners: Mr D Levin & Mr J Levin
Times: 12-2.30/7-11, Closed 25 Dec D
Prices: Fixed L £29.50, Fixed D £55, Coffee £5, Min/Water £3.95, Service added but optional 12.5%
Wine: 800 bottles over £20, 20 bottles under £20, 16 by the glass (£6.50-£18.50)
Notes: Fixed L 3 courses, Dégustation menu £68, Vegetarian menu, Dress Restrictions, No jeans or trainers
Seats: 35, Pr/dining room 24
Smoking: N/Sm in restaurant, Air con
Children: Portions
Rooms: 49 (49 en suite) ★★★★★ TH
Directions: Nearest station: Knightsbridge Off Sloane St, beside Harrods
Parking: 10

LONDON SW3 *continued*

Manicomio

Italian

Modern Italian cuisine in stylish surroundings

☎ 020 7730 3366 85 Duke of York Square, Chelsea SW3 4LY Plan 4-F2
e-mail: manicomio@btconnect.com
web: www.manicomio.co.uk

The name means 'madhouse', but that's not a reflection on the current restaurant, rather on its history as a military asylum! Today you'll find rustic chic with exposed brickwork, oak tables and flooring and red leather seating. The huge terrace is complemented by a private conservatory style dining room with private courtyard drinking area. Authentic Italian dishes are prepared simply using fresh ingredients. Home-made pastas and grill classics are the cornerstones of an interesting and wide-ranging menu. Try the likes of chargrilled cuttlefish with chilli and lemon to start, followed by buckwheat tagliatelle with braised wild boar. Classic desserts include tiramisù and panettone bread-and-butter pudding.

Chef: Bobby Cabral & Tom Salt **Owners:** Ninai & Andrew Zarach **Times:** noon-3/6.30-10.30, Closed Xmas & New Year **Prices:** Starter £7.50-£13, Main £12.25-£21, Dessert £6-£7.50, Coffee £2.15, Min/Water £3.50, Service added but optional 12.5% **Wine:** 63 bottles over £20, 9 bottles under £20, 21 by the glass (£3.50-£6.75) **Notes:** Vegetarian available **Seats:** 70, Pr/dining room 30 **Smoking:** N/Sm area, No pipes, No cigars, Air con **Children:** Portions **Parking:** on street

Nathalie

Modern French

Modern French cuisine in intimate surroundings

☎ 020 7581 2848 3 Milner St SW3 2QA Plan 4-F3
e-mail: eric@nathalie-restaurant.co.uk
web: www.nathalie-restaurant.co.uk

Tucked away in a quiet Chelsea street, this relaxed, family-run restaurant is named after the owners' first daughter. The atmosphere is cosy and discreet, ideal as we hear that members of the Royal Family have been known to visit. Service is friendly and personalised with the chef-patron and his wife very hands-on. Good traditional French dishes are served here with a modern twist. A simple carte features the likes of tart of smoked haddock and leeks with a saffron sauce to start, or interesting main courses like guinea fowl casserole with diced bacon and caramelised chicory tart. French tradition extends to desserts like coffee and chocolate opera gâteau.

Chef: Eric Chatroux **Owners:** Eric Chatroux, Anne Jensen **Times:** 12-2/7-10, Closed Xmas, New Year, Easter, end of Aug, BHs, Sun & Mon **Prices:** Fixed L £14.50, Starter £5.75-£11.50, Main £15.75-£19.50, Dessert £5.50-£6.50, Coffee £2.50, Min/Water £3.50, Service added but optional 12.5% **Wine:** 100 bottles over £20, 10 bottles under £20, 4 by the glass (£3.75-£4.50) **Notes:** Fixed L 6 courses, Vegetarian available **Seats:** 22, Pr/dining room 16 **Smoking:** N/Sm in restaurant **Directions:** Nearest station: Sloane Sq Parallel to Walton St. Between Fulham Rd and King's Rd **Parking:** Pay at meter

Nozomi

Japanese NEW

Chic, Knightsbridge modern Japanese

☎ 020 7838 0181 14 - 15 Beauchamp Place, Knightsbridge SW3 1NQ Plan 4-E4

Located on fashionable Beauchamp Place in upmarket Knightsbridge, Nozomi is a place to see and be seen. The interior is chic and modern, with wooden floors, plain colours and contemporary prints, while service is professional, friendly and knowledgeable. There's a correspondingly modern approach to the Japanese cuisine, too, though methods are traditional and authentic, delivering high-quality produce and clean, fresh flavours. The lengthy, enticing selection is perfect to mix and match from a menu laid out in divisions of small dishes, fish, meat and poultry, tempura, side orders, sushi, maki roll and temaki, and desserts. Expect black cod (this version served with Nozomi miso and pickled daikon), salmon koshiyaki, or lamb shoga to revitalise the taste buds.

Times: 12-3/6.30-11.30

Racine

Traditional French

Busy, popular French brasserie upholding the bourgeois culinary tradition

☎ 020 7584 4477 239 Brompton Rd SW3 2EP Plan 4-E3

Located across the road from Knightsbridge's Brompton Oratory, this establishment is dedicated to French bourgeois cooking. This stylish, traditional brasserie is popular with Knightsbridge shoppers and foodies alike. The trick is in the detail. Formally-attired waiters provide correct, unfussy service whilst the curtained entrance, leather banquette seating and crisply clothed tables add further sentimental allure to a menu of French culinary classics. Start with warm garlic and saffron mousse with mussels before a main course of calf's head with sauce Ravigote or skate Normande. To finish there's the chestnut Mont Blanc or vanilla ice cream with Valrhona chocolate sauce.

Chef: Henry Harris, Chris Handley **Owners:** Eric Garnier, Henry Harris **Times:** 12-3/6-10.30, Closed 25 Dec **Prices:** Fixed L £15.50, Fixed D £17.50, Starter £5.25-£12.50, Main £12.50-£20.50, Dessert £5-£6.50, Coffee £2, Min/Water £3, Service added but optional 14.5% **Wine:** 75 bottles over £20, 16 bottles under £20, 14 by the glass (£3.65-£9.80) **Notes:** Fixed D 6-7.30 only, Vegetarian available **Seats:** 75, Pr/dining room 18 **Smoking:** N/Sm in restaurant, Air con **Children:** Portions **Directions:** Nearest station: Knightsbridge, South Kensington Restaurant opposite Brompton Oratory

Rasoi Restaurant

see page 292

Restaurant Gordon Ramsay

see page 293

Tom Aikens

see page 294

England

England

LONDON SW3 *continued*

Toto's

Italian **NEW**

Popular, friendly Italian restaurant

☎ 0871 332 7293 Walton House, Walton St SW3 2JH Plan 4-F3

Tucked away at the back of Knightsbridge, this lovely white-painted corner property has a patio/courtyard area where you can lunch alfresco. Inside a mezzanine overlooks the main dining room, taking in the sunny yellow walls, petrol blue chairs and fresh flowers, while a Venetian chandelier makes a striking centrepiece. The friendly service and great Italian cooking make this a very popular destination, packed with locals and those lucky enough to get a table by chance. The extensive menu offers modern Italian cuisine with classical undertones. Carpaccio of milk lamb with basil and white celery hearts sits comfortably alongside gratinated home-made veal cannelloni.

Prices: Food prices not confirmed for 2007. Please telephone for details

Tugga

Portuguese **NEW**

Popular, funky and fun Portuguese

☎ 020 7351 0101 312 King's Rd SW3 5UH Plan 1-D1
e-mail: tugga@tugga.com
web: www.tugga.com

The décor's vibrant and fun - though some might consider it quite mad - at this popular King's Road Portuguese. A few tables spill out onto the pavement, there's a busy bar and more formally laid tables towards the back. Huge flowers come painted on pink backgrounds, while striped pink-and-purple tabletops, aubergine ceilings (with flashes of silver) and dark floorboards fuse with a backing track of funky music. The simple but vibrant, well-executed, Portuguese-influenced cooking hits just the right note; oven-baked wild sea bream with an onion, tomato and thyme marinade or confit of duck with Parmentier potatoes infused with black truffle perhaps.

Chef: R Mourao & F Fevereiro **Owners:** Pedro Romos **Times:** 12-3/6.30-11, Closed Xmas & New Year, Mon **Prices:** Fixed L £12-£30, Fixed D £18-£40, Starter £3.50-£7.50, Main £10.50-£22, Dessert £2-£6.50, Coffee £2, Min/Water £3.50, Service added but optional 12.5% **Wine:** 22 bottles over £20, 8 bottles under £20, 11 by the glass (£4.50-£9) **Notes:** Vegetarian available, Dress Restrictions, Smart casual **Seats:** 85, Pr/dining room 12 **Smoking:** N/Sm area, Air con **Parking:** On street

Rasoi Restaurant

LONDON SW3

Indian V

Elegant townhouse Indian restaurant - simply one of the best

☎ 020 7225 1881 10 Lincoln St SW3 2TS Plan 4-F2
e-mail: rasoi.vineet@btconnect.com
web: www.vineetbhatia.com

Discreetly tucked away down a side street off the King's Road close to Sloane Square, this elegant Chelsea townhouse (where you have to ring the doorbell to gain entry) is home to the much-lauded Vineet Bhatia's rasoi (kitchen). Bhatia's modern, progressive attitude to Indian cuisine is echoed in the décor, rich in vibrant Eastern styling that sets the scene for an intimate, relaxed but sophisticated experience. Sandy-beige and chocolate-brown tones, silk cushions, woodcarvings and a bewitching array of tribal masks create an exotic atmosphere, alongside specially-sourced, contemporary cutlery and crockery, crisp white linen and a pleasant marriage of Western and Indian front-of-house service. There's a snug front room overlooking the street, while the back room is bathed in daylight from a conservatory-style skylight. Vineet Bhatia's contemporary, thoroughly evolved cuisine redefines the concept of Indian food and dining, and makes a visit here a real experience. There's an elegance to the kitchen's technical skill, with fine clarity and balance to vibrant flavours and textures, while presentation is refined, cultured and eye-catching. Luxury ingredients parade on an enticing range of menu options that includes a stunning seven- or nine-course Rasoi Gourmand menu (with or without wine selection). This is a must visit for lovers of modern Indian cuisine!

Chef: Vineet Bhatia **Owners:** Vineet & Rashima Bhatia **Times:** 12-2.30/6.30-10.30, Closed Xmas, New Year, BHs, Sun, Closed L Sat **Prices:** Fixed L fr £19, Starter £9-£16, Main £16-£32, Dessert £8-£12, Coffee £4.50, Min/Water £4, Service added but optional 12.5% **Wine:** 210 bottles over £20, 4 bottles under £20, 8 by the glass (£5-£12) **Notes:** Tasting menu 7 courses £58, 9 courses £69, Vegetarian menu, Dress Restrictions, Smart casual **Seats:** 35, Pr/dining room 24 **Smoking:** N/Sm in restaurant, Air con **Directions:** Nearest station: Sloane Square Near Peter Jones and Duke of York Sq **Parking:** on street

Restaurant Gordon Ramsay

LONDON SW3

French, European V NOTABLE WINE LIST

London's finest and Britain's most famous chef

☎ 020 7352 4441 68 Royal Hospital Rd SW3 4HP Plan 4-F1
e-mail: reservations@gordonramsay.com
web: www.gordonramsay.com

Gordon Ramsay may have gone global, with a burgeoning TV career and ever-expanding restaurant empire, but his Chelsea temple of gastronomy - opened back in 1998 - still remains the mothership of his London operations, delivering the best cooking in the capital. Ramsay's hallmark purple discreetly marks out the restaurant's entrance, while the extensive refurbishment by design guru David Collins of the intimate, elegant dining room is wonderfully stylish and sophisticated. Service here is as good as it gets; slick, professional and polished, charmingly orchestrated by maître d' Jean-Claude Breton, who manages to make you feel like you're the only guests in the room. Enthusiastic explanations of dishes increase anticipation, while there's plenty of help navigating the fabulous wine list, too. Royal Hospital Road remains as popular as ever, thus bookings can only be made a month in advance, so be ready to hang on the end of the 'phone to secure that table. You certainly won't be disappointed! Classical dishes with contemporary spin grace the kitchen's tantalising fixed-price repertoire of lunch, carte and seven-course Menu Prestige, which come studded with luxury. Simplicity, integrity and lightness of touch are hallmarks of the approach, coupled with innovation, flair, stunning ingredients, precision and depth of flavour. The superlatives may roll on, but the skills on display are as good as they come, with consistency and execution nigh faultless. So expect to be wowed by the likes of best end of Cornish lamb with confit shoulder, provençale vegetables, baby onions, walnuts and a creamed morel sauce, or perhaps pan-fried John Dory fillets served with Cromer crab, caviar, crushed new potatoes and a basil vinaigrette, while a chocolate and amaretti biscuit soufflé - teamed with cinnamon ice cream - might take the eye at dessert. And do wallow in the experience, it's one of life's musts!

Notable Wine List: An extensive and immaculate wine list offering depth in every area, a thoughtful selection by the glass and an informative sommelier selection.

Chef: Gordon Ramsay
Owners: Gordon Ramsay Holdings Ltd
Times: 12-2.30/6.45-11, Closed 2 wks Xmas, BHs, Sat, Sun
Prices: Fixed L £40-£90, Fixed D £70, Coffee £5, Min/Water £4, Service added but optional 12.5%
Wine: 950 bottles over £20, 30 bottles under £20, 18 by the glass (£5-£49)
Notes: Fixed L 7 courses, 7 course prestige menu £90, Vegetarian menu, Dress Restrictions, Jacket preferred, no jeans or trainers
Seats: 44
Smoking: N/Sm in restaurant, Air con
Children: Portions
Directions: Nearest station: Sloane Square Near Royal Army Museum
Parking: On street

England

Tom Aikens

LONDON SW3

Modern French V NOTABLE WINE LIST

Gastronomic big-hitter of class and distinction

☎ 020 7584 2003 43 Elystan St SW3 3NT Plan 4-E2
e-mail: info@tomaikens.co.uk
web: www.tomaikens.co.uk

Chef: Tom Aikens
Owners: T & L Ltd
Times: 12-2.30/6.45-11, Closed 2 wks Xmas & N Year, Ist 2 wks Aug & BHs, Sat & Sun
Prices: Fixed L £29, Fixed D £60, Coffee £5, Min/Water £4.50, Service added but optional 12.5%
Wine: 500 bottles over £20, 10 bottles under £20, 20 by the glass (£6-£20)
Notes: Fixed L 3 courses, Tasting menu £75, Vegetarian menu, Dress Restrictions, Smart dress, no jeans/T-shirts, jacket pref
Seats: 60
Smoking: N/Sm in restaurant, Air con
Children: Portions
Directions: Nearest station: South Kensington Off Fulham Rd (Brompton Rd end)
Parking: Parking meters outside

This much-heralded Chelsea temple to the serious foodie - surprisingly tucked away in a quiet residential street - has put Tom Aikens up there among the top London kitchens. It's an understated, discreet setting for a premier leaguer, a one-time pub transformed by Anouska Hempel's design into a dining room dedicated to the theatre of fine dining. Dark wooden floors and window shutters, black leather chairs and white walls dotted with modern artwork set the interior's minimalist, self-confident lines. Bamboo screens, table lamps set high into window frames and sumptuous flower displays further distinguish the room, alongside the crockery, cutlery and slate serving plates and well-directed, professional and knowledgeable service. Aikens' fixed-priced menu repertoire (lunch, dinner and tasting option) follows the theme of the clean-lined surroundings, with dishes eye-catchingly laid out under their main ingredient; take 'Piglet', which translates as roasted cutlet and loin with pork lasagne, braised trotter and baby squid. But it's the successful marriage of classical roots, modern interpretation, first-class ingredients and flamboyant presentation that makes Aikens' food stand out from the crowd. Attention to detail dominates every aspect with its sheer quality, with ancillaries like breads, amuse-bouche, pre-dessert and petits fours (of afternoon-tea proportions) hitting top form. Technical skill and intricate design and presentation pepper inventive, generous-portioned, vibrant dishes, their innovative combinations showering the senses with visual and flavour sensations. Take roasted John Dory with sautéed squid, capers, coriander and pickled red pepper, or perhaps roasted milk-fed lamb cutlet and braised leg with onion tart fine and sheep's cheese to wow the taste buds.

Notable Wine List: An extensive and serious wine list expertly chosen, with particularly strong Rhone and Burgundy lists.

LONDON SW3 *continued*

Brasserie St Quentin

☎ 020 7589 8005 243 Brompton Rd SW3 2EP
web: www.theaa.com/restaurants/111887.html

Good value French inspired dishes (and wines) in stylish brasserie dining room.

Cross Keys

☎ 020 7349 9111 1 Lawrence St, Chelsea SW3 5NB
web: www.theaa.com/restaurants/113931.html
Gastro-pub with a very popular conservatory eating area. Modern Mediterranean menu.

Haandi

☎ 020 7823 7373 136 Brompton Rd SW3 1HY
web: www.theaa.com/restaurants/114001.html

Northern Frontier Indian cuisine often served in haandis (narrow-necked cooking pots). The chefs can be seen hard at work.

The Pig's Ear

☎ 020 7352 2908 35 Old Church St, Chelsea SW3 5BS
web: www.theaa.com/restaurants/113978.html
Bistro-style gastro pub with candlelit dining room offering robust dishes and comforting desserts.

Riccardos

☎ 020 7370 6656 126 Fulham Rd SW3 6HU
Elegant Italian food with a modern twist.

Shikara

☎ 020 7581 6555 87 Sloane Av SW3
Wholesome Indian fare and earthly dishes of the tandoor.

Spiga Chelsea

☎ 020 7351 0101 312 Kings Rd SW3 5UH
Contemporary but classic Italian with superior pasta and pizza. Sister of Spiga W1.

LONDON SW4

® Tsunami

Japanese

Contemporary neighbourhood Japanese restaurant

☎ 020 7978 1610 5-7 Voltaire Rd SW4 6DQ Plan 1-E3
web: www.tsunamijapaneserestaurant.co.uk

Tucked away down a side street near Clapham Station, this buzzy, stylish neighbourhood Japanese restaurant is a honey pot for a cool crowd. Contemporary seating and lighting, colourful flower displays, an open kitchen and black-clad staff create a vibrant platform for the modern Japanese fusion cuisine. Tempura, sashimi, sushi and oysters have their own section on the lengthy menu, with the quality ingredients and imaginative presentation also showing in specials like prime fillet beef with sea urchin and foie gras butter or steamed sea bass with sake and soy.

Chef: Ken Sam **Owners:** Ken Sam **Times:** 12.30-11/6-11, Closed 25 Dec-4 Jan, Closed L Mon-Fri **Prices:** Starter £3.50-£9.95, Main £6.50-£16.50, Dessert £3.95-£5.95, Min/Water £3, Service added but optional 12.5% **Wine:** 23 bottles over £20, 18 bottles under £20, 9 by the glass (£3.75-£5.50) **Notes:** Vegetarian available **Seats:** 100 **Smoking:** N/Sm area, No pipes, No cigars, Air con **Children:** Portions **Directions:** Nearest station: Clapham North Off Clapham High St Telephone for directions **Parking:** On street

Morel Restaurant

☎ 020 7627 2468 14 Clapham Park Rd, Clapham SW4 7BB
web: www.theaa.com/restaurants/114007.html

Trendy modern décor, modern French food, and a relaxed atmosphere.

San Marco

☎ 020 7622 0452 126 Clapham High St SW4 7UH
Attractively simple pizzeria with checked tablecloths and house wine drunk out of tumblers.

Strada

☎ 020 7627 4847 102-104 Clapham High St, Clapham SW4 7UL
Superior pizza from quality ingredients cooked in wood-fired ovens.

LONDON SW5

Cambio De Tercio

Modern Spanish

Authentic Spanish cuisine in a lively atmosphere

☎ 020 7244 8970 163 Old Brompton Rd SW5 0LJ Plan 4-C2
web: www.cambiodetercio.co.uk

Just round the corner from Earl's Park in Old Brompton Road, what appears initially to be a small restaurant is actually rather large inside with tables stretching back and a bar on one side. Wooden flooring and red cotton-covered chairs set off the white tablecloths while lively Spanish music creates a buzzing atmosphere. Authentic Spanish cuisine is the order of the day, with dishes like fresh cod confit with spinach purée and garlic mousseline on a menu written in both Spanish and English. For dessert try the chocolate fondant with coconut ice cream.

Times: 12-2.30/7-11.30, Closed Xmas, New Year **Directions:** Nearest station: Gloucester Road Close to junction with Drayton Gardens

Kare Kare

☎ 020 7373 0024 152 Old Brompton Rd SW5 0BE
web: www.theaa.com/restaurants/113945.html
Modern, romantic, atmospheric location for a contemporary, healthy Indian. Special children's menu.

Strada

☎ 020 7835 1180 237 Earls Court Rd SW5
Superior pizza from quality ingredients cooked in wood-fired ovens.

Tendido Cero

☎ 020 7370 3685 174 Old Brompton Rd SW5 0BA
Simpler sister of Cambio de Tercio with good tapas.

LONDON SW6

Blue Elephant

Traditional Thai V NEW

Truly extravagant Fulham Thai

☎ 020 7385 6595 4-6 Fulham Rd SW6 1AA
Plan 1-D3
e-mail: london@blueelephant.com
web: www.blueelephant.com

From bustling Fulham Broadway, this extravagant Thai restaurant instantly transports you to another world - the experience is almost like dining in a tropical rainforest. Think lush plants, trickling fountains, bridges spanning koi carp-filled ponds, an ornate bar and truly welcoming Thai staff. Candles twinkle, while the scent of tropical flowers mingles with the heady aroma of exotic herbs and spices flown in fresh to service an equally flamboyant, lengthy menu. Expect paneng nua (a rich curry of beef and coconut milk with basil leaves), or perhaps kho samui (a mélange of seafood, spiked with fresh green peppercorns and garlic).

Chef: Somphang Sae-Jew **Owners:** Blue Elephant International Group **Times:** 12-2.30/7-12, Closed Xmas, Closed L Sat **Prices:** Fixed L £10, Fixed D £32-£35, Starter £5.25-£12, Main £10.25-£28, Dessert £5.50-£11.50, Coffee £2.75, Min/Water £2.30, Service added but optional 12.5% **Wine:** 80 bottles over £20, 9 bottles under £20, 14 by the glass (£5-£7.85) **Notes:** Vegetarian menu, Dress Restrictions, Smart casual **Seats:** 350, Pr/dining room 14 **Smoking:** Air con **Directions:** Nearest station: Fulham Broadway Please telephone for directions

Deep

Seafood NEW

A real treat for fish and shellfish enthusiasts in contemporary surroundings

☎ 020 7736 3337 The Boulevard, Imperial Wharf SW6 2UB Plan 1-E3
e-mail: info@deeplondon.co.uk
web: www.deeplondon.co.uk

Stunning waterside location in Imperial Wharf, the luxurious dining room has floor to ceiling windows to make the most of the view, while alfresco dining can be enjoyed on two terraces complete with café-style chrome tables and chairs. The friendly, switched-on team give attentive service. An interesting combination of mainly French, with Baltic and Scandinavian cooking influences feature on a menu dominated by fish and shellfish. Carefully sourced produce is demonstrated in the amazing range of starters that include Scottish langoustines, Norwegian prawns, Irish rock oysters or mussels and Arctic caviar. The perch and zander are from a freshwater lake in Sweden and may appear in dishes such as roast fillet of zander with seared brisket and sauce aigre-doux and fennel purée.

Chef: Mr C Sandefeldt & Mr F Bolin **Owners:** Christian & Kerstin Sandefeldt **Times:** 12-3/7-11, Closed Mon, Closed L Sat, D Sun **Prices:** Fixed L fr £15.50, Starter £6.50-£19, Main £13.50-£19.75, Dessert £4-£6, Coffee £2.50, Min/Water £3.50, Service added but optional 12.5% **Wine:** 65 bottles over £20, 12 bottles under £20, 11 by the glass (£4-£7.50) **Notes:** Tasting menu £50, Sun L buffet £29.50, Vegetarian available, Dress Restrictions, Smart casual **Seats:** 120 **Smoking:** N/Sm in restaurant, Air con **Directions:** Nearest station: Fulham Broadway From Fulham Broadway Underground Stn take Harwood Rd then Imperial Rd **Parking:** Public car park, street parking after 5.30

Saran Rom

Thai V NEW

Luxury riverside Thai restaurant specialising in authentic cuisine

☎ 020 7751 3111 Imperial Wharf, The Boulevard, Town Mead Rd SW6 2UB Plan 1-E3
e-mail: info@saranrom.com
web: www.saranrom.com

No expense has been spared in creating the lavish interior of this authentic Thai restaurant. The celebrated Thai interior designer behind the Bangkok Oriental Hotel and Siam Paragon Five Star Hotel has created sumptuous décor with silk hangings, 19th-century antiques and teak carvings. Add a ground floor bar and outside terrace and it all adds up to a fantastic location to enjoy some traditional Thai hospitality. The cuisine aims to be 'fit for Kings' and the setting is certainly reminiscent of Bangkok's finest palaces. Try starters like duck spring rolls or chor ladda (steamed Thai dumplings filled with chicken and prawns). For a main course you might opt for Mussaman lamb or perhaps the stunning green chicken curry with green peppercorns on the vine. The wine list makes a good read and there's an excellent selection by the glass.

Chef: Yupa Sontisup **Owners:** Mr Kobenor Negoypaiboon **Times:** 12/midnight **Prices:** Fixed L £11.90-£14.95, Fixed D £30-£40, Starter £3.95-£6.50, Main £7.95-£14.95, Dessert £4.50-£6.50, Coffee £1.95, Min/Water £3.75, Service added but optional 12.5% **Wine:** 30 bottles over £20, 21 bottles under £20, 38 by the glass (£3.75-£9.75) **Notes:** Vegetarian menu **Seats:** 200, Pr/dining room 100 **Smoking:** N/Sm area, Air con **Children:** Portions **Directions:** Nearest station: Fulham Broadway Please telephone for directions **Parking:** 100

Wizzy

Korean NEW

Unassuming, simple, authentic and rare Korean restaurant

☎ 020 7736 9171 616 Fulham Rd SW6 5RP Plan 1-D3

A shop front-style entrance on the Fulham Road picks out this unassuming authentic Korean named after its chef-patron, Hwi Shin (nicknamed Wizzy). Clean, simple and plain, the décor keeps the focus on the food, with a few ceramic faces hung on pale grey walls, wooden tables and cream, plastic-moulded chairs. Modern, authentic Korean cuisine is the style, based around three cooking methods - steaming, barbecuing and marinating, with the combination of multiple flavours and ingredients at its heart. You might start with marinated baby crab in rice topped with tobiko caviar, and grilled bulgogi (thin slices of beef in soy, herb and fruit sauce) with chilli pickled vegetables to follow.

Times: 12-3/6-10.30 **Prices:** Food prices not confirmed for 2007. Please telephone for details **Directions:** Telephone for directions

Yi-Ban Chelsea

Japanese, Chinese NEW

Stylish modern Oriental dining at Chelsea Wharf-side location

☎ 020 7731 6606 No 5 The Boulevard, Imperial Wharf, Imperial Rd SW6 2UB Plan 1-E3
e-mail: michael@yi-ban.co.uk
web: www.yi-ban.co.uk

A stylish, contemporary restaurant on the new development at Imperial Wharf, Chelsea. The dining area is located beyond a funky bar and teppan-yaki counter, where voile curtains and dark wood give a moody, modern feel. The contemporary oriental cuisine here encompasses teppan-yaki and Chinese food, the former cooked at a counter where diners can watch the chef in action. For an oriental restaurant there is a good selection of desserts, the most enticing of which may be Oriental steam cup cake in Cointreau syrup and orange Chantilly served with caramelised pineapple and lemon curd.

Chef: Hiroki Takemura/Andy Chung **Owners:** N Mach & D Quang **Times:** 6-11, Closed 1 wk from 22 Dec, Sun, Closed L all week **Prices:** Fixed L £15-£35, Fixed D £45-£55, Starter £4-£12, Main £8-£28, Dessert £4-£12, Coffee £1.80, Min/Water £4, Service added 13.5% **Wine:** 12 bottles over £20, 3 bottles under £20, 2 by the glass (£4.50-£6) **Notes:** Vegetarian available **Seats:** 80 **Smoking:** N/Sm area, No pipes, Air con **Directions:** Nearest station: Fulham Broadway Please telephone for directions **Parking:** Underground car park & street after 5

The Farm

☎ 020 7381 3331 18 Farm Ln SW6 1PP

Possibly the UK's first cash free restaurant. European food with a spicy ethnic twist.

1492 Latin Fusion

☎ 020 7381 3810 404 North End Rd, Fulham Broadway SW6 1LU
web: www.theaa.com/restaurants/113892.html

Wide ranging Latin American cuisine, orange walls and dark wood set the scene.

Strada

☎ 020 7731 6404 175 New Kings Rd, Parsons Green SW6 4SW

Superior pizza from quality ingredients cooked in wood-fired ovens.

LONDON SW7

The Bentley Kempinski Hotel

see page 299

Brunello

Modern Italian

An opulent setting for classy Italian cuisine

☎ 020 7368 5700 Baglioni Hotel, 60 Hyde Park Gate, Kensington Rd SW7 5BB Plan 4-C4
e-mail: l.virgilio@baglionihotels.com
web: www.baglionihotels.com

Chic, opulent and decadent perfectly describes the Brunello restaurant, which lives up to its fashionable location in a sophisticated and buzzy Italian townhouse hotel, overlooking Hyde Park. Both hotel and dining room ooze luxury and style, the latter decorated with black glass chandeliers, huge gilt mirrors, black and gold velvet, and intimate candlelight. The formal service comes with Italian enthusiasm, charm and character. The carte is divided into antipasti, soups, pasta, risotto, fish and meat courses, and lists modern Italian and regional dishes, some based on classics like veal chop Milanese, while others are more innovative such as venison saddle with mashed celeriac and chocolate sauce. Ingredients are superb, pasta a highlight and the Italian wine list is unrivalled.

AA Hotel of the Year for England

Chef: Stefano Stecca **Owners:** Baglioni Hotels **Times:** 12-2.30/7-10.45 **Prices:** Fixed L £20, Fixed D £48, Starter £10-£18, Main £21-£30, Dessert £8-£14, Coffee £4, Min/Water £4.50, Service added but optional 12.5% **Wine:** 500 bottles over £20, 3 bottles under £20, 17 by the glass (£5-£20) **Notes:** Vegetarian available **Seats:** 70, Pr/dining room 60 **Smoking:** No pipes, Air con **Children:** Portions **Rooms:** 88 (88 en suite) ★★★★★ TH **Directions:** Nearest station: Kensington High Street Hotel entrance on Hyde Park Gate facing park & Kensington Palace. **Parking:** NCP (Young St)

Cafe Lazeez

Indian

Friendly local Indian restaurant

☎ 020 7581 9993 93-95 Old Brompton Rd SW7 3LD Plan 4-D2
e-mail: southkensington@cafelazeez.com
web: www.cafelazeez.com

A popular Indian restaurant with a regularly changing menu. Staff are friendly, helpful and enthusiastic about the food on offer. There are lots of vegetarian choices that are marked on the menu. Interesting appetisers include Indian potato and pomegranate chaat (tangy potatoes and pomegranate in a poppadom shell). Main courses offer a choice of traditional dishes like prawn masala, or evolved dishes like coriander and pepper-crusted lamb chops. Take away food is an option here, with home delivery across most of London.

Chef: Avneet Bhutani **Owners:** Seasons Restaurant Ltd **Times:** 11/12.30 **Prices:** Fixed L £15-£20, Fixed D £20-£25, Starter £4.75-£12.50, Main £10-£16.25, Dessert £4-£5.50, Service added but optional 12.5% **Wine:** 28 bottles over £20, 13 bottles under £20, 10 by the glass (£3-£7.50) **Notes:** Vegetarian available **Seats:** 130, Pr/dining room 50 **Smoking:** N/Sm area, Air con **Children:** Menu, Portions **Directions:** Nearest station: South Kensington Please telephone for directions **Parking:** Pay & display nearby

LONDON SW7 *continued*

L'Etranger

French, Japanese

Stylish setting for classy fusion cuisine

☎ 020 7584 1118 36 Gloucester Rd SW7 4QT
Plan 4-C4
e-mail: annabel@etranger.co.uk
web: www.circagroupltd.co.uk

Part of a complex with an adjacent wine shop and basement cocktail bar, L'Etranger is a chic and sophisticated operation. Rich colours and fresh orchid displays add to the sophisticated atmosphere of the restaurant, where service is attentive and professional. A strong French influence dictates the Asian fusion menu, with high quality core ingredients given a twist with oriental spicing and sound cooking methods applied to innovative dishes such as tuna spring roll with ginger and coriander to start, followed by caramelised black cod with miso and a trio of lavender, saffron and wasabi crèmes brûlée.

Chef: Jerome Tauvron **Owners:** Ibi Issolah **Times:** 12-3/6-11, Closed Sun, Closed L Sat **Prices:** Fixed L £14.50, Fixed D £16.50-£45, Starter £7.50-£14.50, Main £15-£49, Dessert £6.50-£9.50, Coffee £3.50, Min/Water £3.50, Service added but optional 12.5% **Notes:** Fixed D 6 courses £65, Vegetarian available **Seats:** 55, Pr/dining room 20 **Smoking:** No pipes, Air con **Children:** Portions **Directions:** Nearest station: Gloucester Rd 5 mins walk from Gloucester Rd tube station at junct of Queens Gate Terrace and Gloucester Rd **Parking:** NCP

Swag and Tails

Modern International

Refined gastro-pub with beautiful interiors

☎ 020 7584 6926 10-11 Fairholt St SW7 1EG Plan 4-E4
e-mail: theswag@swagandtails.com
web: www.swagandtails.com

Set in a quiet mews just across the road from Harrods, this inviting restaurant has exquisite interiors created by the owner who also trained as an interior designer. Original wood panelling in the spacious bar area complements the more modern feel in the dining room and conservatory, which are adorned with attractive prints from different eras. Service from the attentive, friendly staff is excellent. The food combines a classic bistro feel with innovative twists - pan-seared foie gras on a granary croute with shallot purée and a rosemary jus, for example, or roast sea bass fillet with capers and spinach purée.

Chef: Alan Jenkins **Owners:** Annemaria & Stuart Boomer-Davies **Times:** 12-3/6-10, Closed Xmas, New Year, BHs, Sat-Sun **Prices:** Starter £5.25-£10.95, Main £10.50-£15.95, Dessert £5.25-£6, Coffee £2.25, Min/Water £3.50, Service added but optional 10% **Wine:** 12 bottles over £20, 22 bottles under £20, 11 by the glass (£3.50-£10.50) **Notes:** Vegetarian available **Seats:** 34 **Smoking:** N/Sm in restaurant **Directions:** Nearest station: Knightsbridge Tube Station Close to Harrods **Parking:** On street

Zuma

Modern Japanese

Stylish, cutting edge Japanese cuisine

☎ 020 7584 1010 5 Raphael St SW7 1DL
Plan 4-F4
e-mail: info@zumarestaurant.com
web: www.zumarestaurant.com

A stone's throw from Harrods and Harvey Nichols in the heart of Knightsbridge, Zuma's cutting edge modernity and stylish design is matched by its fashionable, glamorous clientele. The innovative Japanese cuisine is conjured from ultra fresh produce to create vibrant flavours in an extensive repertoire of beautifully presented dishes served from the main kitchen, the sushi bar or the robata grill as they are cooked. This parade of dishes is ideal for sharing: fried soft shell crabs with wasabi, mayonnaise and mizuna or tuna tartare with miso, myoga and lotus root crisps. Desserts such as dark chocolate pudding with a passionfruit centre are also impressive.

Times: 12-2.30/6-10, Closed 25-26 Dec, 1 Jan, Closed D 24 Dec **Directions:** Nearest station: Knightsbridge Telephone for directions

The Bombay Brasserie

☎ 020 7370 4040 Courtfield Close,
Courtfield Rd SW7 4UH
web: www.theaa.com/restaurants/114068.html

A palatial restaurant with a bright, airy conservatory. Relaxed, elegant and a perennial favourite with smart curry fans.

continued

England

The Bentley Kempinski Hotel

LONDON SW7

French, European

Fine-dining experience in ornate restaurant

☎ 020 7244 5555 27-33 Harrington Gardens SW7 4JX
Plan 4-C2
e-mail: info@thebentley-hotel.com
web: www.thebentley-hotel.com

Discreetly set in the heart of Kensington, no expense has been spared on this luxury townhouse hotel that oozes lavish opulence. Yellows and golds and wall-to-wall marble add an almost Louis XV edge to proceedings, while service - by an international team - is appropriately slick and professional. The setting for the fine-dining dinner-only 1880 restaurant (named after the date of the building) is an equally palatial affair that offers a real sense of occasion. Think elaborate ceilings, crystal chandeliers, silk wall panels and richly coloured carpets and furnishings. Next door, also on the hotel's lower-ground floor and accessed by the same sweeping circular staircase from the lobby, is the Malachite Bar, replete with jade-green marble counter and leopard-skin furnishings - just the place for pre-dinner drinks. The 1880's sophisticated and contemporary cooking is notable for its grazing-concept menus, with six-, seven-, eight- and nine-course options all miniature versions of dishes on the substantial, fixed-price carte. Expect seared Celtic sea scallops with cauliflower and courgette, sultanas and capers, and desserts like an 'emphasis on chocolate'. Save room for breads and petits fours, they're beautifully made, too.

Owners: International Luxury Hotels **Times:** 12-2.30/6-10, Closed Easter & Xmas, BHs, Sun-Mon **Prices:** Fixed L £19.50, Fixed D £49, Coffee £4, Min/Water £4, Service optional, Group min 10 service 12.5% **Wine:** 100% bottles over £20, 30 by the glass (£6.50-£14.50) **Notes:** Grazing menus from £53 for 7 courses, Vegetarian available, Dress Restrictions, Smart casual, jacket/shirt, Civ Wed 60 **Seats:** 45, Pr/dining room 60 **Smoking:** N/Sm in restaurant, Air con **Children:** Menu, Portions **Rooms:** 64 (64 en suite) ★★★★★ HL **Directions:** Nearest station: Gloucester Road Off A4 Cromwell Rd, opposite Gloucester Hotel **Parking:** on street & car park

The Delhi Brasserie

☎ 020 7370 7617 134 Cromwell Rd SW7 4HA
web: www.theaa.com/restaurants/114009.html

Elegant, authentic Indian restaurant. The menu includes slightly more unusual dishes as well as old favourites.

FireHouse

☎ 020 7584 7258 3 Cromwell Rd SW7 2HR
web: www.theaa.com/restaurants/113998.html

Stylish, three storey restaurant opposite Natural History Museum serving British and European dishes.

Two Rosettes
The best local restaurants, which aim for and achieve higher standards, better consistency and where a greater precision is apparent in the cooking. There will be obvious attention to the selection of quality ingredients.

One Rosette
Excellent local restaurants serving food prepared with care, understanding and skill, using good quality ingredients. These restaurants stand out in their local area.

LONDON SW8

The Food Room

French

Stylish modern Battersea dining

☎ 020 7622 0555 123 Queenstown Rd SW8 3RH
Plan 1-E3

Minimalist, modern French eatery in Battersea, decorated in warm, soft colours with stylish mirrors, metal and abstract art. This spacious, airy venue comes with relaxed, friendly service. Classic French and Mediterranean dishes are produced using fresh seasonal produce with the emphasis on clear but subtle flavours. The carte offers a good choice of imaginative dishes like lobster bisque with raviole of spinach and smoked salmon to start. Main courses might include crispy sea bass served with sautéed spinach and vanilla sauce. Traditional desserts feature the likes of praline fragilite served with coffee and caramel.

Chef: Mr E Guignard **Owners:** Eric & Sarah Guignard **Times:** 12-2.30/7-10.30, Closed Mon, Closed L Sat, D Sun **Prices:** Fixed L fr £13.50, Fixed D fr £24.50, Starter £5.75-£7.50, Main £11.75-£15.75, Dessert £6-£6.25, Coffee £2.20, Min/Water £2.95, Service added but optional 12.5% **Wine:** 35 bottles over £20, 16 bottles under £20, 9 by the glass (£3.50-£5.75) **Notes:** Vegetarian available, Smart casual **Seats:** 60 **Smoking:** N/Sm area, No pipes, No cigars, Air con **Children:** Portions **Directions:** Nearest station: Queenstown Road 10 min from Clapham Junction **Parking:** on street

LONDON SW10

Aubergine

see opposite

Chutney Mary Restaurant

Indian

Seductive Indian restaurant offering refined Indian cuisine

☎ 020 7351 3113 535 Kings Rd, Chelsea SW10 0SZ
Plan 1-E3
e-mail: chutneymary@realindianfood.com
web: www.realindianfood.com

Contemporary ethnic style defines this fine dining Indian restaurant. Clever use of mirrors and seductive Indian craftsmanship combine with dramatic lighting and 1840s sepia etchings to create a romantic setting. You will find refined Indian food on offer from diverse regions, created by a team of master chefs. Service is relatively relaxed with knowledgeable waiters able to help you choose food and wines.

continued

Typical starters include tokri chaat - a potato basket filled with street food favourites, strained yogurt and chutneys. Main courses might feature lobster makhani - lobster pieces with tomato and brandy sauce, served in the shell. For dessert you might try dark chocolate fondant with orange blossom lassi.

Chutney Mary Restaurant

Chef: Nagarajan Rubinath **Owners:** Masala World, R Mathrani, N Panjabi **Times:** 12.30-3/6.30-11.30, Closed D Xmas **Prices:** Fixed L £17, Starter £7.25-£13.75, Main £16-£26.25, Dessert £5.75-£7, Coffee £2.50, Min/Water £3.70, Service added but optional 12.5% **Wine:** 76 bottles over £20, 10 bottles under £20, 12 by the glass (£4.50-£10.30) **Notes:** Tasting menu 7 courses £55, Fixed L 3 courses Sat & Sun, Vegetarian available **Seats:** 110, Pr/dining room 24 **Smoking:** N/Sm area, Air con **Directions:** Nearest station: Fulham Broadway On corner of King's Rd and Lots Rd; 2 mins from Chelsea Harbour. **Parking:** Parking meters outside

Osteria dell'Arancio

Italian

Fashionable Italian in lively Chelsea setting

☎ 020 7349 8111 383 King's Rd SW10 0LP Plan 1-E3
e-mail: info@osteriadellarancio.co.uk
web: www.osteriadellarancio.co.uk

With its name painted in large letters down the cream wall outside, you can't miss this vibrant little Italian osteria in a one-time pub on the King's Road. Bench seating, bright lighting and funky artwork lend a cheerful Mediterranean tone, while service is relaxed and Italian. Authentic Italian cuisine is the style, the modern, sensibly-compact and appealing menus come typically written in Italian with English translations and ooze Latin panache. Look out for beef tagliata with rocket and parmesan crisps, Venetian-style calves' liver, or campofilone pasta with fresh anchovies.

Times: 12-3/6.30-11

The Painted Heron

Modern Indian

Good value and unusual modern Indian cuisine

☎ 020 7351 5232 112 Cheyne Walk SW10 0DJ
Plan 1-E3
e-mail: thepaintedheron@btinternet.com
web: www.thepaintedheron.com

A blue awning and glass frontage picks out this modern Chelsea Indian close to Battersea Bridge. Dark wood and leather upholstered chairs, dark slatted blinds and plain white walls deliver a contemporary edge to the split-level restaurant, with a hint of the nautical reflecting its Thameside location via blond-wood floors, rope-lined skirting boards and metal handrails lining steps. There is a small walled terrace

continued on page 302

England

Aubergine

LONDON SW10

French

Accomplished and refined cooking from eminent Chelsea eatery

☎ 020 7352 3449 11 Park Walk, Chelsea SW10 0AJ Plan 4-C1
e-mail: info@auberginerestaurant.co.uk
web: www.auberginerestaurant.co.uk

The namesake-coloured canopy and front door make this renowned, well-heeled Chelsea fixture easy to spot on its side street just off the Fulham Road bustle, where William Drabble's modern French cuisine continues to shine. Aubergine cruets, dress plates and menus continue the theming inside at generous-sized, white-clothed tables with chocolate undercloths, where the room's muted, subtle tones create a relaxed, understated, stylish mood. Floors are light wood, walls beige ragged-effect hung with abstract artworks, and comfortable high-backed chairs come in cream, apricot and dark red. There's a stunning floral display at the entrance and a small seating area to enjoy aperitifs.

The predominantly Gallic service is professional, attentive and friendly, providing the perfect support act for William Drabble's refined modern cooking that comes underpinned by a classical theme. Intelligently simple, stylish and self confident, it focuses around the use of the highest-quality ingredients (including luxury items), with dishes impressively uncomplicated by unnecessary embellishment. It's accurate, delicate, perfectly timed and balanced and oozes clean, clear flavours. Think poached lobster tail served with cauliflower purée and a truffle butter sauce to start, perhaps an ice honey chiboust with blood orange to finish and, in between, a loin of veal served with boulangère potatoes and foie gras sauce. The repertoire's delivered via a fixed-price menu format of lunch (this three courses affair - with half bottle of wine, half bottle of still mineral water, coffee and petits fours - is considered a bargain not to be missed), plus an enticing carte and seven-course gourmand option, while peripherals like bread, amuse-bouche and petits fours all hit form, too.

Chef: William Drabble
Owners: A-Z Restaurants
Times: 12-2.30/7-11, Closed 2 wks Xmas, BHs, Easter, Sun, Closed L Sat
Prices: Fixed L fr £34, Fixed D fr £64, Coffee £5.50, Min/Water £4, Service added but optional 12.5%
Notes: Tasting menu 7 courses £77, Fixed L incl wine & water, Vegetarian available, Dress Restrictions, Smart casual preferred
Seats: 60
Smoking: N/Sm in restaurant, Air con
Directions: Nearest station: South Kensington, Fulham Broadway W along Fulham Rd, close to Chelsea and Westminster Hospital
Parking: Local parking available

LONDON SW10 *continued*

at the rear for summer alfresco dining. The kitchen delivers high quality modern Indian cooking, with traditional dishes given a contemporary spin and presentation, focusing on fresh ingredients and intelligently subtle spicing. Think tandoori lamb chops, nutmeg and mace flower to start, followed by roasted duck breast in a green herb chutney sauce with coconut, or tandoor-grilled monkfish tail with green chillies and garlic.

Times: 12-3/6.30-11, Closed Xmas & Easter, Closed L Sat
Directions: Nearest station: South Kensington Telephone for directions

Vama

Indian V

Upmarket Indian restaurant on the Kings Road

☎ 020 565 8500 & 7565 8500 438 King's Rd SW10 0LJ Plan 1-E3
e-mail: manager@vama.co.uk
web: www.vama.co.uk

After nine years in business the restaurant underwent an extensive refurbishment in 2006. There is a separate party room, bar and waiting area and the restaurant is stylishly decorated in warm colours. Large floor tiles, carved wooden chairs with cushioned seats and large wooden framed pictures give a comfortable modern feel. Classical North West Indian food is showcased here using traditional recipes cooked in a clay oven with traditional marinades. Typical dishes include tandoori jhinga, matar methi malai and adaraki gosht, the latter being beautifully tender cubes of lamb in a medium hot sauce. A typical dessert would be kulfi aam ki - Indian mango ice cream with fresh fruit and mango and raspberry sauce.

Chef: Andy Varma **Owners:** Andy Varma, Arjun Varma **Times:** 12-4/6.30-12, Closed 25-26 Dec, 1 Jan **Prices:** Fixed L £10, Fixed D £17.50, Starter £5.50-£14.50, Main £6.50-£22, Dessert £6-£7.50, Coffee £3.75, Min/Water £3.95, Service added 12.5%, Group min 6 service 12.5% **Wine:** 15 bottles over £20, 8 bottles under £20, 6 by the glass (£5-£7) **Notes:** Sun brunch £15, Gourmand £45, Vegetarian menu, Dress Restrictions, Smart casual **Seats:** 120, Pr/dining room 35 **Smoking:** No pipes, Air con **Directions:** Nearest station: Sloane Square About 20 mins walk down King's Rd **Parking:** 25

Friends

☎ 020 7376 3890 6 Hollywood Rd SW10 9HY
Rustic pizzeria.

LONDON SW11

The Greyhound at Battersea

Modern British 

Trendy, stylish gastro-pub with top-notch cuisine and wines

☎ 020 7978 7021 136 Battersea High St SW11 3JR Plan 1-D3
e-mail: eat@thegreyhoundatbattersea.co.uk
web: www.thegreyhoundatbattersea.co.uk

The transformation of an old down-at-heels pub on bustling Battersea High Street to smart, trendy local and dining room presses all the right quality buttons. Large flash bar, leather seating, polished-wood floors, with crystal glasses and expensive table appointments place it a cut above your average gastro-pub. Service is attentive, friendly and relaxed, and product knowledge is excellent. Great quality, serious skill and some innovative dishes show the kitchen's fine pedigree and prove a match for the fabulous wine list. Clear flavours, fine presentation, seasoning and balance all hit a high note. Expect main dishes such as Duke of Berkshire pork loin, black pudding, braised Brussels tops and roasted pineapple or line-caught Cornish hake fillet, courgette, aubergine and prawn ravioli.
Notable Wine List: An exciting and enthusiastic wine list with stunning selections throughout, categorised by grape type.

Chef: Matthew Foxon **Owners:** Mark & Sharlyn Van der Goot **Times:** 12-2.30/7-9.30, Closed 23-26 Dec, 31 Dec-3 Jan, Mon, Closed D Sun **Prices:** Fixed D £31, Starter £3.50-£6.50, Main £6.50-£10, Dessert £3-£5.50, Coffee £1.80, Min/Water £2.75, Service added but optional 10% **Wine:** 350 bottles over £20, 120 bottles under £20, 16 by the glass (£2.10-£12) **Notes:** Sun L 2 courses £15, 3 courses £18.50, Dress Restrictions, Smart casual **Seats:** 55, Pr/dining room 25 **Smoking:** N/Sm in restaurant **Children:** Min L only, Portions **Directions:** Nearest station: Clapham Junct Located near Battersea Bridge and Clapham Junction **Parking:** On street

Ransome's Dock

Modern British NOTABLE WINE LIST

Simple seasonal cooking in waterside setting

☎ 020 7223 1611 & 7924 2462 Battersea SW11 4NP Plan 1-E3
e-mail: chef@ransomesdock.co.uk
web: www.ransomesdock.co.uk

This welcoming waterside restaurant is located in a former ice cream factory close to Albert Bridge. With its cornflower blue walls and modern artwork, this friendly, relaxed place is unpretentious and informal, with snacks, coffee and juices available in the bar area. Outside dining is available in summer. One of the forerunners in showcasing local, seasonal produce - much of it organic - the menus are governed by what's in season, with many producers and animal breeds given name checks. Norfolk smoked eel with beetroot and herb salad, Shorthorn sirloin steak and chips with green peppercorn sauce and hot prune and Armagnac soufflé with Armagnac custard show the style.
Notable Wine List: A wine list of pure passion and enthusiasm by the chef-patron, with much interest and diversity including a great sherry listing.

Chef: Martin Lam, Vanessa Lam **Owners:** Mr & Mrs M Lam **Times:** 12/6-11, Closed Xmas, Closed D Sun **Prices:** Fixed L £15, Starter £5-£12.50, Main £11-£22.50, Dessert £5-£8.50, Coffee £2.75, Min/Water £3.50, Service added but optional 12.5% **Wine:** 350 bottles over £20, 20 bottles under £20, 8 by the glass (£3.75-£8.50) **Notes:** Brunch menu Sat & Sun, Vegetarian available **Seats:** 55 **Smoking:** N/Sm area, No pipes, Air con **Children:** Portions **Directions:** Nearest station: Sloane Square/Clapham Junction Between Albert Bridge & Battersea Bridge **Parking:** 20

Black Pepper

☎ 020 7978 4863 133 Lavender Hill, Clapham SW11 5QJ
web: www.theaa.com/restaurants/113988.html

Friendly, family-run restaurant, popular with locals and offering a choice of Italian or Persian menus.

Chez Manny

☎ 020 7223 4040 145 Battersea High St SW11 3JS
web: www.theaa.com/restaurants/113994.html
Extremely friendly restaurant with a genuine welcome. Very relaxed atmosphere for enjoying French dishes.

Gourmet Burger Kitchen

☎ 020 7228 3309 44 Northcote Rd SW11 1N7
New Zealand inspired burger joint using top notch beef.

Matilda

☎ 020 7228 6482 74/76 Battersea Bridge Rd SW11
Relaxed pub dining with emphasis on traditional and home-made dishes.

Osteria Antica Bologna

☎ 020 7978 4771 23 Northcote Rd SW11 1NG
Rustic Italian restaurant serving authentic food with an emphasis on fresh and seasonal produce.

Strada

☎ 020 7801 0794 11-13 Battersea Rise SW11 1HG
Superior pizza from quality ingredients cooked in wood-fired ovens.

LONDON SW13

MVH

Classical

Theatrical décor, in heaven or hell, with divine cuisine

☎ 020 8392 1111 5 Whitehart Ln, Barnes SW13 0PX
Plan 1-D3

Images of heaven and hell are created on the two floors of this out-of-the-ordinary eatery in a residential area of Barnes. The upstairs is a devilish red with darkwood and leather, eastern artefacts and images of men in various poses. Downstairs is all sweetness and light, in cream and white, with angelic images of women alongside wire or metal sculptures of the female form. A real mixture of food styles offers classical, ethnic and European-influenced dishes. Examples are a

continued

full-flavoured chicken in coconut milk with lime risottini and Thai basil, and fillet of cod with sweet miso, vanilla potatoes and beetroot purée.

Times: 12-2.30/6-10.30, Closed L Mon, Tue, Wed

Sonny's Restaurant

Modern British

Imaginative cooking in modern venue

☎ 020 8748 0393 94 Church Rd, Barnes SW13 0DQ
Plan 1-D3
e-mail: barnes@sonnys.co.uk
web: www.sonnys.co.uk

The designer décor at this chic restaurant manages to be both minimalist and attractive. Tucked away in a row of smart shops, stylish frosted windows hide a trendy café bar and, to the rear, a bright, modern and bustling restaurant with interesting artwork on the walls. It's a relaxing place to dine, the service is casual and friendly, and the food is contemporary yet wholesome, with generous servings of imaginative modern British dishes. Expect first-class seasonal ingredients and some exciting combinations, resulting in robust, full-flavoured dishes, such as Dorset crab remoulade with ginger and orange jelly, bresaola with ricotta and pickled walnuts, pheasant saltimbocca with sage and lemon risotto.

Chef: David Massey **Owners:** Rebecca Mascarenhas, James Harris **Times:** 12.30-2.30/7.30-11, Closed BHs, Closed D Sun **Prices:** Fixed L £13.50, Fixed D £19.50, Starter £4.75-£8.50, Main £11.50-£16.50, Dessert £5-£6.50, Coffee £2.25, Min/Water £3, Service added but optional 12.5% **Wine:** 42 bottles over £20, 16 bottles under £20, 16 by the glass (£3.50-£10) **Notes:** Sun L 3 courses £21.50, Vegetarian available **Seats:** 100, Pr/dining room 26 **Smoking:** No pipes, Air con **Children:** Menu, Portions **Directions:** Nearest station: Barnes/Hammersmith From Castelnau end of Church Rd on left by shops **Parking:** On street

Strada

☎ 020 8392 9216 375 Lonsdale Rd SW13 9PY
web: www.theaa.com/restaurants/109777.html
Good value traditional Italian food in a grand, airy old brick building overlooking the Thames.

LONDON SW14

The Depot Waterfront Brasserie

Modern British

Riverside brasserie

☎ 020 8878 9462 Tideway Yard, Mortlake High St SW14 8SN Plan 1-D3
e-mail: info@depotbrasserie.co.uk
web: www.depotbrasserie.co.uk

With a Thames-side location, situated in what used to be a stable block, this brasserie has a rustic appearance that lends it both character and style. Simple bare tables, neutral shades and high ceilings complement the look. The menu consists of a good selection of simply-constructed dishes, including typical modern British favourites which are enhanced with Mediterranean ingredients in dishes such as chargrilled tuna with Jerusalem artichokes, spinach and red wine jus.

Times: 12-3.30/6-12, Closed 24-26 Dec **Directions:** Nearest station: Barnes Bridge train station Between Barnes Bridge & Mortlake stations

England

LONDON SW14 *continued*

Redmond's

Modern British

Slick, consistent cooking from an experienced chef

☎ 020 8878 1922 170 Upper Richmond Rd West SW14 8AW Plan 1-D3
e-mail: pippa@redmonds.org.uk
web: www.redmonds.org.uk

After establishing a fairly formidable reputation - and earning a sack full of plaudits - for his eponymous restaurant near Cheltenham, Redmond relocated lock, stock and barrel in 1997 to this location in Richmond. The dining room has a chic, understated feel with a clientele drawn from regular, neighbourhood visitors and fans of long-standing. While the residents of this leafy suburb may be blissfully unaware of the restaurant's Cotswold connections, it's reassuring to know that the food is still just as consistent as it was twenty years ago, applying the same high standards to conception, delivery and presentation. A typical starter might be seared marinated pigeon breast with butternut squash polenta, while for mains you might choose fillet of bream with king prawns and stir-fried vegetables.

Chef: Redmond Hayward **Owners:** Mr R Hayward, Mrs P Hayward **Times:** 12-2.30/7-10, Closed 4 days Xmas, BH Mon's, Closed L Mon-Sat, D Sun **Prices:** Fixed L £18.50, Fixed D £16.95-£32, Coffee £2.50, Min/Water £3.25, Service optional, Group min 6 service 10% **Wine:** 5 by the glass (£4.95-£5.95) **Notes:** Special events usually £60 3 courses incl wine & coffee **Seats:** 48 **Smoking:** N/Sm in restaurant, Air con **Children:** Menu, Portions **Directions:** Nearest station: Mortlake Located half way between Putney and Richmond. On the South Circular Road at the Barnes end of Sheen **Parking:** Street parking after 7 pm

The Victoria

Modern European

Good simple food in friendly gastro-pub

☎ 020 8876 4238 10 West Temple Sheen SW14 7RT Plan 1-C2
e-mail: reservations@thevictoria.net
web: www.thevictoria.net

Tucked away in a quiet residential area close to Sheen High Street, this stylish gastro-pub is a firm favourite with locals, and has seven comfortable bedrooms for foodies from further afield. This bright and airy pub has white walls, white painted floorboards and leather armchairs, with the conservatory restaurant containing well spaced tables, clean lines and a wood-burning stove. French doors open out on to a patio for alfresco summer dining. The confident modern British cuisine has French and Spanish influences in the straightforward, fuss-free dishes. Seasonality is key and a typical early spring menu may include lamb sweetbreads with potato gnocchi and morel cream, steamed sea trout with English asparagus and new potatoes and vanilla pot with Yorkshire rhubarb and ginger sticks.

Chef: Darren Archer **Owners:** Mark Chester & Darren Archer **Times:** 12-2.30/7-10, Closed 4 days Xmas **Prices:** Starter £4.95-£11.95, Main £8.95-£19.95, Dessert £3.95-£6.95, Coffee £1.75, Min/Water £2.95, Service added but optional 12.5% **Wine:** 45 bottles over £20, 20 bottles under £20, 8 by the glass (£3.45-£4.45) **Seats:** 70, Pr/dining room 45 **Smoking:** N/Sm in restaurant **Children:** Menu, Portions **Rooms:** 7 (7 en suite) ◆◆◆◆ **Directions:** Nearest station: Mortlake Between upper Richmond Road and Richmond Park, halfway between Putney and Richmond **Parking:** 18

LONDON SW15

Enoteca Turi

Italian NOTABLE WINE LIST

Seasonal, regional Italian cooking in Putney

☎ 020 8785 4449 28 Putney High St SW15 1SQ Plan 1-D3
e-mail: enoteca@tiscali.co.uk
web: www.enotecaturi.com

With its warm, rustic Tuscan colours, wooden floors and wine racks, this charming restaurant brings a genuine taste of Italy to the southern corner of Putney High Street. Seasonal ingredients form the backbone of the regional Italian cooking, which is executed with confidence and flair and presented with care. Try the antipasto Pugliese before tucking into spaghetti with fresh crab, rocket, garlic and chilli or roast breast of guinea fowl with peverada, black cabbage and cannellini beans. A large selection of after-dinner drinks includes an impressive range of grappas and amaros.
Notable Wine List: Superb Italian wine list with detailed and great tasting notes.

Chef: Mr B Fantoni **Owners:** Mr G & Mrs P Turi **Times:** 12-2.30/7-11, Closed 25-26 Dec, 1 Jan, Sun **Prices:** Fixed L fr £13.50, Starter £6.50-£9.50, Main £10.50-£17.50, Dessert £5.50-£6.50, Coffee £2.95, Min/Water £3.50, Service added but optional 12.5% **Wine:** 300 bottles over £20, 21 bottles under £20, 10 by the glass (£3.50-£7.50) **Notes:** Vegetarian available **Seats:** 85, Pr/dining room 28 **Smoking:** N/Sm area, No pipes, No cigars, Air con **Children:** Portions **Directions:** Nearest station: Putney Opposite Odeon Cinema near bridge **Parking:** Putney Exchange car park

Spencer Arms

British NEW

Putney gastro-pub serving food with flair

☎ 020 8788 0640 237 Lower Richmond Rd SW15 1HJ Plan 1-D3

This cosy gastro-pub on the edge of Putney Common is making a splash with Adrian Jones ex Shibden Mill Inn and Jamie Sherriff at the helm. Great British food is freshly prepared and the menu offers popular choices from duck burger with goat's cheese to a rower's breakfast or weekend brunch. Staff are rushed off their feet to meet demand at busy times, but service is friendly and the food's worth the wait. Try a main course like osso buco of pork served with purple broccoli and garlic potato.

Times: 12-2.30/6.30-10 **Prices:** Food prices not confirmed for 2007. Please telephone for details **Seats:** 70 **Directions:** Telephone for directions

Talad Thai

Thai

Hearty cooking at a popular Thai restaurant

☎ 020 8789 8084 320 Upper Richmond Rd, Putney SW15 6TL Plan 1-D3

A relaxed and friendly Thai restaurant in a quiet part of Putney, with its own Thai supermarket a few doors away. The very modern set up includes wooden tables packed closely together, so this is not somewhere to share intimate secrets. The lengthy traditional menu offers a journey through Thai cuisine, with food listed by type, such as stir fries, curry dishes, noodle dishes etc, and authentic ingredients are

continued

brought in fresh from Thailand. Expect the likes of green curry with pork, prawns, beef, chicken or vegetables, pad Thai noodles or fried fish with minced pork.

Chef: Suthasinee Pramwew **Owners:** Mr Sa-ard Kriangsak **Times:** 11.30-3/5.30-11, Closed 25 Dec, 1 Jan **Prices:** Food prices not confirmed for 2007. Please telephone for details **Notes:** Vegetarian available **Seats:** 40, Pr/dining room 40 **Smoking:** N/Sm area, Air con **Directions:** Nearest station: Putney/East Putney Please telephone for directions **Parking:** On street opposite

Emiles

☎ 020 8789 3323 96 Felsham Rd, East Putney SW15 1DQ
web: www.theaa.com/restaurants/113996.html

Unpretentious and friendly restaurant, very popular with locals serving modern British dishes.

Gourmet Burger Kitchen

☎ 020 8789 1199 333 Putney Bridge Rd, Putney SW15 2PG

New Zealand inspired burger joint using top notch beef.

Isola del Sole

☎ 020 8785 9962 16 Lacy Rd SW15 1NL
web: www.theaa.com/restaurants/113939.html

Delicious, healthy and genuine Italian food, with a bias for Sardinian regional dishes; excellent service and terrific value for money.

Louhannah

☎ 020 8780 5252 30 Putney High St, Putney SW15 1SQ
web: www.theaa.com/restaurants/113951.html

Popular with shoppers and cinema goers this eatery has a modern continental menu and laid-back atmosphere.

LONDON SW17

Chez Bruce

see below

Chez Bruce

LONDON SW17

Modern British NOTABLE WINE LIST

Memorable dining at Wandsworth big-hitter

☎ 020 8672 0114 2 Bellevue Rd, Wandsworth Common SW17 7EG Plan 1-E2
e-mail: enquiries@chezbruce.co.uk
web: www.chezbruce.co.uk

This small, unassuming place - that looks more like a bistro from outside rather than Wandsworth's culinary big-hitter - is set in a parade of shops overlooking the common, and is heaving most of the time. First-timers should look out for the large maroon-coloured planter bursting with flowers outside, or just follow the savvy crowd who are full of admiration for Bruce Poole's memorable cuisine. Inside cuts a relaxed, modern edge, with wooden floors, muted restful beiges and caramels, soft lighting and a collection of prints. The effect is simple but pleasing, though space is at a premium, and with no drinks area diners are shown straight to white-linen clad tables, where service proves friendly, eager, attentive and knowledgeable. The kitchen's accomplished modern approach pays due respect to classical and regional France, but remains pleasingly unfussy while focusing on the highest quality ingredients with an eye for seasonality. Noteworthy flavours, perfect balance and impeccable skill make for a notable experience. Expect the likes of crisp fillet of bream served with mussel, saffron and almond broth, or perhaps côte de boeuf (for two) classically teamed with hand-cut chips and a béarnaise sauce. Classic crème brûlée or tarte fine aux pommes provides a perfect finish, while an impressive wine list (and sommelier) completes a class act.
Notable Wine List: The wine list shows pure enthusiasm throughout with quality selections on every page combined by expert guidance from Canadian sommelier Terry Threlfall.

Chef: Bruce Poole, Matt Christmass **Owners:** Bruce Poole, Nigel Platts-Martin **Times:** 12-2/6.30-10.30, Closed 24-26 Dec,1 Jan, Closed L 27,31 Dec & 2nd Jan **Prices:** Fixed L £18.50-£25, Fixed D £37.50, Coffee £3.50, Min/Water £3.50, Service added but optional 12.5% **Wine:** 450 bottles over £20, 8 bottles under £20, 21 by the glass (£4.50-£13.50) **Notes:** Dress Restrictions, Smart casual **Seats:** 75, Pr/dining room 16 **Smoking:** N/Sm in restaurant, Air con **Children:** L only, Menu, Portions **Directions:** Nearest station: Wandsworth Common/Balham Near Wandsworth Common train station **Parking:** On street, station car park

LONDON SW17 *continued*

Kastoori

Indian V

Indian vegetarian with fresh and imaginative fare

☎ 020 8767 7027 188 Upper Tooting Rd SW17 7EJ Plan 1-E2

Worth the trek from further into London or the suburbs if you're not a local, this welcoming vegetarian Indian presents an assuming face with its bright, closely packed tables and relaxing colour scheme of yellow, white, grey and blue. A delightful choice of Gujarati dishes is threaded with East African flavours in main dishes like green pepper curry in a sesame and peanut sauce, green leaf curry with coriander, fennel and spinach or chilli banana with mild chillies and spicy tomato sauce. Remember to ask for the chef's choices and daily specials.

Chef: Manoj Thanki **Owners:** Mr D Thanki **Times:** 12.30-2.30/6-10.30, Closed 25,26 Dec, Closed L Mon & Tue **Prices:** Food prices not confirmed for 2007. Please telephone for details **Wine:** 1 bottle over £20, 19 bottles under £20, 2 by the glass (£2.25) **Notes:** Vegetarian only **Seats:** 82 **Smoking:** Air con **Children:** Portions **Directions:** Nearest station: Tooting Bec & Tooting Broadway. Situated between two stations. **Parking:** On street

LONDON SW18

Ditto

☎ 020 8877 0110 55-57 East Hill, Wandsworth SW18 2QE
web: www.theaa.com/restaurants/113932.html

Expect generous portions of modern European dishes and a switched-on team at this bright, modern restaurant.

LONDON SW19

The Light House Restaurant

Modern International

Simple modern cooking in upmarket Wimbledon

☎ 020 8944 6338 75-77 Ridgway, Wimbledon SW19 4ST Plan 1-D2
e-mail: lightrest@aol.com
web: www.lighthousewimbledon.com

Set in a small row of shops in Wimbledon's upmarket village, this relaxed eatery does a brisk trade, particularly at weekends, so reservations are advised. A minimalist modern décor of wooden floors and sand-coloured walls provides a low-key background for some great food; dishes are simple, rustic creations rooted in Italian cuisine, with influences from further afield, particularly Asia. Mains might include red lentil and sweet potato curry, or pan-fried sea bass with roast butternut squash, bok choy and saffron cream, while puddings are contemporary concoctions such as wild berry jelly with lemon shortbread, or passionfruit tart with crème fraîche and blueberries.

Chef: David Winton **Owners:** Mr Finch & Mr Taylor **Times:** 12-2.30/6.30-10.30, Closed 24-26 Dec, 1 Jan, Etr Sun & Mon, Closed D Sun **Prices:** Fixed L fr £14.50, Starter £5-£8.50, Main £11-£16.50, Dessert £5.20, Coffee £2.25, Min/Water £3, Service added but optional 12.5% **Wine:** 60 bottles over £20, 17 bottles under £20, 13 by the glass (£3.25-£6.75) **Notes:** Vegetarian available **Seats:** 80 **Smoking:** N/Sm area, No pipes, No cigars **Children:** Menu, Portions **Directions:** Nearest station: Wimbledon Telephone for directions

San Lorenzo

☎ 020 8946 8463 Worple Rd Mews, Wimbledon SW19

Reliable neighbourhood restaurant.

Strada

☎ 020 8946 4363 91 High St SW19 5EG

Superior pizza from quality ingredients cooked in wood-fired ovens.

LONDON W1

Alastair Little Restaurant

Modern European

Harmonious flavours and vibrant colours in Soho

☎ 020 7734 5183 49 Frith St W1V 5TE Plan 3-B2

This small shop-front restaurant, unassumingly tucked away in the heart of Soho is easy to walk past. But don't, it's quite a little gem. Inside reflects the admirably uncomplicated style of the cuisine, with wood floors, simple blue chairs and smartly set tables. Bold pictures add a splash of colour and the wacky ceiling lighting proves a feature. It's popular and relaxed, with a warm atmosphere and friendly service, while the kitchen's intelligently straightforward modern cooking delivers clear, well-balanced flavours using fresh, high-quality produce; think roast lamb served with spinach and flageolets, and a rhubarb crème brûlée finish.

Chef: Sue Lewis & Juliet Peston **Owners:** K Pedersen, M Andre-Vega **Times:** 12-3/6-11.30, Closed Xmas, BHs, Sun, Closed L Sat **Prices:** Fixed L £33, Fixed D £38, Coffee £1.50, Min/Water £3.75, Service optional, Group min 8 service 12.5% **Wine:** 43 bottles over £20, 4 bottles under £20, 4 by the glass (£5.50-£6.50) **Notes:** Fixed L 3 courses **Seats:** 42, Pr/dining room 25 **Smoking:** No pipes, No cigars, Air con **Children:** Portions **Directions:** Nearest station: Tottenham Court Rd Near Ronnie Scott's Jazz Club **Parking:** Brewer St, Poland St

Alloro

Italian

A taste of Italy in the heart of Mayfair

☎ 020 7495 4768 20 Dover St W1S 4LU Plan 3-A1

A classy décor of wood and tiled flooring, big mirrors and red and cream leather chairs, and smartly attired staff mark out this stylish Italian venue. Modern Italian cooking tours the country's regions, the style being honest and unfussy with rustic presentation. Simplicity, quality ingredients and great flavours prevail here, from its selection of antipasti, fresh pasta (Gragnano spaghetti with lobster, garlic and sweet chilli sauce) and risotto to tempting desserts such as millefeuille with caramelised fruits. Main courses may take in beef entrecôte with Ligurian olives and aromatic herbs.

Chef: Daniele Camera **Owners:** A-Z Restaurant Ltd **Times:** 12-2.30/7-10.30, Closed Xmas, 4 days Etr & BH's, Sun, Closed L Sat **Prices:** Fixed L £26, Fixed D £33, Coffee £2.50, Min/Water £3.50, Service added but optional 12.5% **Wine:** 500 bottles over £20, 2 bottles under £20, 9 by the glass (£4.50-£14) **Notes:** Vegetarian available, Dress Restrictions, No shorts or sandals **Seats:** 60, Pr/dining room 16 **Smoking:** No pipes, No cigars, Air con **Children:** Portions **Directions:** Nearest station: Green Park To the right of Green Park Station

England

Angela Hartnett at The Connaught

LONDON W1

Italian, Mediterranean NOTABLE WINE LIST

Mayfair opulence meets refined, contemporary cooking

☎ 020 7592 1222 Carlos Place W1K 2AL Plan 2-G1
e-mail: reservations@angelahartnett.com
web: www.angelahartnett.com

Magnificent, rich, modern and swish all rolled into one, the beautifully refurbished, Nina Campbell designed, Menu dining room integrates the Connaught's grandeur and classicism with a feeling of welcome, warmth, light and intimacy. Darkwood panelling, blinds, bold modern oil paintings and classic napery give a nod to the contemporary cooking of Angela Hartnett. And, if you want to get close to the action, there's a chef's table in the kitchen seating up to ten. Service at the Menu is sharp, prompt and well informed, but approachable and friendly, too. Hartnett's highly refined, Ramsay-influenced cuisine delivers much more excitement and oomph than the normal hotel restaurant. The modern approach draws on her Italian background to create enticing combinations on a fixed-price repertoire that includes a tasting option. High skill, tip-top quality produce, bold flavours, clean-cut presentation and intelligent simplicity score on the plate. Anjou pigeon served with chestnuts and Puy lentils, girolle mushrooms and a chestnut velouté might feature as a main course, followed by a dessert of a slow confit quince with crème Catalan, pain d'épice, coffee oil and liquorice ice cream. A tome of a wine list rounds off a class act, with a strong by-the-glass selection, while an elegant terrace provides the opportunity for alfresco dining.

Notable Wine List: An extensive and well chosen wine list full of high-quality wines.

Chef: Angela Hartnett **Owners:** Gordon Ramsay Holdings Ltd **Times:** 12-3/5.45-11 **Prices:** Fixed L £30-£55, Fixed D £55-£70, Service added but optional 12.5% **Wine:** 735 bottles over £20, 15 bottles under £20, 12 by the glass (£5-£39) **Notes:** Fixed L 3 courses, Vegetarian available, Dress Restrictions, No jeans or trainers, smart, jacket preferred **Seats:** 70, Pr/dining room 50 **Smoking:** N/Sm in restaurant, Air con **Children:** Menu, Portions **Rooms:** 92 (92 en suite) ★★★★★ **Directions:** Nearest station: Bond Street/Green Park Please telephone for directions **Parking:** Adams Row

Archipelago

Modern International

Unique and adventurous dining experience

☎ 020 7383 3346 110 Whitfield St W1T 5ED Plan 3-B3

You set out on a journey of exploration when you eat here, seeking out exotic and innovative dishes using ingredients like crocodile, kangaroo and peacock. Even the menu is unusual, a sealed scroll with an ancient map on the back is broken open to reveal the treats in store. Choose from exotically named dishes like Rajasthan Strut, described as peacock-on-a-date with a tomato and vanilla confit, to start. Horizon granites are palate-cleansing ices to take before a main course like the Berber Banquet. This is spicy, ground Ethiopian lamb with Injera pancake and exotic fruit sambal. Desserts are no less exciting, try the Colombian Fix, serious therapy for chocoholics! The surroundings are equally unusual, an eclectic netherworld surrounded by golden Buddhas, giant peacock feathers and dwarf palm trees. If you're looking for a unique dining experience then look no further.

continued

Chef: Daniel Creedon **Owners:** Bruce Alexander **Times:** 12-2.30/6-11, Closed Xmas, BHs, Sun, Closed L Sat **Prices:** Fixed L fr £12.50, Starter £6.50-£10.50, Main £13.50-£19.50, Dessert £6-£7, Coffee £2.50, Min/Water £3.50, Service added but optional 12.5% **Wine:** 23 bottles over £20, 4 bottles under £20, 4 by the glass (£5) **Notes:** Vegetarian available **Seats:** 32 **Smoking:** N/Sm in restaurant, Air con **Directions:** Nearest station: Warren Street From underground south along Tottenham Court Rd. 1st right into Grafton Way. 1st left into Whitfield St **Parking:** NCP, street

Athenaeum Hotel, Bullochs at 116

British, Mediterranean

Intimate dining experience and great service in Mayfair

☎ 020 7499 3464 116 Piccadilly W1J 7BJ Plan 4-H5
e-mail: info@athenaeumhotel.com
web: www.athenaeumhotel.com

The Athenaeum is discreet in every way but the interior of the building, despite limited space, is all charm and quality. The restaurant, accessed via the hotel's main reception area, is a pleasant room with low lighting, tiled floor and secluded areas for dining. Food is refreshing, understated and simple, using the finest organic produce: shellfish bisque; pan-fried Scotch beef fillet with seared foie gras, creamed parsnip and Madeira jus, and date and toffee pudding with vanilla ice cream. Service is of the highest level, superbly hosted and supervised.

Times: 12.30-2.30/5.30-10.30, Closed L Sat & Sun **Rooms:** 157 (157 en suite) ★★★★★ **Directions:** Nearest station: Hyde Park Corner, Green Park Telephone for directions

England

LONDON W1 *continued*

Automat

American NEW

Stylish dining in American brasserie

☎ 020 7499 3033 33 Dover St W1S 4NF Plan 3-A1
e-mail: info@automat-london.com
web: www.automat-london.com

This elegant diner-themed restaurant delivers good-value comfort food to Mayfair. Up front there's a café edge, in the middle a quality diner buzz with banquette seating and wooden panels, while at the back there's an open kitchen, long bar and tables set on different levels. It's light, bright and fun, set to a backing track of Frank Sinatra music. The food is uncomplicated and precise, allowing ingredients to speak for themselves. The short carte features some stereotypical Stateside diner favourites, but dishes benefit from modern interpretations. Perhaps fish chowder or chicken noodle soup, New York strip steak with fries and Mississippi mud pie.

Chef: Peter Templehoff **Owners:** Carlos Almada **Times:** noon/1am **Prices:** Starter £6-£10, Main £6-£24, Dessert £6, Coffee £2.15, Min/Water £3.50, Service added but optional 12.5% **Wine:** 55 bottles over £20, 6 bottles under £20, 10 by the glass (£3.95-£6.25) **Notes:** Brunch available Sat & Sun, Vegetarian available **Seats:** 110 **Smoking:** N/Sm area, No pipes, No cigars, Air con **Directions:** Nearest station: Green Park Telephone for directions

Bam-Bou

French, Vietnamese, Pan Asian

Lively restaurant inspired by Indo-China

☎ 020 7323 9130 1 Percy St W1T 1DB Plan 3-B3
e-mail: sthompson@bam-bou.co.uk
web: www.bam-bou.co.uk

Located in a Georgian townhouse, once the retreat of Ezra Pound's Vorticist Movement, Bam-Bou is a discreet Asian-style restaurant with a French colonial feel. Intimate rooms, replete with authentic artefacts, wood floors, candlelight and jazzy music, provide the setting for sampling a vibrant ethnic menu that draws on Thai, Vietnamese and Chinese cuisine with a strong Western influence. Menu choice is not over elaborate and sound cooking results in full-flavoured dishes. Service is informal and friendly, with good suggestions on how to enjoy the food. Hot and sour soup with tiger prawn and seared scallops, sweet pork, pickled choy shoots are typical.

Chef: Gary Lee **Owners:** Caprice Holdings **Times:** 12-3/6-11, Closed 25-26 Dec, BH Mon's, Sun, Closed L Sat **Prices:** Starter £5.50-£7, Main £9-£15.50, Dessert £4.50-£5.50, Coffee £2.25, Min/Water £3.50, Service added but optional 12.5% **Wine:** 59 bottles over £20, 4 bottles under £20, 10 by the glass (£3.75-£9) **Notes:** Express menu available, Vegetarian available, Smart casual **Seats:** 80, Pr/dining room 20 **Smoking:** N/Sm in restaurant, Air con **Children:** Portions **Directions:** Nearest station: Tottenham Court Rd/Goodge St 1 min from Oxford St **Parking:** On street parking

Bellamy's

French

Classy brasserie in quiet mews

☎ 020 7491 2727 18-18a Bruton Place W1J 6LY Plan 2-H2
e-mail: gavin@bellamysrestaurant.co.uk

There's a buzz to this French brasserie that's very appealing - come at lunchtime or for dinner and it's perennially popular. Tightly packed tables foster a sense of occasion, and the staff keep the conversation and service flowing despite the pressure. The food is classic French brasserie fare, simply but competently prepared from top notch ingredients and delivered with all due ceremony. Expect mains such as fillet of sole with oil, lemon and pommes vapour, or standard menu favourites like boeuf bourguignon and tarte au citron, along with oysters, lobster, caviar and whatever delights the short set menu du jour offers.

Chef: Stephane Pacoud **Owners:** Gavin Rankin Syndicate **Times:** 12-3/7-10.30, Closed BHs, Sun, Closed L Sat **Prices:** Fixed L £24, Fixed D £27, Starter £7-£18, Main £17.50-£24, Dessert £6.50, Coffee £3.75, Min/Water £3.90, Service added but optional 12.5% **Wine:** 44 bottles over £20, 2 bottles under £20, 13 by the glass (£5-£20) **Notes:** Vegetarian available **Seats:** 70 **Smoking:** No pipes, Air con **Children:** Portions **Directions:** Nearest station: Green Park/Bond St Off Berkeley Sq, parallel with Bruton St **Parking:** On street, NCP

Benares

Indian

Fine-dining Indian with striking design and top-notch cooking

☎ 020 7629 8886 12 Berkeley Square W1J 6BS Plan 2-H1
e-mail: reservations@benaresrestaurant.com
web: www.benaresrestaurant.com

Discreetly set on Berkeley Square, Benares puts on a classy Mayfair performance with its striking contemporary design. A wide staircase sweeps up to a cool bar with a series of water-filled ponds decorated with brightly coloured floating flowers. The slick dining room is decked out with lime-stone flooring, dark leather banquettes and ebony-coloured chairs with creamy white upholstery. The modern Indian cuisine is as sophisticated as the surroundings. Highly lauded chef-patron Atul Kochhar (previously at Tamarind) produces eye-catching food, utilising tip-top, luxury European-style produce. Vibrant cooking, subtle spicing and authenticity triumphantly fuse East and West. Expect dishes such as squid salad, coconut shavings and coriander sprigs to begin, with marinated John Dory, tomatoes and shiitake mushrooms to follow.

Times: 12-2.30/5.30-11, Closed 1 Jan, 25-26 Dec, Closed L Sat **Directions:** Nearest station: Green Park E along Piccadilly towards Regent St. Turn left into Berkeley St and continue straight to Berkeley Square

Bentley's Oyster Bar & Grill

British, European

Classic seafood powerhouse

☎ 020 7734 4756 11/15 Swallow St W1B 4DG Plan 3-B1
e-mail: cyril.lommaert@bentleys.org
web: www.bentleysoysterbarandgrill.co.uk

The allure of this traditional oyster bar remains as strong as ever. The downstairs booths upholstered in green leather or the more formal tables upstairs provide the perfect setting for grazing on native or rock oysters in the shell. Starters include home-cured herrings with potato salad or smoked sturgeon with crème fraîche and chives. There's fish pie, Dover sole, plaice or, more exotically, zander with smoked eel and pickled cabbage to follow. Finish with rhubarb and custard or a savoury of Guinness rarebit. Black-clad staff provide professional service.

Chef: Brendan Fyldes **Owners:** Richard Corrigan **Times:** 12/11.30 **Prices:** Starter £5.75-£14, Main £12-£25, Dessert £5.75-£6, Coffee £2.20, Min/Water £3.25, Service added but optional 12.5%, Group service 15% **Wine:** 100 bottles over £20, 40 bottles under £20, 7 by the glass (£4.25-£9.75) **Notes:** Vegetarian available, Dress Restrictions, Smart casual **Seats:** 90, Pr/dining room 14 **Smoking:** N/Sm in restaurant **Children:** Portions **Directions:** Nearest station: Piccadilly Circus 2nd right after Piccadilly Circus **Parking:** 10 yds away

The Berkeley Square

see below

Blandford Street

Modern British, European NOTABLE WINE LIST

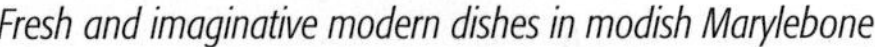

Fresh and imaginative modern dishes in modish Marylebone

☎ 020 7486 9696 5-7 Blandford St, Marylebone W1U 3DB Plan 2-G3
e-mail: info@blandford-street.co.uk
web: www.blandford-street.co.uk

Beautifully refurbished restaurant, just off Marylebone High Street, which can certainly hold its own in an area rich in competition. Points to note are the exquisite hand-painted wallpaper and stylish pavement terrace. There's also a room at the rear, which is available for private dining or meetings. A passion for great ingredients is evident in the dishes offered. These include daily fresh fish, aged Scottish rib-eye steak (only from grass-fed herds, hung for a minimum of 21 days) served with proper chips and sauce béarnaise, free-range chicken leg stuffed with shiitake mushrooms and ginger, bok choy and Chinese spices, and Riesling choucroute with British rare breed pork belly, Ventrèche bacon, Morteau sausage and Dijon mustard.
Notable Wine List: An interesting and carefully chosen wine list. Every wine has detailed and informative tasting notes.

Chef: Martin Moore **Owners:** Nicholas Lambert **Times:** 12-2.30/6.30-10.30, Closed Xmas, New Year, Easter, BHs, Sun, Closed L Mon, Sat **Prices:** Fixed L £19.95, Starter £5.95-£14.95, Main £9.95-£23.95, Dessert £5.95, Coffee £2, Min/Water £3.25, Service added but optional 12.5% **Wine:** 8 by the glass (£4-£7.50) **Notes:** Vegetarian available **Seats:** 55, Pr/dining room 18 **Smoking:** N/Sm area, No pipes, Air con **Children:** Portions **Directions:** Nearest station: Bond Street Turn right out of Oxford St exit, cross road and down Marylebone Ln to Marylebone High St. Onto Blandford St, restaurant on left **Parking:** NCP: Weymouth Street

The Berkeley Square

LONDON W1

Modern European V NOTABLE WINE LIST

Mayfair fine dining without the pomp

☎ 020 7629 6993 7 Davies St, Berkeley Square W1K 3DD Plan 2-H1
e-mail: info@theberkeleysquare.com
web: www.theberkeleysquare.com

A blue canopy and small shop-front terrace, with a few fair-weather tables alfresco, pick out this intimate but relaxed two-floor restaurant on the square. The interior design follows a stylish contemporary vogue with a blend of soft purples - mulberry carpet, soft mauve wall and aubergine curtains - while chairs are brown leather and banquettes a vibrant lime, the walls enlivened with bright, modern abstract artworks. Service is knowledgeable and professional but nicely relaxed. Chef-patron Steven Black shows his pedigree in confident, classy and polished modern dishes. Tip-top produce, a lightness of touch and elegant presentation parade on a repertoire of fixed-price menus, which includes a seven-course surprise option. Expect the likes of roasted monkfish served with a mussel tortellini, globe artichoke, fine beans, parmesan crisp and a saffron and mussel foam, while a caramelised Granny Smith apple, teamed with an apple beignet and walnut and sage ice cream, might feature at dessert.

Notable Wine List: A well chosen and enthusiastic wine list.

Chef: Steven Black **Owners:** John De Stefano **Times:** 12-2.30/6-10, Closed Xmas, New Year, BHs, last 2 wks Aug, Sun, Sat **Prices:** Fixed L £17.95, Coffee £2, Min/Water £3.50, Service added but optional 12.5% **Wine:** 190 bottles over £20, 4 bottles under £20, 10 by the glass (£6-£9.50) **Notes:** Set ALC 2-3 course £42.95-49.95, Tasting menu 7 courses £55, Vegetarian menu **Seats:** 70, Pr/dining room 14 **Smoking:** N/Sm area, No pipes or cigars, Air con **Children:** Menu, Portions **Directions:** Nearest station: Bond Street, Green Park NW end of Berkeley Sq **Parking:** On street

LONDON W1 *continued*

Brian Turner Mayfair

Modern British

Back to basics British cooking in upmarket hotel

☎ 020 7596 3444 Millennium Hotel, 44 Grosvenor Square, Mayfair W1K 2HN Plan 2-G1
e-mail: annie.mckale@mill-cop.com
web: www.brianturneronline.co.uk

In contrast to the other smart eateries in this swanky Mayfair hotel, Brian Turner's split-level restaurant boasts understated retro-chic, decked out in contemporary shades and natural materials. Famed for his interest in traditional British comfort food, cooking is based on simple, wholesome and satisfying British classics, yet dishes are given a light and modern touch. The kitchen delivers bangers and mash with onion gravy alongside braised ox cheek, celeriac and horseradish mash and smoked bacon, and Dover sole with lemon hollandaise. Leave room for a nursery pud like hazelnut sponge with toffee sauce and hazelnut ice cream.

Chef: Brian Turner & Paul Bates **Owners:** Millennium Hotels **Times:** 12.30-2.30/6.30-10.30, Closed BHs, Sun, Closed L Sat **Prices:** Fixed L £23.50, Starter £7.95-£14, Main £14.50-£28, Dessert £7.25, Coffee £3, Min/Water £3.95, Service added but optional 12.5% **Wine:** 90 bottles over £20, 6 by the glass (£6.50-£8) **Notes:** Vegetarian available, Civ Wed 100 **Seats:** 86, Pr/dining room 60 **Smoking:** N/Sm area, No pipes, Air con **Children:** Portions **Rooms:** 348 (348 en suite) ★★★★ **Directions:** Nearest station: Bond Street, Green Park Central London, close to Oxford St, Bond St and Park Ln **Parking:** NCP next door

Butler's

Traditional British

Traditional dining in elegant Mayfair retreat

☎ 020 7491 2622 Chesterfield Mayfair Hotel, 35 Charles St, Mayfair W1J 5EB Plan 4-H6
e-mail: fandbch@rchmail.com
web: www.redcarnationhotels.com

The Chesterfield hotel exudes quiet elegance and exclusivity appropriate to its prestigious Mayfair address. The feeling is maintained in the African-themed Butlers restaurant, with its sumptuous red and gold décor. Dine here or in the light and airy Conservatory, which has access to the walled garden, where the traditional British menu offers a good range of dishes based on fine-quality ingredients. Imaginative dishes like baked haddock with saffron mash and mussel broth jostle for attention alongside the traditional chargrilled meats and the carving, salmon and wine trolleys. Service is excellent.

continued

Chef: Stephen Henderson **Owners:** Red Carnation Hotels **Times:** 12.30-2.30/5.30-10.30 **Prices:** Fixed L fr £14.50, Fixed D fr £22.50, Starter £6-£13.95, Main £12.95-£25, Dessert £5.95-£6.95, Coffee £3.75, Service added but optional 12% **Wine:** 65 bottles over £20, 8 bottles under £20, 10 by the glass (£3.95-£11) **Notes:** Sun L 2 courses from £14.50, Vegetarian available, Civ Wed 100 **Seats:** 65, Pr/dining room 24 **Smoking:** N/Sm area, No pipes, Air con **Children:** Menu, Portions **Rooms:** 110 (110 en suite) ★★★★ HL **Directions:** Nearest station: Green Park From N side exit of tube station turn left and then first left into Berkeley St. Continue down to Berkeley Sq and then left heading towards Charles St **Parking:** NCP - 5 minutes

Camerino

Italian

Elegant Italian restaurant where everything is made on the premises

☎ 020 7637 9900 16 Percy St W1T 1DT Plan 3-B3
e-mail: info@camerinorestaurant.com
web: www.camerinorestaurant.com

Smartly presented Italian restaurant in a side street off Tottenham Court Road, with bold red drapes and floral swirls decorating the walls (a camerino is an actress's changing room). Ingredients come directly from Smithfield, Billingsgate and New Covent Garden and are used in a range of Italian regional dishes. There is a set lunch and pre-theatre menu, and dishes from the main carte include veal with tuna sauce, casunziei tortelli (pasta filled with beetroot, ricotta, butter and poppy seeds), and lamb neck braised in wine, with balsamic and red onions served with mashed potato. Dessert might be gianduia fondant.

Chef: Valerio Daros **Owners:** Paolo Boschi **Times:** 12-3/6-11, Closed 1 wk Xmas, 1st Jan, Etr Day, most BHs, Sun, Closed L Sat **Prices:** Food prices not confirmed for 2007. Please telephone for details **Wine:** 54 bottles over £20, 4 bottles under £20, 9 by the glass (£3.75-£6.50) **Notes:** Vegetarian available, Dress Restrictions, Smart casual preferred **Seats:** 70 **Smoking:** No pipes, No cigars, Air con **Directions:** Nearest station: Tottenham Court Rd, Goodge St Please telephone for directions **Parking:** Goodge St

Cecconi's

Traditional Italian

Modern Italian cuisine and cutting-edge design

☎ 020 7434 1500 5a Burlington Gardens W1X 1LE Plan 3-A1
web: www.cecconis.co.uk

Enzo Cecconi was the youngest ever manager of the famous Cipriani restaurant in Venice so when he opened Cecconi's in London in 1978 it became an overnight success. Refurbished in 2005 it has been

continued

taken back to its Venetian roots and is now a chic, stylish modern restaurant attracting a hip crowd. An extensive all-day menu means you can come in at any time and enjoy a great range of simple, well-presented dishes offering good value for money. Start from 7am with breakfast served until 12, or brunch at weekends from 12 until 5. Pop in for a light lunch with choices like lobster and potato salad with crispy pancetta, or indulge in a leisurely dinner. Main courses include new variations on Italian classics, try lobster spaghetti or veal Milanese.

Chef: Andrea Cavaliere **Owners:** Soho House Ltd **Times:** 12/midnight, Closed Xmas, New Year **Prices:** Starter £4-£12, Main £15-£24, Dessert £7, Coffee £2.50, Min/Water £3.50, Service optional **Wine:** 280 bottles over £20, 11 bottles under £20, 14 by the glass **Notes:** Vegetarian available **Seats:** 80 **Smoking:** Air con **Children:** Portions **Directions:** Nearest station: Piccadilly Circus/Oxford Circus Burlington Gdns between New Bond St and Savile Row **Parking:** On street

China Tang

Chinese V NEW

Sophisticated Chinese set in luxurious surroundings

☎ 020 7629 9988 The Dorchester, Park Ln W1A 2HJ Plan 4-G6
e-mail: reservations@chinatanglondon.co.uk

Lavish, opulent and stunning are just a few words to describe this ultra-deluxe Chinese setting in the basement of The Dorchester, (formerly the Dorchester Club), where no expense has been spared. There's a lavish cocktail bar and spacious dining room, the decor a mix of art deco and traditional Chinese. Interior design is mirrored pillars, stunning glass-fronted artworks, tables with marble inset tops laid with heavy silver chopsticks, hand-carved chairs and deep banquette seating. The classic Cantonese cooking, utilizing top-quality produce, parades on dim sum and carte menus that come dotted with luxuries. Take lobster braised in ginger and spring onions, classic Peking duck or perhaps sautéed pork in a black bean sauce.

Chef: Ringo Chow **Owners:** David Tang **Times:** 11/midnight, Closed 25 Dec **Prices:** Starter £4-£22, Main £10-£60, Dessert £7-£15, Coffee £3, Min/Water £5, Service added but optional 12.5% **Wine:** 400 bottles over £20, 18 by the glass (£5-£25) **Notes:** Vegetarian available, Dress Restrictions, Smart casual **Seats:** 120, Pr/dining room 80 **Smoking:** No pipes, Air con **Children:** Portions **Directions:** Nearest station: Hyde Park Corner Please telephone for directions

Cipriani

Italian

A dazzling piece of Venice in Mayfair

☎ 020 7399 0500 25 Davies St W1E 3DE Plan 2-H2
web: www.cipriani.com

Arrigo Cipriani's first venture outside Venice - haunt of the fashionable, rich and famous - is ideally located just off Berkeley Square. The modern glass-fronted exterior leads to a large, stylish dining room, where impeccable art deco style meets beautiful Murano chandeliers, and white-jacketed staff offer slick and attentive service. Low, leather-upholstered seating and magnolia tablecloths provide added comfort. Classic, accurate, straightforward Italian cooking - with lots of Cipriani touches, authentic, top-quality ingredients and unfussy presentation - hits the mark in dishes such as tagliatelle with fresh peas starter, followed by beef medallions alla Rossini. Do save room for the dessert selection of cakes and fine breads.

continued

Chef: Guiseppe Marangi **Owners:** Cipriani Family **Times:** 12-3/6-11.45, Closed 25 Dec **Prices:** Fixed L £28-£35, Fixed D £35-£40, Starter £7-£21, Main £17-£33, Dessert £8-£11, Coffee £3.50, Min/Water £5.50, Service added but optional 12.5% **Wine:** 6 by the glass (£3.50-£10) **Notes:** Fixed L 3 courses, Vegetarian available, Dress Restrictions, No shorts **Seats:** 140, Pr/dining room 32 **Smoking:** Air con **Children:** Portions **Directions:** Nearest station: Bond Street Please telephone for directions

Cocoon

Pan Asian

Happening pan-Asian restaurant

☎ 020 7494 7600 65 Regents St W1B 4EA Plan 3-B1
e-mail: reservations@cocoon-restaurants.com
web: www.cocoon-restaurants.com

It's essential to book a table at this unreservedly popular restaurant, even on a weekday. The loud clamour of after-work conversation is minimised by the careful siting of tables in hidden nooks and crannies, with the clever use of net curtains effectively screening groups away from each other. You can dine at the sushi bar and watch the chefs at work, or pick and choose from a comprehensive menu that takes in the best of the Asian culinary world. Dim sum, sashimi, teriyaki, tempura, green miso soup are all there, along with some interesting fusion dishes.

Chef: Andrew Lassetter **Owners:** Matt Hermer, Paul Demming **Times:** 12-2.45/5.30-11.30, Closed 25-26 Dec, 1 Jan **Prices:** Fixed L £19.50, Fixed D £19.50, Starter £3.50-£15, Main £10.50-£52, Dessert £6.50-£9, Min/Water £4.50, Service added 12.5% **Wine:** 100% bottles over £20, 14 by the glass (£4.50-£9.50) **Notes:** Vegetarian available, Dress Restrictions, Smart casual **Seats:** 180, Pr/dining room 14 **Directions:** Nearest station: Piccadilly Circus 1 min walk from Piccadilly Circus **Parking:** NCP Brewer St

Crescent Restaurant at The Montcalm Nikko London

Modern European

A peaceful sanctuary in the heart of the city

☎ 020 7402 4288 Great Cumberland Place W1H 7TW Plan 2-F2
e-mail: montcalm@montcalm.co.uk
web: www.montcalm.co.uk

It's hard to believe you're only minutes from Marble Arch when eating at this idyllic Georgian restaurant, originally built in 1787 for the Marquis de Montcalm. Located in a secluded crescent, the noise and bustle are barely evident - the English country garden murals, bright and airy feel to the dining room and cricketing theme seem more like

continued

LONDON W1 *continued*

a country house. The food aspires to modern European, with a leaning toward Italy; on this bistro-style menu expect starters similar to green pea and ricotta soup with basil oil and mains like confit duck leg with cassoulet of white beans, braised pork and chorizo. Lunch is particularly good value.

Crescent Restaurant at The Montcalm Nikko

Chef: Tristan Kenworthy **Owners:** Nikko Hotels (UK) Ltd **Times:** 12.30-2.30/6.30-10.30, Closed L Sat, Sun & BHs **Prices:** Fixed L £21, Fixed D £29.50, Coffee £3.50, Min/Water £3.50 **Wine:** 16 bottles over £20, 3 bottles under £20, 9 by the glass (£4-£8) **Notes:** Fixed price L & D incl 1/2 bottle of wine per person, Vegetarian available, Dress Restrictions, Smart casual **Seats:** 70, Pr/dining room 60 **Smoking:** N/Sm area, No pipes, No cigars, Air con **Children:** Menu, Portions **Rooms:** 120 (120 en suite) ★★★★ HL **Directions:** Nearest station: Marble Arch Telephone for directions **Parking:** 9

The Cumberland - Rhodes

Modern British NEW

Exciting concept at Rhodes W1

☎ 0870 333 9280 Great Cumberland Place W1A 4RF
Plan 2-F2
e-mail: enquiries@thecumberland.co.uk
web: www.guoman.com

Chef, restaurateur and author Gary Rhodes has moved to the West End to open Rhodes W1 at The Cumberland Hotel in Marble Arch. The high-ceilinged restaurant is split into two dining areas either side of a bar, creating a modern and impressive backdrop for some exciting cuisine. Expect European dishes with Gary's British influence, simply and well prepared, easy to eat. The menu offers pleasing classics and new dishes, try French onion soup to start, main courses like braised oxtail with mashed potato or salmon with leek and parmesan risotto and fried baby squid, with classic desserts like bread-and-butter pudding or warm rum baba with rhubarb fool.

Chef: Gary Rhodes **Times:** 12-2.30/6-10.15 **Prices:** Food prices not confirmed for 2007. Please telephone for details **Seats:** 140 **Rooms:** 1015 (1005 en suite) ★★★★ HL **Directions:** Telephone for directions

Deya at Mostyn Hotel

Indian V

Hip restaurant with contemporary Indian food

☎ 020 7224 0028 34 Portman Square W1H 7BY
Plan 2-F2
e-mail: info@deya-restaurant.co.uk
web: www.deya-restaurant.co.uk

Located just behind Oxford Street, the Mostyn Hotel was originally built as a residence for Lady Black, a lady-in-waiting at the court of George II. Deya is the fashionable restaurant and offers traditional Indian food with a contemporary twist. The décor is discreet and modern with a subtle Indian theme most evident in the murals on the wall divisions - there's also a trendy bar, which attracts a sophisticated crowd for cocktails and chatter. Among the highlights on the menu are scallops three ways (poached in coconut milk and lime leaf, pan-fried with sesame seeds, with poppy seeds and with cardamom and coriander), lamb shank rogan josh and snapper masala. Don't miss the excellent breads.

Chef: Virappan Muragappan **Owners:** Claudio Pulze/Raj Sharma/Sir Michael Caine **Times:** 12-2.45/6.30-10.45, Closed Xmas, New Yr, BHs, Sun, Closed L Sat **Prices:** Fixed L £14.95, Starter £6.50-£9.95, Main £11.50-£15.50, Dessert £4.50-£7.50, Coffee £2, Min/Water £3, Service added but optional 12.5% **Wine:** 135 bottles over £20, 15 bottles under £20, 10 by the glass (£5.50-£7.50) **Notes:** 3 tasting menus available, Vegetarian menu Dress Restrictions, Smart casual **Seats:** 80 **Smoking:** N/Sm in restaurant, Air con **Children:** Portions **Rooms:** 121 (121 en suite) ★★★ HL **Directions:** Nearest station: Marble Arch/Bond St On the corner of Seymour St and Portman St **Parking:** NCP Bryanston St

Embassy London

Modern European

Modern, sophisticated Mayfair restaurant and club

☎ 020 7851 0956 29 Old Burlington St W1S 3AN
Plan 3-A1
e-mail: embassy@embassylondon.com
web: www.embassylondon.com

Set behind a modern glass frontage in the heart of the West End, this Mayfair restaurant is as stylish and sophisticated as its address. The ground-floor dining room is a contemporary, split-level affair, with chi bar, floor-to-ceiling windows and small alfresco terrace at the front. Soothing creams and browns, white linen, mirrored surfaces and stunning flower displays cut an understated, upmarket edge. Attentive black-clad staff, a vibrant atmosphere and enticing modern European cooking all fit the bill, too. Expect clear, clean-cut flavours and presentation, balanced combinations and tip-top produce to deliver the likes of roasted halibut with black noodles and Cornish crab, or a chocolate and Amaretto fondant with praline ice cream. Dine before descending to the nightclub below.

Chef: Garry Hollihead **Owners:** Mark Fuller & Garry Hollihead **Times:** 12-3/6-11.30, Closed 25-26 Dec, 1 Jan, Good Fri, Sun-Mon, Closed Oct-Apr & Sat **Prices:** Fixed L £19.50, Fixed D £22.50-£39.50, Starter £6-£19.50, Main £14-£28, Dessert £8, Coffee £1.90, Min/Water £4, Service added but optional 12.5% **Wine:** 58 bottles over £20, 6 bottles under £2(6 by the glass (£4.50-£6.50) **Notes:** Fixed L summer only, Vegetarian available, Dress Restrictions, Smart casual, no trainers, smart jeans only **Seats:** 120 **Smoking:** No pipes, Air con **Directions:** Nearest station: Green Park, Piccadilly Circus Just off Burlington Gardens, running between Bond and Regent St **Parking:** NCP

L'Escargot - The Ground Floor Restaurant

Modern French

Soho institution combining a classy venue with breathtaking artwork

☎ 020 7439 7474 48 Greek St W1D 4EF Plan 3-C2
e-mail: sales@whitestarline.org.uk
web: www.lescargotrestaurant.co.uk

Probably London's first designer restaurant, dating from 1927, L'Escargot is popular with theatre-goers and renowned for its art collection, with works by some of the most celebrated artists of the 20th century, including Miró, Chagall, Warhol, Hockney and Matisse. Professional service copes well with the crowds and the atmosphere is fabulous. An appealing menu written in Franglais offers plenty of variety, with old favourites such as escargots en coquille 'bordelaise' alongside lasagne of crab with sauce Américaine, navarin of venison with pilaff rice and glazed root vegetables, and coconut crème brûlée. There's a full carte at lunch and dinner and a good-value menu du jour for lunch and pre-theatre dinner.

Chef: Dominic Teague **Owners:** Jimmy Lahoud & Marco Pierre White **Times:** 12-2.30/6-11.30, Closed 25-26 Dec, 1 Jan, Sun, Closed L Sat **Prices:** Fixed L £15, Fixed D £18, Starter £7.50, Main £12.50-£14.95, Dessert £6.50, Coffee £3.50, Min/Water £3.50, Service added but optional 12.5% **Wine:** 350 bottles over £20, 15 bottles under £20, 8 by the glass (£4-£5.85) **Notes:** Pre theatre menu available, Vegetarian available, Smart casual **Seats:** 70, Pr/dining room 60 **Smoking:** No pipes, Air con **Children:** Portions **Directions:** Nearest station: Tottenham Court Rd, Leicester Square Telephone for directions **Parking:** NCP Chinatown, on street parking

L'Escargot - The Picasso Room

see page 314

Fino

Spanish

Fashionable tapas with an authentic range

☎ 020 7813 8010 33 Charlotte St W1T 1RR Plan 3-B3
e-mail: info@finorestaurant.com
web: www.finorestaurant.com

An upmarket and lively Spanish restaurant hidden away in a surprisingly bright and airy basement on chic Charlotte Street. High ceilings, pale wood floors, red leather chairs and a contemporary mezzanine bar area set the stylish scene for sampling some skilfully cooked tapas dishes. Great for grazing and groups' dining, order between three and four dishes each off the daily menu that lists both classic and contemporary dishes, and watch them being prepared in the open-to-view kitchen. Expect rustic and robust dishes such as milk-fed lamb cutlets, crisp pork belly roasted to perfection, marinated grilled quail, and some excellent seafood, perhaps clams with sherry and ham and crisp fried squid. Extremely helpful staff.

Chef: Jean Phillipe Patruno **Owners:** Sam & Eddie Hart **Times:** 12-2.30/6-10.30, Closed Xmas & BH, Sun **Prices:** Fixed L £17.95-£28, Fixed D £23.95-£34, Starter £3.50-£9, Main £8-£16, Dessert £5.50 £6.50, Coffee £2, Min/Water £4, Service added but optional 12.5% **Wine:** 110 bottles over £20, 10 bottles under £20, 18 by the glass (£3.50-£8.50) **Notes:** Vegetarian available **Seats:** 80 **Smoking:** N/Sm area, No pipes, No cigars, Air con **Directions:** Nearest station: Goodge St/Tottenham Court Rd Entrance on Rathbone St

Four Seasons Hotel London

Modern European

Relaxed, contemporary dining with views of Hyde Park and Park Lane

☎ 020 7499 0888 Hamilton Place, Park Ln W1A 1AZ Plan 4-G5
e-mail: fsh.london@fourseasons.com
web: www.fourseasons.com

This is sophisticated dining just a stone's throw from Hyde Park. The well-known Lanes Restaurant is a lovely dark dining room oozing understated luxury - stained glass, wood panelling and marble. Spotlights illuminate each table and the wall to ceiling shelves showcase some beautiful glassware. Service here is seamless yet unpretentious, with obvious attention to detail. The cosmopolitan menu has Asian influences from the chef's time in the Far East, seen in dishes like roast sea bass fillet with wasabi. It also includes traditional British favourites like roast rib of Blairmore beef and Yorkshire pudding.

Chef: Bernhard Mayer **Owners:** Four Seasons Hotels & Resorts **Times:** 12-3/6-11 **Prices:** Fixed L £29, Fixed D £36, Starter £9-£20, Main £24-£36, Dessert £9, Coffee £4.40, Min/Water £3.80, Service included **Wine:** all bottles over £20, 15 by the glass (£6.40-£11) **Notes:** Fixed L 3 courses, Sun L £38 incl 1/2 bottle wine, Civ Wed 300 **Seats:** 90, Pr/dining room 300 **Smoking:** N/Sm area, No pipes, Air con **Children:** Menu, Portions **Rooms:** 219 (219 en suite) ★★★★★ HL **Directions:** Nearest station: Green Park/Hyde Park Corner Hamilton Place, just off Hyde Park corner end of Park Lane **Parking:** 50

England

L'Escargot - The Picasso Room

LONDON W1

French V

Accomplished French cuisine in intimate dining room above L'Escargot

☎ 020 7439 7474 48 Greek St W1D 4EF Plan 3-C2
e-mail: sales@whitestarline.org.uk
web: www.lescargotrestaurant.co.uk

A separate dining room above the Ground Floor restaurant, dedicated to Picasso and displaying his prints and ceramics. The L-shaped room has comfortable leather seating and quality table settings, while service is formal but discreet and relaxed.

A very traditional French menu offers the likes of snails, frogs' legs and smoked foie gras among the starters in various guises. If that doesn't take your fancy, you could go for roasted Cornish scallop with squid ink sauce and deep fried calamari. Main courses feature lots of top British produce like Dorset lobster, Suffolk chicken and Wyn Valley lamb, demonstrating the careful sourcing of ingredients to suit each dish.

Cooking style ranges from a simple pot au feu of Dorset lobster with thyme butter sauce to a more complex dish like roasted Anjou pigeon with buttered Puy lentils, celeriac cream and a millefeuille of confit duck. Desserts stick to the Gallic theme with the likes of parfait of bananas with warm chocolate fondant and chocolate sauce. An extensive wine list, dominated by the main French regions, echoes the quality of the food.

Chef: Warren Geraghty
Owners: Jimmy Lahoud & Marco Pierre White
Times: 12-2/6-11, Closed 2 wks from 24 Dec & Aug, Sun-Mon, Closed L Sat
Prices: Fixed L fr £20.50, Fixed D £42, Coffee £4, Min/Water £3.50, Service added but optional 15%
Wine: 35 bottles over £20, 15 bottles under £20, 8 by the glass (£4-£5.85)
Notes: Vegetarian available, Smart casual
Seats: 30
Smoking: No pipes, Air con
Children: Min 8 yrs
Directions: Nearest station: Tottenham Court Rd, Leicester Square Telephone for directions
Parking: NCP or street parking

LONDON W1 *continued*

Frankie's at Criterion Grill

Modern Italian

Simple Italian food amidst Byzantine splendour

☎ 020 7930 0488 224 Piccadilly W1J 9HP Plan 3-B1
e-mail: sales@whitestarline.org.uk
web: www.whitestarline.org.uk

The Criterion has become the third addition to the group of Frankie's Italian family restaurants, the result of an inspired collaboration between chef Marco Pierre White and jockey Frankie Dettori. London's only neo-Byzantine restaurant is distinguished by its canopied entrance in Piccadilly Circus. The interior is breathtaking with a gold mosaic ceiling and marble floor. In contrast, the style of food is simple, with plenty of popular pizza and pasta, but the elegant choice might be mozzarella di buffala caprese, escalope of veal alla Milanese, and mascarpone crème brûlée.

Chef: Yacine Sadadou **Owners:** Marco Pierre White, Jimmy Lahoud & Frankie Dettori **Times:** 12/11, Closed 24-26 Dec **Prices:** Fixed L £14.95, Fixed D £20.50-£33, Starter £5.50-£10, Main £9.50-£16.50, Dessert £5.50, Coffee £2.50, Min/Water £3.50, Service added but optional 12.5%, Group min 20 service 15% **Wine:** 37 bottles over £20, 11 bottles under £20, 12 by the glass (£3.95-£8.75) **Notes:** Pre-theatre menu available, Vegetarian available **Seats:** 150 **Smoking:** No pipes, Air con **Children:** Portions **Directions:** Nearest station: Piccadilly Circus Telephone for directions **Parking:** Chinatown NCP

Galvin at Windows

Rosettes not confirmed at time of going to press

Modern French

Exciting new destination restaurant in the heart of Mayfair

☎ 020 7493 8000 London Hilton on Park Ln, 22 Park Ln W1K 1BE Plan 4-G5

This exciting new restaurant had just opened as we went to press. Galvin at Windows is the new venture on the 28th floor of the London Hilton on Park Lane, which has been transformed into a modern French restaurant and renamed. Chris Galvin, who recently opened an eponymous restaurant with his brother on Baker Street (see Galvin - Bistrot de Luxe, below), will be chef-patron in the joint venture with the hotel. The glamorous interior is designed to evoke the golden age of the 1930s with a 21st-century theme, and offers peerless views over London. The cuisine style is modern French with a bit of glamour mixed with bourgeois cooking. It will open from breakfast through dinner and is set to become one of London's destination restaurants. Chris has a long pedigree and is an acclaimed chef - previous to Galvin - Bistrot de Luxe, his most recent appearance has been at the Wolseley, W1. Watch our website for an update and click the link to Pubs and Restaurants.

Chef: Chris Galvin, André Garrett **Times:** 7-10.30 **Prices:** Food prices not confirmed for 2007. Please telephone for details **Notes:** **Seats:** 108

Galvin - Bistrot de Luxe

French V NOTABLE WINE LIST **NEW**

AA Restaurant of the Year for London

☎ 020 7935 4007 66 Baker St W1U 7DH Plan 2-G3
e-mail: info@galvinbistrotdeluxe.co.uk
web: www.galvinbistrotdeluxe.co.uk

The Galvin name above its grey awning and glass frontage gives the only clue to the pedigree of this relaxed little gem midway up Baker

continued

Street. The brothers Galvin (Chris and Jeff) have worked in some of London's top kitchens before setting up their family affair here; it's very Parisian bistro and classy. Panelled walls, black leather banquettes, simple chairs and crisp white linen provide the look. Fans whirl overhead, mirrors and foodie prints adorn walls, while there are tantalizing glimpses into the kitchen. Fittingly, the highly accomplished cooking is unmistakably Gallic, with great ingredients and superb flavours at value-for-money prices, especially the prixe fixe menu. Escargots bourgignonne, then choucroute of fish with Reisling, and tarte au citron show off the style.

Notable Wine List: A predominately French-based wine list full of interest and quality.

Chef: Chris & Jeff Galvin **Owners:** Chris & Jeff Galvin **Times:** 12-2.30/6-11, Closed 25 & 26 Dec, 1 Jan **Prices:** Fixed L £15.50, Fixed D £17.50, Starter £6-£10.50, Main £11-£18.50, Dessert £5-£6.75, Coffee £2.50, Service added but optional 12.5% **Wine:** 88 bottles over £20, 17 bottles under £20, 12 by the glass (£3.95-£7.25) **Notes:** Fixed L 3 courses, Fixed D 6-7pm only, Vegetarian available **Seats:** 95 **Smoking:** No pipes, No cigars, Air con **Children:** Portions **Directions:** Nearest station: Baker Street Please telephone for directions **Parking:** On street & NCP

Le Gavroche Restaurant

see page 316

Gordon Ramsay at Claridge's

see page 316

The Greenhouse

see page 317

The Grill

Traditional English, Continental

Fine dining at the famous London hotel

☎ 020 7518 4060 Brown's Hotel, Albemarle St W1S 4BP Plan 3-A1
e-mail: reservations.brownshotel@roccofortehotels.com
web: www.roccofortehotels.com

The Grill is the main restaurant at Browns, offering a combination of English and Continental cuisine. New look décor, by interior designer Olga Polizzi, features moss green leather banquette booth seating, cream linen Roman blinds and 1930s Italian lights. The carving trolley and original wood panelling hint at the historic roots of this the first public dining room in London, within a very famous and well-loved hotel. Simple classical dishes and the use of fine ingredients ensure the continued popularity of the restaurant menu. Here you will find daily-changing plats du jour and a traditional carte, featuring the likes of seared tuna with oriental vegetable salad, followed by tournedos of Scottish beef Rossini. From the grill you could try English lamb cutlets or perhaps darne of Scottish salmon with parsley butter. The hotel is renowned for its afternoon tea, served in Brown's English Tea Room.

Chef: Laurence Glayzer **Owners:** Rocco Forte Hotels **Times:** 12.30-2.30/7-10.30 **Prices:** Fixed L £25, Fixed D £45, Starter £9.50-£16.50, Main £12.75-£28, Dessert £8.50, Coffee £4.50, Min/Water £4.50, Service optional **Wine:** 350 bottles over £20, 12 by the glass (£5.50-£8) **Notes:** Vegetarian available, Dress Restrictions, Jackets requested for gents, Civ Wed 70 **Seats:** 85, Pr/dining room 70 **Smoking:** No pipes, Air con **Rooms:** 117 (117 en suite) **Directions:** Nearest station: Green Park Near Piccadilly Circus **Parking:** Valet/Burlington St

England

Le Gavroche Restaurant

LONDON W1

French

Mayfair's bastion of French tradition

☎ 020 7408 0881 & 7499 1826
43 Upper Brook St W1K 7QR Plan 2-G1
e-mail: bookings@le-gavroche.com
web: www.le-gavroche.co.uk, www.michelroux.co.uk

Entering Le Gavroche is like being transported into a timeless hospitable world, epitomising a style of classic French cooking and service that is close to unique on this side of the Channel. The crown of Britain's best cooking may long have been relinquished to innovation across town or up river at Bray's Fat Duck (see entry), but the exacting standards of its kitchen and service - in the safe hands of Michel Roux Jr - remain impeccable, while this gilt-edged venue never fails to let you know you're somewhere very special indeed. The Roux brothers' first British venture, Le Gavroche may be almost 40 years old, but its packed tables testify to its enduring appeal and popularity. Cosseting and opulent, the basement dining room comes awash with legions of dedicated staff and decorated with rich fittings and furnishings, while tables are set with crisp linen and lavish crystal and silver, all setting the tone for a truly classical French experience. Like the décor, Michel Jr's superb, skilful cooking drips with luxuries (you'll have to dig deep into your pockets), while blending classical dishes with others that show a lighter touch and more contemporary taste. Roast saddle of rabbit with crispy potatoes and parmesan, or a Gavroche signature omelette Rothschild (aka apricot and Cointreau soufflé), is rounded off perfectly with l'assiette du chef - showing what the kitchen can really do with desserts. A tasting Menu Exceptional and a serious, French-dominated wine list wraps up this classy Gallic act.

Chef: Michel Roux Jr **Owners:** Le Gavroche Ltd **Times:** 12-2/6.30-11.00, Closed Xmas, New Year, BHs, Sun, Closed L Sat **Prices:** Fixed L £46, Starter £18.60-£44.80, Main £26.20-£42.80, Dessert £12.80-£30.60, Coffee £6.40, Min/Water £4, Service added but optional 12.5% **Wine:** 2000 bottles over £20, 20 bottles under £20, 4 by the glass (£4-£10) **Notes:** Fixed L 3 courses incl 1/2 bottle of water & wine, Vegetarian available, Dress Restrictions, Jacket required. No jeans **Seats:** 60 **Smoking:** N/Sm in restaurant, Air con **Children:** Portions **Directions:** Nearest station: Marble Arch From Park Lane into Upper Brook St, restaurant on right **Parking:** NCP - Park Lane

Gordon Ramsay at Claridge's

LONDON W1

French, European V NOTABLE WINE LIST

Elegant dining and gastronomic flair

☎ 020 7499 0099 Brook St W1K 4HR Plan 2-H2
e-mail: gordonramsay@claridges.co.uk
web: www.gordonramsay.com

Once renowned as the resort of kings and princes, Claridge's today continues to set the standards by which other hotels are judged, while its marriage with Gordon Ramsay has elevated it to one of London's most popular dining venues. The restaurant exudes 1930s sophistication, from its dramatic three-tiered light shades to its delicate etched glass panels. The elegant, high-ceilinged room - restored to its former art deco glory by designer and architect Thierry Despont - is all very grand. Service is expectedly slick and professional and tables elegantly appointed, while there's an intimate bar area, and, for the ultimate experience, a chef's table in the heart of the kitchen. Chef Mark Sargeant's highly accomplished, modern haute-European cuisine focuses around top-class seasonal ingredients, the fixed-price repertoire of lunch, carte and six-course tasting option dotted with luxury, the cooking fitting perfectly under the Ramsay stable umbrella. There's an intelligent simplicity and integrity that allows main ingredients to shine in clean-flavoured dishes; perhaps West Country pork cheeks cooked in honey and cloves and accompanied by grain mustard pomme mousseline and braising juices, and maybe an assiette of orange three-ways finish - parfait, tart and jelly. Save room for all the extra touches (tasters, inter-courses, petits fours and alike), while a galaxy of stars populate the serious wine list.

Notable Wine List: An extensive and immaculate wine list offering depth in every area.

Chef: Mark Sargeant **Owners:** Gordon Ramsay Holdings Ltd **Times:** 12-3/5.45-11 **Prices:** Fixed L £30-£70, Fixed D £60, Coffee £5, Min/Water £3.50, Service added but optional 12.5% **Wine:** 800 bottles over £20, 10 bottles under £20, 15 by the glass (£5-£15) **Notes:** Fixed L 3 courses, Prestige menu 6 courses £70, Vegetarian menu, Dress Restrictions, Smart, jacket preferred, no jeans/trainers **Seats:** 100, Pr/dining room 60 **Smoking:** N/Sm in restaurant, Air con **Children:** Portions **Rooms:** 203 (203 en suite) ★★★★★ HL **Directions:** Nearest station: Bond Street At the corner of Brook & Davies St **Parking:** On street

England

The Greenhouse

LONDON W1

Modern European NOTABLE WINE LIST

Fine dining at a discreet Mayfair address

☎ 020 7499 3331 27a Hay's Mews W1J 5NY
Plan 4-H6
e-mail: reservations@greenhouserestaurant.co.uk
web: www.greenhouserestaurant.co.uk

A chic, modern Mayfair-mews restaurant, with a subtle botanical theme - in keeping with its name - comes stylishly kitted out in neutral tones and natural textures, and dotted with a classy collection of art nouveau decorative glass. The entrance is via a smartly furnished terrace garden with wooden decking between tables and pot plants, while inside it's smart, calm and softly lit. Talented chef Antonin Bonnet (formerly of Morton's, London) has taken over from Bjorn van der Horst and heads-up the highly accomplished kitchen at The Greenhouse in fine style. His modern approach is inspired by the highest-quality produce from the markets, putting a creative spin to French and Mediterranean classics on a fixed-price repertoire of lunch, carte and a brace of seven-course tasting options. Expect a rump of Limousin veal, perhaps served with bitter praline and salsify gratin, or braised and roasted pork with polenta and parmesan foam, and to finish, maybe a black truffle pannacotta with pear and pistachio.

Notable Wine List: Probably one of the largest wine lists in the UK with high-quality listings in every area.

Chef: Antonin Bonnet **Owners:** Marlon Abela Restaurant Corporation **Times:** 12-2.30/6.45-11, Closed 25-26 Dec, 1 Jan, BHs, Sun, Closed L Sat **Prices:** Fixed L £28-£55, Fixed D £60, Coffee £5, Min/Water £5, Service added but optional 12.5% **Wine:** 2331 bottles over £20, 8 bottles under £20, 18 by the glass (£6-£24) **Notes:** Tasting menu £75, Inspirational menu £85, Vegetarian available **Seats:** 65, Pr/dining room 10 **Smoking:** N/Sm in restaurant, Air con **Children:** Portions **Directions:** Nearest station: Green Park, Hyde Park, Bond St Behind Dorchester Hotel just off Hill St **Parking:** NCP, Meter Parking

Hakkasan

LONDON W1

Chinese

Exotic Chinese dining in central London

☎ 020 7927 7000 No 8 Hanway Place W1T 9DH
Plan 3-B3
e-mail: reservation@hakkasan.com

Secreted away in a back street off Tottenham Court Road, this dramatic, trendy basement Cantonese restaurant (brainchild of the now infamous Allen Yau) is accessed by an Indian slate stairwell (once you've cleared the on-duty doorman that is) and delivers exceptional Chinese cuisine. Dark and with a club-like atmosphere, Hakkasan is a bustling, incredibly popular restaurant and bar that attracts an adoring crowd. Yau's brief to his designer Christian Liagre was to 'bring back the dragon', the result is a dazzling modern, ethnic interior reflecting the wealth of Chinese culture. Think black lacquer and red calligraphy, delicate Balinese latticework to divide up seating areas and low-slung spotlights. Then add close-set, darkwood-polished tables and leather banquette seating, club-style music, a long bar and attentive, knowledgeable staff to the upbeat picture.

The lengthy menu is built on Cantonese foundations, with influences from other regions, and aptly suits the surroundings. Clean, distinct flavours, high-quality ingredients and authentic technical skills from an accomplished kitchen deliver on dim sum and carte menus. Think roasted silver cod with champagne and Chinese honey, or stir-fry black pepper rib-eye beef with merlot. There's a great cocktail list too.

Chef: C Tong Chee Hwee **Owners:** Alan Yau **Times:** 12-2.45/6-12.30, Closed 25 Dec, Closed L 26 Dec, 1 Jan, D 24 Dec **Prices:** Fixed L £30-£70, Fixed D £50-£100, Starter £5.50-£19, Main £12.50-£52, Dessert £6-£13.50, Coffee £2.50, Min/Water £4.50, Service added but optional 13% **Wine:** 340 bottles over £20, 10 by the glass **Notes:** Dim sum offered at lunchtimes, Vegetarian available, Dress Restrictions, No jeans, shorts, trainers, caps or vests **Seats:** 225 **Smoking:** Air con **Directions:** Nearest station: Tottenham Court Rd From station take exit 2, then 1st left, 1st right, restaurant straight ahead **Parking:** Valet parking (dinner only), NCP

LONDON W1 *continued*

The Grill Room (Dorchester Hotel)

British

Splendid food in opulent surroundings

☎ 020 7629 8888 The Dorchester, Park Ln W1A 2HJ Plan 4-G6
e-mail: thegrillroom@thedorchester.com
web: www.thedorchester.com

Newly redecorated, this grand hotel dining room has a whimsical feel to it. Highlanders on the walls and tartan on the floor make a striking statement, but the luxurious ambience and formal settings make this a wonderful venue to sample reliable dishes, new and old, from menus that change each Tuesday. As you would expect service is traditional, discreet and efficient. Seared scallops with cauliflower purée, citrus vinaigrette and mimolette crisps join established favourites like lobster soup to start. Rabbit leg with calves' sweetbreads and ceps or ragout of John Dory, lobster and mussels join perfectly roasted Aberdeen Angus rib as main course choices. Try the honey roast pear with cardamom custard to finish.

Chef: Olivier Couillaud **Owners:** The Dorchester Collection **Times:** 12.30-2.30/6-11 **Prices:** Fixed L £25, Fixed D fr £28, Starter £9.50-£18.50, Main £21.50-£30, Dessert £10.50, Coffee £4.90, Min/Water £4.75, Service added but optional 12.5% **Wine:** All bottles over £20, 15 by the glass (£8.50-£17) **Notes:** Fixed D 6-7.30pm, Sun L 3 courses £32.50, Vegetarian available, Dress Restrictions, Smart casual, Civ Wed 450 **Seats:** 81 **Smoking:** N/Sm in restaurant, Air con **Children:** Menu, Portions **Rooms:** 250 (250 en suite) ★★★★★ HL **Directions:** Nearest station: Hyde Park Corner On Park Ln, overlooking Hyde Park **Parking:** South Audley St

Hakkasan

see page 317

Kai Mayfair

Chinese

Luxurious venue for authentic Chinese cooking

☎ 020 7493 8988 65 South Audley St W1K 2QU Plan 4-G6
e-mail: kai@kaimayfair.co.uk
web: www.kaimayfair.co.uk

A setting of comfortable opulence is provided at this upmarket restaurant, with a décor of rich reds and muted gold and silver. Staff are dressed in military-style jackets finished with a Swarovski crystal emblem of the restaurant's name in Chinese characters. The kitchen prides itself on authenticity with some fairly traditional dishes, but new flavours are created and the repertoire adapted by including non-traditional ingredients, even ostrich. Eye-catching options are wasabi prawn tempura with mango salsa and basil seed, and braised abalone with Chinese broccoli and white truffle reduction.

Chef: Alex Chow **Owners:** Bernard Yeoh **Times:** 12-2.15/6.30-11, Closed 25-26 Dec, New Year **Prices:** Fixed L £23, Fixed D £50, Starter £7-£18, Main £13-£68, Dessert £5-£9.50, Coffee £3, Min/Water £4.50, Service added but optional 12.5% **Wine:** 100% bottles over £20, 10 by the glass (£4.90-£8.10) **Notes:** Tasting menu £75-100, Vegetarian available **Seats:** 110, Pr/dining room 12 **Smoking:** Air con **Directions:** Nearest station: Marble Arch Telephone for directions **Parking:** Directly outside

see advert opposite

Kilo

Traditional French V NEW

Contemporary French dining in chic Mayfair location

☎ 020 7629 8877 3-5 Mill St W1S 2AU Plan 3-A2
e-mail: reception@kilo-mayfair.co.uk
web: www.kilo-mayfair.co.uk

Newly refurbished Mayfair restaurant offering informal but chic dining behind huge plate glass windows. The décor is eclectic, with cork and wood effect flooring, polished wood tables and intricate black screens, while pink and brown flower murals add interest. Cooking style is modern French with an emphasis on fresh fish sold and priced by the kilo, hence the restaurant's name. Choices on the carte or the good-value menu du jour may include juicy scallops on tomato concasse, and red mullet with basil purée and sauce vièrge.

Chef: Renaud Marin **Owners:** Soren Jessen **Times:** 10-4/6-11, Closed 25 & 26 Dec, BHs, Sun **Prices:** Food prices not confirmed for 2007. Please telephone for details **Wine:** 30 bottles over £20, 15 bottles under £20, 6 by the glass (£4-£6) **Notes:** Dress Restrictions, Smart casual **Seats:** 60 **Smoking:** Air con **Children:** Portions **Directions:** Nearest station: Oxford Circus 2 mins walk from underground station, just off Conduit St

Latium

Italian NEW

Fresh, authentic Italian cooking

☎ 020 7323 9123 21 Berners St, Fitzrovia W1 Plan 3-B3
e-mail: info@latiumrestaurant.com
web: www.latiumrestaurant.com

Given the Latin name for the chef-patron's home town (Latina), this restaurant provides such authentic tastes and recipes you'll feel as though you were in Italy. The chef's unique passion for Italian cuisine means a great seasonal menu and authentic produce cooked with real flair and flavour. Ravioli is a particular speciality, taken to a new level with a separate menu offering a choice of five fresh filled pasta dishes as starters and five as mains. Try pumpkin ravioli with butter and sage to start, or a main course like artichoke ravioli with prawn. Grilled loin of veal with sautéed potato and Swiss chard shows the style.

Chef: Maurizo Morelli **Prices:** Food prices not confirmed for 2007. Please telephone for details

Levant

Lebanese, Middle Eastern V

Lebanese food in highly atmospheric setting

☎ 020 7224 1111 Jason Court, 76 Wigmore St W1H 9DQ Plan 2-G3
e-mail: info@levant.co.uk
web: www.levant.o.uk

Packed with Eastern promise - including belly dancers some evenings - this highly atmospheric basement restaurant is great fun. Descend the stone staircase into a dark and colourful world of rich tones, lanterns and candlelight, silk fabrics and Arabic artefacts. Polished-wood tables lend an unpretentious touch, there's a bar up front, and staff are friendly, knowledgeable and cheery. The menus offer a balanced selection of colourful Lebanese-style food, at its core the

continued on page 320

LONDON W1 *continued*

traditional mezze, made for sharing and eaten with fingers or excellent warm pitta - houmous, falafel, baba ghannuge (grilled aubergine dip, tahini and lemon juice). The lamb kafta showcases the accomplished cooking and deft seasoning with affordable prices.

Levant

Chef: Mike Smith **Owners:** Tony Kitous **Times:** 12/midnight, Closed 25-26 Dec **Prices:** Fixed L £6.95-£9.95, Fixed D £26.50-£42, Starter £4.75-£7, Main £12.50-£26, Dessert £5.75-£6.75, Coffee £2.75, Min/Water £3.50, Service added 12.5% **Wine:** 34 bottles over £20, 6 bottles under £20, 6 by the glass (£4.25-£8.50) **Notes:** Tasting menu £40, Vegetarian menu, Dress Restrictions, Smart casual **Seats:** 120, Pr/dining room 12 **Smoking:** No pipes, No cigars, Air con **Directions:** Nearest station: Bond Street From Bond St station, walk through St Christophers Place, reach Wigmore St, restaurant across road **Parking:** On street

Lindsay House Restaurant

see opposite

Locanda Locatelli

see page 322

Maze

see opposite

Memories - The Langham Hotel

Modern European **NEW**

British cuisine with a continental twist in grand surroundings

020 7973 7544 1c Portland Place W1B 1JA Plan 2-H4
e-mail: lonmemories@langhamhotels.com
web: www.langhamhotels.com

Built in 1865 and lavishly restored to its original splendour, this grandiose Victorian pile stretches across the bottom end of Portland Place. Memories restaurant has a grand-style old atmosphere, with high, hand-painted ceilings, impressive columns and a real colonial feel that takes you back to the days of the British Empire. Tables are elegantly set and service slick, knowledgeable and attentive. Cooking is modern British with French and continental influences and fixed-prices menus list a broad range of well-balanced dishes that make good use of quality seasonal ingredients. Mackerel fillets with aubergine foam, wild sea bass on a scallop risotto, roulade of braised lamb shank with white haricot beans and fennel, and pineapple pannacotta with Charentais melon carpaccio and watermelon granité show the style.

Chef: David Collard **Owners:** Langham Hotels **Times:** 12-2.30/6-10.30 **Prices:** Fixed L £20-£30, Fixed D £36.50-£45, Starter £8-£14, Main £14-£45, Dessert £6.50-£7.50, Coffee £4.25, Min/Water £5.25, Service added but optional 12.5% **Wine:** 350 bottles over £20, 24 by the glass (£5.50-£14.50) **Notes:** Sun L 3 courses £38.50, Vegetarian available, Dress Restrictions, Smart casual, Civ Wed 220 **Seats:** 70, Pr/dining room 30 **Smoking:** N/Sm area, No pipes, No cigars, Air con **Children:** Menu, Portions **Rooms:** 427 (427 en suite) ★★★★★ HL **Directions:** Nearest station: Oxford Circus On north end of Regent St, by Oxford Circus **Parking:** On street & NCP

Mirabelle

French

Classic French cuisine with Mayfair glamour

020 7499 4636 56 Curzon St W1J 8PA Plan 4-H6
e-mail: sales@whitestarline.org.uk
web: www.whitestarline.org.uk

The seductive glamour of Mirabelle continues to draw well-dressed crowds. It wears all the hallmarks of the Marco Pierre White empire well, with its easy cosmopolitan feel, art deco mirrors, resident pianist and displays of art. Professional plated service is slick with experienced French staff. Traditional Gallic cooking with notable simplicity and flavour maintains the restaurant's deserved reputation. Try a starter of dressed crab with sauce mayonnaise and melba toast, or a main course like grilled lobster with herbs and garlic and béarnaise sauce or

continued on page 323

England

Lindsay House Restaurant

LONDON W1

Modern British V

Vibrant flavours and top-notch ingredients in a Soho townhouse

☎ 020 7439 0450 21 Romilly St W1D 5AF Plan 3-C2
e-mail: richardcorrigan@lindsayhouse.co.uk
web: www.lindsayhouse.co.uk

This well-known Soho restaurant is discreetly tucked away behind the doors of an elegant townhouse. The four-storey building dates back to 1740 and instead of the restaurant frontage you might expect in Soho, it's all very low key and you have to ring the doorbell on arrival. Inside you'll find elegant traditional-style dining rooms on the ground and first floors, plus a private dining room called the Chef's Library on the second floor. Diners can choose from an array of menus at lunch and dinner including theatre, garden (vegetarian) and tasting menus to suit the occasion. The cooking style relies on carefully sourced top-quality ingredients and robust simple flavours, hallmarks of Richard Corrigan's Irish roots. It's hard to choose from all the delights on the menu. Simple dishes with wonderful ingredients include the likes of poached organic duck egg, spinach and girolles, and impressive technical skills are evident in dishes like duck five ways (duck ham, rillettes, roast foie gras, gizzards and crouton of own liver). Great flavour combinations are demonstrated in the likes of smoked eel and foie gras terrine with sour apple, or a dessert like the seasonal chocolate plate.

Chef: Richard Corrigan **Owners:** Searcy Corrigan **Times:** 12-2.30/6-11, Closed 2 wks Xmas, 1 wk Etr, BHs, Sun, Closed L Sat-Sun, D Sun **Prices:** Fixed L £27, Fixed D £52, Service added but optional 12.5%, Group min 8 service 15% **Notes:** Tasting menu 7 courses £69, Vegetarian menu, Dress Restrictions, Smart casual **Seats:** 50, Pr/dining room 40 **Smoking:** N/Sm area, No pipes, No cigars, Air con **Children:** Portions **Directions:** Nearest station: Leicester Square Just off Shaftesbury Avenue, off Dean Street **Parking:** NCP

Maze

LONDON W1

French, Asian 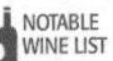 NOTABLE WINE LIST

Grazing in elegance at the heart of Mayfair

☎ 020 7107 0000 10-13 Grosvenor Square W1K 6JP Plan 2-G2
e-mail: maze@gordonramsay.com
web: www.gordonramsay.com

The latest addition to the Gordon Ramsay stable isn't difficult to find, with entrances from the imposing London Marriott Hotel Grosvenor Square or directly off Grosvenor Square. Contemporary and bright, the extensive dining area follows the maze theme, decked out in split-levels with the lowest at the centre, surrounded by a glass screen featuring the restaurant's maze motif. Tables are simply laid, while service exudes style and panache, from its professional demeanour to its knowledge. There is also a chef's table overlooking the main pass. Executive chef Jason Atherton, hot-foot from Ramsay's Dubai venture, Verre, delivers a modern French approach with Asian influences, via a fashionable, grazing-style menu featuring an impressive and appealing array of innovative, complex and highly accomplished tapas-style dishes that come dressed to thrill and showcase the best seasonal ingredients (with six to eight dishes recommended per head). There's also a traditional carte, essentially based on larger portions of the grazing options, plus a chef's menu - grazing dishes chosen by the kitchen. Expect the likes of Cornish crab mayonnaise with avocado, sweetcorn sorbet and Oscietra caviar to start, followed by grilled lamb with braised lamb neck, Cos lettuce, bacon and onions and ras el hanout. The 'flights of wines' innovation epitomises the attention to detail throughout, offering three glasses based on a country or grape variety, which ideally suits the grazing concept.

Notable Wine List: A well-chosen high-quality wine list including a diverse range by the glass, and an interesting wines by flight section which offers a trio of 125ml glasses.

Chef: Jason Atherton **Owners:** Gordon Ramsay Holdings Ltd **Times:** 12-2.45/6-11 **Prices:** Starter £6-£9, Main £6-£9, Dessert £3-£6.50, Coffee £4, Min/Water £4, Service added but optional 12.5% **Wine:** 266 bottles over £20, 5 bottles under £20, 18 by the glass (£5-£17) **Notes:** Fixed D 6-10 courses £37-£60, Vegetarian available, Dress Restrictions, Smart casual **Seats:** 90, Pr/dining room 10 **Smoking:** N/Sm in restaurant, Air con **Children:** Portions **Rooms:** 221 (221 en suite) ★★★★ HL **Directions:** Nearest station: Bond Street Hotel entrance in on Duke St, off Oxford St **Parking:** Grosvenor Sq

England

Locanda Locatelli

LONDON W1

Italian NOTABLE WINE LIST

Inspired Italian cuisine in chic contemporary setting that attracts a celebrity crowd

☎ 020 7935 9088 8 Seymour St W1H 7JZ Plan 2-F2
e-mail: info@locandalocatelli.com
web: www.locandalocatelli.com

Tucked away off Portman Square, a stone's throw from Marble Arch, this slick, sophisticated and much-vaunted Italian - about the best in the country - is set in the back of the Hyatt Regency Churchill Hotel and is the haunt of a well-heeled, celebrity crowd. Cream leather banquette seating, concave mirrors and subdued lighting (in the evenings) set the scene at this buzzy, classy David Collins' designed restaurant. Its retro yet stylish interior features parquet flooring, grained-wood walls, glass dividers and modern artworks, including pieces by Paul Simonan (of the Clash pop band) and Damien Hirst. The service is as sleek as the décor, Italian staff court customers with flair and passion, while chef Giorgio Locatelli glides between tables surveying his clientele and ensuring his delicious food is being enjoyed with the passion shown in its creation.

The ingredients are the absolute best, and the breads (think foccacio, pane carasau, grissini, etc) and pasta are phenomenal. The style is modern northern Italian, and there's a real freshness about the cooking, enhanced by great combinations while nothing is over-worked or too complicated, so flavours sing out. The traditionally laid-out menu offers plenty of choice, so do come hungry and set to go four rounds - antipasta, pasta, main and dessert - to do the ultimate justice to Giorgio's inspired cooking ... it doesn't come better in the Italian format. Think superb home-made egg pasta served with red mullet and black olives, perhaps roast rabbit leg with Parma ham, polenta and radicchio, or roast monkfish teamed with walnuts and caper sauce, and, maybe heading-up desserts, a signature tasting of Amedei chocolate with pine kernel ice cream. A sommelier is on hand to help navigate the impressive regionally-focused, all-Italian wine list with its superb vintages from Tuscany and Piemonte. But do book well in advance as it's always busy. This is one not to be missed.

Notable Wine List: An extensive and very high-quality Italian wine list.

Chef: Giorgio Locatelli
Owners: Plaxy & Giorgio Locatelli
Times: 12-3/7-11, Closed Xmas, New Year, BHs, Sun
Prices: Starter £7.50-£18, Main £12-£29.50, Dessert £6-£8.50, Coffee £2.20, Min/Water £3.50, Service optional
Wine: 400 bottles over £20, 3 bottles under £20, 10 by the glass (£3.50-£10)
Notes: Vegetarian available
Seats: 70
Smoking: No pipes, No cigars, Air con
Children: Portions
Rooms: 445 (445 en suite) ★★★★★ HL
Directions: Nearest station: Marble Arch Please telephone for directions
Parking: NCP adjacent, parking meters

England

LONDON W1 *continued*

pigeon from Bresse with foie gras, green cabbage and Madeira sauce. Simple classic desserts feature the likes of lemon tarte or raspberry soufflé. Private dining has a separate menu and there are great value set lunches.

Chef: Igor Timchishin **Owners:** Marco Pierre White, Jimmy Lahoud **Times:** 12-2.30/6-11.30, Closed 26 Dec & 1 Jan **Prices:** Fixed L £17.50, Starter £10.50-£20, Main £16.50-£27.50, Dessert £8.50, Coffee £3.50, Min/Water £3.50, Service added but optional 12.5%, Group min 12 service 15% **Wine:** 335 bottles over £20, 3 bottles under £20, 12 by the glass (£5-£10) **Notes:** Sun L 3 courses £22, Dress Restrictions, Smart dress **Seats:** 120, Pr/dining room 48 **Smoking:** No pipes, Air con **Children:** Portions **Directions:** Nearest station: Green Park Telephone for directions. Parking on street **Parking:** Berkeley Sq on street

Mosaico

Italian

Stylish Italian restaurant in a stylish London location

☎ 020 7409 1011 13 Albermarle St W1S 4HJ Plan 3-A1
e-mail: mosaico-restaurant.co.uk

This effortlessly chic Italian has an equally stylish location in the heart of Mayfair - beneath DKNY and opposite Brown's Hotel, just round the corner from The Ritz. Smart, predominantly Italian staff are skilled and attentive. Mirrors create an illusion of space so it doesn't feel like a basement, while red leather banquettes and chairs, and lots of wood create an air of luxury. The cooking style is fairly modern and speaks with a northern Italian accent, including some traditional dishes reinterpreted with a twist. Accurate cooking results in textbook risotto and the quality of the ingredients is allowed to shine through. Pasta, bread, grissini and ice creams are all home-made. A serious, all-Italian wine list.

continued

Times: 12-2.30/6.30-10.45, Closed Sunday, Closed L Sat, Sun, Xmas, Easter, BHs **Directions:** Telephone for further details

Nicole's

Modern Mediterranean

Fashionable restaurant for the chic & well-heeled

☎ 020 7499 8408 158 New Bond St W1Y 9PA Plan 3-A1
e-mail: nicoles@nicolefarhi.com
web: www.nicolefarhi.com

A wide stone staircase leads down to a split-level dining room located below the Nicole Farhi fashion store in an exclusive Bond Street location. The upper area has a steel and glass bar, while oak and leather predominates in the lower level, which is designed for more leisurely dining. Meals offered range through breakfast, lunch and dinner, plus a bar food option. Dishes are simple in style - think baked lemon and garlic crusted cod with crab mashed potatoes, or grilled spiced lamb rump with chickpea fries - based on high-quality seasonal ingredients.

Chef: Annie Wayte **Owners:** Stephen Marks **Times:** 12-3.30/6.30-10.30, Closed BHs, Sun **Prices:** Starter £6-£10.25, Main £18.95-£25, Dessert £7, Service added but optional 15% **Wine:** 47 bottles over £20, 4 bottles under £20, 20 by the glass (£5-£10.75) **Notes:** Vegetarian available **Seats:** 65, Pr/dining room 80 **Smoking:** N/Sm in restaurant, Air con **Directions:** Nearest station: Green Park, Bond St Between Hermes shop & Asprey

Nobu

LONDON W1

Japanese

Stylish, minimalist, upmarket Japanese with outstanding cuisine

☎ 020 7447 4747 Old Park Ln W1Y 4LB Plan 4-G5
e-mail: ecb@ecbpr.co.uk
web: www.noburestaurants.com

Taking up the whole of the first floor of the hip Metropolitan Hotel, Nobu (short for Nobuyuki Matsuhisa, the owner, who also has other restaurants in London, LA and New York) has international standing and woos a glamorous, fashion-conscious clientele, celebrities and foodies alike. The interior is stylish, ultra sleek and minimalist, its clean lines decked out in cool neutral colours, stark tiled floors, leather banquettes and chairs, while vast plate-glass windows deliver superb views over Park Lane and Hyde Park. It's still one of the most fashionable venues in town, so tables are fairly closely set, while a small bar-reception area comes with leather tub chairs. Black-clad staff are attentive, friendly and necessarily knowledgeable to guide the uninitiated through the lengthy, flexible-styled menu, predominantly aimed at grazing on smaller dishes and to share with dining companions. The accomplished kitchen's style is clearly Japanese but is enlivened by a twist of South America here and there. Dishes focus on exceptionally fresh produce, with defined and vibrant flavours and impressive presentation, as in black cod with miso, pan-fried Dover sole with red chilli shiso salsa, and beef 'toban' yaki. There's also a sushi bar to round up a class act. (See entry for sister Nobu Berkeley, also in W1, and Ubon by Nobu, E14.)

Chef: Mark Edwards **Owners:** Nobuyuki Matsuhisa, Robert de Niro, Drew Nieporent **Times:** 12-2.15/6-10.15, Closed 25-26, Dec, 31 Jan, BHs **Prices:** Starter £4-£16, Main £8.50-£35, Dessert £5.50-£9, Coffee £1.75, Min/Water £5, Service added but optional **Wine:** 200 bottles over £20, 16 by the glass (£5.50-£8) **Notes:** Tasting menu 7 courses £70, Vegetarian available **Seats:** 150, Pr/dining room 40 **Smoking:** N/Sm area, No pipes, No cigars, Air con **Directions:** Nearest station: Hyde Park, Green Park Please telephone for directions **Parking:** On street

England

LONDON W1 *continued*

Nobu Berkeley Street

Japanese NEW

Fun modern restaurant with a serious approach to food

☎ 020 7290 9222 15 Berkeley St W1J 8DY Plan 5-A6
e-mail: ecb@ecbpr.co.uk
web: www.noburestaurants.com

Sister of the famous Nobu restaurant off Park Lane, Nobu Berkeley is equally popular. Downstairs a large, stylish bar serves drinks till the early hours. The upstairs restaurant is open for dinner only and features a sushi bar with an open kitchen, a wood-burning oven and 12-seater hibachi table (a Nobu first), where guests can cook their own food with a chef's assistance. Décor is attractively designed with soft colours and tactile materials. Knowledgeable staff will happily guide you through the menus. Choose between the carte/grazing menu or the six-course tasting menu. Crispy Gloucester Old Spot pork with spicy miso is a hit, as is chocolate harumaki (spring rolls) with passionfruit dipping sauce.

Chef: Mark Edwards **Owners:** Nobu Natsuhisa, Robert de Niro **Times:** 6-1am, Closed 25 & 26 Dec, Closed L all week **Prices:** Starter £5-£16, Main £8.50-£26, Dessert £7.50-£9, Min/Water £4, Service added but optional 15% **Wine:** 10 by the glass (£5.50-£12) **Notes:** Vegetarian available **Seats:** 120 **Smoking:** N/Sm in restaurant, Air con **Directions:** Nearest station: Green Park Telephone for directions **Parking:** Mayfair NCP

No 6 Restaurant

Modern British

Combination of old and new, shop and restaurant turned food emporium

☎ 020 7935 1910 6 George St W1U 3QX Plan 2-G3

This upmarket deli-cum-restaurant just off the bottom end of Marylebone High Street draws an appreciative crowd. Beyond the shop under an atrium roof you can sit at one of a few wooden tables. The cream walls are hung with foodie pictures to whet your appetite as you browse the daily-changing menu. Everything is made in-house with the focus on fresh produce in the likes of a starter of chargrilled squid with chickpea purée and roasted pepper and lemon salsa. Try a main course of goat's cheese soufflé with lettuce, beetroot and walnut salad, and finish off with apple crumble and ginger ice cream.

Chef: Emma Miller **Owners:** Emma Miller **Times:** 8/6, Closed 10 days in Aug, Xmas & New Year & BHs, Sat-Sun, Closed D Mon-Fri **Prices:** Starter £5.50-£7.95, Main £10.50-£14.50, Dessert £4.95-£5.50, Coffee £2.95, Min/Water £3.25, Service optional **Wine:** 12 bottles over £20, 14 bottles under £20, 6 by the glass (£3.50-£3.75) **Notes:** Vegetarian available **Seats:** 30 **Smoking:** N/Sm in restaurant, Air con **Children:** Portions **Directions:** Nearest station: Bond St Just off Marylebone High St **Parking:** NCP, parking meters outside

Two Rosettes

The best local restaurants, which aim for and achieve higher standards, better consistency and where a greater precision is apparent in the cooking. There will be obvious attention to the selection of quality ingredients.

Orrery

Rosettes not confirmed at time of going to press

Modern European V

Flagship Conran offering stunning food and service in equal measures

☎ 020 7616 8000 55-57 Marylebone High St W1U 5RB Plan 2-G4
e-mail: oliviere@conran-restaurants.co.uk
web: www.orrery.co.uk

Aptly perched above the Conran shop, this first-floor restaurant is all cool, clean lines and sophisticated simplicity, with an etched glass screen at the far end depicting the namesake orrery - a mechanical model of the solar system. Flagship of the Conran galaxy of eateries and one of London's most prestigious dining venues, it's set on the high street in Marylebone village in what was once the site of Henry VIII's hunting lodge. The pedigree of the Conran design is unmistakable, contemporary, streamline and typically understated, it comes flooded by light from large arched windows and skylights. Two long rows of tables lined with banquettes and chairs fill the narrow, bright room, where service is as stylish as the surroundings, appropriately professional, hospitable and attentive. A small, intimate lounge bar for pre-meal drinks allows the opportunity to peruse the menu choice, which embraces a great-value three-course lunch jour (the Sunday dinner version includes a glass of champagne), lunch and dinner cartes, and a tasting Menu Gourmand and vegetarian option Menu Potager (both including the alternative of selected wines by the glass). The cooking style is suitably innovative and creative, light and contemporary, with its roots firmly in the classics. Meticulous presentation, highly accomplished technical skills, clean flavours and top-notch produce (including luxury items) pepper a repertoire set to thrill. Think tournedos of Scottish beef served with escargots bourguignon, or a tronçon of Cornish turbot with baby leaf spinach, girolle and sauce hollandaise, while a classic raspberry soufflé teamed with milk ice cream might head-up desserts. A suitably extensive wine list matches the stature of the cooking, while peripherals like canapés, amuse-bouche, pre-desserts and breads all hit top form, too, and add to the impressive experience factor.

We learned that there was a change of chef as we went to press.

Owners: Conran Restaurants **Times:** 12-2.30/6.30-10.30, Closed 25-26 Dec, New Year, Good Friday, Closed D 24 Dec **Prices:** Fixed L £23.50, Starter £9.50-£16.50, Main £18-£28, Dessert £6.50-£10, Coffee £3.50, Min/Water £3.75, Service added but optional 12.5% **Wine:** 960 bottles over £20, 2 bottles under £20, 18 by the glass (£3.75-£13.50) **Notes:** Tasting menu £55 (incl wine £90) Sun D 3 courses £30, Vegetarian menu **Seats:** 80 **Smoking:** N/Sm area, No pipes, Air con **Children:** Portions **Directions:** Nearest station: Baker St, Regents Park At north end of Marylebone High St **Parking:** NCP, 170 Marylebone Rd

Ozer

Turkish

A Turkish delight just a stone's throw from Oxford Street

☎ 020 7323 0505 5 Langham Place W1N 7DD
Plan 3-A3
web: www.sofra.co.uk

Handily positioned off Oxford Street and an ideal pitstop for those exhausted by shopping, this elegant Turkish restaurant has a comfortable bar area with brightly coloured cushions and low seating, leading through to the high-ceilinged dining room, with beautiful copper and marble effect walls. There's a busy, buzzy atmosphere at dinner but you never feel rushed, and the attentive staff are more than happy to advise and recommend. The menu is the same at lunch and dinner and offers a wide range of traditional cuisine, including excellent meze, as well as more unusual dishes. The cooking is simple and unfussy, with stylish, modern presentation. Try the seafood meze followed by tender marinated lamb or salmon bugulama, a delicious bulgar risotto with perfectly cooked salmon.

Times: noon/mdnt **Directions:** Nearest station: Oxford Circus 2 min walk towards Upper Regent Street.

Passione

Italian

Wonderful flavours from an intimate, lively Italian

☎ 020 7636 2833 10 Charlotte St W1T 2LT Plan 3-B3
web: www.passione.co.uk

Its pinkish-terracotta and glass frontage seem somewhat unremarkable for a widely esteemed Italian, though the name on the awning perfectly sums up this small but big-hearted restaurant, epitomizing chef-patron Gennaro Contaldo's love affair with great food. Green walls are hung with food photographs, while blond-wood floors and chairs add a modern edge to closely set tables and a lively, informal atmosphere. It's not difficult to see why Gennaro is a Jamie Oliver mentor, his regional Italian cooking driven by fresh, high quality seasonal produce, herbs and simple, clean-flavoured style. Think wild sorrel risotto, grilled turbot with a purée of carrot and celeriac mash and vegetables, or rabbit with rosemary, garlic and sauté potatoes.

Chef: Gennaro Contaldo & Mario Magli **Owners:** G Contaldo, G D'Urso, Liz Przybyuski **Times:** 12.30-2.15/7-10.15, Closed 1 wk Xmas, BHs, Sun, Closed L Sat **Prices:** Starter £9.50-£15, Main £21-£26, Dessert £7, Coffee £2.50, Service added but optional 12.5% **Wine:** 28 bottles over £20, 5 bottles under £20, 2 by the glass (£4) **Notes:** Vegetarian available **Seats:** 40, Pr/dining room 18 **Smoking:** No pipes, No cigars, Air con **Children:** Portions **Directions:** Nearest station: Goodge Street 5 min walk from underground station **Parking:** Nearby pay & display

Patterson's

Modern European

Delightful cuisine in an elegant setting

☎ 020 7499 1308 4 Mill St, Mayfair W1S 2AX
Plan 3-A2
e-mail: pattersonsmayfair@btconnect.com
web: www.pattersonsrestaurant.com

Situated near Savile Row, Patterson's provides an elegant setting for fine dining, with slick, professional service. The bar area leads to a spacious dining room with oak flooring, well-spaced tables and high-backed leather chairs. You can relax here and peruse the modern British menu, founded on carefully sourced local and organic produce. Father-and-son team Raymond and Tom produce dishes that surprise and delight with their flavour and presentation. Try a starter like crab lasagne with basil and shellfish cappuccino, or a main course of loin of lamb in filo pastry with spring vegetables and a purée of butter beans. Desserts offer some unusual combinations like nougatine torte with poached pineapple, almond cream and honeycomb.

Chef: Raymond & Thomas Patterson **Owners:** Raymond & Thomas Patterson **Times:** 12-3/5.30-11, Closed 25-26 Dec, 1 Jan, Good Fri & Etr Mon, Sun, Closed L Sat **Prices:** Fixed L £15, Starter £12, Main £17-£19, Dessert £11, Coffee £2.50, Min/Water £2.50, Service added but optional 12.5% **Wine:** 70 bottles over £20, 15 bottles under £20, 6 by the glass (£3.50-£7.50) **Seats:** 50, Pr/dining room 30 **Smoking:** N/Sm area, No pipes, Air con **Children:** Menu, Portions **Directions:** Nearest station: Oxford Circus Located off Conduit St opposite Savile Row entrance **Parking:** Savile Row

Pied à Terre

see page 326

The Providores

Fusion

A unique style of operation and fusion food

☎ 020 7935 6175 109 Marylebone High St W1U 4RX
Plan 2-G3
e-mail: anyone@theprovidores.co.uk
web: www.theprovidores.co.uk

The Providores provides an all-day café, wine/ tapas bar downstairs and a fine dining restaurant upstairs. Enjoy breakfast, brunch, great coffee and a fascinating menu of snacks and more substantial fare in the Tapa Room below, and an extensive choice of fusion food in the dining room above. Both menus change frequently according to produce and inspiration, but the food remains innovative and exciting: seared kangaroo fillet on butternut squash and tarragon fritter with babaganoush, kumquat relish and warrigals, for example, or roast black pepper and wattleseed-crusted New Zealand venison loin on umeboshi braised chicory and courgettes with salsify and sultana, caper and pistachio salsa.

Chef: Peter Gordon **Owners:** P Gordon, M McGrath, J Leeming **Times:** from 12-10.30, Closed 25-26, 31 Dec, 1 Jan **Prices:** Starter £5.60-£13.50, Main £17.60-£24, Dessert £8.60, Coffee £2.20, Min/Water £3, Service added but optional 12.5% **Wine:** 78 bottles over £20, 7 bottles under £20, 28 by the glass (£5.50-£8.50) **Notes:** Vegetarian available **Seats:** 38 **Smoking:** N/Sm in restaurant, Air con **Children:** Portions **Directions:** Nearest station: Bond St Baker St Regents Park From Bond St station cross Oxford St, down James St, into Thayer St then Marylebone High St

England

Pied à Terre

LONDON W1

Modern French V NOTABLE WINE LIST

Outstanding, highly refined modern cooking

☎ 020 7636 1178 34 Charlotte St W1T 2NH Plan 3-B3
e-mail: info@pied-a-terre.co.uk
web: www.pied-a-terre.co.uk

There have been dramatic changes since its closure following a fire and subsequent rebuild and refurbishment, which sees this class-act return from the ashes and step up a gear with some superlative and exciting cooking. The frontage of the intimate venue is as unassuming as ever, while the interior refurbishment is fittingly stylish and glamorous. Four large crescent-shaped booths line one side of the room, while smaller tables for two or four flank the other. The décor is contemporary and oozes understated luxury, with cream suede rosewood furniture and architectural glass combining harmoniously. There's also a newly created bar upstairs to allow diners more time to chill out both pre- and post-meal, featuring leather seats and art by Hamilton, Blake and Hodgkin. Oz-born chef Shane Osborn has a new redesigned kitchen from which to deliver his brand of stylish and creative modern French cuisine, which has, like the décor, stepped up a notch. It's sophisticated, refined and brimful of emphatic flavours and class, using tip-top quality ingredients and innovation - technically superb it ticks all the boxes. The tantalizing fixed-price repertoire of lunch, carte and eight-course tasting option promotes an agony of choice, delivering top-drawer dishes.
Think roasted cod served with a ragout of lentils and root vegetables, celery purée, oxtail and red wine, while dessert might feature a mango rice pudding with poached pineapple and coconut sorbet. A stunning range of ancillaries.

Notable Wine List: A wine list full of passion, depth and top quality complemented by an excellent wine team.

Chef: Shane Osborn
Owners: David Moore & Shane Osborn
Times: 12-2.45/6.15-11, Closed 2 wks Xmas & New Year, Sun, Closed L Sat
Prices: Fixed L £24.50-£49.50, Fixed D £60, Coffee £4.50, Min/Water £4, Service added but optional 12.5%
Wine: 700 bottles over £20, 10 bottles under £20, 12 by the glass (£5-£12)
Notes: Tasting menu £75, Vegetarian menu
Seats: 40, Pr/dining room 12
Smoking: N/Sm in restaurant, Air con
Directions: Nearest station: Goodge Street S of BT Tower and Goodge St
Parking: Cleveland St

England

LONDON W1 *continued*

Quo Vadis

Modern Italian

Showcase for authentic Italian cuisine and modern art

☎ 020 7437 9585 26-29 Dean St W1D 3LL Plan 3-B2
e-mail: sales@whitestarline.org.uk
web: www.whitestarline.org.uk

Although Karl Marx once lived in this building, one of the oldest in Soho, its real claim to fame has been as 'Leo Quo Vadis', one of London's most respected Italian restaurants, founded in the 1930s by Peppino Leoni. The ground floor restaurant has stained glass windows and a simply restored interior displaying striking works of art by artists like Damien Hirst, Andy Warhol and Modigliani. The modern Italian cuisine is just as impressive, serving up antipasti, pasta, risottos, fish, meat and salad dishes on an authentic and varied Italian menu. Try marinated salmon in Jamaican coffee and seasonal fruit salad to start, perhaps followed by ravioli filled with lobster, mandarin and vanilla sauce. Fish dishes include interesting combinations like pan-fried John Dory with wild asparagus fondue of fennel and orange powder.

Chef: Fernando Corradazzi **Owners:** Jimmy Lahoud, Marco Pierre White **Times:** 12-2.30/5.30-11.30, Closed 24-25 Dec, 1 Jan, Sun, Closed L Sat **Prices:** Fixed L £14.95, Fixed D £19.95, Starter £7-£11, Main £9-£18.50, Dessert £5, Coffee £3.50, Min/Water £3.50, Service added but optional 12.5% **Wine:** 34 bottles over £20, 3 bottles under £20, 6 by the glass **Notes:** Pre-theatre and tasting menu available, Vegetarian available **Seats:** 80, Pr/dining room 90 **Smoking:** No pipes, Air con **Parking:** On street or NCP

Rasa Samudra

Indian V

Authentic Keralan seafood and vegetarian restaurant

☎ 020 7637 0222 5 Charlotte St W1T 1RE Plan 3-B3
e-mail: dasrasa@hotmail.com
web: www.rasarestaurants.com

The showy pink exterior stands out in this street of restaurants, but inside it's surprisingly traditional, with several different rooms decorated with exotic Indian art, and statues of Hindu gods and goddesses. Friendly staff bring delicious poppadoms and pickles while you choose from the entirely seafood and vegetarian menu. Don't expect regular Indian food. Keralan dishes like Kappayum Meenum - mild king fish curry with a turmeric and cassava sauce, Crab Varuthathu - crab cooked with ginger, curry leaves, chilli and mustard seeds, and masala dosa - paper-thin pancake filled with spicy potatoes, onions and ginger, served with sambar and coconut chutney, bring the authentic flavour of this Indian region to London.

continued

Chef: Prasad Mahadevan Nair **Owners:** Das Shreedharan **Times:** 12-3/6-11, Closed 2 wks Dec, Closed L Sun **Prices:** Fixed L £22.50-£30, Fixed D £22.50-£30, Starter £4.25-£7.50, Main £6.25-£12.95, Dessert £2.75-£3.50, Coffee £1.95, Min/Water £3, Service added but optional 12.5% **Wine:** 6 bottles over £20, 6 bottles under £20, 1 by the glass (£2.95) **Notes:** Fixed L 3 courses, Vegetarian menu **Seats:** 100, Pr/dining room 70 **Smoking:** N/Sm in restaurant, Air con **Directions:** Nearest station: Tottenham Court Road, Goodge Street Telephone for directions

Rasa W1

Indian V

Impressive South Indian cuisine from Kerala

☎ 020 7629 1346 6 Dering St W1S 1AD Plan 2-H2
e-mail: dasrasa@hotmail.com
web: www.rasarestaurants.com

This pleasant Indian restaurant is tucked away just off New Bond and Oxford streets. It's an offshoot of the mini-group created by Das Shreedharan that has put regional Keralan cuisine on the capital's eating-out map. While inside continues the theme of classical Indian décor and temple atmosphere, its highly authentic, village-style Southern Indian cooking of the Kerala draws the crowds. Vegetarian food maybe a speciality, but lamb, chicken and fish have their place too, as does a splendid array of pre-meal snacks and pickles. Expect vibrant, fresh flavours and diverse textures, perhaps lamb puff to start, followed by chicken curry roasted in coriander and coconut, with banana dosa to finish.

Chef: Sasidharan Nair **Owners:** Das Shreedharan **Times:** 12-3/6-11, Closed 24-30 Dec, 1 Jan, Sun **Prices:** Fixed L £19.50-£25, Fixed D £19.50-£25, Starter £4.25-£7.50, Main £6.25-£12.95, Dessert £2.50-£3.50, Coffee £1.95, Min/Water £3, Service added but optional 12.5% **Wine:** 6 bottles over £20, 6 bottles under £20 **Notes:** Fixed L 3 courses, Vegetarian menu, Casual **Seats:** 75 **Smoking:** N/Sm area, No pipes, No cigars, Air con

The Red Fort

Mughal Court

Stylish, elegant and contemporary Soho Indian

☎ 020 7437 2525 77 Dean St W1D 3SH Plan 3-B2
e-mail: info@redfort.co.uk
web: www.redfort.co.uk

The listed, red-painted, carved-timber façade of this stalwart Soho Indian might suggest it's lost in a time warp, but don't be fooled, this is a stylish, contemporary, upmarket affair. The entrance leads to either its subterranean Akbar Bar or ground-floor dining room, where restful, neutral tones set the scene alongside walls adorned with authentic artefacts. At the back, there's a water feature and open kitchen. Banquettes line walls, tables are laid with white linen and staff are smartly turned out. The menu embodies the theme, while dishes are primarily Mughal Court/North Western in style and utilise top-notch ingredients. Think Gressingham duck with pineapple, lemongrass, cinnamon and tamarind sauce.

Chef: Iqbal Ahamad **Owners:** Amin Ali **Times:** 12-2.15/5.45-11.15, Closed 24-26 Dec, Closed L Sat & Sun **Prices:** Fixed L £20-£45, Fixed D £35-£45, Starter £6-£9.50, Main £14-£29.50, Dessert £6-£7, Coffee £2.50, Min/Water £4.95, Service added but optional 12.5% **Wine:** 30 bottles over £20, 5 bottles under £20, 9 by the glass (£4.75-£5.50) **Notes:** Set L £12, pre theatre £16, Vegetarian available, Dress Restrictions, No shorts or sports clothes **Seats:** 84 **Smoking:** N/Sm area, No pipes, No cigars, Air con **Directions:** Nearest station: Leicester Square Walk north on Charing Cross Rd. At Cambridge Circus turn left into Shaftesbury Ave. Dean St is 2nd road on right

LONDON W1 *continued*

The Ritz

British, European NOTABLE WINE LIST

Sumptuous cuisine from a Piccadilly grandee

☎ 020 7493 8181 150 Piccadilly W1J 9BR Plan 5-A6
e-mail: enquire@theritzlondon.com
web: www.theritzlondon.com

Renowned as one of the most beautiful dining rooms in Europe, the Ritz restaurant is an opulent confection of Louis XVI furnishings, gold chandeliers, and trompe d'oeil frescos. Dressing up is de rigueur, so break out the glad rags and make the most of the occasion by booking ahead for a table overlooking the patio and park. The menu is as grand as the setting; rooted in classical French cuisine with the odd nod to modern trends, it's crammed with luxury ingredients, and offers an array of choice that's sure to cause pleasurable dithering. Butter-poached Cornish lobster scented with cardamom and coriander is a typical main, while desserts might include cinnamon sablé with raspberry cream, honeycomb croquant and lemon sorbet.
Notable Wine List: A classic and well chosen wine list full of depth and quality.

Chef: John T Williams **Owners:** Ritz Hotel (London) Ltd **Times:** 12.30-2.30/6-11 **Prices:** Fixed L £35-£37, Fixed D £65-£80, Starter £14-£28, Main £19-£47, Dessert £13-£28, Coffee £6, Min/Water £5.50, Service included **Wine:** 725 bottles over £20, 8 by the glass (£9-£11) **Notes:** Fixed L 3 courses, Fixed D 4 courses, Menu Sonata £90, Vegetarian available, Dress Restrictions, Jacket & tie requested, no jeans or trainers, Civ Wed 50 **Seats:** 90, Pr/dining room 14 **Smoking:** Air con **Children:** Menu, Portions **Rooms:** 133 (133 en suite) ★★★★★ HL
Directions: Nearest station: Green Park 10-minute walk from Piccadilly Circus or Hyde Park Corner **Parking:** NCP on Arlington Street

Roka

Japanese

Stylish and friendly Japanese grill

☎ 020 7580 6464 37 Charlotte St W1T 1RR Plan 3-B3
e-mail: info@rokarestaurant.com
web: www.rokarestaurant.com

With its floor-to-ceiling windows overlooking Charlotte Street, and a mix of wood, stainless steel and glass, Roka is a modern and funky place matched by some seriously good cooking. A centrally located robata grill dominates proceedings and the bar-style seating allows diners to watch the chefs in the open kitchen. The menu is designed around the Japanese robatayaki grill cuisine, as well as an impressive selection of fresh, vibrant sushi and sashimi dishes. A rice hot pot with king crab and wasabi tobiko, wagyu beef with fresh wasabi and Japanese mushrooms or pork and golden scallop dumplings are typical offerings.

Chef: Rainer Becker, Nic Watt **Owners:** Rainer Becker, Arjun Waney **Times:** 12-2.30/5.30-11.30, Closed 25-26 Dec, 1 Jan, Closed L Sun **Prices:** Starter £2.60-£10.60, Main £8.90-£18.60, Dessert £5.60-£8.90, Coffee £2.50, Min/Water £3.90, Service added but optional 12.5% **Wine:** 99% bottles over £20, 1% bottles under £20, 10 by the glass (£4.75-£10) **Notes:** Tasting menus 5-12 courses fr £15, Vegetarian available **Seats:** 90 **Smoking:** N/Sm in restaurant, Air con **Children:** Portions **Directions:** Nearest station: Goodge St/Tottenham Court Rd 5 min walk from Goodge St **Parking:** on street

Salt Yard

Mediterranean NEW

Tapas restaurant offering vibrant dishes combined with friendly service

☎ 020 7637 0657 54 Goodge St W1T 4NA Plan 3-B4
e-mail: info@saltyard.co.uk
web: www.saltyard.co.uk

Enjoy relaxed informal dining in the ground-floor bar area with its deep red walls and comfortable seating, or go downstairs to the non-smoking restaurant area where you have a view of the kitchen. Décor is simple with bare wood tables and comfortable high-backed chairs. Lunch and dinner menus are the same, the tapas menu offers a range of bar snacks, charcuterie, cheese and excellent breads. The well-constructed main menu is based around a good selection of Spanish and Italian influenced meat, fish and vegetable tapas, focussing on seasonal ingredients and interesting combinations. Dishes to look out for are courgette flowers stuffed with Monte Enebro goat's cheese and drizzled with honey or confit of pork belly with cannellini beans. Service is relaxed, friendly and informative.

Chef: Brian Villahermosa **Owners:** Sanja Morris & Simon Mullins **Times:** 12-3/6-11, Closed BHs, 25 Dec & 1 Jan, Sun, Closed L Sat **Prices:** Main £2.75-£12, Dessert £4.50-£5.50, Coffee £2, Min/Water £2.75, Service added but optional 10% **Wine:** 25 bottles over £20, 12 bottles under £20, 9 by the glass (£2.95-£5.95) **Notes:** Tapas menu prices, Vegetarian available **Seats:** 60 **Smoking:** N/Sm area, Air con **Directions:** Nearest station: Goodge St Near Tottenham Court Rd **Parking:** NCP Cleveland St, meter parking Goodge Place

Sartoria

Italian NEW

Modern Italian with a 'tailored' theme at the heart of Saville Row

☎ 020 7534 7000 & 7534 7030 20 Savile Row W1S 3PR Plan 3-A2
e-mail: sartoriareservations@conran-restaurants.co.uk
web: www.conran.com

Part of the Conran empire, this sophisticated Italian restaurant is true to its Savile Row location with a tailoring theme. This extends from the suited mannequins to 'tape measure' ashtrays, and crockery with a button logo. Even the seats are embroidered with a needle and thread motif. Don't let this distract you from the menu though, where there is plenty of good seasonal Italian food on offer. The style is sophisticated yet artisan using quality ingredients in dishes like roasted monkfish with baked radicchio and raspberry and amaretti pannacotta. The extensive regional Italian wine list is well worth a look and the pre-theatre menu is great value.

continued

Chef: Pasquale Amico **Owners:** Sir Terence Conran **Times:** 12-3/6-11, Closed 25-26 Dec, Sun, Closed L Sat **Prices:** Fixed L £19.50, Fixed D £24.50, Starter £6.50-£10.50, Main £16.50-£22.50, Dessert £5.50-£6.50, Coffee £2, Min/Water £3.50, Service added but optional 12.5% **Wine:** 340 bottles over £20, 10 bottles under £20, 12 by the glass (£4.50-£13.50) **Notes:** Vegetarian available, Dress Restrictions, Smart casual preferred **Seats:** 90, Pr/dining room 45 **Smoking:** Air con **Directions:** Nearest station: Oxford Circus/Green Park Tube to Oxford Circus, take exit 3, turn left down Regent St towards Piccadilly Circus, take 5th right into New Burlington St, end of street on left **Parking:** On street

Sherlock Holmes Hotel

Modern Mediterranean

Traditional methods for inspirational cuisine

☎ 020 7486 6161 Sherlock Holmes Hotel, 108 Baker St W1U 6LJ Plan 2-F4
e-mail: shh.fb@parkplazahotels.co.uk
web: www.sherlockholmeshoteluk.com

Situated in a chic boutique hotel there's no mistaking the links to the famous fictional detective with paintings and a bronze cast to remind diners of his Baker Street roots. The décor is chic and unfussy with warm colours and modern styling. Interestingly, a mesquite wood-burning stove and a charcoal grill are the main methods of cooking here. The emphasis is on quality ingredients with international inspiration for the various dishes. Try teriyaki marinated Scottish salmon fillet with sautéed bok choy and spring onion noodles for example.

Chef: Rachid Hammoum **Owners:** Park Plaza Hotels **Times:** 12-2.30/6-10.30 **Prices:** Fixed L fr £12.50, Starter £7.50-£10.50, Main £11.50-£26, Dessert £6-£7, Coffee £2.50, Min/Water £4.25, Service added 12.5% **Wine:** 31 bottles over £20, 3 bottles under £20 **Notes:** Vegetarian available, Civ Wed 60 **Seats:** 50, Pr/dining room 50 **Smoking:** N/Sm in restaurant, Air con **Children:** Portions **Rooms:** 119 (119 en suite) ★★★★ **Directions:** Nearest station: Baker Street Located on Baker Street, close to the tube station **Parking:** Chiltern street

Shogun, Millennium Hotel Mayfair

Japanese

Authentic Japanese food in the heart of Mayfair

☎ 020 7629 9400 Grosvenor Square W1A 3AN Plan 2-G1

This well established, Japanese restaurant is located in the lavishly decorated basement of the Millennium Hotel Mayfair, an impressive Georgian fronted building overlooking Grosvenor Square. From its discreet entrance, a winding staircase sweeps its way down to the attractive restaurant and a small sushi bar on the left. The simple wooden tables are set with bamboo place mats and at one end of the room a substantial shrine has been set up, complete with a large samurai figure. Shogun produces some of the best Japanese food in the capital, with a number of good-value set dinners and zenzai, dobin-mushi, sashimi, tempura, teriyaki and dessert options.

Times: 6-11, Closed Mon

Sketch (Lecture Room & Library)

see page 330

Le Soufflé, InterContinental London

Rosettes not confirmed at time of going to press

Modern French

Luxurious dining with a French theme

☎ 020 7409 3131 1 Hamilton Place, Hyde Park Corner W1J 7QY Plan 4-G5
e-mail: london@interconti.com
web: www.london.interconti.com

Centrally located, overlooking Hyde Park and the London skyline, this much-loved landmark provides luxury facilities and a high standard of service to an international clientele. Le Soufflé is the hotel's elegant restaurant serving modern French cuisine in sophisticated surroundings. *At the time of going to press the hotel was undergoing a refurbishment, due to reopen in autumn 2006.*

Times: 12.30-3/7-10.30, Closed 1st wk Jan, BHs, Sun & Mon, Closed L Sat **Rooms:** 451 (451 en suite) ★★★★★ **Directions:** Nearest station: Hyde Park Corner Telephone for directions

Spiga

Italian

Perennially popular, crowd-pleasing modern Italian

☎ 020 7734 3444 84/86 Wardour St W1V 3LF Plan 3-B2
web: www.spigasoho.co.uk

Bustling, glass-fronted Soho Italian high on decibels with simple contemporary décor and busy, efficient staff that strut their stuff in long black aprons. Tiled floors, close-set laminated wooden tables, diner-style booths with leather banquette seating or modern chairs, walls decked out in colourful posters and a buzzy, youthful clientele set the scene. A wood-burning oven and glass-fronted kitchen add to the theatre, turning out crowd-pleasing pizzas and pastas dishes, alongside more upmarket offerings like chargrilled tuna steak with

continued on page 331

England

Sketch (Lecture Room & Library)

LONDON W1

French V NOTABLE WINE LIST

Technical wizardry offers a unique experience

☎ 0870 777 4488 9 Conduit St W1S 2XG Plan 3-A2
web: www.sketch.uk.com

Unassuming from outside, with its white-shuttered windows and iron railings, the un-savvy might easily walk on by, save for the evening doorman outside to catch the attention. Once inside though, this one-time HQ of Christian Dior comes brimful of surprises. A collaboration between Mourad Mazouz and Parisian super-chef Pierre Gagnaire that offers a multi-level food-based extravaganza, which includes the vibrant, ground-floor Gallery brasserie plus a cool tea room by day, hyper-trendy bar by night. Throughout, fashionable international designers have created specially commissioned signature pieces that catch the eye. The fine-dining Lecture Room and Library upstairs is opulently decorated in shades of orange with pale leather-tiled panels on walls, while brightly coloured carpets and long lampshades cut a somewhat Middle Eastern edge. Service is professional, attentive and necessarily knowledgeable, and there's a small lounge to enjoy the champagne trolley. Dishes bear the unmistakable creative genius of consultant Pierre Gagnaire's distinctive culinary style. Innovative and technically superb, the very best quality fresh produce is transformed into an enormous range of textures and flavours. It's complex and deeply French, with dishes combining many elements, as in 'Langoustines Addressed in Four Ways', perhaps a main's fillet of venison, served with a marmalade of red cabbage and cranberry, quince purée and saffron, and horseradish cream and chestnut ice cream, while to finish, 'Grand Desserts' could arrive as seven dishes. Be prepared to be wowed by the experience and sheer theatre of the place.
Notable Wine List: A beautifully chosen wine list full of quality wines throughout, complete with tasting notes.

Chef: P Gagnaire, P Sanchez
Owners: Pierre Gagnaire, Mourad Mazouz
Times: 12-2.30/7-10.30, Closed 25 Dec, Sun-Mon, Closed L Sat
Prices: Fixed L £35, Starter £34-£52, Main £46-£56, Dessert £18-£34, Service added but optional 12.5%
Wine: 500 bottles over £20, 10 bottles under £20, 20 by the glass (£5-£24)
Notes: Fixed 6 course D £65-£90, Vegetarian menu
Seats: 50
Smoking: N/Sm area, Air con
Directions: Nearest station: Oxford Circus 4 mins walk from Oxford Circus tube station, take exit 3, down Regent St, Conduit St is 4th on right
Parking: Cavendish Sq

rocket, fresh tomatoes and roasted potatoes, or pan-fried beef fillet with a potato rösti and sautéed ceps.

Chef: Nick Bell **Owners:** Vince Power **Times:** 12/12, Closed Xmas, New Year, Closed L Sun **Prices:** Fixed L £15.50, Fixed D £15.50-£19.50, Starter £3.95-£11.50, Main £8-£19.50, Dessert £6.95, Coffee £1.80, Min/Water £2.80, Service added but optional 12.5% **Wine:** 15 bottles over £20, 12 bottles under £20, 8 by the glass (£3.50-£8) **Notes:** Vegetarian available **Seats:** 120 **Smoking:** No pipes, No cigars, Air con **Directions:** Nearest station: Oxford Street At Shaftesbury Ave end of Wardour St

❀ *Spoon at Sanderson*

Modern European V

Alain Ducasse mix-and-match concept

☎ 020 7300 1444 50 Berners St W1T 3NG Plan 3-B3
e-mail: spoon@morganshotelgroup.com
web: www.morganshotelgroup.com

A cool restaurant in a hip, cutting-edge, Philippe Starck-designed hotel that delivers real wow factor, with striking 80 foot onyx Long Bar and Courtyard Garden that provides a leafy oasis for alfresco dining. The food is as trendy as the décor. Lunch offers a grazing-style concept of small dishes, while dinner introduces further potential to the mix-and-match approach; follow the chef's recommended compositions, or choose your own combination such as crab cake with honey vinaigrette and manzanilla sorbet to start, followed by pan-seared tuna with satay sauce and wok-sautéed vegetables, finishing with exotic square.

Times: 12 2.30/6-11 **Directions:** Nearest station: Oxford Circus Restaurant on Berners St off Oxford St

❀❀❀ The Square

see below

❀❀ Sumosan Restaurant

Modern Japanese

Authentic Japanese cooking at an upmarket Mayfair address

☎ 020 7495 5999 26 Albermarle St, Mayfair W1S 4HY Plan 3-A1
e-mail: info@sumosan.com
web: www.sumosan.com

This cosmopolitan Japanese restaurant is located in the heart of Mayfair, surrounded by exclusive jewellers, designer clothes shops and fine art vendors. It's a popular venue both with the local business community and those looking for authentic cuisine, and has a pared down modern décor of cool clean lines, parquet flooring, and polished darkwood tables. All the bases are covered, from teppan-yaki and tempura to sushi and sashimi; you can choose from an extensive carte, or plump for the seven-course lunch selection which is exceptional value. Kick off with baby squid in teriyaki sauce perhaps, or sea bream carpaccio, before tucking into the likes of beef teppan-yaki, or chicken yakitori.

Chef: Bubker Belkhit **Owners:** Janina Wolken **Times:** 12-3/6-11.30, Closed Xmas, New Year, BHs, Closed L Sat-Sun **Prices:** Starter £3.50-£19, Main £7.50-£55, Dessert £6-£8.50, Coffee £2.50, Min/Water £3.75, Service added but optional 12.5% **Wine:** 87 bottles over £20, 3 bottles under £20, 9 by the glass (£4-£9) **Notes:** Tasting menu L £45, D 65, Vegetarian available **Seats:** 115, Pr/dining room 40 **Smoking:** N/Sm area, No pipes, Air con **Children:** Portions **Directions:** Nearest station: Green Park Please telephone for directions

❀❀❀
The Square

LONDON W1

French NOTABLE WINE LIST

A class culinary act in the heart of Mayfair

☎ 020 7495 7100 6-10 Bruton St W1J 6PU Plan 3-A1
e-mail: info@squarerestaurant.com
web: www.squarerestaurant.com

Style and sophistication lurk beyond the glass frontage of this discreet, chic restaurant just off fashionable Bond Street. The expansive dining room is furnished in contemporary style, with terracottas, rich browns, steely blues and creams all harmonising. Parquet floors are set out with clothed tables, their rich brown, floor-length undercloths topped-off with crisp white linen, while striking, vibrant abstract artworks add a splash of colour to the neutral tones.

A superb wine list and Philip Howard's bright, intense cooking prove more than a match for the elegant surroundings and professional service. His modern approach is underpinned by a classical French theme; the repertoire, which includes an eight-course tasting option, is dotted with luxury items.

Cultured dishes display an emphasis on well-sourced, top-notch ingredients and strong, clear flavours, and come dressed to thrill. Take a signature starter of Cornish crab lasagne with a cappuccino of shellfish and basil, perhaps followed by saddle of lamb with shallot purée, while a classic tarte Tatin of pineapple with lime ice cream might round things off.

Notable Wine List: A top-class wine list full of first-class growers and vintages.

Chef: Philip Howard **Owners:** Mr N Platts-Martin & Philip Howard **Times:** 12-3/6.30-10.45, Closed 24-26 Dec,1 Jan, Closed L Sat & Sun, BHs **Prices:** Fixed L £25-£50, Fixed D £60, Coffee £5, Min/Water £4.25, Service added but optional 12.5% **Wine:** 1200 bottles over £20, 10 bottles under £20, 14 by the glass (£4.95-£15) **Notes:** Tasting menu £75, Vegetarian available **Seats:** 70, Pr/dining room 18 **Smoking:** N/Sm in restaurant, Air con **Directions:** Nearest station: Bond Street, Green Park Telephone for directions

England

LONDON W1 *continued*

Taman Gang

South East Asian

Vivacious, upmarket basement venue with late opening and elegant cuisine

☎ 020 7518 3160 141 Park Ln W1K 7AA Plan 2-F2
e-mail: info@tamangang.com
web: www.tamangang.com

Leave the chaos of Marble Arch behind and descend to this exotic, dimly lit, split-level basement bar and dining room packed with Eastern promise. Hand-carved limestone walls, mahogany furniture, lanterns and low banquettes evoke the look and feel of ancient Indonesia. Flickering candles, white orchids, contemporary music and youthful, knowledgeable and attentive black-clad staff add to the trendy, atmospheric vibe. The cuisine fits the surroundings, a fashionable, modern, sophisticated Pan-Asian mix, kind of Chinese by way of Japan and Thailand. Stunning presentation, tip-top ingredients, vibrant flavours and skilful handling from a repertoire that promotes sharing. Expect dishes like dim sum platter starter, followed by marinated black cod and fresh hoba miso and black bean. Don't miss the Oriental-inspired cocktail list.

Times: 12-3.30/6-1, Closed L Mon-Sat

Tamarind

Indian

Contemporary, classy Indian in Mayfair

☎ 020 7629 3561 20 Queen St, Mayfair W1J 5PR Plan 4-H6
e-mail: manager@tamarindrestaurant.com
web: www.tamarindrestaurant.com

The entrance may be a simple door leading on to a staircase, but it delivers you to this sophisticated and glamorous, designer-styled basement Indian in the heart of Mayfair, decked out in contemporary, minimalist style and graced by elegantly attired, attentive and friendly staff. Muted metallic colours, low lighting and a glass theatre kitchen add to the sense of style, with the kitchen delivering a medley of traditional and contemporary cuisine - focused around the tandoor oven - and cooked in authentic north-west Indian style. Expect neatly presented, subtle dishes to grace an appealing menu; perhaps tender lamb cutlets marinated with raw papaya, garlic, paprika and star anise, or supreme of chicken marinated with mint, coriander, green chillies and pomegranate seeds.

Chef: Alfred Prasad **Owners:** Indian Cuisine Ltd. **Times:** 12-2.45/6-11, Closed 25-26 Dec,1 Jan, Closed L Sat, BHs **Prices:** Fixed L fr £16.95, Fixed

continued

D fr £48, Starter £6.50-£12, Main £12.95-£24, Dessert £6-£7.50, Coffee £2.50, Min/Water £4.50, Service added but optional 12.5% **Wine:** 138 bottles over £20, 4 bottles under £20, 12 by the glass (£4-£12) **Notes:** Pre-theatre 6-7pm fixed D 2 courses £22.50, Dress Restrictions, No jeans, no shorts **Seats:** 90 **Smoking:** No pipes, No cigars, Air con **Directions:** Nearest station: Green Park Towards Hyde Park, take 4th right into Half Moon St to end (Curzon St). Turn left, Queen St is 1st right **Parking:** NCP

Teca

Modern, Traditional Italian

Classy Italian in fashionable Mayfair

☎ 020 7495 4774 54 Brook's Mews WIK 4EG Plan 2-H2
web: www.tecarestaurant.com

A stylish, modern Italian restaurant, tucked away behind Claridges in well-heeled Mayfair. The wide glass frontage gives way to a spacious restaurant with light wooden floors, crisply clothed tables and quality table settings. The food is simplicity itself, focusing on traditional Italian ingredients of the highest quality. The Italian and English menu is extensive, so take some time to choose from dishes like home-made strozzapreti pasta with black olives and guinea fowl ragout, or osso buco lamb stew with puréed potatoes. Classic desserts include peach and Amaretto charlotte with caramel sauce and there is a good selection of Italian cheeses, served with home-made bread and chutney.

Chef: Luca Conti **Owners:** Teca Restaurant Ltd **Times:** 12-2.30/7-10.30, Closed Xmas, New Year, Easter, BHs, Sun, Closed L Sat **Prices:** Fixed D £32.50, Starter £8-£15, Main £9-£15, Dessert £7, Coffee £3, Min/Water £3.50, Service added but optional 12.5% **Wine:** 320 bottles over £20, 4 bottles under £20, 14 by the glass (£4-£8) **Notes:** Vegetarian available, Dress Restrictions, Smart casual **Seats:** 55 **Smoking:** No pipes, No cigars, Air con **Children:** Portions **Directions:** Nearest station: Bond Street Please telephone for directions **Parking:** Brooks St

La Trouvaille

French

Classic French with a modern twist

☎ 020 7287 8488 12a Newburgh St W1F 7RR Plan 3-A2
e-mail: contact@latrouvaille.co.uk
web: www.latrouvaille.co.uk

Set among the cobbled pedestrian lanes and boutiques off Carnaby Street, this restaurant is quite a find, as the name suggests. Refurbished to create a first-floor dining room offering modern style and a relaxed atmosphere, the ground floor is now a chic wine bar with a short snack menu. The menu is seriously French, with starters like marinated frogs' legs with parsnip gratin and cream of cauliflower. For the main course, perhaps try 'bavette de boeuf Galloway marinée', marinated skirt of Galloway beef served with traditional accompaniments like red wine and shallot sauce, gratin dauphinoise and green beans. 'Crème brûlée du moment' needs no translation.

Chef: Mr Pierre Renaudeau **Owners:** T Bouteloup **Times:** 12-3/6-11, Closed Xmas, BHs, Sun **Prices:** Fixed L £15, Fixed D £33, Coffee £2.25, Min/Water £2.95, Service added but optional 12.5% **Wine:** 40 bottles over £20, 9 bottles under £20, 11 by the glass (£3.50-£7.50) **Notes:** Vegetarian available **Seats:** 45, Pr/dining room 30 **Smoking:** N/Sm in restaurant **Children:** Portions **Directions:** Nearest station: Oxford Circus Off Carnaby St by Liberty shop **Parking:** NCP (off Broadwick St)

England

Umu

see below

Vasco & Piero's Pavilion Restaurant

Italian

Genuine taste of Umbria in intimate, family-run restaurant

☎ 020 7437 8774 15 Poland St W1F 8QE Plan 3-B2
e-mail: vascosfood@hotmail.com
web: www.vascosfood.com

Conveniently tucked away close to the London Palladium and Liberty, this cosy corner restaurant looks somewhat unassuming from outside, but don't be deceived. Once inside the bijou, family-run eatery, the wonders of real Umbrian food and warm hospitality come to life. Closely packed tables, subtle lighting, a warm terracotta colour scheme and attentive, helpful Italian service add to the authenticity. The chef-patron hails from Umbria and imports many speciality products direct from the region, while the kitchen's intelligently simple treatment of high-quality ingredients is key here. Menus may change daily but clear, vivid flavours reign supreme in dishes like hand-made tagliatelle with black truffles, or perhaps calves' liver and sage with spinach.

Chef: Vasco Matteucci **Owners:** Tony Lopez, Paul Matteucci & Vasco Matteucci **Times:** 12-3/6-11, Closed BHs, Sun, Closed L Sat **Prices:** Fixed D fr £26, Starter £5-£9.50, Main £9.50-£18.50, Dessert £6.75, Coffee £2.50, Min/Water £3.40, Service added but optional 12.5% **Wine:** 20 bottles over £20, 10 bottles under £20, 6 by the glass (£4-£7) **Notes:** Vegetarian available, Dress Restrictions, No shorts **Seats:** 50, Pr/dining room 36

continued

Smoking: No pipes, Air con **Children:** Min 5 yrs, Portions **Directions:** Nearest station: Oxford Circus From Oxford Circus turn right towards Tottenham Court Rd, continue for 5min and turn right into Poland St. On corner of Great Marlborough St & Noel St **Parking:** NCP car park opposite

Veeraswamy Restaurant

Indian

Sophisticated Indian with refined traditional cooking

☎ 020 7734 1401 Mezzanine Floor, Victory House, 99 Regent St W1B 4RS Plan 3-B1
e-mail: veeraswamy@realindianfood.com
web: www.realindianfood.com

Plush, Mogul-style carpets sit on gleaming black Indian granite or darkwood floors, shimmering chandeliers and vibrant coloured lanterns hang from ceilings, adding to the sophisticated, chic

continued

Umu

LONDON W1

Japanese

Sophisticated Japanese offering high-quality Kyoto cuisine

☎ 020 7499 8881 14-16 Bruton Place W1J 6LX Plan 2-H2
web: www.umurestaurant.com

You need to keep an eye out for this classy Mayfair Japanese, tucked away just off Berkeley Square. There are no flashing lights or large signs, its discreet frontage is almost club-like, a touch button sliding open the wooden front door onto welcoming staff and a sophisticated modern interior. Award-winning designer Tony Chi has created his vision of opulent Kyoto styling, with high-quality wood and mirrors, banquette seating and a chef's central sushi table. Staff are attentive, necessarily knowledgeable and helpful in guiding diners through the menu maze.

The cooking - from chef Ichiro Kubota - suits the surroundings and offers both classic and contemporary interpretations of Kyoto cuisine, delivered via fixed-price lunch option, extensive carte, a separate sushi menu, and six tasting options. The carte itself splits neatly into appetisers, sashimi, main courses, soups and rices, and desserts. The sheer quality of ingredients and the freshness, clarity, vibrancy and combinations of flavours strike through in every dish and combine with great attention to detail in superb presentation. So dig deep into the pockets and expect to be wowed by the likes of grilled toro teriyaki with yuzu-flavoured grated radish and fresh wasabi, or perhaps kuwayaki-roasted duck in a rich soy sauce.

Chef: Ichiro Kubota **Owners:** Marlon Abela Restaurants Corporation **Times:** 12-2.30/6-11, Closed Between Xmas & New Year, BHs, Sun **Prices:** Fixed L £22-£44, Fixed D £60-£130, Starter £5-£16, Main £8-£45, Dessert £6-£8, Coffee £3, Min/Water £4, Service added but optional 12.5% **Wine:** 480 bottles over £20, 2 bottles under £20, 14 by the glass (£6-£18) **Notes:** Fixed L 3 courses, Fixed D 4-6 courses, Tasting menu avail, Vegetarian available **Seats:** 60, Pr/dining room 12 **Smoking:** N/Sm in restaurant, Air con **Directions:** Nearest station: Green Park/Bond St Off Bruton St & Berkeley Sq

LONDON W1 *continued*

atmosphere at London's oldest Indian restaurant, now restored to its glamorous, former 1920's glory. Latticed silver screens, silver banquettes or upholstered chairs and large tables ooze comfort, alongside views over Regent Street. Classic Indian dishes from the north and west coast grace its menu, authentically and freshly prepared with quality ingredients. Take a Kashmiri rogan josh, or Kerala recipe sea bass fillets with red spices cooked in a banana leaf.

Chef: Gopal Kochak **Owners:** R Mathrani, C Panjabi & N Panjabi **Times:** 12-2.30/5.30-11.30, Closed D Xmas **Prices:** Fixed L fr £16, Starter £5.50-£10.50, Main £10.50-£26, Dessert fr £5.50, Coffee £2.50, Min/Water £3.95, Service added 12.5% **Wine:** 64 bottles over £20, 3 bottles under £20, 11 by the glass (£4.30-£8.60) **Notes:** Fixed L 3 courses, Vegetarian available **Seats:** 114, Pr/dining room 36 **Smoking:** N/Sm area, No pipes, No cigars, Air con **Directions:** Nearest station: Piccadilly Entrance near junct of Swallow St and Regent St, in Victory House

Villandry

Modern International

Impressive restaurant, quality foodstore and bar

☎ 020 7631 3131 170 Great Portland St W1W 5QB Plan 3-A4
e-mail: contactus@villandry.com
web: www.villandry.com

You can enter directly into the restaurant from the street or via its buzzy bar but, as Villandry prizes the quality of its ingredients, entering through its upmarket foodstore really whets the appetite. The glass-fronted, high-ceilinged room is clean and modishly minimalist, plain white with stone floors and crisp white linen. The modern approach, accurate cooking and simple presentation makes the most of quality, seasonal produce via appealing, brasserie-style menus that change twice daily (at lunch and dinner). Main dishes include smoked haddock and cod fishcake, sautéed spinach and parsley sauce, or grilled calves' liver with bubble and squeak, sauce diable and crispy bacon.

Chef: David Rood **Owners:** Jamie Barber **Times:** 12-3/6-10.30, Closed 23 Dec-2 Jan, BHs, Closed D Sun **Prices:** Starter £5.75-£9.75, Main £11.50-£19.75, Dessert £4.50-£5.75, Coffee £2.25, Min/Water £3, Service added but optional 12.5% **Wine:** 120 bottles over £20, 22 bottles under £20, 12 by the glass (£3.75-£9.50) **Notes:** Vegetarian available **Seats:** 100, Pr/dining room 18 **Smoking:** N/Sm in restaurant, Air con **Children:** Menu, Portions **Directions:** Nearest station: Great Portland Street/Oxford Circus Restaurant entrance at 91 Bolsover St **Parking:** Outside restaurant

Westbury Hotel

Modern French

Accomplished cooking at an exclusive Mayfair hotel

☎ 020 7629 7755 & 8382 5450 Bond St W1S 2YF Plan 3-A2
e-mail: restaurant@westburymayfair.com
web: www.westburymayfair.com

Built in 1955, the hotel is styled on the Westbury in New York and is home to the renowned Polo Bar. The restaurant overlooks Conduit Street, with its own street entrance, and has a contemporary classic look with panelled walls and an attractive fireplace. Breakfast, lunch and dinner are served, and afternoon tea in the lounge is recommended. A range of modern dishes includes caramelised fillet of monkfish Polonaise, and best end of new season lamb with pressed shoulder and fricassee of sweetbreads. Staff are friendly, knowledgeable and impeccably professional.

Chef: Daniel Hillier **Owners:** Cola Holdings Ltd. **Times:** 12-2.30/6-10.30, Closed Sun, Closed L Sat **Prices:** Fixed L fr £24.95, Starter £8.50-£13.50, Main £17.50-£23.50, Dessert £6-£7.50, Coffee £4.45, Min/Water £4, Service added 12.5% **Wine:** 240 bottles over £20, 6 bottles under £20, 12 by the glass (£5.50-£11) **Notes:** Vegetarian available **Seats:** 70, Pr/dining room 16 **Smoking:** N/Sm in restaurant, Air con **Children:** Menu, Portions **Rooms:** 247 (247 en suite) ★★★★ **Directions:** Nearest station: Oxford Circus, Piccadilly Circus, Green Park Telephone for directions **Parking:** Burlington St

The Wolseley

European

Bustling domed brasserie offering stylish all-day dining

☎ 020 7499 6996 160 Piccadilly W1J 9EB Plan 5-A6
web: www.thewolseley.com

This European café-style phenomenon continues to be a crowd-pleaser. The former Wolseley car showroom has been reinvented as a buzzing restaurant with a glass-domed roof. The show never stops from 7am to midnight - the menus range from breakfasts to all-day snacks and afternoon tea packages, right through to a full carte including soups, starters, crustacea and caviar, salads, eggs and pasta, fish, entrées, grills, dish of the day and desserts. Whatever and whenever you want to eat you're sure to find something to suit a busy lifestyle here.

Chef: Cyrus Cato, Alex Scrimgeour **Owners:** Chris Corbin & Jeremy King **Times:** 7am-mdnt, Closed 25 Dec,1 Jan, Aug BHs, Closed D 24 Dec, 31 Dec **Prices:** Starter £5.25-£17.25, Main £9.50-£28.50, Dessert £4-£7, Service optional **Wine:** 40 bottles over £20, 7 bottles under £20, 28 by the glass (£4.25-£11.25) **Notes:** Vegetarian available **Seats:** 150 **Smoking:** N/Sm area, No pipes, No cigars, Air con **Children:** Portions **Directions:** Nearest station: Green Park 500mtrs from Underground station

Yauatcha

Chinese V

Oriental cuisine with formal service

☎ 020 7494 8888 15 Broadwick St W1F 0DL
Plan 3-B2
e-mail: reservations@yauatcha.com

This Soho restaurant is found in 'The Igeni' building, designed by Richard Rogers, with the interior by Christian Liagre. Features include fish tanks embedded in several walls and one that creates the bar. Two distinct spaces mean a tranquil upstairs tea house serving over 150 teas and various pastries, and a more atmospheric basement Dim Sum restaurant with low seating. Traditional Cantonese cooking, some Japanese and other Oriental specialities are on offer. Relaxed and friendly formal Asian service means well-informed waiters who can create a bespoke menu for you. Try baked and grilled dishes like stir fry black pepper venison or roast silver cod with baby leek in Chinese honey and Shaio Hsing wine.

Chef: Mr Wong **Owners:** Alan Yau **Times:** 12/11.30, Closed 24-25 Dec, Closed L 26 Dec, 1 Jan **Prices:** Fixed L £30, Fixed D £50-£60, Starter £3.50-£14.50, Main £5.50-£38, Dessert £3.95-£13.50, Coffee £2.60, Min/Water £4.50, Service added but optional 13% **Wine:** 71 bottles over £20, 5 bottles under £20, 8 by the glass (£4.20-£5.90) **Notes:** Vegetarian available **Seats:** 109 **Smoking:** N/Sm in restaurant, Air con **Directions:** Nearest station: Tottenham Ct Rd, Piccadilly Circ, Oxford Circ On the corner of Broadwick and Berwick St **Parking:** Poland Street - 100 yds

YMing

Chinese

Chinese regional specialities in Theatreland

☎ 020 7734 2721 35-36 Greek St W1D 5DL
Plan 3-C2
e-mail: cyming2000@blueyonder.co.uk
web: www.yming.co.uk

This stylish restaurant is less frenetic than its Chinatown neighbours. Duck-egg blue walls with jade carvings surround well-spaced and crisply clothed tables. Helpful staff guide the uninitiated through set and à la carte menus of Cantonese and regional and historic dishes like Ta T'sai (an 18th-century lamb dish from the Qian Long court). Try Mo Shu Pork or nymph mushroom (poor man's abalone) to start, followed by steamed fish of the day, Hunanese Dongan chicken or Szechuan shredded pork and crisp, fresh snow peas, Chinese leaves or choi sum.

Chef: Aaron Wong **Owners:** Christine Yau **Times:** noon-11.45, Closed 25-26 Dec, 1 Jan, Sun (ex Chinese New Year) **Prices:** Fixed L £10-£20, Fixed D £15-£20, Starter £3-£7, Main £6.50-£16, Dessert £2.50-£5.50, Coffee £1.60, Min/Water £3.60, Service added 10% **Wine:** 24 bottles over £20, 20 bottles under £20, 8 by the glass (£3.50-£6.50) **Notes:** Vegetarian available, clean and tidy dress **Seats:** 60, Pr/dining room 25 **Smoking:** N/Sm area, Air con **Parking:** China town car park

Yumi Restaurant

Japanese

Authentic Japanese restaurant

☎ 020 7935 8320 110 George St W1H 5RL Plan 2-G3

Staff are friendly and helpful here and one of the menus is in picture form so guests have an idea of what to order. The rest of the menu is

continued

in Japanese and English. Service is formal Japanese with kimono-clothed staff keeping vigil over the predominantly Japanese customers. The main dining area is in the basement with a few private dining areas off the main room. With an array of sushi, sashimi, tempura and terriyaki dishes to choose from, typical main dishes include grilled king fish marinated in miso paste or chicken yakitori.

Times: 5.30-10.30 **Directions:** Telephone for further details

Carluccio's Caffè

☎ 020 7629 0699 Fenwick, New Bond St W1A 3BS
Quality Italian chain.

Carluccio's Caffè

☎ 020 7636 2228 8 Market Place, Oxford Circus W1N 7AG

Carluccio's Caffè

☎ 020 7935 5927 St Christopher's Place W1U 1AY

Chor Bizarre

☎ 020 7629 9802 & 7692 8542 16 Albermarle St, Mayfair W1S 4HW
web: www.theaa.com/restaurants/112193.html

Regional Indian cuisine with emphasis on lighter Kashmir dishes.

The Delhi Brasserie

☎ 020 7437 8261 44 Frith St W1D 4SB
web: www.theaa.com/restaurants/114011.html

Handy location off Soho Square. Traditional, elegant decor, and lots of old favourites on the menu.

England

LONDON W1 *continued*

Eat & Two Veg

☎ 020 7258 8595 50 Marylebone High St W1U 5HN
web: www.theaa.com/restaurants/113933.html

A super modern diner straight from a cosmopolitan vegetarian's dining dream. Open for breakfast, lunch and dinner seven days a week, serving delicious meat-free food in a lively, light-hearted atmosphere.

Elena's L'Etoile

☎ 020 7636 1496 30 Charlotte St W1T 2NG
web: www.theaa.com/restaurants/113934.html
Immerse yourself in old-fashioned bistro style and bistro cooking. Elena herself makes the rounds to be sure you're being cared for. The menu includes the classics as well as more contemporary dishes.

The Gay Hussar

☎ 020 7437 0973 2 Greek St, Soho W1D 4NB
web: www.theaa.com/restaurants/114054.html
A mainstay of Soho for decades, the menu is original, authentic and unlike any other you will find in the capital. Favourite dishes include chilled wild cherry soup and the Kolozsvari Toltott Kaposzta, or Transylvanian stuffed cabbage with sauerkraut and smoked bacon and sausage.

Marsala Zones

☎ 020 7287 9966 9 Marshall St W1F 7ER
Modern Indian with a balanced approach.

Michael Moore Restaurant

☎ 020 7224 1898 19 Blandford St, Marylebone W1U 3DH
web: www.theaa.com/restaurants/113952.html
Fine global cuisine in a warm, intimate restaurant, filled with natural light.

New World Chinese Restaurant

☎ 020 7434 2508 1 Gerrard Place W1D 5PA
In the heart of London's Chinatown, dim sum is a favourite here.

Patara

☎ 020 7437 1071 15 Greek St W1D 4DP
The fourth London branch of this popular modern Thai concept chain.

La Porte des Indes

☎ 020 7224 0055 32 Bryanston St W1H 7EG
web: www.theaa.com/restaurants/113567.html
Indian eatery with eclectic menu in former Edwardian ballroom.

Sardo

☎ 020 7387 2521 45 Grafton Way W1P 5LA
Authentic and satisfying Sardinian specials in a relaxed setting.

Signor Zilli

☎ 020 7734 3924 40 & 41 Dean St W1D 4PR
Fashionable Italian at the heart of medialand. Expect celebrities and good fish.

Strada

☎ 020 7287 5967 15-16 New Burlington St W1S 3BJ
Superior pizza from quality ingredients cooked in wood-fired ovens.

Strada

☎ 020 7580 4644 9-10 Market Place W1W 8AQ
Superior pizza from quality ingredients cooked in wood-fired ovens.

Wagamama

☎ 020 7292 0990 10a Lexington St W1R 3HS
Informal noodle bars with no booking.

Wagamama

☎ 020 7409 0111 101a Wigmore St W1H 9AB

Yo! Sushi

☎ 020 7287 0443 52 Poland St
Sushi, sashimi, noodles and more.

Yo! Sushi

☎ 020 7318 3944 Selfridges Food Hall, 400 Oxford St W1A 1AB

Zilli Fish

☎ 020 7734 8649 36-40 Brewer St W1F 9TA
Fish with an Italian accent from the ebullient Aldo Zilli.

LONDON W2

 Assaggi

Italian V

A popular buzzing restaurant with Sardinian/Italian cuisine

☎ 020 7792 5501 39 Chepstow Place W2 4TS
Plan 2-A2
e-mail: nipi@assaggi.demon.co.uk

Located in a Victorian townhouse in Notting Hill, this bright, colourful restaurant is above the fashionable Chepstow Pub. Large windows give the dining room a fresh, airy feel and its unpretentious décor makes diners feel right at home, the friendly staff ensuring a warm welcome and invaluable help with translating the menu. It's a great place for people-watching but the food shouldn't be overlooked - this is quality Italian with a leaning toward regional Sardinian cooking. Try dishes like pecorino con carpegna e ruculo (light, crisp breads with grilled pecorino cheese, rocket and wafer-thin Italian ham) or fritto misto - a mixture of fried fish and seafood. Simple classics, done well.

continued

Chef: Nino Sassu **Owners:** Nino Sassu, Pietro Fraccari **Times:** 12.30-2.30/7.30-11, Closed 2 wks Xmas, BHs, Sun **Prices:** Starter £8.50-£12.90, Main £17.50-£19.90, Dessert £6.70, Coffee £1.90, Min/Water £2.90, Service optional **Wine:** 24 bottles over £20, 3 bottles under £20, 6 by the glass (£4.50-£5.50) **Notes:** Vegetarian available **Seats:** 35 **Smoking:** No pipes, No cigars, Air con **Children:** Portions **Directions:** Nearest station: Notting Hill Gate Telephone for directions

Island Restaurant & Bar

Modern British

Contemporary hotel restaurant with a relaxing atmosphere

☎ 020 7551 6070 Royal Lancaster Hotel, Lancaster Ter W2 2TY Plan 2-D2
e-mail: eat@islandrestaurant.co.uk
web: www.islandrestaurant.co.uk

Relaxed, contemporary hotel restaurant that can be entered via the salubrious reception area or directly from the street. Huge plate glass windows overlooking the park opposite bring plenty of light, and comfy chairs and solicitous waiting staff make it easy to linger. There is a split level bar and open-plan kitchen. In the evening, crisp white tablecloths and dramatic lighting bring an extra touch of glamour. Quality seasonal ingredients are handled with skill to produce daily changing menus, presented in a pleasingly minimalist style. A good balance between fish and meat can bring a simple whole lemon sole with herb and brown shrimp butter or caramelised pork belly, pork cheek ravioli, black pudding and butter bean broth.

Chef: Leigh Biggins **Owners:** Lancaster Landmark Hotel Co Ltd. **Times:** 12-3/6-10.45 **Prices:** Fixed L £12, Fixed D £15-£22, Starter £4.50-£9.50, Main £10.50-£40, Dessert £6-£10, Coffee £2.50, Min/Water £3.50, Service added but optional 12.5% **Wine:** 22 bottles over £20, 4 bottles under £20, 6 by the glass (£4-£16) **Notes:** Dress Restrictions, Smart casual **Seats:** 90 **Smoking:** N/Sm area, Air con **Children:** Menu, Portions **Parking:** 50

Nipa Thai Restaurant

Thai

Fine authentic Thai cuisine overlooking Hyde Park

☎ 020 7551 6039 The Royal Lancaster Hotel, Lancaster Ter W2 2TY Plan 2-D2
e-mail: nipa@royallancaster.com
web: www.royallancaster.com

Situated on the first floor of the large Royal Lancaster Hotel, this is a surprisingly intimate affair, decked out in authentic Thai fashion with teak panelling and original artefacts, while picture windows overlooking Hyde Park and efficient, friendly service add to the experience. Its Thai chefs produce quality dishes - including regional specialities - on a lengthy, reasonably priced menu, where chilli symbols helpfully indicate spicing levels. Think roasted duck in red curry, or baked prawns and glass noodles mixed with galangal, mushrooms and coriander root, and simple desserts like Thai coconut ice cream.

Chef: Nongyao Thoopchoi **Owners:** Lancaster Landmark Hotel Co Ltd **Times:** 12-2/6.30-10.30, Closed Xmas, New Year, BHs, Sun, Closed L Sat **Prices:** Fixed D £27-£30, Starter £5.85-£7.25, Main £9.40-£14.35, Dessert £5.90-£6.50, Coffee £2.80, Min/Water £4.50 **Wine:** 28 bottles over £20, 1 bottle under £20, 2 by the glass (£4.25) **Notes:** Fixed D 4 courses, Dress Restrictions, Smart casual **Seats:** 55 **Smoking:** Air con **Children:** Portions **Rooms:** 416 (416 en suite) ★★★★ HL **Directions:** Nearest station: Lancaster Gate Opposite Hyde Park on Bayswater Rd. On 1st floor of hotel **Parking:** 30

Royal China

Chinese

Ever-popular, traditional Bayswater Chinese

☎ 020 7221 2535 13 Queensway W2 4QJ Plan 2-B1
e-mail: royalchina@btconnect.com
web: www.royalchinagroup.co.uk

Don't be deceived by the smallish shop front, the large dining room extends way back, decked out in black-and-gold lacquered walls, mirrors, and etched glass and teak screens that create more intimate areas. Lots of Chinese diners are a testimony to its success. Classic Chinese food, with quality ingredients, especially seafood, clean-cut dishes and flavours. The extensive menu is bolstered by several set options, with dim sum a favourite and available daily. A typical meal might include deep-fried soft-shell crab and spicy salt or steamed scallop with soy and coriander to start with sautéed beef with chilli and black bean sauce to follow.

Chef: Kevin Man **Owners:** Pearl Investments LTD **Times:** 12/11, Closed 25-26 Dec **Prices:** Fixed D fr £30, Starter £4.50-£18, Main £7.50-£28, Dessert £4.20-£6.50, Coffee £2, Min/Water £3.50, Service added but optional 13% **Wine:** 40 bottles over £20, 6 bottles under £20, 6 by the glass (£4.50-£8) **Notes:** Fixed D 4 courses, Vegetarian available **Seats:** 180, Pr/dining room 20 **Smoking:** Air con **Directions:** Nearest station: Bayswater, Queensway Stn Please telephone for directions **Parking:** NCP opposite

Chair

☎ 020 985 0400 98 Westbourne Grove W2 5RU
web: www.theaa.com/restaurants/113993.html

Café-style restaurant and designer furniture show room all in one. Modern British menu and staff who are keen to please.

Levantine

☎ 020 7262 1111 26 London St, Paddington W2 1HH
Authentic Lebanese restaurant in the heart of Paddington.

Yo! Sushi

☎ 020 7727 9392 Unit 218, Whiteleys Shopping Centre W2 6LY
Sushi, sashimi, noodles and more.

Yo! Sushi

☎ 020 7706 9550 Unit R07, The Lawn, Paddington Station W2 1HB
Sushi, sashimi, noodles and more.

England

LONDON W4

Sam's Brasserie & Bar

European NEW

All-day stylish brasserie with friendly service and quality food

☎ 020 8987 0555 11 Barley Mow Passage W4 4PH Plan 1-C3
e-mail: info@samsbrasserie.co.uk
web: www.samsbrasserie.co.uk

Just off the Chiswick High Road down a narrow passageway, this large, airy former paper factory plays host to a bustling bar and brasserie. Patron Sam (Harrison) himself, worked as general manager to Rick Stein's Padstow empire, while chef Rufus Wickham has an impressive track record, too. Designed in New York loft style, the high ceilings, exposed pipe-work, pillars and white walls cut a trendy, timeless industrial edge, while the abstract artwork adds colour. There's a bar at

continued

the back, split-level restaurant, semi-open kitchen, friendly service and a relaxed vibe. The cooking fits the bill perfectly - intelligently simple, and focusing on quality seasonal ingredients and clear flavours. Fish here is superb. Grilled red mullet with rocket and salsa verde or roast cod with apple and potato gratin, followed by the comfort of apple crumble and custard perhaps.

Chef: Rufus Wickham **Owners:** Sam Harrison **Times:** 12-3/6.30-10.30 **Prices:** Fixed L £11.50, Starter £4.75-£12, Main £8.75-£17.50, Dessert £4.75-£6, Coffee £2, Min/Water £3, Service added but optional 12.5% **Wine:** 43 bottles over £20, 21 bottles under £20, 19 by the glass (£3.25-£6.75) **Seats:** 100 **Smoking:** N/Sm in restaurant, Air con **Children:** Menu **Directions:** Nearest station: Chiswick Park/Turnham Green Behind Chiswick High Rd, next to the green **Parking:** Metered parking

La Trompette

see below

Le Vacherin

French

Smart Parisian-style bistro serving uncomplicated French cuisine

☎ 020 8742 2121 76-77 South Pde W4 5LF Plan 1-C3
e-mail: malcolm.john4@btinternet.com
web: www.levacherin.co.uk

Full-length windows and a green frontage pick out this slice of leafy Chiswick that's forever France. Blond-wood floors, mirror-frieze lined walls, foodie pictures and posters, French staff clad in long white

continued

La Trompette

LONDON W4

European NOTABLE WINE LIST

French-inspired cuisine at chic, popular restaurant

☎ 020 8747 1836 5-7 Devonshire Rd, Chiswick W4 2EU Plan 1-C3
e-mail: reception@latrompette.co.uk
web: www.latrompette.co.uk

Set on a quiet side street in fashionable Chiswick, La Trompette sings its own praises, with a more flamboyant frontage than its neighbours that singles it out from the crowd. Potted box trees and an awning cordon off the small outside dining area with a certain style, replete with heaters and white cloths. The tinted-glass, sliding-door frontage adds a further classy, self-assured note, and, with Nigel Platts-Martin and Bruce Poole as its owners (of Chez Bruce fame), there's no doubting this brasserie-style outfit's pedigree. A muted colour scheme prevails over a sophisticated, relaxing interior, decked out in chocolate leather banquettes, smartly dressed tables and light-oak floors. Efficient, knowledgeable and friendly French service adds a reassuring note, while an award-winning wine list provides a star turn (complete with sommelier) alongside a bustling but unpretentious atmosphere. The accomplished modern European cooking continues the evolved take on French cooking under the assured wing of James Bennington (ex Chez Bruce), delivered via appealing, daily-changing, fixed-price menus. Simple, brasserie-style dishes, with fresh, quality ingredients take centre stage, showcasing clean, clear flavours and fine balance. Superb breads (in at least three flavours) accompany a class act. Expect the likes of foie gras and chicken liver parfait with toasted brioche to start, followed by mains of halibut with Jerusalem artichoke mushroom duxelle, Serrano ham and veal jus, with pear and almond tart to finish.

Notable Wine List: An extensive and well laid out wine list with a comprehensive offering from all the major wine producing areas of the world.

Chef: James Bennington **Owners:** Nigel Platts-Martin, Bruce Poole **Times:** 12-2.30/6.30-10.30, Closed 3 days at Xmas **Prices:** Fixed L £23.50, Fixed D £35, Coffee £3.50, Min/Water £3.50, Service added but optional 12.5% **Wine:** 500 bottles over £20, 20 bottles under £20, 14 by the glass (£4.50-£13.25) **Seats:** 72 **Smoking:** N/Sm in restaurant, Air con **Children:** Portions **Directions:** Nearest station: Turnham Green From station follow Turnham Green Tce to junct with Chiswick High Rd. Cross road & bear right. Devonshire Rd 2nd left **Parking:** On street aprons and a backing track of Gallic music, evoke the atmosphere of a Parisian bistro. The cooking follows suit, with simple, classic French brasserie fare. Specials bolster the carte, including the namesake soft mountain cows' milk cheese, Vacherin in season (November - February). Otherwise, expect grilled 28-day hung Scotch beef fillet with chips and béarnaise, or grilled lamb cutlets with tomato hollandaise and boulangère potatoes.

Chef: Malcolm John **Owners:** Malcolm & Donna John **Times:** 12-3/6-11, Closed 25 Dec, BHs, Mon **Prices:** Fixed L £15, Starter £5.95-£8.95, Main £11.95-£19, Dessert £5.95-£7.50, Coffee £2.50, Min/Water £3.50, Service added but optional 12.5% **Wine:** 20 bottles over £20, 15 bottles under £20, 5 by the glass (£5) **Notes:** Vegetarian available **Seats:** 72, Pr/dining room 30 **Smoking:** N/Sm area, No pipes **Children:** Portions **Directions:** Nearest station: Chiswick Park Turn left and restaurant, 400mtrs on left

Gravy

☎ 020 8998 6816 142 Chiswick High Rd W4 1PU
Cosy family owned restaurant and bar where emphasis is on friendly atmosphere.

LONDON W5

Momo

Japanese

Popular restaurant serving traditional Japanese cuisine

☎ 020 8997 0206 14 Queens Pde, Ealing W5 3HU Plan 1-C4

This Japanese restaurant is hidden away in a quiet residential area of North Ealing, behind the shop front of an urban precinct. It enjoys an excellent reputation with locals for its traditional Japanese cooking. The restaurant has exotic décor and you can have a traditional Japanese cooking pot (nabemono) at your table if you wish. The menu, in Japanese and English, is divided into sections covering set meals; sushi; sashimi; various appetisers; seafood including king prawns, squid and mackerel dishes; meat and poultry dishes featuring pork, chicken and beef; vegetable or soybean dishes; and an extensive choice of rice and noodle dishes, all at very reasonable prices.

Chef: Shigeru Kondo **Owners:** Mr Kondo **Times:** 12-3/6-11, Closed 2 wk Xmas, 1 wk Aug, Sun **Prices:** Fixed L £8.80-£16.50, Fixed D £19.50-£27, Starter £3.90-£16, Main £8.80-£25, Dessert £2.30-£4.50, Coffee £2.20, Min/Water £3.50, Service added 12% **Wine:** 4 bottles over £20, 4 bottles under £20, 2 by the glass (£3.20) **Notes:** Vegetarian available **Seats:** 30 **Smoking:** No cigars, Air con **Children:** Menu **Directions:** Nearest station: North Ealing 0.2m from North Ealing station **Parking:** On street

Carluccio's Caffè

☎ 020 8566 4458 5-6 The Green, Ealing W5 5DA
Quality Italian chain.

Charlotte's Place

☎ 020 8567 7541 16 St Matthews Rd, Ealing Common W5 3JT
web: www.theaa.com/restaurants/110884.html
Minimalist interior, tempting menu of British and French classics. Extra buzzy at weekends with live jazz.

LONDON W6

Agni

Indian V **NEW**

Modern Indian cuisine in stylish surroundings

☎ 020 8846 9191 160 King St W6 0QU Plan 1-D3
e-mail: info@agnirestaurant.com
web: www.agnirestaurant.com

Set over two floors, with a relaxed bistro style, Agni comes decked out in yellow and gold with a clear Indian theme. This new-kid-on-the-block has pedigree too, with Gowtham Karingi (ex head chef at Zaika and Veeraswamy) and Neeraj Mittra (ex manager at Chutney Mary) at the helm, and service is professional and very friendly. Modern Indian is the style reflecting the progression of regional Indian food from its ancient roots, with emphasis on quality ingredients and clever spicing. Bags of choice, from the street food of Delhi and beachside snacks of Mumbai to kebabs from Lucknow and hyderabad biryani pots (meat dishes cooked in sealed pots).

Chef: Gowtham Karingi **Owners:** Neeraj Mittra & Gowtham Karingi **Times:** 12-2.30/6-11, Closed 25 Dec to 1 Jan, Closed L Sat **Prices:** Fixed L £5.50-£8.50, Fixed D £11-£24, Starter £2.95-£5.50, Main £5.50-£10.95, Dessert £2.50-£4, Coffee £2, Min/Water £2.50, Service added but optional 10% **Wine:** 4 bottles over £20, 12 bottles under £20, 6 by the glass (£2.75-£4.25) **Notes:** Chef's table £35, Vegetarian menu **Seats:** 45, Pr/dining room 30 **Smoking:** N/Sm in restaurant, Air con **Children:** Menu, Portions **Directions:** Nearest station: Hammersmith Broadway, Ravenscourt Park Telephone for directions **Parking:** Meter parking on street, Kings Mall

Anglesea Arms

Modern British

Trendy gastro-pub offering simple, robust food

☎ 020 8749 1291 35 Wingate Rd W6 0UR Plan 1-D3
e-mail: anglesea.events@gmail.com

Plenty of hustle and bustle is always guaranteed at this shabby-chic Hammersmith gastro-pub, popular with trendy locals and students alike. A log fire, wooden floors, Victorian décor and an open-plan - sometimes boisterous - kitchen all add to its laid-back charm. Seasonal produce is evident on the daily-changing blackboard menu, which serves up good, hearty and robust food that hits the mark every time.

Times: 12.30-2.45/7-10.30, Closed 24-31 Dec **Directions:** Nearest station: Goldhawk Road, Ravenscourt Park. Off Goldhawk Road.

England

LONDON W6 *continued*

The Brackenbury

Modern European

Unfussy, enjoyable, urban bistro

☎ 020 8748 0107 129-131 Brackenbury Rd W6 0BQ Plan 1-D3
e-mail: lisa@thebrackenbury.fsnet.co.uk

Tucked away in a residential street, this cosy bistro has been converted from two small houses. The décor is in quiet, natural colours that work well with the polished tables and modern wooden chairs. It has the feeling of a 'brasserie du quartier' about it with its relaxed and welcoming atmosphere and helpful, unstuffy service. The menu of modern European dishes changes constantly. Begin with bresaola celeriac, pear remoulade and Olio Santo, followed by wild mushroom risotto, pesto and aged balsamic and finish with banoffee cheesecake, caramelised banana and toffee sauce.

Chef: Noel Capp **Owners:** Lisa Inglis **Times:** 12.30-2.45/7-10.45, Closed 24-26 Dec, 1 Jan, Easter Mon, Aug BH Mon, Closed L Sat, D Sun **Prices:** Fixed L fr £12.50, Starter £4-£7.50, Main £9.50-£15, Dessert £4-£7, Coffee £1.85, Min/Water £2.90, Service added but optional 12.5% **Wine:** 34 bottles over £20, 20 bottles under £20, 8 by the glass (£3.30-£4.50) **Notes:** Vegetarian available **Seats:** 60 **Smoking:** N/Sm in restaurant **Children:** Portions **Directions:** Nearest station: Goldhawk Road, Hammersmith Telephone for directions **Parking:** On street

Chez Kristof

French

Rustic French cooking in neighbourhood bistro

☎ 020 8741 1177 111 Hammersmith Grove W6 0NQ Plan 1-D4
e-mail: info@chezkristof.co.uk
web: www.chezkristof.co.uk

Situated on a corner site in a quiet part of Shepherd's Bush, this bustling neighbourhood restaurant is often packed with a youngish crowd, drawn by the simple, rustic French cooking. Squeeze on to one of the closely packed tables and tuck into well executed Gallic classics such as sautéed frogs' legs with garlic and parsley, braised duck and pork stew with white beans and apple tarte Tatin with vanilla ice cream. A visit to the restaurant's own delicatessen next door is a must for diners who also want to eat great French food at home.

Chef: Richard McLellan **Owners:** Jan Woroniecki **Times:** 12-3/6-11.15, Closed 24-26 Dec, 1 Jan **Prices:** Fixed L £12, Starter £4-£8, Main £12.50-£16, Dessert £5-£6, Coffee £2, Min/Water £3, Service added 12.5% **Wine:** 46 bottles over £20, 16 bottles under £20, 8 by the glass (£3.75-£6.50) **Notes:** Vegetarian available **Seats:** 100, Pr/dining room 45 **Smoking:** N/Sm area **Children:** Menu, Portions **Directions:** Nearest station: Hammersmith Please telephone for directions **Parking:** On street

The Gate

Modern Vegetarian V

Vegetarian restaurant offering inventive cuisine

☎ 020 8748 6932 51 Queen Caroline St W6 9QL Plan 1-D3
e-mail: hammersmith@gateveg.co.uk
web: www.thegate.tv

This is a vegetarian restaurant in an unusual listed building, approached via a church entrance hall. Once inside the room, formerly an artist's studio, it is bright and airy with high ceilings, large windows and dramatic art. The cooking is an inspired alternative to the usual vegetarian choices. It seeks out bold flavours, inventive combinations and fresh ingredients to produce simple but ingenious dishes. Worldwide influences and modern techniques make this a great choice for vegetarians, vegans and those in search of new tastes. Try quince and goat's cheese salad, aubergine schnitzel or roasted almond and cauliflower korma for example.

Chef: Adrian Daniel, Joe Tyrrell **Owners:** Adrian Daniel, Michael Daniel **Times:** 12-3/6-11, Closed 23 Dec-3 Jan, Easter Mon, BHs, Sun, Closed L Sat **Prices:** Fixed L £18, Fixed D £21, Starter £4.50-£6, Main £8.50-£13.50, Dessert £4.50-£6, Coffee £1.25, Min/Water £2.50, Service added but optional 12.5% **Wine:** 10 bottles over £20, 14 bottles under £20, 12 by the glass (£3-£4.50) **Notes:** Annual Fungi Festival 6 course menu (mid Oct), Vegetarian only **Seats:** 60 **Smoking:** N/Sm in restaurant, Air con **Children:** Portions **Directions:** Nearest station: Hammersmith Telephone for directions **Parking:** On street

The River Café

see opposite

Sagar

Vegetarian, Indian V

South Indian vegetarian restaurant

☎ 020 8741 8563 157 King St, Hammersmith W6 9JT Plan 1-D3

A modern glass frontage picks out this unpretentious Indian from the crowd among the shops on a busy Hammersmith street. Decked out with close-set lightwood tables and chairs, blood-wood floorboards and plain walls dotted with Indian artefacts, the atmosphere's bustling and high on decibels on busy days. Service is informed, while the kitchen's lengthy vegetarian repertoire incorporates dosas (a must try), uthappams (lentil pizza) and puri to curries and thalis. Skilfully crafted dishes with clean-cut presentation and fresh distinct flavours and character are the forte. Think a paper paneer dosa (crisp rice and lentil pancake served with mild spicy vegetables and home-made cottage cheese), vegetable biriyani or kurma, and a ras malai (sponge milk pudding) dessert.

Times: 12-2.45/5.30-10.45

Snows-on-the-Green Restaurant

Modern British, Mediterranean

Enjoyable dining in this vibrant West London restaurant

☎ 020 7603 2142 166 Shepherd's Bush Rd, Brook Green, Hammersmith W6 7PB Plan 1-D3
e-mail: sebastian@snowsonthegreenfreeserve.co.uk
web: www.snowsonthegreen.co.uk

This double-fronted restaurant with its busy location between Hammersmith and Shepherds Bush offers a generous choice of rustic, Mediterranean fare served by some of the friendliest staff in the capital. The dining room décor has a chic New York feel to it and a lively ambience. Uncomplicated, well-seasoned dishes keep media-types coming back for lunch. Using the best of seasonal produce, enjoy main courses such as roast rabbit saddle en croûte with morcilla sausage or daube of beef cheeks with snails and artichoke purée before finishing with fig tart fines and lavender ice cream.

continued

England

The River Café

LONDON W6

Italian

Famous Italian Thames-side trendsetter

☎ 020 7386 4200 Thames Wharf, Rainville Rd W6 9HA Plan 1-D3
e-mail: info@rivercafe.co.uk
web: www.rivercafe.co.uk

Twenty years on people still flock to Rose Gray and Ruth Rogers' famous Hammersmith Italian at the edge of the Thames. The place almost needs no description; a spacious, modern, minimalist white room with plenty of steel and glass and an urban vibe that successfully mixes a bustling, informal atmosphere with a fine-dining experience. Light floods in through floor-to-ceiling windows (opening up to the terrace in summer), and there's a long stainless-steel open kitchen with wood-burning oven, lively cocktail bar and close-set tables to add to the buzz.

Menus change twice daily, so there's a sense of spontaneity to the flavour-driven cooking. The authentic, unfussy Italian cuisine - mainly Tuscan and Lombardian influenced - doesn't come cheap, but uses only the very best, freshest produce (with many ingredients specifically sourced for their rarity, locality and seasonality) simply treated with skill and panache. Take roast middle white pork loin on the bone with porcini, juniper, marjoram and Pinot Grigio, delivered with erbette saltate, Savoy cabbage, cicoria, cima and rocket, and perhaps a chocolate nemesis or lemon tart to finish.

Chef: R Gray, R Rogers, Theo Randall **Owners:** Rose Gray, Ruth Rogers **Times:** 12.30-3/7-11, Closed 24 Dec-1 Jan, Easter, BHs, Closed D Sun **Prices:** Starter £10-£17, Main £24-£32, Dessert £7-£8, Min/Water £1.60, Service added but optional 12.5% **Wine:** 200 bottles over £20, 6 bottles under £20, 12 by the glass (£4.25-£17.25) **Notes:** Vegetarian available **Seats:** 108 **Smoking:** N/Sm in restaurant **Children:** Portions **Directions:** Nearest station: Hammersmith Restaurant in converted warehouse. Entrance on S side of Rainville Rd at junct with Bowfell Rd **Parking:** 29

Chef: Sebastian Snow **Owners:** Sebastian Snow **Times:** 12-3/6-11, Closed 24-29 Dec, BHs, Sun, Closed L Sat **Prices:** Fixed L £13.50, Starter £6-£8.75, Main £14-£16, Dessert £5-£6, Coffee £2, Min/Water £1.35, Service optional, Group min 6 service 12.5% **Wine:** 20 bottles over £20, 20 bottles under £20, 10 by the glass (£3.65-£6.95) **Notes:** Vegetarian available **Seats:** 80, Pr/dining room 30 **Smoking:** N/Sm area, No pipes, No cigars, Air con **Children:** Menu, Portions **Directions:** Nearest station: Hammersmith Broadway 300yds from station **Parking:** On street

Azou

☎ 020 8563 7266 375 King St, Hammersmith W6 9NJ
web: www.theaa.com/restaurants/113985.html

Small, family-run restaurant serving Moroccan, Tunisian and Algerian dishes.

Los Molinos

☎ 020 7603 2229 127 Shepherds Bush Rd W6 7LP

Tapas and raciones in authentic, bustling surroundings.

LONDON W8

The Ark

Italian

Relaxed, generously-priced Italian dining in the heart of Kensington

☎ 020 7229 4024 122 Palace Gardens Ter W8 4RT Plan 4-A6
e-mail: natwalls@aol.com
web: www.thearkrestaurant.co.uk

This small Italian restaurant has mirror-clad walls, cerise cushions on the banquette seating and toe-tapping background music. There are fifteen or so well-spaced tables and service is efficient and friendly. Well-priced set and à la carte menus of Italian regional dishes make this a fun dining destination. Start with melted fontina fondue with poached egg and black truffle before a main course of boned quail on faro risotto, osso buco bianco or perhaps lamb cutlets with braised aubergine. Crowd-pleasing desserts include tiramisù and zabaglione al Marsala.

Chef: Steve Moran **Owners:** Louise Mayo **Times:** 12-3/6.30-12, Closed Xmas, BHs, Sun, Closed L Mon **Prices:** Fixed L fr £15, Starter £6.50-£11.50, Main £10.50-£19.50, Dessert £6-£7, Coffee £2.50, Min/Water £4, Service added but optional 12.5% **Wine:** 35 bottles over £20, 12 bottles under £20, 16 by the glass (£3.75-£6.50) **Notes:** Vegetarian available **Seats:** 50 **Smoking:** No pipes, Air con **Children:** Portions **Parking:** On street

Babylon

Modern International 

Minimalist chic, rooftop gardens and extraordinary views

☎ 020 7368 3993 The Roof Gardens, 99 Kensington High St W8 5SA Plan 4-B4
e-mail: babylon@roofgardens.virgin.co.uk
web: www.virgin.com/limitededition

Panoramic views over the London skyline from the decked terrace and sleek, glass-sided dining room and framed by the lush greenery from the Roof Gardens below, prove a winning Kensington formula. Contemporary styling, booths, white linen and a small bar with fish-tank walls provide the stylish backcloth for slick, friendly service and those capital views. The menu suits the surroundings, is modern and accomplished, with a colourful nod to the Mediterranean and beyond

continued

England

LONDON W8 *continued*

in starters like pan-fried diver-caught scallops with curried apple and parsnip purée and mains such as fillet of spring lamb with lamb casserole, spring vegetables and Chardonnay jus.

Chef: Oliver Smith **Owners:** Sir Richard Branson **Times:** 12-3/7-11, Closed 25 Dec & selected dates in Dec-Jan, Closed D Sun **Prices:** Fixed L £16-£18.50, Fixed D £42.50, Starter £8.50-£14.50, Main £15-£26.50, Dessert £6.75-£13, Coffee £2.50, Min/Water £3.50, Service added but optional 12.5% **Wine:** 70 bottles over £20, 9 bottles under £20, 11 by the glass **Notes:** Tasting menu available, Vegetarian available, Dress Restrictions, Smart casual **Seats:** 120, Pr/dining room 12 **Children:** Menu, Portions **Directions:** Nearest station: High Street Kensington From High St Kensington tube station, turn right, then right into Derby St **Parking:** 15

Belvedere

Modern British, French

Jewel in Holland Park, with stunning interior and garden views

☎ 020 7602 1238 Abbotsbury Rd, Holland House, Holland Park W8 6LU Plan 1-D3
e-mail: sales@whitestarline.org.uk
web: www.belvedererestaurant.co.uk

Set in the beautiful old orangery inside tranquil Holland Park, this elegant, romantic restaurant oozes glamorous, elegant good looks. Once the summer ballroom to the Jacobean mansion of Holland Park, the Belvedere's inspiring interior styling is the work of design guru David Collins. Think vaulted ceiling and high windows, elaborate pillars, parquet flooring and huge oyster-shell shaped lights. Add leafy green plants, brown leather seating, white linen, a marble-topped bar and intimate mezzanine and terrace, and the result is dramatic. The kitchen's simple but classic modern British and French brasserie cooking hits just the right note; think a fillet of beef au poivre with French beans and fries, and a chocolate and honeycomb parfait with raspberry sorbet.

continued

Chef: Billy Reid **Owners:** Jimmy Lahoud **Times:** 12-2.30/6-10.30, Closed 26 Dec, 1 Jan, Closed D Sun **Prices:** Fixed L fr £14.95, Fixed D fr £17.95, Starter £6.50-£12, Main £8.50-£19.95, Dessert £6.50, Coffee £3, Min/Water £3.50, Service added but optional 12.5%, Group min 13 service 15% **Wine:** 60 bottles over £20, 1 bottle under £20, 11 by the glass (£4-£7.25) **Notes:** Fixed D 6-7m only, weekend L 3 courses £22.50, Vegetarian available **Seats:** 90 **Smoking:** No pipes, Air con **Directions:** Nearest station: Holland Park On the Kensington High St side of Holland Park **Parking:** 50

Cheneston's Restaurant

Modern British V NOTABLE WINE LIST

Intimate restaurant in elegant townhouse hotel

☎ 020 7917 1000 Milestone Hotel, 1 Kensington Court W8 5DL Plan 4-B4
e-mail: bookms@rchmail.com
web: www.milestonehotel.com

Located opposite Kensington Palace and Gardens, this Victorian mansion has been transformed into a hotel of style and class, with many restored original features. Expect stunning bedrooms, luxurious lounges and a sumptuous dining room with leaded Victorian windows and shining crystal and silverware. As befits the surroundings and the clientele, food is classically based and both cooking style and presentation are simple and unfussy. Typical dishes include potted confit of duck, apple and blackberry chutney, roast guinea fowl, parsnip mash and red wine reduction, and steamed treacle pudding. Service is formal and professional from an international team. **Notable Wine List:** A classic wine list under the guidance of a enthusiastic young sommelier.

Chef: David Smith **Owners:** The Red Carnation Hotel **Times:** 12-3/5.30-11 **Prices:** Fixed L £18.50, Fixed D £23.50, Starter £6.25-£27.50, Main £12.50-£33.50, Dessert £7.50-£10.25, Coffee £5, Min/Water £4.50, Service added but optional 12.5% **Wine:** 250 bottles over £20, 5 bottles under £20, 10 by the glass (£6.50-£40) **Notes:** Sun L available, Vegetarian menu, Dress Restrictions, Smart casual, Civ Wed 30 **Seats:** 40, Pr/dining room 8 **Smoking:** N/Sm in restaurant, Air con **Children:** Menu, Portions **Rooms:** 57 (57 en suite) ★★★★★ HL **Directions:** Nearest station: High St Kensington M4/Hammersmith flyover, take 2nd left into Gloucster Rd, left into High St Kensington, 500mtrs on left **Parking:** NCP

Clarke's

Modern Mediterranean

The freshest food simply treated with reverence

☎ 020 7221 9225 124 Kensington Church St W8 4BH Plan 4-A5
e-mail: restaurant@sallyclarke.com
web: www.sallyclarke.com

Set amongst the well-known antique shops of Kensington Church Street and Notting Hill, you'll find the neat shop front for the restaurant, adjacent to Sally Clarke's famous bread shop. Minimalist décor is chic and modern with crisply starched table linen. Staff are friendly when invited to be but remain professional and diligent. The restaurant now offers a choice of two, three or four courses at dinner and also brunch on Saturdays from 11 until 2 so there are opportunities for less expensive eating, but the four course set dinner remains the classic choice. The menus change weekly and are posted on their website each Monday so you can take a look before booking Ingredients, skill and artistry take priority here, and it is this that make the cooking so successful and enduring. Modern European-style dishes might include salad of buffalo mozzarella with grapes, blood

continue

England

oranges and toasted hazelnuts, bitter leaves, sprouting grains and thyme slipper bread. An interesting main course might be roasted breast of corn fed chicken with horseradish and green herb cream, steamed choi sum, winter vegetables and wild rice.

Chef: Sally Clarke, Liz Payne **Owners:** Sally Clarke **Times:** 12.30-2/7-10, Closed 8 days Xmas & New Year, Sun, Closed D Mon **Prices:** Fixed D £49.50, Starter fr £12, Main fr £24, Dessert fr £8, Service included **Wine:** 86 bottles over £20, 10 bottles under £20, 8 by the glass (£4.50-£8.50) **Notes:** Fixed D 4 courses, Vegetarian available **Seats:** 90, Pr/dining room 40 **Smoking:** N/Sm in restaurant, Air con **Directions:** Nearest station: Notting Hill Gate Telephone for directions **Parking:** On street

Eleven Abingdon Road

Modern European NEW

A hidden gem off High Street Kensington

☎ 020 7937 0120 11 Abingdon Rd, Kensington W8 6AH Plan 4-A4

e-mail: eleven@abingdonroad.co.uk

This light, modern restaurant in a little side street off High Street Kensington is quite a find. The airy décor, lovely art collection and friendly feel make it a great location for a quick bite or a more relaxed meal. Open from 8am until 11pm you could stop by for breakfast or take afternoon tea away from the shops. Staff dressed in jeans and long aprons present a menu of modern European and trusty British dishes using top-notch ingredients. Great balance of flavours and use of seasonal ingredients are a giveaway that there's some serious talent in the kitchen. Try the likes of skate with mash, spinach and beurre noisette, or hold out for a lovely bitter chocolate mousse.

Chef: David Stafford **Owners:** Rebecca Mascarenhas **Times:** 12.30-2.30/6.30-11, Closed 25 Dec, BHs **Prices:** Food prices not confirmed for 2007. Please telephone for details **Seats:** 80 **Directions:** Nearest station: Kensington High St. Telephone for directions

Kensington Place

Modern British

Busy brasserie-style restaurant with vibrant colour and atmosphere

☎ 020 7727 3184 201-5 Kensington Church St W8 7LX Plan 4-A6

e-mail: kpparty@egami.co.uk

web: www.egami.co.uk

Popular, prominently located restaurant, where passers-by get a good look in through the long plate glass fascia. A revolving door leads into a small bar area and the restaurant proper is decorated with bright murals. Tables are closely packed and the colourful wooden chairs are reminiscent of the schoolroom. Well executed brasserie food, simple and precise, using top-quality seasonal produce, with old favourites offered alongside more imaginative creations. Fish is a speciality, with dishes like griddled scallops with pea purée and mint vinaigrette, and sea bass with citrus fruits and olive oil. The restaurant has its own fish shop next door to help with your private catering needs.

Chef: Rowley Leigh **Owners:** Place Restaurants Ltd. **Times:** 12-3.30/6.30-11.45, Closed 24-26 Dec, 1 Jan **Prices:** Fixed L £19.50, Fixed D £24.50-£39.50, Starter £7-£15, Main £15-£24.50, Dessert £6.50-£12.50, Coffee £2.25, Min/Water £3.50, Service added but optional 12.5% **Wine:** 212 bottles over £20, 6 bottles under £20, 16 by the glass (£5.50-£8.50) **Notes:** Set Sun lunch £24.50, Vegetarian available **Seats:** 140, Pr/dining room 45 **Smoking:** Air con **Children:** Menu, Portions **Directions:** Nearest station: Notting Hill Gate Telephone for directions **Parking:** On street

continued

Launceston Place Restaurant

British

Uncomplicated cuisine in a genteel setting

☎ 020 7937 6912 1a Launceston Place W8 5RL Plan 4-C4

e-mail: lpr@egami.co.uk

web: www.egami.co.uk

Wrapped around a street corner in a leafy part of Kensington, this upmarket eatery has a genteel air. It's housed in a series of small townhouse rooms, each decked with gilt mirrors, colourful prints and crisply clad tables, and caters to a well-heeled crowd of locals, suits and lunching ladies. An accomplished kitchen adopts a modern British line - with a nod to the Mediterranean - and delivers a menu of straightforward contemporary dishes; twice baked goat's cheese soufflé with red wine poached pears followed by sea bass with aubergine caviar, or roast chump of lamb with a mint jus perhaps. The fixed-price lunch menu is great value.

Chef: Philip Reed **Owners:** Christopher Bodker **Times:** 12.30-2.30/6-11, Closed Xmas, New Year, Easter, Closed L Sat **Prices:** Fixed L fr £16.50, Fixed D fr £18.50, Starter £5.50-£10, Main £15.50-£18, Dessert £6-£7, Coffee £2.75, Min/Water £3.25, Service added but optional 12.5% **Wine:** 88 bottles over £20, 7 bottles under £20, 13 by the glass (£4.50-£9.50) **Notes:** Vegetarian available **Seats:** 85, Pr/dining room 14 **Smoking:** No pipes, No cigars, Air con **Directions:** Nearest station: Gloucester Road Just south of Kensington Palace

Royal Garden Hotel, Tenth Floor Restaurant

see page 344

Timo

Italian V

Chic, authentic Italian dining

☎ 020 7603 3888 343 Kensington High St W8 6NW Plan 1-D3

e-mail: timorestaurant@tiscali.co.uk

Situated in a calmer area of the ever-trendy Kensington High Street, this restaurant is worth seeking out for its authentic regional Italian cooking. Décor is smart but relaxed with tan suede chairs and crisply dressed tables; huge prints add a splash of colour. The menu is traditional Italian style with starters, second courses, mains and desserts, priced for flexibility and with side orders to supplement the dishes if you've got a big appetite. Classical cooking style and presentation, try a starter of tuna tartare and perhaps a main like tagliata with caramelised onions.

Chef: Mr M Squillance & Mr S Pacini **Owners:** Piero Amodio **Times:** 12-2.30/7-11, Closed Xmas, New Year, BHs, Closed L Sat **Prices:** Starter £6-£12, Main £11.50-£17.50, Dessert £5.50-£7.50, Coffee £3.50, Min/Water £3.75, Service added 12.5%, Group min 10 service 15% **Wine:** 120 bottles over £20, 4 bottles under £20, 8 by the glass (£4-£8.50) **Notes:** Vegetarian menu **Seats:** 55 **Smoking:** N/Sm area, No pipes, No cigars, Air con **Children:** Portions **Directions:** Nearest station: Kensington High St 5 mins walk towards Hammersmith, after Odeon Cinema, on left of street **Parking:** 3

England

Royal Garden Hotel, Tenth Floor Restaurant

LONDON W8

International V

Fantastic views and imaginative cuisine

☎ 020 7361 1910 2-24 Kensington High St W8 4PT Plan 4-B5
e-mail: tenthrestaurant@royalgardenhotel.co.uk
web: www.royalgardenhotel.co.uk

The hotel is built on the site of the former Kensington Palace vegetable plot, hence its name. You get fantastic views of Kensington Gardens and Hyde Park from the Tenth Floor Restaurant. With its huge windows to exploit the views and allow light to flood in, this ultra-modern, elegant dining room has its own bar and a cabaret area.

However, it's the food that's centre-stage here. Modern European cuisine brings together a fusion of traditional cooking techniques and modern twists, with a generous sprinkling of quality ingredients like lobster, foie gras, truffles, saffron and oysters, cast across an interesting menu. A separate vegetarian and six-course tasting menu are available. A starter of twice-baked smoked haddock soufflé might be followed by a main course of poached fillet of red mullet with Fine de Claire oysters and lemongrass sauce. Desserts tempt with the likes of a trio of passionfruit with chocolate Macadamia nut brownie, or warm banana financier with white chocolate and hazelnut parfait.

There are gastronomic events with guest chefs throughout the year.

Chef: Norman Farquharson
Owners: Goodwood Group
Times: 12-2.30/5.30-11, Closed 2 wks Aug, 2 wks Jan, Sun, Closed L Sat
Prices: Fixed L fr £17.25, Starter £6.50-£13.50, Main £16.50-£36, Dessert fr £6.50, Coffee £3.25, Min/Water £3.75, Service optional, Group min 8 service 10%
Wine: 95 bottles over £20, 9 bottles under £20, 7 by the glass (£4.50-£9)
Notes: Vegetarian menu, Dress Restrictions, Smart casual, Civ Wed 100
Seats: 110
Smoking: N/Sm area, Air con
Children: Portions
Rooms: 396 (396 en suite) ★★★★★ HL
Directions: Nearest station: Kensington High Street Next to Kensington Palace, Royal Albert Hall
Parking: 200

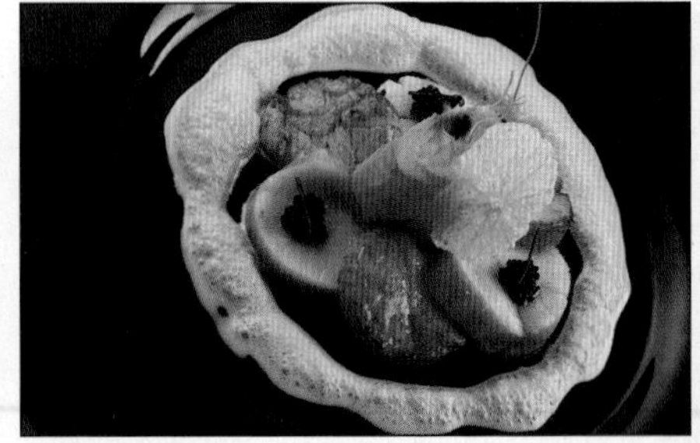

LONDON W8 *continued*

Zaika

Indian

Lively restaurant serving carefully prepared modern Indian cuisine

☎ 020 7795 6533 1 Kensington High St W8 5NP
Plan 4-B4
e-mail: info@zaika-restaurant.co.uk
web: www.zaika-restaurant.co.uk

Zaika occupies a former bank building opposite Kensington Palace and retains many of the original features. High ceilings, double-height stone windows and carved arches grace the panelled, airy interior, brightened by a rich palette of vibrant colours - which includes the contemporary chairs and banquettes. Blond-wood floorboards, Indian artefacts, modern lighting and a bar at the front add to the sophisticated styling, while professional, informed service and an impressive wine list complete the upbeat vibe. The kitchen's innovative menu of refined modern-Indian cuisine delivers well-executed, vibrant-flavoured and creatively presented dishes from quality ingredients. Think Tandoori monkfish accompanied by a cauliflower and curry leaf risotto with crispy cauliflower florets, spiced lobster jus, sour spices and cocoa.

Chef: Sanjay Dwivedi **Owners:** Claudio Pulze, Raj Sharma (Cuisine Collection) **Times:** 12-2.45/6-10.45, Closed BHs, Xmas, New Year, Closed L Sat **Prices:** Fixed L £15, Starter £6.25-£12.50, Main £12.50-£19, Dessert £6-£12.50, Coffee £2, Min/Water £3.50, Service added but optional 12.5% **Wine:** 500 bottles over £20, 9 bottles under £20, 10 by the glass (£5-£12.50) **Notes:** Vegetarian available, Dress Restrictions, Smart casual preferred **Seats:** 84 **Smoking:** N/Sm in restaurant, Air con **Children:** Portions **Directions:** Nearest station: Kensington High Street Opposite Kensington Palace

Bellini

☎ 020 7937 5520 47 Kensington Court W8 5DA
web: www.theaa.com/restaurants/113986.html

Welcoming haunt of many newspaper journalists. Mediterranean and Italian dishes. Excellent set menus before 7pm.

Wagamama

☎ 020 7376 1717 26a High St Kensington W8 4PW

Informal noodle bars with no booking.

LONDON W9

The Waterway

☎ 020 7266 3557 54-56 Formosa St, Little Venice W9 2JU
web: www.theaa.com/restaurants/113981.html

Great views with waterfront terrace. Relaxed atmosphere and British-French menu.

LONDON W11

E&O

Pan Asian

Buzzy Oriental restaurant

☎ 020 7229 5454 14 Blenheim Crescent W11 1NN
Plan 1-D4
e-mail: info@eando.nu
web: www.eando.nu

A former pub close to Notting Hill and Portobello Road, this fashionable bar-restaurant mixes oriental style with modern, minimalist décor of slatted wood and discreet mirrors. Tables are simply set with a bamboo pot for cutlery and chopsticks, and staff are relaxed and knowledgeable. The modern Asian cuisine draws inspiration from the Pacific Rim, with an extensive menu covering all the usual bases of dim sum, soups, salads, tempura, curries, sashimi, futo maki rolls and roasts. Specials include chilli-crusted tofu with black bean, chicken pad Thai and lobster and tiger prawns with sweet ginger noodles.

Chef: Simon Treadway **Owners:** Will Ricker **Times:** 12-3/6-11, Closed 25 & 26 Dec, 1 Jan & Aug BH **Prices:** Starter £4.50-£6.50, Main £9.50-£27, Dessert £5.50-£6.50, Coffee £1.80, Min/Water £3, Service added but optional 12.5% **Wine:** 78 bottles over £20, 7 bottles under £20, 20 by the glass (£3.50-£9) **Seats:** 86, Pr/dining room 18 **Smoking:** N/Sm in restaurant, Air con **Directions:** Nearest station: Notting Hill Gate At tube station turn right, at mini rdbt turn into Kensington Park Rd, restaurant 10min down hill **Parking:** Street parking available

Edera

Modern Italian

Good value friendly Italian

☎ 020 7221 6090 148 Holland Park Av W11 4UE
Plan 1-D4
e-mail: edera@btconnect.com

Kitted out with light wooden floors, deep red pillars and sandstone walls, Edera is a stylish, friendly place with the feel of a classic Italian eatery. Popular with locals, booking is strongly recommended and diners should allow extra time to find parking in the nearby streets. This chic restaurant draws inspiration from all regions of Italy and the creative menu delivers accomplished cooking at very reasonable prices. Seasonality is key and typical dishes may include tuna carpaccio with fresh artichokes, pan-fried veal cutlet Milanese style with rocket and parmesan, followed by a classic tiramisù or grappa-flavoured pannacotta with grapes poached in red wine.

Chef: Carlo Usai **Owners:** A-Z Ltd/Mr Pisano **Times:** 12-2.30/6.30-11, Closed 25-26 & 31 Dec **Prices:** Starter £7-£14, Main £12-£22, Dessert £5-£8, Coffee £2, Min/Water £3, Service added but optional 12.5% **Wine:** 150 bottles over £20, 8 bottles under £20, 10 by the glass (£4-£10.50) **Notes:** Vegetarian available, Smart casual appreciated **Seats:** 70, Pr/dining room 20 **Smoking:** Air con **Children:** Portions **Directions:** Nearest station: Holland Park Please telephone for directions **Parking:** Street parking

see page 346

England

England

The Ledbury

LONDON W11

Modern French NOTABLE WINE LIST

Highly accomplished cooking in fashionable, residential Notting Hill

☎ 020 7792 9090 127 Ledbury Rd W11 2AQ
Plan 1-D4
e-mail: info@theledbury.com
web: www.theledbury.com

This latest and much-awaited offering from Nigel Platts-Martin and Philip Howard (who together also own The Square in Mayfair, see entry) has a smart, refined vibe, and is set in the heart of residential Notting Hill. The interior is contemporary, sophisticated and luxurious, with cream leather chairs alongside long dark curtains and polished-wood floors. Tables are relatively closely set, but the room doesn't feel cramped, helped by a clever use of mirrors and a terrace with additional tables covered by parasols and a canopy. Service is professional and attentive without being stuffy or overbearing, directed by maitre d' Helena Hell. Accomplished, sophisticated cooking from Philip Howard protégé, Oz-born Brett Graham, delivers high technical skill through modern dishes underpinned by a classical French theme, with fine visual presentation, interesting combinations and textures. Peripherals like bread, amuse-bouche, pre-desserts and petits fours are all top form. Fixed-price lunch, carte and eight-course tasting option, and all accompanied by a high-class wine list. Expect starters such as roast scallops with pumpkin purée and pumpkin gnocchi, or lasagne of rabbit and chanterelles with main courses like assiette of lamb with borlotti beans and artichokes, or English partridge with Serrano ham, endive and a mushroom and artichoke tarte.

Notable Wine List: A top-class wine list full of carefully chosen and interesting wines.

Chef: Brett Graham **Owners:** Nigel Platts-Martin & Philip Howard **Times:** 12-2/6.30-11, Closed 24-26 Dec, 1 Jan, Aug BH wk end **Prices:** Fixed L £24.50, Fixed D £45, Coffee £4, Min/Water £3.95, Service added but optional 12.5% **Wine:** 530 bottles over £20, 20 bottles under £20, 14 by the glass (£4.50-£10.50) **Notes:** ALC 3 courses £45, Tasting menu 8 courses £55, Vegetarian available **Seats:** 95 **Smoking:** N/Sm in restaurant, Air con **Directions:** Nearest station: Westbourne Park & Notting Hill Gate 5 min walk along Talbot Rd from Portobello Rd, on corner of Talbot and Ledbury Rd **Parking:** Talbot Rd, metered

Notting Hill Brasserie

LONDON W11

Modern French

Chic food, chic décor, chic location

☎ 020 7229 4481 92 Kensington Park Rd W11 2PN
Plan 4-D4
e-mail: enquiries@nottinghillbrasserie.com

Converted from three Edwardian townhouses, this brasserie oozes quality with its mix of stylish good looks and period features. The swish minimalist décor, modern African art, stunning flower arrangements and confident, friendly service are further enhanced by a separate cocktail bar with lashings of live jazz.

The accomplished kitchen impresses with both classic and original twists, while keeping things intelligently simple on crisply-scripted menus. Here you might find a classic Chateaubriand roasted in a salt crust with hand-made chips and béarnaise sauce, or pan-fried halibut fillet paired with baby artichokes, pancetta and roasting juices, and perhaps a hot chocolate fondant with lavender ice cream to round things off in style. Excellent breads, too.

Chef: Mark Jankel **Owners:** Carlo Spetale **Times:** 12-4/7-1, Closed D Sun **Prices:** Fixed L £16.50, Starter £7-£13.50, Main £19-£24.50, Dessert £6.50, Coffee £2.50, Min/Water £3.50, Service optional, Service added but optional 12.5% **Wine:** 62 bottles over £20, 8 bottles under £20, 14 by the glass (£3.50-£7.50) **Notes:** Tasting menu £ 65, Sun L £25-£30, Vegetarian available **Seats:** 110, Pr/dining room 44 **Smoking:** N/Sm in restaurant, Air con **Children:** Portions **Directions:** Nearest station: Notting Hill Gate 3 mins walk from Notting Hill station **Parking:** On street

England

LONDON W11 *continued*

Lonsdale

Fusion, Modern Asian

Chic lounge-style eatery with a cool clientele

☎ 020 7727 4080 48 Lonsdale Rd W11 2DE
Plan 1-D4
e-mail: reception@thelonsdale.co.uk
web: www.thelonsdale.co.uk

An appropriately discreet red awning and frosted-glass windows pick out this fashionable lounge-style bar-restaurant (replete with stylish retro décor and brightly lit cocktail bar) on its upmarket residential street. The interior design is bold, the atmosphere buzzy and trendy, and staff youthful, informal but professional. The intimate seating area strips away all the formalities of fine-dining, with its close-set, low dark wood tables and square leather stalls with zebra print cushions. The kitchen follows the contemporary trend, its modern approached studded with Asian influence; think steamed sea bass with ginger, spring onions and pak choi, or perhaps, twice-cooked pork belly with butternut squash purée and chilli pickles.

Chef: Ian Atkinson **Owners:** Adam & Charles Breeden **Times:** 6-12, Closed 25-26 Dec, 1 Jan, Closed L all week **Prices:** Starter £7-£9, Main £10-£16, Dessert £6.50-£7.50, Service added 12.5% **Seats:** 100 **Smoking:** Air con **Children:** Min 5 yrs **Directions:** Nearest station: Notting Hill/Ladbroke Grove One street parallel N Westbourne Grove between Portobello Rd and Ledbury Rd

Notting Hill Brasserie

see opposite

Essenza

☎ 020 7792 1066
210 Kensington Park Rd W11 1NR
web: www.theaa.com/restaurants/109732.html

Smart and intimate trattoria, serving fresh, seasonal Italian dishes.

Notting Grill

☎ 020 7229 1500 123a Clarendon Rd,
Holland Park W11 4JG
web: www.theaa.com/restaurants/113959.html

Antony Worrall Thompson's eatery featuring quality meat dishes and produce from his own garden.

LONDON W14

Cibo

Italian

Beautiful Italian food of local renown

☎ 020 7371 2085 3 Russell Gardens W14 8EZ Plan 1-D3
e-mail: ciborestaurant@aol.com
web: www.ciborestaurant.co.uk

This cosy, neighbourhood restaurant has a hard-earned reputation for providing solid, reliable and - let's not be coy - delicious Italian food to a clientele that consists largely of Kensington residents who come here in their droves. The décor is striking and unusual, with artwork on the walls and a real sense of intimacy that's enhanced by a genuine warm welcome and engaging service. Pasta dishes and fish are the specialities on this intriguing and appealing menu - try carpaccio di pesce spade e branzino al timo (thinly sliced raw swordfish and sea bass in thyme and olive oil) to start and then spaghetti all'aragosta in salsa (spaghetti with lobster in its own sauce).

Times: 12.15-2.30/7-11, Closed Xmas, Easter BHs, Closed L Sat, D Sun **Directions:** Nearest station: Olympia/Shepherds Bush Russell Gardens is a residential area off Holland Road, Kensington (Olympia) Shepherd's Bush

LONDON WC1

Jurys Great Russell Street

Modern

Elegant 1930s setting for relaxed dining

☎ 020 7347 1000 16-22 Great Russell St WC1B 3NN
Plan 3-C3
e-mail: great_russell@jurysdoyle.com
web: www.jurysdoyle.com

This impressive neo-Georgian listed building - designed by the renowned architect Sir Edwin Lutyens in the 1930s - retains many of its original features and houses a smart, spacious restaurant (named after said architect) tucked away in the basement. Its clean, traditional lines are in keeping with the surroundings, as is the adjacent, small, classic cocktail bar for aperitifs. The crowd-pleasing menu fits the bill, too, with the likes of fillet of Brittany sea bass served with a langoustine mousse, truffled cabbage and sauce cardinal, or lamb shank with English root vegetables and couscous. Desserts might include pears poached in cranberry juice and port.

Chef: Paul O'Brien **Owners:** Jurys Doyle **Times:** 6-10, Closed L all week **Prices:** Fixed L £19.50-£25, Fixed D £25.50-£32, Starter £6-£10, Main £10-£22, Dessert £5-£8, Service included **Notes:** Vegetarian available, Smart casual **Seats:** 120, Pr/dining room 26 **Smoking:** N/Sm in restaurant, Air con **Children:** Portions **Rooms:** 170 (170 en suite) ★★★★ HL **Directions:** Nearest station: Tottenham Court Road Short walk from Tottenham Court Rd and Tube Station **Parking:** NCP opposite the Hotel

England

LONDON WC1 *continued*

Matsuri High Holborn

Japanese

Traditional Japanese in contemporary setting

☎ 020 7430 1970 Mid City Place, 71 High Holborn WC1V 6EA Plan 3-E3
e-mail: eat@matsuri-restaurant.com
web: www.matsuri-restaurant.com

Futuristic Japanese restaurant occupying a corner site on bustling High Holborn. Expect big glass windows, an austere interior and a choice of three dining areas that showcase the various styles of cuisine - the sushi counter, the teppan-yaki room and the main dining room with open-plan kitchen. The Japanese ex-pats frequenting this restaurant are a clue to the quality and authenticity of the cooking. Menus are lengthy, yet good ingredients are simply prepared and well presented, with lots of memorable fresh fish. The teppan-yaki set menus provide an overall flavour of Japanese cuisine.

Chef: H Sudoh, T Aso, S Mabalot **Owners:** Matsuri Restaurant Group **Times:** 12-2.30/6-10, Closed 25-26 Dec, 1 Jan, BHs, Sun **Prices:** Fixed L £8.50-£22, Fixed D fr £20, Starter £3.50-£12, Main £15-£35, Dessert £3-£6, Coffee £3, Min/Water £4.75, Service added but optional 12.5% **Wine:** 30 bottles over £20, 4 bottles under £20, 2 by the glass (£3.75) **Seats:** 120, Pr/dining room 10 **Smoking:** N/Sm area, Air con **Directions:** Nearest station: Holborn On the corner of Red Lion St. Opposite the Renaissance Chancery Court Hotel **Parking:** On Street (pay & display)

The Montague on the Gardens

Modern British

Stylish hotel restaurant with modern cuisine

☎ 020 7637 1001 15 Montague St, Bloomsbury WC1B 5BJ Plan 3-C4
e-mail: bookmt@rchmail.com
web: www.montaguehotel.com

continued

A swish boutique hotel in the heart of Bloomsbury, the Montague has two dining options - the Blue Door bistro or the fine dining restaurant, the Chef's Table. The latter is a light, airy space with panoramic views over London on three sides. Mahogany panelled walls and homely touches of décor make for an intimate dining atmosphere, with attentive staff on hand to make guests feel at ease. Cooking is modern English with hints of Mediterranean flavours. So expect to be more than satisfied with dishes such as grilled scallops with chilli pumpkin and lemon pesto, and seared sea bass, kohlrabi, parsnip purée and raspberry sauce.

Chef: Neil Ramsey **Owners:** Red Carnation Hotels **Times:** 12.30-2.30/5.30-10.30 **Prices:** Fixed L £12.50, Fixed D £19.50, Starter £6.25-£9.90, Main £13.95-£28.95, Dessert £5.50-£7.50, Coffee £3.95, Min/Water £4.50, Service added but optional 12.5% **Wine:** 49 bottles over £20, 19 bottles under £20, 17 by the glass (£4.50-£11) **Notes:** Sun L 3 courses £16.50, Vegetarian available, Civ Wed 90 **Seats:** 45, Pr/dining room 100 **Smoking:** N/Sm in restaurant, Air con **Children:** Menu, Portions **Rooms:** 99 (99 en suite) ★★★★ HL **Directions:** Nearest station: Russell Square 10 minutes from Covent Garden, adjacent to the British Museum **Parking:** Bloomsbury Square

Pearl Restaurant & Bar

Modern French

Stylish, city-orientated, destination restaurant with modern French menu

☎ 020 7829 7000 252 High Holborn WC1V 7EN Plan 3-D3
e-mail: info@pearl-restaurant.com
web: www.pearl-restaurant.com

The old Pearl Assurance Building has been transformed into a glamorous, metropolitan, destination restaurant. The achingly chic interior includes original marble pillars and lots of cream leather chairs, expensive settings and a huge wooden wine cave. Staff - including a sommelier - provide attentive service. The skilful kitchen produces classical dishes but with a wide range of influences from around the globe. Start with a beautifully presented dish of caramelised scallops with herb-crusted frogs' legs, parsley purée and garlic foam. Main courses might include carefully prepared veal cooked four ways with a pea, broad bean, macaroni and pea shoot vinaigrette. To finish there's Valrhona chocolate brownie with pear granite.

Chef: Jun Tanaka **Owners:** Hotel Property Investors **Times:** 12-2.30/6-10, Closed Dec, 10 Jan, BHs (except Xmas), 2 wks Aug, Sun, Closed L Sat **Prices:** Fixed L £23.50, Fixed D £45, Coffee £3.25, Min/Water £3.95, Service added but optional 12.5% **Wine:** 440 bottles over £20, 15 bottles under £20, 42 by the glass (£4.80-£39) **Notes:** Tasting menu 6 courses £55, £100 with wines, Vegetarian available **Seats:** 74, Pr/dining room 12 **Smoking:** N/Sm area, Air con **Rooms:** 356 (356 en suite) ★★★★★ HL **Directions:** Nearest station: Holborn 200 mtrs from Holborn tube station **Parking:** NCP

Cigala

☎ 020 7405 1717 54m Lambs Conduit St WC1N 3LW
web: www.cigala.co.uk
Appealing Spanish restaurant with tapas bar.

Wagamama

☎ 020 7930 7587 14a Irving St WC1H 7AF
Informal noodle bars with no booking.

England

Wagamama

☎ 020 7323 9223 4a Streatham St WC1A 1JB
Informal noodle bars with no booking.

Yo! Sushi

☎ 020 7636 0076 Myhotel, 11-13 Bayley St WC1B 3HD
Sushi, sashimi, noodles and more.

LONDON WC2

The Admiralty Restaurant

Modern European

Full-flavoured fare in a stunning setting

☎ 020 7845 4646 Somerset House, The Strand WC2R 1LA Plan 3-D2
e-mail: maria@somerset-house.org.uk
web: www.somerset-house.org.uk

The restaurant is part of the Somerset House complex, a fine 18th-century building close to the River Thames, with accompanying art galleries, a skating rink and the spectacular Fountain Court. Beautiful galleon-shaped chandeliers recall the building's former life as Naval Headquarters. Cooking is refined and demonstrates flashes of great skill. The same menu is offered for all meals on a rolling basis with a few items refreshed at a time. Robustly flavoured dishes include oxtail ravioli, roast saddle of rabbit with morel cannelloni, and pistachio soufflé with chocolate sauce.

Chef: Daniel Groom **Owners:** Leiths **Times:** 12-2.15/6-10.15, Closed 24-27 Dec, Closed D Sun **Prices:** Fixed L fr £17.50, Fixed D £36.50-£37, Starter £7-£11.90, Main £19.50-£23, Dessert £7-£13.50, Coffee £3, Min/Water £3.75, Service added but optional 12.5% **Wine:** 96 bottles over £20, 13 by the glass (£4-£16.50) **Notes:** Tasting menu £39.50-49.50, pre theatre avail, Vegetarian menu **Seats:** 55, Pr/dining room 60 **Smoking:** N/Sm area, No pipes **Children:** Portions **Directions:** Nearest station: Temple, Covent Garden Telephone for directions

Albannach

Modern Scottish

Highland chic meets city bustle with contemporary twists on Scottish favourites

☎ 020 7930 0066 66 Trafalgar Square WC2N 5DS Plan 5-C6
e-mail: info@albannach.co.uk
web: www.albannach.co.uk

continued

Purple sprouting heather in the windows, kilted staff and, of course, the name are all major clues that you're in a Scottish-themed restaurant. Overlooking Trafalgar Square, the walls of this fabulous mezzanine restaurant are adorned with beautiful Scottish photographs. The darkwood, open-plan dining areas are perhaps more like a bar or a nightclub than a fine dining restaurant but it's a style that works, creating an atmospheric destination to imbibe generous amounts of whiskey or enjoy a full-on foray into eclectic, modern Scottish cuisine with Caledonian produce championed with William Wallace-style fervour. Try a mousse of Arbroath smokies with a salad of tomato and courgettes and a lemongrass and tomato vinaigrette, then follow up with thyme-roasted Buccleuch beef fillet with morel sauce.

Chef: Thijmen Peters **Owners:** Dan Sullam, Niall Barnes **Times:** 12-3/5-10, Closed 25-26 Dec, 1 Jan, Sun **Prices:** Fixed L fr £16.50, Fixed D £35.75-£45.75, Starter £5.50-£7.50, Main £13-£19.25, Dessert £5.75-£8.25, Coffee £2.75, Min/Water £3.50, Service added but optional 12.5% **Wine:** 30 bottles over £20, 7 bottles under £20, 9 by the glass (£5.50-£10) **Notes:** Vegetarian available **Seats:** 65, Pr/dining room 20 **Smoking:** N/Sm in restaurant, Air con **Children:** Min 8 yrs, Portions **Directions:** Nearest station: Charing Cross SW corner of Trafalgar Sq, opposite Canada House **Parking:** NCP

Asia de Cuba

Asian, Cuban

Funky fusion experience

☎ 020 7300 5588 St Martin's Hotel, 45 St Martin's Ln WC2N 4HX Plan 3-C1
e-mail: restaurant.resuk@morganshotelgroup.com
web: www.asiadecuba-restaurant.com

You'll want to bring some friends or family along with you to this restaurant as the huge portions are all designed for sharing. It's a lively setting with loud Latin music and a buzzy atmosphere in the Philippe Starck designed split-level dining room, with bare light bulbs and pillars stacked with books, prints and plants. The fusion of Asian and Latin cuisine provides some interesting combinations like Asian pesto-grilled prawns with wok-charred tropical fruit and crisp lotus root chips. Get stuck into the cocktails too.

Chef: Owen Stewart **Owners:** China Grill Restaurant-Jefferey Chawdorow **Times:** 12-2.30/5.30-12 **Prices:** Food prices not confirmed for 2007. Please telephone for details **Wine:** 122 bottles over £20, 19 by the glass (£5-£14) **Notes:** Pre theatre menu £22 **Seats:** 180, Pr/dining room 100 **Smoking:** Air con **Children:** Menu, Portions **Directions:** Nearest station: Leicester Sq Please telephone for directions **Parking:** 80

Bank Aldwych Restaurant

Modern European

Metropolitan dining in theatreland

☎ 020 7379 9797 1 Kingsway WC2B 6XF Plan 3-D2
e-mail: aldres@bankrestaurants.com
web: www.bankrestaurants.com

Set in the heart of theatreland, this celebrated metropolitan brasserie has a vibrant modern interior that strikingly combines glass, mirrors, lightwood, black stone and vivid colour blocks. It's a bustling, buzzy place, with a popular front bar, glass-screened open-to-view kitchen, and a huge, lively restaurant that opens all day, serving power breakfasts, good-value lunches and sound modern brasserie dishes at

continued

LONDON WC2 *continued*

dinner. Sample the likes of fish soup, crab linguine, rib-eye steak with béarnaise, and passionfruit tart. Staff are friendly, sharply dressed and well organised.

Chef: Damien Pondevie **Owners:** Bank Restaurant Group plc **Times:** 12-2.45/5.30-11, Closed 25-26 Dec, 1-2 Jan, BHs, Closed D Sun **Prices:** Fixed L £13.50, Fixed D £16, Starter £6.50-£12.50, Main £12.50-£32, Dessert £5-£7.50, Coffee £2.25, Min/Water £3 **Wine:** 66 bottles over £20, 20 bottles under £20, 25 by the glass (£3.80-£8.20) **Notes:** Fixed D before 7pm/after 10pm, Vegetarian available, Dress Restrictions, Smart casual **Seats:** 230, Pr/dining room 30 **Smoking:** Air con **Children:** Menu, Portions **Directions:** Nearest station: Holborn, Charing Cross, Temple 2 mins from The Strand **Parking:** NCP Drury Lane

Christophers

Contemporary American

Victorian grandeur meets contemporary styling

☎ 020 7240 4222 18 Wellington St, Covent Garden WC2E 7DD Plan 3-D2
e-mail: coventgarden@christophersgrill.com
web: www.christophersgrill.com

A sweeping stone staircase provides an intriguing curtain raiser at this fascinating Victorian building, once London's first licensed casino and convenient for the Royal Opera House or theatre. High, decorative ceilings and tall windows blend with contemporary chic, via bold colours, polished-wood floors and striking accessories. The contemporary American cooking displays a sophisticated edge to match the surroundings, with dishes likes New York shrimp cocktail, oysters Rockefeller, New England clam bake, blackened salmon, Napa cabbage, chorizo, Maytag blue cheese dressing and Maine lobster backed by an array of steak options.

Times: 12-3/5-11, Closed 24 Dec-2 Jan, 25-26 Dec, 1 Jan, Closed D Sun **Directions:** Nearest station: Embankment/Covent Garden Just by Strand, overlooking Waterloo Bridge

Imperial China

Chinese V

Sophisticated Cantonese cooking with a delicate touch

☎ 020 7734 3388 White Bear Yard, 25a Lisle St WC2H 7BA Plan 3-B2
e-mail: mail@imperial-china.co.uk
web: www.imperial-china.co.uk

A large, busy restaurant off Lisle Street, where elegantly dressed staff keep the food moving efficiently between white-clothed tables and panelled pillars. A magnet for Chinese Londoners and ideal for private functions, there is now a waterfall complete with bridge and koi fish pond to enjoy. The light, delicate and sophisticated Cantonese cooking offers a comprehensive dim sum menu and both favourites and unfamiliar choices among the lengthy selection from southern China. Sip jasmine tea from a delicate cup while you work through the food descriptions. Why not start with steamed scallop with dong choi and vermicelli, then enjoy fried sliced pork with lotus root in red bean paste.

Chef: Mr Wing Kei Wong **Times:** 12/11.30, Closed Xmas **Prices:** Fixed L fr £14.95, Fixed D £18.95-£28.50, Starter £2.80-£34.95, Main £5.95-£23.95, Dessert £2.95-£4.25, Coffee £1.50, Min/Water £3.50, Service added but optional 12.5% **Wine:** 10 bottles over £20, 20 bottles under £20, 1 by the

continued

glass (£3) **Notes:** Vegetarian menu, Civ Wed 50 **Seats:** 350, Pr/dining room 50 **Smoking:** N/Sm area, Air con **Directions:** Nearest tube: Leicester Sq. From station into Little Newport St, straight ahead into Lisle St and right into White Bear Yard **Parking:** Chinatown car park

Incognico

French, Italian

Stylish brasserie in the heart of theatreland

☎ 020 7836 8866 117 Shaftesbury Av, Cambridge Circus WC2H 8AD Plan 3-C2
e-mail: incognicorestaurant@gmail.com
web: www.incognico.com

A discreet glass frontage - just a few paces from Cambridge Circus - picks out Incognico, its stylish good looks and atmosphere reminiscent of a classic French brasserie. The dark and moody, brown-toned interior is the work of design guru David Collins, replete with dark leather banquettes, oak panelling, stripped wooden floor and soft up-lighting. While the legacy of retired Nico Ladenis still lives on in the restaurant's witty name, the cooking's style continues to follow the same intelligent approach that allows ingredients to shine. Expect French/Italian dishes like escalope of foie gras with orange, perhaps veal milanese, and a pear and almond tart or pannacotta with poached strawberries to finish.

Chef: Jeremy Brown **Owners:** Sergio Rebecchi **Times:** 12-3/5.30-11, Closed 10 days Xmas, 4 days Easter, BHs, Sun **Prices:** Starter £5.50-£10.50, Main £12.50-£18.50, Dessert £4.50-£5.50, Coffee £3, Min/Water £3.50, Service added but optional 12.5% **Wine:** 50 bottles over £20, 6 bottles under £20, 12 by the glass (£4.50-£8.75) **Notes:** Vegetarian available, Dress Restrictions, Smart casual **Seats:** 85, Pr/dining room 20 **Smoking:** No pipes, Air con **Directions:** Nearest station: Leicester Sq Behind Cambridge Circus **Parking:** NCP

The Ivy

British, International

London theatreland legend, booking essential!

☎ 020 7836 4751 1 West St, Covent Garden WC2H 9NQ Plan 3-C2

One of London's most famous restaurants and a fixture of the gossip columns, this legendary dining destination is frequented by many of the world's biggest stars, and those hoping some A-list glamour will rub off onto them. As you might expect it's high-volume and hectic, though service is efficient. No-nonsense favourites like shepherd's pie and fishcakes feature on the long brasserie menu, alongside classics like tournedos Rossini and eggs Benedict, with the odd innovation thrown in to keep the gastronomes happy.

Chef: Alan Bird, Mark Hix **Owners:** Richard Caring Signature Restaurants **Times:** 12-3/5.30-12, Closed 25-26 Dec, 1 Jan, Aug BH, Closed L 27 Dec, D 24 Dec **Prices:** Fixed L £21.50, Starter £6.75-£15.75, Main £9.75-£35, Dessert £6.25-£8.50, Coffee £2.75, Min/Water £3.75, Service optional **Wine:** 112 bottles over £20, 7 bottles under £20, 14 by the glass (£5-£11.50) **Notes:** Fixed L 3 courses, Vegetarian available **Seats:** 100, Pr/dining room 60 **Smoking:** Air con **Children:** Portions **Directions:** Nearest station: Leicester Square Telephone for directions **Parking:** NCP, on street

England

Jaan Restaurant

LONDON WC2

Modern French, Asian

Impressive cuisine in smart Thameside hotel

☎ 020 7836 3555 Swissotel London, The Howard, Temple Place WC2R 2PR Plan 3-E2
e-mail: london@swissotel.com
web: www.london.swissotel.com

This smart hotel enjoys wonderful views across the London skyline from its Thames-side location, with the Jaan restaurant and bar opening out on to a delightful courtyard garden to offer alfresco dining in fair weather. Inside, there's a modern, contemporary edge to the spacious, stylish, clean lines of the Jaan. Wooden floors, luxurious silks, antique Asian artwork and friendly, yet formal service create the ambience. The kitchen's approach is inspired by modern French cuisine and enhanced by the delicate flavours of Asia, which blends perfectly with the surroundings. The enticing repertoire is delivered via a fixed-price medley, which includes value Business Lunch, five- or seven-course tasting options and carte. Top-class ingredients, consistency, sparkling technical artistry and presentation, balance and clarity and intensity of flavours all find their place. Expect a stylish composite starter like scallop and duck 'two ways' to show off the accomplished skills, with a sashimi of scallop, ponzu dressing, tobiko and duck consommé, plus seared scallop and confit of duck, complete with waiter instructions on the order in which it should be eaten. Mains might see a rack of lamb teamed with bok choy, baby aubergine, miso sauce and lamb jus, with another tasting-style dish, perhaps an 'Emphasis on Peach' to finish, delivering peach crumble with chilli, peach sorbet, jelly and spring roll.

Chef: Simon Duff **Owners:** New Ray Ltd **Times:** 12-2.30/5.45-10.30, Closed Sun, Closed L Sat **Prices:** Fixed L fr £19, Fixed D fr £38, Coffee £4, Min/Water £4, Service added 12.5% **Wine:** 1 bottle under £20, 12 by the glass (£5-£11) **Notes:** Tasting menu £45, Dress Restrictions, smart, casual, Civ Wed 100 **Seats:** 56 **Smoking:** No pipes, No cigars, Air con **Children:** Menu, Portions **Rooms:** 189 (189 en suite) ★★★★★ HL **Directions:** Nearest station: Temple Telephone for directions **Parking:** 30

J. Sheekey

Fish, Seafood V

Seafood restaurant in theatreland, favoured by celebrities

☎ 020 7240 2565 St Martin's Court WC2N 4AL Plan 3-C2
e-mail: reservations@j-sheekey.co.uk
web: www.j-sheekey.co.uk

This long-established restaurant proves ever popular for its dedication to seafood, in fact there's often a queue outside. Once past the doorman there's a dining bar and three separate rooms with closely set tables and photographs of the stars who have eaten here. Expect a bistro-like menu with separate sections for shellfish, crab, oysters and caviar before the rest of the dishes are listed. The main courses are all fish choices but there's a separate vegetarian and vegan menu. The cooking has a light touch, as in the perfectly timed piece of cod served with langoustine and sea purslane risotto.

Chef: Martin Dickenson **Owners:** Caprice Holdings **Times:** 12-3/5.30-12, Closed 25-26 Dec, 1 Jan, Aug BH, Closed D 24 Dec **Prices:** Starter £6.50-£15.25, Main £10.75-£29.75, Dessert £5.50-£8.50, Service optional **Wine:** 21 by the glass (£5-£9.50) **Notes:** Vegetarian menu **Seats:** 105 **Smoking:** No pipes, No cigars, Air con **Children:** Portions **Directions:** Nearest station: Leicester Square Telephone for directions **Parking:** On street

Maggiore's

French, Mediterranean 

Modern European cuisine in buzzy, Covent Garden restaurant

☎ 020 7379 9696 33 King St, Covent Garden WC2E 8JD Plan 3-C2
e-mail: enquiries@maggiores.uk.com
web: www.maggiores.uk.com

A red canopy and colourful flower boxes pick out this bistro from the Covent Garden crowd. Two intimate dining rooms - one with a large, conservatory-style skylight which opens fully in the summer - are laid out with wooden floors, elegantly laid tables and smoked mirrors, all backed by friendly and professional, mainly French, service. Modern focused and underpinned by a classical French theme, the classy, ambitious cooking uses high-quality ingredients in an eclectic repertoire of European dishes. Presentation is simple, portions

continued

England

LONDON WC2 *continued*

generous and flavours bold, accompanied by a superb wine list. Start with pan-fried foie gras, truffle honey and tarte Tatin of parsnip, followed by slow-cooked fillet of Cornish cod, casserole of Tarbais beans with shrimp, oyster and champagne velouté.

Notable Wine List: One of the largest wine lists in the UK with around 2,000 bins offering great depth and quality throughout.

Chef: Marcellin Marc **Owners:** Tyfoon Restaurants Ltd **Times:** 12-2.30/5-11, Closed 24-26 Dec & 1 Jan **Prices:** Fixed L £20.50, Fixed D £25.50, Starter £6.50-£12.50, Main £15.50-£18.50, Dessert £7.50, Coffee £4, Min/Water £4.50, Service added but optional 12.5% **Wine:** 1906 bottles over £20, 10 bottles under £20, 15 by the glass (£4-£9) **Notes:** Tasting menu £65, Vegetarian available, Civ Wed 150 **Seats:** 70, Pr/dining room 30 **Smoking:** N/Sm in restaurant, Air con **Children:** Portions **Directions:** Nearest station: Covent Garden 1 min walk from The Piazza and Royal Opera House **Parking:** NCP, on street

Mela

Indian

Classical Indian cooking in theatreland

☎ 020 7836 8635 152-156 Shaftesbury Av WC2H 8HL Plan 3-C2
e-mail: info@melarestaurant.co.uk
web: www.melarestaurant.co.uk

Handy for theatreland at the top end of Shaftesbury Avenue, this is a busy well-established Indian restaurant. The ground-floor dining area is bright and spacious with an eye-catching Indian mural lit by fairy lights. Smartly attired staff in dark tunics provide attentive and enthusiastic service. The carte is available at lunch and dinner and there is also a great value lunch menu offering snack-type dishes like stuffed parathas, open breads and curries. The simple, classical Indian cooking also includes some Western produce such as quail, soft shell crab, sea bass, rabbit and scallops.

Chef: Kuldeep Singh, Uday Seth **Owners:** Kuldeep Singh **Times:** 12-3/5.30-11.30, Closed Xmas **Prices:** Fixed L £15, Starter £3.50-£6.25, Main £5.95-£21.95, Dessert £3.50-£4.50, Service added but optional 12.5% **Wine:** 3 bottles over £20, 20 bottles under £20, 5 by the glass (£3.25-£3.95) **Notes:** Vegetarian menu **Seats:** 105, Pr/dining room 35 **Smoking:** N/Sm area, Air con **Parking:** NCP, Chinatown

Mon Plaisir

French

A Francophile's delight in central London

☎ 020 7836 7243 21 Monmouth St WC2H 9DD Plan 3-C2
e-mail: eatafrog@mail.com
web: www.monplaisir.co.uk

About as French as you can get this side of the Channel, this cosy network of rooms is decked out with modern abstracts and interesting artefacts. The atmosphere buzzes with pre- and post-theatre diners, muffling the conversation from closely packed neighbours. Everything on the classic and modern French menus is freshly cooked, including very traditional rustic dishes like foie gras or pork terrine, French onion soup, coq au vin and raisin tart. All desserts are hand made by the chef patissier. Friendly professional Gallic waiters glide smoothly between the neatly clothed tables.

Chef: Frank Raymond **Owners:** Alain Lhermitte **Times:** 12-2.15/5.45-11.15, Closed Xmas, New Year, BHs, Sun, Closed L Sat **Prices:** Fixed L £13.95, Fixed

continued

D £14.50, Starter £5.95-£12.95, Main £14.50-£21.50, Dessert £5.75, Coffee £2.05, Min/Water £2.95, Service added but optional 12.5% **Wine:** 40 bottles over £20, 9 bottles under £20, 14 by the glass (£3.75-£6.90) **Notes:** Regional menu available monthly £23.50, Vegetarian available, Dress Restrictions, Smart casual **Seats:** 100, Pr/dining room 28 **Smoking:** No pipes, No cigars, Air con **Children:** Portions **Directions:** Nearest station: Covent Garden, Leicester Square Off Seven Dials

The Neal Street Restaurant

Traditional Italian

Famous restaurant run by renowned, mushroom-loving celebrity chef

☎ 020 7836 8368 26 Neal St WC2H 9QW Plan 3-D2
e-mail: gianluca@nealstreet.co.uk
web: www.carluccios.com

After 34 years Antonio Carluccio's much-loved and popular Covent Garden restaurant still remains a magnet for lovers of authentic, regional Italian food. The stylish interior sets modern art (Hockneys and Paolozzis) and a distinctive collection of walking sticks against white brick walls. Closely packed tables, a buzzy atmosphere (particularly in the evenings) and efficient Italian staff complete the front-of-house picture. Sophisticated simplicity and authentic, high-quality ingredients are the menu's common thread, in season focusing on Carluccio's passion - mushrooms and truffles. The appealing repertoire delivers an enticing range of traditional dishes from every region of Italy; take risotto with white truffle, a classic lobster linguine, or perhaps calves' liver with caramelised onions Venetian style, all backed by excellent breads.

Chef: Maurilio Molteni **Owners:** Antonio Carluccio, Priscilla Carluccio **Times:** 12-2.30/6-11, Closed 25 Dec-2 Jan, Easter Mon, BHs, Sun **Prices:** Fixed L fr £21, Fixed D fr £25, Starter £7.50-£14, Main £15-£23, Dessert £5.50-£8, Coffee £2.50, Min/Water £3.50, Service added but optional 12.5% **Wine:** 104 bottles over £20, 5 bottles under £20, 10 by the glass (£5-£8.50) **Notes:** Vegetarian available, Dress Restrictions, Smart casual **Seats:** 65, Pr/dining room 24 **Smoking:** N/Sm in restaurant, Air con **Children:** Portions **Directions:** Nearest station: Covent Garden Short walk from tube station **Parking:** Shelton Street

One Aldwych - Axis

European

Dramatic dining venue in the heart of theatreland

☎ 020 7300 0300 1 Aldwych WC2B 4RH Plan 3-D2
e-mail: axis@onealdwych.com
web: www.onealdwych.com

A double-height ceiling and abstract cityscape mural give this hip and trendy metropolitan restaurant its wow-factor. Its amazing muted

continued

colours, black leather upholstery and the occasional live jazz band. Staff make dining here far from an impersonal experience with helpful table service. Good ingredients are skilfully prepared in the modern British style with Asian, American and European influences, like starters of crispy duck noodle salad and the roasted Canadian halibut provençale main course. Puddings are less far-ranging with old favourites like baked chocolate pot with Black Forest cherry compôte or prune and Armagnac soufflé with Chantilly cream.

Chef: Mark Gregory **Owners:** Gordon Campbell-Gray **Times:** 12-2.45/5.45-10.45, Closed Xmas, New Year, Sun, Closed L Sat **Prices:** Fixed L £16.75, Fixed D £19.75, Starter £5.75-£11.25, Main £13.95-£27.75, Dessert £5.50-£7.95, Coffee £3.25, Min/Water £3.95, Service added but optional 12.5% **Wine:** 187 bottles over £20, 3 bottles under £20, 13 by the glass (£4.95-£9.25) **Notes:** Vegetarian available, Civ Wed 60 **Seats:** 120, Pr/dining room 40 **Smoking:** No cigars, Air con **Children:** Menu, Portions **Directions:** Nearest station: Covent Garden At point where Aldwych meets the Strand opposite Waterloo Bridge. On corner of Aldwych & Wellington St, opposite Lyceum Theatre **Parking:** NCP - Wellington St

One Aldwych - Indigo

Modern European

Trendy mezzanine dining

☎ 020 7300 0400 1 Aldwych WC2B 4RH Plan 3-D2
e-mail: indigo@onealdwych.com
web: www.onealdwych.com

The epitome of modern chic and contemporary styling, this sophisticated restaurant is set on a balcony overlooking the buzzy hotel lobby bar below, making it the perfect spot for people-watching.

continued

Spotlights zoom down onto tables, seats are comfortable, service is focused and the atmosphere fashionable and relaxed. The kitchen follows the theme, with cosmopolitan, flavour-driven, clean-cut dishes delivered on creatively flexible menus that play to the gallery. There's the option to create your own pasta or salad dish, others can be taken as a starter or main course, while the more structured fine-dining options might deliver Gloucestershire Old Spot pork fillet with a cashew nut crust, goat's cheese and an apple and Calvados Tatin.

One Aldwych - Indigo

Chef: Alex Wood **Owners:** Gordon Campbell-Gray **Times:** 12-3/6-11.15 **Prices:** Fixed L £16.75, Fixed D £19.75, Starter £5.75-£10.25, Main £8.25-£21.50, Dessert £6.50-£8.95, Coffee £3.25, Min/Water £3.95, Service added but optional 12.5% **Wine:** 69 bottles over £20, 2 bottles under £20, 15 by the glass (£4.95-£9.75) **Notes:** Vegetarian available, Civ Wed 60 **Seats:** 62 **Smoking:** No pipes, No cigars, Air con **Children:** Menu, Portions **Rooms:** 105 (105 en suite) ★★★★★ **Directions:** Nearest station: Covent Garden, Charing Cross Located where The Aldwych meets The Strand opposite Waterloo Bridge **Parking:** Valet parking

Origin

LONDON WC2

***Modern European* NEW**

Theatreland grazing menus in contemporary surroundings

☎ 020 7170 9200 The Hospital, 24 Endell St, WC2H 9HQ
web: www.origin-restaurant.com

Set in The Hospital multimedia centre on Endell Street slap bang in the middle of Covent Garden, this new restaurant (opened late 2005) is a replacement for Thyme. The grazing-concept cooking at Origin remains in the safe hands of chef Adam Byatt, while the restaurant's name gives a clue to Adam's criteria for sourcing traceable produce and using independent suppliers for the tip-top quality ingredients used in the kitchen.

The restaurant itself hasn't a street frontage but is housed within The Hospital building, and is something of a mezzanine box, with small windows along one side and a glass wall that looks into an internal atrium at the back. It's decorated in dark blue and white, while darkwood panels separate the dining room from the bar area. Spotlights peer down on tables and modern art adds a cool feel to the contemporary space, while service is efficient and unfussy.

Adam's style is modern, refined, high-skilled precision cooking, the approach via standard three-course menus with the option of smaller, light, starter-sized grazing dishes (the concept that made his name at Thyme) at mains and dessert - it's a fashionable way to try more dishes and sample different flavour combinations. The cooking's foundation has a classical theme, but oozes innovation and creativity, with accurate flavours, texture interest and excellent presentation. Think roast rib of beef with celeriac dauphinoise, pot-roast vegetables and a port jus, or perhaps prune-stuffed rabbit teamed with pumpkin purée and russet apple jus. For dessert, how about chestnut bavarois with grape jelly and biscotti ice cream, while the elegant wine list is specifically designed to pair easily with the grazing-concept menu.

Chef: Adam Byatt **Times:** 12-2.30/6-10.30 **Seats:** 30

LONDON WC2 *continued*

Origin

see page 353

Orso Restaurant

Modern Italian

Italian food in a buzzing basement

☎ 020 7240 5269 27 Wellington St WC2E 7DB Plan 3-D2
e-mail: info@orsorestaurant.co.uk
web: www.orsorestaurant.co.uk

A discreet, street-level entrance leads downstairs to the cavernous basement dining room (once an orchid warehouse) at this long-established, all-day Covent Garden Italian that reverberates with energy, conversation and the clinking of glasses and cutlery. Herringbone floors, pastel tablecloths, fanciful frescoes and friendly staff - constantly flitting about - add to the lively, informal atmosphere. The crowd-pleasing bilingual menu showcases regional Italian cooking and offers bags of choice, from pizza to pot-roast lamb with tomato, black olives and white beans. A pre-theatre menu and weekend brunch offer excellent value.

Chef: Martin Wilson **Owners:** Orso Restaurants Ltd **Times:** noon/midnight, Closed 24 & 25 Dec **Prices:** Fixed D £18, Starter £5.50-£9.50, Main £14-£16, Dessert £6, Min/Water £3.50, Service optional, Group min 8 service 12.5% **Wine:** 37 bottles over £20, 9 bottles under £20, 15 by the glass (£6.50-£11.50) **Notes:** Fixed D is pre-theatre, Vegetarian available **Seats:** 100 **Smoking:** N/Sm area, No pipes, No cigars, Air con **Directions:** Nearest station: Covent Garden Telephone for directions **Parking:** On street

The Portrait Restaurant

Modern British

Stylish, contemporary dining with rooftop views

☎ 020 7312 2490 National Portrait Gallery, St Martins Place WC2H 0HE Plan 3-C1
e-mail: portrait.restaurant@searcys.co.uk
web: www.searcys.co.uk

Offering a stunning London landscape from the rooftop restaurant of the National Portrait Gallery, this light, sleek and contemporary affair is decked out in grey with a wall of glass windows that lets those views do the talking. It's high on volume though, with minimalist hard surfaces and a small bar cranking up the decibels. Light, colourful, clean-cut, bistro-styled dishes - with the occasional Mediterranean slant - provide an accomplished accompaniment to the London skyline. Begin with caramelised beetroot tart, roast pine nuts and balsamic treacle, then enjoy braised lamb shank, confit baby onions, winter vegetables and mashed potatoes.

Chef: Katarina Todosijevic **Owners:** Searcys **Times:** 11.45-2.45/5.30-8.30, Closed 24-26 Dec, 1 Jan, Good Fri, Closed D Sat-Wed **Prices:** Fixed L £17.95-£33.95, Starter £5.95-£9.95, Main £11.95-£23.95, Dessert £6.50-£6.95, Coffee £2.25, Min/Water £3, Service added but optional 12.5% **Wine:** 25 bottles over £20, 10 bottles under £20, 15 by the glass (£3.75-£7) **Notes:** Pre theatre menu £13.95-£16.95, brunch menu £19.50-£24.50, Vegetarian available **Seats:** 100 **Smoking:** N/Sm area, Air con **Children:** Menu, Portions **Directions:** Nearest station: Leicester Square, Charing Cross Just behind Trafalgar Square **Parking:** NCP - Orange St

The Savoy Grill

LONDON WC2

British, French  

Flawless cooking at re-styled legendary restaurant

☎ 020 7592 1600 The Savoy, Strand WC2R 0EU Plan 3-D1
e-mail: savoygrill@marcuswareing.com
web: www.marcuswareing.com

Modernisation has brought a successful balance between the traditional and contemporary in Barbara Barry's redesign of this much-loved institution, while Marcus Wareing has ushered the menu into the present day, though with the odd affectionate nod to its past tradition, as in Scottish smoked salmon and gravad lax carved at the trolley, or the lunchtime dessert trolley. The historic art deco character has been retained but with a lighter touch, mixing semi-circular banquette seating in sleek tobacco, nougat and black stripe with more traditional chairs, while the shimmering gold-leaf effect ceiling and crisp white linen combine to create understated richness. Service fits the bill, too, and is professional and slick without being overbearing. The kitchen's modern approach - underpinned by classical French roots - is based around superb-quality ingredients, precise technical skills and great attention to detail. Clear, clean flavours, seasonality and fine balance parade on a repertoire of fixed-price menus (oozing luxury) that includes a tasting option. Think roast rack of Cornish lamb with confit shoulder, celery leaf gnocchi, baby leeks and carrots and lamb jus, while a warm Valrhona chocolate truffle comes with vanilla ice cream and a sweet basil sauce. A serious wine list and a chef's table in the heart of the kitchen wrap up a class package. (See also Marcus Wareing's restaurant, Pétrus, SW1.)

Notable Wine List: A classic and extensive wine list with a comprehensive offering from around the world.

Chef: Lee Scott **Owners:** Marcus Wareing at the Savoy Grill Ltd **Times:** 12-3/5.45-11 **Prices:** Fixed L fr £30, Fixed D £55, Service added but optional 12.5% **Wine:** 440 bottles over £20, 1 bottle under £20, 12 by the glass (£5-£19.50) **Notes:** Fixed L 4 courses, Early supper £30, Sun L available, Vegetarian menu, Smart, jacket preferred, no jeans/trainers **Seats:** 70, Pr/dining room 60 **Smoking:** N/Sm in restaurant, Air con **Children:** Menu, Portions **Directions:** Nearest station: Charing Cross/Covent Garden Please telephone for directions **Parking:** on street

Belgo

☎ 020 7813 2233 50 Earlham St WC2H 9HP
Belgian style, extending to strong beer, good seafood (mussels of course) and staff in habits.

Café du Jardin

☎ 020 7836 8769 28 Wellington St WC2E 7BD
Mediterranean-style dishes at this bustling split-level restaurant.

Loch Fyne Restaurant, Covent Garden

☎ 020 7240 4999 2-4 Catherine St WC2B 5JS
Quality seafood chain.

Strada

☎ 020 7405 6293 6 Great Queen St WC2B 5DH
Superior pizza from quality ingredients cooked in wood-fired ovens.

The Terrace

☎ 020 430 9115 Lincoln's Inn Field, Holborn WC2A 3LJ
web: www.theaa.com/restaurants/114069.html

Surrounded by mature trees and landscaped lawns this is an eco-friendly building using recycled or 100% recyclable materials. British cuisine with Caribbean touches.

Tuttons Brasserie

☎ 020 7836 4141 11-12 Russell St, Covent Garden WC2B 5HZ
web: www.theaa.com/restaurants/114013.html

British and European menus at a relaxed, friendly, child friendly, watch-the-world-go-by location.

Wagamama

☎ 020 7836 3330 1 Tavistock St, Covent Garden WC2E 7PG
Informal noodle bars with no booking.

LONDON, GREATER

BARNET MAP 06 TQ29

Dylan's

Modern European **NEW**

Modern surroundings for cutting-edge global cuisine

☎ 020 8275 1551 21 Station Pde, Cockfosters EN4 0DW
e-mail: dylan@dylansrestaurant.com
web: www.dylansrestaurant.com

This modern high street restaurant stands out with its glass frontage, leading to a modern interior and a trendy grey, white and burgundy colour scheme. The modern cuisine is confidently prepared and cooked with a deftness of touch. Imaginative dishes might include organic smoked salmon with onion Scotch pancake and baby gem salad to start, followed by breast of duck with apple mash, braised chicory and roasted salsify. Add in a side order like roasted carrots with thyme, or hold out for a delicious dessert like fig and almond pudding with clotted cream.

Chef: Richard O'Connell **Owners:** Dylan Murray, Richard O'Connell **Times:** 12-2.30/6-10 **Prices:** Fixed L £12.50, Fixed D £15.50, Starter £4.90-£8.90, Main £10.50-£16.75, Dessert £5-£6.50, Coffee £2.25, Min/Water £2.50, Service added but optional 12.5% **Wine:** 14 bottles over £20, 16 bottles under £20, 16 by the glass (£3.25-£6.95) **Notes:** Sun Jazz L, 2 courses £18.50, 3 courses £22.50, Vegetarian available, Dress Restrictions, Smart casual **Seats:** 90, Pr/dining room 8 **Smoking:** N/Sm in restaurant, Air con **Children:** Menu, Portions **Directions:** M25 junct 24, follow A111 towards Cockfosters for 3m, Dylan's on left hand side of Cockfosters Rd **Parking:** On street

---

BECKENHAM

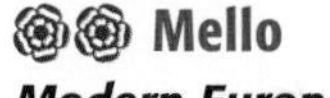

Mello

Modern European

Fashionable dining near suburban high street

☎ 020 8663 0994 2 Southend Rd BR3 1SD
e-mail: info@mello.uk.com
web: www.mello.uk.com

continued

BECKENHAM *continued*

Not quite where you might expect to find somewhere delivering such imaginative, clear-flavoured cuisine, but this ambitious modern restaurant - located in a Victorian listed building - is well worth uncovering. High-backed leather and suede chairs, contemporary art on lemon walls, white table linen and a deep-red carpet cut a simple but effective style. The kitchen clearly has skill and potential, with presentation elegant and sophisticated and ingredients of high quality. The appealing, well-priced repertoire cuts a modern European line, with starters, mains and desserts all one-priced, save a few supplements for the more luxury items; perhaps ham hock, wood pigeon and foie gras terrine or an assiette of Barbary duck served with potted cabbage, Lyonnaise potato and thyme jus. One to watch.

Chef: Christopher Bower **Owners:** A Demirtas **Times:** 12-2.30/6-10, Closed D Sun **Prices:** Starter £4.50-£7, Main £13.50-£17.50, Dessert £4.50-£7, Coffee £1.90, Min/Water £3, Service added but optional 12.5% **Wine:** 34 bottles over £20, 22 bottles under £20, 4 by the glass (£3.50) **Notes:** Tasting menu £60, Sun L £17, Vegetarian available, Dress Restrictions, Smart casual **Seats:** 90, Pr/dining room 36 **Smoking:** No pipes, Air con **Children:** Portions **Directions:** 0.5m from Beckenham town centre, directly opposite Beckenham train station **Parking:** 26

BROMLEY
See LONDON SECTION Plan 1-G1

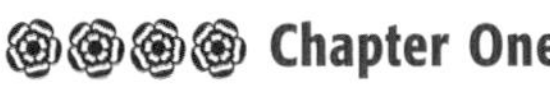

Chapter One

see opposite

Tamasha

☎ 020 8460 3240 131 Widmore Rd BR1 3AX
web: www.theaa.com/restaurants/113911.html

Indian restaurant with Raj-inspired décor and a comprehensive collection of cricketing memorabilia. Live entertainment early in the week.

ENFIELD MAP 06 TQ39

Royal Chace Hotel

International

Airy hotel brasserie

☎ 020 8884 8181 The Ridgeway EN2 8AR
e-mail: reservations@royalchacehotel.co.uk
web: www.royal-chace.com

Privately-owned hotel set in open countryside not far from Enfield. Its spacious brasserie is a tasteful concoction of polished wood, leafy plants and muted shades, and draws a mix of locals, guests and suits with a wide-ranging menu of classic and modern dishes. Start with foie gras and chicken parfait perhaps, served with figs and Parma ham, and then tuck into seared scallops and bacon with a vegetable and citrus salsa and Japanese dressing, or heavier fare such as beef with béarnaise sauce, or venison with beetroot fondant, sautéed cabbage, red wine and chocolate sauce.

Royal Chace Hotel

Chef: Chris Jenkins **Owners:** R Nicholas **Times:** 7-10, Closed Xmas, Closed L Mon-Sat, D Sun **Prices:** Fixed D fr £29.95, Starter £4.25-£8.25, Main £9.45-£16.95, Dessert fr £4.50, Coffee £1.75, Min/Water £2.60, Service added but optional 10% **Wine:** 7 bottles over £20, 36 bottles under £20 **Notes:** Vegetarian available, Dress Restrictions, No jeans or trainers, Civ Wed 220 **Seats:** 120, Pr/dining room 50 **Smoking:** N/Sm in restaurant, Air con **Children:** Menu, Portions **Rooms:** 92 (92 en suite) ★★★ HL **Directions:** 3m from M25 junct 24, 1.5m to Enfield **Parking:** 220

HADLEY WOOD MAP 06 TQ29

West Lodge Park Hotel, The Cedar Restaurant

Modern British

Solid cooking in a splendid hotel

☎ 020 8216 3900 Cockfosters Rd EN4 0PY
e-mail: westlodgepark@bealeshotels.co.uk
web: www.bealeshotel.co.uk

Located just inside the M25, this stunning country house with magnificent grounds (including a well-known arboretum) was visited by both Elizabeth I and King James I and contains a collection of paintings by Mary Beale. Converted into a hotel in 1921, it is now decorated with a luxurious balance of modern and traditional themes. The Cedar Restaurant is fairly traditional both in its formal style of service and in the cuisine, which looks to British classics for inspiration, with contemporary flourishes adding zest. You might start with game pie with a bramble and port coulis, then continue with pan-fried sea bass with champ and a white wine sauce. Quirky dishes such as strawberry consommé with fig jelly (as a pre-dessert) really spice things up.

Chef: Wayne Turner **Owners:** Beales Ltd **Times:** 12.30-2/7-10, Closed L Sat **Prices:** Starter £6.50-£10.50, Main £17.50-£24.95, Dessert £7.50, Coffee £2.95, Min/Water £3.85, Service optional **Wine:** 110 bottles over £20, 14 bottles under £20, 13 by the glass (£5.05-£9.85) **Notes:** Vegetarian available, Dress Restrictions, Smart casual, jacket & tie recommended, Civ Wed 72 **Seats:** 70, Pr/dining room 54 **Smoking:** N/Sm in restaurant, Air con **Children:** Portions **Rooms:** 59 (59 en suite) ★★★★ HL **Directions:** On the A111, 1m S of M25 junct 24 **Parking:** 75

continued

England

Chapter One

BROMLEY See LONDON SECTION Plan 1-G1

Modern European

Sophisticated cooking at unbeatable prices

☎ 01689 854848 Farnborough Common, Locksbottom BR6 8NF
e-mail: info@chaptersrestaurants.com
web: www.chaptersrestaurants.co.uk

Chef: Andrew McLeish
Owners: Selective Restaurants Group
Times: 12-2.30/6.30-10.30, Closed 1-4 Jan
Prices: Fixed L fr £16.50, Starter £5.95, Main £15.50, Dessert £5.50, Coffee £2.50, Min/Water £3, Service added but optional 12.5%
Wine: 120 bottles over £20, 36 bottles under £20, 14 by the glass (£3.75-£5.50)
Notes: Tasting menu with wine £60, Sun D 3 courses £22.95, Dress Restrictions, No shorts, jeans or trainers
Seats: 120, Pr/dining room 55
Smoking: N/Sm in restaurant, Air con
Children: Portions
Directions: Situated on A21, 3m from Bromley. From M25 junct 4 onto A21 for 5m
Parking: 90

With its mock-Tudor appearance Chapter One is handily located on the A21 and home to Andrew McLeish's much-acclaimed cooking. The front door opens into a world of refinement, from the spacious dining room with its metropolitan styling and serene pastel tones to the suave, professional and welcoming service. Wooden floors, dark blue upholstered chairs and crisp linen continue the theme, while a separate brasserie with a louder buzz and more casual edge, attracts a wised-up crowd looking for culinary thrills at cheaper prices.

McLeish's confident and accomplished cooking aptly suits the surroundings and takes a modern European approach based on classical techniques, with dishes displaying plenty of innovation alongside distinct flavours, balanced combinations and high skill. Quality ingredients are certainly handled with consummate integrity here. Think slow-roast belly of Suffolk pork teamed with Savoy cabbage, potato fondant and a foie gras and caramelised apple purée, while pan-fried, line-caught sea bass might be accompanied by a risotto of clam and chorizo sausage, and to finish, perhaps an organic lemon tart served with a crème fraîche sorbet and millefeuille of passionfruit. The appealing repertoire is a fixed-price affair (one-price starters, mains and desserts) and reads like central London luxury with suburban prices - lunch offering fantastic value at this level. The wine list shows admirable pedigree, too, while its sister restaurant over in Blackheath is perhaps predictably called Chapter Two (see entry) and is worth checking out.

England

HARROW ON THE HILL

Incanto

☎ 020 8426 6767 41 High St HA1 3HT
web: www.theaa.com/restaurants/114010.html

Southern Italian food in welcoming former post office.

HEATHROW AIRPORT
See LONDON SECTION Plan 1-A3

Simply Nico

French

French brasserie-style cuisine in stylish surroundings

☎ 0870 400 9140 Crowne Plaza London - Heathrow, Stockley Rd UB7 9NA
e-mail: heathrow.simplynico@corushotels.com
web: www.london-heathrow.crowneplaza.com

An elegant restaurant with high ceiling, art-deco lighting, canary yellow walls and well-spaced tables - the perfect setting for modern French brasserie cuisine. The theatre-style kitchen behind glass gives diners a window on the workings behind the scenes. The fixed-price

continued

menu lists three selected dishes for each course. The main menu offers an excellent choice with quality seafood and some luxury ingredients and intense flavours. Look out for classics like pan-fried calves' liver with crispy pancetta and spring onion pomme purée or puddings such as chocolate and raspberry roulade with chocolate sauce.

Chef: Patrick Power **Owners:** Corus Hotel **Times:** 5-11, Closed BHs, Sun **Prices:** Fixed D £23.50-£42.40, Starter £4.95-£12.95, Main £12.95-£23.95, Dessert £5-£5.50, Service added but optional 10% **Wine:** 21 bottles over £20, 12 bottles under £20, 11 by the glass (£4.25-£7.25) **Notes:** Vegetarian available **Seats:** 120 **Smoking:** N/Sm in restaurant, Air con **Children:** Portions **Rooms:** 458 (458 en suite) ★★★★ HL **Directions:** From M25 junct 15 take M4. At junct 4 take A408, straight on at lights, hotel on slip road on left **Parking:** 50

KEW See LONDON SECTION Plan 1-C3

The Glasshouse

see opposite

KINGSTON UPON THAMES
See LONDON SECTION Plan 1-C1

Ayudhya Thai Restaurant

Thai

Authentic, neighbourhood Thai in the heart of suburbia

☎ 020 8546 5878 0208 5495984
14 Kingston Hill KT2 7NH

A charmingly authentic, long-established Thai, unassumingly set in a small parade of shops. Once inside, you're transported to another world, via dark-wood panelled walls, pitched roof lines, Thai royal family pictures, wood carvings and original artefacts. Oriental music and polite, authentically costumed staff complete the traditional picture. An extensive menu of Thai staples follows the décor's theme. Dishes are colourful and light, with good texture interest and deft seasoning that will certainly get those taste buds tingling. Try green papaya salad 'Ayudhya' to begin, then follow with deep-fried monkfish with ginger. Handy menu notes and a few set options aid the novice, and there's a takeway service, too.

Times: 12-2.30/6.30-11, Closed Xmas, BHs, Closed L Mon
Directions: 0.5m from Kingston town centre on A308, and 2.5m from Robin Hood rdbt at junction of A3.

England

The Glasshouse

KEW
See LONDON SECTION Plan 1-C3
Modern British 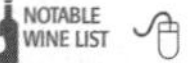
Local favourite with a light touch

☎ 020 8940 6777 14 Station Rd TW9 3PZ
e-mail: info@glasshouserestaurant.co.uk
web: www.glasshouserestaurant.co.uk

Glass-fronted in keeping with its name (and probably inspired by its neighbour, the Royal Botanic Gardens), this sophisticated, smart and buzzy local restaurant - set in a parade of Kew Village shops close to Kew Bridge tube station - is a class act and sister to Chez Bruce, the well-known Wandsworth restaurant (see entry). Its sleek, contemporary décor has a light-and-airy appeal, drawing a loyal crowd of devotees with its vibrant atmosphere and bustling mix of diners. An eclectic mix of furniture, antiques, cushions and drapes blends with well-spaced tables and the appropriately relaxed and friendly yet professional service. The precision cooking is impressive, too, taking an unfussy modern and seasonal approach, distinguished by a light touch and clean, clear flavours. Think slow-roast pork belly served with Morteau sausage, apple tarte fine, choucroute, prunes and crispy ham, or perhaps crisp sea bass accompanied by creamed white polenta, shrimps, mussels and caramelised endive, and to finish, a hot chocolate fondant teamed with pistachio ice cream. The appealing menu repertoire comes at fixed prices (and includes a seven-course tasting option), while the wine list is a notable affair, with many available by the glass.

Notable Wine List: A superb all-round wine list, beautifully presented with quality selections in every area.

Chef: Anthony Boyd **Owners:** Larkbrace Ltd **Times:** 12-2.30/7-10.30, Closed Xmas, New Year **Prices:** Fixed L £18.50, Fixed D £35, Coffee £3.50, Min/Water £3.50, Service added but optional 12.5% **Wine:** 468 bottles over £20, 9 bottles under £20, 15 by the glass (£4-£11) **Notes:** Tasting menu 7 courses £45, Vegetarian available **Seats:** 60 **Smoking:** N/Sm in restaurant, Air con **Children:** Menu, Portions **Directions:** Telephone for directions **Parking:** On street; metered

Carluccio's Caffè

☎ 020 8549 5898 Charter Quay KT1 1HT
Quality Italian chain.

Frère Jacques

☎ 020 8546 1332 10 -12 Riverside Walk, Bishops Hall KT1 1QN
web: www.frerejacques.co.uk
Simple French fare in a relaxed riverside bistro.

Strada

☎ 020 8974 8555 1 The Griffin Centre, Market Place KT1 1JT
web: www.theaa.com/restaurants/114033.html
One of the newest additions to this perennially popular chain of modern Italian restaurants, occupying two floors of a grand listed building near the Thames.

Wagamama

☎ 020 8546 1117 16-18 High St KT1 1EY
Informal noodle bar with no booking.

Two Rosettes
The best local restaurants, which aim for and achieve higher standards, better consistency and where a greater precision is apparent in the cooking. There will be obvious attention to the selection of quality ingredients.

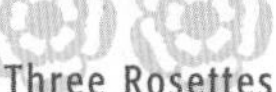

Three Rosettes
Outstanding restaurants that demand recognition well beyond their local area. Timing, seasoning and the judgement of flavour combinations will be consistently excellent, supported by other elements such as intelligent service and well-chosen wine list.

PINNER MAP 06 TQ18
SEE LONDON SECTION PLAN 1-B5

Friends Restaurant

Modern British

Good suburban brasserie dining

☎ 020 8866 0286 11 High St HA5 5PJ
e-mail: info@friendsrestaurant.co.uk
web: www.friendsrestaurant.co.uk

This high street restaurant with its black-and-white timber frontage lures impulse diners into the comfortably appointed, two-floor interior. Smartly dressed staff - under the eye of the chef-proprietor - move between the leather-clad seating and smartly dressed tables dispensing light starters of Shetland salmon marinated in whisky and lime. Main courses are more robust including a generous confit duck leg and breast with garlic mash and red wine sauce or jugged Berkshire hare. Finish with apple and macaroon crumble served with cinnamon ice cream.

Chef: Terry Farr **Owners:** Mr Farr **Times:** 12-3/6.30-10.30, Closed 25 Dec, BHs, Mon in summer, Closed D Sun **Prices:** Fixed L £14.50, Fixed D £25.50, Starter £6.25-£7.50, Main £15.95-£28.50, Dessert £6.75-£7.50, Coffee £2.75, Min/Water £3.50, Service added but optional 10% **Wine:** 40 bottles over £20, 6 bottles under £20, 7 by the glass (£4-£5.50) **Notes:** Vegetarian available **Seats:** 40 **Smoking:** N/Sm in restaurant, Air con **Children:** Portions **Directions:** In centre of Pinner, 2 mins walk from underground station **Parking:** Nearby car parks x3

RICHMOND (UPON THAMES) MAP 06 TQ17
SEE LONDON SECTION PLAN 1-C3

Bingham Hotel, Restaurant & Bar

Modern British

Romantic dining by the banks of Old Father Thames

☎ 020 8940 0902 61-63 Petersham Rd TW10 6UT
e-mail: reservations@thebingham.co.uk
web: www.thebingham.co.uk

Enjoying a wonderful riverside location, this Georgian townhouse now houses a boutique hotel and its romantic riverside restaurant. Black wallpaper, river views and custom-made chandeliers provide contemporary atmosphere in spades. For summer evenings, there are balcony tables. Simple, attractively presented classic British and European dishes use lots of British ingredients such as the baked river trout starter with new potatoes and rocket salad and the main course of Scottish fillet of beef with duchess potatoes and shallot and red wine butter. Side orders include gratinated cauliflower, ratte potato wedges and colcannon. Excellent table service.

Chef: Bruce Wright **Owners:** Ruth & Samantha Trinder **Times:** 12.30-4/7-10, Closed 26 Dec-early Jan, Closed D Sun **Prices:** Fixed L £17-£20, Fixed D £25-£38, Coffee £2.50, Min/Water £3.50, Service added 12.5% **Wine:** 22 bottles over £20, 10 bottles under £20, 7 by the glass (£4-£7) **Notes:** Civ Wed 50 **Seats:** 40, Pr/dining room 30 **Smoking:** N/Sm in restaurant **Children:** Menu, Portions **Rooms:** 23 (23 en suite) ★★★ HL **Directions:** Please telephone for directions **Parking:** 12

La Buvette

French

Stylish French bistro

☎ 020 8940 6264 6 Church Walk TW9 1SN
e-mail: info@brulabistrot.com
web: www.la-buvette.com

Sister restaurant to Brula in Twickenham (see entry), this is a unique property, built in York stone within an old church refectory. The courtyard seats 40 in summer and is protected from the elements by brick walls, a canopied entrance and enormous umbrella. Inside the sunny yellow walls give a Mediterranean feel. The classical French bistro-style menu features the likes of fricassée of snails or whole baked Vacherin Mont d'Or to share as starters, while mains might include tenderloin of pork with macaroni à l'ancienne. The formula is popular with discerning locals who return to savour the taste of France.

Chef: Buck Carter & Toby Williams **Owners:** Lawrence Hartley & Bruce Duckett **Times:** 12-3/6-11, Closed 25-26 Dec, 1 Jan, Good Fri **Prices:** Fixed L £11, Starter £4.50-£8.50, Main £11.50-£15.25, Dessert £4.75, Coffee £2.50, Min/Water £3, Service optional **Wine:** 20 bottles over £20, 10 bottles under £20, 8 by the glass (£3.25-£7.50) **Notes:** Sun L 3 courses from £15, Menu Rapide available **Seats:** 50 **Smoking:** N/Sm in restaurant **Children:** Menu, Portions **Directions:** 3 mins from train station, opposite St Mary Magdelene church

® Ma Cuisine Le Petit Bistrot

Traditional French

Rustic French cooking in an atmospheric bistro

☎ 020 8332 1923 The Old Post Office, 9 Station Approach, Kew TW9 3QB

Sister restaurant to the Twickenham eatery of the same name, Ma Cuisine is set in a bank of shops next to Kew station, not far from the famous gardens. Checked tablecloths, posters and a black and white tiled floor give it a French bistro feel, while a large picture window lets in plenty of light. The lunch menu is good value and teams a short range of formal choices with sandwich and breakfast selections, but dinner is the main event - expect classic French dishes such as bouillabaisse, poitrine de porc (pork belly with Morteau sausage), cassoulet and coq au vin, with quality ingredients to the fore.

Chef: Tim Francis **Owners:** John McClements/Dominique Sejourne **Times:** 12-2.30/6.30-11 **Prices:** Fixed L £15, Starter £4.95-£7, Main £11.50-£14.95, Dessert £3.95-£4.50, Coffee £2, Min/Water £2.75, Service added but optional 10% **Wine:** 13 bottles over £20, 23 bottles under £20, 12 by the glass (£3.50-£7) **Seats:** 45 **Smoking:** N/Sm in restaurant **Children:** Menu, Portions **Directions:** From Kew Garden Station follow signs to Royal Botanical Gardens. At fork in road keep to the right. Restaurant is 50 mtrs on right **Parking:** On street

®® Restaurant at The Petersham

Modern British

Sophisticated dining and breathtaking Thames views

☎ 020 8940 7471 The Petersham, Nightingale Ln TW10 6UZ
e-mail: enq@petershamhotel.co.uk
web: www.petershamhotel.co.uk

Perched on affluent Richmond Hill, this elegant hotel offers magnificent views over a curving stretch of the Thames. The restaurant matches the classic-meets-contemporary style, with walnut panelling, mirrors and well-spaced tables, while the bright room's full-length windows make the best of those river views, and the planes making their way into nearby Heathrow. A modern British approach, underpinned by French influences and plenty of luxury, graces the appealing, sensibly compact and clearly constructed carte. The sophisticated, accomplished cooking shows a commitment to high-quality produce, and perfectly suits the setting and ambience. Start with seared scallops and smoked eel, and continue with baked sea bass with seaweed or roasted saddle of lamb en croûte.

Chef: Alex Bentley **Owners:** The Petersham Hotel Ltd. **Times:** 12.15-2.15/7-9.45, Closed Xmas, New Year, 25-26 Dec, 1 Jan, Closed D 24 Dec **Prices:** Fixed L £18.50, Starter £5.50-£12, Main £12-£24, Dessert £5-£5.50, Coffee £2.50, Min/Water £3.50, Service added but optional 10% **Wine:** 93 bottles over £20, 12 bottles under £20, 8 by the glass (£4.50-£7) **Notes:** Vegetarian available, Dress Restrictions, Smart casual, Civ Wed 40 **Seats:** 70, Pr/dining room 26 **Smoking:** N/Sm in restaurant, Air con **Children:** Menu, Portions **Rooms:** 61 (61 en suite) ★★★★ HL **Directions:** Telephone for directions **Parking:** 60

®® Richmond Gate Hotel

Traditional

Elegant restaurant in a prestigious hotel

☎ 020 8940 0061 Richmond Hill TW10 6RP
e-mail: richmondgate@foliohotels.com
web: www.foliohotels.com/richmondgate

As its name suggests, this stylish and imposing Georgian hotel, perched atop Richmond Hill and the Thames Valley, sits opposite the royal park gates. Its intimate Gates on the Park Restaurant continues the theme, with high vaulted ceilings, elegant table appointments and attentive and friendly service. There's an adjacent cocktail bar and smart lounge for pre- or post-meal drinks. The dishes are modern interpretations of classically-based ideas and the kitchen makes sound use of quality ingredients, keeping things intelligently simple to focus on clean, clear flavours. Take a breast of Gressingham duck and confit leg with an apple and bacon rösti and juniper jus, with perhaps a tarte Tatin of figs with honey ice cream to finish.

Chef: Nenad Bibic **Owners:** Folio Hotels **Times:** 12.30-2/7-9.30, Closed L Sat, BHs **Prices:** Fixed L £19.50, Fixed D £28, Starter £6.50-£12.50, Main £15.50-£22.50, Dessert £6.50, Coffee £3.50, Min/Water £3.95, Service optional **Wine:** 36 bottles over £20, 24 bottles under £20, 8 by the glass (£5-£6.50) **Notes:** Vegetarian available, Civ Wed 70 **Seats:** 30, Pr/dining room 70 **Smoking:** N/Sm in restaurant, Air con **Children:** Menu, Portions **Rooms:** 68 (68 en suite) ★★★★ **Directions:** At top of Richmond Hill, opposite Star and Garter, just opposite Richmond Park **Parking:** 50

Chez Lindsay

☎ 020 8948 7473 11 Hill Rise TW10 6UQ

Popular neighbourhood restaurant known for its crêpes.

Strada

☎ 020 8940 3141 26 Hill St TW1 1TW

Superior pizza from quality ingredients cooked in wood-fired ovens.

England

RUISLIP

Hawtrey's Restaurant at the Barn Hotel

French

Imaginative, sophisticated cuisine in a smart hotel

☎ 01895 636057 & 679999 The Barn Hotel, West End Rd HA4 6JB
e-mail: info@thebarnhotel.co.uk
web: www.thebarnhotel.co.uk

This former farm with 3 acres of grounds has in recent years grown to include a whole complex of buildings with the restaurant styled as a Jacobean baronial hall with tasteful mahogany panelling, chandeliers and gilt-framed oil paintings on the walls. Skilful cooking and attention to detail characterises the modern French menu with the five-course prestige tasting menu being undoubtedly the best way to sample the talents of this Gordon Ramsay alumnus. Begin with an amuse of roast pumpkin velouté, a starter of pressed foie gras layered with smoked duck, confit duck and pickled girolles, then proceed with pan-fried sea bream fillet with cod brandade and Matelote sauce, or pot-roasted venison loin with braised spiced beetroot, before finishing with Muscat-scented rice pudding.

Chef: Jean Luc Sainlo **Owners:** Pantheon Hotels & Leisure **Times:** 12-2.30/7-10.30, Closed L Sat, D Sun **Prices:** Fixed L fr £16.50, Fixed D £29-£42.50, Min/Water £3.50, Service added but optional 10% **Wine:** 52 bottles over £20, 58 bottles under £20, 9 by the glass (£3.75-£4.95) **Notes:** Prestige tasting menu £49.50, Dress Restrictions, Smart casual, Civ Wed 24 **Seats:** 44, Pr/dining room 20 **Smoking:** N/Sm in restaurant, Air con **Children:** Menu, Portions **Rooms:** 59 (59 en suite) ★★★ HL **Directions:** From M40/A40 - exit at Polish War Memorial junct and follow A4180 towards Ruislip. After 2m turn right at mini rdbt into hotel entrance **Parking:** 50

SURBITON
See LONDON SECTION Plan 1-C1

The French Table

French

Modern cuisine in warm, friendly local restaurant

☎ 020 8399 2365 85 Maple Rd KT6 4AW
web: www.thefrenchtable.co.uk

Set in a small parade of shops just a street back from the Thames, this pretty looking restaurant with stained-glass windows is a popular, intimate, friendly, neighbourhood-style affair. The interior is bold, with black tiled floor, banquette seating or simple wooden chairs, plum-coloured walls, modern art and a large mirror to add a feeling of

continued

space. The enjoyable, good-value, creative French/Mediterranean cooking hits just the right note, too, and focuses on using fresh seasonal produce. Think a trilogy of pork belly with artichoke and chorizo, or perhaps roast monkfish served with parsnip purée, smoked vegetables, bayonne ham and a morel jus.

The French Table

Chef: Eric Guignard **Owners:** Eric & Sarah Guignard **Times:** 12-2.30/7-10.30, Closed 25-26 Dec, 10 days Jan, Mon, Closed L Sat, D Sun **Prices:** Fixed L fr £13.50, Starter £5.20-£9.90, Main £10.50-£16.20, Dessert fr £4.95, Coffee £1.95, Min/Water £2.95, Service added but optional 12.5% **Wine:** 35 bottles over £20, 16 bottles under £20, 9 by the glass (£3.50-£5.75) **Notes:** Sun L 3 courses £18.50, Vegetarian available, Dress Restrictions, Smart casual **Seats:** 48 **Smoking:** N/Sm in restaurant, Air con **Children:** Portions **Directions:** 5 min walk from Surbiton Station, 1m from Kingston **Parking:** On street

---

TWICKENHAM
See LONDON SECTION Plan 1-C2

La Brasserie Ma Cuisine Bourgeoise

French

Brasserie classics in suburban Twickenham

☎ 020 8744 9598 2 Whitton Rd TW1 1BJ
e-mail: johnmac21@aol.com

Discreetly located in a modest parade of shops, this brasserie continues to build its reputation as a venue for good French food. Plain walls with a hint of lavender, dark polished tables, plain wooden floorboards, a fully stocked cheese table; there is little here to distract from the menu. Helpful staff are on hand to assist. The menu comprises simple dishes, prepared and cooked well. This allows you to rediscover old brasserie and Burgundian favourites like the starter of parmentier of pig's feet with sauce gribiche and main courses like steamed chicken in a pouch with champagne and morels. Finish with an exemplary lemon tarte.

Chef: John McClements **Owners:** John McClements/Dominique Sejourne **Times:** 12-2.30/7-11, Closed Sun **Prices:** Fixed L £20, Starter £6-£8.50, Main £15-£25, Dessert £5.50-£7, Coffee £3.50, Min/Water £3.50, Service added but optional 10% **Notes:** Fixed L 3 courses **Seats:** 40, Pr/dining room 12 **Smoking:** N/Sm in restaurant, Air con **Children:** Min 9 yrs **Directions:** Close to Twickenham Station **Parking:** On street/train station

Brula

French

Bucolic French dining in deepest Twickenham

☎ 020 8892 0602 43 Crown Rd TW1 3EJ
e-mail: info@brulabistrot.com
web: www.brulabistrot.com

This Victorian sweet shop became a neighbourhood bistro in the 1970s, although the parquet floor, canopied entrance and stained glass retain a 1920s feel. *Poirot* has been filmed here to strengthen its Jazz age credentials. Polite staff deliver keenly-priced French regional dishes to eager diners seated at plain wooden tables. Grandmère would have approved of starters such as rustic fish soup or game terrine with onion marmalade and delightfully simple main courses like braised ham and parsley sauce or Onglet steak with garlic butter. Finish with a heart-stopping petit pot au chocolat.

Chef: Jamie Russel & Rebecca Murfett **Owners:** Lawrence Hartley, Bruce Duckett **Times:** 12-3/6-10.30, Closed Xmas, BHs **Prices:** Fixed L £11, Starter £4.50-£8.50, Main £11.50-£15.25, Dessert £4.75, Coffee £2.50, Min/Water £3, Service optional **Wine:** 20 bottles over £20, 10 bottles under £20, 8 by the glass (£3.25-£7.50) **Notes:** Sun L 3 courses from £15, Menu Rapide available **Seats:** 40, Pr/dining room 21 **Smoking:** N/Sm in restaurant **Children:** Menu, Portions **Directions:** Join A305, go straight at traffic lights over the A3004, turn left onto Baronsfield Rd. Restaurant is at the end of the T-junct, immediately on the right **Parking:** On street & parking meters

Ma Cuisine Le Petit Bistrot

Traditional French

French bistro cuisine

☎ 020 8607 9849 6 Whitton Rd TW1 1BJ
e-mail: johnmac21@aol.com

Very much the traditional French-style bistro, with its trademark checked tablecloths, black-and-white tiled floors and posters on the walls. The food is reassuringly simple, you will find classic, rustic dishes produced from high-quality ingredients. Try a straightforward fish stew to start, perhaps followed by pork belly with Morteau sausage and choucroute. Desserts are also along traditional lines with crêpes Suzette, crème brûlée, pot au chocolate and tarte au citron all vying for your attention.

Chef: John McClements **Owners:** John McClements/Dominique Sejourne **Times:** 12-2.30/6.30-11, Closed Sun **Prices:** Fixed L £15, Starter £4.95-£7, Main £11.50-£14.95, Dessert £3.95-£4.50, Coffee £2, Min/Water £2.75, Service added but optional 10% **Wine:** 13 bottles over £20, 23 bottles under £20, 12 by the glass (£3.50-£7) **Notes:** Vegetarian available **Seats:** 70 **Smoking:** N/Sm in restaurant **Children:** Menu, Portions **Directions:** 2 min walk from Twickenham station

Loch Fyne Restaurant & Oyster Bar

☎ 020 8255 6222 175 Hampton Rd TW2 5NG
Quality seafood chain.

UXBRIDGE MAP 06 TQ08

Masala

☎ 01895 252925 61 Belmont Rd UB8 1QT
web: www.theaa.com/restaurants/113902.html
Dining here is more than an experience, it's an education. Learn first-hand about the different cooking styles of India's various regions.

WEST DRAYTON For restaurant details see Heathrow Airport (London)

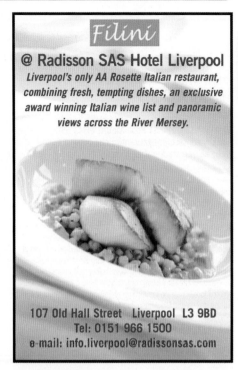

MERSEYSIDE

BIRKENHEAD MAP 15 SJ38

Fraiche

see page 364

LIVERPOOL MAP 15 SJ39

Radisson SAS Hotel Liverpool - Filini

Modern Italian

Stylish modern setting for authentic Italian cuisine

☎ 0151 966 1500 107 Old Hall St L3 9BD
e-mail: info.liverpool@radissonsas.com
web: www.radissonsas.com

continued

England

Fraiche

BIRKENHEAD MAP 15 SJ38

Modern French

Intimate and elaborate fine dining in Merseyside

☎ 0151 652 2914 11 Rose Mount CH43 5SG
e-mail: contact@restaurantfraiche.com
web: www.restaurantfraiche.com

Designed by chef-patron Marc Wilkinson himself and inspired by the views of the shore from his home, this intimate, modern and relaxing little restaurant (of some dozen or so tables) is well-worth tracking down. Soft muted beiges in linen and suede create warmth and subtlety; there's a seating area at the front for aperitifs and original artwork on the walls, which all create a simple backdrop for the well-trained, friendly service and elaborate, highly skilled cooking. Expect the concise, crisply-scripted repertoire of fixed-priced menus (including a tasting option) to excite and surprise the palate and senses, with plenty of twists of flavours, colour, texture and temperature. The stimulating compositions feature tip-top produce, sourced locally or from the markets of France; think a fillet of brill with parsley quinoa and red wine reduction, or perhaps black face Suffolk lamb with crisp sweetbread and apricot and white bean purée, while a study of rhubarb, sorbet, pastilla, 'ginger air', poached with saffron, could head-up desserts. And for those dining alone, or the out-and-out foodie, there's a 'culinary box' brimful of the latest cookery books, articles, magazines, menus from great restaurants etc, to peruse.

Chef: Marc Wilkinson **Owners:** Marc Wilkinson **Times:** 12-1.30/7-9.30, Closed 25 Dec, 1 Jan, Sun-Mon, Closed L Tue-Thur **Prices:** Fixed L £21, Fixed D £34, Coffee £3.25, Min/Water £3, Service optional **Wine:** 160 bottles over £20, 26 bottles under £20, 5 by the glass (£4.50-£5.25) **Notes:** Fixed L 3 courses, Tasting menu L £35, D £45, ALC fr £26, Vegetarian available **Seats:** 20, Pr/dining room 20 **Smoking:** N/Sm in restaurant **Children:** Min 8 yrs, Portions **Directions:** M53 junct 3 towards Prenton. Follow for 2m then take left towards Oxton, Fraiche on right **Parking:** On street

LIVERPOOL *continued* MAP 15 SJ39

Formerly St Paul's Eye Hospital, this hotel has the city's largest suite, The River Suite, and boasts ocean- and urban-themed bedrooms. The restaurant here, named Filini, was created by restaurateur and commentator Roy Ackerman. Authentic Sardinian dishes on an Anglo-Italian menu are on offer here in stylish surroundings, with panoramic views over the River Mersey. The modern Italian cuisine makes good use of the best local and Italian produce in dishes like seared scallops with tossed fregola grossa, or porcini pancake with truffle foam. The White Bar provides an alternative eating option, offering antipasti, Italian and traditional English dishes.

Chef: Chris Marshall **Owners:** Beetham Organisation Ltd **Times:** 12-2.30/6-10.30, Closed Sun **Prices:** Fixed L £11.50, Starter £5.50-£8.50, Main £12.95-£19.50, Dessert £5.50, Service optional, Group min 10 service 10% **Wine:** 23 bottles over £20, 10 bottles under £20, 8 by the glass (£3.65-£4.95) **Notes:** Vegetarian available, Civ Wed 100 **Seats:** 90, Pr/dining room 140 **Smoking:** N/Sm in restaurant, Air con **Children:** Menu, Portions **Rooms:** 204 (204 en suite) ★★★★ **Directions:** Telephone for directions **Parking:** 25 see advert on page 363

Simply Heathcotes

Modern British

Modern eatery with extensive brasserie-style menu

☎ 0151 236 3536 Beetham Plaza, 25 The Strand L2 0XL
e-mail: liverpool@heathcotes.co.uk
web: www.heathcotes.co.uk

This spectacular contemporary restaurant - decked out in glass, granite and cherry wood with Philippe Starck bucket chairs - is the Liverpudlian outpost of Paul Heathcote's culinary empire. The cooking suits the surroundings, delivering an extensive, crowd-pleasing, brasserie-style repertoire to the Heathcote formula and range, using plentiful seasonal, Lancashire produce and accomplished skill. Think roasted chump of fell-bred lamb with potato gnocchi, oven-dried tomatoes, fresh greens and mint sauce, or perhaps roasted monkfish with mussels and curried leeks, and, to finish, the signature Heathcote's bread-and-butter pudding with a compôte of apricots and clotted cream.

Simply Heathcotes

Chef: Phillip Sinclair **Owners:** Heathcotes Restaurants **Times:** 12-2.30/6-10, Closed 1-2 Jan BHs, Closed L 3 Jan **Prices:** Fixed L £12, Starter £3.75-£6.50, Main £8.50-£22, Dessert £4-£6.50, Coffee £1.80, Min/Water £3.25, Service optional, Group min 8 service 10% **Wine:** 48 bottles over £20, 18 bottles under £20, 10 by the glass (£3.85-£5.25) **Notes:** Sun L 2 courses £14.50, 3 courses £17, Vegetarian available, Dress Restrictions, Smart casual **Seats:** 108, Pr/dining room 30 **Smoking:** N/Sm in restaurant, Air con **Children:** Menu, Portions **Directions:** Opposite pier head, located on The Strand, near Princes Dock

England

60 Hope Street Restaurant

Modern British

Former gentleman's residence offering smart modern dining

☎ 0151 707 6060 60 Hope St L1 9BZ
e-mail: info@60hopestreet.com
web: www.60hopestreet.com

A Grade II listed building located in an avenue between Liverpool's two cathedrals, at the hub of the creative quarter. The décor here is right up-to-date with minimalist modern finishes, simple styling and seasonal flowers. Likewise, a modern menu features British dishes such as seared scallops with crushed Jersey royals and gremolata to start. Follow that with roast breast of Goosnargh chicken with Parisienne potatoes, baby leeks and 'Lomo' pork with rocket foam. For dessert, try something different like a deep-fried jam sandwich perhaps! A pre-theatre menu is available. Dining options include the large main restaurant, separate relaxed bistro and a private dining room.

Chef: Sarah Kershaw **Owners:** Colin & Gary Manning **Times:** 12-2.30/6-10.30, Closed BHs, Sun, Closed L Sat **Prices:** Fixed L £13.95, Fixed D £16.95, Starter £5.50-£12.95, Main £10.50-£40, Dessert £5.95-£9.95, Coffee £1.75, Min/Water £3.25, Service optional, Group min 8 service 10% **Wine:** 70 bottles over £20, 12 bottles under £20, 6 by the glass (£4.25-£5.95) **Notes:** Vegetarian available **Seats:** 90, Pr/dining room 30 **Smoking:** N/Sm in restaurant, Air con **Children:** Portions **Directions:** From M62 follow city centre signs, then brown tourist signs for cathedral. Hope St near cathedral **Parking:** On street

The Lower Place

☎ 0151 210 1955 Philharmonic Hall, Hope St L1 9BP
web: www.theaa.com/restaurants/114015.html

Modern international cuisine in a relaxing atmosphere - all in the midst of the art deco splendour of the Philharmonic Hall. Early evenings are busy with the post-work, pre-concert crowd, then things slow down to a more relaxing pace.

SOUTHPORT MAP 15 SD31

Warehouse Brasserie

International

Chic destination sprinkled with global flavours

☎ 01704 544662 30 West St PR8 1QN
e-mail: info@warehousebrasserie.co.uk
web: www.warehousebrasserie.co.uk

This startlingly stylish, buzzy and eye-catching glass-and-chrome restaurant moulded from a former warehouse - complete with theatre

continued

kitchen and chefs on show - hits a contemporary note and draws a fashionable crowd of fun seekers and well-heeled business types. The cooking follows the modern theme, with a global repertoire of refreshingly unpretentious, well-presented dishes that might deliver confit duck spring roll with mango salsa, or Malaysian fried halibut, roasted tomato and chilli sambal. Classics like fillet steak with béarnaise or homely fish 'n' chips with mushy peas and tartare sauce, find a place, too. The fixed-price, Early Doors menu bolsters the crowd-pleasing carte.

Warehouse Brasserie

Chef: Marc Verite, Darren Smith **Owners:** Paul Adams **Times:** 12-2.15/5.30-10.45, Closed 25-26 Dec, 1 Jan, Sun **Prices:** Fixed L £11.95, Fixed D £15.95, Starter £3.95-£8.95, Main £8.95-£17.50, Dessert £4.50-£12.95, Coffee £1.60, Min/Water £2.50, Group min 8 service 10% **Wine:** 28 bottles over £20, 23 bottles under £20, 5 by the glass **Notes:** Vegetarian available **Seats:** 110, Pr/dining room 18 **Smoking:** N/Sm in restaurant, Air con **Children:** Portions **Directions:** Telephone for directions **Parking:** NCP - Promenade

THORNTON HOUGH MAP 15 SJ38

Thornton Hall Hotel

Modern British

Sound British cooking at a charming country hotel

☎ 0151 336 3938 Neston Rd CH63 1JF
e-mail: reservations@thorntonhallhotel.com
web: www.thorntonhallhotel.com

A popular choice for weddings, this Victorian manor sits in delightful gardens within easy reach of Liverpool and Chester. Its extensive facilities include a choice of restaurants - both the bar and health club serve a range of snacks, but the real draw is the Italian Room restaurant, an imposing affair with a magnificent hand-tooled leather ceiling, inlaid with mother of pearl. Modern British cooking is the order of the day; kick off with a dish of slow-roast belly pork perhaps, served with apple black pudding, before tucking into pepper-crusted breast of duck, or supreme of cod with mixed bean casserole and champagne butter sauce.

Chef: Brian Herron **Owners:** The Thompson Family **Times:** 12-2.30/7-9.30, Closed 1 Jan, Closed L Sat **Prices:** Fixed L £10.95, Fixed D £28, Starter £5.95-£7.50, Main £16.50-£21.50, Dessert £5.95, Min/Water £3.95, Service included **Wine:** 21 bottles over £20, 32 bottles under £20, 8 by the glass (£3.45-£4.85) **Notes:** Sun L £17.50, Sun D £35 per couple, Vegetarian available, Dress Restrictions, Smart casual, no T-shirts or jeans, Civ Wed 400 **Seats:** 45, Pr/dining room 24 **Smoking:** N/Sm in restaurant **Children:** Portions **Rooms:** 63 (63 en suite) ★★★★ HL **Directions:** M53 junct 4 onto B5151 & B5136 and follow brown tourist signs (approx 2.5m) to Thornton House Hotel **Parking:** 250

England

NORFOLK

ALBURGH MAP 13 TM28

The Dove Restaurant with Rooms

French, European NEW

Family-run restaurant with a classic menu

☎ 01986 788315 Holbrook IP20 0EP
e-mail: info@thedovenorfolk.co.uk

This former inn turned restaurant with rooms is run by a husband-and-wife team who pride themselves on making the most of quality local and home-grown ingredients. Dishes are straightforward and not overworked; you might start with a terrine of chicken liver pâté wrapped in Black Forest ham with red onion chutney, move on to roast Barbary duck breast with Puy lentils, or pan-fried fillet of sea bass with a mussel ratatouille and basil butter sauce, and finish up with raspberry Pavlova or crêpes Suzette. Service is relaxed but professional, and there's a cosy lounge for pre- or post-dinner drinks.

Chef: Robert Oberhoffer **Owners:** Robert & Conny Oberhoffer **Times:** 12-2/7-9, Closed Mon-Tue, Closed L Wed-Sat, D Sun **Prices:** Fixed L £13.45, Starter £4.25-£5.95, Main £12.75-£18.95, Dessert £4.95, Coffee £2, Min/Water £2.50, Service optional **Wine:** 7 bottles over £20, 22 bottles under £20, 3 by the glass (£3.25) **Notes:** Sun L 2 courses £11.45, 3 courses £13.45, Vegetarian available, Dress Restrictions, Smart casual **Seats:** 50 **Smoking:** N/Sm area, No pipes, No cigars **Children:** Portions **Rooms:** 2 (1 en suite) ◆◆◆◆ **Directions:** Between Harleston and Bungay, by A143, at junct of B1062 **Parking:** 20

BLAKENEY MAP 13 TG04

The Blakeney Hotel

Traditional British

Quayside hotel with a wide-ranging menu

☎ 01263 740797 The Blakeney Hotel, The Quay NR25 7NE
e-mail: reception@blakeney-hotel.co.uk
web: www.blakeney-hotel.co.uk

Situated on the quayside, this attractive brick and flint hotel offers panoramic views across the estuary and salt marshes to Blakeney Point. It has two comfortable lounges for pre-dinner drinks, one with a log fire for the winter months and the other a sun room that makes the most of the charm of the north Norfolk coast. The elegant restaurant offers a lengthy menu firmly rooted in British cuisine, and features old favourites (pan-fried calves' liver with bacon and mash; grilled Dover sole), as well as more sophisticated fare such as braised lamb shank on minted creamed potato and roasted vegetables.

Owners: Michael Stannard **Times:** 12-2/6.30-8.45, Closed 24-27 Dec, Closed D 31 Dec **Prices:** Fixed L £14.70-£25.50, Fixed D fr £22.50, Starter fr £5.50, Main fr £17.50, Dessert fr £4, Coffee £2, Min/Water £2.50, Service optional **Wine:** 26 bottles over £20, 23 bottles under £20, 7 by the glass (£2.70-£4.85) **Notes:** Vegetarian available, Dress Restrictions, Smart casual for D **Seats:** 100, Pr/dining room 100 **Smoking:** N/Sm in restaurant **Children:** Min 5 yrs D, Portions **Rooms:** 64 (64 en suite) ★★★ HL **Directions:** From the A148 between Fakenham and Holt at Letheringsett, take the B1150 to hotel **Parking:** 60

Morston Hall

BLAKENEY MAP 13 TG04

Modern British NOTABLE WINE LIST

Inspired set-menu cooking in small country house

☎ 01263 741041 Morston, Holt NR25 7AA
e-mail: reception@morstonhall.com
web: www.morstonhall.com

Tucked away on the north Norfolk coast, this small, flint-and-brick Jacobean country-house hotel is set in attractive gardens and offers a set-menu repertoire that will delight at every course. Morston's not just well known for its chef-patron, Galton Blackiston, it's something of a food lover's paradise, too, with a whole range of cookery demonstrations, courses and wine tastings on offer. Inviting lounges - with roaring log fire on winter days - lead through to the airy, elegant restaurant, resplendent with its bright new conservatory. Galton's inspired cooking suits the surroundings and is delivered via a daily-changing, no-choice, four-course dinner menu, served in a single sitting for all diners at the set time of 7.30 for 8pm. The style aims for skilful and intelligent simplicity, with the focus on fresh, high-quality, local seasonal produce and clean, clear flavours. Think roast breast of guinea fowl stuffed with a wild mushroom farcie and served with Parmentier potatoes, French beans, young carrots and guinea fowl jus, while dessert might feature a warm local rhubarb soufflé with ginger ice

cream. Lovely home-made rolls and petits fours add to the class act. **Notable Wine List:** A well chosen wine list categorised by grape variety with detailed tasting notes for each wine.

Chef: Galton Blackiston **Owners:** T & G Blackiston **Times:** 12.30/7.30, Closed 2 wks Jan, Closed L Mon-Sat (ex party booking) **Prices:** Fixed L £30, Fixed D £44, Min/Water £3, Service optional **Wine:** 13 by the glass (£3-£8) **Notes:** Fixed L 3 courses, Fixed D 4 courses, coffee incl, Vegetarian available, Dress Restrictions, Smart casual, no jeans or trainers **Seats:** 35, Pr/dining room 20 **Smoking:** N/Sm in restaurant **Children:** Menu, Portions **Rooms:** 7 (7 en suite) ★★★ HL **Directions:** On A149 coast road **Parking:** 40

The Moorings

Modern British NEW

Small, relaxed predominantly fish-based bistro

☎ 01263 740054 High St NR25 7NA
e-mail: reservations@blakeney-moorings.co.uk
web: www.blakeney-moorings.co.uk

Aptly named, relaxed, seaside-style bistro situated on a busy side road adjacent to the quayside. Yellow walls, oiled wooden boards, closely-packed clothed tables and relaxed service all hit the mark. Unsurprisingly, the menu comes awash with the fruits of the sea, with fish (much of it sourced locally) dominating the fixed-price menu. Cooking is straightforward and accurate, with simple dishes and presentation that don't stint on flavour. Try spicy Norfolk crab cake starter, followed by a main course of panaché of scallops, monkfish, angoustine, wilted spinach and saffron nage or roast sea bass fillet, emon, parsley and pine nut crust and tapenade dressing.

Chef: Richard & Angela Long **Owners:** Richard & Angela Long **Times:** 10.30-5/7-9.30, Closed 3 weeks before and after Xmas, Mon-Thu (Nov-Mar), Closed D Sun & Mon **Prices:** Starter £4.75-£6.95, Main £10.95-£16.95, Dessert £4.50-£4.75, Coffee £1.75, Min/Water £3.50, Service optional **Wine:** 4 bottles over £20, 20 bottles under £20, 4 by the glass **Notes:** Sun L 3 courses £12.95 **Seats:** 50 **Smoking:** N/Sm in restaurant, Air con **Children:** Menu, Portions **Directions:** Off A149 where High St runs N to the quay **Parking:** On street, car park 50mtrs

Morston Hall

see opposite

BRANCASTER STAITHE MAP 13 TF74

The White Horse

Modern, Traditional

Seafood beside the tidal marsh

☎ 01485 210262 PE31 8BY
e-mail: reception@whitehorsebrancaster.co.uk
web: www.whitehorsebrancaster.co.uk

Its location on the edge of the tidal marshes could not be improved, and the views from the conservatory restaurant with adjoining dining area are truly memorable. Tourists and locals alike flock here throughout the year, and relax in comfort. If you want a window seat, it would be wise to book very early. Locally sourced fish and shellfish are the lure here, and their simple handling allows the impeccably fresh flavours a full expression - Cyril's Brancaster mussels poached in white wine, cream and parsley, for example. The menus change frequently to take maximum advantage of what's available, and that always includes meat - roast rump of English lamb with sweet onion confit and fondant potato - as well as seafood.

Chef: Nicholas Parker **Owners:** Cliff Nye **Times:** 12-2/6.45-9 **Prices:** Starter £3.95-£6.25, Main £9.25-£16.95, Dessert £3.95-£4.95, Coffee £1.90, Min/Water £1.50, Service optional **Wine:** 17 bottles over £20, 34 bottles under £20, 12 by the glass (£2.80-£4.95) **Notes:** Vegetarian available **Seats:** 100 **Smoking:** N/Sm in restaurant **Children:** Menu, Portions **Rooms:** 15 (15 en suite) ★★ HL **Directions:** On A149 coast road, midway between Hunstanton & Wells-next-the-Sea **Parking:** 85

BRUNDALL MAP 13 TG30

The Lavender House

Modern British V

Quintessential English thatched cottage offering a gourmet experience

☎ 01603 712215 39 The Street NR13 5AA
web: www.thelavenderhouse.co.uk

This thatched cottage with heavy oak beams dates from around 1540. Sympathetically restored and extended, it now offers a light modern interior. There are comfortable sofas in the bar and high backed wicker dining chairs and crisp white table settings in the restaurant areas. The modern British cooking takes advantage of products from local artisan suppliers. An appetiser to start and taster dishes between courses give you a chance to try an enormous selection of wonderful delicacies. Starters like steamed Norfolk game pudding with beetroot, black pepper and sour cream might be followed by a main course of fillet and shin of Barnard's beef with roasted root vegetables, Binham Blue cheese fritter, port wine and béarnaise sauces. The selection of English farmhouse cheeses is extensive.

Chef: Richard Hughes, Richard Knights **Owners:** Richard & Sue Hughes **Times:** 6.30-12, Closed 24 Dec-30 Dec, Sun & Mon, Closed L all week **Prices:** Fixed D £34, Coffee £2.95, Min/Water £3, Service optional **Wine:** 43 bottles over £20, 33 bottles under £20, 8 by the glass (£3.50-£6.50) **Notes:** Fixed D 6 courses, Vegetarian menu **Seats:** 50, Pr/dining room 36 **Smoking:** N/Sm in restaurant **Children:** Portions **Directions:** 4m from Norwich city centre **Parking:** 16

England

BURNHAM MARKET MAP 13 TF84

Fishes Restaurant

Modern British

A fish lover's paradise

☎ 01328 738588 Market Place PE31 8HE
e-mail: info@fishesrestaurant.co.uk
web: www.fishesrestaurant.co.uk

As the name suggests, this is the place to come for the catch of the day. Superb quality locally sourced fish and shellfish are simply cooked and garnished letting the flavours speak for themselves. Impressive starter combinations might include seared seven spice tuna, octopus and noodle salad and sweet chilli dipping sauce. If that doesn't whet your appetite, how about a main course of local smooth hound shark, deep fried in a crisp beer batter and served with home-made chips and fresh tartare sauce. All this can be enjoyed in the relaxed, brasserie-style surroundings of a double-fronted shop, next door to the Hoste Arms.

Chef: Matthew Owsley-Brown & Kieron Hales **Owners:** Matthew & Caroline Owsley-Brown **Times:** 12-2.15/6.45-10, Closed Xmas for 10 days, 3 wks Jan, Mon, Closed D Sun **Prices:** Fixed L £19-£24.75, Fixed D £37-£49.95, Coffee £2, Min/Water £3.50, Service optional, Group min 8 service 10% **Wine:** 63 bottles over £20, 12 bottles under £20, 14 by the glass (£5.50-£10) **Seats:** 42, Pr/dining room 12 **Smoking:** N/Sm in restaurant **Children:** Min before 8pm, Portions **Directions:** From Fakenham take B1065. 8m to Burnham Market, restaurant on the green **Parking:** On street

Hoste Arms Hotel

Modern European, Pacific Rim NOTABLE WINE LIST

Stylish inn with wide-ranging impressive menu

☎ 01328 738777 The Green PE31 8HD
e-mail: reception@hostearms.co.uk
web: www.hostearms.co.uk

Choose between the gallery and the garden room at this very relaxed inn close to the north Norfolk coast, and you'll get the same easygoing but professional service. A brand new cellar has been created to house wines and an ornate room for wine tasting. There is also further private dining and an orangery. Local man Lord Nelson was once a regular visitor, but he'd hardly recognise this stylish place now. The walled garden is designed with Indian and Moroccan touches, with all-year-round alfresco dining a bonus. The modern British menu with Pacific Rim influences covers a broad spectrum that includes quality snacks and fine dining. Choose from starters that double as main courses, fish, meat and salads all stamped with locally-sourced quality - half a dozen Burnham Creek oysters are not to be missed.

Notable Wine List: A beautifully chosen wine list which offers quality throughout and a partcularly strong South African listing.

continued

Chef: Rory Whelan **Owners:** Paul Whittome **Times:** 12-2/7-9, Closed D 25 Dec, 31 Dec **Prices:** Fixed L £16.50-£30, Fixed D £19.25-£40, Starter £4.25-£11.50, Main £9.25-£17.50, Dessert £5.50-£7.95, Coffee £1.40, Min/Water £2.75, Service optional **Wine:** 210 bottles over £20, 23 bottles under £20, 22 by the glass (£2.95-£11.80) **Notes:** Vegetarian available **Seats:** 140, Pr/dining room 24 **Smoking:** N/Sm area, No pipes, No cigars, Air con **Children:** Menu **Rooms:** 36 (36 en suite) ★★★ HL **Directions:** 2m from A149 between Burnham & Wells **Parking:** 45

CROMER MAP 13 TG24

Elderton Lodge Hotel & Langtry Restaurant

Modern British NEW

Romantic retreat serving the best Norfolk produce

☎ 01263 833547 Gunton Park NR11 8TZ
e-mail: enquiries@eldertonlodge.co.uk
web: www.eldertonlodge.co.uk

This delightful former shooting lodge set in 6 acres of gardens was once a retreat of Lillie Langtry, hence the name of the hotel's Langtry Restaurant. Here warm Tuscan terracotta walls, high-backed chairs and complementing carpet provide the comforts, while aperitifs are taken in the cosy hotel bar as a prelude to a candlelit dinner. The kitchen's uncomplicated, modern interpretations make intelligent use of quality produce from the abundant local larder, so expect the likes of medallions of venison served with a forest mushroom sauce, or breast of pheasant wrapped in pancetta and filo pastry.

Chef: Richard Park **Owners:** Rachel Lusher & Patrick Roofe **Times:** 12-2/7-9 **Prices:** Fixed L £10, Fixed D £27, Coffee £2.25, Min/Water £3, Service optional **Wine:** 14 bottles over £20, 21 bottles under £20, 5 by the glass (£3.50-£3.75) **Notes:** Vegetarian available, Civ Wed 55 **Seats:** 50, Pr/dining room 25 **Smoking:** N/Sm in restaurant **Children:** Portions **Rooms:** 11 (11 en suite) ★★★ HL **Directions:** On A149 (Cromer/North Walsham road), 1m S of village **Parking:** 100

GREAT BIRCHAM MAP 13 TF73

The Kings Head Hotel

British NEW

Great food in stylish village hotel

☎ 01485 578265 PE31 6RJ
e-mail: welcome@the-kings-head-bircham.co.uk
web: www.the-kings-head-bircham.co.uk

Situated in a peaceful little village close to Sandringham, The Kings Head may look like a very well kept inn, but this stylish hotel and restaurant is one of the new gems of Norfolk. The contemporary restaurant overlooks

continued

England

a sheltered courtyard which is perfect for alfresco dining in summer months. Lots of local, seasonal produce appears on the simple, no-fuss menu of British and Mediterranean dishes: pressed ham, parsley and garlic terrine, roast fillet of haddock with pea purée, confit potatoes and tartare sauce, followed by plum and cinnamon crumble.

Chef: Ben Handley **Owners:** William Powle **Times:** 12-2.30/7 **Prices:** Food prices not confirmed for 2007. Please telephone for details **Rooms:** 9 (9 en suite) ★★★ HL **Directions:** Telephone for directions

---

GREAT YARMOUTH MAP 13 TG50

Imperial Hotel

Modern, Traditional

Family-run seaside hotel serving quality cuisine

☎ 01493 842000 North Dr NR30 1EQ
e-mail: reception@imperialhotel.co.uk
web: www.imperialhotel.co.uk

An imposing hotel with a separate external restaurant entrance leading down to the Rambouillet Restaurant on the lower ground floor. During the war the restaurant was used as an army telephone exchange. These days it's calling diners in for simple classical cooking and friendly service. Traditional dishes are simply prepared and presented with the focus on fresh ingredients. Typical starters might include Imperial Caesar salad or prawn cocktail. A main course of poached wing of Longshore skate is served with a straightforward accompaniment of foaming brown butter and capers. Formal table service is combined with a relaxed friendly approach from staff.

Chef: Stephen Duffield **Owners:** Mr NL & Mrs A Mobbs **Times:** 12-2/6.30-10, Closed L Mon-Sat **Prices:** Fixed D £20-£21, Starter £4-£8, Main £9-£25, Dessert £5-£7.50, Coffee £1.60, Min/Water £3.50, Service optional **Wine:** 10 bottles over £20, 40 bottles under £20, 6 by the glass (£2-£7) **Notes:** Vegetarian available, Dress Restrictions, Smart-casual No shorts or trainers, Civ Wed 140 **Seats:** 60, Pr/dining room 140 **Smoking:** N/Sm in restaurant, Air con **Children:** Portions **Rooms:** 39 (39 en suite) ★★★ **Directions:** North end of Great Yarmouth seafront **Parking:** 45

GRIMSTON MAP 12 TF72

Congham Hall

Modern British V

Imaginative, seasonal cooking in Georgian setting

☎ 01485 600250 Lynn Rd PE32 1AH
e-mail: info@conghamhallhotel.co.uk
web: www.conghamhallhotel.co.uk

A beautifully proportioned, elegant Georgian manor house set in 30 acres of mature grounds which includes a noteworthy herb garden.

continued

Traditional features have been maintained, as has a style of décor throughout the inviting and tastefully furnished public rooms. Imaginative cooking is served in the Orangery Restaurant, an intimate, summery room with French windows looking out over the garden. Local and seasonal produce feature prominently on classically inspired dinner menus and on the simpler lunchtime 'du jour' menu, which offers especially good value. Dishes may include roast duck with celeriac mousse and thyme jus, wild sea bass with mussel and chive chowder, and hot chocolate fondant with fig ice cream.

Chef: Jamie Murch **Owners:** von Essen Hotels **Times:** 12-1.45/7-9.15 **Prices:** Fixed L fr £15.50, Fixed D fr £44, Coffee £5, Min/Water £4, Service optional **Wine:** 115 bottles over £20, 9 bottles under £20, 10 by the glass (£3.75-£4.25) **Notes:** Sun L 3 courses £22.50, Gourmand menu 7 courses £58, Vegetarian menu, Dress Restrictions, No jeans, shorts or trainers, Civ Wed 100 **Seats:** 50, Pr/dining room 18 **Smoking:** N/Sm in restaurant **Children:** Min 7 yrs D, Portions **Rooms:** 14 (14 en suite) ★★★ HL **Directions:** 6m NE of King's Lynn on A148, turn right towards Grimston. Hotel 2.5m on left (do not go to Congham) **Parking:** 50

HEACHAM MAP 12 TF63

Rushmore's

British

Traditional British food cooked with an assured touch

☎ 01485 579393 14 High St PE31 7ER
e-mail: norfolkchef@ukonline.co.uk
web: www.heacham.fsnet.co.uk

This traditional English restaurant was once the village shop before conversion in the early 1990s. The eponymous chef-patron hails from Norfolk and he clearly has a love of his home county as the food relies heavily on local ingredients - shellfish from the coast and game from Sandringham, for example. Utterly British in style, this is simple, effective cooking with a classic feel - chicken terrine with smoked bacon pâté for example, or sautéed wood pigeon breasts, Savoy cabbage and wild mushroom sauce. Desserts are rib-stickingly delicious.

Chef: Colin Rushmore **Owners:** P Barrett, D Askew **Times:** 12-2/6.30-9.30, Closed Mon, Closed L Tue & Sat, D Sun **Prices:** Fixed L £12.70-£15, Fixed D £23.50-£29.75, Starter £5.20-£6.25, Main £12.75-£19.70, Dessert £4.95-£5.50, Coffee £1.80, Min/Water £2.95, Service optional **Wine:** 6 bottles over £20, 15 bottles under £20, 2 by the glass (£2.95) **Notes:** Vegetarian available **Seats:** 42, Pr/dining room 6 **Smoking:** N/Sm in restaurant **Children:** Min 5 yrs, Portions **Directions:** A149 towards Hunstanton. At Heacham, turn left at Lavender Fields. Follow into village, take 1st left into High St **Parking:** 25

England

HETHERSETT MAP 13 TG10

Park Farm Hotel

British NEW

Attractive new restaurant serving a relaxed style of food

☎ 01603 810264 NR9 3DL
e-mail: enq@parkfarm-hotel.co.uk
web: www.parkfarm-hotel.co.uk

What was once a farm many years ago has now evolved into a substantial hotel. The new restaurant, overlooking the garden, has a smart orangery-style roof. Plain white walls are hung with bright, unframed canvases, and tables are neatly clothed and laid with contemporary crockery and cutlery. There is a set-price menu for lunch and dinner, and dishes make good use of local seasonal produce. Enjoyable dishes include succulent chargrilled rib-eye steak with herb butter, and a decent baked cheesecake flavoured with almond and served with Amaretto ice cream.

Chef: David Bell **Owners:** David Gaving **Times:** 12-2/7-9.30 **Prices:** Food prices not confirmed for 2007. Please telephone for details **Notes:** Vegetarian available **Seats:** 60 **Rooms:** 42 (42 en suite) ★★★ HL **Directions:** 6m S of Norwich on B1172

HOLKHAM MAP 13 TF84

The Victoria at Holkham

British, French

Norfolk hideaway with an interesting colonial feel

☎ 01328 711008 Park Rd NR23 1RG
e-mail: victoria@holkham.co.uk
web: www.victoriaatholkham.co.uk

Part of the Holkham Estate, home to the Earls of Leicester since the 1700s, this converted Victorian property has a colonial feel inspired by a sikh maharajah, who visited the estate in the 1800s. It's been updated sensitively into a stylish restaurant with rooms, maintaining the ethnic theme in its current contemporary look. The restaurant has definitely benefited from a new conservatory, which adds plenty of natural light. Simple, classic British food abounds on the menu with dishes that stress the inclusion of local ingredients - Thornham mussels, with cider cream and gremolata (an award-winning recipe from their sous-chef) or their legendary Holkham game platters - simply roasted wild duck, partridge, pheasant or woodcock, with roasted root vegetables, game chips and watercress.

Chef: Neil Dowson **Owners:** Viscount & Viscountess Coke **Times:** 12-2.30/7-9.30 **Prices:** Starter £5.50-£8, Main £12-£17, Dessert £6, Coffee £1.70, Min/Water £3.50, Service optional, Group min 6 service 10% **Wine:** 54 bottles over £20, 19 bottles under £20, 10 by the glass (£3.20-£5)

continued

Notes: Vegetarian available, Dress Restrictions, Smart casual, Civ Wed 80 **Seats:** 80, Pr/dining room 20 **Smoking:** N/Sm in restaurant **Children:** Menu, Portions **Rooms:** 10 (10 en suite) ★★ HL **Directions:** 3m W of Wells-next-the-Sea on A149. 12m N of Fakenham **Parking:** 50

HOLT MAP 13 TG03

Yetman's

Modern British

A popular and friendly haunt, excellent local produce

☎ 01263 713320 37 Norwich Rd NR25 6SA
web: www.yetmans.net

With a pretty rear garden and an airy, easy appeal, this smartly painted restaurant was formed from two adjoining cottages. Fresh flowers and friendly staff are just some of the reasons this is such a popular venue with locals and tourists alike. The house speciality is chargrilling and local produce is treated with simplicity on a concise menu. Expect plenty of fresh, skilfully selected fish, meat and poultry, as in venison, pheasant and field mushroom pie, or grilled fillet of halibut with a spiced sweet potato mash.

Times: 12.30-2/7-9.30, Closed 25-26 Dec, 3wks in Nov, Mon-Tue, Closed D Sun **Directions:** on A418 (Norwich road), on outskirts of Holt

---

HORNING MAP 13 TG31

Taps

British

Reassuring and consistent cooking from an intimate local restaurant

☎ 01692 630219 25 Lower St NR12 8AA

Located in the picturesque village of Horning on the Norfolk Broads, this friendly neighbourhood restaurant draws clientele from far and wide, with diners drawn to the easy-going informality of the service, the low-key warmth of the décor, revitalised with a recent refurbishment, and - of course - the accurate cooking, keen sense of flavour and fair prices offered by the menu. With good quality, local produce high on the agenda this is food designed to satisfy the palate with tried and tested combinations that never fail to deliver. Try roast belly pork in five spice with pickled pears to start and then roast cod fillet with a lemon butter sauce.

Times: 12-2/7-9.30, Closed Mon, Closed D Sun **Directions:** From Norwich follow signs to The Broads on A1151. Through Wroxham and turn right to Horning & Ludham. After 3m turn right into Horning, Lower Street 500yds on left

---

HUNSTANTON MAP 12 TF64

The Neptune Inn & Restaurant

British, French NEW

Intimate and stylish inn serving quality locally sourced produce

☎ 01485 532122 85 Old Hunstanton Rd PE36 6HZ
e-mail: reservations@theneptune.co.uk
web: www.theneptune.co.uk

This former coaching inn has been given a New England style makeover with stunning results. Imagine yourself in Maine, North

continued

Norfolk, while you relax and dine amid Lloyd Loom furniture, white-painted panelling and replica boats. The monthly-changing menu offers seasonal and local fresh produce in dishes with a French influence. Herb-crusted loin of lamb with Puy lentils, dauphinoise potatoes and a red wine jus, or braised halibut, colcannon potato with a yellow and red pepper confit show the style. Take time out for the American-style Sunday brunch.

The Neptune Inn & Restaurant

Chef: Jon Cleland **Owners:** Paul & Hilary Berriff **Times:** 12-3/7-11 **Prices:** Starter £6.50-£7.50, Main £16.50-£22, Dessert £4.50, Coffee £2, Min/Water £2.50, Service optional **Wine:** 19 bottles over £20, 20 bottles under £20, 6 by the glass (£3.50-£4.95) **Seats:** 28 **Smoking:** N/Sm in restaurant **Children:** Min 10 yrs **Rooms:** 7 (7 en suite) ◆◆◆◆ **Directions:** Please telephone for directions **Parking:** 8

NORTH WALSHAM MAP 13 TG23

⊛⊛ Beechwood Hotel

British, Mediterranean

A passion for local produce in elegant surroundings

☎ 01692 403231 Cromer Rd NR28 0HD
e-mail: enquiries@beechwood-hotel.co.uk
web: www.beechwood-hotel.co.uk

Agatha Christie was a frequent visitor to this gracious ivy-clad property, and fans can see letters to the family displayed in the hallway. The Beechwood has a strong focus on food, offering a daily 'ten-mile' dinner with ingredients drawn from within a ten-mile radius of the hotel: notably shellfish from Cromer, Sheringham, Thornham and Morston as well as local meat and vegetables. Modern British dishes with a Mediterranean influence are served in the smartly appointed restaurant, such as Walsingham cheese tart with mustard and smoked bacon ice cream, Sheringham lobster, and pineapple tarte Tatin. Drinks can be taken in the garden or the clubby lounge bar.

Chef: Steven Norgate **Owners:** Don Birch & Lindsay Spalding **Times:** 12-1.45/7-9, Closed L Mon-Sat **Prices:** Fixed L £18, Fixed D £34, Min/Water

continued

£3, Service optional **Wine:** 220 bottles over £20, 10 bottles under £20, 5 by the glass (£4.20) **Notes:** Dress Restrictions, Smart casual **Seats:** 60, Pr/dining room 20 **Smoking:** N/Sm in restaurant **Children:** Min 10 yrs, Portions **Rooms:** 17 (17 en suite) ★★★ **Directions:** From Norwich on B1150, 13m to N Walsham. Turn left at lights and next right. Hotel 150 mtrs on left **Parking:** 25

see advert above

NORWICH MAP 13 TG20

⊛⊛ Adlard's Restaurant

Modern French, Italian NOTABLE WINE LIST

Chic city-centre restaurant with serious approach to food and wine

☎ 01603 633522 79 Upper St Giles St NR2 1AB
e-mail: info@adlards.co.uk
web: www.adlards.co.uk

In a quiet street close to the city centre stands one of Norwich's most enduring restaurants hosted by the affable David Adlard. Inside it's a chic, modern affair, decked out with pine floors, white-clothed tables and impressive oil paintings on cream-beige walls. It's intimate and cheerful, with a light and airy feel engendered by the décor and light from its street windows. The kitchen takes a serious line by carefully sourcing quality seasonal ingredients and delivering clear flavours in dishes that are underpinned with a French theme. Perhaps roasted partridge with confit cabbage, pomme fondant and chestnut sauce, or a coffee and hazelnut cake with chocolate sorbet, coffee jelly and chocolate sauce. A classy wine list accompanies.
Notable Wine List: A carefully chosen wine list with personal tasting notes throughout.

continued

England

NORWICH *continued* MAP 13 TG20

Chef: Roger Hickman **Owners:** David Adlard **Times:** 12.30-1.45/7.30-10.30, Closed 1st wk Jan, Sun/Mon **Prices:** Fixed L £17, Starter £9-£12, Main £19-£23, Dessert £9, Coffee £3.25, Min/Water £3.50, Service optional **Wine:** 275 bottles over £20, 15 bottles under £20, 4 by the glass (£4.50) **Seats:** 40 **Smoking:** N/Sm in restaurant, Air con **Children:** Portions **Directions:** City centre, 200yds behind the City Hall **Parking:** On street

Ah-So Japanese Restaurant

Japanese

The land of rising sun landed in Norwich

☎ 01603 618901 16 Prince of Wales Rd NR1 1LB
e-mail: booking@ah-so.co.uk
web: www.ah-so.co.uk

This smart, modern restaurant specialises in teppan-yaki, where meals are cooked in front of you on a large polished stainless steel griddle. Popular with business types, a surprisingly relaxed atmosphere pervades considering the bustle of staff preparing dishes at the table - indeed the chefs can even provide a little culinary theatre if you ask them. Dishes are authentically Japanese, generally assembling fresh ingredients simply - miso soup with tofu for example, or chicken yakitori with fried rice, grilled vegetables and dipping sauces. Set meals at a range of prices allow for flexible dining - and a chance to sample a number of dishes in one sitting.

Chef: Efren Eddsell **Owners:** Marcus Rose **Times:** 12-9/6-12, Closed L Mon-Sat **Prices:** Fixed D £11.95-£29.95, Starter £2.50-£6, Main £7.45-£24, Service optional, Group min 10 service 5% **Wine:** 6 bottles over £20, 11 bottles under £20, 2 by the glass (£3.95-£5.95) **Notes:** Vegetarian available **Seats:** 50, Pr/dining room 32 **Smoking:** N/Sm in restaurant, Air con **Children:** Menu, Portions **Directions:** From station, cross bridge and straight for 600 yds, restaurant on right, near Anglia TV

Annesley House Hotel

Modern British

Conservatory dining in charming surroundings

☎ 01603 624553 6 Newmarket Rd NR2 2LA
e-mail: annesleyhouse@bestwestern.co.uk
web: www.bw-annesleyhouse.co.uk

You can easily walk into the city centre from this smart Grade II listed hotel in landscaped grounds. The conservatory restaurant is furnished with Mediterranean-style décor and ornate white and black cast iron chairs (cushioned for comfort), with views over the water garden and waterfall. The modern British food with European influences benefits from straightforward handling that allows the quality ingredients to shine. On the short fixed price menu you might find starters like Szechuan pork with a pepper salad or king prawns marinated in ginger lemongrass and chilli, followed by pan-fried skate wing with warm tartare sauce, and raspberry and elderflower spritzer jelly.

Chef: Philip Woodcock **Owners:** Mr & Mrs D Reynolds **Times:** 12-2/6-10, Closed Xmas & New Year **Prices:** Fixed D £20, Starter £4.75-£6.75, Main £17-£19.25, Dessert £5.25-£5.75, Coffee £2.50, Min/Water £4.50, Service optional **Wine:** 7 bottles over £20, 23 bottles under £20, 7 by the glass (£3.95-£4.95) **Notes:** Vegetarian available **Seats:** 40, Pr/dining room 18 **Smoking:** N/Sm in restaurant **Children:** Portions **Rooms:** 26 (26 en suite) ★★★ HL **Directions:** On A11, close to city centre **Parking:** 25

Arlington Grill & Brasserie

Modern European

Enjoyable dining at historic city-centre venue

☎ 01603 617841 The George Hotel, 10 Arlington Ln, Newmarket Rd NR2 2DA
e-mail: reservations@georgehotel.co.uk
web: www.georgehotel.co.uk

A city-centre location makes the George Hotel a popular dining venue. Behind the frosted glass frontage lies a contemporary dining room with leather banquette seating, darkwood panelling and mirrors which give a bright but intimate atmosphere - the open-plan grill adds a touch of theatre. Friendly, uniformed staff offer formal service. Dishes use fresh, local and seasonal produce such as starters of Morston mussels steamed with shallots, parsley, white wine, garlic and cream, and main courses of local pheasant with root vegetables, celeriac mash and Madeira glaze. Desserts include poached pear with red wine and cinnamon syrup.

Chef: Paul Branford **Owners:** David Easter/Kingsley Place Hotels Ltd **Times:** 12-2/6-10 **Prices:** Fixed L £7.95-£10.95, Fixed D £19.95, Starter £4.35-£5.25, Main £9.95-£16.95, Dessert £4.50-£5.95, Coffee £2.25, Min/Water £3.75, Service optional **Wine:** 3 bottles over £20, 20 bottles under £20, 5 by the glass (£2.95-£3.10) **Notes:** Sun L 2 courses £10.50, 3 courses £13, Vegetarian available **Seats:** 44, Pr/dining room 60 **Smoking:** N/Sm in restaurant, Air con **Children:** Menu, Portions **Rooms:** 43 (43 en suite) ★★★ HL **Directions:** 1/2m from Norwich City Centre, 2m from Norwich City station, 30m from A14 **Parking:** 40

Beeches Hotel & Victorian Gardens

Modern International

A varied menu and delightful Victorian premises

☎ 01603 621167 2-6 Earlham Rd NR2 3DB
e-mail: beeches@mjbhotels.com
web: www.mjbhotels.com

The hotel is made up of three beautifully restored Grade II listed houses in a conservation area next to the Roman Catholic Cathedral. A walk down between the hotel's Victorian buildings leads you to the 3-acre Plantation Gardens, developed and maintained by the Plantation Preservation Trust, with free admission to hotel residents - perfect for a stroll before dinner. The menu, priced for two or three courses, might offer crayfish and celeriac remoulade, beef medallions with mushroom duxelle, potato rösti and Madeira sauce, and vanilla cheesecake with mango coulis.

continued

Chef: Chris Allen **Owners:** Mrs M Burlingham **Times:** 6.30-9.30, Closed L all week **Prices:** Fixed D £22.95, Coffee £1.80, Min/Water £2.60, Service optional **Wine:** 3 bottles over £20, 19 bottles under £20, 3 by the glass (£2.10-£3.90) **Notes:** Vegetarian available **Seats:** 32 **Smoking:** N/Sm in restaurant **Children:** Min 12 yrs, Portions **Rooms:** 41 (41 en suite) ★★★ HL **Directions:** W of City on B1108, behind St Johns R C Cathedral **Parking:** 50

Brummells Seafood Restaurant

International

Quaint medieval restaurant for fresh seafood

☎ 01603 625555 7 Magdalen St NR3 1LE
e-mail: brummell@brummells.co.uk
web: www.brummells.co.uk

A rustic but chic restaurant with exposed beams and stonework, Brummells is housed in a 17th-century building in the oldest part of Norwich. Service is formal but the atmosphere is relaxed, and quite romantic in the evening by candlelight. Accurately cooked seafood takes on an international flavour with dishes ranging through creamed fish soup with coconut milk, local mussels with white wine, cream and garlic, sea bass steamed with prawn butter, ginger and leeks, and chargrilled tuna with a compôte of fruity curry marmalade. Meat and vegetarian options are also offered, such as roast lamb neck fillet with snails, shallots and streaky bacon or pancakes filled with wild mushrooms and spinach.

hef: A Brummell, J O'Sullivan **Owners:** Mr A Brummell **Times:** 12-lexible/6-Flexible, Closed L Bookings only **Prices:** Starter £6-£14, Main 16-£35, Dessert £5.50, Coffee £3.50, Min/Water £4, Service optional, roup min 7 service 10% **Wine:** 58 bottles over £20, 32 bottles under 20, 3 by the glass (£3.45-£3.75) **Notes:** Bookings only for L **Seats:** 30 **moking:** N/Sm in restaurant, Air con **Children:** Portions **Directions:** In ty centre, 2 mins walk from Norwich Cathedral, 40yds from Colegate

By Appointment

British, European

Dinner in Aladdin's cave

☎ 01603 630730 27-29 St George's St NR3 1AB

By Appointment occupies three 15th-century merchants' houses with a labyrinth of corridors leading to a multitude of nooks and crannies. There are four intimate dining rooms, all very theatrical, with the added luxury of two comfortable drawing rooms. The whole house is filled with antique furniture, and tables are embellished with Victorian silver-plated cutlery and fine china. Dishes are classically English with continental influences, such as lobster bisque with croûtons and garlic rouille, and succulent breast of duck with cranberry and orange relish, parsnip shavings and port and thyme sauce.

Chef: Timothy Brown **Owners:** Timothy Brown, R Culyer **Times:** 7.30-9.30, Closed 25 Dec, Sun-Mon, Closed L all Week **Prices:** Starter £6.25-£7.95, Main £19.95, Dessert £6.50, Coffee £2.50, Min/Water £2.75, Service optional **Wine:** 40 bottles over £20, 20 bottles under £20, 3 by the glass (£3.95) **Notes:** Vegetarian available **Seats:** 50, Pr/dining room 36 **Smoking:** N/Sm in restaurant **Children:** Min 12 yrs **Directions:** City centre. Entrance rear of Merchants House **Parking:** 4

De Vere Dunston Hall

Modern European

Accomplished cuisine in grand hotel

☎ 01508 470444 Ipswich Rd NR14 8PQ
e-mail: dhreception@devere-hotels.com
web: www.devereonline.co.uk

An imposing Grade II listed building set in 170 acres of landscaped grounds, just a short drive from the city centre. The La Fontaine restaurant offers an extensive carte showcasing modern interpretations of French classics. Try a starter of tian of crab and potato salad with aïoli and coriander, followed perhaps by peppered duck breast on a sweet potato fondant with celery and ginger-scented jus. Vegetarians are well catered for and desserts include warm rice pudding with spiced fruits.

Chef: Paul Murfitt **Owners:** De Vere Hotels **Times:** 7-10, Closed Sun, Closed L Mon-Sun **Prices:** Starter £5.50-£8.50, Main £11.95-£17.95, Dessert £4.95-£8.50, Coffee £3.75, Min/Water £3.75, Service included **Notes:** Vegetarian available, Dress Restrictions, Smart, no jeans **Seats:** 45, Pr/dining room **Smoking:** N/Sm in restaurant, Air con **Children:** Menu, Portions **Rooms:** 130 (130 en suite) ★★★★ HL **Directions:** On A140 between Norwich & Ipswich **Parking:** 300

The Georgian House Hotel

European, Italian NEW

Local produce and regional beers in an immaculate small hotel

☎ 01603 615655 32-34 Unthank Rd NR2 2RB
e-mail: reception@georgian-hotel.co.uk
web: www.georgian-hotel.co.uk

This independently owned hotel is set in wooded grounds within easy walking distance of the city centre. Public areas include a choice of lounges, a small bar serving real ales from the St Peter's Brewery in Suffolk, and a smartly presented restaurant. Local produce is used to good effect in a starter of marinated seafood salad flavoured with roasted romano peppers, bay leaves and garlic, followed by local lamb leg steak charred pink, with roasted butternut squash and a rosemary jus. Home-made desserts include a white and dark chocolate delice.

Times: 6-9 **Rooms:** 28 (28 en suite) ★★★ HL **Directions:** Outskirts of town centre, opposite St Johns Roman Catholic cathedral.

England

NORWICH *continued* MAP 13 TG20

Marriott Sprowston Manor Hotel

International

Fine dining in elegant hotel

☎ 01603 410871 Sprowston Park, Wroxham Rd NR7 8RP
e-mail: debbie.phillips@marriotthotels.com
web: www.marriott.co.uk/nwigs

Surrounded by open parkland, this imposing property is set in attractively landscaped gardens with golf and leisure facilities. The hotel is built around a house that dates back 450 years and many original features have been retained. Dine in the informal Café Zest or in the elegant Manor Restaurant with its crystal chandeliers and mahogany reeded columns. The menus are traditional with British and French influences: Norfolk crab cake with dill and mustard dressing, Norfolk beef fillet with creamed spinach and mushroom tartlet and sweet waffles, sautéed bananas and pecan and maple ice cream.

Chef: Paul Danabie **Owners:** Marriott International **Times:** 12.30-2/6-10, Closed L Sat, D Sun **Prices:** Fixed L £13.95, Fixed D £22.50, Starter £6.45-£7.45, Main £18.95-£25.95, Dessert £5.45-£5.95, Coffee £2.85, Min/Water £3.95, Service optional **Wine:** 37 bottles over £20, 29 bottles under £20, 18 by the glass (£4.90-£7.45) **Notes:** Sun L £16.95, Vegetarian available, Dress Restrictions, Smart casual, no shorts, Civ Wed 300 **Seats:** 70, Pr/dining room 150 **Smoking:** N/Sm in restaurant **Children:** Menu, Portions **Rooms:** 94 (94 en suite) ★★★★ HL **Directions:** From A47 take Postwick exit onto Norwich outer ring road, then take A1151. Hotel approx 3m and signed **Parking:** 170

Old Rectory

Modern British

A Georgian haven in the heart of Norwich

☎ 01603 700772 & 750772 103 Yarmouth Rd, Thorpe St Andrew NR7 0HF
e-mail: enquiries@oldrectorynorwich.com
web: www.oldrectorynorwich.com

This Georgian house sits in pretty grounds overlooking the River Yare just a few minutes' drive from the centre of Norwich. Deep sofas and comfortable armchairs beckon in the lounge - enjoy a pre-dinner drink, and then move through to the restaurant, a period room lit by candles, with a concise menu that changes daily. Dishes are mostly modern British in style, with a winning emphasis on flavour and good quality local ingredients; kick off with a pork, duck, pheasant and prune terrine perhaps, before tucking into partridge with nutmeg mash, cabbage, bacon and jus, or black treacle marinated roasted Attleborough pork tenderloin with rosemary-baked butternut squash. Service is attentive and thoughtfully paced.

Chef: James Perry **Owners:** Chris & Sally Entwistle **Times:** 7-10.30, Closed Xmas & New Year, Sun, Mon, Closed L all week **Prices:** Fixed D £25, Coffee £1.95, Min/Water £2.95, Service included **Wine:** 10 bottles over £20, 12 bottles under £20, 5 by the glass (£2.60-£3.75) **Notes:** Vegetarian available **Seats:** 18, Pr/dining room 16 **Smoking:** N/Sm in restaurant **Children:** Portions **Rooms:** 8 (8 en suite) ★★ HL **Directions:** From A47 take A1042 to Thorpe, then A1242. Hotel right after 1st lights **Parking:** 16

1 Up

Modern British

Contemporary restaurant and modern food above a popular pub

☎ 01603 627687 The Mad Moose Arms & 1Up, 21, Warwick St NR2 3LD
e-mail: madmoose@animalinns.co.uk

Aptly named, '1 Up' sits upstairs above this trendy, bustling gastro-pub and provides its fine-dining arm at dinner only. A relaxed brasserie-style look of mustard walls, deep blues and natural woods cuts an appealing modern edge, fittingly backed by appropriately casual but professional service. The food fits the bill too, the accomplished cooking is big on flavour and balance, and committed to the use of high-quality seasonal ingredients. Warm smoked duck with roast squash, chicory and candied hazelnuts or rump of English lamb, rosemary cocotte potatoes, grilled figs and creamed goat's cheese might appear, and perhaps banana bavarois, lime and lemongrass sorbet and mango coulis to finish. In addition a substantial bar menu is offered downstairs.

Chef: Eden Derrick **Owners:** Mr Henry Watt **Times:** 12-3/7-9.30, Closed 25-26 Dec, 1 Jan, Closed L Mon-Sat, D Sun **Prices:** Fixed D £15-£18, Starter £4-£7.95, Main £8-£14.50, Dessert £4.50-£5.50, Coffee £1, Min/Water £2, Service optional **Wine:** 15 bottles over £20, 30 bottles under £20, 4 by the glass (£2.50-£5.50) **Notes:** Sun L available, Vegetarian available **Seats:** 48 **Smoking:** N/Sm in restaurant **Children:** Portions **Directions:** Telephone for directions **Parking:** On street

St Benedicts Restaurant

Modern British

Imaginative cuisine in a relaxed, contemporary setting

☎ 01603 765377 9 St Benedicts St NR2 4PE
e-mail: stbens@ukonline.co.uk

The contemporary interior and blue leather seating give an inviting feel to this local restaurant. You'll find simple table decorations, and original church pews with two popular central booths. The staff are casually dressed, relaxed but professional. Cooking is imaginative with an emphasis on quality, flavour and good ingredients sourced locally whenever possible. Enjoy some unusual taste sensations like haunch of venison with spiced pears and bitter chocolate jus and slow-cooked crispy duck with braised chicory and persimmon. More traditional dishes might include grilled rib-eye steak, celeriac rösti, flat mushrooms and red wine shallot sauce. You could try the English fruit liqueurs, made by a husband-and-wife team in Devon.

Chef: Nigel Raffles **Owners:** Nigel & Joyne Raffles **Times:** 12-2/7-10, Closed 25-31 Dec, Sun-Mon **Prices:** Fixed D £15.95, Starter £4.25-£5.50, Main £10.50-£12.95, Dessert £4.75, Coffee £1.45, Min/Water £2.25, Service optional, Group min 10 service 10% **Wine:** 30 bottles over £20, 32 bottles under £20, 8 by the glass (£3.60-£4.50) **Notes:** Vegetarian available **Seats:** 42, Pr/dining room 24 **Smoking:** N/Sm in restaurant **Children:** Portions **Directions:** Just off inner ring road. Turn right by Toys R-Us, 2nd right into St Benedicts St. Restaurant is on left by pedestrian crossing **Parking:** On street, West Wick Pay & Display

Shiki

Japanese

Sushi with style whether you want to eat in or take away

☎ 01603 619262 5 Tombland NR3 1HE
e-mail: bookings@shikirestaurant.co.uk
web: www.shiki.co.uk

This clean, minimalist restaurant is very much in the style of other urban Japanese eateries with cream coloured walls, stripped pine floors and bench seating. Sushi is the central attraction - on display at the chilled counter as you enter, and on the main menu where it's joined by other Japanese specialities such as tempura, teriyaki or tonkatsu. Good ingredients and clear flavours more than live up to expectations. Try the tapas-style menu which allows you to sample smaller portions of the main dishes so you can get a real taster of what's on offer.

Times: 12-2/5.30-10

Stower Grange

British, French

Relaxing and elegant surroundings for an enjoyable meal

☎ 01603 860210 School Rd, Drayton NR8 6EF
e-mail: enquiries@stowergrange.co.uk
web: www.stowergrange.co.uk

A 17th-century, ivy-clad property in a quiet residential area. The restaurant overlooks the rear gardens and grounds providing a relaxing venue for diners. Tables are neatly laid with crisp linen, crockery and plain white cutlery, and the hands-on owner and management ensure a warm welcome and efficient service. Cooking is straightforward and reassuring, with just about everything made on the premises. You might start with grilled brochette of salmon, prawn and tuna on a rocket salad, followed by breast of chicken with a chorizo and mushroom sauce. The owners are enthusiastic about wine and where possible source bottles directly from growers and producers in France.

Times: 12-2.30/7-9.30, Closed 26-30 Dec, Closed L Sat, Sun, D Sun **Rooms:** 11 (11 en suite) ★★ HL **Directions:** Telephone for directions

Tatlers

Modern British

Relaxed and stylish brasserie dining

☎ 01603 766670 21 Tombland NR3 1RF
e-mail: info@tatlers.com
web: www.tatlers.com

A converted Victorian townhouse close to Norwich Cathedral is the setting for this long-established and bustling brasserie-style restaurant. Period features abound, as do wooden floors, scrubbed tables and wall panelling painted soothing shades of terracotta and sage green. The striking upstairs bar doubles as a gallery for changing contemporary exhibitions. Expect a friendly, low-key atmosphere and a daily menu listing modern British dishes, although some show classic French undertones. Dishes utilise good local ingredients and may include salt cod fishcakes with red onion and tarragon relish for starters, followed by sirloin steak with wild mushroom and truffle butter, with rhubarb and vanilla crème brûlée or a plate of British cheese to finish.

continued

Chef: Brendan Ansbro **Owners:** Annelli Clarke **Times:** 12-2/6.30-10, Closed 25-26 Dec, Sun **Prices:** Fixed L fr £14, Starter £5-£8.50, Main £11-£17, Dessert £6.50-£7.50, Coffee £2.25, Min/Water £2.70, Service optional, Group min 10 service 10% **Wine:** 25 bottles over £20, 10 bottles under £20, 9 by the glass (£3.45-£4.65) **Seats:** 75, Pr/dining room 30 **Smoking:** N/Sm area, No pipes, No cigars **Children:** Portions **Directions:** In city centre in Tombland. Next to Erpingham gate by Norwich Cathedral **Parking:** Law courts, Elm Hill, Colegate

Loch Fyne Restaurant

☎ 01603 723450 30-32 St Giles St NR2 1LL
Quality seafood chain.

RINGSTEAD MAP 12 TF74

The Gin Trap Inn

British

Charming 17th-century inn turned gastro-pub

☎ 01485 525264 6 High St PE36 5JU
e-mail: info@gintrap.co.uk
web: gintrapinn.co.uk

Located in a peaceful village on the outskirts of Hunstanton, this charming 17th-century coaching inn is very much a gastro-pub these days. The bar is quite rustic with plain wooden tables, a huge fireplace with wood-burning stove, exposed brickwork and beams adorned with traps. The candlelit restaurant has neatly clothed tables with crisp napkins and relaxed but attentive service. The menu draws on good quality produce, some of which is locally sourced. Dishes are neatly presented with clear flavours, as in baked line-caught halibut or succulent grilled rib-eye steak. The bar menu is worth looking at too and there is an interesting children's menu, both featuring fresh produce.

Times: 12-2/6-9 **Rooms:** 3 (3 en suite) ◆◆◆◆

SHERINGHAM MAP 13 TG14

Dales Country House Hotel

Traditional, International

Country-house hotel in National Trust parkland

☎ 01263 824555 NR26 8TJ
e-mail: dales@mackenziehotels.com
web: www.mackenziehotels.com

The National Trust parkland of Sheringham Park, and its own extensive gardens contains this Victorian country-house hotel. The intimate Upchers restaurant, in keeping with the house style, is relaxed and smart. The kitchen is well supplied with game from local estates, fish from the north Norfolk coast, and quality meats, ideally displayed on

continued

England

SHERINGHAM *continued* MAP 13 TG14

the contemporary carte and daily specials. The simple cooking style yields excellent flavours. With a fireside lunch menu available, a typical evening meal may start with a salad of grilled Mediterranean vegetables and pine nuts, continue with Pernod pork fillet strips with tarragon shallots, forest mushrooms and vermicelli noodles, and finish with iced soufflé of mandarin and Cointreau.

Chef: Howard Bowen **Owners:** Mr & Mrs Mackenzie **Times:** 12-2/7-9.30 **Prices:** Fixed L £14.95-£20.95, Starter £4.20-£6.95, Main £9.95-£19.95, Dessert £4.55-£6.95, Coffee £1.65, Min/Water £3.50, Service optional **Wine:** 11 bottles over £20, 26 bottles under £20, 8 by the glass (£3-£6.50) **Notes:** Fixed L 3 courses, Sun L 3 courses £16.50, Vegetarian available, Dress Restrictions, No shorts or sportswear **Seats:** 50, Pr/dining room 40 **Smoking:** N/Sm in restaurant **Children:** Portions **Rooms:** 17 (17 en suite) ★★★★ HL **Directions:** On B1157, 1m S of Sheringham. From A148 Cromer to Holt road, take turn at entrance to Sheringham Park. Restaurant 0.5m on left **Parking:** 50

SHIPDHAM MAP 13 TF90

Bay Tree Brasserie at Pound Green Hotel

British, International

Rosettes not confirmed at time of going to press

☎ 01362 820940 Pound Green Ln IP25 7LS
web: www.poundgreenhotel.co.uk

This small privately owned hotel is situated in a quiet residential area in the village. The large restaurant offers an interesting choice of dishes from the blackboard menu including daily changing specials. Good cooking skills are used to get the very best from seasonal produce. Diners can enjoy flavoursome starters like smoked duck with pickled red cabbage and walnut salad and straightforward mains like pot roast belly pork on apricot and herb stuffing or baked cod fillet on spinach with creamy prawn sauce. Service is friendly and welcoming. *As we went to press we learned that there was a change of hands.*

Times: 12-2/7-9, Closed First 2 wks Jan **Rooms:** 11 (7 en suite) ◆◆◆ **Directions:** A47 to Dereham. A1075 5m to Shipdham. Take left at brown hotel sign into Pound Green Lane

---

SNETTISHAM MAP 12 TF63

🏵 The Rose & Crown

Modern, Traditional

Bustling local with culinary verve

☎ 01485 541382 Old Church Rd PE31 7LX
e-mail: info@roseandcrownsnettisham.co.uk
web: www.roseandcrownsnettisham.co.uk

Behind the rose-covered façade of this thriving local inn lurks a cosy warren of nooks and crannies, uneven floors and log fires. A colourful contemporary décor extends throughout the range of dining areas that includes a garden room opening on to a walled garden with a children's play area. Novel combinations make the menu an exciting read, and dishes don't disappoint; your choice might include seared marinated mackerel with warm potato salad, tempura tiger prawns and bouillabaisse, or grilled lamb and stilton sausages with bubble-and-squeak, red wine and mint sauce. Book ahead.

Chef: Andrew Bruce **Owners:** Anthony & Jeanette Goodrich **Times:** 12-2/6.30-9 **Prices:** Fixed L £10, Starter £4.50-£6.25, Main £7.95-£14.50, Dessert £4.50, Coffee £1.50, Min/Water £3, Service optional, Group min 10

continued

service 10% **Wine:** 10 bottles over £20, 20 bottles under £20, 10 by the glass (£3.25-£4.25) **Notes:** Vegetarian available **Seats:** 60, Pr/dining room 30 **Smoking:** N/Sm in restaurant **Children:** Menu, Portions **Rooms:** 11 (11 en suite) ★★ HL **Directions:** From King's Lynn take A149 N towards Hunstanton. After 10m into Snettisham to village centre, then into Old Church Rd towards church. Hotel is 100yds on left **Parking:** 70

STOKE HOLY CROSS MAP 13 TG20

🏵🏵 The Wildebeest Arms

Modern British NOTABLE WINE LIST

Modern take on a traditional pub with enticing menus

☎ 01508 492497 82-86 Norwich Rd NR14 8QJ
e-mail: mail@animalinns.co.uk

A fresh, bright, modern, open-plan pub setting mixes beams, panelling, open fire and bare floorboards with fresh flowers and African motifs and artefacts. The haunt of Norwich movers and shakers, the food mixes comforting English classics like sausages with creamed cabbage and roast beets and French brasserie favourites like onion and Yorkshire blue cheese tart. Staff are friendly and well informed about the locally sourced food and drink on offer. Menus are competitively priced for cooking of this calibre. To start, expect seared scallops with apple boudin, Alsace bacon, guacamole and pea shoots. Main courses could include local sea bass with ratte potatoes, tomato fondue and grilled courgettes. Finish with coconut pannacotta. **Notable Wine List:** A well constructed wine list with useful and informative tasting notes.

Chef: Daniel Smith **Owners:** Henry Watt **Times:** 12-3.30/6-11.30, Closed 25-26 Dec **Prices:** Fixed L £11.95-£14.95, Fixed D £18.50-£20.95, Starter £4.50-£8.95, Main £10.95-£18.50, Dessert £5.50-£6.50, Coffee £1.50, Min/Water £2.75, Service optional **Wine:** 60 bottles over £20, 70 bottles under £20, 10 by the glass (£3.25-£4.35) **Notes:** Vegetarian available **Seats:** 60 **Smoking:** N/Sm area, No pipes, Air con **Children:** Portions **Directions:** From A47, take A140 turn off towards Ipswich. Turn first left signposted byway to Dunston. Continue to end of the road and turn left at the T-junct, restaurant on right **Parking:** 40

THORNHAM MAP 12 TF74

🏵 Lifeboat Inn

Traditional, International

Fish features strongly at this historic alehouse

☎ 01485 512236 Ship Ln PE36 6LT
e-mail: reception@lifeboatinn.co.uk
web: www.lifeboatinn.co.uk

Enjoy superb views across open meadows to Thornham Harbour from this 16th-century smugglers' alehouse, now more of a gastro-pub with rooms. There is plenty of character inside with open fires and oak beams. The smart restaurant with white clothed, candlelit tables offers an interesting daily changing carte while a bar snack menu is available too. Fish is naturally a highlight with fresh starters like baked Cromer crab or a huge bowl of Brancaster mussels and interesting mains such as oven-roasted monkfish on a seafood risotto. For the meat-eaters there might be a hearty dish of Gressingham duck breast on a chorizo and black pudding cassoulet.

Chef: Michael Sherman **Owners:** A J Leisure **Times:** 7-9.30, Closed L all week **Prices:** Fixed D £28, Coffee £1.60, Min/Water £2.75, Service optional **Wine:** 16 bottles over £20, 24 bottles under £20, 12 by the glass (£3-£6) **Notes:** Vegetarian available **Seats:** 70, Pr/dining room 18 **Smoking:** N/Sm in restaurant **Children:** Portions **Rooms:** 13 (13 en suite) ★★ HL **Directions:** Take A149 from King's Lynn to Hunstanton, follow coast road to Thornham, take 1st left **Parking:** 100

The Orange Tree

British NEW

Popular gastro-pub on the North Norfolk coast

☎ 01485 512213 High St PE36 6LY
e-mail: email@theorangetreethornham.co.uk
web: www.theorangetreethornham.co.uk

A traditional gastro-pub dating back to around 1640, with a contemporary twist to the décor. Choose to dine in the bar with its inglenook fireplace and beams or in one of the two restaurant areas with their plush leather dining chairs. Either way, the waiting staff are relaxed and professional. Tossed linguini arrabiata, Italian style meatballs and white bean brushetta might sit alongside pan-fried skate, hand-cut chips and mint pea purée on a menu featuring international and modern British cuisine. Local produce includes Thornham Creek oysters, Brancaster mussels and local crab.

Chef: Phil Milner **Owners:** Chris Hinde **Times:** 12-2.30/6-9.30 **Prices:** Food prices not confirmed for 2007. Please telephone for details **Rooms:** 6 (6 en suite) ★★★ INN **Directions:** On A149 between Holme-Next-The-Sea and Brancaster Staithe

---

TITCHWELL MAP 13 TF74

Titchwell Manor Hotel

Modern International

Coastal weekend retreat with good seafood

☎ 01405 210221 PE31 0BB
e-mail: margaret@titchwellmanor.com
web: www.titchwellmanor.com

This 19th-century farmhouse is now a family-run hotel overlooking a salt marsh reserve. Modern décor of white walls, wooden floors and leather furniture goes well with the seaside atmosphere. Meals can be taken in the bar or in the attractively presented conservatory dining room with its neatly clothed tables and relaxing atmosphere. Service is professional. Local and seasonal ingredients are skilfully prepared to produce dishes with interesting combinations and clear flavours. Local seafood is used extensively. Expect starters of Brancaster mussels in white wine, cream and herbs and a main course of beef fillet, onion compôte, wild mushrooms and foie gras spring rolls.

Chef: Eric Snaith **Owners:** Titchwell Manor Hotel **Times:** 12-2.30/6-9.30 **Prices:** Starter £5-£9, Main £8-£20, Dessert £5-£7, Coffee £3, Min/Water £3.50, Service optional, Group min 8 service 10% **Wine:** 22 bottles over £20, 27 bottles under £20, 7 by the glass (£3.85-£4.95) **Notes:** Sun L 3 courses £15, Vegetarian available, Smart casual **Seats:** 50 **Smoking:** N/Sm in restaurant, Air con **Children:** Min 7 yrs D, Menu, Portions **Rooms:** 15 (15 en suite) ★★ HL **Directions:** On the A149 coast road between Brancaster and Thornham **Parking:** 25

WELLS-NEXT-THE-SEA MAP 13 TF94

The Crown Hotel

Pacific Rim

Great location for modern cooking

☎ 01328 710209 The Buttlands NR23 1EX
e-mail: reception@thecrownhotelwells.co.uk
web: www.thecrownhotelwells.co.uk

This historic former coaching inn dates back to the 16th century and retains original features such as the ancient beams in the bar and the lovely open fireplace. Just a few minutes from the beach, you can sit outside in fine weather and soak up some rays on the sheltered sun deck. Inside, the warm conservatory restaurant offers modern classic dishes using an abundance of local produce. Try sweetcorn and clam chowder to start, perhaps followed by brill en papillote with mussel ragout. Desserts feature iced rum, raisin and caramelised banana parfait.

Chef: Chris Coubrough **Owners:** Chris Coubrough **Times:** 7-9, Closed L all week **Prices:** Fixed D £29.95, Min/Water £2.95, Service optional **Wine:** 40 bottles over £20, 24 bottles under £20, 11 by the glass (£2.95-£4.85) **Notes:** Coffee incl. Price also incl. canapés and amuse-bouche, Vegetarian available **Seats:** 30, Pr/dining room 22 **Smoking:** N/Sm in restaurant **Children:** Menu, Portions **Directions:** 9m from Fakenham. At the top Buttlands Green

---

WYMONDHAM MAP 13 TG10

Number Twenty Four Restaurant

Modern, Traditional

Sound cooking in listed townhouse

☎ 01953 607750 24 Middleton St NR18 0AD
web: www.number24.co.uk

There's nothing pretentious or stuffy about this relaxed, friendly, family-run restaurant located in a row of listed terraced cottages. Low-key style, pale cream walls and well-spaced, neatly clothed tables hit just the right note. The sensibly compact menu takes a modern approach, with a nod to international influences. Changing daily to reflect quality market choice, the selection includes a vegetarian option. The cooking is straightforward with clear flavours. Look out for crispy confit shredded duck salad with spiced kumquat chutney and warm brioche, followed by grilled fillet of brill with king prawns on parsnip mash with crayfish and saffron cream sauce.

Chef: Jonathan Griffin **Owners:** Jonathan Griffin **Times:** 12-2/7-9, Closed 26 Dec, 1 Jan, Mon, Closed L Tue, D Sun **Prices:** Fixed L £13.95, Fixed D £23.50, Coffee £1.75, Min/Water £2.95 **Wine:** 12 bottles over £20, 20 bottles under £20, 6 by the glass (£3.95-£4.25) **Notes:** Sun L 2 courses

continued

WYMONDHAM *continued* MAP 13 TG10

£12.95, 3 courses £14.95, Vegetarian available, Dress Restrictions, Smart casual, no shorts **Seats:** 60, Pr/dining room 20 **Smoking:** N/Sm in restaurant **Children:** Portions **Directions:** Town centre opposite war memorial **Parking:** On street opposite. In town centre car park

Casablanca

☎ 01953 607071 2 Middleton St NR18 0AD

High street restaurant serving great value Moroccan food.

NORTHAMPTONSHIRE

CASTLE ASHBY MAP 11 SP85

Falcon Hotel

Modern British

Country hotel with an emphasis on good food

☎ 01604 696200 NN7 1LF

e-mail: falcon.castleashby@oldenglishinns.co.uk

web: www.falcon-castleashby.com

This family-run hotel is located in the heart of the village and occupies a large stone-built property and two neighbouring cottages dating from the 16th century. The pretty restaurant overlooks the garden, and dishes are based on fresh local produce including vegetables from the garden. There's a set-price menu for lunch and dinner plus an à la carte selection offering the likes of griddled wild boar and apple sausages with apple mash and red wine jus, and lightly baked fillet of sea bass layered with spinach.

Times: 12-2.30/7-9.30, Closed D 24 Dec **Rooms:** 16 (16 en suite) ★★

DAVENTRY MAP 11 SP56

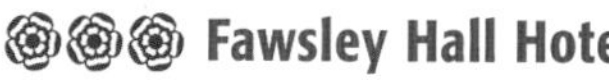

Fawsley Hall Hotel

see opposite

EYDON MAP 11 SP54

The Royal Oak @ Eydon

Modern British NEW

Refurbished village pub with style

☎ 01327 263167 6 Lime Av NN11 3PG

Everything here has been done well, yet without losing the original bonhomie and character, from flagstone floors to inglenook and leaded windows. A good choice of hand-pumped ales is matched by quality wines by the glass, including champagne, which sums up that stylish edge. The menu's approach is modern focused, backed by a specials board. Fish plays a key role, though there's plenty for meat eaters, too. The accomplished cooking is intelligently simple, accurate and with depth of flavour, allowing high-quality ingredients to shine. Typical main dishes include pan-fried Cornish monkfish tail with chorizo, oven-roasted rack of lamb with mint and pine nut crust, or a choice of first class steaks with accompaniments.

Chef: Justin Lefevre **Owners:** Justin Lefevre **Times:** 12-2/7-9 **Prices:** Food prices not confirmed for 2007. Please telephone for details **Directions:** Telephone for directions

FOTHERINGHAY MAP 12 TL09

The Falcon Inn

British, Italian NOTABLE WINE LIST

Vibrant cooking in rural Northamptonshire

☎ 01832 226254 Huntsbridge PE8 5HZ

e-mail: falcon@huntsbridge.co.uk

web: www.huntsbridge.com

The Falcon manages to combine its role as friendly village local with that of renowned pub-restaurant. Located in the mellow stone-built village where Mary, Queen of Scots ended her days, the pub has immense character and a lovely garden with views of the church. While British classics are served in the bar, the restaurant menu is Anglo-Italian, kicking off with warm olives and foccacia and offering the likes of stinco di maiale - pork shin slow braised with vegetables, herbs and white wine, served with saffron risotto, parmesan and gremolata.

Notable Wine List: An expertly chosen wine list full of interest and quality, personal tasting notes and great value for money.

Owners: John Hoskins **Times:** 12-2.15/6.15-9.30 **Prices:** Fixed L £13.50, Starter £4.95-£8.95, Main £12.95-£19.95, Dessert £4.75-£6.95, Coffee £1.70, Min/Water £2.95, Service optional, Group min 10 service 10% **Wine:** 80 bottles over £20, 40 bottles under £20, 16 by the glass (£3.50-£9) **Notes:** Vegetarian available **Seats:** 45, Pr/dining room 25 **Smoking:** N/Sm in restaurant **Children:** Menu, Portions **Directions:** Off A605 follow signpost Fotheringhay **Parking:** 50

England

Fawsley Hall Hotel

DAVENTRY MAP 11 SP56

British, Mediterranean V

A grand Tudor manor with sublime food

☎ 01327 892000 Fawsley NN11 3BA
e-mail: reservations@fawsleyhall.com
web: www.fawsleyhall.com

This majestic country house set in an awe-inspiring 2,000 acres of rolling hills and parkland has a history stretching back over 700 years. It's a stunning place that manages to carefully balance tasteful period charm with modern luxury, with a recent renovation adding a new spa. The Great Hall, with its wood panelling, candlelight and cavernous ceilings, is a particularly spectacular room and is currently used as a lounge - pre-dinner drinks here are wholeheartedly advised. The restaurant itself is comfortably appointed with well-spaced tables and attractive table settings. Service is assured and without the unnecessary fuss sometimes associated with hotels of this kind.

The kitchens continue to maintain their high standards, producing dishes with an intelligent simplicity allowing ingredients to speak for themselves both in their flavour and in the uncluttered presentation. Dishes might include terrine of quail and foie gras with lentil and hazelnut dressing, followed by seared fillet of red mullet with langoustines and saffron potatoes.

Chef: Philip Dixon
Owners: Fawsley Hall Hotel Ltd
Times: 12-2.30/7-9.30, Closed L Mon-Fri
Prices: Fixed D £35-£49.50, Starter £7-£12.50, Main £17.50-£25, Dessert £7.50-£12, Min/Water £3, Service added but optional 12.5%
Wine: 163 bottles over £20, 24 bottles under £20, 12 by the glass (£4.50-£6.25)
Notes: Fixed D 4 courses, Vegetarian menu, Civ Wed 140
Seats: 85, Pr/dining room 140
Smoking: N/Sm in restaurant
Children: Menu, Portions
Rooms: 43 (43 en suite) ★★★★ HL
Directions: From M40 junct 11 take A361, follow for 12m. Turn right towards Fawsley Hall
Parking: 100

HELLIDON MAP 11 SP55

Hellidon Lakes

Contemporary

An impressive setting for imaginative cuisine

☎ 01327 262550 NN11 6GG
e-mail: hellidon@marstonhotels.com
web: www.hellidonlakes.com

Set in 220 acres of countryside, including 27 holes of golf and 12 lakes, it would be difficult not to have a great view from the fine dining restaurant, but why not ask for a window seat anyway. The menu is extensive with some supplements for speciality dishes. Modern international cuisine can be enjoyed with the likes of pork and spinach terrine or French-style confit of duck leg with sauté potatoes and Puy lentil cassoulet. The global wine list offers some more unusual wines and a good selection of half bottles and wines by the glass.

Chef: Charles Anderson **Owners:** Marston Hotels **Times:** 12-2/7-9.45, Closed L Sat & Sun **Prices:** Fixed L £13.50-£15.95, Starter fr £5.50, Main fr £15, Dessert fr £5, Coffee £2.50, Min/Water £3.50, Service optional **Wine:** 31 bottles over £20, 18 bottles under £20, 20 by the glass (£3.80-£7.95) **Notes:** Sun carvery £10.95, Vegetarian available, Dress Restrictions, Smart dress, no jeans, trainers or T-shirts **Seats:** 60, Pr/dining room 50 **Smoking:** N/Sm in restaurant **Children:** Menu, Portions **Rooms:** 110 (110 en suite) ★★★★ HL **Directions:** M40 junct 11 onto A361 towards Charwelton, turn right, hotel 2m

HORTON MAP 11 SP85

The New French Partridge

Modern British, French V

Confident cooking in stylish country-house restaurant

☎ 01604 870033 Newport Pagnell Rd NN7 2AP
e-mail: info@newfrenchpartridge.co.uk
web: www.newfrenchpartridge.co.uk

continued

Situated in private grounds in the lovely Northamptonshire village of Horton, this former coaching inn was built in 1622. The current owners have restored it to its original splendour, including ten luxurious and individually designed bedrooms and a bar in the vaulted cellar. A well-balanced menu of modern French and British dishes makes good use of high quality ingredients. You may start with poached quail breast with baby beetroot, broad beans and sautéed chorizo or risotto nero with buttered squid and follow with seared zander, asparagus and shiitake salad or home-cured free-range pork belly with baby vegetable cassoulet and glazed lamb sweetbreads.

Chef: Wayne Farmer, Ian Oakenfull, Simon Addison **Owners:** Ian Oakenfull, Tanya Banerjee **Times:** 11.30-2.30/6.30-10.30, Closed L Sat, D Sun **Prices:** Fixed L £17.50-£25, Coffee £3.50, Min/Water £3.90 **Wine:** 40 bottles over £20, 10 bottles under £20, 10 by the glass (£4.50) **Notes:** Tasting menu £65, Sun L £27.50, Fixed D 5 courses £41.50, Vegetarian menu, Dress Restrictions, Smart casual, Civ Wed 70 **Seats:** 70, Pr/dining room 12 **Smoking:** N/Sm in restaurant **Children:** Portions **Rooms:** 10 (10 en suite) ★★ HL **Directions:** On B526 between Milton Keynes and Northampton, in village of Horton **Parking:** 35

KETTERING MAP 11 SP87

Kettering Park Hotel

Modern British

Modern British cuisine in a smart hotel restaurant

☎ 01536 416666 Kettering Parkway NN15 6XT
e-mail: kpark.reservations@shirehotels.com
web: www.shirehotels.com

This modern hotel combines old world charm with up-to-date comfort. In the split-level Langberry's restaurant you'll find traditional décor with subtle lighting, a welcoming fire in winter and formal table service from well-trained staff; there's an outdoor terrace for alfresco eating in warmer months. An interesting menu delivers British dishes including confit of Barbary duck risotto and sage oil to start, with mains of honey-roasted belly of Lincolnshire pork. Desserts might feature a classical lemon tart. Heart symbols on the menu indicate lighter and simply prepared dishes.

Chef: Dougie **Owners:** Shire Hotels **Times:** 12.30-2.30/7-9.30, Closed Xmas & New Year (ex residents), Closed L Sat, Sun **Prices:** Starter £6-£10, Main £12-£22, Dessert £6-£8, Coffee £3.25, Min/Water £3.50, Service optional **Wine:** 14 bottles over £20, 14 bottles under £20, 15 by the glass (£4-£9) **Notes:** Vegetarian available, Civ Wed 100 **Seats:** 90, Pr/dining room 40 **Smoking:** N/Sm in restaurant **Children:** Menu, Portions **Rooms:** 119 (119 en suite) ★★★★ HL **Directions:** Off A14 junct 9 **Parking:** 200

ROADE MAP 11 SP75

Roade House Restaurant

Modern British

Popular village restaurant serving simple lunches and more serious dinners

☎ 01604 863372 16 High St NN7 2NW
e-mail: info@roadehousehotel.co.uk
web: www.roadehousehotel.co.uk

Originally a stone-built pub dating back to the 18th century, it has been sympathetically extended and renovated to provide a large, comfortable lounge bar with open fire, and a non-smoking restaurant. Special dining evenings are held throughout the year. The set price menus are good value at lunch and dinner. With sound depth of flavours, starters might include ravioli of smoked sheep's milk ricotta or rabbit terrine while expect mains along the lines of roast monkfish with lightly curried mussels or seared duck breast with confit leg, kumquats and orange and red wine sauce.

Chef: Chris Kewley **Owners:** Mr & Mrs C M Kewley **Times:** 12-2/7-9.30, Closed 1 wk Xmas, Sun, Closed L Sat **Prices:** Fixed L £20, Fixed D £30-£33, Coffee £2.50, Min/Water £3, Service optional **Wine:** 30 bottles over £20, 20 bottles under £20, 2 by the glass (£3.50-£4) **Notes:** Dress Restrictions, No shorts for men **Seats:** 50 **Smoking:** N/Sm in restaurant, Air con **Children:** Portions **Directions:** M1 junct 15 (A508 Milton Keynes) to Roade, left at mini rdbt, 500yds on left **Parking:** 20

TOWCESTER MAP 11 SP64

Vine House Restaurant

Modern British

Fresh local ingredients in a home-from-home atmosphere

☎ 01327 811267 100 High St, Paulerspury NN12 7NA
e-mail: info@vinehousehotel.com
web: www.vinehousehotel.com

This 300-year-old cottage is now a homely restaurant run by husband-and-wife team Marcus and Julie Springett. The emphasis is on relaxed, informal dining in a friendly atmosphere. Décor is traditional cottage-style and guests are made to feel really welcome in the cosy dining room. The menu is based firmly on local produce and the best available ingredients with lots of home-made items. Try the hot treacle roasted organic Scottish salmon with watercress and orange salad, or perhaps home-made duck liver pâté as starters. Main courses might include local Sussex chicken and bacon sausages with bread sauce, herb stock and beef dripping chips. Desserts include the likes of Bramley apple crumble with clotted cream.

Chef: Marcus Springett **Owners:** Mr M & Mrs J Springett **Times:** 12-1.45/6-10 **Prices:** Fixed L fr £26.95, Fixed D fr £29.95, Coffee £2.50, Min/Water £3.50, Service added 12.5% **Notes:** Vegetarian available **Seats:** 26, Pr/dining room 10 **Smoking:** N/Sm in restaurant **Directions:** 2m S of Towcester, just off A5 **Parking:** 20

WHITTLEBURY MAP 11 SP64

Whittlebury Hall Hotel & Spa

British European

Fine-dining restaurant dedicated to Formula 1 commentator Murray Walker

☎ 01327 857857 NN12 8QH
e-mail: sales@whittleburyhall.co.uk
web: www.whittleburyhall.co.uk

Just around the corner from Silverstone, Murray's Restaurant is named after Murray Walker and is home to a series of Formula 1 anecdotes from his commentary years, as well as photos from F1 drivers and teams. It provides an intimate, sophisticated dining venue with formal service and smart casual dress code, offering modern European cooking with classical influences. Try a starter like pistachio nut-crusted roulade of foie gras with banana bread and sweet chilli jus. Main courses might feature scallops and lobster in vermouth nage and fettuccini. Desserts are 'The Finale' on the menu and include the likes of pineapple parfait wrapped in a tuile parcel.

Chef: Peter Manner **Owners:** Macepark (Whittlebury) Ltd **Times:** 7-10, Closed 24 26, 31 Dec, 1-7 Jan, Sun, Mon, Closed L all wk **Prices:** Fixed L fr £15.50, Fixed D fr £29.95, Starter £6-£12, Main £18-£24, Dessert £6-£12, Coffee £2.95, Min/Water £3.50, Service optional **Wine:** 60 bottles over £20, 40 bottles under £20, 16 by the glass (£3.50-£8.50) **Notes:** Vegetarian available, Dress Restrictions, Smart casual, no jeans, trainers or shorts, Civ Wed 200 **Seats:** 48, Pr/dining room 400 **Smoking:** N/Sm in restaurant **Children:** Min 12 yrs, Menu, Portions **Rooms:** 211 (211 en suite) ★★★★ **Directions:** M3/M13 to Whittlebury, through village, hotel at far end on right **Parking:** 300

NORTHUMBERLAND

CORNHILL-ON-TWEED MAP 21 NT83

Tillmouth Park Hotel

Modern British

Modern cuisine in Victorian elegance

☎ 01890 882255 TD12 4UU
e-mail: reception@tillmouthpark.force9.co.uk
web: www.tillmouthpark.co.uk

Set on the banks of the River Till in secluded woodland, this imposing Victorian manor recalls a leisurely country-house age. Think stone and marble fireplaces, stained glass, oil paintings, chandeliers, antiques and fishing objets d'art, all backed by relaxed but attentive service. The intimate, wood-panelled Library Dining Room with its crisp white linen overlooks the garden, while aperitifs are served in the stunning galleried lounge or elegant drawing room. In such surroundings, the kitchen's modern spin on traditional dishes shows flair and imagination. Expect a loin of venison teamed with rösti potato, roasted shallots, pea mash and a Puy green lentil sauce, and date and toffee sponge with toffee sauce to close.

Chef: Gerard Boylan, Tony McKay **Times:** 12-2/7-8.45, Closed 26-28 Dec, Closed L Mon-Sat **Prices:** Fixed D £32.50, Min/Water £4.50, Service optional **Wine:** 34 bottles over £20, 34 bottles under £20, 10 by the glass (£3.75-£5.95) **Notes:** Coffee incl, Dress Restrictions, Smart casual, no jeans, Civ Wed 60 **Seats:** 40, Pr/dining room 20 **Smoking:** N/Sm in restaurant **Children:** Portions **Rooms:** 14 (14 en suite) ★★★ HL **Directions:** A698, 3m E from Cornhill-on-Tweed **Parking:** 50

England

HEXHAM MAP 21 NY96

De Vere Slaley Hall

British, French

Fresh flavours and quality ingredients at this impressive hotel

☎ 01434 673350 Slaley NE47 0BX
e-mail: slaley.hall@devere-hotels.com
web: www.devereonline.co.uk

Equally attractive to leisure or corporate guests, this large hotel - an original hall with lots of modern extensions - has a renowned golf course, spa facilities and 1,000 acres of parkland. Comfortable lounges include the recently refurbished bar and clubhouse and more traditional library lounge, and the restaurant is light and attractive in autumnal shades. Food is offered from a daily market menu and a brasserie-style carte with dishes such as a pressed terrine of confit duckling with foie gras and truffle wrapped in Bayonne ham, a trio of deep-fried fresh fish, chunky chips, peas and fresh ketchup, and chargrilled sirloin steak with sauce béarnaise.

Times: 1-3/7-9.30, Closed L Mon-Sat **Rooms:** 139 (139 en suite) ★★★★ HL **Directions:** A1 from S to A68. Follow signs for Slaley Hall From N A69 to Carbridge then take A68 S and follow signs to Slaley Hall

LONGHORSLEY MAP 21 NZ19

Macdonald Linden Hall

Modern British

Grade II listed country property set amid extensive parkland

☎ 01670 500000 NE65 8XF
e-mail: stay@lindenhall.co.uk
web: www.lindenhall.co.uk

Georgian mansion set in 450 acres of park and woodland surrounded by beautiful Northumberland countryside. Facilities include a golf course, a country pub and conference suites. There are lovely views from the hotel's Dobson Restaurant, and here the civilised formalities are observed in terms of dress. The menu is priced for two or three courses with an optional intermediary sorbet (home-made fresh daily). The same format applies for lunch and dinner, with a more extensive choice in the evening. Typical of the style are dishes of grilled red mullet with herb salad and sauce gazpacho, and pan-fried chicken supreme with wild mushroom duxelle and sesame seed pastry.

Times: 12-2.30/7-9.30 **Rooms:** 50 (50 en suite) ★★★ **Directions:** Located between Longhorsley and Longframlington off A697

MATFEN MAP 21 NZ07

Matfen Hall

Modern British

Satisfying dining in elegant country-house surroundings

☎ 01661 886500 NE20 0RH
e-mail: info@matfenhall.com
web: www.matfenhall.com

Set in 250 acres of classic parkland, this imposing Regency mansion - still owned by the Blackett family who built it - boasts its own championship golf course as well as high-tech spa and leisure facilities. The elegant, spacious, book-lined Library and adjoining Print Room Restaurant ooze atmosphere, especially by candlelight, with floor-length tablecloths, fine glassware and lovely views. The cuisine is modern British - underpinned by French influences - featuring accurate, balanced and intelligently uncomplicated dishes that allow well-sourced, fresh local produce and flavour to shine. Take chargrilled medallions of fillet steak paired with Lyonnaise potato and a foie gras butter sauce, or a warm, liquid-centred chocolate cake with coconut ice cream to illustrate the style.

Chef: Phil Hall **Owners:** Sir Hugh & Lady Blackett **Times:** 12.15-2.30/7-10, Closed L Mon-Sat **Prices:** Fixed D £25, Starter £6.45-£8.25, Main £14.95-£21.50, Dessert £5.50-£6.25, Coffee £2.50, Min/Water £3.50, Service optional **Wine:** 42 bottles over £20, 33 bottles under £20, 8 by the glass (£3.25-£5) **Notes:** Sun L 3 courses £16.95, Vegetarian available, Dress Restrictions, Smart casual, Civ Wed 160 **Seats:** 90, Pr/dining room 120 **Smoking:** N/Sm in restaurant **Children:** Portions **Rooms:** 53 (53 en suite) ★★★★ HL **Directions:** A69 signed Hexham, leave at Heddon on the Wall. Then B6318, through Rudchester & Harlow Hill. Follow signs on right for Matfen **Parking:** 120

PONTELAND MAP 21 NZ17

Café Lowrey

British, French

Good value bistro-style eating

☎ 01661 820357 35 The Broadway, Darras Hall, Ponteland NE20 9PW
web: www.cafelowrey.co.uk

A modern bistro-style restaurant within a small shopping precinct in a residential area of Ponteland, not far from Newcastle airport. The extensive menu features modern British and French style dishes using local produce. Early evening specials are on offer Monday to Friday from 5.30-7pm and Saturday lunchtime. The menu offers the likes of smoked chicken and king prawn salad with walnut dressing to start, followed perhaps by sesame crusted salmon with egg noodles and soy and ginger dressing. Desserts are simple like crème brûlée or warm chocolate brownie with chocolate fudge sauce.

continued

Café Lowrey

Chef: Ian Lowrey **Owners:** Ian Lowrey **Times:** 12-2/5.30-10, Closed BHs, Sun, Closed L Mon-Fri **Prices:** Fixed L £12.50, Fixed D £15.50, Starter £4.50-£10.50, Main £9.50-£20, Dessert £4-£5.50, Coffee £2.10, Min/Water £2.50, Service optional, Group min 10 service 10% **Wine:** 10 bottles over £20, 10 bottles under £20, 4 by the glass **Notes:** Vegetarian available, Dress Restrictions, Smart casual **Seats:** 68 **Smoking:** N/Sm area, No pipes, No cigars **Children:** Portions **Directions:** From A696, follow signs for Darras Hall. Left at mini rdbt, restaurant in 200yds **Parking:** On street

NOTTINGHAMSHIRE

LANGAR MAP 11 SK73

❀❀ Langar Hall

Traditional British

European cooking in tranquil country-house setting

☎ 01949 860559 NG13 9HG
e-mail: imogen@langarhall.co.uk
web: www.langarhall.com

This Victorian country house has a secluded setting overlooking gardens and ancient fishponds to the fields and hamlet beyond. The lounges, library and elegant dining room are furnished with antiques. The classical formality of it all falls short of intimidating thanks to a warm welcome and helpful service. The comfortable, candlelit dining room is the perfect setting for dinner which comprises contemporary, seasonal British dishes. To start, roast wood pigeon is accompanied by rabbit fillet, lentils and Madeira sauce. Main courses include steamed fillet of turbot and braised fennel with mussel sauce. Be there at the right time of year and you could finish with the rhubarb plate - poached Yorkshire rhubarb, crème fraîche mousse, blood orange and rhubarb jelly with a ginger biscuit.

Chef: Toby Garratt, Gary Booth **Owners:** Imogen Skirving **Times:** 12-2/7-10 **Prices:** Fixed L fr £13.50, Fixed D £26-£37, Starter £5-£16.50, Main £13.50-£20, Dessert £7.50, Coffee £2.50, Min/Water £2.50, Service added but optional 10% **Wine:** 14 bottles under £20, 7 by the glass (£4.75) **Notes:** Sun L 2 courses £20, 3 courses £25, Vegetarian available, Dress

continued

Restrictions, Smart casual, Civ Wed 40 **Seats:** 30, Pr/dining room 20 **Smoking:** N/Sm in restaurant **Children:** Portions **Rooms:** 12 (12 en suite) ★★★ HL **Directions:** Off A46 & A52 in village centre (behind church) **Parking:** 40

NOTTINGHAM MAP 11 SK53

❀❀ Hart's Restaurant

Modern British V

Skilfully prepared dishes in a modern, urban, brasserie setting

☎ 0115 988 1900 Standard Hill, Park Row NG1 6FN
e-mail: ask@hartsnottingham.co.uk
web: www.hartsnottingham.co.uk

Hart's Restaurant fits comfortably into what used to be part of Nottingham's old General Hospital building. Situated 30 metres from the hotel, the newly refurbished dining room has new booths and banquettes, warmer colours and a new lighting scheme that highlights the contemporary art. Retaining its lively atmosphere, the restaurant is now more comfortable, intimate and sophisticated. Skilfully prepared modern British dishes are the norm here with extensive use of local produce whenever possible. Subtle presentation only augments the pleasure of starters like home-made black pudding, wild mushrooms and poached egg and main courses of fallow deer loin, celeriac purée and port and juniper sauce. Finish with chocolate pudding with Jersey milk ice cream.

Chef: Alan Gleeson **Owners:** Tim Hart **Times:** 12-2/7-10.30, Closed 26 Dec & 1 Jan, Closed L 31 Dec, D 25 Dec **Prices:** Fixed L £12.95-£14, Starter £5-£12.50, Main £13.95-£20.50, Dessert £7.50-£9.50, Coffee £1.50, Min/Water £2.95, Service added but optional 12% **Wine:** 50 bottles over £20, 25 bottles under £20, 6 by the glass (£4.25-£5.95) **Notes:** Sun D 2 courses £12.95, 3 courses £15.95, Vegetarian menu, Civ Wed 75 **Seats:** 80, Pr/dining room 90 **Smoking:** N/Sm in restaurant **Children:** Portions **Rooms:** 32 (32 en suite) ★★★★ HL **Directions:** M1 junct 24, follow A453 to city centre. Follow signs to the Castle. Once on Maid Marion Way turn left at the Gala Casino, continue to top of the hill and turn left through black gates **Parking:** 17

England

NOTTINGHAM *continued* MAP 11 SK53

The Lobster Pot

***Seafood* NEW**

A gem of a seafood restaurant

☎ 0115 947 0707 199 Mansfield Rd NG1 3FS

It may not be much to look at from the outside, but misjudge this little seafood restaurant at your peril! The simple space features fish-themed objets d'art and Middle Eastern carvings, and the chunky wooden tables are quickly filled so booking is advised. The food leaves a powerful impression long after the last mouthful, with subtle saucing that doesn't dominate the main ingredient. King scallops pan-fried in garlic butter, balsamic vinegar and white wine sauce is a fine example of the fare, served by charming and knowledgeable hosts.

Chef: Mr & Mrs Pongsawang **Owners:** Mr & Mrs Pongsawang **Times:** 12-2/6-10.30, Closed BHs, Mon, Closed L Sun **Prices:** Starter £3.50-£4.50, Main £7.95-£12.95, Dessert £3, Coffee £1, Min/Water £2.20, Service optional **Wine:** 2 bottles over £20, 28 bottles under £20, 3 by the glass (£1.95) **Seats:** 40 **Smoking:** N/Sm in restaurant, Air con **Children:** Portions **Directions:** From Nottingham town centre N on A60 for 0.5m, restaurant on left at the lights where Huntingdon St joins Mansfield Rd

Merchants Restaurant & Bar

British, French NOTABLE WINE LIST

Classic French brasserie with chic interior

☎ 0115 958 9898 Lace Market Hotel, 31 High Pavement NG1 1HE
e-mail: dine@merchantsnottingham.co.uk
web: www.merchantsnottingham.co.uk

This Grade II listed Georgian warehouse conversion has found a new lease of life as a classic brasserie restaurant. The chic relaxed interior was designed by David Collins. Waiting staff are relaxed but attentive, serving up a two- or three-course lunch menu and one carte for both lunch and dinner. Cuisine is classic French brasserie style with British elements. Try a starter of seared diver scallops and tomato confit salad. For a main course try lamb rump on braised Savoy cabbage with dark olive jus. **Notable Wine List:** An interesting and well chosen wine list with an emphasis on small producers.

Chef: Patrick Tweedie **Owners:** Lace Market Hotel Ltd **Times:** 12-2.30/7-10.30, Closed 26 Dec, 1 Jan, Sun, Closed L Sat & Mon **Prices:** Fixed L £11.95, Fixed D £29.50, Starter £5.50-£11.50, Main £16.50-£19.95, Dessert £6.50-£7, Coffee £2.10, Min/Water £3, Service added but optional 10% **Wine:** 52 bottles over £20, 12 bottles under £20, 7 by the glass (£4-£6.50) **Notes:** Vegetarian available, Civ Wed 60 **Seats:** 64, Pr/dining room 18 **Smoking:** N/Sm in restaurant, Air con **Rooms:** 42 (42 en suite) ★★★★ **Directions:** Follow town centre signs for Galleries of Justice, entrance is opposite **Parking:** On street. NCP adjacent

Restaurant Sat Bains with Rooms

see opposite

Sonny's

Modern, European

Cutting-edge city-centre cuisine

☎ 0115 947 3041 3 Carlton St, Hockley NG1 1NL
e-mail: nottingham@sonnys.co.uk
web: www.sonnys.co.uk

Closed

Housed in a listed former print works, Sonny's occupies a beautiful, airy space with a contemporary interior featuring an extensive private art collection. The atmosphere is bustling yet relaxed. Shoppers continuously pass by and through the large floor-to-ceiling mirrors on one wall adding to the general hustle and bustle. Different cooking styles are drawn on to create a modern European menu, and dishes are cooked to order using the freshest ingredients. Starters might feature crab bisque or pumpkin risotto, while mains might see Vincisgrassi - an 18th-century recipe of baked pasta with Parma ham, porcini and truffles - alongside Italian fish stew (brodetto adriatico) or nearer to home, rack of Derbyshire lamb.

Chef: Steven Robbins **Owners:** Ms R Mascarenhas **Times:** 12-2.30/7-10.30, Closed BHs **Prices:** Fixed L £11.50-£13.50, Starter £4.95-£8.50, Main £10.50-£19.50, Dessert £5.50-£6.95, Coffee £2, Min/Water £3, Service added but optional 10% **Wine:** 10 bottles over £20, 20 bottles under £20, 10 by the glass (£2.95-£7) **Notes:** Sun L 2 courses £13.50, 3 courses £16.50, Vegetarian available **Seats:** 80 **Smoking:** N/Sm in restaurant, Air con **Children:** Menu, Portions **Directions:** City centre **Parking:** Fletcher Gate car park

World Service

Modern British NOTABLE WINE LIST

Globetrotting eatery on the way up

☎ 0115 847 5587 Newdigate House, Castle Gate NG1 6AF
e-mail: enquiries@worldservicerestaurant.com
web: www.worldservicerestaurant.com

A Nottingham favourite, this chic eatery is designed to look like the home of an eccentric traveller, and teams country-house comfort with exotic artefacts to create a relaxed contemporary décor. Entry is via an oriental garden to a lounge where gilt armchairs, a roaring fire and coconut shell tables await, plus a decadent list of cocktails. The food is rooted in modern British cuisine, but occasionally picks up on the international vibe; the menu changes daily and features mains like pork belly with black pudding and Boston baked beans.

continued on page 386

England

Restaurant Sat Bains with Rooms

NOTTINGHAM MAP 11 SK53

European NOTABLE WINE LIST

AA Restaurant of the Year for England

☎ 0115 986 6566 Lenton Ln, Trentside NG7 2SA
e-mail: info@restaurantsatbains.net
web: www.restaurantsatbains.com

Tucked away down a quiet lane this delightful, sympathetically converted Victorian farmhouse sits on the banks of the Trent. Smartly refurbished and fashionably attired, quality reigns supreme, from the restaurant's high-backed leather seats to the spacious tables and first-class tableware - complete with the chef-patron's monogrammed signature. The lounge offers champagne and oysters, and after-dinner relaxing. Exposed beams, veneered flagstone floors, jazz backing track and expressionist modern art all conspire to create a smooth, classy and restrained backdrop for some flamboyant cooking. Service is delightfully friendly, with genuine warmth and a willingness to please, while Sat Bains' culinary odyssey is not to be missed - this is modern cooking on the edge from a highly-skilled pioneer.

Abruptly scripted dish descriptions and combinations stretch the imagination and dazzle with a host of innovative techniques, textures and bright, fresh flavours that explore the palate and sensations, delivering bold, distinctive, precise and imaginative cooking of such calibre that the tasting dégustation or surprise menus are almost a requisite. So expect the likes of Anjou pigeon 'poche-roti', melon, feta, mint, parfait of innards and grapefruit jus, or perhaps a chocolate and polenta biscuit with parsnip ice cream to wow on the carte, or the likes of 'emulsified' foie gras, raisin-maple purée, macadamia and gingerbread, or langoustine with confit belly pork and sweet peppers to raid the senses on the tasting menu. This is a rare style of cooking, something out-of-the-ordinary, new and exciting, so hang on for the ride, or perhaps stay overnight in one of the attractively presented bedrooms to recover from the culinary sojourn.

Notable Wine List: A beautifully presented wine list; split into three main, broad categories of fresh, smooth and rich, with detailed tasting notes.

Chef: Sat Bains
Owners: Sat Bains, Amanda Bains
Times: 7-9.30, Closed 2 wks Jan & 2wks Aug, Sun, Mon, Closed L all week
Prices: Fixed D £40, Coffee £2.50, Min/Water £4.50, Service added 12.5%
Wine: 110 bottles over £20, 10 by the glass (£6-£40)
Notes: Tasting menu 10 courses £65, Bespoke menu £85 24hrs notice, Vegetarian available, Dress Restrictions
Seats: 40, Pr/dining room 14
Smoking: N/Sm in restaurant, Air con
Rooms: 8 (8 en suite) ★★★ HL
Directions: From M1 junct 24 take A453 for approx 8 m. Through Clifton, road divides into 3 - take middle lane signed 'Lenton Lane Industrial Estate', then 1st left and left again - brown signpost Restaurant Sat Bains
Parking: 22

England

NOTTINGHAM *continued* MAP 11 SK53

Notable Wine List: A well chosen and interesting wine list with good coverage from around the world.

Chef: Preston Walker **Owners:** Daniel Lindsay, Phillip Morgan, Ashley Walter, Chris Elson **Times:** 12-2.15/7-10, Closed Jan 1-7 **Prices:** Fixed L £12, Starter £5-£13.50, Main £13.50-£19.50, Dessert £5.25-£8.50, Coffee £1.75, Min/Water £2.95, Service added but optional 10% **Wine:** 64 bottles over £20, 27 bottles under £20, 8 by the glass (£3.50-£6) **Notes:** Vegetarian available **Seats:** 80, Pr/dining room 34 **Smoking:** N/Sm in restaurant **Children:** Min 12 yrs D, Menu, Portions **Directions:** 200m from Nottingham town centre **Parking:** NCP

Loch Fyne Restaurant & Oyster Bar

☎ 0115 988 6840 17 King St NG1 2AY

Quality seafood chain.

Wagamama

☎ 0115 924 1797 The Cornerhouse, Burton St NG1 4DB

Informal noodle bars with no booking.

OXFORDSHIRE

ARDINGTON MAP 05 SU48

The Boar's Head

British, French

Relaxed dining in charming village setting

☎ 01235 833254 Church St OX12 8QA
e-mail: info@boarsheadardington.co.uk
web: www.boarsheadardington.co.uk

The Boar's Head once came under the scrutiny of Lord Wantage, who, as he disapproved of alcohol, encouraged the sale of tea and soup instead! Happily today there's far more flexibility and choice. Set in the delightful Downland village of Ardington, this pub cum restaurant extends a friendly welcome whether you're just relaxing over a quiet drink, enjoying a light bar snack or taking a meal in the rustic-style restaurant. The straightforward carte menu, based on seasonal and local ingredients, certainly delivers. For instance, a terrine of foie gras with poached pears in chilli and saffron, followed by duck breast with wild rabbit croustade and apple galette. The Grand Marnier soufflé with iced chocolate cream makes an excellent finish.

Chef: Bruce Buchan **Owners:** Boar's Head (Ardington) Ltd **Times:** 12-2/7-10, Closed 4 days between Xmas & New Year **Prices:** Fixed L fr £14.50, Starter £5.95-£10.50, Main £14.50-£19.50, Dessert £6.50-£7.50, Coffee £2.50, Min/Water £3, Service optional **Wine:** 40 bottles over £20, 30 bottles under £20, 10 by the glass (£3.20-£5.50) **Notes:** Sun L 3 courses £20, Vegetarian available **Seats:** 40, Pr/dining room 24 **Smoking:** N/Sm in restaurant **Children:** Portions **Rooms:** 3 (3 en suite) ◆◆◆◆ **Directions:** 2 m E of Wantage on A417 **Parking:** 20

continued

BICESTER MAP 11 SP52

Bignell Park Hotel

British, French V

Creative cooking in country setting

☎ 01869 326550 Chesterton OX26 1UE
e-mail: enq@bignellparkhotel.co.uk
web: www.bignellparkhotel.co.uk

Sixteenth century charm and character combine well with modern facilities at this small hotel situated in a peaceful country setting near Bicester Shopping Village. Housed in a converted barn, with a dramatic gallery as a backdrop, the oak-beamed and painting-packed restaurant is the setting for imaginative fixed-price dinners. Daily menus offer value for money and a varied choice of confidently cooked modern dishes and traditional favourites. Examples include herb-crusted cod with shallot and crab risotto, lamb rump with tarragon and tomato liquor, and Baileys rice pudding.

Chef: Chris Coates **Owners:** Caparo Hotels **Times:** 12-2/7-9.30 **Prices:** Fixed D £21.95, Coffee £2, Min/Water £2.50, Service optional **Wine:** 20 bottles over £20, 15 bottles under £20, 6 by the glass (£2.50-£4) **Notes:** Vegetarian menu, Civ Wed 60 **Seats:** 60, Pr/dining room 20 **Smoking:** N/Sm in restaurant **Children:** Menu, Portions **Rooms:** 23 (23 en suite) ★★★ HL **Directions:** M40 junct 9, follow A41 towards Bicester, turn off at Chesterton and hotel is signed at turning **Parking:** 50

BRITWELL SALOME MAP 05 SU69

The Goose

British, European

18th-century gastro-pub offering accomplished cuisine

☎ 01491 612304 OX49 5LG
e-mail: thegooseatbritwellsalome@fsmail.net

A warm, characterful village pub with cosy bar area at the front and main dining room at the rear. Quality table settings and attentive service from an enthusiastic young team contribute to a great overall experience. Serious gastro-pub cookery is offered here with simple presentation and high-quality seasonal produce. Cooking skills are accomplished, demonstrated in dishes like the ballotine of free-range chicken, filled with morels and calves' sweetbreads with beetroot jus, or roast fillet of Oxfordshire beef, potato purée and wild mushrooms as well as accompaniments like the lovely home-made bread. Evening menus are more extensive, while a daily-changing set lunch menu is complemented by an inviting bar menu.

Times: 12-3/6.30-11, Closed D Sun **Directions:** M40 junct 6 take B4009 to Watlington and on towards Benson. Pub on right, 1.5m

---

BURFORD MAP 05 SP21

The Bay Tree Hotel

British, European

Historic inn with an appealing modern menu

☎ 01993 822791 12-14 Sheep St OX18 4LW
e-mail: bookings@cotswold-inns-hotels.co.uk
web: www.cotswold-inns-hotels.co.uk

Delightful 16th-century inn of honey-coloured stone located in the Cotswold town of Burford. Relax with a drink in the Woolsack bar, with its open fire and comfy leather armchairs, before dining in the elegant restaurant. Here there are tapestries, flagstone floors and leaded windows looking out over the hotel's walled garden and patio area. Produce is locally sourced and features in dishes of pan-fried sirloin with chorizo dauphinoise, béarnaise sauce and rosemary velouté, and whole grilled Bibury trout with new potatoes and caper beurre noisette.

Times: 12-2/7-9.30 **Rooms:** 21 (21 en suite) ★★★ **Directions:** From Oxford, A40, take right at Burford rdbt. Continue half way down the hill and turn left into Sheep St. Bay Tree 200yds on right

Jonathan's at the Angel

Modern European

Simple, effective brasserie fare in a pretty village

☎ 01993 822714 14 Witney St OX18 4SN
e-mail: jo@theangel-uk.com
web: www.theangel-uk.com

Wrapped in a cocoon of stone cottages at the edge of a quiet, picturesque village, this bijou restaurant is a delicious haven of rustic elegance complete with sunny courtyard and walled garden. Inside, the white-painted walls create a bright and breezy feel with open stonework and a host of interesting artefacts to let the eye wander over while eating. The excellent brasserie-style cooking offers up good flavours, with varied and appropriate presentation and simple garnishes. Dishes are well balanced with due attention given to seasonality. Baked gnocchi with wild mushroom sauce would be a good example of a starter, while pot-au-feu of mixed seafish and shellfish cooked with vegetables and potatoes shows the style of main courses.

Chef: Jonathan Lewis **Owners:** Jonathan & Josephine Lewis **Times:** 12-2/7-9.30, Closed 18 Jan-11 Feb, Mon, Closed D Sun **Prices:** Fixed L £14.50, Fixed D £18.50, Starter £5.50-£8.50, Main £13.95-£21.50, Dessert £5.95, Coffee £2.25, Min/Water £2.50, Service included, Group min 15 service 10% **Wine:** 20 bottles over £20, 8 bottles under £20, 11 by the glass (£3.50-£4.75) **Notes:** ALC & Sun L 2 courses £18.50, 3 courses £21.50, Dress Restrictions, Smart casual **Seats:** 34, Pr/dining room 18 **Smoking:** N/Sm in restaurant **Children:** Min 9 yrs, Portions **Rooms:** 3 (3 en suite) ◆◆◆◆◆ **Directions:** From A40, turn off at Burford rdbt, down hill 1st right into Swan Lane, 1st left to Pytts Lane, left at end into Witney St **Parking:** On street

The Lamb Inn

Modern British

Traditional coaching inn with saddlebags of Cotswold charm

☎ 01993 823155 Sheep St OX18 4LR
e-mail: info@lambinn-burford.co.uk
web: www.cotswold-inns-hotels.co.uk/lamb

A spacious restaurant overlooking a lovely courtyard with typical Cotswold-stone walls and a seating area that positively hums in the summer. Inside, cream walls, mullioned windows and frosted skylights make for a bright, cheerful room decorated with food-related pictures, wooden tables and chairs and large floral displays. Food is imaginative and flavours are concise and well balanced using the best of local produce such as Gloucestershire Old Spot pork, Hereford beef, Bibury trout and Cerney goat's cheese. Expect starters such as grilled mackerel with saffron pickled vegetables, while a tempting main of duo of slow cooked beef with pomme fondant and sautéed mushrooms would undoubtedly live up to expectations. Desserts are no less exciting - walnut pie with maple syrup ice cream, for example.

Chef: Sean Ducie **Owners:** Cotswold Inns & Hotels **Times:** 12-2.30/7-9.30 **Prices:** Fixed D £32.50, Coffee £2.50, Min/Water £3.85, Service added but optional 10% **Wine:** 40 bottles over £20, 18 bottles under £20, 9 by the glass (£3.85-£8.80) **Notes:** Sun D menu **Seats:** 55 **Smoking:** N/Sm in restaurant **Children:** Portions **Rooms:** 15 (15 en suite) ★★★ HL **Directions:** 1st left as you descend on the High St **Parking:** Care of Bay Tree Hotel

continued

England

BURFORD *continued* MAP 05 SP21

The Navy Oak Restaurant & Bar

Modern British, Mediterranean

Traditional surroundings, inventive modern dishes

☎ 01993 878496 Lower End, Leafield OX29 9QQ
e-mail: thenavyoak@aol.com
web: www.thenavyoak.co.uk

One of the first buildings built in the village, the main bar area is 400 years old. The open-plan kitchen means that diners can see the chef at work while they enjoy their meal. Open fires and cosy lighting contribute to a traditional country inn feel. The cooking style draws on a range of influences to create interesting modern dishes. The lunch menu includes baguettes and snacks, while the dinner menu focuses on more complex fare. Starters might include game terrine, while mains range from pan-fried sirloin steak to braised garlic sausage with Puy lentils, pork belly and bocconcini.

Chef: Alastair Ward & Timothy Pile **Owners:** Alastair & Sarah Ward **Times:** 12.30-2.30/7-9.30, Closed 1-18 Jan, Mon, Closed D Sun **Prices:** Fixed L £12, Fixed D fr £19, Starter £4.50-£6.50, Main £8.50-£16, Dessert £5-£6.50, Coffee £1.60, Min/Water £2.75, Service optional **Wine:** 20 bottles over £20, 14 bottles under £20, 8 by the glass (£2.75-£6) **Notes:** Gastronomic £37.50 (6 courses, 6 wines) **Seats:** 60, Pr/dining room 30 **Smoking:** N/Sm in restaurant **Children:** Portions **Directions:** Telephone for directions **Parking:** 25

CHARLBURY MAP 11 SP31

The Bell Hotel

Modern British

Warm ambience and fine cuisine

☎ 01608 810278 Church St OX7 3PP
e-mail: reservationsatthebell@msn.com
web: www.bellhotel-charlbury.co.uk

This privately-owned 18th-century coaching inn of mellow Cotswold stone is set in over an acre of grounds. The cosy, traditional oak-beamed bar and lounge offer a warm welcome and the dining room has a friendly, informal ambience. Modern English cooking here has European influences and makes use of local produce on the monthly changing menus. Typical dishes include a starter of duck and chestnut ravioli on a bed of spinach with Jerusalem artichoke sauce. Main courses might include loin of Cornbury venison with red wine, black pepper and thyme, on braised red cabbage.

Chef: Pete Southey **Owners:** Martin Lyall **Times:** 12-2.30/7-9.30 **Prices:** Starter £5.25-£7.95, Main £11.95-£18.25, Dessert £3.95-£5.95, Coffee £1.20, Min/Water £2.10, Service optional, Group min 8 service 10% **Wine:** 4 bottles over £20, 17 bottles under £20, 6 by the glass (£2.95-£3.95) **Notes:** Vegetarian available **Seats:** 30, Pr/dining room 20 **Smoking:** N/Sm in restaurant **Children:** Menu, Portions **Rooms:** 11 (11 en suite) ★★ **Directions:** Situated 3m off A44 between Oxford and Chipping Norton 5m NW of Woodstock. From London via M40 follow signs for Blenheim Palace, then A44 N. Hotel is in centre of town **Parking:** 40

CHECKENDON MAP 05 SU68

Wheelers of St James's at The Highwayman

British, French NEW

Marco Pierre White transformation of a 17th-century pub

☎ 01491 682020 Exlade St RG8 0UA
e-mail: wheelers@marcopierrewhite.org
web: marcopierrewhite.org

A country pub with a sophisticated interior, The Highwayman is tucked away off the main road to Reading on the outskirts of the village. Fixtures and fittings are from the old Wheeler's of St James in London, so expect wood panelling, dark walls, comfortable leather chairs and banquette seating, generous sized tables (some solid marble), and an abundance of black and white photos. It's bigger than you think, with a bar, first dining area, lounge area and main dining room. Food is traditional British with a French twist - soft roes on toast or potage of mussels Billy-By to start, followed by Dover sole meunière or honey-roast belly pork Marco Polo with butter beans - with some dishes revealing their origins - Mirabelle potted salmon and Pierre Koffman au chocolate Amer.

Chef: Matthew Brown **Owners:** Marco Pierre White **Times:** 12-2.30/6-10.30 **Prices:** Fixed L £12.50, Fixed D fr £15.50, Starter £5.50-£8.50, Main £9.50-£25, Dessert £5, Coffee £2.95, Min/Water £3, Service included **Wine:** 59 bottles over £20, 16 bottles under £20, 18 by the glass (£4-£9.50) **Notes:** Sun supper 2 course £12.50, 3 course £14.50 **Seats:** 80 **Smoking:** N/Sm in restaurant **Children:** Portions **Directions:** Telephone for directions **Parking:** 40

CHINNOR MAP 05 SP70

Sir Charles Napier

Modern British NOTABLE WINE LIST

Country inn of great character

☎ 01494 483011 Sprigg's Alley OX39 4BX
web: www.sircharlesnapier.co.uk

Huge fires in winter and comfortable sofas, exposed beams and flagstone floors create a welcoming atmosphere at this popular old country inn. Various unusual sculptures dotted around the bar and dining room provide a talking point for visitors, and there's a vine-shaded terrace outside (with more sculptures) for summer dining. A straightforward menu of hearty rustic choices shows a dedication to good produce and clean, accurate flavours. Rack of lamb with herb crust, cauliflower purée, black olives, horseradish and Madeira, turbot with Savoy cabbage, purple potatoes, crayfish and crab butter, and pot roast pigeon with red wine, lentils and baby root vegetables reflect an

continued

enthusiasm that takes in fish, meat and game, with a vegetarian choice also available.

Notable Wine List: A wine list full of interest put together with much thought and care; includes some really interesting New World wines.

Chef: Richard Burkert **Owners:** Julie Griffiths **Times:** 12/6.30, Closed 25-27 Dec, Mon, Closed D Sun **Prices:** Fixed L £14-£15, Starter £6.75-£12.50, Main £11.50-£21.50, Dessert £6.75, Coffee £2, Min/Water £3, Service added but optional 12.5% **Wine:** 10 by the glass (£3.75-£5.95) **Notes:** Vegetarian available **Seats:** 75, Pr/dining room 45 **Smoking:** N/Sm area, No pipes, No cigars, Air con **Children:** Min 6 yrs D, Menu, Portions **Directions:** M40 junct 6 to Chinnor. Turn right at rdbt, up hill for 2m to Sprigg's Alley **Parking:** 60

CHOLSEY MAP 05 SU58

The Sweet Olive

French

French restaurant in charming pub

☎ 01235 851272 Baker St OX11 9DD

Quintessential English pub meets Gallic charm and what a match! This country restaurant pulls in crowds of diners who enjoy the good honest cooking from a mainly French team. The rustic interior is a combination of simple country inn and French restaurant with wine cases and bottles decorating the walls. Thankfully, this is one pub where there is still a bar, so you can have a drink and eat in the bar if you choose. Expect starters like duck terrine and main courses like onglet of beef with white wine and shallots. British puds make an appearance alongside classics like crème brûlée.

Times: Telephone for details

CHURCH ENSTONE MAP 11 SP32

The Crown Inn

Modern British

Good, honest cooking and genuine friendliness

☎ 01608 677262 Mill Ln OX7 4NN
web: www.crowninnenstone.co.uk

With a history of hostelry dating back to the 16th century, the Crown still welcomes visitors into its warm, friendly and rustic atmosphere. There are two restaurant areas - the light, bright conservatory and the red-walled, beamed dining room. The short, no-fuss, daily-changing menus deliver dishes of equal honesty, and the commitment to using local produce is fundamental. Try the cured meat platter, brie and olives, followed by pheasant breast with chipolatas, bacon and cranberry sauce or beer battered cod, chips and salad. All puddings are home made. Leave space for warm chocolate pudding with fudge sauce and ice cream.

Chef: Tony Warburton **Owners:** Mr & Mrs Warburton **Times:** 12-2/7-9, Closed 24 & 26 Dec, Mon, Closed D Sun **Prices:** Starter £3.75-£8.25, Main £7.95-£16.50, Dessert £4.50, Coffee £1.40, Min/Water £3, Service optional **Wine:** 5 bottles over £20, 16 bottles under £20, 7 by the glass (£2.75-£3.50) **Notes:** Vegetarian available **Seats:** 42, Pr/dining room 18 **Smoking:** N/Sm in restaurant **Children:** Menu, Portions **Directions:** Telephone for directions **Parking:** 8

DEDDINGTON MAP 11 SP43

Deddington Arms

Modern British

Traditional but stylish coaching inn offering fine food

☎ 01869 338364 Horsefair OX15 0SH
e-mail: deddarms@oxfordshire-hotels.co.uk
web: www.deddington-arms-hotel.co.uk

This Cotswold stone coaching inn off the market square has an original oak beamed bar with flagstone floor and cosy fireplace. The restaurant has been updated with air-conditioning and features carved wood panelling and archways. You'll find traditional British fare on the menu with Mediterranean influences. Typical dishes might include seared scallops with carrot butter sauce and plumped sultanas to start, followed by fillet of beef with onion and orange marmalade and port jus. Desserts might feature frangipane tart with prune and Armagnac ice cream.

Chef: Nick Porter **Owners:** Oxfordshire Hotels Ltd **Times:** 12-2/6.30-9.45 **Prices:** Fixed L fr £7.50, Starter £5.75-£7.25, Main £13.75-£17.75, Dessert £5.75, Coffee £1.60, Min/Water £2.70, Service optional **Wine:** 13 bottles over £20, 27 bottles under £20, 8 by the glass (£2.95-£4.30) **Notes:** Sun L 3 courses £16.95, Vegetarian available **Seats:** 60, Pr/dining room 30 **Smoking:** N/Sm in restaurant, Air con **Children:** Menu, Portions **Rooms:** 27 (27 en suite) ★★★ HL **Directions:** Telephone for directions **Parking:** 36

DORCHESTER (ON THAMES) MAP 05 SU59

George Hotel

Traditional

Classic coaching inn serving traditional food with a twist

☎ 01865 340404 25 High St OX10 7HH
e-mail: thegeorgehotel@fsmail.net
web: www.thegeorgedorchester.co.uk

A centrally located 15th-century inn next door to Dorchester Abbey, the George has plenty of historic character with beams and inglenook fireplaces. The dining room boasts its own secret garden and water feature. Cooking is skilled with an interesting take on some generally traditional fare, such as apple and red wine crumble - unusual but effective. Other options are monkfish cheeks with a cockle, lemon and caper dressing, and pan-fried calves' liver with seared sprouts and parsnips and wholegrain mustard cream. Food is also served in the Potboys bar.

Chef: Jan Wood **Owners:** Neville & Griffin Ltd **Times:** 12-2.15/7-9.30, Closed Xmas, New Year, Mon, Closed L Tue-Sat **Prices:** Fixed D fr £29.95, Coffee £1.70, Min/Water £4.50 **Wine:** 30 bottles over £20, 80 bottles under £20, 150 by the glass (£2.60-£5.10) **Notes:** Vegetarian available **Seats:** 35, Pr/dining room 30 **Smoking:** N/Sm in restaurant **Children:** Portions **Rooms:** 17 (17 en suite) ★★★ HL **Directions:** In town centre, 8m south of Oxford **Parking:** 70

England

DORCHESTER (ON THAMES) *continued*
MAP 05 SU59

White Hart Hotel

British, French

Historic coaching inn serving fine cuisine

☎ 01865 340074 High St OX10 7HN
e-mail: whitehart@oxfordshire-hotels.co.uk
web: www.oxfordshire-hotels.co.uk

This 17th-century coaching inn retains its original façade with wooden gates, beams and brickwork. Inside, the décor is warm and inviting, complementing the flagstone floors and stone fireplaces. The lunchtime special menu is great value and Sunday lunch is a popular option too. The carte demonstrates a serious approach to cuisine with simple presentation and fine fresh produce. A typical main course might be glazed suckling pig stuffed with rosemary and apricots and served with dauphinoise potato and port sauce. Try warm fig and orange frangipane tart with vanilla anglaise for dessert.

Times: 12-2.30/6.30-9.30 **Rooms:** 26 (26 en suite) ★★★ HL **Directions:** Village centre. Just off A415/ A4074. 3m from Wallingford, 6m from Abingdon

---

FARINGDON MAP 05 SU29

The Lamb at Buckland

British, French

Charming country inn with hearty food

☎ 01367 870484 Buckland SN7 8QN
e-mail: enquiries@thelambatbuckland.co.uk
web: www.thelambatbuckland.co.uk

Set in a scenic village, this 18th-century inn can be tricky to find at night, but rewards the effort. The bar is a quiet and cosy place for a drink, while the beamed restaurant draws a loyal local crowd with a tried and tested menu of old favourites. Mains range from beef and kidney pie, to roast breast of Gressingham duck with an apple and Calvados sauce, while desserts might include steamed syrup sponge or bread and butter pudding. A blackboard menu complements the carte and lighter options are available at lunchtime.

Chef: Paul Barnard **Owners:** The Lamb at Buckland Ltd **Times:** 12-3/7-11, Closed 23 Dec-6 Jan, Mon, Closed D Sun **Prices:** Fixed L £10, Fixed D £15, Starter £4-£8.95, Main £6.95-£21.95, Dessert £4-£5.25, Min/Water £3, Service optional **Wine:** 21 bottles over £20, 15 bottles under £20, 13 by the glass (£2.95-£7.45) **Notes:** Vegetarian available **Seats:** 65, Pr/dining room 18 **Smoking:** N/Sm in restaurant **Children:** Menu, Portions **Directions:** Midway between Oxford and Swindon on A420. 4m E of Faringdon **Parking:** 40

GORING MAP 05 SU68

The Leatherne Bottel

British

Unique Thames-side location for enjoyable eating

☎ 01491 872667 RG8 0HS
e-mail: leathernebottel@aol.com
web: www.leathernebottel.co.uk

Right on the Thames in a gloriously tranquil setting, the Leatherne Bottel is the perfect location for alfresco dining when the weather is favourable. But inside is no less inviting. The dining room overlooks the river and has strikingly vibrant artwork and fresh flower displays that brighten any mood, and there is a separate bar area. The chef adds Pacific Rim ideas, inspired by her time in New Zealand, to the modern British and European dishes. Perhaps try roast boneless quail, wild rice salad, currant and grape sauce, or marinated pork shoulder, braised in cider with sweet and sour beetroot, potato purée and anis jus. The pudding menu has temptations like lemongrass and coconut pannacotta and a sunken chocolate soufflé cake with brandied cherries.

Chef: Julia Storey **Owners:** Croft Chase Ltd **Times:** 12-2/7-9, Closed 31 Dec, Closed D Sun **Prices:** Food prices not confirmed for 2007. Please telephone for details **Wine:** 47 bottles over £20, 8 bottles under £20, 2 by the glass (£3.50-£3.95) **Notes:** Vegetarian available **Seats:** 45 **Smoking:** No pipes **Children:** Min 10 yrs **Directions:** M4 junct 12 or M40 junct 6, signposted from B4009 towards Wallingford **Parking:** 40

Five Rosettes

The finest restaurants in the British Isles where the cooking stands comparison with the best in the world. These restaurants will have highly individual voices, exhibit breathtaking culinary skills and set the standard to which others aspire

Le Manoir aux Quat' Saisons

GREAT MILTON MAP 05 SP60

Contemporary French V NOTABLE WINE LIST

An absolute dream of a place

☎ 01844 278881 OX44 7PD
e-mail: lemanoir@blanc.co.uk
web: www.manoir.com

Whatever the season, a visit to Raymond Blanc's mellow stone, 15th-century manor house hotel, set in beautiful grounds, is one of life's not-to-be-missed experiences - it's the epitome of luxury and good taste, where modern style and classic virtues combine with truly memorable cooking and exemplary service. The dining room is in three parts, with the principal rooms a conservatory extension and the Grand Salle which continue the contemporary theme. Take a stroll round the stunning gardens dotted with life-size bronze statues, a Japanese garden and tea house and the all-important organic potager. Producing some 90 types of vegetables and over 70 varieties of herbs, it's fundamental to the Blanc philosophy of freshness, quality and seasonality. Expect classic French dishes in a modern, light, fresh style with clear, precise flavours, balance and subtlety, delivered with breathtaking skill and immaculate presentation. Take roasted loin and braised cheek of suckling pig with apple compôte and crispy Asian pork belly, or to finish, perhaps caramelised William pear baked in thin brioche with cinnamon and vanilla ice cream. The number of chefs who have learned their trade here is a testament to Raymond's supreme commitment to training and ultimately a tribute to the man and the high esteem in which his kitchen and renowned hotel are held.

Notable Wine List: A superb classical list offering a real depth of vintages and a predominate focus towards French wines.

Chef: Raymond Blanc & Gary Jones
Owners: Mr R Blanc
Times: 12.15-2.30/7.15-9.45
Prices: Fixed L £45, Starter £30-£34, Main £36-£38, Dessert £19, Coffee £4.95, Min/Water £3.95, Service optional
Wine: All bottles over £20, 14 by the glass (£6.50-£18.50)
Notes: Tasting menu 7 courses £95, Fixed L 3 courses, Vegetarian menu, Dress Restrictions, No jeans, trainers or shorts, Civ Wed 50
Seats: 100, Pr/dining room 50
Smoking: N/Sm in restaurant, Air con
Children: Menu, Portions
Rooms: 32 (32 en suite) ★★★★★ HL
Directions: M40 junct 7 follow A329 towards Wallingford. After 1m turn right, signed Great Milton and Le Manoir aux Quat' Saisons
Parking: 70

England

HENLEY-ON-THAMES MAP 05 SU78

The Cherry Tree Inn

Modern British, French

Popular inn with a modern menu

☎ 01491 680430 Stoke Row RG9 5QA
e-mail: info@thecherrytreeinn.com
web: www.thecherrytreeinn.com

Set in the sleepy hamlet of Stoke Row not far from Henley, this 400-year-old inn is a popular local haunt. Beams and flagstone floors provide an old-world backdrop for contemporary furnishings, while a nearby barn has been converted into four chic bedrooms. Dinner brings hearty portions of modern British fare; kick off with a crab, ginger and leek tartlet perhaps, and then tuck into the likes of fillet of roast salmon salad with grilled artichokes, or roast Gressingham duck with braised red cabbage, and a Cassis and green peppercorn jus. Roast on Sundays.

Chef: Richard Coates **Owners:** Paul Gilchrist & Richard Coates **Times:** 12-3/7-10, Closed 25-26 Dec **Prices:** Starter £4.95-£6.50, Main £9.50-£14.95, Dessert £4.10-£6.50, Coffee £1.50, Min/Water £2.95, Service optional **Wine:** 12 bottles over £20, 27 bottles under £20, 11 by the glass (£2.95-£6.50) **Notes:** Vegetarian available **Seats:** 76 **Smoking:** N/Sm throughout **Children:** Menu, Portions **Rooms:** 4 (4 en suite) ◆◆◆◆ **Directions:** On the A4155 from Henley-on-Thames exit B481 to Sonning Common. Follow signs for Stoke Row, turn right for pub **Parking:** 25

Number 28 at the White Hart

Modern British

Historic inn with contemporary style and flavour

☎ 01491 649000 28 High St, Nettlebed RG9 5DD
e-mail: sales@number-28.co.uk
web: www.number-28.co.uk

The hotel has a stylish modern restaurant with a distinctive designer feel, ideal for romantic evenings. The menu follows the seasons and modern trends, selecting the finest local organically grown produce. The aim is to offer fresh, crisp colourful creations, described by the kitchen as food they would cook for their best friends. Recommendations are seared hand-dived Scottish scallops served with marinated peppers, chorizo crisps and tomato fondue as a starter, then seared best end of Chiltern lamb with butternut squash, baby vegetables, sweetbreads and basil froth as a main course. A particularly interesting dessert is ravioli of chocolate with caramelised banana, chocolate-stuffed dates and vanilla pod cappuccino.

Number 28 at the White Hart

Chef: Nick Seckington **Owners:** Robyn & Tim Jones **Times:** 12-2.30/7-9.30, Closed Mon-Wed, Closed L all week, D Sun **Prices:** Fixed D £35, Coffee £2.80, Min/Water £3.50, Service optional **Wine:** 46 bottles over £20, 24 bottles under £20, 10 by the glass (£3.50-£6.95) **Notes:** Tasting menu 5 courses £55, Sun L menu available, Vegetarian available, Dress Restrictions, Smart dress **Seats:** 30, Pr/dining room 18 **Smoking:** N/Sm in restaurant **Children:** Menu, Portions **Rooms:** 12 (12 en suite) RR **Directions:** From Henley take A4130 towards Wallingford. Approx 5m **Parking:** 50

Loch Fyne Restaurant & Oyster Bar

☎ 01491 845780 20 Market Place RG9 2AH

Quality seafood chain.

KINGHAM MAP 10 SP22

Mill House Hotel

Modern British V

Fine country-house dining

☎ 01608 658188 OX7 6UH
e-mail: stay@millhousehotel.co.uk
web: www.millhousehotel.co.uk

continued

Mill House Hotel

The Cotswold-stone mill house dates back to the time of the Domesday Book and was rebuilt in 1770. Set in ten acres of lawned gardens with a trout stream, it makes a relaxing setting for country-house dining. Modern British dishes make good use of fresh ingredients. Local touches are highlighted on the menu, like the pan-fried pork cutlet, produced by pig farmer of the year, Jimmy Butler. There is a separate vegetarian menu and extensive cheese menu featuring regional favourites. The extensive wine cellar holds over 120 bins from the old and new worlds. The gastro-pub style food is served in the Mill Stream Bar and Terrace.

Chef: Paul Harris **Owners:** John Parslow **Times:** 12-2/6.30-10 **Prices:** Fixed L fr £12.50, Fixed D £28-£34, Starter £3.95-£5.95, Main £10-£12.50, Dessert fr £4.50, Coffee £2, Min/Water £3, Service optional **Wine:** 50 bottles over £20, 27 bottles under £20, 5 by the glass (£5-£5.25) **Notes:** Sun L 2 courses £15.50, courses £17.50, Vegetarian menu, Smart-casual, Civ Wed 80 **Seats:** 70, Pr/dining room 50 **Smoking:** N/Sm in restaurant **Children:** Menu, Portions **Rooms:** 23 (23 en suite) ★★★ HL **Directions:** Just off B4450, between Chipping Norton and Stow-on-the-Wold. On S outskirts of village **Parking:** 60

OXFORD MAP 05 SP50

Blanc Brasserie

Modern French, Mediterranean

Confident brasserie dining in fashionable suburb

☎ 01865 510999 71-72 Walton St OX2 6AG
e-mail: oxford@lepetitblanc
web: www.lepetitblanc.co.uk

A busy yet relaxed French-style brasserie located in the fashionable Oxford quarter of Jericho. The spacious, two-roomed restaurant has a smart, contemporary décor, with wooden floors, modern furnishings and colourful prints, while floor to ceiling windows allow natural light to flood in. Expect a buzzy atmosphere and brisk but friendly service from black-clothed staff - children are positively welcomed. As its

continued

name suggests, food here is rooted in French culinary excellence with Asian and Mediterranean influences, yet utilises the best British ingredients. Authentic brasserie dishes, listed on the carte and the excellent value fixed-price menu, take in deep-fried goat's cheese with French bean salad, roast breast of corn-fed chicken with fondant potato and truffle-scented celeriac purée, and caramelised apples with Calvados sabayon.

Chef: Thierry Errante **Owners:** Raymond Blanc & Loch Fyne Group **Times:** 12-2.30/6-11, Closed 25 Dec **Prices:** Fixed L £12, Fixed D £14.50, Starter £3.50-£7.50, Main £9.50-£18.50, Dessert £3.50-£5.50, Coffee £1.75, Min/Water £3, Group min 6 service 10% **Wine:** 15 bottles over £20, 18 bottles under £20, 16 by the glass (£3.25-£5.75) **Notes:** Vegetarian available **Seats:** 134, Pr/dining room 14 **Smoking:** N/Sm in restaurant, Air con **Children:** Menu, Portions **Directions:** From city centre. N along St Giles, left into Little Clarendon St and right at end of Walton St **Parking:** Gloucester Green/St Giles

Cotswold Lodge Hotel

Modern British

Elegant, traditional dining near city centre

☎ 01865 512121 66a Banbury Rd OX2 6JP
e-mail: aa@cotswoldlodgehotel.co.uk
web: www.cotswoldlodgehotel.co.uk

Situated near the city centre, this family-run Victorian hotel has a comfortable lounge and elegant public areas. The dining room is decorated with murals of college scenes, which can be enjoyed from the comfort of high-backed chairs. Modern British dishes are the focus of a simple menu here. Starters might include celeriac and Stilton soup, while main courses feature the likes of chicken supreme with roasted leeks and Pommery mustard sauce. Try a classic dessert like pear and almond tart to finish.

Chef: Garin Chapman **Owners:** Mrs O Peros **Times:** 12-2.30/6.30-10 **Prices:** Starter £4.25-£8, Main £11.50-£17.50, Dessert £4-£5.25, Coffee £2.75, Min/Water £3, Service included **Wine:** 10 bottles over £20, 10 bottles under £20, 8 by the glass (£3-£8) **Notes:** Vegetarian available, Dress Restrictions, Smart casual **Seats:** 48, Pr/dining room 140 **Smoking:** N/Sm in restaurant **Children:** Menu, Portions **Rooms:** 49 (49 en suite) ★★★★ **Directions:** Take A4165 (Banbury Road) off A40 ring road, hotel 1.5m on left. **Parking:** 30

Gee's Restaurant

Modern British

Modern cooking in Victorian conservatory

☎ 01865 553540 61 Banbury Rd OX2 6PE
e-mail: info@geesrestaurant.co.uk
web: www.gees-restaurant.co.uk

continued

England

OXFORD *continued* MAP 05 SP50

The Victorian conservatory setting for this restaurant a few minutes from St Giles makes it a romantic dinner venue. The large carte offers a wide choice including a set menu and individually priced dishes, plus a six-course seafood tasting menu offered on Wednesday and Thursday. Pre-theatre dinners include a glass of house wine, while post-theatre dinners of Gee's burger and Zuni Caesar salad are on offer on Friday and Saturday from 11pm to midnight. Cooking is simple and straightforward, based around classic combinations such as grilled line-caught Jersey sea bass with lemon and thyme butter sauce. The jazz night every Sunday has become something of an institution.

Chef: Michael Wright **Owners:** Jeremy Mogford **Times:** 12-2.30/6-11.30, Closed 27-28 Dec **Prices:** Fixed L £12.95, Fixed D £23, Starter £5-£13, Main £10-£22, Dessert £5-£9.50, Coffee £2, Min/Water £2.95, Service optional, Group min 5 service 10% **Wine:** 14 bottles over £20, 6 bottles under £20, 16 by the glass (£4-£10) **Notes:** Seafood tasting menu £45, Sun L 2-3 courses £18-£22, Vegetarian available **Seats:** 85 **Smoking:** N/Sm in restaurant, Air con **Children:** Portions **Directions:** M40 junct 8. From northern ring road, follow signs to city centre through Summertown. Gee's opp Parktown on Banbury Rd **Parking:** Street parking, car park opposite

❀ *The Lemon Tree*

Modern, Mediterranean

Attractive restaurant with a Mediterranean feel

☎ 01865 311936 268 Woodstock Rd OX2 7NW
e-mail: info@thelemontreeoxford.co.uk
web: www.thelemontreeoxford.co.uk

There's a warm, settling ambience to this spacious restaurant - the comfortable bar and the attractive rear gardens being as much a part of that sensation as the tranquil dining room. The latter's flagstone flooring, wicker chairs, large ferns and conservatory style ceiling give an impression of sunnier Mediterranean, even Californian climes. Influences from the Med crop up on the brasserie-style menu too, but most of the food tends toward comforting home-grown fare - potted trout with pickled cucumber, for example, or roast pork belly with parsnips, apple relish and mustard sauce - all nicely balanced and full of flavour.

Times: Closed 24-31 Dec, Closed L Mon-Thurs **Directions:** 1.5m from city centre heading N

❀❀ Macdonald Randolph

Modern, Traditional

Classic Oxford dining experience

☎ 0870 400 8200 Beaumont St OX1 2LN
e-mail: randolph@macdonald-hotels.co.uk
web: www.macdonaldhotels.co.uk

Situated in the heart of Oxford opposite the Ashmolean Museum, the hotel was built in 1864 and recently underwent a £6 million refurbishment. The richly furnished and comfortable restaurant combines tradition with elegance and gives diners wonderful views of the city. Modern British cuisine is on offer using seasonal ingredients, simply prepared and beautifully presented. Try a classic starter like cream of Jerusalem artichoke soup with spinach purée and truffle oil. Main courses feature modern interpretations of traditional dishes with combinations like pan-fried fillet of sea bass with fennel purée and langoustine sauce, or chump of lamb with leek and celeriac tagliatelle and basil mash.

continued

Chef: Tom Birks **Owners:** Macdonald Hotels PLC **Times:** 12-2.30/5.30-10 **Prices:** Fixed L £19-£22, Fixed D £24-£27, Starter £6-£9, Main £17-£28, Dessert £6.95-£9, Coffee £3.95, Min/Water £4.85, Service optional **Wine:** 80 bottles over £20, 24 bottles under £20, 12 by the glass (£4.80-£5.90) **Notes:** Vegetarian available, Dress Restrictions, Smart casual, Civ Wed 300 **Seats:** 90, Pr/dining room 30 **Smoking:** N/Sm in restaurant **Children:** Menu, Portions **Rooms:** 150 (150 en suite) ★★★★ HL **Directions:** M40 junct 8 onto A40 towards Oxford, follow signs towards city centre, leads to St Giles, hotel is on right **Parking:** 50

❀ Quod Restaurant & Bar

Modern European

Buzzing city-centre spot serving brasserie fare

☎ 01865 202505 Old Bank Hotel, 92-94 High St OX1 4BN
e-mail: quod@oldbank-hotel.co.uk
web: www.quod.co.uk

A huge oval zinc-topped bar, modern art, stone floor and wooden tables fill the sleek, modern interior of this bustling, lively, all-day bar/brasserie set within the chic and stylish Old Bank Hotel. Youthful, attentive service and a sun-deck terrace add value, while the crowd-pleasing, brasserie-style cooking hits just the right note. Menus take in the classics alongside a fashionable nod to the Mediterranean - chargrilled rib-eye with chips, slow-roast lamb shank with mint pesto and Tuscan vegetable caponata, and perhaps banoffie pie or pecan pie to finish. Or choose pasta, risotto or salads.

Chef: Mark Forman **Owners:** Mr J Mogford **Times:** noon/11, Closed 25-26 Dec **Prices:** Fixed L £8.95, Starter £3.95-£6.95, Main £9.95-£16.50, Dessert £4.35-£4.75, Coffee £1.95, Min/Water £2.95, Service optional, Group min 5 service 10% **Wine:** 5 bottles over £20, 9 bottles under £20, 14 by the glass (£4.25-£5.95) **Notes:** Sun L available, Vegetarian available **Seats:** 150, Pr/dining room 24 **Smoking:** N/Sm area, No pipes, No cigars, Air con **Children:** Menu, Portions **Rooms:** 42 (42 en suite) ★★★★ HL **Directions:** Approach city centre via Headington. Over Magdalen Bridge into High St. Hotel 75yds on left **Parking:** 40

Cherwell Boathouse Restaurant

☎ 01865 552746 60 Bardwell Rd OX2 6ST
web: www.theaa.com/restaurants/114017.html
Enjoy international dishes at this small and intimate restaurant, right on the banks of the Isis in a truly scenic spot.

Edamame

☎ 01865 246 916 15 Holywell St OX1 3SA
Japanese canteen-style dining.

Fishers Seafood Restaurant 

☎ 01865 243003 36-37 St Clements OX4 1AB
web: www.theaa.com/restaurants/114016.html

Fresh fish is shipped in daily to ensure a wide choice of fresh seasonal shellfish platters, and the atmospheric interior resembles a stylish ship's cabin, with wooden floors, benches and lanterns.

Loch Fyne Restaurant

☎ 01865 292510 55 Walton St OX2 6AE

Quality seafood chain.

STADHAMPTON MAP 05 SU69

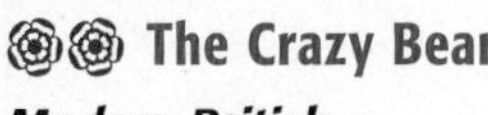

The Crazy Bear

Modern British

Impressive cooking in imaginative surroundings

☎ 01865 890714 Bear Ln OX44 7UR
e-mail: enquiries@crazybear-oxford.co.uk
web: www.crazybeargroup.co.uk

Not your normal makeover of a traditional 16th-century inn but certainly striking with lots of mirrors, leather, atmospheric lighting combined with original features. The bedrooms are dramatically decorated making stopping overnight after dinner an attractive option. It's a relaxing and popular place with well-informed and friendly staff. Modern British dishes with lots of international influences are prepared using the best ingredients from near and far. Dishes are simply but effectively presented. Start with shrimp and crayfish cocktail before a main course of Torbay sole meunière or tournedos Rossini with Perigord truffles and Malmsey sauce. Finish with pineapple tart Tatin with coconut ice cream.

Chef: Martin Gallon **Owners:** Jason Hunt **Times:** 12-3/6-10 **Prices:** Fixed L £12.50, Fixed D £15.50, Starter £6.50-£14, Main £11.50-£24, Dessert £6.50, Coffee £2.50, Min/Water £3.50, Service added but optional 12.5% **Wine:** 90 bottles over £20, 20 bottles under £20, 15 by the glass (£3.85-£8.50) **Notes:** Sun L 1-3 courses £11.50-£19, Vegetarian available, Dress Restrictions, Smart casual, no jeans/trainers, Civ Wed 100 **Seats:** 40, Pr/dining room 50 **Smoking:** N/Sm area, No pipes, Air con **Children:** Menu, Portions **Rooms:** 12 (12 en suite) ★★★★★ GA **Directions:** From London leave M40 at junct 7 turn left onto A329, continue for 4m, left after petrol station & left again into Bear Lane **Parking:** 50

Thai Thai

Thai V

Truly authentic Thai cuisine in the heart of rural Oxfordshire

☎ 01865 890714 Crazy Bear Hotel, Bear Ln OX44 7UR
e-mail: enquiries@crazybear-oxford.co.uk
web: www.crazybeargroup.co.uk

Expect the unexpected here - it's a bit of culture shock really - for all intents and purposes you eat in a Bedhouin tent while enjoying some of the best Thai food in the UK. Part of a 16th-century inn that certainly has a style all of its own and never ceases to surprise at every turn, Thai Thai has become renowned for the authenticity of its cuisine. Using only seasonal, organic ingredients, including some flown in from the Far East, the Thai chefs produce the genuine tastes of their country. The long menu guides you through the options that include a section for dim sum (meaning 'touch the heart') and there are tasting menus for the adventurous. Start with Shanghai hot and sour soup perhaps, followed by slow pot roast of ox cheek, Chinese mushrooms and spring onions. Desserts are decidedly Western Hemisphere - expect the likes of vanilla cheesecake with sautéed blueberries.

Chef: Anusak Thepdamrongchaikagul **Owners:** Jason Hunt **Times:** 12-3/6-10, Closed L Sun **Prices:** Fixed L £12, Fixed D £15, Starter £6, Dessert £6.50, Coffee £2.50, Min/Water £3.50, Service added but optional 12.5% **Wine:** 90 bottles over £20, 20 bottles under £20, 15 by the glass (£3.85-£8) **Notes:** Tasting menu available, Vegetarian menu, Civ Wed 100 **Seats:** 25 **Smoking:** N/Sm in restaurant **Children:** Menu, Portions **Directions:** From London leave M40 junct 7 turn left onto A329, continue for 4 miles, left after petrol station and 2nd left again into Bear Lane **Parking:** 70

SWERFORD MAP 11 SP33

The Mason's Arms

Modern British

Country restaurant with skilfully produced dishes

☎ 01608 683212 Banbury Rd OX7 4AP
e-mail: themasonschef@hotmail.com
web: www.masonsarms.co.nr

The owners searched long and hard before putting down roots at this country pub and restaurant which dates back to the 1700s. With a background of working in top London restaurants, the chef-proprietor is committed to sourcing local ingredients for his innovative British-based cuisine with some Asian and European influences (light bites and fixed price at lunch, and carte in the evening). The carte showcases dishes such as poached belly of Gloucestershire Old Spot pork, crispy crackling and sweet potato purée in a rich jus with beans,

continued

SWERFORD *continued* MAP 11 SP33

or chargrilled marlin steak, warm potato, chorizo and artichoke salad with salsa verde and caper dressing, and honey and Drambuie crème brûlée with raspberry sorbet.

Chef: Bill Leadbeater **Owners:** B & C Leadbeater, Tom Aldous **Times:** 12-3/7-11, Closed 25-26 Dec, Closed D 24 Dec **Prices:** Fixed L £9.95-£10.95, Starter £5-£8, Main £10-£18, Dessert £5.50-£6, Coffee £1.90, Min/Water £2.70, Service optional, Group min 10 service 10% **Wine:** 12 bottles over £20, 23 bottles under £20, 6 by the glass (£3.25-£5.30) **Notes:** Vegetarian available **Seats:** 75, Pr/dining room 40 **Smoking:** N/Sm in restaurant **Children:** Menu, Portions **Parking:** 60

THAME MAP 05 SP70

Spread Eagle Hotel

Modern V

Brasserie hotel dining in appealing market town

☎ 01844 213661 Cornmarket OX9 2BW
e-mail: enquiries@spreadeaglethame.co.uk
web: www.spreadeaglethame.co.uk

A traditional-looking former coaching inn presiding over the main street of this delightful market town. Fothergills brasserie is named after the diarist and raconteur who owned the hotel in the 1920s. The restaurant today caters very well for all tastes, with special vegetarian and children's menus. Local Oxfordshire beef is used in traditional dishes like Chateaubriand or steaks. A house speciality is the chocolate mud dessert, Mr J. Fothergill's authentic 1920s recipe, comprising a rich dark chocolate mousse set on a crème anglaise.

Chef: Alisdair Dudley **Owners:** Mr D & Mrs S Barrington **Times:** 12.30-2.30/5.30-9 **Prices:** Fixed L £18.45, Fixed D £22.45, Starter £4.30-£9.95, Main £8.65-£20.95, Dessert £5, Coffee £2, Min/Water £2.80, Service included **Wine:** 10 bottles over £20, 26 bottles under £20, 6 by the glass **Notes:** Vegetarian menu, Civ Wed 200 **Seats:** 65, Pr/dining room 20 **Smoking:** N/Sm in restaurant, Air con **Children:** Menu, Portions **Rooms:** 33 (33 en suite) ★★★ **Directions:** M40 - junct 6 from S, junct 8 from N. Town centre on A418 (Oxford to Aylesbury road) **Parking:** 80

The Swan at Tetsworth

Modern, Traditional British

Elizabethan coaching inn with a timeless atmosphere

☎ 01844 281182 High St, Tetsworth OX9 7AB
e-mail: Restaurant@theswan.co.uk
web: www.theswan.co.uk/restaurant.htm

Tracing its history back to 1482, The Swan retains all its old world and rustic charm, and today combines its business as both a restaurant and renowned antiques centre. There's nothing dated about the menus however. Whether eating in the garden in the summer or enjoying a cosy candlelit dinner, guests can expect an internationally inspired, seasonal menu. Start with scallops and black pudding with mango and ginger dressing perhaps, followed by corn-fed chicken supreme in a borlotti bean, chorizo and cabbage broth, or wild mushroom tagliatelle with garlic and chilli cream. Sticky toffee pudding with caramel sauce and vanilla ice cream or coffee and mascarpone torte could tempt for dessert.

The Swan at Tetsworth

Chef: David Whiteside **Times:** 11.30-2.30/6-10.30, Closed 26 Dec, Closed D Sun **Prices:** Fixed L £15.95, Fixed D £18.95, Starter £4.75-£8.50, Main £11-£18, Dessert £4.75-£6.50, Coffee £1.85, Min/Water £3.50, Service added but optional 10% **Wine:** 22 bottles over £20, 30 bottles under £20, 13 by the glass (£3.75-£8) **Notes:** Vegetarian available **Seats:** 55, Pr/dining room 12 **Smoking:** N/Sm area, No pipes, No cigars **Children:** Portions **Directions:** From London - 3m from M40 junct 6. From Birmingham - 5m from M40 junct 8 **Parking:** 120

WALLINGFORD MAP 05 SU68

Lakeside Restaurant

Modern, Traditional

A popular restaurant in an attractive setting

☎ 01491 836687 The Springs Hotel & Golf Club, Wallingford Rd, North Stoke OX10 6BE
e-mail: info@thespringshotel.com
web: www.thespringshotel.com

Built in 1874 in Victorian mock-Tudor style, the Springs Hotel overlooks a scenic spring-fed lake and delightful grounds - King Edward VIII was once a frequent visitor. Inside there is plenty of period detail - crackling fires in open hearths, comfortable lounges and exposed oak beams. The Lakeside Restaurant is set in the glass-enclosed Winter Garden and offers the attentiveness of formal service with a friendly, unobtrusive feel. The food has a foot in the twin camps of British and European styles - you might expect rump steak with grain mustard sauce or iced spiced parfait with fruit coulis.

Chef: André Roux **Owners:** Lakeside Restaurant **Times:** 12-2.30/7-9.45 **Prices:** Fixed L £12.95, Fixed D fr £27.95, Starter £6.95-£8.95, Main £15.95-£22.50, Dessert £5.95-£6.95, Coffee £2.50, Min/Water £3.75, Service optional, Group min 10 service 10% **Wine:** 32 bottles over £20, 12 bottles under £20, 14 by the glass (£3.75-£4.10) **Notes:** Sun L £22.50 incl 2 glasses wine, Vegetarian available, Dress Restrictions, No denim, trainers or T-shirts, Civ Wed 90 **Seats:** 80, Pr/dining room 30 **Smoking:** N/Sm in restaurant **Children:** Portions **Rooms:** 32 (32 en suite) ★★★ HL **Directions:** Edge of village of North Stoke **Parking:** 150

continued

WESTON-ON-THE-GREEN MAP 11 SP51

Weston Manor Hotel

British, European

Modern cuisine in impressive medieval manor house hotel

☎ 01869 350621 OX25 3QL
e-mail: reception@westonmanor.co.uk
web: www.westonmanor.co.uk

During World War II, Weston Manor served as an officer's mess for American airmen, who must have been impressed by this historic medieval manor. Soon afterwards it was converted into a hotel, maintaining beautiful grounds and many original features. The restaurant is really a baronial dining hall with a high-vaulted ceiling, oak panelling and the old minstrels' gallery, and you can easily see why these features make it a popular venue for weddings and functions. A small, regularly-changing menu offers seasonal produce in dishes like crispy leg of duck on a bed of spinach with caramelised onions.

Times: 12-2/7-9.30, Closed L Sat - Sun **Rooms:** 35 (35 en suite) ★★★ HL **Directions:** 2 mins from M40 junct 9, via A34 (Oxford) on Weston-on-Green; hotel in village centre

WOODCOTE MAP 05 SU68

Ricci's on the Green

French, European

Relaxed bistro style

☎ 01491 680775 Goring Rd RG8 0SD
e-mail: michelricci@waitrose.com
web: www.chezricci.co.uk

You might spot a game of cricket across on the village green, but inside this restaurant you could be back in provincial France. Stripped tables, exposed beams and cheerful Provençale colours give a relaxed feel, while a log fire ensures cosiness in winter. The cooking is traditional bistro-style, making good use of simple quality ingredients. Hearty country-style dishes might include chicken livers with buttered fettuccini or duck breast in honey and orange sauce. Book a terrace table for lazy summer afternoons to enjoy the cricket.

Chef: Stuart Sheperd **Owners:** Michel Ricci **Times:** 12-2.30/7-21.30, Closed Mid Feb, 2 wks Aug, 1 wk Nov, Mon & Tue **Prices:** Food prices not confirmed for 2007. Please telephone for details **Wine:** 5 bottles over £20, 8 bottles under £20, 2 by the glass (£3.50-£4.95) **Notes:** Vegetarian available **Seats:** 60 **Children:** Portions **Parking:** 30

WOODSTOCK MAP 11 SP41

Feathers Hotel

Modern British

Accomplished modern British cuisine at a sophisticated town-house hotel

☎ 01993 812291 Market St OX20 1SX
e-mail: enquiries@feathers.co.uk
web: www.feathers.co.uk

Set in a busy market town not far from Blenheim Palace, this chic little hotel offers a choice of two eateries. Lighter fare is available in the bar or bistro, but the restaurant is the main draw, a stylish, wood-panelled affair comprised of three interconnecting rooms decorated in rich plums and creams, with traditional fittings and elegantly appointed tables. Expect a modern British menu of dishes such as Cornish halibut with cabbage, mussels and bacon, or rump of Welsh heather-fed lamb with salsa verdi, rounded off by divine desserts including lemon posset with sweet pesto, prune and Armagnac pudding, or dark chocolate decadence with cherry ripple.

Chef: Simon Garbutt **Owners:** Empire Ventures Ltd. **Times:** 12.30-2.30/7-9.30, Closed D Sun **Prices:** Fixed D £35-£45, Coffee £2.50, Min/Water £3.50, Service added but optional 10% **Wine:** 80 bottles over £20, 20 bottles under £20, 14 by the glass (£4-£7.50) **Notes:** Vegetarian available, Dress Restrictions, Smart casual. No jeans/trainers **Seats:** 54, Pr/dining room 30 **Smoking:** N/Sm in restaurant **Children:** Menu, Portions **Rooms:** 20 (20 en suite) ★★★ HL **Directions:** 8m from Oxford on A44. Follow signs Evesham & Blenheim Palace. In Woodstock take 2nd left into the town. Hotel 20mtrs on left **Parking:** On street

Kings Head Inn

International

Friendly inn with Pacific Rim-inspired dining

☎ 01993 811340 Chapel Hill, Wootton OX20 1DX
e-mail: t.fay@kings-head.co.uk
web: www.kings-head.co.uk

Originally two small cottages in the formerly busy High Street, the inn is listed and the street is now a quiet backwater of the conservation village of Wootton. Open fires, stone walls and beamed ceilings create a welcoming atmosphere. Fresh local ingredients are prepared here in dishes with an international flavour, taking inspiration from the Pacific Rim. Most of the menu is gluten-free and includes the likes of Cantonese braised leg and pink roasted breast of Gressingham duck with a duck sherry gravy.

Chef: Tony Fay **Owners:** Mr & Mrs T Fay **Times:** 12-2/7-9, Closed Xmas, Mon (ex BHs), Closed D Sun **Prices:** Starter £3.95-£5.95, Main £9.25-£17.95, Dessert £4.95, Coffee £2, Min/Water £3.50 **Wine:** 24 bottles over £20, 23 bottles under £20, 7 by the glass (£2.95-£4.25) **Notes:** Vegetarian available **Seats:** 30 **Smoking:** N/Sm in restaurant **Children:** Min 12 yrs **Rooms:** 3 (3 en suite) ◆◆◆◆ **Directions:** On A44 2m N of Woodstock turn right to Wootton. The inn is located near church, village shop and school on Chapel Hill **Parking:** 7

Macdonald Bear Hotel

Modern British

Modern cooking in historic inn

☎ 0870 4008202 Park St OX20 1SZ
e-mail: bear@macdonald-hotels.co.uk
web: www.bearhotelwoodstock.co.uk

continued

WOODSTOCK *continued* MAP 11 SP41

Dating back to the 13th century, this ivy-clad hotel on the main street is one of England's oldest coaching inns, brimful of traditional character and atmosphere, and once the hideaway of Richard Burton and Elizabeth Taylor during their on-off love affair. The smart, inviting restaurant, like the rest of the building, oozes character, with oak beams, stone walls and an open fireplace, while service is warm, relaxed and friendly. The kitchen takes a modern-European direction on its seasonal menus, combining skill with quality ingredients. Take roast partridge served with Savoy cabbage and foie gras galette, sage butter and pan gravy, with perhaps a brioche bread and butter pudding with vanilla ice cream to close.

Chef: Imad Abdul-Razzak **Owners:** Macdonald Hotels PLC **Times:** 12.30-2/7-9.30 **Prices:** Fixed L £16.95, Fixed D £25.95, Starter £5-£12, Main £16-£25, Dessert £6-£7.50, Coffee £2.95, Min/Water £4.35, Service optional **Wine:** 53 bottles over £20, 27 bottles under £20, 12 by the glass (£4.25-£5.25) **Notes:** Vegetarian available **Seats:** 80, Pr/dining room 30 **Smoking:** N/Sm in restaurant **Children:** Menu, Portions **Rooms:** 54 (54 en suite) ★★★ HL **Directions:** Town centre, facing the market square **Parking:** 45

RUTLAND

CLIPSHAM MAP 11 SK91

The Olive Branch

British, European

Stone-flagged gastro-pub presenting the best local produce

☎ 01780 410355 Main St LE15 7SH
e-mail: info@theolivebranchpub.com
web: www.theolivebranchpub.com

Old village inn furnished with a mixture of antiques, French monastery pews, pine tables and open fires. The atmosphere is relaxed and informal with service provided by a knowledgeable young team. Skilfully prepared and presented food with a variety of traditional and innovative dishes created from local ingredients. Fresh fish and game are well represented. Good examples are home-cured bresaola from local beef with celeriac remoulade, braised fillet of turbot with chive mash and white wine and mussel velouté, roast pollack, mushroom rarebit and smoked bacon sauce, and breast of pheasant with pearl barley risotto. Desserts include ginger sponge pudding with marmalade ice cream and baked white chocolate cheesecake and blueberry compôte.

Chef: Sean Hope **Owners:** Sean Hope, Marcus Welford, Ben Jones **Times:** 12-2/7-9.30, Closed 26 Dec, 1 Jan, Closed L 31 Dec, D 25 Dec **Prices:** Fixed L £14, Starter £4.50-£8.95, Main £10.50-£19.50, Dessert £4.50-£7, Coffee £2, Min/Water £2.75, Service optional, Group min 12 service 10% **Wine:** 30 bottles over £20, 30 bottles under £20, 10 by the glass (£2.75-£5.50) **Notes:** Sun L £19.50, Vegetarian available **Seats:** 45, Pr/dining room 28 **Smoking:** N/Sm in restaurant **Children:** Menu, Portions **Directions:** 2m from A1 at Stretton junct, 5m N of Stamford **Parking:** 15

OAKHAM MAP 11 SK80

Barnsdale Lodge Hotel

Modern British, European

Attractively converted farmhouse hotel on the shores of Rutland Water

☎ 01572 724678 The Avenue, Rutland Water, North Shore LE15 8AH
e-mail: enquiries@barnsdalelodge.co.uk
web: www.barnsdalelodge.co.uk

This stylish hotel built around a courtyard was once a 17th-century farmhouse. Original features like bread ovens and stone floors go well with the country-house style furnishings. There's a choice of three dining rooms or the courtyard. Staff are young and helpful. Dishes are modern British in style with Italian influences and good use is made of seasonal, local ingredients. Start with fried king scallops or eggs Benedict and try the oven-baked Rutland trout with lime and parsley. Puddings include a wonderful banana and date pudding with a warm caramel sauce.

Chef: Richard Carruthers **Owners:** The Hon Thomas Noel **Times:** 12.15-2.15/7-9.30 **Prices:** Fixed L fr £11.95, Starter £4.95-£5.25, Main £9.95-£15.50, Dessert £4.50-£5.25, Coffee £2.95, Min/Water £2.95, Service added but optional 10% **Wine:** 45 bottles over £20, 36 bottles under £20, 8 by the glass (£2.95-£4.95) **Notes:** Sun L £18.95, Vegetarian available, Civ Wed 100 **Seats:** 120, Pr/dining room 50 **Smoking:** N/Sm area, No pipes, No cigars **Children:** Menu, Portions **Rooms:** 45 (45 en suite) ★★★ **Directions:** Turn off A1 at Stamford onto A606 to Oakham. Hotel 5m on right. (2 miles E of Oakham) **Parking:** 250

Four Rosettes

Amongst the very best restaurants in the British Isles, where the cooking demands national recognition. These restaurants will exhibit intense ambition, a passion for excellence, superb technical skills and remarkable consistency. They will combine appreciation of culinary traditions with a passionate desire for further exploration and improvement.

Hambleton Hall Hotel

OAKHAM MAP 11 SK80

British V NOTABLE WINE LIST

Romantic retreat serving the best of English country-house cuisine

☎ 01572 756991 Hambleton LE15 8TH
e-mail: hotel@hambletonhall.com
web: www.hambletonhall.com

Set in sweeping landscaped grounds overlooking Rutland Water, Hambleton Hall is the epitome of the English country-house hotel. As soon as you arrive, Hambleton weaves its spell. The intimate dining room is dressed in warm traditional colours, with heavy brocade drapes and oil paintings, enhanced by the lovely backdrop of the garden and lake. Service is professional and friendly and the wine list appropriately extensive, while chef Aaron Patterson's inspired cooking delivers a superb, subtly modern take on classic country-house cooking. His style echoes that of his mentor, Raymond Blanc, in its focus on the finest quality produce, seasonality and clarity of flavour, together with the use of the freshest vegetables, herbs and salads from the hotel's own kitchen garden. Local game is a speciality, while luxury items pepper the sophisticated repertoire of fixed-price menus where technical excellence reigns supreme. The menu might offer loin of fallow venison with caramelised endive and a cocoa-flavoured sauce, perhaps an assiette of rabbit with carrot purée, or fillet of turbot with a risotto of Jerusalem artichoke and clams. Finish with an assiette of pineapple, or maybe a classic passionfruit soufflé with a passionfruit and banana sorbet.
Notable Wine List: A super list full of enthusiasm and expertise, including an interesting 'wines of the moment' section which offers popular wines that are drinking particularly well.

Chef: Aaron Patterson
Owners: Mr T Hart
Times: 12-1.30/7-9.30
Prices: Fixed L fr £18.50, Fixed D £40-£50, Starter £12-£24, Main £20-£39, Dessert £9-£18, Coffee £5, Min/Water £3, Service included
Wine: 350 bottles over £20, 20 bottles under £20, 8 by the glass (£4-£8)
Notes: Tasting menu £65, Sun L 3 courses £37.50, Vegetarian menu, Dress Restrictions, Smart dress, no jeans, T-shirts or trainers, Civ Wed 64
Seats: 60, Pr/dining room 24
Smoking: N/Sm in restaurant
Children: Portions
Rooms: 17 (17 en suite) ★★★★
Directions: 8m W of the A1 Stamford junct (A606), 3m E of Oakham
Parking: 36

England

UPPINGHAM MAP 11 SP89

Lake Isle Restaurant & Town House Hotel

British, French

Quality food in a sleepy market town

☎ 01572 822951 16 High St East LE15 9PZ
e-mail: info@lakeislehotel.com
web: www.lakeislehotel.com

Formerly a shop, this small hotel in the quiet market town of Uppingham retains many of its original features, including panelled walls and mahogany shop fittings with heavy wooden tables complementing the otherwise chic, up-to-date interiors. Clean, simple and fresh flavours abound, with an emphasis on quality ingredients. The cooking is excellent and all the dishes on the menu invariably live up to their descriptions. Typical dishes might be duck liver parfait with sunflower seed focaccia and spiced apricot compôte or a notably good Cromer crab tartlet to start, or paupiette of salmon and trout with lime crème fraîche dressing for mains. The desserts, like honey and Norfolk lavender pannacotta, are also worthy of note, as is the wine list.

Times: 12-2.30/7-9.30, Closed L Mon, D Sun **Rooms:** 12 (12 en suite) ★★ HL **Directions:** Located on main High St

SHROPSHIRE

CHURCH STRETTON MAP 15 SO49

Stretton Hall Hotel

British

Country-house cooking with local appeal

☎ 01694 723224 All Stretton SY6 6HG
e-mail: enquiries@strettonhall.co.uk
web: www.strettonhall.co.uk

This stunning Georgian house sits in a quiet village in the south Shropshire countryside and offers imposing views across meadows to the slopes of Caer Caradoc. The Lemon Tree restaurant is decorated in simple country style, and draws a loyal local clientele with hearty portions of straightforward fare using quality ingredients locally sourced whenever possible. Expect dishes such as foie gras ravioli starter, with mains ranging from pan-fried venison steak with a bitter chocolate and port sauce, to sea bass cooked en papillote with white wine, lemon and herbs. Vegetarian options are also available.

Owners: Mr C Baker **Times:** 12.30-2/7-9 **Prices:** Starter £4-£8.45, Main £12-£18, Dessert £4-£6.95, Coffee £1.50, Min/Water £2, Service optional

continued

Wine: 14 bottles over £20, 29 bottles under £20, 8 by the glass (£2.70-£3.25) **Notes:** Vegetarian available, Civ Wed 72 **Seats:** 40, Pr/dining room 14 **Smoking:** N/Sm in restaurant **Children:** Portions **Rooms:** 12 (12 en suite) ★★★ HL **Directions:** Off A49 Ludlow to Shrewsbury Road, in village of All Stretton **Parking:** 40

The Studio

Modern British

Imaginative food in a former art studio

☎ 01694 722672 59 High St SY6 6BY

An interesting collection of art and ceramics reflects the restaurant's former life as an artist's studio. The original paint palette sign still swings at the front of the building, a small welcoming bar is positioned by the front door and there is a lovely patio garden overlooking the Shropshire hills for alfresco dining. Bistro-style food is served and all the dishes are made in-house using well sourced local produce and the classical and traditional skills of the husband and wife team. Recommendations include pan-fried haunch of venison steak with celeriac purée and a red wine and raspberry sauce.

Chef: Tony Martland **Owners:** Tony & Sheila Martland **Times:** 7-9, Closed 1 wk Jan, 2 wks Nov, Sun & Mon, Closed L all week **Prices:** Starter £4.50-£7.50, Main £14-£17.50, Dessert £5, Coffee £1.75, Min/Water £2.50, Service optional **Wine:** 10 bottles over £20, 29 bottles under £20, 7 by the glass (£3.75) **Seats:** 34 **Smoking:** N/Sm in restaurant **Children:** Portions **Directions:** Off A49 to town, left at T-junct onto High Street, 300 yds on left **Parking:** On street parking available

LLANFAIR WATERDINE MAP 09 SO27

The Waterdine

Modern British

Charming countryside dining

☎ 01547 528214 LD7 1TU

The Waterdine is a former drover's inn, dating back over 400 years. Set in wonderful Shropshire countryside, it's full of charm and character. Friendly, efficient hospitality from the owners puts you at your ease immediately. Here you'll find an experienced chef making great use of quality local produce, including fruit and vegetables from the inn's own garden. The menu is seasonal and changes regularly.

Times: 12-1.45/7-9, Closed 1 wk spring, 1 wk autumn, Closed D Sun, Mon **Rooms:** 3 (3 en suite) ◆◆◆◆◆

LUDLOW MAP 10 SO57

The Clive Restaurant with Rooms

Modern British

Bright, modern restaurant in former farm house

☎ 01584 856565 & 856665 Bromfield SY8 2JR
e-mail: info@theclive.co.uk
web: www.theclive.co.uk

Once the home of Clive of India, this roadside farmstead is now a stylish restaurant with rooms. Decoration of the lounge bar, café bar and bright, modern restaurant is in a contemporary style. Lightwood modern furniture, mirrors and large windows create space and light,

continued

vith pink, yellow and grey walls adorned with black and white hotos. The buzzy café bar can be quite noisy when full. Dishes using ocal produce are cooked in a modern British style with some Aediterranean influences. Mushrooms stuffed with mozzarella and vhite truffle oil might be followed by sautéed guinea fowl with citrus auce, fine beans provençale, and prune and Armagnac Baba to nish.

The Clive Restaurant with Rooms

hef: Peter Gartell **Owners:** Paul & Barbara Brooks **Times:** 12-3/7-9.30, losed 25-26 Dec **Prices:** Fixed L fr £25, Fixed D fr £25, Starter £4.95-7.95, Main £13.95-£15.95, Dessert £5.50-£5.95, Coffee £2.25, Min/Water 2.80, Service optional **Wine:** 30 bottles over £20, 49 bottles under £20, by the glass (£2.80-£4.95) **Notes:** Fixed L 3 courses, Sun L 3 courses 16.75, Vegetarian available **Seats:** 35 **Smoking:** N/Sm in restaurant **hildren:** Portions **Rooms:** 15 (15 en suite) ◆◆◆◆ **Directions:** 2m of Ludlow on A49, near Ludlow Golf Club and Race Course **arking:** 80

Dinham Hall Hotel

Aodern British

omfortable townhouse in the gastronomic centre

☎ 01584 876464 By the Castle SY8 1EJ
-mail: info@dinhamhall.co.uk
veb: www.dinhamhall.co.uk

uilt in 1792, this mellow stone townhouse hotel is situated just off e main square, with lovely gardens and wonderful views across the alley beyond. The best outlook can be enjoyed from the Georgian-yle restaurant, where warm yellow walls create a welcoming nbience. A well-deserved reputation for good food ensures a steady ream of local enthusiasts, drawn to the quality seasonal produce, urced from a broad range of suppliers, handled with confidence and nagination. Look out for beetroot gravad lax with potato tian starter, llowed by Gloucestershire Old Spot pork tenderloin with wild ushrooms and Armagnac fondant potato, cauliflower purée and urple sprouting, and a classic chocolate fondant. Service is ofessional and even flamboyant.

hef: Dean Banner **Owners:** Mr J Mifsud **Times:** 12.30-1.45/7-8.45, osed D 25 Dec **Prices:** Fixed L £18-£23, Fixed D £38.50-£47, Coffee .50, Min/Water £3.50, Service optional **Wine:** 60 bottles over £20, 8 ottles under £20, 8 by the glass (£4.50) **Notes:** Vegetarian available, Civ ed 140 **Seats:** 30, Pr/dining room 80 **Smoking:** N/Sm in restaurant **hildren:** Min 8 yrs, Menu, Portions **Rooms:** 13 (13 en suite) ★★★ HL **irections:** Town centre, off Market Place

The Feathers Hotel

Modern British

Historic building with up-to-the-minute food

☎ 01584 875261 The Bull Ring SY8 1AA
e-mail: enquiries@feathersatludlow.co.uk
web: www.feathersatludlow.co.uk

Described by Nikolaus Pevsner in *The Buildings of England* as 'that prodigy of timber-frame houses' and more recently in The New York Times as 'the most handsome inn in the world', this Jacobean hotel is widely renowned and is blessed with olde worlde charm in spades. The kitchen here balances traditional and innovative concepts in their cooking with most dishes offering well-conceived flavours with lovely ingredients - smoked eel, foie gras terrine, salsify compote and a lobster and red wine reduction, or breast of mallard with tempura leg and vanilla mash.

Chef: Jonathan Thomas **Owners:** Ceney Developments **Times:** 12-2.30/6.30-9.30, Closed L Mon-Sat **Prices:** Fixed D £29.95-£32, Coffee £1.75, Min/Water £4.25, Service optional, Group min 12 service 10% **Wine:** 25 bottles over £20, 20 bottles under £20, 9 by the glass (£3.25-£5.75) **Notes:** Sun L 2 courses £13.95, 3 courses £16.95, Vegetarian available, Dress Restrictions, Smart casual, Civ Wed 80 **Seats:** 60, Pr/dining room 30 **Smoking:** N/Sm in restaurant **Children:** Menu, Portions **Rooms:** 40 (40 en suite) ★★★ **Directions:** Town centre hotel in th middle of Ludlow. Approximately 40 minutes from Hereford **Parking:** 36

Hibiscus

see page 402

Mr Underhills

see page 403

Overton Grange Country House & Restaurant

see page 403

England

England

Hibiscus

LUDLOW MAP 10 SO57

Modern French NOTABLE WINE LIST

Exciting and memorable modern cooking in charming atmosphere

☎ 01584 872325 17 Corve St SY8 1DA
web: www.hibiscusrestaurant.co.uk

Chef: Claude Bosi
Owners: Claude Bosi & Claire Bosi
Times: 12.30-1.30/7-10, Closed 2 wks Jan, 1 wk Aug, Sun & Mon, Closed L Tue
Prices: Fixed L £21.50, Fixed D £45, Coffee £3.25, Min/Water £3, Service optional
Wine: 300 bottles over £20, 30 bottles under £20, 8 by the glass (£3.75-£7.50)
Notes: Tasting menu £67.50
Seats: 36
Smoking: N/Sm in restaurant
Children: Portions
Directions: Town centre, bottom of hill below Feathers Hotel
Parking: 6

For a gastronomic premier-leaguer, Hibiscus doesn't really shout its whereabouts that loudly, so look out for the low-key sign on the town's Corve Street for Claude and Claire Bosi's stylish, sophisticated but unassuming restaurant, set in what was once a 17th-century coaching inn. Here ancient oak-panelled walls contrast with exposed stone, contemporary artwork and modern seating, while the handful of much-in-demand, formally dressed tables are looked after with charm by Claire, who takes care of front of house, where service is professional, but relaxed and unobtrusive, and catches the mood perfectly. Claude's cooking doesn't stand still; it's innovative and exciting and stands out from the crowd. An apprenticeship in some of France's top kitchens has brilliantly born fruit here in Ludlow. His adventurous, inventive and creative cooking is based around his classic Lyonnaise training, but his modern French approach exudes daring, imagination and intriguing combinations that show a loyalty to seasonality. The freshest local ingredients are brought together with style, a deftness of touch and passion to create striking flavour and texture combinations. Think roast Mortimer Forest venison teamed with a smoked chocolate sauce, chilled chicken liver parfait, roasted shallots and bitter clementine marmalade, or perhaps Cornish turbot poached in a coffee and cardamom broth with creamed Savoy cabbage, roast quince and spiced quince purée. A pannacotta of Earl Grey tea served with a warm emulsion of gingerbread and ginger cookie, or Claude's assiette of mini desserts, might provide the finish. A lightness of touch makes the nine-course tasting option un-daunting.
Notable Wine List: The wine list offers a really fine selection from the world's top growers.

Mr Underhills

.UDLOW MAP 10 SO57

Aodern International

Inpretentious dining on the riverbank

☎ 01584 874431 Dinham Weir SY8 1EH

veb: www.mr-underhills.co.uk

his historic building - now the Bradley's restaurant with rooms - was riginally part of the castle corn mill and comes attractively set on the anks of the wooded River Teme overlooking the weir and in the lee f the brooding castle ramparts. Its small but pretty courtyard garden ffers an ideal vantage point, as does the bright-and-airy dining oom's large picture windows, allowing views over both garden and e fast-flowing Teme, while the small reception room is the place for peritifs. Dinner is a fixed-price tasting affair of six courses plus coffee nd petits fours, but there's no choice before dessert. Chef-patron hris enquires about dietary requirements or dislikes when booking, en on the day you are advised on what the main menu dishes will e. The style keeps things intelligently simple, concentrating on ringing the best out of prime, seasonal ingredients, the emphasis on eshness and natural flavours rather than cutting-edge cuisine. Begin ith a starter of day-boat halibut served on shredded vegetables with coriander, lemongrass and ginger broth, followed by a mains of ow-roasted fillet of beef with braised beef sauce and ox cheek pie. The choice of desserts includes the likes of lemon tart with orange and mascarpone ice cream. Service, with wife Judy as host, is suitably relaxed and friendly though precise, and there's an endearing feeling of going to a private dinner party with friends about the whole experience. A notable wine list rounds things off in style.

Chef: Christopher Bradley **Owners:** Christopher & Judy Bradley **Times:** 7.30-8.30, Closed 1 wk Jan, 1 wk July, Tue, Closed L all wk, D Mon-Tue **Prices:** Main £45, Min/Water £2.20, Service optional **Wine:** 140 bottles over £20, 20 bottles under £20, 10 by the glass (£2.80-£6) **Notes:** Tasting menus only, Vegetarian available, Dress Restrictions, Smart casual **Seats:** 30 **Smoking:** N/Sm in restaurant **Children:** Portions **Directions:** From Castle Square: with castle in front, turn immediately left, proceed round castle, turn right before bridge, restaurant on left **Parking:** 7

Overton Grange Country House & Restaurant

.UDLOW MAP 10 SO57

Aodern British, French

evitalised country house with classy cooking

☎ 01584 873500 Old Hereford Rd SY8 4AD

-mail: info@overtongrangehotel.com

veb: www.overtongrangehotel.com

anding in mature grounds on the outskirts of Ludlow with lovely ews across the Shropshire countryside, this handsome Edwardian untry-house hotel is certainly one of the highlights to savour for the wn's gastro-tourists. Quintessential country house it may be on the itside, but inside a new look has created a more contemporary ge. The dining room is in two parts at the rear, with plenty of itural light flooding through large lead-light windows dressed with man blinds. Aubergine and cream is the modern colour theme, bles are elegantly laid, chairs are high-backed suede and service ghly polished, professional and European. Chef Olivier Bossut's oking perfectly matches the surroundings, elegantly blending odern and classical French cuisine with superb technical skill, tip-top oduce and bold flavours. Presentation is intricate and appealing to e eye and combinations work in harmony on the palate via a pertoire of crisply scripted menus, with the eight-course tasting gustation option offering a great introduction to the chef's pedigree and best dishes. Expect the likes of steamed squab pigeon accompanied by creamy Savoy cabbage and a périgourdine truffle sauce, and to finish, perhaps a bitter chocolate soufflé with pistachio sauce and white chocolate ice cream. An extensive, well-chosen wine list offers the perfect accompaniment, as does a pre-meal stroll on the lawns in summer, or beside a blazing fire in one of two small lounges or bar for aperitifs on colder days.

Chef: Olivier Bossut **Owners:** Indigo Hotels Ltd **Times:** 12-2.30/7-10, Closed 27 Dec-7 Jan, Closed L Sun-Wed, D Sun (ex residents) **Prices:** Fixed L £32.50-£42.60, Fixed D £42.50-£59.50, Starter £9.50-£12.50, Main £20-£25, Dessert £9.50-£12.50, Coffee £3.50, Min/Water £3.50, Service added 10% **Wine:** 170 bottles over £20, 12 bottles under £20, 8 by the glass (£4.95-£7.50) **Notes:** Fixed L 3 courses, fixed D 4 courses, Vegetarian available, Dress Restrictions, Smart casual, Civ Wed 30 **Seats:** 40, Pr/dining room 24 **Smoking:** N/Sm in restaurant **Children:** Min 6 yrs **Rooms:** 14 (14 en suite) ★★★ HL **Directions:** M5 junct 5. On B4361 approx 1.5m from Ludlow towards Leominster **Parking:** 50

England

LUDLOW *continued* MAP 10 SO57

The Roebuck Inn Restaurant

Traditional British

Welcoming atmosphere in ancient inn

☎ 01584 711230 Brimfield SY8 4NE
web: www.theroebuckinn.com

Fifteenth-century village inn it may be, but the focus here is on the more modern setting of its bright-and-airy dining room, with linen tablecloths, fresh flowers and winter log fires. The old front bar has been refurbished too, while the kitchen's approach mixes traditional and more modern ideas, utilising the freshest local seasonal produce. Everything's made in-house from bread and pasta to petits fours, the menu bolstered by blackboard specials. Think roast chicken breast with crispy herb risotto cake and a smoked garlic and red wine sauce, and, to finish perhaps, the ubiquitous bread-and-butter pudding, but this version made with brioche, croissant and apricot conserve laced with vanilla sauce and apricot coulis.

Chef: Jonathan Waters **Times:** 11.30-2.30/6.30-9.30, Closed 25-26 Dec **Prices:** Starter £4-£6.50, Main £7-£17.50, Dessert £5, Coffee £2.25, Min/Water £2.50, Service optional **Notes:** Vegetarian available, Dress Restrictions, Smart casual **Seats:** 45 **Smoking:** N/Sm in restaurant **Children:** Portions **Rooms:** 3 (3 en suite) ◆◆◆◆ **Directions:** Just off A49 between Ludlow & Leominster **Parking:** 20

MARKET DRAYTON MAP 15 SJ63

The Cottage Restaurant at Ternhill Farm House

Modern British NEW

Local fresh produce served in cottage-style restaurant

☎ 01630 638984 Ternhill TF9 3PX
e-mail: jo@ternhillfarm.co.uk
web: www.ternhillfarm.co.uk

A former Georgian farmhouse and coaching inn, Ternhill was extended in Victorian times and the former farm buildings now provide secure parking. The cottage-style restaurant has well spaced rustic tables, high-backed leather chairs and a huge inglenook fireplace. Cooking is modern British in style with international influences and lots of fresh seasonal produce. Expect imaginative flavour combinations and contrasts and good use of spices in dishes like banana wrapped in cured ham, baked with tomatoes, coriander, cumin, turmeric, chilli, ground ginger and cream, or fillet of red mullet pan-fried in a basil and roasted pinenut butter.

Chef: Michael Abraham **Owners:** Michael & Joanne Abraham **Times:** 7-9, Closed Sun & Mon, Closed L all week **Prices:** Starter £4.25-£5.95, Main £9.25-£16.25, Dessert £4.25-£5.25, Coffee £2.45, Min/Water £2.50, Service optional **Wine:** 5 bottles over £20, 22 bottles under £20, 6 by the glass (£1.85-£4.95) **Notes:** Vegetarian available, Dress Restrictions, Smart casual **Seats:** 20, Pr/dining room 14 **Smoking:** N/Sm in restaurant **Children:** Min before 8pm **Rooms:** 5 (5 en suite) ◆◆◆◆ **Directions:** On x-rds of A41 & A53, 3m W of Market Drayton **Parking:** 12

Goldstone Hall

Modern British

Modern cooking amidst period charm

☎ 01630 661202 Goldstone TF9 2NA
e-mail: enquiries@goldstonehall.com
web: www.goldstonehall.com

Set in impressive gardens and mature woodland, Goldstone Hall is a jewel of Tudor architecture. Beams, exposed timbers and open fires abound and many rooms, including the elegant dining room, have original panelled walls. The daily menus are based on seasonal and local produce, notably home-grown herbs and vegetables. Fixed-price dinner menus and the light supper choice list simple, contemporary British dishes - spring chicken and apricot terrine with green peppercorn mayonnaise, duck with fig and port glaze, and grilled fillet steak with red wine and shallot glaze show the style.

Chef: Carl Fitzgerald-Bloomer **Owners:** Mr J Cushing & Mrs H Ward **Times:** 12-2.30/7.30-11 **Prices:** Fixed D fr £29, Starter fr £5.50, Main fr £18 Dessert fr £5.50, Coffee £2.40, Min/Water £3.50, Service included **Wine:** 13 bottles over £20, 57 bottles under £20, 7 by the glass (£3.50-£5) **Notes:** Fixed D Gastronome 6 courses £40, Sun L £18.95, Vegetarian available, Dress Restrictions, Smart casual, Civ Wed 100 **Seats:** 40, Pr/dining room 20 **Smoking:** N/Sm in restaurant **Children:** Portions **Rooms:** 11 (11 en suite) ★★★ HL **Directions:** From A529, 4m S of Market Drayton, follow signs for Goldstone Hall Hotel **Parking:** 40

Rosehill Manor

Traditional

Traditional country-house style restaurant

☎ 01630 638532 & 637000 Rosehill, Ternhill TF9 2JF
web: www.rosehillmanorhotel.co.uk

A 17th-century manor house set in 1.5 acres of mature gardens. Privately owned and personally run, the emphasis is on freshly prepared traditional cooking complemented by professional service. The restaurant has garden views and a relaxing atmosphere, with an open fire in winter. The bar has lovely exposed beams reflecting the character of the original house. Typical dishes include a starter of filo basket filled with mushrooms and bacon with stilton, and a main course of breast of duck with Grand Marnier sauce; or rack of Shropshire lamb with minted gravy.

Chef: Jane Eardley **Owners:** Mr & Mrs P Eardley **Times:** 12-2/7-9.30, Closed L Mon-Sat, D Sun **Prices:** Fixed L fr £16.50, Fixed D fr £19.50, Starter fr £4.50, Main £13.50-£16.50, Dessert fr £4.50, Coffee £1.75, Min/Water £3.50, Service optional **Wine:** 10 bottles over £20, 15 bottles under £20 **Notes:** Fixed L 3 courses, Smart Casual, Civ Wed 100 **Seats:** 70, Pr/dining room 30 **Smoking:** N/Sm in restaurant **Children:** Portions **Rooms:** 8 (8 en suite) ★★ HL **Directions:** On A41 4m from Market Drayton **Parking:** 60

MUCH WENLOCK MAP 10 SO69

Raven Hotel

British, Mediterranean

Fresh cooking in historic location

☎ 01952 727251 30 Barrow St TF13 6EN
e-mail: enquiry@ravenhotel.com
web: www.ravenhotel.com

This town-centre hotel brings together several 15th-century almshouses and a medieval great hall, with a coaching inn at its heart. The cosy warren of rooms is dotted with oak beams and open fires and the airy restaurant looks out over an inner courtyard where you can eat outside on warm summer evenings. Local produce and fresh ingredients are the key to cooking here, using herbs from the kitchen garden. Classic dishes are given modern European interpretations, along the lines of supreme of chicken with Shropshire blue cheese, smoked bacon and creamed leeks. A bar menu is also available.

Times: 12-2.30/6.45-9.30, Closed 25 Dec **Rooms:** 15 (15 en suite) ★★★ **Directions:** 10m SW from Telford on A4169, 12m SE from Shrewsbury. In town centre

NORTON MAP 10 SJ70

Hundred House Hotel

British, European

Historic backdrop and quirky charm meets modern cuisine.

☎ 01952 730353 Bridgnorth Rd TF11 9EE
e-mail: reservation@hundredhouse.co.uk
web: www.hundredhouse.co.uk

Principally Georgian, but with parts dating back to the 14th century, this endearing one-time coaching inn and courthouse is now a friendly, family-run hotel, set in pretty grounds complete with herb and flower gardens. Indoors is rich in original features, with a wealth

continued

Hundred House Hotel

of exposed beams, open fires, quality rustic furnishings and memorabilia, with aromatic herbs and flowers suspended overhead. With formal or informal rooms for dining and friendly, well-informed service, dishes are modern British in essence, but with some traditional favourites, too. Fresh, well-sourced produce and clear flavours parade in dishes intelligently not over embellished. Expect a breast of Gressingham duck with grapefruit and orange puff pastry and a savoury sauce to be followed by hot treacle tart with home-made custard.

Chef: Stuart Phillips **Owners:** Mr H Phillips, Mrs S Phillips, Mr D Phillips, Mr SG Phillips **Times:** 12-2.15/6-9.30, Closed D 26 Dec **Prices:** Starter £4.95-£8.95, Main £10.95-£23.95, Dessert £4.95-£5.95, Coffee £1.95, Min/Water £3.50, Service optional, Group min 7 service 10% **Wine:** 14 bottles over £20, 21 bottles under £20, 15 by the glass (£3.30-£4.65) **Notes:** Fixed L Sun only 2 courses £16.95, 3 courses £19.95, Vegetarian available, Dress Restrictions, Smart casual **Seats:** 60, Pr/dining room 30 **Smoking:** N/Sm area, No pipes, No cigars **Children:** Menu, Portions **Rooms:** 10 (10 en suite) ★★ HL **Directions:** Midway between Telford & Bridgnorth on A442. In centre of Norton village **Parking:** 30

OSWESTRY MAP 15 SJ22

The Bradford Arms Hotel

Modern British NEW

Innovative, modern cooking in traditional surroundings

☎ 01691 830582 Llanymynech SY22 6EJ
e-mail: info@bradfordarmshotel.com
web: www.bradfordarmshotel.com

Formerly a coaching inn on the Earl of Bradford's estate, this sympathetically renovated property has a traditional-style bar and two light and airy dining areas, one a conservatory, the other a more formal room. A serious commitment to providing accomplished, innovative, modern British cuisine with an international flair, utilising quality, locally sourced produce - perhaps local Welsh Black beef or Welsh spring lamb - is the kitchen's style. Menus are bolstered by evening specials such as chargrilled fillet of beef, pomme purée, caramelised parsnips and a wild mushroom and blue cheese sauce.

Chef: Simon Hough **Owners:** Fiona & Bud Winter **Times:** 12-2/7-9, Closed 25 & 26 Dec, Sun & Mon **Prices:** Food prices not confirmed for 2007. Please telephone for details **Wine:** 14 bottles over £20, 29 bottles under £20, 6 by the glass (£1.90-£3.60) **Notes:** Vegetarian available **Seats:** 26, Pr/dining room 24 **Smoking:** N/Sm in restaurant **Children:** Portions **Rooms:** 5 (5 en suite) ◆◆◆◆ **Directions:** 5.5m S of Oswestry on A483 in Llanymynech **Parking:** 20

England

OSWESTRY *continued* MAP 15 SJ22

Pen-y-Dyffryn Country Hotel

British

Top-notch cooking in hillside haven

☎ 01691 653700 Rhydycroesau SY10 7JD
e-mail: stay@peny.co.uk
web: www.peny.co.uk

Built as a rectory in 1845, this alluring stone building stands isolated amid lush and beautiful grounds in a stunning valley, with glorious rolling country views. There's a homely feel about the place and the hospitality is warm and welcoming, which is augmented by the real fires in the comfortable lounges and traditionally-styled dining room. The dinner menu offers four options at each course and fresh local produce, much of it organic, underpins the kitchen's philosophy for sourcing quality ingredients. Follow pheasant terrine and quince jelly, with best end of Welsh lamb with thyme jus, and round off with plum and almond tart or a plate of local cheeses.

Chef: David Morris **Owners:** MJM & AA Hunter **Times:** 6.45-11, Closed 20 Dec-21 Jan, Closed L all week **Prices:** Fixed D £30-£32, Coffee £2.95, Min/Water £3.95, Service optional **Wine:** 50 bottles over £20, 30 bottles under £20, 2 by the glass (£3.95-£4.95) **Notes:** Vegetarian available **Seats:** 25 **Smoking:** N/Sm in restaurant **Children:** Min 3 yrs, Menu, Portions **Rooms:** 12 (12 en suite) ★★★ HL **Directions:** 3m W of Oswestry on B4580 **Parking:** 18

Wynnstay Hotel

European, International NEW

Modern cooking in elegant, period-style surroundings

☎ 01691 655261 Church St SY11 2SZ
e-mail: info@wynnstayhotel.com
web: www.wynnstayhotel.com

This listed Georgian property was once a coaching inn and posting house, and surrounds a unique 200-year-old crown bowling green. The hotel's elegant Four Seasons Restaurant comes decorated in pastel shades along with hues of yellow and gold, backed by equally smartly turned-out staff who prove suitably attentive, professional and friendly. A mixture of traditional dishes with modern interpretations incorporating international and Italian influences is the kitchen's style, supported by good use of the best available produce, as much as possible locally sourced. You might start with parmesan basket filled with wild mushrooms, followed by fillet of lamb wrapped in leeks and served with herb-roasted shallots and tarragon jus, with cherry and almond torte with Calvados custard to finish.

Chef: David Braddick **Owners:** Mr N Woodland **Times:** 12-2/7-9.30, Closed D Sun **Prices:** Fixed L £14.50, Fixed D £19.75, Starter £5.25-£6.95, Main £11-£17.95, Dessert £4.95-£5.05, Coffee £1.30, Min/Water £3, Service optional **Wine:** 10 bottles over £20, 32 bottles under £20, 8 by the glass (£3.60-£4.60) **Notes:** Vegetarian available, Dress Restrictions, Smart casual, Civ Wed 90 **Seats:** 46, Pr/dining room 200 **Smoking:** N/Sm in restaurant, Air con **Children:** Menu, Portions **Rooms:** 29 (29 en suite) ★★★ HL **Directions:** In centre of town, opposite the church **Parking:** 80

SHREWSBURY MAP 15 SJ41

Albright Hussey Manor Hotel & Restaurant

Modern British

A truly historic setting for fine dining

☎ 01939 290571 & 290523 Ellesmere Rd SY4 3AF
e-mail: info@albrighthussey.co.uk
web: www.albrighthussey.co.uk

This moated manor house, built in 1524, was mentioned in the Domesday Book. While the hotel has been modernised and extended in parts, the restaurant remains full of original character with a wealth of oak beams, panelling and lead-lined windows. Some of the seating is in quirky nooks and crannies providing plenty of privacy. The cooking style is an imaginative blend of traditional and modern dishes using good local ingredients. Typical starters like wild mushroom risotto with grilled asparagus might be followed by roast loin of local venison or noisettes of Frodesley lamb.

Chef: Michel Nissten **Owners:** Franco, Vera & Paul Subbiani **Times:** 12-2.15/7-10 **Prices:** Fixed L £15.95-£21.95, Starter £5.25-£12.50, Main £10.50-£22, Dessert £5.25-£6.95, Coffee £1.90, Min/Water £3.30, Service optional, Group min 6 service 10% **Wine:** 80 bottles over £20, 20 bottles under £20, 15 by the glass (£2.65-£10) **Notes:** Fixed L 3 courses, Vegetarian available, Dress Restrictions, No jeans, trainers or T-shirts, Civ Wed 200 **Seats:** 80, Pr/dining room 40 **Smoking:** N/Sm in restaurant, Air con **Children:** Portions **Rooms:** 26 (26 en suite) ★★★★ HL **Directions:** On A528, 2m from centre of Shrewsbury **Parking:** 100

Mytton & Mermaid Hotel

Modern British

Historic riverside inn serving contemporary cuisine

☎ 01743 761220 Atcham SY5 6QG
e-mail: admin@myttonandmermaid.co.uk
web: www.myttonandmermaid.co.uk

Casual country-house hotel, convenient for Shrewsbury, striving for excellence in food and service while maintaining a comfortable, friendly environment. The Grade II listed building dates from 1735, enjoying spectacular views over the River Severn, and was owned by architect Sir Clough Ellis of Portmeirion fame during the 1930s. The restaurant is furnished with antique oak tables and adorned with candles and fresh flowers. Local produce is used where possible in dishes such as assiette of duck (duck confit, seared duck breast, and smoked duck), fillet of rare-breed Shropshire beef and gratin of wild mushrooms, and warm chocolate tart with roasted pear and pear and crème fraîche sorbet.

Chef: Adrian Badland **Owners:** Mr & Mrs Ditella **Times:** 11.30-2.30/6.30-10, Closed 25 Dec, Closed D 26 Dec **Prices:** Fixed D £27.50, Starter £6.25-£7.95, Main £11.95-£20, Dessert £5.95-£7.25, Coffee £2, Min/Water £3.75, Service optional **Wine:** 23 bottles over £20, 30 bottles under £20, 14 by the glass (£3-£4) **Notes:** Sun D 3 courses & live jazz £18.95, Vegetarian available, Civ Wed 75 **Seats:** 100, Pr/dining room 15 **Smoking:** N/Sm in restaurant **Children:** Menu, Portions **Rooms:** 18 (18 en suite) ★★★ HL **Directions:** Just outside Shrewsbury on the B4380 (old A5). Opposite Attingham Park **Parking:** 80

Rowton Castle Hotel

Modern British

ine dining in a welcoming hotel

☎ 01743 884044 Halfway House SY5 9EP
-mail: post@rowtoncastle.com
eb: www.rowtoncastle.com

ituated in 17 acres of grounds, this Grade II listed building dates back
parts to 1696. The Cedar Restaurant features a 17th-century carved
ak fireplace and offers a seasonal menu of two or three courses. Oak
anelling adds to the warm and intimate ambience. Typical starters
night include home-made seasoned venison sausage, sliced on to
arm field mushrooms, with a rich red wine jus. For main courses
xpect dishes such as pan-fried pork fillet with blue cheese dumplings,
age scented sauce and crispy prosciutto ham. Try the interesting
easonal desserts to finish.

imes: 12-2/7-9.30 **Rooms:** 19 (19 en suite) ★★★ HL
irections: From Birmingham take M6 west. Follow M54 & A5 to
hrewsbury. Continue on A5 and exit at 6th rdbt. Take A458 to Welshpool.
owton Castle 4m on right

TELFORD MAP 10 SJ60

Best Western Valley Hotel & Chez Maws

Modern International

Imaginative menus in historic surroundings

☎ 01952 432247 TF8 7DW
e-mail: info@thevalleyhotel.co.uk
web: www.chezmawrestaurant.co.uk

Situated in the World Heritage site of Ironbridge, this listed Georgian building is surrounded by parkland and stands on the banks of the River Severn. It was once the home of the Maws family who manufactured ceramic tiles and Chez Maws, the bright and contemporary-style restaurant, is named after them. Imaginative and good use of quality local and seasonal ingredients shine through daily-changing dishes that span the globe. From an eclectic menu, try Thai spiced duck and sesame cakes with a chilli dip, herb-crusted Welsh lamb with Puy lentil and vegetable casserole, or whole lemon sole with sautéed chilli and lime prawns. Service is friendly and efficient.

Chef: Barry Workman **Owners:** Philip & Leslie Casson **Times:** 12-2/7-9.30, Closed 26 Dec-2 Jan, Closed L Sat & Sun **Prices:** Fixed L £11-£19, Fixed D £18-£26, Starter £4.50-£6.95, Main £15.50-£18.50, Dessert £4-£6, Coffee £1.70, Min/Water £3.75, Service optional **Wine:** 6 bottles over £20, 14 bottles under £20, 4 by the glass (£3-£4.50) **Notes:** Fixed L/D for groups only, Vegetarian available, Dress Restrictions, Smart casual, Civ Wed 120 **Seats:** 50, Pr/dining room 30 **Smoking:** N/Sm in restaurant **Children:** Menu, Portions **Rooms:** 35 (35 en suite) ★★★ HL **Directions:** From M6 on to M54, take junct 6 and follow A5223 to Ironbridge for 4m. At mini island turn right, hotel 80 yds on left **Parking:** 100

Old Vicarage Hotel and Restaurant

VORFIELD MAP 10 SO79

lodern British

uality cooking in one-time vicarage

☎ 01746 716497 WV15 5JZ
-mail: admin@the-old-vicarage.demon.co.uk
eb: www.oldvicarageworfield.com

is red-brick Edwardian vicarage turned elegant, small, family-run
tel is set in 2 acres of grounds and reflects the peace and quiet of
village setting. The interior features polished-wood floors and
bles, fresh flowers, a relaxing lounge (perfect for pre-dinner drinks),
d a new, light-and-airy Orangery restaurant, which offers lovely
ews over the surrounding Shropshire countryside. Service is as
endly and unobtrusive as the atmosphere. The highly
complished, modern-focused kitchen's emphasis is firmly driven by
vour and intelligent simplicity rather than over-complexity, which
tly suits the surrounding. The refreshing style allows seasonal, high-
ality regional produce to shine via a confident light touch. Expect
e likes of a chump of Shropshire lamb, roasted with garlic and
companied by sweet and sour red cabbage, or perhaps shallow
n-fried Black Angus fillet, with braised Puy lentils, roasted shallots
d red wine sauce, while a blackcurrant parfait served with raspberry
ampagne jelly and a blueberry sorbet might feature at dessert.

Chef: Martyn Pearn **Owners:** Mr & Mrs D Blakstad **Times:** 12-2/7-9, Closed L Mon Tue Sat (lunch by reservation only), D 24-26 Dec **Prices:** Fixed L £19.50, Starter £6.95-£11.95, Main £18.95-£26.95, Dessert £6.95, Coffee £3, Min/Water £3.25, Service included **Wine:** 75 bottles over £20, 11 bottles under £20, 9 by the glass (£4.55-£5.95) **Notes:** Sun L 3 courses £21.50, Vegetarian available, Smart casual **Seats:** 64, Pr/dining room 20 **Smoking:** N/Sm in restaurant **Children:** Menu, Portions **Rooms:** 14 (14 en suite) ★★★ HL **Directions:** From Wolverhampton take A454 (Bridgnorth road), from M54 junct 4 take A442 towards Kidderminster **Parking:** 30

England

TELFORD *continued* MAP 10 SJ60

Hadley Park House

Mediterranean, Pacific Rim

Conservatory restaurant offering modern cuisine

☎ 01952 677269 Hadley Park TF1 6QJ
e-mail: info@hadleypark.co.uk
web: www.hadleypark.co.uk

This Georgian mansion was built by Thomas Telford's chief engineer. The airy conservatory dining room complements the traditional oak-panelled bar. Modern British cooking is displayed through an eclectic range of dishes, making good use of quality locally-sourced ingredients. The menu changes seasonally but you might find a starter like cream of natural smoked haddock and chive soup, topped with a poached egg. Follow this with a main course like poached fillets of lemon sole with crushed potato, leek and carrot spaghetti and roast shellfish sauce.

Chef: Tim Wesley **Owners:** Mark & Geraldine Lewis **Times:** 12-2/7-9.30, Closed 1-7 Jan, Closed L Sat, D Sun **Prices:** Fixed L £12-£16, Starter £4.50-£7.50, Main £10.95-£18.50, Dessert £5, Coffee £1.95, Min/Water £4 **Wine:** 13 bottles over £20, 25 bottles under £20, 7 by the glass (£4.25-£4.40) **Notes:** Vegetarian available, Civ Wed 80 **Seats:** 80, Pr/dining room 12 **Smoking:** N/Sm in restaurant, Air con **Children:** Menu, Portions **Rooms:** 12 (12 en suite) ★★★ HL **Directions:** M54 junct 5 take A5 Rampart Way, at rdbt take A442 towards Hortonwood, over double rdbt, next rbdt take 2nd exit, hotel at end of this lane **Parking:** 30

WORFIELD MAP 10 SO79

Old Vicarage Hotel and Restaurant

see page 407

SOMERSET

BATH MAP 04 ST76

The Bath Priory Hotel and Restaurant

see opposite

Combe Grove Manor Hotel & Country Club

International

Georgian country-house hotel dining

☎ 01225 834644 Brassknocker Hill, Monkton Combe BA2 7HS
e-mail: julianebbutt@combegrovemanor.com
web: www.combegrovemanor.com

A delightful hotel with magnificent views and a wealth of leisure and therapy treatments to tempt guests. The Eden Bistro (open for lunch and dinner daily) is located in the basement with adjoining terrace and gardens where guests can dine alfresco in summer. The main restaurant - the elegant Georgian Dining Room - with its high ceiling and large windows, has notable countryside views and offers finer dining in a more traditional style. Open on Thursday, Friday and Saturday evenings only, its menu includes the likes of a wonderful mushroom risotto with rocket and truffle oil.

continued

Chef: Elvis Myers **Owners:** Paul Morgan **Times:** 12-2/7-9.30, Closed Mon-Wed, Closed L Thu-Sat, D Sun **Prices:** Food prices not confirmed for 2007. Please telephone for details **Wine:** 25 bottles over £20, 38 bottles under £20, 6 by the glass (£3.50-£4) **Notes:** Vegetarian available, Dress Restrictions, No trainers or jeans, Civ Wed 50 **Seats:** 40, Pr/dining room 90 **Smoking:** N/Sm in restaurant **Children:** Min 12 yrs **Rooms:** 42 (42 en suite) ★★★★ **Directions:** Telephone for directions **Parking:** 100

Macdonald Bath Spa Hotel, Vellore Restaurant

British, International

Regency elegance, attentive service and accomplished cuisine

☎ 0870 400 8222 Sydney Rd BA2 6JF
e-mail: sales.bathspa@macdonald-hotels.co.uk
web: www.bathspahotel.com

One of the city's most luxurious hotels, this sumptuously elegant hotel is rich with neo-classical stylings, from the grandiose entrance to the murals that adorn the two restaurants - the conservatory style Alfresco and the opulent fine-dining venue, The Vellore. Dinner at the latter is the best showcase for the kitchen's culinary skills and for the efficient and entertaining service: there's a sommelier on hand to guide your choice of wine, while bread is carved from the trolley, for example. Food is both accomplished and appealing - you might expect a starter of smoked fish blinis, sour cream and keta caviar, followed by wild cod fillet with Jerusalem artichoke, cauliflower cream and red wine essence.

Chef: Andrew Hamer **Owners:** Macdonald Hotels PLC **Times:** 12-2/7-9.45, Closed L Mon-Sat **Prices:** Fixed L £14.95, Fixed D £37.50, Starter £10-£13, Main £22-£30, Dessert £7-£10, Coffee £4.95, Min/Water £4, Service optional **Wine:** all bottles over £20, 6 by the glass (£7.20-£9.95) **Notes:** Vegetarian available, Dress Restrictions, No jeans preferred, Civ Wed 120 **Seats:** 80, Pr/dining room 120 **Smoking:** N/Sm in restaurant **Children:** Menu, Portions **Rooms:** 104 (104 en suite) ★★★★★ HL **Directions:** A4 and follow city centre signs for 1m. At lights turn left towards A36. Turn right after pedestrian crossing then left into Sydney Place. Hotel 200yds on right **Parking:** 160

The Bath Priory Hotel and Restaurant

BATH MAP 04 ST76

French NOTABLE WINE LIST

Intimate country-house restaurant with innovative cooking

☎ 01225 331922 Weston Rd BA1 2XT
e-mail: mail@thebathpriory.co.uk
web: www.thebathpriory.co.uk

Although only a few minutes from the city, set on a tree-lined residential road behind high walls, you'll find all the trappings of a country-house retreat at this Gothic-style mansion set in 4 acres of impeccably maintained gardens. The style is luxurious and sophisticated, with a collection of oil paintings adorning walls, deep sofas and roaring winter fires, yet the mood is thoroughly relaxed with a friendly but professional approach from staff. The intimate, formal restaurant continues the theme, with white-clothed tables, deep burgundy and gold soft furnishings, high ceilings and views over the gardens.

The kitchen, under chef Chris Horridge, (ex Le Manoir aux Quat' Saisons, see entry) shows pedigree, delivering innovative dishes created and presented with imagination and flair. Tip-top ingredients, interesting combinations, clean flavours and high skill deliver on the contemporary French repertoire. Perhaps slow-poached saddle of fallow deer with sweet potato, liquorice reduction and lovage oil, brill with lentils, bacon, fennel purée and fennel pollen foam, and to finish - nougatine leaves with manuka honey and lavender truffled goat's cheese with arugula cream.

Notable Wine List: A beautifully presented extensive wine list with good tasting notes throughout, organically produced wines highlighted and a notable half-bottle list.

Chef: Chris Horridge
Owners: Mr A Brownsword
Times: 12-1.45/7-9.45
Prices: Fixed L £20-£25, Fixed D £52-£57, Starter £8-£13, Main £12-£17, Dessert £5-£10, Coffee £4, Min/Water £3, Service optional
Wine: 380 bottles over £20, 30 bottles under £20, 7 by the glass (£5-£10)
Notes: Tasting menu £70, Dress Restrictions, No jeans or T-shirts, Civ Wed 64
Seats: 60, Pr/dining room 64
Smoking: N/Sm in restaurant
Children: Menu, Portions
Rooms: 31 (31 en suite) ★★★★ HL
Directions: Telephone for directions
Parking: 40

BATH *continued* MAP 04 ST76

The Olive Tree at the Queensberry Hotel

Modern British NOTABLE WINE LIST

Enjoyable restaurant dining in stylish hotel

☎ 01225 447928 Russel St BA1 2QF
e-mail: reservations@thequeensberry.co.uk
web: www.thequeensberry.co.uk

The Queensberry is a stylish, 18th-century townhouse hotel hidden in the centre of Georgian Bath. Less formal than the hotel, The Olive Tree restaurant has modern décor with wooden floors and soft grey walls hung with modern artworks. Skilful lighting belies this dining room's basement location. Brown leather banquettes and unclothed tables add to the relaxed feel. Attentive service from polo-shirted staff is notable. Modern British dishes are given a Mediterranean accent. Expect flavour-filled starters of scallops, squash, parmesan purée and chorizo oil and some eclectic combinations such as the venison loin with Devils on Horseback. Flavours are well managed and clear throughout. Puddings include a rich prune and Calvados crème brûlée.

Notable Wine List: An interesting and personal selection of wines categorised by drinking styles.

Chef: Marc Salmon **Owners:** Mr & Mrs Beere **Times:** 12-2/7-10, Closed L Mon **Prices:** Fixed L £14.50, Starter £6.25-£9.50, Main £15.50-£23.95, Dessert £7, Coffee £2.95, Min/Water £3.25, Service optional, Group min 10 service 10% **Wine:** 157 bottles over £20, 26 bottles under £20, 12 by the glass (£3.75-£9.95) **Notes:** Vegetarian available **Seats:** 60, Pr/dining room 30 **Smoking:** N/Sm in restaurant, Air con **Children:** Portions **Rooms:** 29 (29 en suite) ★★★ HL **Directions:** City centre. 100yds N of Assembly Rooms in Lower Lansdown **Parking:** Residents' valet parking; Street pay/display

continued

Royal Crescent Hotel - Pimpernels

see below

Sakura Restaurant

Japanese

Cook-it-yourself Nabe cuisine, authentic Japanese elegance

☎ 01225 422100 The Windsor Hotel, 69 Great Pulteney St BA2 4DL
e-mail: sales@bathwindsorhotel.com
web: www.bathwindsorhotel.com

A lovely Georgian building retaining much charm and character. The Sakura Restaurant is downstairs with windows that look out across the Japanese Zen garden to parkland beyond. In keeping with an authentic, specialist restaurant, there is an element of 'cook-it-yourself' choosing from beef, tofu and vegetables or a seafood option all cooked as a Japanese-style fondue. The special Nabe tables are made of white wood with a central gas hob and iron cooking pot where you do the cooking. Authentic Japanese drinks include specialist beers, hot or cold sake served in a wooden box and Japanese plum wine.

continued

Royal Crescent Hotel - Pimpernels

BATH MAP 04 ST76

British

Contemporary fine dining in Georgian splendour

☎ 01225 823333 16 Royal Crescent BA1 2LS
e-mail: info@royalcrescent.co.uk
web: www.royalcrescent.co.uk

The sweeping curve of the city's internationally famous Royal Crescent - John Wood the Younger's masterpiece of Georgian architecture - provides the sublime setting for this elegant hotel. Discreetly secreted away, it's recognisable by the liveried doorman, while inside continues the fanfare of Georgian splendour, with impressive paintings and artefacts. The fine-dining Pimpernel's restaurant matches the elegance and is set in the former dower house that overlooks the peaceful gardens, where, on warm summer evenings, one can dine alfresco. Service is commendable, professional and attentive and includes the helpful skills of a sommelier, while the kitchen's contemporary British approach lives up to the billing, is highly accomplished and packed with interest. Fine textures, balanced combinations, clean unfussy flavours and precision parade on a thoroughly appealing fixed-price repertoire. Take slow-braised shoulder of lamb with roast lamb rump accompanied by aubergine caviar and provençale vegetables, or perhaps roast John Dory with cod brandade, caramelised salsify and a

Sauternes butter sauce, and to finish, maybe try the hot chocolate fondant served with white chocolate sauce.

Chef: Steven Blake **Owners:** von Essen Hotels **Times:** 12.30-2.30/7-10.30, Closed times vary at Xmas & New Year **Prices:** Fixed L £18, Fixed D £55, Coffee £3.75, Min/Water £3.75, Service included **Wine:** 227 bottles over £20, 12 by the glass (£5.50-£9) **Notes:** Sun L £25, Vegetarian available, Dress Restrictions, Smart casual, no jeans, Civ Wed 60 **Seats:** 65 Pr/dining room 36 **Smoking:** N/Sm in restaurant, Air con **Children:** Menu **Rooms:** 45 (45 en suite) ★★★★★ **Directions:** Please telephone for directions **Parking:** 17

Chef: Sachiko Bush **Owners:** Cary & Sachiko Bush **Times:** 6-9.30 (Last Orders 11), Closed Xmas, Sun-Mon, Closed L all week **Prices:** Fixed D £27-£30, Coffee £2.50, Min/Water £3.50 **Wine:** 8 bottles over £20, 8 bottles under £20, 2 by the glass (£2.50-£3.50) **Seats:** 24 **Smoking:** N/Sm in restaurant **Children:** Min 12 yrs **Rooms:** 14 (14 en suite) ★★★ TH **Directions:** From E & N take M4 junct 18 towards Bath. From S & W approach Bath on A36 **Parking:** 10

Woods Restaurant

British, French

Peaceful setting for relaxed city dining

☎ 01225 314812 9-13 Alfred St BA1 2QX
web: www.woods.co.uk

This well-established restaurant is a short walk from the historic town centre. It has a small reception area leading to the restaurant which is a large wooden-floored room decorated with horse racing prints on the walls. The cooking style is simple and uncluttered, making good use of well-sourced produce in the likes of rich lamb casserole with fresh rosemary, garlic and winter root vegetables and basil-marinated sardine fillets with yellow peppers and red onion pipérade. Service is relaxed, and there is a short lunch menu and a more extensive carte to choose from.

Times: 6-10, Closed 26 Dec, 1 Jan, Sun **Directions:** Telephone for directions

Fire House Rotisserie

☎ 01225 482070 2 John St BA1 2JL

Grills, gourmet pizzas and vegetarian dishes in a relaxed setting.

Fishworks

☎ 01225 448707 Green St BA1 2JY

Exciting fish dishes from this café above a fishmonger's.

Loch Fyne Restaurant

☎ 01225 750120 24 Milsom St BA1 1DG

Quality seafood chain.

No. 5 Bistro

☎ 01225 444499 5 Argyle St BA2 4BA
web: www.theaa.com/restaurants/114056.html

Modern British cooking in a relaxed, informal atmosphere. Specials change daily, main menu changes seasonally. There's a great 'bring your own wine' offer - no corkage - on Monday and Tuesday evenings.

Tilleys Bistro

☎ 01225 484200 North Pde, Passage BA1 1NX

Tremendous variety, including an extensive vegetarian choice.

BRIDGWATER MAP 04 ST23

Walnut Tree Hotel

Modern British

Relaxed dining in a restored coaching inn

☎ 01278 662255 & 0845 370 6000 Fore St, North Petherton TA6 6QA
e-mail: info@walnuttreehotel.com
web: www.walnuttreehotel.com

An inn has been on this site since at least 1620 and the present day version is a lovingly restored 18th-century coaching inn. Inside, the décor is Mediterranean in style with soft yellows and blues. Formal dining is in the Lemon Tree dining room, while the more casual eating option is the contemporary Duke's Bistro. The restaurant menu features a mix of traditional and modern British and European cooking, simply cooked and carefully presented. A typical main course might be braised shank of lamb with parsnip purée, roasted root vegetables, rosemary and redcurrant jus.

Chef: Nathan Brown **Owners:** Acorn Hotels Ltd **Times:** 12-2/6.30-9.30 **Prices:** Starter £3.75-£7.95, Main £9.95-£15.95, Dessert £4.50, Coffee £1.75, Min/Water £3.50, Service optional **Wine:** 8 bottles over £20, 26 bottles under £20, 11 by the glass (£2.95-£6.25) **Notes:** Sun L 2 courses £9.95, 3 courses £12.95, Civ Wed 80 **Seats:** 90, Pr/dining room 100 **Smoking:** N/Sm in restaurant, Air con **Children:** Portions **Rooms:** 33 (33 en suite) ★★★ **Directions:** M5 junct 24 follow North Petherton, 1st rdbt turn left, 1m on right in village **Parking:** 70

BRUTON MAP 04 ST63

Bruton House Restaurant

British V NEW

Fine dining and contemporary style in historic village

☎ 01749 813395 High St BA10 0AA
e-mail: info@brutonhouse.co.uk
web: www.brutonhouse.co.uk

The spacious bar and drawing room area are comfortably furnished with sofas and armchairs so you can relax before or after dining. The elegant restaurant retains character features including a large stone fireplace and oak beams, along with more contemporary touches such as bright artwork, wood flooring, and leather chairs. Service is formal but also friendly. The accomplished and passionate chef-proprietors are making a strong reputation for themselves here. There is a clear focus on simple, seasonal cuisine with commitment to local producers. British produce such as sirloin of Bromham beef and Applecross Bay langoustines feature on the menu. Expect mains such as loin of Clarendon Estate venison with caramelised endive and celeriac purée.

Chef: Scott Eggleton & James Andrews **Owners:** Christie-Miller Andrews Ltd **Times:** 12-2/7-9.30, Closed 1 Jan, Sun-Mon **Prices:** Fixed D £35, Starter £4.50-£7, Main £10.95-£16, Dessert £5-£7, Coffee £1.75, Min/Water £3.50, Service optional, Group min 8 service 10% **Wine:** 12 bottles under £20, 12 by the glass (£3.50-£5) **Notes:** Vegetarian menu **Seats:** 30 **Smoking:** N/Sm in restaurant **Children:** Portions **Directions:** A303, exit signed Bruton, follow signs to Bruton, restaurant at end of High St, opposite pharmacy **Parking:** on street

England

BRUTON *continued* MAP 04 ST63

Truffles

British

Creeper clad, intimate restaurant in a charming village

☎ 01749 812255 95 High St BA10 0AR
e-mail: mark@trufflesbruton.co.uk
web: www.trufflesbruton.co.uk

It may have two floors but this pleasant rural restaurant is economical with its tables, no doubt to ensure that guests have a comfortable dining experience and the proprietors have more time to spend giving an extremely friendly service. The cooking has a modern British feel using local ingredients wherever possible with influences coming from all over the world - Middle Eastern, for example, in a confit duck leg glazed with pomegranate molasses starter. A typical main from the more serious evening menu might include fillet of wild sea bass with celeriac dauphinoise and bouillabaisse sauce.

Chef: Mark Chambers **Owners:** Mr & Mrs Chambers **Times:** 12-2/7-9.30, Closed Mon, Closed L Tue-Wed, D Sun **Prices:** Fixed L fr £12.95, Fixed D fr £28.95, Coffee £2, Min/Water £3.25, Service optional **Notes:** Vegetarian available, Dress Restrictions, Smart casual preferred **Seats:** 30, Pr/dining room 10 **Smoking:** N/Sm in restaurant, Air con **Children:** Portions **Directions:** Near A303, in town centre, at start of one-way system, on left **Parking:** On street opposite

---

CHARD MAP 04 ST30

Bellplot House Hotel & Thomas's Restaurant

Modern European

Handsome Georgian property offering West Country fare

☎ 01460 62600 High St TA20 1QB
e-mail: info@bellplothouse.co.uk
web: www.bellplothouse.co.uk

This Grade II listed townhouse originally stood on a bell-shaped piece of land - hence the name. It was built for four spinster sisters and owned for over 250 years by mostly ladies (who give their names to the bedrooms). There is an emphasis on good friendly service in the Georgian-style dining room, where guests enjoy drinking from Royal Brierley cut-glass crystal. Dishes, based on fresh, local (suppliers are listed on the back of the menu) and seasonal ingredients, offer traditional flavours with a modern twist: tenderloin of pork on a bed of cannellini beans, dates, hazelnuts and mustard.

Chef: Thomas Jones **Owners:** Dennis Betty, Thomas Jones **Times:** 7-9, Closed Sun, Closed L all week **Prices:** Starter £4.50-£6.75, Main £12.50-£15.75, Dessert £4.50-£6.25, Coffee £2.10, Min/Water £1, Service optional **Wine:** 3 bottles over £20, 12 bottles under £20, 3 by the glass (£3.10) **Notes:** Vegetarian available **Seats:** 30 **Smoking:** N/Sm in restaurant **Children:** Menu, Portions **Rooms:** 7 (7 en suite) ◆◆◆◆◆ **Directions:** M5 junct 25,/A358 signposted Yeovil. At rdbt take 4th exit A358 from Taunton, follow signs to Chard town centre. 500 mtrs from Guildhall **Parking:** 12

CREWKERNE MAP 04 ST40

Kempsters Restaurant

Modern British V NEW

Restored Somerset longhouse providing excellent cooking using local produce

continued

☎ 01935 881768 Lower St, West Chinnock TA18 7PT
e-mail: debbie@kempsters.fslife.co.uk

A lovingly restored Somerset longhouse with heavy new oak doors, old beams, pine and slate floors and Somerset country life black and white photographs on the walls. Comfortable furnishings and warm décor reflect the high standards and warm welcome offered here. Cooking is accomplished making excellent use of predominantly locally and regionally sourced ingredients, right down to local tea and coffee merchants. At dinner, enjoy canapés on arrival then tuck into a starter of hand-dived seared scallops and main course of rack of Dorset lamb with mustard grain mash. Vegetarians are well catered for and there is a good selection of cider brandy.

Chef: Charles Kempster, Sarah Hunt **Owners:** Charles & Debbie Kempster **Times:** 12-3/7-11.30, Closed 2 wks after 14 Feb, Mon, Closed D Sun **Prices:** Fixed L £11.95-£12.95, Starter £4.50-£7.95, Main £14.95-£19.95, Dessert £4.50-£4.95, Coffee £2.75, Min/Water £3.50, Service optional, Group min 10 service 10% **Wine:** 29 bottles over £20, 19 bottles under £20, 8 by the glass (£3.50-£5.95) **Notes:** Sun L 1 course £8.95, Vegetarian menu, Dress Restrictions, Smart dress **Seats:** 27 **Smoking:** N/Sm in restaurant **Children:** Min 12 yrs, Portions **Rooms:** 3 (1 en suite) ◆◆◆◆ **Directions:** From A303 take Crewkerne junct, follow A356 to Chiselborough/West Chinnock, turn left, over hill into West Chinnock **Parking:** 15

DULVERTON MAP 03 SS92

Tarr Farm Inn

Modern British, Mediterranean

Historic inn with focus on excellent eating

☎ 01643 851507 Tarr Steps, Exmoor National Park TA22 9PY
e-mail: enquiries@tarrfarm.co.uk
web: www.tarrfarm.co.uk

Almost hidden away from the outside world, this riverside inn really is the place to escape from it all. Dating back to the 16th century the inn sits in a wooded valley at Exmoor's heart, and offers its guests relaxed and informal dining in addition to stylish accommodation. Any meal here is memorable and the short menus are full of locally sourced ingredients, as in a starter of seared River Fowey scallops, cauliflower purée and mild curry cappuccino, followed by pan-fried fillet of Exmoor beef with tomato Tatin. Enticingly, puddings come with dessert wine recommendations.

Chef: Jerzy Rozputynski **Owners:** Richard Benn & Judy Carless **Times:** 12-3/6.30-12 **Prices:** Starter £4.50-£7.95, Main £11.95-£17.95, Dessert £3.50-£4.95, Coffee £1.85, Min/Water £1, Service optional **Wine:** 61 bottles over £20, 39 bottles under £20, 7 by the glass (£3.50-£4.50) **Notes:** Monthly Seafood night, 5 courses £30 **Seats:** 45, Pr/dining room 20 **Smoking:** N/Sm area **Children:** Min 14 yrs D, Portions **Rooms:** 9 (9 en suite) ◆◆◆◆◆ **Directions:** Leave M5 junct 27, signed Tiverton. Follow signs to Dulverton, from Dulverton take B3223 signed Tarr Steps for approx 6.5m **Parking:** 40

Woods Bar & Dining Room

British NEW

Woodman's retreat with a passion for good food and wine

☎ 01398 324007 4 Banks Square TA22 9BU

Food-lovers are beating a path to this charming pub-cum-restaurant where the passion for good food and wine is obvious. Inside, a

continued

ovely log fire warms the cosy interior, which is split-level with a bar ıt the top of the restaurant. Clean, accurate cooking is the draw here vith a great choice of eating options from simple starters or light unches, rustic rolls, woodman's lunch or the full carte. Typical dishes nclude a main course of loin of Somerset pork, slow roasted belly vith black pudding, apple jam and port jus. Desserts are to die for, ry assiette of citrus fruit - lemon posset, orange pannacotta, lime ranita. Ask for help in choosing a wine and you won't be lisappointed.

wners: Paddy Groves **Times:** 12-2.30/7-9.30 **Prices:** Food prices not onfirmed for 2007. Please telephone for details **Directions:** Telephone or directions

)UNSTER MAP 03 SS94

The Luttrell Arms Hotel

raditional British

listoric setting for interesting dishes using fresh local roduce

01643 821555 High St TA24 6SG
-mail: info@luttrellarms.fsnet.co.uk
veb: www.luttrellarms.co.uk/main.htm

he historic setting lends plenty of character to the restaurant within ais 15th-century hotel. The slightly split-level restaurant has a ontemporary, quality feel with attractive styling and comfortable eating while the bar area has some lovely old features and interesting ooks and crannies. Friendly local staff offer professional service. The ıenu changes every few weeks and is supplemented by a daily pecial and vegetarian option. Dishes are straightforward using good ombinations with the emphasis on fresh local produce. You can try shes using Exmoor venison, Somerset prawns, local pheasant or xmoor beef, depending on the season.

mes: 12-3/7-10 **Rooms:** 28 (28 en suite) ★★★ HL **Directions:** A39 Minehead, Turn S towards Tiverton on the A396. Hotel is in centre of unster Village

XFORD MAP 03 SS83

Crown Hotel

lodern British

/ell-loved country inn

01643 831554 Park St TA24 7PP
-mail: info@crownhotelexmoor.co.uk
/eb: www.crownhotelexmoor.co.uk

continued

The country sports set frequents this famous old hotel set in lovely gardens in the middle of Exmoor. Others find it irresistible too, and the welcome is warm and genuine. Reputedly the moor's oldest coaching inn, it has a cocktail bar, and romantic candlelit dining room and formal table settings where the traditional menus are perused. Exmoor lamb is sure to be found, perhaps served as pot-baked shoulder with pea purée, along with pan-fried loin of local deer with plum sauce and honey roast figs. Starters like seared west coast scallops, cep cream, pancetta and buttered leeks are a special strength, and old favourites such as sticky toffee pudding still have their fervent supporters. Finish with coffee and chocolate truffle.

Chef: David Errington **Owners:** Mr C Kirkbride & S & D Whittaker **Times:** 7-9, Closed L all week **Prices:** Fixed D £32.50, Coffee £2.50, Min/Water £3.95, Service optional **Wine:** 21 bottles over £20, 19 bottles under £20, 8 by the glass (£3.95-£6.25) **Notes:** Vegetarian available, Dress Restrictions, Smart casual, no jeans, T-shirts, swimwear **Seats:** 30, Pr/dining room 14 **Smoking:** N/Sm in restaurant **Children:** Min 7 yrs, Portions **Rooms:** 17 (17 en suite) ★★★ HL **Directions:** From Taunton take A38 to A358. Turn left at B3224 & follow signs to Exford **Parking:** 30

HINTON CHARTERHOUSE MAP 04 ST75

Homewood Park

Traditional British

Fine food in a country-house setting

☎ 01225 723731 BA2 7TB
e-mail: info@homewoodpark.co.uk
web: www.homewoodpark.co.uk

All the delights associated with country-house life are experienced to the full at Homewood Park: stunning grounds, comfortable lounges, attentive service and a dining room with garden views. Here, high-backed chairs and fine cutlery, china and glassware enhance the culinary experience. It is clear from the menus that food is a major focus: seared foie gras with ratte potatoes and fantastic truffle sauce, and an accomplished baked turbot in pastry with parsley purée, lobster and bordelaise sauce. Dishes are inventive, cooking is precise and the presentation very appealing to the eye. Lighter meals are also available in the bar and lounges.

Chef: Graham Chatham **Owners:** von Essen Hotels **Times:** 12-2.30/7-11 **Prices:** Fixed L £13.50-£18.50, Fixed D fr £39.50, Starter £12.50, Main £23.50, Dessert £8, Coffee £2.75, Min/Water £2.75, Service optional **Wine:** 213 bottles over £20, 21 bottles under £20, 17 by the glass (£5-£6) **Notes:** Tasting menu £47.50, Sun L 3 courses £22.50, Vegetarian available, Dress Restrictions, Smart casual, no jeans or trainers, Civ Wed 50 **Seats:** 60, Pr/dining room 40 **Smoking:** N/Sm in restaurant **Children:** Portions **Rooms:** 19 (19 en suite) ★★★ HL **Directions:** 6m SE of Bath off A36, turn left at second sign for Freshford **Parking:** 50

England

HOLFORD MAP 04 ST14

Combe House Hotel

Modern British

Punchy flavours and fresh local ingredients in a relaxed and comfortable dining room

☎ 01278 741382 TA5 1RZ
e-mail: info@combehouse.co.uk
web: www.combehouse.co.uk

Tucked away in a quiet valley in the Quantock Hills, this peaceful Somerset country-house hotel is set in 4 acres of tranquil gardens with an organic kitchen garden providing the chef with vegetables and soft fruit. Other ingredients are sourced locally - meat and game from local farms and shoots, fish from Brixham and of course Somerset cheeses. The menu is modern British in style with international influences dotted throughout - seared scallops and baked oysters Florentine to start, for example, then slow-braised shoulder of lamb with apple and mint jelly as a main.

Chef: Lawrence Pratt **Owners:** Andrew Ryan **Times:** 12-2.30/7-9 **Prices:** Starter £4.95-£8.50, Main £14.95-£18.95, Dessert £4.95, Coffee £2, Min/Water £2.75, Service optional **Wine:** 6 bottles over £20, 15 bottles under £20, 2 by the glass (£4) **Notes:** Vegetarian available, Civ Wed 40 **Seats:** 40, Pr/dining room 8 **Smoking:** N/Sm in restaurant **Children:** Portions **Rooms:** 17 (16 en suite) ★★ HL **Directions:** Telephone for directions

HUNSTRETE MAP 04 ST66

Hunstrete House Hotel

Modern French

Contemporary dining in an English country-house setting

☎ 01761 490490 BS39 4NS
e-mail: reception@hunstretehouse.co.uk
web: www.hunstretehouse.co.uk

continued

A deer park on the edge of the Mendips, a Georgian mansion, period paintings and furniture come together to create a quintessential country house atmosphere. The elegant Regency dining room has white linen and formal settings. An adjoining, enclosed courtyard is used for dining in summer. Cooking is contemporary in style and uses the best of local, seasonal ingredients. Menus comprise well thought-out dishes, accurately executed. Start with ham hock and foie gras terrine with pea purée and crispy bacon salad, before a main course of poussin with pancetta gnocchi, consommé and broad beans. Finish with a trio of griottine cherries with clotted cream and warm cherry soup.

Chef: Matthew Lord **Owners:** Culloden Associates **Times:** 12-2/7-9.30 **Prices:** Fixed L fr £15.95, Fixed D fr £47.95, Service added but optional 5% **Wine:** 15 bottles under £20, 8 by the glass (£4.50-£8.50) **Notes:** Tasting menu £49.95, Sun L £24.95, Vegetarian available, Dress Restrictions, No jeans smart casual, Civ Wed 60 **Seats:** 35, Pr/dining room 50 **Smoking:** N/Sm in restaurant **Children:** Menu, Portions **Rooms:** 25 (25 en suite) ★★★ CHH **Directions:** On A368 - 8 miles from Bath **Parking:** 50

MIDSOMER NORTON MAP 04 ST65

The Moody Goose at The Old Priory

Modern British NEW

Charming, characterful setting to enjoy innovative flavours and combinations

☎ 01761 416784 & 410846 Church Square BA3 2HX
e-mail: info@theoldpriory.co.uk
web: www.theoldpriory.co.uk

Dating back to 1152, the Old Priory is reputedly one of the oldest houses in Somerset, and is tucked away in a quiet square. Period features have been lovingly restored and include inglenook fireplaces, flagstone floors and oak beams. The main restaurant has pale walls adorned with French watercolours creating a bright, airy feel. The menus are designed with an emphasis firmly on fresh seasonal produce, locally sourced where possible. Herbs, fruit and vegetables come from the Priory's own kitchen garden. Classical French cuisine influences the cooking with interesting dishes such as parfait of foie gras with pickled wild mushrooms and quince jelly, and rondel of Aberdeen Angus beef fillet with a crepinette of oxtail and Madeira jus.

Chef: Stephen Shore **Owners:** Stephen & Victoria Shore **Times:** 12-1.30/7-9.30, Closed 1 Jan, BHs except Good Friday, Sun **Prices:** Fixed L £13.50-£21.50, Fixed D fr £23.50, Starter £8-£11, Main £17-£19.50, Dessert £6.50, Coffee £2.50, Min/Water £3, Service optional **Wine:** 79 bottles over £20, 16 bottles under £20, 9 by the glass (£3.50-£4.75) **Notes:** Vegetarian available **Seats:** 36, Pr/dining room 16 **Smoking:** N/Sm in restaurant, Air con **Children:** Portions **Rooms:** 7 (7 en suite) ★★ **Directions:** Down Midsomer Norton High Street, right at lights, right at rdbt in front of church **Parking:** 14

Andrews on the Weir

PORLOCK MAP 03 SS84

Modern European V

Great local produce in superb bayside location

☎ 01643 863300 Porlock Weir TA24 8PB
e-mail: information@andrewsontheweir.co.uk
web: www.andrewsontheweir.co.uk

In a delightful setting right on the water's edge overlooking Porlock Bay and the weir, Andrews is the epitome of the restaurant-with-rooms genre, a charming Georgian building decorated in classic country-house mode with a singular dedication to serving fine food and freshest ingredients that make the dining experience memorable. The restaurant itself is light and elegant with a relaxed, informal atmosphere and large windows providing splendid views over the harbour. Service is welcoming, attentive and friendly yet precise, in tune with the atmosphere and kitchen's approach.

Chef-patron Andrew Dixon's modern European cooking style is underpinned by classical roots and inspired by carefully sourced, high-quality local produce that's intelligently simply prepared with flair to let clear, clean flavours shine without unnecessary over-complication. High skill, attention to detail, balanced combinations and spot-on execution parade on the fixed-price repertoire of lunch, carte and vegetarian menus. Expect Exmoor lamb, braised for eight hours and perhaps served with pan-fried sweetbreads, confit onions, creamed potatoes and braising juices, while a rich Valrhona chocolate tart with mascarpone cream might provide the finish.

Chef: Andrew Dixon
Owners: A Dixon, Rodney Sens
Times: 12-3/6.30-10, Closed Jan, Mon, Tue
Prices: Fixed L fr £15.50, Fixed D fr £38.50, Coffee £3.50, Min/Water £2.50, Service optional, Group min 7 service 10%
Wine: 42 bottles over £20, 22 bottles under £20, 7 by the glass (£3.60-£6.05)
Notes: Tasting menu £55, Sun L £24.50, Vegetarian menu
Seats: 40
Smoking: N/Sm in restaurant
Children: Min 12 yrs, Portions
Rooms: 5 (5 en suite) ★★★★ RR
Directions: From M5 junct 25 follow A358 towards Williton, then A39 through Porlock & onto Porlock Weir. Hotel in 1.5m
Parking: 5

England

PORLOCK MAP 03 SS84

Andrews on the Weir

see page 415

The Oaks Hotel

British, French

Elegant Edwardian house dining with sea views

☎ 01643 862265 TA24 8ES
e-mail: info@oakshotel.co.uk
web: www.oakshotel.co.uk

A small hotel overlooking Porlock towards the sea, The Oaks is personally run by a husband and wife team, Tim and Ann Riley. The restaurant is light with large windows enabling virtually every table to enjoy the splendid view. The daily-changing menu places the emphasis firmly on local produce in simply prepared dishes. A smoked bacon, mushroom and goat's cheese starter is particularly enjoyable, in crisp, thin, buttery pastry served with mixed leaves. Roast fillet of Devon beef and a selection of local fish are popular main courses.

Times: 7-8, Closed Nov-Mar **Rooms:** 8 (8 en suite) ★★★
Directions: At bottom of Dunstersteepe Road, on left on entering Porlock from Minehead.

SHEPTON MALLET MAP 04 ST64

Charlton House

Rosettes not confirmed at time of going to press

Modern British V

Innovative cuisine in wonderfully elegant surroundings

☎ 01749 342008 Charlton Rd BA4 4PR
e-mail: enquiries@charltonhouse.com
web: www.charltonhouse.com

continued

It's no surprise that this chic country-house hotel set in delightful grounds exudes style and atmosphere, owned as it is by the founders of the internationally acclaimed design label Mulberry. Decorated with imagination and theatrical panache, exquisite Mulberry fabrics and leather furnishings abound, while the smart and spacious conservatory-style Mulberry Restaurant comes with quality table settings and overlooks the manicured lawns. The kitchen pays due respect to high-quality local produce, much from the hotel's own organic and rare breed farm, Sharpham Park. Dishes impress with their intelligent simplicity, skill, innovation and execution. Take a loin of Sharpham venison with winter fruit couscous, braised haunch and chestnut suet pudding and kidney with sage and bacon, or soft-poached rabbit loin, cannelloni of leg and dates, with squash purée and a ragout of pearl barley and vegetables. Single Estate dark chocolate, passionfruit and textured chocolate dessert or the tangerine tasting plate of jelly, ice, posset and tart might follow. A seven-course tasting menu and vegetarian menu bolster the carte. The wine list is extensive and personally chosen by the proprietor. Service is attentive and professional. Afternoon tea is a tradition here and the spa the ultimate in pampering, rounding off the experience.
At the time of going to press a new chef was in the process of being appointed. Fine hotel standards are destined to remain the same.

Owners: Roger Saul **Times:** 12.30-2.30/7.30-10.15 **Prices:** Fixed L £22-£24, Fixed D £45-£60, Starter £8-£10, Main £12-£14, Dessert £6-£8, Coffee £4.50, Min/Water £3, Service optional, Group min 8 service 10% **Wine:** 121 bottles over £20, 7 bottles under £20, 11 by the glass (£4.80-£9 **Notes:** Tasting menu 7 courses £65, £90 with wine for each course, Vegetarian menu, Civ Wed 120 **Seats:** 84, Pr/dining room 70 **Smoking:** N/Sm in restaurant, Air con **Children:** Menu, Portions **Rooms:** 26 (26 en suite) ★★★★ HL **Directions:** On A361. Hotel is located 1m before Shepton Mallet **Parking:** 70

STOKE SUB HAMDON MAP 04 ST41

The Priory House Restaurant

Modern British NEW

Smart high street restaurant for relaxed, enjoyable dining

☎ 01935 822826 1 High St TA14 6PP
e-mail: reservations@theprioryhouserestaurant.co.uk
web: www.theprioryhouserestaurant.co.uk

A high street 'shop front' location painted in an attractive blue. Inside the blue and beige colour scheme continues with a small bar and lounge area in addition to the smart restaurant with pretty garden terrace. Accomplished modern British cooking makes good use of local meat and game. Typical choices include seared hand-dived scallops, smoked bacon, baby capers and beurre noisette to start, followed by loin of West Country wild venison with celeriac rösti and blueberry sauce, baked Brixham wild sea bass fillet, or pink roasted breast of free-range Devonshire duck. Wines are supplemented by ar interesting selection of Somerset cider brandies. Try the local Somers cheeses.

Chef: Peter Brooks **Owners:** Peter & Sonia Brooks **Times:** 12-2/7-9.30, Closed 25 Dec, BH, 1 wk May, 2wks Nov, Sun & Mon, Closed L Tue-Fri **Prices:** Fixed L £14.50, Starter £5.50-£12.50, Main £15.50-£19.50, Dessert £6, Coffee £2.50, Min/Water £2.50, Service optional **Wine:** 36 bottles ove £20, 12 bottles under £20, 6 by the glass (£4.50-£5) **Notes:** Vegetarian available **Seats:** 25 **Smoking:** N/Sm in restaurant **Children:** Min 7 yrs **Directions:** 0.5m from A303 in the centre of Stoke Sub Hamdon **Parking:** Free car park 200yds & street parking

STON EASTON MAP 04 ST65

Ston Easton Park

British, French

Fine dining in a Palladian mansion

☎ 01761 241631 BA3 4DF
e-mail: info@stoneaston.co.uk
web: www.stoneaston.co.uk

Very much a country house operation, amply justified by the grandeur of the property. The house dates from 1740 and is close to Bath, set amid parklands and landscaped gardens created by Humphrey Repton. The library and state rooms are magnificent, and the Cedar Tree Restaurant is the main dining room. The Print Room and Regency-style Yellow Dining Room are available for private parties, and the terrace is a popular alternative for a summer lunch. Imaginative modern dishes include warm fig and stilton tartlet with red pepper sorbet, pan-seared red snapper with grilled polenta, and tropical fruit and coconut sushi. Fresh vegetables are supplied by the Victorian kitchen garden.

Chef: Michael Parke **Owners:** von Essen Hotels **Times:** 12-2/7-9.30 **Prices:** Fixed L £17.50, Fixed D £44.50, Starter fr £12, Main fr £22.50, Dessert fr £10, Coffee £2.75, Min/Water £3, Service included **Notes:** Menu du Marche £55, Vegetarian available, Dress Restrictions, Smart casual, Civ Wed 100 **Seats:** 40, Pr/dining room 80 **Smoking:** N/Sm in restaurant **Children:** Min 7 yrs, Menu, Portions **Rooms:** 23 (23 en suite) **Directions:** Follow A39 from Bath for approx. 8m. Turn onto A37 (Shepton Mallet), Ston Easton is next village **Parking:** 100

TAUNTON MAP 04 ST22

Corner House Hotel

Modern

Enjoyable bistro dining in tastefully updated Victorian surroundings

☎ 01823 284683 Park St TA1 4DQ
e-mail: res@corner-house.co.uk
web: www.corner-house.co.uk

The impressive turrets and stained glass of this Victorian building conceal a contemporary hotel interior. The 4DQ bistro combines modern comfort with original features to produce a dining venue that has a pleasing, relaxed ambience. Simple, well-executed dishes are based on fresh Somerset ingredients. Start with duck spring roll with plum sauce before a main course of 4DQ fishcake signature dish with buttered spinach, butter sauce and frites or pork fillet stuffed with smoked Applewood cheese. The caramelised rice pudding with apple brandy is a great way to finish the meal.

Owners: Hatton Hotels **Times:** 12-2.30/6.30-9.45 **Prices:** Fixed L £11.95-£24.45, Fixed D £20.95-£29.95, Starter £3.50-£6.95, Main £8.45-£17.50, Dessert £3.45-£5.50, Coffee £1.85, Min/Water £2.50, Service optional **Wine:** 30 bottles over £20, 18 bottles under £20, 12 by the glass (£2.95-£9.20) **Notes:** Sun L 3 courses £11.95, Vegetarian available **Seats:** 100, Pr/dining room 55 **Smoking:** N/Sm area, No pipes, No cigars **Children:** Menu, Portions **Rooms:** 28 (28 en suite) ★★★ HL **Directions:** Telephone for details **Parking:** 40

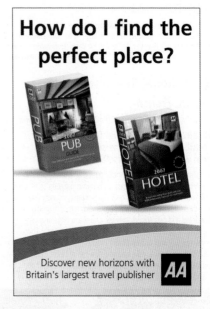

Farthings Hotel & Restaurant

Modern British

Somerset country-house elegance

☎ 01823 480664 Hatch Beauchamp TA3 6SG
e-mail: info@farthingshotel.com
web: www.farthingshotel.com

Overlooking the village green, this delightful hotel dates back over 200 years. The two rooms forming the elegant restaurant have recently been refurbished and enjoy views over the extensive gardens. Guests can expect traditional country-house style dining in a calm and relaxed atmosphere. Dinner service is attentive and the British cooking with European influences features the best quality local ingredients, prepared and presented with care. Expect dishes like pan-seared Blackdown Hills chicken with mango spring roll and spicy plum sauce or pan-fried Cornish sea bass with crayfish mash, spinach and mussel cream. Excellent selection of South West country cheeses.

Chef: John Cameron **Owners:** David & Jacky Forbes **Times:** 12-3/7-11, Closed D Sun (residents only) **Prices:** Fixed D £31.95, Starter £4.50-£6.95, Main £13.95-£18.95, Dessert £5.50-£7.50, Coffee £2.95, Min/Water £2.95, Service optional **Wine:** 11 bottles over £20, 21 bottles under £20, 4 by the glass (£3.95-£5.60) **Notes:** Dress Restrictions, Smart casual, Civ Wed 44

continued

TAUNTON *continued* MAP 04 ST22

Seats: 30, Pr/dining room 10 **Smoking:** N/Sm in restaurant **Children:** Portions **Rooms:** 10 (10 en suite) ★★ **Directions:** From M5 take A358 towards Ilminster, 3m to sign for Hatch Beauchamp & brown tourist sign for Farthings. In village 300yds after pub on right **Parking:** 20

Mount Somerset Hotel

British, French

Elegant Regency property with interesting contemporary food

☎ 01823 442500 Henlade TA3 5NB
e-mail: info@mountsomersethotel.co.uk
web: www.mountsomersethotel.co.uk

An Italian-designed Regency house retaining all of its original grandeur, The Mount Somerset, as its name suggests, is set on top of a hill with magnificent views over the Somerset countryside. The recently refurbished restaurant is splendid, with a magnificent central chandelier and two superb mirrors. Chairs are large and very comfortable and tables are smartly appointed with crisp linen, sparkling silver and contemporary crockery. The likes of a collection of crab (tian, spring roll, cake and soup), a trio of beef (good fillet, faggot and tartlet), and several peripheral courses (canapés and petits fours) all add to the sense of occasion.

Chef: Stefan Warwick **Owners:** von Essen Hotels **Times:** 12-2/7-9.30 **Prices:** Fixed L £14.50, Fixed D £27.50-£36, Starter £5-£8, Main £18-£22, Dessert £4.50-£6, Coffee £2, Min/Water £2.95, Service optional **Wine:** 30 bottles over £20, 30 bottles under £20, 6 by the glass (£3.75-£6.50) **Notes:** Vegetarian available, Dress Restrictions, Smart casual; no jeans or trainers, Civ Wed 60 **Seats:** 40, Pr/dining room 20 **Smoking:** N/Sm in restaurant **Children:** Menu, Portions **Rooms:** 11 (11 en suite) ★★★ HL **Directions:** From M5 junct 25 take A358 (Chard); turn right in Henlade (Stoke St Mary), then turn left at T-junct. Hotel 400yds on right **Parking:** 50

The Willow Tree Restaurant

Modern British

Imaginative regional cooking in a period restaurant

☎ 01823 352835 3 Tower Ln TA1 4AR

Having worked for the Roux brothers for 12 years and run a successful restaurant in London, Darren Sherlock delights in sourcing the finest local ingredients from local suppliers. Everything is made in-house - stocks, bread, pasta, pastry and ice cream - and is served in the delightful little restaurant. Exposed beams and an inglenook fireplace set the scene inside, while outside there is a charming waterside terrace. The menu makes good reading with dishes of sea bass fillet with a fennel and gruyère lasagne and caviar cream sauce, or calotte of beef served with sautéed salsify, artichokes, black olives and truffle mash. The cheeseboard is also well worth investigation.

continued

Chef: Darren Sherlock **Owners:** Darren Sherlock & Rita Rambellas **Times:** 6.30-10, Closed Jan, Aug, Sun-Mon, Closed L all week **Prices:** Fixed D £22.50-£29.50, Coffee £1.95, Min/Water £2.50, Service optional, Group min 7 service 10% **Wine:** 30 bottles over £20, 15 bottles under £20, 4 by the glass (£3.75-£3.95) **Notes:** Dress Restrictions, Smart casual **Seats:** 25, Pr/dining room 16 **Smoking:** N/Sm in restaurant **Children:** Min 10 yrs **Directions:** 200 yds from Taunton bus station **Parking:** 20yds 300 spaces

WELLINGTON MAP 03 ST12

Bindon Country House Hotel & Restaurant

Traditional British

Classic cuisine in attractive country retreat

☎ 01823 400070 Langford Budville TA21 0RU
e-mail: stay@bindon.com
web: www.bindon.com

Set in its own grounds with views towards the Blackdown Hills, this Grade II listed Baroque country house boasts a Victorian interior and several open fireplaces. In summer, enjoy a drink on the terrace with views of the formal lawns. Service in the elegant Wellesley Restaurant is formal yet friendly and tables are laid with the best linen. Clean flavours are created from plenty of local produce on a menu that is unashamedly traditional and English. Typical dishes may include chicken liver parfait with walnut toast and home-made chutney, sautéed Brixham sea bass with crushed new potatoes and chive cream sauce or a selection of mini rhubarb desserts.

Chef: Michael Davies **Owners:** Lynn & Mark Jaffa **Times:** 12-1/7-9.30 **Prices:** Fixed L £12.95-£16.95, Fixed D £35, Coffee £1.95, Min/Water £2.95, Service optional **Wine:** 137 bottles over £20, 28 bottles under £20, 6 by the glass (£4-£4.75) **Notes:** Dress Restrictions, No jeans or T-shirts, Civ Wed 50 **Seats:** 30, Pr/dining room 16 **Smoking:** N/Sm in restaurant **Children:** Min 7 yrs, Menu, Portions **Rooms:** 12 (12 en suite) ★★★ CHH **Directions:** From Wellington B3187 to Langville Budville, through village & right towards Wiveliscombe, right at junct, past Bindon Farm, right after 450yds **Parking:** 25

WELLS MAP 04 ST54

Goodfellows

Mediterranean, European NEW

A contemporary and eclectic combination of restaurant, fishmonger, pâtisserie and deli

☎ 01749 673866 5 Sadler St BA5 2RR
e-mail: goodfellows@btconnect.com

The mulberry-coloured shop front of this establishment houses an informal pâtisserie and deli counter. Downstairs provides a modern, bright main restaurant with open-plan kitchen that shares a cold-fish counter where the chef sells fresh fish and offers cooking tips. There is further restaurant space upstairs with a glass atrium and an adjoining courtyard. Accomplished and versatile cooking can be seen at the open stove. The modern European cuisine offers seafood with Mediterranean influences - a light style with intense flavours from oils and vinaigrettes using the likes of black olives, capers and anchovy or truffle oil. Expect dishes such as seared tuna carpaccio with mustard and herbs or fillet of sea bass with fennel, salami, red and pepper and cardamom coulis.

continued

Goodfellows

Chef: Adam Fellows **Owners:** Adam & Martine Fellows **Times:** 12-2.30/6.30-9.30, Closed 25 Dec, 1 Jan & 1st 2 wks in Jan, Sun & Mon, Closed D Tue & Wed **Prices:** Fixed L fr £12.50, Fixed D fr £29, Starter £4.50-£9.50, Main £6.50-£22, Dessert £3.50-£4.50, Coffee £2, Min/Water £2.50, Service optional, Group min 8 service 8% **Wine:** 38 bottles over £20, 13 bottles under £20, 11 by the glass (£2.95-£7) **Seats:** 40, Pr/dining room 18 **Smoking:** N/Sm in restaurant, Air con **Children:** Portions **Directions:** Town centre near Market Place

Swan Hotel

Traditional British

Generous and imaginative dishes in a traditional setting

☎ 01749 836300 Sadler St BA5 2RX
e-mail: swan@bhere.co.uk
web: www.bhere.co.uk

A 15th-century coaching inn with stunning views from the front over Wells Cathedral. The long, narrow dining room, with linen-fold oak panelling and interesting antiques, provides a very traditional setting with a formal style of service. Imaginative dishes, presented on the seasonally changing carte and the chef's market menu, are served in good country portions. Expect the likes of terrine of guinea fowl, wild mushrooms and smoked bacon, or haunch of venison with potato pancakes and bitter chocolate jus, and to finish lime and ricotta cheesecake with gin and tonic ice cream. Cooking is careful with good use made of local produce.

Chef: Paul Mingo-West **Owners:** Christopher Chapman **Times:** 12.30-2/7-9.30 **Prices:** Fixed L fr £12, Fixed D fr £25.50, Starter £7.50-£9.25, Main £18.50-£22, Dessert £6.75-£6.95, Coffee £2.50, Min/Water £2.65, Service optional **Wine:** 27 bottles over £20, 15 bottles under £20, 5 by the glass (£3.65-£5.80) **Notes:** Vegetarian available, Civ Wed 90 **Seats:** 60, Pr/dining room 100 **Smoking:** N/Sm in restaurant **Children:** Menu, Portions **Rooms:** 50 (50 en suite) ★★★ HL **Directions:** A39, A371, opposite Cathedral **Parking:** 30

WEST CAMEL MAP 04 ST52

The Walnut Tree Hotel

Modern British, French NEW

Fine food in friendly village hotel

☎ 01935 851292 Fore St BA22 7QW
e-mail: info@thewalnuttreehotel.com
web: www.thewalnuttreehotel.com

This small hotel has all the character and atmosphere of a village inn. There is a family-orientated restaurant, with a different kitchen and team to the fine-dining Rosewood Restaurant. Here lightwood panelling and white table settings give a clean, airy feel. Accomplished cooking sees good use of carefully sourced produce and sound techniques. Typical starters might include potted wild salmon and shrimp with herb aioli, cucumber and caviar. Main courses feature modern British dishes like poached lamb noisettes with grilled aubergine, mint onions and Madeira sauce.

Chef: Neil Cadle **Times:** Noon/8.45 **Prices:** Food prices not confirmed for 2007. Please telephone for details **Rooms:** 13 (13 en suite) ★★ HL

WILLITON MAP 03 ST04

White House Hotel

British Mediterranean

Friendly, family-run Georgian hotel

☎ 01984 632306 632777 Long St TA4 4QW

Run by husband-and-wife team Richard and Kay Smith, this charming little Georgian hotel has a relaxed atmosphere. Decorated in autumnal shades with exposed stone walls and wooden tables, the restaurant has a warm and unpretentious feel. Menus are hand-written, offering a concise but tempting range of dishes, notable for their use of fresh local produce. Typical mains might include pan-fried guinea fowl supreme with caramelised apples, or lamb with a roasted garlic and crème fraîche sauce.

Times: 7.30-9, Closed early Nov-mid May **Rooms:** 10 (9 en suite) ★★ HL **Directions:** On A39 in centre of village

---

WINCANTON MAP 04 ST72

Holbrook House Hotel

Traditional British

Elegant hotel with stylish restaurant

☎ 01963 824466 Holbrook BA9 8BS
e-mail: reception@holbrookhouse.co.uk
web: www.holbrookhouse.co.uk

A handsome country-house hotel with the feel of a private manor house, standing in 23 acres of parkland and formal gardens, not far from Wincanton. Plush leather sofas in the tastefully decorated lounges invite guests to linger over a drink before moving into the elegant restaurant, where the warm colour scheme creates a calming atmosphere. The innovative food is also worth savouring, with the short set menu, regularly changed to reflect the season's fresh yield, offering dishes like hand-dived Cornish scallops with black pudding and cauliflower purée, and rump of Dorset lamb with celeriac gratin with roasted root vegetables. The hotel's leisure facilities are also worth a visit.

continued

England

WINCANTON *continued* MAP 04 ST72

Chef: Kevin Hyde **Owners:** Mr & Mrs J McGinley **Times:** 12.30-2/7-9, Closed L Sat, D Sun **Prices:** Fixed L £15.95, Starter £6.95-£9.50, Main £15.95-£22.50, Dessert £6.50-£7.95, Coffee £2.95, Min/Water £2.95 **Wine:** 40 bottles over £20, 8 bottles under £20, 10 by the glass (£4.95-£9.50) **Notes:** Dress Restrictions, Smart casual, Civ Wed 120 **Seats:** 49, Pr/dining room 140 **Smoking:** N/Sm in restaurant **Children:** Portions **Rooms:** 21 (21 en suite) ★★★ CHH **Directions:** From A303 at Wincanton, turn left on A371 towards Castle Cary & Shepton Mallet **Parking:** 100

WINSFORD MAP 03 SS93

Karslake House

Modern British

Fresh local produce in charming country-house style

☎ 01643 851242 Halse Ln TA24 7JE
e-mail: enquiries@karslakehouse.co.uk
web: www.karslakehouse.co.uk

A former malthouse, the spacious dining room retains charm and character along with modern comforts. Open for non-residents on Friday and Saturday evenings or by prior arrangement. There is a clear dedication to the use of fresh, locally sourced produce, much of which is Exmoor's fish, meat and game. Enjoy main dishes such as confit of organic Exmoor duck with parsnip and celeriac mash with blackberry sauce, or grilled Brixham sea bass on a bed of stir-fried vegetables with white wine and soy sauce. Unusually, some of the hotel's own grapes are used for one of the wines listed.

Chef: Juliette Mountford **Owners:** Mr & Mrs F.N.G. Mountford **Times:** 7.30-8.30, Closed Nov-Apr, Closed D Sun-Thu (ex residents) **Prices:** Fixed D £29.50, Coffee £2.50, Min/Water £1.95, Service optional **Wine:** 10 bottles over £20, 22 bottles under £20, 2 by the glass (£4.40-£4.80) **Notes:** Vegetarian available **Seats:** 18 **Smoking:** N/Sm in restaurant **Children:** Min 12 yrs **Rooms:** 6 (5 en suite) ◆◆◆◆ **Directions:** A396 to Winsford, then left up the hill **Parking:** 12

YEOVIL MAP 04 ST51

Helyar Arms

Modern British

Accomplished cooking in a Somerset haven

☎ 01935 862332 Moor Ln, East Coker BA22 9JR
e-mail: info@helyar-arms.co.uk
web: www.helyar-arms.co.uk

Made famous by T.S. Eliot in the poem of the same name, East Coker is one of Somerset's prettiest villages. Its inn dates back to the 15th

continued

century, and boasts its very own skittle alley as well as attractive gardens for alfresco dining. Modern British cooking is the order of the day; expect straightforward dishes distinguished by excellent technical skills, such as glazed slow-roast pork belly with roast sweet potato and parsnip crisps, or steak and kidney suet pudding with buttered leeks and stock pot gravy. Ingredients are from local producers whenever possible.

Chef: Mathieu Eke **Owners:** Ian McKerracher **Times:** 12-2.30/6.30-9.30, Closed 25 Dec **Prices:** Starter £4-£7, Main £8-£16, Dessert £5-£7, Coffee £2, Service optional **Wine:** 15 bottles over £20, 18 bottles under £20, 31 by the glass (£2.30-£15.75) **Notes:** Vegetarian available **Seats:** 55, Pr/dining room 40 **Smoking:** N/Sm area **Children:** Menu, Portions **Rooms:** 6 (6 en suite) ◆◆◆◆ **Directions:** 3m from Yeovil. Take A37 or A30. Follow signs for East Coker. Helyar Arms is 50 mtrs from church **Parking:** 30

Lanes

Modern British, European NEW

Imaginative, modern cooking in contemporary surroundings

☎ 01935 862555 West Coker BA22 9AJ
e-mail: stay@laneshotel.net
web: www.laneshotel.net

Recently re-opened after a £1.5 million refurbishment, Lanes was once a Victorian vicarage. The brasserie-style restaurant is housed in a stylish contemporary extension with floor-to-ceiling windows, wooden floors and modern art on plain white walls. The menu evolves with the seasons and offers an imaginative range of dishes and includes options in smaller or larger portions. Using local produce where possible, a sample meal might begin with carpaccio of marinated venison, juniper and raspberry vinegar dressing, potato and wasabi salad, and continue with traditional Irish pickled beef, braised Savoy cabbage and new potatoes.

Chef: Jason Eland **Owners:** John & Alison Roehrig **Times:** 12-2.30/7-10 **Prices:** Starter £3.75-£6, Main £7.50-£15, Dessert £4.25-£5, Coffee £1.50, Min/Water £2.50, Service optional **Wine:** 23 bottles over £20, 24 bottles under £20, 7 by the glass (£2-£2.60) **Notes:** Sun L 3 courses £14, Vegetarian available **Seats:** 74, Pr/dining room 40 **Smoking:** N/Sm in restaurant, Air con **Children:** Portions **Rooms:** 10 (10 en suite) ★★★ HL **Directions:** 2m outside Yeovil, A30 towards Crewkerne **Parking:** 40

England

Little Barwick House Ltd

YEOVIL MAP 04 ST51

Modern British NOTABLE WINE LIST

Delightful house, wonderful grounds, unfussy service and great food

☎ 01935 423902 Barwick Village BA22 9TD
e-mail: reservations@barwick7.fsnet.co.uk
web: www.littlebarwickhouse.co.uk

Set in 3.5 acres of enchanting gardens, this listed Georgian dower house has been tastefully restored by the owners to achieve a balance of period charm and modern interior design sensibilities that shows real discernment. Sumptuous fabrics, Farrow and Ball colours and sympathetic modern touches provide an unobtrusive backdrop for good eating and drinking, which of course are paramount for this locally renowned restaurant with rooms.
The lack of fuss in the cooking belies a complexity of approach and a sophistication of palate that clearly indicates the touch of a highly experienced chef: subtlety and consistency are the watchwords here. Forget undue ceremony - just enjoy the symphony of flavours created throughout this concise menu: start with pan-fried Cornish scallops on a tomato compote and crispy bacon, a main course of saddle of wild roe deer on a wild mushroom risotto and Pedro Ximenez sherry sauce, and finish with a dessert of warm dark chocolate tart with vodka granite and passionfruit ice cream.
Notable Wine List: An interesting and well chosen wine list categorised by drinking style.

Chef: Timothy Ford **Owners:** Emma & Timothy Ford **Times:** 12-2/7-9.30, Closed New Year, 2wks Jan, Mon, Closed L Tues, D Sun **Prices:** Fixed L £18.95, Fixed D £34.95, Starter £7.95-£12.95, Main £19.95-£24.95, Dessert £5.95-£6.25, Coffee £3.25, Min/Water £3.50, Service optional **Wine:** 144 bottles over £20, 25 bottles under £20, 4 by the glass (£5-£5.95) **Seats:** 40 **Smoking:** N/Sm in restaurant, Air con **Children:** Min 5 yrs, Portions **Rooms:** 6 (6 en suite) ★★★★★ RR **Directions:** Turn off A371 Yeovil to Dorchester opp Red House rdbt, 0.25m on left **Parking:** 25

Yeovil Court Hotel Limited

Modern British

Enjoyable dining in a modern, family-run hotel

☎ 01935 863746 West Coker Rd BA20 2HE
e-mail: unwind@yeovilhotel.com
web: www.yeovilhotel.com

With its modern décor and convivial bar area, this friendly, family-run hotel has a welcoming ambience. The dining room is also decorated in a modern style with white tablecloths and good quality settings. After your meal, the helpful staff will lead you to a comfortably furnished lounge. Dishes are modern British in style with the occasional French influence. Starters could include open wood pigeon pie with Savoy cabbage, baby onions and smoked bacon or confit duck leg and Puy lentil terrine served with mango and chilli chutney. For mains expect the likes of herb-crusted Welsh lamb with provençale vegetables, or saddle of Malmesbury rabbit with grilled chorizo and wild mushroom and parmesan risotto. Finish with a passionfruit semi-fredo with crisp coconut biscuit.

Chef: Lincoln Jones **Owners:** Brian & Carol Devonport **Times:** 12-1.45/7-9.30, Closed 24 Dec, 26-28 Dec, 1-2 Jan, Closed L Sat **Prices:** Fixed L £12.95-£14.95, Starter £3.95-£6.95, Main £11.25-£17.95, Dessert £4.25, Coffee £2.50, Min/Water £2.75, Service optional **Wine:** 17 bottles over £20, 33 bottles under £20, 6 by the glass (£3.20-£3.80) **Notes:** Vegetarian available **Seats:** 50, Pr/dining room 75 **Smoking:** N/Sm in restaurant, Air con **Children:** Portions **Rooms:** 30 (30 en suite) ★★★ HL **Directions:** On A30, 2.5m W of town centre **Parking:** 65

continued

Two Rosettes
The best local restaurants, which aim for and achieve higher standards, better consistency and where a greater precision is apparent in the cooking. There will be obvious attention to the selection of quality ingredients.

STAFFORDSHIRE

BURTON UPON TRENT MAP 10 SK22

Meynell and Deer Park Restaurant

Modern British

Handsome inn with a very rural location

☎ 01283 575202 Hoar Cross DE13 8RB
e-mail: info@themeynell.co.uk
web: www.themeynell.co.uk

The Meynell is a brick-built country inn standing at a quiet village crossroads. It has a traditional pub interior with exposed beams in several rooms, oak floors and open fires. A comprehensive menu is offered in the Deer Park Restaurant featuring some timeless classics with international influences. Expect dishes such as sautéed chicken livers with sun-dried tomato and potato salad to begin, followed by chargrilled Staffordshire beef fillet with rösti potato, roasted fine beans and almonds and a wild mushroom café au lait sauce, then brioche bread-and-butter pudding with crème anglaise.

Chef: Tony Holland **Owners:** Mike and Jane Chappell **Times:** 12-2.30/7-9.30, Closed D Sun **Prices:** Fixed L £15-£20, Fixed D £17.50-£22, Starter £4-£7, Main £11.50-£20, Dessert £4.50-£6, Coffee £1.95, Min/Water £3, Service optional **Wine:** 12 bottles over £20, 6 bottles under £20, 4 by the glass (£2.95-£4.50) **Notes:** Vegetarian available, Dress Restrictions, Smart casual **Seats:** 30, Pr/dining room 44 **Smoking:** N/Sm in restaurant **Children:** Portions **Directions:** 7m W of Burton on Trent, 2 minute drive off the A515 main road between Lichfield on the A50 **Parking:** 50

CHEADLE MAP 10 SK04

Thornbury Hall Rasoi

British, Indian

Striking setting for authentic Pakistani cooking

☎ 01538 750831 Lockwood Rd ST10 2DH
e-mail: info@thornburyhall.com
web: www.thornburyhall.com

A fine Georgian manor house in a country location with extensive grounds is the setting for this unique restaurant serving Pakistani food. The restaurant is richly decorated with red and gold wallpaper, terracotta tiled floor, red and white linen, cane furniture and gold decorative pieces. The menu offers the kind of food that would be served to honoured guests in Pakistan. Diners are made to feel very welcome with a high level of service, and main courses are silver served. House specialities include Karhai Murg Dhali, chicken or lamb pieces cooked with combinations of lentils.

Times: 12-2/6-10 **Directions:** 7m from Stoke-on-Trent

LEEK MAP 16 SJ95

Number 64

British

Modern British food in an elegant Georgian townhouse

☎ 01538 381900 64 St Edwards St ST13 5DL
e-mail: enquiries@number64.com
web: www.number64.com

Situated in the heart of a historic market town, this Grade II listed building has been sympathetically renovated to provide a restaurant with rooms, wine bar, speciality food shop, coffee shop and a patisserie. Inside the décor is pleasantly traditional - stripped floors, floral curtains and plenty of light from the tall windows. The menu is uncomplicated, modern British in style - simple but effective dishes using quality ingredients. A typical starter might be confit duck with Puy lentils and dried Parma ham followed by guinea fowl with rhubarb chutney, potato boulangère and confit shallots.

Times: 12-2/7-9, Closed D Sun **Rooms:** 3 (3 en suite) ★★★★ RR **Directions:** In town centre near junct of A520 and A53, at bottom of hill

Three Horseshoes Inn

International

Traditional inn offering an oriental twist to a modern British menu

☎ 01538 300296 Buxton Rd, Blackshaw Moor ST13 8TW
e-mail: mark@threeshoesinn.co.uk
web: www.threeshoesinn.co.uk

A traditional ivy-clad inn in immaculate grounds, run by a friendly family. The food operation is divided between an informal brasserie and an elegant restaurant on a lower level. Exposed beams, polished brass and rustic furniture abound throughout. A commitment to good food cooked from locally sourced seasonal produce is evident, with some Thai flavours influencing the international menu. The likes of Moroccan lamb shank, braised belly of pork, and steamed monkfish tail with coconut sticky rice are accurately cooked and well flavoured. A final mention goes to 'Sweet Sensation' - a chocolate and liqueur fondue with marshmallows for dipping - wicked!

Chef: Mark & Stephen Kirk **Owners:** Bill, Jill, Mark & Stephen Kirk **Times:** 12.30-2/6.30-9, Closed 26 Dec-30 Dec, Closed L Mon-Sat **Prices:** Food prices not confirmed for 2007. Please telephone for details **Seats:** 100 **Smoking:** N/Sm in restaurant **Rooms:** 6 (6 en suite) ★★ HL **Directions:** M6 junct 15 or 16 onto A500. Exit A53 towards Leek. Turn left onto A50 (Burslem) **Parking:** 100

England

LICHFIELD MAP 10 SK10

Bratz

Modern European

Minster house with great views and appealing modern cuisine

☎ 01543 253788 Minster House, Pool Walk WS13 6QT
web: www.bratzrestaurant.co.uk

Located in a Georgian building with lovely views of Minster Pool and the cathedral, this restaurant's crooked staircases and low ceilings are complemented by light, contemporary décor. In keeping with the setting, the menu offers a sophisticated pairing of traditional and contemporary, with a European edge. Dishes range through home-cured salmon and horseradish pancakes with shallot and caper dressing, breast of Barbary duck with beetroot fondant, grilled potatoes and balsamic jus, and warm chocolate brownie with scented cherries and pistachio ice cream. A good vegetarian choice is also available.

Times: 12-2/7-10, Closed Mon, Closed L Tue-Sat, D Sun **Directions:** City centre. Please phone for further directions.

The Four Seasons Restaurant

Modern European

Stunning mansion and impressive cuisine

☎ 01543 481494 Swinfen Hall Hotel, Swinfen WS14 9RE
e-mail: info@swinfenhallhotel.co.uk
web: www.swinfenhallhotel.co.uk

Set in 100 acres of parkland including a deer park, guests might gasp when they arrive at the stunning entrance hall to this beautiful 18th-century country-house hotel, but there is more to come. The lavishly decorated public rooms, including carved ceilings and impressive oil

continued

The Four Seasons Restaurant

paintings, soon exhaust the superlatives. Despite the high style, the place is welcoming and comfortable. A three-course fixed price menu showcases the classical cooking in the oak-panelled Four Seasons Restaurant, with locally sourced, often luxury ingredients taking pride of place. Seared salmon smoked over oak chips, with crab ravioli and caviar butter sauce fit comfortably into the country-house style of starters, with marinated wild boar, spicy apple compôte and caramelised shallots making a stylish main dish.

Chef: Neil Peers **Owners:** Helen & Vic Wiser **Times:** 12.30-2.30/7-9.30, Closed L Sat, D Sun **Prices:** Fixed L fr £16.95, Fixed D fr £39.50, Coffee £3.50, Min/Water £3.50, Service optional **Wine:** 75 bottles over £20, 11 bottles under £20, 6 by the glass (£4.25-£6.50) **Notes:** Sun L 2 courses £24.50, 3 courses £29.50, Dress Restrictions, No trainers or jeans, Civ Wed 120 **Seats:** 50, Pr/dining room 20 **Smoking:** N/Sm in restaurant **Children:** Portions **Rooms:** 19 (19 en suite) ★★★★ HL **Directions:** 2m S of Lichfield on A38 between Weeford rdbt and Swinfen rdbt. Follow A38 to Lichfield, hotel is 0.5m on right **Parking:** 80

Chandlers

☎ 01543 416688 Corn Exchange Buildings, Conduit St WS13 6JU
Large brasserie with modern British menu.

RUGELEY MAP 10 SK01

The Plum Pudding Brasserie

Modern British

Innovative cooking, canal-side location

☎ 01543 490330 Rugeley Rd, Armitage WS15 4AZ
e-mail: enquiries@theplumpudding.co.uk
web: www.theplumpudding.co.uk

A modern brasserie in a canal-side pub, with a large terrace alongside the canal. The atmosphere is relaxed and intimate and service is friendly. Modern British food is cooked with fresh, locally sourced

continued

RUGELEY *continued* MAP 10 SK01

produce from organic meats through to local cheeses. Typical dishes include a starter of pressed lamb shank and Toulouse sausage terrine with home-made piccalilli. Main courses might feature a 250g (8oz) Staffordshire fillet steak served with braised oxtail tartlet, tomato and tarragon ravioli and shiitake jus. Innovative desserts include the likes of Toblerone soufflé with Amaretto ice cream.

Chef: Richard Light & Steven Kirkham **Owners:** Mr & Mrs J Takhar **Times:** 12-3.30/6-11.30, Closed 1 Jan **Prices:** Fixed L fr £12, Fixed D fr £15, Starter £3.95-£6.75, Main £9.95-£16.95, Dessert £4.95, Coffee £1.50, Min/Water £1.95, Service optional **Wine:** 10 bottles over £20, 34 bottles under £20, 7 by the glass (£2.75-£4.50) **Notes:** Fixed D not available Fri & Sat, Vegetarian available **Seats:** 70 **Smoking:** N/Sm in restaurant **Children:** Portions **Rooms:** 4 (4 en suite) ◆◆◆◆ **Directions:** M6 junct 11 follow signs for Cannock to Rugeley. Situated on A513 through Rugeley to Lichfield **Parking:** 50

STAFFORD MAP 10 SJ92

Moat House

Modern British

Cutting-edge menu meets conservatory dining in canal-side hotel

☎ 01785 712217 Lower Penkridge Rd, Acton Trussell ST17 0RJ
e-mail: info@moathouse.co.uk
web: www.moathouse.co.uk

Aptly named, this well-restored hotel occupies a 15th-century, Grade II listed property - a moated former manor house - with a striking canal-side setting. The main building is full of oak panelling and exposed beams, while the spacious and stylish conservatory restaurant is a modern, luxurious affair with high-back seating and generous-sized tables, set to a backdrop of barges plying the canal. The enticing menu is dotted with luxury items, promoting an agony of choice on a classically based, modern-focused repertoire. Fresh, high-quality seasonal ingredients combine with a sense of flair to deliver skilfully crafted, flavour-driven dishes that show the kitchen's pedigree; for example, take a pavé of turbot paired with a fondue of leeks, langoustines and salsify.

Times: 12-2/7-9.30, Closed 25 Dec, 1-2 Jan **Rooms:** 32 (32 en suite) ★★★★ HL **Directions:** M6 junct 13 towards Stafford, 1st right to Acton Trussell, hotel by church

The Swan Hotel

British

Innovative cooking in town centre contemporary brasserie

☎ 01785 258142 46 Greengate St ST16 2JA
e-mail: info@theswanstafford.co.uk
web: www.theswanstafford.co.uk

A former coaching inn, this is quite a dining destination locally and an impressive venue. The split-level brasserie with its timber frame and stylish modern décor appeals to discerning locals and residents alike. The restaurant retains a historic feel with polished wooden or marble tables, crisp napery, candles and leather banquette or cane seating. The cooking style is precise with clear flavours and smart presentation. Popular dishes might include the likes of chicken and bacon fettuccini, roast sea bass or rack of lamb with a choice of side dishes.

Times: 12-2.30/5.30-10, Closed 25-26 Dec **Rooms:** 31 (31 en suite) ★★★ HL **Directions:** M6 junct 13//14 then to town. Follow signs to rail station, turn right after station at mini rdbt. 1st left into Water St. Hotel on left. (Access via Mill St)

STOKE-ON-TRENT MAP 10 SJ84

The Elms, Passion of India

Indian

Welcoming Indian restaurant serving healthy dishes

☎ 01782 266360 Snowhill, Shelton ST1 4LY

The building was once home to the pottery owner John Ridgeway, becoming a pub during the Victorian era. It is now a handsome Indian restaurant, warm and friendly, and richly decorated featuring gold cornices and crisp linen. A healthy approach is taken to the cooking using Ayurvedic principles, with every ingredient carefully balanced to produce tasty and wholesome dishes, such as local speciality Staffordshire oatcakes stuffed with paneer, spring onions, herbs and spices, or lamb pepper fry (tender lamb cooked with peppercorns and coconut milk), and sumptuous home-made gajjar ka halva (carrot dessert).

Chef: Harish Kumar **Owners:** Pritpal Singh Nagi **Times:** 6-11.30, Closed 25 Dec, Sun, Closed L Mon-Sat, D Sun **Prices:** Fixed D £25-£35, Starter £3.95-£14.99, Main £8.95-£13.95, Dessert £3.95-£4.25, Coffee £1.95, Min/Water £3.95, Service optional **Wine:** 8 bottles over £20, 15 bottles under £20, 1 by the glass (£3.45) **Notes:** Vegetarian available, Dress Restrictions, Smart casual **Seats:** 120, Pr/dining room 30 **Smoking:** N/Sm in restaurant **Children:** Portions **Directions:** Telephone for directions **Parking:** 80

Haydon House Hotel

British, European

Family-run hotel with a sound reputation

☎ 01782 711311 Haydon St, Basford ST4 6JD
e-mail: enquiries@haydon-house-hotel.co.uk
web: www.haydon-house-hotel.co.uk

This late Victorian townhouse is set in the Etruria district of Stoke-on-Trent, which played home to the workforce of Josiah's Wedgwood's celebrated pottery for 200 years. It retains many original features, including a ghost, and is also a popular haunt for locals lured by a gracious décor and reputation for quality cuisine in the Townhouse Restaurant. The carte and flambé (prepared at your table) menus change seasonally, with a weekly changing fixed price menu. Expect mains such as sea bass with French beans and a vanilla cream sauce, or rack of Welsh lamb with fondant potato, caramelised shallots and a smoked red wine sauce.

continued

Chef: Michael Hall **Owners:** Mr J F Machin **Times:** 12-2/7-10, Closed 26 Dec, 1 Jan, Closed L Sat & Sun **Prices:** Fixed L £12.50-£14.50, Fixed D £17.50-£19.50, Starter £4.50-£8.50, Main £12.95-£25.50, Dessert £4.25-£5.25, Coffee £1.95, Min/Water £3, Service optional **Wine:** 20 bottles over £20, 16 bottles under £20, 2 by the glass (£2.40-£3.40) **Notes:** Coffee incl fixed L & D, Vegetarian available, Dress Restrictions, Smart casual, Civ Wed 80 **Seats:** 45, Pr/dining room 76 **Smoking:** N/Sm in restaurant **Children:** Portions **Rooms:** 23 (23 en suite) ★★★ HL **Directions:** From M6 take either junct 15 or 16, follow A500 to A53, take A53 signed Newcastle, take 2nd left before lights **Parking:** 42

UTTOXETER MAP 10 SK03

Restaurant Gilmore at Strine's Farm

Modern British

Friendly, family-run farmhouse restaurant

☎ 01889 507100 Beamhurst ST14 5DZ
e-mail: paul@restaurantgilmore.com
web: www.restaurantgilmore.com

The building is a converted three-storey farmhouse set in acres of open grounds, including cottage gardens, herb and vegetable plots, making it a popular venue for weddings. It's the second incarnation of Restaurant Gilmore, the first was in Birmingham a few years ago. The farmhouse version occupies three separate dining rooms, each with its own character. The kitchen takes its role seriously, sourcing the finest produce from all markets, and the cooking incorporates traditional techniques and a modern approach. There is an emphasis on flavours throughout the regularly changing menu, with dishes of pan-fried Orkney scallops and vanilla risotto, or pot-roasted loin of moorland lamb, baked shallots and sweet potato.

Chef: Paul Gilmore **Owners:** Paul & Dee Gilmore **Times:** 12.30-2/7.30-9, Closed 2 wks Aug, 1 wk Easter, 1 wk Jan, Mon & Tue, Closed L Sat, D Sun **Prices:** Fixed L £16.50, Fixed D £32.50, Coffee £3.50, Min/Water £3.75, Service optional, Group min 8 service 10% **Wine:** 38 bottles over £20, 20 bottles under £20, 6 by the glass (£4) **Notes:** Sun L 3 courses incl coffee £24, Vegetarian available, Dress Restrictions, Smart casual **Seats:** 24 **Smoking:** N/Sm in restaurant **Children:** Portions **Directions:** 1.5m N of Uttoxeter on A522 to Cheadle. Set 400yds back from the road along a fenced farm track **Parking:** 12

SUFFOLK

ALDEBURGH MAP 13 TM45

152 Aldeburgh

Modern European

Well-tuned cooking in popular resort

☎ 01728 454594 152 High St IP15 5AX
e-mail: info@152aldeburgh.co.uk
web: www.152aldeburgh.co.uk

Located through an archway from the High Street to the beach, this succinctly named, bustling brasserie exactly fits the Aldeburgh bill. Light and clean-cut, its stripped wooden floors, cream panelling, pine tables and chairs, fresh flowers and informal, helpful and cheerful service, create a relaxed, friendly atmosphere that ticks all the right boxes. The innovative, compact seasonal menus make fine use of quality ingredients from local suppliers (especially fish), and the intelligently straightforward, modern approach delivers clear flavours via accurately cooked dishes. Take tuna carpaccio with red pepper

continued

chutney and basil oil, or perhaps monkfish with spinach, celeriac and saffron potatoes, and finish with Cox apple tarte Tatin.

152 Aldeburgh

Chef: Garry Cook **Owners:** Garry Cook/Andrew Lister **Times:** 12-3/6-10 **Prices:** Fixed L £14-£15, Fixed D £17.50, Starter £5-£9.75, Main £10.50-£18, Dessert £5.25-£6.25, Coffee £1.80, Min/Water £2.50, Service included **Wine:** 12 bottles over £20, 35 bottles under £20, 8 by the glass (£2.75-£6.65) **Notes:** Vegetarian available **Seats:** 56 **Smoking:** N/Sm in restaurant **Children:** Portions **Parking:** On-street parking on High St. & Kings St.

The Brudenell

Modern British

A refreshingly modern brasserie only a few steps from the sea

☎ 01728 452071 The Parade IP15 5BU
e-mail: info@brudenellhotel.co.uk
web: www.brudenellhotel.co.uk

Only a few steps from the beach, this glass-fronted brasserie makes the most of a fabulous location on an unspoiled stretch of Suffolk coast in the beautiful seaside town of Aldeburgh. The split-level restaurant is a chic affair: wooden tables, pastel shades and Mediterranean shutters give it an informal feel where ambience is as important as the food. French, Italian, Asian and British influences sit comfortably alongside one another on this fairly extensive menu that side-steps the usual bistro fare with clever variations on a theme - how about crayfish cocktail or pink pigeon with port and shallot reduction followed by monkfish, salmon and crab Thai curry? On sunnier days dining on the terrace is thoroughly enjoyable.

Chef: Mark Clements **Owners:** Thorpeness & Aldeburgh Hotels Ltd **Times:** 12-2.30/6-10 **Prices:** Fixed L fr £12.95, Fixed D £25, Starter £3.95-£11.25, Main £7.95-£19.95, Dessert £4.95-£5.95, Coffee £1.60, Min/Water £3.50, Service optional **Wine:** 35 bottles over £20, 21 bottles under £20, 20 by the glass (£3.50-£9.95) **Notes:** Fixed L Sun only, Vegetarian available, Smart casual **Seats:** 80 **Smoking:** N/Sm in restaurant **Children:** Menu, Portions **Rooms:** 42 (42 en suite) ★★★ HL **Parking:** 15

see advert on page 427

England

ALDEBURGH *continued* MAP 13 TM45

Regatta Restaurant

Traditional British

Busy, bistro-style restaurant featuring locally caught fish

☎ 01728 452011 171 High St IP15 5AN
e-mail: regatta.restaurant@aldeburgh.sagegost.co.uk
web: www.regattaaldeburgh.com

Nautical murals pay tribute to Aldeburgh's maritime tradition at this bistro-style restaurant, as well as highlighting the mainstay of fish and seafood on offer. A chalked blackboard gives a daily update on the freshly caught offerings, while the menu lists the alternatives. Walls are plain cream, tables are stripped pine and there is bench seating along the walls and across the front of the window. Staff are stylishly dressed in black polo shirts with black trousers and aprons, and service is very relaxed. Food is simply cooked and presented with clear flavours from the wonderfully fresh ingredients. Expect dishes such as Regatta's own oak-smoked salmon with caper berries or local lobster thermidor. As we went to press the proprietor informed us that the restaurant was about to receive a refurbishment, splitting the operation into fine dining and a bistro for casual and family dining.

Chef: Robert Mabey **Owners:** Mr & Mrs R Mabey **Times:** 12-2/6-10, Closed L 25-26 Dec, D Sun (Nov-Feb) **Prices:** Fixed L £8, Starter £3.50-£6, Main £8.50-£14, Dessert £3.50-£4.50, Coffee £1.80, Min/Water £2.50 **Wine:** 10 bottles over £20, 30 bottles under £20, 3 by the glass (£3.25-£3.50) **Notes:** Gourmet D 6 courses 6 wines £35, Vegetarian available **Seats:** 90, Pr/dining room 30 **Smoking:** N/Sm in restaurant, Air con **Children:** Menu, Portions **Directions:** Middle of High St, town centre

Wentworth Hotel

Modern British

Traditional values with modern twists in seaside hotel

☎ 01728 452312 Wentworth Rd IP15 5BD
e-mail: stay@wentworth-aldeburgh.co.uk
web: www.wentworth-aldeburgh.com

Overlooking the beach at the quiet end of town, this reassuringly traditional hotel is popular with returning guests, and boasts staff who create a friendly and informal ambience. In this family-friendly atmosphere, the smart dining room, elegantly decorated in Etruscan red, is a beacon of excellence locally, with its mixture of firm favourites and upbeat modern ideas. Seasonal changes and local suppliers keep the food fresh and interesting, with Brancaster mussels flavoured with ginger, white wine and chilli perhaps, followed by chargrilled sea bream with coriander butter, or a technically assured pan-fried breast of guinea fowl with herb potato cake and port wine sauce. Given the restaurant's popularity, booking is essential at busy times.

continued

Chef: Graham Reid **Owners:** Wentworth Hotel Ltd/Michael Pritt **Times:** 12-2/7-9 **Prices:** Fixed L fr £12.50, Fixed D £12.50-£17.50, Coffee £2, Min/Water £3.25, Service optional **Wine:** 26 bottles over £20, 39 bottles under £20, 11 by the glass (£2.50-£7) **Seats:** 90, Pr/dining room 20 **Smoking:** N/Sm in restaurant **Children:** Menu, Portions **Rooms:** 35 (35 en suite) ★★★ HL **Directions:** From A12 take A1094 to Aldeburgh. In Aldeburgh straight on at mini-rdbt, turn left at x-roads into Wentworth Rd. Hotel on right **Parking:** 33

White Lion Hotel

Traditional British

Elegant dining by the sea

☎ 01728 452720 Market Cross Place IP15 5BJ
e-mail: info@whitelion.co.uk
web: www.whitelion.co.uk

Dating in part back to 1563, this popular hotel is situated at the quiet end of town, overlooking the sea. There are two lounges, and an elegant restaurant where locally caught fish and seafood feature on the menu. Service here, from smartly uniformed staff, is professional and friendly. Good local produce, and fish purchased from fishermen on the beach make for the freshest of dishes. Try seared king scallops, parsnip purée, crisp pancetta with lime butter sauce, or a main course of sea bass with oyster mushroom, pine nut and rocket tagliatelle. The modern brasserie offers an alternative dining choice.

Chef: Eleanor Richmond **Owners:** Thorpness and Aldeburgh Hotels Ltd **Times:** 12-2.30/6.30-9.30 **Prices:** Fixed L £10.95-£12.95, Fixed D £22.50-£25, Starter £4.95-£7.95, Main £8.95-£14.95, Dessert £4.95-£5.95, Coffee £2, Min/Water £3.60, Service optional **Wine:** 33 bottles over £20, 26 bottles under £20, 20 by the glass (£4.95-£7.95) **Notes:** Vegetarian available, Civ Wed 90 **Seats:** 60, Pr/dining room 50 **Smoking:** N/Sm in restaurant **Children:** Menu, Portions **Rooms:** 38 (38 en suite) ★★★ HL **Directions:** Please telephone for directions **Parking:** 15

BARNBY MAP 13 TM48

The Swan Inn

Seafood NEW

Unpretentious pub serving a stunning array of fresh fish

☎ 01502 476646 Swan Ln NR34 7QF

A traditional inn with its distinctive pink walls and village bar, the Swan is also very well known for its fish restaurant called the Fisherman's Cove. In this low-beamed room, the nautical memorabilia includes the bow of a small dinghy mounted on the wall, where blackboards list the day's choice. Owned by a family of Lowestoft fish merchants, it offers a variety of the freshest fish, simply pan fried, grilled or cooked in batter, and served with chips or new potatoes, salads or peas. Expect jellied eels, home-smoked fish and shellfish among the superb choice.

Chef: Dawn Cartwright **Owners:** Danny Cole **Times:** 12-2/7-9 **Prices:** Food prices not confirmed for 2007. Please telephone for details **Directions:** Telephone for directions

BECCLES MAP 13 TM48

Swan House

Modern International

Informal venue for good food with music and art

☎ 01502 713474 By The Tower NR34 9HE
e-mail: info@swan-house.com
web: www.swan-house.com

Scrubbed tables, wooden floors and crackling winter log fires set the informal scene at this wine bar-style restaurant in the town's market place. Live musicians and art exhibitions also feature, plus special events such as wine-tasting dinners. A fairly eclectic, modern selection of dishes offers simplicity combined with excellent ingredients. Menus list key suppliers and offer helpful tips on wines to accompany each main course. Dishes range from crab and coriander tart with balsamic dressing for starters to main courses of duck confit with burnt orange sauce, and baked monkfish with lemongrass dressing.

Chef: Lesley Dumphie **Owners:** M R Blunk, Ms L Dumphie **Times:** 12-2.45/6.45-10, Closed 26 Dec, 1 Jan, Closed L 25 Dec **Prices:** Fixed D fr £21.50, Starter £4.20-£6.90, Main £11.90-£18.90, Dessert £4.50-£5.30, Coffee £1.70, Min/Water £2.60, Service optional, Group min 8 service 10% **Wine:** 10 bottles over £20, 41 bottles under £20, 10 by the glass (£2.90-£6.50) **Notes:** Sun L 2 courses £14.90, 3 courses £17.90, Fixed D Tue-Thur, Vegetarian available **Seats:** 40 **Smoking:** N/Sm in restaurant **Children:** Min 14 yrs **Directions:** Next to church tower in town centre **Parking:** On street & nearby car parks

BILDESTON MAP 13 TL94

The Bildeston Crown

Modern British **NEW**

Accomplished cooking in a stylish country inn

☎ 01449 740510 104 High St IP7 7EB
e-mail: hayley@thebildestoncrown.co.uk
web: www.thebildestoncrown.co.uk

Located in wonderful Suffolk countryside, this 16th-century coaching inn has been skilfully renovated to provide comfortable dining and accommodation. Beams, ancient brickwork, oak floors, leather chairs, imposing artwork and open fires all set the tone, while friendly, helpful staff move between elegantly set tables in the bar, dining room and, in summer, the terrace. Fresh local produce is used extensively to produce classic-style dishes with some French influences. Cooking is skilful and not afraid to offer simple starters like herring roe on toast as well as intriguing main course combinations like sea bass with oxtail faggot and red wine risotto, or Whitstable crab and Jerusalem artichoke ravioli. Finish maybe with lemongrass pannacotta.

Chef: Chris Lee **Owners:** Mr Buckle **Times:** 12-3/7-10 **Prices:** Starter £4-£20, Main £9-£32, Dessert £5-£20, Coffee £2, Min/Water £2.85 **Wine:** 36 bottles over £20, 28 bottles under £20, 15 by the glass (£2.95-£5.50) **Notes:** Tasting menu 8 courses £50, Sun L 1-3 courses £12-£20, Civ Wed 30 **Seats:** 40, Pr/dining room 16 **Smoking:** N/Sm in restaurant **Children:** Portions **Directions:** Telephone for directions **Parking:** 30

BROME MAP 13 TM17

The Snailmakers at Brome Grange

European

Accomplished cooking in luxurious surroundings

☎ 01379 870456 IP23 8AP
e-mail: bromegrange@fastnet.co.uk
web: www.bromegrange.co.uk

Although newly refurbished, the restaurant has all the atmosphere of an old inn, with its warm burnt-red walls, oak panelling, impressive curtains and rich upholstery. Smartly dressed staff offer professional service. The traditional British menu has French and Asian influences offering well-executed dishes and some luxury ingredients. Typical main courses include fillet of beef on a bed of bubble and squeak with a whisky and stilton cream sauce, or wild Scottish salmon served on crushed sweet chilli potatoes, or seafood filo. There is plenty of choice and good use of seasonal produce. The bar menu is also worth a look.

continued

England

BROME *continued* MAP 13 TM17

Chef: J Osborne & R Woodrow **Owners:** Paul A Meredew **Times:** 12-2.30/6.30-9.30 **Prices:** Fixed L £12.95-£17.95, Fixed D £24.95-£27.95, Starter £4.50-£6.50, Main £17.95-£24.95, Dessert £5.95, Coffee £1.50, Min/Water £3.50 **Wine:** 15 bottles over £20, 29 bottles under £20, 8 by the glass (£3.50-£4.50) **Notes:** Vegetarian available, Civ Wed 100 **Seats:** 34, Pr/dining room 90 **Smoking:** N/Sm in restaurant **Children:** Portions **Rooms:** 19 (19 en suite) ★★★ HL **Directions:** A12 take A140 towards Norwich, approx 20m on left **Parking:** 60

BUNGAY MAP 13 TM38

Earsham Street Café

Modern British, Mediterranean

Modern fare in unpretentious café

☎ 01986 893103 11-13 Earsham St NR35 1AE
e-mail: www.earshamstcafe@aol.com

Busy, bustling and informal, this great café restaurant is a hit with locals for afternoon tea and cakes, rustic Mediterranean inspired lunches and inventive weekend dinners. There's often a queue out the door, so be sure to book a table. A bright interior with scrubbed tables sets the scene in which to savour duck with pan-fried foie gras, or pork with black pudding and roasted apples. Dishes are well executed and the reliable kitchen makes good use of fresh local ingredients, particularly fish - baked halibut, pea and parmesan risotto and pesto dressing.

Chef: Stephen David,Christopher Rice **Owners:** Rebecca Mackenzie, Stephen David **Times:** 9.30-4.30/7-9, Closed Xmas, New Year, BHs, Sun, Closed D ex last Fri & Sat of month 7-9 **Prices:** Starter £4.25-£10.50, Main £6.95-£19, Dessert £4.25-£6, Coffee £1.10, Min/Water £2.50, Service optional **Wine:** 30 bottles over £20, 21 bottles under £20, 15 by the glass (£2.65-£8.40) **Notes:** Jazz supper 3 courses & glass champagne £30, Vegetarian available **Seats:** 55, Pr/dining room 16 **Smoking:** N/Sm in restaurant **Children:** Menu, Portions **Directions:** In the centre of Bungay **Parking:** Parking opposite

---

BURY ST EDMUNDS MAP 13 TL86

Angel Hotel - Abbeygate & Vaults Restaurants

Modern British

Imposing hotel fine dining near the cathedral

☎ 01284 714000 Angel Hill IP33 1LT
e-mail: sales@theangel.co.uk
web: www.theangel.co.uk

Charles Dickens reputedly wrote part of his *Pickwick Papers* whilst staying here, and indeed the setting in a pretty square looking across to the cathedral remains inspirational today. The impressive old coaching inn may have a rich history going back several centuries, but its comforts and services are bang up to date. Both the elegant main Abbeygate Restaurant and the Vaults restaurant below the ground floor are relaxed in style, and serve accomplished food along modern British lines. For starters, hot smoked salmon with horseradish ice cream, and a main dish of fillet of British beef with a seasoned mash, roasted shallots and red wine sauce show sound technical skills.

Chef: Simon Barker **Owners:** Robert Gough **Times:** 12-2/7-9.30, Closed Sun at Vaults, Closed L all week at Abbeygate **Prices:** Fixed L £13.90-£22.90, Starter £5.25-£8.95, Main £12.95-£21.95, Dessert £5.95, Coffee £2.50, Min/Water £3, Service optional **Wine:** 20 bottles over £20, 23 bottles under £20, 24 by the glass (£3.25-£12.95) **Notes:** Vegetarian available, Smart casual, Civ Wed 85 **Seats:** 85, Pr/dining room 80 **Smoking:** N/Sm in restaurant **Children:** Portions **Rooms:** 76 (76 en suite) ★★★ HL **Directions:** Town centre, right from Northgate St traffic lights **Parking:** 30

Best Western Priory Hotel

Modern British

Accomplished manor house hotel dining

☎ 01284 766181 Mildenhall Rd IP32 6EH
e-mail: reservations@prioryhotel.co.uk
web: www.prioryhotel.co.uk

A Grade II listed property in a pretty setting just outside town, built on the remains of a 13th-century priory. Beyond the landscaped gardens is the smart hotel restaurant where modern artwork and an up-to-date décor create a comfortable environment. After pre-dinner drinks in the lounge, the well-executed cooking based on quality ingredients, local where possible, ensures an accomplished meal. The flavours in oven-baked goat's cheese wrapped in peppered pastrami, and served with a cucumber and lime relish, are balanced by a pan-roasted rump of lamb with rösti potato, ratatouille and redcurrant glaze. Still hungry? A richly-flavoured chocolate and mixed nut brownie with home-made rum and raisin ice cream and a decent cup of coffee should satisfy the heartiest appetites.

Chef: Jon Ellis **Owners:** Priory Hotel Ltd. **Times:** 12.30-2/7-10, Closed L Sat **Prices:** Fixed L £18-£21, Fixed D £31-£35, Min/Water £2.95, Service added but optional 10% **Wine:** 44 bottles over £20, 43 bottles under £20, 4 by the glass (£3.25-£4.50) **Notes:** Coffee incl, Vegetarian available **Seats:** 74, Pr/dining room 26 **Smoking:** N/Sm in restaurant **Children:** Portions **Rooms:** 39 (39 en suite) ★★★ HL **Directions:** From Bury St. Edmunds follow signs for Mildenhall A1011. 1m out of town centre **Parking:** 60

continued

England

Clarice House

Modern European

Upmarket health and beauty spa with modern menu

☎ 01284 705550 Horringer Court, Horringer Rd IP29 5PH
e-mail: enquiry@claice-bury.fsnet.co.uk
web: www.clarice.co.uk

This neo-Jacobean mansion is now a small country-house health and beauty spa. The restaurant offers a Club menu with lots of healthy options like salads and grilled dishes, alongside hot or cold baguettes and side orders like bread, potatoes and rice. The fixed-price lunch and dinner menus offer a range of dishes with starters like wild mushroom tagliatelle with basil oil and mains of honey-roasted Suffolk ham hock served on a bed of crushed root vegetables.

Chef: Steve Winser **Owners:** King Family **Times:** 11-3/6-11, Closed Xmas, Boxing Day, New Year's day **Prices:** Fixed L £14.95, Fixed D £21.95, Coffee £1.50, Min/Water £3, Service optional **Wine:** 6 bottles over £20, 22 bottles under £20, 4 by the glass (£2-£3) **Notes:** Vegetarian available, for dinner **Seats:** 40, Pr/dining room 20 **Smoking:** N/Sm in restaurant, Air con **Rooms:** 13 (13 en suite) ◆◆◆◆◆ **Directions:** From Bury St Edmunds on A143 towards Horringer and Haverhill, hotel 1m from town centre on right **Parking:** 82

The Leaping Hare Restaurant & Country Store

Modern British

Seasonal and local produce served in a vineyard restaurant

☎ 01359 250287 Stanton IP31 2DW
e-mail: info@wykenvineyards.co.uk
web: www.wykenvineyards.co.uk

This is a vineyard restaurant, part of Wyken Hall estate, set in a 400-year-old Suffolk barn with high ceilings, old beams, wooden flooring and paintings and tapestries of leaping hares. The barn is divided between the restaurant and café. Modern simple cooking here makes use of good quality local produce. Try Wyken pheasant broth to start, or mains like braised faggots, clapshot and Savoy cabbage or rack of Suffolk lamb. The wine list naturally features the estate-made Wyken wines amongst others. The adjacent Country Store, and farmers' market every Saturday morning, are well worth a visit.

Chef: Peter Harrison **Owners:** Kenneth & Carla Carlisle **Times:** 12-2.30/7-9, Closed 2 wks Xmas, Closed D Sun-Thu **Prices:** Fixed L £16.95, Starter £4.95-£6.95, Main £11.95-£15.95, Dessert £4.95, Coffee £1.95, Min/Water £2.95, Service optional **Wine:** 10 bottles over £20, 12 bottles under £20, 5 by the glass (£3.50-£3.95) **Notes:** Vegetarian available **Seats:** 55 **Smoking:** N/Sm in restaurant **Children:** Portions **Directions:** 8m NE of Bury St Edmunds, 1m off A143. Follow brown signs at Ixworth to Wyken Vineyards **Parking:** 50

Maison Bleue

French

Upbeat French seafood brasserie

☎ 01284 760623 30-31 Churchgate St IP33 1RG
e-mail: info@maisonbleue.co.uk
web: www.maisonbleue.co.uk

Recently refurbished, this French seafood restaurant has had a modern, stylish make-over. With professional and friendly service, a dedicated local crowd creates a lively atmosphere. Seafood is treated simply and served as freshly as possible by the charming French staff.

continued

A bargain 'plat du jour with coffee' lunch is not to be missed, though the main menus are well priced too. Book ahead for the plateau de fruits de mer. Sample dishes include Mediterranean fish soup with rouille for starters, and mains of whole grilled Dover sole or pan-fried fillet of sea bass with a port sauce and foie gras.

Chef: Pascal Canevet **Owners:** Regis Crepy **Times:** 12-2.30/7-9.30, Closed Jan, 2 wks in summer, Sun-Mon **Prices:** Fixed L £10.95-£13.95, Fixed D £24.95, Starter £4.95-£9.95, Main £10.50-£18.95, Dessert £4.95, Coffee £1.95, Min/Water £2.95, Service optional **Wine:** 44 bottles over £20, 64 bottles under £20, 10 by the glass (£2.25-£2.65) **Notes:** Vegetarian available **Seats:** 65, Pr/dining room 35 **Smoking:** N/Sm in restaurant **Children:** Portions **Directions:** Town centre, Churchgate St is opposite cathedral **Parking:** On street

Ravenwood Hall Hotel

Traditional, International

Tudor hall with traditional food

☎ 01359 270345 Rougham IP30 9JA
e-mail: enquiries@ravenwoodhall.co.uk
web: www.ravenwoodhall.co.uk

With its origins in the reign of Henry VIII, this historic hall is set in 7 acres of tranquil countryside a couple of miles outside Bury St Edmonds. The hall itself has been restored over the years but retains an ornate carved oak structure and rare 16th-century wall paintings. Accommodating staff and easy-going food make dining here a truly relaxed and unpretentious affair, while the menu tends toward familiar classics with own-smoked fish and meats and herbs from the garden adding a homely touch. Start with Suffolk white onion and cumin soup, then continue with roast rack of lamb with rosemary dumplings.

Chef: David White **Owners:** Craig Jarvis **Times:** 12-2/7.30-9.30 **Prices:** Fixed D £24.95, Coffee £2.50, Min/Water £2.80, Service optional **Wine:** 55 bottles over £20, 32 bottles under £20, 10 by the glass (£3-£6.50) **Notes:** ALC 3 courses £35, Sun L 3 courses £24.95, Vegetarian available, Civ Wed 130 **Seats:** 50 **Smoking:** N/Sm in restaurant **Children:** Menu, Portions **Rooms:** 14 (14 en suite) ★★★ HL **Directions:** 3m from Bury St Edmunds, just off A14 junct 45 **Parking:** 150

DEBENHAM MAP 13 TM16

The Angel Inn

Modern British, French

Flavourful cooking in rustic restaurant with rooms

☎ 01728 860954 5 High St IP14 6QL
e-mail: dgiven@btconnect.com
web: www.theangelinn-debenham.org

Set in the heart of the peaceful village, this charming, 16th-century former inn turned restaurant with rooms has stayed true to its roots. Whitewashed walls, beams, pictures of country scenes and heavy wooden tables and chairs develop the restaurant's rustic air. The cooking though, is modern (the seasonal carte supplemented by daily blackboard specials), delivering fresh local produce with good depth of flavour. Take a medallion of beef fillet served with black pudding mash, beetroot crisps and Madeira jus.

Chef: Jonathan Watson **Owners:** Darren Given **Times:** 12-2.30/6.30-9.30, Closed D Sun **Prices:** Fixed L £11.95, Starter £4.75-£6.75, Main £11.25-£15.95, Dessert £3.50-£4.50, Coffee £1.50, Min/Water £2.75 **Wine:** 2 bottles over £20, 18 bottles under £20, 7 by the glass (£2-£3) **Notes:** Vegetarian available **Seats:** 32, Pr/dining room 24 **Smoking:** N/Sm in restaurant **Children:** Portions **Rooms:** 3 (3 en suite) ★★★ RR **Directions:** Telephone for directions **Parking:** 12

England

FRESSINGFIELD MAP 13 TM27

Fox & Goose Inn

Modern British

Pub turned restaurant in a pretty village setting

☎ 01379 586247 IP21 5PB
e-mail: foxandgoose@uk2.net
web: www.foxandgoose.net

The Fox & Goose is a country inn next door to the church in a classic village location. All the comforting features are there - exposed timbers and open fires - with a handsome bar and two dining rooms set off by modern art and a background of light jazz. On offer is a good-value lunch, a tasting menu of many courses in the evening (for whole tables only), and a great choice from the carte. The modern British dishes with French influences read beautifully, with various elements blending harmoniously together: pork fillet topped with a stilton rarebit, served on sprouting broccoli, with fondant potato, artichoke and peppercorn purée, pear tarte Tatin and roast pork jus.

Chef: P Yaxley, M Wyatt **Owners:** Paul Yaxley **Times:** 12-2/7-9, Closed 27-30 Dec, 2nd wk Jan for 2 weeks, Mon **Prices:** Fixed L £11.95-£13.50, Starter £4.50-£8.50, Main £11.95-£17.95, Dessert £4.50-£5.50, Coffee £1.95, Min/Water £2.50, Service optional **Wine:** 22 bottles over £20, 30 bottles under £20, 6 by the glass (£2.95-£3.50) **Notes:** Tasting menu £38, Vegetarian available **Seats:** 48, Pr/dining room 25 **Smoking:** N/Sm in restaurant **Children:** Min 9 yrs D, Portions **Directions:** A140 & B1116 (Stradbroke) left after 6m - in village centre by church **Parking:** 15

HINTLESHAM MAP 13 TM04

Hintlesham Hall

see below

HORRINGER MAP 13 TL86

The Ickworth Hotel

International

Modern, eclectic cooking in National Trust owned hotel

☎ 01284 735350 IP29 5QE
e-mail: ickworth@luxuryfamilyhotels.com
web: www.ickworthhotel.com

One of a small group of family friendly hotels, The Ickworth Hotel is the former home of the Hervey family and is now owned by the National Trust. The hotel boasts eclectic décor and numerous facilities including a crèche, children's play area, tennis courts and spa, with grounds designed by Capability Brown. The Inferno, a Mediterranean café concept, is aimed at families while more formal dining is available in the main restaurant. Here the menu boasts the likes of poached free-range chicken and root vegetables in a barley broth starter with a plate of local Suffolk pork (loin, cheek and belly) or a nage of mullet, lobster and shellfish to follow.

Times: 12-2/7-9.30 **Rooms:** 38 (38 en suite) ★★★★
Directions: From A14 take 1st exit for Bury St Edmunds (Junct 42). Follow signs for Westley & Ickworth Estate

Hintlesham Hall

HINTLESHAM MAP 13 TM04

Modern European V

Fine dining in outstanding country house

☎ 01473 652334 IP8 3NS
e-mail: reservations@hintleshamhall.com
web: www.hintleshamhall.com

You'll find plenty of comfortable lounges, open fires and fine pieces of art and china at this magnificent 16th-century country-house hotel set in 175 acres of grounds and landscaped gardens. The fine-dining Salon restaurant is a truly grand and formal affair (a jacket will be readily provided to those unaware of the dress code), with its high domed ceiling decorated with gold leaf, ornate cornices, a huge branched chandelier and large windows that look out onto the grounds. There are no surprises about the formal-styled, efficient table service. The kitchen takes a modern approach, though underpinned by a classical theme. Top-quality ingredients, sound execution and good depth of flavour abound. This is classic country-house cooking, consistent, accomplished and pleasing rather than cutting-edge, and aptly suited to the surroundings. For mains, perhaps choose sliced chump of lamb served with sweet potato, spring onion mash and a Gewürztraminer sauce, or perhaps a confit delice of brill teamed with crab tortellini and a shellfish reduction, and to finish a vanilla soufflé

with maple syrup ice cream. Mid-week lunch offers exceptional value and there's a serious wine list, too, with a good selection by the glass and a great selection of half bottles.

Chef: Alan Ford **Owners:** Ms Dee Ludlow **Times:** 12-1.30/7-9.30, Closed L Sat **Prices:** Fixed L fr £29.50, Fixed D £32.50-£47.50, Starter £10-£18, Main £22-£29.50, Dessert £8-£11, Coffee £3, Min/Water £3.50, Service optional **Wine:** 200 bottles over £20, 65 bottles under £20, 12 by the glass (£3.95-£8) **Notes:** Fixed L 3 courses, Vegetarian menu, Dress Restrictions, Tailored jacket at D; smart casual at L, Civ Wed 100 **Seats:** 80, Pr/dining room 80 **Smoking:** N/Sm in restaurant **Children:** Min at D **Rooms:** 33 (33 en suite) ★★★★ HL **Directions:** 5m W of Ipswich on A1071

IPSWICH MAP 13 TM14

❀ Il Punto

French

Solid brasserie cooking in full sail!

☎ 01473 289748 Neptune Quay IP4 1AX
e-mail: info@ilpunto.co.uk
web: www.ilpunto.co.uk

Climb aboard this vintage Dutch barge moored at Neptune Quay, a short walk from the town centre, and you'll find the dining room is split between the two decks. A suitably nautical feel has been created by the polished wood and blue and white fabrics, but the food is more French brasserie. Well-executed dishes are attractively presented and there are well-defined flavours in home-made ravioli of salmon and crayfish with asparagus sauce, pan-fried whole Dover sole meunière with parsley, lemon and butter sauce and iced nougat glacé with apricot coulis.

Chef: Frederic Lebrun **Owners:** Mr R Crepy **Times:** 12-2.30/7-9.30, Closed Jan, Sun-Mon, Closed L Sat **Prices:** Fixed L £12.95, Fixed D £24.95, Starter £5.20-£7.10, Main £13.50-£17.50, Dessert £4.95, Coffee £1.80, Min/Water £2.50, Service optional **Wine:** 37 bottles over £20, 44 bottles under £20, 8 by the glass (£1.60-£3.75) **Notes:** Vegetarian available **Seats:** 80, Pr/dining room 30 **Smoking:** N/Sm in restaurant **Children:** Menu, Portions **Directions:** Telephone for directions **Parking:** NCP

❀❀ Salthouse Harbour Hotel

Modern Mediterranean

Relaxed contemporary brasserie overlooking the marina

☎ 01473 226789 No 1 Neptune Quay IP4 1AX
e-mail: staying@salthouseharbour.co.uk
web: www.salthouseharbour.co.uk

A smart mix of contemporary minimalism and original features is the impressive styling at this 48-bedroomed hotel set in a renovated, early 19th-century warehouse overlooking the trendy area of Neptune Marina. The busy ground-floor brasserie comes decked out in sleek lines, with a stylish intimate bar, leather banquette seating, bold artwork, huge windows and a relaxed atmosphere. Its modern brasserie cooking perfectly fits the bill, with well-executed, clear-flavoured dishes using quality locally sourced produce. Think braised shank of lamb with leek chestnut mash and rosemary jus, or perhaps fillet of cod with a cranberry and thyme risotto. On warm summer days, you can dine alfresco and enjoy all the atmosphere of the marina.

Chef: Tim Keeble **Owners:** Robert Gough **Times:** 12-3/6-10 **Prices:** Starter £3.95-£8.95, Main £8.95-£18.95, Dessert £3-£7.25, Coffee £2.35, Min/Water £3.10, Service optional **Wine:** 11 bottles over £20, 22 bottles under £20, 32 by the glass (£3.25-£12.95) **Notes:** Fixed price Sun menu, Vegetarian available, Civ Wed 80 **Seats:** 60 **Smoking:** N/Sm in restaurant **Children:** Menu, Portions **Rooms:** 43 (43 en suite) ★★★★ TH **Directions:** A14 junct 53, A1156 to town centre and harbour, off Key St **Parking:** 30

IXWORTH MAP 13 TL97

❀ Theobalds Restaurant

Modern British

Village restaurant serving seasonal ingredients with natural flavours

☎ 01359 231707 68 High St IP31 2HJ
web: www.theobaldsrestaurant.co.uk

Theobalds is a smartly presented 16th-century property on the main street of the small village; a long established business run by husband and wife team Simon and Geraldine Theobald. The oak-beamed restaurant is simply decorated and hung with paintings by local artists. Here the seasonal menu might offer twice-baked cheese soufflé, followed by roast best end of lamb with candied aubergines and a rosemary and Madeira sauce. There is a separate lounge area with an inglenook fireplace and a pretty patio garden, both used for pre-meal drinks and coffee.

Chef: Simon Theobald **Owners:** Simon & Geraldine Theobald **Times:** 12.15-1.30/7-9, Closed 10 days in Summer, Mon, Closed L Tues, Thurs, Sat, D Sun **Prices:** Fixed L £19.50, Fixed D £26, Starter £6.50-£8.95, Main £14.95-£18.95, Dessert fr £6.75, Coffee £2.25, Min/Water £2.50, Service optional **Wine:** 44 bottles over £20, 17 bottles under £20, 5 by the glass (£2.95-£3.75) **Notes:** Fixed D price for midweek, Sun L 3 courses £24.50 **Seats:** 42, Pr/dining room 16 **Smoking:** N/Sm in restaurant **Children:** Min 8 yrs D, Portions **Directions:** 7m from Bury St Edmunds on A143 Bury/Diss Rd **Parking:** On street

LAVENHAM MAP 13 TL94

❀ Angel Hotel

Modern British

Medieval inn with lip-smacking food

☎ 01787 247388 Market Place CO10 9QZ
e-mail: angellav@aol.com
web: www.theangelhotel.com

First licensed in 1420 the Angel is at the centre of one of England's finest medieval villages and is replete with traditional period décor - including oak beams, inglenook fireplace and plain wooden chairs and tables. The cuisine is largely of the traditional kind with recent culinary innovations from the continent and even Asia making their way onto this attractive menu - crab and prawns with chilli and herb rösti to start, for example, then pheasant breast with braised red cabbage. Desserts (steamed syrup sponge would be typical) are served with a choice of cream, custard or ice cream.

Chef: Michael Pursell **Owners:** Mr & Mrs R Whitworth & Mr J Barry **Times:** 12-2.15/6.45-9.15, Closed 25-26 Dec **Prices:** Starter £3.95-£6.95, Main £7.25-£16.95, Dessert £4.25, Coffee £1.50, Min/Water £3, Service optional, Group min 10 service 10% **Wine:** 9 bottles over £20, 36 bottles under £20, 9 by the glass (£3-£3.75) **Notes:** Vegetarian available, Dress Restrictions, Smart casual **Seats:** 100, Pr/dining room 15 **Smoking:** N/Sm in restaurant **Children:** Portions **Rooms:** 8 (8 en suite) ★★ HL **Directions:** From Bury St Edmunds towards Sudbury on A134, then A1141 to Lavenham. In town centre, near Tourist Information **Parking:** 50

England

LAVENHAM *continued* MAP 13 TL94

Great House Restaurant

Traditional French

Gallic charm in Tudor setting

☎ 01787 247431 Market Place CO10 9QZ
e-mail: info@greathouse.co.uk
web: www.greathouse.co.uk

The Great House is a resolutely French restaurant (with rooms) with French staff in the most English of settings. The 15th-century house with a Georgian façade stands just opposite the historic Guildhall in this well-preserved medieval town. The beamed Tudor dining room boasts a huge inglenook, smell of logs, oak floors and uneven walls, making a splendid setting for high-quality rural French cuisine. An accomplished kitchen favours well-sourced luxury ingredients and an elaborate style, so expect to find duck foie gras and magret terrine with port jelly, herb-crusted rack of lamb with rosemary jus, turbot with vanilla sauce, and iced orange and Grand Marnier parfait on the menu.

Chef: Regis Crepy **Owners:** Mr & Mrs Crepy **Times:** 12-2.30/7-9.30, Closed Jan, Mon, Closed D Sun **Prices:** Fixed L fr £15.95, Fixed D fr £25.95, Starter £6-£9.50, Main £11-£22.50, Dessert £4.75-£6.75, Coffee £1.95, Min/Water £2.50, Service optional, Group min 10 service 10% **Wine:** 68 bottles over £20, 78 bottles under £20, 10 by the glass (£2.50-£7.50) **Notes:** Sun lunch £25.95, Vegetarian available **Seats:** 40, Pr/dining room 12 **Smoking:** N/Sm in restaurant **Children:** Portions **Rooms:** 5 (5 en suite) ♦♦♦♦ **Directions:** In Market Place (turn onto Market Lane from High Street). **Parking:** Market Place

The Swan Hotel

British

Dine surrounded by medieval splendour

☎ 01787 247477 High St CO10 9QA
e-mail: info@theswanatlavenham.co.uk
web: www.theswanatlavenham.co.uk

Once having an important connection to the town's wool trade, this 14th-century hotel stands out even amongst its medieval and Tudor village setting. A collection of delightful listed buildings, the interior is a riot of oak beams, panelled walls and leaded lights. With a minstrels' gallery, the elegant medieval great hall is populated by well-spaced tables, comfortably upholstered chairs, expensive table linen and formal settings. Attentive staff serve modern British and European dishes such as a starter of fresh crab risotto with elderflower and shisoo cress jelly and main courses of seared sea bass fillet with rosemary mash, caramelised salsify and lemongrass beurre blanc. The Rothschild omelette soufflé with apricot sauce is a rich and satisfying dessert.

Chef: Stuart Conibear **Owners:** Thorpeness & Aldeburgh Hotels Ltd **Times:** 12-2.30/7-9.30, Closed L Sat **Prices:** Fixed L £13.95, Fixed D

continued

£28.95, Starter £6.50-£12.75, Main £17.25-£19.25, Dessert £6.50-£8.75, Coffee £2.50, Min/Water £3.50, Service optional **Wine:** 100 bottles over £20, 35 bottles under £20, 9 by the glass (£3.75-£8.50) **Notes:** Sun L 3 courses £22, Vegetarian available, Dress Restrictions, No jeans or trainers, Civ Wed 80 **Seats:** 80, Pr/dining room 30 **Smoking:** N/Sm in restaurant, Air con **Children:** Min 10 yrs, Portions **Rooms:** 51 (51 en suite) ★★★★ HL **Directions:** From Bury St Edmunds take A134 for 6m. Lavenham is 6m along B1071 **Parking:** 50

see advert opposite

LONG MELFORD MAP 13 TL84

The Black Lion Hotel

Traditional Mediterranean

Stylish hotel dining on village green

☎ 01787 312356 Church Walk, The Green CO10 9DN
e-mail: enquiries@blacklionhotel.net
web: www.blacklionhotel.net

Overlooking the green, this delightful, stylish hotel successfully mixes Georgian charm with contemporary furnishings and modern dining. Crisp white linen and soft lighting mingle with antiques and oil paintings in the restaurant, while the cosy bar is more informal. British and Mediterranean cooking permeates the menu, with plenty of local produce used in flavoursome dishes like smoked organic salmon ravioli with dill and lime sauce, Long Melford sausage and mash with caramelised onions and chocolate brownies with black cherry ice cream. In summer, enjoy cream teas in the Victorian walled garden.

Chef: Annette Beasant **Owners:** Craig Jarvis **Times:** 12-2/7-9.30 **Prices:** Starter £4.25-£5.95, Main £10.95-£16.50, Dessert fr £4.95, Coffee £1.95, Min/Water £2.80, Service optional **Wine:** 55 bottles over £20, 32 bottles under £20, 10 by the glass (£3-£6.50) **Notes:** Vegetarian available **Seats:** 50, Pr/dining room 20 **Smoking:** N/Sm in restaurant **Children:** Menu, Portions **Rooms:** 10 (10 en suite) ★★★ HL **Directions:** From Bury St Edmunds take A134 to Sudbury. Turn right onto B1064 to Long Melford. Right onto A1092 to Cavendish. Black Lion on the green **Parking:** 10

Scutchers Restaurant

Modern British

Friendly bistro serving imaginative fare

☎ 01787 310200 Westgate St CO10 9DP
e-mail: eat@scutchers.com
web: www.scutchers.com

A bright, lively bistro where coloured fabrics, pine furnishings, lots of pictures and modern lighting combine seamlessly with the old beams in this ancient building, which dates from the 16th century. It may look smart but the atmosphere is relaxed and friendly. Modern British cooking gets positive treatment, the style being simple, with the quality and freshness of the raw ingredients enhancing competently cooked dishes. Typical choices on the extensive carte include grilled fillet of halibut on crushed potatoes with crab butter sauce, roast breast of Gressingham duck with caramelised apple compôte and Marsala gravy and white, dark and milk chocolate truffle terrine with coffee bean sauce. A good-value fixed-price weekday menu is also available.

Chef: Nicholas Barrett **Owners:** Nicholas & Diane Barrett **Times:** 12-2/7-9.30, Closed 25 Dec, 2wks Mar, last wk Aug, Sun-Mon **Prices:** Fixed L £15, Starter £6-£11, Main £14-£22, Dessert £6, Coffee £2.50, Min/Water £2.50, Service optional **Wine:** 100 bottles over £20, 14 bottles under £20, 12 by the glass (£2.80-£3.60) **Notes:** Vegetarian available **Seats:** 70 **Smoking:** N/Sm in restaurant, Air con **Children:** Portions **Directions:** About 1m from Long Melford towards Clare **Parking:** 12

LOWESTOFT MAP 13 TM59

The Crooked Barn

Modern European

Characterful dining in restful Broads setting

☎ 01502 501353 Ivy House Country Hotel, Ivy Ln, Oulton Broad NR33 8HY
e-mail: aa@ivyhousecountryhotel.co.uk
web: www.ivyhousecountryhotel.co.uk

This converted 18th-century thatched barn - complete with creaking floorboards and crooked beams - makes a delightful dinner venue with its beautiful garden views and ornamental lily ponds. Local artists' works hang on the wall and tables are clad in pale green with crisp linen napkins. Outside there is a courtyard for summer dining. Uniformed staff are friendly and helpful. Modern British and European dishes - made with fresh, predominantly local ingredients - revel in their simplicity, freshness and colour. Try the well-presented starter of monkfish and king prawn tempura or the main course of perfectly cooked Suffolk lamb with garlic mash, bean cassoulet and chorizo. Finish with the hot sticky toffee and orange pudding with a caramel sauce.

Chef: Richard Pye **Owners:** Caroline Coe **Times:** 12-1.45/7-9.30, Closed 24 Dec- 8 Jan **Prices:** Fixed L £13.95-£15, Fixed D £25-£29, Starter £3.95-£9.95, Main £13.95-£20.95, Dessert £4.95-£8.95, Coffee £2.95, Min/Water £3.50, Service optional **Wine:** 15 bottles over £20, 20 bottles under £20, 4 by the glass (£2.50-£3.25) **Notes:** Vegetarian available, Dress Restrictions, Smart casual, no shorts, Civ Wed 100 **Seats:** 45, Pr/dining room 16 **Smoking:** N/Sm in restaurant **Children:** Portions **Rooms:** 19 (19 en suite) ★★★ HL **Directions:** A146 into Ivy Lane **Parking:** 50

MILDENHALL MAP 12 TL77

Riverside Hotel

British, French

Popular hotel dining with lovely gardens

☎ 01638 717274 Mill St IP28 7DP
e-mail: bookings@riverside-hotel.net
web: www.riverside-hotel.net

Built in around 1720, this imposing red-brick Georgian hotel has been renovated to a high standard. It offers a choice of dining venues; The Terrace Bar is one option, where you can enjoy informal dining with alfresco eating weather permitting. The bright conservatory-style Terrace Restaurant is the more formal setting for dining; open-plan, it has glass doors along one side offering lovely views of the gardens, leading down to the river. Freshly prepared food is served from both fixed-price and carte menus. The setting makes this hotel a popular venue for weddings and events.

Times: 12-2/6.30-9.00 **Rooms:** 23 (23 en suite) ★★★
Directions: From M11 junct 9 take A11 for Norwich. At Fiveways Rdbt take A1101 into town. Left at mini-rdbt, hotel last on left before bridge

NAYLAND MAP 13 TL93

The White Hart Inn

British, French

First-rate gastro-pub cuisine with a French twist

☎ 01206 263382 High St CO6 4JF
e-mail: nayhart@aol.com
web: www.whitehart-nayland.co.uk

This ancient, smartly turned-out inn - set in a charming, quintessentially English village in the heart of Constable country - comes brimful of character. Think heavy wooden beams, tiled floors and feature fireplaces, while the restaurant (formally laid at dinner) is a more elegant affair, and there's a terrace for alfresco summer dining, too. The kitchen's French flair - as well as the polished, friendly and mostly Gallic service - reflects Michel Roux's ownership, with seasonality and quality local produce distinguishing accomplished, assured dishes on the lengthy repertoire. Expect classics like a rich shellfish bisque or terrine of foie gras to open, perhaps a casserole of tender lamb with spring vegetables to follow, and a pistachio crème brûlée to close. Lunchtimes see a lighter selection.

Chef: Christophe Lemarchand **Owners:** Mr M Roux **Times:** 12-2.30/6.30-9.30, Closed 26 Dec-9 Jan, Mon **Prices:** Fixed L £11.50, Starter £4.60-£12.80, Main £9.60-£16.20, Dessert £3.90-£4.60, Coffee £1.90, Min/Water £2.80, Service optional, Group min 6 service 10% **Wine:** 75 bottles over £20, 50 bottles under £20 **Notes:** Vegetarian available, Dress Restrictions, Smart casual, Civ Wed 70 **Seats:** 55, Pr/dining room 36 **Smoking:** N/Sm in restaurant **Children:** Portions **Rooms:** 6 (6 en suite) ◆◆◆◆ **Directions:** 6m N of Colchester on A134 towards Sudbury **Parking:** 22

NEWMARKET MAP 12 TL66

Bedford Lodge Hotel

Modern International

A perfect place to dine during Newmarket races

☎ 01638 663175 Bury Rd CB8 7BX
e-mail: info@bedfordlodgehotel.co.uk
web: www.bedfordlodgehotel.co.uk

Based around an 18th-century Georgian hunting lodge, Bedford Lodge is a popular destination for the racing crowd who enjoy its combination of refined period elegance and leisurely informality as well as the proximity to the gallops at Newmarket races. The Orangery restaurant has been decorated in keeping with the period and features a large menu populated by simple, tasty dishes that draw influences from all over the world, from the Far East (king prawn tempura) to modern British (pan-fried supreme of pheasant, casserole of winter vegetables with a port and sage liquor).

Chef: Adrian Doughty **Owners:** Barnham Broom Golf Club **Times:** 12-2.30/7-9.30, Closed L Sat **Prices:** Fixed L £15-£30, Starter £6-£14, Main £9-£25, Dessert £6-£10, Coffee £4.50, Min/Water £4, Service optional **Wine:** 40 bottles over £20, 8 bottles under £20, 12 by the glass (£4-£10) **Notes:** Vegetarian available, Dress Restrictions, No shorts, sandals, vests, Civ Wed 120 **Seats:** 47, Pr/dining room 150 **Smoking:** N/Sm in restaurant, Air con **Children:** Menu, Portions **Rooms:** 55 (55 en suite) ★★★★ HL **Directions:** From town centre follow A1303 towards Bury St Edmunds for 0.5m **Parking:** 100

Star Inn

☎ 01638 500275 The Street, Lidgate CB8 9PP
Catalan-influenced cooking from Mediterranean fish soup to tortillas.

ORFORD MAP 13 TM45

The Crown & Castle

Modern British

Fun and quality fine dining on the Suffolk coast

☎ 01394 450205 IP12 2LJ
e-mail: info@crownandcastle.co.uk
web: www.crownandcastle.co.uk

Put on the map as a foodie haven by its proprietor, food writer Ruth Watson, this Victorian, red-brick inn is set on Orford's old market square next to the castle keep and overlooking the estuary. Contemporary touches make a stylish statement, while stripped floors, simply set, closely positioned wooden tables offer a delightfully relaxed atmosphere that epitomises the gastro-pub genre. The cooking delivers a modern approach, showcasing fresh, locally sourced

continued

produce, with many of the dishes featured in Ruth's cookbooks. Skill, creativity and quality are high-end; the fixed-price menu divides into raw, cold and hot dishes plus desserts, such as Orford-caught skate, sautéed grapes, toasted almonds and nut brown butter.

Chef: Ruth Watson, Max Dougal **Owners:** David & Ruth Watson **Times:** 12.15-2.15/7-9.30, Closed 19-21 Dec & 3-4 Jan **Prices:** Fixed L £16.50-£19.50, Fixed D £35, Starter £3.95-£9.50, Main £13.95-£19.50, Dessert £5.50, Coffee £1.75, Min/Water £2.75, Service optional, Group min 8 service 10% **Wine:** 72 bottles over £20, 37 bottles under £20, 16 by the glass (£3.50-£7.50) **Notes:** Fixed D Sat & BHs only, Vegetarian available **Seats:** 60, Pr/dining room 10 **Smoking:** N/Sm in restaurant **Children:** Min 8 yrs D, Menu, Portions **Rooms:** 18 (18 en suite) ★★ **Directions:** 9m E of Woodbridge, off A12 **Parking:** 20

The Butley-Orford Oysterage

☎ 01394 450277 Market Hill IP12 2LH
Salmon, eels, cod roe, mackerel and kippers smoked on the premises.

SAXMUNDHAM

Pistachio Restaurant

Traditional British NEW

Relaxed, enjoyable dining in 17th-century surroundings

☎ 01728 604444 Main Rd, Kelsale IP17 2RF
web: www.pistachio-restaurant.com

New chef/owner, new name and new menu, but little has changed within this early 17th-century timber-framed cottage. The cosy beamed dining room has an old brick floor and open fireplaces, while crisp white linen and white crockery complement the mahogany furnishings. Good value lunch and dinner menus aim to offer sincere and unpretentious British food, with six choices per course. Choices range from crottin of goat's cheese with red onion marmalade or carrot and lentil soup for starters, to pheasant breast wrapped in Parma ham or Pistachio grill - Suffolk belly pork, lamb neck fillet, Gloucester Old Spot sausage, rösti and mushrooms.

Chef: Graham Ball **Owners:** Graham Ball **Times:** 12-2.30/6-9.30, Closed 3 days Xmas, Mon, Closed D Sun **Prices:** Fixed D £17.95-£20.95, Starter £4.95-£8.25, Main £8.95-£15.95, Dessert £4.95-£5.50, Coffee £1.20, Min/Water £2.50, Service optional **Wine:** 15 bottles over £20, 24 bottles under £20, 12 by the glass (£2.75-£8.75) **Notes:** Sun L 2 courses £9.95, 3 courses £14.95, Vegetarian available **Seats:** 55, Pr/dining room 25 **Smoking:** N/Sm in restaurant **Children:** Portions **Directions:** On A12, 0.5m N of Saxmundham near Kelsale junct **Parking:** 20

SOUTHWOLD MAP 13 TM57

The Crown

Modern British

Coaching inn offering modern city-style cuisine

☎ 01502 722275 90 High St IP18 6DP
e-mail: crown.reception@adnams.co.uk
web: www.adnams.co.uk

An original early 19th-century coaching inn with a wonderful panelled snug back bar, casual front bar and small formal restaurant. Service is relaxed and friendly throughout. The main bar is lively with a cosmopolitan feel and offers informal eating options, from a simple soup and a roll to local oysters, fish, Basque stew or steak. Ingredients are sourced locally wherever possible and food is freshly cooked to order. The restaurant offers city-style cuisine with the likes of locally

continued

smoked fish to start, followed perhaps by Suffolk chicken with red peppers and black beans or grilled rib-eye steak with hand-cut fries, mushrooms, onions and tomatoes.

Chef: Sue Miles **Owners:** Adnams PLC **Times:** 12-2/6.30-9.30 **Prices:** Fixed D £29, Starter £3.75-£6.50, Main £11.50-£16.50, Dessert £5.50-£6.50, Coffee £1.80, Min/Water £2.75, Service optional **Wine:** 154 bottles over £20, 86 bottles under £20, 17 by the glass (£2.30-£6.10) **Notes:** Sun roast available, Vegetarian available **Seats:** 30, Pr/dining room **Smoking:** N/Sm in restaurant **Children:** Menu, Portions **Rooms:** 14 (13 en suite) ★★ HL **Directions:** Take A1095 from A12; hotel in the middle of the High Street **Parking:** 15

The Randolph

Modern, Traditional

Stylish gastro-pub meets upmarket restaurant

☎ 01502 723603 41 Wangford Rd, Reydon IP18 6PZ
e-mail: reception@randolph.co.uk
web: www.therandolph.co.uk

This welcoming restaurant with rooms is a great base to explore the Suffolk coast. Once a pub, it still retains a traditional bar but modern wicker and leather furniture have now been added. With a lounge bar with comfortable leather sofas, the dining room has wooden tabletops with simple settings. Modern British dishes with European influences span the pub/brasserie divide with starters of smoked salmon and capers with bread or bubble and squeak with black pudding and pancetta to start and main courses of fish and chips or sea bass with smoked salmon and linguine. Finish with chilled rice pudding mousse with caramelised banana. A children's menu is available.

Chef: Martin Page **Owners:** David Smith **Times:** 12-2/6.30-9, Closed D 25 Dec **Prices:** Starter £3.50-£6.95, Main £7.95-£13.95, Dessert £4.50-£5.90, Coffee £1.75, Min/Water £3, Service optional **Wine:** 2 bottles over £20, 15 bottles under £20, 6 by the glass (£2.80-£3.20) **Notes:** Vegetarian available **Seats:** 65 **Smoking:** N/Sm in restaurant **Children:** Menu, Portions **Rooms:** 12 (4 en suite) RR **Directions:** 1m from Southwold **Parking:** 40

Swan Hotel

Modern British

Accomplished cooking in a seaside inn

☎ 01502 722186 Market Place IP18 6EG
e-mail: swan.hotel@adnams.co.uk
web: www.adnamshotels.co.uk

A former 17th-century coaching inn set on the market square at the heart of this pretty seaside town it may be, but today's Swan oozes cosy, contemporary styling. There's a comfortable drawing room, bar and lounge, while the elegant, bay-fronted restaurant looks out over the square. The accomplished kitchen's modern approach pays due reverence to quality local produce from the abundant local larder in well-executed dishes; perhaps a chicken liver parfait with home-made chutney and toasted brioche to open, and roast fillet of salmon served on creamed leeks with salsa verdi to follow. There's an excellent wine list and range of Adnams ales, too, while if staying over, the Admiral's Room comes complete with telescope to survey the sea.

Chef: Ian Howell **Owners:** Adnams PLC **Times:** 12-2.30/7-9.30 **Prices:** Fixed L £15, Fixed D £35, Starter £3.95-£6, Main £10.50-£14, Dessert £5.50-£6.50, Coffee £2, Min/Water £3, Service optional **Wine:** 60 bottles over £20, 75 bottles under £20, 8 by the glass (£2.35-£6) **Notes:** Dress

continued

Restrictions, Smart casual - no jeans, Civ Wed 40 **Seats:** 65, Pr/dining room 36 **Smoking:** N/Sm in restaurant **Children:** Min 12 yrs D, Menu, Portions **Rooms:** 42 (42 en suite) ★★★ HL **Directions:** Turn right off A12 signed Southwold/Reydon, continue for 4m into Southwold. Follow main street into Market Place, hotel on left **Parking:** 36

STOKE-BY-NAYLAND MAP 13 TL93

The Angel Inn

Modern British, Mediterranean

Traditional coaching inn with innovative cooking

☎ 01206 263245 Polstead St CO6 4SA
e-mail: theangel@tiscali.co.uk
web: www.horizoninns.co.uk

A traditional 16th-century oak beamed coaching inn, The Angel is part of the family-owned Horizon Inns collection. The emphasis here is on a relaxed style combining old and new, so you'll find period features alongside the modern art and leather sofas. The menu includes a few dishes served either as a starter or a main course, like steamed mussels in a white wine and cream sauce. Vegetarian choices include innovative options like baked tower of polenta, beef steak tomato and mozzarella with tomato coulis and salad. Other dishes feature local produce and might include wild boar and apple sausages or whole griddled sardines.

Chef: Neil Bishop **Owners:** Horizon Inns **Times:** 12-2/6.30-9.30 **Prices:** Starter £3.25-£6.95, Main £9.75-£16.50, Dessert £4.25, Coffee £1.50, Min/Water £2.35, Service optional **Wine:** 4 bottles over £20, 21 bottles under £20, 10 by the glass (£2.65-£7) **Notes:** Vegetarian available **Seats:** 28 **Smoking:** N/Sm in restaurant **Children:** Portions **Rooms:** 6 (6 en suite) ◆◆◆◆ **Directions:** From A12, take Colchester right turn, then A135, 5m to Nayland from A125, take B1068 **Parking:** 20

WALBERSWICK MAP 13 TM47

The Anchor

Modern British NEW

Gastro-pub serving unpretentious global- and traditional-influenced food

☎ 01502 722112 Main St IP18 6UA
e-mail: info@anchoratwalberswick.com
web: www.anchoratwalberswick.com

Very much in the gastro-pub mould, the Anchor comes with wooden seating, tables and floors and a typically relaxed atmosphere. The food is as unpretentious as the service, but strikes an unusual global path with influences from far and wide, while playing to the gallery with simpler comfort food, too. Rather interestingly, each dish is matched with a beer or wine, while the kitchen works with quality locally-sourced produce - many items admirably home grown on the owner's allotments. Expect the accomplished cooking to take in the likes of a feijoada - a pork and bacon stew with small red beans, rice and a fresh tomato salsa - and perhaps a vanilla and rosemary pannacotta or classic toffee-and-date pudding to finish.

Chef: Sophie Dorber **Owners:** Sophie & Mark Dorber **Times:** 11-4/6-11 **Prices:** Starter £4.50-£7.25, Main £9.25-£14.50, Dessert £4.50-£5.50, Coffee £1.50, Min/Water £2.50, Service optional **Wine:** 43 bottles over £20, 25 bottles under £20, 16 by the glass (£3-£5.75) **Notes:** Vegetarian available **Seats:** 70 **Smoking:** N/Sm in restaurant **Children:** Menu, Portions **Directions:** On entering village the Anchor is on the right **Parking:** 60

England

WESTLETON MAP 13 TM46

The Westleton Crown

British, Mediterranean

Great, British food in a Great British setting

☎ 01728 648777 The Street IP17 3AD
e-mail: reception@westletoncrown.co.uk
web: www.westletoncrown.co.uk

A traditional coaching inn with origins in the 12th century, The Westleton Crown manages to retain the rustic charm of its heritage with the comfort you'd expect of contemporary dining. Dine in the cosy parlour, elegant dining room, atmospheric conservatory or - when fine - on the terrace. Diners choose from a fairly extensive menu, with daily specials, offering classics with a twist - haggis spring roll with neeps and tattie fritters anyone? There are the barest hints of the Mediterranean and Asia, but this is largely of the modern British school - and jolly well done it is too. Mains might include oven-roasted fillet of beef with root vegetable broth or smoked fish platter with home-made relishes.

Chef: Richard Bargewell **Owners:** Agellus Hotels Ltd **Times:** 12-2.30/7-9.30 **Prices:** Fixed L £12-£24, Fixed D £17-£29, Starter £4-£5.50, Main £8.50-£17, Dessert £4.95, Coffee £1.35, Service optional **Wine:** 13 bottles over £20, 16 bottles under £20, 6 by the glass (£2.60-£5.20) **Notes:** Vegetarian available **Seats:** 80, Pr/dining room 40 **Smoking:** N/Sm in restaurant **Children:** Portions **Rooms:** 25 (25 en suite) ★★ **Directions:** From Ipswich head N on A12, turn right past Yoxford, follow tourist signs for 2m **Parking:** 30

WOODBRIDGE MAP 13 TM24

Seckford Hall Hotel

British, International

Sound cooking amid Elizabethan splendour

☎ 01394 385678 IP13 6NU
e-mail: reception@seckford.co.uk
web: www.seckford.co.uk

Queen Elizabeth I is rumoured to have visited this 16th-century manor and it still has a stately feel today with its imposing red-brick façade and carved oak entrance. Inside it's a warren of comfortable public rooms, including an elegant oak-panelled restaurant decorated with tapestries and fresh flower displays, where a lengthy menu of modern British cuisine is served. The accomplished kitchen makes good use of local produce, and dishes range from classy interpretations of familiar fare (sautéed calves' liver with mustard mash and crispy pancetta) to more adventurous combinations: pan-fried lamb with a boudin of Parma ham, apricot and foie gras perhaps, or roast pavé of cod with a pumpkin and spinach risotto.

continued

Chef: Mark Archer **Owners:** Mr & Mrs Bunn **Times:** 12.30-1.45/7.30-9.30, Closed 25 Dec, Closed L Mon **Prices:** Fixed L £16.50-£22, Coffee £2.75, Min/Water £3.50, Service included **Wine:** 40 bottles over £20, 45 bottles under £20, 10 by the glass (£3.25-£6.50) **Notes:** ALC 3 courses £29.50-£38.50, Vegetarian available, Dress Restrictions, No jeans or trainers, Civ Wed 125 **Seats:** 70, Pr/dining room 100 **Smoking:** N/Sm in restaurant, Air con **Children:** Menu, Portions **Rooms:** 32 (32 en suite) ★★★ CHH **Directions:** Hotel signposted on A12 (Woodbridge by-pass). Do not follow signs for town centre **Parking:** 100

YAXLEY MAP 13 TM17

The Bull Auberge

British, International

Family-run restaurant serving traditional fare

☎ 01379 783604 Ipswich Rd IP23 8BZ
e-mail: deestenhose@fsmail.net
web: www.the-auberge.co.uk

This roadside inn dating from 1453 has been converted by the current owners into a restaurant with rooms. Public areas have a wealth of original features, such as exposed brickwork and beams. The dining room is small and cosy with a relaxed and friendly atmosphere, and tables set with linen, candles and lemon bowls. The emphasis is on local produce served in rustic dishes, perhaps porcetta - Norfolk pork belly rolled around garlic and herbs, slowly roasted and served on braised red cabbage with parsnip mash and pan juices - or seafood casserole in an aromatic vegetable and saffron broth with potato gnocchi. For dessert, try cinnamon bread, custard and fudge pudding.

Chef: John Stenhouse **Owners:** John & Dee Stenhouse **Times:** 12-2/7-9.30, Closed Xmas, Sun & Mon, Closed L Sat **Prices:** Fixed L £12, Fixed D £19.50, Starter £3.50-£7.95, Main £11.75-£19.50, Dessert £4.95, Coffee £2.40, Min/Water £3, Service optional **Wine:** 10 bottles over £20, 35 bottles under £20, 9 by the glass (£2.75-£4.25) **Notes:** Vegetarian available **Seats:** 30, Pr/dining room 20 **Smoking:** N/Sm in restaurant, Air con **Children:** Portions **Rooms:** 4 (4 en suite) ◆◆◆◆◆ **Directions:** 5m S of Diss on A140 **Parking:** 25

YOXFORD MAP 05 TM36

Satis House Hotel

Malaysian

Listed 18th-century country house serving authentic Malaysian food

☎ 01728 668418 IP17 3EX
e-mail: yblackmore@aol.com

continued

Satis House Hotel

Charming privately owned hotel set amid landscaped grounds just off the A12. Charles Dickens was once a regular visitor and the property's name features in his book *Great Expectations*. A decent sized menu of Malaysian cuisine offers a good range of dishes from mild and spicy to pretty hot, and can be quite inexpensive, according to choice. An enjoyable chicken satay comprises tender pieces of chicken chargrilled and served with peanut dipping sauce and a good salad of shiitake mushrooms and rice noodles. Superbly flavoured, tender lamb curry made with yogurt and cinnamon is served with steamed rice and stir-fried vegetables in garlic. A great dish packed with flavour.

Chef: Ms D Ferrance, Mrs C Blackmore **Owners:** Mrs Y C Blackmore **Times:** 7-9.30, Closed 25 Dec-3 Jan, Sun, Closed L (by arrangement only) **Prices:** Starter £3.95-£10, Main £8.50-£16.95, Dessert £5, Coffee £1.75, Min/Water £2.95, Service optional, Group min 12 service 10% **Wine:** 8 bottles over £20, 20 bottles under £20, 3 by the glass (£3.75) **Notes:** Malaysian banquet 4 courses £25, Dress Restrictions, Smart casual **Seats:** 30, Pr/dining room 16 **Smoking:** N/Sm in restaurant **Children:** Min 5 yrs, Portions **Rooms:** 8 (8 en suite) ★★ HL **Directions:** Between Ipswich and Lowestoft on A12, N of village **Parking:** 30

SURREY

ABINGER HAMMER MAP 06 TQ04

Drakes on the Pond

Modern British, European

Skilful cooking in a classy village restaurant

☎ 01306 731174 Dorking Rd RH5 6SA
e-mail: info@drakesonthepond.com

Located on the edge of the village in a cottage-style building with views of the Surrey hills. Well-spaced tables are placed in a light and airy room decorated in yellows and golds with crisp linen, blue glassware and fresh flowers. Personally run by the friendly proprietors, the restaurant has a cheerful and upbeat atmosphere. Gentleness and sureness of touch characterises the cooking, with dishes of fresh white crab tian and creamed coconut with spice-coated soft shell crab and curry oil, slow-cooked loin of rabbit, confit leg, beetroot and potato dauphinoise and braised salsify, and glazed slow-roasted pineapple, soft sugar and ginger parfait with coconut tuiles.

Chef: Jonathan Clarke **Owners:** John Morris & Tracey Honeysett **Times:** 12-2/7-10, Closed 2 wks Aug-Sep, Xmas, New Year, BHs, Sun, Mon, Closed L Sat **Prices:** Fixed L fr £18.50, Starter £8.50-£16, Main £21-£25, Dessert £8-£9, Coffee £3.50, Min/Water £3.50, Service optional, Group min 8 service 10% **Wine:** 70 bottles over £20, 20 bottles under £20, 15 by the glass (£4.50-£5.75) **Notes:** Vegetarian available, Dress Restrictions, Smart casual **Seats:** 32 **Smoking:** N/Sm in restaurant, Air con **Children:** Min 10 yrs **Directions:** On the A25 between Dorking and Guildford **Parking:** 20

BAGSHOT MAP 06 SU96

Pennyhill Park Hotel & The Spa

see page 438

CAMBERLEY MAP 06 SU86

Macdonald Frimley Hall Hotel & Spa

Modern European

Smart country-house dining

☎ 0870 400 8224 Lime Av GU15 2BG
e-mail: gm.frimleyhall@macdonald-hotels.co.uk
web: www.macdonaldhotels.co.uk

This country-house hotel has been refurbished with impressive results, and although the décor is modern, traditional elements are retained. The Linden Restaurant is decorated in a fresh and contemporary style with lighting atmospheric with candles in the evening, and includes a large alcove area with four tables, which provides a more intimate dining area. Service is relatively formal but friendly. Modern European cooking is represented in fairly classical dishes such as chargrilled beef fillet with oxtail risotto, wild mushrooms and thyme jus or poached halibut with baby vegetables and lemon beurre blanc. Maybe a dessert of espresso crème brûlée with Amaretto ice cream would round the meal off nicely.

Chef: Max Pettini **Owners:** Macdonald Hotels PLC-Linden Restaurant **Times:** 12.30-2/7-9.45, Closed L Sat **Prices:** Fixed L £15.95-£24.50, Fixed D £27.50-£44.95, Starter £6.95-£9.50, Main £14-£24.95, Dessert £6.50-£7.50, Coffee £2.95, Min/Water £4.50, Service added but optional 12.5% **Wine:** 52 bottles over £20, 26 bottles under £20, 12 by the glass (£4.25-£6.35) **Notes:** Vegetarian available, Civ Wed 120 **Seats:** 70, Pr/dining room **Smoking:** N/Sm in restaurant, Air con **Children:** Menu, Portions **Rooms:** 96 (96 en suite) ★★★★ HL **Directions:** From M3 junct 3 follow signs for Bagshot. Turn left onto A30 signed Camberley/Basingstoke. At rdbt branch left onto A325, then right into Conifer Dr & Lime Ave to hotel **Parking:** 100

CHARLWOOD MAP 06 TQ24

For restaurant details see under Gatwick Airport (London), (Sussex, West)

DORKING MAP 06 TQ14

Macdonald Burford Bridge Hotel

International

Historic hotel offering contemporary design and dining

☎ 0870 400 8283 Burford Bridge, Box Hill RH5 6BX
e-mail: burfordbridge@macdonald-hotels.co.uk
web: www.macdonald-hotels.co.uk

Sitting at the foot of beautiful Box Hill, the hotel dates back to the 16th century and is reputedly where Lord Nelson and Lady Hamilton met for the last time before the Battle of Trafalgar. Today, it's a smart, contemporary hotel, with comfortable armchairs and sofas in the bar and an elegant modern restaurant with low ceilings and candlelit tables overlooking the gardens. The modern cooking, underpinned by a classical theme, encompasses quality produce alongside simple

continued on page 439

England

Pennyhill Park Hotel & The Spa

BAGSHOT MAP 06 SU96

Modern British NOTABLE WINE LIST

Innovative cuisine in luxurious five-star setting

☎ 01276 471774 London Rd GU19 5EU
e-mail: enquiries@pennyhillpark.co.uk
web: www.exclusivehotels.co.uk

Set in 120 acres of grounds, there's a nostalgic grandeur to the exterior of this ivy-clad Victorian manor now delightful country-house hotel, with state-of-the-art spa and the fine-dining Latymer restaurant. Set in the original part of the house, the Latymer is classical and classy, small and intimate. Think oak panelling, leaded windows and wooden beams teamed with heavy tapestries, innovative flower displays and beautifully presented tables. And, while the setting may be a touch traditional for some tastes, the food's certainly a more contemporary affair.

Expect innovative and elaborate modern cuisine underpinned by a classical theme on a fixed-price repertoire centred around tip-top, fresh produce with clean, clear flavours. Mains might comprise a slow-cooked fillet of beef teamed with horseradish mash and morels, or perhaps John Dory served with crushed potato and a velouté of thyme and foie gras, while a lemongrass crème brûlée matched with thyme ice cream and chocolate milkshake might catch the eye at dessert. As anticipated, service is formal yet friendly, while a jacket and tie are preferred.

Notable Wine List: The wine list is extensive and offers numerous wines by the glass, with examples to suit each dish on the menu.

Chef: Andrew Turner
Owners: Exclusive Hotels
Times: 12-2.30/7-10, Closed BHs, Closed L Sat, D Open D Sat-Sun, L & D Mon-Fri from 1 July
Prices: Fixed L £20, Fixed D fr £55, Coffee £3.95, Min/Water £3.95, Service optional
Wine: 250 bottles over £20, 12 bottles under £20, 272 by the glass (£4-£150)
Notes: Tasting menu available Tue-Sat, Vegetarian available, Civ Wed 160
Seats: 36, Pr/dining room 160
Smoking: N/Sm in restaurant, Air con
Children: Min 12 yrs, Portions
Rooms: 123 (123 en suite) ★★★★★
Directions: On A30 between Bagshot & Camberley
Parking: 500

England

DORKING *continued* MAP 06 TQ14

presentation. Take roast fillet of peppered beef with a millefeuille of aubergine, onion mousse and spicy langoustine provençale for example.

Chef: Clifford McCrea **Owners:** Macdonald Hotels **Times:** 12-2.30/7-9.30 **Prices:** Fixed L £19.50, Fixed D £28.95, Starter £7-£11.50, Main £16-£26.50, Dessert £7.50, Coffee £2.95, Min/Water £4.50, Service added but optional 12.5% **Wine:** 38 bottles over £20, 10 bottles under £20, 12 by the glass **Notes:** Vegetarian available, Dress Restrictions, No jeans, T-shirts or trainers, Civ Wed 200 **Seats:** 70, Pr/dining room 18 **Smoking:** N/Sm in restaurant **Children:** Menu, Portions **Rooms:** 57 (57 en suite) ★★★★ HL **Directions:** M25 junct 9. Towards Dorking, the hotel is on the A24 at the Burford Bridge rdbt **Parking:** 140

Two To Four

Mediterranean, Pacific Rim NEW

Eclectic dining in chic new town-centre restaurant

☎ 01306 889923 2-4 West St RH4 1BL
e-mail: eliterestaurants@hotmail.com

A charming Grade II listed building tucked away between boutiques and antique shops in the town centre is the setting for this interesting new restaurant venture. With dining on three floors, expect a chic, minimalist feel, with bare wooden tables, ceramic tiled floors and natural decorations with a friendly, bustling atmosphere and professional service. The eclectic carte and chalkboard specials list French classics combined with Asian influences, as seen in seared scallops with coconut and lemongrass risotto and a coriander and lime pesto, or fresh crab mayonnaise with crispy potato cake and a mango and pepper vinaigrette. Typical main course options include peppered beef fillet with truffle and thyme jus and herb-crusted rack of lamb with confit garlic mash.

Chef: Rob Gathercole **Owners:** Elite Restaurants **Times:** 12-2.30/6-10.30, Closed Xmas, Easter, BHs, 2wks Aug, Sun-Mon **Prices:** Fixed L £12, Fixed D £28.50-£33.50, Starter £7.50, Main £17.95, Dessert £6.50-£7.50, Coffee £2, Min/Water £3, Service added but optional 10% **Wine:** 32 bottles over £20, 12 bottles under £20, 6 by the glass (£4-£5) **Notes:** Vegetarian available **Seats:** 70, Pr/dining room 18 **Smoking:** N/Sm in restaurant, Air con **Children:** Portions **Directions:** M25, exit at Leatherhead junct, follow signs to Dorking town centre **Parking:** West St car park

EGHAM MAP 06 TQ07

The Oak Room at Great Fosters

Modern British NOTABLE WINE LIST

Regal Elizabethan setting for accomplished cuisine

☎ 01784 433822 Stroude Rd TW20 9UR
e-mail: enquiries@greatfosters.co.uk
web: www.greatfosters.co.uk

Steeped in history, this once moated, former royal retreat and now majestic Elizabethan manor hotel, sits in acres of celebrated landscaped grounds. Darkwoods, deep sofas and magnificent tapestries blend with exquisite period features in its stately interior, while the elegant, aptly named, Oak Room restaurant cleverly blends modern design with more traditional features. Think vaulted oak-beamed ceiling, open fire and mullioned windows versus high-backed chairs, large contemporary tapestry and friendly, polished service. The kitchen's modern approach flirts with the classical, delivering accomplished dishes showcasing quality produce. Expect a fillet of Buccleuch beef with braised shin, truffle mash and foie gras bonbon, and perhaps a bitter chocolate and pear tart with mascarpone sorbet to finish.

Notable Wine List: A well balanced wine list offering a wide range of quality wines; a good selection by the glass and a page of seasonal offerings.

The Oak Room at Great Fosters

Chef: Christopher Basten **Owners:** Great Fosters (1931) Ltd **Times:** 12.30-2/7-9.30, Closed L Sat **Prices:** Fixed L fr £19.50, Fixed D fr £32.50, Starter £9-£12, Main £22-£25, Dessert £7.50-£9, Coffee £3.75, Min/Water £3.75, Service added but optional 10% **Wine:** 250 bottles over £20, 4 bottles under £20, 15 by the glass (£4-£7) **Notes:** Sun L 3 courses £27.50, Vegetarian available, Civ Wed 170 **Seats:** 60, Pr/dining room 20 **Smoking:** N/Sm in restaurant **Children:** Portions **Directions:** 1m from town centre **Parking:** 200

EPSOM MAP 06 TQ26

Chalk Lane Hotel

Modern British, French V

Accomplished, simple cooking close to Epsom racecourse

☎ 01372 721179 Chalk Ln, Woodcote End KT18 7BB
e-mail: smcgregor@chalklanehotel.com
web: www.chalklanehotel.com

continued

England

EPSOM *continued* MAP 06 TQ26

Tucked down a little lane within a short walk of Epsom races and within a conservation area, this endearing listed hotel can be hard to find, so make sure you ring ahead for directions. There's a relaxed air of refinement here with guest comfort clearly a priority, and the engaging, informed and well-organised service is definitely part of the appeal of this intimate restaurant. Food has an unforced simplicity - don't expect fireworks, just great ingredients cooked with obvious technical ability. Starters might include risotto with razor clams, baby leeks and sweet basil shoots, while steamed sea bass with chilli ginger dressing would be a representative main course. Separate vegetarian menu available.

Chef: Greg Lewis **Owners:** Steven McGregor **Times:** 12.30-2.30/7-10, Closed L Sat **Prices:** Fixed L £10-£19.50, Starter £6-£12, Main £15-£25, Dessert £5.50-£8.50, Coffee £2.50, Min/Water £3.50, Service added but optional 12.5% **Wine:** 70 bottles over £20, 30 bottles under £20, 12 by the glass (£3.50-£4.75) **Notes:** Vegetarian menu, Dress Restrictions, Smart casual **Seats:** 40, Pr/dining room 20 **Smoking:** N/Sm in restaurant **Children:** Portions **Rooms:** 22 (22 en suite) ★★★ HL **Directions:** M25 junct 9 then A24 towards Ashtead & Epsom. Just in Epsom turn right at BP garage, then left into Avenue Road & follow hotel signs **Parking:** 60

FARNHAM MAP 05 SU84

Bishop's Table Hotel

Modern British V

Friendly formal dining in elegant surroundings

☎ 01252 710222 27 West St GU9 7DR
e-mail: welcome@bishopstable.com
web: www.bishopstable.com

In a convenient central location in the lovely market town of Farnham, the hotel restaurant offers a formal setting for dining. The building was once the home of the Marquise of Lothian, then a school for clergy, before its current incarnation as a hotel - complete with resident ghost known as 'William'. Don't let that put you off enjoying a combination of French classical cuisine and English cooking with modern twists, all using fresh ingredients. Try a starter of crab ravioli with sweet wine carrots and shellfish sauce, and a main course of cannon of lamb wrapped in tarragon mousse with rocket mash for example. Desserts might include an orange chocolate soufflé.

Chef: James Cooper **Owners:** Mr K Verjee **Times:** 12.30-1.45/7-9.45, Closed 26 Dec-5 Jan, Closed L Mon **Prices:** Fixed L £15-£17.50, Starter £6.20-£9.50, Main £16.20-£21.50, Dessert £6.20-£6.80, Coffee £2.50, Min/Water £3.60, Service optional **Wine:** 27 bottles over £20, 21 bottles under £20, 7 by the glass (£3.20-£5.20) **Notes:** Fixed L 3 courses, Vegetarian menu, Dress Restrictions, Smart casual, no jeans or T shirts **Seats:** 55, Pr/dining room 36 **Smoking:** N/Sm in restaurant **Children:** Portions **Rooms:** 17 (17 en suite) ★★★ HL **Directions:** A331 to town centre, next to public library **Parking:** Street parking, pay & display (300 yds)

GODALMING MAP 06 SU94

La Luna

Modern Italian

Stylish two-tone Italian restaurant

☎ 01483 414155 10 Wharf St GU7 1NN
e-mail: laluna@tiscali.co.uk
web: www.lalunarestaurant.co.uk

Sophisticated Italian restaurant with striking black-and-white décor - black high-backed chairs and crisp white-clothed tables - set on wooden floors. The recently appointed young head chef brings a new touch to the seasonal cooking. Special dishes include hand-made crab ravioli served with prawn bisque and capers, and pork fillet wrapped in ham and mushroom, rolled in puff pastry and served with sautéed Tuscan cavolo nero. Appetising vegetarian options - cannelloni bean soup with parmesan crostini, and delicate porcini and pumpkin risotto drizzled with truffle oil - are clearly marked on the menu. Tasting menu available.

Chef: Valentino Gentile **Owners:** Daniele Drago & Orazio Primavera **Times:** 12-2/7-10, Closed early Jan, 2 wks in Aug, Mon, Closed D Sun **Prices:** Fixed L fr £11.95, Starter £5.95-£9.50, Main £17.95, Dessert £4.75-£5.95, Coffee £2, Min/Water £3.75 **Wine:** 150 bottles over £20, 11 bottles under £20, 4 by the glass (£5) **Notes:** Fixed D 4 courses incl wine, Vegetarian available **Seats:** 58, Pr/dining room 24 **Smoking:** N/Sm in restaurant, Air con **Children:** Portions **Directions:** In centre of Godalming, junction of Wharf St & Flambard Way **Parking:** Public car park behind restaurant see advert opposite

---

GUILDFORD MAP 06 SU94

Café de Paris

French

Informal restaurant with an authentic French flavour

☎ 01483 534896 35 Castle St GU1 3UQ
e-mail: cafedeparis35@aol.co.uk
web: www.cafedeparisguildford.co.uk

This recently expanded restaurant has the avowed intention of providing a taste of Paris in the heart of Guildford. It is a large building with a stone-built Georgian frontage located opposite the castle grounds in the back streets along with many other bistro-style eateries. Cooking is very Parisienne, with lots of fish and a blend of traditional and creative dishes. Think duck foie gras sautéed with grapes and Armagnac, monkfish tail braised in mussel juice with white wine, mussel and saffron cream sauce, and tarte Tatin flambéed with Calvados and served with crème Chantilly.

Chef: Eddie Willen, Davide Creuzet **Owners:** Frank & Maya Kraus/Cafe De Paris Ltd **Times:** 12-2.30/6.00-10.30, Closed Xmas wk, BHs, Sun

continued

Prices: Fixed L £12.50, Starter £4.95-£11.50, Main £8.50-£24, Dessert £4.95-£5.95, Coffee £1.50, Min/Water £2.95, Service added but optional 10% **Wine:** 32 bottles over £20, 23 bottles under £20, 7 by the glass (£3-£4) **Notes:** Pre-theatre D £12.50, Vegetarian available, Smart casual **Seats:** 80, Pr/dining room 50 **Smoking:** N/Sm area, No pipes, Air con **Children:** Portions **Directions:** Guildford town centre, corner of Castle and Chapel Streets **Parking:** NCP

HASLEMERE MAP 06 SU93

Lythe Hill Hotel

Modern European

Sumptuous hotel dining in Surrey countryside

☎ 01428 651251 Petworth Rd GU27 3BQ
e-mail: lythe@lythehill.co.uk
web: www.lythehill.co.uk

Lythe Hill has been created from a collection of distinctive farm buildings, which include a splendid Elizabethan house, plus stylish, newer additions, each furnished in a style that complements the age of the property, and all set in 30 acres of glorious parkland. The Auberge de France restaurant is located in the timbered farmhouse and oozes historic charm, with mellow oak panelling and ancient beams creating an evocative dining ambience. The French-based menu acknowledges modern-day trends and classic dishes are given a fusion twist. Expect seared scallops with wild mushrooms, spinach and scallop velouté, roast monkfish with chorizo froth, and a classic lemon tart. The contemporary Italian Garden restaurant offers lighter dishes.

Chef: Neil Wackrill **Owners:** Lythe Hill Hotels **Times:** 12.30-2.15/7.15-9.45, Closed 25-26, 31 Dec, Closed L Mon-Sat **Prices:** Starter £6-£12, Main £15-£30, Dessert £6-£8, Coffee £3.50, Min/Water £4.75, Service optional **Wine:** 200 bottles over £20, 7 bottles under £20, 6 by the glass (£4.50-£11) **Notes:** Sun L 3 courses £14.95, Vegetarian available, Dress Restrictions, Smart casual, Civ Wed 130 **Seats:** 60, Pr/dining room 35 **Smoking:** N/Sm in restaurant **Children:** Menu, Portions **Rooms:** 41 (41 en suite) ★★★★ **Directions:** 1 mile E of Haslemere on B2131 **Parking:** 150

HORLEY For restaurant details see Gatwick Airport (London), (Sussex, West)

OCKLEY MAP 06 TQ14

Bryce's Seafood Restaurant

British, Seafood V

Rural fish destination with pub and restaurant options

☎ 01306 627430 The Old School House RH5 5TH
e-mail: bryces.fish@virgin.net
web: www.bryces.co.uk

Former boys' boarding school dating from around 1750, split into a pub area and more formal restaurant. The place is not on a main road and can be difficult to spot in the dark, but provides a welcoming environment with well-trained staff. The main menu is all fish, backed up by a blackboard, offering a modern take on fresh British seafood. Typical dishes are seared king scallops and calves' liver with black pudding fritters and sweet beetroot, or pan-fried fillets of gilthead bream with salmon risotto and chestnut mushrooms.

Chef: B Bryce and Richard Attkins **Owners:** Mr B Bryce **Times:** 12-2.30/7-9.30, Closed 25 Dec, 1 Jan **Prices:** Fixed L £23, Fixed D £29, Coffee £1.75, Min/Water £3.50, Service optional, Group min 8 service 10% **Wine:** 12 bottles over £20, 15 bottles under £20, 15 by the glass (£1-£15) **Notes:** Vegetarian menu **Seats:** 50 **Smoking:** N/Sm in restaurant **Children:** Portions **Directions:** From M25 junct 9 take A24, then A29. 8m S of Dorking on A29 **Parking:** 35

PEASLAKE MAP 06 TQ04

Hurtwood Inn Hotel

Modern British

An inviting village inn

☎ 01306 730851 Walking Bottom GU5 9RR
e-mail: sales@hurtwoodinnhotel.com
web: www.hurtwoodinnhotel.com

Set in the heart of a pretty Surrey village, this hotel dates back to the 1920s and still retains many original features. Oscar's restaurant occupies an oak-panelled dining room which is candlelit by night and boasts well-spaced tables, crisp linen and an abundance of fresh flowers. Choose from a menu of modern English dishes delivered by a

continued

PEASLAKE *continued* MAP 06 TQ04

long-standing team who know their stuff; pan-seared scallops are a typical starter, served with black pudding and creamed leeks, while mains might include pancetta-wrapped guinea fowl with root vegetable rösti, or a parcel of halibut with pea purée and saffron cream sauce.

Chef: Gerry Dee **Owners:** Mr & Mrs S Best **Times:** 12-2/7-9.30, Closed 26-30 Dec, 1 Jan, Closed L Mon, Fri, Sat, D Sun **Prices:** Starter £5.25-£6.75, Main £9.95-£18.95, Dessert £4.95-£5.25, Coffee £2, Min/Water £2.95, Service optional **Wine:** 22 bottles over £20, 15 bottles under £20, 7 by the glass (£2.75-£3.95) **Notes:** Sun L 2-3 courses £14.95-£16.95, Gastronomic menu £32.50, Vegetarian available, No trainers or shorts **Seats:** 30, Pr/dining room 25 **Smoking:** N/Sm in restaurant **Children:** Portions **Rooms:** 21 (21 en suite) ★★★ HL **Directions:** Leave A25 in Gomshall, follow signs to Peaslake, turn opposite Jet Garage, follow hotel signs **Parking:** 22

REDHILL MAP 06 TQ25

Nutfield Priory - Cloisters Restaurant

Modern European V

A unique setting for ambitious cuisine

☎ 01737 824400 Nutfield RH1 4EL
e-mail: nutfieldpriory@handpicked.co.uk
web: www.handpicked.co.uk

Built in the late 19th century as an extravagant folly, this stately priory is bedecked with elaborate carving, ornate stonework and stunning stained glass. The Cloisters House restaurant offers secluded spaces for special celebrations and panoramic views across three counties. It's an imposing affair and the food doesn't let the side down; the capable kitchen has a sensitive touch and delivers ambitious creations such as an assiette of sea bass, salmon and mahi with Puglia fennel risotto and saffron-infused mussel cream, or roasted Balmoral pheasant breast with bubble-and-squeak and a Madeira and sage jus, followed by a gratin of poached pear with wasabi ice cream and hazelnut nougatine.

Chef: Mark Bradford **Owners:** Hand Picked Hotels **Times:** 12-2/7-9.30, Closed L Sat **Prices:** Fixed L £18.50-£22.50, Fixed D £35-£40, Starter £6.50-£13.50, Main £20-£30, Dessert £6.50-£11, Coffee £3.75, Min/Water £4, Service optional **Wine:** 78 bottles over £20, 10 bottles under £20, 8 by the glass (£4.75-£11) **Notes:** Vegetarian menu, Dress Restrictions, No jeans, Civ Wed 80 **Seats:** 60, Pr/dining room 100 **Smoking:** N/Sm in restaurant **Children:** Portions **Rooms:** 60 (60 en suite) ★★★★ HL **Directions:** On A25, 1m E of Redhill, off M25 junct 8 **Parking:** 130

REIGATE MAP 06 TQ25

The Dining Room

Modern British V

Inspirational cooking in stylish Surrey

☎ 01737 226650 59a High St RH2 9AE

This modern, stylish restaurant brings a touch of the London scene to Reigate. The new bar with leather sofas and soft lights is creating a stir as a fabulous location for pre- and post-dinner drinks. In the restaurant, Tony Tobin continues to offer imaginative British dishes using fresh ingredients. His cooking draws inspiration from the Mediterranean and further afield Thailand and Australia. Seared sea scallops with cauliflower purée, curried beignets and curry oil offer a spicy option to start. Follow this with a modern dish like seared fillet of beef with foie gras wontons, truffle mash and red wine sauce. A more traditional combination for dessert might be hot chocolate fondant with pistachio shortbread and pistachio ice cream.

Chef: Tony Tobin **Owners:** Tony Tobin **Times:** 12-2/7-10, Closed Xmas & BHs, Closed L Sat, D Sun **Prices:** Fixed L £28.50, Fixed D £28.50-£34, Starter £10.50, Main £18, Dessert £7.95, Coffee £3.50, Min/Water £3.50, Service added but optional 12.5% **Wine:** 61 bottles over £20, 16 bottles under £20, 10 by the glass (£4.50-£12.50) **Notes:** Fixed D 2 courses, Tasting menu £42.00, Vegetarian menu, Dress Restrictions, Smart casual **Seats:** 75, Pr/dining room 28 **Smoking:** N/Sm in restaurant, Air con **Children:** Portions **Directions:** 1st floor restaurant on Reigate High St **Parking:** On street, car park

RIPLEY MAP 06 TQ05

Drake's Restaurant

see opposite

SHERE MAP 06 TQ04

Kinghams

Modern British

Local produce showcased in attractive cottage restaurant surroundings

☎ 01483 202168 Gomshall Ln GU5 9HE
e-mail: paul@kinghams-restaurant.co.uk
web: www.kinghams-restaurant.co.uk

Built in the 1620s, this pretty red-brick cottage enjoys a picturesque Surrey village setting. The interior has a welcoming feel with low ceilings and beams, crisp white linen and well-trained staff attending to customers' needs. There is a heated gazebo in the garden for summer months. Cooking is imaginative with excellent presentation and uses lots of local, seasonal farm produce. Fresh fish is delivered daily so you could start with soused mackerel in orange, carrot and fennel before moving on to a main course of grilled Dover sole with lemon and lime butter. Carnivores might prefer pan-fried lamb rump stuffed with shallots and black pudding. To finish, there's warm banana and Jersey black butter pudding on sage parfait.

Chef: Paul Baker **Owners:** Paul Baker **Times:** 12.15-2.30/7-9.30, Closed 25 Dec-4 Jan, Mon, Closed D Sun **Prices:** Fixed L £14.95, Fixed D £21.90, Starter £5.95-£8.95, Main £10.95-£18.95, Dessert £4.95-£5.95, Coffee £3, Min/Water £3.50, Service optional, Group min 8 service 10% **Wine:** 18 bottles over £20, 26 bottles under £20, 6 by the glass (£3.50-£7.95) **Notes:** Vegetarian available **Seats:** 48, Pr/dining room 24 **Smoking:** N/Sm in restaurant **Children:** Portions **Directions:** On A25 between Guildford and Dorking. 12 mins from M25 junct 10 **Parking:** 16

continued

Drake's Restaurant

RIPLEY MAP 06 TQ05

Modern French

Skilled, artisan cooking in village restaurant

☎ 01483 224777 The Clock House, High St GU23 6AQ
web: www.drakesrestaurant.co.uk

An imposing, red-brick Georgian house, with its old restored clock set above the doorway, picks out this Surrey culinary high-flyer. Home to chef-patron Steve Drake (ex Drakes on the Pond at Abinger Hammer), the eponymous restaurant has fine pedigree and goes from strength to strength, driven by a dedicated young team who show clear dedication and passion to their craft. A green and lemon colour scheme (green carpet, lemon walls, green upholstered chairs) is complemented by interesting artwork, the open-plan space having an unstuffy vibe, smart but in an unpretentious and relaxed way. Tables are formally laid and there's a small seating area for aperitifs, plus the bonus of a pretty walled garden for summer drinks. Steve's cooking takes a modern approach (he likes to describes it as 'artisan cooking') and oozes skill, flair and finesse, creating dishes presented with elegant simplicity and clean, clear flavours from the freshest, high-quality seasonal produce. Think venison saddle with 'chou farci' and sauté of girolle and artichoke, with perhaps a chilled mint and cardamom soup served with a cardamom biscuit to finish. And do save room for the cracking petits fours, too, just don't fight over them. Definitely one to watch.

Chef: Steve Drake **Owners:** Steve & Serina Drake **Times:** 12-1.30/7-9.30, Closed 2 wks Xmas, 2 wks Aug, Sun, Mon, Closed L Sat **Prices:** Fixed L fr £19.50, Fixed D fr £39.50, Coffee £3.50, Min/Water £3.50, Service optional **Wine:** 100 bottles over £20, 22 bottles under £20, 8 by the glass (£4-£6) **Notes:** Tasting menu £58, Smart casual **Seats:** 34, Pr/dining room 10 **Smoking:** N/Sm in restaurant **Children:** Min 12 yrs **Directions:** M25 junct 10/A3 towards Guildford. Follow Ripley signs off A3, restaurant in centre of village. **Parking:** 2

STOKE D'ABERNON MAP 06 TQ15

Woodlands Park Hotel

Modern European

Grand retreat with country-house style

☎ 01372 843933 Woodlands Ln KT11 3QB
e-mail: woodlandspark@handpicked.co.uk
web: www.handpicked.co.uk

Originally built for the Bryant family, the matchmakers, this beautiful Victorian mansion enjoys an attractive setting in 10.5 acres of Surrey countryside. The original house retains many period features including a grand hall, minstrels' gallery and impressive staircase. You can enjoy a pre-dinner drink in the cocktail bar while you decide where to dine. Contemporary cuisine is on offer in the informal brasserie as an alternative to the more formal main oak-panelled dining room. The focus here is on carefully prepared dishes using high-quality ingredients. A simple combination of modern European influences results in imaginative cooking, complemented by fine wines.

Times: 12-2.30/7-10, Closed Mon, Closed L Mon-Sat, D Sun **Rooms:** 57 (57 en suite) ★★★★ **Directions:** From M25 junct 10, A3 towards London. Through Cobham centre and Stoke D'Abernon, left at garden centre into Woodlands Lane. Hotel 0.5m on left

TADWORTH MAP 06 TQ25

Gemini

International V

Relaxed urban restaurant with appealing menus

☎ 01737 812179 28 Station Approach KT20 5AH
e-mail: comments@gemini-restaurant.com
web: www.gemini-restaurant.com

This well-established restaurant is located in a modest parade of shops and has developed a loyal local following over the years. The separate bar area and the dining room have a relaxed feel to them with traditional table settings and friendly and attentive service. The notable technical skills of the kitchen combined with high quality ingredients produce dishes that draw on French, British and Asian traditions. Start with the duck and ginger spring rolls and noodle salad served with Thai sauce before a main course of beef rib-eye with vine tomatoes, roquefort and port sauce with field mushrooms. Finish with warm blackberry and apple crumble with vanilla ice cream.

Chef: Graham Clark **Owners:** Claire Wigzell **Times:** 12-2/7-9.30, Closed L Sat, D Sun **Prices:** Fixed L £11-£15, Starter £3.95-£9.50, Main £11.50-£18.50, Dessert fr £5.50, Coffee £2.80, Min/Water £3.20, Service added 10% **Wine:** 29 bottles over £20, 12 bottles under £20, 2 by the glass (£3.50-£4.50) **Notes:** Sun L 3 courses £25, Vegetarian menu, Dress Restrictions, Smart casual **Seats:** 50 **Smoking:** N/Sm in restaurant
Children: Portions **Directions:** M25 junct 8, at rdbt turn right to Sutton, on 3rd rdbt take 2nd exit to Tadworth at lights turn right, restaurant on left
Parking: On street

England

SUSSEX, EAST

BATTLE MAP 07 TQ71

Powder Mills Hotel

Modern English V

Modern British menu in a well-appointed conservatory dining room

☎ 01424 775511 Powdermill Ln TN33 0SP
e-mail: powdc@aol.com
web: www.powdermillshotel.com

This stunning 18th-century country-house hotel nestles in 200 acres of beautiful parkland - guests can enjoy walks through the many woodland trails. Originally the site of a gunpowder works, Powdermills has now been skilfully converted into a fascinating hotel. The conservatory restaurant is sumptuously Georgian with marble floors, Greek statues and huge windows looking out onto the terrace and swimming pool. The food however is resolutely modern with dishes like ginger seared scallops with a feuilleté of tomato fondue, pan roasted turbot with a tagliatelle of baby leek and truffle, or a dark chocolate and walnut mousse with walnut ice cream demonstrating an ambitious and generally well-executed cooking style.

Chef: James Penn **Owners:** Mr & Mrs D Cowpland **Times:** 12-2/7-9 **Prices:** Fixed L £14, Fixed D £29.50, Starter £7.50-£10, Main £20-£30, Dessert £7.50-£10, Coffee £2, Min/Water £2.75, Service added but optional 10% **Wine:** 60 bottles over £20, 40 bottles under £20, 4 by the glass (£2.80-£3.50) **Notes:** Vegetarian menu, Dress Restrictions, Smart casual, no jeans, shorts or T-shirts, Civ Wed 100 **Seats:** 90, Pr/dining room 16 **Smoking:** N/Sm in restaurant **Children:** Menu, Portions **Rooms:** 40 (40 en suite) ★★★ HL **Directions:** A21/A2100 past Battle Abbey. Turn into Powder Mill Lane, first right **Parking:** 100

BRIGHTON MAP 06 TQ30

Due South

British, European

Seaside dining, committed to organic and local produce

☎ 01273 821218 139 Kings Rd Arches BN1 2FN
e-mail: eat@duesouth.co.uk
web: www.duesouth.co.uk

A modern glass-fronted restaurant set into an old archway right on the seafront. There is an outside terrace for alfresco dining while inside the dining area is upstairs. Brown banquette seating and polished pine tables give a modern feel. The restaurant is popular locally and has a strong commitment to the environment and renewable resources. The menu focuses on local, seasonal produce from organic and free-range

continued

sources, 80% sourced within a 20-mile radius. Dishes like local wild rabbit kebabs and grilled fish of the day reflect this philosophy. Wines are English and European to cut down on long import distances.

Chef: James Jenkins **Owners:** Robert Shenton **Times:** 12-4/6-9.30, Closed 2 wks Xmas & New Yr, Closed D Sun **Prices:** Starter £5.50-£8.50, Main £11.50-£18.95, Dessert £5-£5.50, Coffee £1.85, Min/Water £3.50, Service added but optional 10%, Group min 6 service 10% **Wine:** 29 bottles over £20, 14 bottles under £20, 8 by the glass (£3.80-£4.75) **Notes:** Vegetarian available **Seats:** 55, Pr/dining room 14 **Smoking:** N/Sm in restaurant **Children:** Min 14 yrs D, Portions **Directions:** On seafront, opposite cinema **Parking:** NCP Churchill Sq

The Gingerman Restaurant

British, French

Straightforward cuisine at a busy Brighton eatery

☎ 01273 326688 21A Norfolk Square BN1 2PD
e-mail: info@gingermanrestaurants.com
web: www.gingermanrestaurants.com

Popular Brighton eatery with an easy-on-the-eye modern décor of stripped pine floorboards, white walls and smartly dressed tables. Lunch is good value, but dinner brings more complex fare; expect a modern European menu created from quality local ingredients, with fresh fish from the boats a daily speciality. Mains might include braised pork belly with cauliflower purée and port sauce, or roast monkfish tail with steamed leeks and a creamy mussel broth, while desserts such as chocolate Jaffa crème brûlée make the perfect finale.

Chef: Ben McKellar/David Keates **Owners:** Ben & Pamela McKellar **Times:** 12.30-2/7-10, Closed 2 wks winter, Sun-Mon **Prices:** Fixed L £13.95-£24, Fixed D £27, Coffee £2.50, Min/Water £3, Group min 6 service 10% **Notes:** Sun L 3 courses £20, Vegetarian available **Seats:** 32 **Smoking:** N/Sm in restaurant, Air con **Children:** Portions **Directions:** Telephone for directions

Hotel du Vin Brighton

British, French NOTABLE WINE LIST

Stylish brasserie dining in Metropolitan hotel setting

☎ 01273 718588 Ship St BN1 1AD
e-mail: info@brighton.hotelduvin.com
web: www.hotelduvin.com

Perfectly located between the seafront and The Lanes shopping area, this stylish landmark hotel and bistro occupies a tastefully converted mock-Tudor building. Décor has a strong wine theme, from the individually designed bedrooms through to the buzzy, split-level bar and the relaxed brasserie-style restaurant, with its wooden floors and subtle lighting. Cooking is classic bistro style. The modern European menu has a pronounced French accent, as seen in foie gras and chicken liver parfait with onion marmalade, coq au vin, cassoulet, and roast cod with parsley beurre blanc.

Notable Wine List: A key hallmark of this group is an extensive wine list, packed full of interest and high-quality wines.

Chef: Rob Carr **Owners:** Marylebone Warwick Balfour **Times:** 12-2/7-10, Closed L Dec 31 lunch only **Prices:** Fixed L £14.50, Starter £4.50-£6.75, Main £14.50-£16.95, Dessert £6.75, Coffee £2.75, Min/Water £3, Service optional **Wine:** 450 bottles over £20, 40 bottles under £20, 16 by the glass (£3.50-£16.10) **Notes:** Fixed L incl glass of wine, Sun L 3 courses £23.50, Vegetarian available **Seats:** 85, Pr/dining room 36 **Smoking:** N/Sm in restaurant **Children:** Menu, Portions **Rooms:** 33 (33 en suite) ★★★★ TH **Directions:** A23 to seafront, at rdbt take right, then right onto Middle St, bear right until Ship St, hotel is at sea end, on the right **Parking:** 10

One Paston Place

Modern Italian

Imaginative, skilful cooking in plush surroundings

☎ 01273 606933 1 Paston Place BN2 1HA
e-mail: info@onepastonplace.co.uk
web: www.onepastonplace.co.uk

The baroque and classical interior comes with wooden floors and walls decked out with mirrors that help lighten the formality of the dining room (as do the very friendly staff). Well-spaced tables and crisp white linen combine with chandeliers and a giant silver ice bucket brimful of champagne and wine. Contemporary European cooking is the style and, with Francesco Furriello at the stove, there's a touch of Italian inspiration about the repertoire, too. There are three menus: an everyday menu, a taster option and more sedate carte. Peripherals like amuse-bouche and pre-desserts add interest. Dishes include a starter of tortelli of lobster with seared haddock and sauternes sauce, followed by venison rossini with foie gras, alba white truffle and Madeira.

Chef: Francesco Furriello **Owners:** Gusto Ltd **Times:** 12-2.30/7-late, Closed Sun-Mon **Prices:** Fixed L fr £16, Fixed D fr £29, Service optional, Group min 25 service 12.5% **Wine:** 144 bottles over £20, 7 bottles under £20, 11 by the glass (£4.50-£6) **Notes:** Vegetarian available, Taster menu £59 **Seats:** 40 **Smoking:** N/Sm in restaurant, Air con **Children:** Min 7 yrs, Portions **Directions:** Between Palace Pier & Marina **Parking:** Street parking available

Sevendials

Modern European

Former bank transformed into a stylish restaurant offering modern cuisine

☎ 01273 885555 1-3 Buckingham Place BN1 3TD
e-mail: sam@sevendialsrestaurant.co.uk
web: www.sevendialsrestaurant.co.uk

This former bank is built in a triangular shape dictated by two roads running either side. It is now a stylish restaurant with high ceilings featuring deep cornicing and beige walls punctuated by dark stained wood window surrounds. Dark wooden tables and modern art contribute to a clubby feel. Simple brasserie-style European cookery can be enjoyed in generous portions with some unusual flavour combinations. Try the likes of confit duck leg with Spanish lentil, tomato and chorizo stew, or Sevendials steak and kidney pie with buttered mash and cabbage. Good selection of champagnes and cocktails.

Chef: Sam Metcalfe **Owners:** Sam Metcalfe **Times:** 12-2.30/7-10.30, Closed Xmas & New Year, Mon **Prices:** Fixed L fr £10, Starter £5-£10, Main £10-£20, Dessert £5.50-£6.50, Coffee £1.40, Min/Water £3, Service added but optional 12% **Wine:** 52 bottles over £20, 21 bottles under £20, 12 by the glass (£3-£4.75) **Notes:** Vegetarian available, Civ Wed 55 **Seats:** 55, Pr/dining room 20 **Smoking:** No pipes, No cigars **Children:** Menu, Portions **Directions:** From Brighton station turn right 0.5m up hill, restaurant situated at Seven Dials rdbt **Parking:** Two mins from restaurant

BRIGHTON *continued* MAP 06 TQ30

Terre à Terre

Modern Vegetarian V

Vegetarian cooking with a unique interpretation

☎ 01273 729051 71 East St BN1 1HQ
e-mail: mail@terreaterre.co.uk
web: www.terreaterre.co.uk

An oasis in Brighton's hectic centre, Terre à Terre stands out for its unswerving devotion to vegetarian cooking. The long, slim space is constantly filled, though the new terrace with tables adds more options in warm weather. The food almost defies description, with its layering of ingredients that makes each dish more like a mezze. Nothing is straightforward, and the kitchen's verve and imagination can be breathtaking. Witty nudges at junk food, like buttermilk-soaked halloumi dipped in chip shop batter, show that vegetarian cooking can be light-hearted and fun. Enjoy a starter of wild side and golden cross risotto, followed by fundamentally fungus soufflé. Best to book, even on weekday evenings.

Times: 12-3/6-10.30, Closed 24-26 Dec, 1 Jan, Mon, Closed L Tue
Directions: Town centre near casino, close to Palace Pier & The Lanes

see advert on page 445

Fringe

☎ 01273 623683 10 Kensington Gardens BN1 4AL
web: www.theaa.com/restaurants/114029.html

Café and bar with simple, rustic food, make-your-own cocktails, live DJ music. Breakfasts served too.

Leonardo Restaurant

☎ 01273 328888 55 Church Rd, Hove BN3 2BD
web: www.theaa.com/restaurants/114018.html
A welcoming, exuberant place with a great atmosphere. The menu is Italian all the way, with a combination of old favourites and new inventions.

Regency Restaurant

☎ 01273 325014 131 Kings Rd BN1 2HH
Classic seafood restaurant dating back to the 1930s.

EASTBOURNE MAP 06 TV69

Grand Hotel (Mirabelle)

British, European

Seaside grandee serving sophisticated cuisine

☎ 01323 412345 King Edward's Pde BN21 4EQ
e-mail: reservations@grandeastbourne.com
web: www.grandeastbourne.com

Tastefully restored to its former glory, this celebrated Victorian hotel is a veteran of the Eastbourne seafront. It's a palatial venue, complete with spacious lounges, a luxurious health club, and a Grand Hall, where afternoon tea is served amid marble-columned splendour. Mirabelle is the swankier of two restaurants, and offers a choice of set menus, plus a seven-course tasting selection for those who really want to do the place justice. British and European dishes predominate; kick off with foie gras parfait perhaps, served with sea urchin cream and pea jelly, and then tuck into roast goose breast with port sauce and pickled plums, or best end of salt marsh lamb with a lamb confit shepherd's pie.

Chef: Keith Mitchell, Gerald Roser **Owners:** Elite Hotels **Times:** 12.30-2/7-10, Closed 1-14 Jan, Sun-Mon **Prices:** Fixed L £17.50, Fixed D £36.50-£44, Min/Water £3, Service added but optional 10% **Wine:** 340 bottles over £20, 17 bottles under £20, 14 by the glass (£3.90-£8) **Notes:** Coffee incl, Tasting menu with wines available, Vegetarian available, Dress Restrictions, Jacket or tie for D, Civ Wed 200 **Seats:** 50 **Smoking:** N/Sm in restaurant, Air con **Children:** Min 12 yrs **Rooms:** 152 (152 en suite) ★★★★★ HL **Directions:** Western end of the seafront **Parking:** 50

FOREST ROW MAP 06 TQ43

Ashdown Park Hotel

British, European NOTABLE WINE LIST

Grand hotel dining in a country-house setting

☎ 01342 824988 Wych Cross RH18 5JR
e-mail: reservations@ashdownpark.com
web: www.ashdownpark.com

Set in over 180 acres of parkland that is the remains of an ancient forest formerly covering all of south east England; the restaurant takes its name from the Roman name for the great forest 'Anderida'. Reached via a long corridor, the restaurant is a grand formal dining room where professional staff put their silver service skills to good use. Cloches are used for the main courses, soups are served from tureens and traditional dishes like Chateaubriand and Dover sole are carved and filleted respectively at the table. The menu is firmly rooted in classical dishes with traditional accompaniments, with the occasional foray into something more adventurous, like marinated rump of South Downs lamb, hotpot potato, black pudding and shallot confit.

Notable Wine List: An extensive wine list with a fine selection, full of interesting wines.

Chef: Graeme Campbell **Owners:** Elite Hotels **Times:** 12-2/7-10 **Prices:** Fixed L £16, Fixed D £35, Coffee £3.25, Min/Water £3, Service added 10% **Notes:** ALC £46, Vegetarian available, Dress Restrictions, Jacket and Tie for gentlemen after 7pm, Civ Wed 150 **Seats:** 120, Pr/dining room 160 **Smoking:** N/Sm in restaurant **Children:** Menu, Portions **Rooms:** 106 (106 en suite) ★★★★ HL **Directions:** A22 towards Eastbourne, pass through Forest Row, continue on A22 for 2m. At Wych Cross turn left, hotel 0.75m on right **Parking:** 120

HASTINGS & ST LEONARDS MAP 07 TQ80

Jali Bar & Restaurant @ The Chatsworth Hotel

Indian

Indian cooking by the sea

☎ 01424 457300 Carlisle Pde TN13 1JG
e-mail: info@chatsworthhotel.com
web: www.jalirestaurant.co.uk

Just a short walk from the old town, this friendly hotel has an enviable seafront location, not far from the pier. Refurbished in contemporary style, the Jali bar and restaurant makes the most of the views, and offers an extensive menu of Indian dishes such as korma gosht (lamb in a yoghurt and cashew sauce), tawa jhinga masala (prawns stir-fried in masala spices with peppers), and meen moilee (salmon in a coconut milk sauce). Tuck in and don't feel too guilty - the caring kitchen team work hard to limit the fat and salt content of their cooking, and avoid any ingredients derived from genetically modified crops. Takeaway available.

Chef: Ramesh Angre **Owners:** Aristel Group of Hotels **Times:** 12-2.30/6.30-11, Closed L Mon-Sat **Prices:** Fixed L £15-£22, Fixed D £20-£24, Starter £4.25-£7.95, Main £4.50-£14.50, Dessert £3.25-£3.75, Coffee £2, Min/Water £2.75, Service added 10% **Wine:** 9 bottles over £20, 13 bottles under £20, 6 by the glass (£4.50) **Notes:** Vegetarian available **Seats:** 52 **Smoking:** N/Sm in restaurant, Air con **Children:** Portions **Rooms:** 52 (52 en suite) ★★ HL **Directions:** On Hastings seafront, near railway station **Parking:** 8

HERSTMONCEUX MAP 06 TQ61

Sundial Restaurant

French

Pretty cottage setting for classic French cuisine

☎ 01323 832217 BN27 4LA
e-mail: sundialrestaurant@hotmail.com
web: www.sundialrestaurant.co.uk

Classic French cooking in a cosy red-brick cottage on the high street in this pretty Sussex village. The newly refurbished interior blends a modern décor with Tudor-style windows and black oak beams. Tables are well appointed with linen and the finest china, silver and glassware. Choose from the carte, monthly and seasonal fixed-price menus or the chef's Menu Dégustation, all in French with English subtitles. From the carte, perhaps choose pan-fried king scallops with cep mushroom ravioli and wild mushroom cream sauce, followed by roast rack of lamb and confit shoulder with herb jus, and plum tarte Tatin to finish.

Chef: Vincent Rongier **Owners:** Mr & Mrs V & Mary Rongier **Times:** 12-2/7-10, Closed Mon, Closed D Sun **Prices:** Fixed L £22, Fixed D £22, Starter £8.50-£19.75, Main £17.75-£19.75, Dessert £5.50-£10.75, Coffee £2.50, Min/Water £3.25, Service added but optional 10% **Wine:** 124 bottles over £20, 13 bottles under £20, 4 by the glass (£3.75-£4.95) **Notes:** Fixed L 3 courses, Menu dégustation £45, Vegetarian available, Dress Restrictions, Smart casual preferred **Seats:** 50, Pr/dining room 22 **Smoking:** N/Sm in restaurant **Children:** Portions **Directions:** In village centre, on A271, between Bexhill & Hailsham **Parking:** 16

JEVINGTON MAP 06 TQ50

Hungry Monk Restaurant

British, French

Charming 14th-century cottage restaurant

☎ 01323 482178 BN26 5QF
web: www.hungrymonk.co.uk

The 14th-century flint house was once a monastic retreat, and original oak beams and log fires continue to set the tone in antique-furnished lounges and the intimate, candlelit dining room. Classic French country cooking draws on wider European influences to offer plenty of choice at each course on the daily fixed-price menu. Choose squid and mussel stew as a starter, followed by roast beef fillet with Burgundy and pancetta sauce or opt for Barbary duck with bean cassoulet, or perhaps rack of lamb with Moroccan spices and polenta. Round off with ginger sponge with vanilla custard.

Chef: Gary Fisher, Matt Comben **Owners:** Mr & Mrs N Mackenzie **Times:** 12-2/6.45-9.45, Closed 24-26 Dec, BHs, Closed L Mon-Sat **Prices:** Fixed L £29.95, Fixed D £30.95, Coffee £2.95, Min/Water £3.50, Group min 8 service 12.5% **Wine:** 85 bottles over £20, 47 bottles under £20, 6 by the glass (£3.40-£7.80) **Notes:** Vegetarian available **Seats:** 38, Pr/dining room 16 **Smoking:** N/Sm in restaurant, Air con **Children:** Min 4 yrs, Portions **Directions:** A22, turn towards Wammock at Polegate x-rds. Continue for 2.5m, restaurant on right **Parking:** 14

LEWES MAP 06 TQ41

Circa

International

Dazzling dining in contemporary setting

☎ 01273 471777 145 High St BN7 1XT
e-mail: eat@circacirca.com
web: www.circacirca.com

continued

Circa

Situated on the ground floor of the Pelham House Hotel, this restaurant has a light, bright interior decorated in the art deco style. Wooden floors, wicker and leather chairs, bold artwork and simply clothed tables set the scene for some exuberant dining. Clipboard menus include a vibrant selection of dishes from around the world. Presentation lives up to vivacious descriptions. Start with blue swimmer crab meat, rainbow congee and goat's cheese samosa before a main course of baked Appleton pork loin, chilli squares and prawn satay. Finish with pistachio kulfi.

Times: 12-2.30/6-10 **Directions:** In town centre

The Shelleys

Modern British

Elegant market town hotel dining

☎ 01273 472361 High St BN7 1XS
e-mail: info@shelleys-hotel-lewes.com
web: www.shelleys-hotel.com

The classically proportioned exterior of this elegant 16th-century hotel is echoed within, with public rooms graced by beautiful chandeliers and fine oil paintings. It takes its name from the poet Shelley whose

continued

family once lived here. The airy, spacious dining room is romantically candlelit and overlooks a peaceful private garden. A confident kitchen sources quality Sussex ingredients and produces simply presented, yet appealing dishes that are listed on a modern British menu that takes influences from across Europe. Examples are pan-fried scallops with wild mushrooms and spiced butter sauce, Angus beef fillet with Borscht consommé and cep ravioli, and lemon and mascarpone tart. Service is professional and friendly and not at all stuffy.

Chef: Simon Thomas **Owners:** Peter & Sylvia Pattenden **Times:** 12-2.15/7-9.15 **Prices:** Fixed L £12.50-£15, Fixed D £30-£35, Min/Water £3.50, Service optional **Wine:** 25 bottles over £20, 20 bottles under £20, 6 by the glass (£2.90-£4) **Notes:** Civ Wed 50 **Seats:** 40, Pr/dining room 40 **Smoking:** N/Sm in restaurant **Children:** Portions **Rooms:** 19 (19 en suite) ★★★ HL **Directions:** From Brighton take A27 towards Eastbourne. Follow signs for Lewes town centre **Parking:** 30

NEWICK MAP 06 TQ42

❀❀ Newick Park Hotel & Country Estate

Modern European

Accomplished cooking in elegant country house

☎ 01825 723633 BN8 4SB
e-mail: Bookings@newickpark.co.uk
web: www.newickpark.co.uk

This delightful Georgian mansion - set in over 200 acres of landscaped gardens and parkland - offers a quintessential country-house experience. Interiors are grand, with tasteful fabrics and gentile colours, while open fires cosset in winter and a terrace beckons in summer. High ceilings, bright summery colours and striking flower displays and artwork grace the elegant restaurant, while the kitchen makes admirable use of fresh local ingredients, including produce from its own organic kitchen garden. The cooking impresses with its highly accomplished execution, modern approach and interpretations of classics. Think roast fillet of turbot with Palourde clam, saffron and

continued

almond broth, or Chateaubriand with hand-cut chips and sauce béarnaise, and perhaps a mint chocolate fondant finish, served with chocolate sauce.

Chef: Chris Moore **Owners:** Mr and Mrs Childs **Times:** 12-2/7-9, Closed New Year **Prices:** Fixed L fr £14.50, Starter £7.50-£10.50, Main £20.50-£27.50, Dessert £7.50-£10.50, Coffee £3.50, Min/Water £3, Service optional **Wine:** 77 bottles over £20, 17 bottles under £20, 4 by the glass (£3.50) **Notes:** Dress Restrictions, Smart casual, Civ Wed 120 **Seats:** 60, Pr/dining room 74 **Smoking:** N/Sm in restaurant **Children:** Menu, Portions **Rooms:** 16 (16 en suite) ★★★ HL **Directions:** From village turn S on A272, continue along lane for 1m, past pubs and garage to T-junct. Turn left and continue to entrance on right **Parking:** 100

❀ Two Seven Two

European, International **NEW**

Accessible cuisine in stylish surroundings

☎ 01825 721272 20/22 High St BN8 4LQ
e-mail: twoseventwo@hotmail.co.uk
web: 272restaurant.co.uk

This former village hardware store has been transformed into a stylish modern restaurant, with a simple cream and buttermilk colour scheme. Polished pine flooring, painted brickwork and hand-made Italian chairs make a smart impression on diners. A simpler, lighter lunch menu complements a more serious modern European dinner menu with international influences. Start with creamy lemon and herb risotto topped with crispy squid rings, or foie gras on toasted walnut bread, then move on to rolled roast pork on basil and tomato macaroni, or venison on onion risotto. Service is relaxed, informal and friendly.

Chef: Neil Bennett **Owners:** Simon Maltby **Times:** 12-2.30/7-9.30, Closed 25-26 Dec, 1-2 Jan, Mon, Closed L Tue, D Sun **Prices:** Fixed L £10.50, Fixed D £19.95, Starter £4.75-£7.25, Main £11.95-£17.75, Dessert £4.95-£6.95, Coffee £2, Min/Water £2.95, Group min 8 service 10% **Wine:** 48 bottles over £20, 38 bottles under £20, 6 by the glass (£3.25-£3.75) **Notes:** Vegetarian available **Seats:** 60 **Smoking:** N/Sm in restaurant, Air con **Children:** Portions **Directions:** On A272, 7m E of Haywards Heath and 7m N of Lewes **Parking:** 10

RYE MAP 07 TQ92

❀ Mermaid Inn

Traditional British, French V

Local legend with a traditional menu

☎ 01797 223065 & 223788 Mermaid St TN31 7EY
e-mail: mermaidinnrye@btclick.com
web: www.mermaidinn.com

continued

RYE *continued* MAP 07 TQ92

Tucked away down a cobbled side street, this impossibly romantic inn dates back to the 15th century and numbers Elizabeth I, Henry James, Richard Burton and Johnny Depp among former guests. Uneven floors and a heavily timbered ceiling are testament to its advanced age, and come teamed with cosy sofas and open fires in winter, while the restaurant is an airy room with graciously appointed tables. Traditional English dishes predominate; smoked quail salad or twice-baked wild mushroom soufflé are typical starters, followed by the likes of poached chicken supreme with baby leeks and carrots, white wine and tarragon velouté.

Chef: Robert Malyon **Owners:** Mrs J Blincow & Mr R I Pinwill **Times:** 12-2.30/7-9.30 **Prices:** Fixed L £18-£18.50, Fixed D £37.50, Starter £6.50-£10.50, Main £15-£31, Dessert £6, Coffee £3.50, Min/Water £5.50, Service added but optional 10% **Wine:** 31 bottles over £20, 21 bottles under £20, 9 by the glass (£4-£5.50) **Notes:** Fixed D 4 courses, Vegetarian menu, Dress Restrictions, No jeans or T-shirts **Seats:** 64, Pr/dining room 12 **Smoking:** N/Sm in restaurant **Children:** Menu, Portions **Rooms:** 31 (31 en suite) ★★★ **Directions:** Rye is situated on A259 between Ashford and Hastings **Parking:** 26

Webbes at The Fish Café

Traditional British

Fish and seafood restaurant in an amiable setting

☎ 01797 222226 17 Tower St TN31 7AT
e-mail: info@thefishcafe.com
web: www.thefishcafe.com

This former toy factory has been tastefully restored with modishly minimal interiors while retaining many of the old warehouse-style features of the original building - the exposed brickwork and high ceilings in particular. The restaurant is laid-out over three floors: a café-style ground floor, a more formal first floor for dinner and a private function room on the second floor. The eclectic menu combines classic fish dishes with contemporary Asian and Mediterranean influences - lobster and Jerusalem artichoke risotto, for example, or roast hake with chorizo sausage, butter beans and a parmesan tuile.

Chef: Paul Webbe **Owners:** Paul & Rebecca Webbe **Times:** 6-9.30, Closed 25-26 Dec, 2-9 Jan, Closed L all week, D Sun-Mon **Prices:** Starter £4-£9, Main £10-£23, Dessert £4-£5.50, Coffee £1.50, Min/Water £3.50, Service optional **Wine:** 29 bottles over £20, 31 bottles under £20, 6 by the glass (£2.75-£3.50) **Notes:** Vegetarian available **Seats:** 52, Pr/dining room 70 **Smoking:** N/Sm in restaurant, Air con **Children:** Menu, Portions **Directions:** Telephone for directions **Parking:** Cinque Port Street

Landgate Bistro

☎ 01797 222829 5-6 Landgate TN31 7LH
web: www.landgatebistro.co.uk
Bustling bistro with varied menu.

TICEHURST MAP 06 TQ63

 Dale Hill Hotel & Golf Club

Modern European

Formal dining in modern golfing hotel

☎ 01580 200112 TN5 7DQ
e-mail: info@dalehill.co.uk
web: www.dalehill.co.uk

Views from the formal Wealden restaurant at this smart, modern golfing hotel take in the 18th green and the broad expanse of the Kentish Weald. The hotel has two golf courses, a swimming pool and gym, a conservatory brasserie and the Spike Bar. The kitchen offers an interesting range of modern British dishes on an extensive carte o a three-course fixed-price menu. Begin with smoked ham hock terrine, move on to confit duck leg with braised root vegetables, or seared tuna loin with basil broth, and finish with warm plum and almond tart.

Chef: Mark Carter **Owners:** Wealden View Restaurant **Times:** 12-2.30/6.30-9, Closed L Mon-Sat **Prices:** Fixed L £19.95-£21, Fixed D £24.95-£26, Starter £4-£8, Main £12-£25, Dessert £4-£8, Coffee £2.50, Min/Water £3.90, Service optional **Wine:** 25 bottles over £20, 25 bottles under £20, 7 by the glass (£2.95-£5.80) **Notes:** Dress Restrictions, Smart casual, Civ Wed 150 **Seats:** 70, Pr/dining room 24 **Smoking:** N/Sm in restaurant, Air con **Children:** Menu, Portions **Rooms:** 35 (35 en suite) ★★★★ **Directions:** At junction of A21 & B2087 follow signs for Ticehurst & Flimwell; Dale Hill is 1m on left **Parking:** 220

UCKFIELD MAP 06 TQ42

Buxted Park

Modern European

Masterful cooking in classical surroundings

☎ 01825 733333 Buxted TN22 4AY
e-mail: buxtedpark@handpicked.co.uk
web: www.handpicked.co.uk

Set in 300 acres of beautiful parkland and formal gardens, this impressive Palladian mansion has been a prime ministerial home and a playground for Hollywood stars. The restaurant is located on the original Victorian orangery and retains many original features whilst still appearing modern and bright. With views over the gardens, it's a stylish and relaxing place in which to dine. Accomplished modern British and European cuisine blends classic and modern ideas and is based around top-quality ingredients. Try the terrine of smoked ham hock and confit rabbit to start or perhaps the rack of Launceston lamb with rosemary truffle froth as a main course, and finish with the rhubarb crumble soufflé.

continued

Chef: Pramod Pillai **Owners:** Hand Picked Hotels **Times:** 12-2.30/7-9.30 **Prices:** Fixed L £12.95-£28.50, Fixed D £28.50-£38.50, Starter £10, Main £19.50, Dessert £9, Min/Water £4, Service optional **Wine:** 100 bottles over £20, 8 by the glass (£5.50-£9.50) **Notes:** Tasting menu available, Vegetarian available, Dress Restrictions, Smart casual, Civ Wed 130 **Seats:** 40, Pr/dining room 120 **Smoking:** N/Sm in restaurant, Air con **Children:** Menu, Portions **Rooms:** 44 (44 en suite) ★★★★ HL **Directions:** Turn off A22 Uckfield by-pass (London-Eastbourne road), then take A272 to Buxted. Cross lights, entrance to hotel 1m on right **Parking:** 100

Horsted Place

Modern British

Opulent country-house restaurant, formal but friendly

☎ 01825 750581 Little Horsted TN22 5TS
e-mail: hotel@horstedplace.co.uk
web: www.horstedplace.co.uk

The house, set in its own 1100-acre estate, was built in 1850, and has interiors designed by Augustus Pugin. In 2006 it celebrated its 20th anniversary as a country-house hotel and the elegant restaurant was redesigned to mark the occasion. The kitchen produces plenty of interest in dishes where flavours can be quite complex, such as ballotine of foie gras, followed by braised fillet of wild sea bass in Savoy cabbage, pancetta and lemon butter sauce, with mascarpone dumplings with lime and crème fraîche ice cream to finish.

Chef: Allan Garth **Owners:** Perinon Ltd **Times:** 12-2/7-9.30, Closed L Sat **Prices:** Fixed L £15.95, Starter £8.50, Main £19.50, Dessert £8, Coffee £2.80, Min/Water £3.50, Service optional **Wine:** 99 bottles over £20, 9 bottles under £20, 7 by the glass (£4) **Notes:** Sun L £25, Vegetarian available, Dress Restrictions, No jeans, Civ Wed 100 **Seats:** 40, Pr/dining room 100 **Smoking:** N/Sm in restaurant **Children:** Min 7 yrs, Portions **Rooms:** 20 (20 en suite) ★★★ **Directions:** 2m S on A26 towards Lewes **Parking:** 50

WADHURST MAP 06 TQ63

The Best Beech Inn

French, European

Good eating in rural Sussex

☎ 01892 782046 Mayfield Ln TN5 6JH
e-mail: roger_felstead@hotmail.com
web: www.bestbeech.net

Found in Sussex's winding lanes this place has, in its time, served the villagers as a butchers, a sweet shop, a petrol station and then of course by providing their requisite pint. Dating from 1680 the inn now mainly reflects the Victorian character of its heyday. The kitchen produces a modern European menu with French influences for the more formal restaurant and something to suit all tastes in the simpler bistro. For starters try the confit of duck terrine with red onion marmalade and balsamic reduction, followed by seared sirloin of beef sat aside a pomme fondant topped with sweet potato crisps and finished with a red wine jus, and for dessert the white wine and cinnamon poached pear glazed with sabayon.

Chef: Stephan Santin **Owners:** Roger Felstead **Times:** 12-2/7-9, Closed 25-26 Dec, Closed D Sun **Prices:** Fixed L £12, Fixed D £19-£25, Starter £4.95-£6.20, Main £10.95-£17.95, Dessert £4.95-£5.95, Coffee £2.50, Min/Water £2.50, Service optional, Group min 6 service 10% **Wine:** 40 bottles over £20, 10 bottles under £20, 6 by the glass (£3.55-£3.95)

continued

Notes: Sun L 2 courses £13.50, 3 courses £17, Vegetarian available, Dress Restrictions, Smart casual **Seats:** 64, Pr/dining room 34 **Smoking:** N/Sm in restaurant **Children:** Min 10 yrs, Portions **Directions:** From Wadhurst take B2100 to Mark Cross, continue for 1m **Parking:** 35

WESTFIELD MAP 07 TQ81

The Wild Mushroom Restaurant

Modern British

Cosy dining in a converted farmhouse

☎ 01424 751137 Woodgate House, Westfield Ln TN35 4SB
e-mail: info@wildmushroom.co.uk
web: www.wildmushroom.co.uk

This converted Victorian farmhouse has a lovely garden and you can enjoy pre-dinner drinks here or in the bar, before moving through to the intimate L-shaped restaurant. Service is formal, but relaxed and welcoming. The dinner menu starts with canapés, followed by an extensive choice at each course. Try scallop, potato and watercress chowder to start, with perhaps aged fillet of Scottish beef with wild mushroom jus and a potato galette to follow. Desserts include the likes of warm chocolate fondant with milk sorbet.

Chef: Paul Webbe/Matthew Drinkwater **Owners:** Mr & Mrs P Webbe **Times:** 12-2.30/7-10, Closed 25 Dec, 2 wks at New Year, Mon, Closed L Sat, D Sun **Prices:** Fixed L £14.95, Starter £5-£7.95, Main £11-£17.95, Dessert £5.50, Coffee £2.25, Min/Water £3.50, Service optional **Wine:** 25 bottles over £20, 39 bottles under £20, 6 by the glass **Notes:** Vegetarian available, Dress Restrictions, Smart casual **Seats:** 40 **Smoking:** N/Sm in restaurant **Children:** Portions **Directions:** From A21 towards Hastings, turn left onto A28 to Westfield. Restaurant 1.5m on left **Parking:** 20

WILMINGTON MAP 06 TQ50

Crossways

British

Small country house with a focus on food

☎ 01323 482455 BN26 5SG
e-mail: stay@crosswayshotel.co.uk
web: www.crosswayshotel.co.uk

Once the home of Elizabeth David's parents, this Georgian country house is set amid well kept gardens in the heart of the Cuckmere Valley. A friendly and relaxed atmosphere is assured by the proprietors and the restaurant is very much the focus of the hotel. Food is prepared with love and affection from fresh ingredients, local where possible. Dishes are offered from a set monthly menu, such as roasted pear with prawns and bacon pâté, and guinea fowl with Madeira, shallot and mushroom sauce. Ice creams, sorbets and petits fours are all home made, as are puddings, including a favourite brandy snap basket with banana and butterscotch.

Chef: David Stott **Owners:** David Stott, Clive James **Times:** 7.30-8.30, Closed 24 Dec-24 Jan, Sun-Mon, Closed L all week **Prices:** Fixed D £35.95, Min/Water £3.50, Service optional **Wine:** 18 bottles over £20, 26 bottles under £20 **Notes:** Fixed D 4 courses, coffee incl, Vegetarian available **Seats:** 24 **Smoking:** N/Sm in restaurant **Children:** Min 12 yrs **Rooms:** 7 (7 en suite) ★★★★ RR **Directions:** On A27, 2m W of Polegate **Parking:** 20

England

SUSSEX, WEST

BOSHAM MAP 05 SU80

Millstream Hotel

Modern British

Indulgent dining in a village setting

☎ 01243 573234 Bosham Ln PO18 8HL
e-mail: info@millstream-hotel.co.uk
web: www.millstream-hotel.co.uk

Set in the pretty village of Bosham, this popular hotel lures a well-heeled sailing crowd from nearby Chichester, thanks to a picture-perfect location and accomplished cooking. Treat yourself to afternoon tea or a snack in the leafy garden if weather permits, but save room for the main event, when an ambitious kitchen pulls out all the stops to deliver a luxurious meal. Quality ingredients abound - start with a terrine of salmon gravad lax and gruyère cheese perhaps, followed by breast of corn-fed chicken with seared foie gras and Périgord truffle, and iced coffee parfait with Amaretto syrup.

Chef: Bev Boakes **Owners:** The Wild Family **Times:** 12.30-2/6.45-9.15 **Prices:** Fixed L £15.50, Fixed D £28.50, Coffee £2.20, Min/Water £3.50, Service optional **Wine:** 90 bottles over £20, 27 bottles under £20, 10 by the glass (£3.75-£6.75) **Notes:** Dress Restrictions, No jeans in the evenings, smart casual, Civ Wed 92 **Seats:** 60, Pr/dining room 92 **Smoking:** N/Sm in restaurant, Air con **Children:** Portions **Rooms:** 35 (35 en suite) ★★★ HL **Directions:** Take A259 exit from Chichester rdbt and in village follow signs for quay **Parking:** 40

BRACKLESHAM MAP 05 SZ89

Cliffords Cottage Restaurant

French

Cosy cottage restaurant close to the sea

☎ 01243 670250 Bracklesham Ln PO20 8JA

Exposed oak beams, some of them skull-crackingly low, attest to the great age of this whitewashed, thatched cottage near the seafront. The small dining room is cosy and welcoming, and staff know many of the clientele by name. Fish features on the menu as you might expect given the location, but there is ample meat and game too, perhaps in the form of pan-fried breast of guinea fowl with red wine jus, or roast sirloin with Yorkshire pudding. Puddings from the trolley are a much-loved Sunday fixture.

Times: 12.30-5/7-9.30, Closed Jan **Directions:** From A27 follow signs for The Witterings. A286 to Birdham, B2198 to Bracklesham

BURPHAM MAP 06 TQ00

George & Dragon

British, French

Idyllically located old inn on the South Downs

☎ 01903 883131 BN18 9RR

Perfectly placed at the end of a lane on the South Downs, and ideal for a walk before or after dinner. Old beams, stone floors and bags of atmosphere attract an eclectic crowd. A lengthy specials board supplements the carte, with familiar dishes like breast and confit leg of duck, and roast rump of lamb dressed up with rich sauces. More innovative cuisine includes seared fresh scallops with creamy spinach risotto or smoked chicken, pigeon breast and baby leek terrine with apple and cider brandy chutney. Bar meals only served at lunchtime.

Chef: C Perrin, A Field, E Cassar **Owners:** Alastaire & Angela Thackeray **Times:** 12-2/7-9, Closed 25 Dec, Closed D Sun **Prices:** Starter £5.50-£7.50, Main £9.95-£18.95, Dessert fr £5.25, Coffee £1.75, Min/Water £3.40, Group service 10% **Wine:** 6 bottles over £20, 18 bottles under £20, 4 by the glass (£3.50-£4.50) **Notes:** Vegetarian available, Smart casual preferred **Seats:** 40 **Smoking:** N/Sm in restaurant **Children:** Portions **Directions:** 2.5m along no-through road signed Burpham off A27, 1m E of Arundel **Parking:** 40

CHICHESTER MAP 05 SU80

Comme Ça

French

Classic French cooking in friendly restaurant

☎ 01243 788724 & 536307 67 Broyle Rd PO19 6BD
e-mail: comme.ca@commeca.co.uk
web: www.commeca.co.uk

A long-established French restaurant on the fringe of Chichester. Inside, there's a mix of Victorian and Edwardian prints with objets d'art. The simple cosy restaurant is decorated in bright, bold colours and there is a garden room with French doors leading on to a patio and sunken garden. A lengthy carte at dinner serves up French classics at every course, mainly true to Normandy roots. The wine list naturally focuses on France, but gives space to other global labels. Try roasted boneless rack of lamb scented with rosemary, served with confit garlic and crushed celeriac.

Chef: Michael Navet, Mark Howard **Owners:** Mr & Mrs Navet **Times:** 12-2/6-10.30, Closed Xmas week & New Year week, BHs, Mon, Closed L Tue, D Sun **Prices:** Food prices not confirmed for 2007. Please telephone for details **Notes:** Vegetarian available, Dress Restrictions, Smart casual preferred **Seats:** 100, Pr/dining room 14 **Smoking:** N/Sm in restaurant **Children:** Menu, Portions **Directions:** On A286 near Festival Theatre **Parking:** 46

Croucher's Country Hotel & Restaurant

Modern European

Former farmhouse offering modern cuisine in bright, characterful surroundings

☎ 01243 784995 Birdham Rd PO20 7EH
e-mail: crouchers@btconnect.com
web: www.crouchersbottom.com

This former farmhouse has been carefully restored to include newly built barn-style public rooms, which house the restaurant and bar. Brown leather sofas offer somewhere to relax in the bar lounge before

continued

dining in the restaurant with its high beamed ceilings. Large windows overlook the courtyard and fields, and pre-dinner drinks can be enjoyed on the terrace in summer. Modern European cooking offers imaginative combinations and fresh flavours in the likes of panaché of roasted sea scallops and Selsey crab ravioli starter, followed by roast rump of veal with creamed shallots.

Chef: G Wilson, N Markey, A Craig **Owners:** Mr L van Rooyen & Mr G Wilson **Times:** 12.30-2.30/7-9.30, Closed 26 Dec, 1 Jan **Prices:** Fixed L £12.50, Fixed D £19.50, Starter £4.95-£8.50, Main £14.95-£19.50, Dessert £6-£7, Coffee £2.50, Min/Water £3.20, Service optional, Group min 12 service 12.5% **Wine:** 15 bottles over £20, 12 bottles under £20, 3 by the glass (£3.50-£5) **Notes:** Vegetarian available, Dress Restrictions, Smart casual **Seats:** 80, Pr/dining room 20 **Smoking:** N/Sm in restaurant **Children:** Menu, Portions **Rooms:** 18 (18 en suite) ★★★ HL **Directions:** From A27, S of Chichester, take A286 to The Witterings. Hotel 2m on left **Parking:** 50

Hallidays

Modern British

A charming traditional village restaurant serving modern cuisine

☎ 01243 575331 Funtington PO18 9LF

Three flint and thatched cottages dating from the 12th century have been transformed to create this intimate two-room restaurant with a wealth of original features, and pale green and yellow décor. It is a family business offering friendly service, rewarded by plenty of local custom. Weekly-changing menus based solely on seasonal ingredients offer a range of modern British dishes like cutlets of South Downs lamb with herb mousse, 21-day aged Aberdeen Angus sirloin, sautéed with mushrooms, tarragon and vin jaune or citrus buttermilk mousse with raspberries and sugared almonds. Excellent mini bread rolls, canapés, such as parmesan sablé and crayfish on crème fraîche, with home-made petits fours to finish.

Chef: Andrew Stephenson **Owners:** Mr A Stephenson & Mr P Creech **Times:** 12-1.45/7-9.45, Closed 2 wks Mar, 1 wk Sep, Mon-Tue, Closed L Sat, D Sun **Prices:** Fixed L £16, Fixed D £31, Starter £5.75-£8, Main £15-£18, Dessert £5-£7.50, Coffee £2.75, Min/Water £2.50, Service optional **Wine:** 25 bottles over £20, 20 bottles under £20, 4 by the glass (£3.50-£4.25) **Notes:** Sun L £21, Vegetarian available, Dress Restrictions, No shorts **Seats:** 26 **Smoking:** N/Sm area **Children:** Portions **Directions:** Telephone for directions **Parking:** 12

Royal Oak Inn

Modern, Traditional

Traditional food and buzzy atmosphere with a sophisticated twist

☎ 01243 527434 Pook Ln PO18 0AX
e-mail: nickroyaloak@aol.com
web: www.sussexlive.co.uk/royaloakinn

Set in the village of East Lavant a few miles outside town, this former coaching inn is a friendly, traditional pub with a sophisticated edge; beams, bare brick walls, fireplaces and an intimate bar area meets leather sofas and armchairs. The restaurant continues the theme, with bare pine tables and tall, modern leather chairs. The crowd-pleasing menu successfully mixes tradition with Mediterranean touches, bolstered by daily blackboard specials and an emphasis on the freshest locally sourced, seasonal produce. Try crispy oriental duck or crab and king prawn cocktail to start, and continue with calves' liver with bubble and squeak, or Royal Oak fishcakes with chorizo and fine bean salad.

continued

Royal Oak Inn

Chef: Malcolm Goble **Owners:** Nick & Lisa Sutherland **Times:** 12-2/6.15-9.30 **Prices:** Starter £4.95-£9.50, Main £10.50-£18, Dessert £5-£6.50, Coffee £2.10, Min/Water £2.90, Service optional **Wine:** 12 bottles over £20, 15 bottles under £20, 10 by the glass (£3.10-£7.50) **Notes:** Sun L avail, Vegetarian available **Seats:** 47 **Smoking:** N/Sm in restaurant, Air con **Children:** Menu, Portions **Rooms:** 6 (6 en suite) ◆◆◆◆◆ **Directions:** From Chichester take A286 towards Midhurst, 2m to mini rdbt take right, signposted East Lavant. Royal Oak on the left **Parking:** 23

CHILGROVE MAP 05 SU81

The Chilgrove White Horse

British, Mediterranean NOTABLE WINE LIST

Accomplished cooking at a pretty Sussex inn

☎ 01243 535219 PO18 9HX
e-mail: info@whitehorsechilgrove.co.uk
web: www.whitehorsechilgrove.co.uk

Located on the edge of the Sussex Downs, this homely 18th-century inn makes a pretty destination, its whitewashed walls decked with blooms of lilac wisteria. Inside there's a friendly bar and lounge with leather sofas and a crackling fire, in addition to a more formal dining area where tables are neatly clothed and set with linen napkins. There's no shortage of skill in the kitchen; flavour combinations are deftly judged and organic ingredients used where possible, with mains along the lines of pheasant in bacon with a Madeira sauce, or baked crab thermidor. Tempting desserts might include citrus tart or hot chocolate fondant. **Notable Wine List:** A well-established wine list which highlights some great vineyards and vintages.

Chef: Juanma Otero **Owners:** C Burton **Times:** 12-2/7-10, Closed Mon, Closed D Sun **Prices:** Starter £7.50-£9.95, Main £14.95-£19.95, Dessert £5.95-£8.95, Coffee £3, Min/Water £2.75, Service added 10% **Wine:** 550 bottles over £20, 50 bottles under £20, 6 by the glass (£2.75-£3.75) **Notes:** Sun L £12.95 **Seats:** 60, Pr/dining room 14 **Smoking:** N/Sm in restaurant, Air con **Children:** Portions **Rooms:** 8 (8 en suite) ◆◆◆◆ **Directions:** 7m N of Chichester on B2141. 3m W of A286 **Parking:** 60

England

CLIMPING MAP 06 SU90

Bailiffscourt Hotel & Health Spa

British, French

A fascinating venue offering creative modern cooking

☎ 01903 723511 BN17 5RW
e-mail: bailiffscourt@hshotels.co.uk
web: www.hshotels.co.uk

Lord and Lady Moyne rescued this estate and then commissioned Amyas Phillips to create an authentic medieval manor house, using reclaimed materials and considerable ingenuity. The result is a truly unique architectural gem. The restaurant has a heavy wooden ceiling, stone window frames with leaded lights and walls adorned with rich tapestries, transporting you back to medieval times. The cooking style is definitely in the present, however, concentrating on simple flavours and straightforward cuisine with French and Italian influences. Starters might include roast quail with cep risotto and sage butter or crab and tarragon raviolo with scallop velouté. Main courses range from seared sweetbreads wrapped in Parma ham with tomato fondue and spring onion gnocchi to slow roasted suckling pig with apple chutney and sage crushed potatoes.

Chef: Russell Williams **Owners:** Pontus & Miranda Carminger **Times:** 12-1.30/7-9.30 **Prices:** Fixed L £11, Fixed D £43.50, Coffee £3.95, Min/Water £4.25, Service optional **Wine:** 152 bottles over £20, 3 bottles under £20 **Notes:** Vegetarian available, Dress Restrictions, Smart casual, Civ Wed 60 **Seats:** 70, Pr/dining room 70 **Smoking:** N/Sm in restaurant **Children:** Menu, Portions **Rooms:** 39 (39 en suite) ★★★ HL **Directions:** From A27 (Arundel), take A284 towards Littlehampton. Continue to the A259, Bailiffscourt is signed towards Climping Beach **Parking:** 60

COPTHORNE For restaurant details see Gatwick Airport (London), (Sussex, West)

CUCKFIELD MAP 06 TQ32

Ockenden Manor

see below

EAST GRINSTEAD MAP 06 TQ33

Gravetye Manor Hotel

see opposite

continued

Ockenden Manor

CUCKFIELD MAP 06 TQ32

Modern French

Olde worlde elegance and refined cuisine

☎ 01444 416111 Ockenden Ln RH17 5LD
e-mail: reservations@ockenden-manor.com
web: www.hshotels.co.uk

As you arrive at this Elizabethan manor house, set in a Tudor village, you may feel you're stepping back in time. Walking through the magnificent gardens it's easy to imagine what it would have been like to live here in days gone by, and as a guest you're welcomed like an old friend. The wood-panelled restaurant with stained-glass windows and ornate painted ceiling provides a formal setting for dinner. Rich red and yellow décor and a warming log fire create a relaxing and intimate environment.

Be prepared for a tempting choice of dishes from the à la carte 'Sussex' and 'Cuckfield' menus, making great use of local produce, or opt for the full gastronomic experience with the seven-course tasting menu. Whichever menu you choose from, you'll find expertly cooked dishes with a distinct French influence and top-quality ingredients. Try a starter like crisp galette of pig's trotter, foie gras and morels with truffled Savoy cabbage, perhaps followed by a main course of sliced saddle of Balcombe venison with roasted butternut squash, parsnip

purée and crisps. Home-made ice cream is a speciality and the wine list is extensive.

Chef: Mr Steve Crane **Owners:** The Goodman & Carminger Family **Times:** 12-2/7-9 **Prices:** Fixed L £14.95-£16.95, Coffee £2, Min/Water £3.75, Service optional, Group min 10 service 10% **Wine:** 12 by the glass (£3.75) **Notes:** Fixed ALC £46, Tasting menu £65, Vegetarian available, Dress Restrictions, No jeans, Civ Wed 74 **Seats:** 40, Pr/dining room 75 **Smoking:** N/Sm in restaurant **Rooms:** 22 (22 en suite) ★★★ HL **Directions:** Village centre **Parking:** 45

England

Gravetye Manor Hotel

EAST GRINSTEAD MAP 06 TQ33

Modern British NOTABLE WINE LIST

Fabulous country-house hotel with historic gardens and memorable cuisine

☎ 01342 810567 RH19 4LJ
e-mail: info@gravetyemanor.co.uk
web: www.gravetyemanor.co.uk

No visit to Gravetye Manor would be complete without exploring some of the 30 acres of garden created by Willam Robinson as the Natural English Garden. Robinson also restored the house, which became a hotel in 1958. The current owners continue the custodianship of house and gardens and the tradition of country-house hospitality with care and affection. The traditional oak-panelled restaurant has a carved white ceiling with winter log fires. Chef Mark Raffan has his culinary roots in classical French cuisine from his time with the Roux brothers, plus a stint as personal chef to the late King Hussein of Jordan. This background and his considerable experience here at Gravetye ensures an interesting and eclectic menu of broadly modern English cuisine. Typical dishes include terrine of local game with red onion and port wine reduction, winter leaves and toast to start; followed perhaps by braised cheek of beef with traditional style accompaniments of lardons, baby onions, button mushrooms, creamed potatoes and red wine.

Notable Wine List: A classic wine list featuring many fine growers.

Chef: Mark Raffan **Owners:** A Russell & M Raffan **Times:** 12.30-1.45/7-9.30, Closed 25 Dec eve (ex residents) **Prices:** Fixed L £19-£22, Fixed D £37-£64, Starter £12-£17, Main £30-£34, Dessert £10, Coffee £4, Min/Water £3.50, Service included **Wine:** 612 bottles over £20, 8 bottles under £20, 9 by the glass (£4-£8) **Notes:** Sun L £35, tasting menu £65, £105 with wines, Vegetarian available, Dress Restrictions, Jacket & tie preferred, Civ Wed 45 **Seats:** 50, Pr/dining room 20 **Smoking:** N/Sm in restaurant **Children:** Min 7 yrs, Portions **Rooms:** 18 (18 en suite) ★★★ HL **Directions:** From M23 junct 10 take A264 towards East Grinstead. After 2m take B2028. After Turners Hill, follow signs **Parking:** 45

GATWICK AIRPORT (LONDON) MAP 06 TQ24

Langshott Manor

Modern European

Fine dining in elegant Elizabethan manor house

☎ 01293 786680 Langshott Ln, Horley RH6 9LN
e-mail: admin@langshottmanor.com
web: www.langshottmanor.com

Ideally located for Gatwick Airport, this timber-framed manor house, dating back to 1580, sits in 3 acres of beautiful mature grounds complete with a pond. The Mulberry restaurant retains many original features such as the leaded windows overlooking the gardens (alfresco dining is recommended when weather permits) complemented by discreetly modern décor. The food is firmly in the modern British camp with a keen eye on quality, seasonal ingredients throughout the menu. You might expect a fresh pea ravioli with morels to start, followed by black pepper monkfish with truffle mash and buttered spinach - an amuse of crab and lobster bisque adds an extra zing to the meal.

Chef: Stephen Toward **Owners:** Peter & Deborah Hinchcliffe **Times:** 12-2.30/7-9.30 **Prices:** Fixed L £19, Fixed D £39, Starter £7-£11, Main £22-£24, Dessert £8-£11, Coffee £3, Min/Water £3.50, Service added 12.5%, Group service 12.5% **Wine:** 95 bottles over £20, 6 bottles under £20, 7 by the glass (£5-£7.50) **Notes:** Vegetarian available, Dress Restrictions, No Jeans, jacket and tie, Civ Wed 60 **Seats:** 55, Pr/dining room 22 **Smoking:** N/Sm in restaurant **Children:** Min 12 yrs, Portions **Rooms:** 22 (22 en suite) ★★★ HL **Directions:** From A23, Horley, take Ladbroke Rd turning off Chequers Hotel rdbt, 0.75m on right **Parking:** 25

Two Rosettes

The best local restaurants, which aim for and achieve higher standards, better consistency and where a greater precision is apparent in the cooking. There will be obvious attention to the selection of quality ingredients.

England

GATWICK AIRPORT (LONDON) *continued*
MAP 06 TQ24

The Old House Restaurant

Modern British

Fine dining in comfortable, traditional surroundings

☎ 01342 712222 Effingham Rd, Copthorne RH10 3JB
e-mail: info@oldhouserestaurant.co.uk
web: www.oldhouserestaurant.co.uk

As the name suggests, this bright, sunny restaurant is a 16th-century house converted into a homely eatery with bags of charm. Tudor style is the prevalent theme in the décor - white walls with black painted beams, diamond-leaded windows and an inglenook fireplace. There is a deep sense of history here and the dining room is suitably grand, in gold, cream and navy, without being intimidating. The food is simple, honest fare with a definite French influence. The menu is strong on traditional favourites cooked accurately with a few modern twists - calves' liver on bubble and squeak with bacon and a red wine jus, pan-roasted breast of chicken with asparagus mousse and vermouth cream, or panaché of salmon and tiger prawns with crushed new potatoes and lobster bisque sauce are good examples of the satisfying mains.

Chef: Alan Pierce **Owners:** Mr & Mrs C Dormon **Times:** 12.15-2/6.30-9.30, Closed Xmas, New Year, 1 wk spring, BHs, Mon, Closed L Sat, D Sun **Prices:** Fixed L £14.50, Fixed D £33-£40, Starter £3.50-£9.25, Main £19.50-£28, Dessert £6-£6.50, Coffee £3, Min/Water £3, Service optional, Group service 10% **Wine:** 70 bottles over £20, 23 bottles under £20, 6 by the glass (£4.25-£5.75) **Notes:** Vegetarian available, Dress Restrictions, Smart casual, no jeans or trainers **Seats:** 80, Pr/dining room 35 **Smoking:** N/Sm in restaurant, Air con **Children:** Min 10 yrs **Directions:** From M23 junct 10 follow A264 to East Grinstead, take 1st left at 2nd rdbt, left at crossroads, restaurant 0.75m on left **Parking:** 45

Restaurant 1881

Modern French, Mediterranean

Fine dining in elegant surroundings

☎ 01293 862166 Stanhill Court Hotel, Stanhill Rd, Charlwood RH6 0EP
e-mail: enquiries@stanhillcourthotel.co.uk
web: www.stanhillcourthotel.co.uk

Surrounded by 35 acres of ancient woodland including an amphitheatre and Victorian walled garden, this attractive country house was built in 1881 and is within easy reach of Gatwick airport. The wood-panelled Restaurant 1881 is elegantly appointed and has cracking views over the grounds. Using quality ingredients, the food is largely classical French in inspiration with European influences offering well presented dishes with some innovative ideas. Start with a pressed cassoulet terrine with oven-roasted fig then continue with cannon of monkfish loin with a chorizo and basil gnocchi, for example.

Chef: Tony Staples **Owners:** Antony Colas **Times:** 12-3/7-11, Closed L Sat **Prices:** Fixed L £12.95, Fixed D £25.95, Starter £4-£8, Main £15-£29, Dessert £5-£7.50, Coffee £2.95, Min/Water £3.95, Service added but optional 10% **Wine:** 80 bottles over £20, 20 bottles under £20, 15 by the glass (£3.50-£4.75) **Notes:** Vegetarian available, No jeans or T-shirts, Civ Wed 180 **Seats:** 120, Pr/dining room 260 **Smoking:** N/Sm in restaurant, Air con **Children:** Portions **Rooms:** 15 (15 en suite) ★★★ HL **Directions:** Telephone for directions **Parking:** 150

GOODWOOD MAP 06 SU80

Marriott Goodwood Park Hotel / Richmond Room

British, European

Sporting and leisure hotel close to Goodwood

☎ 0870 400 7225 PO18 0QB
web: www.marriott.co.uk

A smart, modern hotel and country club with extensive facilities including a golf course and spa. The Goodwood Sports Café offers international bistro-style cuisine, overlooking the golf course and swimming pool. The cocktail bar is the ideal place to relax before dinner and take in the memorabilia of Goodwood's motorsport heritage. The Richmond Room restaurant is the fine-dining option, decorated with a barn theme making the most of the high, beamed ceiling with stencilled patterns. A range of modern and traditional dishes are on offer here, using fresh local ingredients. The cooking style is elaborate with lots of flavour and stylish presentation.

Times: 12.30-2/7-10 **Rooms:** 94 (94 en suite) ★★★★ **Directions:** Just off A285, 3m NE of Chichester. Follow signs for Goodwood, once in estate follow signs for hotel

HAYWARDS HEATH MAP 06 TQ32

Jeremy's at Borde Hill

Modern European

Attractive restaurant with a creative kitchen

☎ 01444 441102 Balcombe Rd RH16 1XP
e-mail: reservations@jeremysrestaurant.com
web: www.jeremysrestaurant.com

This converted stable-block restaurant sits in the grounds of the Borde Hill Estate and overlooks a Victorian walled garden - where the

continued

kitchen's herbs are grown - and a lovely terrace that provides a fair-weather bonus. Inside it's a vibrant contemporary affair, with wooden floors, high-backed leather chairs and large pictures, which perfectly match the kitchen's modern European cooking built around fresh seasonal produce. Expect the likes of roasted monkfish tail - served with Jerusalem artichoke and haricot bean stew and prawn bisque sauce - to be backed by friendly and professional service and a relaxed atmosphere.

Chef: J & V Ashpool, Mr R Gleadow **Owners:** Jeremy & Vera Ashpool **Times:** 12-2.30/7-9.30, Closed 1st wk Jan, Mon, Closed D Sun **Prices:** Fixed L £17.50, Fixed D £22.50, Starter £6.50-£10, Main £13.50-£22, Dessert £6-£7.50, Coffee £2.50, Min/Water £3, Service optional, Group min 8 service 10% **Wine:** 60 bottles over £20, 11 bottles under £20, 6 by the glass (£3.50-£4.50) **Notes:** Tasting menu Tue night £30 (£45 with wine), Vegetarian available, Civ Wed 55 **Seats:** 55 **Smoking:** N/Sm in restaurant **Children:** Portions **Directions:** 1.5m N of Haywards Heath. From M23 junct 10a take A23 through Balcombe **Parking:** 20

HORSHAM MAP 06 TQ13

Les Deux Garçons

Modern French

Charming French restaurant

☎ 01403 271125 Piries Place RH12 1DF
e-mail: info@lesdeuxgarcons.com
web: www.lesdeuxgarcons.com

The Restaurant at LDG, as it is known, offers modern, stylish surroundings, split into two areas. The separate Terrace offers an alfresco area for French-style pavement dining, with the same menus and service throughout. Thoroughly French, the menus offer a range from the gastronomic carte to a market menu and lovely children's menu. There is a huge choice of dishes presenting traditional French flavours and style with a modern twist. Try ravioli of crab claw with rich crab bisque and truffle oil to start, perhaps followed by poached fillet of halibut, filo pastry wrapped king prawns and fish velouté sauce.

Chef: James Villiers **Owners:** Bob Emmott **Times:** 12-3/7-11, Closed Xmas wk, Sun, Mon **Prices:** Fixed L £9.90, Fixed D £11.90, Starter £6-£12, Main £12-£25, Dessert £6, Coffee £1.90, Min/Water £2.50, Service optional, Group min 9 service 10% **Wine:** 30 bottles over £20, 17 bottles under £20, 9 by the glass (£3.50-£4) **Notes:** Dégustation menu 6 courses £39, Vegetarian available **Seats:** 60, Pr/dining room 20 **Smoking:** N/Sm in restaurant, Air con **Children:** Menu, Portions **Directions:** Follow town centre signs, then sign for Piries Place & car park, situated bottom of car park at entrance to Piries Place **Parking:** Parking adjacent to restaurant

---

LICKFOLD MAP 06 SU92

The Lickfold Inn

Modern British

Ancient inn with thoroughly modern food

☎ 01798 861285 Lickfold GU28 9EY
e-mail: thelickfoldinn@aol.com
web: www.thelickfoldinn.co.uk

Dating back to the 15th century, this delightful old inn is built in a herringbone brick pattern and possesses an abundance of original features - a large inglenook fireplace and sturdy wooden beams to name but two. It's a very popular, family-run place with cheerful staff and a great atmosphere - particularly in summer, when the patio is used to full effect. Food is served in generous portions with an emphasis on fish and seafood, and a menu of crowd-pleasers such as risotto of crayfish, peas and langoustine in a chive velouté, with chicken wrapped in pancetta with mozzarella, followed by raspberry crème brûlée to finish.

Chef: Simon Goodman **Owners:** James Hickey & Andrea Hickey **Times:** 12-2.30/7-9.30, Closed 25-26 Dec, Mon, Closed D Sun **Prices:** Starter £5.95-£10.95, Main £9.95-£21.95, Dessert £5.95-£7.95, Coffee £1.75, Min/Water £3.50, Service optional **Wine:** 25 bottles over £20, 14 bottles under £20, 8 by the glass (£3.45) **Notes:** Sun L available, Dress Restrictions, No football shirts **Seats:** 40, Pr/dining room 40 **Smoking:** N/Sm in restaurant **Children:** Portions **Directions:** Signposted from A272, 6m E of Midhurst. From A285 6m S of Haslemere, follow signs for Lurgashall Winery and continue on to Lickfold village **Parking:** 40

LOWER BEEDING MAP 06 TQ22

The Camellia Restaurant at South Lodge Hotel

see page 458

MANNINGS HEATH MAP 06 TQ22

Mannings Heath Golf Club

Modern European

Traditional cuisine at an elegant golf club

☎ 01403 210228 Hammerpond Rd RH13 6PG
e-mail: enquiries@manningsheath.com
web: www.manningsheath.com

Mannings may be a members-only golf course, but its elegant restaurant is open to all and offers superb views of the green. Dine on the terrace if weather permits, or take shelter in the wood-panelled

continued on page 459

The Camellia Restaurant at South Lodge Hotel

LOWER BEEDING MAP 06 TQ22

Modern British V

Country-house cuisine overlooking the South Downs

☎ 01403 891711 Brighton Rd RH13 6PS
e-mail: enquiries@southlodgehotel.co.uk
web: www.exclusivehotels.co.uk

A haven of gracious living, this impeccably presented Victorian country-house hotel stands in 90 acres of mature gardens and grounds and offers stunning views over the South Downs. With its wood panelling, oil paintings, heavy fabrics and sense of space, it was built to impress and it certainly does. The sumptuous, candlelit restaurant - named after the 100-year-old camellia which still grows against the terrace wall - continues the theme, with ornate ceilings, wood panelling and floors and crisp white tablecloths, while large windows offer views over the downs. Service is formal but appropriately friendly.

The kitchen's approach is intelligently simple, with the emphasis on allowing tip-top produce to shine. The style is modern-focused and underpinned by a classical theme, with the fixed-price menu repertoire refreshingly unpretentious. Dishes are delivered with flair and a lightness of touch and enjoy well-defined flavours and combinations. For mains, take a fillet of Sussex beef served with roasted garlic mash, shiitaki mushrooms and a sweetbread sauce, or a seared fillet of wild sea bass paired with saffron potato and white wine cream, and for dessert, perhaps a hot chocolate pudding with raspberry and chocolate millefeuille.

Chef: Lewis Hamblet
Owners: Exclusive Hotels & Golf Clubs
Times: 12-2/7-10
Prices: Fixed L £14-£20, Fixed D £46-£55, Coffee £3.95, Min/Water £3.95, Service optional
Wine: 197 bottles over £20, 7 bottles under £20, 204 by the glass (£7.50)
Notes: Sun L £26, Vegetarian menu, Dress Restrictions, Smart casual - no sportswear, Civ Wed 160
Seats: 40, Pr/dining room 130
Smoking: N/Sm in restaurant
Children: Menu
Rooms: 45 (45 en suite) ★★★★ CHH
Directions: On A23, left onto B2110, take a right turn through Handcross to A281 junct
Parking: 190

MANNINGS HEATH *continued* MAP 06 TQ22

Goldings dining room with its inglenook fireplace and beamed ceiling. In keeping with the traditional décor, the Waterfall and Kingfisher menus (named after the two golf courses) feature a concise range of classical dishes with European influences. Braised faggot of local rabbit is a typical starter, while mains might include chargrilled veal chop with Madeira jus and sautéed potatoes, or rack of lamb with herb crust and basil jus.

Chef: Robby Pierce **Owners:** Exclusive Hotels **Times:** 12.30-2.30/7-9, Closed L Mon, D Sun-Wed **Prices:** Fixed L £12.50-£18, Fixed D £16.95-£22.45, Coffee £1.25, Min/Water £3, Service optional **Wine:** 20 bottles over £20, 14 bottles under £20, 4 by the glass (£3.75) **Notes:** Sun L 3 courses £13.50, Dress Restrictions, No jeans or trainers, collared shirt required, Civ Wed 100 **Seats:** 43, Pr/dining room 12 **Smoking:** N/Sm in restaurant **Children:** Menu, Portions **Directions:** From Horsham A281, for 2m. Approaching Mannings Heath, left at the Dun Horse. Follow road to T-junct, left then follow road past village green. At T-junct, right then right again **Parking:** 120

MIDHURST MAP 06 SU82

Spread Eagle Hotel and Health Spa

Modern British

Accomplished modern cooking in character setting

☎ 01730 816911 South St GU29 9NH
e-mail: reservations@spreadeagle-midhurst.com
web: www.hshotels.co.uk/spread/spreadeagle-main.htm

This beautiful old property, parts of which date back to 1430, occupies a prime position at the foot of the town, yet enjoys the seclusion of its own delightful grounds. The building itself retains many original features, including ancient beams, sloping floors and oak panelling. Two interconnecting rooms make up the restaurant, separated by a large stone fireplace complete with copper canopy adorned with old copper pots. The hospitality here is renowned while the food is similarly spot-on, with appealing dishes delivered with good technical skill and clear flavours. Expect starters such as terrine of smoked ham with home-made piccalilli, mains like sea bass with confit potato and pancetta, and desserts of pear tarte Tatin with honey ice cream and hazlenut caramel.

Chef: Gary Moreton-Jones **Owners:** The Goodman Family **Times:** 12.30-2/7-9.30 **Prices:** Fixed L £15-£17, Fixed D £35-£37.50, Coffee £2.65, Min/Water £3, Service optional **Wine:** 50 bottles over £20, 20 bottles under £20, 15 by the glass (£4-£7) **Notes:** Vegetarian available, Dress Restrictions, Smart casual, Civ Wed 80 **Seats:** 50, Pr/dining room 12 **Smoking:** N/Sm in restaurant **Children:** Menu, Portions **Rooms:** 39 (39 en suite) ★★★ HL **Directions:** Town centre **Parking:** 70

ROWHOOK MAP 06 TQ13

Neals Restaurant at The Chequers Inn

British, Mediterranean

Enjoyable rustic pub dining

☎ 01403 790480 RH12 3PY
e-mail: thechequers1!@aol.com
web: www.nealsrestaurants.biz

This 15th-century rural village pub is traditionally decorated with open fires, oak beams, flagstones and rustic wooden tables. There's a separate dining area and terrace for summer dining. Modern British dishes are simply but effectively presented like the warm terrine of Sussex goat's cheese with balsamic, olive oil and cress. For a main course, try the grilled cod with its rich saffron, mussel and clam chowder and finish with either the chocolate and raspberry tart or the excellent selection of British regional cheeses.

Times: 12-2/7-9, Closed D Sun **Directions:** From Horsham take A281 towards Guildford. At rdbt take A29 signposted for London. After 200 mtrs turn left, follow signs for Rowhook

---

RUSPER MAP 06 TQ23

Ghyll Manor

Modern European NEW

Creative and accomplished cooking at peaceful country-house hotel

☎ 0845 345 3426 High St RH12 4PX
e-mail: reception@ghyllmanor.co.uk
web: www.ghyllmanor.co.uk

Set in the sleepy village of Rusper, this historic mansion house - now country-house hotel - retains many original features and is set in 45 acres of idyllic, peaceful grounds that include a lake. The restaurant - in the original part of the house - exudes a warm, cosy ambience and comes with oak beams, well-proportioned seating and spacious tables, while service takes an efficient and friendly, professional approach. The kitchen's modern European style is delivered via fixed-price dinner, carte and the chef's six-course tasting menus. Expect seared wild sea bass served with buttered baby fennel, lobster ravioli and lobster essence, and perhaps a glazed iced coconut parfait with warm citrus and mango salad to finish.

Prices: Food prices not confirmed for 2007. Please telephone for details
Rooms: 29 (29 en suite) ★★★ CHH

STORRINGTON MAP 06 TQ01

Old Forge

Modern International

Fine food and wine in historic setting

☎ 01903 743402 6 Church St RH20 4LA
e-mail: contact@oldforge.co.uk
web: www.oldforge.co.uk

This collection of old-world cottages with low ceilings and wooden beams houses a forge dating back to the 16th century. Husband-and-wife team Cathy and Clive Roberts offer a warm welcome and invite guests to enjoy modern cooking based on traditional ingredients, accompanied by some fine wines. The menu changes regularly to keep up with seasonal availability, but a typical main course might be a parcel of braised lamb with roasted aubergines and coriander couscous. For dessert expect the likes of chocolate and griottine clafoutis.

Chef: Cathy Roberts **Owners:** Mr & Mrs N C Roberts **Times:** 12.15-1.30/7.15-9, Closed Xmas-New Year, 2 wks spring, 2 wks autumn, Mon-Wed, Closed L Sat, D Sun **Prices:** Fixed L £14, Min/Water £2.50, Service included **Wine:** 30 bottles over £20, 16 bottles under £20, 10 by the glass (£3.25-£4) **Notes:** Coffee incl, ALC 2 courses £26, 3 courses £34, Smart casual **Seats:** 34, Pr/dining room 12 **Smoking:** N/Sm in restaurant **Children:** Portions **Directions:** On side street in village centre **Parking:** On street

England

TURNERS HILL MAP 06 TQ33

Alexander House Hotel & Utopia Spa

Modern European

Country-house grandeur and imaginative cuisine

☎ 01342 714914 East St RH10 4QD
e-mail: info@alexanderhouse.co.uk
web: www.alexanderhouse.co.uk

This Victorian mansion house was once a retirement home for clergy. These days it offers well-proportioned rooms including a relaxing lounge with ornate carved mantelpiece and comfortable sofas. The bar and brasserie have leather seating and darker décor where simple light dishes are served here. The restaurant is in the oldest part of the hotel and offers country house grandeur with formal table service, but in a relaxed and friendly atmosphere. The cooking style is classical French with some European influences. Starters might include pan-fried diver scallops with cauliflower purée and a grape and caper dressing. Typical mains are pan-fried fillet of beef with braised potato and wild mushroom compote, or noisette of lamb with baby fondant potato, spinach and ratatouille. If you're staying in the hotel you might like to try Lord or Lady Alexander's traditional afternoon tea.

Chef: Kirk Johnson **Owners:** Alexander Hotels Ltd **Times:** 12-3/7-9.30, Closed L Mon-Sat, D Sun-Tue **Prices:** Fixed D £39.50, Coffee £3.50, Min/Water £3.50, Service added but optional 12.5% **Wine:** 130 bottles over £20, 15 bottles under £20, 8 by the glass (£5-£8.50) **Notes:** ALC 3 courses £49.50 Sun L 3 courses £26, Vegetarian available, Dress Restrictions, No jeans or trainers, Civ Wed 90 **Seats:** 40, Pr/dining room 16 **Smoking:** N/Sm in restaurant **Children:** Min 7 yrs, Portions **Rooms:** 32 (32 en suite) ★★★★ **Directions:** On B2110 between Turners Hill & East Grinstead; 6m from M23 junct 10 **Parking:** 150

WORTHING MAP 06 TQ10

Ardington Hotel

International

Contemporary cuisine by the sea

☎ 01903 230451 Steyne Gardens BN11 3DZ
web: www.ardingtonhotel.co.uk

In contrast to the character and age of the building - set near the seafront in a pretty garden square - the Ardington's Indigo restaurant is a bright, airy, contemporary affair, decked out with vibrant abstract artwork and high-backed chairs. The kitchen delivers some adventurous dishes alongside straightforward offerings. Perhaps Southdown lamb served with a potato cake, pancetta and Puy lentils lining up beside classics like cod fillet in beer batter with fries and home-made tartare sauce, or a range of grills with choice of sauce and classic trimmings.

Chef: John Gettings **Owners:** Mr & Mrs B Margaroli **Times:** 12-2/7-8.45, Closed 23 Dec-7 Jan, Closed L Mon-Tue **Prices:** Fixed L £9.85, Starter £5.95, Main £11-£17, Dessert £5.95, Coffee £2.10, Min/Water £3.25, Service optional **Wine:** 3 bottles under £20, 6 by the glass (£2.90) **Notes:** Vegetarian available **Seats:** 70, Pr/dining room 50 **Smoking:** N/Sm in restaurant **Children:** Menu, Portions **Rooms:** 45 (45 en suite) ★★★ HL **Directions:** Telephone for directions

TYNE & WEAR

GATESHEAD MAP 21 NZ26

Eslington Villa Hotel

Modern British, French

Modern cooking in a charming setting

☎ 0191 487 6017 & 420 0666 8 Station Rd, Low Fell NE9 6DR
e-mail: eslingtonvilla@freeuk.com
web: www.eslingtonvillahotel.com

Built around 1902, the building retains Edwardian features such as high ceilings, fireplaces and cornices. The conservatory dining room is decorated in a more contemporary style with tartan carpets and thistle drapes. Modern, British and French influenced cuisine is served in relaxed, friendly surroundings. Traditional starters use a range of quality ingredients in dishes with clear flavours, like potato and leek soup with poached haddock, chives and truffle oil. Main courses offer authentic Italian dishes like saltimbocca of veal with sage and truffle risotto, parmesan tuile and rocket; or closer to home the likes of mixed grill featuring Cumberland sausage, or mouthwatering fillet of Scottish beef with rösti, braised cabbage and crispy bacon.

continued

Chef: Andy Moore **Owners:** Mr & Mrs N Tulip **Times:** 12-2/7-9.45, Closed 25-26 Dec, 1 Jan, BHs, Closed L Sat, D Sun **Prices:** Fixed L £14, Fixed D £20, Starter £4.50-£8.50, Main £15-£19, Dessert £4-£8, Coffee £2, Min/Water £3.25, Service optional **Wine:** 17 bottles over £20, 24 bottles under £20, 7 by the glass (£3.35-£4.50) **Notes:** Vegetarian available, Smart casual **Seats:** 80, Pr/dining room 30 **Smoking:** N/Sm in restaurant **Children:** Portions **Rooms:** 17 (17 en suite) ★★★ HL **Directions:** From A1 (M) turn off to Team Valley Trading Estate, up Eastern Avenue. Turn left at PDS car showroom. Hotel is 100 yds on left **Parking:** 30

Riverside Restaurant & Bar - Baltic Mill

☎ 0191 440 4942 Baltic Centre, for Contemporary Art, South Shore Rd NE8 3BA
web: www.theaa.com/restaurants/114019.html

Making the most of the setting beside the Tyne with floor to ceiling windows across the length of the restaurant, and offering lunches from light meals to three courses (midday to 4.30pm). It reopens two hours later with a full modern British menu.

NEWCASTLE UPON TYNE MAP 21 NZ26

Blackfriars Restaurant

Modern British

Modern dining in ancient surroundings

☎ 0191 261 5945 Friars St NE1 4XN
e-mail: info@blackfriarscafebar.co.uk
web: www.blackfriarscafebar.co.uk

Once the refectory of an early 13th-century priory, this eatery may have the oldest dining room in the UK. Massive stone walls, ancient beams, and inglenooks lit by huge flickering candles set a Gothic tone. But you can escape to the peaceful courtyard for summer dining. Friendly, efficient staff serve modern British dishes based on local ingredients. An adventurous starter of nettle and wild garlic soup may be followed by grilled local salmon, mash and basil jus, finishing with boozy prune and chocolate truffle tart with toffee sauce. Vegetarians can expect good options.

Chef: Chris Slaughter & Simon Brown **Owners:** Andy & Sam Hook **Times:** 12-2.30/6-12, Closed BHs except Good Fri, Mon, Closed D Sun **Prices:** Fixed L £10.50, Fixed D £15, Starter £4-£6, Main £12-£18, Dessert £5-£6, Coffee £1.70, Min/Water £2.80, Service optional, Group min 6 service 10% **Wine:** 12 bottles over £20, 18 bottles under £20, 6 by the glass (£3.25-£4.50) **Notes:** Vegetarian available **Seats:** 70, Pr/dining room 20 **Smoking:** N/Sm in restaurant, Air con **Children:** Portions **Directions:** Take the only small cobbled road off Stowel St (China Town). Blackfriars 100yds on left **Parking:** Car park next to restaurant

Café 21 Newcastle

French, International V

Busy bistro in Newcastle's trendy Quayside area

☎ 0191 222 0755 Quayside NE1 3UG
e-mail: bh@cafetwentyone.co.uk

City-centre bistro with contemporary colour and style. The walls are hung with large mirrors, little pictures and old French recipes. White clothed wooden tables are set on wooden floors, each with a bowl of olives, tea lights, and branded crockery with the Café 21 logo. Well presented and accurately cooked French bistro dishes with British and Asian influences, with regularly changing specials, are based on local produce where possible. Try cheese and spinach soufflé, fishcakes with chips and parsley sauce or peppered saddle of venison with creamed celeriac and blue cheese fritter. There's also a selection of farmhouse cheeses. Service is informal and friendly.

Chef: Christopher Dobson **Owners:** Mr and Mrs T Laybourne **Times:** 12-2.30/6-10.30, Closed Xmas, BHs, Sun **Prices:** Fixed L fr £14, Starter £5.50-£11, Main £12.50-£22.50, Dessert £5.50-£7, Coffee £2.20, Min/Water £3, Service added but optional 10% **Wine:** 42 bottles over £20, 18 bottles under £20, 8 by the glass (£3.40-£4.80) **Notes:** Vegetarian menu **Seats:** 60 **Smoking:** N/Sm area, No pipes, Air con **Children:** Portions **Directions:** Telephone for directions **Parking:** On street, NCP

Fisherman's Lodge

British, French

Tranquil setting for imaginative cooking

☎ 0191 281 3281 Jesmond Dene, Jesmond NE7 7BQ
e-mail: enquiries@fishermanslodge.co.uk
web: www.fishermanslodge.co.uk

Occupying a wonderfully secluded parkland location, this restaurant is within easy reach of the city centre. Formerly Lord Armstrong's private dwelling, the décor is in the style of a smart, shooting lodge but with lots of modern comfort. Fine linen and glassware add extra sparkle to the dining room. Service is relaxed but efficient. Carefully presented, modern British dishes have clear flavours. Expect starters of confit corn-fed chicken and foie gras terrine with foie gras beignets and fig chutney. Main courses might include roast Cornish brill, shallot confit, truffle tortellini and baby leeks, or roast loin of venison, confit cabbage and fondant potato. Finish with caramelised banana, millefeuille of banana mousse and banana parfait with a honeyed tuile.

Chef: Jamie Walsh **Owners:** Tom and Jocelyn Maxfield **Times:** 12-2/7-10.30, Closed 25 Dec, BHs, Sun, Closed L 31 Dec, D Sun **Prices:** Fixed L £17.50-£22.50, Coffee £3.95, Min/Water £3.75, Service optional **Wine:** 205

continued

England

NEWCASTLE UPON TYNE *continued*
MAP 21 NZ26

bottles over £20, 8 bottles under £20, 12 by the glass (£4.25-£7.25) **Notes:** Fixed L 3 courses, ALC 2 courses £40, 3 courses £50, Vegetarian available, Smart casual, Civ Wed 60 **Seats:** 60, Pr/dining room 40 **Smoking:** N/Sm in restaurant **Children:** Portions **Directions:** 2.5m from city centre, off A1058 (Tynemouth road). Turn into Jesmond Rd then 2nd right on Jesmond Dene Rd. Follow signs **Parking:** 40

Jesmond Dene House

Modern British NEW

Fashionable new hotel restaurant with a keen eye on contemporary food trends

☎ 0191 212 3000 Jesmond Dene Rd NE2 2EY
e-mail: info@jesmonddenehouse.co.uk
web: www.jesmonddenehouse.co.uk

Built in the early 1820s, this Georgian house overlooking the wooded valley of Jesmond Dene has plenty of rural charm yet it's only five minutes from the centre of town. Recently converted into a hotel, the décor throughout understandably looks pristine, with comfortable wood-panelled lounges and a restaurant split into two dining areas - a former music room with a dramatic colour scheme and the oak-floored garden room. The cooking is generous and skilful, with a seasonally-inspired menu concentrating on well-matched flavours with dashes of thoughtful experimentation - crab lasagne with shellfish cappuccino and basil to start, for example, followed by Aberdeen Angus plate with two types of celery (slow-cooked shoulder, rare fillet, braised celery, celeriac cream and bone marrow).

Chef: Terry Laybourne/Jose Graziosi **Owners:** Terry Laybourne/Peter Candler **Times:** 12-2.30/7-10.30 **Prices:** Fixed L £17-£18, Starter £6.50-£14.50, Main £17.50-£24.50, Dessert £4-£9.50, Coffee £2.20, Min/Water £3, Service added 10% **Wine:** 195 bottles over £20, 26 bottles under £20, 18 by the glass (£4.10-£9.90) **Notes:** Tasting menu £65, Dress Restrictions, Smart casual, Civ Wed 100 **Seats:** 60, Pr/dining room 18 **Smoking:** N/Sm in restaurant **Children:** Menu, Portions **Rooms:** 40 (40 en suite) ★★★★ HL **Directions:** From Newcastle City Centre follow A167 to junct with A184. Turn right towards Matthew Bank. Turn right into Jesmond Dene Rd. **Parking:** 64

Malmaison Hotel

French  

Good brasserie dining in trendy location

☎ 0191 245 5000 Quayside NE1 3DX
e-mail: newcastle@malmaison.com
web: www.malmaison.com

Former warehouse, now a chic modern hotel on the trendy and popular Newcastle quayside, with stunning views of the Millennium Bridge. Enjoy drinks in the first-floor bar overlooking the river Tyne, with its stripped wood floors, oversized sofas and bustling atmosphere, then move through to the equally contemporary brasserie-style restaurant. Bold colours, moody lighting and giant picture windows set the relaxing scene for sampling some traditional brasserie classics like salmon fishcake with parsley sauce, steak frites, duck confit with braised Puy lentils and thyme jus, and crème brûlée. **Notable Wine List:** A really high quality wine list, with concise tasting notes throughout and offering an interesting and diverse mix of wines.

continued

Chef: Gareth Marks **Owners:** MWB **Times:** 12-2.30/6-11 **Prices:** Fixed L £12.95, Fixed D £25-£40, Starter £4.50-£7.25, Main £10.95-£23.95, Dessert £4.95-£6.95, Coffee £1.95, Min/Water £3.30, Service optional, Group **Wine:** 127 bottles over £20, 18 bottles under £20 **Notes:** Vegetarian menu **Seats:** 84, Pr/dining room 20 **Smoking:** N/Sm in restaurant, Air con **Children:** Portions **Rooms:** 120 (120 en suite) ★★★ HL **Directions:** Telephone for directions **Parking:** 60

Newcastle Marriott Hotel, Gosforth Park

Traditional European

Formal hotel dining room overlooking Gosforth Park

☎ 0191 236 4111 High Gosforth Park, Gosforth NE3 5HN
e-mail: frontdesk.gosforthpark@marriotthotels.co.uk
web: www.marriott.co.uk

This smart modern hotel is located on the outskirts of the city amid 12 acres of woodland. The Park Restaurant is richly decorated, with marble-tiled and carpeted floors, heavy drapes and upholstered seating. Lunches tend to be geared to conferences and include a buffet offering. At dinner there is a daily fixed-price menu of fairly straightforward dishes and a more ambitious carte studded with luxury items such as truffles, foie gras, scallops and lobster. Representative dishes are pot roast breast of pigeon with parmentier vegetables and port thyme jus, lobster medallion and scallop with chive caviar sauce and iced orange parfait with citrus syrup.

Chef: Simon Devine **Owners:** Marriott International **Times:** 12.30-2/7-10, Closed 31 Dec, Closed L Sat (Mon-Fri for conferences only) **Prices:** Fixed L £16.95, Fixed D £21-£28, Starter £5.50-£9.25, Main £13.50-£25.50, Dessert £5.50, Coffee £2.85, Min/Water £3.95, Service optional **Wine:** 19 by the glass (£5.15-£7.85) **Notes:** Vegetarian available, Civ Wed 200 **Seats:** 120, Pr/dining room 30 **Smoking:** N/Sm in restaurant, Air con **Children:** Menu, Portions **Rooms:** 178 (178 en suite) ★★★★ HL **Directions:** From A1 take A1056 (Killingworth/Wideopen) 3rd exit to hotel ahead. **Parking:** 300

Treacle Moon

Modern Mediterranean

Chic dinner venue near the quay

☎ 0191 232 5537 5-7 The Side NE1 3JE
e-mail: john@treaclemoonrestaurant.co.uk
web: www.treaclemoonrestaurant.com

Modern images of the city and its connecting bridges grace the walls of this modern restaurant near the quayside. Chic tables with fresh flowers and tall glassware are candlelit at night for an extra touch of romance. Friendly and attentive staff make it a welcoming venue for dinner. Cuisine is modern Mediterranean in style, with five choices of dish at each course. Try a starter like hot charred king prawns with Asian salad, sweet chilli and sesame. For a main course, you might choose roast loin of venison with celeriac purée, poached pear, wild mushrooms and red wine sauce. Desserts feature favourites like apple and pear crumble with cinnamon ice cream.

Chef: Paul Martin **Owners:** Tom & Jocelyn Maxfield **Times:** 6-10.30, Closed Xmas, 2 wks Aug, BHs, Sun, Closed L all week **Prices:** Fixed D fr £36, Coffee £2.95, Min/Water £3.50, Service optional **Wine:** 50 bottles over £20, 8 bottles under £20, 4 by the glass (£4.50-£8.50) **Notes:** Vegetarian available, Dress Restrictions, Formal Modern **Seats:** 30 **Smoking:** N/Sm in restaurant, Air con **Children:** Portions **Directions:** On the quayside **Parking:** Dene Street

Vermont Hotel

British, European

Great location for quayside dining

☎ 0191 233 1010 Castle Garth NE1 1RQ
e-mail: info@vermont-hotel.co.uk
web: www.vermont-hotel.com

This hotel enjoys a brilliant central location next to the castle and close to the bustling quayside. Formerly the County Hall, the grand old building has views over the Tyne and Millennium bridges. The aptly named Bridge restaurant is the fine-dining option here and is decorated in classic, elegant style with bench and cane seating, fine glassware and linen napkins. The cooking style is Anglo-French with European influences on a varied menu. Service is relaxed and attentive, and the Blue Room is available for private dining.

Chef: Gary Cook **Owners:** Lincoln Group **Times:** 12-2.30/6-11 **Prices:** Fixed L £14, Fixed D £24, Coffee £2.80, Min/Water £3.50 **Wine:** 50 bottles over £20, 40 bottles under £20, 8 by the glass (£3.40-£5.60) **Notes:** Sun L 2 courses £14, 3 courses £17, Vegetarian available, Dress Restrictions, Very smart; no casual dress, no jeans, Civ Wed 150 **Seats:** 80, Pr/dining room 80 **Smoking:** N/Sm in restaurant, Air con **Children:** Portions **Rooms:** 101 (101 en suite) ★★★★ **Directions:** City centre, by high level bridge and castle keep **Parking:** 70

Barn Again Bistro

☎ 0191 281 7179 21a Leazes Park Rd NE1 4PF
Fun, safari-tinged surroundings with a global menu to match.

TYNEMOUTH MAP 21 NZ36

Sidney's Restaurant

Modern British

Buzzing bistro in Tyneside town centre

☎ 0191 257 8500 & 213 0284
3-5 Percy Park Rd NE30 4LZ
e-mail: bookings@sidneys.co.uk
web: www.sidneys.co.uk

Once a Victorian butcher's shop, Sidney's is now a cosy, stylish, modern bistro. Wooden floors, leather benches and unclothed tables with simple settings are the background to the buzzy atmosphere helped along by friendly and efficient staff. Modern British is the house style here, but with the occasional Mediterranean or Asian influences such as starters of rare beef salad served with capers and lemon, and main courses of red mullet with mango and chilli salsa or beetroot risotto with shaved parmesan. Apple crumble with ice cream or English and Irish cheeses to finish perhaps.

Chef: Steve McDonnell **Owners:** Andy & Sam Hook **Times:** 12-2.30/6-12, Closed BHs ex Good Friday, Sun **Prices:** Fixed L £9, Fixed D £15, Starter £4.25-£6.50, Main £11.50-£16.95, Dessert £4.25-£4.50, Coffee £1.70, Min/Water £2.80, Service optional, Group min 6 service 10% **Wine:** 13 bottles over £20, 19 bottles under £20, 6 by the glass (£3.25-£4.10) **Notes:** Vegetarian available **Seats:** 50, Pr/dining room 20 **Smoking:** N/Sm in restaurant, Air con **Children:** Menu, Portions **Directions:** From Newcastle take A1058 to Tynemouth. Restaurant on corner of Percy Park Rd & Front St **Parking:** On street

WARWICKSHIRE

ABBOT'S SALFORD MAP 10 SP05

Salford Hall Hotel

Modern, Traditional

Modern food in a historic setting

☎ 01386 871300 WR11 5UT
e-mail: reception@salfordhall.co.uk
web: www.salfordhall.co.uk

The hotel has an interesting history having first been a retreat for the Abbot of Evesham, then a family home in the Tudor period and finally a nunnery before becoming a hotel. The restaurant is very traditional with oak panelling, a large fireplace and mullioned windows. The modern British menu offers simple dishes - confit of Barbary duck leg with wok-fried vegetables, tenderloin of pork and apple tarte Tatin with sage fondant and Madeira jus, or wild mushroom and parmesan cheese risotto - using the best of fresh ingredients, locally sourced where appropriate.

Chef: Paul Napper **Owners:** Charter Hotels Ltd **Times:** 12.30-2/7-10, Closed Xmas, Closed L Sat **Prices:** Fixed L fr £12, Fixed D £29.50-£36, Service optional **Wine:** 100 bottles over £20, 22 bottles under £20, 25 by the glass (£3.75-£6.75) **Notes:** Vegetarian available, Dress Restrictions, No jeans or trainers, Civ Wed 80 **Seats:** 50, Pr/dining room 50 **Smoking:** N/Sm in restaurant **Children:** Min 2 yrs, Portions **Rooms:** 33 (33 en suite) ★★★ HL **Directions:** Off A46 between Stratford Upon Avon & Evesham. Take road signed Salford Priors, Abbots Salford 1.5m on left **Parking:** 60

ALCESTER MAP 10 SP05

Kings Court Hotel

Modern, Traditional

Modern cooking in old-world setting

☎ 01789 763111 Kings Coughton B49 5QQ
e-mail: info@kingscourthotel.co.uk
web: www.kingscourthotel.co.uk

This privately-owned hotel - originally a Tudor farmhouse - is situated in the village where the infamous Gunpowder Plot was hatched. The spacious Courtyard restaurant has a warm and friendly atmosphere, there's a walled courtyard garden for warm-weather aperitifs and the Twisted Boot Bar for colder days. The kitchen's modern approach pays due respect to traditional tastes and well-sourced produce, with the restaurant delivering the likes of tournedos of fillet, perhaps served with wild mushrooms and a port glaze, and homely desserts like bread-and-butter pudding with vanilla sauce.

Chef: David Price **Owners:** Thomas Aldous **Times:** 12-2/7-10, Closed Xmas, Closed L Sat **Prices:** Fixed L £8.95-£9.50, Starter £3.95-£5.95, Main £10.95-£14.95, Dessert £3.95, Coffee £1.50, Min/Water £2.50, Service optional **Wine:** 2 bottles over £20, 18 bottles under £20, 12 by the glass (£2.55-£4.70) **Notes:** Vegetarian available, Civ Wed 100 **Seats:** 70, Pr/dining room 100 **Smoking:** N/Sm in restaurant **Children:** Menu, Portions **Rooms:** 41 (41 en suite) ★★★ HL **Directions:** 1m N of Alcester on the A435, 8m outside of Stratford-upon-Avon **Parking:** 100

England

ALDERMINSTER MAP 10 SP24

Ettington Park Hotel

British

Dine in Gothic splendour

☎ 01789 450123 CV37 8BU
web: www.handpicked.co.uk

The stately oak-panelled dining room, with its original 18th-century rococo ceiling and wall panels embossed with family crests, epitomises the glamour and character at this imposing Victorian Gothic mansion set in 40 acres of parkland. Tables clothed in formal white linen, polished glassware and cutlery, and views across the garden to the 12th-century family chapel set a traditional note. By contrast, there's a sense of adventure about the cooking, though the food remains classically French based, with the skilled kitchen delivering some complex cooking. Maybe fillet of Scotch beef served with a watercress rouille, gâteau of celeriac and spinach and shallot red wine sauce, or Bramley apple soufflé with Calvados ice cream.

Chef: Giles Stonehouse **Owners:** Hand Picked Hotels **Times:** 12-2/7-9.30, Closed L Mon-Fri **Prices:** Fixed L £14.95-£38, Fixed D £35-£47.50, Starter £8.50-£11.50, Main £21.50-£26.50, Dessert £8.50-£9.50, Coffee £3.95, Min/Water £4, Service optional **Wine:** 108 bottles over £20, 2 bottles under £20, 10 by the glass (£4.50-£9.50) **Notes:** Tasting menu £55, with wine £85, Sun L £19.50, Vegetarian available, Smart casual, Civ Wed 96 **Seats:** 50, Pr/dining room 80 **Smoking:** N/Sm in restaurant **Children:** Menu, Portions **Rooms:** 48 (48 en suite) ★★★★ HL **Directions:** M40 junct 15/A46 towards Stratford-upon-Avon, then A439 into town centre onto A3400 5m to Shipston. Hotel 1/2m on left **Parking:** 80

ATHERSTONE MAP 10 SP39

Chapel House Hotel

British, French

Elegant surroundings for imaginative cooking

☎ 01827 718949 Friar's Gate CV9 1EY
e-mail: info@chapelhousehotel.co.uk
web: www.chapelhousehotel.co.uk

Formerly the dower house to Atherstone Hall, Chapel House was built in 1729 as an elegant town house, and Florence Nightingale was a frequent visitor here. Extended and upgraded over the years, it retains many period features. The restaurant is a light, elegant Georgian dining room with well-spaced tables, crisp white linen ware and silver cutlery. The cooking style is mainly classical French but with a modern, lighter touch. The chef uses fresh local produce as much as possible and the menu features the likes of king prawn and mushroom brioche to start, with local Grendon lamb au Porto as a main course.

Chef: Richard Henry Napper **Owners:** Richard & Siobhan Napper **Times:** 7-9, Closed 24 Dec-3 Jan, Etr week, late Aug-early Sep, Sun, Closed L all week **Prices:** Starter £4.95-£9.85, Main £18-£22.50, Dessert £4.95-£7.75, Coffee £2.85, Min/Water £2.95, Service optional **Wine:** 60 bottles over £20, 40 bottles under £20, 8 by the glass (£2.95-£4.45) **Notes:** Dress Restrictions, Smart casual **Seats:** 24, Pr/dining room 12 **Smoking:** N/Sm in restaurant **Children:** Portions **Rooms:** 12 (12 en suite) ★★ **Directions:** Off Market Sq in Atherstone, behind High St **Parking:** On street

BRANDON MAP 11 SP47

Macdonald Brandon Hall Hotel & Spa

British, French NEW

Modern restaurant in large country hotel

☎ 0870 400 8105 Main St CV8 3FW
e-mail: general.brandonhall@macdonald-hotels.co.uk
web: www.macdonald-hotels.co.uk

Set in 17 acres of well-tended lawns and woodland, this one-time hunting lodge is now a large country hotel with excellent leisure facilities. Its spacious, modern-styled restaurant is smartly laid out with a host of mirrors, with clientele a mix of locals and leisure and conference crowd. Simplicity is the keynote to the kitchen's success, with an appealing repertoire that holds the interest through to the end. Chicken liver parfait, red onion chutney and melba toast; lamb shank with red wine jus, minted mash and red cabbage; and chocolate bread and butter pudding show off the accomplished style.

Chef: Mr Simon Johnson **Owners:** Macdonald Hotels PLC **Times:** 12.30-2.30/7-9.30 **Prices:** Fixed L fr £16.95, Fixed D fr £24.95, Starter £3-£11.50, Main £10.50-£18.95, Dessert £6.50-£9.50, Coffee £3.85, Min/Water £4.55, Service optional **Wine:** 53 bottles over £20, 38 bottles under £20, 12 by the glass (£4.25-£7) **Notes:** Sun L £14.95, Vegetarian available, Civ Wed 80 **Seats:** 90, Pr/dining room 280 **Smoking:** N/Sm in restaurant, Air con **Children:** Menu, Portions **Rooms:** 120 (120 en suite) ★★★★ HL **Directions:** From A46 follow signs on A428 towards Binley Woods/Brandon, turn right at village green, hotel 500yds on right **Parking:** 260

FARNBOROUGH MAP 11 SP44

The Inn at Farnborough

French, Mediterranean

Skilful cooking in the heart of a small village

☎ 01295 690615 Main St OX17 1DZ
e-mail: enquiries@innatfarnborough.co.uk
web: www.innatfarnborough.co.uk

Dating from around 1700 this former butcher's shop is now a restaurant and pub all in one. The old and the contemporary sit happily together creating a really relaxed atmosphere in which to eat and drink - service comes with a smile! Essentially French, the menu is based on much locally sourced produce and comes up with some interesting choices. Dishes such as sautéed king scallops with crispy Parma ham, rocket salad and toasted hazelnut and tarragon dressing, followed by confit of Oxfordshire lamb with dauphinoise potato, pea and mint purée and rosemary jus, then baked apple tart with caramel ice cream show the style.

Chef: Anthony Robinson **Owners:** Oyster Inns Ltd **Times:** 12-3/6-10, Closed 25 Dec **Prices:** Fixed L £10.95, Fixed D £12.95, Starter £5.50-£9.95, Main £10.95-£16.95, Dessert £5.50, Coffee £2.25, Min/Water £2.50, Service optional **Wine:** 11 bottles over £20, 24 bottles under £20, 14 by the glass (£3.35-£6) **Notes:** Vegetarian available **Seats:** 80, Pr/dining room 16 **Smoking:** N/Sm in restaurant **Children:** Portions **Directions:** M40 junct 11 - (Banbury). 3rd rdbt turn right onto A423 to Southam. After 4m turn left down road signed Farnborough. After 1m turn right into the village - the Inn at Farnborough is on right **Parking:** 40

KENILWORTH MAP 10 SP27

Simply Simpsons

French

tylish bistro serving classically-based modern dishes

01926 864567 101-103 Warwick Rd CV8 1HL
-mail: info@simplysimpsons.com
veb: www.simplysimpsons.com

contemporary bistro on the main street of the pretty town of enilworth. The fashionable restaurant has quarry-tiled floors, polished vooden tables, artwork and painted bricks. Sister restaurant to impsons in Edgbaston, here you'll find simpler cooking and friendly nformal service. Fresh local produce and stylish presentation combine n wonderful dishes like confit of duck leg on a mixed leaf salad with eetroot to start. Main courses might feature the likes of roast fillet of nonkfish with Indian spices, chickpeas and gremolata or slow roast elly of pork with rösti potato, glazed apple and Calvados sauce. For essert, try the home-made sticky toffee pudding served with toffee auce.

imes: 12.30-2/7-10, Closed Last 2 wks of Aug, BHs, Sun, Mon
irections: In main street in Kenilworth centre

Raffles

01926 864300 57 Warwick Rd CV8 1HN
web: www.theaa.com/restaurants/114020.html

Malaysian cuisine, including Indian and Chinese. Colonial atmosphere and Singapore Slings a must.

Mallory Court Hotel

LEAMINGTON SPA (ROYAL) MAP 10 SP36

Modern British

xquisitely prepared dishes in sumptuous country-house plendour

01926 330214 Harbury Ln, ishop's Tachbrook CV33 9QB
-mail: reception@mallory.co.uk
veb: www.mallory.co.uk

nis elegant, Lutyens-style country manor house is quite the little ece of England; an idyllic, impeccable retreat set in 10 acres of ndscaped grounds and immaculate lawns. Contemporary country-ouse splendour is the style, where pampered relaxation comes easy sumptuous lounges over aperitifs or coffee, the mellow, homely mosphere cultivated by an efficient, dedicated and enthusiastic team. ne small dining room continues the theme, with oak panelling, aded-light and mullioned windows, and crisp white linen. The ccomplished modern British cooking approach is underpinned by a assical French theme and is surprisingly more urban than country; its gh standards and sophistication would meet the exacting demands the London set. Top-class ingredients, skilful combinations and esentation, clear flavours, and a lightness of touch all find their ace. The fixed-price menu repertoire is intelligently compact and enticing; take a trio of Lighthorn lamb with minted fennel purée, and perhaps a chocolate samosa with orange pannacotta and sweet orange jam to finish. There's a new brasserie for lighter meal options, too, while a stroll in the lovely gardens is the perfect prelude to dinner, or for a post-lunch amble.

Chef: Simon Haigh **Owners:** Sir Peter Rigby **Times:** 12-1.45/6.30-9 **Prices:** Fixed L fr £20, Fixed D fr £39.95, Coffee £3.50, Min/Water £3.50, Service optional **Wine:** 300 bottles over £20, 3 bottles under £20, 15 by the glass (£5.50-£6.50) **Notes:** Vegetarian available, Dress Restrictions, No jeans or sportswear, Civ Wed 160 **Seats:** 50, Pr/dining room 27 **Smoking:** N/Sm in restaurant **Children:** Min 9 yrs, Portions **Rooms:** 33 (33 en suite) ★★★ HL **Directions:** M40 junct 13 N-bound. Turn left, and left again towards Bishops Tachbrook. Continue for 0.5m and turn right up Harbury Lane. M40 junct 14 S-bound. Follow A452 for Leamington. At 2nd rdbt take left into Harbury Lane **Parking:** 50

LEAMINGTON SPA (ROYAL) *continued*
MAP 10 SP36

 Solo

European

Accomplished cooking in modern restaurant

☎ 01926 422422 23 Dormer Place CV32 5AA
e-mail: solorestaurant@hotmail.com
web: www.solorestaurant.co.uk

Situated opposite the park and just around the corner from The Parade, this intimate, tastefully modernised eatery has subtle lighting, trendy prints and an art deco feel. Ian Wallace has taken the helm at another establishment, but retains ownership here and the cooking maintains its freshness and vibrancy. Seafood is a speciality with dishes like Salcombe crab pasta with lemon oil to start. Accomplished cooking is exhibited in main courses like loin of Finnebrogue baby deer with a chocolate scented jus. Irresistible desserts include the likes of sticky toffee pudding or chocolate fondant.

Times: 12-2/7-9.30, Closed Xmas, BHs, Sun, Mon **Directions:** Telephone for directions

---

STRATFORD-UPON-AVON MAP 10 SP25

Billesley Manor Hotel

British, European

Modern food in a fine historic setting

☎ 01789 279955 Billesley, Alcester B49 6NF
e-mail: enquiries@billesleymanor.co.uk
web: www.billesleymanor.co.uk

Lovely Elizabethan manor house set in 11 acres of grounds close to Stratford-upon-Avon. Shakespeare was a guest in his time and is believed to have written part of *As You Like It* here. The Stuart Restaurant is a splendid oak-panelled room with a huge stone fireplace, chandeliers and silver pheasants. It also offers views of the garden and fountain - the yew topiary is worth a viewing. A modern approach is taken to food and ingredients are carefully sourced. Local game is layered with foie gras in a terrine served with pickled walnuts, and could be followed by warm escabèche of grey mullet in a carrot and garlic galette.

Chef: Christopher Short **Owners:** Paramount **Times:** 12.30-2/7-9.30 **Prices:** Fixed D £27.95-£41.20, Starter £6.45-£9.70, Main £15.50-£22, Dessert £6-£9.50, Service added but optional 5% **Wine:** 42 bottles over £20, 17 bottles under £20, 6 by the glass (£3.95-£5.45) **Notes:** Dress Restrictions, No denims, trainers or T-shirts, Civ Wed 73 **Seats:** 42, Pr/dining room 40 **Smoking:** N/Sm in restaurant **Children:** Menu, Portions **Rooms:** 72 (72 en suite) ★★★★ HL **Directions:** M40 junct 15, then take A46 S towards Stratford/Worcester. Follow the A46 E over three rdbts. Continue for 2m then take a right for Billesley **Parking:** 100

Fox and Goose

British

Delightfully rustic village inn serving locally sourced produce

☎ 01608 682293 Armscote CV37 8DD
e-mail: email@foxandgoose.co.uk
web: www.foxandgoose.co.uk

Originally two cottages and a blacksmith's forge, this privately owned inn has been totally refurbished. There's now a smart dining room, a cosy bar, a private dining room and four idiosyncratic bedrooms. A knowledgeable team of friendly staff create a relaxed and informal atmosphere. The daily-changing blackboard offers a range of classic Britis dishes with some Mediterranean influences, such as duo of smoked tun and salmon with cracked black pepper and lime juice, Herefordshire bee Wellington with red wine jus and white chocolate crème brûlée.

Chef: Nick Rowberry **Owners:** Paul Stevens **Times:** 12-2.30/7-9.30, Closed 25 Dec **Prices:** Starter £4.95-£6.50, Main £9.95-£17.95, Dessert £4.95-£5.95, Coffee £1.60, Min/Water £3.95, Service optional **Wine:** 11 bottles over £20, 20 bottles under £20, 6 by the glass (£3.15-£4.50) **Notes:** Vegetarian available **Seats:** 45, Pr/dining room 20 **Smoking:** N/S area **Children:** Portions **Rooms:** 4 (4 en suite) ◆◆◆◆ **Directions:** From Stratford-upon-Avon take A3400 S for 7m. After Newbolc on-Stour turn right towards Armscote (signed). 1m to village **Parking:** 20

Macdonald Alveston Manor

Modern British NEW

Modern dining in Elizabethan manor

☎ 01789 205478 Clopton Bridge CV37 7HP
e-mail: events.alvestonmanor@macdonald-hotels.co.uk
web: www.macdonald-hotels.co.uk/alvestonmanor

A striking red-brick and half-timbered façade, well-tended grounds an a giant cedar, under which it is said that *A Midsummer Night's Drean* was first performed, all contribute to the charm of this well-establishe hotel. The main house retains much of its Elizabethan charm, with leaded light windows and splendid original panelling. In the traditional, country-house style restaurant you can enjoy reliable modern British dishes, perhaps pork belly with ham and pear terrine, seared calves' liver with black pudding and truffled mash, and vanilla pannacotta with poached pear and cardamom syrup.

Chef: David Grindrod **Owners:** Macdonald Hotels PLC **Times:** 12-2.30/ 9.30, Closed L Mon-Sat **Prices:** Fixed D £32.50, Starter £5.95-£9.95, Main £14.95-£22.50, Dessert £5.50-£7.95, Coffee £2.95, Min/Water £4.85, Servic included **Wine:** 69 bottles over £20, 14 bottles under £20, 15 by the glas (£4.60-£8) **Seats:** 110, Pr/dining room 40 **Smoking:** N/Sm in restaurant **Children:** Menu, Portions **Rooms:** 113 (113 en suite) ★★★★ HL **Directions:** 6m from M40 junct 15, just on edge of town, across Clopton Bridge towards Banbury **Parking:** 120

Macdonald Shakespeare

Modern British

Modern cooking behind a Tudor-timbered façade

☎ 0870 400 8182 Chapel St CV37 6ER
e-mail: general.shakespeare@macdonald-hotels.co.u
web: www.macdonaldhotels.co.uk

This 17th-century building is just what you would expect to see in Shakespeare's home town, with its Tudor timbered façade. Inside it's just as authentic, with lots of original beams and open fires, lit in winter. The smart décor uses rich, deep fabrics giving a traditional fe throughout. The cooking, however, is right up to the minute. You car get a taste of the excellent fresh ingredients in dishes like pork and smoked bacon terrine with apricot and sage dressing to start. Follow that with filo wrapped loin of English lamb, served with a polenta ca and poached garlic jus. Classic desserts might include raspberry Eton mess with spiced raspberry sorbet.

Chef: Chris McPherson **Owners:** Macdonald Hotels PLC **Times:** 12-2/6- 9.30, Closed L Mon-Sat (on request) **Prices:** Fixed L £14.95, Fixed D £26, Starter £5.50-£9.50, Main £15.50-£22.95, Dessert £6, Coffee £2.95, Min/Water £4.70, Service optional **Wine:** 52 bottles over £20, 27 bottles

continued

ınder £20, 12 by the glass (£4.25-£5.25) **Notes:** Civ Wed 100 **Seats:** 80, ʼr/dining room 25 **Smoking:** N/Sm in restaurant **Children:** Portions ₹ooms: 74 (74 en suite) ★★★★ HL **Directions:** Follow signs to town :entre. Round one-way system, into Bridge St. At rdbt turn left. Hotel ːOOyds on left **Parking:** 35

Stratford Manor

Traditional British

ıssured cooking in a contemporary environment

☎ 01789 731173 Warwick Rd CV37 0PY
e-mail: stratfordmanor@marstonhotels.com
web: www.marstonshotels.com

ʼhe Stratford Manor is a modern purpose-built hotel located 3 miles ʼom Stratford-upon-Avon in attractive countryside. It offers a range of ıcilities including conference rooms, a leisure centre with a gym, ›ool, spa, sauna and tennis courts. The stylish dining room is lecorated in calm colours; the atmosphere is relaxed and the service olished. The menus offer interesting, well executed dishes, such as ame terrine with chutney, roast rump of lamb with ratatouille and yonnaise potatoes, and chocolate crème brûlée with cherries. Light neals are served in the Terrace Bar.

imes: 12-2.30/6-9.30, Closed L Sat **Rooms:** 104 (104 en suite) ★★★★

Stratford Victoria

British, European

raditional hotel serving classic cuisine

☎ 01789 271000 Arden St CV37 6QQ
e-mail: stratfordvictoria@marstonhotels.com
web: www.marstonshotels.com

ı old-fashioned red telephone box makes a curious statement in this therwise modern hotel with a Victorian appearance, an easy walk om the town centre and all its attractions. Inside you'll find leather ıesterfields, exposed beams and a relaxing décor. The food remains liably good, with presentation taken seriously, in the Traditions staurant. From the set menu with additional carte prices, the British ıd European range might include prawn, crab and avocado tian, and ɔnfit of duck wrapped in streaky bacon, buttered Savoy and puréed ɔtato. Desserts like iced banana parfait with caramelised banana and ɔached William pear with mango sorbet maintain the same high andards.

hef: Mark Grigg **Owners:** Marston Hotels **Times:** 12.30-2/6-9.45 **rices:** Fixed L £14.50, Fixed D £25.95-£32.75, Starter £5.50-£7.75, Main 4.95-£19.50, Dessert £5.50, Coffee £2.50, Min/Water £3.75, Service cluded **Wine:** 31 bottles over £20, 20 bottles under £20, 19 by the glass 3.65-£6.10) **Notes:** Sun L carvery, 4 courses incl coffee £16.95, getarian available, Civ Wed 160 **Seats:** 90, Pr/dining room 90 **noking:** N/Sm in restaurant, Air con **Children:** Menu, Portions **ooms:** 100 (100 en suite) ★★★★ **Directions:** From town centre, llow A3400 to Birmingham. Turn left at lights towards Arden Street, hotel 0yds on right **Parking:** 102

ambs of Sheep Street

☎ 01789 292554 12 Sheep Streeet CV37 6EF
odern British fare handy for the theatre.

he Opposition

☎ 01789 269980 13 Sheep St CV37 6EF
lated (literally) to Lambs above and similar in style.

WARWICK MAP 10 SP26

Ardencote Manor Hotel

Modern International

Refurbished lakeside restaurant

☎ 01926 843111 Lye Green Rd CV35 8LS
e-mail: hotel@ardencote.com
web: www.ardencote.com

The Lodge restaurant has been refurbished in 21st-century style - it now has a more open-plan layout and a modern bistro look. Diners can choose between the traditional carte and the 'La Plancha' menu which offers simple grilled dishes with a choice of sauces. Interpretations of classical English dishes like shepherd's pie sit alongside more elaborate French classics like tournedos of beef fillet. Whatever the dish, seasonality and fresh produce are clearly important and everything on the menu is made from scratch. Typical dishes might include fillet of Scottish beef with a sliver of dolcelatte, wrapped in pancetta and served with a wild thyme jus.

Chef: Lee Childs **Owners:** TSB Developments Ltd **Times:** 12-3/6-11 **Prices:** Fixed L £10-£15, Starter £5.75-£6.95, Main £15.25-£19.25, Dessert £4.95-£6.25, Coffee £2.50, Min/Water £2.95, Service included **Wine:** 27 bottles over £20, 38 bottles under £20, 7 by the glass (£2.50-£5.25) **Notes:** Sun L 1-3 courses, max £19.95, Vegetarian available, Civ Wed 150 **Seats:** 70, Pr/dining room 28 **Smoking:** N/Sm in restaurant **Children:** Menu, Portions **Rooms:** 75 (75 en suite) ★★★★ **Directions:** 4m from Warwick. Off A4189 (Warwick/Henley-in-Arden road). In Claverdon follow signs for Shrewley and brown tourist signs for Ardencote Manor. Approx 1.5m **Parking:** 250

Robbie's Restaurant

☎ 01926 400470 74 Smith St CV34 4HU
web: www.theaa.com/restaurants/114021.html
More like a dinner party than a formal restaurant, Robbie's is friendly, with chatty staff, an upbeat atmosphere, and a monthly-changing modern British menu.

England

WISHAW MAP 10 SP19

The De Vere Belfry

European

Fine cooking at celebrated golf hotel

☎ 01675 470301 B76 9PR
e-mail: enquiries@thebelfry.com
web: www.thebelfry.com

The busy hotel complex is geared up for top-level golfing, leisure and international conference needs, with three championship golf courses set in 370 acres of grounds. The luxuriously furnished restaurant is intimately located within the original part of the hotel and is well suited to the fine dining theme, offering simple, classical and modern cooking. Menus range from a short fixed-price option, through to a carte, a tasting menu and a good-value Sunday lunch menu. Dinner could include ham hock terrine, partridge with thyme jus, and Valrhona chocolate millefeuille for dessert.

Chef: Ian Boden **Owners:** Quinn Group **Times:** 12.30-2/7.30-10, Closed L Mon-Sat **Prices:** Fixed D £34.95, Starter £9.95-£15.95, Main £22.95-£29.50, Dessert £7.95, Coffee £2.95, Min/Water £3.50 **Wine:** 37 bottles over £20 **Notes:** Sun L £19.95, Dress Restrictions, No jeans or T-shirts, jacket & tie preferred, Civ Wed 70 **Seats:** 70 **Smoking:** N/Sm in restaurant, Air con **Children:** Min 14 yrs **Rooms:** 324 (324 en suite) ★★★★ **Directions:** At junct of A446 & A4091, 1m NW of M42 junct 9 **Parking:** 915

WEST MIDLANDS

BALSALL COMMON MAP 10 SP27

Haigs Hotel

Modern British

Friendly, popular modern restaurant

☎ 01676 533004 Kenilworth Rd CV7 7EL
e-mail: info@haigsemail.co.uk
web: www.haigshotel.co.uk

A smart, black and white half-timbered exterior hides the chic modern interior of this popular hotel and restaurant. Privately-owned and family-run, the hotel prides itself on its levels of comfort and service. The modern British cuisine draws praise from regulars and visitors alike, offering some interesting combinations. Sunday lunch is a big occasion with an extensive menu on offer. The carte changes seasonally and there are always vegetarian options to choose from. A global wine list produces an interesting selection of fine wines and champagnes.

Chef: Paul Kelly **Owners:** Bill & Diane Sumner **Times:** 12.30-2.30/7-9.30, Closed L Mon-Sat, D Sun **Prices:** Fixed L fr £13.95, Fixed D fr £22.50, Starter £5.95-£7, Main £11-£19.95, Dessert £5-£6.50, Coffee £1.75, Min/Water £3, Service optional **Wine:** 36 bottles over £20, 59 bottles under £20, 10 by the glass (£3.25-£5.99) **Notes:** Vegetarian available **Seats:** 60, Pr/dining room 28 **Smoking:** N/Sm in restaurant **Children:** Portions **Rooms:** 23 (23 en suite) ★★★ **Directions:** On A452, 6m SE of NEC/airport, on left before village centre **Parking:** 25

Nailcote Hall

Modern

Delightful cooking in an attractive country house with great facilities

☎ 024 7646 6174 Nailcote Ln, Berkswell CV7 7DE
e-mail: info@nailcotehall.co.uk
web: www.nailcotehall.co.uk

This 17th-century house set in 15 acres of grounds boasts a nine-hole championship golf course and a Roman bath-style swimming pool. The Oak Room restaurant is spacious and comfortable, the tartan-carpeting and dark oak beams perfectly in keeping with the style of the house. Service is attentive and professional with a sommelier on hand to guide guests toward the right wine selection. The food is both ambitious and accomplished with surprising flavour combinations delivered confidently - seared king scallops with leek mash and a duo of Clonakilty puddings, for example, or a main of roasted halibut with braised oxtail ravioli, Puy lentils and truffle dressing. Extras such as an amuse of pea velouté with truffle foam, home-made bread, a pre-dessert and petits fours add a definite wow-factor to the meal.

Chef: Neil Oates **Owners:** Mr R W Cressman **Times:** 12-2/7-9.30, Closed L Sat, D Sun **Prices:** Fixed L fr £19.50, Fixed D fr £31.50, Starter £6-£12.75, Main £19.95-£28, Dessert £6.90-£8.25, Coffee £1.90, Min/Water £3.50, Service optional **Wine:** 80 bottles over £20, 23 bottles under £20, 5 by the glass (£3.90-£6.75) **Notes:** Sun L 2 courses £23.95, 3 sourses £25.95, Vegetarian available, Dress Restrictions, Smart casual, no jeans or trainers, Civ Wed 120 **Seats:** 45, Pr/dining room 140 **Smoking:** N/Sm in restaurant **Children:** Menu, Portions **Rooms:** 40 (40 en suite) ★★★★ HL **Directions:** On B4101 towards Tile Hill/Coventry, 10 mins from NEC/Birmingham Airport **Parking:** 100

BARSTON MAP 10 SP27

The Malt Shovel at Barston

Modern European

Popular local foody pub in a rural setting

☎ 01675 443223 Barston Ln B92 0JP
web: www.themaltshovelatbarston.com

Old country pub surrounded by fields, with stripped wooden floors, chunky tables, open fires, lime green paintwork and heavy fabrics. A separate dining area is slightly more formal. Portions are plentiful and the quality sound, with fish of all kinds featuring strongly. The bar menu is supplemented by blackboard specials from the restaurant. Typically a starter of seared scallops, Parma ham and rocket and parmesan salad, followed by roast cod with braised red cabbage and parsnip fritters, and to finish chocolate truffle cake with pistachio ice cream. Vegetarians have interesting options too.

continue

:hef: Max Murphy **Owners:** Caroline Furby & Chris Benbrook **Times:** 12-.30/6.30-9.30, Closed 25 Dec, Closed D Sun **Prices:** Fixed D £25-£29, tarter £2.95-£6.50, Main £9.95-£17.95, Dessert £5.50, Coffee £1.45, Ain/Water £2.70, Service optional, Group min 6 service 10% **Wine:** 10 ottles over £20, 15 bottles under £20, 7 by the glass (£2.10-£4.40) **Notes:** Vegetarian available **Seats:** 40 **Smoking:** N/Sm in restaurant, Air on **Children:** Min 10 yrs, Portions **Directions:** M42 junct 5, take turn owards Knowle. 1st left on Jacobean Lane, right turn at T-junct (Hampton ane). Sharp left into Barston Lane. Restaurant 0.5m **Parking:** 30

3IRMINGHAM MAP 10 SP08

Bank Restaurant & Bar

Modern European V

:ontemporary canal-side cuisine

☎ 0121 633 4466 4 Brindley Place B1 2JB
:-mail: birmres@bankrestaurants.com
veb: www.bankrestaurants.com

.llied to the smart London restaurants of the same name, this chic anal-side eatery does a brisk trade with shoppers and suits alike. It's n airy venue conjured from glass and steel, with red leather seating, uality tableware, and a long bar for pre-dinner drinks. Modern uropean dishes predominate, plus a few old favourites. Fish-lovers e particularly well served, but the brasserie menu is extensive and aters to most tastes including vegetarians. Expect salt cod fritters, onfit belly pork with buttered Savoy cabbage and carrot purée ollowed by a warm Valrhona cake.

hef: Stephen Woods **Owners:** Bank Restaurant Group Plc **Times:** 12-45/5.30-10.30, Closed 1-2 Jan, 1 May, BHs **Prices:** Fixed L £12.50, Fixed D 15, Starter £4.20-£9.25, Main £10.50-£32, Dessert £4.50-£5.45, Coffee £2, in/Water £2.50, Service added but optional 12.5% **Wine:** 45 bottles over 20, 23 bottles under £20, 15 by the glass (£3.10-£6.85) **Notes:** Vegetarian vailable, Smart casual **Seats:** 150, Pr/dining room 100 **Smoking:** N/Sm ea, No pipes, Air con **Children:** Menu, Portions **Directions:** Located off oad St (A456) **Parking:** 100 yds away (Sheepcoat St)

Birmingham Marriott

1odern British V

'egant brasserie in traditional hotel

☎ 0121 452 1144 12 Hagley Rd, Five Ways B16 8SJ
-mail: pascal.demarchi@marriotthotels.co.uk
'eb: www.marriott.co.uk/bhxbh

ıis large Edwardian hotel is located on the outskirts of the city centre. ere's a real feel of fin-de-siècle elegance throughout. Comfortable, ell-presented public areas include an informal restaurant, West 12, pular with the city's businessmen and leisure guests alike. Service is pically up-front and helpful for the UK's second city. The brasserie-le menu comprises traditional dishes with some modern influences. art with the crab and leek tart with poached egg before trying either e 35-day aged Scotch rib-eye or calves' liver served with bubble-and-ueak and Madeira sauce. Finish with banana and rosemary tarte Tatin.

ıef: Toby Bult **Owners:** Marriot International Ltd **Times:** 12-2.30/6-10, osed L Sat **Prices:** Starter £6-£8, Main £12-£24, Dessert £5-£7, Coffee £3, n/Water £4, Service optional **Wine:** 20 bottles over £20, 12 bottles der £20, 10 by the glass (£4.90-£9) **Notes:** Sun L £15.50, Vegetarian ailable, Smart casual, Civ Wed 80 **Seats:** 60, Pr/dining room 60 **noking:** N/Sm in restaurant **Children:** Menu, Portions **Rooms:** 104)4 en suite) ★★★★ HL **Directions:** City end of A456, at the Five ays rdbt **Parking:** 60

Chung Ying Garden

Traditional Chinese

Cantonese restaurant with amazing choice of dishes

☎ 0121 666 6622 & 622 1668 17 Thorp St B5 4AT
e-mail: chungyinggarden@aol.com
web: www.chungying.co.uk

Former war-time barracks are pressed into service these days as a large restaurant for over 380 people on two levels. Seating is divided into separate areas according to need and there are function rooms, a dance floor, DJ facilities and in-house karaoke and disco, an authentic taste of Hong Kong in Birmingham. Cuisine is traditional Cantonese with a vast menu (said to be the largest in England) with around 400 dishes including sweet and sours, sizzlers and live seafood. If you're overwhelmed by choice, try the crispy aromatic duck with pancakes or sizzling fillet of beef in black pepper sauce, with red bean pancakes for dessert.

Chef: Mr Siu Chung Wong **Owners:** Mr S C Wong **Times:** noon/midnight, Closed 25 Dec **Prices:** Fixed L £14-£32, Starter £2.20-£36, Main £5-£36, Dessert £1.50-£5, Coffee £1.40, Min/Water £3.50, Service optional **Wine:** 2 by the glass (£2.80) **Notes:** Vegetarian available, Smart casual preferred **Seats:** 380, Pr/dining room 200 **Smoking:** Air con **Directions:** City centre, just off Hurst St, near Hippodrome Theatre & shopping centre, just off A38 **Parking:** 50

Goldsmiths

Modern British

Upmarket cooking at a city-centre hotel

☎ 0121 200 2727 Copthorne Hotel Birmingham, Paradise Circus B3 3HJ
e-mail: reservations.birmingham@mill-cop.com
web: www.millenniumhotels.com

Conveniently located in the heart of the city centre, this modern hotel

continued

England

BIRMINGHAM *continued* MAP 10 SP08

offers a choice of two eating venues. Goldie's brasserie is an informal haunt with a nice line in light meals and snacks, while Goldsmiths restaurant delivers an upmarket menu of classier fare. Expect accomplished cooking distinguished by both quality ingredients and more than a dash of imagination; your choice of mains might include a warm mushroom cappuccino, followed perhaps by baked fillet of sea bass with calamari and tomato jam, or tournedos of Scotch beef with galette potato and truffle jus.

Chef: John Stephens **Owners:** Millennium Hotels and Resorts **Times:** 12-2.30/6-10.30, Closed 25 Dec, Closed L Sat **Prices:** Fixed L £14-£20, Fixed D £18-£30, Starter £6.50-£8.50, Main £10.95-£20, Dessert £6.50-£8.50, Coffee £2.50, Min/Water £3.95 **Wine:** 27 bottles over £20, 33 bottles under £20, 15 by the glass (£3.50-£8.95) **Notes:** Vegetarian available, Civ Wed 200 **Seats:** 85, Pr/dining room 30 **Smoking:** N/Sm in restaurant, Air con **Children:** Menu, Portions **Rooms:** 212 (212 en suite) ★★★★ **Directions:** In city centre, telephone for further directions **Parking:** 80

Hotel Du Vin

British, French V

Stylish conversion of an old hospital with classic bistro food

☎ 0121 200 0600 25 Church St B3 2NR
e-mail: info@birmingham.hotelduvin.com
web: www.hotelduvin.com

Originally an eye hospital, the hotel building dates from the early Victorian era and is located in the city's Jewellery Quarter. Fine original features have been retained including a sweeping staircase and granite pillars. The Bistro upholds the Hotel Du Vin philosophy of quality food cooked simply with fresh ingredients, and classic bistro dishes include smoked salmon with a traditional garnish, chargrilled rib-eye steak with béarnaise sauce and pommes frites, and for pudding crème brûlée. There is an emphasis on wine, naturally, and wine-related events are held throughout the year.

Chef: Nick Turner **Owners:** MWB **Times:** 12-2/6-10 **Prices:** Fixed L £30.50, Fixed D £34.50, Starter £7.75-£8.50, Main £14.50-£15.75, Coffee £2.50, Min/Water £3, Service optional **Wine:** 600 bottles over £20, 200 bottles under £20, 20 by the glass (£3.50-£11.50) **Notes:** Sun L £22.50, Vegetarian available, Civ Wed 80 **Seats:** 85, Pr/dining room 120 **Smoking:** N/Sm in restaurant **Children:** Menu, Portions **Rooms:** 66 (66 en suite) ★★★★ TH **Directions:** Telephone for directions **Parking:** 20

Jessica's

Modern British

Discreet suburban dining meets bold, accomplished cooking

☎ 0121 455 0999 1 Montague Rd, Edgbaston B16 9HN
web: www.jessicasrestaurant.co.uk

Jessica's discreet, pretty courtyard entrance just off the busy Hagley Road in a leafy, residential suburb offers an unexpected private feel. Inside the airy, conservatory-style restaurant has a modern, minimalist edge, decked out with pale-wood floors, white walls hung with modern art and rich purple chairs that contrast with white-clothed tables and views over the garden. The kitchen takes food seriously, its modern approach - underpinned by a classical theme - comes cloaked in high-level technical skill and innovative combinations that use tip-top ingredients. As in cod teamed with pig's trotter ravioli, pineapple, asparagus and lentils, while a lavender crème caramel might have a support cast of apricots and pistachios. Freshly baked bread and petits fours keep standards high through to the end.

continued

Chef: Glynn Purnell **Owners:** Mr K & Mrs D Stevenson, Glynn Purnell **Times:** 12.30-2.30/7.00-10.30, Closed 1 wk Xmas, 1 wk Etr, last 2 wks Jul, Sun, Closed L Sat & Mon **Prices:** Fixed L £15, Service added but optional 12.5%, Group min 6 service 12.5% **Wine:** 75 bottles over £20, 26 bottles under £20, 9 by the glass (£4.75-£5.75) **Notes:** Tasting menu 5 courses £36.50, 7 courses £42.50, Vegetarian available **Seats:** 36 **Smoking:** N/Sm in restaurant, Air con **Children:** No Children **Parking:** On street

Malmaison Birmingham

British, French

Buzzing brasserie in the heart of Birmingham's Mailbox

☎ 0121 246 5000 1 Wharfside St, The Mailbox B1 1RD
e-mail: birmingham@malmaison.com
web: www.malmaison.com

Malmaison Birmingham is part of the Mailbox complex, a 1960s former Royal Mail sorting office, along with a host of designer stores. The hotel's public rooms include a stylish bar and brasserie, where great, fresh ingredients are simply prepared and offered at affordable prices. House specialities are eggs Benedict, the Mal burger (made from ground beef served on an onion bap, with bacon, gruyère cheese, home-made relish and fries), and crème brûlée. Classic Sunday brunch includes prawn cocktail, pancakes, corned beef hash and Sunday roast, with Buck's fizz and Bloody Mary.

Chef: Nigel Grantham **Owners:** Malmaison Ltd **Times:** 12-2.30/6-10.30 **Prices:** Fixed L £12.50, Fixed D fr £14.50, Starter £4.50-£7.25, Main £10.95-£23.95, Dessert fr £4.95, Coffee £2, Min/Water £2.95, Service added but optional 10% **Wine:** 127 bottles over £20, 10 bottles under £20, 10 by the glass (£4.95-£7.25) **Notes:** Fixed L incl wine, Vegetarian available **Seats:** 155, Pr/dining room 40 **Smoking:** N/Sm in restaurant, Air con **Children:** Portions **Rooms:** 189 (189 en suite) ★★★ **Directions:** M6 junct 6, follow the A38 towards Birmingham, hotel is located within The Mailbox **Parking:** Mailbox carpark

Opus Restaurant

Modern British NEW

Chic eatery with crustacea counter

☎ 0121 200 2323 54 Cornwall St B3 2DE
e-mail: restaurant@opusrestaurant.co.uk
web: www.opusrestaurant.co.uk

This spacious, contemporary restaurant is close to the City Chambers in Birmingham city centre. Wood flooring, wine racks and a crustacea counter at the centre set the scene for fresh modern dining with shellfish a speciality. Try a starter of warm lobster and crab cake with red pepper mayonnaise, perhaps followed by a main course of Jimmy Butler's free-range pork collar with polenta bubble-and-squeak and parsley sauce. Desserts feature modern interpretations of traditional favourites, like baked egg custard with warm cinnamon doughnuts and apricot sorbet.

Chef: Dean Cole **Times:** 12-3/6-10.30, Closed Sun, Closed L Sat **Prices:** Food prices not confirmed for 2007. Please telephone for details **Directions:** Telephone for directions

England

Simpsons

BIRMINGHAM MAP 10 SP08

Modern French V NOTABLE WINE LIST

serious restaurant with excellent food

0121 454 3434 20 Highfield Rd B15 3DU

-mail: info@simpsonsrestaurant.co.uk

veb: www.simpsonsrestaurant.co.uk

et in a Grade II listed Georgian building in Edgbaston, Simpsons is videly regarded as one of the best restaurants in the Birmingham rea. It's the epitome of good taste - chic and subtle hues of cream nd beige, artful floral arrangements in the bar and salon, and ontemporary artwork adorning the walls. There are four individually iemed dining rooms - French, Venetian, Oriental and Colonial - dding a hint of the theatrical to the surroundings - with sense of ccasion heightened by discreetly attentive service from professional aff who demonstrate their skill admirably when advising on this erious wine list.

he modern French menu focuses on quality ingredients from the est UK sources (Salcombe crab, Aberdeenshire beef, Loch Fyne noked salmon) presented in dishes cooked with a high degree of ilinary expertise by a talented chef. A typical meal might start with eared foie gras with black pudding, pomme purée and Madeira auce, then continue with roast calves' sweetbreads, daube ravioli, carrot and orange purée and a dessert - usually nothing less than exquisite - of coffee pannacotta with tiramisù ice cream and chocolate sugar.

Notable Wine List: A well presented and extensive wine list with strong Bordeaux and Burgundy sections and an interesting monthly selection.

Chef: Andreas Antona, Luke Tipping **Owners:** Andreas & Alison Antona **Times:** 12.30-2/7-10, Closed 24-26, 31 Dec, 1-2 Jan, BHs, Closed D Sun **Prices:** Fixed L £22.50, Fixed D £30, Starter £11-£16.50, Main £21-£32.50, Dessert £7.95, Coffee £3.75, Min/Water £3.50, Service added but optional 12.5% **Wine:** 500 bottles over £20, 10 by the glass (£5-£21) **Notes:** Sun L 3 courses £27.50, Tasting menu 6 courses £65, Vegetarian menu, Dress Restrictions, Smart casual **Seats:** 70, Pr/dining room 18 **Smoking:** N/Sm in restaurant, Air con **Children:** Menu, Portions **Directions:** 2m from city centre, opposite St Georges Church, Edgbaston **Parking:** 15

Thai Edge Restaurant

hai

uthentic Thai cooking in a contemporary setting

0121 643 3993 Brindley Place B1 2HS

-mail: manager777@btconnect.com

veb: www.thaiedge.co.uk

ntemporary, minimalist design meets subtle lighting, cool marble ed floors, well-spaced white-linen dressed tables and smart, thentically-attired staff in this spacious, open-plan, oriental-inspired staurant. Authentic Thai cooking from all four regions of the country each with its own distinctive flavour combinations - is the style, with shes ideal for sharing. As there is no running order to the Thai meal, the dishes are served together. The typically lengthy repertoire mes with clear translations - backed by helpful, well-informed staff - d there's a series of set options for novices, pairs or groups, plus od choices for vegetarians.

continued

Thai Edge Restaurant

Chef: Mit Jeensanthia **Owners:** Harish Nathwani **Times:** 12-2.30/5.30-11, Closed 25-26 Dec, 1 Jan **Prices:** Fixed L £9.90, Starter £5-£8.50, Main £6-£28, Dessert £4.50, Min/Water £3, Service added but optional 10% **Notes:** Sun buffet available, Vegetarian available **Seats:** 100 **Smoking:** N/Sm area, Air con **Directions:** Brindley Place is just off Broad St (approx 0.5m from B'ham New Street station) **Parking:** Brindley Place

BIRMINGHAM *continued* MAP 10 SP08

La Toque d'Or

French

Top-notch French cuisine in the Jewellery Quarter

☎ 0121 233 3655 27 Warstone Ln, Hockley B18 6JQ
e-mail: didier@latoquedor.co.uk
web: www.latoquedor.co.uk

Francophiles should make a beeline for Birmingham's jewellery quarter to search out this gem of a restaurant. Tucked away along a narrow alley, it's a chic creation; rough quarry floors and exposed brick walls teamed with stained glass, heavy red velour furnishings and crisply clothed tables. And the food's good too - a modern French menu designed to please suits, shoppers and serious foodies alike, conjured from a combination of imported and fresh local produce. To start, a chicken and tarragon terrine perhaps, followed by venison with lentils, bacon and star anise jus, or red mullet with creamed leeks and a smoked salmon butter sauce. Excellent service.

Chef: Didier Philipot **Owners:** SSPG Consulting Ltd **Times:** 12.30-1.30/7-9.30, Closed 1 wk Xmas, 1 wk Etr, 2 wks Aug, Sun-Mon, Closed L Sat **Prices:** Fixed L £16.50, Fixed D £24.50, Coffee £2.75, Min/Water £3.20, Service included **Wine:** 35 bottles over £20, 12 bottles under £20, 5 by the glass (£3.20-£4.80) **Notes:** Vegetarian available **Seats:** 36 **Smoking:** No pipes, No cigars, Air con **Children:** Portions **Directions:** 1m N of city centre, 400mtrs from clock tower (in Jewellery Quarter). Across from police station **Parking:** NCP - Vyse Street

The Bucklemaker

☎ 0121 200 2515 30 Mary Ann St,
St Paul's Square B3 1RL
web: www.theaa.com/restaurants/114025.html
Tucked into a former Georgian silversmiths workshop, this delightful restaurant is traditional, contemporary and welcoming all at once. The atmosphere is businessy at lunch, romantic in the evenings, with modern European menus and a friendly, buzzy bar area.

Henry's Cantonese Restaurant

☎ 0121 200 1136 27 St Paul's Square B3 1RB
web: www.theaa.com/restaurants/114022.html
A topflight, slightly formal Cantonese restaurant. Bright and spacious with a relaxed atmosphere, Henrys is popular with a professional crowd. You'll find all your favourites, plenty of veggie dishes and five set menus.

Imran's Balti

☎ 0121 449 1370 264-266 Ladypool Rd,
Sparkbrook B12 8JU
Longstanding balti famous for its family-sized naan.

Maharaja

☎ 0121 622 2641 23-25 Hurst St B5 4AS
Indian serving superior versions of familiar dishes.

Metro Bar and Grill

☎ 0121 200 1911 73 Cornwall St B3 2DF
web: www.theaa.com/restaurants/114023.html
A sumptuous, modern meeting and eating place that attracts a loyal crowd of regulars. The bright, slightly rustic modern European menu seems to please just about everyone, and there are daily blackboard specials.

San Carlo

☎ 0121 633 0251 4 Temple St B2 5BN
Traditional Italian with pizzas, pasta and good fish.

Thai Edge

☎ 0121 643 3993 7 Oozells Square,
Brindley Place B1 2HL
web: www.theaa.com/restaurants/114024.html
A smart, modern restaurant, with white décor and masses of flowers which are flown in from Thailand. Dishes are beautifully served and you'll find all your Thai favourites on the menu.

COVENTRY MAP 10 SP37

Brooklands Grange Hotel

Traditional

Quality cooking in traditional hotel

☎ 024 7660 1601 Holyhead Rd CV5 8HX
e-mail: info@brooklands-grange.co.uk
web: www.brooklands-grange.co.uk

Behind its Jacobean façade - formerly a 16th-century farmhouse - Brooklands Grange is a well-run, modern and comfortable hotel. Its traditionally styled, elegant restaurant - with attached conservatory - offers formal dining but in a relaxed and friendly style, and, while the kitchen's approach maybe thoroughly modern, it doesn't forget conventional tastes. Expect assured cooking and skilful presentation ir well-flavoured dishes, perhaps pan-roasted monkfish stuffed with feta and basil crumble and wrapped in prosciutto, served with lemon, her and wilted rocket couscous. Finish with a warm English gooseberry cobbler with gooseberry and elderflower ice cream.

Chef: Jonathan Beard **Owners:** Brooklands Grange Ltd **Times:** 12-2/7-9.30, Closed BHs, Closed L Sat **Prices:** Fixed L £16.95-£25.95, Fixed D £16.95-£25.95, Starter £3.95-£7.25, Main £9.95-£18.95, Dessert fr £4.95, Coffee £1.65, Min/Water £3.95 **Wine:** 11 bottles over £20, 30 bottles und £20, 6 by the glass (£3.25-£4.85) **Notes:** Fixed L 3 courses, Vegetarian available, Dress Restrictions, Smart casual, no T-shirts **Seats:** 70, Pr/dining room 16 **Smoking:** N/Sm in restaurant **Children:** Portions **Rooms:** 31 (31 en suite) ★★★ HL **Directions:** From M42 junct 6 take A45 towards Coventry. Then A4114 (Pickford Way) and 3rd exit at rdbt (continue on A4114). Hotel on left **Parking:** 52

DORRIDGE MAP 10 SP17

Forest Hotel

Modern Mediterranean

Reliable cooking in a modern, boutique hotel

☎ 01564 772120 25 Station Approach B93 8JA
e-mail: info@forest-hotel.com
web: www.forest-hotel.com

Just over the road from the railway station in this south-eastern

continu

;uburb of Birmingham, the red-brick, boutique-style Forest Hotel :uts a sophisticated modern edge with its stylish designer décor and ight and airy downstairs restaurant and bar. The crowd-pleasing, ɔroadly European style of cooking suits the contemporary ;urroundings, delivered via an extensive range of dish and menu ɔptions that include a Menu Rapide lunch, prix-fixe dinner and carte. Quality seasonal ingredients, precision and intelligent simplicity :ombined with good presentation in well-conceived dishes, like grilled halibut with parmesan risotto and white wine cream. Competitive pricing and informal, professional service hit just the 'ight note, too.

Chef: Dean Grubb **Owners:** Gary & Tracy Perkins **Times:** 12-2.30/6.30-0, Closed 25 Dec, Closed D Sun **Prices:** Fixed L fr £12, Fixed D fr £15, Starter £3.95-£7.95, Main £8.50-£18.95, Dessert £4.50-£6.50, Coffee £1.40, Min/Water £2.95, Service added but optional 10%, Group min 8 service 10% **Wine:** 15 bottles over £20, 25 bottles under £20, 9 by the glass (£3.50-£4.50) **Notes:** Fixed L&D Mon-Fri, Sun L 2 courses £14.50, 3 courses £17.50, Vegetarian available, Civ Wed 100 **Seats:** 70, Pr/dining room 150 **Smoking:** N/Sm in restaurant, Air con **Children:** Menu, Portions **Rooms:** 12 (12 en suite) ★★★★ RR **Directions:** From M42 junct 5, go through Knowle village, right to Dorridge village, turn left before bridge **Parking:** 40

HOCKLEY HEATH MAP 10 SP17

Nuthurst Grange Country House Hotel

British French

Fine dining with all the trimmings in country-house style

☎ 01564 783972 Nuthurst Grange Ln B94 5NL
e-mail: info@nuthurst-grange.com
web: www.nuthurst-grange.com

An imposing country house with a tree-lined drive and lovely views over extensive landscaped gardens and woodland. In the sunny dining room guests are comfortably seated at large round tables set with crystal glassware and orchids. Menus follow the old traditions with lots of intermediary courses, and canapés, breads and petits fours are all home made. Cheese and digestif trolleys are indicative of the gastronomic air. A range of highly imaginative classic and modern, French and British cuisine is offered from a choice of fixed-price menus, with a separate vegetarian selection. Accurately cooked duck comes with green beans and sweet potato purée, followed by a good hazelnut and pistachio soufflé.

Times: 12-2/7-9.30, Closed 25-26 Dec, Closed L Sat **Rooms:** 15 (15 en suite) ★★★ **Directions:** Off A3400, 0.5 mile S of Hockley Heath, turn at sign into Nuthurst Grange Lane

---

MERIDEN MAP 10 SP28

Manor Hotel

British, French

Satisfying food cooked with skill in Georgian manor

☎ 01676 522735 Main Rd CV7 7NH
e-mail: reservations@manorhotelmeriden.co.uk
web: www.manorhotelmeriden.co.uk

This sympathetically extended Georgian manor house is located in the heart of this sleepy village within easy reach of the National Exhibition Centre and close to the medieval cross that supposedly marks the centre of England. There are two dining options - the informal Triumph Buttery for light lunches and snacks and the more formal Regency Restaurant for fine dining. The latter specialises in traditionally inspired dishes with a light, modern touch - fillet of salmon with red onion jam and dill butter sauce or roast duck breast with apple fondant and caramelised endive, for example.

continued

Chef: Peter Griffiths **Owners:** Mr R Richards **Times:** 12-2/7-9.45, Closed 27-30 Dec, Closed L Sat **Prices:** Fixed L £23-£25, Fixed D £25-£27, Starter £6.50-£10.50, Main £12.95-£22.95, Dessert £4.95-£5.25, Coffee £2.95, Service included **Wine:** 20 bottles over £20, 28 bottles under £20, 6 by the glass (£3-£3.95) **Notes:** Vegetarian available, Civ Wed 120 **Seats:** 150, Pr/dining room 220 **Smoking:** N/Sm in restaurant, Air con **Children:** Menu, Portions **Rooms:** 110 (110 en suite) ★★★ **Directions:** M42 junct 6 take A45 towards Coventry then A452, signed Leamington. At rdbt join B4102, signed Meriden, hotel 0.5m on left **Parking:** 180

SOLIHULL MAP 10 SP17

The Town House Restaurant & Bar

Modern European

Cosmopolitan city-centre bar and brasserie

☎ 0121 704 1567 727 Warwick Rd B91 3DA
e-mail: hospitalityengineers@btinternet.com
web: www.thetown-house.com

A cosmopolitan brasserie-style dining venue housed in an elegant, refurbished building, opposite the main shopping centre. Expect a contemporary, open-plan interior, beautifully designed and furnished with an abundance of leather, steel, stylish objets d'art, fresh flowers, and gleaming glasses on polished wooden tables. A relaxed and informal atmosphere prevails for light meals, serious dining, or just a glass of wine. Modern, classic bistro-style cooking takes in open sandwiches, set and Sunday lunch menus, a taster menu, and a carte offering risotto with scallops, roast cod with clam chowder, and lamb Wellington followed by caramelised pear, Baileys crème brûlée and honeycomb ice cream.

Chef: Rob Wear **Owners:** John & Jayne O Malley/John & Heidi Billane **Times:** 12-3/6-10, Closed 1 Jan **Prices:** Fixed L £13-£14, Fixed D £15.50-£17, Starter £5-£7, Main £12.50-£17, Dessert £5-£6.50, Coffee £2, Min/Water £3, Service added but optional 8% **Wine:** 16 bottles over £20, 18 bottles under £20, 13 by the glass (£3.75-£7.50) **Notes:** Tasting menu £34.95, Sun L/D 2-3 courses £16-£20, Vegetarian available **Seats:** 95, Pr/dining room 60 **Smoking:** N/Sm in restaurant **Children:** Menu, Portions **Directions:** Centre of Solihull **Parking:** 45

England

WALSALL MAP 10 SP09

The Fairlawns at Aldridge

Modern British, European

Elegant hotel with robust modern cooking

☎ 01922 455122 178 Little Aston Rd, Aldridge WS9 0NU
e-mail: welcome@fairlawns.co.uk
web: www.fairlawns.co.uk

Part of an extended Victorian house attractively set in 9 acres of landscaped gardens, Fairlawns is a popular rural hotel, particularly with locals. Contemporary elegance sums up the restaurant, replete with cream décor, rich woods, crisp white linen and well-spaced tables, while service proves relaxed and friendly with traditional values. The accomplished kitchen produces imaginative interpretations of predominantly British dishes, using fresh, quality, seasonal ingredients - many from local producers. Take English lamb three ways (braised shoulder, home-made sausage and cutlet) served with cauliflower fritters, for instance, or perhaps seared calves' liver with dry-cured bacon and bubble and squeak, and rhubarb pannacotta to close.

Chef: Mark Bradley **Owners:** John Pette **Times:** 12-2/7-10, Closed 1 Jan, Gd Fri, Estr Mon, May Day, Whit Mon, Closed L Sat, D 25 & 26 Dec **Prices:** Fixed L £16.50-£25, Fixed D £22.50-£32.50, Min/Water £1.95, Service optional **Wine:** 40 bottles over £20, 40 bottles under £20, 4 by the glass (£3.75-£4.50) **Notes:** Coffee incl, Sun L 3 courses £18.50, Vegetarian available, Dress Restrictions, No jeans, trainers, sports clothing, Civ Wed 100 **Seats:** 80, Pr/dining room 100 **Smoking:** N/Sm in restaurant, Air con **Children:** Menu, Portions **Rooms:** 50 (50 en suite) ★★★ **Directions:** Outskirts of Aldridge, 400 yds from junction of A452 (Chester Rd) & A454 (Little Aston Road) **Parking:** 120

WIGHT, ISLE OF

FRESHWATER MAP 05 SZ38

Farringford

Modern British

Country-house hotel overlooking Tennyson Downs

☎ 01983 752500 Bedbury Ln PO40 9TQ
e-mail: enquiries@farringford.co.uk
web: www.farringford.co.uk

Set in 33 acres of mature parkland, this former home of Alfred, Lord Tennyson remains a relaxed and sophisticated country-house retreat, with its cosy log fires in winter and marvellous views all year round. The restaurant brings a modern touch to the period property, with its large picture windows and attentive, friendly young staff. Generous portions of the modern British cooking are served from the carte menu, with separate fish and meat sections to appeal to all tastes. Roast monkfish with new potatoes, Parma ham, baby bok choy and chive beurre blanc is a typical seafood offering, with perhaps passionfruit and orange tart, clotted cream and guava sorbet to follow.

Chef: Ross Hastings **Owners:** Lisa Hollyhead **Times:** 12-2/6.30-9 **Prices:** Fixed D £27-£31, Starter £4.50-£7.95, Main £14-£19, Dessert £3.95-£7.95, Coffee £2, Min/Water £3.25, Service optional **Wine:** 28 bottles over £20, 12 bottles under £20, 4 by the glass (£3-£5) **Notes:** Sun L available, Vegetarian available, Dress Restrictions, No sports clothes or denim, Civ Wed 150 **Seats:** 100, Pr/dining room 20 **Smoking:** N/Sm in restaurant **Children:** Menu, Portions **Rooms:** 18 (18 en suite) ★★★ **Directions:** Follow signs for Yarmouth, over bridge for 1m, take left at Pixie Hill. Continue for 2m. At rdbt take left into Afton Rd. Turn left at the bay. Turn into Bedbury Ln. Farringford is 0.5m from bay **Parking:** 50

SEAVIEW MAP 05 SZ69

Priory Bay Hotel

Modern V

Lovely country-house hotel with fine views

☎ 01983 613146 Priory Dr PO34 5BU
e-mail: enquiries@priorybay.co.uk
web: www.priorybay.co.uk

Set amid 70 acres of lovely grounds which include a private beach, a 9-hole golf course and mature woodlands, this tranquil country house once a priory in the 14th century which housed a community of monks, enjoys views of the Solent and Spithead. Relaxed and candlelit the elegant dining room makes for a romantic dinner setting and offers fantastic views of the gardens and the sea. Sumptuous food demonstrates undoubted technical skill combined with a flair for

continued

flavour combinations. Dishes tend to allow good quality ingredients to speak for themselves - try White Island tomato soup with asparagus ravioli to start, then move on to Highland beef fillet with wild mushrooms, creamed celeriac mash and Madeira jus.

Chef: Chris Turner **Owners:** Mr R Palmer & Mr J Palmer **Times:** 12.30-2.15/7-9.30 **Prices:** Fixed L £15.50, Fixed D £29.50, Coffee £2.30, Min/Water £3.50, Service optional **Wine:** 21 bottles over £20, 14 bottles under £20, 5 by the glass **Notes:** Vegetarian available, Dress Restrictions, Smart/smart casual recommended, Civ Wed 100 **Seats:** 70, Pr/dining room 50 **Smoking:** N/Sm in restaurant **Children:** Menu, Portions **Rooms:** 31 (31 en suite) ★★★ HL **Directions:** On B3330 to Nettlestone, 0.5 miles from St Helens **Parking:** 50

Seaview Hotel & Restaurant

British **NEW**

Bright and lively hotel with a choice of restaurants

☎ 01983 612711 High St PO34 5EX
e-mail: reception@seaviewhotel.co.uk
web: www.seaviewhotel.co.uk

A charming hotel with a timeless quality tucked away from the seafront but offering glimpses of the Solent from selected vantage points. There are two dining options - the cosy Front Restaurant that is traditional and quaint, or the smart Sunshine Restaurant and Regatta Room, a brasserie styled in a nautical blue and white. The seasonally inspired menus, including a five-course gastronomic menu, list the modern choices: fillet of local bass, fennel tagliatelle with crab and watercress sauce through to a dessert of mulled poached pear with Stilton crème brûlée are among the carefully-cooked choices. The smartly dressed staff provide excellent service.

Chef: Michael Green **Owners:** Techaid Facilities Ltd **Times:** 12-2.30/7.30-9.45, Closed 3 days at Xmas **Prices:** Starter £5.95, Main £15.50, Dessert £5.95, Coffee £2.95, Min/Water £2.95, Service optional **Wine:** 49 bottles over £20, 20 bottles under £20, 2 by the glass (£2.95) **Notes:** Sun L £16.95, Vegetarian available **Seats:** 80, Pr/dining room 100 **Smoking:** N/Sm in restaurant, Air con **Children:** Menu, Portions **Rooms:** 17 (17 en suite) ★★★ HL **Directions:** Take B3330 from Ryde to Seaview, left into Puckpool Hill & follow signs for Hotel **Parking:** 12

VENTNOR MAP 05 SZ57

Hambrough Hotel

British, European **NEW**

Skilful cooking in stylishly renovated seaside hotel

☎ 01983 856333 Hambrough Rd PO38 1SQ
e-mail: info@thehambrough.com
web: www.thehambrough.com

Extensive refurbishment has transformed this former Victorian villa, set on a hillside overlooking Ventnor with views out to sea, into a stylish hotel and restaurant. The interior is modern and stylish, decorated in minimalist style in creams, fawns and browns, with well-equipped and comfortable bedrooms. Both the bar and restaurant enjoy sea views, the latter being the venue for some skilful and imaginative cooking. The short fixed-price menu makes good use of quality ingredients and the kitchen's passion for food is revealed in a starter of tender, almond-glazed sweetbreads with a creamy smoked garlic velouté, followed by roast lamb loin served with artichoke purée, merguez sausage and an accurate lamb jus.

Chef: Simon McKenzie **Times:** 12-2.30/7-9.30 **Prices:** Food prices not confirmed for 2007. Please telephone for details **Rooms:** 7 (7 en suite) ★★ HL **Directions:** Telephone for directions

The Pond Café

European

Accomplished restaurant in a scenic village setting

☎ 01983 855666 Bonchurch Village Rd, Bonchurch PO38 1RG
e-mail: info@thepondcafe.com
web: www.thepondcafe.com

The pond in the title is just across the road from this Victorian property, and on fine days it can be admired from the patio tables. Inside, the pastel decorations and wooden flooring are pleasantly understated, and the young French manager leads her friendly team with confidence. There's an exciting element to the uncomplicated modern European cooking, thanks to the skills of the kitchen. The imaginative preparation and presentation of dishes like glazed goat's cheese, salad of French beans, hazelnuts, sun-blushed tomatoes and balsamic syrup, or roast fillet of beef, braised cheek and wild mushroom jus, are what bring people back.

Chef: Simon McKenzie **Owners:** Frederic Sol **Times:** 12-2.30/7-9.30, Closed 2 wks in Nov, Mon (Nov-Mar), Closed L Tue (Nov-Mar), D Sun (Nov-Mar) **Prices:** Starter £4.50-£7.95, Main £9.95-£17.95, Dessert £4.50-£6.50, Coffee £2.20, Min/Water £3.60, Service optional **Wine:** 20 bottles over £20, 6 by the glass (£5-£7) **Notes:** Vegetarian available **Seats:** 26, Pr/dining room 20 **Smoking:** N/Sm in restaurant **Children:** Menu, Portions **Directions:** Telephone for directions **Parking:** On street

The Royal Hotel

British, French

Sophisticated cuisine in smart surroundings

☎ 01983 852186 Belgrave Rd PO38 1JJ
e-mail: enquiries@royalhoteliow.co.uk
web: www.royalhoteliow.co.uk

The Victorian-style décor of the restaurant is in keeping with the rest of the hotel, making the most of imposing high ceilings with crystal chandeliers and large oil paintings. It is quite formal, with a sophisticated atmosphere and smartly attired staff. Modern English and French influenced cuisine makes the best use of fine local produce like asparagus from the Arreton Valley, local Ventnor lobster and Godshill free-range chicken. You could try a starter of pan-fried escalope of wild salmon, served with buttered crab iceberg and aïoli dressing. Main courses include flavoursome options like wild mushroom linguini served with broccoli, confit tomatoes and stilton and truffle cream.

Chef: Alan Staley **Owners:** William Bailey **Times:** 12-1.45/6.45-9, Closed 2 wks Jan, Closed L Mon-Sat in Apr-Oct **Prices:** Fixed L £19.50, Fixed D £32.50-£47.50, Min/Water £3, Service optional **Wine:** 29 bottles over £20, 26 bottles under £20, 6 by the glass (£3.50-£6.70) **Notes:** Coffee incl, fixed L Sun only, Vegetarian available, Dress Restrictions, Smart casual, no shorts, Civ Wed 150 **Seats:** 100, Pr/dining room 40 **Smoking:** N/Sm in restaurant **Children:** Min 5 yrs, Portions **Rooms:** 55 (55 en suite) ★★★★ HL **Directions:** On A3055 coastal road, into Ventnor. Follow the one way system, turn left at lights into Church St. At top of hill bear left into Belgrave Rd, hotel on right **Parking:** 50

England

George Hotel

YARMOUTH MAP 05 SZ38

European

Romantic and dramatic dining by the Solent

☎ 01983 760331 Quay St PO41 0PE
e-mail: res@thegeorge.co.uk
web: www.thegeorge.co.uk

One-time home to the island's governor, the George is set by the water's edge close to the ferry terminal in the heart of the bustling yachting village and harbour, with lovely sea views. Built in the 17th century, it's a haven of rich character and pleasing period charm, enhanced by bold design and colours. There's a cosy bar, inviting lounge with log fire, or sunny, informal brasserie awash with the colours and view of the ocean for openers. But, it's the intimate, romantic, dinner-only George Restaurant, with its candlelight, polished wood and deep red panelling that delivers the dramatic fine-dining course. Chef Kevin Mangeolles has been at the kitchen's helm for more than a decade, keeping the restaurant at the forefront of the island's fine-dining scene. His modern approach is influenced by France, the intelligently compact, appealing, fixed-price menus showcasing top-notch ingredients and luxury, with the emphasis on dramatic presentation and meticulous cooking. Free-range duck with nougatine, endive, dauphine potato and jasmine tea sauce, or perhaps halibut with leeks and langoustine puntette risotto might appear, while a classic hot chocolate fondant, served with orange rice pudding and orange ice cream, could be the closing choice.

Chef: Kevin Mangeolles **Owners:** Mr J Willcock, Mr J Illsley **Times:** 7-9.30, Closed L all week, D Sun-Mon (Brasserie open all day, all wk) **Prices:** Fixed D £46.50, Service included **Wine:** 60 bottles over £20, 20 bottles under £20, 13 by the glass (£3.95) **Notes:** Vegetarian available, Civ Wed 100 **Seats:** 40, Pr/dining room 25 **Smoking:** N/Sm in restaurant, Air con **Children:** Min 10 yrs **Rooms:** 17 (17 en suite) ★★★ HL **Directions:** Adjacent to fort **Parking:** Pay & Display

WILTSHIRE

BRADFORD-ON-AVON MAP 04 ST86

The Georgian Lodge Restaurant

International

Enjoy modern British dishes in relaxed surroundings

☎ 01225 862268 25 Bridge St BA15 1BY
e-mail: georgianlodge@btconnect.com
web: www.georgianhotel.co.uk

Situated by the river, changes are afoot at this Georgian establishment with refurbishment giving a quality feel. Guests can dine in the comfort and style provided by mahogany furniture and leather upholstery. The modern British menu has international influences, with straightforward dishes that rely on high-quality ingredients and technical cooking skills. Expect mains such as roasted Cornish monkfish, sweet potatoes, Thai asparagus and sorrel fish sauce, or roast rack of lamb with apricot couscous, sauté lamb's kidneys and sweetbreads. Service is relaxed and efficient.

Times: 12-2.30/6.30-10 **Directions:** In town centre, just off town bridge

The Tollgate Inn

Modern British, Mediterranean

Traditional character inn offering notable cooking

☎ 01225 782326 Ham Green BA14 6PX
e-mail: alison@tollgateholt.co.uk
web: www.tollgateholt.co.uk

This roadside inn has two restaurant areas - downstairs is an intimate dining room with a wood burning stove, furnished with pews and cushions, once a weaver's shed. The first-floor restaurant is larger with an open fire, wooden beams and high-backed leather chairs, and was the adjoining Baptist church for the workers. The fine modern British cuisine with Mediterranean influences specialises in local produce and each item is carefully sourced with every effort made to trace each ingredient to its origin. All this makes for some excellent dishes leaving diners spoilt for choice with the likes of ham hock and foie gras terrine with gribiche dressing to start, or a main of classic lobster themidor.

continued

The Tollgate Inn

Chef: Alexander Venables **Owners:** Alexander Venables, Alison Ward-Baptiste **Times:** 11-2.30/5.30-11, Closed Dec 25-26, Mon, Closed D Sun **Prices:** Fixed L £10.95, Starter £4.50-£7, Main £12.50-£17, Dessert £3.75-£5.75, Coffee £2.50, Min/Water £2.50, Service optional, Group min 6 service 10% **Wine:** 7 bottles over £20, 21 bottles under £20, 7 by the glass (£3.25-£4.50) **Notes:** Vegetarian available **Seats:** 60, Pr/dining room 38 **Smoking:** N/Sm in restaurant, Air con **Children:** Min 12 yrs **Rooms:** 4 (4 en suite) ◆◆◆◆ **Directions:** M4 junct 18, take A46 and follow signs for Bradford-on-Avon, take A363 then turn left onto B3105, in Holt turn left onto B3107 towards Melksham. The Tollgate Inn is 100 yds on right **Parking:** 40

Widbrook Grange

Traditional British

Imaginative British cooking in comfortable country house

☎ 01225 864750 Trowbridge Rd, Widbrook BA15 1UH
e-mail: stay@widbrookgrange.com
web: www.widbrookgrange.com

Nestling by the Kennet and Avon Canal near the delightful town of Bradford-on-Avon, this family-owned 18th-century Georgian country house is relaxed, friendly and classy. The recently refurbished Medlar Tree restaurant is named after an ancient tree in the gardens and offers an intimate fine dining experience. High quality ingredients are sourced by a kitchen that concentrates on simple British dishes like venison and pheasant terrine wrapped in Wiltshire smoked bacon, grilled fillet of cod served on spinach and tagliatelle and home-made bread and butter pudding filled with apples and sultanas and served with Calvados anglaise.

Chef: Robert Harwood **Owners:** Peter & Jane Wragg **Times:** 7-11, Closed 24-31 Dec, Sun, Closed L Mon-Sat **Prices:** Fixed D £23.50, Starter £5-£7.50, Main £15.50-£18.50, Dessert £5.50, Coffee £2, Min/Water £3.50, Service included **Wine:** 14 bottles over £20, 13 bottles under £20, 4 by the glass (£3.50) **Notes:** Vegetarian available, Dress Restrictions, No jeans or tracksuits, Civ Wed 50 **Seats:** 45 **Smoking:** N/Sm in restaurant **Children:** Portions **Rooms:** 20 (20 en suite) ◆◆◆◆◆ **Directions:** 1m S of Bradford-Upon-Avon on A363 **Parking:** 50

Woolley Grange

Modern British

Child-friendly atmosphere and excellent dining

☎ 01225 864705 Woolley Green BA15 1TX
e-mail: info@woolleygrangehotel.co.uk
web: www.woolleygrangehotel.co.uk

This splendid Cotswold manor house is set in attractive, peaceful gardens amid beautiful countryside. Children are made especially welcome - with a trained nanny on duty in the nursery and other child-friendly facilities. The restaurant is split into two rooms - the Orangery leading on to the garden, and the main dining room, which abounds with pictures of life at Woolley. The food is modern with international influences and boasts fresh, zingy flavours - sirloin with braised oxtail, rosti potato, red cabbage and horseradish soufflé, or pan roast pork cutlet with gherkin and caper sauce and an ultra-fresh sauté of spring cabbage, for example.

Chef: Adrian Ware **Owners:** Luxury Family Hotels & von Essen Hotels **Times:** 12-2/7-9.30 **Prices:** Fixed D £35.50, Starter £10, Main £20.50, Dessert £5, Coffee £2.50, Min/Water £3.50, Service optional **Wine:** 71 bottles over £20, 10 bottles under £20, 8 by the glass (£4.75-£6.75) **Notes:** Sun L £21.50 **Seats:** 40, Pr/dining room 22 **Smoking:** N/Sm in restaurant **Children:** Menu, Portions **Rooms:** 26 (26 en suite) ★★★ **Directions:** Telephone for directions **Parking:** 25

CASTLE COMBE MAP 04 ST87

The Bybrook Restaurant at Manor House

see page 478

COLERNE MAP 04 ST87

Lucknam Park

see page 479

DONHEAD ST ANDREW MAP 04 ST92

Forester Inn

British, European NEW

Enjoy carefully sourced and prepared dishes in a charming country inn

☎ 01747 828038 Lower St SP7 9EE
e-mail: enquiries@foresterinndonheadstandrew.co.uk
web: www.foresterinndonheadstandrew.co.uk

A quintessentially English thatched country inn, sympathetically extended with wooden beams and areas of natural stonework throughout. A variety of wooden tables and chairs, leather sofas and two wood fires contribute to the relaxed feel. The emphasis at this inn is firmly on the food with plenty of choice from lunch and dinner menus, carte and blackboard specials. The gastro-pub style cooking with traditional and international influences is clean with vibrant flavours making good use of local, organic and free-range products where possible. Possible menu choices include a starter of salt and pepper squid with mixed leaf salad and sweet chilli dressing, followed by oven-roasted sea bass on a bed of sauté fennel and artichoke hearts.

Chef: Tom Shaw, Roger Rumsey **Owners:** Martin & Christine Hobbs **Times:** 12-2/6.30-9 **Prices:** Starter £4-£8.25, Main £8.95-£16.95, Dessert £4.95-£6.95, Coffee £2, Min/Water £3, Service optional **Wine:** 42 bottles over £20, 33 bottles under £20, 16 by the glass (£2.50-£10) **Notes:** Vegetarian available **Seats:** 50, Pr/dining room 50 **Smoking:** N/Sm in restaurant **Children:** Menu, Portions **Rooms:** 2 (2 en suite) ◆◆◆◆ **Directions:** A30 at Ludwell take road signed The Donheads. T junct turn right, take next right, T junct turn left **Parking:** 30

The Bybrook Restaurant at Manor House

CASTLE COMBE MAP 04 ST87

Traditional British

Innovative cooking in imposing surroundings

☎ 01249 782206 SN14 7HR
e-mail: enquiries@manor-housecc.co.uk
web: www.exclusivehotels.co.uk

Peacefully located in the pretty village of Castle Combe, this 14th-century manor is a luxurious haven of good taste. Curl up with a book by the fire or work up an appetite with a round of golf or croquet, and then take a seat in the restaurant, an atmospheric room hung with tapestries and portraits with an imposing stained glass window.
The food lives up to the setting - expect accomplished modern cuisine complemented by an extensive range of wines by the glass from a kitchen with no shortage of talent or flair. Mains are artful creations such as pot-roast pork with Earl Grey-infused prune purée, glazed beets and liquorice-scented jus, or rolled shoulder of braised Cornish lamb with curly kale, pomme purée and button onions.

Chef: David Campbell **Owners:** Exclusive Hotels **Times:** 12-2.30/7-10.30, Closed L Sat **Prices:** Fixed L £20-£25, Coffee £4.50, Min/Water £3.95, Service optional **Wine:** 143 bottles over £20, 112 by the glass (£5.25-£237.50) **Notes:** Tasting menu 6-8 courses £95-110, Vegetarian available, Civ Wed 100 **Seats:** 90, Pr/dining room 90 **Smoking:** N/Sm in restaurant

Children: Menu, Portions **Rooms:** 48 (48 en suite) ★★★★ CHH **Directions:** M4 junct 17, follow signs for Castle Combe **Parking:** 100

LITTLE BEDWYN MAP 05 SU26

The Harrow at Little Bedwyn

see page 480

LOWER CHICKSGROVE MAP 04 ST92

Compasses Inn

Modern British **NEW**

Carefully prepared, quality produce in delightful country inn

☎ 01722 714318 SP3 6NB
e-mail: thecompasses@aol.com
web: www.thecompassesinn.com

This 14th-century thatched inn comes brimful of character and atmosphere. Its original beams derive from decommissioned galleons, while stone walls, uneven flagstones and high settle booths add further charm, and, with only two windows, candlelight adds to the timeless quality, punctuated with helpings of relaxed and friendly service. The cooking's certainly not stuck in a time warp, the modern approach making intelligent use of carefully sourced produce, including fish from Brixham. Menus come chalked up on blackboards, changing regularly to focus on seasonal and local availability, perhaps mussels in a bacon, white wine, garlic cream sauce, and slow-roasted lamb shoulder with port and redcurrant jus.

Chef: Toby Hughes, Ian Chalmers **Owners:** Alan & Susie Stoneham **Times:** 12-3/6-11, Closed 25 & 26 Dec, Mon, Closed D Sun **Prices:** Starter

continued

£4.95-£6.95, Main £7.95-£16.95, Dessert £4.50, Coffee £1.50, Min/Water £2.50, Service optional **Wine:** 13 bottles over £20, 24 bottles under £20, 6 by the glass (£2.75-£3.50) **Notes:** Sun roast £8.95, Vegetarian available **Seats:** 50, Pr/dining room 14 **Smoking:** N/Sm area **Children:** Menu, Portions **Rooms:** 4 (4 en suite) ◆◆◆◆ **Directions:** On A30 W of Salisbury, take 3rd right after Fovant, after 1/2m turn left into Lagpond Lane, Inn 1m on left **Parking:** 35

MALMESBURY MAP 04 ST98

Old Bell Hotel

Traditional British

Skilful cooking in elegant Edwardian surroundings

☎ 01666 822344 Abbey Row SN16 0BW
e-mail: info@oldbellhotel.com
web: www.oldbellhotel.com

continued on page 481

Lucknam Park

COLERNE MAP 04 ST87

Modern British

Faultless country-house cuisine

☎ 01225 742777 SN14 8AZ
e-mail: reservations@lucknampark.co.uk
web: www.lucknampark.co.uk

The mile-long drive lined with mature beech and elm trees creates a wonderful first impression and raises expectations of the delights in store at this magnificent Palladian mansion - now country-house hotel - set in 500 acres of parkland and beautiful gardens. A choice of lounge areas, from the luxurious splendour of the 17th-century drawing room with its chandeliers, ornate cornicing, oil paintings and deep sofas to the atmospheric library, deliver the anticipated comforts and luxury. The formal dining room, in the mansion's former ballroom, is an elegant bow-fronted affair with lovely views across the estate, gardens and that avenue of trees. Well-spaced tables, crisp napery and fine glassware fit the bill, as does the attentive, professional and knowledgeable service, while chef Hywel Jones's highly accomplished, clean-cut cooking more than matches expectations.

The approach is modern-focused, underpinned by a classical French theme, with great emphasis placed on sourcing high-quality seasonal ingredients. The fixed-price menus come dotted with luxury; think roast Scottish diver scallops, braised pork belly, langoustine and butternut squash purée to start, followed by a loin of Wiltshire lamb with fondant potato, provençale vegetables and Niçoise olives, or perhaps roast turbot fillet with cep dumplings, caramelised root vegetables and an Italian truffle jus, while a passionfruit tart, served with a yogurt sorbet and exotic fruit brochette, might head-up desserts.

Chef: Hywel Jones
Owners: Lucknam Park Hotels Ltd
Times: 12.30-2.30/6.45-10, Closed L Mon-Sat
Prices: Fixed D £60-£65, Coffee £4.50, Min/Water £3.75, Service included
Wine: 300 bottles over £20, 2 bottles under £20, 6 by the glass (£4.50-£7)
Notes: Sun L 3 courses £35, Vegetarian available, Dress Restrictions, Smart casual, no denim or trainers, Civ Wed 64
Seats: 80, Pr/dining room 30
Smoking: N/Sm in restaurant
Children: Min 5 yrs, Menu, Portions
Rooms: 41 (41 en suite) ★★★★★ HL
Directions: From M4 junct 17 take A350 to Chippenham, then A420 towards Bristol for 3m. At Ford turn towards Colerne. After 4m turn right into Doncombe Ln, then 100yds on right
Parking: 80

England

The Harrow at Little Bedwyn

LITTLE BEDWYN MAP 05 SU26

Modern NOTABLE WINE LIST

Emphasis on stunning seafood and wine

☎ 01672 870871 SN8 3JP
e-mail: bookings@harrowinn.co.uk
web: www.harrowinn.co.uk

It may look more like a small village pub from the outside, secreted away down winding country lanes in the hamlet of Little Bedwyn, but don't be fooled, this country restaurant is a class act. The dining room - split into two sections - is bright and contemporary, featuring dark-leather high-backed chairs and neatly dressed tables laid with Riedel glasses and colourful Villeroy crockery. Service, led by Sue Jones, is friendly and relaxed, and husband Roger mans the stove. There's also a small garden at the rear for summer alfresco dining and aperitifs.

Roger's approach in the kitchen is equally modern, with much emphasis placed on the freshness and sourcing of quality ingredients. Fish is caught on day boats landed at Brixham, while meat is from specialist farmers and butchers (perhaps 28-day hung Aberdeen Angus from Moray) and salads and herbs are specifically grown in North Devon. Thus Roger's cooking style is intelligently straightforward, allowing ingredients to shine with clean-cut flavours. Expect the likes of grilled fillet of line-caught turbot with wild mushrooms and mash, and perhaps a traditional lemon tart with fresh Guernsey double cream to finish. A stunning wine list of passion and high quality, plus an excellent range of cheeses, provide exceptional accompaniment.

Notable Wine List: Last year's wine award winner for England and overall winner.

Chef: Roger Jones
Owners: Roger & Sue Jones
Times: 12-3/7-11, Closed 3 wks Jan & Aug, Mon-Tue, Closed D Sun
Prices: Fixed L £20-£25, Starter £9-£12, Main £18-£24, Dessert £7.50, Coffee £2, Min/Water £2.50, Service optional
Wine: 800 bottles over £20, 100 bottles under £20, 12 by the glass (£4-£10)
Notes: Fixed L 3 courses, Tasting menu incl wine £75, Vegetarian available, Dress Restrictions, Smart casual
Seats: 34
Smoking: N/Sm in restaurant
Children: Menu, Portions
Directions: Between Marlborough & Hungerford, well signed
Parking: On street

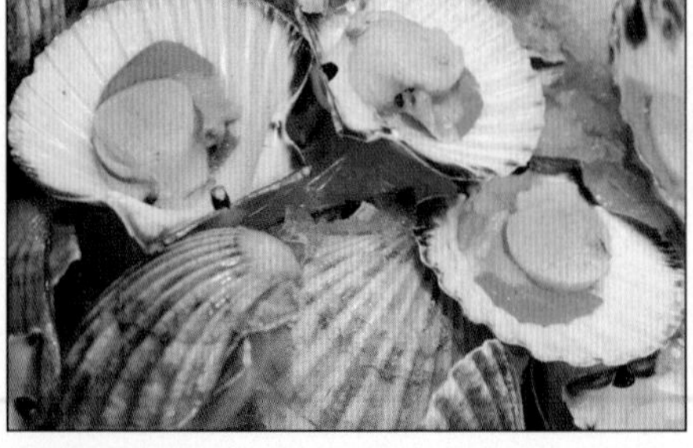

MALMESBURY *continued* MAP 04 ST98

Reputedly the oldest purpose-built hotel in England, The Old Bell has provided rooms and food since 1220. Visitors will note that facilities have improved greatly since then! Older rooms are furnished with antiques - new ones have a more contemporary feel. Service is friendly and efficient. The dining room is an elegant Edwardian addition offering imaginative dishes using local ingredients. Try the stilton, pear and endive salad with glazed walnuts and parmesan or the marinated smoked salmon and crab with spring onion, ginger and lemon to start followed by the Scottish beef fillet, rösti potatoes, broad beans, morels and truffle jus. Comforting desserts include bread and butter pudding, warm chocolate fondant or an 'indulgence' of all five dessert offerings.

Chef: Tom Rains **Owners:** The Old Bell Hotel Ltd **Times:** 12-2.30/7-9.30 **Prices:** Starter £4.50-£8.50, Main £14.50-£21.50, Dessert £5.75-£6.50, Coffee £2, Min/Water £2.75, Service optional **Wine:** 72 bottles over £20, 8 bottles under £20, 10 by the glass (£3.75-£5.75) **Notes:** Tasting menu £45, Dress Restrictions, Smart dress preferred, Civ Wed 80 **Seats:** 60, Pr/dining room 24 **Smoking:** N/Sm in restaurant **Children:** Menu, Portions **Rooms:** 31 (31 en suite) ★★★ HL **Directions:** In town centre, next to Abbey. 5 m from M4 junct 17 **Parking:** 31

The Rectory Hotel

British

Traditional country-house hotel with a close eye on contemporary style

☎ 01666 577194 Crudwell SN16 9EP
e-mail: info@therectoryhotel.com
web: www.therectoryhotel.com

Under new ownership since 2005, the original Cotswold stone-built rectory dates from the 16th century but has additional Victorian additions. Three acres of walled gardens provide a delightful setting beside the village church. The hotel is elegant with stylish period furnishings and sympathetic décor. The restaurant overlooks the attractive gardens and features some impressive wood panelling. The dinner menu features British cuisine with some good straightforward dishes accurately cooked. Try some local produce with the likes of Bathhurst Estate venison with blackberry jus and celeriac gratin. Desserts are traditional and delicious, who wouldn't be tempted by a baked egg custard with nutmeg ice cream?

Chef: Peter Fairclough **Owners:** Mr & Mrs Standing **Times:** 12-2/7-9.30, Closed L 31 Dec **Prices:** Starter £5-£7.50, Main £12.50-£18.50, Dessert £4.50-£6.50, Coffee £2.50, Min/Water £3, Service optional **Wine:** 89 bottles over £20, 28 bottles under £20, 6 by the glass (£3.25-£9.50) **Notes:** Vegetarian available, Civ Wed 60 **Seats:** 30, Pr/dining room 36 **Smoking:** N/Sm in restaurant **Children:** Menu, Portions **Rooms:** 12 (12 en suite) ★★★ HL **Directions:** Follow A429 to Cirencester. Rectory is in Crudwell village centre, next to church **Parking:** 35

Whatley Manor

MALMESBURY MAP 04 ST98

Modern French NOTABLE WINE LIST

French-cuisine in new-style, luxury country-house hotel

☎ 01666 822888 Easton Grey SN16 0RB
e-mail: reservations@whatleymanor.com
web: www.whatleymanor.com

Nestling in 12 acres of gardens, meadows and woodland, this stunning Cotswold-stone country house has been lovingly renovated to provide the highest levels of luxury. Designed to soothe and restore, there are luxurious furnishings and fabrics, and a magnificent spa, while service is professional but understated. There's a choice of restaurants: Le Mazot (named after and reflecting the old-fashioned Swiss mountain chalet) is the more informal brasserie (though suitably sophisticated in its own right with an appealing menu); while the elegant Dining Room is the intimate, dinner-only fine-dining option, resplendent in silk-clad walls and luxurious table settings. Its cuisine is classic French with a contemporary theme, focusing on top-class produce, and, like everything else here, luxury. Light, complex, beautifully presented dishes are delivered via a fixed-price carte and tasting option. You might take a main course of Dutch veal prepared two ways (fillet roasted and glazed, breast slowly braised, wrapped in pasta and topped with a rosemary foam and cep cream), and to finish, perhaps

a prune and Armagnac soufflé served with its own ice cream.

Notable Wine List: A developing wine list which is beautifully presented and offers a good mix of established wines and some lesser known producers.

Chef: Martin Burge **Owners:** Christian Landolt **Times:** 7-10, Closed Mon-Tues, Closed L all week **Prices:** Fixed D fr £60, Coffee £2.95, Min/Water £2.50, Service added but optional 10% **Wine:** 276 bottles over £20, 17 by the glass (£4.50-£8) **Notes:** Tasting menu £75, Vegetarian available **Seats:** 40, Pr/dining room 20 **Smoking:** N/Sm in restaurant **Children:** Min 12 yrs, Portions **Rooms:** 23 (23 en suite) ★★★★★ HL **Directions:** Please telephone for directions **Parking:** 100

OAKSEY MAP 04 ST99

The Wheatsheaf Inn

Modern British **NEW**

Friendly gastro-pub in tranquil village setting

☎ 01666 577348 Wheatsheaf Ln SN16 9TB

Dating back to the 14th century, this Cotswold stone pub has a big inglenook fireplace, wooden fronted bar and dark beams. The restaurant has a light, modern feel with sisal carpet, wooden tables and painted walls decorated with wine racks and jars of preserved vegetables. The kitchen team offers modern British pub food with a strong commitment to local produce. Starters include smoked chicken, bacon and black pudding salad, which may be followed with flavoursome breast of Barbary duck, red cabbage, parmesan mash and port sauce, or chargrilled tuna with Chinese spices, sauté potatoes and herb salad.

Chef: Tony Robson-Burrell **Owners:** Tony & Holly Robson-Burrell **Times:** 12-2/6.30-9.30, Closed Mon, Closed D Sun **Prices:** Fixed D £15.95, Starter £4.50-£7.50, Main £7.50-£14.95, Dessert £4.95-£6, Coffee £1.75, Min/Water £2.50, Service optional **Wine:** 6 bottles over £20, 18 bottles under £20, 6 by the glass (£3.10-£3.60) **Notes:** Vegetarian available **Seats:** 44, Pr/dining room 8 **Smoking:** N/Sm in restaurant **Children:** Portions **Directions:** Off A429 towards Cirencester, near Kemble **Parking:** 15

PURTON MAP 05 SU08

The Pear Tree at Purton

Modern British

Charming Cotswold stone hotel with superior food

☎ 01793 772100 Church End SN5 4ED
e-mail: stay@peartreepurton.co.uk
web: www.peartreepurton.co.uk

Surrounded by rolling Wiltshire farmland, this 15th-century former vicarage, belonging to the unique twin towers church of St Mary's in Purton, looks out over 7.5 acres of well-tended gardens. The airy conservatory restaurant perfectly complements the serene setting with fine linen and elegant tableware adding to the air of gentile refinement. The menu adds influences from around the world to a solidly British foundation with good ingredients - many locally sourced - cooked simply, marrying flavours with obvious expertise. Pressed salmon terrine marinated with teriyaki, lime and ginger would be a typical starter, while wood pigeon breast with wine, black treacle and sherry vinegar dressing is a good example of the main courses here.

Chef: Alan Postill **Owners:** Francis and Anne Young **Times:** 12-2/7-9.15, Closed 26-30 Dec, Closed L Sat **Prices:** Fixed L £18.50, Fixed D £33.50, Min/Water £3, Service optional **Wine:** 62 bottles over £20, 29 bottles under £20, 12 by the glass (£4.50-£7.50) **Notes:** Coffee incl, Fixed L 3 courses, Fixed D 4 courses, Vegetarian available, Dress Restrictions, No jeans or shorts, Smart casual, Civ Wed 50 **Seats:** 50, Pr/dining room 50 **Smoking:** N/Sm in restaurant **Children:** Portions **Rooms:** 17 (17 en suite) ★★★ HL **Directions:** From M4 junct 16, follow signs to Purton. Turn right at Spa shop, hotel 0.25m on right **Parking:** 70

REDLYNCH MAP 05 SU22

Langley Wood Restaurant

Traditonal British

Country dining room with a loyal following

☎ 01794 390348 SP5 2PB
e-mail: therestaurant@langleywood.freeserve.co.uk

In a small country house dating back to the 17th-century, the traditional dining room, dominated by a huge fireplace (lit on cooler days), is a great favourite locally. The setting is delightful, with lawned gardens surrounded by forest. There may be few surprises on the well-established, balanced menu, but Mediterranean flavours bring a real zest to the quality ingredients, lifting them several notches above the ordinary. Begin the meal with roast fillet of salmon with sun-dried tomato tapenade followed by breast of chicken stuffed with basil and mozzarella, wrapped in Prosciutto ham and served in a creamy tomato sauce. The chocolate and Amaretto truffle torte on the wonderful dessert trolley makes a perfect finale.

Chef: Sylvia Rosen **Owners:** David and Sylvia Rosen **Times:** 12.30-2.30/7-10.30, Closed Xmas-New Year, Mon & Tue, Closed L Wed-Fri, D Sun **Prices:** Fixed L £17.75, Starter £4.75-£7.25, Main £10.75-£16.25, Dessert £4.75, Min/Water £2.50, Service optional **Wine:** 24 bottles over £20, 46 bottles under £20, 5 by the glass (£2.75-£3.50) **Notes:** Fixed L is Sun 3 courses, Vegetarian available, Dress Restrictions, Smart casual **Seats:** 30 **Smoking:** N/Sm in restaurant **Directions:** Between A338 Salisbury to Ringwood road and A36 Salisbury to Southampton road **Parking:** 30

ROWDE MAP 04 ST96

George & Dragon

British, European

Charming old pub with a relaxed gastro-pub atmosphere

☎ 01380 723053 High St SN10 2PN
e-mail: thegandd@tiscali.co.uk

continue

The bar is the first room of entry at the George & Dragon, with four wooden tables around a large open fire. The restaurant also has wooden furniture and there are dark wooden beams throughout. The carte menu is substantially supplemented by blackboard specials, with fish as a speciality - grilled cod fillet on a bacon and new potato compote; lobster linguine with chilli tomato sauce. An interesting alternative is duck shepherd's pie followed by a choice of traditional puddings: sticky toffee, apple and rhubarb crumble, and Eton mess.

Chef: Christopher Day **Owners:** Mr & Mrs Hale & Mr C Day **Times:** 12-3/6-11, Closed L Mon, D Sun **Prices:** Fixed L fr £11, Coffee £2, Min/Water £3, Service optional **Wine:** 16 bottles over £20, 17 bottles under £20, 8 by the glass (£2.90-£4.65) **Notes:** Set 3 course Sun L £15.50, Vegetarian available **Seats:** 35 **Smoking:** N/Sm in restaurant **Children:** Portions **Directions:** 1.5m out of Devizes towards Chippenham on A342 **Parking:** 12

SALISBURY MAP 05 SU12

Anokaa

Modern Indian NEW

Contemporary Indian cuisine in colourful, stylish surroundings

☎ 01722 414142 60 Fisherton St SP2 7RB
e-mail: enquiry@anokaa.com
web: www.anokaa.com

Large-plate glass windows front this modern split-level restaurant, giving you a peek at the delights in store. The décor is unfussy with only subtle references to India visible while service is slick and confident - both factors very much in keeping with the forward-looking approach of the food. Dishes are all freshly prepared and each is distinctively spiced - jinga zafrani, for example, a dish of king prawns in spices, fennel and coriander, or duck jalsha, with the meat crisped on charcoal and served in a sauce of apricot, ginger and bay leaf. The lunch menu is a real bargain - and ensures tables are full, so get there early!

Chef: Ram Chandra Banjade **Owners:** Mohammed Odud, Solman Farsi **Times:** 12-2/5.30-10 **Prices:** Fixed L £7.25-£10.25, Fixed D £22.95-£42.50, Starter £3.55-£15, Main £7.95-£26, Dessert £2.95-£5.95, Coffee £1.55, Min/Water £4.10, Group min 10 service 10% **Wine:** 9 bottles over £20, 18 bottles under £20, 6 by the glass (£3.55-£4.25) **Notes:** Vegetarian available, Dress Restrictions, Smart casual **Seats:** 80 **Smoking:** N/Sm in restaurant, Air con **Children:** Min 5 yrs **Directions:** Adjoined to The Salisbury Playhouse & City Hall **Parking:** Main car park to rear of restaurant

Red Lion Hotel

French NEW

Imaginative cooking in eclectic surroundings

☎ 01722 323334 Milford St SP1 2AN
e-mail: reception@the-redlion.co.uk
web: www.the-redlion.co.uk

The old and the new mingle cheerfully at this relaxed hotel which is full of character. There is a wattle and daub wall dating from the early 13th century in the Vine Restaurant that makes a talking point amongst the elegant settings. Using fresh, local produce whenever possible, the menu, too, blends an interesting mix of modern and traditional styles. Expect well presented hearty main courses such as roast rump of lamb with caramelised root vegetables, garlic and thyme jus or cassoulet of confit duck with Puy lentils and chorizo sausage.

Times: 7-9.30 **Rooms:** 51 (51 en suite) ★★★ HL

SWINDON MAP 05 SU18

The Ridge Restaurant

Traditional British

Interesting food in opulent surroundings

☎ 01793 721701 Blunsdon House Hotel, Blunsdon SN26 7AS
e-mail: info@blunsdonhouse.co.uk
web: www.blunsdonhouse.co.uk

A sprawling corporate hotel in large, well-tended grounds with a choice of eating options, including the fine dining Ridge Restaurant. This Regency-style room is panelled in walnut, and boasts chandeliers, heavy gold and turquoise drapes, and unusual table settings. The British food is served by very attentive staff; perhaps loin of lamb in a potato and herb crust with truffle sauce, or seared fillet of sea bass with creamed leeks, asparagus and morel sauce. A small, cosy bar is perfect for a pre-dinner drink.

Chef: Lloyd Nichols **Owners:** Mr & Mrs P Clifford and Family **Times:** 12.15-2/7-10, Closed L Mon-Sat, D Sun **Prices:** Starter £5.50-£8, Main £16.50-£26.50, Dessert £5.50, Coffee £2.20, Min/Water £2.75, Service included **Wine:** 17 bottles over £20, 16 bottles under £20 **Notes:** Sun L 3 courses £15 incl coffee, Vegetarian available, Dress Restrictions, Smart casual, no jeans or sleeveless T-shirts, Civ Wed 100 **Seats:** 65, Pr/dining room 16 **Smoking:** N/Sm in restaurant, Air con **Children:** Menu, Portions **Rooms:** 117 (117 en suite) ★★★★ HL **Directions:** M4 junct 15, 200 yds off A419. Northern edge of Swindon at Blunsdon **Parking:** 300

Pagoda Palace

☎ 01793 877888 Pepperhill Box, Meadway, Peatmoor SN5 5YZ
web: www.theaa.com/restaurants/114026.html

An impressive traditional-style temple overlooking the tranquil Peatmoor Lagoon in West Swindon. The menu lists a feast of specialty Szechwan, Cantonese and Peking dishes. Excellent dim sum.

TROWBRIDGE MAP 04 ST85

The Linnet

Modern British

Cosy country inn down a quiet lane

☎ 01380 870354 Great Hinton BA14 6BU

Tucked away unsignposted down a quiet country lane, this charming inn appears to be a well-kept secret, frequented by discerning locals. The relaxed informal surroundings and simple décor are enhanced by candlelight in the evenings so you can settle in and enjoy the atmosphere. Cooking and presentation are to a high standard using good quality ingredients and interesting combinations in modern British dishes with international influences. Try the likes of baked tenderloin of pork filled with prunes and spinach wrapped in smoked bacon on a wild mushroom sauce or salt and vinegar battered pollack fillet on dill mushy peas and caper cream. Good value Sunday lunch menu.

Chef: Neil Clark **Owners:** Jonathan Furby **Times:** 12-2/6.30-9.30, Closed 25, 26 Dec, 1 Jan, Mon **Prices:** Fixed L fr £11.75, Fixed D £21.25-£29, Starter £4.25-£5.95, Main £12.25-£18.25, Dessert £4.25-£6.50, Coffee £1.95, Min/Water £1.75, Service optional **Wine:** 12 bottles over £20, 32 bottles under £20, 9 by the glass (£2.60-£5.75) **Notes:** Vegetarian available **Seats:** 40 **Smoking:** N/Sm in restaurant, Air con **Children:** Portions **Directions:** Off A342, 4m W of Devizes, 3m E of Trowbridge **Parking:** 45

England

WARMINSTER MAP 04 ST84

Bishopstrow House Hotel

British

Enjoyable food in pleasant country-house environs

☎ 01985 212312 BA12 9HH
e-mail: info@bishopstrow.co.uk
web: www.bishopstrow.co.uk

Part of the von Essen group of hotels, this cosy Georgian country house is set in 27 acres of landscaped grounds and possesses one of the biggest collections of antique firearms in the country, as well as a host of period features complemented by a sensitive, modern approach to décor. The modern menu consists largely of tried and tested combinations delivered with consummate skill and technical accuracy with the classical French influence never far from view. Asparagus, quail's egg and black truffle salad to start and honey-glazed confit duck leg with braised red cabbage and lentils would both be representative of the rewarding food on offer.

Chef: Frank Bailey **Owners:** von Essen Hotels **Times:** 12.15-2/7.30-9.30 **Prices:** Fixed L £12.50, Fixed D £41, Starter £4.50-£7.50, Main £6.50-£17, Dessert £4.50-£7.50, Coffee £2.75, Min/Water £3.80, Service added but optional 15% **Wine:** 180 bottles over £20, 6 bottles under £20, 16 by the glass (£2.50-£12) **Notes:** Tasting menu 7 courses £50, Vegetarian available, Dress Restrictions, Smart casual, Civ Wed 70 **Seats:** 65, Pr/dining room 28 **Smoking:** N/Sm in restaurant **Children:** Menu, Portions **Rooms:** 32 (32 en suite) ★★★★ HL **Directions:** From Warminster take B3414 (Salisbury). Hotel is signed **Parking:** 100

WHITLEY MAP 04 ST86

The Pear Tree Inn

British, European

Attractive inn serving local produce

☎ 01225 709131 Top Ln SN12 8QX
e-mail: enquiries@thepeartreeinn.com
web: www.thepeartreeinn.com

The inn was once a farm and the décor reflects its history, using old farming implements and simple wooden tables. The mellow stone building has been transformed with a rustic yet contemporary feel and is set in lovely grounds. The interior is divided into a bar, dining area and garden room. Modern British cuisine with European influences and locally sourced seasonal produce are the draw here. Dishes are straightforward and the menu offers a good choice. Try the likes of Jerusalem artichoke soup with truffle oil to start, followed by a main course of pan-fried turbot with celeriac purée, sprouting broccoli and mussel and olive dressing. Puddings include sticky gingerbread with poached quince and cardamom ice cream.

continued

Chef: Marc Robertson **Owners:** Martin & Debbie Still **Times:** 12-2.30/6.30-9.30, Closed 25-26 Dec, 1 Jan **Prices:** Fixed L £13.50-£15.50, Starter £4.50-£8, Main £11.50-£19, Dessert £5.50, Coffee £2.50, Min/Water £2.95, Service optional **Wine:** 32 bottles over £20, 23 bottles under £20, 10 by the glass (£3.35-£5.50) **Notes:** Vegetarian available **Seats:** 60, Pr/dining room 40 **Smoking:** N/Sm in restaurant **Children:** Menu, Portions **Rooms:** 8 (8 en suite) ★★★★★ RR **Directions:** Telephone for directions **Parking:** 60

WORCESTERSHIRE

ABBERLEY MAP 10 SO76

The Elms Hotel & Restaurant

Modern British

Grand surroundings meet contemporary country-house cooking

☎ 01299 896666 Stockton Rd WR6 6AT
e-mail: info@theelmshotel.co.uk
web: www.theelmshotel.co.uk

Built in 1710 by Gilbert White (a pupil of Sir Christopher Wren), this stunning Queen Anne house overlooks beautifully manicured lawns to the countryside beyond. The lavish interiors are very much in keeping with the grandiose exteriors, with ornate plaster ceilings, carved fireplaces, antique furnishings and stained-glass windows evoking a sense of historical glamour. The food here is firmly in the modern British camp with creatively updated versions of classic dishes and interesting use made of ingredients. You might expect a starter of terrine of confit duck, apple chutney and toasted brioche, followed by pan-roasted cod with herb risotto, sesame and prawn tortellini with a lemon grass and saffron foam.

Chef: Daren Bale **Owners:** von Essen Hotels **Times:** 12-2.30/7-9.30 **Prices:** Fixed L £13.50, Fixed D £35, Starter £9.50, Main £23.75, Dessert £8.50, Coffee £2.75, Min/Water £4, Service optional **Wine:** 200 bottles over £20, 20 bottles under £20, 4 by the glass (£4.25-£4.75) **Notes:** Sun L £24.95, tasting menu 7 courses £57.50, Vegetarian available, Dress Restrictions, Smart casual, no jeans, no T-shirts, Civ Wed 70 **Seats:** 50, Pr/dining room 50 **Smoking:** N/Sm in restaurant **Children:** Menu, Portions **Rooms:** 21 (21 en suite) ★★★ HL **Directions:** Located on A443 near Abberley, 11m NW of Worcester **Parking:** 40

BROADWAY MAP 10 SP03

Dormy House Hotel

British, French

Enjoyable dining at this luxurious Cotswold retreat

☎ 01386 852711 Willersey Hill WR12 7LF
e-mail: reservations@dormyhouse.co.uk
web: www.dormyhouse.co.uk

This sympathetically converted 17th-century farmhouse overlooks the Cotswold town of Broadway. Luxurious rooms and a traditional approach to dining make a winning combination. Smart dress is required but there is no stuffiness here. Those looking for a less formal meal can always opt for the gastro-pub menu in the Barn Owl bar. Staff throughout provide excellent, friendly service. High-quality, locally sourced produce are used to create simple yet elegant traditional dishes with the occasional contemporary twist. Pheasant and pistachio timbale with Madeira cream sauce precedes roast fillet of Cornish beef, oxtail faggot and foie gras ravioli served with horseradish mash. Finish with the banana and chocolate crème brûlée with banana sorbet.

Times: 12-2/7-9.30, Closed 24-27 Dec, Closed L Mon-Sat **Rooms:** 47 (47 en suite) ★★★ HL **Directions:** From A44 take turn signed 'Saintbury', after 0.5m turn left

The Lygon Arms

Modern British

Grandiose Cotswold hotel with gratifying food

☎ 01386 852255 High St WR12 7DU
e-mail: info@thelygonarms.co.uk
web: www.thelygonarms.co.uk

This 500-year-old yellow limestone country house is in one of the most picturesque of the Cotswold villages and is blessed with a multitude of original features. The restaurant itself is set within the Great Hall, a magnificent room with a grand open fireplace as its centrepiece and an impressive barrel-vaulted ceiling - it is the epitome of traditional British style and service. The food has similar characteristics, boasting fine local ingredients, robust flavours and technically complex dishes - terrine of duck rillette with lentils, shallots and red wine dressing, for example, or roast breast of guinea fowl with ballotine of the leg and a wild mushroom and foie gras sauce.

Chef: Martin Lovell **Owners:** Paramount Hotels **Times:** 12-2.30/7-9.30 **Prices:** Fixed L £15, Fixed D fr £39.50, Starter £6.95-£16.95, Main £22.50-£26.50, Dessert £8.50-£9.75, Coffee £3.60, Min/Water £3.25, Service optional **Wine:** 148 bottles over £20, 1 bottle under £20, 10 by the glass (£4.50-£7.50) **Notes:** Gastro D menu available Thur-Sat, Dress Restrictions, Smart casual, No jeans, T-shirts, trainers, Civ Wed 80 **Seats:** 90, Pr/dining room 80 **Smoking:** N/Sm in restaurant, Air con **Children:** Min 12 yrs, Menu, Portions **Directions:** A40 to Burford, then A424 through Stow-on-the-Wold, continue A44 **Parking:** 100

Russell's

Modern British

Indulgent cuisine in a restaurant with rooms

☎ 01386 853555 20 High St WR12 7DT
e-mail: info@russellsofbroadway.com
web: www.russellsofbroadway.com

On the high street of a picturesque village, this chic restaurant with rooms blends period features with muted modern décor and contemporary art. A stone fireplace takes centre stage in the front room, but rather than having a real fire, it is used as a showcase for the hotel's fine wines. In summer you can eat outside on the sunny terrace. The fixed-price menu and carte offer a good range of contemporary British dishes with international influences, using carefully chosen ingredients. Try a starter of Enoki mushroom and egg noodle laksa with spiced chicken dumplings, pak choi and a quail egg for example. Main courses feature the likes of pan-fried halibut with creamed salsify and buttered spinach. Save some room for dessert though, where you can enjoy delicious steamed pecan and maple syrup sponge with butterscotch sauce and clotted cream.

Times: 12-2.30/6-9.30 **Rooms:** 4 (4 en suite) RR

BROMSGROVE MAP 10 SO97

The Bromsgrove Hotel

Modern

Mediterranean-themed hotel

☎ 01527 576600 Kidderminster Rd B61 9AB
e-mail: banqueting.bromsgrove@hanover-international.com
web: www.hanover-international.com

A striking modern hotel with an airy, Mediterranean feel in a rural setting, yet only 2 miles from the M5 (J4/5) and M42 (J1), hence its popularity with a mainly business clientele. Facilities include a well-equipped leisure club, a courtyard garden, and the Parador restaurant, with its Spanish-style terracotta tiles and big rugs. Expect an appealing blend of traditional and modern cuisine. Daily fixed-price menus may include ham hock and chorizo terrine with celeriac and horseradish remoulade, braised shank of lamb with caramelised red onion jus, and lemon pannacotta.

Chef: Graham Sutton **Owners:** Pedersen Ltd **Times:** 12.30-2/7-9, Closed Xmas, Closed L Sat **Prices:** Fixed L fr £15.50, Fixed D £19.50, Starter £3.40-£7.90, Main £8-£16, Dessert £3.50-£4.50, Coffee £2.50, Min/Water £3.60, Service optional **Wine:** 8 bottles over £20, 21 bottles under £20, 5 by the glass (£3.25-£4.90) **Notes:** Vegetarian available, No Jeans, Civ Wed 200 **Seats:** 100, Pr/dining room 200 **Smoking:** N/Sm in restaurant, Air con **Children:** Menu, Portions **Rooms:** 109 (109 en suite) ★★★★ **Directions:** On A448 Kidderminster road 1m W of Bromsgrove centre **Parking:** 200

Epic Bar Brasserie

Modern British NEW

Stylish, modern brasserie with high-quality cooking

☎ 01527 871929 68 Hanbury Rd, Stoke Prior B60 4DN
e-mail: epic.bromsgrove@btconnect.com
web: www.epicbrasserie.co.uk

The stylish and retro-modern interior of this converted roadside inn delivers leather seating, stripped wooden floors, spotlights, polished-wood tables and friendly service to this local hub of gastronomy. The extensive menu is fashionable, flexible (many dishes can be ordered as a starter or main course) and appealing with an international note, where Pacific Rim dishes could rub shoulders with British stalwarts. For example, a starter of deep-fried wonton prawns could be followed by smoked haddock and chive risotto with poached egg and hollandaise. Cooking is direct, unfussy and flavour driven, presentation simple yet striking.

Chef: Jason Lynas **Owners:** Patrick McDonald **Prices:** Food prices not confirmed for 2007. Please telephone for details **Directions:** Telephone for directions

England

BROMSGROVE *continued* MAP 10 SO97

Grafton Manor Restaurant

British. Indian

Modern cuisine dotted with Indian dishes in elegant period setting

☎ 01527 579007 Grafton Ln B61 7HA
e-mail: stephen@graftonmanorhotel.co.uk
web: www.graftonmanorhotel.co.uk

This impressive 16th-century manor house - once the seat of the Earl of Shrewsbury - is set in manicured grounds and retains many original features. Moulded ceilings, open fires and a sumptuous period drawing room for aperitifs and coffees set the style, together with the tastefully furnished dining room that comes replete with crisp white linen and uniformed staff. Surprising perhaps, but the modern British menu comes dotted with the occasional authentic Indian dish; take first-class railway lamb infused with coconut, for instance. Otherwise, expect a loin of lamb with fennel and morel emulsion and fondant potato, while a separate vegetarian menu keeps all-comers happy.

Chef: Simon Morris/Tim Waldon **Owners:** The Morris Family **Times:** 12.30-1.30/7-9.30, Closed BHs, Closed L Sat, D Sun **Prices:** Fixed L £18.50-£20.50, Fixed D £27.85, Coffee £2.65, Min/Water £3.25, Service optional **Wine:** 43 bottles over £20, 27 bottles under £20, 3 by the glass **Notes:** Fixed L 3 courses, Vegetarian menu, Dress Restrictions, Smart casual, Civ Wed 120 **Seats:** 60, Pr/dining room 60 **Smoking:** N/Sm in restaurant **Children:** Portions **Directions:** Off B4091, 1.5m SW of Bromsgrove **Parking:** 60

CHADDESLEY CORBETT MAP 10 SO87

Brockencote Hall

French, International

French provincial county-house dining

☎ 01562 777876 DY10 4PY
e-mail: info@brockencotehall.com
web: www.brockencotehall.com

This converted Victorian family residence now houses a comfortable hotel. Decorated in French country-house style, there are lots of pastel shades, chandeliers, fireplaces and a large conservatory. With its formal settings and attractive views across the grounds, the elegant dining room is popular with business and tourist customers alike. Ingredients are sourced locally and also direct from the chef's home country of France. The menu features such Gallic provincial starters as ballotine of confit shoulder pork with Parma ham and poached pear and main courses of sea bass in vine leaves with champagne and shallot cream. Puddings include a honey-glazed plum on Breton sablé. There is also a six-course tasting menu.

continued

Brockencote Hall

Chef: Colin Layfield **Owners:** Mr & Mrs Petitjean **Times:** 12-1.30/7-9.30 **Prices:** Fixed L £14, Fixed D £28.30, Starter £6.80-£15, Main £15.50-£22.50, Dessert £6-£9.50, Coffee £3.20, Min/Water £3, Service included **Wine:** 80 bottles over £20, 30 bottles under £20, 5 by the glass (£3.50-£9) **Notes:** Sun L £24.50, Vegetarian available, Dress Restrictions, Smart casual, no jeans, Civ Wed 60 **Seats:** 60, Pr/dining room 30 **Smoking:** N/Sm in restaurant **Children:** Menu, Portions **Rooms:** 17 (17 en suite) ★★★ HL **Directions:** On A448 just outside village, between Kidderminster & Bromsgrove **Parking:** 45

EVESHAM MAP 10 SP04

The Evesham Hotel

Varied NOTABLE WINE LIST

Relaxed Regency style, weekly-changing menu surprises

☎ 01386 765566 Coopers Ln, Off Waterside WR11 1DA
e-mail: reception@eveshamhotel.com
web: www.eveshamhotel.com

Built in 1540 as a fine Tudor farmhouse and modernised in 1810 in Georgian style, this is not your run-of-the-mill hotel. Owned and managed by the Jenkinson family since the mid-1970s it delivers a slightly eccentric but always innovative experience. The Cedar Restaurant, an elegant Georgian room that looks out onto a180-year-old Cedar of Lebanon tree, has a menu that is deliberately wide-ranging and unique, and is supplemented by whatever local produce becomes available at the time. Theme nights include an 'Archers' night, in honour of the long-running radio series from the area, featuring produce like loin of local wild venison, pan-fried and served with a juniper berry sauce and rowanberry jelly.
Notable Wine List: Possibly the wackiest wine list in the world and a highly individual list.

Chef: Sue James **Owners:** John Jenkinson **Times:** 12.30-2/7-9.30, Closed 25-26 Dec **Prices:** Starter £3.50-£8.75, Main £13-£20, Dessert £3.75-£5.50, Coffee £2.50, Min/Water £2.50, Service included **Wine:** 335 bottles over £20, 268 bottles under £20 **Notes:** Buffet lunch available £9.20, Vegetarian menu **Seats:** 55, Pr/dining room 12 **Smoking:** N/Sm in restaurant **Children:** Menu, Portions **Rooms:** 40 (40 en suite) ★★★ HL **Directions:** Coopers Lane is off road along River Avon **Parking:** 45

Riverside Hotel

Traditional British

Fine dining with fabulous river views

☎ 01386 446200 The Parks, Offenham Rd WR11 8JP
e-mail: info@river-side-hotel.co.uk
web: www.river-side-hotel.co.uk

Beautifully located hotel overlooking the River Avon, set amid 3 acres of gardens in the ancient deer park of Evesham Abbey. Smart public areas include the lounge, where a live pianist plays, and the luxuriously appointed restaurant. A meal on the terrace watching the boats go by is a treat in fine weather. Fresh ingredients, organic where possible, form the basis of the menu, with good fresh fish (whole grilled sea bass on crushed potatoes with sweet chilli sauce) and chargrilled Hereford prime rib-eye steak. At lunch you can choose between the carte and a lighter option. Themed events are a regular occurrence, such as Italian, Greek, wine and champagne evenings.

Chef: Racheal Taylor **Owners:** Deborah Sinclair **Times:** 12-2/7-9, Closed L Mon, D Sun **Prices:** Food prices not confirmed for 2007. Please telephone for details **Wine:** 20 bottles over £20, 20 bottles under £20, 7 by the glass (£3.95-£6.65) **Seats:** 48 **Smoking:** N/Sm in restaurant **Children:** Portions **Rooms:** 10 (7 en suite) ★★ HL **Directions:** From A46 Evesham follow signs for Offenham, then take a right onto B4510. Hotel 0.5m on left down private drive **Parking:** 20

KIDDERMINSTER MAP 10 SO87

The Granary Hotel & Restaurant

Modern European

Modern cuisine in a setting to match

☎ 01562 777535 Heath Ln, Shenstone DY10 4BS
e-mail: info@granary-hotel.co.uk
web: www.granary-hotel.co.uk

continued

A major refurbishment has given this modern hotel a striking new bar in a bold black and white colour scheme. The restaurant is largely unchanged - an airy, contemporary room, it's decorated in dark woods and muted colours, and furnished with Lloyd Loom chairs and well-spaced tables. A carvery is served on weekday lunchtimes, but evenings bring a tempting modern menu; black pudding and sweet apple in pancetta is a typical starter, while mains are well-judged combinations such as lamb with minted mash and a rosemary and redcurrant jus.

Chef: Tom Court **Owners:** Richard Fletcher **Times:** 12-2.30/7-11, Closed L Mon/Sat, D Sun **Prices:** Fixed L £9.50, Fixed D £17.50, Starter £4.95-£7.75, Main £10.95-£19.95, Dessert £3.50-£4.95, Coffee £1.95, Min/Water £3.50, Service optional **Wine:** 10 bottles over £20, 31 bottles under £20, 8 by the glass (£2.80-£4.80) **Notes:** Vegetarian available, Civ Wed 200 **Seats:** 60, Pr/dining room 40 **Smoking:** N/Sm in restaurant, Air con **Children:** Portions **Rooms:** 18 (18 en suite) ★★★ HL **Directions:** Situated on A450 between Worcester and Stourbridge. 2m outside Kidderminster **Parking:** 95

MALVERN MAP 10 SO74

Cottage in the Wood and Restaurant

British NOTABLE WINE LIST

Country retreat with stunning views

☎ 01684 575859 Holywell Rd,
Malvern Wells WR14 4LG
e-mail: proprietor@cottageinthewood.co.uk
web: www.cottageinthewood.co.uk

A relaxing, family-run hotel in a glorious setting, with arguably the 'best view in England', looking out over the Severn Plain from high on the steep wooded slopes of the Malvern Hills. The cottage is a cluster of three white-painted buildings, with the classically decorated restaurant located in the elegant Georgian dower house. Views from window tables are stunning but the ambitious cooking does its best to

continued

England

MALVERN *continued* MAP 10 SO74

distract, with a modern British menu that focuses on seasonal local produce. Scallops with lobster tortellini and venison with fig and chestnut ravioli and juniper jus show the style. The thoughtfully compiled wine list is packed with interest, enthusiasm and a refreshing lack of pretension.

Notable Wine List: Full of enthusiasm, this list offers over 500 wines, personal tasting notes, a useful fast track list and extensive selection of half-bottles.

Chef: Dominic Pattin **Owners:** The Pattin Family **Times:** 12.30-2/7-9.30 **Prices:** Fixed L £16.75, Starter £8.50-£11, Main £17.50-£22, Dessert £8.95, Coffee £2.75, Min/Water £3 **Wine:** 384 bottles over £20, 72 bottles under £20, 10 by the glass (£3.95-£4.50) **Notes:** Sun L 3 courses incl coffee £23, Vegetarian available, Dress Restrictions, Smart casual preferred. No jeans, trainers **Seats:** 70, Pr/dining room 20 **Smoking:** N/Sm in restaurant, Air con **Children:** Portions **Rooms:** 31 (31 en suite) ★★★ HL **Directions:** 3m S of Great Malvern off A449. From Great Malvern, take 3rd turning on right after Railway pub **Parking:** 40

Foley Arms Hotel

Modern British, European

Traditional coaching inn with great views

☎ 01684 573397 14 Worcester Rd WR14 4QS
e-mail: reservations@foleyarmshotel.com
web: www.foleyarmshotel.co.uk

Royalty stayed here during Malvern's heyday as a spa town, and left their crest to prove it. The hotel remains elegant to this day, especially in the restaurant where bay windows highlight the stunning Severn Valley views. There is a modern European approach to cooking where using local ingredients, colour and presentation play an important part in dishes such as field mushrooms stuffed with haggis and topped with mozzarella starter, smoked oven-baked duck breast with spinach mash and orange and plum sauce, or pan-fried medallions of pork loin layered with black pudding and apple.

Chef: Will Dickie **Owners:** Nigel & Helen Thomas **Times:** 12-2/7-9.15, Closed L Sat **Prices:** Fixed L fr £12.50, Fixed D £15-£19.95, Coffee £2.50, Min/Water £3.50, Service optional **Wine:** 20 bottles over £20, 25 bottles under £20, 10 by the glass **Notes:** Fixed D 2 courses, Vegetarian available, Smart casual, Civ Wed 100 **Seats:** 50, Pr/dining room 25 **Smoking:** N/Sm in restaurant **Children:** Menu, Portions **Rooms:** 28 (28 en suite) ★★★ HL **Directions:** M5 junct 8 from south (junct 7 from north). Follow signs for Upton/Malvern, approx 8m from motorway on A449, in centre of town **Parking:** 60

Holdfast Cottage Hotel

Modern, Traditional NEW

Beautifully simple, quality dishes in a lovely cottage setting

☎ 01684 310288 Marlbank Rd, Welland WR13 6NA
e-mail: enquiries@holdfast-cottage.co.uk
web: www.holdfast-cottage.co.uk

A delightful country cottage at the foot of the Malvern Hills. The manicured lawns and wisteria-clad façade complement the wonderful gardens. The charming restaurant continues the cottage feel, with wooden tables, simple cutlery and glassware. Service is relaxed and welcoming. The set four-course menu includes a freshly-made sorbet, and vegetarians are well catered for. Simple presentation and clear quality cooking with attention to seasonality are evident in dishes like oven-roasted salmon on crushed potatoes with avocado purée and lime and coriander salsa, or fillet of Herefordshire beef on buttered colcannon and panaché of baby vegetables.

Chef: Adam Cambridge **Owners:** Guy & Annie Dixon **Times:** 12/7 **Prices:** Fixed L fr £19.95, Fixed D fr £27.50, Coffee £1.95, Min/Water £2.50, Service optional **Wine:** 6 bottles over £20, 36 bottles under £20, 2 by the glass (£3.60) **Notes:** Fixed D 4 courses, Sun L 2 courses £15.95, 3 courses £18.95, Vegetarian available, Civ Wed 30 **Seats:** 30, Pr/dining room 18 **Smoking:** N/Sm in restaurant **Children:** Portions **Rooms:** 8 (8 en suite) ★★ **Directions:** On A4104 midway between Welland & Little Malvern **Parking:** 20

Seasons Restaurant at Colwall Park Hotel

Modern British

Stylish restaurant serving excellent local produce

☎ 01684 540000 Walwyn Rd, Colwall WR13 6QG
e-mail: hotel@colwall.com
web: www.colwall.com

An attractive hotel with a country-house look, Colwall Park is located at the heart of a small village with views of the Malvern Hills from the gardens. In contrast to the generally traditional décor in the public rooms, the restaurant is quite contemporary in shades of cream with light oak panelling and bespoke artwork. Dishes can tend towards the complicated but are technically well executed, with good use made of seasonal produce and local producers acknowledged. Typical options are pressed terrine of confit duck and foie gras, roast loin of Cotswold venison, and mulled pear tarte Tatin. There is also an impressive British cheeseboard.

Chef: James Garth **Owners:** Mr & Mrs I Nesbitt **Times:** 12.30-2.30/7.30-9, Closed L all week ex by arrangement **Prices:** Fixed L £15.95, Fixed D £24.95, Starter £6.25-£7.95, Main £17.25-£19.95, Dessert £6.75-£7.50, Coffee £2, Min/Water £3.25, Service included **Wine:** 80 bottles over £20, 20 bottles under £20, 8 by the glass (£3.15-£4.50) **Notes:** Vegetarian available **Seats:** 40, Pr/dining room 100 **Smoking:** N/Sm in restaurant **Children:** Menu, Portions **Rooms:** 22 (22 en suite) ★★★ HL **Directions:** On B4218, off A449 from Malvern to Ledbury **Parking:** 40

OMBERSLEY MAP 10 SO86

The Venture In Restaurant

British, French

Modern British dining in medieval draper's house

☎ 01905 620552 Main Rd WR9 0EW

Dating back to 1430, this restaurant has a wealth of beamed ceilings and inglenooks as well as a resident ghost. Fresh flowers and gentle colours make this an inviting and comfortable dining venue with

continued

attentive and thoughtful service. The excellent breads, ice creams and petits fours are made in-house. Dishes use best quality ingredients, skilfully prepared and simply garnished. Precede the main course of roasted squab with sweet pickled red cabbage and red wine sauce with a starter of seared Cornish scallops with buttered noodles, leeks and bouillabaisse froth. To finish, there's a port-poached pear served with stilton ice cream or delicious iced banana parfait, caramelised banana and chocolate sorbet.

Chef: Toby Fletcher **Owners:** Toby Fletcher **Times:** 12-2/7-9.30, Closed 25 Dec-1 Jan, 2wks summer & 2wks winter, Mon, Closed D Sun **Prices:** Fixed L £18.95, Fixed D £33-£36.50, Min/Water £3, Service optional **Wine:** 40 bottles over £20, 19 bottles under £20, 5 by the glass (£3.75-£4.75) **Notes:** Dress Restrictions, Smart casual **Seats:** 32, Pr/dining room 32 **Smoking:** N/Sm in restaurant, Air con **Children:** Min 12 yrs D **Directions:** From Worcester N towards Kidderminster - A449 (approx 5m). Turn left at Ombersley turning - 0.75m on right **Parking:** 15

TENBURY WELLS MAP 10 SO56

Cadmore Lodge

British, French

Enjoyable dining in rural retreat

☎ 01584 810044 Berrington Green, St Michaels WR15 8TQ
e-mail: info@cadmorelodge.co.uk
web: www.cadmorelodge.co.uk

This friendly, family-run hotel has a country-style restaurant with great lake and valley views, warm colours and a log fire. The surrounding 70-acre estate gives this restaurant a peaceful and relaxing atmosphere helped by friendly, welcoming staff. There's a daily-changing dinner menu of traditional dishes with some French and oriental influences. To start, there's home-made pâté with main courses of sirloin steak au poivre or venison fillet with a port reduction and roasted beetroot and horseradish mash. Finish with fresh strawberries and a raspberry brandy snap basket.

Chef: Mark Griffiths, Mark Bore **Owners:** Mr & Mrs J Weston **Times:** 12-2/7-9.15, Closed 25 Dec, Closed L Mon **Prices:** Fixed L £9.50-£11.50, Fixed D £22.50, Coffee £1.20, Min/Water £1.10 **Wine:** 4 bottles over £20, 22 bottles under £20, 4 by the glass (£2.20-£2.90) **Notes:** Vegetarian available, Civ Wed 100 **Seats:** 50, Pr/dining room 50 **Smoking:** N/Sm in restaurant, Air con **Children:** Menu, Portions **Rooms:** 15 (14 en suite) ★★ **Directions:** Off A4112 from Tenbury Wells to Leominster. 2m from Tenbury Wells, turn right opposite St Michaels Church **Parking:** 100

UPTON UPON SEVERN MAP 10 SO84

White Lion Hotel

British, European

Historic coaching inn with appealing food

☎ 01684 592551 21 High St WR8 0HJ
e-mail: info@whitelionhotel.biz
web: www.whitelionhotel.biz

This former coaching inn dates back to 1510 and has a colourful history, not least as the place where Henry Fielding wrote parts of his novel, *Tom Jones*. Period details - exposed timbers, lathe and plaster walls - have been sensitively incorporated into the modern décor which maintains a traditional feel. Food is classically based with Mediterranean twists. Slick presentation and good ingredients are a major factor in the appeal of dishes such as smoked Scottish venison

continued

wafers with sweet cherry balsamic dressing or, as a main, baked hake with smoked salmon and tomato butter sauce.

Chef: Jon Lear, Richard Thompson **Owners:** Mr & Mrs Lear **Times:** 12-2/7-9.15, Closed 1 Jan **Prices:** Starter £5.95-£7.45, Main £14.95-£18.55, Dessert fr £5.75, Coffee £1.40, Min/Water £2.75, Service optional **Wine:** 5 bottles over £20, 28 bottles under £20, 3 by the glass (£3.75-£5) **Notes:** Sun L 2 courses £13.25, 3 courses £16, Vegetarian available **Seats:** 45 **Smoking:** N/Sm in restaurant **Children:** Portions **Rooms:** 13 (13 en suite) ★★★ HL **Directions:** From A422 take A38 towards Tewkesbury. After 8m take B4104 for 1m, after bridge turn left to hotel **Parking:** 16

WORCESTER MAP 10 SO85

Brown's Restaurant

Modern British

Interesting modern cooking in former corn mill

☎ 01905 26263 The Old Cornmill, South Quay WR1 2JJ

This former Victorian corn mill retains some of its original architectural features in its new incarnation as a restaurant. The chic, modern décor is in line with the modern British cuisine. International influences can also be seen in the varied menu that makes good use of locally-sourced fresh ingredients. Look out for a starter of chilli-spiced pear, red onion and goat's cheese tart with a walnut and rocket salad. Try fish of the day for a main course, or perhaps something more exotic, like Thai spiced roast butternut squash with noodles, coriander and coconut broth.

Chef: Gary Phipps **Owners:** Mr R Everton **Times:** 12.30-1.45/7.30-9.45, Closed 1wk Xmas, Mon, Closed L Sat, D Sun **Prices:** Fixed L £29.50, Fixed D £33.50, Starter £4.95-£8.95, Main £9.95-£20.95, Dessert £5.50, Coffee £2.50, Min/Water £3.50, Service optional **Wine:** 80 bottles over £20, 26 bottles under £20, 8 by the glass (£5.45-£7.50) **Notes:** Fixed L 5 courses, ALC prices L, Dress Restrictions, Smart casual preferred **Seats:** 110 **Smoking:** N/Sm in restaurant **Children:** Portions **Directions:** From M5 junct 7 to city centre. At lights turn into Copenhagen St, car park adjacent to restaurant **Parking:** Large car park adjacent to the Restaurant

YORKSHIRE, EAST RIDING OF

BEVERLEY MAP 17 TA03

The Manor House

Modern British

City style in country-house setting

☎ 01482 881645 Northlands, Walkington HU17 8RT
e-mail: info@walkingtonmanorhouse.co.uk
web: www.walkingtonmanorhouse.co.uk

Late Victorian country-house hotel standing in well-tended gardens, with two different style dining rooms making up its restaurant. The Blue Room boasts crystal chandeliers and silk walls, while the larger, airier conservatory overlooks the south terrace and manicured lawns. Both have elegant table settings and comfortable seating, and deliver the same fine-dining experience. As well as two dining rooms, there are two fixed-price menus to match, both delivering a traditional theme with modern overtones. Quality ingredients, clear flavours and technical skill hit the mark in dishes such as seared scallops with sauté of baby leek and sauce vièrge starter, fillet of Yorkshire beef with truffle and fresh horseradish gnocchi with a finale of warm apple galette, chocolate and lavender sorbet and butterscotch sauce.

continued

England

BEVERLEY *continued* MAP 17 TA03

Chef: Neil Armstrong **Owners:** Ann Pickering **Times:** 11.30-2.30/6-9.15, Closed L Sat, D Sun **Prices:** Fixed L £9.95, Fixed D £13.75-£19.95, Coffee £2.50, Min/Water £3, Service optional **Wine:** 31 bottles over £20, 22 bottles under £20, 4 by the glass (£3.50) **Notes:** Fixed ALC £34.50, Vegetarian available, Civ Wed 50 **Seats:** 60, Pr/dining room 30 **Smoking:** N/Sm in restaurant **Children:** Portions **Rooms:** 7 (7 en suite) ★★ HL **Directions:** From Hull towards York, at end of Beverley bypass left at rdbt towards Walkington, right at x-rds, on left **Parking:** 30

®® Tickton Grange Hotel

British

Elegant Georgian country-house retreat with exciting dining

☎ 01964 543666 Tickton HU17 9SH
e-mail: info@ticktongrange.co.uk
web: www.ticktongrange.co.uk

This charming Georgian country-house hotel dates from the 1820s and has 4 acres of private grounds and attractive gardens. There's an elegant dining room with bay windows and hill views. Staff are both efficient and friendly. Suppliers of local produce are listed prominently. Carefully selected ingredients are skilfully transformed into modern British dishes notable for imaginative combinations, clear flavours and attractive presentation. Expect starters of poached Cuckoo Marran hen's egg, mixed bean salad and sauce vièrge followed by pan-fried Sat Carr rainbow trout fillet, green beans, black olives and cherry tomatoes To finish there's kir royale roulade, crème fraîche and blueberry basket and the wonderful Tickton truffles. For a really special occasion, there is the Taittinger champagne dinner.

Chef: David Nowell **Owners:** Mr & Mrs Whymant **Times:** 12-2/7-9.30 **Prices:** Fixed L £15, Fixed D £35, Starter £5.50-£6.95, Main £14.95-£22.95, Dessert £6.50-£8.50, Coffee £1.60, Service optional **Wine:** 33 bottles over £20, 32 bottles under £20, 8 by the glass (£3.25-£6.50) **Notes:** Fixed D 4 courses, Vegetarian available, Civ Wed 150 **Seats:** 45, Pr/dining room 20 **Smoking:** N/Sm in restaurant **Children:** Menu, Portions **Rooms:** 17 (17 en suite) ★★★ HL **Directions:** From Beverley take A1035 towards Bridlington. After 3m hotel on left, just past Tickton **Parking:** 75

WILLERBY MAP 17 TA03

®® Willerby Manor Hotel

Modern European

Quality cooking in a slick, modern setting

☎ 01482 652616 Well Ln HU10 6ER
e-mail: willerbymanor@bestwestern.co.uk
web: www.willerbymanor.co.uk

Originally the home of a wealthy shipping merchant, this attractive manor house is now a busy hotel renovated in modern style, although the older parts of the hotel retain many original features. There are two dining options - the Everglades brasserie in a sunny conservatory, or the more formal Icon restaurant in a thoroughly contemporary dining room. The latter leans heavily toward Italy and France in style - langoustine and vegetable terrine with saffron vinaigrette or grilled turbot with calamari and sauce Nero would be good examples. Rather than the traditional separation into starters and mains, the menu gives the option of small or large portions for several of the dishes - a nice idea.

Chef: David Roberts, Ben Olley **Owners:** Alexandra Townend **Times:** 12.30-2.30/7-9.30, Closed 1st wk Jan, last 2 wks Aug, BHs, Sun, Closed L Mon-Sat, D Sun **Prices:** Fixed D £21.50, Starter £4.40-£5.95, Main

continued

£12.65-£14.40, Dessert £4.30-£4.60, Coffee £1.80, Min/Water £3.20, Service optional **Wine:** 7 bottles over £20, 23 bottles under £20, 4 by the glass (£3.95-£4.95) **Notes:** Vegetarian available, Civ Wed 300 **Seats:** 40, Pr/dining room 40 **Smoking:** N/Sm in restaurant, Air con **Children:** Portions **Rooms:** 51 (51 en suite) ★★★ HL **Directions:** M62/A63, follow signs for Humber Bridge, then signs for Beverley until Willerby Shopping Park. Hotel signed from rdbt next to McDonald's **Parking:** 200

YORKSHIRE, NORTH

ALDWARK MAP 19 SE46

®® *Aldwark Manor*

British, European

19th-century manor house with a contemporary dining room

☎ 01347 838146 838251 YO61 1UF
e-mail: reception@aldwarkmanor.co.uk
web: www.marstonhotels.com

The manor house dates from 1865 and is set amid 100 acres of parkland, including an 18-hole golf course, within striking distance of both York and Harrogate. The restaurant, located in a new wing, is bright, airy and fully air-conditioned. Modern pictures of wine bottles on huge canvases dominate the room, and tables are neatly clothed with crisp napkins. Staff are smartly uniformed, and service is both professional and attentive. A regularly changing set-price menu of three courses is offered. Dishes are fairly simple with a modern approach with good saucing; perhaps risotto of smoked haddock with saffron and parmesan, or crisp duck breast with fondant potato, orange sauce and roasted parsnips.

Times: 12-2.30/7-9.30 **Rooms:** 60 (60 en suite) ★★★★ HL **Directions:** From A1, A59 towards Green Hammerton, then B6265 towards Little Ouseburn, follow signs Aldwark Bridge/Manor. A19 through Linton on Ouse to Aldwark.

ARNCLIFFE MAP 18 SD97

®® Amerdale House Hotel

British, European

Imaginative modern cuisine in a gorgeous Dales village

☎ 01756 770250 BD23 5QE
e-mail: amerdalehouse@littondale.com
web: www.amerdalehouse.co.uk

The setting here is a big wow-factor - this charming Victorian manor house is within an area of outstanding natural beauty and surrounded by immaculately maintained gardens. The house itself retains many original features, beautiful décor and period furniture, while the dining room tends more toward a Regency style. The daily-changing menu is very much influenced by seasonality and freshness with home-grown and local ingredients making appearances throughout. The chef's modern British approach leans toward the traditional with consistently well-cooked and thoughtful dishes - roast lion of Dales lamb on minted couscous, for example, or the delicious dessert of Yorkshire curd tart and liquorice ice cream.

Chef: Nigel Crapper **Owners:** Paula & Nigel Crapper **Times:** 7.30-8.30, Closed mid Nov-mid Mar, Closed L all week **Prices:** Fixed D £34.50, Min/Water £2.50, Service included **Wine:** 50 bottles over £20, 46 bottles under £20, 2 by the glass (£3) **Seats:** 24 **Smoking:** N/Sm in restaurant **Children:** Min 8 yrs **Rooms:** 11 (11 en suite) ★★ **Directions:** On the outskirts of village. **Parking:** 20

ASENBY MAP 19 SE37

Crab and Lobster Restaurant

French, British

Character restaurant serving mainly seafood

☎ 01845 577286 Dishforth Rd YO7 3QL
e-mail: enquiries@crabandlobster.co.uk
web: www.crabandlobster.co.uk

Quirky and unconventional are just two words that come to mind when describing the décor at this thatched restaurant. From its low-ceilinged bar to dining room and pavilion conservatory, all is festooned in a riot of 'collectable anything' memorabilia ... some of it planned, some not. And, as the name suggests, seafood is the speciality of the lengthy, crowd-pleasing modern-themed repertoire that cleverly merges the traditional and more unusual. Take a threesome; baked queenies with gruyère, garlic and lemon; roast cod, Thai crab risotto, lime and ginger coulis; and homely sticky toffee pudding. Dishes are accomplished and well conceived, portions generous and the atmosphere's relaxed, while the guys should checkout the Marilyn Monroe themed men's room before they leave.

Times: 12-2.30/7-9.30 **Directions:** From A19/A168 take A167, drive through Topcliffe follow signs for A1. On left, 8m from Northallerton

AUSTWICK MAP 18 SD76

The Austwick Traddock

Modern British

Organic cooking at a charming country-house hotel

☎ 015242 51224 Nr Settle LA2 8BY
e-mail: info@austwicktraddock.co.uk
web: www.austwicktraddock.co.uk

Certified by the Soil Association, this cosy candlelit restaurant prides itself on only using organic and wild ingredients. The menu offers modern British dishes, such as rack of Mansergh Hall lamb with Lyonnaise potatoes and caramelised shallots, and much loved desserts - sticky toffee pudding with butterscotch sauce for example. And the setting? An intimate Georgian country-house hotel in the midst of the Yorkshire Dales National Park. Relax by the fire with a book or board game in one of two comfortable lounges, or sally out into the stunning countryside for a walk.

Chef: Selena Quinn **Owners:** Bruce & Jane Reynolds **Times:** 12.30-3/6.45-11, Closed L Mon-Sat **Prices:** Fixed L £14-£18, Fixed D £25-£30, Coffee £3, Min/Water £2.50, Service optional **Wine:** 13 bottles over £20, 27 bottles under £20, 8 by the glass (£2.20-£5.10) **Seats:** 36, Pr/dining room 16 **Smoking:** N/Sm in restaurant **Children:** Portions **Rooms:** 10 (10 en suite) ★★ SHL **Directions:** From Skipton take A65 towards Kendal, 3m after Settle take right signed Austwick, cross hump back bridge, hotel 100yds on left **Parking:** 20

BILBROUGH MAP 16 SE54

The Three Hares Country Inn

Modern British

Traditional inn with supremely satisfying food

☎ 01937 832128 Main St YO23 3PH
e-mail: threehares@ukf.net
web: www.thethreehares.co.uk

This traditional stone-built inn is the only pub in the village so serves the dual purpose of cosy local combined with superior gastro-pub. There are three distinct areas to the Three Hares - a comfortable, modern bar, the Red Room that has a definite racing theme and the Old Village Forge with its attractive stone-flagged floor. The modern British menu keeps things relatively simple with successful updates or revisions of classic dishes cooked with undeniable skill. Try oxtail bourguignon with Yorkshire rarebit and toasted brioche as a main,

continued on page 494

England

Wine Award Winner and Overall Winner

The Devonshire Arms

Country House Hotel & Spa

page 493

England

The Devonshire Arms Country House Hotel & Spa

BOLTON ABBEY MAP 19 SE05

Modern French WINE AWARD ENGLAND & OVERALL WINNER

AA Wine Award Winner for England & Overall Winner

☎ 01756 710441 BD23 6AJ

e-mail: res@devonshirehotels.co.uk

web: www.devonshirehotels.co.uk

This classic country-house hotel has stunning views of the Wharfedale countryside. Originally a 17th-century coaching inn, it oozes the atmosphere of a private country mansion. The fine-dining Burlington Restaurant, with its refined, traditional edge, has large, highly-polished antique tables which come appropriately set with the finest table appointments and service is professional but friendly. The dining room extends into the conservatory, with its wicker chairs and stone floor and views over the Italian courtyard garden. Executive Head Chef Michael Wignall brings an impressive track record to his highly accomplished kitchen, with time spent with Paul Heathcote, Marco Pierre White and John Burton Race and previously at Cliveden's Waldo's. His carefully crafted, complex but elegantly light dishes ooze modern French influence - underpinned by high-level technical skill - and come littered with top-notch, luxury ingredients and precise, intense flavours. The appealing, fixed-price carte and ten-course tasting option are backed up by an excellent list of cheeses, a stunning range of a dozen or more petits fours and vast wine list. Expect the likes of loin of estate hare, cannelloni of osso buco with langoustines, chervil root purée and braised artichokes, followed by semi-dried fig tarte Tatin, cardamom ice cream and caramelised rice.

Notable Wine List: A truly outstanding list which is full of top-class producers, amazing verticals, good introductions and an impressive half-bottle listing.

Chef: Michael Wignall
Owners: Duke & Duchess of Devonshire
Times: 12.30-2.30/7-10, Closed Mon, Closed L Tue-Sat
Prices: Fixed L fr £33, Fixed D fr £58, Service added but optional 10%
Wine: 2128 bottles over £20, 51 bottles under £20, 12 by the glass (£6-£13)
Notes: Fixed L 3 courses, Fixed D 4 courses, Tasting menu £68, Vegetarian available, Smart casual, no jeans, no trainers, Civ Wed 90
Seats: 70, Pr/dining room 90
Smoking: N/Sm in restaurant
Children: Menu
Rooms: 40 (40 en suite) ★★★★ HL
Directions: On B6160 to Bolton Abbey, 250 yds N of junct with A59 rdbt junct
Parking: 100

England

BILBROUGH *continued* MAP 16 SE54

with a rather naughty sticky toffee pudding with home-made pistachio ice cream as a pudding.

Chef: Lee Wood **Owners:** Charles Oliver **Times:** 12-2/7-9, Closed 2 wks at start of year, Mon (ex BHs), Closed D Sun **Prices:** Starter £4.95-£8.95, Main £9-£16.95, Dessert £5, Coffee £2.95, Min/Water £3, Service optional **Wine:** 4 bottles over £20, 18 bottles under £20, 8 by the glass (£3.25-£6) **Notes:** Sun L available, Vegetarian available **Seats:** 34, Pr/dining room 16 **Smoking:** N/Sm in restaurant **Children:** Portions **Directions:** From York take A64 towards Leeds and follow signs for Bilbrough on right **Parking:** 35

see advert on page 491

BOLTON ABBEY MAP 19 SE05

The Devonshire Arms Country House Hotel & Spa

see page 493

BOROUGHBRIDGE MAP 19 SE36

The Dining Room

Modern British, European

Quality cooking in relaxed surroundings

☎ 01423 326426 20 St James Square YO51 9AR
e-mail: thediningrooms@wanadoo.co.uk

Behind this establishment's bow-fronted, shop-style frontage there's a traditional-style lounge and bar for aperitifs, while in contrast, the eponymous dining room is a modern affair, with plain white walls and eye-catching artwork, decked out with beams, high-backed chairs, linen-dressed tables and quality crockery. Chef-patron Chris Astley is passionate about his cooking, his intelligently compact menus (bolstered by specials) deliver fresh, clean-flavoured dishes utilising quality ingredients and superb presentation skills. Take lightly curried smoked haddock chowder with seared king scallop, a fillet of line-caught cod on a leek and chive butter sauce, or classic warm chocolate mousse with liquid chocolate centre and espresso ice.

Chef: Christopher Astley **Owners:** Mr & Mrs C Astley **Times:** 12-2/7-9.30, Closed 25-27 Dec, Mon, Closed L Tue-Sat, D Sun **Prices:** Fixed D £25, Starter £4.95-£6.95, Main £13.50-£19.50, Dessert £4.95-£7.95, Coffee £2.70, Min/Water £3, Service optional **Wine:** 40 bottles over £20, 40 bottles under £20, 9 by the glass (£3.95-£7.50) **Notes:** Vegetarian available **Seats:** 32 **Smoking:** N/Sm in restaurant **Children:** Min 3 yrs, Portions **Directions:** A1(M), Boroughbridge junct, sign to town. Opposite fountain in the town square **Parking:** On street/Private on request

BURNSALL MAP 19 SE06

Red Lion Hotel

Modern British

Picturesque old inn serving hearty favourites

☎ 01756 720204 By the Bridge BD23 6BU
e-mail: redlion@daelnet.co.uk
web: www.redlion.co.uk

This delightful, 16th-century Dales village inn - beside a five-arch bridge over the River Wharfe - has avoided the trend to modernise, and retains real charm and character. Think flagstone floors, hand-pump ales, roaring fires, low ceilings and exposed beams. Dine in the elegant restaurant, or more casually in the oak-panelled bar. The cooking is straightforward, bold and value-driven from a committed kitchen. Fresh local ingredients enhance traditional fare with its modern twist and eye-catching daily specials. Look out for Red Lion fish soup, steak and kidney pie, or sea bass with celeriac mash.

Chef: James Rowley **Owners:** Andrew & Elizabeth Grayshon **Times:** 12-2.30/6-9.30 **Prices:** Fixed L £19.95-£21.95, Fixed D £29.95-£32.95, Starter £4.95-£8.95, Main £13.95-£18.95, Dessert £5.95-£8.95, Coffee £2, Min/Water £2.95, Service optional **Wine:** 12 by the glass **Notes:** Fixed L 3 courses, Vegetarian available, Smart casual, Civ Wed 125 **Seats:** 50, Pr/dining room 90 **Smoking:** N/Sm in restaurant **Children:** Menu, Portions **Rooms:** 15 (15 en suite) ★★ HL **Directions:** 10m from Skipton on B6160 **Parking:** 70

CRATHORNE MAP 19 NZ40

Crathorne Hall Hotel

British

Edwardian country house with impressive cuisine

☎ 01642 700398 TS15 0AR
e-mail: crathornehall@handpicked.co.uk
web: www.handpicked.co.uk

Step back in time and savour the period elegance and grandeur of Crathorne Hall, a magnificent Edwardian former stately home set in 15 acres of grounds with views of the Leven Valley and the Cleveland Hills. Glowing wood panelling, an impressive carved stone fireplace, ornate ceilings and imposing oil paintings are just some of the original features in the formal Leven restaurant. Impressive modern European cooking is characterised by interesting combinations, high-quality ingredients and an accomplished simplicity. Take a stroll through the glorious grounds before an enjoyable dinner, perhaps crab roulade with shellfish cream, followed by roast Highland venison with bitter chocolate sauce, and hot Grand Marnier soufflé to finish.

continued

Chef: Peter Fleming **Owners:** Hand Picked Hotels **Times:** 12.30-2.30/7-10 **Prices:** Fixed L £15, Fixed D £30, Starter £6.75-£11.50, Main £13.50-£17.95, Dessert £4.50-£6.50, Coffee £2.95, Min/Water £3.50, Service optional **Wine:** 78 bottles over £20, 6 bottles under £20, 8 by the glass (£4.75-£6.25) **Notes:** Vegetarian available, Civ Wed 120 **Seats:** 45, Pr/dining room 26 **Smoking:** N/Sm in restaurant **Children:** Min 2 yrs D, Menu, Portions **Rooms:** 37 (37 en suite) ★★★★ HL **Directions:** Off A19, 2m E of Yarm. Access to A19 via A66 or A1, Thirsk **Parking:** 80

ESCRICK MAP 16 SE64

The Parsonage Country House Hotel

British V

Quality service and cooking in a delightful country house

☎ 01904 728111 York Rd YO19 6LF
e-mail: sales@parsonagehotel.co.uk
web: www.parsonagehotel.co.uk

This 19th-century former parsonage with beautiful grounds has been lovingly restored and extended. Inside, there are comfortable lounges, a bar and the elegant fine dining restaurant. Here diners are a mix of residents and visitors, all enjoying well sourced produce from the 'Yorkshire Farmers' menu. Dishes are nicely presented, and might include a starter of breast of partridge on a roast parsnip and apple salad with cranberry dressing, followed by breast of Harome duckling with balsamic-scented rhubarb and concluding with hot chocolate fondant with spiced pear fritters and ginger sabayon.

Chef: Neal Birtwell **Owners:** P Smith **Times:** 12-2/7-9, Closed L Sat **Prices:** Fixed L fr £10, Fixed D fr £25, Starter £5-£7.50, Main £15-£21, Dessert £5-£11.50, Coffee £2.50, Min/Water £3.10 **Wine:** 10 by the glass (£2.50-£5.20) **Notes:** Vegetarian available, Dress Restrictions, No jeans, Civ Wed 100 **Seats:** 50, Pr/dining room 20 **Smoking:** N/Sm in restaurant **Children:** Portions **Rooms:** 48 (48 en suite) ★★★ HL **Directions:** S from York on A19, Parsonage on right, 4m out of town in Escrick village **Parking:** 80

GUISBOROUGH MAP 19 NZ61

Macdonald Gisborough Hall

Modern British **NEW**

Well-prepared local produce at an elegant Victorian house

☎ 0870 400 8191 Whitby Ln TS1 6PT
e-mail: general.gisboroughhall@macdonald-hotels.co.uk
web: www.macdonald-hotels.co.uk

A grand Victorian country house on the edge of Guisborough, with stunning views of the Cleveland hills. The smart dining room has a traditional feel and overlooks the formal gardens. Service is friendly and the menus (including a seasonal menu) feature classically-based cuisine with a modern slant. Monkfish millefeuille with Parma ham, broad beans and dill cream sauce is an excellent dish, with plump, well-timed medallions of fish and wafer thin slices of crisp ham.

Prices: Food prices not confirmed for 2007. Please telephone for details **Rooms:** 71 (71 en suite) ★★★★ HL

Pinchinthorpe Hall

Modern British

Cooking with a punch in a vibrant bistro setting

☎ 01287 630200 Pinchinthorpe TS14 8HG
e-mail: nybrewery@pinchinthorpe.wanadoo.co.uk
web: www.pinchinthorpehall.co.uk

Take a stroll around the grounds of this 17th-century manor and you'll find an organic micro brewery in the coach house conjuring tasty tipples from local spring water. Next door is the Brewhouse Bistro, an unpretentious venue with flagstone floors, bare brick walls and unclothed timber tables. There's an early bird menu, but it's worth waiting for the carte, which delivers bold dishes at competitive prices. Flavours are as big as the portions, with mains along the lines of Dexter beef sirloin steak served pink with sauce béarnaise, or Whitby cod, crab and roast pepper fishcakes set on garden kale with a creamed tartare velouté.

Chef: Kevin Mulraney **Owners:** George Tinsley, John Warnock & Alison Foster **Times:** 12/9.30 **Prices:** Fixed L £8.95, Starter £3.95-£6.95, Main £9.95-£17.95, Dessert £4.50-£5.95, Coffee £1.95, Min/Water £2.95, Service optional **Wine:** 35 bottles over £20, 25 bottles under £20
Notes: Earlybird menu 3 courses £10.95, Mon-Fri, 4.30-6.30pm, Vegetarian available, Smart casual, Civ Wed 80 **Seats:** 45, Pr/dining room 40 **Smoking:** N/Sm in restaurant **Children:** Portions **Rooms:** 6 (6 en suite) ★★★★ RR **Directions:** 10m S of Middlesbrough **Parking:** 150

HAROME MAP 19 SE68

The Star Inn

Traditional British NOTABLE WINE LIST

Creative cuisine at a popular inn

☎ 01439 770397 YO62 5JE
e-mail: starinn@bt.openworld.com
web: www.thestaratharome.co.uk

A gastronomic haven, this pretty thatched inn is always busy with an appreciative crowd of locals and foodies from further afield. Run by a committed family team, it's a cosy haunt full of candle-lit nooks, ancient beams and open fires, and although the bar can be cramped when busy, the restaurant is quieter and there's also a comfortable coffee loft. The cooking is British in style with an emphasis on ingredients from the region. Expect innovative creations from a chef who likes to put an array of flavours on the plate; roe deer with venison shepherd's pie perhaps, or grilled black pudding with pan-fried foie gras, apple and vanilla chutney and a scrumpy reduction. Desserts are worth a look too - how about the 'celebration of forced Yorkshire rhubarb'?

Notable Wine List: A well-thought out wine list with good tasting notes.

Chef: Andrew Pern **Owners:** A & J Pern **Times:** 11.30-3/6.30-11, Closed 25 Dec, 2 wks early spring, BHs, Mon, Closed D Sun **Prices:** Starter £6.50-£11.95, Main £12.50-£22.50, Service optional **Wine:** 60% bottles over £20, 40% bottles under £20, 10 by the glass (£3.50-£4.95) **Notes:** Sun L menu 12-6pm, Civ Wed 50 **Seats:** 36, Pr/dining room 10 **Smoking:** N/Sm in restaurant **Children:** Portions **Directions:** From Helmsley take A170 towards Kirkbymoorside, after 0.5m turn right towards Harome. After 1.5m Inn is 1st building on right

England

HARROGATE MAP 19 SE35

The Boar's Head Hotel

Modern British

Charming British setting and food

☎ 01423 771888 Ripley Castle Estate HG3 3AY
e-mail: reservations@boarsheadripley.co.uk
web: www.boarsheadripley.co.uk

A former coaching inn with an aristocratic elegance, the Boar's Head is set in the private village of Ripley belonging to the Ripley Castle Estate. It's owned by the current castle occupiers Sir Thomas and Lady Ingilby, who donated some of their paintings, including those of past Ingilby ancestors. The dining room walls fetchingly come in a vibrant deep red, while comfortable seating and well-trained staff all fit the bill. The kitchen's modern approach is fittingly inspired by traditional British cuisine and uses fresh, quality ingredients with flair in well-presented dishes. Think pan-fried Yorkshire beef fillet with a rich red wine sauce and grilled queenie scallops. (The Bistro here offers less formal surroundings and a simpler menu.)

Chef: Marc Guilbert **Owners:** Sir Thomas Ingilby & Lady Ingilby **Times:** 12-2/7-9 **Prices:** Fixed L fr £16.95, Fixed D £34-£40, Coffee £2, Min/Water £3, Service optional **Wine:** 120 bottles over £20, 30 bottles under £20, 10 by the glass (£3.50-£5.50) **Notes:** Fixed D 4 courses, Vegetarian available, Civ Wed 150 **Seats:** 40, Pr/dining room 40 **Smoking:** N/Sm in restaurant **Children:** Menu, Portions **Rooms:** 25 (25 en suite) ★★★ HL **Directions:** On A61 (Harrogate/Ripley road). In village centre **Parking:** 45

Clocktower

Modern British

Elegant hotel with excellent dining

☎ 01423 871350 Rudding Park, Follifoot HG3 1JH
e-mail: sales@ruddingpark.com
web: www.ruddingpark.com

continued

You'll find the newly refurbished Clocktower restaurant in the converted stable block of Rudding Park House an elegant and stylish modern hotel set in 200-year-old landscaped parkland. The striking, contemporary dining room has bare wood tables with good quality settings and glassware, modern artwork on the walls, and an adjacent lively bar area. A relaxed and happy air prevails and staff are both friendly and professional. The seasonal menu uses fresh local produce and offers modern British dishes with a twist, indicating a degree of creative energy - pan-fried king scallops with pesto linguine, Nidderdale lamb shank with thyme jus, Home Farm venison with sloe gin sauce, and rhubarb and vanilla cheesecake.

Chef: Stephanie Moon **Owners:** Simon Mackaness **Times:** 12-3/7-9.30 **Prices:** Starter £6-£9, Main £13-£20, Dessert £6-£9, Coffee £3.20, Min/Water £3.50, Service included **Wine:** 35 bottles over £20, 25 bottles under £20, 15 by the glass (£3.50-£4.50) **Notes:** Vegetarian available, Civ Wed 180 **Seats:** 170, Pr/dining room 250 **Smoking:** N/Sm in restaurant, Air con **Children:** Menu, Portions **Rooms:** 49 (49 en suite) ★★★★ HL **Directions:** A61 at rdbt with A658 follow signs 'Rudding Park' **Parking:** 250

The Courtyard

Modern British

Trendy venue in a former stable block

☎ 01423 530708 1 Montpellier Mews HG1 2TQ

This former Victorian stable block in an attractive courtyard or trendy shops is complete with original Jacob's ladder leading to the hayloft upstairs. Nowadays the restaurant boasts contemporary pastel décor, beech furniture and candlelight in the evening. You can dine outside in the cobbled courtyard garden in summer. The menu offers contemporary British cuisine with classical influences and local and seasonal produce is sourced whenever possible. Expect dishes like seared sea bass fillet with basil and goat's cheese risotto and sauce vièrge or Cumbrian chicken breast filled with tarragon mousse. Supplemented by daily specials, early bird menus are also available.

Chef: Ryan Sadler **Owners:** Martin Wilks **Times:** 12-2/6-9.30, Closed 25-26 Dec, 1 Jan, Sun **Prices:** Fixed L fr £9.95, Fixed D fr £12.95, Starter £4.95-£8.50, Main £11.95-£19.95, Dessert £4.95-£7.50, Coffee £2.25, Min/Water £3.25, Service added 10% **Wine:** 60 bottles over £20, 20 bottles under £20, 8 by the glass (£3.50-£8) **Notes:** Vegetarian available **Seats:** 28 **Smoking:** N/Sm in restaurant **Children:** Portions **Directions:** Please telephone for directions **Parking:** On street

Harrogate Brasserie with Rooms

British, French

A great place to eat and enjoy some jazz

☎ 01423 505041
28-30 Cheltenham Pde HG1 1DB
e-mail: info@brasserie.co.uk
web: www.brasserie.co.uk

This continental-style restaurant with rooms has live jazz nights on Wednesday, Friday and Sunday. The brasserie extends through three cosy, richly decorated dining areas, all adorned with artefacts, mainly with a jazz theme. The menu, supplemented by daily specials from the blackboard, offers modern British cooking. Typical starters might include chicken liver parfait or deep-fried brie, while mains extend to crispy duck confit with a honey orange sauce or slow-roasted lamb joint with a red wine jus.

Times: 6-9.45, Closed 26 Dec, 1 Jan, BHs, Closed L all week (ex residents) **Rooms:** 17 (17 en suite) ★★★ RR **Directions:** In town centre, 500 mtrs from railway station, behind theatre, 150mtrs from Conference Centre

Hotel du Vin & Bistro

British, Mediterranean

Luxurious surroundings for fine food and wine

☎ 01423 856800 Prospect Place HG1 1LB
e-mail: info@hotelduvin.com
web: www.hotelduvin.com

Originally created from a row of eight Georgian-styled houses, which have operated as a hotel since the 1930s, Hotel du Vin Harrogate provides a luxurious experience. Food and wine are very important, the bistro menu changes daily and is available throughout the day. Classic dishes are featured, supporting the HdV philosophy of quality food cooked simply, with the freshest of local ingredients. This might include dishes like seared scallops with saffron risotto and Parma ham to start, or a main course of baked fillet of sea bass with fennel salad. The wine list is carefully selected and wine events are held throughout the year.

Times: 12-1.45/6.30-9.45 **Rooms:** 43 (43 en suite) ★★★★ TH **Directions:** From A1 follow signs for Harrogate & town centre. Take 3rd exit on Prince of Wales rdbt (marked town centre). Hotel is 400yds on right

Quantro

Modern European

Stylish restaurant with good-value cooking

☎ 01423 503034 3 Royal Pde HG1 2SZ
e-mail: info@quantro.co.uk
web: www.quantro.co.uk

A sister business to the Leeds eatery of the same name, this glass-fronted town-centre restaurant is modern and sophisticated, with a lime and aubergine interior, banquettes and ambient lighting. The modern European style of food is delivered with panache and there is good use of quality ingredients. Expect goat's cheese and fig tart with glazed beetroot, corn-fed duck breast with caramelised apples, fennel and vanilla purée, followed by chocolate and peppermint pot

continued

with pistachio shortbread. The cheaper light lunch and early evening menus offer exceptionally good value.

Chef: Neil Ballinger **Owners:** T & K Burdekin **Times:** 12-2/6-10, Closed 25-26 Dec, 1 Jan, Sun, Closed D Sun (ex trade shows) **Prices:** Fixed L fr £9.95, Starter £3.90-£5.90, Main £9.20-£14.90, Dessert £3.50-£4.50, Service added but optional 10% **Wine:** 12 bottles over £20, 37 bottles under £20, 13 by the glass (£3-£6) **Notes:** Vegetarian available, Smart casual preferred **Seats:** 40 **Smoking:** N/Sm in restaurant, Air con **Children:** Min 8 yrs **Directions:** Telephone for directions **Parking:** On street

HOVINGHAM MAP 19 SE67

Worsley Arms Hotel

Traditional British

A good traditional spa hotel restaurant

☎ 01653 628234 High St YO62 4LA
e-mail: worsleyarms@aol.com
web: www.worsleyarms.com

A 19th-century, village centre hotel with a history dating back to the time when Sir William Worsley decided it would be a good idea to turn the village into a spa town - sadly an enterprise that failed. The restaurant, decorated in soothing reds and greens, has well-spaced tables and service is efficient and friendly. Good, locally sourced ingredients are used extensively in dishes like the starter of black pudding with pineapple chutney, poached rhubarb and a parmesan crisp. Main courses include a matured rib-eye steak with hand-cut chips and sauce béarnaise. Finish with sticky toffee pudding, toffee sauce and banana ice cream.

Chef: Jonathon Murray **Owners:** Mr & Mrs A Finn **Times:** 12-2/7-9.45, Closed L Mon-Sat **Prices:** Fixed L £10-£20, Fixed D £25-£30, Starter £3-£8, Main £9.95-£25, Dessert £3-£8, Coffee £2.50, Min/Water £5, Service optional **Wine:** 35 bottles over £20, 12 bottles under £20, 6 by the glass (£4-£10) **Notes:** Vegetarian available, Civ Wed 90 **Seats:** 70, Pr/dining room 40 **Smoking:** N/Sm in restaurant **Children:** Portions **Rooms:** 20 (20 en suite) ★★★ **Directions:** 20 mins N of York on the B1257, between Malton and Helmsley **Parking:** 30

England

England

KIRKHAM MAP 19 SE76

Stone Trough Inn

Modern British

Satisfying gastro-pub dining

☎ 01653 618713 Kirkham Abbey, Whitwell on the Hill YO60 7JS
e-mail: info@stonetroughinn.co.uk
web: www.stonetroughinn.co.uk

This red-roofed, yellow-stoned country inn occupies a wonderful elevated position close to romantic ruins. Log fires, flagstone floors, walls full of bric-à-brac and comfortable seating make this a popular dining destination. Service is thoughtful and friendly. The hard-working kitchen produces starters of sautéed wild mushrooms, foie gras and peppercorn brioche followed by roast Flaxton lamb, fondant potatoes, spinach and mild mushrooms rounded off with a passionfruit posset and tuile biscuit. Home-made breads, brioches and petits fours encourage the loyal, local following.

Chef: Adam Richardson **Owners:** Adam & Sarah Richardson **Times:** 12-2.15/6.45-9.30, Closed 25 Dec, 2-5 Jan, Mon, Closed L Tue-Sat, D Sun **Prices:** Starter £4.50-£7.95, Main £10.95-£16.95, Dessert fr £4.75, Coffee £1.95, Min/Water £2.95, Service optional, Group min 25 service 10% **Wine:** 15 bottles over £20, 25 bottles under £20, 10 by the glass (£2.90-£4) **Notes:** Vegetarian available **Seats:** 55 **Smoking:** N/Sm in restaurant **Children:** Menu, Portions **Directions:** 1.5m off the A64, between York & Malton **Parking:** 100

KNARESBOROUGH MAP 19 SE35

General Tarleton Inn

Modern British

Foodie destination in North Yorkshire countryside

☎ 01423 340284 Boroughbridge Rd, Ferrensby HG5 0PZ
e-mail: gti@generaltarleton.co.uk
web: www.generaltarleton.co.uk

The restaurant was originally a land-locked boatyard, but you would never guess from its smart, comfortable seating, exposed brickwork and beamed ceiling. Owned by the team behind the Angel Inn at Hetton (see entry), it's a destination for food-lovers trying exciting pub dining in the bar brasserie, or enjoying the more formal atmosphere of the dining room restaurant. Here you will find honest modern British cooking with the emphasis firmly on seasonal local and regional produce. A typical main course might be roast halibut layered with grain mustard, mushroom duxelle, tomato fondue and soft herb crust. For dessert you could try an old favourite, warm cobble

continued

pudding, which is spiced Yorkshire carrot and walnut cake filled with apple compôte and served with creamed Wensleydale, orange and lemon syrup.

General Tarleton In

Chef: John Topham, Robert Ramsden **Owners:** John & Claire Topham **Times:** 12-1.45/6-9.15, Closed L Mon-Sat, D Sun **Prices:** Fixed L £18.95, Fixed D £29.50, Coffee £1.60, Min/Water £3, Service optional **Wine:** 50 bottles over £20, 26 bottles under £20, 12 by the glass (£2.25-£4.55) **Notes:** Fixed L 3 courses, Vegetarian available, Dress Restrictions, Smart casual **Seats:** 64, Pr/dining room 36 **Smoking:** N/Sm in restaurant **Children:** Menu, Portions **Rooms:** 14 (14 en suite) ★★★ **Directions:** From A1 junct 48 take A6055 towards Knaresborough. Continue for 4 mins, Inn is situated on right in the village of Ferrensby **Parking:** 40

Restaurant 48

European

Simple cooking in a relaxed hotel setting

☎ 01423 863302 Dower House Hotel, Bond End HG5 9AL
e-mail: enquiries@bwdowerhouse.co.uk
web: www.bwdowerhouse.co.uk

This is the restaurant of the Dower House Hotel, an extended 15th-century property of some character standing in pleasant gardens on the outskirts of town. Public rooms comprise a cosy bar and lounge, and the restaurant, which overlooks the garden and terrace. Nicely presented dishes might include Moroccan spiced sausages with butternut squash and mint yogurt, sea bass with braised fennel and saffron potatoes, and an unusual but successful blueberry cheesecak with crème brûlée and fig and lemon sorbet. The hotel also has two function rooms and a health and leisure club.

Chef: Michael Wright **Owners:** Ashdale UK Ltd, Martin Wicks **Times:** 12-2/7-9.30 **Prices:** Fixed L £9-£19, Fixed D £17-£29, Starter £3.95-£6.75, Ma £9-£19, Dessert £3.50-£6, Coffee £2.50, Min/Water £2.75, Service optional **Wine:** 12 bottles over £20, 30 bottles under £20, 8 by the glass (£2.78-£5.50) **Notes:** Vegetarian available, Dress Restrictions, No shorts, T-shirts. Smart casual preferred, Civ Wed 70 **Seats:** 100, Pr/dining room 20 **Smoking:** N/Sm in restaurant **Children:** Menu, Portions **Rooms:** 31 (3 en suite) ★★★ **Directions:** 2m W of Harrogate on A59. At Harrogate end of Knaresborough High Street **Parking:** 100

England

MALTON MAP 19 SE77

Burythorpe House Hotel

Traditional British

Cosy country house to suit all tastes

☎ 01653 658200 Burythorpe YO17 9LB
e-mail: reception@burythorpehousehotel.com
web: www.burythorpehousehotel.com

Set in pretty woodland, this charming country-house hotel dates back to the 18th century and boasts an extensive range of facilities including a leisure suite, swimming pool and two restaurants. Choose the Conservatory for lighter meals (steak and kidney pudding, gammon steak and pineapple) or the wood-panelled Oak Room for classier fare, such as roast duckling with an orange and Grand Marnier sauce, or chicken with a wild mushroom duxelle, then round off the evening with a game of billiards or a whisky by the fire.

Chef: Mr & Mrs T Austin **Owners:** Mr & Mrs T Austin **Times:** 12-2/7-9.30, Closed Xmas week (except 25 Dec L) **Prices:** Fixed D £21, Starter £3.75-£6.75, Main £7.75-£14.95, Dessert £4.25, Coffee £2.30, Min/Water £2.60, Service optional **Wine:** 12 bottles over £20, 46 bottles under £20, by the glass (£3.20-£4.20) **Notes:** Dress Restrictions, Smart casual **Seats:** 60, Pr/dining room 20 **Smoking:** N/Sm in restaurant, Air con **Children:** Min 7 yrs, Menu, Portions **Rooms:** 16 (16 en suite) ★★★ HH **Directions:** Edge of Burythorpe village, 4m S of Malton **Parking:** 30

MARTON MAP 19 SE78

The Appletree Country Inn

Modern British

Quality food in cosy, country gastro-pub

☎ 01751 431457 YO62 6RD
e-mail: appletreeinn@supanet.com
web: www.appletreeinn.co.uk

The pub was a working farm some 100 years ago, with the farmer's wife serving beer from earthenware jugs in the living room. Today it's still a true country inn, but with a separate bar and dining room. Retaining that rustic pub atmosphere, the restaurant exudes charm with dark-red walls, polished wood tables and masses of candles. It's naturally a thoroughly warm, cosy and friendly affair, too. The cooking fits the bill, simple and unfussy while making good use of local seasonal produce. Take roasted haunch of wild red deer venison with mustard mash and a chocolate-redcurrant jus.

Chef: TJ Drew **Owners:** TJ & Melanie Drew **Times:** 12-2/6.30-9.30, Closed Xmas, 2 weeks Jan, Mon-Tue **Prices:** Starter £4-£8, Main £9-£18, Dessert £4-£6.50, Coffee £2.20, Service optional **Wine:** 39 bottles over £20, 79 bottles under £20, 14 by the glass (£3-£8) **Notes:** Booking essential, Mineral water complimentary, Vegetarian available **Seats:** 24, Pr/dining room 8 **Smoking:** N/Sm in restaurant **Children:** Portions **Directions:** 2m from Kirkbymoorside on A170 towards Pickering, turn right to Marton **Parking:** 30

Swinton Park

MASHAM MAP 19 SE28

Modern British

Elegant and atmospheric luxury castle hotel

☎ 01765 680900 HG4 4JH
e-mail: enquiries@swintonpark.com
web: www.swintonpark.com

Though extended during the Victorian and Edwardian eras, the original part of this castle hotel dates from the 17th century and comes complete with turrets, gatehouse, sweeping drive and a 200-acre estate. Everything about Swinton Park oozes elegance; beautiful day rooms, huge windows, high ceilings, heavy drapes, antiques and portraits, and swish sofas. There's a real sense of grandeur, and Samuel's restaurant doesn't disappoint, with its ornate gold-leaf ceiling, comfortable seating, crisp white linen, impeccable service and views over lake and parkland. The cooking draws heavily on fresh produce from the walled kitchen garden and estate, particularly game, herbs and vegetables. Clean distinct flavours, fine combinations and balance, seasonality and luxury parade on the fixed-price menu repertoire, which at dinner includes a carte (supplemented by a classic 'Provenance' choice at each turn) and nine-course tasting option. So expect a haunch of estate venison with braised faggot, Savoy cabbage, shallot Tatin, celeriac purée and bay leaf jus, and perhaps a hot

chocolate fondant finish, teamed with a blood orange shot and natural yogurt ice cream. There's an impressive cheese trolley, too.

Chef: Andrew Burton **Owners:** Mr and Mrs Cunliffe-Lister **Times:** 12.30-2/7-9.30 **Prices:** Fixed L £14, Fixed D £40, Coffee £3, Min/Water £3.95, Service optional **Wine:** 140 bottles over £20, 35 bottles under £20, 12 by the glass (£5-£7.95) **Notes:** Provenance menu, Tasting menu & Sun L avail, Civ Wed 100 **Seats:** 60, Pr/dining room 20 **Smoking:** N/Sm in restaurant **Children:** Min 8 yrs D, Menu, Portions **Rooms:** 30 (30 en suite) ★★★★ HL **Directions:** On B6267, from Masham follow brown signs for Swinton Park **Parking:** 80

MIDDLESBROUGH MAP 19 NZ41

The Highfield Hotel

French, International NEW

French brasserie-style restaurant

☎ 01642 817638 335 Marton Rd TS4 2PA
e-mail: info@thehighfieldhotel.co.uk
web: www.thehighfieldhotel.co.uk

The La Terrasse restaurant within the hotel has Parisian prints and photographs on the walls, with café style chairs and linen cloths, creating an authentic brasserie feel. Like the décor, the cuisine is classic French brasserie style with international influences and a strong emphasis on seafood. Expect the likes of trio of halibut, mackerel and smoked salmon to start, followed by pan-fried duck breast on vegetable spaghetti with pink peppercorn and honey sauce. There is also a carvery at Sunday lunch and an adjoining brasserie.

Chef: Stephen Wilson/Ivan Lux **Owners:** Oakwell Leisure **Times:** 12-2.30/6-10.30 **Prices:** Fixed L £15, Starter £5.95-£8.95, Main £14.50-£20, Dessert £5.95, Coffee £2, Min/Water £2.95, Service included **Wine:** 30 bottles over £20, 30 bottles under £20, 14 by the glass (£2.85-£4.70) **Notes:** Vegetarian available, Civ Wed 70 **Seats:** 80, Pr/dining room 25 **Smoking:** N/Sm in restaurant **Children:** Menu, Portions **Rooms:** 23 (23 en suite) ★★★ HL **Directions:** Telephone for directions **Parking:** 100

PICKERING MAP 19 SE78

Fox & Hounds Country Inn

Modern British

Village pub with enticing menu

☎ 01751 431577 Main St, Sinnington YO62 6SQ
e-mail: foxhoundsinn@easynet.co.uk
web: www.thefoxandhoundsinn.co.uk

This 18th-century coaching inn in a quiet village setting has an old mounting block outside the front door, and some of the original window frames bear old inscriptions, often on risqué topics. The old bar is comfortable and informal, while the dining room has upholstered chairs and white table linen. Service is attentive. The restaurant is at its best with traditional dishes. Starters of king scallops, black pudding, pork belly and scallions precede a trio of pork comprising roast fillet, home-made pie and a faggot, followed by a dessert of lemon tart.

Chef: Mark Caffrey **Owners:** Mr & Mrs A Stephens **Times:** 12-2/6.30-9, Closed 25-26 Dec **Prices:** Starter £4.25-£6.75, Main £9.75-£15.75, Dessert £4.65, Coffee £1.95, Min/Water £2.50, Service optional **Wine:** 3 bottles over £20, 22 bottles under £20, 6 by the glass (£3) **Notes:** Vegetarian available, Dress Restrictions, Smart casual, No shorts **Seats:** 40, Pr/dining room 12 **Smoking:** N/Sm in restaurant **Children:** Menu **Rooms:** 10 (10

continued

en suite) ★★ HL **Directions:** In centre of Sinnington, 300 yds off A170 between Pickering & Helmsley **Parking:** 35

The White Swan Inn

British NOTABLE WINE LIST

Welcoming inn with pleasing food

☎ 01751 472288 Market Place YO18 7AA
e-mail: welcome@white-swan.co.uk
web: www.white-swan.co.uk

This charming 16th-century coaching inn has been in the Buchanan family for over 20 years and was taken over by the current generation in 1996. It's a place of great character with flagstone floors, log fires and a cosy, intimate dining room - it also has a colourful past as a refuge for salt smugglers. The menu features classic gastro-pub style cooking using locally sourced ingredients - ginger pig from Levisham, for example. Dishes include Levisham Longhorn beef shin and kidney pudding with horseradish and parsley mash.

Notable Wine List: The wine list is full of interest with great detail, focusing on drinking styles and an opening section dedicated to pinot noir.

Chef: Darren Clemmit **Owners:** The Buchanan Family **Times:** 12-2/7-9 **Prices:** Fixed L fr £10, Starter £4.25-£8.95, Main £10.95-£16.95, Dessert £3.95-£5.25, Coffee £2, Min/Water £2.50, Service optional **Wine:** 97 bottles over £20, 43 bottles under £20, 7 by the glass (£3.35-£7.85) **Notes:** Sun L 3 courses £17.95, Vegetarian available, Civ Wed 60 **Seats:** 60, Pr/dining room 18 **Smoking:** N/Sm in restaurant **Children:** Menu, Portions **Rooms:** 21 (21 en suite) ★★ HL **Directions:** A1/A19 towards Thirsk, then A170 to Pickering. Between the church and steam railway station **Parking:** 35

RAMSGILL MAP 19 SE17

Yorke Arms

see opposite

RICHMOND MAP 19 NZ10

Frenchgate Hotel

Modern British V

Restored gentleman's residence with a robust modern menu

☎ 01748 822087 59-61 Frenchgate DL10 7AE
e-mail: info@thefrenchgate.co.uk
web: www.thefrenchgate.co.uk

The hotel is a three-storey Georgian townhouse set in a quiet cobbled street. The building has been beautifully restored, and there are lovel

continued on page 50

Yorke Arms

RAMSGILL MAP 19 SE17

Modern NOTABLE WINE LIST

Character restaurant dedicated to quality

☎ 01423 755243 HG3 5RL
e-mail: enquiries@yorke-arms.co.uk
web: www.yorke-arms.co.uk

Dominating its tiny Dales hamlet, this attractive, creeper-clad former shooting lodge and pub overlooks the village green. Now styling itself a restaurant with rooms, it oozes character and charm. Inside there's wonderful stone flooring, the little back snug still lives on and there's a comfy lounge. As well as the main dining room, there's a cosier, smaller affair for quieter nights, with a roaring fire in the winter months. The main room is equally welcoming with a sophisticated, antique mood, dominated by exposed beams and a huge mirror, while polished floorboards, rugs, a large oak dresser and wooden furniture provide plenty of traditional charm. Service is suitably professional and attentive from a young team. Frances Atkins' highly accomplished, modern-focused cooking comes underpinned by a suitably classical theme. There's great emphasis here on quality throughout, with tip-top local produce from the abundant country larder. Expect clean flavours and an intelligently straightforward and balanced approach that lets ingredients shine, backed by refreshingly simple presentation. The appealing carte includes dishes of the day and there's a six-course tasting option. Expect herb-crusted roast hake served with mussels, peas and a bacon rösti, or perhaps roasted squab pigeon with lentils, roots and a red wine jus, and to finish, how about a Grand Marnier soufflé with chocolate truffle and orange salad.

Notable Wine List: A well chosen and presented wine list with a balanced offering from both Old and New Worlds.

Chef: Frances Atkins, Roger Olive
Owners: Mr & Mrs G Atkins
Times: 12-2/7-9, Closed D Sun (ex residents)
Prices: Fixed L £17.50-£26, Starter £5.95-£11.50, Main £17.50-£24, Dessert £6-£9.95, Coffee £3.50, Min/Water £3.50, Service optional
Wine: 7 bottles under £20, 15 by the glass (£3-£6.50)
Notes: Tasting menu 6 courses £50, Vegetarian available, Dress Restrictions, No jeans or trainers, jacket & tie preferred
Seats: 60, Pr/dining room 20
Smoking: N/Sm in restaurant
Children: Min 12 yrs
Rooms: 14 (14 en suite) ★★★★★ RR
Directions: From Pateley Bridge, turn right onto Low Wath road and continue for 5m, turn right into Ramsgill, Yorke Arms is beside village green
Parking: 20

England

RICHMOND *continued* MAP 19 NZ10

period features, antique furniture throughout, and stunning works of art by five different artists. Modern British cooking with a continental twist includes confit of home-cured bacon with baked beans and poached quail's egg, and fillet of local beef with braised oxtail and thyme jus, with warm coconut rice pudding and mango ice cream to finish. Everything is made on site, including sauces, stocks, ice creams, breads, chocolate and patisserie.

Chef: Matt Allen **Owners:** David & Luiza Todd **Times:** 12-2.30/7-10 **Prices:** Fixed L £10-£15, Fixed D £56, Starter £5-£7, Main £10-£18, Dessert £5-£9, Coffee £1.75, Min/Water £2.90, Service optional **Wine:** 37 bottles over £20, 48 by the glass (£3.35-£10) **Notes:** Vegetarian menu, Dress Restrictions, Smart casual **Seats:** 24, Pr/dining room 16 **Smoking:** N/Sm in restaurant **Children:** Min 6 yrs D, Portions **Rooms:** 8 (8 en suite) ★★ HL **Directions:** Please telephone for details **Parking:** 12

RIPON MAP 19 SE37

The Old Deanery

British, European NEW

A historic setting for memorable dining

☎ 01765 600003 Minster Rd HG4 1QS
e-mail: reception@theolddeanery.co.uk
web: www.theolddeanery.co.uk

Adjacent to one of the oldest cathedrals in England, the Old Deanery dates back to 1625 and is on the site of a former monastery of St Wilfrid. The restaurant combines the original character of the building with sleek modern leather chairs, wooden tables and crystal chandeliers. Served on stylish tableware, diners enjoy succulent British and European fare often sourced from the local area, cooked in a skilful way. Start with slow roast belly of pork with cloves and acacia honey, then move on to roast fillet of salmon, lemon couscous and anchovy beignet. The sophisticated urban bar looks out onto the terraced gardens.

Chef: Barrie Higginbotham **Owners:** Express Terminals Ltd **Times:** 12-2/7-10, Closed 25 Dec, Closed D some Sun evenings **Prices:** Fixed L £7.50, Starter £4.95-£9.95, Main £10.50-£19.50, Dessert £6.25, Coffee £1.85, Min/Water £3, Service optional **Wine:** 10 by the glass (£3.65-£5.65) **Notes:** Sun L 2 courses £12.75, 3 courses £15.75, Vegetarian available, Civ Wed 50 **Seats:** 50, Pr/dining room 30 **Smoking:** N/Sm in restaurant **Children:** Portions **Rooms:** 11 (11 en suite) ★★★ HL **Directions:** A1(M) junct 48 follow A168. At 2nd rdbt take B6265 to Ripon. Past racecourse continue into Ripon for 0.5m to rdbt. Take 3rd exit to Bedern Bank and onto Minster Rd **Parking:** 20

SCARBOROUGH MAP 17 TA08

Beiderbecke's Hotel

Modern International

Buzzing atmosphere with jazz music while you eat

☎ 01723 365766 1-3 The Crescent YO11 2PW
e-mail: info@beiderbeckes.com
web: www.beiderbeckes.com

Marmalade's restaurant in the hotel offers international cuisine with a modern twist. It hosts live music acts at weekends, including the resident jazz band. This is reflected in the décor with red walls setting off jazz pictures and a stage for the musicians. Diners can enjoy the lively atmosphere while they choose from an extensive menu and range of daily specials on the blackboard. Typical dishes include chicken bang bang with spicy peanut sauce to start, followed by stuffed lamb saddle or perhaps Gressingham duck. Desserts might include banana fritters or baked Alaska.

Times: 6-9.30 **Rooms:** 27 (27 en suite) ★★★ HL **Directions:** In town centre, 200 mtrs from rail station

SUTTON-ON-THE-FOREST MAP 19 SE56

The Blackwell Ox Inn

British, Mediterranean NEW

Gastro-pub cooking in refurbished village inn

☎ 01347 810328 & 690758 Huby Rd YO61 1DT
e-mail: enquiries@blackwelloxinns
web: www.blackwelloxinn.co.uk

Dating back to the 1820s, the inn is named after a famous Shorthorn Teeswater ox weighing in at 2,278lb. Today the inn has been modernised and refurbished to provide a bar, lounge bar and smart restaurant. Based on regional cookery from France with a Spanish influence, the menu offers big rustic flavours, rich stews, light shellfish dishes and a great range of charcuterie and cheeses. Sample dishes include sea bass with crab and roast pepper risotto and gazpacho sauce, or confit of pork, cassoulet and vanilla apple salad. Sandwiches and tapas are also available at lunch.

Chef: Steven Holding **Owners:** Blackwell Ox Inns (York) Ltd **Times:** 11.30-2/6-9.30 **Prices:** Fixed L £7.50, Fixed D £13.50, Starter £3.50-£6.50, Main £8.50-£16, Dessert £3.95-£5.95, Coffee £1.95, Min/Water £3, Service included **Wine:** 19 bottles over £20, 38 bottles under £20, 6 by the glass (£3-£3.50) **Notes:** Tasting menu 7 courses £35-40, Sun L 2/3 course from £11.50, Vegetarian available **Seats:** 36, Pr/dining room 16 **Smoking:** N/Sm in restaurant **Children:** Portions **Rooms:** 5 (5 en suite) ♦♦♦♦ **Directions:** A1237 take B1363 to Sutton-on-the-Forest, turn left at T-junct, Inn 50mtrs on right **Parking:** 19

see advert opposite

Rose & Crown

Modern Seafood

Village pub restaurant serving upmarket modern food

☎ 01347 811333 Main St YO61 1DP

A former roadside pub in a village setting midway between York and Helmsley. Relaxed and comfy, the simple beamed interior has open fires, wooden floors and tables. There is a garden at the rear where you can enjoy your meal or a drink during the warmer months. Cooking is French and Mediterranean bistro style. Expect the likes of braised ham rillette and roast Whitby cod with Toulouse sausage and haricot bean cassoulet. The blackboard menu is complemented by

continued

specials with a good choice of fish dishes. Early bird and lunch menus offer good value for money.

Rose & Crown

Chef: Andrew Middleton **Owners:** Andrew & Caroline Middleton
Times: 12-2/6-9.30, Closed 1st 2wks Jan, Mon, Closed D Sun
Prices: Starter £3.95-£9.50, Main £9.50-£26.50, Dessert £4.50-£6.50, Coffee £2.50, Min/Water £2.70, Service optional **Wine:** 35 bottles over £20, 25 bottles under £20, 8 by the glass (£3.50-£6) **Notes:** Sun L 3 courses 17.95, Vegetarian available **Seats:** 44, Pr/dining room 6 **Smoking:** N/Sm n restaurant **Children:** Portions **Directions:** 8m N of York towards Helmsley on B1363 **Parking:** 12

TADCASTER MAP 16 SE44

❀❀ Restaurant Anise

British, French

Modern restaurant in a converted castle hotel

☎ 01937 535317 Hazlewood Castle, Paradise Ln, Hazlewood LS24 9NJ
e-mail: info@hazlewood-castle.co.uk
web: www.hazlewood-castle.co.uk

he hotel has been imaginatively converted from a 950-year-old castle nd stands in 77 acres of parkland. Yet Restaurant Anise is not quite what you'd expect from a castle dining room - a funky, stylish, nodern, eye-catching, bold-coloured brasserie incorporating a bar. nclothed black tables, formally clad staff and views over the elightful gardens and woodland complete an upbeat picture. The itchen's assured cooking displays an emphasis on freshness and avour, while delivering intelligently simple, refined harmonious ishes that admirably lack ostentatious frills. As in boeuf bourguignon ith traditional garnish and cocotte potatoes, or perhaps a tagine of mb with preserved lemon and fluffy couscous. A Cointreau and anilla crème brûlée might finish the meal in style.

hef: Valerie Hamelin **Owners:** Hazlewood Castle Ltd **Times:** 12-2/6-9, losed 25 Dec **Prices:** Fixed D £25-£31, Starter £4.50-£7.95, Main £5.50-5.95, Dessert £4.95, Coffee £2.25, Min/Water £3 **Wine:** 34 bottles over

continued

£20, 7 bottles under £20, 3 by the glass (£5-£8.50) **Notes:** Sun L 1 course £10.95, Civ Wed 120 **Seats:** 50 **Smoking:** N/Sm in restaurant **Children:** Menu, Portions **Rooms:** 21 (21 en suite) ★★★ **Directions:** Signed from A64, W of Tadcaster, 0.5m from A1/M1 **Parking:** 120

WEST WITTON MAP 19 SE08

❀ The Wensleydale Heifer

British **V** **NEW**

Great new seafood restaurant in the Dales

☎ 01969 622322 DL8 4LS
e-mail: info@wensleydaleheifer.co.uk
web: www.wensleydaleheifer.co.uk

Behind the coach house inn frontage is a smart, modern restaurant, with a 'heifer' theme running throughout in the form of pictures and

continued

England

WEST WITTON *continued* MAP 19 SE08

ornaments. Modern art and red flowers on the tables make a bold, colourful statement against the bare white walls. Good quality fresh fish is handled with great simplicity and cooked accurately, served from a fixed price lunch menu plus specials, and an evening carte. The fish soup is a must, though the likes of whole grande dorade baked with crab and prawns, or Whitby cod, crackling Black Sheep beer batter with goose fat chips and posh mushy peas could be hard to resist. Meat dishes are available using local organic suppliers.

Chef: David Moss **Owners:** David & Lewis Moss **Times:** 12-2.30/6.15-9.30 **Prices:** Fixed L £11.95-£14.95, Fixed D £14.50-£16.50, Starter £4.50-£12, Main £9.75-£22, Dessert £5, Coffee £2.50, Min/Water £3, Service added but optional 10% **Wine:** 15 bottles over £20, 31 bottles under £20, 11 by the glass (£3.50-£4.50) **Notes:** Sunday lunch 2 courses £14.50, 3 courses £16.95, Vegetarian menu **Seats:** 70 **Smoking:** N/Sm in restaurant **Children:** Portions **Rooms:** 9 (9 en suite) ★★ HL **Directions:** On A684 (3m W of Leyburn) **Parking:** 30

see advert opposite

WHITBY MAP 19 NZ81

Dunsley Hall

Modern British V

Modern culinary delights in a fine country house

☎ 01947 893437 Dunsley YO21 3TL
e-mail: reception@dunsleyhall.com
web: www.dunsleyhall.com

Reassuringly elegant and comfortable, this fine country house is located amid acres of gardens on the Whitby coastline. The original wooden panelling and fireplaces have been carefully preserved, and the atmosphere is relaxed and friendly. An amuse-bouche and an intermediate course inject an unhurried feel, and the modern menus with French influences are well worth lingering over. An enthusiastic team makes the most of the fine produce harvested locally from the land and sea. A sample menu offers starters of deep-fried spiced squid or sautéed Whitby scallops with a raisin and caper salad, while mains include grilled silver hake with dill velouté and wilted greens or rack of Dales lamb with parsnip purée, roast chestnuts and barley jus.

Chef: Mike Boyle Cook **Owners:** Mr & Mrs W Ward **Times:** 12-2/7.30-9.30, Closed L Mon-Sat **Prices:** Fixed D £29.95, Starter £6-£8.50, Main £18.50, Dessert £6.50, Coffee £2, Min/Water £3.50, Service optional **Wine:** 21 bottles over £20, 37 bottles under £20, 10 by the glass (£3.50) **Notes:** Fixed D 6 courses, Vegetarian menu, Dress Restrictions, Smart dress, no jeans or shorts, Civ Wed 75 **Seats:** 85, Pr/dining room 30 **Smoking:** N/Sm in restaurant **Children:** Min 5 yrs, Menu, Portions **Rooms:** 18 (18 en suite) ★★★ CHH **Directions:** 3.5m from Whitby off A171 Teeside road **Parking:** 18

Estbek House

Modern British, European

Good seafood dining in an attractive, historic, village restaurant

☎ 01947 893424 East Row, Sandsend YO21 3SU
e-mail: reservations@estbekhouse.co.uk
web: www.estbekhouse.co.uk

Situated in an 18th-century building on the village seafront, this fish restaurant offers alfresco dining in its cobbled courtyard or inside in full view of the open-plan kitchen and small bar. Attentive staff advise on wine and the ever-changing fish menu with lots of locally smoked fish. Start with the herb-scented lobster cheesecake served with sections of lobster claw meat before a main course of delicate lemon sole with sauvignon blanc cream sauce and bouquetière vegetables. Finish with the crispy topped, fruity bread-and-butter pudding with a jug of crème anglaise.

Chef: Tim Lawrence **Owners:** D Cross, T Lawrence **Times:** 6-9, Closed L all week **Prices:** Starter £4.95-£7.95, Main £13.95-£23.95, Dessert £5.50, Coffee £2.25, Min/Water £3.45, Service optional **Wine:** 27 bottles over £20, 30 bottles under £20, 6 by the glass (£3.25-£6.25) **Notes:** Vegetarian available **Seats:** 40, Pr/dining room 22 **Smoking:** N/Sm in restaurant **Children:** Portions **Rooms:** 5 (4 en suite) ★★★★ RR **Directions:** From Whitby follow A174 towards Sandsend, Estbek just befor bridge **Parking:** 6

see advert opposit

The White Horse & Griffin

Modern, Traditional European

Bistro fare in historic coaching inn

☎ 01947 825026 & 604857 Church St YO22 4BH
e-mail: info@whitehorseandgriffin.co.uk
web: www.whitehorseandgriffin.co.uk

continue

Steeped in history, this one-time coaching inn dates back to the 17th century and has played host to many celebrities through the years. It still retains many original features and includes three unpretentious dining areas all with different moods. The kitchen appropriately delivers crowd-pleasing bistro cooking, using locally-sourced meat and fish direct from the boats; a variety of breads are made here each day. Expect dishes such as moules marinière, or, from the day's catch, perhaps Dover sole, halibut or lobster, and to finish an apple and Armagnac prune crumble with crème anglaise.

Chef: S Perkins, K Healy, B Davies **Owners:** June & Stewart Perkins **Times:** 12-3/5-9, Closed D 25 Dec **Prices:** Starter £4.70-£8.95, Main £12.95-£22, Dessert £5.95-£9.50, Coffee £2, Min/Water £2.95 **Wine:** 10 by the glass **Notes:** Vegetarian available **Seats:** 75, Pr/dining room 36 **Smoking:** N/Sm area **Children:** Menu, Portions **Rooms:** 10 (10 en suite) ◆◆◆ **Parking:** 3

Magpie Café

☎ 01947 602058 14 Pier Rd YO21 3PU

Overlooking Whitby harbour, this is an ideal location to enjoy local fish, seafood and Magpie Café specialities.

YARM MAP 19 NZ41

Judges Country House Hotel

Modern French

Delightful conservatory restaurant offering bold cooking

☎ 01642 789000 Kirklevington TS15 9LW
e-mail: enquiries@judgeshotel.co.uk
web: www.judgeshotel.co.uk

Built in 1881 the house was privately owned before becoming an army HQ in WWII, then in the 1980s it was the formal lodging for circuit court judges, hence its name. The classical décor and friendly atmosphere make it a memorable place to visit. Culinary highlights in the dining room include the 'Stinking Bishop' soufflé starter. Main courses reflect the use of local produce with the likes of local hare, local fillet of beef and local lamb in a variety of guises. A break with all that is classical and traditional sees the appearance of a way-out American-style dessert, 'The Elvis', featuring peanut butter ice cream with pancetta, strawberry jelly, brioche and banana - and why not?

Chef: John Lyons **Owners:** Mr M Downs **Times:** 12-2/7-9.30 **Prices:** Fixed L £17.50-£29.50, Fixed D £37.50-£45, Coffee £3.75, Min/Water £4.50, Service optional **Wine:** 150 bottles over £20, 18 bottles under £20, 8 by the glass (£4.75-£8.25) **Notes:** Fixed L 3 courses, Vegetarian available, Dress Restrictions, Jacket & tie preferred, No jeans, Smart dress, Civ Wed 200 **Seats:** 60, Pr/dining room 50 **Smoking:** N/Sm in restaurant **Children:** Menu, Portions **Rooms:** 21 (21 en suite) ★★★ HL **Directions:** 1.5m from junct W A19, take A67 towards Kirklevington, hotel 5m on left **Parking:** 110

England

England

YORK MAP 16 SE65

Blue Bicycle

Modern European

Popular bistro-style city-centre restaurant

☎ 01904 673990 34 Fossgate YO1 9TA
e-mail: info@thebluebicycle.com
web: www.thebluebicycle.com

One of York's best-loved restaurants, this buzzy city centre eatery is popular with locals and tourists alike. You'll easily spot the blue bicycle propped up outside the bright shop-front style window and entrance to the restaurant. The chef brings creative touches to popular dishes, delivering a wide-ranging modern European menu with an emphasis on local ingredients, including fish and game in season. The lunch menu offers a choice of lighter dishes like Thai crab cakes, or more substantial dishes and grills. Dinner offers a weightier choice and more complex dishes like brie and cranberry Wellington.

Chef: Simon Hirst **Owners:** Lawrence Anthony Stephenson **Times:** 12-2.30/6-9.30, Closed 25-26 Dec, 1-2 Jan, Closed L 24, 31 Dec **Prices:** Starter £5-£9.75, Main £14.50-£19.75, Dessert £6.50-£9, Coffee £2.50, Min/Water £3.20, Service added but optional 10% **Wine:** 38 bottles over £20, 36 bottles under £20, 19 by the glass (£3.50-£5.50) **Notes:** Fixed D parties of over 20 only, Vegetarian available **Seats:** 83, Pr/dining room **Smoking:** N/Sm in restaurant **Directions:** Located in centre of York, just off Parliament St **Parking:** On street & NCP

D.C.H

Modern British

Fine dining with great views of York Minster

☎ 01904 625082 Duncombe Place YO1 7EF
e-mail: sales@deancourt-york.co.uk
web: www.deancourt-york.co.uk

Originally built to house the clergy, this smart hotel enjoys an enviable location overlooking the Minster. It's been sensitively refurbished in an elegant, contemporary style and offers two dining options - the popular D.C.H. restaurant for fine dining and the café-bistro, The Court. The former offers a fairly extensive menu with a wonderful array of modern British favourites cooked expertly - beef carpaccio with horseradish remoulade or warm quiche of Whitby crab to start, for example, followed by lamb shank with cardamom sauce or the chef's signature dish of monkfish and scallops in a chilli broth. The excellent presentation, obvious use of fresh, local produce and assured cooking make this a place worth repeat visits - as does the selection of desserts.

D.C.H.

Chef: Andrew Bingham **Owners:** Mr B A Cleminson **Times:** 12.30-2/7-9.30, Closed L 31 Dec, D 25 Dec **Prices:** Fixed L £13.50-£14, Starter £6.25-£10, Main £15-£21, Dessert £5.75-£7.50, Coffee £2.10, Min/Water £2.85 **Wine:** 80 bottles over £20, 8 bottles under £20, 20 by the glass (£3.75-£10) **Notes:** Vegetarian available, Civ Wed 54 **Seats:** 60, Pr/dining room 40 **Smoking:** N/Sm in restaurant, Air con **Children:** Menu, Portions **Rooms:** 37 (37 en suite) ★★★ HL **Directions:** City centre, directly opposite York Minster **Parking:** Hotel parking

The Grange Hotel

Modern British

Creative modern cooking in a Regency townhouse

☎ 01904 644744 1 Clifton YO30 6AA
e-mail: info@grangehotel.co.uk
web: www.grangehotel.co.uk

Located within walking distance of the city centre, this smart townhouse hotel offers a choice of three eateries, boasting a brasserie and seafood bar, in addition to its fine dining restaurant. The latter is the main draw, a lavishly decorated venue known as the Ivy Brasserie, which makes good on the promise of an ambitious menu by delivering top-notch French and Mediterranean cuisine. Classics and old favourites shore up the selection, but are brought up to date with modish ingredients and imaginative twists. You might start with jellied knuckle of ham with sauce gribiche, and then tuck into roast duck with

continued

creamed cabbage and chicory tart, or Yorkshire rib with watercress purée. Save room for a dessert - perhaps roast figs with fudge parfait.

The Grange Hotel

Chef: Philip Upton **Owners:** Jeremy & Vivien Cassel **Times:** 12-2/6-10, Closed L Mon-Sat, D Sun **Prices:** Fixed L fr £14.95, Fixed D £19.95-£25.95, Starter £4.50-£7.50, Main £11.50-£17.50, Dessert £5-£6.50, Coffee £2, Min/Water £3, Service optional **Wine:** 18 bottles over £20, 23 bottles under £20, 14 by the glass (£3.50-£5) **Notes:** Sun L 2 courses £12.95, 3 courses £15.95, Smart casual preferred, Civ Wed 60 **Seats:** 60, Pr/dining room 60 **Smoking:** N/Sm in restaurant **Children:** Portions **Rooms:** 30 (30 en suite) ★★★ HL **Directions:** A19 York/Thirsk road, approx 400 yds from city centre **Parking:** 30

Melton's

British

Carefully prepared modern dishes in a family-run carefree setting

☎ 01904 634341 7 Scarcroft Rd YO23 1ND
e-mail: greatfood@meltonsrestaurant.co.uk
web: www.meltonsrestaurant.co.uk

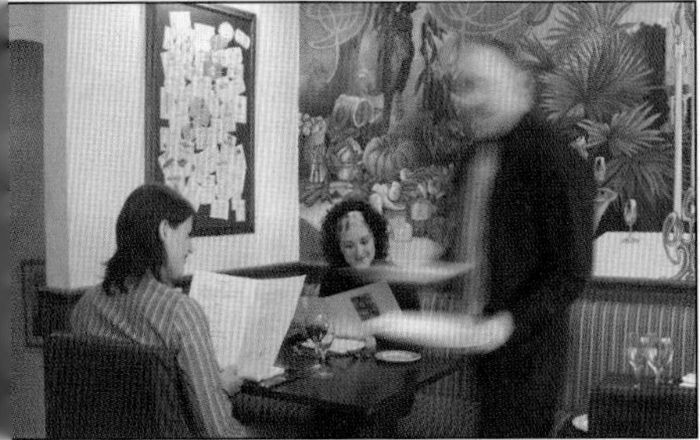

The Victorian terraced frontage conceals a bright and modern dining room with a bustling ambience. The walls are covered with mirrors

continued

and murals depicting a chef and his customers going about their business. Unclothed tables, simple settings and friendly service contribute to the relaxing and enjoyable atmosphere. Simple dishes are carefully prepared and cooked in the modern British style with French and Italian influences. Flavour here is everything. Try the Whitby crab and smoked salmon with devilled toast and cucumber relish to start, followed by roast cod fillet with salsa verde. Desserts are comforting and old-fashioned such as creamy rice pudding with home-made raspberry jam ripple ice cream.

Chef: Michael Hjort, Annie Prescott **Owners:** Michael & Lucy Hjort **Times:** 12-2/5.30-10, Closed 3 wks Xmas, 1wk Aug, Sun, Closed L Mon **Prices:** Food prices not confirmed for 2007. Please telephone for details **Wine:** 58 bottles over £20, 37 bottles under £20, 6 by the glass (£3.75) **Notes:** Min water included **Seats:** 30, Pr/dining room 16 **Smoking:** N/Sm in restaurant, Air con **Children:** Portions **Directions:** South from centre across Skeldergate Bridge, restaurant opposite Bishopthorpe Road car park **Parking:** Car park opposite

Middlethorpe Hall & Spa

see page 508

One 19 The Mount

British

Quality cooking in a popular hotel

☎ 01904 619444 Mount Royale, The Mount YO24 1GU
web: www.mountroyale.co.uk

Its position in a hotel close to the town centre makes this an ideal dining venue for tourists, locals and business people alike. Delightful gardens overlooked by a bright, modern restaurant and separate bar have their own appeal, while a beauty therapist, swimming pool, sauna and hot tub are attractions for residents. The menu offers a good balance with daily specials and vegetarian choices, and the modern cooking is based on sound ingredients and good technical skills. Expect the likes of sautéed king scallops or Thai fishcakes to start, with mains such as sea bass provençale or succulent rack of lamb.

Times: 12-2.30/6-9.30, Closed 1-6 Jan, Sun **Rooms:** 24 (24 en suite) ★★★ HL **Directions:** W on B1036, towards racecourse

York Pavilion Hotel

Traditional Mediterranean

Relaxed, brasserie-style dining in Georgian surroundings

☎ 01904 622099 45 Main St, Fulford YO10 4PJ
e-mail: reservations@yorkpavilionhotel.com
web: www.yorkpavilionhotel.com

Set in an elegant Grade II Georgian house just over a mile from the city walls, the Pavilion's Langton Brasserie is just what its name suggests, a true brasserie-style affair, with floorboards, polished-wood tables and lots of prints and pictures. It's light and airy, too, thanks to high ceilings and large garden windows, while nightfall brings candlelight. The imaginative, sensibly compact menu - bolstered by daily specials - hits just the right note, the up-to-date approach sprinkled with classical touches. So expect the likes of breast of magret duck glazed with balsamic and served with orange truffle crushed potatoes and pancetta, and passionfruit soufflé with tarragon crème brûlée and almond tuile.

continued on page 509

England

Middlethorpe Hall & Spa

YORK MAP 16 SE65

Modern British 

Luxurious dining in an historic setting

☎ 01904 641241 Bishopthorpe Rd, Middlethorpe YO23 2GB
e-mail: info@middlethorpe.com
web: www.middlethorpe.com

Built for a prosperous cutler keen to play the gentleman, Middlethorpe is a magnificent example of a William and Mary country house. It sits in red-brick splendour adjacent to York racecourse amid 20 acres of carefully tended estate that includes a kitchen garden, ha-ha and luxury spa. Afternoon tea in the drawing room is a genteel treat, but save room for the main event - dinner in the wood-panelled restaurant, where quality glassware sparkles in the candlelight and long windows overlook the grounds.

Expect imaginative cooking rooted in classical cuisine and studded with a liberal sprinkling of luxury ingredients; seared diver scallops to start perhaps, served with smoked bacon, parsley risotto and red wine jus, followed by mains such as pork loin and belly with pease pudding, morel custard and baby carrots, or Barbary duck breast with oak-smoked pomme purée, pak choi, turnips and Agen prunes. Diet-breaking desserts might include lemongrass pannacotta with roast pineapple or poppy seed tuile, or butterscotch parfait with caramelised banana and honey syrup.

Notable Wine List: A classic wine list with useful introductions to each section and extensive tasting notes on each wine.

Chef: Lee Heptinstall
Owners: Historic House Hotels Ltd
Times: 12.30-2.15/7-9.45
Prices: Fixed L fr £17, Fixed D fr £39, Coffee £3.50, Min/Water £4, Service included
Notes: Tasting menu 6 courses £55 coffee incl, Sun L £24.50, Vegetarian available, Dress Restrictions, Smart, no trainers, tracksuits or shorts, Civ Wed 56
Seats: 60, Pr/dining room 56
Smoking: N/Sm in restaurant
Children: Min 6 yrs
Rooms: 29 (29 en suite) ★★★★
Directions: 1.5m S of York, beside York racecourse
Parking: 70

YORK *continued* MAP 16 SE65

Chef: Luke Richards **Owners:** Irene & Andrew Cossins **Times:** 12-2/6.30-9.30 **Prices:** Fixed L £12.95-£14.95, Fixed D £25-£30, Starter £4.95-£7.95, Main £13.50-£16.50, Dessert £4.95-£7.95, Coffee £2.20, Min/Water £4, Service optional **Wine:** 36 bottles over £20, 12 bottles under £20, 10 by the glass (£3.50-£7) **Notes:** Vegetarian available, Civ Wed 90 **Seats:** 60, Pr/dining room 150 **Smoking:** N/Sm in restaurant **Children:** Menu, Portions **Rooms:** 57 (57 en suite) ★★★ HL **Directions:** S from York city centre on A19 (Selby), hotel 2m on left. On A1 from N or S take A64 to York, then take Selby/York City Centre A19 junct **Parking:** 50

The Lime House

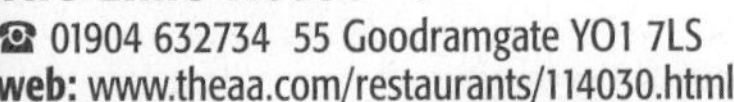

☎ 01904 632734 55 Goodramgate YO1 7LS
web: www.theaa.com/restaurants/114030.html

Excellent food and wine, a relaxed and friendly atmosphere and a regularly changing menu with an international flavour. Good vegetarian choices too.

YORKSHIRE, SOUTH

CHAPELTOWN MAP 16 SK39

Greenhead House

British, European

Exciting food of consistent quality out of the city centre

☎ 0114 246 9004 84 Burncross Rd S35 1SF

A small country house on the outskirts of Sheffield set in a large garden with its own wood oven. Inside you'll find country-style furnishings, a comfortable lounge, oak beams and an open fire. Cooking is inspired but carefully prepared by a skilled kitchen team. Fancy presentation is eschewed; this is good, tasty food served hot as soon as it's ready. The set monthly-changing menu might offer polenta with pan-roasted quails stuffed with Italian sausage, or grilled fillet of skate served on a bed of crushed cauliflower.

Chef: Neil Allen **Owners:** Mr & Mrs N Allen **Times:** 12-1/7-9, Closed Xmas-New Year, 2wks Etr, 2wks end Aug, Sun-Tue, Closed L Wed, Thu & Sat **Prices:** Fixed D £39.95-£44, Starter £4.95-£5, Main £10-£11, Dessert £5.75-£6, Coffee £2.25, Min/Water £2.50, Service included **Wine:** 30 bottles over £20, 10 bottles under £20, 6 by the glass (£4.25-£6.50) **Notes:** ALC L only **Seats:** 32 **Smoking:** N/Sm in restaurant **Children:** Min 7 yrs, Portions **Directions:** 1m from M1 junct 35 **Parking:** 10

ROSSINGTON MAP 16 SK69

Best Western Mount Pleasant Hotel

British, International

Solid, traditional cooking in country-house hotel

☎ 01302 868696 & 868219 Great North Rd, Rossington DN11 0HW
e-mail: reception@mountpleasant.co.uk
web: www.mountpleasant.co.uk

Set in 100 acres of wooded parkland and well-tended gardens, this comfortable country-house hotel is spacious, with a restaurant decorated in tapestries and Grecian-style lighting. The cooking is traditional, with well-cooked, flavoursome dishes like a starter of twice-baked goat's cheese soufflé, followed by a more ambitious fillet of beef with potato galette, white onion ice cream and liquorice jus and a more time-honoured classic like apple tarte Tatin with Calvados syllabub and mint apple ice cream. Finish your dinner by relaxing in one of the hotel's many characterful lounges.

Chef: Dave Booker **Owners:** Richard McIlroy **Times:** 12-2/6.45-9.30, Closed 25 Dec **Prices:** Fixed L fr £15.95, Fixed D £25.75-£33.95, Starter £5.50-£6.95, Main £14.95-£18.95, Dessert £5.25-£7.95, Coffee £2.25, Min/Water £3.95 **Wine:** 24 bottles over £20, 17 bottles under £20, 8 by the glass (£3.25-£6.50) **Notes:** Sun L 3 courses £16.50, Sun D 3 courses £21.95, Vegetarian available, Dress Restrictions, Smart casual preferred, Civ Wed 150 **Seats:** 72, Pr/dining room 200 **Smoking:** N/Sm in restaurant, Air con **Children:** Menu, Portions **Rooms:** 57 (57 en suite) ★★★★ HL **Directions:** Located S of Doncaster, adjacent to Robin Hood Airport, on A638 between Bawtry and Doncaster **Parking:** 100

SHEFFIELD MAP 16 SK38

Artisan

Rosettes not confirmed at time of going to press

Classical **NEW**

Classic chic Parisian-style bistro

☎ 0114 266 6096 32-34 Sandygate Rd, Crosspool S10 5RY
web: www.artisanofsheffield.com

Richard Smith has long been Sheffield's most renowned chef. Five years as Smiths of Sheffield were followed by five years as Thyme (three Rosettes). There were further developments in 2006, with Thyme replaced by two new restaurants, the seafood restaurant Catch (see entry) and Artisan. With décor influenced by Parisian bistro-chic, Artisan offers rustic, hand-crafted food with the emphasis on quality of produce, flavour and taste. Expect the likes of rillettes à la fermière to start, with a main course of Artisan cassoulet and for dessert, a classic tarte Tatin. *The Rosette rating was unconfirmed as we went to press, so please visit our website for the latest update.*

Chef: Simon Wild, Ian Robley, Richard Smith **Owners:** Richard & Victoria Smith **Times:** 12-2.30/6-10 **Prices:** Fixed L £10, Fixed D £25, Starter £5-£15, Main £10-£25, Dessert £4-£8, Coffee £2.50, Min/Water £3, Service included **Wine:** 50 bottles over £20, 50 bottles under £20, 10 by the glass (£3-£7) **Notes:** Tasting menu & Sun L available, Vegetarian available, Dress Restrictions, Casual **Seats:** 60, Pr/dining room 30 **Smoking:** N/Sm in restaurant, Air con **Directions:** Just off A57, in Crosspool suburban shopping centre **Parking:** On street

SHEFFIELD *continued* MAP 16 SK38

Catch

Modern, Traditional NEW

Modern and exciting seafood café

☎ 0114 266 6096 32-34 Sandygate Rd, Crosspool S10 5RY
web: www.catchofsheffield.com

Located upstairs in what was formerly Richard Smith at Thyme restaurant (now refurbished and split into two venues, with Richard's classic Parisian bistro 'Artisan' downstairs), the aptly named Catch is modelled as a modern seafood café, vibrantly stylish, modern and exciting. The interior design has a fish market feel, with metal-topped tables, white-tiled walls and daily-changing blackboard menus suspended from metal racks by meat hooks. Its kitchen is dedicated to delivering fresh, high-quality seafood and has its own in-house fishmonger who buys-in daily. The concept's bold, the cooking accomplished with influences from around the globe; think fish finger butty with tartare sauce to mini fish tapas, or Portuguese fisherman's stew with chorizo and squid to luxury fruits de mer.

Chef: Jack Baker **Owners:** Richard & Victoria Smith **Times:** 12-3/6-10 **Prices:** Fixed L £10, Fixed D £15, Starter £3-£12, Main £9-£30, Dessert £5-£6, Coffee £2, Min/Water £3, Service optional **Wine:** 10 bottles over £20, 10 bottles under £20, 6 by the glass (£3-£6) **Seats:** 30, Pr/dining room 30 **Smoking:** N/Sm in restaurant, Air con **Children:** Portions **Directions:** Please telephone for directions **Parking:** On street

Rafters Restaurant

Modern British, European

Popular neighbourhood restaurant in a leafy area

☎ 0114 230 4819 220 Oakbrook Rd, Nethergreen S11 7ED
web: www.raftersrestaurant.co.uk

continued

Rafters Restaurant

The restaurant is located above a row of shops in a well known suburb of Sheffield. Original rafters, oak beams and exposed brickwork feature, along with contemporary soft furnishings and overhanging lighting, creating a bright and cosy atmosphere. The menu is modern European with influences from around the world in dishes of wonton leaves layered with dressed white crab meat and served with a compôte of apple, sunblush tomato and crayfish tail as a starter, and a main course of pan-fried fillet of Angus beef with sautéed foie gras, autumn mushrooms and Shiraz wine jus. The perfect finish is the bread and butter pudding layered with dried fruits.

Chef: Marcus Lane, Michael Sabin **Owners:** Marcus Lane, Michael Sabin **Times:** 7-10, Closed 25-26 Dec, 1wk Jan, 2 wks Aug, Sun, Tue, Closed L all week **Prices:** Fixed D £27.95, Coffee £2.95, Min/Water £3, Service optional, Group min 8 service 10% **Wine:** 25 bottles over £20, 27 bottles under £20, 6 by the glass (£3.50-£3.95) **Notes:** Vegetarian available, Smart casual **Seats:** 38 **Smoking:** N/Sm in restaurant, Air con **Children:** Min 5 yrs, Portions **Directions:** 5 mins from Eccleshall road, Hunters Bar rdbt **Parking:** 15

Staindrop Lodge Hotel

British, European

Art deco-style brasserie in a smart hotel

☎ 0114 284 3111 Ln End, Chapeltown S35 3UH
e-mail: info@staindroplodge.co.uk
web: www.staindroplodge.co.uk

Bar, brasserie and hotel occupying an extended and refurbished 200-year-old building on the north side of the city, handy for the M1. The split-level restaurant is in art deco style with lots of glass and a solid floor. The menu reflects influences from around the world, with dishes such as duck wontons with a spaghetti of cucumber, sliced spring onions and hoi sin sauce, and cannon of English lamb with potato and mint soufflé and sautéed pak choi. A similar menu is also available in the bar.

Times: 12/9.30 **Rooms:** 32 (32 en suite) ★★★ **Directions:** Take A629 towards Huddersfield, go straight at first rdbt, at mini rdbt take right fork. Restaurant is 0.5 miles on the right

England

YORKSHIRE, WEST

CLIFTON MAP 16 SE12

The Black Horse Inn

Modern British

Welcoming Yorkshire coastal inn with enjoyable dining

☎ 01484 713862 HD6 4HJ
e-mail: mail@blackhorseclifton.co.uk
web: www.blackhorseclifton.co.uk

A traditional village inn with a cheerful pub atmosphere and good coastal views. The modern facilities might seem out of place in this former Luddite meeting house. Gone are Roy Orbison, Danny La Rue and other cabaret stars of the 1970s. Today's guests come here for traditional dishes with the occasional European or Asian flourish, such as confit pig cheek with shiitake mushroom broth, lobster and fennel risotto, or Yorkshire lamb noisettes with pommes Anna. To finish try the apple and rhubarb crumble with crème anglaise.

Chef: Kevin Grady/Darren Marshall **Owners:** Andrew & Jane Russell **Times:** 12-5.30/5.30-9.30, Closed D 25-26 Dec **Prices:** Fixed D £16.95, Starter £4.25-£7.95, Main £10.50-£18.95, Dessert £4.95-£7.50, Coffee £1.85, Min/Water £2.85, Service optional **Wine:** 70 bottles over £20, 40 bottles under £20, 22 by the glass (£3.20-£6.95) **Notes:** Fixed D 5.30-7pm, Vegetarian available, Civ Wed 60 **Seats:** 80, Pr/dining room 60 **Smoking:** N/Sm in restaurant **Children:** Menu, Portions **Directions:** M62 junct 25, Brighouse and follow signs **Parking:** 60

DEWSBURY MAP 16 SE22

Healds Hall Hotel

Modern British

Charming, 18th-century family-run hotel with bistro and restaurant

☎ 01924 409112 Leeds Rd, Liversedge WF15 6JA
e-mail: enquire@healdshall.co.uk
web: www.healdshall.co.uk

This attractive, stone-built 18th-century country house set in peaceful gardens was formerly a mill owner's grand house and has links to the Brontë family. There's a lively, modern bistro and cosy bar, but it's the classic, fine-dining Harringtons Restaurant that's at its heart. The cooking has a strong emphasis on using local produce; take grilled fillet of beef topped with Yorkshire blue cheese, crispy shallot fritters and a port wine sauce. Daily blackboard specials, a good range of Yorkshire cheeses and polite, friendly service bolster the act.

continued

Chef: Phillip McVeagh, David Winter **Owners:** Mr T Harrington **Times:** 12-2/6-10, Closed 1 Jan, BHs, Closed L Sat, D Sun (ex residents) **Prices:** Fixed L £7.50, Starter £3.95-£6.50, Main £12-£17.50, Dessert £4.25-£4.75, Coffee £1.70, Min/Water £3.20, Service optional **Wine:** 21 bottles over £20, 31 bottles under £20, 8 by the glass (£2.75-£3.50) **Notes:** Sun L £16.50, Vegetarian available, Smart casual, Civ Wed 100 **Seats:** 46, Pr/dining room 30 **Smoking:** N/Sm in restaurant, Air con **Children:** Portions **Rooms:** 24 (24 en suite) ★★★ HL **Directions:** M1 junct 40, A638, From Dewsbury take the A652 (signed Bradford). Turn left at A62 and then 50 yds on right **Parking:** 90

HALIFAX MAP 19 SE02

Holdsworth House Hotel

Modern British

Magnificent Jacobean manor-house dining

☎ 01422 240024 Holdsworth HX2 9TG
e-mail: info@holdsworthhouse.co.uk
web: www.holdsworthhouse.co.uk

This delightful 17th-century manor house set in well-tended gardens is an oasis of calm, even though it's set on the outskirts of town. The interior is warm and welcoming with bags of period features; think exposed beams, crooked floors, real fires and oil paintings. The restaurant comprises three interconnecting, aptly named rooms - the oak-panelled Panel Room, the Mullion Room with its leaded windows, and the more informal Stone Room - all laid out with smart table appointments that lend an air of elegance. The kitchen makes creative use of quality local produce as in braised shoulder of Swaledale lamb with creamy Savoy cabbage and sweet potato purée or pan-fried loin of Grizedale venison with home-made black pudding. Desserts include pecan pie with vanilla and walnut ice cream.

Chef: Garry Saunders **Owners:** Gail Moss, Kim Wynn **Times:** 12-2/7-9.30, Closed Xmas, Sun, Closed L Sat **Prices:** Fixed L fr £13.95, Starter £4.95-£8.25, Main £13.75-£19.25, Dessert £6-£10.95, Coffee £2.95, Min/Water £3.25, Service optional, Group min 10 service 10% **Wine:** 40 bottles over £20, 30 bottles under £20, 11 by the glass (£3.25-£6.95) **Notes:** Vegetarian available, Dress Restrictions, Smart casual, no shorts, Civ Wed 120 **Seats:** 45, Pr/dining room 120 **Smoking:** N/Sm in restaurant **Children:** Portions **Rooms:** 40 (40 en suite) ★★★ HL **Directions:** From Halifax take A629 (Keighley), 2m turn right at garage to Holmfield, hotel 1.5m on right **Parking:** 60

England

HALIFAX *continued* MAP 19 SE02

The Old Bore at Rishworth

Modern British V NEW

Traditional coaching inn with a growing reputation for fine food

☎ 01422 822291 Oldham Rd, Rushworth HX6 4QU
e-mail: info@oldbore.co.uk
web: www.oldbore.co.uk

This recently converted 200-year-old coaching inn has a roadside location in pretty countryside. The traditional décor is replete with flagstone floors, stuffed animals and antler chandeliers while the high-backed leather chairs and white linen add a more contemporary touch. The well-conceived menu puts a strong emphasis on seafood, fish and game with a modern British bias to the cooking style Ingredients are sourced from a strong network of local suppliers. A typical starter might be pan-fried hand-dived scallops with cep mushroom risotto, while expect mains like prime Scottish fillet medallion with a parcel of braised oxtail and kidney accompanied by creamy celeriac and horseradish mash.

Chef: Scott Hessel **Owners:** Scott Hessel **Times:** 12-2.15/6-9.30, Closed 25 Dec, 2 wks in Jan, Mon **Prices:** Fixed L fr £9.95, Starter £4.45-£10.95, Main £8.95-£19.95, Dessert £5.45, Coffee £2.45, Min/Water £2.95, Service optional **Wine:** 85 bottles over £20, 30 bottles under £20, 15 by the glass (£2.25-£4.75) **Notes:** Sun L, 2 course £12.95. 3 course £16.95, Vegetarian menu **Seats:** 80, Pr/dining room 20 **Smoking:** N/Sm in restaurant **Children:** Portions **Directions:** M62 junct 22 take A672 towards Halifax, 3m on left after reservoir **Parking:** 20

Shibden Mill

Modern British, European

Secluded inn with a menu to draw the crowds

☎ 01422 365840 Shibden Mill Inn, Shibden Mill Fold, Shibden HX3 7UL
e-mail: enquiries@shibdenmillinn.com
web: www.shibdenmillinn.com

A world away from the hustle and bustle of Halifax, this popular 17th-century inn enjoys an appealing and peaceful setting in the Shibden Valley beside Red Beck. You can dine in both the beamed lounge-style bars, warmed by log fires, and the candlelit loft conversion beneath a raftered ceiling with chandeliers, or outside on the riverside terrace in summer. Expect an exciting menu with imaginative modern twists to classic combinations, as in a starter of roast woodpigeon with beetroot risotto and main courses like venison with spiced red cabbage, vanilla mash and chocolate sauce, and calves' liver, fig and smoked cheese polenta. Good puddings and quality bar meals complete the culinary picture.

Chef: Steve Evans **Owners:** Mr S D Heaton **Times:** 12-2/6-9.30, Closed 25 Dec(Eve), Closed D 26 Dec, 31 Dec **Prices:** Fixed L £8.95, Starter £4.25-£5.75, Main £8.75-£14.95, Dessert £4.50-£4.95, Coffee £1.30, Min/Water £1.90, Service optional **Wine:** 12 bottles over £20, 45 bottles under £20, 13 by the glass (£1.90-£5) **Notes:** Vegetarian available **Seats:** 50, Pr/dining room 10 **Smoking:** N/Sm in restaurant **Children:** Menu, Portions **Rooms:** 12 (12 en suite) ◆◆◆◆ **Directions:** Telephone for directions **Parking:** 100

HAWORTH MAP 19 SE03

Weavers Restaurant with Rooms

Modern, Traditional British

Friendly family-run place with a Northern flavour

☎ 01535 643822 15 West Ln BD22 8DU
e-mail: weaversinhaworth@aol.com
web: www.weaversmallhotel.co.uk

Situated close to the Brontë Parsonage Museum, Weavers is an informal family-run bar and restaurant converted from 18th-century hand loom weavers' cottages. An eccentric collection of mismatched furniture sets the scene and the atmosphere is very relaxed. Northern regional food is on offer, including new ideas, traditional dishes and old favourites the customers won't let them drop. Using ingredients sourced from excellent local suppliers, typical options are butter-basted Goosenargh chicken with minestrone of vegetables and crispy roast potatoes, and chocolate and ginger biscuit cake with Yorkshire tea ice cream. Service is provided by young, friendly staff.

Chef: Colin, Tim & Jane Rushworth **Owners:** Colin & Jane Rushworth (+Family) **Times:** 11.30-2.30/6.30-9.30, Closed 1 wk Xmas, Mon, Closed L Tue & Sat, D Sun **Prices:** Fixed L £10.95, Fixed D £16.95, Starter £5-£6.50, Main £10.50-£17, Dessert £4.95-£6, Coffee £1.95, Min/Water £2.75, Service optional, Group min 6 service 10% **Wine:** 11 bottles over £20, 44 bottles under £20, 10 by the glass (£3.50-£5.50) **Notes:** Sun L 3 courses £16.95 (£19.95 Dec/Mothers Day), Vegetarian available, Dress Restrictions, Clean & tidy **Seats:** 65, Pr/dining room 14 **Smoking:** N/Sm in restaurant, Air con **Children:** Portions **Rooms:** 3 (3 en suite) ★★★ RR **Directions:** From A629 take B6142 towards Haworth, follow signs for Brontë Parsonage Museum use museum car park **Parking:** Brontë Museum car park (free 6pm-8am)

HUDDERSFIELD MAP 16 SE11

The Weavers Shed Restaurant with Rooms

Modern British NOTABLE WINE LIST

Enjoyable regional dining in a contemporary setting

☎ 01484 654284 88 Knowl Rd, Golcar HD7 4AN
e-mail: info@weaversshed.co.uk
web: www.weaversshed.co.uk

This converted 18th-century wool mill has recently undergone refurbishment. Contemporary in style, there are still plenty of original features, including stone and bare wood. The comfortable lounge leads on to an atmospheric dining room. There's a wonderful kitchen garden, which provides fowl, fruit, vegetables and over 70 varieties of wild edibles. Dishes are cooked in the modern British style and based almost without exception on home-grown and local produce. Try the

continued

red onion strudel with white truffle vinaigrette and seasonal leaves and herbs to start. Follow with chargrilled Limousin beef with deep-fried béarnaise and wilted greens. For dessert, try the clafoutis of Forelle pear with crumble ice cream.

Notable Wine List: The wine list shows much effort and thought, with good tasting notes and a focus on smaller, less well known producers.

Chef: S Jackson,I McGunnigle,C Sill **Owners:** Stephen & Tracy Jackson **Times:** 12-2/7-9, Closed 25 Dec-7 Jan, Sun, Mon, Closed L Sat **Prices:** Fixed L fr £13.95, Starter £7.25-£12.95, Main £15.95-£25.95, Dessert £7.95-£9.95, Coffee £2, Min/Water £2.50, Service optional **Wine:** 55 bottles over £20, 26 bottles under £20, 6 by the glass (£3.50) **Seats:** 26, Pr/dining room 16 **Smoking:** N/Sm in restaurant **Rooms:** 5 (5 en suite) ◆◆◆◆ **Directions:** 3m W of Huddersfield off A62. (Please telephone for further directions) **Parking:** 30

ILKLEY MAP 19 SE14

Box Tree see below

Rombalds Hotel & Restaurant

Modern European

Modern international cuisine in a relaxing atmosphere

☎ 01943 603201 11 West View, Wells Rd LS29 9JG
e-mail: reception@rombalds.demon.co.uk
web: www.rombalds.co.uk

An elegantly furnished Georgian townhouse, located in a peaceful terrace between the town and the moors. Local produce features heavily on a menu which draws inspiration from modern English, French and international cooking. Starters range from a simple home-made soup of the day, to braised pig's cheek with celeriac purée and Calvados jus. Main courses are similarly diverse with Cullen skink and melba toast on the one hand, and seared red mullet on a bed of crispy noodles with Thai-style stir-fried vegetables on the other. For dessert why not try a delicious prune and Armagnac brûlée with butter shortbread or the baked Alaska 'Cerise'.

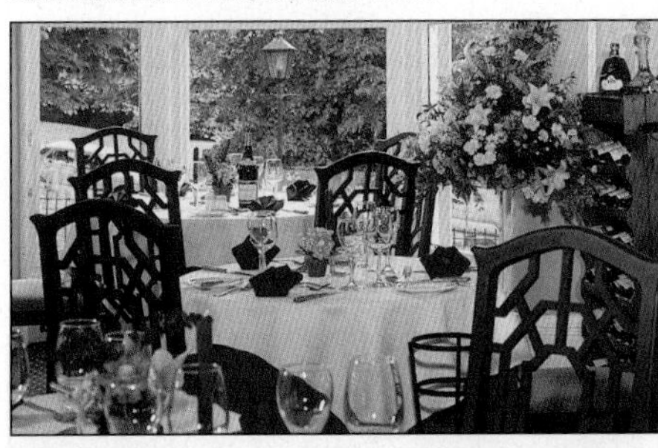

Rombalds Hotel & Restaurant

Chef: Steve Leary **Owners:** Colin & Jo Clarkson **Times:** 12-2/6.30-9, Closed 28 Dec-2 Jan **Prices:** Fixed L £9.95-£12.95, Fixed D £14.95-£17.95, Starter £4.95-£5.95, Main £12.95-£19.50, Dessert £5.25, Coffee £1.95, Min/Water £2.75, Service optional **Wine:** 61 bottles over £20, 56 bottles under £20, 10 by the glass (£2.25-£3.50) **Notes:** Sun L £14.95, Vegetarian available, Smart casual, Civ Wed 70 **Seats:** 34, Pr/dining room 50 **Smoking:** N/Sm in restaurant **Children:** Menu, Portions **Rooms:** 15 (15 en suite) ★★★ HL **Directions:** From Leeds take A65 to Ilkley. At 3rd main lights turn left & follow signs for Ilkley Moor. At junct take Wells Rd, by bank. Hotel 600yds on left **Parking:** 22

Box Tree

ILKLEY MAP 19 SE14

Traditional French (NOTABLE WINE LIST)

Superb cooking in legendary restaurant

☎ 01943 608484 35-37 Church St LS29 9DR
e-mail: info@theboxtree.co.uk
web: www.theboxtree.co.uk

The legendary Box Tree is now safe in the experienced hands of chef Simon Gueller. The 300-year-old, cottage-style restaurant - close to the town centre - is a classical affair, warm and intimate thanks to the cosy dining room's low ceilings, huge stone fireplace, exposed beams and collection of art and antiques. Plush high-backed seating provides comfort, while the elegant, professional service has a genuine friendliness.

Simon's smartly engineered dishes are simply constructed so flavours are strikingly bold and clear, while utilising the freshest seasonal produce. A value prix-fixe lunch and dinner is bolstered by an appealing carte that comes dotted with luxury. Perhaps Anjou squab pigeon breast with quince purée, confit legs, roast foie gras, fondant potatoes and watercress, then a classic hot prune and Armagnac soufflé with fresh vanilla ice cream to finish. Peripherals like breads, canapés and petits fours all hit form, and there's an extensive wine list to enjoy, too.

Notable Wine List: An extensive and well established wine list with a comprehensive offering across all the key wine producing areas.

Chef: Mr S Gueller **Owners:** Mrs R Gueller **Times:** 12-2/7-9.30, Closed Xmas-New Year, 1-5 Jan, Mon, Closed L Tue-Thur, D Sun **Prices:** Fixed L fr £18, Fixed D fr £28, Starter £9-£16, Main £22-£28, Dessert fr £8.50, Coffee £4, Min/Water £3.50 **Wine:** 335 bottles over £20, 11 bottles under £20, 6 by the glass (£5-£6.50) **Notes:** Tasting menu upon request, Vegetarian available, Dress Restrictions, Smart casual **Seats:** 50, Pr/dining room 16 **Smoking:** N/Sm in restaurant, Air con **Children:** Min 10 yrs Sun **Directions:** On A65 from Leeds through Ilkley, main lights approx. 200 yds on left **Parking:** NCP

England

KEIGHLEY MAP 19 SE04

The Harlequin Restaurant

Modern British

Popular cosmopolitan cooking served in style

☎ 01535 633277 139 Keighley Rd, Cowling BD22 0AH

A modern stylish restaurant in a traditional Yorkshire stone converted Victorian house. Comfortable banquette seating and spacious, well-dressed tables set the scene. Style and simplicity are the watchwords here. Flavours are straightforward and enjoyable, drawing diners from near and far. Expect mains such as rack of new season lamb with provençale vegetables and redcurrant and rosemary jus, or traditional roast Norfolk duckling with bilberry and gin sauce. Desserts are a particular highlight, so leave some room to enjoy the likes of rhubarb parfait with ginger tuiles.

Chef: Mr R Gilbert **Owners:** Mr T Zebedee & Ms F McGowan **Times:** 12-3/5.30-11, Closed 4 days at Xmas, BHs, Mon-Tue **Prices:** Starter £4.75-£6.95, Main £10.95-£17.50, Dessert £4.75-£5.50, Coffee £2.50, Min/Water £2.50 **Wine:** 65 bottles over £20, 103 bottles under £20, 14 by the glass (£3-£6) **Notes:** Sun L 3 courses £15.45-£16.95, Vegetarian available **Seats:** 42 **Smoking:** N/Sm in restaurant **Children:** Min 6 yrs D, Portions **Directions:** On A6068 in Cowling village, between Crosshills and Colne. 6m from M65 **Parking:** 10

LEEDS MAP 19 SE23

Anthony's Restaurant

see opposite

Brasserie Forty 4

British, European

Buzzing brasserie overlooking the canal

☎ 0113 234 3232 44 The Calls LS2 7EW
e-mail: info@brasserie44.com
web: www.brasserie44.com

Converted from an old grain store, this bustling eatery is situated on the waterfront with a balcony overlooking the canal. The stylish décor is based around a modern colour scheme of cream and terracotta, creating a warm, welcoming feel that - coupled with this bold, interesting menu and informal, friendly service - is clearly a hit with a wide cross-section of Leeds' diners. The menu offers brasserie standards (Caesar salad, fish cakes, confit duck leg, steak and béarnaise) and places them alongside more original offerings - butter-poached turbot with razor clam vinaigrette for example - all cooked with consummate skill and with an interesting wine list to complement the food.

continued

Chef: David Bukowicki **Owners:** Steve Ridealgh **Times:** 12-2/6-10.30, Closed BHs, Sun, Closed L Sat **Prices:** Fixed L £12.50, Fixed D £19.95, Starter £4.50-£6.75, Main £12.50-£17.50, Dessert £5, Coffee £1.90, Min/Water £1.95, Service added but optional 10% **Wine:** 139 bottles over £20, 34 bottles under £20, 5 by the glass (£3.65-£6.50) **Notes:** Fixed earlybird D incl 1/2 bottle wine **Seats:** 130, Pr/dining room 50 **Smoking:** N/Sm area, No pipes, No cigars, Air con **Children:** Portions **Directions:** From Crown Point Bridge, left past Church, left into High Court Lane. On river **Parking:** On street, NCP

Brontë Restaurant

British, European

Grand dining room offering classic cuisine

☎ 0113 282 1000 De Vere Oulton Hall, Rothwell Ln, Oulton LS26 8HN
e-mail: oulton.hall@devere-hotels.com
web: www.devereonline.co.uk

A Grade II listed mansion dating back over 150 years, carefully restored to combine traditional features and modern comforts. The impressive scale of the hotel can be seen in the grand Brontë restaurant with its cream, dark red and claret décor. English and international cooking is on offer here on an extensive menu littered with fine ingredients. Signature dishes and matching wines are recommended at each course; try langoustine and foie gras ravioli served with lobster jus to start. Main courses might include grilled steaks from the late Queen Mother's estate in the Castle of Mey.

Chef: Steve Collinson **Owners:** De Vere Hotels **Times:** 12.30-2/7-10 **Prices:** Fixed L fr £13.50, Fixed D £25-£35, Starter £6.50-£8.50, Main £14-£28, Dessert £5.50-£8, Coffee £3, Min/Water £3.55 **Wine:** 29 bottles over £20, 20 bottles under £20, 20 by the glass (£4.25-£16.95) **Notes:** Vegetarian available, Dress Restrictions, Smart casual, no T-shirts or shorts, Civ Wed 100 **Seats:** 180, Pr/dining room **Smoking:** N/Sm in restaurant, Air con **Children:** Menu, Portions **Rooms:** 152 (152 en suite) ★★★★★ **Directions:** M62 junct 30 signed Rothwell, or M1 junct 44 signed Pontefract **Parking:** 200

Haley's Hotel & Restaurant

Modern British

Convivial restaurant in a conservation area

☎ 0113 278 4446 Shire Oak Rd, Headingley LS6 2DE
e-mail: info@haleys.co.uk
web: www.haleys.co.uk

A former manor house, this handsome Grade II listed building is located in leafy Headingley a couple of miles from the city centre. The restaurant's traditional décor is in keeping with the setting, with starched white linen, silver cutlery and floral arrangements. Service is

continued

England

Anthony's Restaurant

LEEDS MAP 19 SE23

European

One of the city's most exciting restaurants

☎ 0113 245 5922 19 Boar Ln LS1 6EA
e-mail: reservations@anthonysrestaurant.co.uk
web: www.anthonysrestaurant.co.uk

Large floor-to-ceiling windows - looking into Anthony's light, chic, ground-floor bar with its large, deep leather sofas - picks out this ambitious city restaurant. Stairs lead down to the curved, basement dining room, decorated in clean, modern minimalist lines, its simple colours of cream and chocolate contrasting well with modern art and high-quality cutlery and glassware that grace well-spaced tables. Chef Anthony Flinn's bold, modern cuisine sits well with the surroundings and comes designed to wow and excite; Anthony has an impressive pedigree, having trained with John Campbell (The Vineyard at Stockcross, see entry) and worked at the internationally acclaimed El Bulli restaurant in Spain. The approach is via a compact, crisply-scripted carte, with the kitchen's superbly presented, light style bursting with flavours and surprise. Think roast squab served with foie gras candy and caramelised apple, or John Dory with cock's crest and crispy chicken skin, while a chocolate pot might head up dessert offerings. Much effort goes into the amazing tasters and inter-courses that pepper the repertoire, with pre-starters, amuse-bouche, pre-desserts, petits fours and breads all hitting top form. There's also a good-value fixed-price lunch option and a tasting menu (for the whole table) to complete the exciting package of this rising star.

Chef: Anthony Flinn **Owners:** Anthony Flinn **Times:** 12-2.30/7-9.30, Closed BH incl Tue, wk in Sep, 25 & 26 Dec, Sun, Mon **Prices:** Fixed L £18.95, Starter £7.25-£10.50, Main £19.50-£24.50, Dessert £6.45-£7.50, Coffee £2, Min/Water £1.85, Service optional **Wine:** 100 bottles over £20, 6 bottles under £20, 14 by the glass (£3.69-£7.50) **Notes:** Tasting menu £55, Vegetarian available **Seats:** 36 **Smoking:** N/Sm in restaurant, Air con **Children:** Portions **Directions:** 500 yds from Leeds Central Station towards The Corn Exchange **Parking:** NCP 20 yrds

Haley's Hotel & Restaurant

very effective, delivered with large helpings of northern hospitality. Careful cooking of quality meals is assured, and the presentation suits the style of the establishment. The daily-changing menu offers a choice of modern British dishes with some French influences. Expect the likes of roulade of pigeon with salsify, cod confit with ravioli of potted crayfish and chocolate marquise with honey nougatine, white chocolate and whisky sorbet.

Chef: Charlie Curran **Owners:** Signature Hotels **Times:** 7-9.30, Closed 26-30 Dec, Closed L Mon-Sat, D Sun **Prices:** Starter £4.95-£7.95, Main £17.20-£24.25, Dessert fr £5.25, Coffee £2.50, Min/Water £4.50, Service optional **Wine:** 90 bottles over £20, 15 bottles under £20, 8 by the glass (£4-£10) **Notes:** Sun L 3 courses £19.50, Vegetarian available, Dress Restrictions, No jeans, Civ Wed 100 **Seats:** 60, Pr/dining room 24 **Smoking:** N/Sm in restaurant, Air con **Children:** Portions **Rooms:** 28 (28 en suite) ★★★ HL **Directions:** 2m N of city centre off A660, between HSBC & Starbucks **Parking:** 29

Malmaison Hotel

Modern, Traditional NOTABLE WINE LIST

Funky French brasserie food in stylish hotel

☎ 0113 398 1000 1 Swinegate LS1 4AG
e-mail: leeds@malmaison.com
web: www.malmaison.com

The Leeds offshoot of the chic modern hotel chain is located in an old converted bus company office on Sovereign Quay. It's a stylish, intimate and fashionable venue, with a smart, contemporary interior that features funky bedrooms and a true brasserie-style dining room with panelling and stone floors. Diners can choose between a substantial snack and a three-course meal on the seasonally-changing menu. Uncomplicated cooking offers dishes like seared scallops with parsnip purée, followed by steak and frites or confit duck with thyme jus, finished off with rice pudding.

Notable Wine List: A really high-quality wine list with concise tasting notes throughout offering an interesting and diverse mix of wines.

Chef: Tom Van Zeller **Owners:** Malmaison **Times:** 12-2.30/6-11 **Prices:** Fixed L £12.50, Fixed D £14.50, Starter £4.50-£7.95, Main £10.50-£23.95, Dessert £4.95, Coffee £1.95, Min/Water £2.75, Service added but optional 10% **Wine:** 118 bottles over £20, 14 bottles under £20, 12 by the glass (£4.75-£7.50) **Notes:** Vegetarian available **Seats:** 95, Pr/dining room 12 **Smoking:** N/Sm in restaurant **Children:** Portions **Rooms:** 100 (100 en suite) ★★★ HL **Directions:** City centre. 5 mins walk from Leeds railway station. On junct 16 of Loop Road, Sovereign St & Swinegate **Parking:** Criterion Place car park

LEEDS *continued* MAP 19 SE23

Quantro

Modern European

Imaginative cooking in chic surroundings

☎ 0113 288 8063 62 St Lane LS8 2DQ
e-mail: info@quantro.co.uk
web: www.quantro.co.uk

A sophisticated interior in shades of lime and aubergine, with chunky banquette seating and dark wood tables, characterises this chic restaurant. The atmosphere is relaxed and unpretentious and the service is polished, yet discreet. Modern European menus are cutting edge as befits its metropolitan setting and offer great interest and variety. Cooking style is crisp and succinct with clear flavours, accurate timings, and minimal seasoning thanks to fresh, vibrantly flavoured produce. Tuck into crayfish, mussel and squid chowder, follow with calves' liver with Madeira jus, and finish with dark chocolate pot.

Chef: Andrew Brooks **Owners:** Tim and Kath Burdekin **Times:** 12-2/6-10, Closed 25-26 Dec, 1 Jan, Sun **Prices:** Fixed L £9.95-£12.95, Starter £3.90-£5.90, Main £9.20-£14.90, Dessert £3.25-£3.85, Coffee £1.95, Service added but optional 10% **Wine:** 12 bottles over £20, 37 bottles under £20, 13 by the glass (£3-£6) **Notes:** Vegetarian available, Dress Restrictions, Smart casual preferred **Seats:** 60 **Smoking:** N/Sm in restaurant, Air con **Children:** Min 8 yrs **Directions:** Near Roundhay Park **Parking:** On Street

Simply Heathcotes Leeds

British

Converted warehouse with a friendly bistro feel

☎ 0113 244 6611 Canal Wharf, Water Ln LS11 5PS
e-mail: leeds@heathcotes.co.uk
web: www.heathcotes.co.uk

This trendy brasserie is located in a former warehouse overlooking the Leeds-Liverpool canal - indeed, in its heyday, canal boats used to travel through the warehouse to unload. Nowadays the old stone walls and exposed beams are complemented by low-key modern décor with an upstairs bar lounge for reclining and imbibing. The food is contemporary British in style with a bistro feel - there's even a section called 'Heathcote's comfort' with dishes like Pendle lamb shepherd's pie or deep-fried black pudding in beer batter with chips. More sophisticated fare is on offer with roast salmon fillet with marinated cucumber salad or confit shoulder of Pendle lamb, but the emphasis is still firmly on big, satisfying flavours.

Chef: Simon Peacock **Owners:** Paul Heathcote **Times:** 12-2.30/6-10, Closed 25-26 Dec, 1-2 Jan, BH Mons **Prices:** Fixed L £12.95, Starter £2.75-£6, Main £8.50-£20, Dessert £4-£4.95, Coffee £1.80, Min/Water £3.50,

continued

Service optional, Group min 8 service 10% **Wine:** 48 bottles over £20, 18 bottles under £20, 10 by the glass (£3.85-£5.50) **Notes:** Fixed D 2 courses until 7pm, Vegetarian available **Seats:** 110 **Smoking:** N/Sm in restaurant, Air con **Children:** Menu, Portions **Directions:** 0.5m from M621 junct 3; follow signs to city centre, turn left into Water Lane, then right on Canal Wharf. On Canal Basin **Parking:** 20

Thorpe Park Hotel & Spa

Modern British

Chic modern dining showcasing local produce

☎ 0113 264 1000 Century Way, Thorpe Park LS15 8ZB
e-mail: thorpepark@shirehotels.com
web: www.shirehotels.com

A modern hotel with state-of-the-art spa and contemporary comforts. The range of dining options includes a spacious open-plan restaurant furnished with lightwood and leather. There is an open fire lit in winter and a large alfresco terrace for summer dining. Cuisine reflects the Yorkshire area with maximum use of seasonal ingredients from local suppliers. Try a starter of Whitby crab and avocado salad, perhaps a main course of honey roasted locally reared belly of saddleback pork or duck shepherd's pie, and follow that up with a dessert like a warm chocolate brownie with espresso ice cream.

Chef: Darren Winder **Owners:** Shire Hotels **Times:** 12-2/6.45-9.30, Closed L Sat & Sun **Prices:** Fixed L fr £14.50, Starter £5-£10, Main £15-£30, Dessert £7-£10, Coffee £3.50, Min/Water £3, Service optional **Wine:** 10 by the glass **Notes:** Vegetarian available, Civ Wed 90 **Seats:** 120, Pr/dining room 50 **Smoking:** N/Sm in restaurant, Air con **Children:** Menu, Portions **Rooms:** 123 (123 en suite) ★★★★ HL **Directions:** Telephone for directions **Parking:** 200

Bibis

☎ 0113 243 0905 Minerva House, 16 Greek St LS1 5RU
Bustling contemporary Italian.

Georgetown

☎ 01926 863645 Dysons Clock Building, 24-26 Briggate LS1 6EP
web: www.theaa.com/restaurants/114032.html

Restored Victorian emporium offering authentic Malaysian menu. The Singapore Slings are a must.

MARSDEN MAP 16 SE01

Hey Green Country House Hotel

Modern British

Modern brasserie in elegant surroundings

☎ 01484 844235 Waters Rd HD7 6NG
e-mail: info@heygreen.com
web: www.heygreen.com

Crowther's Brasserie is situated in the oldest part of the hotel, with a superb flagstone floor and open fire burning throughout winter. An archway leads into little dining areas creating a sense of intimacy. The imaginative modern British menu draws inspiration from around the world, so expect an eclectic choice. The selection changes frequently reflecting the seasons and market trends. Dishes are innovative in their conception, with exquisite flavour combinations in simple unfussy dishes like guinea fowl with wild mushroom risotto and Madeira jus, or cod with champ potatoes, salsify and red wine sauce. Wonderfully fresh ingredients are carefully sourced and cooked with flair and respect.

Chef: Nigel Skinkis **Owners:** S Hunter, M Dolman **Times:** 12-2.30/7-9.30, Closed 2-5 Jan, Closed L Mon-Sat **Prices:** Fixed L £12.95-£14.95, Fixed D £15-£20, Coffee £1.50, Min/Water £2.50, Service optional **Notes:** Dress Restrictions, Smart casual, no jeans or T-shirts, Civ Wed 120 **Seats:** 44, Pr/dining room 20 **Smoking:** N/Sm in restaurant **Children:** Min 12 yrs, Menu, Portions **Rooms:** 12 (12 en suite) ★★ **Directions:** Telephone for directions **Parking:** 70

see advert on this page

Olive Branch

Modern British NEW

Popular restaurant featuring seasonal produce

☎ 01484 844487 Manchester Rd HD7 6LU
e-mail: mail@olivebranch.uk.com
web: www.olivebranch.uk.com

Formerly an old coaching inn, the Olive Branch is a popular restaurant with rooms and a bar, offering friendly, relaxed service. The surrounding countryside has many historic attractions and pleasant walking. The fixed two- or three-course modern menu offers the best of seasonal and local produce cooked with flair and enthusiasm. Expects mains such as blackened salmon fillet with creamy lime sauce, crispy confit duck leg with onion sultana marmalade and red wine jus, or loin of venison, wild mushrooms, port wine cream and celeriac mash. The wine list is quite extensive.

Chef: Paul Kewley **Owners:** Paul Kewley & John Lister **Times:** 12-2/6.30-9.30, Closed 1st 2 wks Jan, 1 wk Summer, Closed L Mon, Tue, Sat **Prices:** Fixed L fr £10.95, Fixed D £18.50, Starter £4.95-£8.95, Main £11.95-

continued

£19.50, Dessert £5.95, Coffee £1.95, Min/Water £3.25, Service optional **Wine:** 50 bottles over £20, 30 bottles under £20, 12 by the glass (£3.25-£4.95) **Notes:** Fixed D before 7.30pm, Vegetarian available **Seats:** 65, Pr/dining room 40 **Smoking:** N/Sm in restaurant **Children:** Portions **Rooms:** 3 (3 en suite) ◆◆◆◆ **Directions:** Located on A62 between Slaithwaite and Marsden **Parking:** 20

OTLEY MAP 19 SE24

Chevin Country Park Hotel

Modern European

Scandinavian-style country hotel offering varied and well presented food

☎ 01943 467818 Yorkgate LS21 3NU
e-mail: reception@chevinhotel.com
web: www.chevinhotel.com

continued

England

OTLEY *continued* MAP 19 SE24

A large Finnish-style hotel built from logs, attractively set around a lake in a woodland setting. Pine walls and ceiling feature in the split-level restaurant, where the black chairs and white table coverings make a striking impact. An extensive choice of food with a bold use of flavours is offered, with a set price for two or three courses. Smoked salmon rosette and garden herb risotto might feature along with roast rump of lamb with parsnip purée mash. To finish, try the assiette of desserts for two followed by the good selection of Yorkshire cheeses.

Chef: David Hampshire **Owners:** Chevin Lodge Limited **Times:** 12-2/6.30-9.15, Closed L Mon, Sat **Prices:** Fixed L £18.50-£20, Fixed D £22.50-£24, Starter £4.95-£7.95, Main £13.50-£21.50, Dessert £4.95-£7.95, Coffee £2.95, Min/Water £3.05, Service included **Wine:** 19 bottles over £20, 36 bottles under £20, 10 by the glass (£2.95-£4.95) **Notes:** Sun L £15.95, Vegetarian available, Dress Restrictions, Smart casual minimum, Civ Wed 120 **Seats:** 70, Pr/dining room 30 **Smoking:** N/Sm in restaurant **Children:** Menu, Portions **Rooms:** 49 (49 en suite) ★★★ HL **Directions:** Take A658 towards Harrogate. Left at 1st turning towards Carlton, turn 2nd left towards Yorkgate **Parking:** 100

PONTEFRACT MAP 16 SE42

Wentbridge House Hotel

British, French

NOTABLE WINE LIST

Classical cuisine in a country-house setting

☎ 01977 620444 Wentbridge WF8 3JJ
e-mail: info@wentbridgehouse.co.uk
web: www.wentbridgehouse.co.uk

A well-established hotel in 20 acres of landscaped gardens, with a choice of dining styles. The Fleur de Lys restaurant offers polished service and a varied menu of interesting dishes; while the brasserie offers a more relaxed alternative. Country-house dining is the order of the day with a combination of modern British and French classics such as lobster thermidor and steak Diane. Produce is well sourced and the cooking shows attention to flavours in dishes such as fillet of Scottish beef with kidney, beets and shallots. The restaurant offers a little 'table theatre' with some dishes prepared in the restaurant.
Notable Wine List: A nicely constructed wine list with good tasting notes.

Chef: Steve Turner **Owners:** Mr G Page **Times:** 7.15-9.30, Closed 25 Dec eve, Closed L Mon-Sat, D Sun **Prices:** Fixed D fr £30, Starter £5-£12.50, Main £17-£30, Dessert £6-£8, Coffee £3.20, Min/Water £3, Service optional **Wine:** 100 bottles over £20, 50 bottles under £20, 10 by the glass (£4-£6) **Notes:** Vegetarian available, Civ Wed 130 **Seats:** 60, Pr/dining room 24 **Smoking:** No pipes, No cigars **Children:** Portions **Rooms:** 18 (18 en suite) ★★★ HL **Directions:** 0.5m off A1, 4m S of M62/A1 junct **Parking:** 100

SHIPLEY MAP 19 SE13

Marriott Hollins Hall Hotel & Country Club

Traditional European

Traditional dining venue with formal service

☎ 01274 530053 Hollins Hill BD17 7QW
e-mail: mhrs.lbags.frontdesk@marriotthotels.com
web: www.marriotthotels.com/lbags

Hollins Hall was built by the first Baron of Park Gate in 1858 in the Elizabethan style and is set in 200 acres of grounds. The cosy restaurant occupies the original drawing room of the house and has views over the garden. A fusion of traditional and contemporary food is offered on the menu, plus regular special dishes. Expect the likes of wild mushroom risotto with a parmesan crisp and olive oil, magret duck breast on honey-roast fennel with orange fumet, and hot sticky toffee pudding with toffee sauce.

Chef: Sean Kelly **Owners:** Marriott International **Times:** 12-2/6.30-9.30, Closed L Sat, D BHs **Prices:** Fixed L £15, Fixed D £27.50, Starter £5-£7.95, Main £16-£22.50, Dessert £5.50-£6.95, Coffee £2.25, Min/Water £3.95, Service optional **Wine:** 35 bottles over £20, 28 bottles under £20, 19 by the glass (£5.10-£7.85) **Notes:** Sun L 2 courses £12.95, 3 courses £15.95, Vegetarian available, Dress Restrictions, Smart casual, Civ Wed 120 **Seats:** 120, Pr/dining room 30 **Smoking:** N/Sm in restaurant, Air con **Children:** Menu, Portions **Rooms:** 122 (122 en suite) ★★★★ HL **Directions:** From A650 follow signs to Salt Mill. At lights in Shipley take A6038. Hotel 3m on left **Parking:** 250

WAKEFIELD MAP 16 SE32

Brasserie Ninety Nine

Modern British

Bright, fresh brasserie in a business park

☎ 01924 377699 Trinity Business Park WF2 8EF
e-mail: brasserie99@parkingroup.co.uk

Stainless steel and glass are the chosen materials for the interior of this ultra-modern restaurant located, unexpectedly, beyond the security gates of a high-tech business park. Within the silver and red colour scheme, the kitchen offers a comprehensive choice of modern European dishes made from the best available produce. Well-informed waiting staff serve up the likes of loin of Rydale pork with apple and rosemary mash, and baked cod with potato and herb gnocchi. There's a more limited choice at lunchtime, with a very flavoursome beef lasagne easily making the grade.

Chef: Alan Gazeley **Owners:** Mr Parkin **Times:** 12-5.30/5.30-9.30, Closed 25 Dec, 1 Jan, BHs, Sun, Closed L Sat, D Mon, Tue **Prices:** Fixed D fr

continued

£14.95, Starter £3.95-£8.95, Main £9.25-£17.95, Dessert £4.50-£5.25, Coffee £1.20, Min/Water £2, Service optional, Group min 10 service 10% **Wine:** 20 bottles over £20, 20 bottles under £20, 7 by the glass (£3-£4.25) **Notes:** Vegetarian available, Dress Restrictions **Seats:** 120, Pr/dining room 40 **Smoking:** N/Sm in restaurant, Air con **Children:** Menu, Portions **Directions:** Please telephone for directions **Parking:** 40

Waterton Park Hotel

Modern European

Simple cooking in idyllic setting

☎ 01924 257911 Walton Hall, The Balk, Walton WF2 6PW
e-mail: watertonpark@bestwestern.co.uk
web: www.watertonparkhotel.co.uk

Set on an island in a wildfowl park, this former private mansion is now a comfortable hotel and a popular choice for wedding functions. Carefully prepared food is served in the refurbished, beamed restaurant, with the modern European cuisine embracing local and international flavours, presented with care and confidence. A starter of Yorkshire pea and ham soup may be followed by medallions of monkfish with lime couscous and a chilli and lemongrass oil. The generous desserts are more traditional, think chocolate sponge pudding and classic orange crème brûlée.

Chef: Armstrong Wgabi **Owners:** The Kaye Family **Times:** 12-2/7-9.30 **Prices:** Fixed L fr £15.50, Fixed D fr £24.95, Starter £5.25-£6.25, Main £12.95-£20.50, Dessert fr £4.25, Coffee £1.80, Min/Water £2.75, Service optional **Wine:** 10 bottles over £20, 50 bottles under £20, 10 by the glass (£2.50-£3.25) **Notes:** Fixed L 3 courses, Vegetarian available, Smart casual, Civ Wed 150 **Seats:** 50, Pr/dining room 35 **Smoking:** N/Sm in restaurant **Children:** Portions **Rooms:** 68 (68 en suite) ★★★ HL **Directions:** From Wakefield follow A61 to Walton and follow brown signs. M1 junct 39, A638 (Crofton) **Parking:** 130

WETHERBY MAP 16 SE44

Wood Hall Hotel

Modern British

Classic country house with modern food and décor

☎ 01937 587271 Trip Ln, Linton LS22 4JA
web: www.handpicked.co.uk

Originally owned by the Vavasour family at the time of the Norman Conquest, Wood Hall has been a family home, a boys' school and even the first pastoral and ecumenical centre for Britain. In many respects it is a classic country house, a striking Georgian hall in 100 acres of parkland, but there is no mistaking the contemporary stamp of the décor, all calm, light and soothing. The modern theme extends to the cooking, with good use of local products and dishes of scallops with caviar velouté, squab pigeon with braised cabbage and thyme jus, and a selection of chocolate miniatures to finish. Special gourmet events are a regular feature.

Chef: Ian Samson **Owners:** Hand Picked Hotels **Times:** 12-2.30/6.30-9.30, Closed L Mon, Tue, Fri, Sat **Prices:** Fixed L £15.50-£17.50, Fixed D £35-£45, Starter £11.50-£14.50, Main £21-£27, Dessert £8-£11, Coffee £3.50, Min/Water £3.50, Service optional **Wine:** 100 bottles over £20, 10 by the glass (£4-£12.50) **Notes:** Tasting menus available, Vegetarian available, Dress Restrictions, Smart casual, no jeans or trainers, Civ Wed 120 **Seats:** 35, Pr/dining room 100 **Smoking:** N/Sm in restaurant **Children:** Menu, Portions **Rooms:** 44 (44 en suite) ★★★★ CHH **Directions:** From Wetherby take A661(Harrogate road) N for 0.5m. Left to Sicklinghall/Linton. Cross bridge, left to Linton/Woodhall, right opp Windmill Inn, 1.25m to hotel, (follow brown signs) **Parking:** 100

CHANNEL ISLANDS GUERNSEY

CASTEL MAP 24

Hotel Hougue du Pommier

Mediterranean, International V

Charming traditional hotel with interesting cuisine

☎ 01481 256531 Hougue du Pommier Rd GY5 7FQ
e-mail: hotel@houguedupommier.guernsey.net
web: www.hotelhouguedupommier.com

Tucked away on a quiet lane on the north side of the island, this pleasant privately run hotel is popular with locals and runs special themed events such as a medieval banquet. The restaurant and bar with their rustic Guernsey farmhouse style décor offer formal yet relaxed service. There are several fireplaces, one of which is used to cook the traditional 'Feu du bois' spit-roast menu. There is a huge choice of dishes; ranging from the assiette of fish and seafood, and caramelised Guernsey scallops, to rack of lamb with rosemary and goat's cheese crust with Mediterranean tomato and basil risotto and brown onion jus.

Chef: Andrew Till **Owners:** Linda Letten **Times:** 12-2.30/6.30-9.30, Closed L Mon-Sat **Prices:** Fixed L £12.95-£18.95, Fixed D £21.95, Starter £3.50-£7.50, Main £9.95-£18.50, Dessert fr £4.95, Coffee £2.95, Min/Water £3.20 **Wine:** 6 bottles over £20, Most bottles under £20, 4 by the glass (£2.80-£3.90) **Notes:** Fixed D 5 courses, Vegetarian menu, Dress Restrictions, Smart dress, no jeans or T-shirts **Seats:** 90 **Smoking:** N/Sm in restaurant **Children:** Menu, Portions **Rooms:** 43 (43 en suite) ★★★ HL **Directions:** 2m W of St Peter Port towards Cobo. Turn at Rue de Friquet **Parking:** 60

COBO MAP 24

Cobo Bay Hotel

British, French

Great views of the bay from this popular restaurant

☎ 01481 257102 GY5 7HB
e-mail: info@cobobayhotel.com
web: www.cobobayhotel.com

A traditional seaside holiday destination overlooking a picture postcard Guernsey bay, Cobo Bay Hotel is comfortable and modern, yet retaining the feel of the golden age of British holiday-making. The food is undoubtedly a highlight for guests who can enjoy contemporary cuisine served with consummate professionalism. Quality produce is a key element in the classically based menu with flashes of creative flair. Seafood - as you might expect from the

continued

England

COBO *continued* MAP 24

location - is undoubtedly a highlight, yet carnivores needn't feel left out. Start with a timbale of hand-picked Chancre crab on a marinated cucumber galette with mustard mayonnaise, then continue on to grilled fillet of Guernsey brill with vermouth cream sauce.

Chef: John Chapman **Owners:** Mr D Nussbaumer **Times:** 12-2/7-9.30, Closed 1st wk Jan-mid Feb, Closed L Mon-Sat **Prices:** Fixed L £15.95, Fixed D £22, Coffee £1.50, Min/Water £2.95, Service optional **Wine:** 20 bottles over £20, 20 bottles under £20, 3 by the glass (£2.50) **Notes:** Fixed L 3 courses, Vegetarian available, Smart casual **Seats:** 120 **Smoking:** N/Sm in restaurant, Air con **Children:** Menu, Portions **Rooms:** 36 (36 en suite) ★★★ HL **Directions:** From St Peter Port follow signs for Castel/Cobo/West Coast. At coast road turn right, Hotel 100m on right **Parking:** 100

PERELLE MAP 24

Atlantique Hotel

Modern European

Modern hotel restaurant with seriously good views

☎ 01481 264056 Perelle Bay GY7 9NA
e-mail: enquiries@perellebay.com
web: www.perellebay.com

You can watch the sun go down over the bay from this modern hotel dining room, and move into the comfortable lounge for a post-dinner coffee. Many diners choose to start the evening in the cocktail bar, where the daily menu, supplemented by a separate grill section, can be perused over a drink. The secret of the much-sung modern British cooking with European influences lies in the simple handling of quality produce by a skilled and adaptable team. The fresh sea flavours of seared scallops on fennel and parmesan risotto speak for themselves, while honey braised belly pork topped with a chilli and crab wonton makes a tasty and succulent main dish. Good home-made petits fours get rave reviews.

Chef: Steve Harrison **Owners:** Carey Olsen Trustees/L'Atlantique 2003 Ltd **Times:** 12-2/6.30-9.30, Closed 1 Jan-end Mar, Closed L Mon-Sat **Prices:** Fixed L £10-£15, Fixed D £15-£22, Starter £4-£12, Main £9-£22, Dessert £4.50-£10.50, Coffee £1.50, Min/Water £3, Service optional **Wine:** 25 bottles over £20, 32 bottles under £20, 4 by the glass (£2.25-£6) **Notes:** Fixed L 3 courses, Fixed D 4 courses, Vegetarian available, Smart casual **Seats:** 80, Pr/dining room 40 **Smoking:** N/Sm in restaurant, Air con **Children:** Portions **Rooms:** 23 (21 en suite) ★★★ HL **Directions:** Off west coast road overlooking Perelle Bay **Parking:** 30

ST MARTIN MAP 24

La Barbarie Hotel

British, French

Quietly placed hotel with a strong local reputation

☎ 01481 235217 Saints Rd, Saints Bay GY4 6ES
e-mail: reservations@labarbariehotel.com
web: www.labarbariehotel.com

An old stone priory houses this delightful small hotel, quietly located in St Martin. Named after 17th-century pirates from the Barbary Coast who kidnapped a previous owner, it promises a peaceful stay in its cosy accommodation and brightly decorated restaurant. The fresh fish and steak board attract a strong local following, with a short carte adding to the variety. The kitchen takes a pride in its output, evidenced by starters like seared Guernsey scallops with local crab risotto and saffron cream, followed by paillard of pan-fried veal with Parma ham, sage and lemon zest, wilted greens and egg noodles. Look out for the photos of visiting celebrity chefs.

Chef: Colin Pearson **Owners:** La Barbarie Ltd **Times:** 12-1.45/6-9.30, Closed 29 Oct-9 Mar **Prices:** Fixed L £10.25, Fixed D £18.95, Starter £4-£7, Main £10.95-£16.95, Dessert £3.50-£5.25, Coffee £1.30, Min/Water £2.50, Service optional **Wine:** 6 by the glass (£2.75-£3.50) **Notes:** Fixed D 4 courses, Vegetarian available, Smart casual **Seats:** 70 **Smoking:** N/Sm in restaurant **Children:** Menu **Rooms:** 22 (22 en suite) ★★★ HL **Directions:** At traffic lights in St Martin take road to Saints Bay - hotel on right at end of Saints Rd **Parking:** 60

Hotel Jerbourg

Modern British

Cliff-top hotel restaurant specialising in seafood

☎ 01481 238826 Jerbourg Point GY4 6BJ
e-mail: stay@hoteljerbourg.com
web: www.hoteljerbourg.com

The aptly named, conservatory-style Les Trois Isles restaurant offers stunning sea views out to Herm, Sark and Jersey at this cliff-top hotel set in pretty landscaped grounds. No surprises either that the kitchen specialises in seafood (though there's plenty of choice for meat eaters, too), with dishes like roast Guernsey sea bass with a crab and chive Gewürztraminer velouté, herb polenta and confit salisify finding a place on the carte. Dining tables are neatly clothed, service is relaxed but professional, and there's an elegant lounge for aperitifs.

Chef: Kristian Gregg **Owners:** Arthenella Guernsey Ltd **Times:** 12-2.30/6.30-9.30, Closed Nov-Mar **Prices:** Fixed L fr £12.95, Fixed D £19.50, Starter £5.50-£10, Main £12-£17, Dessert £5-£7.95, Coffee £1.50, Min/Water £2.75, Service optional **Wine:** 6 bottles over £20, 30 bottles under £20, 2 by the glass (£2-£2.95) **Notes:** Fixed L 3 courses, Vegetarian available **Seats:** 80, Pr/dining room 20 **Smoking:** N/Sm in restaurant, Air con **Children:** Menu, Portions **Rooms:** 32 (32 en suite) ★★★ HL **Directions:** From St Peter Port follow signs for St Martin, at lights by Manor stores turn left. Hotel at end of road on right **Parking:** 30

ST PETER PORT MAP 24

The Absolute End

Italian, International

Fisherman's cottage restaurant serving fresh fish straight from the boat

☎ 01481 723822 Longstore GY1 2BG
e-mail: theabsoluteend@cwgsy.net

This converted fisherman's cottage is opposite the sea on the road out of town. The main restaurant has half-panelled walls painted cream on rough plaster, and dotted with small paintings, while upstairs the private dining room has a covered terrace for alfresco dining. In the evening, candles and tablecloths lend a more formal feel. The Italian chef concentrates on fresh fish along with specials from his homeland, and the straightforward results go down well with a well-established clientele. Starters like coquilles St Jacques or linguini with hand-picked crab might be followed by fresh turbot with hollandaise sauce, lobster thermidor or sea bass baked with Italian herbs.

Chef: Antonio Folmi **Owners:** Antonio Folmi **Times:** 12-2/7-10, Closed 'an, Sun **Prices:** Fixed L £15, Fixed D £20, Starter £4.50-£11, Main £9.50-£18.50, Dessert £3.95, Coffee £2, Min/Water £2.50 **Wine:** 30 bottles over £20, 36 bottles under £20, 4 by the glass (£2.75) **Notes:** Vegetarian available, Civ Wed 50 **Seats:** 55, Pr/dining room 22 **Smoking:** N/Sm in restaurant, Air con **Children:** Portions **Directions:** Less than 1m from town centre, going N on seafront road to St Sampson **Parking:** On street

Da Nello

Modern Italian, Mediterranean

Bustling popular Italian just off the High Street

☎ 01481 721552 46 La Pollet GY1 1WF
e-mail: danello@cwgsy.net
web: www.where2eatguernsey.com

Like Dr Who's Tardis, the narrow frontage of this old granite town house opens out into a series of dining areas, leading ultimately to the pièce de résistance, a covered Mediterranean-style piazza decked out in marble and terracotta. This 500-year-old building (on the site of an ancient Roman encampment with pottery finds to prove it) has been much extended and smartly renovated, and remains a popular venue for locals and tourists. The lengthy menu takes in modern and traditional Italian favourites like beef carpaccio, saltimbocca, and plenty of affordable pasta, plus a separate fish section. Pasta and risotto dishes, like assagini di pasta and risotto mare e monti, can be taken as either starter or main. All desserts are made in-house.

continued

Da Nello

Chef: Tim Vidamour **Owners:** Nello Ciotti **Times:** 12-2/6.30-10, Closed 25 Dec-2 Jan **Prices:** Fixed L £10.50, Fixed D £22.95, Starter £3.75-£9.50, Main £8.95-£19.50, Dessert £4.50-£4.95, Coffee £1.55, Min/Water £2.75, Service optional **Wine:** 25 bottles over £20, 32 bottles under £20, 3 by the glass (£2.95-£4.50) **Notes:** Vegetarian available **Seats:** 90, Pr/dining room 20 **Smoking:** N/Sm area, No pipes, No cigars, Air con **Children:** Portions **Directions:** In town centre, 100 yds from North beach car park **Parking:** 900

La Frégate

Traditional French

Relaxed, elegant dining with sea views and seafood

☎ 01481 724624 Les Cotils GY1 1UT
e-mail: enquiries@lafregatehotel.com
web: www.lafregatehotel.com

This unique hotel combines modernity with the charm of an 18th-century manor house, and, from its lofty position, offers stunning views over the island's capital and across to Sark, Herm and Jersey. The dining room continues the contemporary styling, with white-clothed tables and cream paintwork, curtains and leather chairs, set against a darkwood floor. Its wall of windows opens the room up to those views, and there's a terrace for alfresco dining. The kitchen makes fine use of fresh local ingredients, especially seafood - lobster bisque, sea bass fillet with steamed spinach, local mussels and a saffron and dill sauce, and a grilled medley of saltwater fish. Meat eaters and vegetarians will find good choices too.

Chef: Neil Maginnis **Owners:** GSH Ltd **Times:** 12-2.30/6.30-9.45 **Prices:** Fixed L £15-£21.50, Fixed D £26.50, Starter £4.50-£9.75, Main £10.95-£18.50, Dessert £4.50-£7.50, Coffee £2.50, Min/Water £2.55, Service optional **Wine:** 80 bottles over £20, 36 bottles under £20, 4 by the glass (£3) **Notes:** Sun L 3 courses £17.95, Vegetarian available **Seats:** 70, Pr/dining room 30 **Smoking:** N/Sm in restaurant, Air con **Children:** Portions **Rooms:** 13 (13 en suite) ★★★ HL **Directions:** Town centre, above St Julian's Ave **Parking:** 25

England

ST PETER PORT *continued* MAP 24

Governor's

French V

Formal dining with views over St Peter Port harbour

☎ 01481 738623 Old Government House Hotel, St Ann's Place GY1 2NU
e-mail: governors@theoghhotel.com
web: www.theoghhotel.com

Dating back to 1748, this was once the residence of the Governor of Guernsey. A hotel since 1857, it enjoys a great location overlooking the harbour and town. The Governor's Restaurant is an intimate, beautifully decorated room full of memorabilia and photographs of former Island Governors. Shaped seating, rich fabrics and patterned wallpaper recollect the glorious décor of the early 19th century. Traditional cooking is influenced by the French chef, typically using light seasoning and sauces. Main courses might include a 'trilogy' of Somerset lamb with thyme jus, leek and carrot bundle and buttered asparagus.

Chef: Jerome Babbancon **Owners:** Kenneth W McVey **Times:** 12-2/7.30-10, Closed L Sat, Sun **Prices:** Fixed L £11.50, Starter £7.50-£9.50, Main £15.50-£19.50, Dessert £5.50-£8.50, Coffee £1.85, Min/Water £3.85, Service optional **Wine:** 23 bottles over £20, 14 bottles under £20, 8 by the glass (£3.25-£3.45) **Notes:** Vegetarian menu **Seats:** 18, Pr/dining room 32 **Smoking:** N/Sm in restaurant, Air con **Children:** Min 12 yrs **Rooms:** 63 (63 en suite) ★★★★ HL **Directions:** Telephone for directions **Parking:** 28

Le Nautique Restaurant

Traditional French, International

Chic, nautical-themed restaurant

☎ 01481 721714 Quay Steps GY1 2LE

As its name suggests, this harbourside restaurant has a nautical theme with lots of character and overlooks the marina, Castle Cornet and islands beyond. The downstairs dining room has a traditional feel, while the upper level is more cosmopolitan and chic. You will need to book well in advance if you want one of the window tables, though this former warehouse is equally agreeable away from the view. An extensive choice on the modern French menu takes in many variations of classical dishes, with simply cooked fresh fish among the menu's strengths. Roast scallops, pineapple carpaccio and herb salad, or seared fillet of sea bass, crushed new potatoes, chorizo and red wine reduction are among several outstanding choices. Lunchtime offers particularly good value.

Chef: Gunter Botzenhardt, John Flemming **Owners:** Gunter Botzenhardt **Times:** 12-2/6.30-10, Closed Sun, Closed L Sat **Prices:** Fixed L fr £12.50, *continued* Starter £5.50-£9.50, Main £9.50-£18.50, Dessert £5.50-£7.50, Coffee £1.80, Min/Water £2.50, Service optional **Wine:** 49 bottles over £20, 26 bottles under £20, 8 by the glass (£2.80-£4.50) **Notes:** Vegetarian available, Dress Restrictions, Smart casual **Seats:** 56, Pr/dining room 30 **Smoking:** N/Sm in restaurant, Air con **Children:** Portions **Directions:** Seafront opposite harbour and Victoria Marina **Parking:** On street

St Pierre Park Hotel

Modern European V

Smart hotel restaurant serving quality local produce

☎ 01481 728282 Rohais GY1 1FD
e-mail: info@stpierreparkhotel.com
web: www.stpierreparkhotel.com

The only true resort hotel in the Channel Islands, St Pierre Park is set in 45 acres of landscaped gardens and has a friendly and relaxed atmosphere throughout. The interior has seen some major refurbishment in both the bedrooms and public areas and a choice of restaurants is available. The fine dining option is the Victor Hugo restaurant; light and airy with well spaced tables. Fresh fish is a speciality of the regularly changing menus: set price, carte and menu gourmand. A good choice is very fresh locally caught sea bass, accompanied by a creamy risotto, and black cherry flambé with pistachio parfait and nougatine tuile for dessert.

Chef: Julian Prosser **Owners:** C I Traders **Times:** 7-9.30, Closed 26 Dec, 1 Jan, Sun, Closed L Mon-Sat **Prices:** Fixed D £23.50, Starter £6.50-£12, Main £10.50-£34, Dessert £4.95-£12, Coffee £2.20, Min/Water £2.75 **Wine:** 50 bottles over £20, 50 bottles under £20, 8 by the glass (£3-£4) **Notes:** Vegetarian menu, Dress Restrictions, Smart casual, no trainers/jeans/sandals **Seats:** 70, Pr/dining room 24 **Smoking:** N/Sm in restaurant, Air con **Children:** Menu, Portions **Rooms:** 131 (131 en suite) ★★★★ HL **Directions:** Located 1.5m from St Peter Port on road to Cobo Bay **Parking:** 150

Saltwater

British

Contemporary, airy restaurant with great harbour views

☎ 01481 720823 Albert Pier GY1 1AD
e-mail: info@saltwater.gg
web: www.saltwater.gg

Overlooking the outer harbour, this popular local restaurant is a real find. Stylish décor with wooden floors, whitewashed wood-panel walls, a bright conservatory and an understated nautical theme give it a chic but unpretentious feel. The menu has a classic, international flavour and as you would expect favours seafood dishes, many of which are of the simple, classic variety - lobster thermidor for example, or plainly grilled fish. For more complexity you could look at dishes such as pan-fried squid with chilli and coriander to start, followed by sea bass with lobster mash and shellfish sauce both cooked using quality produce and obvious technical skill.

Chef: Anthony Jeans **Owners:** Jenny Meeks, Joanna Baker **Times:** 12-2/6-10, Closed 23 Dec-5 Jan, Sun, Closed L Sat **Prices:** Fixed L £10-£25, Fixed D £10-£25, Min/Water £2.50, Service optional **Wine:** 30 bottles over £20, 10 bottles under £20, 5 by the glass (£2.80-£5.95) **Notes:** Fixed L 3 courses, Vegetarian available **Seats:** 70 **Smoking:** N/Sm in restaurant, Air con **Children:** Menu, Portions

JERSEY

GOREY MAP 24

Jersey Pottery, The Garden Restaurant

French, International

Convivial conservatory restaurant

☎ 01534 850850 Gorey Village JE3 9EP
e-mail: enquiries@jerseypottery.com
web: www.jerseypottery.com

The classier of two eateries at this Jersey institution, the Garden Restaurant has a convivial café ambience and is always busy with a mix of lunching ladies, family gatherings, and chattering couples. Take a tour around the pottery, snap up a bargain in the shop, and then tuck into the likes of herb-marinated fillet of pork in pancetta with grilled black pudding, parsnip and lentil purée and Madeira jus, or apple charlotte with Calvados crème anglaise. Seafood dishes are a speciality; bring friends and share a platter of Jersey lobster, oysters, langoustine and Chancre crab.

Chef: Tony Dorris **Owners:** The Jones Family **Times:** 12-2.30, Closed Xmas, Jan, Mid Feb, Mon, Closed D (private functions only) **Prices:** Fixed L £15.50, Fixed D £21-£40, Starter £5.50-£7.50, Main £9.95-£28.50, Dessert £5.50-£5.95, Coffee £2.65, Min/Water £2.95, Service included **Wine:** 25 bottles over £20, 10 bottles under £20, 8 by the glass (£2.75-£6.95) **Notes:** Civ Wed 180 **Seats:** 180, Pr/dining room 180 **Smoking:** N/Sm in restaurant **Children:** Menu, Portions **Directions:** On main road to Gorey Castle. Turn left before Gorey Village. Follow signs **Parking:** 300

Suma's

Modern Mediterranean

Sea views, skilful cuisine and excellent service

☎ 01534 853291 Gorey Hill JE3 6ET

A superb location delivering outstanding views from inside and from the terrace - over Mont Orgueil Castle and Gorey's attractive fishing harbour - prove an irresistible drawcard at this baby sibling of Longueville Manor (see entry). Its simple, modern décor is as bright and refreshing as the food-and-wine-themed paintings and collages adorning the walls, while the mood is suitably relaxed and friendly. The kitchen's contemporary approach, with its nod to the Mediterranean, perfectly suits the surroundings. Expect high-quality local produce and light, intelligently simple, clear-flavoured dishes like poached local brill with shellfish chowder and saffron potatoes, and a hot Valrhona chocolate fondant with Baileys ice cream or assiette of miniature desserts to finish.

Chef: Daniel Ward **Owners:** Ms S Dufty & Mr M Lewis **Times:** 12-2.30/6.30-9.30, Closed 20 Dec-20 Jan **Prices:** Fixed L fr £12.50, Fixed D fr £30, Starter £7.75-£11.50, Main £13.75-£21, Dessert £7.50-£10, Coffee £2.25, Min/Water £3.75, Service included **Wine:** 41 bottles over £20, 29 bottles under £20, 11 by the glass (£2.75-£4.75) **Notes:** Fixed D Sun-Thurs, Vegetarian available, Dress Restrictions, Smart casual **Seats:** 40 **Smoking:** Air con **Children:** Menu, Portions **Directions:** Take A3 E, continue for 4m from St Helier to Gorey. Before castle take sharp left. Restaurant 100 yds before harbour on left **Parking:** On street

The Village Bistro

British, Mediterranean

Friendly restaurant in village surroundings

☎ 01534 853429 Gorey Village JE3 9EP
e-mail: thevillagebistro@yahoo.co.uk
web: www.village-bistro.com

This popular bistro in a converted church - located in the centre of the pretty seaside village - is a relaxed, family-run affair, with husband Sean front of house while wife Sarah cooks. It's simply furnished and decorated, with the bonus of alfresco dining in the front garden (under parasol or heater) and friendly French service. The cuisine has a careful, rustic style with the emphasis on quality produce and value for money. Fish has its say, perhaps pan-fried skate wing with lemon and tarragon vinaigrette, chunky chips and crispy mixed salad.

Chef: Sarah Copp **Owners:** Sean & Sarah Copp **Times:** 12-2.30/7-10.30, Closed Mon, Closed D Sun **Prices:** Fixed D £13.50, Starter £4.95-£8.50, Main £12.50-£16.50, Dessert £4.95-£5.25, Coffee £1.65, Min/Water £2.50, Service optional, Group min 8 service 10% **Wine:** 12 bottles over £20, 15 bottles under £20, 4 by the glass (£2.75-£3) **Notes:** Fixed D 4 courses, Sun L £17.50, Vegetarian available, Dress Restrictions, Smart casual **Seats:** 40 **Smoking:** N/Sm in restaurant **Children:** Portions **Directions:** Take A3 E from St Helier to Gorey. Restaurant in village centre **Parking:** On street and public car park

England

ROZEL MAP 24

Château La Chaire

British, French

Luxurious surroundings for a gastronomic delight

☎ 01534 863354 Rozel Bay JE3 6AJ
e-mail: res@chateau-la-chaire.co.uk
web: www.chateau-la-chaire.co.uk

Originally a traditional Victorian mansion house, the château lends itself to its current incarnation as a hotel. The architecture and original features such as oak panelling and ornate plasterwork are truly impressive. The creative menu combines French romance and culinary techniques with traditional English dishes and ingredients. Tempting starters might include a terrine of venison with mulled wine jelly and pain d'épice ice cream. Mains feature fish and seafood prominently, but also the likes of roast breast of Gressingham duck with a little pie of its leg, braised red cabbage and fondant potato. You get the impression that time stands still here, so relax and enjoy a wonderful meal in these opulent surroundings.

Chef: Simon Walker **Owners:** The Hiscox Family **Times:** 12-3/7-10 **Prices:** Fixed L £15.95, Fixed D £27.95-£29.95, Starter £6.95-£9.95, Main £14.95-£24.95, Dessert £7.95, Coffee £2.60, Min/Water £2.90, Service added but optional 10% **Wine:** 47 bottles over £20, 29 bottles under £20, 15 by the glass (£2.95-£12.25) **Notes:** Fixed D 4 courses, Vegetarian available, Dress Restrictions, No jeans. Jackets required evening, Civ Wed 60 **Seats:** 60, Pr/dining room 28 **Smoking:** N/Sm in restaurant **Children:** Portions **Rooms:** 14 (14 en suite) ★★★ HL **Directions:** From St Helier NE towards Five Oaks, Maufant, then St Martin's Church & Rozel; 1st left in village, hotel 100mtrs **Parking:** 30

ST AUBIN MAP 24

Hotel La Tour

European, Pacific Rim V NEW

Impressive setting for fine dining

☎ 01534 743770 La Rue du Crocquet JE3 8BZ
e-mail: enquries@hotellatour.com
web: www.hotellatour.com

A historic building of architectural significance, refurbished in contemporary style. The split-level High Street Restaurant allows diners a superb view through large picture windows. The formal atmosphere in the dining room befits the smart white-clothed tables and attentive service. French cuisine is offered on both bistro and carte menus making good use of local produce and seafood; there is also a separate vegetarian menu. Typical dishes might include a starter of pan-fried Jersey scallops served with English black pudding and orange jus. Expect main courses like traditional braised beef bourguignon with steamed Jersey Royals, or whole Jersey plaice, simply grilled with meunière sauce.

Prices: Food prices not confirmed for 2007. Please telephone for details **Notes:** Vegetarian menu **Rooms:** 26 (26 en suite) ★★★ HL

Somerville Hotel

Modern International

Stunning views over the bay, and modern cooking

☎ 01534 741226 Mont du Boulevard JE3 8AD
e-mail: somerville@dolanhotels.com
web: www.dolanhotels.com

The settings don't come much better than this: on the hillside overlooking St Aubin's Bay, with glorious views all the way to St Helier enjoyed from both the lounge and the restaurant. Service is formal and reserved, and the smart table settings are in keeping with this serious approach to dining. The extensive choice on the modern international menu takes in plenty of fresh fish from the surrounding waters, plus a decent range of quality meats, among them grilled calves' liver with smoked bacon, pomme purée and braised gem lettuce, or roast rack of lamb with pithivier of kidneys and root vegetable boulangère. Desserts are very moreish, whether it's a gloriously simple warm dark chocolate tart, or baked mango and pineapple Alaska.

Chef: Wayne Pegler **Owners:** Mr W Dolan **Times:** 12.30-2/7-9 **Prices:** Fixed L fr £10, Fixed D £19.50-£22.50, Starter £5.50-£9.25, Main £10.95-£16.50, Dessert £4.95-£5.95, Coffee £1.40, Min/Water £2.95, Service optional **Wine:** 21 bottles over £20, 28 bottles under £20, 7 by the glass (£2.65-£3.70) **Notes:** Fixed D 4 courses, Sun L 4 courses £17.50, Vegetarian available, Dress Restrictions, Smart casual at D, Civ Wed 40 **Seats:** 120 **Smoking:** N/Sm in restaurant, Air con **Children:** Portions **Rooms:** 59 (59 en suite) ★★★ HL **Directions:** From village follow harbour, then take Mont du Boulevard **Parking:** 30

ST BRELADE MAP 24

Hotel La Place

Modern British

Classic cooking in a beamed dining room

☎ 01534 744261 Route Du Coin, La Haule JE3 8BT
e-mail: hotlaplace@aol.com
web: www.hotellaplacejersey.com

This 16th-century farmhouse has been transformed into a comfortable hotel, and makes a good base for exploring the island. Take an aperitif in the cocktail bar overlooking the pool if the weather's clement, or by the log fire in the lounge in winter, and then head through to the restaurant, a traditional, beamed affair which overlooks a pretty private courtyard. The menu suits the setting and makes good use of local produce - tuck into pan-fried sea bass with asparagus, mash and mussel cream perhaps, or breast of chicken with potato rösti, swede purée, spinach and red wine jus.

hef: Steven Walker **Owners:** Mylncroft Trading Ltd **Times:** 12-2/7-9 **rices:** Fixed L £15-£22, Fixed D £20-£30, Starter £6-£9, Main £6-£19, essert £6-£8, Coffee £2.50, Service added 10% **Wine:** 30 bottles over 20, 20 bottles under £20, 6 by the glass (£3-£5) **Notes:** Sun L £15, egetarian available, No shorts or T-shirts, Civ Wed 100 **Seats:** 80, /dining room 50 **Smoking:** N/Sm in restaurant **Children:** Menu, ortions **Rooms:** 42 (42 en suite) ★★★★ HL **Directions:** Telephone r directions **Parking:** 100

Hotel L'Horizon, The Grill

International

Intimate dining room overlooking the bay

☎ 01534 743101 Route de la Baie JE3 8EF
e-mail: lhorizon@handpicked.co.uk
web: www.handpicked.co.uk

Plenty of glass and mirrors create an impression of light and space at this stylish hotel restaurant, while clever use of partitions and alcoves helps to impart an air of intimacy. A sliding glass door opens to reveal the wonderful views of the bay. Crisp white linen and small flower arrangements add a touch of formality. A classical base underpins the cooking, though the interpretation of most dishes is modern and light, especially when it comes to seafood. Quality produce, local where possible, is evident in the likes of tian of Jersey crab, baked Dover sole with lobster mousse, and roasted pine nut and pear caramel tart with red wine ice cream.

Chef: Kevin Clark **Owners:** Hand Picked Hotels **Times:** 7-9.45, Closed Xmas, Sun-Mon, Closed L all wk **Prices:** Fixed D £37, Min/Water £3, Service included **Wine:** 40 bottles over £20, 18 bottles under £20, 14 by the glass (£4-£6.95) **Notes:** Sun, Vegetarian available, Smart casual, Civ Wed 200 **Seats:** 46, Pr/dining room 250 **Smoking:** N/Sm in restaurant, Air con **Children:** Min 12 yrs, Menu, Portions **Rooms:** 106 (106 en suite) ★★★★ HL **Directions:** 2m from Jersey Airport, 5m from St Helier **Parking:** 150

Ocean Restaurant at the Atlantic Hotel

see page 526

ST CLEMENT MAP 24

Green Island Restaurant

Mediterranean

Contemporary beachside café with alfresco tables

☎ 01534 857787 Green Island JE2 6LS
e-mail: greenislandrestaurant@jerseymail.co.uk
web: www.greenislandrestaurant.com

A jazzed-up beach café/restaurant with pine tables, modern seating and colourful matting on the floor. It is very popular locally, especially in the summer, and the takeaway window serving quality food does a roaring trade. The views out over Green Island are well worth savouring, as is the stylish modern Mediterranean cooking which draws much of its produce from the sea. Baked fillet of plaice simply cooked, and baked fillet of brill with an orange and herb crust might follow after an impressive wild mushroom risotto, available as a starter or main dish. Staff in white T-shirts and jeans are a relaxed and pleasant bunch.

Times: 12-2.30/7-9.30, Closed 21 Dec-Mar, Mon, Closed D Sun **Directions:** Telephone for directions

ST HELIER MAP 24

Bohemia

see page 527

England

Ocean Restaurant at the Atlantic Hotel

ST BRELADE MAP 24

Modern British V

Sophisticated dining with Atlantic views

☎ 01534 744101 Le Mont de la Pulente JE3 8HE
e-mail: info@theatlantichotel.com
web: www.theatlantichotel.com

Adjoining the manicured fairways of the La Moye championship golf course, this elegant, luxury, privately-owned hotel enjoys a peaceful setting amid sub-tropical gardens and with breathtaking views over St Ouen's Bay. The air of understated luxury continues in the refurbished and sophisticated Ocean restaurant, its modern design offering a nod to its coastal setting, while service achieves that perfect balance between professionalism and friendliness.
The kitchen's modern approach - from a chef of pedigree - combines intelligent simplicity alongside tip-top produce from the abundant local Jersey larder, including the fruits of the sea. The cooking's accurate, consistent, innovative and full of flavour; think thyme roasted fillet of sea bass paired with a chorizo casserole, seared scallops and fish bubbles, or salt-cod brandade served with confit pork belly, candied shallots and a shellfish foam, and perhaps an assiette of passionfruit to finish (jelly, sorbet, mousse and hot soufflé), while peripherals like amuse-bouche, breads and petits fours all hold form through to the end.

Chef: Mark Jordan
Owners: Patrick Burke
Times: 12.30-2.30/7-10, Closed 5 Jan-8 Feb
Prices: Fixed L fr £15, Fixed D £37.50, Service optional
Wine: 60 bottles over £20, 20 bottles under £20, 8 by the glass (£4.50-£8.50)
Notes: 3 course ALC £47.50, Tasting menu 5 courses £57.50, Vegetarian menu
Seats: 65, Pr/dining room 20
Smoking: N/Sm in restaurant
Children: Menu, portions
Rooms: 50 (50 en suite) ★★★★ HL
Directions: From St Brelade take the road to Petit Port, turn into Rue de Sergente and right again, signed to hotel
Parking: 60

Bohemia

ST HELIER MAP 24

Modern British, French NOTABLE WINE LIST

Classical cooking in contemporary Jersey restaurant

☎ 01534 880588 The Club Hotel & Spa, Green St JE2 4UH
e-mail: bohemia@huggler.com
web: www.bohemiajersey.com

The Club Hotel & Spa - a swish, contemporary townhouse close to the centre of town - plays host to the island's most trendy, and highly rated restaurant, Bohemia, with its chef Shaun Rankin delivering some seriously accomplished cuisine. A long, trendy bar runs the length of its plate glass windows and attracts an equally trendy crowd, and behind it sits the restaurant. Decorated in shades of earthy brown, there's lots of wood, leather, Lalique glass, fresh flowers and elegant table appointments. Service is appropriately polished and attentive, yet unstuffy, from a friendly international team (with a super restaurant manager and sommelier). A buzzing venue with a vibrant see-and-be-seen vibe, its cuisine outshines anything on the island.

Shaun Rankin's kitchen takes a modern approach underpinned by a classical French theme; this is refined, top-notch, creative cooking at its best. Expect great use of seasonal and local produce from sea and land, bags of luxury (crab, lobster, scallops, oysters, Périgord truffles, caviar, foie gras), great technical skills and lovely clean, clear flavours with fine textural combinations. Think a confit of belly pork with glazed pig cheek, apple pavé, roast foie gras and langoustine brochette, or perhaps grilled local turbot teamed with braised frogs' legs, garlic confit and herb gnocchi, while an apple and vanilla assiette might take the eye at dessert. The repertoire is a fixed-price affair and includes a tasting option, while the fresh Jersey seafood proves a drawcard and peripherals, like tasters and inter-courses and fabulous petits fours, complete the experience The hotel's Club Café upstairs serves less elaborate food, there are luxury rooms and a wonderful spa.

Notable Wine List: A well chosen wine list with many fine vintages.

Chef: Shaun Rankin
Owners: Laurence Huggler
Times: 12-2.30/6.30-10.30, Closed Sun, Closed L Sat
Prices: Fixed L £16.50, Fixed D £45, Starter £15, Main £25, Dessert £7.50, Coffee £2.50, Min/Water £3.50, Service added but optional 10%
Notes: Tasting menu 7 courses £55, incl wine £95, Vegetarian available, Dress Restrictions, Smart casual
Seats: 40, Pr/dining room 6
Smoking: N/Sm in restaurant, Air con
Children: Portions
Rooms: 46 (46 en suite) ★★★★
Directions: Located on Green St in centre of St Helier
Parking: 20

England

ST HELIER *continued* MAP 24

La Petite Pomme

International

Convivial dining with good views

☎ 01534 880110 Liberation Square JE1 3UF
e-mail: enquiries@pommedorhotel.com
web: www.pommedorhotel.com

La Petite Pomme restaurant, the hotel's fine dining option, occupies the first floor of an historic hotel and overlooks Liberation Square and St Helier harbour. The décor is rich and so are the clientele who expect the best of food and service. Well-spaced tables with expensive linen and settings make this a popular venue with local businessmen. Dishes are modern, imaginative and skilfully prepared. Try the sautéed scallop salad with warm pancetta and a chilli lemon dressing to start and follow with a main course of veal escalope with sauté king prawns, pressed limes and red wine cordon. Desserts include cappuccino and whiskey crème brûlée or chocolate fondant with glazed apricots and zest of citrus fruits.

Chef: James Waters **Owners:** Seymour Hotels **Times:** 7-10, Closed 26-30 Dec, Sun, Closed L all week **Prices:** Fixed D £26.50, Coffee £1.40, Min/Water £2.50, Service optional **Wine:** 24 bottles over £20, 45 bottles under £20, 14 by the glass (£2.75-£4.10) **Notes:** Fixed D 1 course £15, Dress Restrictions, Smart casual **Seats:** 50, Pr/dining room 50 **Smoking:** N/Sm in restaurant, Air con **Children:** Menu, Portions **Rooms:** 143 (143 en suite) ★★★★ HL **Directions:** 5m from Airport, 0.5m from ferry terminal **Parking:** 100 yds from Hotel

TRINITY MAP 24

Water's Edge Hotel

Modern British

Stunning setting for enjoyable cuisine

☎ 01534 862777 Bouley Bay JE3 5AS
e-mail: mail@watersedgehotel.co.je
web: www.watersedgehotel.co.je

This privately-owned art deco style hotel lives up to its name with stunning views over Bouley Bay even as far as the distant French coastline. The split-level restaurant makes a wonderful setting to enjoy carefully prepared dishes. Formal service and crisp white table linen complete the clean modern dining experience; try to get a window sea to make the most of the view. The menu offers well executed dishes such as a lobster chervil risotto followed by roasted best end of lamb rolled in mint and coriander seed. Take a look at the Fruits of the Sea

continued

Longueville Manor

ST SAVIOUR MAP 24

Modern British NOTABLE WINE LIST

Historic manor with sophisticated cuisine

☎ 01534 725501 JE2 7WF
e-mail: info@longuevillemanor.com
web: www.longuevillemanor.com

This handsome, wisteria-clad manor house dates from the 13th century and stands in 15 acres at the foot of its own wooded valley, complete with lake. It is decorated throughout in elegantly understated country-house style and provides guests with high standards of comfort and service. The two dining rooms cater for different moods, from the Jacobean dark-panelled Oak Room to the more relaxed and modern Garden Room, rich in fabrics and antiques. Cooking is confident and accomplished, demonstrating culinary flair and skill, with harmonious combinations of top-notch local ingredients, including herbs and vegetables from the kitchen garden, producing interesting, carefully balanced flavours. Classically-based dishes are given a contemporary twist and might include an assiette of local scallops with a cep, rocket and Périgord truffle salad, seared red mullet with marinated crab, pink grapefruit and a lemongrass foam, braised belly pork with truffled potato fondant, shallots and baby leeks, and baked apple tarte Tatin with Jersey black butter ice cream.

Notable Wine List: A large, traditional list, offering over 400 wines including an extensive half-bottle list.

Chef: Andrew Baird **Owners:** Malcolm Lewis **Times:** 12.30-2/7-10 **Prices:** Fixed L £12.50, Starter £12.50-£15.50, Main £28-£30, Dessert £8.75-£10, Coffee £4, Min/Water £3.50, Service included **Wine:** 378 bottles over £20, 28 bottles under £20, 31 by the glass (£4.50-£15) **Notes:** Tasting menu 6 courses £55, 7 courses £65, with wine £95, Vegetarian available, Dress Restrictions, Smart casual, jacket minimum, Civ Wed 40 **Seats:** 65, Pr/dining room 22 **Smoking:** N/Sm area **Children:** Menu, Portions **Rooms:** 30 (30 en suite) ★★★★ **Directions:** From St Helier take A3 t Gorey, hotel 0.75m on left **Parking:** 45

menu too. The wine list offers over 80 wines and a small selection of half bottles. The adjoining Black Dog Bar is an alternative eating option.

Chef: Stephen Hill **Owners:** M Wavell/Water's Edge Hotel Ltd **Times:** 12.30-2/7-9.15, Closed Oct-Apr, Closed L Mon-Sat **Prices:** Fixed L £16-£22, Fixed D £21-£23.50, Starter £4-£10, Main £16.50-£34, Dessert £6-£8, Coffee £1.50, Min/Water £2.75, Service included **Wine:** 32 bottles over £20, 6 bottles under £20, 14 by the glass (£2.50-£5.50) **Notes:** Fixed L 3 courses, Fixed D 4 courses, Vegetarian available, Dress Restrictions, Smart casual, no trainers, jeans or T-shirts, Civ Wed 100 **Seats:** 100, Pr/dining room 40 **Smoking:** N/Sm in restaurant **Children:** Min 7 yrs, Menu, Portions **Rooms:** 50 (50 en suite) ★★★ HL **Directions:** 10-15 mins from St Hellier, A9 N to the A8 to the B31, follow signs to Bouley Bay **Parking:** 20

SARK

SARK MAP 24

Hotel Petit Champ

Modern British **NEW**

Relaxed, country-house dining with amazing sea views

☎ 01481 832046 GY9 0SF
e-mail: info@hotelpetitchamp.co.uk
web: www.hotelpetitchamp.co.uk

Why not arrange to arrive by horse and carriage at this secluded hotel on Sark's West coast? Built over 100 years ago, the hotel was formerly a private home, boatyard and German observation post during the Occupation, but nowadays guests come here to relax and enjoy the magnificent sea views and sunsets. The restaurant offers a mixture of traditional and modern British cookery with international influences in a relaxed country-house atmosphere. Fresh lobster and crab dishes, Sark scallops with a leek and crab risotto and pork tenderloin with breaded pork belly confit are typical dishes.

Chef: Tony Atkins **Owners:** Chris & Caroline Robins **Times:** 12.15-1.45/8, Closed Oct-Easter **Prices:** Fixed D £20.25, Starter £3.50-£7.25, Main £10.50-£18.75, Dessert £3.40-£4.25, Min/Water £2.10, Service optional **Wine:** 8 bottles over £20, 67 bottles under £20, 4 by the glass (£2-£2.25) **Notes:** Sun L 4 courses £12, Fixed D 5 courses, coffee incl, Vegetarian available, Dress Restrictions, Smart casual **Seats:** 50 **Smoking:** N/Sm in restaurant **Children:** Min 7 yrs D, Menu, Portions **Rooms:** 10 (10 en suite) ◆◆◆◆ **Directions:** 20 min walk from village, signed from Methodist Chapel

La Sablonnerie

International

An idyllic location well worth the journey

☎ 01481 832061 GY9 0SD

continued

La Sablonnerie

French sophistication and rustic simplicity rub shoulders in this charming 400-year-old converted farmhouse and cottages. On the southernmost tip of the idyllic, car free island, access is by the hotel's own horse and carriage. The restaurant retains the original style and charm of the farmhouse; diners can also choose to eat alfresco in the attractive gardens. Smartly dressed, formal staff make good use of their silver service skills. Fresh produce from the hotel's own farm and gardens is transformed into elegant international dishes with a strong French influence, such as warm salad of confit duck leg or pan-fried sea bass with a soft herb velouté. Fresh fish and lobster feature strongly on the lunch and dinner menus.

Chef: Martin Cross **Owners:** Elizabeth Perrée **Times:** 12-2.30/7-9.30, Closed mid Oct-Etr **Prices:** Fixed L £16.80-£22.30, Fixed D £23.60-£30.10, Starter £5.80-£7.80, Main £11-£14.50, Dessert £5.80-£6.80, Coffee £1, Min/Water £2.20, Service added 10% **Wine:** 9 bottles over £20, 41 bottles under £20, 6 by the glass (£2-£3.50) **Notes:** Vegetarian available **Seats:** 39 **Smoking:** N/Sm area, No pipes, No cigars **Children:** Menu, Portions **Directions:** On southern part of island. Horse & carriage is transport to hotel

ISLE OF MAN

DOUGLAS MAP 24 SC37

Sefton Hotel

Modern European

Fine-dining beside the sea

☎ 01624 645500 Harris Promenade IM1 2RW
e-mail: info@seftonhotel.co.im
web: www.seftonhotel.co.im

A seafront hotel with a modern, comfortable fine-dining restaurant, decorated with bright artwork. Modern cooking is the order of the day with fine ingredients in European-style dishes, like twice-baked goat's cheese soufflé with peppered salad leaves and plum and fig jam to start. Main courses include a wide choice of meat, fish, flambé and vegetarian dishes featuring the likes of pan-seared sea bass with cassoulet of white beans and cherry tomatoes napped with lobster foam. Try a delicious dessert like lemon and lime pannacotta with passionfruit ice cream and Bellini syrup.

Chef: Johan Bonjus/Chris Swinden **Owners:** Sefton Hotel Plc **Times:** 12-2/6-10, Closed L Sun **Prices:** Fixed D fr £21, Starter £5.75-£8.50, Main £14-£21, Dessert £4.75-£6.25, Coffee £1.75, Min/Water £3.25, Service optional **Wine:** 13 bottles over £20, 16 bottles under £20, 6 by the glass (£3.50) **Notes:** Vegetarian available, Dress Restrictions, Smart casual **Seats:** 25 **Smoking:** N/Sm in restaurant **Children:** Portions **Rooms:** 96 (96 en suite) ★★★★ **Directions:** 1m along Promenade from the sea terminal **Parking:** 20

England

Scotland

ABERDEEN CITY

ABERDEEN MAP 23 NJ90

Copthorne Hotel Aberdeen

British

Traditional hotel restaurant serving simple British cuisine

☎ 01224 630404 122 Huntly St AB10 1SU
e-mail: reservations.aberdeen@mill-cop.com
web: www.copthorne.com

This granite building is a former grain warehouse found in the city's West End shopping district. A traditional hotel restaurant here, Poachers, serves high quality, simply prepared dishes, using the best local and Scottish ingredients. Service is relaxed and friendly so take your time to peruse the menu. You'll find the carte supplemented by options from the chargrill and side orders like sliced olive and herb potatoes. Typical starters include bradan rost mango and avocado salsa, or traditional Cullen skink. Main courses might include pan-seared fillet of monkfish wrapped in Parma ham on a creamy Loch Fyne mussel chowder. Cheese and Scottish oatcakes make an alternative to desserts like iced tiramisù parfait.

Chef: Colin Milne **Owners:** Copthorne **Times:** 7-9, Closed 25-26 Dec, Closed L all week **Prices:** Starter £4.50-£6.50, Main £8.50-£19, Dessert £4.95, Coffee £2.50, Min/Water £4.95, Service optional **Wine:** 30 bottles over £20, 31 bottles under £20, 15 by the glass (£3.10-£7.60) **Notes:** Civ Wed 100 **Seats:** 80, Pr/dining room 12 **Smoking:** N/Sm in restaurant, Air con **Children:** Menu, Portions **Rooms:** 89 (89 en suite) ★★★★ HL **Directions:** City centre. 200yds off Union St, at top of Huntly St **Parking:** 16

Marcliffe Hotel and Spa

Modern British NOTABLE WINE LIST **NEW**

Enjoy the best of Scottish beef and seafood at this privately-owned hotel

☎ 01224 861000 North Deeside Rd AB15 9YA
e-mail: enquiries@marcliffe.com
web: www.marcliffe.com

A split-level conservatory restaurant set in the tree-studded landscaped grounds of a privately owned hotel. Recently refurbished in contemporary style, the bright, open restaurant has Lloyd Loom chairs and specially spun Scottish curtains. The modern Scottish cooking is all about getting the best out of quality produce such as fish, shellfish, meat and game. As well as a fabulous choice of steaks from the char-grill, main courses may include grilled pavé of sea bass with roasted vegetables or roast loin of Buchan lamb with fondant potato and parsnip purée. Wines are noteworthy and there are over 100 malt whiskies to choose from.

AA Hotel of the Year for Scotland

Notable Wine List: An interesting and well-presented wine list offering great value throughout.

Chef: Mike Stoddart **Owners:** J Stewart Spence **Times:** 12.30-2.30/6.30-10 **Prices:** Starter £8.90-£14.90, Main £14.90-£24.90, Dessert £6.90, Coffee £3.90, Min/Water £4.50, Service included **Wine:** 260 bottles over £20, 6 bottles under £20, 40 by the glass (£6.50-£16.50) **Notes:** Sun L 3 courses incl coffee £26.50, Vegetarian available, Dress Restrictions, Smart casual, no T-shirts or hats, Civ Wed 450 **Seats:** 72, Pr/dining room 50 **Smoking:** N/Sm in restaurant **Children:** Min 8 yrs, Menu, Portions **Rooms:** 42 (42 en suite) ★★★★ HL **Directions:** Turn West at A93 direction Braemar. 1m on right **Parking:** 160

The Mariner Hotel

Modern British, Seafood V **NEW**

Established hotel with a crowd-pleasing menu

☎ 01224 588901 349 Great Western Rd AB10 6NW
e-mail: info@themarinerhotel.co.uk
web: www.themarinerhotel.co.uk

Family-run hotel to the west of the city centre. Dine in the Atlantis restaurant, a split-level affair with a subtle nautical theme and a wide-ranging menu that includes lobster and steak selections. Portions are hearty and a light touch lets the quality of regional produce speak for itself, with mains along the lines of chargrilled salmon with carrot and ginger purée, grilled loin of pork with apple fritters, or steamed sea bass with potato ratatouille. Save room for comfort puds such as sticky toffee pudding, lemon posset and steamed syrup pudding.

Chef: George Bennett **Owners:** The Edwards Family **Times:** 12-2/6-9.30, Closed 26 Dec, 1-2 Jan, Closed L Sat **Prices:** Fixed L £15, Fixed D £18, Starter £3-£7.50, Main £12-£32.50, Dessert £4.50, Coffee £2, Min/Water £2.95, Service optional **Wine:** 24 bottles over £20, 20 bottles under £20, 3 by the glass (£3-£4) **Notes:** Sun L 3 courses £14.50, Vegetarian menu **Seats:** 50 **Smoking:** N/Sm in restaurant **Children:** Portions **Rooms:** 25 (25 en suite) ★★★ HL **Directions:** From S, 400yds right off A90 at Great Western Rd lights **Parking:** 50

Maryculter House Hotel

Traditional European

Cosy dining in historic mansion house

☎ 01224 732124 AB12 5GB
e-mail: info@maryculterhousehotel.com
web: www.maryculterhousehotel.com

Set in 5 acres of woodland on the banks of the River Dee, Maryculter House was once a seat of the Knights Templar and dates back to 1225. These days it's a busy country-house hotel and guests can feast by candlelight in the stone-walled Priory restaurant, where a modern Scottish menu - with a hint of French - lists prime local produce, especially beef and salmon. Typically, choose langoustine bisque for starters, move on to beef fillet with brandy, peppercorn and cream sauce, and finish with apple and cinnamon tart with rich caramel sauce.

Chef: Sebastian Schroeder **Owners:** James Gilbert **Times:** 7-9.30, Closed Sun, Closed L all week **Prices:** Starter £2.95-£5.50, Main £13.95-£17.25, Dessert £4.25-£4.95, Coffee £2, Min/Water £3.75, Service optional **Wine:** 20 bottles over £20, 16 bottles under £20, 1 by the glass (£2.65) **Notes:** Vegetarian available, Dress Restrictions, Smart casual, no jeans or T shirts, Civ Wed 150 **Seats:** 40, Pr/dining room 180 **Smoking:** N/Sm in restaurant **Children:** Min 4 yrs, Menu, Portions **Rooms:** 23 (23 en suite) ★★★ HL **Directions:** Off A90 to S of Aberdeen and onto B9077. Hotel is located 8m on right, 0.5m beyond Lower Deeside Caravan Park **Parking:** 150

Norwood Hall

British, European

Fine dining on a grand scale

☎ 01224 868951 Garthdee Rd, Cults AB15 9FX
e-mail: info@norwood-hall.co.uk
web: www.norwood-hall.co.uk

An imposing Victorian mansion with oak-panelled restaurant, named the Tapestry Restaurant, after the ornate tapestry work on the walls. Well-spaced candlelit tables grace this richly furnished dining room, displaying fine crockery and glassware befitting the magnificent scale of the house. A selection of traditional and more adventurous dishes is on offer here, making good use of fine local ingredients. The setting makes the restaurant popular for special occasions and there are private dining suites available too.

Times: 12-2.30/7-9.45 **Rooms:** 37 (37 en suite) ★★★★ HL **Directions:** From S, off A90 at 1st rdbt cross bridge and turn left at rdbt into Garthdee Road, continue 1.5m

The Silver Darling

French, Seafood

Romantic seafood restaurant with stunning harbour views

☎ 01224 576229 Pocra Quay, North Pier AB11 5DQ

The location here is almost as good a talking point as the food. It occupies the old customs house that stands at the entrance to Aberdeen harbour and you can watch passing ships and, if you're lucky, dolphins through the large windows in this first-floor

continued

conservatory restaurant. Given the name (a reference to herring), it's no surprise what drives the kitchen, namely freshly caught, locally landed seafood. The sophisticated evening menu is strongly French influenced and typified by seared scallops with truffle jus and pan-fried sea bass with mushroom risotto, confit carrots and mushroom cappuccino. Lunch is a simpler affair but there's no compromising the quality of ingredients, flavours and cooking skills.

Chef: Didier Dejean **Owners:** Didier Dejean & Karen Murray **Times:** 12-2/6.30-9.30, Closed Xmas-New Year, Sun, Closed L Sat **Prices:** Starter £5.50-£12.50, Main £10.50-£21.50, Dessert £5.50-£7.50, Coffee £2.25, Min/Water £3.20, Service optional, Group min 10 service 10% **Wine:** 41 bottles over £20, 9 bottles under £20, 7 by the glass (£3.95-£4.95) **Seats:** 50 **Smoking:** N/Sm in restaurant **Children:** Portions **Directions:** Situated at Aberdeen Harbour entrance beside Harbour Pilots Round Tower in Footdec **Parking:** on quayside

Howies Restaurant - Chapel Street

☎ 01224 639500 50 Chapel St AB10 1SN
web: www.theaa.com/restaurants/114034.html

The Aberdeen member of the successful Edinburgh-based group of modern Scottish restaurants. Monthly-changing menus of fantastic seasonal and local food made on the premises every day.

ABERDEENSHIRE

BALLATER MAP 23 NO39

Scotland

Darroch Learg Hotel

BALLATER MAP 23 NO39

Modern Scottish

Flawless cooking in stunning setting

☎ 013397 55443 Braemar Rd AB35 5UX
e-mail: info@darrochlearg.co.uk
web: www.darrochlearg.co.uk

There are fine views to be enjoyed over Royal Deeside from this renowned 19th-century country-house hotel, perched high above the village in extensive wooded grounds. Inside there are two comfortable, welcoming lounges, one with a crackling log fire, while the smart restaurant extends into a conservatory to make the best of those views. Decorated in bright modern style, with splashes of colour from contemporary prints, its well-appointed tables come dressed in white linen, while the mood is relaxed and service knowledgeable and friendly, with the Franks themselves (the owners) involved with great effect. The kitchen's modern approach is delivered via appealing carte and seven-course tasting options that place great emphasis on high-quality produce from the abundant local Scottish larder, including venison, beef, salmon and scallops. The accurate, intelligently simple approach and light touch allows the quality ingredients to speak for themselves with clean, clear flavours and limited fuss. Take a breast of guinea fowl served with tagliatelle, broad beans and morels, and a

classic lemon tart finish, accompanied by a berry sauce. And do take time to explore the wine list, as there's some great-value drinking to be enjoyed.

Chef: David Mutter **Owners:** The Franks Family **Times:** 12.30-2/7-9, Closed Xmas, last 3wks Jan, Closed L Mon-Sat **Prices:** Fixed L £22, Fixed D fr £40 **Notes:** Vegetarian available, Dress Restrictions, Smart casual **Seats:** 48 **Smoking:** N/Sm in restaurant **Rooms:** 17 (17 en suite) ★★★ SHL **Directions:** On A93 at the W end of village

BALLATER *continued* MAP 23 NO39

Glen Lui

☎ 013397 55402 Invercauld Rd AB35 5RP

Delightful country house set in lovely grounds.

BANCHORY MAP 23 NO69

Raemoir House Hotel

French, Scottish NOTABLE WINE LIST

Romantic and historic setting for accomplished cuisine

☎ 01330 824884 Raemoir AB31 4ED
e-mail: relax@raemoir.com
web: www.raemoir.com

A romantic setting in 3,500 acres of parkland and forest. The original 'Ha Hoose' is of great historical importance and has been restored to become an annex to the main house, a hotel since 1943. The sense of history is everywhere here, but nowhere more so than in the amazing Oval Dining Room, now used as the restaurant. Here the unique tapestry-lined walls, curved doors and blazing log fire give out tremendous warmth and character. Cuisine is Scottish with French influences. Sample a starter of roast quail with bubble-and-squeak, crispy Parma ham and mustard sauce, followed by a sorbet or soup. Fillet of Aberdeen Angus beef with aubergine Parisienne potatoes, wild mushrooms and Puy lentils could prove irresistible as a main course, although there are lots of other interesting choices.
Notable Wine List: An impressive wine list categorised by grape varieties with extensive and informative tasting notes.

Chef: Grant Walker **Owners:** Mr & Mrs D Webster **Times:** 12-2/7-9 **Prices:** Fixed L £8-£23, Fixed D fr £33, Coffee £2.50, Min/Water £3.50, Service optional **Wine:** 35 bottles over £20, 25 bottles under £20, 6 by the glass (£3.50-£7.50) **Notes:** Vegetarian available, Civ Wed 40 **Seats:** 40, Pr/dining room 35 **Smoking:** N/Sm in restaurant **Children:** Portions **Rooms:** 20 (20 en suite) ★★★ **Directions:** A93 to Banchory then A980, hotel at x-rds after 2.5 m **Parking:** 50

Milton Restaurant

☎ 01330 844566 On A493 Royal Deeside Rd, E of Banchory AB31 5YR

Modish roadside restaurant with craft shop.

OLDMELDRUM MAP 23 NJ82

Meldrum House Hotel Golf & Country Club

Traditional British **NEW**

Elegant dining in a splendid country mansion

☎ 01651 872294 AB51 0AE
e-mail: enquiries@meldrumhouse.com
web: www.meldrumhouse.com

A baronial country mansion set in 350 acres of woodland and parkland with a golf course as the centrepiece. The hotel has been tastefully restored to highlight its original character. The traditional Scottish cooking with international twists has a flare for presentation in well constructed dishes such as pressed duck and liver parfait with pear chutney and oatcakes, followed by a breaded trio of lamb cutlets with redcurrant and rosemary sauce. Desserts like white chocolate bavarois with boozy fruits are also well executed.

Chef: Gary Christie **Owners:** Sylvia Simpson **Times:** 12-2.30/6.30-9.30 **Prices:** Fixed L £16.50, Fixed D £32.50, Coffee £2.50, Min/Water £4.50, Service optional **Wine:** 31 bottles over £20, 29 bottles under £20, 6 by the glass (£3.70-£4.50) **Notes:** Fixed L 3 courses, Fixed D 4 courses, Dress Restrictions, Smart casual, Civ Wed 80 **Seats:** 40, Pr/dining room 16 **Smoking:** N/Sm in restaurant **Children:** Menu, Portions **Rooms:** 9 (9 en suite) ★★★ **Directions:** 11m N of Aberdeen, from Aberdeen to Dyce, follow A947 towards Banff, through Newmachen along outskirts of Oldmeldrum, main entrance is large white archway **Parking:** 60

STONEHAVEN MAP 23 NO88

Tolbooth

Modern, Seafish

Straight from the sea to the plate

☎ 01569 762287 Old Pier Rd AB39 2JU
web: www.tolbooth-restaurant.co.uk

The harbour wall makes a scenic setting for this former prison and excise house, now a popular restaurant. Accessed via an outside staircase, its whitewashed stone walls conceal a modern interior with pretty table settings and local artists' work on the walls. You'll find wonderfully fresh seafood on the menu and blackboard, though not to the exclusion of meat dishes. A beautifully presented lemon sole stuffed with scallop and brown crab meat mousse might result from the fisherman's catch, or grilled lobster with a light garlic and lemon butter. Inviting desserts and lovely home-made bread are further delights.

Chef: Robert Cleaver & Craig Sumers **Owners:** Robert Cleaver **Times:** 12-2/6-9.30, Closed 3 wks after Xmas, Sun & Mon **Prices:** Fixed L £12, Starter £3.95-£7.95, Main £9.84-£18.95, Dessert £5.95-£6.50, Coffee £1.95, Min/Water £2.50, Service optional **Wine:** 18 bottles over £20, 13 bottles under £20, 2 by the glass (£3.25) **Notes:** Vegetarian available **Seats:** 46 **Smoking:** N/Sm in restaurant **Children:** Portions **Directions:** 15m S of Aberdeen on A90, located in Stonehaven harbour **Parking:** Public car park, 100 spaces

ANGUS

BRIDGEND OF LINTRATHEN MAP 23 NO25

 Lochside Lodge & Roundhouse Restaurant

Modern British

Imaginative dishes in unique farm steading

☎ 01575 560340 DD8 5JJ
e-mail: enquiries@lochsidelodge.com
web: www.lochsidelodge.com

This 150-year-old farm steading alongside Lintrathen Loch has been beautifully converted to house a spacious restaurant and bar area displaying farming and sporting memorabilia. The Roundhouse restaurant is home to modern, imaginative cooking using local Angus and Perthshire market produce, combined with international flavours and colours. Start with an interesting dish like Dunsyre blue cheese brûlée glazed with Dunsyre blue, served with red onion chutney. Next you could sample roast saddle of Angus lamb with roasted parsnips and three-bean casserole and mint-flavoured reduction. Finally why not round off a lovely meal with chocolate and Drambuie tart with home-made white chocolate sorbet.

Chef: Graham Riley **Owners:** Graham & Gail Riley **Times:** 12-1.30/6.30-9.30, Closed 1-25 Jan, 25-26 Dec, Mon, Closed D Sun **Prices:** Fixed L £12-18.50, Fixed D £30-£32, Coffee £1.50, Min/Water £3, Service optional, Group min 20 service 10% **Wine:** 15 bottles over £20, 20 bottles under £20, 4 by the glass (£2.60-£3.90) **Notes:** Dress Restrictions, Smart casual, no jeans **Seats:** 35, Pr/dining room 48 **Smoking:** N/Sm in restaurant

continued

Children: Portions **Rooms:** 6 (6 en suite) ★★★★ RR
Directions: From Kirriemuir, take B591 towards Glenisla for 7m, turn left towards Lintrathen and follow to village, restaurant on left
Parking: 40

GLAMIS MAP 21 NO34

 Castleton House Hotel

see below

INVERKEILOR MAP 23 NO64

Gordon's

Modern Scottish

Scottish cooking by a friendly family team

☎ 01241 830364 Main St DD11 5RN
e-mail: gordonsrest@aol.com
web: www.gordonsrestaurant.co.uk

The name of this family-run establishment only tells part of the story, as the eponymous Gordon is joined in the kitchen by son Garry, while wife and mum, Maria runs front of house. It's a cosy affair with bags of character - beamed ceiling, huge open fire and rugs on wooden floors, and there's even a small lounge. The imaginative, modern cooking is underpinned by a classical theme and makes good use of seasonal produce from the abundant Scottish larder on its appealing, sensibly compact menus. Herb-crusted fillet of Angus beef with a celeriac purée, kohlrabi fondant and pinot noir jus, or a Valrhona

continued

Castleton House Hotel

GLAMIS MAP 21 NO34

British French

Victorian country house with culinary flair

☎ 01307 840340 Castleton of Eassie DD8 1SJ
e-mail: hotel@castletonglamis.co.uk
web: www.castletonglamis.co.uk

The tall trees that surround this charming 100-year old house create such a sense of exclusivity and tranquillity that once here it's difficult to imagine ever being able to leave. There is a croquet lawn and animals - ducks, chickens and pigs - roaming around these beautiful grounds complete with moat. With vegetables and herbs coming from the gardens too, the British cooking with French influences relies heavily on the quality - and provenance - of the ingredients, which if not home grown or home-reared are sourced from the surrounding region. The flawlessly timed dishes might include a starter of tortellini of Usan lobster with wilted greens and saffron cream, followed by a chain of carved fillet of local Scottish beef with dauphinoise potatoes, baby spinach and shallot jus, and a dessert of iced vanilla parfait with rhubarb compôte and dark chocolate sauce.

Chef: Andrew Wilkie **Owners:** David & Verity Webster **Times:** 12-2/6.30-9, Closed New Year **Prices:** Fixed L £30, Fixed D £35, Starter £4.50-£8, Main £11-£22.50, Dessert £4.95-£5.25, Service optional **Notes:** Smart

casual **Seats:** 50, Pr/dining room 35 **Smoking:** N/Sm in restaurant **Children:** Menu **Rooms:** 6 (6 en suite) ★★★ **Directions:** On A94 midway between Forfar & Coupar Angus, 3m W of Glamis **Parking:** 50

Scotland

INVERKEILOR *continued* MAP 23 NO64

chocolate and orange fondant finish, with apricot compôte and basil ice cream might be just the thing.

Chef: Gordon Watson & Garry Watson **Owners:** Gordon & Maria Watson **Times:** 12-1.45/7-9, Closed 1st 3 wks Jan, Mon, Closed L Tues, D Sun **Prices:** Fixed L £25, Fixed D £38, Coffee £2.25, Min/Water £3, Service optional **Wine:** 18 bottles over £20, 23 bottles under £20, 4 by the glass (£3.25-£4) **Notes:** Fixed L 3 courses, Fixed D 4 courses, Vegetarian available, Dress Restrictions, Smart casual **Seats:** 24, Pr/dining room 8 **Smoking:** N/Sm in restaurant **Children:** Min 12 yrs **Rooms:** 3 (2 en suite) ◆◆◆◆ **Directions:** On A92, turn off at signs for village of Inverkeilor, between Arbroath and Montrose **Parking:** 6

Scotland

MONTROSE MAP 23 NO75

Best Western Links Hotel

Modern European

French bistro cuisine in relaxed hotel restaurant

☎ 01674 671000 Mid Links DD10 8RL
e-mail: reception@linkshotel.com
web: www.bw-linkshotel.co.uk

An impressive Edwardian building dating back to 1875, this stylishly refurbished hotel is within walking distance of Montrose beach. In the restaurant, there is the air of a bustling French bistro as friendly front-of-house staff bring dishes from the kitchen, which has a semi-opaque screen that enables diners to watch the chefs in action. The menu has a strong French influence and plenty of Scottish produce is used to create big flavours in complex dishes like seafood terrine with lemon, dill and cucumber dressing, or roasted fillet of venison in oatmeal and herb crust with red cabbage and fresh grape essence.

Chef: Franc Rivault **Owners:** Casper Ninteman **Times:** 12-2.30/6-9 **Prices:** Fixed L £9.95-£12.75, Fixed D £19-£25, Starter £3.75-£7.75, Main £9.50-£17.50, Dessert £5.50, Coffee £1.50, Min/Water £4.10, Service optional **Wine:** 10 bottles over £20, 19 bottles under £20 **Notes:** Vegetarian available, Dress Restrictions, Smart casual, Civ Wed 250 **Seats:** 48, Pr/dining room 24 **Smoking:** N/Sm in restaurant **Children:** Menu, Portions **Rooms:** 25 (25 en suite) ★★★ HL **Directions:** From town centre turn into John St, at end turn right, then right again into car park **Parking:** 45

ARGYLL & BUTE

ARDUAINE MAP 20 NM71

Loch Melfort Hotel

British, European

Wonderful views and a menu specialising in fresh seafood

☎ 01852 200233 PA34 4XG
e-mail: reception@lochmelfort.co.uk
web: www.lochmelfort.co.uk

Enjoying one of the finest locations on the West Coast, this popular, family-run hotel has outstanding views across Asknish Bay towards the islands of Jura, Scarba and Shuna. The setting is the perfect complement to the wonderful seafood on offer in the attractive dining room. An alternative dining choice, popular with visiting yachtsmen, the Skerry Bistro offers blackboard specials. Skilful cooking makes excellent use of local produce, particularly fresh fish and shellfish like Asknish Bay crab and langoustines from Luing Split. As well as inviting mains like baked fillet of turbot with herb crust, crab and dill tagliatelle, meat-eaters are also catered for with the likes of roast gigot of Barbreck lamb with mashed potatoes, diced ratatouille and redcurrant jus. The well-chosen wine list is worth a look.

Loch Melfort Hotel

Chef: Colin Macdonald **Owners:** Kyle & Nigel Schofield **Times:** 7-9, Closed 2 Jan-15 Feb, Closed L all week **Prices:** Fixed D £26.50, Min/Water £3, Service optional **Wine:** 25 bottles over £20, 40 bottles under £20, 4 by the glass (£2.90-£3) **Notes:** Coffee incl, seafood buffet Sun eve (in season), Vegetarian available, Dress Restrictions, Smart casual, no jeans **Seats:** 75 **Smoking:** N/Sm in restaurant **Children:** Menu, Portions **Rooms:** 27 (27 en suite) ★★★ HL **Directions:** From Oban, 20 m S on A816; from Lochgilphead, 19 m N on A816 **Parking:** 65

CLACHAN MAP 20 NR75

Balinakill Country House Hotel

Scottish, French

Victorian setting for contemporary cuisine

☎ 01880 740206 PA29 6XL
e-mail: info@balinakill.com
web: www.balinakill.com

Built by William Mackinnon, founder of the British India Line, this magnificient house was used as a school during World War II, came close to demolition in the 1970s, became a family home and was then rescued in its current incarnation as a hotel. There is little evidence of this varied past in the beautiful Victorian plasterwork and panelling. The cooking is classical Scottish and French style, making use of free-range, organic and local produce. Try pan-fried Kintyre Sika venison with a claret reduction, or rack of Skipness lamb.

Chef: Angus MacDiarmid **Owners:** Angus & Susan MacDiarmid **Times:** 7-9, Closed L all week **Prices:** Fixed D £28.95, Coffee £1.90, Min/Water £2.95, Service optional **Wine:** 8 bottles over £20, 25 bottles under £20, 2 by the glass (£2.50) **Notes:** Vegetarian available **Seats:** 24 **Smoking:** N/Sm in restaurant **Children:** Min 12 yrs, Portions **Rooms:** 10 (10 en suite) ★★ CHH **Directions:** 10m S of Tarbert Loch Fyne. The entrance is located on the left off A83 travelling S towards Campbeltown **Parking:** 20

CLACHAN-SEIL MAP 20 NM71

Willowburn Hotel

Traditional French, Scottish

riendly country cottage hotel offering local produce and fine lining

☎ 01852 300276 PA34 4TJ
e-mail: willowburn.hotel@virgin.net
web: www.willowburn.co.uk

his welcoming hotel enjoys a glorious setting with grounds running lown to the water's edge of Clachan Sound. You can watch the vildlife from the dining room window. Service is friendly and nobtrusive, with Jan Wolfe seeing to the front of house and Chris Volfe doing the cooking. Guests are offered canapés before dinner nd a chance to meet one another. Cuisine is a mixture of French, cottish and British cooking styles, producing good clean flavours. Try starter like home-smoked duck with onion marmalade and Grand Aarnier sauce, followed by a main course of loin of pork with fennel ollen, served with sweet potato and apple rösti and peach chutney.

hef: Chris Wolfe **Owners:** Jan & Chris Wolfe **Times:** 7-8.30, Closed Dec-Feb **Prices:** Fixed D £36, Min/Water £2.25, Service optional **Vine:** 50 bottles over £20, 47 bottles under £20, 4 by the glass (£3.75) **lotes:** Coffee incl, Fixed D 4 courses **Seats:** 20 **Smoking:** N/Sm in estaurant **Children:** Min 8 yrs **Rooms:** 7 (7 en suite) ★★ **irections:** 11m S of Oban via A816 and B844 (Easdale) over Atlantic ridge, restaurant 0.5m after bridge on left **Parking:** 20

ERISKA MAP 20 NM94

Isle of Eriska

see below

KILCHRENAN MAP 20 NN02

The Ardanaiseig Hotel

French, British V

An idyllic lochside location, with a rugged romantic feel and awesome food

☎ 01866 833333 by Loch Awe PA35 1HE
e-mail: info@ardanaiseig.com
web: www.ardanaiseig.com

Designed by the prominent 19th-century Scottish architect William Burn, Ardanaiseig is situated on the shores of Loch Awe, where the slopes of Ben Cruachan meet the water, amid truly breathtaking scenery. Interiors are very much in keeping with the period, with gorgeous antiques and fine art, all very understated and uncluttered. The kitchen produces innovative food, faultlessly cooked with good use made of local produce - the chef even picks his own wild mushrooms and grows his own herbs. Dinner is a complete experience with little surprise extras really rounding off the meal - your five courses might include a soufflé of Roquefort cheese, venison saddle with red onion confit and juniper essence, followed by espresso and chocolate ice cream bombe with bananas, vanilla and rum anglaise. Exquisite.

continued

Isle of Eriska

ERISKA MAP 20 NM94

Modern British NOTABLE WINE LIST

lmost flawless blend of service, style and good food in xurious surroundings

☎ 01631 720371 PA37 1SD
-mail: office@eriska-hotel.co.uk
web: www.eriska-hotel.co.uk

here can be few places in the UK to rival the Isle of Eriska as a estination for eating and drinking. First off, it's a private island with at uniquely West Coast feel - mists and heather, stunning sea views nd awesome sunsets. Secondly there's the house - a Scottish baronial ile decorated in an opulent yet tasteful style with heavy curtains, rich olours and plenty of dark, polished wood (both wall-panelling and ntique furniture) and with the thoroughly modern addition of a xurious spa. The restaurant continues the fine balance of old school rmality and current dining sensibilities with highly professional staff ffering knowledgeable and friendly service, particularly the ommelier. The menu could be described as modern but perhaps a ore informative description would be classical French with ontemporary touches and some of the finest Scottish produce. errine of home-cured organic salmon, potato and Comté cheese llowed by roast haunch of West Highland venison with juniper jelly and gravy would be good examples of what's on offer. Don't miss the badgers who come to feed at the terrace door in the evening.
Notable Wine List: This well-presented wine list shows real interest with well-chosen wines throughout.

Chef: Robert MacPherson **Owners:** Mr Buchanan-Smith **Times:** 12.30-1.30/8-9, Closed Jan **Prices:** Fixed D £38.50, Coffee £2, Min/Water £3, Service optional **Wine:** 150 bottles over £20, 45 bottles under £20, 2 by the glass (£3.50) **Notes:** Fixed D 4 courses, Vegetarian available, Dress Restrictions, Jacket & tie, Civ Wed 110 **Seats:** 40, Pr/dining room 20 **Smoking:** N/Sm in restaurant, Air con **Children:** Menu, Portions **Rooms:** 17 (17 en suite) ★★★★★ CHH **Directions:** A82 from Glasgow to Tyndrum. A85 towards Oban; at Connel bridge take A828 to Benderloch village for 4m **Parking:** 50

KILCHRENAN *continued* MAP 20 NN02

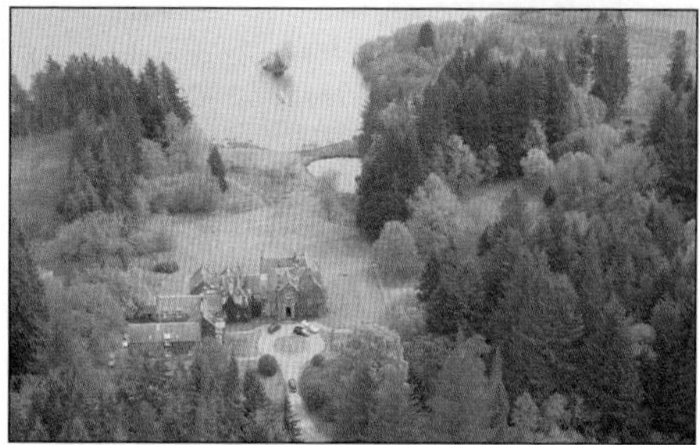

The Ardanaiseig Hotel

Chef: Gary Goldie **Owners:** Bennie Gray **Times:** 12.00-2/7-9, Closed 2 Jan-10 Feb **Prices:** Fixed D £45, Coffee £2.50, Min/Water £3.50, Service optional **Wine:** 94 bottles over £20, 4 bottles under £20, 16 by the glass (£4-£9) **Notes:** Fixed D 4 courses, Vegetarian menu, Dress Restrictions, Smart casual, no jeans or trainers, Civ Wed 50 **Seats:** 36 **Smoking:** N/Sm in restaurant **Children:** Min 9 yrs, Portions **Rooms:** 16 (16 en suite) ★★★ **Directions:** Take A85 to Oban. At Taynuilt turn left onto B845 towards Kilchrenan. In Kilchrenan turn left by pub. Hotel in 3m **Parking:** 16

❀❀ Taychreggan Hotel

British

Imaginative dining in Highland country house

☎ 01866 833211 833366 PA35 1HQ
e-mail: info@taychreggan.co.uk
web: www.taychregganhotel.co.uk

Surrounded by stunning Highland scenery, this stylish and superbly presented hotel enjoys an idyllic setting in 40 acres of grounds on the shores of Loch Awe. A former ferry and cattle drovers' inn, the hotel has a separate bar and traditionally presented dining room with its huge arched windows. Service is courteous and winningly old fashioned. Skilfully prepared contemporary dishes make extensive use of Scottish and locally-sourced ingredients. Start with slow-braised spiced pork belly with spring cabbage and pancetta jus. To follow, there's saddle of prime Scottish lamb with Anna potatoes, ratatouille, braised shallots and mustard seed and garlic jus. Finish with vanilla rice pudding with caramelised pear.

Times: 7.30-8.45 **Rooms:** 20 (20 en suite) ★★★ **Directions:** W from Glasgow on A82 to Crainlarich. W on A85 to Taynuilt. On B845 to Kilchrenan & Taychreggan

LOCHGILPHEAD MAP 20 NR88

❀ Cairnbaan

British, European

Fresh cooking beside the canal

☎ 01546 603668 Crinan Canal, Cairnbaan PA31 8SJ
e-mail: info@cairnbaan.com
web: www.cairnbaan.com

Delightfully located small hotel on the Crinan Canal, with wide picture windows making the most of the views. While alfresco dining is popular in the warmer months, winter is made cosy by the tartan décor in the restaurant, and a wealth of creature comforts. Fresh seafood is a powerful draw throughout the seasons, though it's not a[n] exclusively fish-based menu. Warm salad of Jura scallops, and grilled jumbo langoustines with garlic butter might share space with roast Barbary duck with mixed berry sauce, and supreme of chicken.

Times: 12-2.30/6-9.30 **Rooms:** 12 (12 en suite) ★★★
Directions: Cairnbaan is 2m N of Lochgilphead on A83, Hotel first on left

LUSS MAP 20 NS39

❀❀ Colquhoun's

Modern British

Stunning loch views and imaginative cuisine

☎ 01436 860201 The Lodge on Loch Lomond, Hotel & Restaurant G83 8PA
e-mail: res@loch-lomondhotel.co.uk
web: www.loch-lomond.co.uk

The Lodge on Loch Lomond boasts a fantastic location, and the restaurant has traditional Scandinavian décor with pinewood walls an[d] pillars. One side is completely made up of windows allowing unrivalled loch views. The food is mostly Scottish, but with international influences. Local produce and fresh ingredients are the cornerstones for dishes like a starter of warm salad of smoked

continue[d]

haddock served with poached quail's eggs, crisp Serrano ham and Arran dressing or Aberfeldy cheese parcel with rocket and parmesan salad and walnut dressing. Main courses are equally mouthwatering, try roasted loin of highland venison with red onion marmalade, redcurrant dressing and gaufrette potatoes.

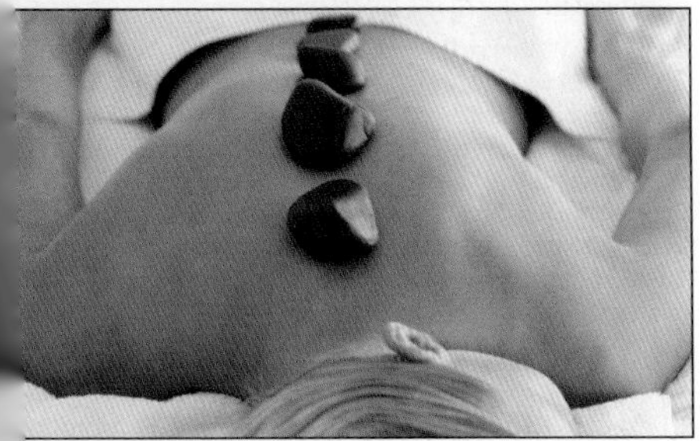

Colquhoun's

Chef: David Friel **Owners:** Niall Colquhoun **Times:** 12-5/6-9.45 **Prices:** Fixed L £16.95-£18.95, Fixed D £26.95-£38.80, Coffee £2.50, Min/Water £4, Service optional **Wine:** 50 bottles over £20, 20 bottles under £20, 6 by the glass (£3.95-£5.45) **Notes:** Fixed L 3 courses, Vegetarian available, Civ Wed 100 **Seats:** 100, Pr/dining room 40 **Smoking:** N/Sm in restaurant **Children:** Menu, Portions **Rooms:** 46 (46 en suite) ★★★ HL **Directions:** 30m N of Glasgow on A82 **Parking:** 70

OBAN MAP 20 NM82

Bachler's Conservatory

French, International **NEW**

Sophisticated dining overlooking Oban Bay

☎ 01631 571115 13 Dalriach Rd PA34 5EQ
e-mail: info@kimberley-hotel.com
web: www.kimberley-hotel.com

continued

The stunning Bachler's Conservatory restaurant overlooks the garden, the harbour and the waters of Oban Bay, with a sophisticated décor of green tablecloths, red striped seating and plenty of fresh flowers. The building was a maternity hospital until 1995, and the hotel name is linked to the South African Kimberley Diamond Mine. The cooking has a distinctly modern French flair but the ingredients are decidedly top-of-the-range Scottish. Seafood straight from the sea is a strength (monkfish roasted in herbal butter with leaf spinach), but local game (roasted venison) and meat (Aberdeen Angus beef and Scottish lamb) are well represented too.

Chef: Walter Bachler **Owners:** K D Nairz, C Kienzl **Times:** 6-10, Closed Nov-Easter, Closed L All wk **Prices:** Starter £3.80-£14.50, Main £15.80-£21.80, Dessert £3.50-£8.20, Coffee £1.80, Min/Water £3.20, Service included **Wine:** 28 bottles over £20, 11 bottles under £20, 11 by the glass (£3-£6.20) **Notes:** Vegetarian available **Seats:** 30 **Smoking:** N/Sm in restaurant **Children:** Portions **Rooms:** 14 (14 en suite) ★★ HL **Directions:** Telephone for directions **Parking:** 10

Eeusk

Seafood

Good simple cuisine and views to die for

☎ 01631 565666 North Pier PA34 5QD
e-mail: eeusk.fishcafe@virgin.net

What a fantastic location, right on one of Oban's piers! The modern building has large glass windows with unrestricted views of the bay and islands. The pier is busy with fishermen and visitors passing by so it's an interesting place to eat and watch the world go by. Simple cuisine makes the best of fine fresh produce, naturally given the location, with a strong emphasis on seafood. Typical dishes might include creamy smoked haddock chowder (a signature dish), or langoustine crème brûlée; but it's difficult to ignore the big bowl of excellent Loch Etive mussels accompanied by crusty bread to dip in the juices.

Chef: Marianne Macdonald **Owners:** The Macleod Family **Times:** 12-2.30/6-9.30, Closed 25-26 Dec, 1 Jan, 2 wks mid Jan **Prices:** Starter £4.95-£8.95, Main £9.95-£19.95, Dessert £3.95-£4.25, Coffee £1.60, Min/Water £3.50, Service optional **Wine:** 17 bottles over £20, 19 bottles under £20, 6 by the glass **Notes:** Vegetarian available **Seats:** 100, Pr/dining room 24 **Smoking:** N/Sm in restaurant **Children:** Min 10 yrs D, Portions **Directions:** 85 miles from Glasgow, North-West A85 **Parking:** Public car park at rear

Manor House Hotel

Traditional British

Quality produce and classical elegance by the sea

☎ 01631 562087 Gallanach Rd PA34 4LS
e-mail: info@manorhouseoban.com
web: www.manorhouseoban.com

continued

Scotland

OBAN *continued* MAP 20 NM82

This genteel Georgian manor house overlooks the harbour and was originally the principal residence on the Duke of Argyll's Oban estate. Today's hotel admirably preserves the elegance of its bygone days, and the small dining room oozes country-house appeal, with deep green walls complemented by heavy drapes and tartan. The kitchen makes fine use of the abundant local larder's quality produce on daily-changing, fixed-priced, five-course dinner menus; take seared skate wing with a leek risotto cake and lemon sauce vièrge, for instance. There's a bar menu only at lunchtimes.

Chef: Patrick Freytag **Owners:** Mr P L Crane **Times:** 12-2.30/6.45-9, Closed 25-26 Dec **Prices:** Fixed L £17.50-£21.50, Fixed D £32.50, Starter £7, Main £18, Dessert £7, Coffee £2, Service optional **Wine:** 20 bottles over £20, 32 bottles under £20, 6 by the glass (£2.50-£3.50) **Notes:** Fixed L 3 courses, Fixed D 5 courses, Dress Restrictions, Smart casual **Seats:** 30 **Smoking:** N/Sm in restaurant **Children:** Min 12 yrs, Portions **Rooms:** 11 (11 en suite) ★★★ HL **Directions:** 300 mtrs W of Oban ferry terminal **Parking:** 20

PORT APPIN MAP 20 NM94

Airds Hotel

see below

STRACHUR MAP 20 NN00

Creggans Inn

Modern British

Local produce showcased in spectacular lochside setting

☎ 01369 860279 PA27 8BX
e-mail: info@creggans-inn.co.uk
web: www.creggans-inn.co.uk

This hotel has a wonderful location on the shores of Loch Fyne. Comfortable bedrooms, open fires and a restaurant that showcases local produce, make this a destination venue. The dining room has stripped floors, terracotta walls and fabulous views. Scottish dishes predominate with starters of juicy Loch Fyne oysters or creamy, smoky Cullen skink served with granary bread. Main courses include pan-seared venison with parsnip purée, grilled fillet of local salmon with langoustine potatoes, or leek, caraway seed and tomato tarte Tatin. Leave room for a dessert of bitter chocolate pavé with Kirsch cherries.

Chef: Calum Williamson **Owners:** The Robertson Family **Times:** 7-9, Closed 25-26 Dec, Closed L all week **Prices:** Fixed D £32, Min/Water £3, Service optional **Wine:** 29 bottles over £20, 29 bottles under £20, 6 by the glass (£3.50) **Notes:** Fixed D 4 courses, coffee incl, Vegetarian available, Dress Restrictions, Smart casual **Seats:** 35 **Smoking:** N/Sm in restaurant **Children:** Min 8 yrs, Menu, Portions **Rooms:** 14 (14 en suite) ★★★ HL **Directions:** From Glasgow A82, along Loch Lomond, then W on A83, onto A815 to Strachur. Or by ferry from Gourock to Dunoon onto A815 **Parking:** 25

Airds Hotel

PORT APPIN MAP 20 NM94

British, European V NOTABLE WINE LIST

Lochside gastronomic treat

☎ 01631 730236 PA38 4DF
e-mail: airds@airds-hotel.com
web: www.airds-hotel.com

The views are stunning from this small, luxury hotel on the shores of Loch Linnhe, originally an 18th-century ferry inn for those in passage to Lismore Island. Inside, country-house comforts meet sophisticated modern chic in a relaxed, intimate atmosphere, with comfortable lounges replete with cosy sofas, log fires and splendid artwork, while the restaurant continues the theme with designer fabrics, candlelit tables and large windows to make the best of those outstanding views. Service is highly professional, but retains a personal and welcoming touch, while the cooking takes a modern approach infused with a Scottish twist. Tip-top ingredients are treated with due respect, the kitchen's intelligently simple, clean-cut style and uncomplicated combinations allowing key ingredient flavours to sing on the daily-changing, fixed-price menus. Think salmon and Dover sole baked in pastry and served with a citrus butter sauce, or perhaps braised turbot and lobster with wilted vegetables and a vermouth velouté, while a prune and Armagnac soufflé or warm date pudding with butterscotch sauce, might feature at dessert.

Notable Wine List: An interesting and well-laid out list featuring a good range of Burgundy wines.

Chef: J Paul Burns **Owners:** Mr & Mrs S McKivragan **Times:** 12-1.45/7.30-9, Closed 5-26 Jan **Prices:** Fixed D £47.50, Starter £3.75-£8, Main £8.50-£17, Dessert £6-£6.50, Min/Water £3.50, Service optional **Wine:** 108 bottles over £20, 12 bottles under £20, 10 by the glass (£4.75-£6.50) **Notes:** Coffee incl. Fixed D 4 courses, Vegetarian menu, Dress Restrictions, Smart casual at D, no jeans/trainers/T-shirts, Civ Wed 40 **Seats:** 36 **Smoking:** N/Sm in restaurant **Children:** Min 8 yrs, Menu, Portions **Rooms:** 12 (12 en suite) ★★★★ HL **Directions:** A828 follow signs for Port Appin. Continue for 2.5m, Airds Hotel on left **Parking:** 20

TARBERT LOCH FYNE MAP 20 NR86

Stonefield Castle Hotel

Modern Scottish

Enjoyable lochside dining in baronial keep

☎ 01880 820836 PA29 6YJ
e-mail: enquiries@stonefieldcastle.co.uk
web: www.stonefieldcastle.co.uk

Built in 1837, this impressive baronial castle sits in its lochside setting surrounded by beautiful woodland gardens. There are elegant public rooms and a dining room with views across Loch Fyne. Service is friendly. Modern Scottish dishes with occasional oriental influences are offered here with good use of local and Scottish ingredients like Buccleuch beef, Argyll lamb, home-grown vegetables and seafood. Try the West Coast scallops with Orkney black pudding and pancetta salad followed by loin of Perthshire lamb. To finish there's bitter chocolate torte and one of the fifty listed malts.

Chef: Gary Mann **Owners:** Stonefield Castle Group **Times:** 12-2/7-9 **Prices:** Fixed D £30-£42.45, Coffee £2, Min/Water £3.50, Service optional **Wine:** 23 bottles over £20, 38 bottles under £20, 6 by the glass (£3.25) **Notes:** Dress Restrictions, Smart casual, Civ Wed 120 **Seats:** 120, Pr/dining room 10 **Smoking:** N/Sm in restaurant **Children:** Menu, Portions **Rooms:** 33 (32 en suite) ★★★ HL **Directions:** 2m N of Tarbert Village **Parking:** 33

TIGHNABRUAICH MAP 20 NR97

The Royal at Tighnabruaich

Modern Scottish

Fresh seafood and game beside the loch side

☎ 01700 811239 Shore Rd PA21 2BE
e-mail: info@royalhotel.org.uk
web: www.royalhotel.org.uk

Just yards from the loch shore, this family-run hotel offers jaw-dropping views over the waters of the Kyles of Bute from a choice of dining areas. The fine-dining Crustacean restaurant has an intimate, candlelit buzz, while there's a more relaxed brasserie-bar option, too. The modern approach has seafood at its heart and native produce its soul - with suppliers admirably named. Seafood straight from the nets, game, or perhaps beef from the Duke of Buccleuch Estate are treated with integrity, the intelligently simple, accurate approach letting the quality, fresh produce do the talking. Start with mousseline of scallops and follow on with grilled Royal lobster or pheasant stuffed with venison forcemeat accompanied by truffle mash.

Chef: R McKie, L McKie **Owners:** Mr & Mrs R McKie **Times:** 12-3/7-8.45, Closed Xmas period, Mon-Tue, Closed L all week (groups by prior arrangement) **Prices:** Fixed D £32.50-£35, Starter £3.95-£10.95, Main £9.95-£26.95, Dessert £3.95-£5.25, Coffee £1.95, Min/Water £3.95, Service optional **Wine:** 40 bottles over £20, 16 bottles under £20, 6 by the glass (£3.95-£4.95) **Notes:** Fixed D 5 courses, Vegetarian available **Seats:** 35, Pr/dining room 20 **Smoking:** N/Sm in restaurant **Children:** Portions **Rooms:** 11 (11 en suite) ★★★ SHL **Directions:** From Strachur, on B886, turn right onto A8003 to Tighnabruaich. Hotel on right at bottom of hill. Dunoon ferry terminal take left onto B8000 to Tighnabruaich **Parking:** 20

AYRSHIRE, EAST

SORN MAP 20 NS52

The Sorn Inn

Modern British

Refurbished coaching inn offering modern cuisine

☎ 01290 551305 35 Main St KA5 6HU
e-mail: craig@sorninn.com
web: www.sorninn.com

A late 18th-century coaching inn on the outside, but bang up-to-date on the inside, with modern styling and a warm, rustic colour scheme throughout. There are two dining options, the Chop House for bistro-style food in a cosy pub area, and the fine-dining restaurant. Here you will find modern British cooking with the emphasis on fresh local produce, particularly game and meat. Try a starter like saddle of rabbit and black pudding with aubergine chutney for example, or a main course of supreme of pheasant, with braised Savoy cabbage, ravioli of its leg confit, wild mushrooms and Puy lentil jus.

Chef: Craig Grant **Owners:** The Grant Partnership **Times:** 12-2.30/6.30-9.30, Closed Mon, Closed D Sun **Prices:** Fixed L £12.95-£14.95, Fixed D £20.50-£24.50, Coffee £1.50, Min/Water £3, Service optional **Wine:** 25 bottles over £20, 30 bottles under £20, 12 by the glass (£3.25-£3.75) **Notes:** Sun menu 12-6.30, Tasting menu, Vegetarian available **Seats:** 42 **Smoking:** N/Sm in restaurant **Children:** Menu, Portions **Rooms:** 4 (4 en suite) ★★★★ RR **Directions:** From A77, take the A76 to Mauchline join B743, 4m to Sorn **Parking:** 9

AYRSHIRE, NORTH

DALRY MAP 20 NS24

Braidwoods

Modern Scottish

Creative flair in a beautiful setting

☎ 01294 833544 Drumastle Mill Cottage KA24 4LN
e-mail: keithbraidwood@btconnect.com
web: www.braidwoods.co.uk

This charming group of old millers' cottages transformed into a modern-looking restaurant with two dining rooms offers rustic dining in a relaxed yet formal environment. A popular venue for 'ladies who lunch', but equally a romantic setting for dinner. Skilled cooking by the chef-patron brings modern Scottish dishes of high quality and good value to the menu. Try a starter of warm timbale of Arbroath smokies using smoked Marbury salmon. Main courses might include the likes of pan-fried loin of Highland red deer, carved on to crushed root vegetables with roast beetroot and thyme essence. To finish off you might sample the old-fashioned bread-and-butter pudding with warm caramel sauce.

Times: 12-1.45/7-9, Closed 25-26 Dec, 1st 3 wks Jan, 1st 2 wks Sep, Mon, Closed L Tue (Sun Etr-Sep), D Sun **Directions:** 1 mile from Dalry on the Saltcoats Road

Scotland

AYRSHIRE, SOUTH

AYR MAP 20 NS32

Fairfield House Hotel

International

Modern, relaxed dining and great views

☎ 01292 267461 12 Fairfield Rd KA7 2AR
e-mail: reservations@fairfieldhotel.co.uk
web: www.fairfieldhotel.co.uk

A luxury seafront hotel with spectacular views across the Firth of Clyde to the Isle of Arran. The magnificent Victorian mansion has been refurbished in a stylish look that blends in with the striking exterior. Martins Bar and Grill has leather seating, Grecian-style pillars and features plants across the bar and restaurant areas, plus an outside deck making the most of the views. The cuisine style is simple using fresh local produce to create popular Scottish dishes with a twist. Try grilled asparagus with pear and rocket salad to start, followed by fillet of Scotch beef with spinach and mushrooms. For dessert try a classic lemon tart. There is a wide selection of fine wines from around the world, plus a good collection of single malts.

Chef: David Stevens **Owners:** G Martin **Times:** 11-9.30 **Prices:** Fixed L £6.95-£20.95, Fixed D £25, Starter £4.95-£8.95, Main £7.95-£21.95, Dessert £3.95-£7.95, Coffee £1.95, Min/Water £3.50, Service optional **Wine:** 30 bottles over £20, 16 bottles under £20, 10 by the glass (£3.50-£6.95) **Notes:** Vegetarian available, Civ Wed 150 **Seats:** 80, Pr/dining room 12 **Smoking:** N/Sm in restaurant, Air con **Children:** Menu, Portions **Rooms:** 44 (44 en suite) ★★★★ HL **Directions:** From A77 to Ayr South. Follow signs for town centre. Left into Miller Rd. At lights turn left, then right into Fairfield **Parking:** 50

see advert opposite

Fouters

Modern Scottish

Intimate basement restaurant and ambitious cooking

☎ 01292 261391 2A Academy St KA7 1HS
e-mail: qualityfood@fouters.co.uk
web: www.fouters.co.uk

It's easy to miss, along a cobbled lane, down a flight of steps to a series of intimate cellar rooms that once operated as a bank vault in the 18th century. The vaulted ceiling, flagstone floors, linen-clothed tables and colourful local seascapes give this family-run place an appealing atmosphere, and the service is relaxed and friendly. Fish landed at the local quay and meat and game from the surrounding hills are skilfully handled and the cooking honest and unpretentious, allowing the fresh flavours to shine through. Dishes might include seared 'melt-in-the-mouth' Scottish scallops with crushed peas and mint, perfectly cooked sea bass with parmesan and herb crust, and vanilla crème brûlée with raspberry sorbet.

Fouters

Chef: Brian Murphy, James Macintosh **Owners:** Mr & Mrs Murphy, Henrietta Fleming **Times:** 12-2.30/5-10, Closed 4-11 Jan, Sun-Mon **Prices:** Starter £3.95-£9.50, Main £14-£22, Dessert £5-£7.50, Coffee £1.60, Min/Water £3.95, Service optional **Wine:** 30 bottles over £20, 12 bottles under £20, 2 by the glass (£2.60-£3.60) **Notes:** Vegetarian available **Seats:** 38, Pr/dining room 24 **Smoking:** N/Sm in restaurant, Air con **Children:** Min 5/10 yrs **Directions:** Town centre, opposite Town Hall, down Cobblestone Lane **Parking:** On street

BALLANTRAE MAP 20 NX08

Glenapp Castle

see opposite

MAYBOLE MAP 20 NS20

Ladyburn

Traditional French

Traditional dining in small country-house hotel

☎ 01655 740585 KA19 7SG
e-mail: jh@ladyburn.co.uk
web: www.ladyburn.co.uk

A 16th-century former dower house, this charming, family-run country house hotel is surrounded by woods, a small burn and gardens with a number of unique rose collections. Oil paintings, silver and other pieces of objet d'art fill the intimate restaurant, which is candlelit and formal. A short, traditional menu utilises the best seasonal produce in a repertoire of British and French dishes, with some ingredients arriving in the kitchen from the hotel's own gardens. Mulligatawny soup could be followed by roast Aylesbury duck served with Cointreau jus and the meal may end with lavender crème brulée.

Times: 12.30-2/7.30-8.30, Closed Xmas, New Year, Mon-Wed **Rooms:** 5 (5 en suite) ★★ HL **Directions:** A77 at Maybole take B7023 to Crosshill. Turn right at war memorial for Dailly & Girvan in 2m turn left, signed Walled Garden campsite, hotel 0.75m on right

continued

PRESTWICK MAP 20 NS32

Restaurant 1933

Modern European

Caledonian cuisine with lovely sea views

☎ 01292 477286 Parkstone Hotel, Esplanade KA9 1QN
e-mail: info@parkstonehotel.co.uk
web: www.parkstonehotel.co.uk

Situated on the seafront in a quiet residential area close to the airport, this family-run hotel caters for business visitors as well as golfers who come to enjoy the many courses in the area. The restaurant - named after the date the hotel was built - is relaxed and informal with views over the Firth of Clyde and the Isle of Arran. Modern European is the declared style of the kitchen with typical dishes including smoked salmon with Arran mustard scone and soured cream, with a main of seared fillet of Bute mackerel on caponata-style vegetables, fish polenta and pesto dressing.

Chef: Kevin Cosgrove **Owners:** Stewart Clarkson **Times:** 12-2/5-9.30 **Prices:** Starter £3-£6.25, Main £9-£16, Dessert £3.95-£5, Coffee £1.95, Min/Water £3.95, Service optional **Wine:** 1 bottle over £20, 20 bottles under £20, 4 by the glass (£2.95) **Notes:** Vegetarian available, Civ Wed 100 **Seats:** 36, Pr/dining room 100 **Smoking:** N/Sm in restaurant **Children:** Menu, Portions **Rooms:** 30 (30 en suite) ★★★ HL **Directions:** From Prestwick Main St, turn W to seafront, hotel 600yds **Parking:** 30

Scotland

Glenapp Castle

BALLANTRAE MAP 20 NX08

Modern British

Elegant castle hideaway offering accomplished, innovative cuisine

☎ 01465 831212 KA26 0NZ
e-mail: info@glenappcastle.com
web: www.glenappcastle.com

A reservation is essential to enter the grounds of this private castle, but it's worth the effort. Beautifully restored in recent years by Fay and Graham Cowan, the castle dates back to 1870 and nowadays offers the perfect luxury retreat. The 30 acres of gardens and woodland are well worth exploring, and guests at the castle can enjoy the terraced formal gardens, Azalea pond and walled garden with impressive 150ft Victorian glasshouses. The dining room takes diners back to an age of elegance with its beautiful proportions, stately window-dressings and immaculately clothed tables. The chef excels himself to produce an original and imaginative set six-course dinner menu each day, demonstrating a superb blend of traditional and modern cuisine. Skilful cooking brings out the best in high quality ingredients with seasonal garnishes and plenty of traditional Scottish produce. Where else could you find a menu interspersed with combinations like Criffel cheese soaked in Bladnoch Whisky and rolled in pinhead oatmeal with grape chutney, or a delicate quenelle of Dunsyre blue cheese with Pinot Noir jelly and white truffle honey? Sublime desserts include the likes of coconut marshmallow with kalamansi parfait, exotic fruits and Pina Colada sauce. A simple lunch menu, on the other hand, offers a variety of dishes with some offered as a starter or main course portion, perhaps featuring a straightforward salad of roasted Isle of Arran langoustines with truffle dressing.

Chef: Matt Weedon **Owners:** Graham & Fay Cowan **Times:** 1-2/7-9, Closed 30 Nov-1 Apr **Prices:** Fixed D £55, Coffee £2.50, Min/Water £3, Service optional **Wine:** 200 bottles over £20, 9 by the glass (£6.50-£13.50) **Notes:** Fixed D 6 courses, Civ Wed 34 **Seats:** 34, Pr/dining room 20 **Smoking:** N/Sm in restaurant **Children:** Min 5 yrs, Menu, Portions **Rooms:** 17 (17 en suite) ★★★★ HL **Directions:** Drive through Ballantrae, over bridge, 1st right - 1m to gates of lodge house **Parking:** 20

TROON MAP 20 NS33

Lochgreen House

see below

MacCallums of Troon

Traditional Mediterranean NEW

Seafood restaurant in harbourside location

☎ 01292 319339 The Harbour KA10 6DH

A stunning location within a working harbour - you can see the fishing fleet come and go (perhaps landing your meal) from this one-time harbour hydraulic pump house. The tastefully converted interior now resembles a spacious boathouse, with high-raftered ceilings and walls brimful of memorabilia of the America's Cup. Wooden floors, darkwood tables and chairs (a few enjoy the views) add to the relaxed atmosphere, while service is friendly from smart, apron-clad staff. It's no surprise that menus come awash with the fruits of the sea, the kitchen taking an intelligently simple approach that lets the freshness of produce shine. Think sea bass with black olives and a pesto mash, or perhaps grilled lobster with garlic butter or thermidor.

Chef: Ewan McAllister, Adele Wylie **Owners:** John & James MacCallums **Times:** 12-2.30/6.30-9.30, Closed Xmas, New Year, Mon, Closed D Sun **Prices:** Starter £3.85-£8.95, Main £9.50-£22.50, Dessert £4.85-£5.85, Coffee £1.20, Min/Water £2.50, Service optional, Group min 12 service 10% **Wine:** 6 bottles over £20, 17 bottles under £20, 4 by the glass (£3.40) **Seats:** 43 **Smoking:** N/Sm in restaurant **Children:** Portions **Directions:** Please telephone for directions **Parking:** 12

TURNBERRY MAP 20 NS20

Malin Court

Scottish

Modern cooking with views of the Firth of Clyde

☎ 01655 331457 KA26 9PB
e-mail: info@malincourt.co.uk
web: www.malincourt.co.uk

Malin Court is situated beside the famous Turnberry golf course with views of the new Kintyre courses. The hotel's restaurant, Cotters, has lounge areas, a real fire in the cooler months and wonderful views along the coast. A lunch and supper menu is offered and a set six-course dinner including canapés and coffee. Modern British dishes are presented alongside traditional Scottish fare, all using quality local ingredients. Typical of these are seared sea bass on roasted fennel with garlic and pesto, and braised shank of Ayrshire lamb on parsnip purée.

Times: 12.30-2/7-9 **Rooms:** 18 (18 en suite) ★★★ HL **Directions:** On A719 one mile from A77 on N side of village.

The Westin Turnberry Resort Hotel

Traditional NOTABLE WINE LIST

Upmarket resort hotel that caters to all tastes

☎ 01655 331000 KA26 9LT
e-mail: turnberry@westin.com
web: www.westin.com/turnberry

Set on a coastal hillside and visible for miles, this imposing hotel

continued

Lochgreen House

TROON MAP 20 NS33

Modern British

Winning country-house hotel and highly rated restaurant

☎ 01292 313343 Monktonhill Rd, Southwood KA10 7EN
e-mail: lochgreen@costleyhotels.co.uk
web: www.lochgreenhouse.co.uk

Set in manicured grounds not far from the coast with views out to Ailsa Craig, Lochgreen was once a family residence that has been sympathetically restored and extended into today's imposing country-house hotel. The light-and-airy, formal Tapestry restaurant comes with a high vaulted ceiling, stunning chandeliers, namesake wall-hung tapestries and furniture to match, and overlooks the fountain garden.

Andrew Costley's cooking is in the classic vein but with a modern approach, his accomplished kitchen's precise handling and finesse with the freshest seasonal produce from the abundant Scottish larder responsible for consistent results. Rich, clear flavours and artistic presentation abound in dishes like seared king scallops with a carrot, sultana and ginger salad and sauce d'épice, or a duo of roast breast of duckling and ravioli of confit leg served with Puy lentils and a fried apple and prune jus. To finish, perhaps warm milk chocolate tart with pistachio ice cream and golden syrup. Lunch is served in the brasserie while a stroll in the carefully tended gardens post- or pre-meal is a Lochgreen requisite.

Chef: Andrew Costley **Owners:** Bill & Cath Costley **Times:** 12-2.30/7-9.3 **Prices:** Fixed L £19.50-£24.50, Fixed D £29.95-£35, Coffee £2.50, Min/Water £4 **Wine:** 82 bottles over £20, 27 bottles under £20, 9 by the glass (£4.15-£7.25) **Notes:** Dress Restrictions, Smart casual, Civ Wed 100 **Seats:** 80, Pr/dining room 30 **Smoking:** N/Sm in restaurant, Air con **Children:** Menu, Portions **Rooms:** 40 (40 en suite) ★★★★ CHH **Directions:** From A77 follow signs for Prestwick Airport, take B749 to Troon, Lochgreen is situated on left 1m from junct **Parking:** 60

makes its presence felt well before you arrive. It's a celebrated resort destination and comes with all mod cons, including a golf academy, spa, and other outdoor pursuits, plus a host of eateries to suit every mood. Book ahead for a window table in the formal restaurant - an elegant room with stunning views of the Isle of Arran and misty Mull of Kintyre - and take your choice from a traditional selection of classic dishes such as game pie or sole meunière, or a six-course 'creative' menu, which features more innovative contemporary cuisine.
Notable Wine List: A classic wine list offering much interest throughout including a notable Penfolds Grange list.

Chef: Ralph Porciani **Owners:** Starwood Hotels & Resorts **Times:** 7-10, Closed Xmas, Closed L Mon-Sun **Prices:** Fixed D £49, Starter £10-£17, Main £25-£39, Dessert £7-£9.50, Coffee £4, Min/Water £4, Service optional **Wine:** 100% bottles over £20, 10 by the glass (£6.50-£12.50) **Notes:** Fixed D 6 courses, Vegetarian available, Smart casual, no jeans, Civ Wed 150 **Seats:** 200, Pr/dining room 16 **Smoking:** N/Sm in restaurant **Children:** Menu, Portions **Rooms:** 221 (221 en suite) ★★★★★ **Directions:** Just off A77 S towards Stranraer, through Maybole. 2m after Kirkoswald turn right & follow signs for Turnberry. Hotel 0.5m on right **Parking:** 200

DUMFRIES & GALLOWAY

AUCHENCAIRN MAP 21 NX75

Balcary Bay Hotel

Modern European V

Great food in a romantic setting

☎ 01556 640217 DG7 1QZ
e-mail: reservations@balcary-bay-hotel.co.uk
web: www.balcary-bay-hotel.co.uk

Built in 1625 by a company of smugglers to import liquor from the Isle of Man, this traditional country-house hotel is in an idyllic setting with a romantic air befitting its origins. The elegant, unstuffy dining room has cracking sea views, professional service with just a touch of formality and a genuinely friendly atmosphere. Food is modern European, with assured technique underpinning such dishes as crab ravioli in saffron fish broth or Parma ham wrapped tenderloin of Galloway pork with braised belly and parsnip purée. The stylish presentation and prominent use of local ingredients only serve to enhance the creative cuisine here. Vegetarians should note the extensive meat-free menu available.

Chef: Andrew Lipp **Owners:** Graeme A. Lamb & Family **Times:** 12-2/7-8.30, Closed Mid Dec-Mid Feb, Closed L Prior booking only Mon-Sat **Prices:** Fixed L £16.25, Fixed D £30.75, Starter £5.25-£8.50, Main £14.50-£18, Dessert £6.25, Coffee £3.25, Min/Water £2.75, Service optional **Wine:** 30 bottles over £20, 65 bottles under £20, 3 by the glass (£2.50-£3.50) **Notes:** Fixed L 3 courses, Fixed D 4 courses, Vegetarian menu, Civ Wed 40 **Seats:** 55 **Smoking:** N/Sm in restaurant **Children:** Menu,

continued

Portions **Rooms:** 20 (20 en suite) ★★★ HL **Directions:** Situated on the A711 between Dalbeattie & Kirkcudbright. On reaching Auhencairn follow signs to Balcary along The Shore Rd for 2m **Parking:** 45

CASTLE DOUGLAS MAP 21 NX76

Plumed Horse Restaurant

Modern British

Destination dining in Scotland

☎ 01556 670333 Main St, Crossmichael DG7 3AU
e-mail: plumedhorse@aol.com
web: www.plumedhorse.co.uk

Not somewhere you are likely to be passing by chance, this restaurant is a destination for foodies who make the effort to reach Crossmichael. Here they will find a simple whitewashed barn conversion with fresh interior décor and simple furnishings. Chef-patron Tony Borthwick continues to offer the best of Scotland's larder from local game and fish to Scottish cheeses. Classic French techniques and modern artistry combine to offer imaginative dishes like confit leg of foie gras duck, salt-crusted breast, sauté of foie gras, orange, compôte of beetroot, Castellino lentils, honey and cloves.

Times: 12.30-1/7-9, Closed 25-26 Dec, 2 wks Jan, 2 wks Sep, Mon, Closed D Sun **Directions:** 3.5 miles NW of Castle Douglas on A713.

Carlo's

☎ 01556 503977 211 King St DG7 1DT
Family-run Italian offering familiar dishes from pizza to shellfish stew.

Designs

☎ 01556 504552 179 King St DG7 1DZ
A popular lunch spot below the shop of the same name. Food has an organic slant.

DUMFRIES MAP 21 NX97

The Linen Room

Modern French NOTABLE WINE LIST NEW

Refreshingly unpretentious restaurant with imaginative food

☎ 01387 255689 53 St. Michael St DG1 2QB
e-mail: enquiries@linenroom.com
web: www.linenroom.com

Unassumingly located on a busy street just a short walk from the town centre, The Linen Room's décor cuts quite an unexpected surprise in its striking simplicity - black walls and carpet setting off fresh white table linen, white cushioned captain's-style chairs and framed black-and-white prints punctuating the walls. Fine dining certainly, but refreshingly unpretentious with friendly, relaxed and informed service. The kitchen shows plenty of pedigree, innovation and sound use of local seasonal produce. Strong flavours and a light touch parade on well-presented, accomplished modern French dishes; take Buccleuch Scottish beef fillet with braised pig's cheek, Beluga lentils and parsnip as a main, and to finish off, a 'distortion of cherry' - surely an intriguing prospect? Two tasting menus and a comprehensive wine list complete an assured package.
Notable Wine List: A well-presented wine list which shows much interest and quality.

Chef: Mr R Robertson & Mr A Wesley **Owners:** P & D Byrne, R Robertson **Times:** 12.30-2.30/7-10, Closed 25 & 26 Dec,1 & 2 Jan,2 wks in Jan & Oct, Mon **Prices:** Fixed L £10.95, Starter £5-£9, Main £13-£18, Dessert £5-£5.50,

continued

Scotland

DUMFRIES *continued* MAP 21 NX97

Coffee £3.50, Min/Water £3.25, Service optional **Wine:** 150 bottles over £20, 60 bottles under £20, 12 by the glass (£3.50-£9) **Notes:** Indulgence menu £45, Tasting menu £39.50, Vegetarian available **Seats:** 32 **Smoking:** N/Sm in restaurant **Parking:** 10

Reivers Restaurant

British, International NEW

Interesting dishes based on local produce from the Borders

☎ 01387 254111 Cairndale Hotel & Leisure Club, English St DG1 2DF
e-mail: sales@cairndalehotel.co.uk
web: www.cairndalehotel.co.uk

Reivers Restaurant is named after the Border Reivers, it tells the story of ongoing feuds between Scottish clans and English families either side of the border between the 13th and 17th centuries. The menu is firmly based around local produce with some interesting combinations of ingredients. For a starter try Isle of Skye scallops with a cauliflower pannacotta and local black pudding. Main courses might feature roast cannon of Border lamb served with a mint and lamb forcemeat and rosemary jus.

Times: 7-9.30, Closed Sun & Mon, Closed L Tue-Sat **Rooms:** 91 (91 en suite) ★★★ HL **Directions:** Telephone for directions

ESKDALEMUIR MAP 21 NY29

Hart Manor

British

Hearty country cooking in a tranquil setting

☎ 013873 73217 DG13 0QQ
e-mail: visit@hartmanor.co.uk
web: www.hartmanor.co.uk

A former shooting lodge, this immaculate establishment sits on a wooded hillside near a rural hamlet. It's a cosy base for hill-walking, photography or a spot of golf, and is run with friendly efficiency by a husband-and-wife team. British country cooking is the speciality; dishes are made to order and full of clean, clear flavours. A stilton and walnut tart is a typical starter, while mains might include roast pork served with crackling, roast apples and a haggis sauce, or alternatively take Lakeland beef and walnut pie. Booking essential.

Chef: Kathleen Leadbeater **Owners:** John & Kathleen Leadbeater **Times:** 7-7.30, Closed Xmas & New Yr **Prices:** Fixed D £30 **Notes:** Fixed D 4 courses, Vegetarian available **Seats:** 12, Pr/dining room 10 **Smoking:** N/Sm in restaurant **Children:** Min 10 yrs **Rooms:** 5 (5 en suite) ◆◆◆◆◆ **Directions:** From M74 junct17 follow signs for Eskdalemuir. Approx 14m. Through Eskdalemuir village, hotel approx 1m left on road to Langholm **Parking:** 10

GATEHOUSE OF FLEET MAP 20 NX55

Cally Palace Hotel

Traditional

Quality British cuisine in a grand setting

☎ 01557 814341 DG7 2DL
e-mail: info@callypalace.co.uk
web: www.callypalace.co.uk

Dating back to 1763 and set in 150 acres of woodland, this country manor is an imposing dinner destination. An opulent décor befits its

continued

stately past. The menu is concise, but changes daily and puts a winning emphasis on quality local ingredients, particularly fish. Expect British cooking; open ravioli of wild mushrooms, asparagus and smoked pancetta, seared salmon, with a sweet chilli and ginger jam, or pan-fried duck with a sage and celeriac purée and Cassis sauce. Those with a sweet tooth should leave room for an indulgent white chocolate crème brûlée.

Cally Palace Hotel

Chef: Jamie Muirhead **Owners:** McMillan Hotels **Times:** 12-1/6.45-9, Closed 3 Jan-early Feb **Prices:** Fixed D fr £28.50, Starter £2.90-£3.75, Main £8-£16, Dessert fr £3.50, Coffee £1.70, Min/Water £3, Service optional **Wine:** 34 bottles over £20, 48 bottles under £20, 7 by the glass (£3.10-£4.90) **Notes:** Fixed D 4 courses, Vegetarian available, Dress Restrictions, Jacket, collar and tie **Seats:** 110 **Smoking:** N/Sm in restaurant, Air con **Children:** Menu, Portions **Rooms:** 55 (55 en suite) ★★★★ HL **Directions:** From A74(M) take A75, at Gatehouse take B727. Hotel on left **Parking:** 70

KIRKBEAN MAP 21 NX95

Cavens

British, French

Hearty cooking at a country-house hideaway

☎ 01387 880234 DG2 8AA
e-mail: enquiries@cavens.com
web: www.cavens.com

Cosy country-house hotel with just eight bedrooms, set in landscaped gardens not far from Dumfries. Reservations are essential, as the dining room is an intimate affair with a limited number of well-spaced tables; expect a concise set menu of dinner party fare, with a choice of two dishes offered at each course plus alternatives on request. Starters might include red onion and goat's cheese tartlet, followed perhaps by grilled Wester Ross salmon with tartare sauce, or fillet of Galloway pork with wild mushrooms, apples, brandy and cream. Ingredients come courtesy of local artisan producers where possible.

Chef: A Fordyce **Owners:** A Fordyce **Times:** 7-8.30, Closed Dec-1 Mar, Closed L all week **Prices:** Fixed D £25, Min/Water £2, Service included **Wine:** 12 bottles over £20, 6 bottles under £20, 2 by the glass (£4.50) **Notes:** Coffee included, Vegetarian available, Dress Restrictions, Smart casual, Civ Wed 100 **Seats:** 14, Pr/dining room 20 **Smoking:** N/Sm in restaurant **Children:** Min 12 yrs **Rooms:** 6 (6 en suite) ★★ HL **Directions:** Telephone for directions **Parking:** 20

LOCKERBIE MAP 21 NY18

Dryfesdale Hotel

Modern British

Country-house hotel serving modern cuisine

☎ 01576 202427 DG11 2SF
e-mail: reception@dryfesdalehotel.co.uk
web: www.dryfesdalehotel.co.uk

Set in manicured gardens, this 18th-century former manse even has a helicopter landing site for those who want to arrive in style. The airy Kirkhill Restaurant, which extends into an attractive terrace, boasts a grand piano in one corner and tables are covered in crisp linen. In the formal dining room, a wide choice of European cuisine is available. Good value dinners may include chicken liver and black pudding pâté, home-made gnocchi with peas and mint dressed with a truffle sabayon and pear tart served with sultana anglaise and a mixed berry compôte.

Chef: Ian Mackenzie **Owners:** Mr G. Wright **Times:** 12-2.30/6-9 **Prices:** Fixed L £12.95-£16.95, Fixed D £25-£29, Starter £3.95-£6.95, Main £8.95-£17.95, Dessert £4.95-£6.95, Coffee £2.50, Min/Water £3.95, Service optional **Wine:** 18 bottles over £20, 14 bottles under £20, 6 by the glass (£4-£6) **Notes:** Vegetarian available, Civ Wed 150 **Seats:** 60, Pr/dining room 80 **Smoking:** N/Sm in restaurant **Children:** Menu, Portions **Rooms:** 16 (16 en suite) ★★★ HL **Directions:** M74 junct 17 (0.5m) to Lockerbie **Parking:** 130

MOFFAT MAP 21 NT00

The Dining Room

Modern Traditional V

Enjoyable dining with commitment to local produce

☎ 01683 220558 Bridge House, Well Rd DG10 9JT
e-mail: info@bridgehousemoffat.co.uk
web: www.bridgehousemoffat.co.uk

Family-run guest house and restaurant in a fine Victorian building on the edge of town, where the owners have an expressed commitment to quality and comfort. Every effort is made to source and use local produce in a fixed-price menu which lists a choice of four dishes at each of three courses, such as a starter of smoked salmon roulade or open tart of wood mushroom with basil pesto, followed by roasted pork fillet filled with oranges and red onions, or sea bass with butter bean and olive tagine, and for dessert almond and cranberry tart with heather ice cream.

Chef: Russell Pearce **Owners:** Russell & Danyella Pearce **Times:** 7-8.30, Closed Xmas, Sun, Closed L all wk, D Mon **Prices:** Fixed D £19.95, Min/Water £2.95, Service optional **Wine:** All bottles under £20, 2 by the glass (£2.45-£2.95) **Notes:** Coffee incl, Vegetarian menu, Dress Restrictions, Smart casual **Seats:** 20 **Smoking:** N/Sm in restaurant **Children:** Menu, Portions **Rooms:** 7 (7 en suite) ◆◆◆◆ **Directions:** Take A109 from Moffat centre, 1st left into Burnside, follow into Well Rd, 0.5m on left **Parking:** 7

NEWTON STEWART MAP 20 NX46

Kirroughtree House

Modern British

Formal dining in Scottish mansion

☎ 01671 402141 Minnigaff DG8 6AN
e-mail: info@kirroughtreehouse.co.uk
web: www.kirroughtreehouse.co.uk

A 17th-century mansion house in 8 acres of grounds where antiques and architectural features abound, including a modesty staircase designed to hide a lady's ankles as she climbs the steps! Opulent, formal decoration extends to the dining rooms where good-quality china, linen and glassware combine with professional and friendly service. The chef seeks out local specialist suppliers to bring the best of Galloway's harvest to his kitchen, such as Kirroughtree venison, Wigtown Bay wildfowl and Cairnsmore cheese. To start, partridge breast wrapped in pancetta with Puy lentils and thyme perhaps, before trying the loin of Scottish lamb wrapped in chicken and tarragon mousse in a rosemary and redcurrant sauce. To finish, there's chocolate pavé with praline and Cointreau sauce.

Chef: Rolf Mueller **Owners:** Mr D McMillan **Times:** 12-1.30/7-9, Closed 2 Jan-mid Feb **Prices:** Fixed L fr £16.50, Fixed D fr £32.50, Starter £2.50-£5.25, Main £10.75-£16.25, Dessert £3.50-£4.75, Coffee £1.75, Min/Water £2.15, Service optional **Wine:** 64 bottles over £20, 28 bottles under £20, 3 by the glass (£4) **Notes:** ALC L Mon-Sat only, Sun L 3 courses £16.50, Vegetarian available, Dress Restrictions, Jacket must be worn after 6.30pm **Seats:** 45 **Smoking:** N/Sm in restaurant **Children:** Min 10 yrs **Rooms:** 17 (17 en suite) ★★★ **Directions:** From A75 turn left onto A712 (New Galloway), hotel entrance 300 yds on left **Parking:** 50

PORTPATRICK MAP 20 NW95

Fernhill Hotel

British, European

Conservatory restaurant with stunning views

☎ 01776 810220 Heugh Rd DG9 8TD
e-mail: info@fernhillhotel.co.uk
web: www.fernhillhotel.co.uk

Set in secluded gardens, this smart hotel overlooks the bustling yacht and fishing village where you can while away the hours in craft shops or a harbourside pub. An airy conservatory houses the restaurant, and with views across to the Irish coast on clear days, it's worth booking ahead for a window table. The concise menu changes daily and offers the likes of pan-fried loin of venison with Valrhona sauce followed by raspberry cranachan. Local Scottish produce is used to good effect, with Mull of Galloway lobster a speciality.

continued

Scotland

PORTPATRICK *continued* MAP 20 NW95

Fernhill Hotel

Chef: Andrew Rankin **Owners:** McMillan Hotels **Times:** 12-1.45/6.30-9, Closed mid Jan-mid Feb **Prices:** Fixed L fr £12.50, Fixed D fr £32.50, Coffee £1.50, Min/Water £3, Service included **Wine:** 12 bottles over £20, 33 bottles under £20, 3 by the glass (£2.75) **Notes:** Fixed D 4 courses, Vegetarian available, Dress Restrictions, No jeans, Civ Wed 40 **Seats:** 70, Pr/dining room 24 **Smoking:** N/Sm in restaurant, Air con **Children:** Menu, Portions **Rooms:** 36 (36 en suite) ★★★ HL **Directions:** A77 from Stranraer, right before war memorial. Hotel 1st left **Parking:** 45

STRANRAER MAP 20 NX06

Corsewall Lighthouse Hotel

Modern Scottish

Stunning lighthouse restaurant

☎ 01776 853220 Corsewall Point, Kirkcolm DG9 0QG
e-mail: info@lighthousehotel.co.uk
web: www.lighthousehotel.co.uk

This unique hotel with dramatic views is attached to a lighthouse, perched on the rocky coastline at the end of a single-track road. Once you've arrived safely, you can relax in the intimate restaurant with close-set tables and attentive service. The dinner menu changes every day, offering a range of fresh Scottish produce. Starters might include the likes of bacon and avocado salad with a heather honey and Arran mustard dressing, while main courses might feature roast Galloway rack of lamb or perhaps roast monkfish fillet with a citrus scented jus.

Chef: A Downie, D McCubbin **Owners:** Gordon, Kay, & Pamela Ward **Times:** 12-2/7-9 **Prices:** Fixed L £10.60-£24.25, Starter £2.85-£5.75, Main £15.95-£19.50, Dessert £5.25, Coffee £1.85, Min/Water £3, Service optional **Wine:** 17 bottles over £20, 27 bottles under £20, 2 by the glass (£3.25) **Notes:** Set D £32.50-£36.25 (5 courses), Vegetarian available, Dress Restrictions, Preferably no jeans, Civ Wed 28 **Seats:** 28 **Smoking:** N/Sm in restaurant **Children:** Portions **Rooms:** 9 (9 en suite) ★★★ HL **Directions:** Take A718 from Stranraer to Kirkcolm, then follow B718 signposted Lighthouse **Parking:** 30

Knockinaam Lodge

PORTPATRICK MAP 20 NW95

Scottish, French NOTABLE WINE LIST

Idyllic location with cooking of real grace and refinement

☎ 01776 810471 DG9 9AD
e-mail: reservations@knockinaamlodge.com
web: www.knockinaamlodge.com

Surrounded by dramatic cliffs, serene woodland, fabulous landscaped gardens and a beautiful cove - not to mention the private beach with the warm waters of the Gulf Stream - Knockinaam Lodge has a simply stunning location. It's a place that revels in its glorious isolation with the Victorian lodge conjuring up the sense of a bygone era, with the charming dining room overlooking the bay. The cooking style is precise with dishes tending to focus on one key element enhanced by complementary flavours; presentation is succinct and unfussy. Many of the vegetables, herbs and flowers that adorn the dining room are home grown and are joined by locally-reared lamb, beef and game and seafood landed nearby. Enjoy the six-course set menu for a true overview of the cooking here: an amuse of salmon tartare, sea bass with red pepper emulsion, scallops with baby spring vegetables, fillet of beef with truffle and thyme glaze, pre-dessert of fresh green grape juice, then pear soufflé with rhubarb soufflé to finish. Exquisite.

Notable Wine List: This well-chosen wine list offers plenty of interest and quality throughout.

Chef: Antony Pierce **Owners:** David & Sian Ibbotson **Times:** 12.30-2/7-9 **Prices:** Fixed L £22.50-£35, Coffee £2, Min/Water £3.50, Service optional **Wine:** 420 bottles over £20, 10 bottles under £20, 10 by the glass (£5-£6) **Notes:** Tasting menu, Fixed L 4 courses, Fixed D 5 courses, Vegetarian available, Dress Restrictions, No jeans, Civ Wed 40 **Seats:** 32, Pr/dining room 18 **Smoking:** N/Sm in restaurant **Children:** Min 12 yrs, Menu **Rooms:** 9 (9 en suite) ★★★ HL **Directions:** From A75, follow signs to Portpatrick, follow tourist signs to Knockinaam Lodge **Parking:** 20

North West Castle Hotel

British **NEW**

Family-run hotel with a traditional menu

☎ 01776 704413 DG9 8EH
e-mail: info@northwestcastle.co.uk
web: www.northwestcastle.co.uk

Built in 1820 for the celebrated arctic explorer Sir John Ross, this imposing manor house overlooks Loch Ryan and is a popular dinner destination for guests and locals alike. Its spacious dining room is decorated in traditional style with well-spaced tables, sparkling chandeliers and elegant mirrors, and is adjoined by a comfy lounge where you'll find leather armchairs and a blazing fire in winter. The menu is in keeping with the setting and features mains such as pan-fried supreme of chicken with neeps, tatties, haggis and whisky cream sauce, or herb-crusted loin of Scottish lamb with bubble-and-squeak potatoes, French beans and rosemary jus.

continued

Chef: Bruce McLean **Owners:** H C McMillan **Times:** 12-2/6.30-9 **Prices:** Fixed L fr £12.50, Fixed D fr £23.50, Starter £2.50-£5, Main £8-£16, Dessert fr £3, Coffee £1.50, Min/Water £2.50, Service included **Wine:** 27 bottles over £20, 59 bottles under £20, 3 by the glass (£2.25-£2.75) **Notes:** Fixed L 3 courses, Fixed D 4 courses, Vegetarian available, Dress Restrictions, No jeans, smart casual, Civ Wed 130 **Seats:** 130, Pr/dining room 180 **Smoking:** N/Sm in restaurant **Children:** Menu, Portions **Rooms:** 72 (72 en suite) ★★★★ HL **Directions:** From Glasgow N take A77 to Stranraer. From S follow M6 to Gretna then A75 to Stranraer. Hotel in town centre opp ferry terminal **Parking:** 50

DUNBARTONSHIRE, WEST

BALLOCH MAP 20 NS38

De Vere Cameron House

see below

CLYDEBANK MAP 20 NS47

Arcoona at the Beardmore

British, French

Stylish modern dining on the banks of the Clyde

☎ 0141 951 6000 Best Western Beardmore Hotel, Beardmore St G81 4SA
e-mail: info@beardmore.scot.nhs.uk
web: www.bw-beardmorehotel.co.uk

This impressive modern hotel is situated on the banks of the Clyde and offers fine dining in the newly refurbished Arcoona restaurant.

continued

De Vere Cameron House

BALLOCH MAP 20 NS38

Modern French NOTABLE WINE LIST

Fine dining on the shores of Loch Lomond

☎ 01389 755565 G83 8QZ
e-mail: reservations@cameronhouse.co.uk
web: www.devere.co.uk

Built in the Scottish baronial style, this mansion house dates back to the 17th century, and in the past has played host to many great statesmen and women, including the likes of Winston Churchill and Queen Victoria. Nestling on the shores of Loch Lomond, no doubt they were smitten by its wonderful views, too, though today it's a leisure-orientated hotel with a host of facilities. The elegant, fine-dining Georgian Room restaurant is a traditional affair, with chandeliers, rich fabrics, oil paintings and pristine table settings. Despite the formality of the efficient service - the obligatory jacket and tie at dinner for gentlemen and staff clad in white gloves and starched aprons - there's a friendly, relaxed feel. The accomplished kitchen's modern approach, underpinned by a classical theme, works well with the surroundings, and makes fine use of the abundant, fresh local produce. Highly creative technical skills, precision and deft execution deliver a fixed-price repertoire that includes a six-course gourmet surprise menu. Expect the likes of pan-fried John Dory served with pomme boulangère, glazed salsify, black trompette and a Sauternes sauce, and perhaps an assiette of petites brûlées five ways teamed with vanilla madeleine to close.

Notable Wine List: The traditional wine list features well-chosen and quality wines throughout with a particularly strong French offering.

Chef: Simon Whitley, Paul Tamburrini **Owners:** De Vere Hotels **Times:** 12-2.30/7-9.30, Closed Mon, Tue, Closed L Wed-Sat **Prices:** Food prices not confirmed for 2007. Please telephone for details **Wine:** 159 bottles over £20, 6 by the glass (£6.50-£9.50) **Notes:** Tasting menu 6 courses £57.50, Vegetarian available, Dress Restrictions, Jacket & tie, Civ Wed 200 **Seats:** 42 **Smoking:** N/Sm in restaurant, Air con **Children:** Min 14 yrs **Rooms:** 96 (96 en suite) ★★★★★ HL **Directions:** M8 junct 30, over toll bridge and follow signs for Loch Lomond (A82). Hotel is on right **Parking:** 250

Scotland

CLYDEBANK *continued* MAP 20 NS47

The restaurant name comes from a passenger ship built by William Beardmore & Co shipbuilders on the site in 1924. It has a light, airy feel with well-spaced tables giving privacy to diners. Décor is chic, contemporary and stylish, while service is friendly and efficient. The menus focuses on modern British and French style cooking with classical elements. Choose carefully as there are lots of extras like home-made vegetable crisps and warm nuts with your aperitif, as well as an impressive selection of home-baked breads, perhaps an amuse-bouche of langoustine thermidor, a pre-dessert of banana consommé with meringue and pistachio nuts, and a small plate of cheeses to taste. All this alongside starters like tortellini of goat's cheese and asparagus with lemon thyme dressing, and mains like organic Shetland salmon with tomato and fennel bouillabaisse.

Arcoona at the Beardmore

Chef: Iain Ramsay **Owners:** Scottish Executive **Times:** 7-10, Closed Festive period, Sun, Mon, Closed L all week **Prices:** Starter £5.25-£6.25, Main £12.50-£18.95, Dessert £4.95, Coffee £1.75, Min/Water £3.85, Service optional **Wine:** 38 bottles over £20, 31 bottles under £20, 12 by the glass (£2.50-£7.95) **Notes:** Vegetarian available, Civ Wed 174 **Seats:** 60, Pr/dining room 16 **Smoking:** N/Sm in restaurant, Air con **Children:** Min 12 yrs, Menu, Portions **Rooms:** 166 (166 en suite) ★★★★ HL **Directions:** M8 junct 19, follow signs for Clydeside Expressway to Glasgow road, then Dumbarton road (A814), then signs for Clydebank Business Park. Hotel on left **Parking:** 400

DUNDEE CITY

DUNDEE MAP 21 NO43

Alchemy Restaurant

French, Scottish

Creative cooking on the quayside

☎ 01382 202404 Apex City Quay Hotel & Spa, 1 West Victoria Dock Rd DD1 3JP
e-mail: reservations@alchemyrestaurant.co.uk
web: www.alchemyrestaurant.co.uk

Stylish modern hotel occupying an enviable position at the heart of Dundee's regenerated quayside. Open-plan public areas offer panoramic views, while first-rate facilities include a decadent spa and range of eateries. Alchemy is the smart choice, a fine dining restaurant with a tempting modern British menu based around quality Scottish produce and a liberal sprinkling of luxury ingredients. The first course might bring scrambled quail egg with oyster and Sévruga caviar, or an Arbroath smokie cappuccino, while mains showcase intriguing combinations such as breast of mallard with beetroot, shallot compôte and onion purée, or sautéed sea bass with truffle purée potato, lime and caper froth. Choose from the carte or a range of fixed price menus.

continued

Chef: Bruce Price **Owners:** Apex Hotels **Times:** 7-9.30, Closed 25 Dec-10 Jan, Sun-Mon, Closed L all week **Prices:** Fixed D £22-£27, Starter £4.90-£8.90, Main £12-£16, Dessert £5-£11, Coffee £2.90, Min/Water £3, Service optional **Wine:** 16 bottles over £20, 2 bottles under £20, 6 by the glass (£5.25-£8.75) **Notes:** Fixed D 4 courses, 3 tasting menus available, Vegetarian available, Dress Restrictions, Smart casual, no jeans or T-shirts, Civ Wed 200 **Seats:** 30, Pr/dining room 12 **Smoking:** N/Sm in restaurant **Children:** Min 14 yrs **Rooms:** 153 (153 en suite) ★★★★ HL **Directions:** A90 from Perth. A85 along riverside for 2m. With Discovery Quay on right, at rdbt follow signs for Aberdeen. At next rdbt turn right into city quay **Parking:** 150

CITY OF EDINBURGH

EDINBURGH MAP 21 NT27

Atrium

Modern European, Scottish

NOTABLE WINE LIST

Modish modern dining in the city centre

☎ 0131 228 8882 10 Cambridge St EH1 2ED
e-mail: eat@atriumrestaurant.co.uk
web: www.atriumrestaurant.co.uk

An atmospheric haunt in the heart of the city, this renowned Edinburgh restaurant is a chic, upmarket dinner destination. Canvas and copper make for a warm and quirky décor, while candlelight flickers in the surfaces of darkwood tables. Ingredients are locally sourced where possible and deftly handled by a kitchen confident in its skills; you might start with a Scottish game terrine with red wine poached fig perhaps, and then move on to venison with spätzle, braised cranberries and red cabbage, or apple tarte fine with caramel sauce and Calvados ice cream. The modern European menu changes daily and is complemented by an extensive and award-winning wine list. Book ahead.

Notable Wine List: An excellent all round wine list with concise tasting notes throughout.

Chef: N Forbes & F Bouteloup **Owners:** Andrew & Lisa Radford **Times:** 12-2/6-10, Closed 25-26 Dec, 1-2 Jan, Sun (apart from Aug), Closed L Sat (apart from Aug) **Prices:** Fixed L fr £13.50, Fixed D £27, Starter £6.50-£12, Main £18-£25, Dessert £6, Coffee £3, Min/Water £3.75, Service optional, Group min 5 service 10% **Wine:** 300 bottles over £20, 12 bottles under £20, 300 by the glass (£4.75-£100) **Notes:** Vegetarian available, Civ Wed 100 **Seats:** 80, Pr/dining room 20 **Smoking:** N/Sm in restaurant, Air con **Children:** Portions **Directions:** From Princes St, turn into Lothian Rd 2nd left & 1st right, by the Traverse Theatre **Parking:** Castle Terrace Car Park and on street

Best Western Bruntsfield Hotel

Modern British

Smart, contemporary hotel restaurant

☎ 0131 229 1393 69/74 Bruntsfield Place EH10 4HH
e-mail: sales@thebruntsfield.co.uk
web: www.bw-bruntsfieldhotel.co.uk

The 'Cardoon' is the modern, brasserie-style restaurant sitting in the basement and conservatory extension of this stylish, townhouse hotel. Lavenders and purples, bay windows and the spacious, funky conservatory set the scene, while European staff, wooden tables and blue drinking glasses all add to the metropolitan edge. The cooking follows the theme, the modern dishes use locally-sourced Scottish produce, its crowd-pleasing carte delivering the likes of a rack of border lamb roasted with honey and thyme, with buttered mash and minted jus, alongside a repertoire of lighter dishes, salads and grills.

Chef: Martyn Dixon **Owners:** Mrs C A Gwyn **Times:** 5.30-9.30, Closed Xmas, Closed L all week **Prices:** Starter £3.65-£8.75, Main £5.95-£19.50, Dessert £5.95, Coffee £2.50, Min/Water £3.50, Service optional **Wine:** 13 bottles over £20, 20 bottles under £20, 6 by the glass (£3.65-£5.15) **Notes:** Vegetarian available, Civ Wed 75 **Seats:** 70, Pr/dining room 65 **Smoking:** N/Sm in restaurant **Children:** Menu, Portions **Rooms:** 71 (71 en suite) ★★★ HL **Directions:** From S enter Edinburgh on A702. Continue for 3m. Hotel overlooks Bruntsfield Links Park. 1m S of the W end of Princes Street **Parking:** 30

 Blue

Modern European, Scottish

One of the first trendy bar/brasseries in the city - and still going strong

☎ 0131 221 1222 Cambridge St EH1 2ED
e-mail: eat@bluebarcafe.com
web: www.bluebarcafe.com

One of Edinburgh's best places to hang out and people watch, Blue is perfectly located for a West End shopping trip or a theatre dinner. The decor is minimal and very much of our time - lots of glass, stainless steel and light oak; service is friendly and without pretence. Food descriptions are short and to the point on the modern European and Scottish monthly-changing menu - whole fish of the day, breast of Borders pigeon with braised Puy lentils, salmon fillet with Asian salad. Flavours are likewise uncluttered, with dishes proving to be pleasing to both the taste buds and the stomach. A deservedly popular restaurant with reliable cooking.

Chef: Neil Forbes, Duncan McIntyre **Owners:** Andrew & Lisa Radford **Times:** 12-2.30/5.30-11, Closed 25-26 Dec, 1-2 Jan, Sun (not Aug) **Prices:** Fixed L fr £9.95, Fixed D £13.95, Starter £4.95-£6.25, Main £8.50-15, Dessert £4-£4.50, Coffee £1.50, Min/Water £2.75, Service optional,

continued

Group min 8 service 10% **Wine:** 16 bottles over £20, 16 bottles under £20, 12 by the glass (£2.95-£6.50) **Notes:** Vegetarian available, Civ Wed 100 **Seats:** 110 **Smoking:** N/Sm in restaurant, Air con **Children:** Menu, Portions **Directions:** From Princes Street turn into Lothian Road, 2nd left, 1st right, above the Traverse Theatre **Parking:** Cambridge Street, & NCP - Castle Terrace

Le Café St Honore

Scottish, French

Rustic French food in genuine bistro

☎ 0131 226 2211 34 NW Thistle St Lane EH2 1EA
web: www.cafesthonore.com

Set in a quiet cobbled side street five minutes from Princes Street, this intimate eatery is the genuine article when it comes to authentic back street Parisian-style bistros. Black and white tiled floors, smoked glass mirrors and wine racks on the walls add to the charming Bohemian atmosphere of the place. As for the food, this isn't a place for faddish cooking, just simple rustic classics created from excellent Scottish ingredients: baked oysters with shrimps and gruyère, saddle of venison with a Dijon crust, beetroot and boudin noir and, of course, crème brulée.

Chef: C Colverson **Owners:** Chris & Gill Colverson **Times:** 12-2.15/7-10, Closed 24-26 Dec, 3 days at New Year **Prices:** Fixed D £19.95, Starter £3.75-£9.95, Main £9.50-£20.50, Dessert £5.50, Coffee £1.50, Min/Water £2.95, Service optional, Group min 8 service 10% **Wine:** 50 bottles over £20, 21 bottles under £20, 8 by the glass (£2.95-£5.25) **Notes:** Pre-theatre menu available, Vegetarian available **Seats:** 56, Pr/dining room 18 **Smoking:** N/Sm in restaurant **Children:** Portions **Directions:** City centre, between Hanover & Frederick St **Parking:** On street - Thistle St

Channings Restaurant

Modern Eclectic

Honest, well prepared food in a bright basement restaurant

☎ 0131 315 2225
15 South Learmonth Gardens EH4 1EZ
e-mail: restaurant@channings.co.uk
web: www.channings.co.uk

Channings is the former home of the polar explorer Sir Ernest Shackleton, a traditional townhouse property offering a peaceful retreat just minutes from the city centre. The modern basement restaurant is next to the bar facing the terraced gardens. The kitchen takes a refreshingly simple approach to the cooking of quality local produce, with uncluttered presentation and an emphasis on flavour. There's no messing about with a wild mushroom risotto of perfectly prepared rice and lightly cooked funghi, succulent saddle of lamb with ratte potatoes and stuffed courgette provençal or a lovely fillet of

continued

EDINBURGH *continued* MAP 21 NT27

Aberdeen Angus cooked just as requested, simply garnished with neatly prepared vegetables, served with a slice of dauphinoise potato.

Chef: Hubert Lamort **Owners:** Mr P Taylor **Times:** 12-2.30/6-10 **Prices:** Fixed L £12, Starter £4-£9, Main £11.50-£16, Dessert £4-£5.50, Coffee £2.50, Min/Water £3.50, Service optional, Group min 10 service 10% **Wine:** 47 bottles over £20, 24 bottles under £20, 12 by the glass (£3.75-£6.75) **Notes:** Sat & Sun L offer 3 courses, bottle wine £60 for 4, Vegetarian available **Seats:** 40, Pr/dining room 30 **Smoking:** N/Sm in restaurant **Children:** Portions **Rooms:** 41 (41 en suite) ★★★★ TH **Directions:** From Princes St follow signs to Forth Bridge (A90), cross Dean Bridge and take 4th right into South Learmonth Ave. Follow road to bottom of hill **Parking:** on street

Scotland

֎֎ Dalhousie Castle and Aqueous Spa

Traditional French

Imaginative cuisine in a truly unique setting

☎ 01875 820153 Bonnyrigg EH19 3JB
e-mail: info@dalhousiecastle.co.uk
web: www.dalhousiecastle.co.uk

This stunning castle is a popular choice for weddings and the atmospheric Dungeon restaurant, in the part that dates back to the 13th century, certainly makes a unique setting for dinner whatever the occasion. Before descending the ancient steps to the restaurant you can enjoy a complimentary glass of champagne, served in the wood-panelled library, which hides a secret bar. The menu showcases modern French cuisine and surprising combinations. Typical dishes might include a starter like ravioli of shredded duck with a bitter chocolate sauce, followed by fillet of Angus beef with a port wine jus and bordelaise potatoes. For dessert you could try iced caramel parfait with warm orange turnovers. The wine list is well chosen.

Chef: Francois Graud **Owners:** von Essen Hotels **Times:** 7-10, Closed L all week **Prices:** Fixed L £17.50-£28, Starter £4.50-£7.85, Main £10.50-

continued

£15.50, Dessert £4.50-£4.25, Coffee £1.60, Min/Water £3.95, Service optional **Wine:** 40 bottles over £20, 20 bottles under £20, 8 by the glass (£5.50-£8.50) **Notes:** Vegetarian available, Smart casual, Civ Wed 100 **Seats:** 45, Pr/dining room 100 **Smoking:** N/Sm in restaurant **Children:** Portions **Rooms:** 33 (33 en suite) ★★★ HL **Directions:** From A720 (Edinburgh bypass) take A7 south, turn right onto B704. Castle 0.5m on right **Parking:** 150

֎ Duck's at Le Marche Noir

International, British NOTABLE WINE LIST

Modern cooking in inviting restaurant

☎ 0131 558 1608 14 Eyre Place EH3 5EP
e-mail: enquiries@ducks.co.uk
web: www.ducks.co.uk

A cosy Edinburgh eatery that can be intimate or vibrant depending on the day's clientele. The friendly but formal table service goes well with the white linen and evening candlelight. Ducks feature everywhere, thanks to owner Malcolm Duck. The good value menu shows a hint of brasserie style with a modern Scottish flavour and European influences, from risotto nero with garlic king prawns starter to corn-fed chicken supreme in Serrano ham, roast sweet potato, red and onion and Madeira jus, taking in Aberdeen Angus beef and confit duck leg with Toulouse sausage and bean casserole on the way.

Notable Wine List: This well-chosen wine list offers plenty of interest and quality throughout.

Chef: David Scouller **Owners:** Mr M K Duck **Times:** 12-2.30/7-10.30, Closed 25-26 Dec, Closed L Sat-Mon **Prices:** Fixed L £12, Fixed D £23-£39, Starter £4.50-£9, Main £12.75-£22, Dessert £5.90-£6.50, Coffee £1.95, Min/Water £3.95, Service optional **Wine:** 200 bottles over £20, 40 bottles under £20, 6 by the glass (£3.50-£7) **Notes:** Vegetarian available **Seats:** 60, Pr/dining room 51 **Smoking:** N/Sm in restaurant **Directions:** Princes St, Hanover St, Dundas St, right at lights **Parking:** On street

֎֎ La Garrigue

French

Authentic French regional cuisine

☎ 0131 557 3032 31 Jeffrey St EH1 1DH
e-mail: lagarrigue@btconnect.com
web: www.lagarrigue.co.uk

A little piece of Languedoc can be found here, recreating a traditional French neighbourhood restaurant, but also featuring Tim Stead furniture and Andrew Walker original South of France paintings. The wooden floor, chunky wooden tables and chairs and cool blue walls give a sophisticated Mediterranean feel. The authentic regional cooking style offers simple, rustic dishes using fresh local produce as well as specialist ingredients sourced by the chef. The atmosphere is

continue

relaxed and friendly but the restaurant is popular so be sure to book ahead. Typical dishes include well-executed classics like fish soup and cassoulet with pork, lamb, duck and Toulouse sausage.

Chef: Jean Michel Gauffre **Owners:** J M Gauffre **Times:** 12-3/6.30-10.30, Closed 25-26 Dec, 1-2 Jan, Sun **Prices:** Fixed L £10.50, Fixed D £24.50, Coffee £1.20, Min/Water £2.50, Service added but optional 10% **Wine:** 12 bottles over £20, 12 bottles under £20, 8 by the glass (£3.50-£7.50) **Notes:** Vegetarian available **Seats:** 48, Pr/dining room 11 **Smoking:** N/Sm area, No pipes **Children:** Portions **Directions:** Halfway down Royal Mile towards Holyrood Palace, turn left at lights into Jeffrey St **Parking:** On street

Hadrians, The Balmoral Hotel

International

Buzzy brasserie with international dishes

☎ 0131 557 5000 1 Princes St EH2 2EQ
e-mail: hadrians@thebalmoralhotel.com
web: www.roccofortehotels.com

Located on the ground floor of the Balmoral Hotel, this slick, urban brasserie has a distinct art deco influence, with walnut floors and walls painted in lime and violet - a combination apparently inspired by the natural landscapes of Edinburgh. A palette of Scottish produce is used to create dishes with international scope - haggis wontons anyone? More conventional fare like brandade of smoked haddock or Scottish chicken breast with roast field mushrooms and truffle mash is also on offer - as well as a traditionally served grilled fish and meats.

Chef: Jeff Bland **Owners:** Rocco Forte Hotels **Times:** 12-2.30/6.30-10.30 **Prices:** Fixed L £13.95, Fixed D £20.95, Starter £5.95-£9.50, Main £8.50-£25, Dessert £5.50-£7.95, Coffee £2.65, Min/Water £3.50, Service optional, Group min 8 service 10% **Wine:** 43 bottles over £20, 25 bottles under £20, 9 by the glass (£3.50-£6.75) **Notes:** Vegetarian available, Dress Restrictions, Smart casual, Civ Wed 60 **Seats:** 100, Pr/dining room 30 **Smoking:** N/Sm in restaurant, Air con **Children:** Menu, Portions **Directions:** Hotel at beginning of Princes Street, next to Waverley Station **Parking:** 40

Haldanes

Modern Scottish

Intimate basement restaurant in an Edinburgh townhouse

☎ 0131 556 8407 13B Dundas St EH3 6QG
e-mail: dinehaldanes@aol.com
web: www.haldanesrestaurant.com

Haldanes has moved premises, to another basement property also in the New Town area. Two tiny eating areas make for cosy dining, with exposed natural stone, Vettriano prints and smart white-clothed tables. There is a small lounge area for a pre-meal drink, while the upstairs bar lounge is used mainly for casual meals during the day, serving coffees, pastries and good-value lunches in the French café-bar style. A monthly menu of modern dishes is based on the finest seasonal Scottish produce simply prepared - exemplified by a dish of fillet of prime Scottish beef topped with a black pepper sabayon and served with a shallot and red wine sauce.

Chef: George Kelso **Owners:** Mr and Mrs G Kelso **Times:** 12-2.15/5.30-10.15, Closed 25 Dec, Mon, Closed L Sun **Prices:** Fixed L fr £15, Fixed D £18.50-£23.50, Starter £5.50-£12.50, Main £16.75-£25, Dessert £6.50-£8.50, Coffee £1.95, Min/Water £3.50, Service optional, Group min 10 service 10% **Wine:** 130 bottles over £20, 22 bottles under £20, 20 by the glass (£3.50-£8) **Notes:** Dress Restrictions, Smart casual preferred **Seats:** 60, Pr/dining room 32 **Smoking:** N/Sm in restaurant **Children:** Portions **Directions:** Telephone for directions **Parking:** On street

The Howard Hotel - The Atholl

Modern Scottish

Stylish elegant townhouse with intimate restaurant

☎ 0131 557 3500 34 Great King St EH3 6QH
e-mail: reserve@thehoward.com
web: www.thehoward.com

The setting in this converted terraced townhouse turned hotel gives an exclusive and clubby feel to The Atholl restaurant. A drawing room with Victorian views over wide cobbled streets steeped with history gives plenty of scope for romance. Traditional Scottish cuisine offers the likes of seared West Coast scallops with a carrot and cardamom purée with chermoula as a starter. Mains might see you enjoying seared fillet of Scottish Aberdeen Angus with wild mushroom and parmesan glaze and colcannon potatoes. For dessert, take a pear and rosemary tarte Tatin with ginger ice cream.

Chef: Steven Falconer **Owners:** Peter Taylor **Times:** 12-2/7-9 **Prices:** Starter £5.50-£9.50, Main £13.50-£22.50, Dessert £6-£7.50, Coffee £2.95, Min/Water £3.95, Service optional **Wine:** 35 bottles over £20, 12 bottles under £20, 9 by the glass (£3.50-£4.50) **Notes:** Civ Wed 35 **Seats:** 18, Pr/dining room 36 **Smoking:** N/Sm in restaurant **Children:** Menu, Portions **Rooms:** 18 (18 en suite) ★★★★ TH **Directions:** Telephone for directions **Parking:** 10

Iggs

Spanish NOTABLE WINE LIST

Convivial and welcoming taste of Spain

☎ 0131 557 8184 15 Jeffrey St EH1 1DR
e-mail: iggsbarioja@aol.com

In a quiet street just off the Royal Mile, this warm-coloured, glass-fronted restaurant delivers a touch of the Mediterranean to the old city. Oils and mirrors adorn the walls, while antique dressers, linen-

continued

Scotland

EDINBURGH *continued* MAP 21 NT27

clad tables and friendly service are set to a backing track of jazzy music. The cooking follows the theme, with simple, well-constructed modern dishes that speak with a Spanish accent, delivering quality ingredients and good flavours via sharp presentation. Think grilled salmon fillet with a cacerola of chickpeas, chorizo and pequillo peppers. There's a patriotic Spanish wine list, and a tapas bar (Barioja) next door.

Notable Wine List: An excellent Spanish wine list; useful tasting notes accompany each wine.

Chef: Andrew MacQueen **Owners:** Mr I Campos **Times:** 12-2.30/6-10.30, Closed Sun **Prices:** Fixed L £12.75-£21, Fixed D £22.50-£27.50, Starter £4-£9, Main £13.50-£27.50, Dessert £5-£8, Coffee £3, Min/Water £3.50, Service optional **Wine:** 85 bottles over £20, 40 bottles under £20, 10 by the glass (£3.50-£5.50) **Notes:** Vegetarian available **Seats:** 80, Pr/dining room 40 **Smoking:** N/Sm in restaurant **Directions:** At the heart of Edinburgh's Old Town 0.5m from castle, just off the Royal Mile **Parking:** On street

Scotland

Macdonald Holyrood Hotel

Scottish, French

Relaxed dining in the shadow of Holyrood Palace

☎ 0131 550 4500 Holyrood Rd EH8 6AU
e-mail: holyrood@macdonald-hotels.co.uk
web: www.macdonaldhotels.co.uk

Just a short walk from the new Scottish Parliament Building, this impressive hotel is located in the heart of Edinburgh's Old Town and offers a full range of modern leisure facilities. The split-level Opus 504 Restaurant showcases a wide range of Scottish produce and keen staff impart detailed knowledge of this. Traditional dishes with a modern twist vie for the diner's attention. Start with the Arbroath smokie risotto with cheddar bites before a main course of roast cod, bubble and squeak and bacon jus. Finish with a fresh fruit salad.

Times: 12-2/6.30-10, Closed L All week (ex group bookings) **Rooms:** 156 (156 en suite) ★★★★ **Directions:** City centre near the Royal Mile

Malmaison Hotel & Brasserie

French, Scottish

Slick style, simple food and friendly service

☎ 0131 468 5000 One Tower Place, Leith EH6 7DB
e-mail: edinburgh@malmaison.com
web: www.malmaison.com

Built in 1883 as a seaman's mission on the water of Leith, this hotel has a castle-like appearance. Inside you'll find slick French style throughout with wooden floors, leather chairs and banquettes. The ground-floor brasserie looks out across a cobbled concourse to the quayside. Candlelight adds to the atmosphere in the evening, as do the walls lined with old wine bottles from France's premier growths. Classic, simple dishes are cooked using fresh local ingredients; try roasted king scallops or confit of duck. Service is relaxed and friendly, you can go for a laid-back Sunday brunch with delicious options like Malmaision eggs Benedict, washed down with a fiery Bloody Mary.

Chef: Yannick Grospellier **Owners:** Malmaison Hotels Ltd **Times:** 12-2/6-10.30, Closed D 25 Dec **Prices:** Fixed L £12.50, Fixed D £13.95, Starter £4.50-£6.50, Main £10.50-£23.95, Dessert £4.95, Service optional, Group min 8 service 10% **Wine:** 136 bottles over £20, 17 bottles under £20, 13 by the glass (£4.75-£10.50) **Notes:** Sun brunch menu, Vegetarian available **Seats:** 62, Pr/dining room 60 **Smoking:** N/Sm in restaurant, Air con

continued

Children: Portions **Rooms:** 100 (100 en suite) ★★★ HL **Directions:** From the city centre follow Leith Docklands, through 3 sets of lights and left into Tower St **Parking:** 48

Marriott Dalmahoy

Modern European

Intimate fine dining in Georgian splendour

☎ 0131 333 1845 Kirknewton EH27 8EB
e-mail: fandb.dalmahoy@marriotthotels.co.uk
web: www.marriott.co.uk/edigs

Many of the original features have been retained in the fine Adam-designed mansion, which is bounded by two championship golf courses, expansive grounds, and the rolling Pentland Hills. In addition, there is an impressive health and beauty spa and a choice of formal and informal drinking and dining options. The smart, classically furnished Pentland Restaurant, overlooking the 18th hole, is where the serious eating takes place. Cooking successfully combines a strong Scottish theme, with the use of quality seafood and game, classic dishes as seen in the retro roast trolley, or perhaps simply grilled Dover sole, and more contemporary dishes, such as lamb with black pudding mash and pulse casserole.

Chef: Alan Matthew **Owners:** Marriott Hotels **Times:** 12.30-2/7-10, Closed L Sat & Sun **Prices:** Fixed L £16-£18, Starter £5-£11, Main £16.50-£30, Dessert £4.95-£7, Coffee £2.85, Min/Water £3.95, Service optional **Wine:** 20 bottles over £20, 14 bottles under £20, 18 by the glass (£5.65-£8.50) **Notes:** Vegetarian available, Dress Restrictions, Smart casual, Civ Wed 200 **Seats:** 120, Pr/dining room 16 **Smoking:** N/Sm in restaurant, Air con **Children:** Menu, Portions **Rooms:** 215 (215 en suite) ★★★★ HL **Directions:** On A71 city bypass. Take Calder exit & follow signs for A71. 7m and hotel clearly signed on left. **Parking:** 350

Melville Castle Hotel

Traditional, European influence

Modern Scottish cuisine in historic cellar venue

☎ 0131 654 0088 Melville Gate,
Gilmerton Rd EH18 1AP
e-mail: reception@melvillecastle.com
web: www.melvillecastle.com

Built in 1786, this dungeon restaurant has everything you would hope to find in a castle, from vaulted ceilings to flagstone floors, brick archways and candle lighting. Smart napery on unclothed polished tables gives an informal feel and service is similarly relaxed. The carte provides a good choice of popular Scottish fare, such as haggis in the form of salt cod fishcakes with aïoli and mixed leaves as a starter. Mains might include free-range chicken pot-au-feu with potato gnocchi and basil. The cooking style is straightforward with refined flavours and slick presentation.

Chef: Karen Mackay **Owners:** The Hay Trust **Times:** 12-2.30/7-9.30 **Prices:** Starter £3.50-£4.75, Main £9.50-£16, Dessert £3-£4, Coffee £1.60, Min/Water £3.75, Service optional **Wine:** 18 bottles over £20, 13 bottles under £20, 8 by the glass (£3.40-£4) **Notes:** Vegetarian available, Dress Restrictions, Smart casual, no jeans, Civ Wed 80 **Seats:** 50, Pr/dining room 70 **Smoking:** N/Sm in restaurant **Children:** Menu, Portions **Rooms:** 32 (32 en suite) ★★★ HL **Directions:** 2 min from city bypass (A720), Sheriffhall rdbt **Parking:** 100

Norton House Hotel

EDINBURGH MAP 21 NT27

Modern British

Small, sophisticated restaurant in elegant hotel

☎ 0131 333 1275 Ingliston EH28 8LX
web: www.handpicked.co.uk

Situated outside the city and convenient for the airport, this extended Victorian mansion is set in 55 acres of parkland. Original features blend with a relaxed, contemporary edge. Visitors to the fine-dining Ushers restaurant can make use of the refurbished drawing room, while hotel brasserie users can relax in the conservatory bar lounge. Ushers is an intimate 22-seat affair, smartly decked out with pale walls, subdued lighting and maroon tablecloths with white runners. The kitchen's modern approach is underpinned by a classical theme, delivered via an appealing, sensibly compact carte. Skilled, precise cooking allows fine-quality Scottish ingredients to shine with deceptive simplicity and clean, clear, balanced flavours. Expect West Coast hand-dived scallops, served with braised pork belly, cauliflower purée and a light curry sauce to tempt at starters, and perhaps a fillet of Buccleuch beef to be accompanied by foie gras 'two ways', truffled pomme purée and root vegetables, while a warm Valhrona chocolate fondant with lavender ice cream, coffee and tonka bean might head up desserts. A good cheese selection, first-class breads and interesting canapés hold up standards, and make a walk around the grounds almost mandatory.

Chef: Graeme Shaw & Glen Bilins **Owners:** Hand Picked Hotels **Times:** 7-9.30, Closed 1 Jan, Sun-Mon, Closed L all week **Prices:** Starter £7.50-£11.95, Main £19.50-£23.95, Dessert £6.50, Coffee £3.50, Min/Water £3.50, Service optional **Wine:** 160 bottles over £20, 6 bottles under £20, 20 by the glass (£4.30-£15) **Notes:** Civ Wed 140 **Seats:** 22, Pr/dining room 40 **Smoking:** N/Sm in restaurant, Air con **Children:** Portions **Rooms:** 47 (47 en suite) ★★★★ HL **Directions:** M8 junct 2, off A8, 0.5m past Edinburgh Airport **Parking:** 100

Number One, The Balmoral Hotel

EDINBURGH MAP 21 NT27

Modern Scottish, French V NOTABLE WINE LIST

Fine dining in luxury hotel

☎ 0131 557 6727 1 Princes St EH2 2EQ
e-mail: numberone@thebalmoralhotel.com
web: www.roccofortehotels.com

This elegant, luxurious hotel enjoys a prestigious address at the top of Princes Street, with fine views over the city and castle. Hotel amenities include a Roman-style health spa, a choice of two bars (one stocking 30 different champagnes) and two very different dining options. Whereas Hadrians is a bustling, informal brasserie, the chic basement restaurant Number One is the place for a romantic meal and some seriously creative cuisine. Styled by Olga Polizzi, rich red walls hold numerous colourful prints and large, well-spaced tables and gold velvet chairs enhance the exclusive feel. Well-drilled staff ensure refined service which is matched by classical French cooking with modern influences.

A large amount of Scottish produce is used in innovative combinations of flavours and textures. A starter of scallops served with chestnut and apple, smoked bacon and parsley root purée may kick off a meal that continues with confit fillet of beef rossini with onion purée, cocotte potatoes and spiced honey jus. Desserts like hot chocolate soufflé with vanilla ice cream and macerated prunes are precise and well executed.
Notable Wine List: An extremely well-presented and laid out wine list with quality selections throughout.

Chef: Jeff Bland **Owners:** Rocco Forte Hotels **Times:** 12-2/7-10, Closed 1st 2 wks Jan, Closed L Mon-Tue, Sat-Sun **Prices:** Fixed L fr £24, Starter £12-£16, Main £25-£29, Dessert £9, Coffee £4, Min/Water £3.95, Service optional, Group min 6 service 12.5% **Wine:** 350 bottles over £20, 8 by the glass (£7-£12.50) **Notes:** Tasting menu 6 courses £65, Vegetarian menu, Dress Restrictions, Smart casual preferred, Civ Wed 60 **Seats:** 50, Pr/dining room 50 **Smoking:** N/Sm in restaurant, Air con **Children:** Portions **Rooms:** 188 (188 en suite) ★★★★★ HL **Directions:** Hotel at E end of Princes St, next to Waverley Station **Parking:** NCP: Greenside/St James Centre

EDINBURGH *continued* MAP 21 NT27

Number One, The Balmoral Hotel

see page 555

Off the Wall Restaurant

Scottish, French

Stylish dining along the Royal Mile

☎ 0131 558 1497 105 High St, Royal Mile EH1 1SG
e-mail: otwedinburgh@aol.com
web: www.off-the-wall.co.uk

Arched leaded-glass windows look out across the Royal Mile from this sophisticated restaurant housed in one of the oldest buildings on this famous thoroughfare. A tasteful, simple décor with plum and white walls create a soothing feel that contrasts with the hustle and bustle of the street below. Cooking is classically based but with a modern approach, using first-class local and seasonal ingredients. Dishes are skilfully cooked and simply presented. Saucing is good and plates are uncluttered allowing key flavours to speak for themselves, as in supreme of squab with onion confit, lentil and port sauce, sea bass, creamed spinach and leeks and parsley sauce, and chocolate torte with mint ice cream. Service is refined and friendly.

Chef: David Anderson **Owners:** David Anderson/Aileen Wilson **Times:** 12-2/6.30-10, Closed 25-26 Dec, 1-2 Jan, Sun **Prices:** Fixed L fr £16.50, Starter £9.95-£11.95, Main £19.95-£21.95, Dessert fr £6.95, Coffee £2, Min/Water £3.50, Service optional **Wine:** 53 bottles over £20, 13 bottles under £20, 7 by the glass (£3.75-£4.95) **Notes:** Pre booked tasting menu £65 **Seats:** 44, Pr/dining room 20 **Smoking:** N/Sm in restaurant **Children:** Portions **Directions:** On Royal Mile near John Knox House - entrance via stairway next to Baillie Fyfes Close (first floor) **Parking:** NCP

The Restaurant at the Bonham

Modern Scottish

Enjoyable dining in stylish urban setting

☎ 0131 274 7444 35 Drumsheugh Gardens EH3 7RN
e-mail: restaurant@thebonham.com
web: www.thebonham.com

Set in the heart of trendy New Town, this converted Victorian townhouse is now home to a spacious and stylish dining room. Wooden floors and panelling sit comfortably with modern furniture, minimalist décor and modern artworks. Attractive wooden tables are set with fine glassware, cutlery, linen napkins and candles. Black-clad staff provide attentive service. The French chef uses his classical training to transform local and seasonal ingredients into dishes with flair and individualism. The short menu avoids the agony of indecision. Simpler starters like pressed confit of duck terrine precede main courses of grilled halibut with roasted salsify and wild mushrooms, rounded off with classic lemon tart.

Chef: Michel Bouyer **Owners:** Peter Taylor, The Town House Company **Times:** 12-2.30/6.30-10 **Prices:** Fixed L fr £13.50, Starter £4.60-£8.50, Main £13-£21.50, Dessert £5-£5.60, Service added but optional 10%, Group min 6 service 10% **Wine:** 22 bottles over £20, 12 bottles under £20 **Notes:** Boozy Snoozy menu 4 people, 3 courses, 2 bottles wine £65, Vegetarian available **Seats:** 60, Pr/dining room 26 **Smoking:** N/Sm in restaurant **Children:** Portions **Rooms:** 48 (48 en suite) ★★★★ TH **Directions:** Located to the W end of Princes St **Parking:** 16

Restaurant Martin Wishart

see opposite page

Rhubarb - the Restaurant at Prestonfield

Traditional, Scottish V

Opulent setting for impressive food

☎ 0131 225 1333 Prestonfield, Priestfield Rd EH16 5UT
e-mail: reservations@prestonfield.com
web: www.rhubarb-restaurant.com

A remarkable period house within its own parkland grounds, the whole interior of Prestonfield is opulence personified. Rhubarb is the luxurious and comfortable restaurant within the hotel and comprises two separate Regency dining rooms, both with fine views and crisp linen on the tables. Four separate rooms available for pre- and post-dinner drinks are as atmospheric and indulgent as the rest of the hotel. The very best Scottish produce is handled with flair and panache in creative European dishes such as pan-seared scallops on horseradish pomme purée with mustard oil and parsley juice, seared fillet of turbot on langoustine crushed potatoes and an assiette of rhubarb desserts.

Chef: Laurence Robertson **Owners:** James Thomson OBE **Times:** 12-3/6-11 **Prices:** Fixed L £16.95, Starter £6-£12, Main £14-£30, Dessert £6-£10, Service optional, Group min 8 service 10% **Wine:** 300 bottles over £20, 17 bottles under £20, 12 by the glass (£4.50-£8.50) **Notes:** Vegetarian available, Civ Wed 500 **Seats:** 90, Pr/dining room 500 **Smoking:** N/Sm in restaurant **Children:** Min 12 yrs, Portions **Rooms:** 24 (24 en suite) ★★★★★ TH **Directions:** Proceed out of city centre on Nicholson St, join Dalkeith Rd. At lights turn left into Priestfield Rd. Prestonfield is on the left. **Parking:** 200

Restaurant Martin Wishart

EDINBURGH MAP 21 NT27

Modern French V NOTABLE WINE LIST

Imaginative, memorable cooking in intimate, fashionable waterfront venue

☎ 0131 553 3557 54 The Shore, Leith EH6 6RA
e-mail: info@martin-wishart.co.uk
web: www.martin-wishart.co.uk

Situated on the fashionable, rejuvenated Leith dockland waterfront this is home to one of Scotland's top chefs and a colossus on the culinary map. Decorated in shades of cream and beige and dotted with eye-catching contemporary artworks, the intimate, modern, minimalist-styled room oozes style and refinement. Crisp white linen, impeccable table appointments, comfortable seating and polished, professional service add class and sophistication. Chef-patron Martin Wishart is a true flavour-smith, his kitchen's modern-French style aptly befits the surroundings, while making fine use of impeccably sourced seasonal produce to deliver sublime, fresh, intense, dynamic flavours. Flawless execution, invention and flair find their place in complex, refined dishes that also pay due homage to texture, balance and combination. The approach is via an eye-catching fixed-price repertoire that comes dotted with luxury and includes a superb-value lunch, plus tasting menu (including a separate vegetarian version and the option of selected wines) and an enticing carte. Think roast halibut served with cauliflower and shrimp gratin, pommes Maxime and a lentil and mushroom jus, or perhaps poached Anjou pigeon and oysters paired with Puy lentils, Savoy cabbage and a foie gras velouté, and, to finish, choose between a confit strawberry mousse with lemongrass jelly and rhubarb sorbet, or classic caramel soufflé with vanilla ice cream.
Notable Wine List: A well-presented wine list, carefully chosen with quality selections throughout.

Chef: Martin Wishart
Owners: Martin Wishart
Times: 12-2/6.30-10, Closed 25 Dec, 1 wk Jan, Sun-Mon, Closed L Sat
Prices: Fixed L £22.50, Fixed D £50, Coffee £4.50, Min/Water £4, Service optional, Group min 6 service 10%
Wine: 200 bottles over £20, 6 bottles under £20, 18 by the glass (£4.50-£8.50)
Notes: Fixed L 3 courses, Tasting menu 7 courses £60, Vegetarian menu, Dress Restrictions, Smart casual
Seats: 50
Smoking: N/Sm in restaurant
Children: Portions
Directions: Telephone for directions/map on website
Parking: On street

Scotland

EDINBURGH *continued* MAP 21 NT27

Santini

Italian

Chic venue for modern Italian food

☎ 0131 221 7788 8 Conference Square EH3 8AN

Santini is a fresh, modern and elegant Italian-themed restaurant and bistro that provides an informal dining venue for the Sheraton Grand's impressive One Spa. The two operations share a spacious entrance dominated by a large cocktail bar, the bistro has diners sitting high on padded stools, while more traditional seating fills the restaurant, a bright, contemporary space with glass, chrome and neutral shades. Dishes are well executed using Scottish ingredients and full of Italian flavours. Menus follow a traditional format (antipasti, primi, pesce and carne), typically including lobster and salmon ravioli and corn-fed chicken with pesto risotto. Expect five-star service from smiling staff.

Chef: Richard Glennie **Owners:** Sheraton Hotel **Times:** 12-2.30/6.30-10.30, Closed 1 Jan, Sun, Closed L Sat **Prices:** Fixed L £21, Starter £7-£14, Main £14-£23, Dessert £6-£7, Coffee £1.50, Min/Water £3.20, Service included **Wine:** 54 bottles over £20, 3 bottles under £20, 7 by the glass (£3.75-£5) **Notes:** Vegetarian available **Seats:** 45 **Smoking:** N/Sm in restaurant, Air con **Children:** Portions **Parking:** 121

The Scotsman

Modern British

Stylish setting for modern fine dining

☎ 0131 556 5565 20 North Bridge EH1 1YT
e-mail: reservations@thescotsmanhotelgroup.co.uk
web: www.thescotsmanhotel.co.uk

Formerly the headquarters of *The Scotsman* newspaper - thus the name - this magnificent Victorian building combines the best of the original features with cutting-edge design. Descend the marble staircase to the stylish, intimate, fine-dining Vermilion restaurant in what was once the newspaper's features room. There are no windows, but pale walls are lined with wine display cabinets, service is friendly and attentive, lighting is soft, and there's even a small lounge area outside. The accomplished kitchen's imaginative output suits the venue (dinner only) and makes good use of quality Scottish produce on its sensibly compact, fixed-price menus. Take roast sea bass with risotto milanese, mussels and a curry foam, and a chocolate marquise to finish.

Chef: Geoff Balharrie **Owners:** The Scotsman Hotel Group **Times:** 7-10, Closed Mon & Tue, Closed L all week **Prices:** Fixed D £28-£35, Starter £9-£14, Main £16-£25, Dessert fr £7, Coffee £2.95, Min/Water £3, Service optional **Wine:** 80 bottles over £20, 3 bottles under £20, 6 by the glass (£5.50-£9.50) **Notes:** Tasting menu Fri, Sat £55, Vegetarian available, Civ

continued

Wed 80 **Seats:** 32, Pr/dining room 80 **Smoking:** N/Sm in restaurant **Children:** Min 12 yrs, Portions **Rooms:** 69 (69 en suite) ★★★★★ HL **Directions:** Town centre, next to railway station

The Sheraton Grand Hotel & Spa

International

Classic Scottish dishes in luxurious surroundings

☎ 0131 221 6422 1 Festival Square EH3 9SR
e-mail: grandedinburgh.sheraton@sheraton.com
web: www.sheraton.com/grandedinburgh

Prices and service are pitched at the same high level whilst décor leaves no doubt as to where you're dining. Tartan walls, oak panelling, Scottish prints and paintings on grand Scottish themes never undermine the intimacy of these crisply dressed tables with formal settings and fresh flowers. Service is formal and polished. Fresh local produce is the basis of well-presented modern and classical dishes. Start with pigeon and confit rabbit terrine with balsamic jus, followed by a main course of smoked roe venison loin with endive tian, roasted chestnut and a red wine sauce. Finish perhaps with pain perdu crostini with poached spiced pear and almond cream.

Chef: Philip Garrod **Owners:** Hotel Corporation of Edinburgh **Times:** 12-2/7-10, Closed Jan, Sun & Mon, Closed L Sat **Prices:** Fixed L £18.50, Starter £6-£12.50, Main £16-£39, Dessert £6.50, Coffee £3, Min/Water £3.90, Service optional **Wine:** 100% bottles over £20 **Notes:** Fixed D 5 courses £50, Vegetarian available, Dress Restrictions, Smart casual, Civ Wed 250 **Seats:** 40 **Smoking:** N/Sm in restaurant, Air con **Children:** No Children **Rooms:** 260 (260 en suite) ★★★★★ HL **Directions:** Off Lothian Road. Entrance to hotel behind Standard Life building **Parking:** 121

Stac Polly

Scottish

Modern Scottish cuisine in relaxed atmosphere

☎ 0131 229 5405 8-10 Grindlay St EH3 9AS
e-mail: enquiry@stacpolly.com
web: www.stacpolly.co.uk

Intimate city-centre eatery close to Edinburgh Castle and within strolling distance of the Princes Street shops (sister to Stac Polly in Dublin Street - see entry). The unassuming shop façade hides a network of charming low-ceilinged rooms, each richly furnished and softly lit to create a relaxed, convivial atmosphere. Modern Scottish cooking dominates the menu, which is the same in both restaurants. The style is crisp and concise, while simple technique allows clear and honest flavours to shine through. This is evident in such dishes as wood pigeon and pickled walnut parfait, seared salmon with pak choi, garlic and spring onion champ, and Clooty dumpling with vanilla ice cream.

continued

Chef: Steven Harvey **Owners:** Roger Coulthard **Times:** 12-2/6-11, Closed 25-26 Dec, 1-2 Jan, Sun, Closed L Sat **Prices:** Fixed L £15.95, Starter £6.25-£8.65, Main £17.95-£20.95, Dessert £6.55, Coffee £2.65, Min/Water £3.65, Service added but optional 10% **Wine:** 34 bottles over £20, 20 bottles under £20, 8 by the glass (£3.75-£5.95) **Notes:** Vegetarian available **Seats:** 50, Pr/dining room 10 **Smoking:** N/Sm area, No pipes, No cigars **Children:** Portions **Directions:** In town centre. Situated beneath the castle, near Lyceum Theatre **Parking:** NCP - Castle Street; parking meters

Stac Polly

Traditional Scottish

Modern Scottish cuisine in atmospheric surroundings

☎ 0131 556 2231 29-33 Dublin St EH3 6NL
e-mail: enquiry@stacpolly.com
web: www.stacpolly.co.uk

Named after a Scottish mountain, there are two restaurants of this name (see above). This restaurant is set at ground and basement level, featuring rough stone-walled cellars combining traditional and modern décor. The menu is the same for both restaurants, and features modern Scottish dishes with a traditional twist. Try a perfectly prepared and beautifully presented starter of basil-marinated baby goat's cheese served with warm garlic-scented garden asparagus and wild mushrooms, or a mouthwatering main course of pan-fried saddle of venison on buttered Savoy cabbage, with an orange, fresh tarragon and green peppercorn sauce.

Chef: Andre Stanislas **Owners:** Roger Coulthard **Times:** 12-2/6-11, Closed 25-26 Dec, 1 Jan, Sun, Closed L Sat **Prices:** Fixed L £15.95, Starter £6.25-£8.65, Main £17.95-£20.95, Dessert £6.55, Coffee £2.65, Min/Water £3.65, Service added but optional 10% **Wine:** 57 bottles over £20, 21 bottles under £20, 8 by the glass (£3.75-£5.95) **Notes:** Vegetarian available **Seats:** 100, Pr/dining room 54 **Smoking:** N/Sm area **Children:** Portions **Parking:** On street - after 6.30 pm

Tower Restaurant & Terrace

Modern British NOTABLE WINE LIST

Cultural and culinary delights combined in one striking venue

☎ 0131 225 3003 Museum of Scotland, Chambers St EH1 1JF
e-mail: reservations@tower-restaurant.com
web: www.tower-restaurant.com

The top floor of the Museum of Scotland is the impressive setting for this elegant, contemporary restaurant. The views across the rooftops to the castle and cathedral are shown to extra advantage from the terrace in summer. The menu is as modern as the setting, serving the likes of beetroot salad with red wine-poached egg and beetroot

continued

grissini, and rolled suckling pig with vegetable strudel and yellow split pea purée. Beef is of a rare quality, grilled in a variety of ways. A couple of light menus at lunchtime and early evening offer terrific value.

Notable Wine List: A well-constructed wine list, usefully divided by price range, with many top producers.

Tower Restaurant & Terrace

Chef: Gavin Elder **Owners:** James Thomson OBE **Times:** 12/12-11, Closed 25-26 Dec **Prices:** Fixed L £11, Starter £6.50-£14.50, Main £14.50-£28, Dessert £5-£9, Coffee £2.25, Min/Water £3.95, Service optional, Group min 8 service 10% **Wine:** 150 bottles over £20, 19 bottles under £20, 12 by the glass (£3.95-£6.75) **Notes:** Vegetarian available **Seats:** 96, Pr/dining room 90 **Smoking:** N/Sm in restaurant, Air con **Directions:** Above the Museum of Scotland building at corner of George IV Bridge & Chambers St, on level 5 **Parking:** On street

The Vintners Rooms

French, Mediterranean

Candlelit restaurant with vintage charm

☎ 0131 554 6767 The Vaults, 87 Giles St, Leith EH6 6BZ
e-mail: enquiries@thevintersrooms.com
web: www.thevintnersrooms.com

Lit only by flickering candles, this romantic restaurant has character aplenty. A former auction room for wine, it's exquisitely adorned with hand-worked stucco, and sits atop cellars that have stored imported barrels of fine tipples from France since the 12th century. There's a touch of the 'auld alliance' about the food too, with modern French dishes conjured from quality Scottish produce - kick off with scallops à la Marseillaise perhaps, and then tuck into venison with a dark chocolate sauce or monkfish with mussels and a saffron broth. This is rustic cuisine, presented with great artistry, and complemented by an extensive wine list.

Chef: P Ginistière **Owners:** Patrice Ginistière **Times:** 12-2/7-10, Closed 1-16 Jan, Sun-Mon **Prices:** Fixed L £15.50, Fixed D £30-£40, Starter £5.50-£10.50, Main £16-£22, Coffee £2, Min/Water £3.20, Service added but optional 10%, Group min 5 service 10% **Wine:** 40 bottles over £20, 12 bottles under £20, 4 by the glass (£3.25-£3.95) **Notes:** Vegetarian available **Seats:** 64, Pr/dining room 34 **Smoking:** N/Sm area **Children:** Portions **Directions:** At the end of Leith Walk; left into Great Junction St, right into Henderson St. Restaurant in old warehouse on right **Parking:** 4

Scotland

EDINBURGH *continued* MAP 21 NT27

The Witchery by the Castle

Traditional Scottish

Destination dining in historic location

☎ 0131 225 5613 Castlehill, Royal Mile EH1 2NF
e-mail: mail@thewitchery.com
web: www.thewitchery.com

Now a renowned hotel destination, The Witchery takes its name from the hundreds of people burnt at the stake as witches on Castlehill in the 16th and 17th centuries. The curious combination of décor reflects the building's interesting past, dating back to 1595. Choose between the rich baroque surroundings of the oak-panelled Witchery, or the elegant charms of the Secret Garden, reached via a stone staircase from the courtyard above. Scottish cuisine using fine ingredients provides top-notch dishes, accompanied by a world-class wine list. Decadent main courses might feature roast loin of Perthshire roe deer with braised red cabbage, grilled Stornoway black pudding and chocolate sauce.

Chef: Douglas Roberts **Owners:** James Thomson OBE **Times:** 12-4/5-11.30, Closed 25-26 Dec **Prices:** Fixed L £12.95, Starter £8-£16, Main £14.50-£29, Dessert £6-£9, Coffee £2.25, Min/Water £3.95, Service optional, Group min 8 service 10% **Wine:** 800 bottles over £20, 25 bottles under £20, 16 by the glass (£4-£10) **Notes:** Vegetarian available **Seats:** 120, Pr/dining room 70 **Smoking:** N/Sm in restaurant, Air con **Children:** Min 12 yrs **Rooms:** 6 (6 en suite) ★★★★★ RR **Directions:** At the gates of Edinburgh Castle, at the top of the Royal Mile

Bellini - Edinburgh

☎ 0131 476 2602 8b Abercromby Place EH3 6LB
web: www.theaa.com/restaurants/114067.html

Regional Italian cuisine in a Georgian dining room in the heart of New Town, with a relaxed and friendly atmosphere.

Circus Cafe

☎ 0131 220 0333 15 North West Circus Place EH3 6SX
web: www.theaa.com/restaurants/114045.html

Former grand art deco bank now a stylish eatery with a deli below. Open all day.

Cosmo

☎ 0131 226 6743 58a North Castle St EH2 3LU
web: www.theaa.com/restaurants/114046.html

The haunt of many celebrities this well established restaurant serves classic Italian cuisine.

Daniel's Restaurant

☎ 0131 553 5933 88 Commercial St EH6 6LX
web: www.theaa.com/restaurants/114035.html
A bright, light warehouse conversion on the lovely Leith waterfront, offering consistently high-quality French and Scottish food and a friendly atmosphere.

David Bann

☎ 0131 556 5888 56/58 St Mary St EH1 1SX
Smart vegetarian restaurant and bar, off the Royal Mile.

First Coast

☎ 0131 313 4404 97-101 Dalry Rd EH11 2AB
web: www.theaa.com/restaurants/114036.html
An intimate, relaxed shop-front restaurant with a frequently-changing modern Scottish menu, offering meat and fowl as well as fish. Short, thoughtful wine list, good vegetarian choices and warm service.

Fishers Bistro

☎ 0131 554 5666 1 The Shore, Leith EH6 6QW
web: www.theaa.com/restaurants/114038.html
A long-time favourite in Leith, with views over the water. From superb raw Loch Fyne oysters, to seared tuna steak with chilli and lime couscous salad, the fish, as you would expect, is excellent.

Fishers in the City

☎ 0131 225 5109 58 Thistle St EH2 1EN
web: www.theaa.com/restaurants/114039.html
A smart, stylish, modern bistro in New Town with all the virtues of the original Fishers Bistro in Leith: superb ingredients, memorable cooking, swift, caring service, and a great atmosphere.

The Gallery Restaurant & Bar

☎ 0131 624 6579 National Gallery, The Mount EH2 2EL
web: www.theaa.com/restaurants/114044.html
A fantastic location and great views in the stunning new Weston link joining the National Gallery and the Royal Scottish Academy. Décor is smart and up to the minute, and so is the modern Scottish menu.

Henderson's Salad Table

☎ 0131 225 2131 94 Hanover St EH2 1DR
Pioneering vegetarian/ health food restaurant with deli and farm shop.

Howies Restaurant - Alva Street

☎ 0131 225 5553 1a Alva St EH2 4PH
web: www.theaa.com/restaurants/114040.html
Monthly-changing menus offer modern Scottish dishes, superb local ingredients and seasonal fare. As much as possible - desserts and warm crusty bread included - is made on the premises.

Howies Restaurant - Victoria Street

☎ 0131 225 1721 10-14 Victoria St EH1 2HG
web: www.theaa.com/restaurants/114041.html
Part of a thriving chain of acclaimed modern Scottish restaurants, this branch is characteristically modern and atmospheric; popular for quick lunches by day, and leisurely candlelit dinners by night. Excellent value.

Howies Restaurant - Waterloo Place

☎ 0131 556 5766 29 Waterloo Place EH1 3BQ
web: www.theaa.com/restaurants/114043.html
This particular Howies occupies a 200-year old Georgian building and reliably serves up the classic Howies mix of a laidback atmosphere and quality, good-value modern Scottish cooking served by friendly staff in bright, light surroundings.

Marque Central

☎ 0131 229 9859 30b Grindlay St EH3 9AX
web: www.theaa.com/restaurants/114057.html
An elegant, understated, restaurant between The Lyceum theatre and Usher Hall. Cooking is modern Scottish with lots of the Mediterranean in the mix, and is ambitious and full of flavour and texture. Pre- and post-theatre menus available.

No.3 Restaurant

☎ 0131 477 4747 3 Royal Ter EH7 5AB
web: www.theaa.com/restaurants/114048.html

A narrow, airy dining room serving great Scottish produce.

The Olive Branch Bistro

☎ 0131 557 8589 91 Broughton St EH1 3RX
web: www.theaa.com/restaurants/114049.html

Lunch, dinner, weekend brunches all from a Mediterranean menu. Informal, relaxed, friendly and romantic.

Scotland

EDINBURGH *continued* MAP 21 NT27

The Stockbridge Restaurant

☎ 0131 226 6766 54 St Stephens St EH3 5AL
web: www.theaa.com/restaurants/114050.html

Romantic basement is an intimate showcase for exciting modern European cooking.

VinCaffe

☎ 0131 557 0088 11 Multrees Walk EH1 3DQ
A popular Italian restaurant offering good range of menu choices.

Waterfront Wine Bar and Bistro

☎ 0131 554 2530 1c Dock Place, Leith EH6 6LU
Former steamship waiting room, now a warren of rooms offering decent food and friendly service.

Zinc

☎ 0131 553 8070 Ocean Terminal, Ocean Dr, Leith EH6 7DZ
Conran grill and bar on the waterfront.

FALKIRK

BANKNOCK MAP 21 NS77

Glenskirlie House Restaurant

Modern British

Elegant dining with both modern and traditional dishes

☎ 01324 840201 Kilsyth Rd FK4 1UF
e-mail: macaloneys@glenskirliehouse.com
web: www.glenskirliehouse.com

Guests at this refined country house are given room to breathe as tables in the smart, Edwardian-style dining room have plenty of space. Luxurious fabrics and striking wallcoverings create an elegant décor. Service is informal and unobtrusive. Using the finest Scottish ingredients, the food combines classic and contemporary influences, often on the same plate - hot carved venison, skirlie wrapped in pistachio mousse and Parma ham with blueberry and mushroom tartlet. For something less complex, you can opt for a traditional steak with mushrooms and onion rings. A wonderful array of desserts is served in time-honoured fashion on a trolley under heavy glass cloches - lemon tart with Calvados ice cream, for example.

Chef: Daryl Jordan **Owners:** John Macaloney, Colin Macaloney **Times:** 12-2/6-9.30, Closed 26-27 Dec, 1-3 Jan, Closed D Mon **Prices:** Fixed L fr £15.95, Starter £7.25-£9.95, Main £18-£20, Dessert £7.95, Coffee £3.25, Min/Water £3.25, Service optional **Wine:** 40 bottles over £20, 30 bottles under £20, 10 by the glass (£2.90-£9.50) **Notes:** Vegetarian available, Civ Wed 94 **Seats:** 54, Pr/dining room 150 **Smoking:** N/Sm in restaurant, Air con **Children:** Menu, Portions **Directions:** From Glasgow take A80 towards Stirling. Continue past Cumbernauld & Auchenkilens rdbt. At junct 4 take A803 signed Kilsyth/Bonnybridge. At T-junct turn right. Hotel 1m on right **Parking:** 100

GRANGEMOUTH MAP 21 NS98

The Grange Manor

British, French

Family-run manor house hotel with innovative cuisine

☎ 01324 474836 Glensburgh FK3 8XJ
e-mail: info@grangemanor.co.uk
web: www.grangemanor.co.uk

This stylish hotel has a smart restaurant for formal dining and Wallace's brasserie serving popular international dishes. The former offers some adventurous cooking with unusual combinations. Seared scallops, lovely and sweet, are served with lavender and pumpkin purée and black pudding dressed with infused raspberry and champagne balsamic. Garlic-crusted supreme of chicken is another elaborate dish (stuffed with a leek and tarragon farce on Chinese

continued

greens with a chive velouté) and the flavours are great. Good quality ingredients are used and much emphasis is placed on presentation. Rich chocolate torte is a light textured dessert served with Chantilly cream and dark chocolate sauce.

Times: 12-2/7-9.30, Closed 26 Dec, 1-2 Jan, Sun, Closed L Sat **Rooms:** 36 (36 en suite) ★★★ HL **Directions:** M9 (eastward) junct 6 200 mtrs on right, M9 (westward) junct 5, then A905 for 2m

FIFE

ANSTRUTHER MAP 21 NO50

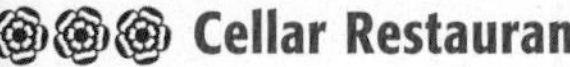

Cellar Restaurant

see page 564

CUPAR MAP 21 NO31

Ostlers Close Restaurant

Modern British

Modern, elegant restaurant making good use of excellent local ingredients

☎ 01334 655574 Bonnygate KY15 4BU
web: www.ostlersclose.co.uk

Tucked away down the eponymous close, this long-established, family-run restaurant attracts a loyal coterie of local food enthusiasts as well as those drawn from further afield by its well-deserved reputation for charming service and assured cooking. The owners have a passion for fresh, local ingredients (many of which are grown in their garden) and in particular for wild mushrooms, which they pick themselves from local woodland. Dishes such as seared hand-dived Skye scallops with stir-fry Glamis seakale pesto, or duck breast with Puy lentils and port wine sauce have a classic feel, though there are touches of the Mediterranean throughout this attractive-sounding menu. Desserts such as pear Tatin with 'Dulce de Leche' ice cream are a must.

Chef: James Graham **Owners:** James & Amanda Graham **Times:** 12.15-1.30/7-9.30, Closed 25-26 Dec, 1-2 Jan, 2 wks Oct, Sun-Mon, Closed L Tue-Fri **Prices:** Starter £5.50-£10.50, Main £10.50-£19.75, Dessert £5.75-£6.75, Coffee £2.25, Min/Water £2.50, Service optional **Wine:** 6 by the glass (£4-4.50) **Seats:** 26 **Smoking:** N/Sm in restaurant **Children:** Min 6 yrs D, Portions **Directions:** In small lane off main street, A91 **Parking:** On street, public car park

DUNFERMLINE MAP 21 NT08

Cardoon

Modern Scottish

Contemporary cooking in relaxed conservatory restaurant

☎ 01383 736258 Best Western Keavil House, Crossford KY12 8QW
e-mail: sales@keavilhouse.co.uk
web: www.keavilhouse.co.uk

A 16th-century former manor house plays host to the Keavil House Hotel and its stylish, conservatory restaurant, Cardoon, which overlooks the gardens and has a terrace for fair-weather aperitifs. Rich colours and a bright, airy, relaxed atmosphere create the mood, while the kitchen's crowd-pleasing, modern, brasserie-style repertoire suits the surroundings, the conventional three-course format enhanced by a range of light dish options and grills. Expect a fillet of turbot on black

continued

spaghetti with tomato, basil and garlic, and perhaps an apple and frangipane tart with Calvados crème anglaise to finish.

Cardoon

Chef: Phil Yates **Owners:** Queensferry Hotels Ltd **Times:** 12-2/6.30-9.30 **Prices:** Fixed L £8-£14, Fixed D £20-£30, Starter £3.25-£7.25, Main £6-£20, Dessert £3.25-£6, Coffee £1.95, Min/Water £3.95, Service optional **Wine:** 20 bottles over £20, 4 by the glass (£3.95-£5.50) **Notes:** Vegetarian available, Dress Restrictions, No football colours, Civ Wed 100 **Seats:** 65, Pr/dining room 22 **Smoking:** N/Sm in restaurant **Children:** Menu, Portions **Rooms:** 47 (47 en suite) ★★★ HL **Directions:** M90 junct 3, 7m from Forth Road Bridge, take A985, turning right after bridge. From Dunfermline, 2m W on A994 **Parking:** 175

ELIE MAP 21 N040

Sangsters

Modern British

AA Restaurant of the Year for Scotland

☎ 01333 331001 51 High St KY9 1BZ
e-mail: bruce@sangsters.co.uk
web: www.sangsters.co.uk

Located in the seaside village centre, Sangsters has a peaceful, relaxed atmosphere with a comfortable front lounge for pre-dinner drinks or after dinner coffees. The restaurant is more of a dining room with bright clean and simple lines and walls adorned with local prints and watercolours. The modern British cooking is precise with attention to detail and considerable skill - modern in style, but without the trappings of over-complex presentation. Enjoy the likes of scallops with slow cooked pork belly, or slow cooked shoulder noisette of lamb with basil pesto, aubergine compôte, buttered spinach and gratin potatoes. Advance booking essential.

Chef: Bruce R Sangster **Owners:** Bruce & Jacqueline Sangster **Times:** 12.30-1.30/7-9.30, Closed 25-26 Dec,early Jan, mid Feb/Oct,mid Nov, Mon, Closed L Tue & Sat, D Sun **Prices:** Fixed L £16.75, Fixed D £30,

continued on page 565

Scotland

Cellar Restaurant

ANSTRUTHER MAP 21 NO50

Scotland

Seafood, European

Superb seafood served in atmospheric restaurant

☎ 01333 310378 24 East Green KY10 3AA

Peter Jukes' well-known seafood restaurant is quite a find, tucked away not far from the harbour. Reached through an archway into a cobbled courtyard, it's actually in the ground-floor cellar of the owner's home. No ordinary house, however, but a 400-year-old former cooperage, steeped in history and full of character features from the flagstone floors, Singer sewing machine bases and roaring log fires to the eclectic décor featuring interesting pieces of art and pottery.

The real draw is of course the food and the restaurant has an established reputation, so it's worth booking in advance. The philosophy is simple and extremely successful, the very best fresh fish and other produce, cooked with care to allow the flavours to shine through. A daily-changing array of dishes use consistently excellent produce - River Forth langoustines, roasted whole with either lemon or garlic butter, or fillet of wild Channel Isle sea bass with crushed potatoes flavoured with chopped black olives, garlic, mint and oregano and Niçoise dressing. There are a few alternatives to seafood as well as some delicious desserts. Front of house, Susan Dukes offers a warm welcome and can help you match suitable wines with the various dishes from a well-chosen list.

Chef: Peter Jukes
Owners: Peter Jukes
Times: 12.30-1.30/7-9.30, Closed Xmas, Sun, Mon, Closed L Tue
Prices: Food prices not confirmed for 2007. Please telephone for details
Wine: 8 by the glass (£4.25-£5.50)
Notes: Fixed D 4 courses (incl. coffee) £35, Vegetarian available
Seats: 40
Smoking: N/Sm in restaurant
Children: Min 8 yrs, Portions
Directions: Located behind Scottish Fisheries Museum
Parking: outside

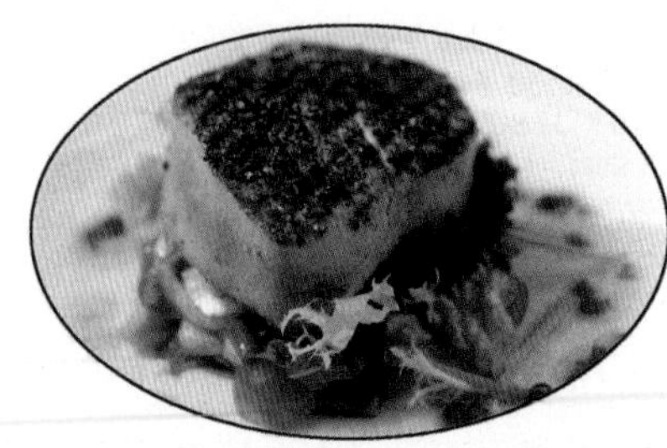

ELIE *continued* MAP 21 N040

Min/Water £2.50, Service optional **Wine:** 31 bottles over £20, 25 bottles under £20, 5 by the glass (£4) **Notes:** Coffee incl, Sun L 3 courses £20, Dress Restrictions, Smart casual **Seats:** 28 **Smoking:** N/Sm in restaurant **Children:** Min 12 yrs **Directions:** From St Andrews on the A917, take the B9131 to Anstruther, turn right at rdbt and follow A917 to Elie. 11m from St Andrews **Parking:** On street

GLENROTHES MAP 21 NO20

Rescobie House Hotel & Restaurant

Modern Scottish

Modern Scottish cuisine in art deco surroundings

☎ 01592 749555 6 Valley Dr, Leslie KY6 3BQ
e-mail: rescobiehotel@compuserve.com
web: www.rescobie-hotel.co.uk

A family-run hotel and restaurant set in secluded gardens on the edge of the village of Leslie. The original house is Grade C listed and dates from 1930, retaining some art deco features. The furnishings and décor are in keeping with the history of the house, providing comfortable and intimate surroundings. Cooking shows flair, offering modern Scottish cuisine with French influences. The dinner menu offers four courses, with main dishes like supreme of guinea fowl stuffed with apple and black pudding, served with sage pomme purée and cider jus. Puddings might feature caramelised citrus tart with clotted cream and fresh berries.

Chef: Paul Higgins **Owners:** Mr & Mrs K Wilkie **Times:** 12-2/6.30-9, Closed 26 Dec-10 Jan, Closed L Mon-Sat **Prices:** Fixed D £25.95-27.95, Coffee £2.25, Min/Water £3.25, Service optional **Wine:** 35 bottles over £20, 22 bottles under £20, 6 by the glass (£3.95-£4.75) **Notes:** Sun L 3 courses £16.95-£18.95, Civ Wed 24 **Seats:** 24, Pr/dining room 10 **Smoking:** N/Sm in restaurant **Children:** Portions **Rooms:** 10 (10 en suite) ★★ SHL **Directions:** From A92 at Glenrothes, take A911 to Leslie. At end of High St follow straight ahead. First left, hotel 2nd on left **Parking:** 12

KIRKCALDY MAP 21 NT29

Dunnikier House Hotel

British

Local flavours in Adam-style dining room

☎ 01592 268393 Dunnikier Park KY1 3LP
e-mail: recp@dunnikier-house-hotel.co.uk
web: www.dunnikier-house-hotel.co.uk

The Oswald Room is an elegant Adam-style dining room in this converted 18th-century manse house. Elegant panelling, efficient service, good quality settings and smart high-backed chairs create a formal backdrop to the contemporary menus. Modern Scottish dishes use lots of local, seasonal produce such as starters of mushroom Provençal in a pastry case and main courses of either peppered venison with grilled vegetables or salmon steak with a sesame seed crust, roasted cherry tomatoes with leek and white wine sauce. Finish with the lemon and blackcurrant crème brûlée.

Times: 12-2/6-9 **Rooms:** 15 (15 en suite) ★★★ HL **Directions:** Turn off A92 at Kirkcaldy West, take 3rd exit at rdbt signed hospital/crematorium, then 1st left past school

MARKINCH MAP 21 NO20

Balbirnie House

Traditional British NOTABLE WINE LIST

Orangery restaurant serving expertly cooked local produce

☎ 01592 610066 Balbirnie Park KY7 6NE
e-mail: info@balbirnie.co.uk
web: www.balbirnie.co.uk

Despite being one of Scotland's most important Grade A listed buildings, the hotel describes itself as 'swanky but not snooty!'. The restaurant is found in a lovely orangery and its traditional décor and delightful ambience make it a welcoming place to eat. The cooking style is also traditional, but with modern and inventive twists. Dinner is a fairly serious affair so come with an appetite. First courses feature East Neuk crab and prawn fettuccine with spiced coconut and coriander cream. Between the starter and main course you can choose a light second course like seafood broth or mulled wine granita. Main courses might include grilled fillet of cod with Arran mustard mash, broccoli, saffron and tomato cream.

Notable Wine List: A nicely presented wine list with good informative tasting notes.

Chef: Ian MacDonald **Owners:** The Russell Family **Times:** 12-2.30/7-9.30 **Prices:** Fixed L fr £11.50, Fixed D fr £32.50, Starter £3.50-£6.95, Main £9.50-£15.50, Dessert £5.50, Service optional **Wine:** 100 bottles over £20, 50 bottles under £20, 10 by the glass (£3.95-£6.30) **Notes:** Fixed D 4 courses, Vegetarian available, Civ Wed 200 **Seats:** 65, Pr/dining room 216 **Smoking:** N/Sm in restaurant, Air con **Children:** Menu, Portions **Rooms:** 30 (30 en suite) ★★★★ HL **Directions:** M90 junct 13, follow signs for Glenrothes and Tay Bridge, right onto B9130 to Markinch and Balbirnie Park **Parking:** 100

Scotland

PEAT INN MAP 21 NO40

The Peat Inn

Rosettes not confirmed at time of going to press

French

The original restaurant with rooms

☎ 01334 840206 KY15 5LH
e-mail: reception@thepeatinn.co.uk
web: www.thepeatinn.co.uk

You only have to step inside this 300-year-old whitewashed coaching inn to discover a gastro-pub that pays serious homage to fine dining. Modest on the outside, inside sumptuous fabrics, gleaming crystal glasses and polished silver cutlery combine with high-backed chairs, tapestries and beams in a smartly decorated dining room. There are three separate dining areas, each with its own character in the style of a French auberge. Created with an emphasis on relaxation and comfort, this is the perfect place to stay overnight in one of the individually styled suites located in an adjacent block, with split-level design and Italian marble bathrooms. *The rosette rating was unconfirmed as we went to press due to a change of hands taking place, so visit our website for the latest update.*

Times: 12.30-1/7-9.30, Closed 25 Dec, 1 Jan, Sun-Mon **Rooms:** 8 (8 en suite) ★★ **Directions:** At junction of B940/B941, 6 miles SW of St Andrews.

ST ANDREWS MAP 21 NO51

Inn at Lathones

Modern European NOTABLE WINE LIST

Local produce in an ancient inn

☎ 01334 840494 Largoward KY9 1JE
e-mail: lathones@theinn.co.uk
web: www.theinn.co.uk

St Andrews' oldest coaching inn is over 400 years old, with lots of historical tales and a resident friendly ghost to prove it! Extended over the years to provide accommodation and meeting rooms, the cosy interior has a country feel with simple décor in the bar and restaurant. Modern European cooking and refined techniques derive the best results from excellent local produce. Starters like tartare of inn-cured salmon with sweet dill and mustard dressing provide clean flavours in a simple combination that works well. Main courses are divided into those from the land and from the sea. Try the likes of roast rack of hill-bred lamb, served with dauphinoise potatoes.

Notable Wine List: A well-presented wine list which shows much passion for high-quality wines.

The Inn at Lathones

Chef: Martin Avey **Owners:** Mr N White **Times:** 12-2.30/6-9.30, Closed 25-26 Dec, 4-18 Jan **Prices:** Fixed D £40-£45, Starter £3.95-£12, Main £11.50-£28.50, Dessert £5.95-£8.50, Coffee £1.50, Min/Water £3, Service optional **Wine:** 15 bottles under £20, 10 by the glass (£4-£8) **Notes:** Fixed D 4 courses, Vegetarian available, Dress Restrictions, Smart casual, Civ Wed 40 **Seats:** 34, Pr/dining room 30 **Smoking:** N/Sm in restaurant **Children:** Menu, Portions **Rooms:** 13 (13 en suite) ★★★★ INN **Directions:** 5m SW of St Andrews on A915. In 0.5m before Largoward on left, just after hidden dip **Parking:** 34

Macdonald Rusacks Hotel

Traditional British

Accomplished cooking in legendary golfing setting

☎ 0870 400 8128 Pilmour Links KY16 9JQ
e-mail: general.rusacks@macdonald-hotels.co.uk
web: www.macdonald-hotels.co.uk

Just a short chip from the 18th hole, this St Andrews' veteran offers unrivalled views of the famous golf course. The food's not bad either tear your eyes away from the green, and you'll find a tempting range of sophisticated contemporary dishes, including mains such as pan-seared monkfish wrapped in pancetta with Puy lentil cassoulet, courgettes and port sauce, or loin of Highland venison served on

continued

butternut squash and parsnip purée, chestnuts and huckleberry jus. There's a grill selection too, and some intriguing vegetarian options; a red onion tarte Tatin shows the style, topped with glazed goat's cheese, and served with a rocket and roast pepper salad, and red wine reduction.

Chef: Craig Beadie **Owners:** Macdonald Hotels PLC **Times:** 12-2.30/6.30-9 **Prices:** Fixed D £32, Coffee £2.95, Service optional **Wine:** 35 bottles over £20, 15 bottles under £20, 13 by the glass (£3.75-£4.75) **Notes:** Vegetarian available, Civ Wed 60 **Seats:** 66, Pr/dining room 65 **Smoking:** N/Sm in restaurant **Children:** Menu, Portions **Rooms:** 68 (68 en suite) ★★★★ HL **Directions:** From M90 junct 8 take A91 to St Andrews. Hotel on left on entering the town **Parking:** 23

The Road Hole Grill

see below

Rufflets Country House

British NOTABLE WINE LIST

Stylish country-house dining in a friendly atmosphere

☎ 01334 472594 Strathkinness Low Rd KY16 9TX
e-mail: reservations@rufflets.co.uk
web: www.rufflets.co.uk

The epitome of style, this Edwardian country house with delightful formal gardens and woodland makes a wonderful retreat. The restaurant features simple and stylish traditional décor with lots of colourful artwork. Service is particularly friendly and attentive making the diner feel really at ease. The chef cooks Scottish cuisine with influences from the Mediterranean, using the freshest local produce

continued

available. Typical dishes include a starter of roast quail stuffed with wild mushroom and wrapped in pancetta. Likewise, a main course might be a seared collop of beef with traditional accompaniments like French beans, dauphinoise potatoes and roast shallots. Scottish cheeses like Iona Cromak, Isle of Mull brie and Lanark Blue might appear on the cheeseboard.

Notable Wine List: A well-chosen, traditional wine list with good tasting notes throughout.

Rufflets Country House

Chef: Jeremy Brazelle **Owners:** Ann Murray-Smith **Times:** 12.30-2/7-9, Closed L Mon-Sat **Prices:** Fixed L £10-£15, Fixed D £30-£39, Coffee £1.75, Min/Water £3.50, Service optional, Group min 20 service 10% **Wine:** 20 bottles over £20, 15 bottles under £20, 8 by the glass (£3.25-£7.50) **Notes:** Vegetarian available, Dress Restrictions, No shorts, Civ Wed 45 **Seats:** 80, Pr/dining room 80 **Smoking:** N/Sm in restaurant **Children:** Menu, Portions **Rooms:** 24 (24 en suite) ★★★★ HL **Directions:** 1.5m W of St Andrews on B939 **Parking:** 50

The Road Hole Grill

ST ANDREWS MAP 21 NO51

British, Scottish

Sumptuous dining in golfing heaven

☎ 01334 474371 Old Course Hotel, Golf Resort & Spa KY16 9SP
e-mail: reservations@oldcoursehotel.co.uk
web: www.oldcoursehotel.co.uk

The luxurious fourth-floor restaurant of the Old Course Hotel, one of the most famous golfing hotels in the world, commands stunning views over the golf course and St Andrews Bay. Luxury and comfort are by-words in the grand hotel, no more so than in this fine-dining venue, with its elegant oak panelling, crisp linen-clothed tables and open-to-view theatre kitchen. Friendly staff deliver exacting service and advice as befits the five-star setting. Well-balanced menus make full use of quality seasonal, local Scottish produce, with a welcome focus on luxury produce from the sea and forests. Foie gras, langoustine, lobster and caviar all feature on the impressive carte. Traditional classics are given a modern twist, from a roast Orkney langoustine soup with trompette mushrooms and a caviar crème fraîche starter, to main course options like rack of Inverness lamb with pea and mint ravioli, aubergine caviar and balsamic, and pan-seared cod on chorizo crushed potatoes with vegetables and mussels and tomato froth.

Puddings include iced banana parfait and a classic crème brûlée.

Chef: Drew Heron **Owners:** Jonathan Stapleton **Times:** 7-10, Closed 23-26 Dec (res only), Closed L all week **Prices:** Fixed D £42.50, Starter £9-£13.95, Main £17.50-£29.50, Dessert £8.50-£12.75, Coffee £3.50, Min/Water £4 **Wine:** 223 bottles over £20 **Notes:** Wine tasting table available, Vegetarian available, Dress Restrictions, Smart dress, no jeans, jacket & tie, Civ Wed 200 **Seats:** 60, Pr/dining room 20 **Smoking:** N/Sm in restaurant **Children:** Menu, Portions **Rooms:** 146 (146 en suite) ★★★★★ HL **Directions:** M90 junct 8, close to A91. 5 mins from St Andrews **Parking:** 100

Scotland

Scotland

ST ANDREWS *continued* MAP 21 NO51

Russell Hotel

French, Scottish

Imaginative cooking in an intimate setting

☎ 01334 473447 26 The Scores KY16 9AS
e-mail: russellhotel@talk21.com
web: www.russellhotelstandrews.co.uk

This comfortable and intimate hotel restaurant prides itself on the sort of convivial atmosphere and closely arranged tables usually only found in Paris bistros. The cooking draws on French and British influences and high quality local ingredients appear in bradan rost kiln-smoked salmon from Loch Fyne, roast loin of Highland venison and roast cannon of Perthshire lamb and lamb's kidneys with sweet potato purée and light Madeira jus. Desserts could include rhubarb and custard cheesecake or pannacotta with a tuille basket and fruit coulis.

Times: 12-2/6.30-9.30, Closed Xmas **Rooms:** 10 (10 en suite) ★★ HL
Directions: Telephone for directions

St Andrews Bay Golf Resort & Spa

Mediterranean

Mediterranean cooking in luxuriously appointed hotel restaurant

☎ 01334 837000 KY16 8PN
e-mail: info@standrewsbay.com
web: www.standrewsbay.com

Overlooking the bay and flanked by its two golf courses, a central atrium is the focal point of this resort hotel. Esperante is the well-presented restaurant overlooking the atrium with an opulent Mediterranean atmosphere, deep ruby and red décor and luxurious upholstery. Staff are professional and friendly. The generous menu is heavily influenced by French and Italian classics with contemporary British touches. Dishes are prepared with skill and care and there is good use of top quality ingredients. Start with the baby leek and asparagus terrine with langoustine and rosemary brochette before a main course of suckling pig on braised cabbage with confit vegetables and a Pommery mustard and tarragon velouté.

Times: 7.30-9.30, Closed Mon-Tues, Closed L all wk **Rooms:** 217 (217 en suite) ★★★★★ HL

St Andrews Golf Hotel

British, French

Modern Scottish fine-dining restaurant

☎ 01334 472611 40 The Scores KY16 9AS
e-mail: reception@standrews-golf.co.uk
web: www.standrews-golf.co.uk

A friendly, family-run hotel with amazing views of the famous golf course and the coastline. Dunes restaurant is a formal wood-panelled dining room where professional staff are on hand, serving at smartly-set tables. Skilful cooking produces pleasingly simple dishes based on fine Scottish produce. A hard day on the golf course will be well rewarded here with hearty portions. Try a starter of warm St Andrews Bay crab cake with rocket and basil salad, sweet chilli dipping sauce and lemon oil that's bound to have your mouth watering. For mains look out for tender braised lamb shank with seasonal root vegetables, mustard mash and rosemary jus. Impressive wine list.

Chef: Mark House **Owners:** Justin Hughes **Times:** 12.30-2/7-9.30, Closed 26-28 Dec **Prices:** Fixed L fr £10, Fixed D £28.50, Starter £4-£6.50, Main £12-£20, Dessert £5, Coffee £2, Min/Water £2, Service optional **Wine:** 40 bottles over £20, 20 bottles under £20, 10 by the glass (£3.75-£6) **Notes:** Dress Restrictions, No jeans, shorts, trainers, baseball caps, Civ Wed 180 **Seats:** 60, Pr/dining room 20 **Smoking:** N/Sm in restaurant, Air con **Children:** Menu, Portions **Rooms:** 21 (21 en suite) ★★★ **Directions:** Enter town on A91, cross both mini rdbts, turn left at Golf Place and 1st right into The Scores. Hotel 200 yds on right **Parking:** 6

Sands Restaurant

Mediterranean

Elegant, stylish restaurant within golf resort hotel complex

☎ 01334 474371 & 468228
The Old Course Hotel, KY16 9SP
e-mail: reservations@oldcoursehotel.co.uk
web: www.oldcoursehotel.co.uk

This hotel borders the 17th fairway of the legendary Old Course, and the Sands Restaurant is one of the dining options. It has stylish décor with lots of darkwood and black leather, and an upbeat atmosphere. Friendly, professional table service is offered by young well-presented staff. The cooking is unpretentious with a fair share of Mediterranean-influenced dishes. Try the likes of dressed crab or seafood soup to start, followed by a main course of crispy fillets of sea bass with celeriac purée and rocket pesto, or the vegetarian choice of tomato, basil and olive polenta with chargrilled courgette, red chard and asparagus.

Chef: Mark Lindsey **Owners:** Kohler Company **Times:** 12-6/6-10, Closed 23-26 Dec (residents only) **Prices:** Starter £6.25-£10.50, Main £14.50-£21.50, Dessert £5.50, Coffee £2.95, Min/Water £4, Service included **Wine:** 24 bottles over £20, 18 by the glass (£4.50) **Notes:** Vegetarian available, Smart casual, Civ Wed 200 **Seats:** 80, Pr/dining room 40 **Smoking:** N/Sm in restaurant **Children:** Menu, Portions **Directions:** M90 junct 8. Situated close to A91 and 5 mins walk from St Andrews **Parking:** 100

The Seafood Restaurant

ST ANDREWS MAP 21 NO51

Modern Seafood WINE AWARD WINNER FOR SCOTLAND

AA Wine Award Winner for Scotland

☎ 01334 479475 The Scores KY16 9AS

e-mail: info@theseafoodrestaurant.com

web: www.theseafoodrestaurant.com

The stern end of an ocean-going liner couldn't offer better uninterrupted views of the sea and coastline than this stunning, modern, glass-walled building, which comes virtually suspended over the bay. Uncompromisingly contemporary and upmarket in style, the bright, clean-lined interior combines traditional high-quality table settings with funkier-styled seating and napery, while a fashionable open-plan kitchen not only proves a striking feature, but allows tantalising aromas to drift into the restaurant and heighten expectancy.

The accomplished, clean, crisp cooking style is flavour-driven, skilfully allowing high-quality, fresh produce to shine on an appealing fixed-price menu repertoire dominated - though not exclusively - by the fruits of the sea and enticing, fashionable fish dishes. Think pan-seared halibut served with a mussel and pancetta chowder and braised pak choi, or pan-seared, hand-dived scallops with soy-braised pork belly and roasted salsify, while an espresso pannacotta with white chocolate and coffee ice cream might take the eye at dessert. (This is sister to The Seafood Restaurant at St Monans, down the coast, where Tim Butler and Craig Millar first joined forces - see entry.)

Notable Wine List: Constructed with a great deal of care and attention, this list offers a beautiful selection of wines at really good prices.

Chef: Craig Millar, Neil Clarke
Owners: Craig Millar, Tim Butler
Times: 12-2.30/6.30-10, Closed 25-26 Dec, Jan 1
Prices: Fixed L fr £20, Fixed D fr £38.50, Coffee £2.75, Min/Water £3.50, Group min 8 service 10%
Wine: 119 bottles over £20, 9 bottles under £20, 10 by the glass (£4-£6.50)
Seats: 60
Smoking: N/Sm area, Air con
Children: Min 12 yrs, Portions
Directions: Please telephone for directions
Parking: 50mtr away

Scotland

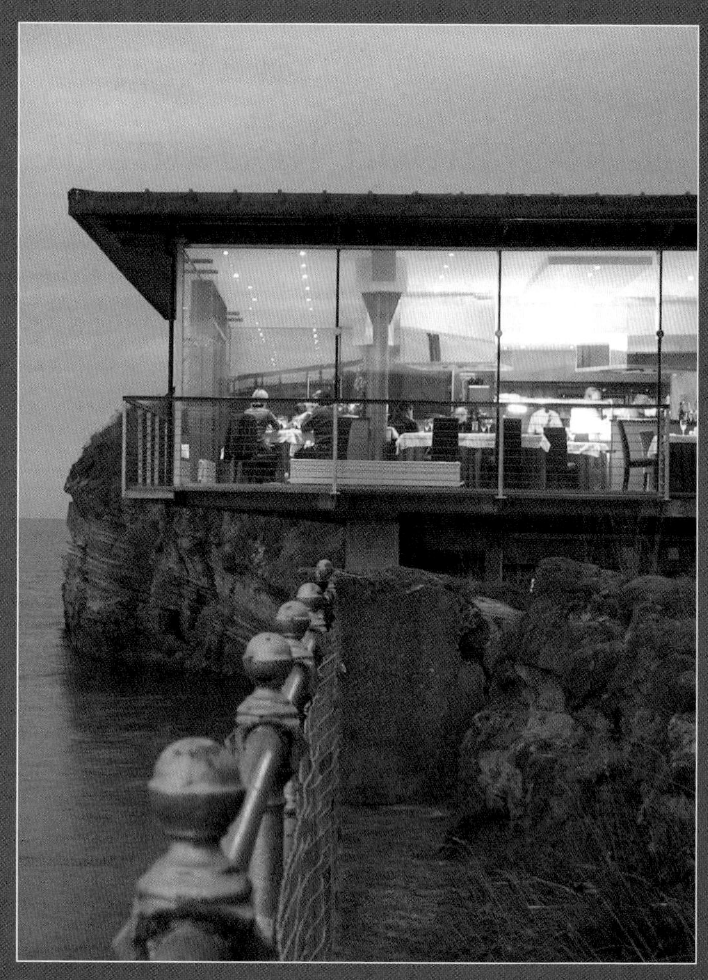

Scotland

Wine Award Winner

The Seafood Restaurant

St Andrews

page 569

ST MONANS MAP 21 NO50

The Seafood Restaurant

Modern Seafood

The freshest seafood by the harbour

☎ 01333 730327 16 West End KY10 2BX
e-mail: info@theseafoodrestaurant.com
web: www.theseafoodrestaurant.com

The restaurant occupies an old fisherman's cottage and features a fresh water well with mythical healing powers. There's an open fire in the Victorian bar, a terrace for sitting outside, and picture windows in the modern restaurant extension overlooking the harbour and the Firth of Forth across the Isle of May. The restaurant, which has always been about the freshest fish simply cooked, has become a little more experimental, but thankfully not too much so. Generally a light touch is applied allowing the fish to dominate the plate. Good to try are smoked haddock and leek tart with saffron aïoli, and hand-dived scallops with linguine and mussel and lobster ragout.

Chef: Andy Simpson **Owners:** Craig Millar, Tim Butler **Times:** 12-2.30/6-9.30, Closed 25-26 Dec,1-2 Jan, Mon, Tues **Prices:** Fixed L £20, Fixed D fr £30, Service included **Wine:** 51 bottles over £20, 14 bottles under £20, 6 by the glass (£4.50-£6) **Seats:** 44 **Smoking:** N/Sm in restaurant **Children:** Portions **Directions:** Take A959 from St Andrews to Anstruther, then head W on A917 through Pittenweem. In St Monans to harbour then right **Parking:** 10

CITY OF GLASGOW

GLASGOW MAP 20 NS56

Abode Hotel Glasgow

Modern British NEW

Concept hotel with stylish décor and accomplished cuisine

☎ 0141 221 6789 572 6000 129 Bath St G2 2SZ

Former Department of Education offices have been substantially redeveloped to create this stylish hotel, with original Edwardian features incorporated into the new look. There's a café bar, with low level lighting, leather seating, table service and a cocktail menu for pre-dinner drinks. Accomplished cooking in the Michael Caines restaurant has a growing reputation. Here you'll find darkwood flooring, comfortable chairs and banquettes, stylish table appointments, and an eye-catching glass-screened wine cave. An impressive dish of ballontine of foie gras with girolles and soused beetroot to start, followed by roast wild sea bass with its super silky texture and cod brandade set the style. The trio of chocolate desserts makes a fabulous finale with its accuracy and great presentation.

continued

Chef: Martin Donnolly **Owners:** Michael Caines Ltd. **Times:** 12-2/7-10, Closed Sun **Prices:** Food prices not confirmed for 2007. Please telephone for details **Rooms:** 63 (63 en suite) ★★★★ HL

Brian Maule at Chardon d'Or

French, British

Confident cooking in a slick city-centre venue

☎ 0141 248 3801 176 West Regent St G2 4RL
e-mail: info@brianmaule.com
web: www.brianmaule.com

A blend of modern and traditional works well in this converted city-centre Georgian townhouse. Attentive, friendly service adds to the relaxed ambience of this restaurant, where French and British cuisine dominate a menu created from high-quality ingredients. Deceptively simple dishes include chicken, foie gras and chorizo roulade with beetroot salad, supreme of duck with creamed celeriac, port and redcurrant jelly jus or extra bitter dark chocolate cheesecake with an orange marmalade and English cream. A popular lunchtime venue for upmarket shoppers and business types attracted by the light specials menu.

Times: 12-2/6-9, Closed 2 wks Jan, 2 wks Summer & BHs, Sun, Closed L Sat **Directions:** 10 minute walk from Glasgow central station

The Buttery

Modern British NOTABLE WINE LIST

Vibrant flavours in Glaswegian grandee

☎ 0141 221 8188 652 Argyle St G3 8UF

This revitalised Glasgow institution - a timbered 19th-century former wine merchant's premises and tavern set in a city tenement - has a surprisingly unassuming exterior. But inside is quite a different matter; its rich and luxurious décor combining original Victorian fittings with fashionable modern touches. Think oak-panelled walls, high ornate ceilings, stained-glass windows, deeply comfortable seating, crisp white linen and a stunning marble-topped bar. The kitchen's modern approach deals in quality ingredients from the abundant Scottish larder, its balanced, appropriately refined dishes showcasing clean, clear flavours. Think a daube of Blairgowrie beef with parsnip mash, roasted root vegetables and pan juices, and an apple and vanilla pannacotta crumble finish, served with rhubarb consommé.
Notable Wine List: A well-balanced, well-chosen wine list with much interest and good tasting notes for each wine.

Chef: Christopher Watson **Owners:** Ian Fleming **Times:** 12-2/7-10, Closed 25-26 Dec, 1-2 Jan, Sun, Mon, Closed L Sat **Prices:** Fixed L £16, Fixed D £38, Coffee £2.50, Min/Water £3, Service optional **Wine:** 87 bottles over £20, 4 bottles under £20, 10 by the glass (£4-£5.50) **Notes:** Vegetarian available **Seats:** 60, Pr/dining room 40 **Smoking:** N/Sm in restaurant, Air con **Children:** Portions **Directions:** From St Vincent St (city centre) first left onto Elderslie St, at rdbt, left onto Argyle St. Restaurant 600 yds on left **Parking:** 36

Café Royale

Modern Scottish NEW

Simple café style in a trendy residential area, serving Scottish produce

☎ 0141 338 6606 340 Crow Rd G11 7HT

Once a bank, this bustling shop-front style establishment has tables on the pavement. Inside you'll find cheery bistro-style décor with blue gingham tablecloths, blue walls and a seafood theme. The food

continued

Scotland

GLASGOW *continued* MAP 20 NS56

ranges from light snacks, a blackboard tapas menu and pre-theatre dinners to an evening carte. Majoring on seafood, a sample evening menu includes langoustines served on shell with home-made lemon mayonnaise for starters, then continues with hand-dived scallops wrapped in Ayrshire bacon with black pudding and mixed leaves, or Buccleuch beef fillet, poached, with whisky pepper butter. Simple cooking that makes the most of fresh, locally sourced produce. Service is relaxed and friendly.

Chef: Claire Mckie **Owners:** The McKie Family **Times:** 11-3/5.30-11.30, Closed 25 & 26 Dec, 1-4 Jan, Mon, Closed D Sun **Prices:** Fixed L £9.95-£25, Fixed D £35-£40, Starter £4.25-£7.95, Main £13.95-£21.95, Dessert £4.95, Coffee £1.70, Min/Water £2.95, Service optional **Wine:** 11 bottles over £20, 9 bottles under £20, 2 by the glass (£3.95) **Notes:** Vegetarian available **Seats:** 40 **Smoking:** N/Sm in restaurant, Air con **Children:** Portions **Directions:** Telephone for directions

étain

Modern French NOTABLE WINE LIST

Rosettes not confirmed at time of going to press

☎ 0141 225 5630 Princes Square G1 3JX
e-mail: etain@conran.com
web: www.etain-restaurant.co.uk

Take the street-side glass elevator directly to this cool, second-floor restaurant or enter through its vibrant Zinc bar and brasserie. Designed by Sir Terence Conran and Partners, the interior is stylish, minimalist and refreshingly simple, full of natural oak, leather and warm, earthy colours, set against shimmering pewter-clad pillars. Floor-to-ceiling glass windows look out over Princes Square, the atmosphere is relaxed and the staff highly skilled, friendly and efficient. The kitchen has pedigree, too. The equally modern approach is underpinned by a French theme, and the aspirational cooking is flavour driven with a focus on high-quality, fresh native produce and dishes dressed to thrill. So expect Glenalmond Estate venison with turnip fondant, braised Savoy cabbage and juniper jus to be backed by an excellent wine list.
We learned that there was a change of chef as the Guide went to press.
Notable Wine List: A classic and well-thought out wine list with a comprehensive offering from around the world.

Owners: Conran Restaurants Ltd **Times:** 12-2.30/7-10, Closed 25 Dec & 1 Jan, Closed L Sat, D Sun **Prices:** Fixed D £27-£32, Coffee £2.85, Min/Water £3.50, Service added but optional 12.5% **Wine:** 180 bottles over £20, 2 bottles under £20, 8 by the glass (£5.25-£6.95) **Notes:** Tasting menu £39, £59 with wine selection, Vegetarian available **Seats:** 65 **Smoking:** N/Sm in restaurant, Air con **Directions:** Please telephone for directions **Parking:** NCP Mitchell Street, street parking available

Gamba

Modern Seafood

One of Glasgow's most established fish restaurants

☎ 0141 572 0899 225a West George St G2 2ND
e-mail: info@gamba.co.uk
web: www.gamba.co.uk

Located right in the centre of the city, this perennial favourite continues to provide attentive service and consistent food in a comfortable basement setting. There's a striking Mediterranean theme to the décor - warm colours and soothing lighting with a cosy cocktail area for pre- or post-prandial drinks. The theme also extends to the food, although other influences - notably Asian - abound on this well-balanced menu. There's a degree of risk-taking with the dishes, but it's classics such as the Gamba fish soup (for which they are deservedly renowned) that win the day. You might follow with grilled langoustine with garlic and herb olive oil, or crisp fried fillets of sea bass on Caesar salad with smoked bacon and prawns.

Gamba

Chef: Derek Marshall, John Gillespie **Owners:** Mr A C Tomkins & Mr D Marshall **Times:** 12-2.30/5-10.30, Closed 25-26 Dec, 1-2 Jan, BHs, Sun **Prices:** Fixed L fr £15.95, Fixed D fr £18.95, Starter £6-£12, Main £12-£24, Dessert £4-£7, Coffee £2.75, Min/Water £3.75, Service optional, Group min 6 service 10% **Wine:** 40 bottles over £20, 10 bottles under £20, 6 by the glass (£4.80-£7) **Notes:** Vegetarian available **Seats:** 66 **Smoking:** N/Sm in restaurant, Air con **Children:** Min 14 yrs **Directions:** Telephone for directions

Ho Wong Restaurant

Chinese NEW

Welcoming Chinese hospitality and an emphasis on seafood

☎ 0141 221 3550 82 York St G2 8LE
e-mail: ho.wong@amserve.com
web: www.ho-wong.com

There's quite a buzz to this popular street-level restaurant close to the city centre, Central Station and the SECC. Friendly, attentive staff, modern décor and impressive surroundings contribute to the relaxed atmosphere. Fish dishes are a real highlight on this sophisticated traditional Cantonese-style menu. If you want to push the boat out, try some fresh lobster, or be adventurous and go for crispy duck with mashed king prawn and crab meat sauce, or monkfish with spring onion and ginger - it's difficult to choose from so many flavoursome dishes. Fish is sourced from the MacCallums of Troon. Set menus are available for groups.

Chef: S Wong **Owners:** David Wong **Times:** 12-2.15/6-11.30, Closed L Sun **Prices:** Fixed L fr £9.50, Fixed D £28-£42.50, Starter £4.50-£7, Main £14.70-£25.70, Dessert £3.50-£3.95, Coffee £1.80, Min/Water £3.50, Service optional, Group min 8 service 10% **Wine:** 33 bottles over £20, 32 bottles under £20, 2 by the glass (£3.20-£3.50) **Notes:** Fixed D 4 courses, Vegetarian available **Seats:** 90, Pr/dining room 35 **Smoking:** Air con **Directions:** Off Argyle St. 2 mins from Glasgow Central Station **Parking:** 8

Killermont Polo Club

Indian

Indian dining in a polo-inspired setting

☎ 0141 946 5412 2002 Maryhill Rd, Maryhill Park G20 0AB
web: www.killermontpoloclub.co.uk

Only ten minutes from the centre of Glasgow, once inside this restaurant, with its unlikely former manse setting, you could be back in the Raj. This stylish Indian restaurant is decked out with dark green walls and polo prints. Service is helpful, especially when explaining the dum pukht house speciality dishes cooked in pastry-sealed containers. All these dishes have their own individual sauces and the method of cooking makes it a multi-flavoured sauce. The cooking is said to be the family food of the Moghul emperors. Other dishes include tandoori, kormas and club specialities.

Times: 12-2.30/5-11.30, Closed New Year **Directions:** Telephone for directions

Langs Hotel

Modern Scottish

Glitzy and unforgettable modern restaurant with contemporary Scottish cuisine

☎ 0141 333 1500 2 Port Dundas Place G2 3LD
e-mail: neil.raw@langshotels.co.uk
web: www.langshotels.co.uk

A sharply styled, modern city-centre hotel whose Aurora restaurant makes a bold and colourful statement set in its own secluded environment. The mood lighting is cool and trendy, enhanced by candles on the spacious tables for a touch of intimacy. Staff are usually uniformed and knowledgeable. The cooking is modern Scottish using the finest local ingredients whenever possible. Careful preparation and eye-catching presentations prepare you for the sumptuous flavours that come from a seriously focused kitchen. An intensely delicious fillet of turbot with langoustine ravioli or fillet of Speyside beef, with a mini cottage pie and dauphinoise potato epitomise the menu's riches.

Chef: Craig Dunn **Owners:** Prestwick Hotels Ltd **Times:** 5-10, Closed Sun, Mon, Closed L all wk **Prices:** Fixed D £17.50, Starter £4.75-£6.50, Main £9.50-£22.50, Dessert £4.75-£5.50, Coffee £1.65, Min/Water £3.50, Service optional **Wine:** 23 bottles over £20, 24 bottles under £20, 12 by the glass (£3.25-£5.95) **Notes:** Vegetarian available, Dress Restrictions, Smart casual preferred, Civ Wed 120 **Seats:** 50, Pr/dining room 14 **Smoking:** N/Sm in restaurant, Air con **Children:** Portions **Rooms:** 100 (100 en suite) ★★★★ HL **Directions:** Telephone for directions **Parking:** 1,200 spaces available, discounted

The Living Room

Modern European

Laid-back bar that aims to please

☎ 0870 220 3028 150 St Vincent St G2 5NE
e-mail: glasgow@thelivingroom.co.uk
web: www.thelivingroom.co.uk

More Manhattan than Glasgow, this achingly chic piano bar is a home from home offering secluded booths, decent music and a menu to suit all comers. Its lengthy selection runs from comfort food to fine cuisine, so whether you're in the mood for bangers and mash or seared sashimi tuna with coconut and lime jus, you'll find something to suit. The food is fresh, flavourful and good value, particularly at lunchtime, and there's an extensive range of cocktails and wines by the glass on offer, plus spirits by the bottle. Sit back and relax.

Chef: Alan Watts **Owners:** Living Ventures **Times:** 11-3/6-11, Closed 25-26 Dec, 1-2 Jan, BHs **Prices:** Starter £3.45-£8.95, Main £7.95-£17.95, Dessert £4.25-£4.95, Coffee £1.95, Min/Water £3.95, Service optional, Group min 6 service 10% **Wine:** 20 bottles over £20, 11 bottles under £20, 10 by the glass (£3.95-£5) **Notes:** Sun brunch available, Vegetarian available, Dress Restrictions, Smart casual, no sportswear **Seats:** 140, Pr/dining room 11 **Smoking:** N/Sm in restaurant, Air con **Children:** Menu, Portions **Directions:** City Centre location between Hope St & Wellington St **Parking:** On street

Lux

Modern Scottish V

Stylish, formal fine dining in a converted railway station

☎ 0141 576 7576 1051 Great Western Rd G12 0XP
e-mail: luxstazione@bt.connect.com
web: www.luxstazione.co.uk

This JJ Burnet-designed Victorian building was once Kelvinside railway station; it was completely renovated and redesigned into two restaurants by the current owners. Situated on the upper floor, Lux is a plush, wood-floored dining room with comfortable leather chairs, subtle lighting and a muted colour scheme. The food is resolutely modern British with a classical influence shining through. Dishes offer unusual combinations of ingredients cooked with obvious technical skill - grilled baby black pudding salad with thyme and strawberry dressing, for example, or Indian sweet potato risotto with hot onion compôte. Finish off with warm individual apple pie with blackcurrant ice cream. Great service is the icing on the cake.

Chef: Stephen Johnson **Owners:** Stephen Johnson **Times:** 6-until late, Closed 25-26 Dec, 1-2 Jan, Sun ex by arrangement, Closed L all week ex by arrangement **Prices:** Fixed D £33.50, Coffee £1.50, Min/Water £3.25, Service optional, Group min 6 service 10% **Wine:** 43 bottles over £20,

continued

Scotland

GLASGOW *continued* MAP 20 NS56

7 bottles under £20, 5 by the glass (£3.95-£7.50) **Notes:** Vegetarian menu, Smart casual **Seats:** 64, Pr/dining room 14 **Smoking:** N/Sm area, No pipes, No cigars, Air con **Children:** Min 12 yrs **Directions:** At traffic lights signed Gartnavel Hospital, on Great Western Rd. 0.25m E of Anniesland Cross **Parking:** 16

Malmaison

Traditional French, British 

French brasserie in a stylish church conversion

☎ 0141 572 1001 278 West George St G2 4LL
e-mail: glasgow@malmaison.com
web: www.malmaison.com

This smart hotel is built around a 19th-century former Greek Orthodox church in the historic Charing Cross area of Glasgow. The restaurant, located in the crypt, is very atmospheric and serves French brasserie-style food. Starters include soups, terrines and moules marinière, while main courses range from the Mal burger to pot-roasted pigeon with cauliflower purée. Quality beef is sourced from the Duke of Buccleuch estate, and steaks from the chargrill come with a choice of sauces. For dessert there's home-made ice cream and sorbet, alongside steamed pudding and Malmaison crème brûlée.
Notable Wine List: A really high-quality wine list with concise tasting notes throughout offering an interesting and diverse mix of wines.

Times: 12-2.30/5.30-10.30 **Rooms:** 72 (72 en suite) ★★★ HL
Directions: From George Square take Vincent Street to Pitt Street. Hotel on corner with West George Street

Millennium Hotel Glasgow

Modern

Superb quality ingredients in modern, stylish brasserie

☎ 0141 332 6711 George St G2 1DS
e-mail: reservations.glasgow@mill-cop.com
web: www.millenniumhotels.com

Smack in the heart of the city in pride of place overlooking George Square, the Millennium's contemporary, minimalist-designed interior comes complete with a stylish, relaxed, eye-catching dining room. Think shades of beiges and browns, stripped wooden floor, leafy palms, smartly appointed tables and friendly, unstuffy service. The modern focus extends to the brasserie-style cuisine, where the emphasis is on quality produce from the abundant Scottish larder. Expect a platter of Loch Fyne mussels, langoustine, scallops, bradan rost, salmon and oysters with a chive beurre blanc, and perhaps a trio of chocolate to finish.

Chef: Stewart Goldie **Owners:** Millennium & Copthorne Hotels
Times: 12-2.15/6-10.15, Closed 25-26 Dec, Closed L Sun **Prices:** Fixed L £8.50, Fixed D £18.45, Starter £3.75-£8.95, Main £12.25-£24, Dessert £4.25-£4.95, Coffee £2.50, Min/Water £3.50, Service optional **Wine:** 20 bottles over £20, 31 bottles under £20, 15 by the glass (£3.50-£7.10)
Notes: Vegetarian available **Seats:** 140, Pr/dining room 40
Smoking: N/Sm in restaurant, Air con **Children:** Menu, Portions
Rooms: 117 (117 en suite) ★★★★ HL **Directions:** M8 junct 15, follow directions to George Sq, brasserie is in Millennium Hotel **Parking:** On street, NCP

No5 Restaurant

British, European

Simple and effective food in a renowned hotel

☎ 0141 339 2001 One Devonshire Gardens Hotel, 1 Devonshire Gardens G12 0UX
e-mail: events@onedevonshiregardens.com
web: www.onedevonshiregardens.com

Made up of five Victorian townhouses, One Devonshire Gardens is set in a tree-lined terrace in Glasgow's West End and has in recent years become one of the city's most fashionable places to stay. The intimate restaurant here is suitably chic with the feel of a refined drawing room and formal yet friendly service to match. The food is modern British with European influences and Scottish produce rightly asserts its presence across this short but punchy menu - boudin of guinea fowl and wood pigeon with an Armagnac jus, for example, or whole grilled West Coast lemon sole and a citrus and chervil butter.

Chef: David Clark **Owners:** Citrus Hotels **Times:** 6.30-9.30, Closed 25-26 Dec, Closed L Private lunches only **Prices:** Fixed D fr £39, Coffee £3.25, Min/Water £3.95, Service optional **Wine:** 70 bottles over £20, 7 by the glass (£5) **Notes:** Vegetarian available, Civ Wed 48 **Seats:** Pr/dining room 50 **Smoking:** N/Sm in restaurant **Children:** Portions **Rooms:** 35 (35 en suite) ★★★★ TH **Directions:** M8 junct 17, follow signs for A82 after 1.5 miles turn left into Hyndland Rd **Parking:** Parking available, residential area

Papingo Restaurant

Modern Scottish

Slick modern cooking in established city-centre bistro

☎ 0141 332 6678 104 Bath St G2 2EN
e-mail: info@papingo.co.uk
web: www.papingo.co.uk

A bright, modern basement restaurant in the city centre with candles on the unclothed wooden tables. Colourful artwork and dimmed light create a warmth to the extensive space. The bright and breezy modern menu concentrates on simple modern Scottish cooking, with the brief lunch menu offering especially good value. Well-defined flavours crop up in menus that may include Papingo fish soup with shrimps, coriander and ginger, saddle of venison with Savoy cabbage and pine nuts in a gin and juniper jus or rum and raisin crème brûlée

Chef: David Clunas **Owners:** Mr Alan Tomkins **Times:** 12-2.30/5-10.30, Closed 25-26 Dec, 1-2 Jan, BH Mon, Closed L Sun **Prices:** Fixed L £8.95-£11.95, Fixed D £11.95-£14.95, Starter £4-£7, Main £7-£19, Dessert £4-£5, Coffee £2.50, Min/Water £3.75, Service optional, Group min 6 service 10%
Wine: 12 bottles over £20, 12 bottles under £20, 7 by the glass (£4-£6)
Notes: Vegetarian available **Seats:** 75 **Smoking:** N/Sm area, No pipes, Air con **Children:** Portions **Directions:** City centre. At junct of Bath St & Hope St **Parking:** NCP 50 yds

Rococo

Modern International

Intimate, stylish place to be seen and enjoy impressive cuisine

☎ 0141 221 5004 202 West George St G2 2NR
e-mail: info@rococoglasgow.co.uk
web: www.rococoglasgow.co.uk

Still one of the most stylish and well-established eateries in the city centre. The charming basement entrance leads to a magical restaurant lit by fibre optics. Modern marble-tiled flooring and stark white walls provide a backdrop for blown glass art and trendy oversized leather seats. The simple lunch menu is excellent value for money, while the carte takes you up a gear in complexity and price. The cooking style is modern Scottish with international influences, producing succinct flavours and using only the finest ingredients. The emphasis on seasonality is impressive and the use of local produce is evident in dishes like roast fillet of Perthshire venison with confit root vegetables and dark chocolate sauce or en papillote of lemon sole and green-lipped mussels flavoured with lemongrass, herbs and white wine.

Chef: Mark Tamburrini **Owners:** Alan & Audrey Brown **Times:** 12-3/5-10, Closed 26 Dec, 1 Jan **Prices:** Fixed L fr £14, Fixed D £39.50-£44.50, Starter £7.25-£8.55, Main £18.95-£25.75, Dessert £7-£7.50, Coffee £2, Min/Water £3.50, Service optional, Group min 6 service 10% **Wine:** 250 bottles over £20, 5 bottles under £20, 8 by the glass (£5-£6.25) **Notes:** Vegetarian available **Seats:** 60, Pr/dining room 30 **Smoking:** N/Sm in restaurant **Children:** Menu **Directions:** City centre **Parking:** On street parking or NCP

see advert on this page

Room

Modern British

Culinary time travel at a modish hotel eatery

☎ 0141 341 0000 1 Devonshire Gardens G12 0UX
e-mail: glasgowreception@roomrestaurants.com
web: www.roomrestaurants.com

Set in one of Scotland's smartest hotels, this lively modern eatery does a brisk trade in retro cuisine, delivering a menu crammed with no-nonsense British dishes such as macaroni cheese with sun-dried tomato and fresh basil, toad in the hole with home-made game sausage, and jam roly poly with home-made strawberry jam. Fashionable ingredients prevent homage sliding into nostalgia, and ensure that the food is in keeping with a funky interior that combines elegant Edwardian features with comfortable modern chic. A concise menu is available at lunchtime, but dinner is the real show, when Room offers an extensive selection of top-notch cuisine.

continued

Chef: Mark Greenaway **Owners:** John Pallagi, Simon Wright **Times:** 11/11 **Prices:** Fixed L £10-£13.95, Starter £5, Main £15-£20, Dessert £5, Coffee £2.50, Min/Water £3, Service added but optional 10% **Wine:** 26 bottles over £20, 15 bottles under £20, 13 by the glass (£3.50-£5.75) **Notes:** Sun L 2 courses £13.95, 3 courses £17.95, Vegetarian available **Seats:** 150, Pr/dining room 50 **Smoking:** N/Sm in restaurant **Children:** Portions **Directions:** 10 mins from city centre, situated in West End district **Parking:** 20

Saint Jude's

Modern British

Popular restaurant and bar complex

☎ 0141 352 8800 190 Bath St G2 4HG
e-mail: reservations@saintjudes.com
web: www.saintjudes.com

A creeper-clad Victorian townhouse conceals this modern first floor restaurant and basement bar complex. It strikes a contemporary note with its minimalist décor and modern art, and service from delightful staff dressed all in black. The food's style and presentation matches the setting, with a short, speedy midday menu giving way to a more expansive dinner carte. Starters and desserts really stand out, with feuillette of fresh autumn berries getting the thumbs up. Innovative main dishes take in seafood (squat lobster, salmon, squid and mussels in a tomato and cayenne broth) and game (roast loin of venison) as well as meat.

Times: 12-2.30/5-10.30, Closed 25 Dec, 1-2 Jan, Closed L Sat-Sun **Directions:** City centre

GLASGOW *continued* MAP 20 NS56

Shish Mahal

British, Indian

Consistently hitting the mark with thirty years serving fine Indian cuisine

☎ 0141 339 8256 & 334 7899 60-68 Park Rd G4 9JF
e-mail: reservations@shishmahal.co.uk
web: www.shishmahal.co.uk

The Shish Mahal continues to go from strength to strength after 30 years under the direction of Ali Aslam. In three sections, including a mezzanine level, the décor has a Moorish theme. Popular with local residents, business people and students, the service is attentive with suited management and smart waiters in black. The cooking style shows great depth of flavour with all the extras meeting the same high standards. Lunch is especially good value from a fixed price menu. Dinner offers a huge selection of chicken, fish, lamb and vegetarian dishes, plus a European selection.

Chef: Mr I Humayun **Owners:** Ali A Aslam, Nasim Ahmed **Times:** 12-2/5-11, Closed Xmas, Closed L Sun **Prices:** Fixed L £5.50-£6.75, Fixed D £14.95-£16.95, Starter £1.95-£6.95, Main £5.95-£14.95, Dessert £1.70-£3.50, Coffee £1.15, Min/Water £3.95, Service optional, Group min 5 service 10% **Wine:** 2% bottles over £20, 98% bottles under £20, 2 by the glass (£2.70) **Notes:** Fixed L 3 courses, Fixed D 4 courses, Vegetarian available **Seats:** 95, Pr/dining room 14 **Smoking:** N/Sm area, Air con **Children:** Portions **Directions:** From M8/A8 take exit towards Dumbarton, drive along Great Western Rd and turn 1st left into Park Rd, restaurant is at number 66-68 **Parking:** Side street, Underground station

Stravaigin

International

Lively basement restaurant with eccentric and eclectic cooking

☎ 0141 334 2665 30 Gibson St G12 8NX
e-mail: bookings@stravaigin.com
web: www.stravaigin.com

continued

Refurbishment has wrought a considerable change at this popular restaurant - as well as new entrance and reception area, the décor is now distinctly modern with a lacquered, tiled floor, stone and leather-covered walls with contemporary art and quirky antiques, and lightwood tables throughout. Whether you're eating in the bar or the main dining area, the wide range of dishes satisfies all tastes and pockets. The food is imaginative and with unusual and exciting fusion dishes you won't find elsewhere in the city; for example, black pepper pappardelle with shredded confit rabbit, roast walnut and parmesan cream to start, followed by braised lamb shoulder stuffed with ricotta, figs and sage, or open ravioli nero with king prawns, roast red pepper and gremolata cream. Desserts like chocolate crusted roast Nashi pear tart with marmalade ice cream taste as good as they sound!

Chef: Daniel Blencowe **Owners:** Colin Clydesdale **Times:** 12-2.30/5-11, Closed 25-26 Dec, 1 Jan, Closed L Tue-Thu **Prices:** Fixed L £9-£11, Fixed D £13-£30, Starter £4-£8, Main £10-£25, Dessert £5-£8, Coffee £1.60, Min/Water £2.85, Service optional **Wine:** 15 bottles over £20, 25 bottles under £20, 15 by the glass (£3-£6) **Notes:** Vegetarian available **Seats:** 76 **Smoking:** N/Sm in restaurant, Air con **Children:** Portions **Directions:** Next to Glasgow University. 200 yds from Kelvinbridge underground **Parking:** On street

Two Fat Ladies

Modern, Seafood NEW

Cosy seafood restaurant offering good-value dishes in the city centre

☎ 0141 847 0088 118a Blytheswood St GL11 6NX

The name of this small street-level restaurant comes from its founding premises at 88 Dumbarton Road (two fat ladies - 88). It has a polished parquet floor and the yellow walls are hung with colourful paintings of coastal scenes. The variety and freshness of the food dictate the style of cooking. Seafood is the speciality, presented in uncomplicated dishes with a degree of innovation. Expect dishes like pan-fried fillet of sea bass with turnip and thyme mash and red wine glaze, halibut fillet on Savoy cabbage with a mussel and chervil cream or king prawns cooked in chilli butter.

Chef: David Monaghan **Owners:** Ryan James **Times:** 12-3/5.30-10.30, Closed Sun **Prices:** Food prices not confirmed for 2007. Please telephone for details **Directions:** Telephone for directions

Ubiquitous Chip

Scottish NOTABLE WINE LIST

Modern Scottish cuisine in a unique setting

☎ 0141 334 5007 12 Ashton Ln G12 8SJ
e-mail: mail@ubiquitouschip.co.uk
web: www.ubiquitouschip.co.uk

A Glasgow institution for over 30 years, this unusual restaurant is a must-see for foodies. It's set in a spectacular glass-covered courtyard in a cobbled mews and has a tropical feel thanks to an array of lush green plants. An extensive redevelopment has added a new mezzanine level overlooking the tables and foliage below, and there's also a more formal dining room, and a cheaper brasserie upstairs. The cooking doesn't disappoint - just as unique as the setting, it brings together top-notch produce in bold combinations that intrigue as much on the plate as the menu. Kick off with prawn and whitefish sausage with green apple mayonnaise perhaps, and then sample Perthshire pork fillet stuffed with prunes and peat-smoked haddie, or Orkney organic salmon with lime and vanilla mash.

continued

Notable Wine List: A large, classic wine list with extensive Bordeaux and German listings.

Chef: Ronnie Clydesdale **Owners:** Ronnie Clydesdale **Times:** 12-2.30/5.30-11, Closed 25 Dec, 1 Jan **Prices:** Fixed L fr £22.80, Fixed D fr £38.95, Min/Water £3.45, Service optional **Wine:** 350 bottles over £20, 18 bottles under £20, 37 by the glass (£2.40-£3.85) **Notes:** Coffee incl, Sun L 3 courses £17.95, Civ Wed 60 **Seats:** 180, Pr/dining room 45 **Smoking:** N/Sm in restaurant, Air con **Children:** Menu, Portions **Directions:** In the West End of Glasgow, off Byres Rd. Beside Hillhead subway station **Parking:** Lilybank gardens (50m)

The Big Blue

☎ 0141 357 1038 445 Great Western Rd G12 8HH
web: www.theaa.com/restaurants/114052.html

The entrance is on one of the West End's busier streets, but this bar is three flights down, in an old archway which opens out onto the Kelvin walkway and overlooks the river. The menu is predominantly Italian with a few seafood dishes thrown in.

Café Gandolfi

☎ 0141 552 6813 65 Albion St G1 1NY

Hugely popular cross between a traditional Glasgow tea room and a continental-style restaurant.

The Cook's Room

☎ 0141 353 0707 13 Woodside Crescent G3 7UL
web: www.theaa.com/restaurants/114053.html

A new location for Tom Battersby's overflowing restaurant. The menu is modern Scottish and extremely well-prepared. Flavours are vivid and the plates beautifully presented.

Red Onion

☎ 0141 221 6000 257 West Campbell St G2 4TT
web: www.theaa.com/restaurants/114051.html

A charming restaurant in the heart of the City, with an eclectic menu and open from breakfast through the day.

HIGHLAND

ACHILTIBUIE MAP 22 NC00

The Summer Isles Hotel

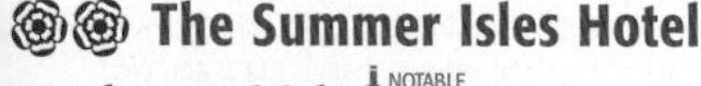

Modern British

Food from land and sea in stunning location

☎ 01854 622282 IV26 2YG
e-mail: info@summerisleshotel.co.uk
web: www.summerisleshotel.co.uk

Dating back to 1850, this former fishing inn has been run as a hotel by the same family since the late 1960s. The restaurant is lined with windows making the most of the spectacular view of the bay and the Summer Isles and the amazing light, with daylight until 10.30pm in summer. Long days spent walking, bird-watching or just relaxing in the tranquil surroundings are rewarded with a leisurely dinner in the restaurant. A fixed menu is served at 8pm, offering local produce capturing the natural flavours of land and sea. Five well-conceived courses might include roast fillet of organic Shetland salmon with mixed herb pesto and warm granary loaf, followed by pan-fried breast of pigeon, served on toasted brioche with duxelle of mushrooms.

continued

Round this off with Summer Isles lobster served with mixed fresh herbs and a warm champagne and butter sauce, followed by fine cheeses and a choice from the sweet trolley.
Notable Wine List: An extensive wine list with particularly strong Bordeaux and Burgundy sections.

Chef: Chris Firth-Bernard **Owners:** Mark & Gerry Irvine **Times:** 12.30-2/8, Closed mid Oct-Easter **Prices:** Fixed D £49, Starter £7-£12, Main £12-£30, Dessert £3.50, Min/Water £2.50, Service included **Notes:** Fixed D 5 courses, Vegetarian available **Seats:** 28 **Smoking:** N/Sm in restaurant **Children:** Min 8 yrs, Portions **Directions:** 10 m N of Ullapool. Turn left off A835 onto single track road. 15m to Achiltibuie. Hotel 100 yds after post office on left **Parking:** 15

Scotland

ALNESS MAP 23 NH66

Teaninich Castle

Modern British **NEW**

Cooking to excite in a romantic Scottish castle

☎ 01349 883231 IV17 0XB
e-mail: info@teaninichcastle.com
web: www.teaninichcastle.com

Fine country house overlooking the Cromarty Firth with a tragic tale of thwarted love and war injuries that left the handsome young master blind. The restaurant provides a formal setting with relaxed and friendly service. Dinner is a complete experience beginning with canapés and ending with coffee and petits fours in the lounge. Quality local produce is cooked with flair. Dishes are not overly embellished but rely on accurate cooking and fresh ingredients. A good combination is salad of seared scallops, roast cannon of Highland venison, and chocolate pecan flan.

Chef: Alasdair Roberston **Owners:** Colux Ltd **Times:** 12.30-2.30/6.30-9 **Prices:** Fixed L £10-£15, Fixed D £31.50-£34, Coffee £1.75, Min/Water £1.50, Service optional, Group min 8 service 10% **Wine:** 24 bottles over £20, 18 bottles under £20, 6 by the glass (£3.50-£5) **Notes:** Dress Restrictions, Smart casual, Civ Wed 40 **Seats:** 40, Pr/dining room 15 **Smoking:** N/Sm in restaurant **Children:** Portions **Rooms:** 6 (6 en suite) ★★ **Directions:** Telephone for directions **Parking:** 20

SOUTH BALLACHULISH MAP 22 NN05

Ballachulish House

Modern Scottish

Magnificent dining in Highland house party setting

☎ 01855 811266 PH49 4JX
e-mail: mclaughlins@btconnect.com
web: www.ballachulishhouse.com

continued

SOUTH BALLACHULISH *continued* MAP 22 NN05

A sympathetically restored 17th-century laird's loch-side residence with superb mountain views, this archetypal country-house hotel has a classic dining room furnished with antiques and crisply clothed tables. The three-hour dining experience has a house party atmosphere. Canapés enjoyed by the drawing room fire are often accompanied by a piper. The five-course menu comprises dishes based on the best Scottish fare. Tried and trusted combinations allow the skilful kitchen to concentrate on keeping flavours fresh and vibrant. The sea-fresh tian of Skye crab with avocado, grapefruit and lemongrass vinaigrette precedes a well-made Jerusalem artichoke and hazelnut cappuccino, a rich slow-cooked pork belly with black pudding, parsnip purée and apple relish and roast loin of Kingairloch venison with spiced red cabbage and pumpkin tortellini. A hot lime soufflé with mango sorbet and coconut sauce brings matters to a close.

Times: 12-2.15/7-8 **Rooms:** 8 (8 en suite) ◆◆◆◆◆ **Directions:** Take A82 to Ballachulish rdbt, then A828 (Oban) for approx 0.25m. Hotel on L & signed

---

BOAT OF GARTEN MAP 23 NH91

Boat Hotel - The Capercaille

British

Scottish cuisine with a modern twist

☎ 01479 831258 Deshar Rd PH24 3BH
e-mail: holidays@boathotel.co.uk
web: www.boathotel.co.uk

This Victorian station hotel has been tastefully modernised, retaining period features like panelling and cornices. The intimate, stylish restaurant is lit by a fire and wall sconces, emphasising the dark blue walls and avant-garde artwork. Traditional Scottish cuisine is prepared with a contemporary twist. Most dishes include local produce and offer interesting combinations, like a starter of smooth Stornoway salmon and cucumber relish parfait. Main courses are similarly tempting such as fillet of Morayshire beef with spinach, sweet mild cheese and fondant potato on a field mushroom and tomato compôte, or baked cannon of Speyside lamb with garlic and herb salt and rosemary potato cake.

Chef: Tony Allcott **Owners:** Ian & Shona Tatchell **Times:** 7-9.30, Closed last 2 wks in Jan, Closed L all week **Prices:** Fixed D fr £32.50, Coffee £2.50, Min/Water £3.35, Service optional **Wine:** 41 bottles over £20, 8 bottles under £20, 4 by the glass **Notes:** Vegetarian available, Dress Restrictions, No jeans **Seats:** 40, Pr/dining room 40 **Smoking:** N/Sm in restaurant **Children:** Min 8 yrs **Rooms:** 22 (22 en suite) ★★★ HL **Directions:** Turn off A9 N of Aviemore onto A95. Follow signs to Boat of Garten **Parking:** 36

BRORA MAP 23 NC90

Royal Marine Hotel

Traditional British

Traditional Highland hotel with reliable cooking

☎ 01408 621252 Golf Rd KW9 6QS
e-mail: info@highlandescape.com
web: www.highlandescape.com

This distinctive Edwardian country house has views over the Dornoch Firth and the Highlands and is popular with those enjoying the many attractions of the area, whether it's shooting and fishing, golf or whisky trails. There are three dining options here - a café bar, the Hunters Lounge and the Lorimer restaurant - the latter offering solid, dependable cooking on the whole. Typical starters include Cullen skink with locally smoked haddock, or a wild mushroom risotto, with mains of saddle of Sutherland venison, finishing with that perennial favourite, sticky toffee pudding.

Chef: Andrew Campbell **Owners:** Duncraggie Ltd **Times:** 12-2/6.30-8.45, Closed L (pre booking only) **Prices:** Fixed L £14-£16, Starter £4-£8, Main £12-£18, Dessert £4-£5, Coffee £1.25, Min/Water £2.95 **Wine:** 27 bottles over £20, 34 bottles under £20, 12 by the glass (£3-£5) **Notes:** Vegetarian available, Civ Wed 60 **Seats:** 50, Pr/dining room 12 **Smoking:** N/Sm in restaurant **Children:** Menu, Portions **Rooms:** 22 (22 en suite) ★★★ HL **Directions:** Turn off A9 in village toward beach and golf course **Parking:** 40

DORNOCH MAP 23 NH78

Dornoch Castle Hotel

Modern British NEW

Refreshing brasserie food in the castle conservatory

☎ 01862 810216 Castle St IV25 3SD
e-mail: enquiries@dornochcastlehotel.com
web: www.dornochcastlehotel.com

Overlooking the garden, the conservatory restaurant is attached to the fine old castle and successfully marries traditional and modern styles. With Dornoch Cathedral just across the road, this is a popular wedding venue. Service is informal, but attentive. The modern Scottish menu offers a straightforward brasserie-style choice using quality ingredients, locally sourced whenever possible. Expect roast rump of Sutherland lamb with dauphinoise potatoes and roast cherry vine tomatoes, roast rack of highland venison, haggis mash and wild mushroom jus, or seared Loch Duart salmon fillet with lemon and dill mash and saffron cream in the evening. A selection of Highland malts from local distilleries is available and there are versatile lunchtime choices in the bar.

Chef: Grant McNicol **Owners:** Colin Thompson, Hugh Anderson **Times:** 12-3/6-9.30 **Prices:** Fixed L £8.95, Starter £5.25-£7.95, Main £13.95-£19.95, Dessert £5.25-£6.25, Coffee £1.65, Min/Water £2.50, Service optional **Wine:** 24 bottles over £20, 20 bottles under £20, 6 by the glass (£3.20-£4.30) **Notes:** Sun L £10.95, Vegetarian available **Seats:** 75, Pr/dining room 25 **Smoking:** N/Sm in restaurant **Children:** Menu, Portions **Rooms:** 21 (21 en suite) ★★★ **Directions:** 2m from A9 in the centre of Dornoch **Parking:** 12

2 Quail Restaurant & Rooms

International

Classic cooking in tiny Highland restaurant

☎ 01862 811811 Inistore House, Castle St IV25 3SN
e-mail: theaa@2quail.com
web: www.2quail.com

With only four tables to its name, you'll definitely need to book ahead to dine at this small book-lined restaurant. Located in a Victorian building, it has a homely feel and as it's run by a husband-and-wife team, you can be sure of personal attention. The focus here is on real food and everything is made in-house. The four-course dinner menu offers a choice between dessert and cheese but the other dishes are fixed. Typically you might start with leek flamiche and chicory salad, then seared scallops with a pea purée, crispy bacon and sesame oil, followed by the main course, perhaps beef fillet with wild mushrooms and sherry gravy. Quality wines are served by the glass or bottle.

Chef: Michael Carr **Owners:** Michael and Kerensa Carr **Times:** 7.30-9.30, Closed Xmas, 2 wks Feb-Mar, Sun-Mon **Prices:** Fixed D £37, Coffee £2.50, Service optional **Notes:** Fixed D 4 courses, Dress Restrictions, Smart casual **Seats:** 14 **Smoking:** N/Sm in restaurant **Children:** Portions **Rooms:** 3 (3 en suite) ◆◆◆◆◆ **Directions:** 200 yds past war memorial on left side of main street, just before Cathedral **Parking:** On street

FORT WILLIAM MAP 22 NN17

Inverlochy Castle Hotel

see below

Moorings Hotel

Modern British

Contemporary cuisine in the heart of the Highlands

☎ 01397 772797 Banavie PH33 7LY
e-mail: reservations@moorings-fortwilliam.co.uk
web: www.moorings-fortwilliam.co.uk

Popular business and tourist hotel located beside Neptune's Ladder, a series of locks on the Caledonian Canal, and boasting magnificent views of Ben Nevis. A four-course dinner is offered in the spacious Jacobean-styled restaurant. The finest locally produce, including West

continued

Inverlochy Castle Hotel

FORT WILLIAM MAP 22 NN17

Modern British NOTABLE WINE LIST

Luxurious Highland castle setting for fine dining

☎ 01397 702177 Torlundy PH33 6SN
e-mail: info@inverlochy.co.uk
web: www.inverlochycastlehotel.com

Nestling in the foothills of Ben Nevis and set in over 500 acres of gardens, this imposing and gracious castle, now luxury hotel, is lavishly appointed in classic country-house style, with aperitifs taken in the sumptuous lounge. The restaurant is decorated with elaborate period furniture and offers stunning mountain views, particularly romantic at sunset. Genuine comfort and luxury abound, while service is highly professional but with a relaxed and friendly note. The kitchen's accomplished modern approach - underpinned by a classical theme - suits the surroundings and makes fine use of the abundant Highland larder as well as produce from the estate's walled garden on its repertoire of daily-changing, five-course dinner and tasting menus. Expect high-level technical skill and clear flavours in dishes like roast monkfish tail with braised pork cheek and a saffron risotto to start, followed by seared escalope of brill served with caviar and Périgord truffle, or roast fillet of veal with morels and violet artichoke, and perhaps a tasting plate of rhubarb to finish.

Notable Wine List: An immaculately presented wine list offering a comprehensive range of wines from around the world; good tasting notes and a notable half-bottle section.

Chef: Matthew Gray **Owners:** Inverlochy Ltd **Times:** 12.30-1.15/6.30-9.15 **Prices:** Fixed L fr £28.50, Fixed D fr £58, Coffee £5.75, Min/Water £3.50, Service optional **Wine:** 270 bottles over £20, 8 by the glass (£5.50-£13) **Notes:** Fixed D 4 courses, Dress Restrictions, Jacket & tie for D, Civ Wed 80 **Seats:** 40, Pr/dining room 20 **Smoking:** N/Sm in restaurant **Children:** Menu, Portions **Rooms:** 17 (17 en suite) ★★★★★ CHH **Directions:** 3m N of Fort William on A82, just past Golf Club **Parking:** 20

Scotland

FORT WILLIAM *continued* MAP 22 NN17

Coast seafood and Highland game, is used to good effect in contemporary British and European dishes. A typical meal may begin with duck confit with onion marmalade or crab and mussel risotto, followed by Aberdeen Angus beef medallions with wild mushroom sauce or herb-crusted salmon with garlic butter sauce. Puddings include raspberry cranachan.

Chef: Paul Smith **Owners:** Mr S Leitch **Times:** 7-9.30, Closed L all week **Prices:** Starter £4.95-£7.95, Main £12.95-£19.95, Dessert £4.50-£5.95, Coffee £1.15, Min/Water £3.10, Service optional **Wine:** 16 bottles over £20, 43 bottles under £20, 4 by the glass (£3.20) **Notes:** Dress Restrictions, Smart casual, Civ Wed 130 **Seats:** 60, Pr/dining room 120 **Smoking:** N/Sm in restaurant **Children:** Portions **Rooms:** 28 (28 en suite) ★★★ HL **Directions:** From A82 take A830 W for 1 mile. 1st right over Caledonian Canal on B8004 **Parking:** 50

GLENFINNAN MAP 22 NM88

The Prince's House

Modern British

Accomplished Scottish cuisine with a warm welcome

☎ 01397 722246 PH37 4LT
e-mail: princeshouse@glenfinnan.co.uk
web: www.glenfinnan.co.uk

Dating back to the 17th century, this traditional country house was allegedly used by Bonnie Prince Charlie at the start of the Jacobite uprising. Family-run and blessed with a marvellous, romantic setting surrounded by mountains and woodland, the house is very strong on hospitality and is simply furnished with natural floor coverings and hardwood panelling on the walls. Simple dishes here are well executed with superb quality ingredients, with local sourcing and seasonality playing a big role in the choice of dishes on this modern menu. Start with Mallaig seafood soup and then move on to Kinlochmoidart venison with celeriac and potato rösti and port wine jus.

Chef: Kieron Kelly **Owners:** Kieron & Ina Kelly **Times:** 7-9, Closed Xmas, Jan-Feb, Low season - booking only, Closed L all wk **Prices:** Fixed D £29-£35, Coffee £1.75, Min/Water £3.25, Service included **Wine:** 20 bottles over £20, 10 bottles under £20, 2 by the glass (£2.95-£3.75) **Notes:** Vegetarian available **Seats:** 30 **Smoking:** N/Sm in restaurant **Children:** Portions **Rooms:** 9 (9 en suite) ★★ **Directions:** From Fort William N on A82 for 2 m. Turn left onto A830 Mallaig Rd for 15 m to Hotel **Parking:** 18

GRANTOWN-ON-SPEY MAP 23 NJ02

Culdearn House

Traditional Scottish, British

Quality local ingredients cooked with flair

☎ 01479 872106 Woodlands Ter PH26 3JU
e-mail: enquiries@culdearn.com
web: www.culdearn.com

This large Victorian villa has beautifully proportioned rooms with high ceilings and many period features. The dining room at the front of the house offers lovely views of the garden from white-clothed tables decorated with fresh flowers. Good quality local ingredients are simply cooked with flair, especially beautifully fresh fish and fully traceable beef. A starter of Mallaig scallops on a bed of asparagus with warm butter might whet your appetite, but be sure to leave room for the Culdearn steak, pan-fried with mushrooms and a creamy Drambuie sauce and the delicious home-made ice creams. Service is efficient but unobtrusive, making this a relaxing place to enjoy a meal. Wine list includes interesting information.

Chef: Feona Laing **Owners:** Mr & Mrs Marshall **Times:** 7, Closed Jan-Feb, Closed L all week **Prices:** Fixed D fr £30, Coffee £2, Min/Water £2.50, Service optional **Wine:** 18 bottles over £20, 18 bottles under £20, 4 by the glass (£3.75) **Notes:** Fixed D 4 courses, Dress Restrictions, Smart casual, no jeans, sportswear/T-shirts **Seats:** 16 **Smoking:** N/Sm in restaurant **Children:** Min 10 yrs **Rooms:** 7 (7 en suite) ★★ SHL **Directions:** Enter Grantown from SW on A95, left at 30mph sign **Parking:** 11

The Glass House Restaurant

European NEW

Delicious food in an intimate setting

☎ 01479 872980 Grant Rd PH26 3LD

This comfortable, minimal restaurant was once a bungalow with the living room and conservatory now making up the dining area. The design follows clean lines, with light colours enhancing the sense of space. The classically based cooking has undoubted ambition, placing good ingredients in simple but effective dishes. The short menu offers baked brie and black pudding spring roll, smoked salmon with pickled cucumber and dill salad and sour cream and chives to start, for example, followed by caramelised duck breast with red wine vinegar sauce. The warm Belgian chocolate tart is highly recommended.

Times: 12-1.45/7-9 **Prices:** Food prices not confirmed for 2007. Please telephone for details **Directions:** Telephone for directions

Muckrach Lodge Hotel

Modern British

Cosy Highland retreat with great cooking

☎ 01479 851257 PH26 3LY
e-mail: info@muckrach.co.uk
web: www.muckrach.co.uk

Snuggled up against the Cairngorms, this former Victorian sporting lodge is set in 10 acres of beautifully landscaped grounds. The cosy bar is popular with sporting clientele and diners can eat in the bistro or the award-winning Finlairg restaurant. The recently appointed head chef is a Gordon Ramsay alumnus who brings with him French and international influences; food is subtle and precisely cooked using top-quality Scottish produce - and the six-course set menu is great value. You can expect a delicate amuse of asparagus velouté with curry oil, followed by wild mushroom risotto with cep powder, and a patchwork of scallop and langoustine, watercress froth and steamed sea bass for mains. For dessert, don't miss the Armagnac parfait on a quince purée. It's also worth ordering the Scottish cheeses.

continued

Chef: Nicolas Poelaert **Owners:** Dawn & James Macfarlane **Times:** 12.15-2/7-9, Closed 4-21 Jan, Mon, Tue (Nov-Mar only) **Prices:** Fixed L fr £20, Fixed D fr £35, Min/Water £2.50, Service optional **Wine:** 102 bottles over £20, 18 bottles under £20, 12 by the glass (£3.50) **Notes:** Coffe incl, Fixed L must be booked, Vegetarian available, Civ Wed 80 **Seats:** 28, Pr/dining room 60 **Smoking:** N/Sm in restaurant **Children:** Menu, Portions **Rooms:** 14 (14 en suite) ★★★ HL **Directions:** From A95 Dulnain Bridge exit follow A938 towards Carrbridge, hotel 500m on right **Parking:** 25

Craggan Mill

☎ 01479 872288 Morayshire PH26 3NT

Converted 18th-century mill serving fresh local produce.

INVERGARRY MAP 22 NH30

Glengarry Castle

British, Scottish

The epitome of Scottish country-house style in a dramatic setting

☎ 01809 501254 PH35 4HW
e-mail: castle@glengarry.net
web: www.glengarry.net

A charming Victorian country house with great views set on the shores of Loch Oich in 50 acres of grounds. A panelled reception hall, marble fireplaces and an elegant dining room are among the luxuries. Service is relaxed and friendly. The traditional Scottish country-house cooking makes good use of local produce such as beef, game, fish and cheeses. Straightforward flavours can be enjoyed in dishes like baked fillet of prime Scottish beef in pastry carved onto red wine sauce, or oven-baked fillet of turbot with Dauphine potato and creamy spinach sauce.

Chef: John McDonald **Owners:** Mr & Mrs MacCallum **Times:** 7-8.30, Closed mid Nov to mid Mar, Closed L Mon-Sun **Prices:** Fixed D £29, Coffee £1.80, Min/Water £3, Service included **Wine:** 24 bottles over £20, 31 bottles under £20, 7 by the glass (£2.80) **Notes:** Fixed D 4 courses **Seats:** 40 **Smoking:** N/Sm in restaurant **Children:** Menu, Portions **Rooms:** 26 (26 en suite) ★★★ CHH **Directions:** 1m S of Invergarry on A82 **Parking:** 30

INVERMORISTON MAP 23 NH41

Glenmoriston Arms Hotel & Restaurant

Traditional Scottish

Friendly country hostelry

☎ 01320 351206 IV63 7YA
e-mail: reception@glenmoristonarms.co.uk
web: www.glenmoristonarms.co.uk

A former drover's inn dating in parts back to 1740, within walking distance of Loch Ness. The simple white building is set back from the road with a lovely garden area. Inside it has all the elements of a great Scottish country hostelry with a smart bar, separate bar/bistro with blackboard menu and an intimate dining room offering a daily-changing fixed price menu. The cooking style is classic Scottish with a modern twist, using herbs and vegetables from the garden, good local meat, fowl and game. Typical dishes might include a traditional tower of haggis, neeps and tatties to start, drizzled with a Highland whisky

continued

sauce. Main courses include the likes of individual beef Wellingtons surrounded by Hunters sauce.

Times: 12-2.30/7-9, Closed Jan & Feb **Rooms:** 8 (8 en suite) ★★ **Directions:** At the junction of A82 & A877

INVERNESS MAP 23 NH64

Bunchrew House Hotel

Modern

Confident simplicity in imposing Highland manor

☎ 01463 234917 Bunchrew IV3 8TA
e-mail: welcome@bunchrew-inverness.co.uk

A fine-looking 17th-century Scottish baronial mansion set alongside the Beauly Firth in 20 acres of woodland and pretty gardens. The stately, well-proportioned restaurant makes the most of the view towards Ben Wyvis and the Black Isle across the water. Book ahead for a window table as the summer sunsets are stunning. There's nothing whimsical about the food or the dedication to combining quality ingredients with sound cooking practices. Contemporary dishes on daily dinner menus may include breast of woodland pigeon with spiced couscous and a Madeira sauce, baked tranche of Thai-dusted Bunchrew salmon with lemongrass sauce, and caramelised lemon tart with Armagnac sauce.

Chef: Walter Walker **Owners:** Terry & Irina Mackay **Times:** 12-1.45/7-8.45, Closed 22-28 Dec **Prices:** Fixed L £25.50, Fixed D £35.50, Coffee £1.75, Min/Water £3.85, Service optional **Wine:** 50 bottles over £20, 26 bottles under £20, 4 by the glass (£3.60) **Notes:** Fixed L 3 courses, Fixed D 4 courses, Vegetarian available, Civ Wed 92 **Seats:** 40, Pr/dining room 14 **Smoking:** N/Sm in restaurant **Children:** Portions **Rooms:** 16 (16 en suite) ★★★ HL **Directions:** 3m W of Inverness on A862 towards Beauly **Parking:** 40

Culloden House Hotel

British, French

Serious Scottish cuisine in historic setting

☎ 01463 790461 Culloden IV2 7BZ
e-mail: info@cullodenhouse.co.uk
web: www.cullodenhouse.co.uk

Step back in time when you enter this opulent Palladian mansion, used by Bonnie Prince Charlie as a lodging and battle headquarters before the battle on Culloden Moor in 1746. In the dining room these days, you'll find fine Scottish produce brought out in a five-course extravaganza. Try tartare of sea trout and smoked salmon with marinated cucumber, followed perhaps by a delicate timbale of haggis, neeps and tatties to set the taste buds going. The main course might be medallions of beef fillet coated with a creamed grain mustard sauce, topped with whole shallots, chestnuts and bacon lardons. For dessert expect the likes of Athole Brose, a confection of honey, cream and whisky sprinkled with toasted caramel. Coffee and hand-made chocolates round off the whole experience.

Times: 12.30-2/7-9, Closed 2 wks Jan/Feb **Rooms:** 28 (28 en suite) ★★★★ **Directions:** From A96, take left turn at junction of Balloch, Culloden, Smithton. Continue for 2m, hotel is on right

INVERNESS *continued* MAP 23 NH64

The Drumossie Hotel

Modern British NEW

Country-house hotel producing high-quality food

☎ 01463 236451 Old Perth Rd IV2 5BE
e-mail: stay@drumossiehotel.co.uk
web: www.drumossiehotel.co.uk

Scotland

An art deco building on a hillside south of Inverness houses this comfortable hotel. It has been refurbished to country-house standard, and features an elegant restaurant with well-dressed tables where the crisp white linen and polished silverware lend a touch of formality. The food is several notches above the ordinary, and has been very well received locally. Notable among the daily-changing set dishes are sautéed scallops with mango and avocado salsa, a subtly imaginative starter, and fricassée of prawn tails and a potato and leek chowder served with grilled lemon sole fillet. The kitchen continues to improve, making this one to watch.

Chef: Graham Singor **Owners:** Ness Valley Leisure **Times:** 12.30-2/7-9.30 **Prices:** Fixed L fr £14.95, Fixed D £35, Coffee £2.95, Min/Water £3.95, Service included **Wine:** 10 by the glass (£3.95-£7.95) **Notes:** Vegetarian available, Smart casual, Civ Wed 400 **Seats:** 90, Pr/dining room 500 **Smoking:** N/Sm in restaurant, Air con **Children:** Menu, Portions **Rooms:** 44 (44 en suite) ★★★★ **Directions:** Telephone for directions **Parking:** 200

Riverhouse

British

Relaxed riverside dining

☎ 01463 222033 1 Greig St IV3 5PT
e-mail: riverhouse@netbreeze.co.uk

This riverside restaurant is situated on the banks of the River Ness, close to the city centre. The wood panelled interior has an intimate atmosphere and there is an opulent feeling to the drapes and décor. Service from enthusiastic young staff is informal but efficient and professional. Classic British dishes are simply prepared using fine local produce, such as smoked salmon, Isle of Harris scallops, haggis and Orkney crab appearing as compound dishes in their own right. You can even watch the chefs cooking in the open kitchen.

Times: 12-2.15/5.30-10.00, Closed Mon, Closed L Sun **Directions:** On corner of Huntly Street and Greig Street

Rocpool

Modern European

Lively cosmopolitan atmosphere meets classic dishes with contemporary twist

☎ 01463 717274 1 Ness Walk IV3 5NE
web: www.rocpool.com

A busy city-centre brasserie with sleek contemporary interior, riverside views and an energetic atmosphere, Rocpool brings a touch of modern style and glamour to town. Lots of wood and glass - with

continued

Glenmoriston Town House Hotel

INVERNESS MAP 23 NH64

French

Refined French dining in elegant townhouse hotel

☎ 01463 223777 20 Ness Bank IV2 4SF
e-mail: reception@glenmoristontownhouse.com
web: www.glenmoristontownhouse.com

Bold contemporary designs blend seamlessly with the classical architecture of this stylish townhouse hotel on the banks of the River Ness. Stylishly-dressed tables, quality glassware, lots of wood and leather, mood lighting and fresh flowers contribute to the modern elegance of the sophisticated restaurant Abstract, which has been recently renovated. Service is friendly and attentive. Come here to experience fine dining with a modern French flavour. High-quality Scottish ingredients are expertly used, with interesting combinations that don't overpower the principal ingredient. Lunch offers good value and there's a sensational eight-course tasting menu. Excellent canapés and appetisers may be followed by a seafood platter of langoustine, oyster, scallops and crab, and a superb fillet of Angus beef with potato and shin terrine, balsamic and beetroot sauce. Roasted baby 'fressinette' banana and toffee and chocolate soup accompanied by a waffle is a noteworthy dessert. Listen to the piano on Friday and Saturday nights.

Chef: Loic Lefebvre **Owners:** Larsen & Ross South **Times:** 12-2/7-9.30, Closed Mon **Prices:** Fixed L £14, Fixed D £42, Dessert £8, Min/Water £3.50, Service optional, Group min 6 service 12.5% **Wine:** 99 bottles over £20, 7 bottles under £20, 10 by the glass (£3.50-£6.20) **Notes:** Vegetarian available, Dress Restrictions, Smart casual **Seats:** 50, Pr/dining room 15 **Smoking:** N/Sm in restaurant **Children:** Menu, Portions **Rooms:** 30 (30 en suite) ★★★ **Directions:** 2 mins from city centre, on river opposite theatre **Parking:** 50

windows down the entire length of the long, slim room - come decked out with wood tables, crisp white linen and leather banquettes, backed by attentive but unobtrusive service. The food is equally fashionable, modern European, delivering quality ingredients cooked with flair. Dishes come attractively presented but sensibly not over embellished as in roast fillet of cod with creamed spinach, baby prawns and a roasted cherry tomato dressing. While the carte cranks things up a gear, the fixed-price lunch and early-evening options offer excellent value.

Rocpool

Chef: Steven Devlin **Owners:** Mr Devlin, Mr Pieraccini **Times:** 12-2.30/5.45-10, Closed 25 Dec, 1 Jan, Sun **Prices:** Fixed L £8.95, Fixed D £10.95, Starter £3.65-£7.45, Main £8.95-£18.50, Dessert £3.90-£5.65, Coffee £1.75, Min/Water £3.65, Service optional **Wine:** 25 bottles over £20, 17 bottles under £20, 11 by the glass (£3.50-£6.95) **Notes:** Fixed D 2 courses, Vegetarian available **Seats:** 55 **Smoking:** N/Sm in restaurant, Air con **Children:** Portions **Directions:** Telephone for details **Parking:** On street

Café 1

☎ 01463 226200 75 Castle St IV2 3EA

Modern-style city centre restaurant with a good range of contemporary dishes.

Harry Ramsdens

☎ 01463 713345 Inshes Retail Park IV2 3TW

Famous fish and chip shop.

KINGUSSIE MAP 23 NH70

The Cross at Kingussie

see page 584

LOCHINVER MAP 22 NC02

The Albannach

Modern Scottish, French NOTABLE WINE LIST

A warm Highland welcome with the finest ingredients

☎ 01571 844407 Baddidarrach IV27 4LP
e-mail: the.albannach@virgin.net
web: www.thealbannach.co.uk

Blessed with stunning sea and mountain views, this intimate restaurant with rooms also has a wealth of style within. Dark red walls, wood panelling, deep brown leather settees, and candlelight make for a romantic setting and the open fires open the palate to the promise of a peaty malt whisky before or after dinner. An impressive wine list is personally selected by the proprietors (who also do the cooking) to suit the food. The menu is accomplished and understated with impressive local ingredients playing a key part in the food's success. Expect pan-fried guinea fowl breast with roast shallot and wild mushroom to start, followed by a perfectly baked fillet of Lochinver halibut with champagne sauce, with perhaps caramelised apple tartlet and Calvados ice cream to finish.

continued

Notable Wine List: An extensive wine list with quality selections in each area.

The Albannach

Chef: Colin Craig, Lesley Crosfield **Owners:** Colin Craig, Lesley Crosfield **Times:** 8, Closed mid Nov-mid Mar, Mon **Prices:** Fixed D fr £45, Min/Water £2.50, Service optional **Wine:** 185 bottles over £20, 85 bottles under £20, 4 by the glass (£4-£9) **Notes:** Coffee incl, Fixed D 5 courses, Vegetarian available, Dress Restrictions, Smart casual **Seats:** 16, Pr/dining room 10 **Smoking:** N/Sm in restaurant **Children:** Min 12 yrs **Rooms:** 6 (6 en suite) ★★★★★ RR **Directions:** From main Ullapool road into Lochinver, turn right over old stone bridge signed Baddidarrach. Continue for 0.5m take left turn after Highland Stoneware Pottery **Parking:** 8

Inver Lodge

British, French

Relaxed fine dining in wonderful location

☎ 01571 844496 IV27 4LU
e-mail: stay@inverlodge.com
web: www.inverlodge.com

Diners at this delightful, modern hotel are treated to spectacular views over the small harbour and the ocean beyond. On a clear day, the Western Isles can be seen through the restaurant's large picture windows. The kitchen makes sound use of the abundant local larder - fish is landed at the quayside below, while excellent Aberdeen Angus beef and Ayrshire lamb might also feature on the fixed-price menu. Descriptions are not short on adjectives and the cooking's equally ambitious. Look out for starters like roasted pears with blue cheese, followed by pan-fried sea bass, red onion and fennel confit with shellfish bisque.

Chef: Peter Cullen **Owners:** Anne & Edmund Vestey **Times:** 7-9, Closed Nov-Mar, Closed L Mon-Sun **Prices:** Food prices not confirmed for 2007. Please telephone for details **Wine:** 24 bottles over £20, 42 bottles under £20, 5 by the glass (£3.50-£4) **Notes:** Fixed D 4 courses, Dress Restrictions, No jeans, shorts, tracksuit trousers, Civ Wed 60 **Seats:** 50 **Smoking:** N/Sm in restaurant **Children:** Min 10 yrs, Portions **Rooms:** 20 (20 en suite) ★★★★ HL **Directions:** A835 to Lochinver, left at village hall, private road for 0.5m **Parking:** 30

Scotland

The Cross at Kingussie

KINGUSSIE MAP 23 NH70

Modern Scottish NOTABLE WINE LIST

Stunning food in converted tweed mill with rooms

☎ 01540 661166 Tweed Mill Brae, Ardbroilach Rd PH21 ILB
e-mail: relax@thecross.co.uk
web: www.thecross.co.uk

Set in woodland beside the tumbling River Gynack, this inviting restaurant with rooms was once a water-powered tweed mill. Here David Young and his wife Katie offer warm hospitality, cosy lounges and comfortable accommodation, but the operation undoubtedly focuses around the restaurant, with its whitewashed stone walls, beams, open fire, modern art and riverside terrace. Major refurbishment and redecoration has installed the likes of natural-wood tables with slate tablemats and Riedel glassware, while service remains relaxed and friendly but efficient and professional. Quality and simplicity are genuine features at The Cross and this extends to the cooking, too, which is refreshingly unfussy and deceptively straightforward, with great focus paid to seasonality and careful sourcing of prime ingredients from the abundant Scottish larder. Expect balanced, clear-flavoured dishes and some sublime combinations from the fixed-price, crisply scripted, daily-changing menus. A loin and belly of pork accompanied by apricots and Rooibosch, broad beans and a chive mash might feature as a main course, or perhaps a fillet of local venison accompanied by bitter chocolate and horseradish dauphinoise. Heading-up desserts, perhaps a crème caramel served with crème brûlée ice cream.
Notable Wine List: An interesting, varied and high-quality wine list. The list begins with a very useful short list page and has other notable features such as a section on second wines of Bordeaux, a personal selection of Tuscan Reds, Rioja and Quinta do Crasto, and a strong half-bottle listing including an excellent selection of pudding wines with several recommended specifically to accompany chocolate.

Chef: Becca Henderson, David Young
Owners: David and Katie Young
Times: 7-8.30, Closed Xmas & Jan (excl New Year), Sun-Mon, Closed L all week
Prices: Fixed D £37-£39, Min/Water £3.50, Service included, Group min 6 service 10%
Wine: 200 bottles over £20, 10 bottles under £20, 2 by the glass (£4.50-£8.50)
Notes: Prices incl nibbles, breads, appetiser, coffee & petits fours
Seats: 20
Smoking: N/Sm in restaurant
Children: Min 10 yrs
Rooms: 9 (9 en suite)
★★★★★ RR
Directions: From lights in centre of Kingussie, uphill along Ardbroilach Rd for 300 mtrs
Parking: 12

MUIR OF ORD MAP 23 NH55

Ord House Hotel

British, French

Home comforts and fresh local produce

☎ 01463 870492 IV6 7UH
e-mail: admin@ord-house.co.uk
web: www.ord-house.co.uk

Built in 1637 as the Laird's house and set in 60 acres of grounds, the property is now a comfortable country-house hotel. Husband-and-wife team John and Eliza Allen offer a warm welcome and encourage guests to enjoy the grounds, which provide some of the fruit, vegetables and herbs used in the cooking. Sporting pursuits are recommended locally and you'll find game, fish and local beef and lamb on the menu. British and French cooking styles are used in dishes like chargrilled venison fillet with redcurrant and port jus, finished off perhaps with raspberry crème brûlée.

Chef: Eliza Allen **Owners:** Eliza & John Allen **Times:** 12-2/7-9, Closed Nov-end Feb **Prices:** Fixed D £22-£24, Starter £6.50-£10.75, Main £8.50-£20, Dessert £4.75, Coffee 95p, Min/Water £1.50, Service included **Wine:** 15 bottles over £20, 30 bottles under £20, 4 by the glass (£2-£4) **Notes:** Vegetarian available **Seats:** 26 **Smoking:** N/Sm in restaurant **Children:** Portions **Rooms:** 12 (12 en suite) ★★ **Directions:** A832 to Muir of Ord. Over x-rd and rail bridge, 1st left signed Ullapool & Ord Distillery. Hotel 1/2m on left **Parking:** 24

NAIRN MAP 23 NH85

The Boath House

see page 586

NETHY BRIDGE MAP 23 NJ02

The Restaurant at The Mountview Hotel

Modern British

Inspired Highland cooking amidst amazing scenery

☎ 01479 821248 Grantown Rd PH25 3EB
e-mail: mviewhotel@aol.com
web: www.mountviewhotelnethybridge.co.uk

Aptly named, this Edwardian country-house hotel offers wonderful views of the Cairngorms from its elevated position on the edge of the village. The light-and-airy, modern restaurant extension has large picture windows to make the most of those views, while bleached-wood tables with simple, stylish settings and relaxed and friendly service add to the comforts. The kitchen's modern approach - underpinned by traditional influences - pays due respect to the best seasonal regional ingredients, including produce from the hotel's organic kitchen garden. Expect imaginative and assured cooking to deliver the likes of pan-fried sirloin of Highland beef with glazed shallots, and perhaps a warm upside-down pear pudding served with vanilla custard to finish.

Chef: Lee Beale **Owners:** Kevin & Caryl Shaw **Times:** 6-11, Closed 25-26 Dec, Mon-Tue, Closed L all week **Prices:** Starter £5-£6.50, Main £14-£18, Dessert £5.25-£5.50, Coffee £2.75, Service optional **Wine:** 3 bottles over £20, 16 bottles under £20, 4 by the glass (£3.25) **Notes:** Vegetarian available **Seats:** 24 **Smoking:** N/Sm in restaurant **Children:** Menu, Portions **Rooms:** 12 (11 en suite) ★★ HL **Directions:** From Aviemore

continued

follow signs for Nethy Bridge, through Boat-of-Garten. In Nethy Bridge over humpback bridge & follow hotel signs **Parking:** 20

ONICH MAP 22 NN06

Lodge on the Loch Hotel

Modern European

Stunning lochside setting for ambitious cuisine

☎ 01855 821237 PH33 6RY
e-mail: reservations@lodgeontheloch.com
web: www.lodgeontheloch.com

This aptly named, idyllically located hotel not only offers fine views over Loch Linnhe, but first-class highland hospitality. Striking design meets country-house comfort (real fires and comfortable lounges), while the formal hotel dining offers friendly, attentive service and those views. Modern Scottish cooking is the style with European influences and Asian seafood, classically rooted, complex and ambitious with clever presentation, while a few dishes for two (perhaps a starter tasting plate or dessert assiette) are featured on the generous menu. Sample dishes start with cranachan of hotel's own smoked fish with honey and wasabi dip, cucumber and sesame lavosh and follow on with oven-baked cod with sausage crust, creamy mash and grain mustard velouté.

Chef: Thomas Petig **Owners:** Daniel Goh **Times:** 12-1.30/6.45-9, Closed Mon-Fri Nov-Easter, (Open 23 Dec-5 Jan), Closed L all week **Prices:** Fixed D fr £20, Starter fr £2.95, Main fr £8.95, Dessert fr £4.95, Service optional **Wine:** 15 bottles over £20, 10 bottles under £20, 3 by the glass (£4.95) **Notes:** Vegetarian available, Dress Restrictions, Smart casual **Seats:** 60 **Smoking:** N/Sm in restaurant **Children:** Min 14 yrs **Rooms:** 15 (15 en suite) ★★★ **Directions:** Off A82 between Glasgow and Inverness **Parking:** 17

Onich Hotel

Traditional

Formal dining with wonderful sea views

☎ 01855 821214 PH33 6RY
e-mail: enquiries@onich-fortwilliam.co.uk
web: www.onich-fortwilliam.co.uk

Stunning views of Loch Linnhe, well-maintained gardens extending to its shores, and genuine hospitality make this hotel an idyllic and welcoming retreat. There's a choice of inviting lounges and contrasting bars, while views of the loch can be enjoyed from the attractive restaurant. The fixed-price menu blends traditional and modern dishes, for example a starter of confit chicken and sweet fennel terrine with red onion marmalade, followed by roast rump of Perthshire lamb

continued on page 587

Scotland

The Boath House

NAIRN MAP 23 NH85

Scottish, French

Stunning food and effortless service in small country-house hotel

☎ 01667 454896 Auldearn IV12 5TE
e-mail: wendy@boath-house.com
web: www.boath-house.com

Chef: Charles Lockley
Owners: Mr & Mrs D Matheson
Times: 12.30-1.45/7-8.30, Closed Xmas, Closed L Mon-Wed
Prices: Fixed L £35, Fixed D £48, Coffee £2.50, Min/Water £3.75, Service optional
Wine: 65 bottles over £20, 11 bottles under £20, 6 by the glass (£5.50)
Notes: Fixed L 4 courses, Fixed D 5 courses, Vegetarian available, Dress Restrictions, Smart casual, no shorts/T-shirts/jeans, Civ Wed 30
Seats: 28, Pr/dining room 8
Smoking: N/Sm in restaurant
Children: Portions
Rooms: 6 (6 en suite) ★★★
Directions: 2 miles E of Nairn on A96 (Inverness to Aberdeen road)
Parking: 20

This lovingly restored, classic Georgian mansion - one of Scotland's finest small hotels - sits in 20 acres of peaceful lawns, mature woodlands and streams. Its walled garden provides produce for chef Charles Lockley's inspired cooking, while ebullient, hands-on owners the Mathesons greet guests and diners like treasured friends. The lake here is stocked with brown and rainbow trout (in the early evening, when the flies are about, they can be seen jumping), while in the grounds, badgers and roe deer can be spotted. Inside, open fires flicker, while lounges and dining room abound with colourful ceramics and vibrant paintings, Boath acting as a permanent exhibition for contemporary Highland art. The elegant, candlelit dining room comes with well-spaced tables, high-quality appointments and comfortable high-backed chairs, and views over garden and lake. Service suits the winning formula here, being attentive, skilled and efficient but suitably relaxed and friendly.

Charles Lockley's modern approach is classically based with a strong Scottish influence, using high-quality produce from the abundant Highland larder. Think a cannon of red deer delivered with roasted pumpkin and parsnip purée, or perhaps roast goose breast with truffle and herb risotto and ceps, while spiced custard teamed with poached mulled pears and an almond tuile might feature at dessert. The approach at dinner is a fixed-price, five-course set affair, but with a choice offered at mains and dessert, the emphasis here on allowing the superb-quality produce to shine. High technical skills, imagination, balance and clean, clear flavours parade in style. Make a night of it and stay in one of six beautiful bedrooms, enjoy a spa treatment, or just stroll in the lovely grounds.

ONICH *continued* MAP 22 NN06

with braised red cabbage and natural jus, and warm chocolate tart with raspberry coulis.

Chef: Alan Pearson **Owners:** Mr S Leitch **Times:** 7-9, Closed Xmas, Closed L all week **Prices:** Fixed D £28, Coffee £1.15, Min/Water £3.10, Service optional **Wine:** 4 by the glass (£3.20) **Notes:** Dress Restrictions, Smart casual **Seats:** 50, Pr/dining room 24 **Smoking:** N/Sm in restaurant **Children:** Menu, Portions **Rooms:** 25 (25 en suite) ★★★ HL **Directions:** Beside A82. Located in village of Onich, 9m S of Fort William **Parking:** 50

POOLEWE MAP 22 NG88

Pool House Hotel

British, French

Stunning location for fine Scottish cuisine

☎ 01445 781272 IV22 2LD
e-mail: enquiries@poolhousehotel.com
web: www.poolhousehotel.com

Set on the shores of Loch Ewe, where the river meets the sea, this former military base may have an unassuming façade, but it boasts a stunning interior. The stylish 'North By North West' dining room has panoramic views of Loch Ewe, where otters and seals can be spotted by diners. A set taste of the Highlands menu is served each evening and the ingredients really speak for themselves. You might find locally made haggis with a Drambuie sauce, medallion of Loch Ewe lobster set on seafood risotto with coconut, green chilli and mussel broth, baked fillet of Kinlochbervie halibut or perhaps fillet of Scottish beef.

Times: 6.30-8.30, Closed Jan **Rooms:** 5 (5 en suite) ★★★ **Directions:** 6M N of Gairloch on A832. Hotel by bridge on River Ewe

ROY BRIDGE MAP 22 NN28

Glenspean Lodge Hotel

Modern British NEW

Crowd-pleasing cuisine at this Highland hotel

☎ 01397 712223 PH31 4AF
e-mail: reservations@glenspeanlodge.com
web: www.glenspeanlodge.com

Built as a hunting lodge in the 1880s and nestled in 5 acres of gardens and woodland, this peaceful country-house hotel offers dramatic panoramas of the Spean Valley and the Nevis range from its spacious dining room. The food looks good too - expect accomplished modern Scottish cooking from a kitchen that aims to please: a tian of haggis with neeps and tatties served with a whisky and grain mustard sauce perhaps, or medallions of roast loin of pork on a bed of buttered cabbage, served with an apple and Arran mustard sauce. A less formal menu is served in the Mackintosh Lounge.

Chef: Paul Draper **Owners:** Alex Fitzpatrick & Brett Hesse **Times:** 5-9, Closed Jan **Prices:** Fixed D fr £25, Starter £3.50-£6, Main £8.50-£16, Dessert £4.50-£5.50, Coffee £1.90, Min/Water £2, Service optional **Wine:** 2 bottles over £20, 15 bottles under £20, 4 by the glass (£2.75) **Notes:** Vegetarian available, Civ Wed 80 **Seats:** 40 **Smoking:** N/Sm in restaurant **Children:** Portions **Rooms:** 15 (15 en suite) ★★★ HL **Directions:** A86, 2m past Roy Bridge **Parking:** 30

SHIELDAIG MAP 22 NG85

Tigh an Eilean Hotel

Modern Scottish

Accomplished cooking in a welcoming hotel

☎ 01520 755251 IV54 8XN
e-mail: tighaneileanhotel@shieldaig.fsnet.co.uk

However long your journey to reach Sheildaig, an 18th-century fishing village perched on the shore of Loch Torridon, you'll know it was worth it when you arrive at this delightful white painted hotel. The restaurant is airy and light, with an atmosphere of relaxed chic, and fabulous views across the loch to the open sea beyond. The hotel centres around the original substantial house, built in around 1800 when the village was constructed using a Government grant. Modern Scottish cuisine with French influences offers straightforward, accurately prepared dishes where nothing is more important than flavour. Daily-changing menus rely on local produce, demonstrating a passion for fine ingredients and a commitment to quality. Typical dishes include risotto of Loch Torridon langoustines to start and perhaps roast loin of Blackface lamb with a tart of chanterelles and sweetbreads as a main course.

Chef: Christopher Field **Owners:** Christopher & Cathryn Field **Times:** 7-8.30, Closed end Oct-mid Mar (except private bookings), Closed L all week **Prices:** Fixed D £41, Min/Water £3.95, Service optional **Wine:** 38 bottles over £20, 18 bottles under £20, 4 by the glass (£3.25-£6.50) **Notes:** Coffee incl, Vegetarian available, Smart casual, Civ Wed 40 **Seats:** 28, Pr/dining room 28 **Smoking:** N/Sm in restaurant **Children:** Menu, Portions **Rooms:** 11 (11 en suite) ★★ **Directions:** From A896 follow signs for Shieldaig. Hotel in village centre on water's edge

SPEAN BRIDGE

Old Pines Hotel

Modern British V NEW

Scandinavian-style setting for Scottish cuisine

☎ 01397 712324 PH34 4EG
e-mail: enquiries@oldpines.co.uk
web: www.oldpines.co.uk

This Scandinavian-style pine chalet hotel enjoys wonderful views of the Ben Nevis range and has a backdrop of ancient pine trees creating a dramatic setting. The restaurant prides itself on offering modern Scottish cuisine using locally sourced ingredients, organic wherever possible. Dinner is a four-course affair starting with home-made canapés and finishing with organic chocolate truffles. In between you might sample crab and basil risotto, strip loin of venison with red wine jus, roasted shallots and braised red cabbage, and dessert of whisky and walnut tart. Service is relaxed, friendly and semi-formal.

continued

SPEAN BRIDGE *continued*

Chef: Ryan Glen **Owners:** Imogen & Ken Dalley **Times:** 12-3/6.30-9 **Prices:** Fixed D £25-£30, Starter £7.50-£9, Main £12.50-£20, Dessert £5-£7.50, Coffee £2, Min/Water £3, Service optional **Wine:** 8 by the glass (£3.25-£5) **Notes:** Vegetarian available, Dress Restrictions, Smart casual, no jeans to D, Civ Wed 30 **Seats:** 30 **Smoking:** N/Sm in restaurant **Children:** Menu, Portions **Rooms:** 8 (8 en suite) ★★ **Directions:** 10m N of Fort William, 400yds from A82 at Commando Memorial **Parking:** 10

Scotland

Smiddy House

Modern British NEW

Top-notch cooking in a convivial setting

☎ 01397 712335 Roy Bridge Rd PH34 4EU
e-mail: enquiry@smiddyhouse.co.uk
web: www.smiddyhouse.co.uk

Prominently located on the ground floor of the old village blacksmith, the candlelit Russell's restaurant seats its diners at tables decked with sparkling glasses, quality china and fresh flowers. It's an intimate venue with warm rustic colours, and a knack for turning the best of local produce into high-quality cuisine. The concise menu stays true to its roots, featuring dishes such as Cullen skink tart, or medallions of venison with colcannon, oatmeal pudding and whisky sauce, as well as more classic fare - citrus baked halibut perhaps, or rhubarb meringue roulade with Turkish delight ice cream. Busy, so book ahead.

Chef: Glen Russell **Owners:** Glen Russell/Robert Bryson **Times:** 12.30-2.30/6-9, Closed 2 days a week (Nov-Apr), Closed L Mon & Sat **Prices:** Fixed D £25.95-£29.95, Coffee £1.75, Min/Water £2.75, Service optional **Wine:** 6 bottles over £20, 22 bottles under £20, 2 by the glass (£3.10-£4.20) **Notes:** Dress Restrictions, Smart casual **Seats:** 38 **Smoking:** N/Sm in restaurant **Children:** Menu, Portions **Rooms:** 4 (4 en suite) ◆◆◆◆ **Directions:** Located in Spean Bridge, 9m N of Fort William, on A82 towards Inverness **Parking:** 15

STEIN MAP 22 NG25

Loch Bay Seafood Restaurant

Seafood

Excellent local seafood in a simple setting

☎ 01470 592235 IV55 8GA
e-mail: david@lochbay-seafood-restaurant.co.uk
web: www.lochbay-seafood-restaurant.co.uk

This simple fisherman's cottage is part of a model fishing village that was never completed, and close to the loch shore near Waternish Point. The wonderfully welcoming atmosphere is another part of its allure, and the need to book for both lunch and dinner really says it all. The blackboard advertises the freshest of seafood from the catch landed at nearby Dunvegan. Everything is simply cooked with almost nothing added to mask the natural flavours. Typical meal includes lobster risotto with shellfish sauce, and grilled Dover sole with citrus and olive oil emulsion.

Chef: David Wilkinson **Owners:** David & Alison Wilkinson **Times:** 12-2/6-9, Closed Nov-Easter (excl. 1wk over Hogmanay), Sun, Closed L Sat **Prices:** Starter £2.95-£8, Main £8.50-£36, Dessert £3.80-£4.75, Coffee £1.30, Min/Water £2.50, Service optional **Wine:** 12 bottles over £20, 19 bottles under £20, 6 by the glass (£2.25-£4.45) **Seats:** 26 **Smoking:** N/Sm in restaurant **Children:** Portions **Directions:** Telephone for directions **Parking:** 6

STRONTIAN MAP 22 NM86

Kilcamb Lodge Hotel

Scottish, French

Tranquil lochside setting for accomplished cuisine

☎ 01967 402257 PH36 4HY
e-mail: enquiries@kilcamblodge.co.uk
web: www.kilcamblodge.co.uk

Used as a barracks during the Highland Clearances, Kilcamb Lodge is now a delightful haven for guests seeking a peaceful retreat in a lovely lochside setting. Accomplished country-house cooking sees careful sourcing of fine fresh ingredients from local suppliers. Typically, you'll find starters like steamed Loch Etive mussels in cider and saffron cream sauce and main courses like roasted loin of Mingarry venison with red cabbage, dauphinoise potatoes and redcurrant jus. Desserts might feature a chocolate trio platter with mango sorbet. Round off an enjoyable meal with freshly ground coffee and petits fours.

Times: 12-2.30/7.30-9.30, Closed 3 Jan-15 Feb, Closed L Mon **Rooms:** 12 (12 en suite) ★★★ CHH **Directions:** Take the Corran ferry off A82. Follow A861 to Strontian. First left over bridge after village.

TAIN MAP 23 NH78

Glenmorangie Highland Home at Cadboll

Modern Scottish, European

Home from home dining from Scotland's larder

☎ 01862 871671 Cadboll, Fearn IV20 1XP
e-mail: relax@glenmorangieplc.co.uk
web: www.glenmorangie.com

More than a country house, this highland home is formed from a 17th-century farmhouse and an 18th-century castle, with its own beach, grounds and two walled gardens providing produce for the house. Guests dine together house-party style here and it's the ideal place to take your own group of friends or family for a truly memorable stay. Modern international cuisine capitalises on the availability of wonderful local produce like fresh seafood and venison from neighbouring estates and suppliers. A typical autumn menu features West Coast scallops, wild mushroom soup, seared pork fillet with potato fondant, braised autumn cabbage and a rich cider jus, followed by hot chocolate chip soufflé with pistachio ice cream.

Chef: David Graham, **Owners:** Glenmorangie Ltd **Times:** 8, Closed 23-26 Dec, 4-27 Jan, Closed L by prior arrangement **Prices:** Fixed D £45, Min/Water £3.50, Service optional **Wine:** 30 bottles over £20, 20 bottles

continued

under £20 **Notes:** Fixed D 4 courses, Dress Restrictions, Smart casual, no jeans or T-shirts, Civ Wed 60 **Seats:** 30, Pr/dining room 30 **Smoking:** N/Sm in restaurant **Children:** Min 16 yrs, Portions **Rooms:** 9 (9 en suite) ★★ HL **Directions:** N on A9, at Nigg Rdbt turn right onto B9175 (before Tain) & follow signs for hotel **Parking:** 60

TONGUE MAP 23 NC55

Ben Loyal Hotel

Modern, Traditional

Food with flair in a magnificent setting

☎ 01847 611216 Main St IV27 4XE
e-mail: benloyalhotel@btinternet.com
web: www.benloyal.co.uk

Arriving here after a stunning highland and coastal drive, guests eating in the restaurant can then take in the magnificent views of the Kyle of Tongue. Local ingredients are expertly cooked in an extensive range of dishes offering something for everyone. You could try a starter of Ben Loyal potted venison or Kyle of Tongue oysters for example, followed by braised lamb shank in red wine sauce, rosemary and fondant potatoes. Then round off with perhaps orange and whisky-scented bread and butter pudding. As well as a children's menu, the bar offers a bistro menu and is a popular choice for locals and tourists.

Chef: Elizabeth Warburton **Owners:** Mr & Mrs P Lewis **Times:** 12-2.30/6-8.30, Closed end Oct-end Mar, Closed L all week **Prices:** Fixed L £9-£15, Fixed D £17-£26, Starter £3.25-£4.95, Main £7-£16, Dessert fr £4.25, Coffee £1.95, Min/Water £2.60, Service optional **Wine:** All bottles under £20, 2 by the glass (£12-£20) **Notes:** Vegetarian available **Seats:** 50, Pr/dining room **Smoking:** N/Sm in restaurant **Children:** Menu, Portions **Rooms:** 11 (11 en suite) ★★ **Directions:** Hotel in centre of village at junction of A836 & A838 **Parking:** 20

Borgie Lodge Hotel

***Modern British* NEW**

Welcoming hotel offering accomplished cooking

☎ 01641 521332 Skerray KW14 7TH
e-mail: info@borgielodgehotel.co.uk
web: www.borgielodgehotel.co.uk

This old Victorian sporting lodge, dating back to the 1800s, continues to provide a welcome retreat for today's sportsmen, mainly fishermen. The atmosphere is very relaxed and friendly with plenty of time for a drink in the Naver Lounge or the Crofter's Bar, where you might hear a few tales about 'the ones that got away'! Cooking is skilful, making good use of local produce in traditional British and Scottish dishes. The menu changes daily depending on what's in season, but you might find roast saddle of Borgie venison or perhaps steamed monkfish with seared scallops as main courses.

Chef: Daniel Stickland **Owners:** RJ, DA & BF Stickland **Times:** 12-2/7-8.30, Closed 25 Dec **Prices:** Fixed D £32, Coffee £3, Min/Water £2, Service included **Wine:** 9 bottles over £20, 18 bottles under £20, 4 by the glass (£3-£4) **Notes:** Fixed D 4 courses, Dress Restrictions, Smart casual, no jeans **Seats:** 16 **Smoking:** N/Sm in restaurant **Children:** Min 12 yrs **Rooms:** 8 (7 en suite) ★★ **Directions:** 0.5m off A836 6m from Tongue **Parking:** 15

TORRIDON MAP 22 NG95

Loch Torridon Country House Hotel

Modern British NOTABLE WINE LIST

Country house with stunning views and accomplished cooking

☎ 01445 791242 IV22 2EY
e-mail: enquiries@lochtorridonhotel.com
web: www.lochtorridonhotel.com

Expect to be wowed by the magnificent lochside setting and awe-inspiring mountain scenery at this beautifully restored Victorian country-house hotel. Once a shooting lodge, it makes a perfect setting for a romantic break or to escape the pressures of life. Original Scottish pine panelling and ornate ceilings cut a formal yet relaxed tone in the restaurant, with its friendly and attentive kilted staff, while the conservatory area takes in the scenery. There's a clubby bar boasting 300 malt whiskies and a serious wine list, too. The modern approach to cooking delivers a progressive take on a classical French theme, with intricate, appealing, accomplished dishes employing top-notch local ingredients, including produce from the hotel's potager. Fricassée of Scottish sea life in ginger, coriander and carrot nage or poached fillet of aged Black Isle beef with tortellini of spinach and roast garlic are fine examples of the fare.
Notable Wine List: A well-presented wine list offering a fine selection of wines.

Chef: Kevin Broome **Owners:** Daniel & Rohaise Rose-Bristow **Times:** 12-2/7-8.45, Closed 2 Jan for 4 wks, Closed L Bar only **Prices:** Fixed D £40, Coffee £4.50, Min/Water £3.75, Service optional **Wine:** 132 bottles over £20, 25 bottles under £20, 8 by the glass (£4-£5) **Notes:** Fixed D 4 courses, Vegetarian available, Dress Restrictions, No jeans or trainers, Civ Wed 42 **Seats:** 38, Pr/dining room 16 **Smoking:** N/Sm in restaurant **Children:** Min 10 yrs, Menu, Portions **Rooms:** 19 (19 en suite) ★★★ **Directions:** From Inverness take A9 N, follow signs to Ullapool (A835). At Garve take A832 to Kinlochewe; take A896 to Torridon. Do not turn off to Torridon Village. Hotel on right after Annat village **Parking:** 20

LANARKSHIRE, SOUTH

BIGGAR MAP 21 NT03

Chancellors at Shieldhill Castle

International, Scottish NOTABLE WINE LIST

Fine food and wine in historic castle setting

☎ 01899 220035 Quothquan ML12 6NA
e-mail: enquiries@shieldhill.co.uk
web: www.shieldhill.co.uk

continued

BIGGAR *continued* MAP 21 NT03

Set in rolling countryside and 7 acres of lawns and woodland, Shieldhill is a fortified mansion that can trace its history from 1199. This imposing building provides a fusion of historic architecture with modern cooking and friendly service. Atmospheric public areas include the oak-panelled lounge and Chancellor's restaurant, a high-ceilinged room resplendent in its baronial furnishings. A technically accomplished kitchen delivers simple, full-flavoured dishes that utilise fresh local produce, including the estate game. You can mix and match dishes from three menus, the carte is available in starter or main course sizes, and choices may include seared pheasant breast with smoked bacon, a classic bouillabaisse, osso buco or speciality steaks.

Notable Wine List: A highly individual list full of enthusiasm and passion for high quality wines.

Chef: Christina Lamb **Owners:** Mr & Mrs R Lamb **Times:** 12-1.45/7-8.45 **Prices:** Fixed L fr £15.95, Fixed D fr £19.95, Starter £6.95-£13.95, Main £13.95-£18.95, Dessert fr £7.95, Coffee £2, Min/Water £3, Service optional, Group min 10 service 5% **Wine:** 20 bottles under £20, 20 by the glass (£4-£16.25) **Notes:** Tasting menu available, Vegetarian available, Civ Wed 150 **Seats:** 32, Pr/dining room 30 **Smoking:** N/Sm in restaurant **Children:** Portions **Rooms:** 16 (16 en suite) ★★★ CHH **Directions:** From Biggar take B7016 to Carnwath. After approx 2.5m turn left onto Shieldhill Road. Castle is 1m on right **Parking:** 60

Fifty Five

Modern Scottish NEW

Contemporary Scottish dining

☎ 01899 2215555 55 High St ML12 6DA
web: www.fiftyfive.uk.com

This High Street restaurant offers contemporary rustic décor where vibrant pictures and prints contrast with bare stonework. Modern Scottish cuisine is on offer; the 55 menu provides a tasting selection for two people, while the carte has a good selection of dishes at each course. Delicate starters include the likes of baked filo of traditional haggis with spiced butternut squash and plum sauce. Prime Scottish beef features among the main course choices, with traditional accompaniments like hand-cut chips, Portobello mushrooms, caramelised onions and tomato, and a choice of sauces.

Chef: Jimmy Guldberg **Times:** 12-2.30/5.30-9, Closed Mon **Prices:** Food prices not confirmed for 2007. Please telephone for details **Directions:** Telephone for directions

EAST KILBRIDE MAP 20 NS65

Macdonald Crutherland House

European

Honest, clear flavours in country-house hotel

☎ 01355 577000 Strathaven Rd G75 0QZ
e-mail: crutherland@macdonald-hotels.co.uk
web: www.macdonaldhotels.co.uk

Set in peaceful countryside just 20 minutes from the centre of Glasgow, this upmarket hotel is deservedly popular with the conference market. Its richly furnished dining room is a haven of elegant good taste and offers an extensive range of dishes. Those on the carte showcase the kitchen's flair, while a fixed-price selection offers simpler choices at keener prices. Expect honest, flavourful cooking - cream of cauliflower soup for example, served with blue cheese and herb dumplings, followed by braised pork belly with pea purée or roast loin of local wild venison with braised red cabbage.

Chef: David Friel **Owners:** Macdonald Hotels PLC **Times:** 12-2.30/7-9.30, Closed L Sat **Prices:** Fixed L £18-£24, Fixed D £29.50-£32, Coffee £2, Min/Water £4, Service optional **Notes:** Fixed L 3 courses, Civ Wed 250 **Seats:** 64, Pr/dining room 36 **Smoking:** N/Sm in restaurant, Air con **Children:** Menu, Portions **Rooms:** 75 (75 en suite) ★★★★ **Directions:** From E Kilbride take A726 towards Strathaven. 1.5m, & beyond Torrance rdbt, hotel on left **Parking:** 200

STRATHAVEN MAP 20 NS74

Rissons at Springvale

Modern Scottish

Relaxed restaurant with modern Scottish cuisine

☎ 01357 520234 18 Lethame Rd ML10 6AD
e-mail: rissons@msn.com

This light and airy, modern-styled restaurant - located just outside the town - comes with an intimate conservatory overlooking the rear garden. The atmosphere is relaxed and friendly, and the service informed, while the kitchen's modern-bistro output matches the mood, delivering simple, unfussy, well-presented dishes that concentrate on flavour and the use of quality produce. Typically shank with bubble-and-squeak and buttered cabbage, or perhaps rib-eye steak with Café de Paris butter and hand-cut chips, while the ubiquitous sticky toffee pudding, served with butterscotch sauce and vanilla ice cream, could be a choice for dessert.

Chef: Scott Baxter, Sandra Law **Owners:** Scott Baxter, Anne Baxter **Times:** 1-7/5.30-9.30, Closed New Year, 1 wk Jan, 1st wk July, Mon-Tue, Closed L Wed-Sat **Prices:** Fixed L £12.95, Fixed D £14.95, Starter £3.75-£7.50, Main £8.95-£16.50, Dessert £4.25-£4.95, Coffee £1.75, Min/Water £3 Service optional **Wine:** 10 bottles over £20, 22 bottles under £20, 6 by the glass (£2.95-£5.50) **Notes:** Vegetarian available **Seats:** 50 **Smoking:** N/Sm in restaurant **Children:** Portions **Rooms:** 11 (11 en suite) ◆◆◆ **Directions:** From M74 junct 8 follow A71, through Stonehouse and onto Strathaven **Parking:** 10

LOTHIAN, EAST

DIRLETON MAP 21 NT58

The Open Arms Hotel

Modern Scottish

Charming country hotel with relaxing atmosphere and enjoyable dining

☎ 01620 850241 EH39 5EG
e-mail: openarmshotel@clara.co.uk
web: www.openarmshotel.com

This well-established hotel lies across the green from Dirleton Castle. The inviting interior includes the popular Deveau's Brasserie and the more formal Library Restaurant. The latter has soft lighting, clothed tables and formal settings. Staff are helpful and friendly, serving carefully prepared modern and traditional dishes like starters of pan-fried herring in oatmeal with lemon beurre blanc and main courses of Ballencrieff organic pork cutlet with sherry, mushroom and cream sauce. Finish with sticky toffee pudding with hot fudge sauce and vanilla ice cream or try the good selection of Scottish cheeses.

Times: 12-2/7-9, Closed D Sun **Rooms:** 10 (10 en suite) ★★★ SHL **Directions:** From A1 (S) take A198 to North Berwick, then follow signs for Dirleton - 2 miles W. From Edinburgh take A6137 leading to A198.

continued

GULLANE MAP 21 NT48

 Greywalls Hotel

ee below

La Potinière

Modern British

mbitious cooking in cottage-style restaurant

☎ 01620 843214 Main St EH31 2AA
web: www.la-potiniere.co.uk

delightful cottage-style restaurant of fairytale proportions, La otinière is a two-partner operation, both sharing the kitchen, while eith also acts as host and wine waiter. Accordingly, the meal is a isurely four-course affair at dinner, plus an amuse-bouche and pre-essert, and three courses at lunch. Smart, crisp linen and quality ableware reinforce the kitchen's serious intent, while the cooking nds a contemporary touch with artistic presentation and makes fine se of local seasonal produce. There are just two choices at each ourse, perhaps featuring smoked salmon soup with grilled oyster, ucculent seared scallop and cucumber and dill salsa, or braised lamb hank with seasonal vegetables, parsnip mash and a reduction of raising juices.

hef: Mary Runciman & Keith Marley **Owners:** Mary Runciman **imes:** 12.30-1.30/7-8.30, Closed Xmas, BHs, Mon-Tue, Closed D Sun (Oct-or) **Prices:** Fixed L £17, Fixed D £38, Min/Water £2.50, Service optional **Vine:** 27 bottles over £20, 8 bottles under £20, 4 by the glass (£3-£4) **otes:** Fixed D 4 courses, Dress Restrictions, Smart casual **Seats:** 30 **moking:** N/Sm in restaurant **Children:** Portions **Directions:** 20m SE of dinburgh. 3m from North Berwick on A198 **Parking:** 10

HADDINGTON MAP 21 NT57

Bonars Restaurant

Contemporary

Clean, contemporary cuisine in former watermill

☎ 01620 822100 Poldrate Mill, Tyne House EH41 4AD
e-mail: info@bonars.co.uk
web: www.bonars.co.uk

An idyllic setting on the riverbank in the refurbished buildings of an old watermill on the River Tyne. Choose between Poldrates brasserie for an informal meal, or Bonars restaurant. Here you will find a Mediterranean-style room with stone walls, spotlights and terracotta tiles. Contemporary cuisine includes starters like curried fishcake with lemongrass and vine tomato dressing. Main courses are straightforward and full of flavour. Try the likes of red wine venison with beignets of haggis for example, or one of the grill dishes on offer. Desserts feature some mouthwatering combinations like twice-baked chocolate torte with bitter chocolate and raspberry ice cream. There are cookery courses and theme nights.

Times: 12-2.30/6-9, Closed Mon, Tues

Waterside Bistro

☎ 01620 825674 1-5 Waterside EH41 4AT

Relatively formal eatery located in a picturesque setting and known for generous portions.

Greywalls Hotel

GULLANE MAP 21 NT48

Modern British

ne cooking in elegant country house

☎ 01620 842144 Muirfield EH31 2EG
-mail: hotel@greywalls.co.uk
web: www.greywalls.co.uk

dignified Lutyens country house with gardens created by Gertrude kyll, Greywalls offers elegant Edwardian comfort in stylish rroundings overlooking the Muirfield Golf Course, with stunning ews of the estuary behind. Features include a wonderful walled rden, tennis courts and croquet lawn, while inside there are mptuous sitting rooms whose deep sofas beckon for pre- and post-nner drinks. The elegant restaurant continues the theme, comprised two calm and peaceful rooms with well-spaced, well-appointed bles and comfortable chairs, and more views over the golf course. aditional formalities mean jackets and ties for gentlemen and formal, ough friendly, unstuffy service.

e kitchen's modern approach comes suitably underpinned by a ssical theme, the cooking focusing on high-quality produce from e abundant Scottish larder. High skill and eye-catching presentation rade on the fixed-price repertoire, as in slow-roast belly of Lothian rk served with braised black pudding, crackling, spring herbs and an apple risotto, or perhaps sea bass on crushed Blue Congo potatoes with wilted spinach and an Avruga caviar champagne velouté, while a cider soufflé, teamed with jelly and crisp, might head-up desserts.

Chef: David Williams **Owners:** Mr & Mrs G Weaver **Times:** 12-2/7-9.30, Closed Jan-Feb, Closed L Mon-Thur **Prices:** Fixed L fr £25, Fixed D £45, Coffee £2.50, Min/Water £3.50, Service optional **Wine:** 250 bottles over £20, 15 bottles under £20, 10 by the glass (£4.50-£9.50) **Notes:** Dress Restrictions, Jacket requested **Seats:** 40, Pr/dining room 20 **Smoking:** N/Sm in restaurant **Children:** Portions **Rooms:** 23 (23 en suite) ★★★ **Directions:** From Edinburgh take A1 to North Berwick slip road, then follow A198 along coast to far end of Gullane - Greywalls in last road on left **Parking:** 40

Scotland

Scotland

LOTHIAN, WEST

LINLITHGOW MAP 21 NS97

Champany Inn

Traditional British, Scottish

Unrivalled steak restaurant in country lodge

☎ 01506 834532 EH49 7LU
e-mail: reception@champany.com
web: www.champany.com

Several cottages and an ancient watermill comprise this unusual hotel. The restaurant itself is an octagonal affair with exposed stone walls and timbered ceiling, while tapestries, gleaming copper and elegant portraits abound. A small lounge boasts leather seating and antiques, while service is efficient and unobtrusive. The extensive wine choice comes stored on a mezzanine floor. A temple to prime beef and the Rolls Royce of steakhouses, Champany specialises in cuts from cattle sourced and prepared by the restaurant's own butchery and hung for three weeks. West Coast seafood also finds its place, but it's the full-flavoured, tender beef that takes pride of place, such as Aberdeen Angus rib-eye with hand-made chips and a selection of vegetables. The farmer's cottage has now been converted into a shop selling Champany produce to enjoy at home.

Chef: C Davidson, D Gibson, C Hart **Owners:** Mr & Mrs C Davidson **Times:** 12.30-2/7-10, Closed 25-26 Dec, Sun, Closed L Sat **Prices:** Fixed L £19.75, Starter £8-£14, Main £18-£35, Dessert £7.50, Coffee £3.75, Min/Water £2.75, Service added 10% **Wine:** 632 bottles over £20, 20 bottles under £20, 5 by the glass (£3.95-£4.95) **Notes:** Vegetarian available, Dress Restrictions, No jeans **Seats:** 50, Pr/dining room 30 **Smoking:** N/Sm in restaurant **Children:** Min 8 yrs **Directions:** 2m NE of Linlithgow. From M9 (N) junct 3, at top of slip road turn right. Champany is 500yds on right **Parking:** 50

Livingston's Restaurant

Modern Scottish, French V

Classical Scottish cooking in a delightful rural restaurant

☎ 01506 846565 52 High St EH49 7AE
e-mail: contact@livingstons-restaurant.co.uk
web: www.livingstons-restaurant.co.uk

Tucked away at the end of a semi-hidden 'ginnel' or lane, Livingston's provides an authentic Scottish experience. Ruby red fabrics, tartan carpets and soft candlelight conspire to create a relaxed and intoxicatingly Caledonian atmosphere that enhances the offerings on a menu which trumpets local ingredients such as Inverurie lamb, Highland venison and Stornoway black pudding. Among the highlights are dishes such as medallions of monkfish wrapped in proscuitto,

continued

curried mussel broth and saffron mash or try saddle of Highland venison, bubble and squeak with bramble jus. The food is complemented by a well-chosen wine list with interesting tasting notes. Diners should make room for the assiette of Livingston's puddings.

Chef: Julian Wright **Owners:** Ronald & Christine Livingston **Times:** 12-2.30/6-9.30, Closed 1 wk Jun, 1 wk Oct, 2wks Jan, Sun-Mon **Prices:** Fixed L fr £15.95, Fixed D fr £33.50, Coffee £2.50, Min/Water £3.50, Service optional, Group min 8 service 10% **Wine:** 35 bottles over £20, 23 bottles under £20, 4 by the glass (£3.50-£4.50) **Notes:** Vegetarian menu, Dress Restrictions, Smart casual **Seats:** 40 **Smoking:** N/Sm in restaurant **Children:** Min 8 yrs, Portions **Directions:** Opposite post office **Parking:** NCP - Linlithgow Cross, on street

Marynka

☎ 01506 840123 57 High St EH49 7ED
Glass-fronted restaurant with modern Scottish cooking.

UPHALL MAP 21 NT07

Macdonald Houstoun House

Traditional European

Fine dining in beautiful surroundings

☎ 0870 194 2107 EH52 6JS
e-mail: houstoun@macdonald-hotels.co.uk
web: www.macdonaldhotels.co.uk/houstoun.house

This historic 17th-century tower house is set in beautifully landscaped grounds and gardens. The choice of dining options includes a vaulted cocktail bar and the elegant period-style dining room. Tables are formally set and service is efficient but also friendly, suiting the mix of business and leisure guests. The fixed price European menu provides good value with traditional choices, while the carte is a little more adventurous. Dishes remain flavour driven through good, honest and uncomplicated cooking using the finest Scottish ingredients. Expect mains like breast of pheasant with celeriac purée, red cabbage, sweetcorn crêpe and port sauce.

Chef: Stephen Frost **Owners:** Macdonald Hotels PLC **Times:** 12-2/7-9.30, Closed L Sat **Prices:** Fixed L fr £15.95, Fixed D fr £22, Starter £5.50-£8.50, Main £15-£22.50, Dessert £5.50-£6.25, Coffee £3.95, Min/Water £4.55, Service optional **Wine:** 60 bottles over £20, 20 bottles under £20, 12 by the glass (£4.25-£7) **Notes:** Vegetarian available, Dress Restrictions, Smart casual, no jeans or trainers, Civ Wed 200 **Seats:** 65, Pr/dining room 30 **Smoking:** N/Sm in restaurant **Children:** Menu, Portions **Rooms:** 71 (71 en suite) ★★★★ HL **Directions:** Please telephone for directions **Parking:** 200

MORAY

ARCHIESTOWN MAP 23 NJ24

Archiestown Hotel

Mediterranean, International NEW

Well-prepared local produce at a small and friendly hotel

☎ 01340 810218 AB38 7QL
e-mail: jah@archiestownhotel.co.uk
web: www.archiestownhotel.co.uk

A small hotel in the heart of the whisky and salmon fishing country of Speyside, noted for its great hospitality and character. The cosy bistro style restaurant offers a seasonally-changing menu full of interesting dishes - home-made spicy prawn and noodle spring rolls with a chill

continued

and ginger dressing makes an impressive start to dinner, followed perhaps by chicken breast stuffed with haggis and wrapped in dry-cured ham served with a whisky and peppercorn sauce. Puddings are satisfyingly traditional.

Times: 12-2/7-9, Closed Xmas & 2wks Jan **Rooms:** 11 (11 en suite) ★★ SHL **Directions:** Turn off A95 onto B9102 at Craigellachie

CRAIGELLACHIE MAP 23 NJ24

Craigellachie Hotel

Traditional Scottish

Formal dining with Scottish flavour and atmosphere

☎ 01340 881204 AB38 9SR
e-mail: info@craigellachie.com
web: www.craigellachie.com

Impressive Victorian hotel in the heart of Speyside's whisky distilling area - no surprises then that the bar features more than 600 malts. Log fires, hunting and fishing paraphernalia, and traditional Scottish décor make for a relaxing experience. The Ben Aigan Restaurant encompasses several rooms, each with its own decorative style, backed by efficient, friendly service. A Scottish approach to cooking, with both French and international influences, delivers excellent flavours via dishes graced by fresh, high-quality produce from the abundant Scottish larder - prime Aberdeen Angus beef, Cabrach lamb, Moray Firth seafood and shellfish, river salmon and game. Braised shank of Cabrach lamb slowly cooked in red wine and sage reduction or fillet of Aberdeen Angus beef on smoked bacon champ, roasted vegetables and whisky jus are fine examples of the fare.

Chef: Addy Daggert **Owners:** Craigellachie Hotel Ltd **Times:** 12-2/6-10 **Prices:** Fixed L £10.70-£15.40, Fixed D £36.20, Coffee £2.50, Min/Water £3.75, Service optional **Wine:** 64 bottles over £20, 30 bottles under £20, 7 by the glass (£2.50-£3) **Notes:** Vegetarian available, Dress Restrictions, Smart casual, Civ Wed 50 **Seats:** 30, Pr/dining room 40 **Smoking:** N/Sm in restaurant, Air con **Children:** Menu, Portions **Rooms:** 25 (25 en suite) ★★★ HL **Directions:** 12m S of Elgin, in the village centre **Parking:** 25

CULLEN MAP 23 NJ56

The Seafield Hotel

Mediterranean

Friendly venue serving top-notch local produce

☎ 01542 840791 Seafield St AB56 4SG
web: www.theseafieldhotel.com

This former coaching inn in the heart of Cullen boasts a split-level restaurant furnished with tartan carpets, Mediterranean-style seating and unclothed tables. Service is relaxed and friendly. There is good

continued

use of local produce here, with the simple cooking style making for unfussy dishes that allow flavours and ingredients to shine. Accompaniments and garnishes are non-intrusive and in harmony with the key elements. Naturally, when dining in Cullen, the world-famous Cullen skink is a must. The hotel has recently had a change of ownership.

Times: 12-2/6-9 **Rooms:** 19 (19 en suite) ★★★ **Directions:** In centre of Cullen, on main thoroughway

ELGIN MAP 23 NJ26

Mansion House Hotel

Modern British, French

Impressive location for good Scottish cuisine

☎ 01343 548811 The Haugh IV30 1AW
e-mail: reception@mhelgin.co.uk
web: www.mansionhousehotel.co.uk

This former mansion house was left to the townspeople of Elgin by the wealthy Bibby family who were in shipping. Huge lawns at the front look out over the Ladyhill monument. The intimate candlelit restaurant recreates the grace of years gone by with white table linen, glittering crystal and fine porcelain. Service is friendly and professional, serving modern Scottish cuisine with a French influence. Good quality ingredients are sourced locally, producing dishes like pan-fried king scallops on black pudding, with saffron butter sauce to start. Tempting mains include pan-seared saddle of venison on a caramelised shallot and celeriac mash with redcurrant jus.

Chef: Kris McKie **Owners:** David Baker **Times:** 12-2/7-9 **Prices:** Fixed L £15-£17, Fixed D £29.95-£32.95, Starter £5.25-£7.55, Main £13.75-£19.95, Dessert £5.25, Coffee £1.50, Min/Water £3.75, Service optional **Wine:** 22 bottles over £20, 27 bottles under £20, 5 by the glass (£3.65) **Notes:** Fixed D 4 courses, Vegetarian available, Dress Restrictions, Smart casual, Civ Wed 150 **Seats:** 50, Pr/dining room 30 **Smoking:** N/Sm in restaurant **Children:** Menu, Portions **Rooms:** 23 (23 en suite) ★★★ **Directions:** In Elgin turn off A96 into Haugh Rd; hotel at end of road by river **Parking:** 100

PERTH & KINROSS

AUCHTERARDER MAP 21 NN91

Andrew Fairlie at Gleneagles

see page 594

Cairn Lodge

Scottish

Stylish dining in comfortable country house

☎ 01764 662634 Orchil Rd PH3 1LX
e-mail: email@cairnlodge.co.uk
web: www.cairnlodge.co.uk

This twin-turreted country house makes a delightful boutique hotel with its wooded grounds close to Gleneagles and dozens of golf courses. The Cairn Bar offers meals throughout the day but the Capercaillie restaurant, with its new, extensive upgrade is the main dining focus here. Comfortable seating, helpful staff, bold décor and silver service set the tone. Modern dishes include starters of smoked

continued on page 595

Andrew Fairlie @ Gleneagles

AUCHTERARDER MAP 21 NN91

Modern French

Dramatic setting, inspired food

☎ 01764 694267 PH3 1NF
e-mail: andrew.fairlie@gleneagles.com
web: www.gleneagles.com

Chef: Andrew Fairlie
Owners: Andrew Fairlie
Times: 7-10, Closed 3 wks Jan, Sun, Closed L all week, D Sun
Prices: Starter £19.50, Main £29.50, Dessert £11, Coffee £2.50, Min/Water £3, Service optional
Wine: 230 bottles over £20, 8 by the glass (£7-£18)
Notes: Tasting Menu £80, Vegetarian available, Dress Restrictions, Smart casual
Seats: 45
Smoking: N/Sm in restaurant, Air con
Children: Min 12 yrs
Directions: Take 'Gleneagles' exit from A9, continue for 1m
Parking: 300

This is fine dining through and through! Set between this luxurious, world-famous golfing hotel's main bar and Strathearn Restaurant, Andrew Fairlie's is an independent business and dinner-only affair that attracts a well-heeled, five-star international clientele. A small bar leads through to the intimate, elegant, high-ceiling dining room that provides the ultimate in discerning interior design. Bold in design with black walls hung with bespoke artworks by Archie Forrest, floor-to-ceiling raw silk drapes and opulent fabrics deliver that expected wow factor. Well-spaced, elegantly-appointed tables with dramatic, strategically placed down-lighters that deliver pools of illumination onto the crisp tableware, and comfortable seating are set to a subtle jazz backing track that helps maintain a smooth buzz to proceedings. The service is pin-sharp and highly professional - the anticipation of the diner's needs is supreme.

The menu and serious wine lists are lavish and user-friendly affairs, their presentation further echoing the décor and sense of occasion. One of Scotland's leading chefs, Andrew Fairlie's modern approach comes underpinned by a classical French theme (classics given a modern makeover) and celebrates the union of dazzling technique and top-notch ingredients. The style is complex and bold, the emphasis on flavour with dishes delivered dressed to thrill. Menus are crisply scripted and come brimful of luxury items, the carte bolstered by a menu dégustation (both fixed-price affairs) that seduce with an agony of choice. Think home-smoked lobster with lime and herb butter, a fillet of John Dory paired with a pea and truffle sauce, braised oxtail Rossini or perhaps a daube of beef served with red onion and marjoram confit, and don't overlook the 'textures of chocolate' dessert with its four different elements, if it finds a place on the menu. Andrew is AA Chefs' Chef 2006-2007 (see page 11).

AUCHTERARDER *continued* MAP 21 NN91

duck breast salad with citrus salsa and main courses of guinea fowl with creamed Savoy cabbage and bacon. For dessert, try glazed poached pear with chocolate sauce and blueberry ice cream.

Times: 12-2/6-9.30 **Rooms:** 10 (10 en suite) ★★ HL **Directions:** From A9 take A824 (Auchterarder). Hotel at S end of town; on road to Gleneagles

Strathearn at Gleneagles

Classic NOTABLE WINE LIST

Classic dining where service is as memorable as the food

☎ 01764 694270 PH3 1NF
e-mail: resort.sales@gleneagles.com
web: www.gleneagles.com

There is only one Gleneagles, but there are several options when it comes to dining. The Strathearn remains a bastion of classical elegance and traditional values. The space is massive with high ceilings and pillars in the grand ballroom style. Formal service is provided by a full brigade in the good old fashioned way, but is absolutely delightful and in no way stuffy. The seasonal menu offers a blend of classical dishes and modern presentation. Take smoked haddock and chive velouté, followed by Highland venison with chestnut dauphinoise, pumpkin and port sauce, for example, with Tamarina chocolate and whisky fondant with clotted ice cream to finish.
Notable Wine List: Classic, well-constructed wine list with a comprehensive offering and depth of vintages.

Chef: Colin Bussey **Owners:** Diageo **Times:** 12.30-2.30/7-10, Closed L Mon-Sat **Prices:** Fixed L £35, Fixed D £47, Coffee £3.95, Service optional **Wine:** 100% bottles over £20, 15 by the glass (£8-£14) **Notes:** Fixed L 3 courses, Vegetarian available, Dress Restrictions, Smart casual, Civ Wed 250 **Seats:** 322 **Smoking:** N/Sm in restaurant **Children:** Menu, Portions **Rooms:** 269 (269 en suite) ★★★★★ **Directions:** Just off A9, well signed. Between Stirling and Perth **Parking:** 1000

COMRIE MAP 21 NN72

Royal Hotel

Traditional British

Traditional food in an elegant environment

☎ 01764 679200 Melville Square PH6 2DN
e-mail: reception@royalhotel.co.uk
web: www.royalhotel.co.uk

The traditional façade of this 18th-century coaching inn belies the style and elegance within. Polished-wood floors, stylish soft furnishings, log fires and antique pieces set the scene, and there's a snug-style bar, colonial-feel conservatory brasserie and more traditional dining room. Traditional Scottish fare is the style, focusing on fresh local produce with skilful preparation. Dishes from a sample menu include haggis hash brown starter, Highland venison steak on roasted vegetables, braised oxtail stew and dumplings, or pan-fried salmon steak with a basil pesto crust.

Royal Hotel

Chef: David Milsom **Owners:** The Milsom Family **Times:** 12-2/6.30-9 **Prices:** Starter £5.30-£8.25, Main £8.50-£17.50, Dessert £4.25-£4.50, Coffee £2, Min/Water £4.50, Service optional **Wine:** 58 bottles over £20, 51 bottles under £20, 4 by the glass (£2.30-£4.50) **Notes:** Vegetarian available **Seats:** 60 **Smoking:** N/Sm in restaurant **Children:** Menu, Portions **Rooms:** 11 (11 en suite) ★★★ HL **Directions:** In main square, 7m from Crieff, on A85 **Parking:** 25

CRIEFF MAP 21 NN82

The Bank Restaurant

British, French

Original features and classic cuisine

☎ 01764 656575 32 High St PH7 3BS
e-mail: mail@thebankrestaurant.co.uk
web: www.thebankrestaurant.co.uk

As the name suggests, this restaurant had a former existence as a banking hall. It is found in an ornate building designed by Washington Brown, who also designed the Caledonian Hotel in Edinburgh. Today, the original wood panelling and cornices can still be seen in the charming restaurant. Diners can enjoy classical French-influenced cuisine in a relaxed and friendly environment. Typical dishes include a main course of rump of Borders lamb with mash, fine beans and a red wine gravy.

Chef: Bill McGuigan **Owners:** Mr B & Mrs L McGuigan **Times:** 12-1.30/7-9.30, Closed 25-26 Dec, 2 wks mid Jan, Mon/Sun **Prices:** Starter £3.50-£6.95, Main £9.95-£15.95, Dessert £3.95-£4.50, Coffee £2, Min/Water £3.25, Service included **Wine:** 31 bottles over £20, 31 bottles under £20, 6 by the glass (£3.10) **Seats:** 22 **Smoking:** N/Sm in restaurant, Air con **Children:** Portions **Directions:** Telephone for directions **Parking:** Parking available 150 yds

DUNKELD MAP 21 NO04

Kinnaird

see below

KILLIECRANKIE MAP 23 NN96

Killiecrankie House Hotel

Modern Scottish NOTABLE WINE LIST

Modern cooking in a delightful country-house hotel

☎ 01796 473220 PH16 5LG
e-mail: enquiries@killiecrankiehotel.co.uk
web: www.killiecrankiehotel.co.uk

A relaxing small country hotel, built as a dower house in 1840, and set in mature landscaped gardens overlooking the River Garry and the Pass of Killiecrankie. Enthusiastically run, the hotel maintains consistently high standards and a sound reputation for accomplished modern Scottish cooking draws a loyal crowd of local diners. The short fixed-price dinner menu changes daily and is built around fresh local produce including herbs and vegetables from the kitchen garden. Typically, begin with seared scallops with orange and vanilla jus, follow with lamb stuffed with tomato and mint mousse, served with a Madeira jus, and finish with vanilla rice pudding. The interesting wine list deserves close study. **Notable Wine List:** Proprietor Tim Waters' knowledge and passion from his previous background as head buyer for Oddbins shines through on this impressive wine list, packed full of interest, personal tasting notes and introductions to each region.

continued

Chef: Mark Easton **Owners:** Mr & Mrs Waters **Times:** 7-11, Closed Jan-Feb, Closed L all week **Prices:** Fixed D fr £28, Starter £6, Main £16, Dessert £6, Coffee £3.50, Min/Water £3.60, Service optional, Group min 6 service 10% **Wine:** 116 bottles over £20, 34 bottles under £20, 4 by the glass (£3.80-£4.50) **Notes:** Vegetarian available, Dress Restrictions, No shorts **Seats:** 30, Pr/dining room 12 **Smoking:** N/Sm in restaurant **Children:** Min 9 yrs, Menu, Portions **Directions:** From A9 take B8079 N of Killiecrankie, hotel is 3m on right, just past village signpost **Parking:** 20

KINCLAVEN MAP 21 NO13

Ballathie House Hotel

Modern Scottish V

Romantic baronial Tayside hotel showcasing local produce

☎ 01250 883268 PH1 4QN
e-mail: email@ballathiehousehotel.com
web: www.ballathiehousehotel.com

continued

Kinnaird

DUNKELD MAP 21 NO04

Modern British

Exquisite country house in remote setting serving innovative food

☎ 01796 482440 Kinnaird Estate PH8 0LB
e-mail: enquiry@kinnairdestate.com
web: www.kinnairdestate.com

An imposing Edwardian baronial mansion on a grand scale, Kinnaird is set in breathtaking countryside in a magnificent 9,000-acre estate overlooking the River Tay valley. A haven of relaxed and civilised charm, it oozes all the lavish trappings of a fine country-house hotel, complete with rare antiques, an impressive collection of art and inviting sitting rooms with deep-cushioned sofas and open fires. The dining room is quite stunning, with original Italianate frescoed walls, marble fireplace, ornate chandelier and breathtaking views through its picture windows. Despite the grandeur, the formality of the service and the obligatory jacket and tie at dinner, the mood is surprisingly unstuffy, tranquil and relaxed. The food is creative, imaginative and exciting to match the surroundings. Classically-based cooking with modern twists deliver on a compact, inspirational menu using the very best of locally-sourced produce from the abundant Scottish larder. There's good emphasis on texture variation and fresh, vibrant, clean flavours. Precision, high skill and accuracy abound in dishes like pot-roasted turbot teamed with ceps, shallots, armandine potatoes and pan juices with sherry vinegar and chives, and to finish, perhaps a vanilla pyramid with a soft sea salt caramel centre, passionfruit sorbet and white chocolate ice cream. An excellent wine list completes the upbeat package.

Chef: Trevor Brooks **Owners:** Mrs C Ward **Times:** 12-1.45/7-9.30 **Prices:** Fixed L £15-£20, Fixed D £55-£60, Coffee £3, Service optional **Wine:** 300 bottles over £20, 3 bottles under £20, 8 by the glass (£4-£10) **Notes:** Vegetarian available, Jacket & tie D, Civ Wed 45 **Seats:** 35, Pr/dining room 20 **Smoking:** N/Sm in restaurant **Rooms:** 9 (9 en suite) ★★★★ **Directions:** From A9 N take B898 for 4.5m. Hotel on right **Parking:** 15

This extensive Victorian shooting lodge was completed around 1850. The friendly and helpful service somehow reflects that it remained a private house until 1970. The traditionally decorated dining room has excellent views across the estate across the tree-lined lawns and down to the River Tay. Ingredients for the traditional menus are either home grown on the estate or Scottish. To start expect delicious roasted squab with truffled white beans and an onion soubise or cured local salmon with dill, lemon and juniper. Main courses include a rack and crusted loin of Perthshire lamb with gratinated potatoes, ratatouille and basil jus. A good selection cheese and excellent wine list complete the offering.

Chef: Kevin MacGillivray **Owners:** Ballathie House Hotel Ltd **Times:** 12.30-2/7-9 **Prices:** Fixed L £16.50, Fixed D fr £39, Coffee £2.75, Min/Water £3, Service optional **Notes:** Daily changing house menu, Vegetarian menu, Dress Restrictions, Jacket and tie preferred, no jeans/T-shirts, Civ Wed 75 **Seats:** 70, Pr/dining room 32 **Smoking:** N/Sm in restaurant **Children:** Min 12 yrs, Portions **Rooms:** 42 (42 en suite) ★★★ CHH **Directions:** From A9 take Luncanty/Stanley exit, follow the B9099 through Stanley, follow signs for Ballathie after 0.5m **Parking:** 100

KINLOCH RANNOCH MAP 23 NN65

Dunalastair Hotel

Traditional British NEW

Accomplished cuisine in traditional Highland hotel with a Scottish baronial feel

☎ 01882 632323 PH16 5PW
e-mail: info@dunalastair.co.uk
web: www.dunalastair.co.uk

Undergoing major redevelopment, this traditional Highland hotel was built as a retreat for soldiers. The magnificent wood-panelled Schiehallion restaurant, complete with roaring log fire and lighting made from red deer antlers, has a Scottish baronial feel. The kitchen adds a modern touch to traditional dishes making use of excellent Scottish ingredients. The cooking and presentation are beautiful in their simplicity with a great balance of flavours and no superfluous elements. Try corn-fed chicken supreme stuffed with leeks, rösti potato and thyme reduction, or grilled halibut fillet on pea and lime risotto with glazed asparagus spears.

Chef: Kevin Easingwood **Owners:** R Gilmour **Times:** 12-2.30/6.30-9 **Prices:** Fixed L £9.95-£17.95, Fixed D £27.50-£32.50, Starter £2.95-£5.95, Main £10.95-£17.95, Dessert £3.50-£5, Coffee £1.40, Min/Water £2 **Wine:** 45 bottles over £20, 25 bottles under £20, 8 by the glass (£2.95-£5.95) **Notes:** Sun L 3 courses £13.95, Vegetarian available, Civ Wed 70 **Seats:** 70, Pr/dining room 20 **Smoking:** N/Sm in restaurant **Children:** Portions **Rooms:** 28 (28 en suite) ★★★ HL **Directions:** From Pitlochry N, take B8019 to Tummel Bridge then B846 to Kinloch Rannoch **Parking:** 50

PERTH MAP 21 NO12

Acanthus Restaurant

British

Enjoyable seasonal cooking in Victorian dining room

☎ 01738 622451 Parklands Hotel,
St Leonards Bank PH2 8EB
e-mail: info@acanthusrestaurant.com
web: www.acanthusrestaurant.com

continued

This one-time home of the Lord Provost has great views across the South Inch. The stylish, Victorian Acanthus Restaurant is the fine dining option. Formal service keeps diners supplied with well-prepared dishes based on local and seasonal ingredients. There's good use of game such as the roast wood pigeon with rabbit beignet, white bean broth and garlic gnocchi, or the celeriac velouté. Inverurie beef is served with breaded ox tongue and Perthshire lamb with kidney merguez. Good rich flavours are finished off with stylish desserts like lemon chiboust.

Chef: Graeme Pallister **Owners:** Scott and Penny Edwards **Times:** 7-9, Closed 26th Dec, 1st & 2nd Jan, Sun-Tue, Closed L Wed-Sat **Prices:** Fixed D £27.95, Service optional, Group min 8 service 8% **Wine:** 30 bottles over £20, 20 bottles under £20, 6 by the glass **Notes:** Dress Restrictions, Smart casual, no shorts or jeans, Civ Wed 30 **Seats:** 36, Pr/dining room 22 **Smoking:** N/Sm in restaurant **Children:** Menu, Portions **Rooms:** 14 (14 en suite) ★★★ HL **Directions:** Adjacent to Perth station, overlooking South Inch Park **Parking:** 25

Deans@Let's Eat

Modern

Vibrant cooking at a quirky bistro

☎ 01738 643377 77/79 Kinnoull St PH1 5EZ
e-mail: enquiries@letseatperth.co.uk
web: www.dean@letseatperth.co.uk

Now owned by a husband-and-wife team, this lively bistro looks set for great things. Housed in a former theatre, it's a cosy and informal venue, decorated in warm colours and lined with bookcases crammed with cookery books. The locals know a good thing when they see it, so book ahead to guarantee your chance to sample modern Scottish cuisine at its best. Kick off with pork and parsley terrine perhaps or warm pigeon salad with fried herb gnocchi and red wine juices, before tucking into the likes of peppered medallions of Blairgowrie beef fillet with white beans, winter roots and truffle cream.

Chef: Willie Deans, Simon Lannan **Owners:** Mr & Mrs W Deans **Times:** 12-2/6.30-9.45, Closed 1 wk Jan, 1 wk summer, Sun-Mon **Prices:** Fixed L £16-£20, Fixed D £22.50-£32.50, Starter £3.75-£7.50, Main £13.75-£18.95, Dessert £5-£6, Coffee £2, Service optional **Wine:** 27 bottles over £20, 16 bottles under £20, 4 by the glass (£3.25-£4.05) **Notes:** Vegetarian available **Seats:** 65 **Smoking:** N/Sm in restaurant **Children:** Portions **Directions:** On corner of Kinnoull Street & Atholl Street, close to North Inch **Parking:** Multi storey car park (300 yds)

Scotland

PERTH *continued* MAP 21 NO12

Huntingtower Hotel

Traditional

Scottish cuisine in wonderful setting

☎ 01738 583771 Crieff Rd PH1 3JT
e-mail: reservations@huntingtowerhotel.co.uk
web: www.huntingtowerhotel.co.uk

Originally built as a mill owner's house in 1892, this is now a country-house hotel, set in 6 acres of magnificent landscaped gardens. Traditional décor and period features are in keeping with the style of the hotel, where the conservatory is used for lunch and the traditional oak-panelled dining room for dinner. Scottish cuisine with a French twist sees dishes like Arbroath smokie soup to start. Main courses might feature roast loin of lamb with stuffed courgettes, aubergine confit, fondant potato and rosemary sauce.

Chef: Bill McNicoll **Owners:** J A Brown & Colin Paton **Times:** 12-2/6-9.30 **Prices:** Fixed L £22-£30, Fixed D £22-£38, Starter £5-£10, Main £14-£19, Dessert £6-£7, Coffee £3.25, Min/Water £5, Service optional **Wine:** 12 bottles over £20, 8 bottles under £20, 4 by the glass (£3.50-£4.75) **Notes:** Civ Wed 200 **Seats:** 70, Pr/dining room 30 **Smoking:** N/Sm in restaurant **Children:** Menu, Portions **Rooms:** 34 (34 en suite) ★★★ **Directions:** 10 minutes from Perth on A85 towards Crieff **Parking:** 200

Murrayshall Country House Hotel

British, French

Scottish dining in country-house golfing destination

☎ 01738 551171 New Scone PH2 7PH
e-mail: lin.murrayshall@virgin.net
web: www.murrayshall.com

This impressive country-house hotel has two beautiful golf courses and views of the Grampian Hills beyond. Inside, the bar serves meals throughout the day whilst the Old Masters restaurant with its well-spaced tables offers more sophisticated fare in the evenings. There's a relaxed, familiar atmosphere here helped by attentive staff. Enjoy simply presented modern Scottish dishes in the refined surroundings. Start with seared Oban scallops with celeriac purée before a main course of succulent duck breast with blueberry jus and rösti potato. Finish with something different like the dark chocolate and dolcelatte fondant with pear and thyme sorbet or the warm vanilla Cape gooseberry risotto with coconut ice cream.

Times: 12-2.30/7-9.45, Closed 26 Dec, Closed L Sat **Rooms:** 41 (41 en suite) ★★★ HL **Directions:** From Perth A94 (Coupar Angus) turn right signed Murrayshall before New Scone

63 Tay Street

British

Chic city dining in Tayside

☎ 01738 441451 63 Tay St PH2 8NN
e-mail: www.63taystreet.co.uk

Accessed via a flight of steps next door to Perth's council offices, the restaurant itself was an office until five years ago, when it was converted by the present owners. Now a smart city dining room, it's a popular haunt for lunch or dinner with friendly staff. Modern Scottish cooking provides a showcase for local produce in dishes like a starter of crab spaghetti with chilli, ginger and coriander. Try a traditional-sounding main course of ox faggot with mash, Savoy cabbage and onion jus, but keep one eye on dessert, as you wouldn't want to miss the chocolate cheesecake with chocolate sauce!

Chef: Jeremy Wares **Owners:** Shona & Jeremy Wares **Times:** 12-2/6.30-9, Closed 1st 2 wk Jan, last wk Jun, 1st wk Jul, Sun, Mon **Prices:** Fixed L £12.95, Fixed D £20.95, Starter £5.95, Main £15.50-£18.50, Dessert £5.50, Coffee £2.25, Min/Water £3, Group min 20 service 10% **Wine:** 60 bottles over £20, 40 bottles under £20, 12 by the glass (£3-£7) **Notes:** Vegetarian available **Seats:** 32 **Smoking:** N/Sm in restaurant **Children:** Portions **Directions:** On the Tay River in centre of Perth **Parking:** On Street

PITLOCHRY MAP 23 NN95

Donavourd House

International

Sound cooking in attractive country house with wonderful views

☎ 01796 472100 PH16 5JS
e-mail: reservations@donavourdhousehotel.co.uk
web: www.donavourdhousehotel.co.uk

Once home to the local laird, this attractive country house sits in its own gardens in a quiet, elevated location overlooking Strathtummel. Decorated in a period style, the dining room has crisp linen and fine glassware, which complements the traditional, classic cooking here. A short menu boasts simple dishes with an emphasis on local produce. A starter of lightly dressed salad greens topped with crumbled stilton, toasted walnuts and sliced pears may be followed by pan-seared breast of duck served with roasted aubergine, chickpea and rice medley and pomegranate molasses sauce.

Times: 6.30-8.30, Closed Jan, Feb, Closed L all week **Rooms:** 9 (9 en suite) ★★ HL **Directions:** Southbound on main rd from Pitlochry, before entrance to A9 follow signs to hotel. Take Pitlochry exit off A6 northbound, turn right under railway bridge and follow signs

Green Park Hotel

British, French

Fine cuisine in a lochside country-house hotel

☎ 01796 473248 Clunie Bridge Rd PH16 5JY
e-mail: bookings@thegreenpark.co.uk
web: www.thegreenpark.co.uk

This family-run country-house hotel enjoys an enviable location on the shore of Loch Faskally. The traditional dining room looks out over gardens towards the loch, providing a relaxing setting for some fine cuisine. The menu makes the most of local and specialist produce and features home-grown seasonal herbs and salads. Game terrine might feature as a starter, with traditional mains such as Scottish sirloin steak or more adventurous combinations like confit of duck topped with a parmesan cheese and oat crust, served with a rich creamy bean and chorizo sausage stew.

Chef: Chris Tamblin **Owners:** Green Park Ltd **Times:** 12-2/6.30-8.30, Closed L all week (ex residents) **Prices:** Fixed D £21, Min/Water £3.20, Service optional **Wine:** 62 bottles over £20, 5 bottles under £20, 6 by the glass (£2.60) **Notes:** Coffee incl, Fixed L £5-15, Vegetarian available, Dress Restrictions, Reasonably smart dress **Seats:** 100 **Smoking:** N/Sm in restaurant **Children:** Menu, Portions **Rooms:** 39 (39 en suite) ★★★ CHH **Directions:** Off A9 at Pitlochry, follow signs **Parking:** 52

Pine Trees Hotel

Modern NEW

Honest food in elegant hotel

☎ 01796 472121 Strathview Ter PH16 5QR
e-mail: info@pinetreeshotel.co.uk
web: www.pinetreeshotel.co.uk

Set within spacious grounds on the edge of the Victorian spa town of Pitlochry, this elegant hotel has a formal dining room overlooking the attractive gardens. The Scottish-influenced food is cooked with expertise and presented with flair, with friendly front-of-house staff clearly taking a pride in their work. The cooking here is confident and simple dishes generate bold flavours: a good country-style chicken and duck liver paté served with brioche and carefully dressed salad, a grilled loin of lamb on a bed of spinach and a chocolate truffle mousse.

Times: 12/6.30, Closed L Mon-Sat **Rooms:** 20 (20 en suite) ★★★ CHH **Directions:** N through Pitlochry to far end of town, turn R into Larchwood Road. Hotel on L just below golf course.

ST FILLANS MAP 20 NN62

The Four Seasons Hotel

Modern European

Breathtaking scenery and bold cuisine

☎ 01764 685333 Loch Earn PH6 2NF
e-mail: info@thefourseasonshotel.co.uk
web: www.thefourseasonshotel.co.uk

Tucked away beneath steeply forested hills on the edge of Loch Earn, this hotel has a range of comfortable lounges, log fires and stunning views where you really can appreciate the seasons throughout the year. Originally built in the early 1800s for the manager of the limekilns, it was also a schoolmaster's house before becoming a hotel. The lochside Meall Reamhar fine-dining restaurant serves up modern Scottish and European dishes based on great Scottish produce. Bold flavours and imaginative combinations produce starters like millefeuille of langoustine and avocado with sorrel and lemon crème fraîche. Soup or sorbet precede main courses like tenderloin of Ayrshire pork with herb and sesame crust, skirlie, Arran mustard and peppercorn cream.

Chef: Peter Woods **Owners:** Andrew Low **Times:** 12-2.30/6-9.30, Closed Jan-Feb **Prices:** Fixed D £32, Min/Water £3.20, Group **Wine:** 71 bottles over £20, 29 bottles under £20, 416 by the glass (£3.75) **Notes:** Coffee incl, Fixed D 4 courses, Vegetarian available, Civ Wed 100 **Seats:** 60, Pr/dining room 20 **Smoking:** N/Sm in restaurant **Children:** Menu, Portions **Rooms:** 18 (18 en suite) ★★★ **Directions:** From Perth take A85 W, through Crieff & Comrie. Hotel at west end of village **Parking:** 30

SPITTAL OF GLENSHEE MAP 23 NO17

Dalmunzie House Hotel

Traditional, British

Cooking worthy of the laird in a highland mansion

☎ 01250 885224 PH10 7QG
e-mail: reservations@dalmunzie.com
web: www.dalmunzie.com

A former Highland laird's mansion, complete with turrets, set on an estate of 6,500 acres. Within easy reach of the ski slopes at Glenshee, this could be the perfect destination after a hard day on the piste. The house is furnished with antiques and fires burn in the original fireplaces. The spacious dining room has well-appointed tables and you can really enjoy the fine dining experience here, or have a more relaxed bite in the bar. Top-quality ingredients are sourced for dishes with classic British influences like a starter of smoked salmon terrine or pavé of smoked Scottish sea trout with horseradish crème fraîche and caper berries. Roast rack of three-bone lamb with a herb crust comes beautifully tender and well presented with wilted greens, finished with a delicate rosemary jus.

Chef: Michelle Mitten **Owners:** Scott & Brianna Poole **Times:** 12-2.30/7-9, Closed 1-28 Dec **Prices:** Fixed D £36, Coffee £2, Min/Water £3, Service included **Wine:** 31 bottles over £20, 37 bottles under £20, 4 by the glass (£3-£3.50) **Notes:** Fixed D 4 courses, Vegetarian available, Dress Restrictions, Smart casual, jacket & tie preferred, Civ Wed 70 **Seats:** 40, Pr/dining room 18 **Smoking:** N/Sm in restaurant **Children:** Portions **Rooms:** 19 (16 en suite) ★★ **Directions:** 15m S of Braemar on A93 at the Spittal of Glenshee **Parking:** 40

RENFREWSHIRE

HOWWOOD MAP 20 NS36

Bowfield Hotel & Country Club

Modern

Stylish modern cooking in old world surroundings

☎ 01505 705225 PA9 1DZ
e-mail: enquiries@bowfield.co.uk
web: www.bowfieldcountryclub.co.uk

Set in a 17th-century bleaching mill, this restaurant oozes character. The atmosphere is very friendly and the staff are keen to please. The cooking style is complex but this is belied by the simple, clear presentation, and tasting the food reveals all the skill and effort behind the preparation of ingredients. Seasonal produce is carefully used and there are lots of Scottish elements, with an emphasis on local fish, game and shellfish. Sea-fresh sweet scallops, perfectly seared and complemented by a beurre blanc and small nest of home-made pasta make for an impressive starter. Seared salmon on parmesan risotto with asparagus may not sound ground-breaking, but the cooking and presentation make this another smash hit.

Chef: Ronnie McAdam **Owners:** Stonefield Castle Group **Times:** 6.30-9, Closed L all week **Prices:** Starter £4.95-£7.50, Main £12.50-£22.50, Dessert £4.50-£5.95, Coffee £2.50, Min/Water £2.50, Service optional **Wine:** 40 bottles over £20, 20 bottles under £20, 10 by the glass (£3.05-£7.50) **Notes:** Fixed 4 courses £25 parties 8+, Dress Restrictions, Smart casual **Seats:** 40, Pr/dining room 20 **Smoking:** N/Sm in restaurant **Children:** Menu, Portions **Rooms:** 23 (23 en suite) ★★★ HL **Directions:** From M8. Take A737 (Irvine Rd), exit at Howwood, take 2nd right up country lane, turn right at top of hill **Parking:** 100

Scotland

Scotland

RENFREWSHIRE, EAST

UPLAWMOOR MAP 10 NS45

Uplawmoor Hotel

Modern Scottish

Friendly inn serving traditional and modern Scottish cuisine

☎ 01505 850565 Neilston Rd G78 4AF
e-mail: enquiries@uplawmoor.co.uk
web: www.uplawmoor.co.uk

An old coaching inn dating back to 1750, this former smugglers' haunt was extended in 1958 by architect James Gray, who added the Charles Rennie Mackintosh-inspired exterior. Subtle lighting and rich furnishings provide a cosy atmosphere, with polished wooden tables and beams giving a rustic feel. Although the simple, traditional bar menu ticks all the boxes, it's the restaurant menu that really sets this place apart. The kitchen sources as much produce from the region as possible for dishes like king scallops, black pudding, crispy bacon and balsamic dressing, fillet steak on a haggis croûton, flambéed in whisky and sticky date pudding with butterscotch sauce.

Chef: Paul Brady **Owners:** Stuart & Emma Peacock **Times:** 6-9.30, Closed 26 Dec, 1 Jan, Closed L all week **Prices:** Fixed L fr £16, Fixed D fr £21, Starter £3.75-£8.50, Main £10.50-£19.50, Dessert £4.50, Coffee £2.50, Min/Water £2.50, Service optional **Wine:** 4 bottles over £20, 18 bottles under £20, 8 by the glass (£2.95-£3.50) **Notes:** Vegetarian available, Dress Restrictions, Smart casual **Seats:** 30 **Smoking:** N/Sm in restaurant **Children:** Min 12 yrs, Menu, Portions **Rooms:** 14 (14 en suite) ★★ HL **Directions:** From Glasgow follow M8 & M77 to junct 2, follow signs for Barrhead & Irvine A736. 5m past Barrhead take village road left signposted to Uplawmoor **Parking:** 38

SCOTTISH BORDERS

JEDBURGH MAP 21 NT62

Jedforest Hotel

French, European

Imaginative cuisine in friendly hotel restaurant

☎ 01835 840222 Camptown TD8 6PJ
e-mail: info@jedforesthotel.com
web: www.jedforesthotel.com

A family-owned Victorian hunting lodge set in 35 acres in the Scottish Borders. The comfortable restaurant has magnificent views and service is friendly and attentive. The emphasis is on Scottish cuisine with French influences, using locally sourced ingredients cooked with flair. Starters might feature asparagus salad with Serrano ham, poached egg and hollandaise sauce. Main courses include the likes of oven-roasted duck breast with potato croquette and orange sauce. For dessert try an interesting combination like yogurt mousse with pineapple compôte and cacao sauce.

Times: 12-2/6.30-9 **Rooms:** 12 (12 en suite) ★★★ HL **Directions:** Just off A68, 3m S of Jedburgh

KELSO MAP 21 NT73

The Roxburghe Hotel

Traditional Scottish

Traditional sporting destination with fine Scottish dining and impressive wine list

☎ 01573 450331 TD5 8JZ
e-mail: hotel@roxburghe.net
web: www.roxburghe.net

Owned by the Duke of Roxburghe, this imposing Jacobean mansion has 500 acres of mature wood and parkland incorporating a championship golf course. The interior is replete with open log fires, high vaulted ceilings and rich and robust fabrics and furnishings. The dining room has quality table appointments and settings with discreet and efficient service. The skilful kitchen uses many ingredients from the estate and provides diners with traditional Scottish starters of confit duck ravioli flavoured with chilli and ginger. Main courses might include pan-fried sea bass with Bashit neeps and wild mushrooms. For dessert, there's butterscotch and pistachio cheesecake with vanilla ice cream.

Times: 12.30-2/7.30-9.45 **Rooms:** 22 (22 en suite) ★★★ HL **Directions:** From A68, 1m N of Jedburgh, take A698 for 5m to Heiton

One Rosette

Excellent local restaurants serving food prepared with care, understanding and skill, using good quality ingredients. These restaurants stand out in their local area.

Two Rosettes

The best local restaurants, which aim for and achieve higher standards, better consistency and where a greater precision is apparent in the cooking. There will be obvious attention to the selection of quality ingredients.

MELROSE MAP 21 NT53

Burt's Hotel

Modern Scottish

Contemporary cooking in a sophisticated setting

☎ 01896 822285 The Square TD6 9PL
e-mail: burtshotel@aol.com
web: www.burtshotel.co.uk

The white painted façade and colourful window boxes make a striking first impression at this family-run hotel in the town's market square. Its hospitality is a byword locally, and the cheerful lounge bar where good pub food can be enjoyed is friendly and welcoming. Dining moves up several notches in the sophisticated restaurant, where a contemporary menu shows an appreciation of straightforward flavours and textures. You might find fillet of sea bass with fennel risotto cake, buttered spinach and vermouth cream, or pan-roasted saddle of venison, plus a choice of grills that boast properly matured Scottish lamb and beef. A terrific cheeseboard offers no fewer than eight speciality products.

Chef: Trevor Williams **Owners:** The Henderson Family **Times:** 12-2/7-9, Closed 26 Dec, 3-5 Jan **Prices:** Fixed L fr £24.75, Fixed D fr £31.75, Coffee £2, Min/Water £3, Service optional **Wine:** 40 bottles over £20, 40 bottles under £20, 8 by the glass (£2.95-£4.60) **Notes:** Fixed L 3 courses, Dress Restrictions, Jacket & tie preferred **Seats:** 50, Pr/dining room 25 **Smoking:** N/Sm in restaurant **Children:** Min 10 yrs, Portions **Rooms:** 20 (20 en suite) ★★★ HL **Directions:** Town centre in Market Sq **Parking:** 40

PEEBLES MAP 21 NT24

Castle Venlaw Hotel

Traditional British

Classical dining in a romantic environment

☎ 01721 720384 Edinburgh Rd EH45 8QG
e-mail: stay@venlaw.co.uk
web: www.venlaw.co.uk

A family-owned 18th-century castle-style hotel in the scenic Borders, overlooking the historic town of Peebles. The hotel was built in 1782 on the site of Old Smithfield Castle. The restaurant is elegant with tall windows, an ornamental fireplace and corniced ceiling; there is also a cosy library bar. Traditional British and Scottish fixed-price menus are given a boost with the occasional Mediterranean influence. Technical skills are demonstrated in accomplished cooking from the kitchen team who deliver dishes that are well balanced and flavoured. House specialities include a starter like pan-fried fillet of red snapper with creamy chive potato salad, red pepper essence and crispy vegetables,

continued

with roast rack of Borders lamb, chargrilled Mediterranean vegetables, fondant potatoes and redcurrant jus to follow. Service is friendly and obliging, while the wine list is thoughtfully prepared and has good tasting notes.

Chef: David Harrison **Owners:** Mr & Mrs J Sloggie **Times:** 12-2.30/7-9 **Prices:** Fixed D £28.50-£32, Coffee £2.25, Min/Water £3, Service optional **Wine:** 75% bottles over £20, 25% bottles under £20, 6 by the glass (£3.50-£7.50) **Notes:** Vegetarian available, Dress Restrictions, Smart casual, Civ Wed 35 **Seats:** 35, Pr/dining room 30 **Smoking:** N/Sm in restaurant **Children:** Min 5 yrs, Menu, Portions **Rooms:** 12 (12 en suite) ★★★ CHH **Directions:** From Peebles at east end of High Street, turn left at rdbt signed A703 to Edinburgh. After 0.75m hotel is signed on right **Parking:** 25

Cringletie House

Modern British V

Enjoyable Scottish dining in Baronial surroundings

☎ 01721 725750 Edinburgh Rd EH45 8PL
e-mail: enquiries@cringletie.com
web: www.cringletie.com

Despite its baronial bearing, this elegant former shooting lodge, with its oak floors, staircases and painted ornamental ceilings retains the warmth of a family home. Most rooms have wonderful views over the countryside including the stately dining room. Expect friendly, well-informed staff to serve modern dishes with distinct Scottish influences based on excellent local produce like Buccleuch beef and hand-dived North Sea scallops. Start with roasted Borders pigeon with smoked garlic potato purée or warm, poached ox tongue with lentils, Madeira and salsa verde and follow with poached and roasted guinea fowl with foie gras choux farcie and artichoke purée. Caramelised lemon tart brings the meal to a satisfying conclusion. An interesting vegetarian menu is offered too.

Chef: Paul Hart **Owners:** Jacob & Johanna van Houdt **Times:** 12-2/6.30-8.30, Closed Jan **Prices:** Fixed L £15, Fixed D £39.50, Coffee £2.50, Min/Water £2.75, Service optional **Wine:** 100 bottles over £20, 22 bottles under £20, 4 by the glass (£4.75) **Notes:** Vegetarian menu, Dress Restrictions, Smart/casual no jeans, no trainers, Civ Wed 45 **Seats:** 60, Pr/dining room 12 **Smoking:** N/Sm in restaurant **Children:** Portions **Rooms:** 14 (14 en suite) ★★★★ HL **Directions:** 2.5m N of Peebles on A703 **Parking:** 30

ST BOSWELLS MAP 21 NT53

Dryburgh Abbey Hotel

Modern Scottish

Scottish cuisine in the breathtaking Borders countryside

☎ 01835 822261 TD6 0RQ
e-mail: enquires@dryburgh.co.uk
web: www.dryburgh.co.uk

This red-stone baronial mansion sits on the banks of the Tweed beside Dryburgh Abbey, the last resting place of Sir Walter Scott. It's an imposing property with a well-earned reputation for hospitality and good food. Enjoy a pre-dinner drink in the newly refurbished lounge, and then move through to the spacious restaurant, which offers a new menu of traditional Scottish dishes every day. Hot smoked trout fillet makes a tempting starter, served with horseradish cream and chive oil, while mains might include roast loin of pork with sage mash and apple compôte, or chargrilled medallions of Buccleuch beef fillet with confit of tomato and basil hollandaise.

continued

ST BOSWELLS *continued* MAP 21 NT53

Chef: Scott Hume & Craig Riddell **Owners:** The Grose Family **Times:** 12-2/7-9.15, Closed L Mon-Sat **Prices:** Fixed D £32.50, Coffee £1.95, Min/Water £3.75, Service included **Wine:** 25 bottles over £20, 30 bottles under £20, 10 by the glass (£4.85-£5.45) **Notes:** Fixed D 4 courses, Sun L from £15.95, Dress Restrictions, No jeans or sportswear, Civ Wed 110 **Seats:** 78, Pr/dining room 40 **Smoking:** N/Sm in restaurant **Children:** Min 12 yrs, Menu, Portions **Rooms:** 38 (38 en suite) ★★★ HL **Directions:** 4m from the A68 **Parking:** 50

SWINTON MAP 21 NT84

❀❀ The Wheatsheaf at Swinton

Modern

Tempting cooking in classic village inn

☎ 01890 860257 The Wheatsheaf at Swinton, Maint St TD11 3JJ
e-mail: reception@wheatsheaf-swinton.co.uk
web: www.wheatsheaf-swinton.co.uk

Although most people know this traditional country inn as a destination food venue, The Wheatsheaf is still very much the hub of the village. A pine-clad conservatory dining room and traditional bar lounge are among the cosy eating areas, which boast log fires in winter. The menu is broad and appeals to all appetites. Fresh local ingredients are the backbone of the cooking here, with fish, seafood, meat, game and vegetables being sourced within the region. Such a keen eye on provenance shows in breast of wood pigeon on black pudding and celeriac and rack of Border lamb with a basil and mustard crust on rosemary-scented juices.

Chef: John Kier **Owners:** Mr & Mrs Chris Winson **Times:** 12-2/6-9, Closed 25-27 Dec, Closed D Sun (Dec, Jan) **Prices:** Starter £4.95-£8.45, Main £10.80-£18.95, Dessert £5.10-£5.45, Coffee £2.60, Min/Water £3.75, Service optional, Group min 12 service 10% **Wine:** 80 bottles over £20, 38 bottles under £20, 10 by the glass (£2.95-£4.75) **Notes:** Civ Wed 50 **Seats:** 45, Pr/dining room 29 **Smoking:** N/Sm in restaurant **Children:** Menu, Portions **Rooms:** 8 (8 en suite) ★★★★ RR **Directions:** From Edinburgh turn off A697 onto B6461. From East Lothian turn off A1 onto B6461 **Parking:** 6

STIRLING

CALLANDER MAP 20 NN60

❀❀❀ Roman Camp Country House Hotel

see opposite

DUNBLANE MAP 21 NN70

❀ *Cromlix House Hotel*

Modern British

Impressive Victorian mansion providing a romantic setting

☎ 01786 822125 Kinbuck FK15 9JT
e-mail: reservations@cromlixhouse.com
web: www.cromlixhouse.com

Built as a family home of grand proportions on a 200-acre estate, Cromlix House is every bit the traditional Scottish hunting lodge. These days it makes a well appointed hotel, now under new ownership, with smart accommodation and friendly service. Two dining rooms offer contrasting styles of décor, and a recommendation from the four-course dinner menu is saddle of Highland venison with red cabbage, gratin potatoes and port sauce. In addition to the comprehensive wine list, there's a good choice of Lowland, Highland and Island malt whiskies.

Times: 12.30-1.15/7-8.30, Closed 1-21 Jan, L by reservation Oct-Apr **Rooms:** 14 (14 en suite) ★★★ HL **Directions:** From A9 take B8033 (Kinbuck), through village, 2nd left after small bridge

STRATHYRE MAP 20 NN51

❀❀ Creagan House

French, Scottish

Impressive food from a local institution

☎ 01877 384638 FK18 8ND
e-mail: eatandstay@creaganhouse.co.uk
web: www.creaganhouse.co.uk

Once a working farm, this 17th-century house has been sympathetically restored, with a large, baronial-style dining hall that manages to balance grandiosity with a romantic intimacy. Service is very friendly, with the owners making every guest feel special. The food is classical French with strong Scottish overtones. Good produce is obviously important to the kitchen team here - all their meat is sourced from farms within Perthshire and herbs are grown in the gardens. Start with Pithiviers of oxtail and foie gras with green tomato chutney, followed by a main course of Mediterranean-spiced Gressingham duck breast, with stuffed leg and cannellini beans. The great selection of whiskeys should not be overlooked.

Chef: Gordon Gunn **Owners:** Gordon & Cherry Gunn **Times:** 7.30-8.30, Closed 21 Jan-9 Mar, 5-23 Nov, Thur, Closed L (ex parties), D Tue-Wed (24 Nov-24 Dec) **Prices:** Fixed D £28.50-£31.50, Coffee £2.50, Min/Water £1.75, Service optional **Wine:** 32 bottles over £20, 42 bottles under £20, 8 by the glass (£2.10-£2.95) **Notes:** Dress Restrictions, Smart casual **Seats:** 15, Pr/dining room 6 **Smoking:** N/Sm in restaurant **Children:** Min 10 yrs, Portions **Rooms:** 5 (5 en suite) ★★★★★ RR **Directions:** 0.25m N of village, off A84 **Parking:** 25

Roman Camp Country House Hotel

CALLANDER MAP 20 NN60

Modern French

Innovative cooking in splendid riverside setting

☎ 01877 330003 FK17 8BG
e-mail: mail@romancamphotel.co.uk
web: www.romancamphotel.co.uk

Set in 20 acres of tranquil woodland gardens and grounds leading down to the River Teith, this charming, long-established country-house hotel has a rich history and was formerly a shooting lodge. Real fires warm the atmospheric public rooms in expected country-house fashion, while decorative tapestries grace the dining room walls. Here well-spaced tables come lit by candlelight and decorated with fresh flowers, while the service is suitably professional yet friendly. The talented kitchen's modern approach is underpinned by a classical theme, the repertoire dominated by high-quality Scottish produce from the abundant local larder that's treated with due reverence.

Expect creative, exciting and innovative dishes with clear flavours, like line-caught sea bass served with a mushroom and scallop ragout and chicken wing jus, and to follow perhaps Goosnargh duck breast teamed with duck confit ravioli and sauté foie gras. Finish off with a dessert of white chocolate parfait accompanied by dark chocolate brioche and mango purée. An extensive wine list and peripherals like canapés, pre-desserts and petits fours hold form through to the end.

Chef: Ian McNaught
Owners: Eric Brown
Times: 12.30-1.45/7-8.30
Prices: Fixed L £20-£25, Fixed D £44-£45, Starter £9.90-£18, Main £27.50-£30, Dessert £8.75-£10.50, Coffee £3.50, Min/Water £2.95, Service optional
Wine: 180 bottles over £20, 20 bottles under £20, 9 by the glass (£3.95-£4.75)
Notes: Vegetarian available, Fixed L 3 courses, Civ Wed 100
Seats: 120, Pr/dining room 36
Smoking: N/Sm in restaurant
Children: Portions
Rooms: 14 (14 en suite) ★★★ HL
Directions: Heading N on A84 through Callander Main St turn right at East End into drive
Parking: 70

Scotland

Scotland

SCOTTISH ISLANDS ARRAN, ISLE OF

BRODICK MAP 20 NS03

Auchrannie Country House Hotel

Modern Scottish

A moveable feast on Arran Isle

☎ 01770 302234 KA27 8BZ
e-mail: info@auchrannie.co.uk
web: www.auchrannie.co.uk

The Isle of Arran is the romantic setting for this imposing country-house hotel, part of a luxury resort complex. The Garden Restaurant is tastefully housed in the conservatory, where beautiful table settings and subtle lighting create an appealing atmosphere for the fine Scottish dining. Traditional recipes are given a modern makeover on the short monthly-changing menu, with a couple of daily specials at each course for added interest. You might find carpaccio of venison with champit potato salad and white truffle oil, or fillet of salmon with leek and Arran Cheddar rarebit, testifying to the local sourcing of ingredients.

Chef: Gregg Russell **Owners:** Mr I Johnston **Times:** 6.30-9.30, Closed L all week **Prices:** Fixed D £26.95-£30.95, Coffee £1.20, Min/Water £3.50, Service optional **Wine:** 24 bottles over £20, 36 bottles under £20, 6 by the glass (£3.75-£4.95) **Notes:** Civ Wed 100 **Seats:** 52, Pr/dining room 22 **Smoking:** N/Sm in restaurant **Children:** Menu, Portions **Rooms:** 28 (28 en suite) ★★★★ HL **Directions:** From Brodick Pier turn right onto main road. Continue for 0.5m turn left at signs for Auchrannie **Parking:** 25

Kilmichael Hotel

Mediterranean, International

Exciting local dining in relaxing country-house surroundings

☎ 01770 302219 Glen Cloy KA27 8BY
e-mail: enquiries@kilmichael.com
web: www.kilmichael.com

This ancient listed property is now a country-house hotel providing a comfortable and relaxing setting to enjoy the best of Arran and Scottish produce. The proprietors aim for a private house feel with interesting collectibles from around the world. The intimate, bright Georgian-style dining room is decked out in red with staff providing a warm and helpful welcome. Cooking is in the contemporary style with strong Mediterranean and international influences. Making extensive use of local and seasonal produce, the short menus are nonetheless well chosen. Start with the roast garlic and chestnut soup before the main course of perfectly timed lamb loin with redcurrant and cream jus, dauphinoise potatoes and broad beans. Finish with the damson gin fool with shortbread.

Times: 7-8.30, Closed Nov-Mar, Tue **Rooms:** 7 (7 en suite) ★★★ **Directions:** Turn right on leaving ferry terminal, through Brodick & left at golf club. Follow brown sign. Continue past church & onto private drive

HARRIS, ISLE OF

SCARISTA

Scarista House

Scottish, French NEW

Fresh Scottish produce in peaceful country house

☎ 01859 550238 HS3 3HX
e-mail: timandpatricia@scaristahouse.com
web: www.scaristahouse.com

A former manse, Scarista House is now a haven for food lovers who seek to explore the magnificent island of Harris. The house enjoys breathtaking views of the Atlantic and is just a short stroll from miles of golden sandy beaches. The newly extended restaurant is a focal point, offering a daily-changing set three or four course menu. Local Scottish produce is evident in dishes like seared Sound of Harris hand-dived scallops with vanilla butter vinaigrette; and roast rack of Lewis lamb with merlot reduction.

Times: 7.30-8, Closed 25 Dec, Mon (ex residents) **Rooms:** 5 (5 en suite) ★★★★ GH **Directions:** On A859 15m S of Tarbert

ISLAY, ISLE OF

BOWMORE MAP 20 NR35

The Harbour Inn

Scottish, International

A must-visit dining experience on this magnificent island

☎ 01496 810330 The Square PA43 7JR
e-mail: info@harbour-inn.com
web: www.harbour-inn.com

The humble exterior of this whitewashed inn in a pretty fishing village belies an interior which houses a sizeable modern restaurant decorated with sympathetic sophistication. The dining room is bustling and atmospheric, conceived with obvious care. The menu relies heavily on premium local produce with many of the dishes focusing around one or two key ingredients, and thus wholly dependent on this picturesque island's great produce including world-class seafood and fish and fantastic cheeses. The wide variety on the menu provides an agony of choice but at a push you might consider smoked beef fillet on potato rösti with wild mushroom and port sauce to start and ragout of seafood with white wine and saffron as a main.

Chef: Paul Lumby **Owners:** Carol Scott, Neil Scott **Times:** 12-2.30/6-9.30 **Prices:** Food prices not confirmed for 2007. Please telephone for details **Notes:** Smart casual **Seats:** 44 **Smoking:** N/Sm in restaurant **Children:** Min 10 yrs, Portions **Rooms:** 7 (7 en suite) ◆◆◆◆◆ **Directions:** Bowmore is situated approx 8m from both ports of Port Ellen & Port Askaig

MULL, ISLE OF

TOBERMORY MAP 22 NM55

Highland Cottage

Modern Scottish, International

A traditional Mull hotel with enticing local menu

☎ 01688 302030 Breadalbane St PA75 6PD
e-mail: davidandjo@highlandcottage.co.uk
web: www.highlandcottage.co.uk

Small, family-run hotel in the conservation area of Tobermory and close to the working fishermen's pier. This restaurant has a loyal local following and, with its country-style décor and large oak fireplace, is perfect for special occasion dining. The resident hosts make every effort on behalf of their guests, and there's a welcoming atmosphere. A commitment to local produce is evident on the menu. After an appetiser of butter bean velouté, start with either the locally smoked haddock or Croig crab cakes with chilli and caper dressing. Main courses include local scallops with scallion and parsnip purée, leeks and herb butter or Ardnamurchan venison with red cabbage and dauphinoise potatoes. Finish with marinated cherries.

Chef: Josephine Currie **Owners:** David & Josephine Currie **Times:** 7-9, Closed mid Oct-mid Nov, Xmas, part Jan-Mar, Closed L all week **Prices:** Fixed D fr £37.50, Min/Water £2.95, Service included **Wine:** 35 bottles over £20, 19 bottles under £20, 10 by the glass (£4.95-£6.50) **Notes:** Coffee incl, Fixed D 4 courses, Dress Restrictions, Smart casual **Seats:** 24 **Smoking:** N/Sm in restaurant **Children:** Min 10 yrs, Portions **Rooms:** 6 (6 en suite) ★★★ SHL **Directions:** Opposite fire station. Main Street up Back Brae, turn at top by White House. Follow road to right, left at next junct **Parking:** On street

Tobermory Hotel

Modern Scottish

Delightful seafront retreat on the Isle of Mull

☎ 01688 302091 53 Main St PA75 6NT
e-mail: tobhotel@tinyworld.co.uk
web: www.thetobermoryhotel.com

With its pretty pink frontage, this friendly, small hotel sits smack on the seafront amid the famous picture-postcard, brightly-coloured cottages overlooking Tobermory Bay. The attractive and aptly named Water's Edge restaurant is laid out with solid-wood furniture, while specially commissioned wall lights on a fish theme prove a talking point. The kitchen follows an intelligent and refreshingly simple modern line, allowing the quality, locally sourced produce to shine. Citrus stuffed sardines with sunblush tomato and spring onion dressing, and Glengorm rack of lamb with roast potatoes, vegetable purée with a rosemary and port jus are typical.

continued

Chef: Helen Swinbanks **Owners:** Mr & Mrs I Stevens **Times:** 7-9, Closed Xmas, Closed L all week **Prices:** Fixed D £27, Coffee £1.80, Min/Water £3.20, Service optional **Wine:** 8 bottles over £20, 31 bottles under £20, 5 by the glass (£3.20) **Seats:** 30 **Smoking:** N/Sm in restaurant **Children:** Menu, Portions **Rooms:** 16 (15 en suite) ★★ HL **Directions:** Telephone for directions **Parking:** On street

The Anchorage

☎ 01688 302313 Main St PA75 6NU

ORKNEY ISLANDS

ST MARGARET'S HOPE MAP 24 ND49

Creel Restaurant

Modern Scottish/Seafood

Family-run seafront restaurant

☎ 01856 831311 Front Rd KW17 2SL
e-mail: alan@thecreel.freeserve.co.uk
web: www.thecreel.co.uk

The Creel is a charming island restaurant with rooms, specialising in local produce. The dining room is informal in style and looks out over the seafront in the pretty village of St Margaret's Hope. A large collection of local artwork is displayed on the walls and in the windows, and the atmosphere is warm and friendly. Fresh and simple is the philosophy behind the cooking and the menu is constantly changing according to the supply of seafood, Orkney meat and vegetables. Seafood, naturally, figures strongly, and favourites are parton bree (crab soup), and roast monkfish and scallops with celeriac confit. For a fitting finish, try the classic lemon tart.

Chef: Alan Craigie **Owners:** Alan & Joyce Craigie **Times:** 7-9, Closed Jan-Mar, Nov, Mon & Tues (Apr, May, Sep, Oct), Closed L all week **Prices:** Starter £7-£8, Main £18-£25, Dessert £6.50-£7.50, Coffee £2.40, Min/Water £1.90, Service optional **Wine:** 14 bottles over £20, 19 bottles under £20, 4 by the glass (£3.50-£5) **Notes:** Vegetarian available **Seats:** 34, Pr/dining room 14 **Smoking:** N/Sm in restaurant **Children:** Portions **Directions:** 13m S of Kirkwall on A961, on seafront in village **Parking:** 12

SKYE, ISLE OF

BREAKISH MAP 22 NG62

The Alba Restaurant

Scottish NEW

French cuisine on a beautiful Scottish island

☎ 01471 822001 Old School House IV42 8PY
e-mail: knox@glenmoriston.fsnet.co.uk

The high windows in this former Victorian schoolhouse were designed to deter daydreaming pupils. Today, blackboards have been replaced by local artwork and fishing paraphernalia, creating a much more inviting interior. The chef's French classical background is evident in the faultless execution of dishes that handles the abundant local game and seafood with accuracy, precision and flair. Lightly grilled sea bass demonstrates just how good fresh fish can be.

Times: 11-5/6.30-8.30, Closed 2 wks Oct, Jan, Feb, Tue, Closed L all week **Directions:** 10 minutes N of Skye Bridge

COLBOST MAP 22 NG24

The Three Chimneys

see page 608

ISLEORNSAY MAP 22 NG71

Hotel Eilean Iarmain

Traditional British

Contemporary cuisine on Skye

☎ 01471 833332 IV43 8QR
e-mail: hotel@eileaniarmain.co.uk
web: www.eileaniarmain.co.uk

This busy hotel is built around a 19th-century inn, set above the beach overlooking the yachts moored in the bay and sea lochs beyond. Enjoy pre-dinner drinks in front of a roaring fire in the cosy lounge before moving into the elegant restaurant. High-quality ingredients are cooked with imagination and flair in dishes like salad of red, green and yellow roasted sweet peppers with capers and olives in a white balsamic dressing, as well as grilled fillet of beef with rosemary garlic jus served with a sauté of forest mushrooms. A baby pineapple stuffed with strawberry ice cream also shows an inspired take on desserts.

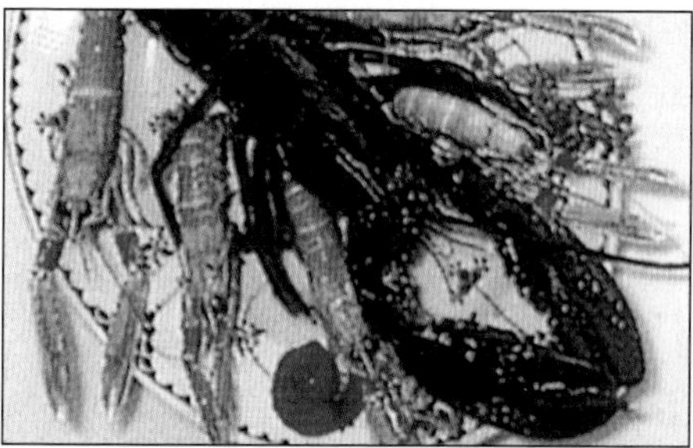

Chef: Steffen Box & Richard Carlton **Owners:** Sir Ian Andrew Noble **Times:** 12-2.30/6.30-8.45, Closed L all week (ex bookings), D (open 6-10 summer) **Prices:** Fixed L fr £10, Fixed D fr £31, Starter £2.25-£5, Main £6.25-£10.50, Dessert £3.95, Coffee £2.50, Min/Water £3.50, Service optional **Wine:** 43 bottles over £20, 8 bottles under £20, 6 by the glass (£3.25) **Notes:** Dress Restrictions, Smart casual, Civ Wed 27 **Seats:** 40, Pr/dining room 22 **Smoking:** N/Sm in restaurant **Children:** Portions **Rooms:** 16 (16 en suite) ★★ **Directions:** Overlooking harbour - cross bridge at Kyle of Lochalsh then take A850 and A851, then to harbour front

Three Rosettes
Outstanding restaurants that demand recognition well beyond their local area. Timing, seasoning and the judgement of flavour combinations will be consistently excellent, supported by other elements such as intelligent service and well-chosen wine list.

Toravaig House Hotel

Modern Scottish NEW

Stylish haven of peace serving Skye's wonderful produce

☎ 01471 820200 & 833231 Knock Bay IV44 8RE
e-mail: info@skyehotel.co.uk
web: www.skyehotel.co.uk

A haven of tranquility, this refurbished, stylish hotel enjoys panoramic views as far as the Knoydart Hills. The elegant Iona Restaurant comes with well-spaced, white-clothed tables, high-backed, dark brown leather chairs and relaxed but efficient service. The emphasis is on the freshest ingredients from the abundant Highland larder. Enjoy Skye's wonderful fish, game or lamb in dishes such as steamed Loch Eishort mussels with cream, white wine and parsley, or venison loin with parsnip purée and wild berry sauce. The style is straightforward, with clear flavours that intelligently allow the quality produce to take centre stage.

Chef: Eddie Shaw/Nick Kock **Owners:** Ken Gunn & Anne Gracie **Times:** 12.30-2/6.30-11.30 **Prices:** Fixed L £10-£20, Fixed D £22-£28, Starter £4-£7.95, Main £12.50-£18.95, Dessert £4.25-£5.25, Coffee £2, Min/Water £2.50, Service included **Wine:** 20 bottles over £20, 30 bottles under £20, 6 by the glass (£3.95-£5.25) **Notes:** Dress Restrictions, Smart casual **Seats:** 30 **Smoking:** N/Sm in restaurant **Children:** Portions **Rooms:** 9 (9 en suite) ★★ **Directions:** Travel to Isle of Skye by bridge, continue towards Boadford for 4m, turn left for Armadale and Sleat. Torvaig is on main A851, 11m beyond this junct **Parking:** 20

see advert opposite

PORTREE MAP 22 NG44

Bosville Hotel

Scottish, French NEW

Masterful cooking using truly local produce

☎ 01478 612846 Bosville Ter IV51 9DG
e-mail: bosville@macleodhotels.co.uk
web: www.macleodhotels.co.uk/bosville

This stylish, popular hotel enjoys fine views over the harbour. Public areas include a smart bar, bistro and the Chandlery Restaurant, which derives its name from the 1700s when a chandler supplied candles, canvas and ships components. The restaurant aims to provide 'the finest cuisine from sea to shore to plate', and this is facilitated by an abundance of fresh local produce, especially seafood and game. The chef is passionate about using seasonal fresh Scottish produce like Isle of Skye shellfish, local organic salads and berries, hand-dived scallops from Loch Sligachan and langoustines direct from Portree Harbour. Great produce is combined with masterful cooking techniques and

continue

inspirational combinations in dishes like skirlie (onion and oatmeal) topped sirloin of Highland beef with a small oxtail bridie.

Times: 6.30-9.30, Closed L all week **Rooms:** 25 (25 en suite) ★★★ HL **Directions:** 200mtrs from bus station, overlooking Portree Harbour

Cuillin Hills Hotel

Traditional French

Highland hotel with stunning views and fine local produce

☎ 01478 612003 IV51 9QU
e-mail: info@cuillinhills-hotel-skye.co.uk
web: www.cuillinhills-hotel-skye.co.uk

There are spectacular views over Portree Bay to the Cuillin Hills beyond from this former MacDonald hunting lodge. The property dates from 1870 and stands in 15 acres of mature grounds. The split-level dining room allows as many tables as possible to enjoy the views from this wonderful location, and drinks on the lawn are a treat in summer. Fresh local produce is used to full advantage, including locally landed seafood and Highland game. Dishes range through the hotel's own cured salmon with lime and coriander, traditional Cullen skink, and saddle of Highland venison with sautéed chanterelle mushrooms, redcurrant and port sauce and parsnip crisps.

Chef: Robert Macaskill **Owners:** Wickman Hotels Ltd **Times:** 12-2/6.30-9, Closed L Mon-Sat **Prices:** Fixed D £32.50, Coffee £1.80, Min/Water £2.95, Service optional **Wine:** 20 bottles over £20, 45 bottles under £20, 7 by the glass (£3.25) **Notes:** Civ Wed 70 **Seats:** 48, Pr/dining room 20 **Smoking:** N/Sm in restaurant **Children:** Menu, Portions **Rooms:** 27 (27 en suite) ★★★ HL **Directions:** 0.25 miles N of Portree on A855 **Parking:** 56

Rosedale Hotel

Traditional Scottish

Local produce by the sea front

☎ 01478 613131 Beaumont Crescent IV51 9DB
e-mail: rosedalehotelsky@aol.com
web: www.rosedalehotelskye.co.uk

This family-run harbourside hotel has good views of the water from the attractive first floor restaurant. It was once a set of fishermen's cottages, and a recent decoration has preserved the intimate atmosphere. Local produce is handled with flair on an imaginative Scottish menu priced by the number of courses. Typical dishes include traditional Cullen skink, or parmesan biscuit with warm salad of leeks and sun-dried tomatoes to start, with fillet of tuna on chargrilled vegetables or pan-fried duck breast on sweet potato and bacon, drizzled with red wine and plum sauce for mains.

Chef: Kirk Moir, Tony Parkyn **Owners:** Mr & Mrs P Rouse **Times:** 7-9, Closed 1 Nov-1 Mar, Closed L all week **Prices:** Fixed D £20-£26.50, Min/Water £3, Service optional **Wine:** 6 bottles over £20, 24 bottles under £20, 7 by the glass (£3) **Seats:** 30 **Smoking:** N/Sm in restaurant **Children:** Menu, Portions **Rooms:** 18 (18 en suite) ★★ HL **Directions:** On harbour front **Parking:** On street

Four Rosettes

Amongst the very best restaurants in the British Isles, where the cooking demands national recognition. These restaurants will exhibit intense ambition, a passion for excellence, superb technical skills and remarkable consistency. They will combine appreciation of culinary traditions with a passionate desire for further exploration and improvement.

The Three Chimneys

COLBOST MAP 22 NG24

Modern Scottish NOTABLE WINE LIST

Foodie hideaway on Skye serving the freshest seafood

☎ 01470 511258 IV55 8ZT
e-mail: eatandstay@threechimneys.co.uk
web: www.threechimneys.co.uk

No matter how long the journey, it's worth the trip out to Skye to visit this magical little restaurant set in glorious wilderness, nestled between the hills and beside Loch Dunvegan. Originally a crofter's cottage and township shop, the whitewashed building's interconnecting rooms pick up on the natural theme to create a feeling of chic simplicity. Take the candlelit restaurant's bare stone walls, low ceilings and polished-wood tables, with their slate tablemats and high-backed chairs. It's intimate and cosy, while service is suitably relaxed and friendly, but professional and well informed.
As you'd expect, the menus change daily to make the best of the abundant local larder, with seafood a highlight. Superb quality produce is simply cooked to let the freshness and quality shine through. The finely-tuned style marries traditional Scottish ideas with a more modern approach, delivering skilful combinations and clean, crisp flavours - as in a fillet of turbot and Skye lobster grilled with coral butter and teamed with garden spinach, a potato rösti and vanilla velouté. For dessert, expect the likes of gingerbread with Agen prunes in a stem ginger syrup with an Armagnac parfait and ginger snap. Add an award-wining wine list and fantastic views that money can't buy, and a walk along the loch to see the seals is a must.

Notable Wine List: A well-balanced wine list which offers much interest and quality, including some useful tasting notes.

Chef: Michael Smith
Owners: Eddie & Shirley Spear
Times: Closed L Sun & winter months
Prices: Fixed L £21, Fixed D £47.50-£50, Coffee £2.25, Min/Water £3.50, Service optional
Wine: 100 bottles over £20, 8 bottles under £20, 8 by the glass (£4.95-£5.95)
Notes: 7 course tasting L £55, Dress Restrictions, Smart casual preferred
Seats: 32
Smoking: N/Sm in restaurant
Children: Min 8 yrs D, Portions
Rooms: 6 (6 en suite)
★★★★★ RR
Directions: 5m W of Dunvegan take B884 to Glendale & Colbost

STRUAN MAP 22 NG33

֍֍ Ullinish Lodge Hotel

Modern French NEW

Tranquillity, candlelit dinners and fresh local produce

☎ 01470 572214 IV56 8FD
e-mail: ullinish@theisleofskye.co.uk
web: www.theisleofskye.co.uk

Set at the end of a track with lochs on three sides and breathtaking views of the Black Cuillins and MacLeods Tables, Ullinish Lodge is quite the haven of peace and boasts Samuel Johnson as a former guest. Sympathetically refurbished, the interior unsurprisingly has a country house feel, with a peaceful lounge and efficient, pleasant service. Tables in the wood-panelled dining room feature pristine white linen, the intimate atmosphere heightened by candlelight. Its kitchen's modern approach makes use of fresh, local produce from the ever-abundant Highland larder; perhaps grilled Loch Bracadale langoustines with triple-cooked chips, Glendale salad and sauce choron, or maybe, braised pig's head with crispy ear loaf, or local estate venison.

Chef: Bruce Morrison **Owners:** Brian & Pam Howard **Times:** 12-2.30/7-8.30, Closed Jan, Mon-Tue (in winter) **Prices:** Fixed D £37.50, Coffee £2.50, Min/Water £3.50, Service optional **Wine:** 10 bottles over £20, 15 bottles under £20 **Notes:** Fixed D 5 courses, Vegetarian available, Dress Restrictions, Smart casual, no T-shirts **Seats:** 22 **Smoking:** N/Sm in restaurant **Rooms:** 6 (6 en suite) ★★ HL **Directions:** 9m S of Dunvegan on A863 **Parking:** 10

continued

Scotland

Wales

ANGLESEY, ISLE OF

BEAUMARIS MAP 14 SH67

Bishopsgate House Hotel

Traditional Welsh

Traditional Welsh cooking in a historic setting

☎ 01248 810302 54 Castle St LL58 8BB
e-mail: hazel@johnson-ollier.freeserve.co.uk
web: www.bishopgatehousehotel.co.uk

An 18th-century Georgian townhouse, believed to have been built as a dower house for a wealthy local family, and now transformed into a small hotel. The popular restaurant offers fresh local produce including fish, salt marsh lamb and beef from the Lleyn Peninsula. Traditional Welsh cooking is epitomised in dishes like lamb shank braised in red wine with a walnut, honey and rosemary jus. Leave some room for a delicious dessert like chocolate and pecan pie served warm with chocolate sauce and vanilla ice cream.

Chef: H Johnson Ollier & I Sankey **Owners:** Hazel Johnson Ollier **Times:** 12.30-2.30/7-10, Closed L Mon-Sat **Prices:** Fixed D £16.95, Starter £4.50-£5.95, Main £9.50-£16.95, Dessert £4.75, Coffee £1.95, Min/Water £4.60, Service optional **Wine:** 11 bottles over £20, 26 bottles under £20, 4 by the glass (£2.90-£3.50) **Notes:** Sun L 2 courses £10.50, 3 courses £12.95, Dress Restrictions, Smart dress, Civ Wed 55 **Seats:** 40 **Smoking:** N/Sm in restaurant **Children:** Portions **Rooms:** 9 (9 en suite) ★★ HL **Directions:** From Britannia Bridge follow A545 into Beaumaris town centre. Hotel is 2nd on left in the main street **Parking:** 10

Ye Olde Bulls Head Inn

British, French

Historic place with punchy food

☎ 01248 810329 Castle St LL58 8AP
e-mail: info@bullsheadinn.co.uk
web: www.bullsheadinn.co.uk

continued

Ye Olde Bulls Head Inn

Charles Dickens and Samuel Johnson were both regular visitors to this historic coaching inn. Originally built in the late 1400s, there are still exposed beams and antique weaponry linking it to its heritage, although the rest of the décor is smart and contemporary, particularly the refurbished Loft restaurant, the more formal of the two dining options. The food is confident, progressive and superbly presented, demonstrating clear ambition and creativity - try the ham hock and Puy lentil terrine with balsamic baby onions to start, then a main of Welsh Black beef with baby vegetables, roasted ceps and Madeira sauce. If the gorgeous apple fritters with green apple purée and caramel sauce isn't their signature dish, it should be!

Chef: Keith Rothwell **Owners:** D Robertson, K Rothwell **Times:** 7-9.30, Closed 25-26 Dec, 1 Jan, Sun, Closed L Mon-Sat **Prices:** Fixed D £35-£37.50, Coffee £2.95, Min/Water £3.75, Service optional **Wine:** 80 bottles over £20, 20 bottles under £20, 4 by the glass (£4.35-£4.75) **Notes:** Sun L on BH's **Seats:** 45 **Smoking:** N/Sm in restaurant **Children:** Min 7 yrs **Rooms:** 13 (13 en suite) ★★ **Directions:** Town centre, main street **Parking:** 10

BRIDGEND

BRIDGEND MAP 09 SS97

The Great House

Modern British

Assured cooking of seasonal produce in historic manor

☎ 01656 657644 Laleston CF32 0HP
e-mail: enquiries@great-house-laleston.co.uk
web: www.great-house-laleston.co.uk

Original mullioned windows, oak beams, elegant inglenooks and old artefacts have been preserved at this restored 16th-century building in the peaceful hamlet of Laleston. Named after the Earl of Leicester, who used the building as a hunting lodge, Leicester's Restaurant is the smart setting for savouring some assured modern British cooking that makes good use of locally-sourced and seasonal ingredients. Local fish, estate-reared venison and Welsh Black beef are specialities. Dishes are not over-worked, resulting in clean, fresh flavours, as evidenced in ham hock ballontine with sauce gribiche, and a well-textured venison loin served with a delicious smoked bacon and apple bavarois and a hibiscus jelly and port wine jus.

Chef: Stuart Bevan, Richard Davies **Owners:** Stephen and Norma Bond **Times:** 12-2/6.45-9.45, Closed 3 days Xmas, BHs, Closed D Sun **Prices:** Fixed L fr £8.50, Starter £3.95-£8.95, Main £7.95-£17.95, Dessert £5.50, Coffee £2.25, Min/Water £3.50, Group min 10 service 10% **Wine:** 38 bottles over £20, 23 bottles under £20, 2 by the glass (£3.40-£5.25) **Notes:** Sun L £17.95, Vegetarian available, Civ Wed 50 **Seats:** 50, Pr/dining room 40 **Smoking:** N/Sm in restaurant, Air con **Children:** Portions **Rooms:** 16 (16 en suite) ★★★ SHL **Directions:** M4 junct 35, A473 then A48 signed Porthcawl & Laleston **Parking:** 40

CARDIFF

CARDIFF MAP 09 ST17

Copthorne Hotel Cardiff-Caerdydd

Modern European

Modern hotel with agreeable fine-dining restaurant

☎ 029 2059 9100 Copthorne Way, Culverhouse Cross CF5 6DH
e-mail: sales.cardiff@mill-cop.com
web: www.copthornehotels.com

Close to the airport, this modern, purpose-built hotel has easy motorway access and, despite being situated among out-of-town shopping centres, the well-tended grounds, pleasant lake and smart appearance give the place a well-groomed countenance, while inside the wood panelling and stained glass create a traditional feel to the Raglans restaurant. The cuisine here is unfussy with generous portions and full flavours - satisfying fare with refined touches. Start with tian of Cornish crab with guacamole for example, then a main of fillet of Scottish halibut with boulangère potatoes and ham hock and cockle broth.

Chef: Manuel Monzon **Owners:** Millennium & Copthorne Hotels **Times:** 12.30-2/6.30-9.45, Closed 25 Dec, Closed L Sat **Prices:** Fixed D £25, Starter £5.50-£8.95, Main £12.95-£39.50, Dessert £5.50, Coffee £2.25, Min/Water £2.95, Service optional **Wine:** 18 bottles over £20, 31 bottles under £20, 14 by the glass (£3.50-£4.90) **Notes:** Vegetarian available, Dress Restrictions, Smart casual, Civ Wed 120 **Seats:** 100, Pr/dining room 180 **Smoking:** N/Sm in restaurant, Air con **Children:** Menu, Portions **Rooms:** 135 (135 en suite) ★★★★ HL **Directions:** M4 junct 33 take A4232 (Culverhouse Cross), 4th exit at rdbt (A48), 1st left **Parking:** 225

Cutting Edge

British, International

Join the Assembly at the Cutting Edge

☎ 029 2047 0780 Discovery House, Scott Harbour, Cardiff Bay CF10 4PJ

This chic modern restaurant is part of a group of Cardiff restaurants including Woods and the Old Post Office. Overlooking the Bay opposite the Welsh Assembly, it's a popular lunch venue for local businesses and Assembly Members, so book ahead or alternatively aim to eat before or after the rush. A simple cooking style allows the quality and flavour of ingredients to shine through. Expect modern British dishes with a hint of the Mediterranean, such as venison and red wine sausages, or Thai fishcakes.

Times: 12-2.30/7-9.30, Closed 25-26 Dec, 31 Dec, BHs, Sun, Closed L Sat, D Mon-Thurs **Directions:** Opposite National Assembly of Wales and Millennium Centre

da Venditto

Italian

Traditional Italian style in modern surroundings in the heart of Cardiff

☎ 029 2023 0781 7-8 Park Place CF10 3DP
web: www.davenditto.com

There may be just a sign and menu case on street-level at this eponymous restaurant, but don't overlook it, as it's something of a hidden gem of an Italian. Inside, the basement premises offer clean contemporary lines, with stainless steel, marble and cherrywood, cutting a chic but casual edge. The classic Italian cooking suits the surroundings, its approach placing emphasis on quality ingredients and clear-flavoured, sophisticated dishes. The fixed-price lunch and traditional but flexible-format carte allows some pasta and risotto options to be taken as starter, intermediate or main course. The crab

continued

CARDIFF *continued* MAP 09 ST17

risotto is especially recommended, and remains one of the best in Wales. Other dishes might include succulent lobster on linguine with garlic and tomato sauce.

da Venditto

Chef: Walter Scoppetta **Owners:** Andrea Venditto **Times:** 12-2.30/5.30-10.45, Closed Xmas, New Yr, BHs, Sun **Prices:** Food prices not confirmed for 2007. Please telephone for details **Notes:** Gourmet nights on various dates, Vegetarian available, Dress Restrictions, Smart casual **Seats:** 60 **Smoking:** N/Sm in restaurant, Air con **Children:** Portions **Directions:** In the city centre, opposite the New Theatre **Parking:** 30

Le Gallois-Y-Cymro

Modern European

Popular culinary venue in Cardiff's Canton district

☎ 029 2034 1264 6-10 Romilly Crescent CF11 9NR
e-mail: info@legallois-ycymro.com
web: www.legallois-ycymro.com

This multi-lingual, Franco-Welsh, family-run restaurant has a loyal following built up over many years by offering menus of carefully cooked dishes in the modern style. The glass shopfront and split-level dining area are decorated in creams, yellows and blues with tables plainly appointed with simple settings. There's a small and busy bar at the rear. Welcoming staff are French and Welsh. Generous menus are based on Welsh and French produce with quality being the guiding factor. Start with slow-cooked peas and squid with garlic, mint, parsley and parmesan. Asian influences are evident in salmon confit with bok choy, mushrooms and roasted garlic cream. Finish with rice pudding with spiced plums.

Chef: Padrig Jones **Owners:** The Jones & Dupuy Family **Times:** 12-2.30/6.30-10.30, Closed Xmas, 1 wk Aug, New Year, Sun & Mon **Prices:** Fixed L fr £16.95, Fixed D fr £35, Coffee £2.50, Min/Water £2.50, Service optional, Group min 6 service 10% **Wine:** 65 bottles over £20, 30 bottles under £20, 11 by the glass (£3.75-£7.25) **Notes:** Vegetarian available, Smart casual **Seats:** 60 **Smoking:** N/Sm area, No pipes, No cigars, Air con **Children:** Portions **Directions:** From town centre follow Cowbridge Rd East. Turn right to Wyndham Crescent, then to Romilly Crescent. Restaurant on right **Parking:** 7

Gilby's Restaurant

Modern European

Enjoyable dining in this Cardiff institution

☎ 029 2067 0800 Old Port Rd, Culverhouse Cross CF5 6DN
e-mail: info@gilbysrestaurant.co.uk
web: www.gilbysrestaurant.co.uk

This converted tithe barn on the outskirts of Cardiff is a local dining destination. Fresh fish are displayed inside cold cabinets and in the background the busy kitchens can be glimpsed. Friendly staff dart between darkwood tables and balustrades which divide up the dining room. The best of local fish and local Welsh produce are emphasised on the British menu with European influences. Follow the peppered yellowfin tuna with caramelised endive and soy, honey and mustard dressing with sea bass and scallops with saffron and chorizo risotto, roasted vine tomatoes, prawn tempura and champagne sauce. Try the queen of puddings to finish. Excellent home-baked breads and good value two-course lunch menu.

Chef: Anthony Armelin, Michael Jones **Owners:** Mr A Armelin **Times:** 12-2.30/5.45-10, Closed 1 wk Jan, 2 wks Sep, BHs, Mon, Closed D Sun **Prices:** Fixed L £14, Fixed D £18.95, Starter £4.50-£12.95, Main £12.95-£20, Dessert £4.50-£5.50, Coffee £2, Min/Water £2.95, Service optional **Wine:** 23 bottles over £20, 18 bottles under £20, 12 by the glass (£3-£3.65) **Notes:** Vegetarian available **Seats:** 100 **Smoking:** N/Sm area **Children:** Min 8 yrs, Portions **Directions:** From M4 junct 33 follow signs for Airport/Cardiff West. Take A4050 Barry/Airport road and right at 1st rdbt **Parking:** 50

The Laguna Kitchen & Bar

Modern International NEW

Enjoyable dining in contemporary surroundings

☎ 029 2011 1103 Park Plaza Cardiff, Greyfriars Rd CF10 3AL
e-mail: ppcres@parkplazahotels.co.uk
web: www.parkplazacardiff.com

A smart, new-build city-centre hotel sporting an eye-catching, contemporary décor and the spacious Laguna Kitchen and Bar. Laguna is far from your typical hotel restaurant, a large modern space with wooden floors, low lighting, unclothed tables, open-plan kitchen at one end and huge windows affording river views. The extensive menu lists simple snacks alongside skilfully prepared dishes, but use of good ingredients is a strength, resulting in fresh and vibrant flavours, as seen in an excellent foie gras and chicken liver parfait with pear chutney and chargrilled Scottish rib-eye steak with béarnaise sauce and great hand-cut chips.

AA Hotel of the Year for Wales

Chef: Mark Freeman **Times:** 12-2.30/5.30-10.30 **Prices:** Fixed L fr £12, Fixed D fr £25, Starter £3.50-£6.50, Main £5-£22.50, Dessert fr £4.50, Coffee £2, Min/Water £3, Service added but optional 10% **Wine:** 31 bottles over £20, 36 bottles under £20, 6 by the glass (£3.25-£9.75) **Notes:** Sun brunch 2 courses £9.50, 3 courses £13.50, Vegetarian available, Civ Wed 140 **Seats:** 110 **Smoking:** N/Sm in restaurant, Air con **Children:** Menu, Portions **Rooms:** 129 (129 en suite) ★★★★ HL **Directions:** City centre, next to New Theatre **Parking:** NCP

Macdonald Holland House

Modern European

Mediterranean cooking in a stylish hotel restaurant

☎ 0870 122 0020 24-26 Newport Rd CF24 0DD
e-mail: revenue.holland@macdonald-hotels.co.uk
web: www.macdonald-hotels.co.uk

There's an exciting buzz at this contemporary city-centre hotel, not least in the First Floor restaurant where there is natural light by day and coloured lights by night cast a glow on the high-quality furnishings and décor. The menu provides plenty of Welsh produce, given cutting-edge appeal by a Mediterranean inspiration that manifests as chicken breast with chorizo pasta and a morel velouté, and fillet of sea bass with saffron-scented potatoes, sautéed baby gem and seafood chowder. Desserts like banana bavarois with caramelised banana and Amaretto ice cream are a highlight of any meal.

Chef: David Woodford **Owners:** Macdonald Hotels PLC **Times:** 12-2/6-10 **Prices:** Fixed L fr £18.50, Fixed D fr £22.50, Starter £5.50-£7.95, Main £9.95-19.95, Dessert £5.25-£6.75, Coffee £2.50, Min/Water £3.75 **Wine:** 18

continued

bottles over £20, 17 bottles under £20, 11 by the glass (£3.75-£7) **Notes:** Vegetarian available, Civ Wed 700 **Seats:** 120, Pr/dining room 500 **Smoking:** N/Sm in restaurant, Air con **Children:** Menu, Portions **Rooms:** 165 (165 en suite) ★★★★ **Directions:** Please telephone for directions **Parking:** 90

Manor Parc Country Hotel

British, Mediterranean

Local dishes in comfortable, country-house surroundings

☎ 029 2069 3723 Thornhill Rd, Thornhill CF14 9UA
e-mail: enquiry@manorparc.com
web: www.manorparc.com

This rather grand, former family home has a light, bright orangery-style restaurant with sumptuous furnishings and silver service. Uniformed staff provide formal service. Traditional menus use local seafood and seasonal produce to produce starters of warm goat's cheese and winter leaf salad or squid grilled with fresh herbs, white wine and lemon butter, while main courses may include fillet of West Wales sea bass with creamy dill potatoes and salsa verde or roast rack of Welsh lamb. Finish your meal with one of the daily choice of home-made desserts from the trolley.

Chef: Mr D Holland, Alun Thomas **Owners:** Mr S Salimeni & Mrs E A Salimeni **Times:** 12-2/6-9, Closed 26 Dec-1 Jan, Closed D Sun **Prices:** Fixed L £16.95, Fixed D £16.95-£22, Coffee £2, Min/Water £4.50, Service optional, Group min 6 service 10% **Wine:** 50 bottles over £20, 4 bottles under £20, 4 by the glass (£3-£5) **Notes:** Sun L 3 courses incl coffee £19, Vegetarian available, Civ Wed 100 **Seats:** 70, Pr/dining room 100 **Smoking:** N/Sm in restaurant **Children:** Portions **Rooms:** 21 (21 en suite) ★★★ HL **Directions:** Off A469 Cardiff-Caerphilly road **Parking:** 85

New House Hotel

British, International

Enjoyable seasonal dining with excellent views

☎ 029 2052 0280 Thornhill CF14 9UA
e-mail: enquiries@newhousehotel.com
web: www.newhousehotel.com

From its elevated position, this country-house hotel has wonderful views of nearby Cardiff and, on clear days, the sea beyond. Good public rooms include a reassuringly traditional, elegantly decorated restaurant that has a patio area for alfresco dining. Specialising in dishes based on local, seasonal produce, there is minimal intervention by the kitchen resulting in simply prepared, effective modern Welsh dishes. Expect starters such as seared pigeon breast with wild mushrooms and cream sauce. Main courses include crab and salmon fishcakes with sautéed spinach, red pepper relish and ginger scallions. Finish with passionfruit crème brûlée.

Times: 12-2/6-9.45, Closed 26 Dec, 1 Jan **Rooms:** 36 (36 en suite) ★★★ HL **Directions:** Take A469 to N of city. Entrance on left shortly after crossing M4 flyover

CARDIFF *continued* MAP 09 ST17

The Old Post Office

British, European

Modern European dining in a contemporary Welsh conservatory setting

☎ 029 2056 5400 Greenwood Ln, St Fagans CF5 6EL
e-mail: heidi.theoldpost@aol.com
web: www.old-post-office.com

Once a village post office, these days there's still a queue at this contemporary Welsh conservatory dining room with its clean lines and distinct lack of clutter. Staff are friendly but service retains an element of formality. Dishes are modern European in style with distinct French influences. Strong, clear flavours allow best-quality ingredients, brought in from near and far, to speak for themselves. Start with poached smoked haddock pavé and brandade with chive dressing before a main course of roasted Welsh rib-eye with pont neuf potatoes, red onion chutney and pancetta creamed leeks. Puddings include port-poached pear with blackberry sorbet and crème fraîche.

Chef: Wesley Hammond **Owners:** Choice Produce **Times:** 12-2/7-9.30, Closed Mon & Tue, Closed L Wed, D Sun **Prices:** Fixed L fr £10, Fixed D fr £35, Coffee £2.50, Min/Water £3.50, Service optional, Group min 6 service 10% **Wine:** 38 bottles over £20, 21 bottles under £20, 8 by the glass (£3.50-£4.75) **Notes:** Vegetarian available **Seats:** 26 **Smoking:** N/Sm in restaurant, Air con **Children:** Menu, Portions **Rooms:** 6 (6 en suite) ★★★★ RR **Directions:** A48 E through Cardiff to St Fagans sign. Right at lights, 1.4m, in village turn right into Croft-y-Genau Rd, right into Greenwood Lane **Parking:** 30

The St David's Hotel & Spa

Modern European

Modern brasserie dining in impressive Cardiff Bay setting

☎ 029 2045 4045 Havannah St, Cardiff Bay CF10 5SD
e-mail: tides@thestdavidshotel.com
web: www.thestdavidshotel.com

Tides Bar & Grill in this modern hotel affords diners dramatic views across Cardiff Bay. A seven-storey atrium, floor-to-ceiling windows, low leather sofas and lower lighting levels give this venue a distinctly modern and minimalist feel. A brasserie-style menu includes starters of wood pigeon ballotine with gooseberry relish or omelette Arnold Bennett followed by lobster Armoricaine, poached turbot with root vegetables and beurre blanc, or calves' liver with Somerset Royal sauce. Finish with golden syrup sponge pudding and brandy custard. Helpful service.

continued

The St David's Hotel & Spa

Chef: Georg Fuchs **Owners:** Rocco Forte Hotels **Times:** 12.30-2.15/6.30-10.30 **Prices:** Fixed L £18.50, Fixed D £22.50, Starter £7.50-£31, Main £15.75-£42, Dessert £7-£8.50, Coffee £3.25, Min/Water £4.50, Service added but optional 10% **Wine:** 5 bottles under £20, 10 by the glass **Notes:** Vegetarian available, Civ Wed 160 **Seats:** 98, Pr/dining room 40 **Smoking:** N/Sm in restaurant, Air con **Children:** Menu, Portions **Rooms:** 132 (132 en suite) ★★★★★ HL **Directions:** From M4 junct 33 take A432, 9m to Cardiff Bay. At rdbt over Queens Tunnel take 1st left, then immediate right **Parking:** 60

Scallops

Mediterranean, Seafood NEW

The freshest fish dishes in a delightful location

☎ 029 2049 7495 Unit 2, Mermaid Quay CF10 5BZ
e-mail: kerryjaynejayne@hotmail.com
web: www.scallopsrestaurant.com

Located in Cardiff Bay on the popular waterfront area, this modern seafood restaurant has a fresh and bright interior with lots of pastel shades, and outside seating in the summer. The seafood and fish dishes here are cooked precisely using the freshest produce imaginable, with many diners coming for the mussels, prawns, lobster or the eponymous scallop. Dishes are subtle and unfussy, never overwhelming the star attraction - the seafood. Open ravioli of king prawns with spinach, pine nuts and shellfish bisque would be a typical starter, followed perhaps by crispy halibut on herb roasted salsify and mange-tout or lobster platter.

Chef: Stefan Nilsson **Owners:** Mrs K Jayne **Times:** 12-2.30/5-10, Closed 1st 2 wks in Jan, Mon (Nov, Jan-Apr), Closed D Sun (in winter) **Prices:** Fixed L £9.95, Starter £3.95-£9.95, Main £11.95-£42, Dessert £4.95-£5.95, Coffee £1.50, Min/Water £3.50, Service optional, Group min 6 service 10% **Wine:** 15 bottles over £20, 18 bottles under £20, 5 by the glass (£3.25-£7.50) **Notes:** Sunday roast L £7.95 **Seats:** 80 **Smoking:** N/Sm in restaurant, Air con **Children:** Menu, Portions **Directions:** Situated on quayside. Follow signs for Cardiff Bay/Mermaid Quay **Parking:** Car park 200yds

Woods Brasserie

Modern European

Buzzy brasserie in Cardiff Bay

☎ 029 2049 2400 Pilotage Building, Stuart St, Cardiff Bay CF10 5BW
web: www.woods-brasserie.com

On the edge of the popular, regenerated Cardiff Bay area, this former customs and excise office dates back to the 1860s. Enormous glass windows help to create a bright and breezy modern feel to the place

continued

and the outdoor seating on the patio makes for essential alfresco dining. There's a heavy French influence on the modern European cooking, the variety of which appeals to shoppers, businessmen and tourists alike. Start with rillette of salmon and frisée salad with vinaigrette dressing and follow it with chargrilled tuna loin on braised fennel, ratatouille and tomato jus.

Chef: Sean Murphy **Owners:** Choice Produce **Times:** 12-2/5.30-10, Closed 25-26 Dec & 1 Jan, Closed D Sun **Prices:** Fixed L £12.50, Starter £4.95-£9.45, Main £9.95-£19.95, Dessert £5.50, Coffee £1.95, Min/Water £1.95, Service optional, Group min 6 service 10% **Wine:** 47 bottles over £20, 21 bottles under £20, 18 by the glass (£3.85-£5.60) **Notes:** Sun L 2 course £14.50, 3 course £17.50, Vegetarian available **Seats:** 90, Pr/dining room 36 **Smoking:** N/Sm area, Air con **Children:** Menu, Portions **Directions:** In heart of Cardiff Bay. M4 junct 33, then towards Cardiff Bay, big stone building on the right **Parking:** Multi-storey car park opposite

Ana Bela

☎ 029 2023 9393 5 Pontcanna St CF11 9HQ
Informal and good fun, with chefs from Argentina.

Juboraj

☎ 029 2062 8894 11 Heol-y-Deri, Rhiwbina CF14 6HA
Interesting and varied Bangladeshi cooking.

La Brasserie

☎ 029 2023 4134 60 Saint Mary St CF1 1FE
Bustling venue offering quality meats and seafood.

Le Monde Fish Bar & Grill

☎ 029 2038 7376 60-62 Saint Mary St CF10 1FE
Seafood restaurant, where food is cooked in a bustling open kitchen.

CARMARTHENSHIRE

CARMARTHEN MAP 08 SN42

Falcon Hotel

British, Mediterranean

Friendly family-run restaurant

☎ 01267 234959 & 237152 Lammas St SA31 3AP
e-mail: reception@falconcarmarthen.co.uk
web: www.falconcarmarthen.co.uk

This friendly small hotel in the centre of Carmarthen has been run by the Exton family for over 45 years. The fully refurbished, air-conditioned restaurant is light, airy and spacious. The cooking style is straightforward and the menu offers a selection of dishes making good use of local produce. Try a starter of locally smoked duck breast with red pepper salad and balsamic dressing, followed perhaps by a main course of braised shank of Towy Valley lamb with redcurrant sauce. Desserts are home-made, with the likes of brioche bread-and-butter pudding with a warm crème anglaise.

Chef: Lubomir Sörm **Owners:** J R Exton **Times:** 12-2.15/6.30-9, Closed 26 Dec, Closed D Sun, 25 Dec **Prices:** Food prices not confirmed for 2007. Please telephone for details **Wine:** 5 bottles over £20, 25 bottles under £20, 3 by the glass (£1.85-£4.50) **Notes:** Sun L £13.95-£15.95, Vegetarian available **Seats:** 100, Pr/dining room 25 **Smoking:** N/Sm in restaurant, Air con **Children:** Portions **Rooms:** 16 (16 en suite) ★★ HL **Directions:** Located in the centre of Carmarthen, 200 yds from bus station **Parking:** 40

LAUGHARNE MAP 08 SN31

The Cors Restaurant

Modern

Great food in a quirky former vicarage

☎ 01994 427219 Newbridge Rd SA33 4SH
e-mail: nickpriestland@hotmail.com
web: www.the-cors.co.uk

Set down a lane, the unremarkable exterior of this former vicarage in the village made famous by Dylan Thomas doesn't prepare first-time visitors for what's inside. With no draught beer, no optics, no credit cards, no printed menus and walls painted with bold colours, this quirky place has a Bohemian air about it. It all makes sense as soon as the food emerges from the kitchen which makes fine use of produce

continued

Wales

LAUGHARNE *continued* MAP 08 SN31

from the region: locally-smoked salmon appears with wild rocket and sweet mustard sauce, roasted rack of Welsh salt marsh lamb arrives with a rosemary garlic crust, and strawberry Pavlova is one of the classic desserts.

The Cors Restaurant

Chef: Nick Priestland **Owners:** Nick Priestland **Times:** 7-9.30, Closed Sun-Wed, 25 Dec **Prices:** Starter £5.95-£6.95, Main £14.50-£19.50, Dessert £4.50-£6, Coffee £1.50, Min/Water £3, Service optional **Wine:** 16 bottles over £20, 10 bottles under £20, 6 by the glass (£3-£6) **Notes:** Vegetarian available **Seats:** 24 **Smoking:** N/Sm in restaurant **Children:** Min 8 yrs **Directions:** From Carmarthen follow A40, turn left at St Clears & 4m to Laugharne **Parking:** 8 see advert page 617

LLANDEILO MAP 08 SN62

The Angel Salem

Modern British

Hearty food in a delightful rural location

☎ 01558 823394 Salem SA19 7LY

It's well worth a trip into the Carmarthenshire countryside to find this welcoming inn, with its big comfy sofas and an interesting mixture of modern and antique furniture. People come for the pleasant surroundings and friendly service, but above all for the carefully prepared food made from quality produce. Contemporary dishes with classical influences are offered from lunchtime blackboard specials and a regularly changing carte. Recommendations are the Angel Inn hors d'oeuvre plate to start, a main course of home-smoked Gressingham duckling, charlotte of apple and duck leg, parsnip purée and juniper jus, and a dessert of apricot and brioche butter pudding with schnapps anglaise. Everything is home-made including the excellent breads.

Chef: Rod Peterson **Owners:** Rod Peterson & Liz Smith **Times:** 12-3/7-9, Closed 2 wks in Jan, Sun-Mon (ex BHs), Closed L Tues **Prices:** Starter £4-

continued

£8, Main £15-£19, Dessert £5.50-£6.50, Service optional **Wine:** 14 bottles over £20, 30 bottles under £20, 3 by the glass (£3.45-£4.40) **Notes:** Vegetarian available **Seats:** 70 **Smoking:** N/Sm in restaurant **Children:** Portions **Directions:** Please telephone for directions **Parking:** 25

LLANELLI MAP 08 SN50

Fairyhill Bar & Brasserie

Modern Welsh NEW

Modern brasserie with views over the Estuary

☎ 01554 744994 Machynys Golf Club, Nicklaus Av SA15 2DG
e-mail: machynys@fairyhill.net
web: www.fairyhill.net

The latest venture of the nearby Fairyhill Hotel (see entry), this stylish bar brasserie is located on the Machynys Peninsula in the impressive new clubhouse of the Jack Nicklaus-designed golf course. Views over the course and bay are excellent and staff make guests feel even more relaxed, with efficient, informal service. Everything on the menu is fairly easy on the pocket with local produce and specialities brought to the fore in dishes such as crispy cockle and laverbread cakes or Machynys fishcakes with tartare sauce. Good hearty fare, guaranteed to please.

Chef: Nick Jones **Owners:** Paul Davies, Andrew Hetherington **Times:** 8-11.30 **Prices:** Food prices not confirmed for 2007. Please telephone for details **Wine:** 9 bottles over £20, 21 bottles under £20, 3 by the glass **Notes:** Vegetarian available **Seats:** 70, Pr/dining room 125 **Smoking:** N/Sm in restaurant **Children:** Min 5 yrs **Directions:** M4 junct 48 onto A4138 towards Llanelli. Follow signs to Machynys **Parking:** 100

CEREDIGION

ABERAERON MAP 08 SN46

Harbourmaster Hotel

Modern Welsh

Modern Welsh cuisine in an historic harbourside hotel

☎ 01545 570755 Pen Cei SA46 0BA
e-mail: info@harbour-master.com
web: www.harbour-master.com

With its dramatic quayside location, this Grade II listed harbourmaster's house has been sympathetically updated. You can eat at the bar tables or in the bright, airy brasserie with its ships' chandlery wall décor and magnificent spiral staircase that dominates the interior. Relaxed, bilingual service delivers modern Welsh dishes based on local produce to eager diners. Start with the Loughor moules marinière before trying a main course of Gower sea bass meunière or chargrilled Welsh Black beef fillet with parsnip dauphinoise, peppercorn and Cognac sauce. Try some excellent Welsh cheeses or the apricot and almond clafoutis to finish.

Chef: Sebastian Bodewes **Owners:** Glyn & Menna Hevlyn **Times:** 12-2/6.30-9, Closed 24 Dec-9 Jan, Closed L Mon, D Sun **Prices:** Fixed L fr £12.50, Starter £4.95-£8.50, Main £13.50-£18.50, Dessert £5, Coffee £2.20, Min/Water £2.75, Service optional, Group min 6 service 10% **Wine:** 25 bottles over £20, 25 bottles under £20, 10 by the glass (£3-£5.50) **Notes:** Sun L 3 courses £16.50 **Seats:** 40 **Smoking:** N/Sm in restaurant **Children:** Portions **Rooms:** 9 (9 en suite) ◆◆◆◆◆ **Directions:** A487 coastal road, follow signs for town-centre tourist information centre **Parking:** 3

Ynyshir Hall

EGLWYSFACH MAP 14 SN69

Modern British NOTABLE WINE LIST

Adventurous and stunning country-house cuisine

☎ 01654 781209 SY20 8TA
e-mail: ynyshir@relaischateaux.com
web: www.ynyshir-hall.co.uk

This charming, white-painted Tudor manor-house hideaway, set in 14 acres of glorious gardens amid the splendour of the Dovey estuary and once owned by Queen Victoria as a shooting lodge, offers one of Wales' great gastronomic and country-house experiences. The original 1,000-acre estate that surrounds the hotel is now an RSPB reserve, while Ynyshir's gardens are ablaze with azaleas and rhododendrons in spring. Owned and personally run by Rob and Joan Reen, Ynyshir is an intimate retreat of high quality, with a country-house theme having a vibrant colour scheme and walls adorned with Rob's bright canvasses. Service, led by Joan, is professional but with that warm, relaxed tone that envelops the house. The restaurant, overlooking the garden, is the epitome of a country-house dining room; small, with generous-sized tables, crisp linen and comfortable high-backed chairs. Head chef Adam Simmonds' cooking has a modern approach underpinned by classical technique and fine use of high-quality Welsh produce, including herbs and salads from Ynyshir's walled garden. His innovative, creative cooking matches those bold colours with clean flavours and fine textures that surprise and delight. Sweet and sour unite and there are lots of foams and sabayons. Expect partridge served with pearl barley, Penderyn whisky, walnuts and ceps, with perhaps a ginger parfait with lime jelly and coconut mousse for dessert. Sensibly compact menus includes an eight-course tasting option.

Notable Wine List: This well presented wine list offers an extensive selection with great depth and an excellent list of half-bottles.

Chef: Adam Simmonds
Owners: Rob & Joan Reen
Times: 12.30-1.30/7-8.45, Closed Jan
Prices: Fixed L fr £21, Fixed D fr £62, Coffee £3.75, Min/Water £3, Service optional
Wine: 300 bottles over £20, 4 bottles under £20, 14 by the glass (£3.50-£8)
Notes: Fixed D 4 courses, Vegetarian available, Dress Restrictions, No jeans, beach-wear or shorts, Civ Wed 40
Seats: 30, Pr/dining room 16
Smoking: N/Sm in restaurant
Children: Min 9 yrs
Rooms: 9 (9 en suite) ★★★ HL
Directions: On A487, 6m S of Machynlleth
Parking: 15

Wales

ABERYSTWYTH MAP 08 SN58

Conrah Hotel

British, International

Family-run hotel offering excellent food in a striking setting

☎ 01970 617941 Ffosrhydygaled, Chancery SY23 4DF
e-mail: enquiries@conrah.co.uk
web: www.conrah.co.uk

Just south of Aberystwyth, this hotel is quite a destination venue in the area with a well-established reputation. Guests enjoy all the trappings of a country-house hotel with lovely gardens and views of Snowdonia. Restaurant diners can also enjoy the experience, enhanced by friendly and professional staff. The menu aims to showcase regional produce in a range of classical and modern dishes. No expense is spared in accompaniments to the main elements with the likes of roast loin of Welsh lamb topped with rosemary crumb, served with dauphinoise potato, sauté cabbage and braised faggot with port jus and roast shallots. Be sure to leave room for one of the luxury desserts like pot-au-chocolat with strawberry and balsamic ice cream and clotted cream.

Times: 12-2/7-9, Closed 1 wk Xmas, Closed D Sun (low season) **Rooms:** 17 (17 en suite) ★★★ **Directions:** On A487, 3m S of Aberystwyth

Harry's

British, French

Classic bistro with French inspired dishes

☎ 01970 612647 40-46 North Pde SY23 2NF
web: www.harrysaberystwyth.com

Close to the shopping area and the seafront, Harry's is a friendly and popular restaurant, and also offers hotel accommodation. Cheerfully reminiscent of a rural French bistro, the rustic interior comprises two dining areas each decked out with chunky wooden furniture, stripped floors and brightly painted walls hung with local artwork. French-inspired menus make good use of local and seasonal produce that bring depth and flavour to the dishes. Typical dishes include mushroom Pithiviers or potted pork and duck with grain mustard dressing to start, followed by seared bass with crab ravioli, tomato and spring onion beurre blanc or pork and leek Wellington with grain mustard dauphinoise.

Chef: Harry Hughes, Chris Williams **Owners:** Harry Hughes **Times:** 12-2.30/6-10.00, Closed 25 Dec **Prices:** Starter £4.80-£6.50, Main £12.50-£16.50, Dessert £4.50, Service included **Seats:** 120, Pr/dining room 40 **Smoking:** N/Sm in restaurant **Children:** Portions **Rooms:** 24 (24 en suite) ★★ HL **Directions:** Town centre **Parking:** 14

EGLWYSFACH MAP 14 SN69

Ynyshir Hall

see page 619

LAMPETER MAP 08 SN54

Falcondale Mansion

Modern British

Mansion house offering fine dining with local produce

☎ 01570 422910 SA48 7RX
e-mail: info@falcondalehotel.com
web: www.falcondalehotel.com

This Victorian mansion is set in 14 acres of gardens containing many rare varieties of exotic and native trees and shrubs. It was originally the country residence of the Harford family, founders of the NatWest bank. Now transformed into a country hotel, you'll find Peterwells Brasserie offering informal eating, while the candlelit restaurant has a daily changing menu using fine local produce. Look out for rack of local Capeli-farmed lamb with mini shepherd's pie and lavender jus, or bara brith butter pudding with Penderyn whisky custard.

Chef: Michael Green, Stephane Biteau **Owners:** Chris & Lisa Hutton **Times:** 12-2/7-9, Closed L 1 Jan **Prices:** Fixed D £32.50, Starter £4.50-£9, Main £12.95-£21.50, Dessert £4.95-£5.95, Coffee £1.95, Min/Water £2.50, Service optional, Group min 10 service 10% **Wine:** 16 bottles over £20, 26 bottles under £20, 12 by the glass (£3.25-£9) **Notes:** Sun L 3 courses £16.50, Dress Restrictions, Smart casual, Civ Wed 60 **Seats:** 40, Pr/dining room 28 **Smoking:** N/Sm in restaurant **Children:** Portions **Rooms:** 20 (20 en suite) ★★★ HL **Directions:** 1m from Lampeter, take A482 to Cardigan, turn right at petrol station, follow for 0.75m **Parking:** 60

CONWY

BETWS-Y-COED MAP 14 SH75

The Royal Oak Hotel

Modern British

Good modern Welsh cooking in comfortable coaching inn setting

☎ 01690 710219 Holyhead Rd LL24 0AY
e-mail: royaloakmail@btopenworld.com
web: www.royaloakhotel.net

This privately-owned, efficiently run, slate-built Victorian hotel has something to offer everyone. Hotel guests breakfast alongside mountain trekkers in the modern bistro. Through the comfortable traditional bar with its antique furniture and original signboard by David Cox, there's a Victorian dining room with ornate plaster ceiling and linen-clothed tables. Helpful staff serve carefully prepared starters of local Welsh Black fillet on noodle salad with chilli and ginger and main courses of baked North Welsh monkfish on squid ink spaghetti with Conwy mussels. Finish with pear and cinnamon crème brûlée.

continued

The Royal Oak Hotel

Chef: Dylan Edwards **Owners:** The Royal Oak Hotel **Times:** 12-2/6.30-9, Closed 25,26 Dec, Mon-Tue, Closed L Wed-Sat, D Sun **Prices:** Fixed L £9.95-£10.95, Fixed D £17.50-£22.50, Starter £4.25-£7.95, Main £12.95-£17.50, Dessert £4.95-£5.75, Coffee £2.75, Min/Water £3.80, Service optional **Wine:** 15 bottles over £20, 38 bottles under £20, 11 by the glass (£3.25-£5.30) **Notes:** Vegetarian available, Dress Restrictions, No jeans, trainers, Civ Wed 85 **Seats:** 60, Pr/dining room 20 **Smoking:** N/Sm in restaurant **Children:** Portions **Rooms:** 27 (27 en suite) ★★★ **Directions:** Situated on A5 trunk road **Parking:** 100

Tan-y-Foel Country House

see below

CONWY MAP 14 SH77

The Castle Hotel

British

An ideal venue for special occasions

☎ 01492 582800 High St LL32 8DB
e-mail: mail@castlewales.co.uk
web: www.castlewales.co.uk

This family-run coaching inn is set in the Unesco World Heritage town of Conwy, which boasts an imposing 13th-century castle. A bar menu offers light meals, but Shakespeare's is the main event, a fine-dining restaurant that takes its name from a set of theatrical scenes painted for the hotel by the distinguished Victorian artist John Dawson-Watson in exchange for his supper. The lengthy carte of modern British dishes features mains such as roasted rump of Welsh lamb with spring onion mash and shallot and tomato jus, or pan-seared fillet of sea bass with Jerusalem artichokes, roast celery and vanilla, parsley and Conwy mussel sauce.

continued

Tan-y-Foel Country House

BETWS-Y-COED MAP 14 SH75

Modern British

Gourmet sanctuary in Snowdonia

☎ 01690 710507 Capel Garmon LL26 0RE
e-mail: enquiries@tyfhotel.co.uk
web: www.tyfhotel.co.uk

'erched in the hills above the pretty town of Betws-y-Coed, this amily-run hotel offers stunning views of the Conwy valley. Its nassuming 17th-century façade conceals a chic and sophisticated nterior which blends country-house comfort with minimalist modern lesign in a series of intimate and individual rooms, including a cosy estaurant which seats only a dozen diners at a time. Daughter Kelly erves, while mum Janet conjures some of the finest cuisine in Wales, llowing quality organic produce to speak for itself in mains such as enderloin of wild boar with sweet potato purée, caramelised apple nd onions, roast root vegetables and cider sauce. The fixed-price nenu changes daily and features a choice of two dishes at each ourse; start with pan-seared pigeon breast with faggot boudin, ancetta and Cumberland sauce perhaps, before tucking into wild urbot with creamy smoked salmon and spring cabbage, celeriac and otato fritter, garden peas and lemon parsley sauce, or hazelnut neringue with framboise cream and fresh raspberries.

Chef: Janet Pitman **Owners:** Mr & Mrs P Pitman **Times:** 7.30-8.15, Closed 1 Dec-1 Feb, Mon-Tue, Closed L all week **Prices:** Fixed D fr £39, Coffee £4, Min/Water £3, Service optional **Wine:** 100 bottles over £20, 4 bottles under £20, 4 by the glass (£3.50-£4.50) **Notes:** Dress Restrictions, No Jeans, trainers, tracksuits, walking boots **Seats:** 12 **Smoking:** N/Sm in restaurant **Children:** Min 7 yrs **Rooms:** 6 (6 en suite) ★★★★★ GH **Directions:** A5 onto A470; 2m N towards Llanrwst, then turning for Capel Garmon. Country House on left before village **Parking:** 14

Wales

CONWY *continued* MAP 14 SH77

The Castle Hotel

Chef: Graham Tinsley **Owners:** Lavin Family & Graham Tinsley **Times:** 12.30-2/7-9.30, Closed L Sat **Prices:** Fixed L £12.95-£14.45, Starter £5.95-£6.75, Main £16.95-£19.95, Dessert £5.75-£6.50, Coffee £2, Min/Water £3.25, Service added but optional 10% **Wine:** 29 bottles over £20, 28 bottles under £20, 12 by the glass **Notes:** Vegetarian available, Dress Restrictions, Smart casual, no collarless T-shirts **Seats:** 50 **Smoking:** N/Sm in restaurant **Children:** Menu, Portions **Rooms:** 28 (28 en suite) ★★★ HL **Directions:** From A55 junct 18 towards town centre. Follow signs for town centre and continue on one-way system. Hotel halfway up High St **Parking:** 36

Wales

The Groes Inn

Traditional

Honest, wholesome food in an intimate inn

☎ 01492 650545 Tyn-y-Groes LL32 8TN
web: www.groesinn.com

With four centuries of providing hospitality for travellers under its belt, this charming inn knows the secret of success. A warm welcome and a cosy warren of nooks and crannies are part of the appeal, enhanced by a beautiful restaurant with a conservatory extending into the garden. Fresh local produce, handled with skill and dedication, sees to the rest, with local seafood, lamb, game and fine Welsh beef providing an irresistible choice. Expect mains such as sweet organic Bryn Dowsi lamb knuckle slowly baked with capers and garlic in a redcurrant jus.

Chef: Gary Mason **Owners:** Dawn & Justin Humphreys **Times:** 12-2.15/6.30-9.00, Closed 25 Dec **Prices:** Fixed D £28, Starter £3.95-£7.50, Main £7.75-£15.75, Dessert £4.50-£4.95, Coffee £1.80, Min/Water £4.65, Service optional **Wine:** 6 bottles over £20, 22 bottles under £20, 10 by the glass (£3.10-£4.95) **Notes:** Fixed D 4 courses, Sun L £16.95, Vegetarian available, Dress Restrictions, Smart casual **Seats:** 54, Pr/dining room 20 **Smoking:** N/Sm in restaurant **Children:** Min 12 yrs **Rooms:** 14 (14 en suite) ★★★ HL **Directions:** In B5106, 3m from Conwy **Parking:** 100

The Old Rectory Country House

see opposite

The Mulberry

☎ 01492 583350 Morfa Dr, Conwy Marina LL32 8EP
Pub with scenic views overlooking the Conwy estuary. Food includes fresh fish and local mussels.

LLANDUDNO MAP 14 SH78

Bodysgallen Hall and Spa

see page 624

Empire Hotel

Modern British

Family-run hotel restaurant offering traditional cuisine

☎ 01492 860555 Church Walks LL30 2HE
e-mail: reservations@empirehotel.co.uk
web: www.empirehotel.co.uk

Built in 1854 as the town's first block of shops, the building was reconstructed in 1904 as the Empire Hotel. The restaurant was formerly a wine and spirits merchants. The cooking is traditional in style but uses modern techniques, with extensive sourcing of quality local produce. Typical dishes include a starter of risotto with wild mushrooms, chicken, fresh cream and parmesan shavings. This might be followed by a traditional slow-cooked shank of lamb spiced with red cabbage and rosemary jus. Try chocolate, almond and pear tart for dessert.

Chef: Michael Waddy, Larry Mutisyo **Owners:** Len & Elizabeth Maddocks **Times:** 12.30-2/6.45-9.30, Closed 16-28 Dec, Closed L Mon-Sat **Prices:** Fixed D £19.95-£25, Coffee £2, Min/Water £3, Service optional **Wine:** 37 bottles over £20, 39 bottles under £20, 7 by the glass (£3.15-£5) **Notes:** Fixed D 4

continued

The Old Rectory Country House

CONWY MAP 14 SH77

British, French

Food to savour in elegant country-house hotel

☎ 01492 580611 Llanrwst Rd, Llansanffraid Glan Conwy LL28 5LF
e-mail: info@oldrectorycountryhouse.co.uk
web: www.oldrectorycountryhouse.co.uk

This charming small hotel - originally Tudor but restyled in Georgian times - has lovely terraced gardens overlooking the Conwy Estuary, Castle and Snowdonia, and is home to an upmarket restaurant serving meals along classic lines using superb quality produce. Owned by committed and sociable resident proprietors, it's a welcoming haven with appropriately friendly and attentive service. Pre-dinner drinks are served in the lounge, while the spacious, elegant dining room comes full of traditional character and charm, and where window seats make the best of those views. Culinary dislikes are discussed on booking, as the daily-changing, fixed-priced, dinner-only menus are a no-choice affair of three courses. Food is carefully prepared, the ingredients of the finest quality from the abundant local Welsh larder. So expect the likes of spiced monkfish tail served with a vanilla risotto and red wine sauce, maybe followed by an anchovy and olive-crusted loin of Welsh mountain lamb from the Conwy Valley accompanied by a leek, laverbread and goat's cheese tart and boulangère potatoes, and to finish, perhaps a trio of desserts (rhubarb pannacotta, hot chocolate fondant and a laverbread and lime sorbet).

Chef: W Vaughan, C Jones **Owners:** M & W Vaughan **Times:** 7.30-11, Closed 15 Dec-18 Jan, Sun, Closed L all week **Prices:** Food prices not confirmed for 2007. Please telephone for details **Wine:** 64 bottles over £20, 50 bottles under £20, 4 by the glass (£3.95-£4.95) **Notes:** Vegetarian available, Dress Restrictions, No jeans, smart casual **Seats:** 14 **Smoking:** N/Sm in restaurant **Children:** Min 5 yrs, Portions **Rooms:** 6 (6 en suite) ★★★★★ GA **Directions:** On A470, 0.5 mile S of junct with A55 **Parking:** 10

courses, Sun L 3 courses £14.50, Vegetarian available, Dress Restrictions, Smart casual **Seats:** 110, Pr/dining room 18 **Smoking:** N/Sm in restaurant, Air con **Children:** Portions **Rooms:** 58 (58 en suite) ★★★ HL **Directions:** From Chester take A55 junct 19 then follow signs towards Llandudno. Follow signs to town centre, head through town centre to Millennium rdbt, take 2nd exit, hotel at end facing main street **Parking:** 44

Imperial Hotel

Modern British

Trustworthy cooking with a Welsh bias

☎ 01492 877466 The Promenade LL30 1AP
e-mail: reception@theimperial.co.uk
web: www.theimperial.co.uk

There's something quintessentially Victorian about this impressively elegant hotel - perhaps it's the seaside location, set back on the promenade in Llandudno, or perhaps it's the grandiose façade. Interiors are decorated in a more unassuming contemporary style. The monthly-changing menu at the Chantrey restaurant offers up dishes, largely British in inspiration, which highlight local produce: walnut and laverbread roulade filled with leeks and Snowdonia Bomber cheese for example, or Welsh lamb with rosemary and caper crust, black pudding and potato cake. Good, reliable cooking with a formal approach to service.

Chef: Arwel Jones **Owners:** Greenclose Ltd **Times:** 12.30-2/6.30-9 **Prices:** Fixed D fr £25, Coffee £2.50, Min/Water £2.50, Service included **Wine:** 16 bottles over £20, 37 bottles under £20, 21 by the glass (£2.50-£5) **Notes:** Sun L 2 courses fr £11.95, 3 courses fr £15, Vegetarian available, Dress Restrictions, Smart casual, Civ Wed 120 **Seats:** 150, Pr/dining room 30 **Smoking:** N/Sm in restaurant **Children:** Menu, Portions **Rooms:** 100 (100 en suite) ★★★ HL **Directions:** On the Promenade **Parking:** 20

Osborne House

Modern British

Small luxury hotel with bistro-style food

☎ 01492 860330 17 North Pde LL30 2LP
e-mail: sales@osbornehouse.com
web: www.osbornehouse.co.uk

This luxurious Victorian townhouse overlooks the seafront at Llandudno and is smartly decorated with rich fabrics, darkwoods and Roman-style pillars adding a Palladian glamour to the dining room. Uniformed staff provide helpful, formal service which despite the grand surroundings manages to feel both personal and pleasantly relaxed. The bistro-style menu consists largely of modern standards, using local ingredients wherever possible - starters might include eggs Benedict or Caesar salad, for example, while typical mains would be sautéed salmon with chunky tomato salsa, a selection of steaks or seared king scallops with smoked bacon and lemon butter.

continued on page 625

Bodysgallen Hall and Spa

LLANDUDNO MAP 14 SH78

Modern NOTABLE WINE LIST

Sumptuous dining in classic country-house setting

☎ 01492 584466 LL30 1RS
e-mail: info@bodysgallen.com
web: www.bodysgallen.com

Starting life as a look-out tower for nearby Conwy Castle, this traditional country-house hotel grew to its current proportions in the 17th century and today still enjoys wonderful views of its extensive grounds and the surrounding countryside. There is a comfortable and welcoming foyer lounge doubling as a bar with two formal yet intimate dining rooms. The well-established service makes this a wonderful dining venue with staff operating like a well-oiled machine.

The best of North Welsh produce is competently showcased on the fixed-price menus of modern British dishes. The 'contrast of red mullet and scallop' starter displays considerable technical skill and an ability to handle delicate flavours. Main courses of John Dory with oxtail ravioli, langoustine and butter sauce are beautifully timed and well sauced. Desserts like the warm chocolate tart with Horlicks ice cream and vanilla foam are exemplary. Special mention has to be made of the canapés and home-made breads.

Notable Wine List: An extensive, well-chosen traditional wine list with tasting notes for most wines.

Chef: John Williams
Owners: Historic House Hotels Ltd
Times: 12.30-1.45/7-9.30
Prices: Fixed L fr £17.50, Fixed D £40, Coffee £3.25, Min/Water £3.75, Service included
Wine: 200 bottles over £20, 25 bottles under £20, 8 by the glass (£3.50-£9)
Notes: Tasting menu £65, Vegetarian available, Dress Restrictions, Smart casual - no jeans/trainers/T-shirts, Civ Wed 55
Seats: 60, Pr/dining room 40
Smoking: N/Sm in restaurant, Air con
Children: Min 6 yrs, Portions
Rooms: 34 (34 en suite) ★★★★ HL
Directions: From A55 junct 19 follow A470 towards Llandudno. Hotel 2m on right
Parking: 40

Wales

LLANDUDNO *continued* MAP 14 SH78

Osborne House

Chef: Michael Waddy & Rob Parry **Owners:** Len & Elizabeth Maddocks **Times:** 12-4/5-10, Closed 16-28 Dec **Prices:** Starter £4-£8.50, Main £9-£18.50, Dessert £4-£5.50, Coffee £1.75, Min/Water £3.50, Service optional **Wine:** 20 bottles over £20, 27 bottles under £20, 6 by the glass (£3.25-£5.50) **Notes:** Sun L 3 courses £14.50 **Seats:** 70, Pr/dining room 18 **Smoking:** N/Sm in restaurant **Children:** Portions **Rooms:** 6 (6 en suite) ★★★★ TH **Directions:** A55 at junct 19, follow signs for Llandudno then Promenade, at War Memorial turn right, Osborne House on left opposite entrance to pier **Parking:** 6

St Tudno Hotel and Restaurant

Modern British V

Accomplished cuisine in elegant surroundings

☎ 01492 874411 The Promenade LL30 2LP
e-mail: sttudnohotel@btinternet.com
web: www.st-tudno.co.uk

erched on the sea front opposite the Victorian pier, this sedate stablishment caters to a genteel clientele, offering classical cuisine and a magnificent afternoon tea. Ornate columns and arches provide glimpses of Lake Como - a mural sadly, but prettily complemented by imposing Italian chandeliers and a working fountain. Quality ingredients are brought together in intriguing combinations to form a seasonal carte plus a list of daily specials; your choice of mains might include pan-roasted salmon with leek and lobster tart, fried courgette flower and red pepper reduction or slow-cooked pork belly with pumpkin purée and piquant sauce, while desserts might include Valrhona chocolate brûlée with Tia Maria cream or iced passionfruit parfait. Vegetarian and eight-course tasting menus available.

Chef: Andrew Williams **Owners:** Mr Bland **Times:** 12.30-1.45/7-9.30 **Prices:** Fixed L fr £15, Fixed D £38.50, Starter £6-£9.50, Main £17.50-£22.50, Dessert £7.50-£8, Coffee £3.75, Min/Water £3.95, Service optional **Wine:** 165 bottles over £20, 42 bottles under £20, 12 by the glass (£3.95-£6.50) **Notes:** Vegetarian menu £35, tasting menu £52.50, Vegetarian menu, Dress Restrictions, Smart casual, no shorts/tracksuits **Seats:** 60 **Smoking:** N/Sm in restaurant, Air con **Children:** Min 6 yrs D, Menu, Portions **Rooms:** 19 (19 en suite) ★★ HL **Directions:** Town centre, on Promenade opposite the pier entrance (near the Great Orme) **Parking:** 9

DENBIGHSHIRE

LLANDRILLO MAP 15 SJ03

Tyddyn Llan

Modern V WINE AWARD WINNER FOR WALES

AA Wine Award Winner for Wales

☎ 01490 440264 LL21 0ST
e-mail: tyddynllan@compuserve.com
web: www.tyddynllan.co.uk

This stylish restaurant with rooms is situated in a quiet corner of North Wales in an elegant Georgian house. Comfortable, thoughtfully furnished rooms and public spaces provide every excuse to stay over. The dining room has particularly attractive views over the surrounding gardens. Service is informal and efficient. The emphasis is on local produce with the chef proprietor offering a straight à la carte menu as well as a popular tasting menu. Expect starters of griddled scallops with vegetable relish and rocket, followed by fillets of sea bass with laverbread butter sauce and for dessert pannacotta and rhubarb or plum soup with blackberries, or alternatively sample the bravura display of British cheese.

Notable Wine List: A wine list which shows much effort and enthusiasm with many interesting food wines categorised by drinking style.

Chef: Bryan Webb **Owners:** Bryan & Susan Webb **Times:** 12.30-2.30/7-9.30, Closed 3 wks Jan/Feb, Closed L Mon-Thu **Prices:** Fixed L fr £19.50, Fixed D fr £40, Coffee £3.50, Min/Water £3.50 **Wine:** 220 bottles over £20, 60 bottles under £20, 15 by the glass (£3.50-£5.80) **Notes:** Sun L £21.50, Tasting menu 7 courses £55, Vegetarian menu, Civ Wed 40 **Seats:** 40, Pr/dining room 40 **Smoking:** N/Sm in restaurant **Children:** Portions **Rooms:** 13 (13 en suite) ★★★★ RR **Directions:** Take B4401 from Corwen to Llandrillo. Restaurant on right leaving village. **Parking:** 20

See also page 626

Wales

Wine Award Winner
Tyddyn Llan

page 625

LLANGOLLEN MAP 15 SJ24

The Wild Pheasant Hotel & Restaurant

Modern British V

Country house with a striking modern wing and beautiful setting

☎ 01978 860629 Berwyn Rd LL20 8AD
e-mail: wild.pheasant@talk21.com
web: www.wildpheasanthotel.co.uk

The Wild Pheasant is a much extended 19th-century country house with views of Castell Dinas Bran, the Berwyn Mountains and the Vale of Llangollen. It is a privately-owned hotel, smartly presented and very hospitable, with wide ranging facilities. Food is served in the Chef's Bar (for snacks) or the Cinnamon Restaurant. Fresh local produce is to the fore in dishes of Welsh lamb chump, Denbighshire best end of lamb, and pheasant wild-style, marinated in juniper berries and cracked pepper and served with one of the chef's favourite sauces.

Chef: Donald Craig **Owners:** P Langhorn **Times:** 12.30-2.30/6.30-9.30, Closed L Mon-Sat **Prices:** Fixed L £11-£13, Fixed D £21.95, Starter £3.95-£5.75, Main £9.85-£13.35, Dessert £4.25-£5.45, Coffee £2.25, Min/Water £3.20, Service optional **Wine:** 15 bottles over £20, 35 bottles under £20, 6 by the glass (£3.25) **Notes:** Fixed D 4 courses, Vegetarian menu, Dress Restrictions, Smart casual, Civ Wed 80 **Seats:** 60, Pr/dining room 120 **Smoking:** N/Sm in restaurant, Air con **Children:** Menu, Portions **Rooms:** 46 (46 en suite) ★★★ HL **Directions:** 1.5m outside Llangollen on the A5 towards Holyhead **Parking:** 200

RHYL MAP 14 SJ08

Barratt's at Ty'N Rhyl

Modern British NEW

Imaginative food in attractive 16th-century house

☎ 01745 344138 & 0773 095 4994 Ty'N Rhyl, 167 Vale Rd LL18 2PH
e-mail: EBarratt@aol.com

A delightful 16th-century house in a secluded location surrounded by mature gardens. The stone-built house is set well back from the road and retains its charm with oak panelling, comfortable sofas and separate bar. The soft lemon-coloured restaurant boasts original wooden floors and well-spaced tables with crisp linen. The daily-changing menu utilises local ingredients and reflects the seasons, with the well-balanced dishes often featuring a maximum of three main ingredients. Expect pan-fried lamb's liver and apple rissoles, lobster, monkfish and crayfish thermidor and glazed banana with buffalo ice cream.

Chef: David Barratt **Owners:** David Barratt **Times:** 7.30-9 **Prices:** Food prices not confirmed for 2007. Please telephone for details **Rooms:** 3 (3 en suite) ◆◆◆◆ **Directions:** Telephone for directions

RUTHIN MAP 15 SJ15

Ruthin Castle

Modern British

Upmarket modern cooking in historic surroundings

☎ 01824 702664 Castle St LL15 2NU
e-mail: reservations@ruthincastle.co.uk
web: www.ruthincastle.co.uk

Dating back to the 13th century, this ancient castle comes complete with a ghostly grey lady with a penchant for strolling the battlements. Now a luxury country-house hotel, it offers its guests a sophisticated British menu in an elegant wood-panelled dining room, delivering upmarket dishes that make the most of local ingredients and include the odd nod to traditional Welsh cuisine. You might start with chicken and rabbit roulade wrapped in Carmarthen ham with onion marmalade, and then tuck into pavé of sea trout with laverbread butter sauce, or braised haunch of local venison with parsnip pomme purée and juniper berry jus.

Chef: James Peter Cooke **Owners:** Mr & Mrs Saintclair **Times:** 12-2/7-9.45, Closed L Sat **Prices:** Fixed L £10.50-£12.50, Fixed D £23.50-£27.50, Starter £4.50-£8.50, Main £15-£18.95, Dessert £4-£6.50, Coffee £2.50, Service optional **Wine:** 60 bottles over £20, 34 bottles under £20, 12 by the glass (£3.75-£6.35) **Notes:** Vegetarian available, Dress Restrictions, Smart casual, Civ Wed 140 **Seats:** 120, Pr/dining room 26 **Smoking:** N/Sm in restaurant **Children:** Portions **Rooms:** 58 (58 en suite) ★★★ **Directions:** Telephone for directions **Parking:** 200

Woodlands Hall Hotel

Traditonal European NEW

Fresh ingredients and fuller flavours in oak-panelled splendour

☎ 01824 705107 Llanfwrog LL15 2AN
e-mail: info@woodlandshallhotel.co.uk
web: www.woodlandshallhotel.co.uk

Standing in 30 acres of parkland, this attractive timber-framed house has lovely views over the Vale of Clwyd. The interior is adorned with intricately carved woodwork, and offers two dining options; the formal, oak-panelled surroundings of Bremner's Restaurant is the serious choice, while there's a relaxed conservatory alternative with lighter menu. The modern approach from a skilled kitchen uses fresh, quality produce to deliver dishes with full flavours on Bremner's sensibly compact, appealing carte. Start with pigeon breast on bubble-and-squeak, continuing with poached cannon of lamb with caramelised red onions or pork teriyaki.

continued

Wales

RUTHIN *continued* MAP 15 SJ15

Chef: Gordon Hogsflesh **Owners:** Gordon Hogsflesh & Tracy Woolliscroft **Times:** 12-2/6.30-9, Closed 2 weeks Jan, Sun, Mon (excl residents) **Prices:** Fixed L £15.50-£18.50, Starter £4.25-£8.50, Main £12.95-£19.50, Dessert £4.75-£6.95, Coffee £1.45, Min/Water £1.60, Service optional **Wine:** 12 bottles over £20, 16 bottles under £20, 13 by the glass (£3.60-£5.60) **Notes:** Sun L 1-3 courses £7.95-15.50, Vegetarian available, Dress Restrictions, Smart casual **Seats:** 20, Pr/dining room 20 **Smoking:** N/Sm in restaurant **Rooms:** 6 (6 en suite) ★★ **Directions:** From Ruthin take B5105, turn right at Cross Keys Inn signed Bontuchel. The hall is signed 0.75m on left **Parking:** 20

The Wynnstay Arms

Modern British NEW

Stylish town-centre brasserie

☎ 01824 703147 Well St LL15 1AN
e-mail: reservations@wynnstayarms.wanadoo.co.uk
web: www.wynnstayarms.com

Extensive renovation has transformed this former pub to provide good quality accommodation as well as an attractive café/bar and the smart Fusions brasserie, which is rapidly earning well deserved respect for its cuisine. Service is informal, but always professional and attentive. The uncomplicated modern cooking style focuses on fresh produce, locally-sourced where possible, to deliver starters such as chicken liver pâté with a toasted herb crustini, and mains of tender pan-fried pork loin steak with black pudding and apple. Desserts tempt with the likes of a delicious vanilla and Amaretto pannacotta with stewed apricots and raspberry coulis, or chocolate truffle ravioli with vanilla pod ice cream.

Chef: Jason Jones **Times:** 12-2/6-9 **Prices:** Food prices not confirmed for 2007. Please telephone for details **Rooms:** 6 (6 en suite) ◆◆◆◆ **Directions:** Telephone for directions

FLINTSHIRE

EWLOE MAP 15 SJ36

De Vere St David's Park

Modern, Traditional

Leisure hotel offering international flavours

☎ 01244 520800 St David's Park CH5 3YB
e-mail: reservations.stdavids@devere-hotels.com
web: www.devereonline.co.uk

An 18-hole championship golf course and spa are among the superb leisure facilities at this purpose-built resort hotel. It is located within easy reach of Chester and Liverpool, and on the edge of beautiful countryside. A choice of dining venues includes the smart Fountains Restaurant with its carte menu and carvery, and the more relaxed Club Café. International flavours are the forte of the former, where diver scallops with minted pea purée and jade sauce, and a trio of pork with apple Tatin and soy jus show off the kitchen's excellent technical skills.

Chef: Stuart Duff **Owners:** De Vere Group Plc **Times:** 12.30-2/7-10, Closed L Sat **Prices:** Fixed L £18.95, Fixed D £23.50, Starter £5.95-£7.95, Main £11.60-£18.50, Dessert £5.95-£6.95, Coffee £2, Min/Water £3.50, Service optional **Wine:** 28 bottles over £20, 30 bottles under £20, 28 by the glass (£4.95-£6.95) **Notes:** Vegetarian available, Dress Restrictions, No trainers, T-shirts, Civ Wed 220 **Seats:** 150, Pr/dining room 45 **Smoking:** N/Sm in restaurant, Air con **Children:** Menu, Portions **Rooms:** 145 (145 en suite) ★★★★ HL **Directions:** 1m from Hawarden station **Parking:** 145

GWYNEDD

ABERDYFI MAP 14 SN69

Penhelig Arms Hotel

Modern British NOTABLE WINE LIST

Fresh fish and local produce at the water's edge

☎ 01654 767215 LL35 0LT
e-mail: info@penheligarms.com
web: www.penheligarms.com

A delightful old inn right at the water's edge in the picturesque resort of Aberdyfi, with lovely views over the tidal Dydi estuary. The bar is a favourite haunt of locals and tourists alike who come for the real ales and great wines by the glass, while those arriving to dine are drawn by the reputation of the fresh fish and quality local meats. Roast loin of cod with creamed spinach, king prawn and saffron velouté is a typically imaginative modern main course, while starters like grilled Pantysgawn goat's cheese with field mushrooms in garlic show the influence of home-grown and local produce, and summer pudding with clotted cream is a seasonal indulgence.
Notable Wine List: An extensive wine list running to almost 300 bins, full of interest and supported by some informative and succinct tasting notes.

Chef: J Griffithe, B Shaw **Owners:** Mr & Mrs R Hughes **Times:** 12-2/6-9.30, Closed 25-26 Dec **Prices:** Fixed D £29, Coffee £2, Min/Water £2.50, Service optional **Wine:** 73 bottles over £20, 185 bottles under £20, 30 by the glass (£3-£7) **Notes:** Sun L 3 courses £18 **Seats:** 36, Pr/dining room 22 **Smoking:** N/Sm in restaurant, Air con **Children:** Portions **Rooms:** 15 (15 en suite) ★★ SHL **Directions:** From Machynlleth take A439 coastal route (9m) **Parking:** 12

ABERSOCH MAP 14 SH32

Neigwl Hotel

British, European

Well-established hotel with a sound reputation

☎ 01758 712363 Lon Sarn Bach LL53 7DY
e-mail: relax@neigwl.com
web: www.neigwl.com

This delightful hotel offers magnificent views over Abersoch Bay from both its restaurant and comfortable lounge. It's privately owned and run, and is located just a short stroll from the town, harbour and beach. Tried and tested favourites are the mainstay of its British

continued

menu with European influences; starters might include duck terrine with poached pears, while mains range from peppered fillet steak with a brandy and cream sauce, to sautéed lamb's liver with onions and bacon, or smoked haddock risotto. Book ahead for a window table.

Chef: Nigel Higginbottom **Owners:** Mark Gauci & Susan Turner **Times:** 7-9, Closed Jan, Closed L all week **Prices:** Fixed D fr £26, Coffee £1.95, Min/Water £4, Service optional **Wine:** 7 bottles over £20, 16 bottles under £20, 5 by the glass (£2.50-£5) **Notes:** Vegetarian available, Dress Restrictions, Smart casual **Seats:** 40 **Smoking:** N/Sm in restaurant **Children:** Menu, Portions **Rooms:** 9 (9 en suite) ★★ **Directions:** A499 from Pwllheli to Abersoch. On entering village turn right at bank. Hotel is 400yds on left **Parking:** 30

Porth Tocyn Hotel

British

Ambitious cooking in country hotel with stunning views

☎ 01758 713303 Bwlch Tocyn LL53 7BU
e-mail: bookings@porthtocyn.fsnet.co.uk
web: www.porth-tocyn-hotel.co.uk

Originally converted from a row of lead miners' cottages, this welcoming hotel has been run by the same family for over 50 years. Marine watercolours adorn the walls of the dining room, with large picture windows providing impressive views over Cardigan Bay and across to Snowdonia. A daily-changing menu is short, contemporary and dictated by local, seasonal produce. Bold flavours can be enjoyed in simple dishes like seared calves' liver with confit cabbage and sultanas with chive jus, roast saddle of Welsh lamb stuffed with tomato and basil or rice pudding with home-made strawberry jam. Service is relaxed and friendly from hands-on owners.

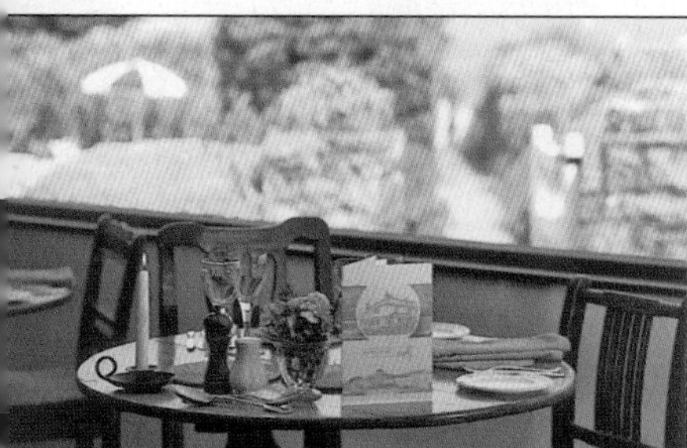

Chef: L Fletcher-Brewer & A Cowling **Owners:** The Fletcher-Brewer Family **Times:** 12.15-2/7.30-9, Closed Mid Nov, wk before Easter, Closed L Mon-Sat **Prices:** Fixed D £38.50, Min/Water £2.75, Service included **Wine:** 48 bottles over £20, 32 bottles under £20, 3 by the glass (£3.25-£5) **Notes:** Sun L buffet £22, Fixed D 4 courses coffee incl, Vegetarian available **Seats:** 50 **Smoking:** N/Sm in restaurant **Children:** Min 7 yrs D, Portions **Rooms:** 17 (17 en suite) ★★★ **Directions:** 2m S of Abersoch, through Sarn Bach & Bwlch Tocyn. Follow brown road signs

BALA MAP 14 SH93

Palé Hall

British, French

Formal dining in delightful mansion

☎ 01678 530285 Palé Estate, Llandderfel LL23 7PS
e-mail: enquiries@palehall.co.uk
web: www.palehall.co.uk

Set in extensive grounds, this enchanting 19th-century mansion is steeped in history and brimming with character. The magnificent entrance hall with its high ceilings and galleried oak staircase is immediately impressive, as are the elegant lounges and smart, oak-panelled restaurant. Service is formal and the cooking is classical, with a good use of local meat and game in season. Dinner may include oxtail and foie gras terrine, followed with a fillet of local Welsh beef with a fricassée of oyster mushrooms and a gratin of exotic fruits flavoured with dates to finish.

Chef: Gilles Mignon **Owners:** Mr Saul Nahed **Times:** 12-1.30/7-8.30 **Prices:** Fixed L fr £14, Fixed D fr £30, Coffee £3, Min/Water £3.50 **Wine:** 45 bottles over £20, 40 bottles under £20, 3 by the glass (£4.50) **Notes:** Dress Restrictions, Smart dress preferred, Civ Wed 40 **Seats:** 28, Pr/dining room 24 **Smoking:** N/Sm in restaurant **Rooms:** 17 (17 en suite) ★★★ **Directions:** Just off B4401, 4m from Llandrillo **Parking:** 40

BARMOUTH MAP 14 SH61

Bae Abermaw

Modern British

Modern cuisine and wonderful sea views

☎ 01341 280550 Panorama Rd LL42 1DQ
e-mail: enquiries@baeabermaw.com
web: www.baeabermaw.com

The Bay View restaurant is aptly named, enjoying stunning views across Cardigan Bay. From the outside, the stern Victorian building gives no hint of its bright, contemporary interior. Wooden floors, fresh white walls, exposed brickwork and modern art prints set the scene. Modern British cuisine with French influences makes good use of local produce on a varied menu. Typical dishes might include pan-fried Welsh Black fillet with dauphinoise potato, port wine sauce and shallots, and a dessert like warm wild blackberry and almond tart with whipped Chantilly cream.

Chef: David Banks **Owners:** Richard & Connie Drinkwater **Times:** 7-9, Closed 2 wks Jan, Mon **Prices:** Fixed D £27-£37, Starter £5.50-£8.50, Main £15.75-£20, Dessert £5.75-£8, Coffee £2.50, Min/Water £3.50, Service optional **Wine:** 33 bottles over £20, 17 bottles under £20, 6 by the glass (£2.80-£4) **Notes:** Dress Restrictions, Smart casual, Civ Wed 80 **Seats:** 28, Pr/dining room 80 **Smoking:** N/Sm in restaurant **Children:** Menu, Portions **Rooms:** 14 (14 en suite) ★★★ HL **Directions:** From Barmouth centre head towards Dolgellau on A496, 0.5m past garage turn left into Panorama Rd, restaurant 100yds **Parking:** 40

CAERNARFON MAP 14 SH46

Seiont Manor

Modern British

Culinary hideaway near Snowdonia

☎ 01286 673366 Llanrug LL55 2AQ
e-mail: seiontmanor@handpicked.co.uk
web: www.handpicked.co.uk

A contemporary take on a traditional Georgian North Welsh farmhouse, original features like stone slabs, exposed brickwork mix easily with exotic fabrics and calming, pastel colours. There's a separate bar for aperitifs and a library for post-prandial relaxation. The beamed Llwyn Y Brain dining room is traditionally appointed with helpful and friendly local staff. Simple cooking and effective presentation allows local produce to really shine. Start with home-made fishcakes with dressed leaves and tarragon and lemon mayonnaise before a main course of pan-seared breast of duck on garlic rösti with a spaghetti of vegetables and sautéed wild mushrooms. To finish there's raspberry pannacotta with cinnamon poached pear and apricot sauce.

continued

Chef: Martin Williams **Owners:** Hand Picked Hotels **Times:** 12-2/7-9.30 **Prices:** Fixed L £13, Fixed D £28.50, Starter £5-£8.50, Main £15-£22, Dessert £6.95, Coffee £2.50, Service optional **Notes:** Vegetarian available, Dress Restrictions, Smart casual, Civ Wed 90 **Seats:** 55, Pr/dining room 20 **Smoking:** N/Sm in restaurant **Children:** Menu, Portions **Rooms:** 28 (28 en suite) ★★★ CHH **Directions:** From Bangor follow signs for Caernarfon. Leave Caernarfon on A4086. Hotel 3m on left **Parking:** 40

CRICCIETH MAP 14 SH53

Bron Eifion Country House Hotel

British

Stylish dining in conservatory restaurant

☎ 01766 522385 LL52 0SA
e-mail: broneifion@bestwestern.co.uk
web: www.broneifion.co.uk

An imposing Grade II listed country house set in peaceful grounds that run down to the sea. Enjoy a pre-dinner drink in the Great Hall, a stately room with minstrels' gallery and lofty timbered roof. Dine in the elegant, candlelit conservatory restaurant in comfortable surroundings enhanced by soft music. British and international cuisine features dishes like fillet steak flambé or venison with chocolate sauce. Flambé dishes served at the table are particularly popular and include desserts like 'banana ponginibio' (sliced bananas cooked in butter with honey and brown sugar, moistened with orange juice and flambéed with Grand Marnier).

Chef: Aled Tomlinson **Owners:** John & Mary Heenan **Times:** 12-2.30/7-9.30 **Prices:** Fixed L £15.95-£19.95, Fixed D £26.95-£29.95, Starter £5.95-£10, Main £23-£35, Dessert £4.95-£7.95, Coffee £2.95, Min/Water £2.75, Service optional **Wine:** 30 bottles over £20, 30 bottles under £20, 5 by the glass (£2.95-£4.95) **Notes:** Sun D £17.95, Vegetarian available **Seats:** 50 **Smoking:** N/Sm in restaurant **Children:** Menu, Portions **Rooms:** 19 (19 en suite) ★★★ HL **Directions:** A497 Between Porthmadog and Pwllheli **Parking:** 50

DOLGELLAU MAP 14 SH71

Dolserau Hall

Traditional

A peaceful setting for enjoyable hotel cuisine

☎ 01341 422522 LL40 2AG
e-mail: welcome@dolserau.co.uk
web: www.dolserau.co.uk

Built in 1863, this impressive country house in a wooded setting has enjoyed a number of uses, from Quaker meeting place to retirement flats, before its current incarnation as a charming hotel.

continued

Food is a major focus for the owners and the daily-changing dinner menu in the Winter Garden Restaurant features Welsh lamb and Black beef, game, fish and locally produced vegetables and fruit. Typical dishes might range from a starter of Welsh farmhouse vegetable soup to a main course of rump of Welsh lamb braised in ale with onions and mushrooms, rounded off with Dolserau bread-and-butter pudding.

Chef: John Charnley **Owners:** Tim & Susan Langdon **Times:** 7-9, Closed Nov-Feb, Closed L all week **Prices:** Fixed D fr £26.95, Coffee £1.50, Min/Water £2.45, Service optional **Wine:** 3 by the glass (£2.25) **Notes:** Fixed D 4 courses, Dress Restrictions, Smart casual, no jeans, sweatshirts, trainers **Seats:** 40 **Smoking:** N/Sm in restaurant **Children:** Min 12 yrs **Rooms:** 20 (20 en suite) ★★★ HL **Directions:** 1.5m from Dolgellau on unclass road between A470/A494 to Bala **Parking:** 20

Penmaenuchaf Hall Hotel

Modern British NOTABLE WINE LIST

Enjoyable dining in Victorian manor

☎ 01341 422129 Penmaenpool LL40 1YB
e-mail: eat@penhall.co.uk
web: www.penhall.co.uk

Nestling in the foothills of Cader Idris, this impressive Victorian manor house, set in 21 acres of terrace gardens and woodland, has splendid views over the Mawddach Estuary. Take a pre-meal stroll in the grounds to soak up the atmosphere, before taking your seat in the smart garden dining room. Here the tables are draped in heavy cream linen, with silver, crystal and fresh flower displays setting the scene, backed up by relaxed and pleasant service from smartly attired staff. Fresh local produce, including herbs from the garden, are delivered with a modern approach, the cooking assured and flavour driven. Take roasted loin of venison with roasted figs, confit cabbage and chocolate jus, or a fillet of sea bass with fennel and red pepper bouillon.

Notable Wine List: The wine list features some useful tasting notes and is well laid out.

Chef: J Pilkington, T Reeve **Owners:** Mark Watson, Lorraine Fielding **Times:** 12-2/7-9.30 **Prices:** Fixed L fr £15.95, Fixed D fr £35, Starter £7.50-£8.50, Main £19.95-£24.50, Dessert £6.75-£8.50, Coffee £2.50, Min/Water £3.50, Service optional **Wine:** 56 bottles over £20, 40 bottles under £20, 5 by the glass (£4-£4.25) **Notes:** Fixed D 4 courses, Vegetarian available, Dress Restrictions, Smart casual, no jeans or T-shirts, Civ Wed 50 **Seats:** 36, Pr/dining room 16 **Smoking:** N/Sm in restaurant **Children:** Min 6 yrs, Portions **Rooms:** 14 (14 en suite) ★★★ HL **Directions:** A493 (Tywyn/Fairbourne), entrance 1.5m on left by sign for Penmaenpool **Parking:** 36

LLANBERIS MAP 14 SH56

Y Bistro

British, French

Well-established restaurant serving modern Welsh cooking

☎ 01286 871278 Glandwr,
43-45 Stryd Fawr (High Street) LL55 4EU
e-mail: ybistro@fsbdial.co.uk
web: www.ybistro.co.uk

This high-street restaurant with attractive frontage has been under the same ownership for 25 years, and it continues to promote fresh Welsh produce in a relaxing atmosphere. The cosy dining room, with high-backed leather chairs, has Tiffany-style lighting and local art and prints. Modern Welsh cooking is influenced by the owner's travels to include Eastern spices and pulses. Dishes are described in Welsh with translations, and portions are hearty. Penfras Welsh is a fillet of cod baked with a 'Welsh' rarebit topping and served with tempura prawns, crispy leeks and roasted cherry tomatoes. When in season, the Welsh lamb is not to be missed.

Y Bistro

Chef: Nerys Roberts **Owners:** Danny & Nerys Roberts **Times:** 7.30-10.15, Closed 2 wks Jan, Sun (Mon in winter), Closed L open for functions, D Sun (Mon in winter) **Prices:** Starter £5.50-£9, Main £14.50-£21, Dessert £6, Coffee £2, Min/Water £3, Service optional **Wine:** 12 bottles over £20, 47 bottles under £20, 5 by the glass (£2.30) **Notes:** Smart casual **Seats:** 40 **Smoking:** N/Sm in restaurant **Children:** Portions **Directions:** In the centre of the village at the foot of Mount Snowdon by Lake Padam **Parking:** On street

---

PORTMEIRION MAP 14 SH53

Castell Deudraeth

Modern

Stylish hotel dining in awe-inspiring North Wales fantasy village

☎ 01766 772400 LL48 6EN
e-mail: castell@portmeirion-village.com
web: www.portmeirion.com

Set in the heart of Clough Williams-Ellis' Italianate village, this castellated hotel has an attractive dining room with garden views shaded in sunny weather with white blinds. Staff speak English and Welsh and the menu is also bi-lingual. Wooden table tops, smartly upholstered chairs and simple settings lend an air of informality to meals here. Using the best of local produce, especially seafood, why not start with a half dozen Menai Straits oysters and follow with the grilled fillet of local sea bass with celeriac mash and a tomato and courgette chutney. To finish there's Williams pear tart layered with white chocolate mousse.

Chef: Peter Hedd Williams **Owners:** Portmeirion Limited **Times:** 12.00-2/6-9.30 **Prices:** Fixed L £15.50-£18.50, Fixed D £29, Service optional **Notes:** Vegetarian available, Civ Wed 40 **Seats:** 80, Pr/dining room 40 **Smoking:** N/Sm area, No pipes, No cigars, Air con **Children:** Menu, Portions **Rooms:** 11 (11 en suite) ★★★★ HL **Directions:** Off A487 at Minffordd. Between Porthmadog & Penryndeudraeth **Parking:** 40

Wales

PORTMEIRION *continued* MAP 14 SH53

Hotel Portmeirion

Modern Welsh

Delightful Italianate setting for good local dining

☎ 01766 770000 LL48 6ET
e-mail: hotel@portmeirion-village.com
web: www.portmeirion-village.com

Built on a river estuary, this main hotel in Clough Williams-Ellis' Italianate village was opened in 1926. Its fame was secured when the cult series, *The Prisoner*, was filmed here in the sixties. The bright curvilinear dining room has columns, large windows and clothed tables with formal settings. Bilingual staff serve modern Welsh dishes based on local produce. Start with the warm chargrilled Caesar salad before a main course of Welsh beef tournedos with Welsh rarebit and champ. Puddings include passionfruit and cherry pannacotta or a good selection of Welsh cheeses.

Chef: David Doughty, Billy Taylor **Owners:** Portmeirion Ltd **Times:** 12-2/6.30-9, Closed 4-16 Jan **Prices:** Fixed L £16.50-£19.50, Fixed D £27.50-£39, Coffee £2.50, Min/Water £3.50, Service optional **Wine:** 50 bottles over £20, 50 bottles under £20, 6 by the glass (£3.50-£5.50) **Notes:** Fixed L 3 courses, Fixed D 4 courses, Vegetarian available, Dress Restrictions, Smart dress, no trainers, jeans, T-shirts, Civ Wed 100 **Seats:** 100, Pr/dining room 30 **Smoking:** N/Sm in restaurant **Children:** Menu, Portions **Rooms:** 51 (51 en suite) ★★★ **Directions:** Off A487 at Minffordd **Parking:** 100

Wales

PWLLHELI MAP 14 SH33

Plas Bodegroes

Modern British

Destination restaurant with rooms on the Llyn Peninsula

☎ 01758 612363 Nefyn Rd LL53 5TH
e-mail: gunna@bodegroes.co.uk
web: www.bodegroes.co.uk

Once a Georgian residence, this sympathetically converted restaurant with rooms occupies a secluded corner of the beautiful Llyn Peninsula. There's a covered terrace, a walled garden and a ha-ha. The elegant, contemporary dining room doubles as a showcase for paintings by famous local artists. Service is personable and efficient. Modern Welsh dishes are cooked with care and flavours are deftly balanced using the best of North Welsh produce. Start with the scallop, crab and laverbread mousseline with crab sauce, before the poached Welsh Black beef with a miniature steak and oyster pie. Finish with chocolate fondant with Baileys ice cream, or good cheeses with lychee sorbet.

Chef: Chris Chown **Owners:** Mrs G Chown & Chris Chown **Times:** 12-2.30/7-9, Closed Dec-Feb, Mon, Closed L Tue-Sat, D Sun **Prices:** Fixed L fr £17.50, Fixed D fr £40, Coffee £2.50, Min/Water £3.50, Service optional **Wine:** 242 bottles over £20, 79 bottles under £20, 2 by the glass (£3.50) **Notes:** Vegetarian available **Seats:** 40, Pr/dining room 16 **Smoking:** N/Sm in restaurant **Directions:** On A497, 1m W of Pwllheli **Parking:** 30

TALSARNAU MAP 14 SH63

Hotel Maes y Neuadd

British, Welsh

NOTABLE WINE LIST

Family-run hotel with fine food

☎ 01766 780200 LL47 6YA
e-mail: maes@neuadd.com
web: www.neuadd.com

With origins in the 14th century, this pretty and enticing manor house has been added to in the 16th, 18th and 20th centuries and yet all parts of the building sit together comfortably. Comfortable and tranquil, the house is furnished with antiques throughout; service is formal but with a friendly, family feel. This unusual menu showcases top-quality Welsh produce, with many of the vegetables and herbs coming from the hotel's extensive gardens. The four-course menu is probably the best way to experience the food here - and the Welsh cheeses should not be overlooked. Starters might include rillette of game with Snowdonia chutney, followed by fillet of salmon with a herb crust, vegetable spaghetti and citrus butter sauce.
Notable Wine List: A well-chosen and nicely presented wine list with concise tasting notes.

Chef: Peter Jackson, John Owen Jones **Owners:** Mr & Mrs Jackson & Mr & Mrs Payne **Times:** 12-1.45/7-8.45 **Prices:** Fixed D £33, Starter £3.50-£7.75, Main £7.50-£11.15, Dessert £4.50-£4.75, Coffee £2.50, Min/Water £3.25, Service optional, Group min 15 service 10% **Wine:** 100 bottles over £20, 74 bottles under £20, 6 by the glass (£3-£5) **Notes:** Thurs Luncheon club 2 courses £12.50, Sun L 3 courses £15.75, Vegetarian available, Smart casual, no denim jeans or sports wear, Civ Wed 65 **Seats:** 50, Pr/dining room 12 **Smoking:** N/Sm in restaurant **Children:** Menu, Portions **Rooms:** 16 (16 en suite) ★★★ HL **Directions:** 3m NE of Harlech, signed off B4573 **Parking:** 60

MONMOUTHSHIRE

ABERGAVENNY MAP 09 SO21

Angel Hotel

Traditional, Modern

Friendly modern restaurant to suit all tastes

☎ 01873 857121 15 Cross St NP7 5EN
e-mail: mail@angelhotelabergavenny.com
web: www.angelhotelabergavenny.com

Combining Georgian elegance with contemporary style, this chic townhouse offers a range of dining options including a candlelit restaurant, comfortable bar, and pretty courtyard in summer. An extensive menu should provoke some pleasurable dithering, and there's no sacrifice of quality to quantity. Expect innovative and accomplished cuisine conjured from top-notch produce; a salad of duck confit with lentils, followed by a crayfish risotto perhaps, or Gloucester Old Spot with cabbage, garlic mash and sage gravy. The prune and Armagnac parfait with poached winter fruits might round things off nicely. Excellent wine list.

Chef: Mark Turton, Paul Tulip **Owners:** Mr & Mrs W J C Griffiths **Times:** 12-2.30/7-10.00, Closed 25 Dec, Closed D 24 & 26 Dec **Prices:** Fixed L £12, Fixed D £27, Starter £4.40-£8, Main £9.60-£16.40, Dessert £4.80, Coffee £2, Min/Water £3, Service optional **Wine:** 35 bottle over £20, 56 bottles under £20, 6 by the glass (£3-£3.50) **Notes:** Sun L 3 courses £16.80, Vegetarian available, Civ Wed 200 **Seats:** 70, Pr/dining room 120 **Smoking:** N/Sm in restaurant **Children:** Portions **Rooms:** 2 (29 en suite) ★★★ HL **Directions:** From A4042/A465/A40 rdbt S of Abergavenny, follow signs for town centre. Continue past railway and bus station on left **Parking:** 40

The Foxhunter

Modern British NOTABLE WINE LIST

A delightful combination of service, surroundings and excellent food

☎ 01873 881101 Nantyderry NP7 9DN
e-mail: info@thefoxhunter.com
web: www.thefoxhunter.com

This charming restaurant is set in an old stationmaster's house that has been sensitively restored and decorated in contemporary style. The Foxhunter has an excellent reputation both locally and nationally with a combination of impressive and imaginative gastro-pub-style food and engaging service. The large menu is difficult to choose from as all the dishes sound equally appealing - you could start with home-salted ox heart, shallot and parsley salad, then move on to roast cod, parsnip purée, mussels and parsnip chips. Save room for the likes of St Emilion of chocolate and mint ice cream.

Notable Wine List: The wine list offers a lovely selection of high-quality wines together with some useful and informative tasting notes.

Chef: Matt Tebbutt **Owners:** Lisa & Matt Tebbutt **Times:** 12-2.30/7-9.30, Closed Xmas, 1 Jan, 2 wks Feb, Sun-Mon (exceptions apply) **Prices:** Fixed L fr £17.95, Starter £5.95-£9.95, Main £11.95-£18.95, Dessert £5.95-£6.95, Coffee £2.75, Min/Water £2.50, Service optional, Group min 8 service 10% **Wine:** 45 bottles over £20, 25 bottles under £20, 4 by the glass (£2.50-£3.50) **Notes:** Vegetarian available **Seats:** 50, Pr/dining room 30 **Smoking:** N/Sm in restaurant **Children:** Portions **Directions:** Just off A4042 between Usk & Abergavenny **Parking:** 25

Llansantffraed Court Hotel

Modern Welsh

Stylish country-house hotel with winning menus

☎ 01873 840678 Llanvihangel Gobion NP7 9BA
e-mail: reception@llch.co.uk
web: www.llch.co.uk

A Grade II listed country-house hotel set in 20 acres of landscaped gardens, this country hotel has lovely views, sumptuous lounges and roaring fires. There's a comfortable bar and a beamed dining room with its country furniture and pretty floral prints. With formal but friendly service, crisp linen, silverware and candles make this a romantic dining venue. The menu comprises classical dishes with unfussy, modern presentation based on high-quality local and home-grown produce. Start with an open ravioli of Argyll scallops and tiger prawns, followed by either fillet of Scottish salmon with Caerphilly and grain mustard crust or flavourful fricassée of Wye Valley chicken.

Chef: Simon King **Owners:** Mr M Morgan **Times:** 12-2/7-8.45 **Prices:** Fixed L £13-£16, Fixed D £29.50, Starter £6-£9, Main £15-£22, Dessert

continued

£6-£9, Coffee £2.50, Min/Water £3.85, Service optional **Wine:** 56 bottles over £20, 38 bottles under £20, 21 by the glass (£3.25-£9.50) **Notes:** Tasting menu £42.50, Sun L £20, Vegetarian available, Civ Wed 150 **Seats:** 50, Pr/dining room 30 **Smoking:** N/Sm in restaurant **Children:** Menu, Portions **Rooms:** 21 (21 en suite) ★★★ CHH **Directions:** From junction of A40 & A465 at Abergavenny, take B4598 signed to Usk. Hotel 4.5m on left (with white gates). 0.5m along drive **Parking:** 250

Llanwenarth Hotel & Riverside Restaurant

Modern British NEW

Riverside dining in stylish restaurant

☎ 01873 810550 Brecon Rd NP8 1EP
e-mail: info@llanwenarthhotel.com
web: www.llanwenarthhotel.com

Situated in the Brecon Beacons National Park, with spectacular views of the Usk Valley, this 16th-century hotel is midway between the market towns of Abergavenny and Crickhowell. The majority of the bedrooms overlook the River Usk, as does the restaurant with its floor-to-ceiling windows, well-spaced tables and terrace. Local, seasonal produce is carefully prepared and there are some well thought out combinations of ingredients and flavours on the lengthy menu: smoked haddock, broccoli and cheddar tartlet, sea bass with crab and rosemary sauce, pear and marzipan tart with cinnamon ice cream.

Chef: Rob Scrimgeour **Owners:** Richard Wallace & Jon West **Times:** 12-2/5.30-9.30, Closed 26 Dec, 1 Jan **Prices:** Fixed L £11.25, Fixed D £14.25, Starter £3.95-£5.95, Main £9.75-£13.95, Dessert £4.25, Coffee £1.75, Min/Water £2.60, Service optional **Wine:** 4 by the glass **Seats:** 60 **Smoking:** N/Sm in restaurant, Air con **Rooms:** 17 (17 en suite) ★★ HL **Directions:** A40 from Abergavenny towards Brecon, hotel 3m past hospital on left **Parking:** 30

Walnut Tree Inn

Italian, Mediterranean

Classic food at the famous inn

☎ 01873 852797 Llandewi Skirrid NP7 8AW
e-mail: francesco@thewalnuttreeinn.com
web: www.thewalnuttreeinn.co.uk

A well-known foodie destination, there has been an inn, pub or restaurant here for about 400 years. It's worth the trip for the location alone, at the foot of the Skirrid Mountain with stunning views of nearby hills and valleys, but of course people really come for the food and you definitely need to book ahead. The restaurant is clean and simple with an unpretentious, relaxed atmosphere. Italian and Mediterranean cuisine centres on great fish and pasta dishes using fresh local produce and a seasonal menu. Starters might feature pan-fried scallops with mixed alliums, then a main course of traditional lasagne alla bolognese or perhaps Vincisgrassi (lasagne with truffle cheese, porcini and Parma ham) - which incidentally are also available to take away. Main courses include roast rack of Welsh lamb with sauté potatoes, rocket and vine cherry tomatoes, but the finale has to be unmissable home-made gelati.

Chef: Spencer Ralph **Owners:** Francesco Mattioli **Times:** 12-3/7-9.30, Closed Mon, Closed D BHs, Sun **Prices:** Starter £6-£14.65, Main £6.25-£19.50, Dessert £5.75-£7, Coffee £1.80, Min/Water £2.95, Service optional **Wine:** 65 bottles over £20, 15 bottles under £20, 8 by the glass (£3.50-£6.50) **Notes:** Vegetarian available **Seats:** 70, Pr/dining room 26 **Smoking:** N/Sm area, No pipes, Air con **Children:** Menu, Portions **Directions:** 3m NE of Abergavenny on B4521 **Parking:** 30

CHEPSTOW MAP 04 ST59

Wye Knot Restaurant

Modern British

Quality dining in friendly cottage restaurant

☎ 01291 622929 The Back NP16 5HH

Overlooking the river Wye, this former holding yard for 19th-century transportees is now an attractive restaurant with its small, friendly bar for aperitifs and simply laid out dining room with linen-clothed tables and assortment of chairs. Expect modern British cooking with Mediterranean influences here. The daily-changing menus reflect local produce and seasonal availability. Strong, clear flavours are artfully combined in starters of gorgonzola tartlette with leek and spinach with a pecan nut and celery dressing and Burgundy poached pear, followed by venison saddle with raspberries and bitter chocolate, roast apples and celeriac. The dessert menu includes a dark chocolate and almond Pithiviers with Amaretto-scented cream. Good home-baked breads.

Chef: Kevin Brookes, Emma Williams **Owners:** Kevin Brookes, Emma Williams **Times:** 12.30-2.30/7-10, Closed 26 Dec, 1 Jan, BHs, Mon-Tues, Closed L Sat **Prices:** Starter £3.50-£8.95, Main £10.95-£18.95, Dessert £4.95, Coffee £2.25, Min/Water £3.50, Service optional, Group min 8 **Wine:** 12 bottles over £20, 18 bottles under £20, 8 by the glass (£3.25-£3.75) **Notes:** Sun L 2 courses £13.95, 3 courses £16.95, Vegetarian available, Dress Restrictions, Smart casual **Seats:** 40 **Smoking:** N/Sm in restaurant **Children:** Menu, Portions **Directions:** From M4 take M48, then onto Chepstow, following signs for Chepstow Castle & Riverbank **Parking:** 8

LLANTRISANT MAP 09 ST39

Brookes Restaurant & Private Dining Room

Modern European V

Welcoming restaurant offering globally-influenced dining

☎ 01443 239600 79-81 Talbot Rd, Talbot Green CF72 8AE
e-mail: staffbrookes@btconnect.com

You can't miss this buzzy eatery, its frontage is painted lilac. Interior décor is equally bold and modern, the large dining room featuring glass block surfaces and striking whitewashed walls adorned with contemporary artwork. Lengthy modern menus scour the globe for inspiration, notably from Europe and Asia. Cooking style is quite rustic, yet dishes are carefully prepared using lots of local produce, as seen in Welsh rib-eye steak with wild mushroom chasseur sauce and loin of monkfish wrapped in Parma ham with crab risotto. The upstairs café is popular with shoppers.

Chef: Craig Brookes **Owners:** Craig & Kevin Brookes **Times:** 12-2.30/7-10.30, Closed 24 Dec, 1 Jan & BHs, Mon, Closed L Sat, D Sun **Prices:** Fixed

continued

L £12.95, Starter £4.50-£8.95, Main £13.95-£18.95, Dessert £5.50, Service optional **Wine:** 16 bottles over £20, 21 bottles under £20, 2 by the glass (£3.25-£4.50) **Notes:** Sun D 2 courses £13.95, 3 courses £16.95, roast £8.95, Vegetarian menu **Seats:** 91, Pr/dining room 26 **Smoking:** No pipes, Air con **Children:** Portions **Directions:** M4 junct 34, follow signs for Llantristant, turn left at 2nd lights **Parking:** On street

---

SKENFRITH MAP 09 SO42

The Bell at Skenfrith

Traditional British NOTABLE WINE LIST

Restaurant with rooms and all-round appeal

☎ 01600 750235 NP7 8UH
e-mail: enquiries@skenfrith.co.uk
web: www.skenfrith.co.uk

Standing beside the River Monnow in a lovely village setting, this stylishly refurbished former coaching inn still retains much charm and character. Beams, flagstone floor and big fires contribute to the understated elegance, backed by relaxed, friendly and efficient service and an impressive wine list. The menu follows a modern British approach, with keen attention to seasonality and the use of quality local produce - all suppliers are admirably listed on the reverse of the menu, with the herbs used in the kitchen's accomplished dishes grown in The Bell's own garden. Thyme-roasted scallops, crispy black pudding and creamed leek compote or braised belly of pork, potato and mustard dauphinoise and creamed spinach are fine examples of the fare. **Notable Wine List:** Interest and quality on every page, and informative and personal tasting notes accompany every wine. Thirteen wines available by the glass are particularly well chosen and offer great value. Half-bottle choices are extensive, as is the separate list of pudding wines and a stunning range of vintage Cognacs.

Chef: David Hill **Owners:** Mr & Mrs W Hutchings **Times:** 12-2.30/7-9.30, Closed New Year, end Jan-beg Feb, Mon (Nov-Mar) **Prices:** Starter £4.50-£9.50, Main £14-£18, Dessert £5.50, Coffee £2.50, Min/Water £2.95, Service optional **Wine:** 167 bottles over £20, 39 bottles under £20, 13 by the glass (£3.50-£4.90) **Notes:** Sun L 2 courses £15.50, 3 courses £19.50, Vegetarian available **Seats:** 55, Pr/dining room 40 **Smoking:** N/Sm in restaurant **Children:** Min 8 yrs **Rooms:** 8 (8 en suite) ★★★★★ RR **Directions:** N of Monmouth on A466 for 4m. Left on B4521 towards Abergavenny, 3m on left **Parking:** 35

USK MAP 09 SO30

The Newbridge

Modern European

Friendly gastro-pub on the banks of the Usk

☎ 01633 451000 Tredunnock NP15 1LY
e-mail: thenewbridge@tinyonline.co.uk
web: www.thenewbridge.co.uk

Idyllically set on the meandering banks of the River Usk, this 200-year old inn has been sympathetically transformed into a spacious restaurant. There's a touch of Tuscany about the place that sets a friendly rustic tone, while smart table settings and efficient service indicate you're in capable hands. Dishes are modern European in sty[le] with the odd nod to more exotic climes. Local meats feature heavily, while a specials board offers fish options direct from the Cornish quayside. Tuck into seared scallops to start perhaps, before sampling Monmouthshire lamb with champ and rosemary jus, or venison on red cabbage with chestnuts and parsnips.

continue[d]

The Newbridge

Chef: Iain Sampson **Owners:** Glen Rick Court Ltd **Times:** 12-2.30/6.30-9.30, Closed 26 Dec **Prices:** Fixed L £18-£26.50, Starter £5-£8, Main £14-£20, Dessert £5-£8, Coffee £1.95, Min/Water £3.10, Service optional **Wine:** 63 bottles over £20, 35 bottles under £20, 9 by the glass (£2.50-£3.95) **Notes:** Sun L 2 courses £15.50, 3 courses £19, Tasting menu £40, Vegetarian available, Dress Restrictions, Smart casual, Civ Wed 60 **Seats:** 80, Pr/dining room 16 **Smoking:** N/Sm in restaurant, Air con **Children:** Portions **Rooms:** 6 (6 en suite) ★★★★ RR **Directions:** A449 towards Usk. Continue through Usk and take B route to Llangibby for approx 5m. From Llangibby continue for approx. 0.5m until sign for Tredunnock. Turn left through Tredunnock to the back of the river **Parking:** 60

◉ Raglan Arms

Modern British

Unpretentious restaurant with substantial portions

☎ 01291 690800 Llandenny NP15 1DL

This friendly, two-storey flint-built inn, located in a beautiful village setting in scenic Monmouthshire, is a cosy, stone-floored pub with restaurant seating around the bar and in a conservatory extension. The solid, unpretentious home cooking keeps an eye on seasonality and uses local, organic produce wherever possible. Come hungry, as portions are substantial - especially bolstering winter dishes like oxtail, beer and root vegetables.

Times: 12-2.30/7-9.30, Closed Mon, Closed D Sun **Directions:** Llandenny is situated halfway between the market towns of Usk and Raglan

◉ Three Salmons Hotel

British, Mediterranean

Lots of choice on the menu at this old coaching inn

☎ 01291 672133 Bridge St NP15 1RY
e-mail: salmonshotel@aol.com
web: www.3-salmons-usk.co.uk

A traditional 17th-century coaching inn turned hotel in the heart of Usk town. Meals can be taken in the bar or restaurant and the staff are relaxed and friendly. All dishes are carefully prepared using seasonal produce and local vegetables, and the blackboard menu offers a good selection of fresh fish. You could be tempted by a ragout of scallops and monkfish with saffron cream, or grilled delice of salmon. If you prefer something meaty, how about medallions of beef and Toulouse sausage and a rich Provençal sauce or breast of guinea fowl on a bed of pak choi and squid ink noodles with mustard and marjoram cream?

Chef: Steven White **Owners:** Tracey Lewis, Clive Hughes **Times:** 12-2.30/7-10, Closed D Sun **Prices:** Fixed L £9.95-£16.95, Fixed D £12.95-£25.95, Starter £4.95-£8.95, Main £9.95-£30, Dessert £3.95-£5.95, Coffee £1.50, Min/Water £3.95, Service optional **Wine:** 25 bottles over £20, 8

continued

bottles under £20, 8 by the glass (£3.25-£6.50) **Notes:** Vegetarian available, Civ Wed 100 **Seats:** 34, Pr/dining room 22 **Smoking:** N/Sm in restaurant **Children:** Menu, Portions **Rooms:** 24 (24 en suite) ★★★ HL **Directions:** M4 junct 24, A449 N, first left A472 to Usk. Hotel in centre of village **Parking:** 40

WHITEBROOK MAP 04 SO50

◉◉ Crown at Whitebrook

Modern British, French

Superb technical skills and exhilarating recipes

☎ 01600 860254 NP25 4TX
e-mail: info@crownatwhitebrook.co.uk
web: www.crownatwhitebrook.co.uk

An old drover's inn set well of the beaten track at the heart of the Wye Valley, but well worth the effort to find it. Many of the original 17th-century features remain, like old beams, now washed white with lime ash, while the elegantly dressed tables and minimalist décor are firmly 21st century. The menu offers a bold interpretation of modern British ideas, strongly influenced by Europe and North America, with some exciting results; lobster and spinach lasagne with seared scallops and coriander risotto is a knockout main dish, and trio of toffee (caramel soufflé, rhubarb and toffee crumble and toffee bombes) makes a superb dessert.

Chef: James Sommerin **Owners:** Well Oiled Ltd **Times:** 12-2/7-9.30, Closed 2 wks Xmas, New Year, Mon, Closed D Sun **Prices:** Fixed L £19.50, Fixed D £37.50, Coffee £2.95, Min/Water £3, Service optional, Group min 6 service 12.5% **Wine:** 130 bottles over £20, 26 bottles under £20, 10 by the glass (£4.75-£6.50) **Notes:** Vegetarian available, Dress Restrictions, Smart casual preferred **Seats:** 36, Pr/dining room 12 **Smoking:** N/Sm in restaurant **Children:** Min 12 yrs **Rooms:** 10 (10 en suite) ★★★★★ RR **Directions:** W off A66 immediately S of Bigsweir Bridge (5m from Monmouth), 2m on unclassified road **Parking:** 20

NEWPORT

NEWPORT MAP 09 ST38

◉◉ The Chandlery

Modern, Traditional

Skilful cooking in historic maritime surroundings

☎ 01633 256622 77-78 Lower Dock St NP20 1EH
web: www.thechandleryrestaurant.com

This Grade II listed Georgian ships' chandlery building in Newport's commercial centre has now been sympathetically converted into a restaurant. Original features mix well with the smart décor. There's a comfortable bar area and well-spaced tables in the light and airy dining rooms. Service is attentive and friendly. European dishes are all

continued

NEWPORT *continued* MAP 09 ST38

carefully prepared and presented in a modern unfussy way using top-quality local and Welsh produce. Try the starter of Jerusalem artichoke, Perl Las cheese and tomato salad with quail's egg and rocket, followed by the Welsh beef fillet with oxtail sauce, celeriac purée and fried potatoes. To finish there's steamed treacle sponge with butterscotch sauce and custard.

Chef: Simon Newcombe, Carl Hammet **Owners:** Simon Newcombe, Jane Newcombe **Times:** 12-2/7-10, Closed 1 wk Xmas, Sun-Mon, Closed L Sat **Prices:** Fixed L £9.95, Starter £3.95-£8.50, Main £9.50-£17.95, Dessert £4.95-£5.95, Coffee £1.50, Min/Water £2.95, Service optional, Group min 6 service 10% **Wine:** 14 bottles over £20, 24 bottles under £20, 6 by the glass (£2.90-£4.05) **Notes:** Tasting menu available, Vegetarian available **Seats:** 80, Pr/dining room 60 **Smoking:** N/Sm area, Air con **Children:** Portions **Directions:** Situated on A48, 0.5m from the Royal Gwent Hospital at the foot of George St Bridge **Parking:** 20

Owens at the Celtic Manor Resort

Modern European V

Fine dining at a luxury resort hotel

☎ 01633 413000 Coldra Woods NP18 1HQ
e-mail: postbox@celtic-manor.com
web: www.celtic-manor.com

Owens is the Resort's fine-dining flagship, an intimate venue serving award-winning food using the finest of Welsh organic produce. A new addition to the restaurant, Owens Lounge Bar, provides a private area for Owens' diners to meet for a drink before dinner, with luxurious black leather chairs set against cool granite and limed oak tables, linking perfectly with the restaurant décor. A wide choice is offered from the carte, the tasting menu and a separate vegetarian carte. Global influences are apparent in the dishes, which include a starter of frogs' legs followed by slow-roasted Welsh beef fillet served with rib meat ravioli, shallot purée and red wine sauce.

Chef: Nicholas Evans **Owners:** Sir Terence Matthews **Times:** 7-10.30, Closed 1-12 Jan, Sun, Closed L all week **Prices:** Fixed D fr £45, Min/Water £4, Service optional **Wine:** 175 bottles over £20, 9 by the glass (£4.75-£10) **Notes:** Tasting menu £60, with wine £95, Surprise 10 courses £60, Vegetarian menu, Dress Restrictions, No jeans, trainers or T-shirts, Civ Wed 100 **Seats:** 45, Pr/dining room 26 **Smoking:** N/Sm in restaurant, Air con **Children:** No Children **Rooms:** 330 (330 en suite) ★★★★★ HL **Directions:** From M4 junct 24 take A48 towards Newport, turn right after 300yds **Parking:** 1000

ST BRIDES WENTLOOGE MAP 09 ST28

The Inn at the Elm Tree

Modern British, European

Modern-style inn serving fresh local produce in peaceful location

☎ 01633 680225 St Brides Wentlooge NP10 8SQ
e-mail: inn@the-elm-tree.co.uk
web: www.the-elm-tree.co.uk

This stylish barn conversion is quite an unexpected find in the tranquil setting of Wentlooge Flats. Its modern restaurant has a cool minimalist note with relaxed, attentive service, and there's a pleasant tropical courtyard for warm summer evenings. The kitchen's modern approach follows the theme and makes good use of fresh local produce, including the fruits of the sea. Expect the likes of a St Brides seafood chowder to start and lemon tart with liquorice ice cream to finish and, in between, braised shank of Welsh lamb with mashed potato and a Madeira sauce.

Chef: David Goddard **Owners:** Shaun Ellis **Times:** 12-2.30/6-9.30 **Prices:** Fixed L £10, Starter £4-£9.95, Main £14-£18.95, Dessert £4.50-£5.95, Coffee £1.50, Min/Water £3.80, Service optional **Wine:** 14 bottles over £20, 28 bottles under £20, 10 by the glass (£3.60-£4.90) **Notes:** Civ Wed 60 **Seats:** 45, Pr/dining room 20 **Smoking:** N/Sm in restaurant **Children:** Min 12 yrs **Rooms:** 10 (10 en suite) ◆◆◆◆◆ **Directions:** From M4 junct 28 take A48 towards Castleton. At 1st rdbt turn left , continue 1.5m, right onto Morgan Way. Turn right at T-junct onto B4239. Inn 2.5m **Parking:** 30

PEMBROKESHIRE

HAVERFORDWEST MAP 08 SM91

Wolfscastle Country Hotel

International

Good freshly cooked food in comfortable surroundings

☎ 01437 741225 & 741688
Wolf's Castle SA62 5LZ
e-mail: info@wolfscastle.com
web: www.wolfscastle.com

This large, stone house with gabled roof dates back to the mid-19th century and enjoys a prominent position in the village. Inside there is a pleasant bar and attractive restaurant with a good reputation for its food. The same menu is available throughout the bar and restaurant, with dishes using fresh local produce where possible. Starters range from home-made soups to salads, terrines and home-made fishcakes. Mains might include pan-fried sirloin of Welsh beef or roast

continued

Pembrokeshire Gressingham duck. A large choice of simple traditional dishes includes scampi, local sausages and fisherman's pie.

Chef: Steve Brown **Owners:** Mr A Stirling **Times:** 12-2/7-9, Closed 24-26 Dec **Prices:** Food prices not confirmed for 2007. Please telephone for details **Wine:** 19 bottles over £20, 43 bottles under £20, 9 by the glass (£2.50-£4.80) **Notes:** Civ Wed 60 **Seats:** 55, Pr/dining room 32 **Smoking:** N/Sm in restaurant **Children:** Menu, Portions **Rooms:** 24 (24 en suite) ★★ CHH **Directions:** From Haverfordwest take A40 towards Fishguard. Hotel in centre of Wolf's Castle **Parking:** 50

PORTHGAIN MAP 08 SM83

The Shed

British, International

Local seafood dining in sea-going surroundings

☎ 01348 831518 SA62 5BN
e-mail: caroline@theshedporthgain.co.uk
web: www.theshedporthgain.co.uk

These slate works offices have served as fisherman's lock-ups and now an atmospheric quayside restaurant in this picturesque port village. Decorated in the flotsam and jetsam style, it looks like a sea captain has just nipped down the shops for some chewing tobacco. In short, a great setting to enjoy local seafood, much of it caught by the owners. Expect starters like Porthgain crab with gazpacho sauce or a main course of line-caught sea bass with vanilla vinaigrette or the delicious local lobster. Finish with walnut tart with Welsh whisky butterscotch sauce and cream.

Chef: Caroline Jones **Owners:** Rob & Caroline Jones **Times:** 11-4.30/7-1.30, Closed Nov-Apr open only weekends, subject to bookings **Prices:** Fixed D £29.95, Starter £4.95-£7.95, Main £16.95-£25.95, Dessert 3.50-£5.95, Coffee £1.80, Min/Water 80p **Wine:** 10 bottles over £20, 20 bottles under £20, 6 by the glass (£3-£3.95) **Notes:** No children under yrs at D Fri & Sat **Seats:** 36 **Smoking:** N/Sm in restaurant **Directions:** 7m from St. Davids. Off A40 **Parking:** On village street

---

ST DAVID'S MAP 08 SM72

Morgan's

British, International

Family-run restaurant serving fresh local fare

☎ 01437 720508 20 Nun St SA62 6NT
e-mail: morgans@stdavids.co.uk
web: www.morgans-in-stdavids.co.uk

Once the home of the village school mistress, Morgan's is right at the heart of Britain's smallest city, its stylish interior providing a showcase for local artists. Tara and David Pitman took over in February 2006

continued

(Tara cooking), offering a classic menu with some Pacific and exotic twists. Ingredients are locally sourced and the blackboard lists daily fish dishes and other specials. Typical are Morgan's antipasto, followed by Welsh Black beef fillet, Montpellier butter and Pembrokeshire dauphinoise. Finish with banana tart, home-made Welsh honey ice cream and butterscotch sauce.

Chef: Tara Pitman **Owners:** David & Tara Pitman **Times:** 11-2.30/6.30-10.30, Closed Jan, Tue **Prices:** Starter £4-£7.50, Main £11-£18, Dessert £4-£6.50, Coffee £2, Min/Water £2.50, Service optional **Wine:** 10 bottles over £20, 10 bottles under £20, 3 by the glass (£2.50-£4)
Notes: Vegetarian available, Smart casual **Seats:** 36, Pr/dining room 12
Smoking: N/Sm in restaurant **Children:** Portions
Directions: Haverfordwest 16m. On A487 to Fishguard, just off main square **Parking:** Car park opposite

Warpool Court Hotel

Modern British

Spacious hotel restaurant with wonderful sea views

☎ 01437 720300 SA62 6BN
e-mail: info@warpoolcourthotel.com
web: www.warpoolcourthotel.com

Built in 1860 to house St David's Cathedral choir, the hotel has an interesting history and a stunning location overlooking one of the most beautiful stretches of coastline in Europe. Of particular note are the 3,000 hand-painted tiles to be found downstairs and in the original bedrooms. The finest available ingredients, locally sourced where possible, are used to create a good choice of imaginative dishes. Examples are steamed langoustine with ginger and leek or spinach and quail egg ravioli, followed by Welsh Black beef fillet, fondant potato, red onion confit and red wine jus or roast brill, globe artichokes, parsley and caper butter. Finish with the chocolate dessert plate with pistachio ice cream.

Chef: Shaun Ellison **Owners:** Peter Trier **Times:** 12-1.45/7-9.15, Closed Jan **Prices:** Fixed L £25, Fixed D £44, Min/Water £3.45, Service included **Wine:** 103 bottles over £20, 18 bottles under £20, 3 by the glass (£3) **Notes:** Vegetarian available, Civ Wed 130 **Seats:** 50, Pr/dining room 22 **Smoking:** N/Sm in restaurant **Children:** Menu, Portions **Rooms:** 25 (25 en suite) ★★★ CHH **Directions:** From Cross Sq in centre of St Davids, left by HSBC Bank into Goat St, at fork follow hotel signs **Parking:** 100

TENBY MAP 08 SN10

Panorama Hotel

European, International

Sea front hotel with homely food

☎ 01834 844976 The Esplanade SA70 7DU
e-mail: mail@tenby-hotel.co.uk
web: www.tenby-hotel.co.uk

Overlooking the sands of Tenby's south beach, this traditional, family-run hotel is not called the Panorama for nothing, blessed as it is with wonderful views of Carmarthen bay and the island of Caldey. The décor has a cosy, homely feel evoking nostalgia for the golden days of the British seaside holiday. The hotel's Robin's restaurant makes the best use of Pembrokeshire produce throughout its lengthy British menu with international influences. Try Thai crab cake as a starter then pork with woodland mushrooms and cream.

Chef: Robin Wright **Owners:** Robin & Carol Wright **Times:** 7-9, Closed Xmas, Sun, Closed L all week, D Sun **Prices:** Fixed D £25, Min/Water £1.95, Service optional **Notes:** Fixed D courses, Vegetarian available, Dress Restrictions, Smart casual **Seats:** 25 **Smoking:** N/Sm in restaurant **Children:** Portions **Rooms:** 7 (7 en suite) ★★ HL **Directions:** From A478 follow South Beach & town centre signs, sharp left at mini-rdbt, under railway and up Greenhill Rd. Along South Parade to Esplanade **Parking:** On street

Wales

Penally Abbey Hotel

Traditional Modern

Enjoy local produce in charming country-house setting

☎ 01834 843033 Penally SA70 7PY
e-mail: penally.abbey@btinternet.com
web: www.penally-abbey.com

This ivy-fronted, country-house hotel is set in five acres of grounds and has impressive views across Carmarthen Bay. Renovation and upgrading has done nothing to diminish the charm of the place. The restaurant is spacious, well decorated with good garden and sea views. Service is pleasant and unhurried. The menu comprises modern British dishes with good use of local produce. To start, try the smoked salmon and trout gâteau with asparagus followed by the Welsh Black beef with stilton and red wine jus. Finish with the crème caramel with red berries.

Times: 12.30-2/7.30-9.30, Closed L (ex by arrangement only) **Rooms:** 12 (12 en suite) ★★★ CHH **Directions:** From Tenby take A4139 to Penally

POWYS

BRECON MAP 09 SO02

The Felin Fach Griffin

British

High-quality dining in a wonderful upland setting

☎ 01874 620111 Felin Fach LD3 0UB
e-mail: enquires@eatdrinksleep.ltd.uk
web: www.eatdrinksleep.ltd.uk

Lying at the junction of the Brecon Beacons and the Black Mountains, the bright red exterior of this dining pub with rooms is difficult to miss. The interior is no less jolly, being divided into dining spaces each with a different theme or colour. Furniture is comfortable, rustic and harlequin. The informal atmosphere, cheerful service and simple menu belie a striving for excellence which is discernable in starters like roasted scallops, cep mushroom marmalade and black pepper butter or main courses of local rib-eye of beef with red onion confit, béarnaise and chips and puddings like crème brûlée. The same care is taken in sourcing the wines and beers.

Chef: Ricardo Van Ede **Owners:** Charles Inkin, Edmund Inkin **Times:** 12.30-2.30/6.30-9.30, Closed 24-25 Dec, few days Jan, Closed L Mon (in winter excl BHs) **Prices:** Fixed L £12.95-£23.50, Fixed D £29.50, Starter £4.90-£9.50, Main £9.50-£16.95, Dessert £5.50-£6, Coffee £1.80, Min/Water £2.80, Service optional **Wine:** 30% bottles over £20, 70% bottles under £20, 10 by the glass (£3-£5.65) **Notes:** Sun L £12.19-21.95, Vegetarian available **Seats:** 45, Pr/dining room 20 **Smoking:** N/Sm in restaurant **Children:** Portions **Rooms:** 7 (7 en suite) ◆◆◆◆ **Directions:** 3.5m N of Brecon on A470. Large terracotta building on left, o edge of village **Parking:** 60

Peterstone Court Hotel

Modern British

Accomplished modern British cooking overlooking the River Usk

☎ 01874 665387 Llanhamlach LD3 7YB
e-mail: info@peterstone-court.com
web: www.peterstone-court.com

Local ingredients are a feature of the menu at this comfortable Georgian manor on the edge of the Brecon Beacons, with livestock supplied direct from the nearby family farm. It's treated sympathetically by a talented kitchen and delivered to the table in flavoursome combinations; roast rump of Welsh lamb arrives with sun-blushed tomato and basil mash, plus a tartlet of lamb's kidneys, while veal is accompanied by calves' liver, bacon, shallots, creamed cabbage and boudin blanc. Desserts are a highlight and might includ apple and rosemary tarte Tatin with Calvados ice cream, or a trio of clever rhubarb creations. Choose from the extensive carte or plump for the seven-course tasting menu to really do the place justice.

Chef: Mr Lee Evans **Times:** 12-2.30/7-9.30 **Prices:** Starter £5.50-£8.95, Main £8.95-£16.95, Dessert £5.95, Coffee £2.25, Min/Water £3.50, Service optional **Wine:** 21 bottles over £20, 29 bottles under £20, 7 by the glass (£3.25-£4.45) **Notes:** Sun L 2 courses £14.50, 3 courses £18.50, Tasting menu £45, Civ Wed 120 **Seats:** 30, Pr/dining room 120 **Smoking:** N/S in restaurant **Children:** Menu, Portions **Rooms:** 12 (12 en suite) ★★★ CHH **Directions:** 2.5m from Brecon on A40 to Abergavenny **Parking:** 40

The Usk Inn

British, French

'maginative menu at a traditional inn

☎ 01874 676251 Station Rd, Talybont-on-Usk LD3 7JE
e-mail: dine@uskinn.co.uk
web: www.uskinn.co.uk

This traditional-looking inn in the quiet village of Talybont-on-Usk was once a bank, but you'd never guess from the open log fires, polished wooden tables and flagstone floors inside. The bright, airy restaurant has a Mediterranean feel, while the bar area is more traditional. Local Welsh produce and seasonal ingredients are used to create an maginative menu supplemented by blackboard specials. Look out for resh figs wrapped in cured ham, stuffed with goat's cheese, and simple dishes like slow-roasted lamb served on mashed potato with diced vegetables and a hint of mint.

hef: Andrew Felix, Sean Gibbs **Owners:** Andrew, Paul & Jillian Felix **imes:** 12-3/6.30-9.30, Closed 25-27 Dec **Prices:** Fixed L £10.95-£16.95, xed D fr £13.95, Starter £3.95-£7.95, Main £8.95-£25, Dessert £2.95-£6, offee £1.50, Min/Water £3.75, Service optional **Wine:** 8 bottles over £20,) bottles under £20, 9 by the glass (£3.25-£6) **Notes:** Vegetarian vailable, Dress Restrictions, No slogan T-shirts, etc **Seats:** 60 **moking:** N/Sm in restaurant, Air con **Children:** Portions **Rooms:** 11 (11 ı suite) ◆◆◆◆ **Directions:** 250 yds off A40, 6m E of Brecon **arking:** 35

The White Swan

Aodern European

aditional pub oozing with character

☎ 01874 665276 LD3 7BZ
-mail: stephen.way@tiscali.co.uk
eb: www.the-white-swan.com

:t in the heart of the Brecon Beacons, this traditional inn overlooks e peaceful St Brynach's churchyard. You can eat casually in the acious bar or more formally in the smaller rustic restaurant, and ke in the vast fireplace, bare stone walls, oak beams and cosy mosphere. Local produce features on the modern British menu, om lunchtime snacks and blackboard specials to the more mprehensive evening carte. Start with breaded wild mushroom otto cake, or smoked bacon, leek and black pudding terrine, then ove on to roast rump of Welsh Mountain lamb, haunch of Brecon nison stuffed with peppery raspberry mousse, or loin of local wild ar topped with apple and onion confit and wrapped in puff stry.

continued

Chef: L Havard, S Howells, S Way **Owners:** Richard Griffiths **Times:** 12-2/7-11.30, Closed 25-26 Dec, 1 Jan, Mon **Prices:** Fixed L fr £12.95, Fixed D fr £17.95, Starter £4.45-£7.95, Main £10.95-£17.95, Dessert £4.25-£5.45, Coffee £1.30, Min/Water £2.50 **Wine:** 10 bottles over £20, 20 bottles under £20, 8 by the glass (£1.95-£2.25) **Notes:** Fixed D 2 courses **Seats:** 60, Pr/dining room 50 **Smoking:** N/Sm in restaurant **Children:** Menu, Portions **Directions:** 3m E of Brecon, off A40. Take B4558 following signs for Llanfrynach **Parking:** 40

BUILTH WELLS

The Drawing Room

Modern British

AA Restaurant of the Year for Wales

☎ 01982 552493 Cwmbach, Newbridge-on-Wye LD2 3RT
e-mail: post@the-drawing-room.co.uk
web: www.the-drawing-room.co.uk

Set in the heart of Wales near to the market town of Builth Wells (home to the Royal Welsh Show), this attractive restaurant with rooms is set in a Georgian country residence which has been refurbished to the highest standards. The dining room has a refined feel with subtle wall colours adorned with eye-catching Mary Loxton prints and an uncluttered atmosphere. The food is French-influenced with clean, unfussy flavours utilising quality local ingredients such as Welsh lamb and Welsh Black beef. A typical starter would be Cardigan Bay crab salad with prawns and avocado, while a main course might be sauté of monkfish with capers and sage, lemon and prawn risotto with a fish velouté.

Chef: Colin and Melanie Dawson **Owners:** Colin and Melanie Dawson **Times:** 12-2/7-9, Closed 2 wks Jan, 2 wks Oct, Mon, Closed D Sun **Prices:** Fixed L £19.50-£25, Starter £7.50-£9.50, Main £18.50-£25, Dessert £6.50-£7.50, Coffee £3, Min/Water £3.50, Service optional **Wine:** 50 bottles over £20, 26 bottles under £20, 8 by the glass (£3.75-£5.25) **Notes:** Fixed L 3 courses, Dress Restrictions, Smart casual **Seats:** 20, Pr/dining room 8 **Smoking:** N/Sm in restaurant **Children:** Min 12 yrs **Rooms:** 3 (3 en suite) ★★★★★ RR **Directions:** From Builth Wells, take A470 towards Rhayader, 3m on left **Parking:** 14

CAERSWS MAP 15 SO09

The Talkhouse

British NOTABLE WINE LIST **NEW**

Classic seasonal cooking at former coaching inn

☎ 01686 688919 Pontdolgoch SY17 5JE
e-mail: info@talkhouse.co.uk
web: www.talkhouse.co.uk

This stone-built, 17th-century inn now has smart décor and furnishings and a warm, friendly and relaxed atmosphere. The bright, traditional-styled dining room has French windows opening on to a secluded garden for alfresco summer dining, while the comfortable sitting room comes with deep sofas and armchairs and a beamed bar with log fire. The classic seasonal cooking makes fine use of fresh local produce as in smoked haddock rarebit, a venison terrine with onion chutney, Welsh fillet of beef with horseradish rösti and rich pan jus, and a steamed chestnut and pear pudding finish.
Notable Wine List: A developing wine list which shows great enthusiasm.

Wales

Chef: Stephen Garratt **Owners:** Stephen & Jacqueline Garratt **Times:** 12-1.30/6.30-8.45, Closed 25-26 Dec, 1st 2 wks Jan, Mon, Closed L Tue (bookings only Wed & Thur), D Sun, Mon **Prices:** Starter £4.50-£6.50, Main £12-£18.95, Dessert £4.50, Coffee £2.50, Min/Water £3, Service optional **Wine:** 40 bottles over £20, 60 bottles under £20, 6 by the glass (£3.25-£4.95) **Notes:** Booking essential, Vegetarian available, Dress Restrictions, Smart casual **Seats:** 40, Pr/dining room 20 **Smoking:** N/Sm in restaurant **Children:** Min 14 yrs **Rooms:** 3 (3 en suite) ◆◆◆◆◆ **Directions:** On A470 6m SW of Newtown, 1.25m W of Caersws **Parking:** 40

CRICKHOWELL MAP 09 SO21

Bear Hotel

British, European

Quaint coaching inn offering imaginative food and a friendly welcome

☎ 01873 810408 High St NP8 1BW
e-mail: bearhotel@aol.com
web: www.bearhotel.co.uk

This historic coaching inn, purportedly built for a wealthy merchant in 1432, is furnished with antiques and retains all its original character. The welcoming bar has cosy sections and there is no need to book a table to eat here. The restaurant, and at weekends the function room, offer a more formal restaurant experience. Here the menu offers British and European dishes using lots of wonderful local produce. Try a main course like fillet of Welsh Black beef served on a spicy pak choi, sweet potato gnocchi and confit shallot purée, with a port sauce.

continued

Sunday lunch is a great experience for all the family with traditional roast beef and alternatives like leg of Welsh lamb.

Bear Hote

Owners: Mrs. J Hindmarsh, Stephen Hindmarsh **Times:** 12-2/7-9.30, Closed 25 Dec, Mon, Closed L Tue-Sat, D Sun **Prices:** Starter £5.95-£8.95, Main £12.95-£19.95, Dessert £5-£6.50, Coffee £1.20, Min/Water £2.50, Service optional **Wine:** 15 bottles over £20, 35 bottles under £20, 16 by the glass (£2.20-£5) **Notes:** Vegetarian available, Dress Restrictions, Smart casual **Seats:** 60, Pr/dining room 30 **Smoking:** N/Sm in restaurant **Children:** Min 9 yrs, Menu, Portions **Rooms:** 26 (26 en suite) ★★★ **Directions:** Town centre, off A40 (Brecon road). 6m from Abergavenny **Parking:** 40 see advert opposit

Gliffaes Hotel Ltd

Modern British

Traditional country house setting with innovative, modern dining

☎ 01874 730371 NP8 1RH
e-mail: calls@gliffaeshotel.com
web: www.gliffaeshotel.com

This Italianate country-house hotel has a long and glorious fly-fishing history. Have a drink in the charming bar before entering the elegant dining room with its rich carpeting, panelled walls and beautiful views over the River Usk and valley. Modern British dishes with French influences are given the occasional Asian touch such as the starter of tempura bay flower courgette stuffed with cream cheese on ratatouille Main courses might include venison steak stuffed with sage and boud blanc or grilled lemon sole with caper and prawn butter sauce and dauphinoise. Finish with ricotta terrine with praline and slow roast figs

Chef: Stephan Trinci **Owners:** Mr/s Brabner & Mr/s Suter **Times:** 12-2.30/7.30-9.15, Closed 2-31 Jan, Closed L Mon-Sat **Prices:** Fixed L fr £27, Fixed D fr £32, Coffee £2, Service included **Wine:** 39 bottles over £20, 38 bottles under £20, 6 by the glass (£3.30-£6) **Notes:** Fixed L 3 courses, Vegetarian available, Dress Restrictions, Smart casual preferred, Civ Wed 4 **Seats:** 70, Pr/dining room 35 **Smoking:** N/Sm in restaurant **Children:** Menu, Portions **Rooms:** 22 (22 en suite) ★★★ HL **Directions:** 1m off A40, 2.5m W of Crickhowell. **Parking:** 30

Manor Hotel

Modern European

Real food from local produce, served simply

☎ 01873 810212 Brecon Rd NP8 1SE
e-mail: info@manorhotel.co.uk
web: www.manorhotel.co.uk

Dating back to the early 1700s, the Manor hotel was the birthplace o Sir George Everest in 1790, former Surveyor General of India. His

continu

name is given to the Everest Dining Room, which enjoys stunning views of the Usk valley. Here you will find exciting modern cooking using fresh local ingredients. Local meats and poultry raised on the Manor's own farm can be found on the menu, alongside fresh seafood and fish delivered daily. Try a main course like home-reared roast duck with roasted sweet onions and dried fruit port sauce.

Times: 12-2/7-9 **Rooms:** 22 (22 en suite) ★★★ HL **Directions:** 0.5m W of Crickhowell on A40, Brecon road

Nantyffin Cider Mill Inn

British, International

Combination of old character and gastro-pub feel

☎ 01873 810775 Brecon Rd NP8 1SG
e-mail: info@cidermill.co.uk
web: www.cidermill.co.uk

Located on the main road between Abergavenny and Brecon, this 16th-century former drover's inn and cider mill is always busy, so book ahead. A chic gastro-pub décor makes the most of original features, while log fires keep things cosy - choose from a menu that draws inspiration from Asia, North Africa and the Mediterranean, as well as closer to home. A great supporter of local suppliers, the owners rear their own livestock from the family farm. Mains might include mixed seafood cassoulet with bruschetta, or roast loin of home-reared Old Spot pork with bubble-and-squeak and onion rings. Lunch is good value.

Chef: Sean Gerrard **Owners:** Glyn Bridgeman & Sean Gerrard **Times:** 12-2.30/6.30-10, Closed 1 wk Jan, Mon, Closed D Sun(winter) **Prices:** Fixed L fr £12.95, Fixed D fr £16.95, Starter £3.95-£8.95, Main £8.95-£16.95, Dessert £5.50-£6.95, Coffee £1.80, Min/Water £3.50, Service optional **Wine:** 20 bottles over £20, 29 bottles under £20, 8 by the glass (£3.25-£4.45) **Notes:** Vegetarian available **Seats:** 65 **Smoking:** N/Sm in restaurant **Children:** Menu, Portions **Directions:** 1m W of Crickhowell on A40 at junct with A479 **Parking:** 40

Ty Croeso Hotel

Traditional Welsh V NEW

Relaxed country-house dining with strong Welsh emphasis

☎ 01873 810573 The Dardy, Llangattock NP8 1PU
e-mail: info@ty-croeso.co.uk
web: www.ty-croeso.co.uk

Translating as 'House of Welcome', Ty Croeso certainly lives up to its name under new ownership. Eat in the relaxed and comfortably refurbished candle-lit restaurant, while summer offers tables on the flower-filled terrace overlooking the Usk. The sensibly compact carte and excellent-value Taste of Wales menus put the emphasis on quality produce – Welsh beef, lamb, game, cheese and vegetables all feature

continued

strongly. Simple, accomplished preparation hits the mark. Roasted red peppers with Pant-Ysgawn (Welsh goat's cheese) or twice-cooked goat's cheese soufflé are typical starters, with pork tenderloin, Welsh mustard sauce, leek and potato rösti to follow. Excellent home-made ice creams make the perfect finale.

Chef: Lisa Grenfell **Owners:** Linda Jarrett **Times:** 7-9, Closed L all week ex BH wknds **Prices:** Fixed D £18, Starter £4.25-£5.75, Main £9.50-£15.50, Dessert £4-£5.50, Coffee £1.80, Service optional, Group min 12 service 10% **Wine:** 2 bottles over £20, 22 bottles under £20, 6 by the glass (£2.70) **Notes:** Vegetarian menu, Dress Restrictions, Smart casual **Seats:** 40 **Smoking:** N/Sm in restaurant **Children:** Portions **Rooms:** 8 (8 en suite) ★★ HL **Directions:** Telephone for directions **Parking:** 16

HAY-ON-WYE MAP 09 SO24

Old Black Lion Inn

Modern British

International cooking in Welsh borders setting

☎ 01497 820841 26 Lion St HR3 5AD
e-mail: info@oldblacklion.co.uk
web: www.oldblacklion.co.uk

This 17th-century inn is full of original architectural features, charm and character. A French window illuminates the dining room and provides access to the patio for alfresco dining in summer. Friendly young staff serve simple starters of goat's cheese and sun-blushed tomato tart, then imaginative main courses of fillet of fallow venison on a parsnip tart with brandy and peppercorn sauce. Satisfying desserts such as Baileys bread-and-butter pudding to finish. There are usually good vegetarian options and some game dishes in season.

continued

Wales

HAY-ON-WYE *continued* MAP 09 SO24

Old Black Lion Inn

Chef: Peter Bridges **Owners:** Dolan Leighton **Times:** 12-2.30/6.30-9.30, Closed 24-26 Dec **Prices:** Starter £4.95-£6.25, Main £9.95-£17.95, Dessert £4.50, Coffee £1.50, Min/Water £2, Service optional **Wine:** 16 bottles over £20, 23 bottles under £20, 6 by the glass (£3.10) **Notes:** Sun roast L 1-3 courses £8.95-£12.95, Vegetarian available **Seats:** 60, Pr/dining room 20 **Smoking:** N/Sm in restaurant **Children:** Min 5 yrs **Rooms:** 10 (10 en suite) ★★ HL **Directions:** 1m off A438. From TIC car park turn right along Oxford Rd, pass Nat West Bank, next left (Lion St), hotel 20 yds on right **Parking:** 20

KNIGHTON MAP 09 SO27

Milebrook House

Modern, International

Family-run hotel with contemporary, fun food

☎ 01547 528632 Milebrook LD7 1LT
e-mail: hotel@milebrook.kc3ltd.co.uk
web: www.milebrookhouse.co.uk

The former home of the explorer Wilfred Sir Thesiger, this 18th-century dower house was once visited by Emperor Haile Selassie. His imperial majesty would have no doubt enjoyed the exquisite formal gardens with its remarkable variety of indigenous and exotic trees and plants and may even have partaken of a game of croquet before dinner. Nowadays the kitchen garden provides virtually all the vegetables served in the restaurant, complementing the local produce that makes its way into this imaginative modern British menu. Food is presented with real flair and panache and has high aspirations - white bean soup with poached scallop and chives would be a representative starter, roast pollack with seared foie gras and red wine fumet, a typically ambitious main.

Chef: Wayne Rimmer **Owners:** Mr & Mrs R T Marsden **Times:** 12-2/7-9, Closed L Mon, D Sun/Mon (open for residents) **Prices:** Fixed L £11.95,

continued

Fixed D £29.50, Starter £3.95-£6.50, Main £12.75-£17.25, Dessert £5.25, Coffee £1.95, Min/Water £2.50, Service optional **Wine:** 31 bottles over £20, 35 bottles under £20, 4 by the glass (£3.50-£4.90) **Notes:** Sun L 3 courses,, Vegetarian available **Seats:** 40, Pr/dining room 16 **Smoking:** N/Sm in restaurant **Children:** Min 8 yrs **Rooms:** 10 (10 en suite) ★★ HL **Directions:** 2m E of Knighton on A4113 (Ludlow) **Parking:** 24

LLANDRINDOD WELLS MAP 09 SO06

Hotel Metropole

Modern British

Stylish redesigned dining room with well-balanced menus

☎ 01597 823700 Temple St LD1 5DY
e-mail: info@metropole.co.uk
web: www.metropole.co.uk

This aptly-named Victorian hotel dominates the centre of the famous spa town, its smartly refurbished dining room exuding rejuvenated style. Relaxed, warm and modern, it comes decked out with contemporary leather and suede high-backed chairs, ivory linen and classic white crockery. The kitchen's modern approach comes with a classical twist. Think pan-roasted loin of Welsh lamb with a smoked cerwyn and celeriac rösti, creamed leeks, aubergine fritters and lemon-thyme jus, or panettone and marmalade bread-and-butter pudding with blood orange and mascarpone ice cream. Skilful preparation and fresh local produce shine.

Chef: Nick Edwards **Owners:** Justin Baird-Murray **Times:** 12.30-1.45/7-9.30 **Prices:** Food prices not confirmed for 2007. Please telephone for details **Wine:** 20 bottles over £20, 40 bottles under £20, 8 by the glass (£2.80-£4.60) **Notes:** Vegetarian available, Civ Wed 200 **Seats:** 200, Pr/dining room 250 **Smoking:** N/Sm in restaurant, Air con **Children:** Menu, Portions **Rooms:** 120 (120 en suite) ★★★ HL **Directions:** In centre of town off A483 **Parking:** 140

LLANFYLLIN MAP 15 SJ11

Seeds

Modern British

Good honest cooking in Grade II listed building

☎ 01691 648604 5 Penybryn Cottage, High St SY22 5AP

In a property built in 1580, Seeds is a low-ceilinged parlour with an intimate dinner party atmosphere. Original beams and slate flooring combine with curios, maps, books and original works of art to provide a truly intriguing setting. Jazz music plays in the background and friendly staff provide relaxed and friendly service. The menu offers up unfussy modern British fare. Try a starter of warm black pudding salad with blackcurrant dressing, a main of roast rack of Welsh lamb or perhaps grilled sea bass. Puddings have a real comfort factor with treacle tart and lemon posset vying for attention.

Chef: Mark Seager **Owners:** Felicity Seager, Mark Seager **Times:** 11-2.15/7-8.30, Closed 2 wk Oct, 25 Dec, Mon-Tue, Closed L Wed in winter, D Sun **Prices:** Fixed D £23.75-£25.70, Starter £3.50-£6.95, Main £8.95-£15, Dessert £4-£4.50, Min/Water £3, Service optional **Wine:** 35 bottles over £20, 89 bottles under £20, 3 by the glass (£3.25-£4.80) **Notes:** Coffee incl **Seats:** 22 **Smoking:** N/Sm in restaurant **Children:** Portions **Directions:** Village centre, on A490, 15 mins from Welshpool, follow signs to Llanfyllin **Parking:** Free car park in town, street parking

LLANGAMMARCH WELLS MAP 09 SN94

Lake Country House Hotel & Spa

British, European NOTABLE WINE LIST

Fine dining and old-fashioned charm

☎ 01591 620202 LD4 4BS
e-mail: info@lakecountryhouse.co.uk
web: www.lakecountryhouse.co.uk

Good old-fashioned values of service and hospitality are a real feature at this comfortable Victorian manor set in extensive grounds. In keeping with tradition, afternoon tea is served in the sitting room, while the spacious dining room continues the theme of comfort and luxury with its white-clothed tables, quality crockery and cutlery, and impeccably directed, old-style service. The kitchen delivers interesting flavour combinations via sensibly compact, four-course, daily-changing dinner menus, which make good use of locally-sourced produce. Perhaps monkfish tail wrapped in Carmarthen ham with anchovy potato purée, a roast fish and red wine shallot sauce, followed by caramelised lemon tart with clove ice cream and lime syrup. **Notable Wine List:** A carefully constructed list showing great enthusiasm for fine wines and great vintages.

Chef: Sean Cullingford **Owners:** J Mifsud **Times:** 12.30-2/7.30-9.15 **Prices:** Fixed L £24.50, Fixed D £39.50, Coffee £3, Min/Water £3.40, Service optional **Wine:** 20 bottles under £20, 7 by the glass (£5.50-£7.50) **Notes:** Fixed L 3 courses coffee incl, Fixed D 4 courses, Vegetarian available, Dress Restrictions, Prefer no jeans; collar at all times, Civ Wed 70 **Seats:** 40, Pr/dining room 30 **Smoking:** N/Sm in restaurant **Children:** Min 8 yrs, Menu, Portions **Rooms:** 19 (19 en suite) ★★★ CHH **Directions:** 6m from Builth Wells on A483 from Garth, turn left for Llangammarch Wells & follow signs to hotel **Parking:** 80

LLANWDDYN MAP 15 SJ01

Lake Vyrnwy Hotel

British

Stunning views and cooking presented to perfection

☎ 01691 870692 Lake Vyrnwy SY10 0LY
e-mail: res@lakevyrnwy.com
web: www.lakevyrnwy.com

Set in 24,000 acres of woodland and moors this fine country-house hotel stands above Lake Vyrnwy. The accommodation makes the most of the views, not least the conservatory restaurant where the yield of local farms and game shoots is given pride of place on the menu. Faultless presentations whet the appetite, with options like loin of local organic lamb wrapped in herb mousse, and chargrilled fillet of Welsh

continued

Black beef following home-smoked trout fillets on horseradish blinis, or the Middle Eastern flavours of Lebanese lamb kofta with aubergine salsa. Look out for the home-made chocolate bread!

Lake Vyrnwy Hotel

Times: 12-2.30/7-9.15 **Rooms:** 35 (35 en suite) ★★★ **Directions:** Follow Tourist signs on A495/B4393, 200 yds past dam at Lake Vyrnwy.

LLANWRTYD WELLS MAP 09 SN84

Carlton House

see page 644

Lasswade Country House Hotel

Modern British

Pro-organic Edwardian country-house dining

☎ 01591 610515 Station Rd LD5 4RW
e-mail: info@lasswadehotel.co.uk
web: www.lasswadehotel.co.uk

An Edwardian house in an idyllic location with wonderful views from the conservatory and lounge. The dining room feels like that of a traditional Edwardian home with embossed wallpaper, polished wooden tables and elegant chandeliers. There is a great emphasis on organic and quality local produce like smoked salmon shipped specially by train from North Wales or the Welsh Black beef produced only a quarter of a mile away. Cooking is simple without any pretension in dishes such as roast rack of Gaer Farm lamb or fillet of Milford cod roast with chilli jam.

Chef: Roger Stevens **Owners:** Roger & Emma Stevens **Times:** 7.30-9.30, Closed 25 Dec **Prices:** Fixed D £28, Min/Water £1.25, Service optional **Wine:** 6 bottles over £20, 25 bottles under £20, 2 by the glass (£2.50-£2.93) **Notes:** Dress Restrictions, Smart casual **Seats:** 20, Pr/dining room 24 **Smoking:** N/Sm in restaurant **Children:** Portions **Rooms:** 8 (8 en suite) ★★ SHL **Directions:** On A483, follow signs for station, opposite Spar shop, adjacent to tourist info office, 400yds on right before station **Parking:** 6

Carlton House

LLANWRTYD WELLS MAP 09 SN84

Modern British

Impressive cooking in friendly restaurant with rooms

☎ 01591 610248 Dolycoed Rd LD5 4RA
e-mail: info@carltonrestaurant.co.uk
web: www.carltonrestaurant.co.uk

This charming and homely restaurant with rooms, set in an attractive three-storey Victorian building, has been a well-established Welsh food destination for many years, and has a personal, lived-in style all of its own. Run by the friendly and enthusiastic Gilchrists, a husband-and-wife team, the sunny and intimate restaurant (with room for just 14 covers) comes with original tongue-and-groove wood panelling from its former role as a gentlemen's outfitters. Cheerful curtains, Rennie Mackintosh-style high-backed chairs, art deco wall lamps and numerous artefacts create a homely, relaxed atmosphere. Diners are diligently and professionally looked after by Dr Gilchrist, while wife Mary Anne looks after the cooking, her one-woman act undertaken with panache, underlining her obvious passion and talent. Though the daily-changing menu may be short (some three-choices at each turn), it's more than compensated for by the focus on using only the highest-quality, local seasonal Welsh produce and delivering clear flavours via traditional-styled, no-frills cuisine. Think roast rack of Irfon Valley lamb in a herb crust served with crushed potatoes, courgettes and a light tomato sauce, and perhaps a warm chocolate fondant with vanilla crème anglaise to finish.

Chef: Mary Ann Gilchrist **Owners:** Dr & Mrs Gilchrist **Times:** 12.30-2/7-9, Closed 10-30 Dec, Sun, Closed L (by reservation only), D Sun **Prices:** Fixed L £25, Fixed D £25, Starter £5.50-£9, Main £22-£27, Dessert £5.50-£8, Min/Water £2.50, Service optional **Notes:** Coffee incl, Fixed L 3 courses **Seats:** 14 **Smoking:** N/Sm in restaurant **Rooms:** 6 (5 en suite) ★★★ RR **Directions:** In town centre **Parking:** On street

LLYSWEN MAP 09 SO13

Llangoed Hall

Traditional British NOTABLE WINE LIST

A classy setting for ambitious cooking

☎ 01874 754525 LD3 0YP
e-mail: enquiries@llangoedhall.co.uk
web: www.llangoedhall.com

A former home to the Laura Ashley dynasty, this majestic Edwardian house has lost none of its grandeur, welcoming guests with a distinctly upmarket décor of luxurious fabrics, duck-egg blue walls, and assorted sketches by Whistler. The staff are deservedly proud of the food, and happy to spill the beans on the provenance of the local ingredients that are a feature of the tempting menu. Mains are along the lines of Welsh Black beef fillet on a horseradish mash with a caramelised shallot tarte Tatin, or roast loin of Breconshire venison on braised red cabbage with beetroot jus, while desserts might include glazed orange and lemon tart with a lemon sorbet. Expect ambitious and accomplished cuisine from a restaurant on its way up.
Notable Wine List: A well-presented wine list with good tasting notes throughout.

Chef: Sean Ballington **Owners:** Sir Bernard Ashley **Times:** 12.30-2.30/7-10.00 **Prices:** Fixed L £25, Fixed D £43, Coffee £2, Min/Water £4.50, Service optional **Wine:** 110 bottles over £20, 9 bottles under £20, 6 by the glass (£5-£6) **Notes:** Fixed L 3 courses, Fixed D 4 courses, Dress Restrictions, Jacket at dinner, no denim jeans, Civ Wed 60 **Seats:** 50, Pr/dining room 54 **Smoking:** N/Sm in restaurant **Children:** Min 8 yrs, Portions **Rooms:** 23 (23 en suite) ★★★★ **Directions:** On A470, 2m from Llyswen towards Builth Wells **Parking:** 50

MONTGOMERY MAP 15 SO29

Dragon Hotel

Traditional

Historic inn serving accomplished restaurant and bar food

☎ 01686 668359 & 668287 Market Square SY15 6PA
e-mail: reception@dragonhotel.com
web: www.dragonhotel.com

Beams and timbers from the nearby castle - destroyed by Cromwell - feature in this black-and-white fronted, 17th-century coaching inn at the heart of town. Its homely, traditional décor extends to the cosy beamed restaurant, which has a fireplace converted from an old bread oven. The cooking - with a nod to the Mediterranean on the way - is via wholesome dishes that make sound use of local produce. Take braised lamb shank with leek-scented mash potato and redcurrant jus, or sunnier grilled swordfish steak with roasted baby tomatoes and pistou dressing.

continued

Wales

Chef: Paul McNall **Owners:** M & S Michaels **Times:** 12-2/7-9, Closed L all week ex by prior arrangement **Prices:** Fixed L £14.45-£20.75, Fixed D £20.75, Starter £3.75-£6, Main £11.75-£19.50, Dessert £3.75, Coffee £1.50, Min/Water £2.50, Service optional **Wine:** 8 bottles over £20, 42 bottles under £20, 5 by the glass (£1.90-£2.25) **Notes:** Vegetarian available **Seats:** 42 **Smoking:** N/Sm in restaurant **Children:** Portions **Rooms:** 20 (20 en suite) ★★ HL **Directions:** Behind the town hall **Parking:** 20

NANT-DDU MAP 09 SO01

Nant Ddu Lodge Hotel

Modern International

Bustling bistro in contemporary hotel

☎ 01685 379111 Cwm Taf, Nant Ddu CF48 2HY
e-mail: enquiries@nant-ddu-lodge.co.uk
web: www.nant-ddu-lodge.co.uk

Family-run, Georgian riverside hotel with bustling bistro. Contemporary décor, vibrant colours, original artwork and a relaxed, informal atmosphere and service hit the right note. Plenty of quality local produce finds its place on the lengthy, crowd-pleasing, modern-focused menu, with a nod to the Mediterranean and far beyond. Daily specials bolster the repertoire of simply-prepared, imaginative dishes, which are also served in bar. Look out for starters like seafood bruschetta, followed by mains like chargrilled pork loin with brandy and peppercorn sauce or grilled halibut steak on steamed mussels with coconut and lemongrass, with fresh fruit and marshmallow fondue to finish.

Chef: Richard Wimmer **Owners:** Mr & Mrs D Ronson **Times:** 12-2.30/6.30-9.30, Closed D Sun **Prices:** Starter £3.50-£5.95, Main £8.95-£14.95, Dessert £3.95, Coffee £1.50, Min/Water £2.95, Service optional **Wine:** 5 bottles over £20, 25 bottles under £20, 8 by the glass (£2.50-£3.95) **Notes:** Vegetarian available **Seats:** 80, Pr/dining room 20 **Smoking:** N/Sm in restaurant **Children:** Menu, Portions **Rooms:** 31 (31 en suite) ★★★ HL **Directions:** 6m N of Merthyr Tydfil, and 12m S of Brecon on A470 **Parking:** 50

RHONDDA CYNON TAFF

MISKIN MAP 09 ST08

Miskin Manor Country Hotel

Modern Traditional

Enjoyable dining in traditional manor house

☎ 01443 224204 Groes Faen CF72 8ND
e-mail: info@miskin-manor.co.uk
web: www.miskin-manor.co.uk

Peacefully set in 22 acres of gardens, this fine Grade II listed country house is steeped in Welsh history, its original features adding much to its charm. The oak-panelled, silver-service restaurant has a romantic air and lovely views over the garden, while the kitchen follows the traditional line - dotted with occasional modern twists - and takes pride in sourcing fresh, quality produce from the abundant Welsh larder. Take a fillet of Welsh Black beef, perhaps partnered by a caramelised shallot tarte Tatin and Dìjon mustard and brandy cream sauce, or seared snapper fillet with steamed pak choi and sesame sauce.

Chef: Mark Beck, Ian Presgrave **Owners:** Mr & Mrs Rosenberg **Times:** 12-2.30/7-10 **Prices:** Fixed L fr £9.95, Fixed D fr £28.50, Starter £5-£8.50, Main £12.95-£20.50, Dessert £5.25-£7.95, Coffee £2.60, Min/Water £2.85, Service added but optional 10% **Wine:** 13 bottles over £20, 35 bottles under £20, 8 by the glass (£3.70-£4) **Notes:** Vegetarian available, Dress Restrictions, Smart casual, Civ Wed 100 **Seats:** 50, Pr/dining room 14 **Smoking:** N/Sm in restaurant **Children:** Portions **Rooms:** 43 (43 en suite) ★★★★ CHH **Directions:** 8m W of Cardiff. M4 junct 34, follow hotel signs **Parking:** 200

SWANSEA

Wales

LLANRHIDIAN MAP 08 SS49

The Welcome to Town

British, French

Country inn serving great local cuisine

☎ 01792 390015 SA3 1EH
web: www.thewelcometotown.co.uk

There's a village-pub feel to this 300-year-old, whitewashed coaching inn overlooking the Gower coast. Mind you, it was once the local court house and jail, though, as the name implies, you can now experience a friendlier welcome. There's a traditional note to the décor, with blackened oak beams, simple whitewashed walls, stone fireplace and central bar. Wooden tables and chairs, floral seat cushions and white linen continue the unpretentious theme, while the accomplished, skilful kitchen's modern approach - underpinned by classical roots - uses only the best local produce. Think a fillet of John Dory served with spinach, vanilla mash and beurre noisette, or pear and blueberry shortbread with sabayon cream and Melba sauce. Good vegetarian options available.

Chef: Ian Bennett **Owners:** Jay & Ian Bennett **Times:** 12-2/7-9.30, Closed 25-26 Dec,1 Jan,last 2 wks Feb,1 wk Oct, Mon, Closed D Sun **Prices:** Fixed L fr £13.50, Fixed D fr £32.50, Coffee £2.95, Min/Water £3, Service optional **Wine:** 13 bottles over £20, 32 bottles under £20, 7 by the glass (£3.25-£4.95) **Notes:** Sun L 2 courses £14.95, 3 courses £19.95, Vegetarian available, Smart casual **Seats:** 40 **Smoking:** N/Sm in restaurant **Children:** Portions **Directions:** 8m from Swansea on the B4231. M4 junct 47 towards Gowerton. From Gowerton take B4295 **Parking:** 12

continued

REYNOLDSTON MAP 08 SS48

 Fairyhill

Modern British  NOTABLE WINE LIST

Stylish woodland retreat with skilful kitchen

☎ 01792 390139 SA3 1BS
e-mail: postbox@fairyhill.net
web: www.fairyhill.net

Hidden away on the Gower Peninsula (Britain's first designated Area of Outstanding Natural Beauty), this Georgian house with beautiful grounds has been restored with great care. A welcoming entrance hall leads on to a comfortably furnished lounge and to a dining room that extends through three rooms. The large terrace allows diners to enjoy the mild Gower climate. Service is attentive and friendly and the accurate and skilful modern Welsh cooking makes the most of locally-sourced, often organic, ingredients. Penclawdd cockles can be served as canapés or the classic combination with bacon and laverbread. Welsh Black beef arrives as a carpaccio with a truffle salad and parmesan. Samphire and salt marsh lamb make seasonal appearances.
Notable Wine List: A superb list with quality selections throughout, including an 'under £20' section and a strong half-bottle collection.

Chef: Paul Davies, Bryony Jones **Owners:** Mr Hetherington, Mr Davies **Times:** 12.30-2/7.30-9, Closed 26 Dec, 3-21 Jan, Closed L Mon (winter only), D Sun (winter only) **Prices:** Fixed L £15.95, Fixed D £37.50, Starter £4.50-£9.25, Main £13.95-£19.50, Dessert £5.50, Coffee £3.50, Min/Water £3.75, Service optional **Wine:** 550 bottles over £20, 40 bottles under £20, 12 by the glass (£3.75-£7.50) **Notes:** ALC L only, Sun L 3 courses £24.50, Vegetarian available **Seats:** 60, Pr/dining room 40 **Smoking:** N/Sm in restaurant **Children:** Min 8 yrs, Portions **Rooms:** 8 (8 en suite) ★★★ CHH **Directions:** M4 junct 47, take A483 then A484 to Llanelli, Gower, Gowerton. At Gowerton follow B4295 for approx 10m **Parking:** 45

SWANSEA MAP 09 SS69

The Grand Hotel

British, European

Modern cooking and surrounds with excellent flavour combinations

☎ 01792 645898 Ivey Place, High St SA1 1NE
e-mail: info@thegrandhotelswansea.co.uk
web: www.thegrandhotelswansea.co.uk

Located next to the railway station, the Grand Hotel has been a landmark hotel in Swansea since the 1930s. Renovation has restored it to the elegance of its heyday with plenty of glass, stainless steel and, in the main restaurant, wood floors and leather, high-backed chairs giving a thoroughly contemporary spin on the original style of the building. Diners can choose between the Beeches Restaurant for fine dining and the Bay Bistro for more informal eating. The former is the best showcase for the capabilities of the kitchen here; there's a strong Mediterranean influence in dishes such as duck ravioli in game and redcurrant broth, or wild mushroom and chestnut risotto, although flavours from Britain and the Far East inevitably creep in.

Times: 6.30-9.30, Closed L all week **Rooms:** 31 (31 en suite) ★★★★ HL **Directions:** M4 junct 42, signed City and Train Station. Hotel opposite train station

The Restaurant

British, French

Harbourside restaurant with an emphasis on fresh fish

☎ 01792 466200 Pilot House Wharf, Trawler Rd, Swansea Marina SA1 1UN
e-mail: therestaurant@aol.com

A harbourside restaurant on the first floor of a striking, boat-shaped building, The menu comes aptly awash with the fruits of the sea. Bright yellow-ochre décor provides a suitably light, uncluttered dining space, where service proves helpful. The location ensures the promise of the freshest fish, displayed on the regularly-changing blackboard specials menu. Meat-lovers are not forgotten, with perhaps the likes of a loin of Welsh lamb finding its place, but the real drawcard here is fresh fish. Expect an uncomplicated, modern approach as in chargrilled sea bass, perhaps served with roasted Mediterranean vegetables.

Times: 12-2/6.30-9.30, Closed L Mon, D Sun

Restaurant 698, Bartram @

Modern European

Vibrant relative newcomer with food that hits the mark

☎ 01792 361616 698 Mumbles Rd SA3 4EH
e-mail: info@698.uk.com
web: www.698.uk.com

From the groovy typographics of the frontage to the chic, modern interiors (high-backed leather chairs, artfully exposed brick, floor-to-ceiling 'feature' radiators), there's a young, funky feel to this relatively new restaurant and coffee shop near the Mumbles which is already earning plaudits locally. As you might expect from a chef who is an alumnus of Anton Mosimann's private dining club, the food has a precise simplicity, clear flavours and uses great produce. The menu is eclectic with dishes that absorb inspiration from around the world and lots of Welsh produce is featured. A typical starter would be smoked salmon with dill-flavoured rösti potato and a beetroot dressing, while a main would be braised chump chop of Welsh lamb with tagliatelle Niçoise-style. Extras like amuse-bouche and a pre-dessert are a nice touch.

Chef: Steven Bartram **Owners:** Steven & Suzette Bartram **Times:** 12-2/6.30-9.30, Closed 25 Dec, Mon (Winter), Closed D Sun **Prices:** Fixed L fr £9.95, Fixed D fr £16.95, Coffee £1.50, Min/Water £3.20 **Notes:** Sun L 2 courses £13.95, 3 courses £16.95, Vegetarian available, Dress restrictions, Smart casual **Seats:** 40 **Smoking:** N/Sm in restaurant **Children:** Menu, Portions **Directions:** From Swansea follow road to Mumbles, at rdbt head towards the pier for approx 1m, restaurant on right **Parking:** On street

Windsor Lodge Hotel & Restaurant

Modern Traditional NEW

Popular city-centre hotel restaurant with a tranquil atmosphere

☎ 01792 642158 & 652744
Mount Pleasant SA1 6EG
e-mail: reservations@windsor-lodge.co.uk
web: www.windsor-lodge.co.uk

A small hotel in a 200-year-old Grade II listed building, Windsor Lodge is located right in the centre of Swansea, yet it manages to

continued

retain an air of calm, echoing a time when it would have been surrounded by countryside. The food is simple in style with fresh, daily ingredients incorporated in an international menu that is strong on Welsh produce - Penclawdd laverbread with bacon and shallot filo 'moneybags' in a sweet pepper sauce to start, followed by Welsh beef with a cream of stilton and whiskey sauce. Home-made breads are worthy of note.

Chef: Katrina Stewart **Owners:** Ron & Pam Rumble **Times:** 12/7.30-9, Closed 23 Dec-3 Jan, Sun, Closed L (ex by prior arrangement) **Prices:** Fixed D £25-£28, Min/Water £3, Service optional **Wine:** 15 bottles over £20, 30 bottles under £20, 2 by the glass (£3) **Notes:** Coffee incl, Vegetarian available **Seats:** 30 **Smoking:** N/Sm in restaurant **Children:** Menu, Portions **Rooms:** 19 (19 en suite) ★★ HL **Directions:** Along Mount Pleasant Hill, close to Swansea Central Police Station, 100yds on left **Parking:** 20

VALE OF GLAMORGAN

BARRY MAP 09 ST16

Egerton Grey Country House Hotel

Modern British

True country-house experience in a lovely wooded valley

☎ 01446 711666 Porthkerry, Rhoose CF62 3BZ
e-mail: info@egertongrey.co.uk
web: www.egertongrey.co.uk

The hotel is a Victorian former rectory where the beautifully restored gardens are a must-see in summer. The restaurant occupies the former billiard room, panelled in antique Cuban mahogany, where chandeliers, fine bone china, crystal and silverware provide a feast for the eye. An oak-panelled dining room is also available for private parties. British fare with European influences includes crab and pink ginger salad with lemon and fennel shavings, and fillet of Welsh Black beef with seared foie gras and rosemary-scented fondant potato.

Chef: Katie Mitchell **Owners:** Mr R Morgan-Price & Huw Thomas **Times:** 12-2/6.30-9 **Prices:** Fixed L fr £10, Fixed D fr £30, Min/Water £3.50, Service optional **Wine:** 37 bottles over £20, 33 bottles under £20, 8 by the glass (£4-£5.50) **Notes:** Vegetarian available, Dress Restrictions, Smart casual, Civ Wed 40 **Seats:** 40, Pr/dining room 16 **Smoking:** N/Sm in restaurant **Children:** Portions **Rooms:** 10 (10 en suite) ★★★ CHH **Directions:** M4 junct 33, follow signs for Airport then Porthkerry, then turn left at hotel sign by thatched cottage **Parking:** 60

HENSOL MAP 09 ST07

La Cucina at The Vale Hotel

Italian, Mediterranean

Modern golf restaurant with traditional pizza oven

☎ 01443 667877 The Vale Hotel CF72 8JY
e-mail: reservations@vale-hotel.com
web: www.vale-hotel.com

Situated in a stunning setting above the hotel and golf course, surrounded by 600 acres of beautiful countryside, part of the Hensol Castle estate, the restaurant is found in the golf clubhouse building. The fresh, polished interior has a vast vaulted wooden ceiling. Tables are well-spaced and covered with sandy coloured linens; you'll find luxurious rattan bucket chairs in the bar and lounge. The simple lunch menu offers a handful of appetisers and mains alongside the wood-

continued

fired pizza menu. The evening menu sees a wider choice with Mediterranean-style main courses, grills and authentic pizzas baked in the wood-burning oven.

Chef: Jamie Duncan **Owners:** Vale Hotel Ltd **Times:** 12.30-2.30/6-10, Closed Sun, Mon, Closed L Tue **Prices:** Fixed D £18.45-£27.50, Starter £3.50-£7.50, Main £8-£17, Dessert £3.50-£5, Coffee £1.75, Min/Water £3.75, Service optional **Wine:** 4 bottles over £20, 20 bottles under £20, 4 by the glass (£2.65-£4.45) **Notes:** Vegetarian available **Seats:** 76 **Smoking:** N/Sm in restaurant, Air con **Children:** Menu, Portions **Directions:** M4, 3 mins from junct 34, follow signs for Vale Hotel **Parking:** 500

WREXHAM

LLANARMON DYFFRYN CEIRIOG
MAP 15 SJ13

West Arms Hotel

Traditional British, Welsh

Historic inn with good food in the beautiful Ceiriog Valley

☎ 01691 600665 600612 LL20 7LD
e-mail: gowestarms@aol.com
web: www.thewestarms.co.uk

This 16th-century drover's inn is full of character with lots of exposed beams, polished brass, inglenooks and ornate fireplaces with open fires. The traditional bar with its alluring menu is popular with locals, and shooting parties also like the traditional dining here so booking is advisable. Classically-inspired and well-executed dishes use local and Welsh produce as in a starter of a warm gravad lax, mussel and leek tart or chargrilled vegetable terrine. For mains, try medallions of Welsh beef served on crushed potatoes and wild mushrooms or the panaché of grilled sea bass, red mullet and seared scallops. Maybe finish with lemon posset with sautéed strawberries.

Chef: Grant Williams **Owners:** Mr & Mrs Finch & Mr G Williams **Times:** 12-2/7-9, Closed L Mon-Sat **Prices:** Fixed D fr £32.90, Starter £4.95-£7.45, Main £8.95-£16.95, Dessert £4.95-£5.50, Coffee £3.50, Min/Water £2.75, Service added but optional 10% **Wine:** 28 bottles over £20, 26 bottles under £20, 10 by the glass (£3.90-£4.60) **Notes:** Sun L menu, Vegetarian available, Civ Wed 70 **Seats:** 34, Pr/dining room 10 **Smoking:** N/Sm in restaurant **Children:** Menu, Portions **Rooms:** 15 (15 en suite) ★★★ HL **Directions:** Exit A483 (A5) at Chirk (mid-way between Oswestry and Llangollen) and follow signs for Ceiriog Valley (B4500) - 11m **Parking:** 20

WREXHAM MAP 15 SJ35

Cross Lanes Hotel

Modern British

Friendly hotel brasserie in beautiful grounds

☎ 01978 780555 Cross Lanes, Bangor Rd, Marchwiel LL13 0TF
e-mail: guestservices@crosslanes.co.uk
web: www.crosslanes.co.uk

Built as a country house in the late 19th century and a hotel since 1959, this elegant building stands in 6 acres of beautiful grounds. Kagan's brasserie-style restaurant is a relaxed and friendly dining venue, with slate and oak floors, rustic tables, old prints of Wrexham, and cosy log fires in winter. The modern British menu, which includes local and seasonal produce, draws inspiration from around the globe. The choice is extensive, offering something for everyone, especially the smoked haddock tartlet with chive sauce and the roast rump of Welsh lamb with leek mash and rosemary sauce.

Chef: Philip Riden **Owners:** Michael Kagan **Times:** 12-3/6.30-9.30, Closed D 25-26 Dec **Prices:** Fixed L £10.50-£14.50, Fixed D £28, Starter £4-£7.95, Main £8-£16, Dessert £4.50-£5.50, Coffee £1.50, Min/Water £3, Service optional **Wine:** 30 bottles over £20, 35 bottles under £20, 16 by the glass (£2.30-£5) **Notes:** Vegetarian available, Civ Wed 140 **Seats:** 50, Pr/dining room 60 **Smoking:** N/Sm in restaurant **Children:** Menu, Portions **Rooms:** 16 (16 en suite) ★★★ HL **Directions:** On A525, Wrexham to Whitchurch Rd, between Marchweil and Bangor-on-Dee **Parking:** 70

Cross Lanes Hotel

Northern Ireland

NORTHERN IRELAND CO ANTRIM

CARNLOUGH MAP 01 D6

Londonderry Arms Hotel

Modern

Fine dining in genteel hotel

☎ 028 2888 5255 20 Harbour Rd BT44 0EU
e-mail: ida@glensofantrim.com
web: www.glensofantrim.com

Built in the mid-19th century for Lady Londonderry - whose grandson, Winston Churchill, also owned the property at one time - this delightful hotel is set in a pretty fishing village overlooking the Antrim coast. Its Georgian architecture, traditional décor and friendly service lend an endearing, genteel charm. The kitchen's modern French approach contrasts with its surroundings, offering a simple, straightforward style in generous portions that makes good use of quality produce from the local larder. Start with choices like oak-smoked salmon on garlic-scented ciabatta, and follow with grilled pork medallions wrapped in smoked bacon with leeks, roast potatoes and sweet chilli jam.

Chef: Manus Jamison **Owners:** Frank O'Neill **Times:** 12.30-2.45/7-8.45, Closed 25 Dec, Closed L Mon-Sat **Prices:** Starter £3.45-£5.75, Main £11.95-£14.50, Dessert £4.25, Coffee £1.20, Min/Water £2.95, Service optional **Wine:** 4 bottles over £20, 25 bottles under £20, 4 by the glass (£3.65) **Notes:** Vegetarian available **Seats:** 80, Pr/dining room 14 **Smoking:** N/Sm area **Children:** Menu, Portions **Rooms:** 35 (35 en suite) ★★★ **Directions:** 14m N of Larne on coast road

CO BELFAST

BELFAST MAP 01 D5

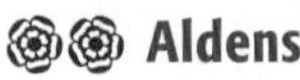

Aldens

Modern European

Stylish restaurant serving imaginative food

☎ 028 9065 0079
229 Upper Newtownards Rd BT4 3JF
e-mail: info@aldensrestaurant.com
web: www.aldensrestaurant.com

A large red canopy outside this suburban restaurant makes an appealing first impression that is fully justified by the stylish interior. The large etched glass screens, which match the windows, provide intimate areas, and the subtle lighting and quality table settings inspire confidence. Smart, well informed staff provide excellent service. There are some traditional favourites (grilled gammon steak with pineapple) on the modern menu (roast breast of duck with green peppercorns and crisp asparagus), while other dishes show a marked Asian influence, like aromatic Thai broth with tofu, bok choi and noodles. Fresh seasonal produce is evident in sautéed veal kidneys with mushrooms and garlic butter, and steamed mussels too.

Chef: Denise Hockey **Owners:** Jonathan Davis **Times:** 12-2.30/6-10, Closed 2 wks Jul, BHs, Sun, Closed L Sat **Prices:** Fixed D fr £21.95, Starter £4-£9, Main £6-£17, Dessert £4-£6, Coffee £1.95, Min/Water £3.50, Service optional, Group min 6 service 10% **Wine:** 73 bottles over £20, 38 bottles under £20, 6 by the glass (£3.50-£4.50) **Notes:** Vegetarian available **Seats:** 70 **Smoking:** N/Sm area, No pipes, No cigars, Air con **Children:** Portions **Directions:** At x-rds with Sandown Rd **Parking:** On street

Beatrice Kennedy

Modern, Traditional V

Imaginative food in busy townhouse near the university

☎ 028 9020 2290 44 University Rd BT7 1NJ
e-mail: reservations@beatricekennedy.co.uk
web: www.beatricekennedy.co.uk

An interior decked out in 1940s-style with rich, warm colours, lazy colonial ceiling fans and the sounds of big-band jazz conspire to create a brasserie atmosphere. Leather chairs, white tablecloths, candles and chandeliers add to the intimate mood. Smartly turned-out staff are well informed and friendly. Good value, modern Irish food with a bistro approach is the style. Fresh local ingredients, simply cooked with flair and imagination. Sample dishes start with open lasagne of asparagus, olive and plum tomatoes, followed by chicken breast with lemon couscous, roasted peppers and harissa.

Chef: Jim McCarthy **Owners:** Jim McCarthy **Times:** 12.30-3/5-10.30, Closed 24-26 Dec, 1 Jan, Easter, Mon, Closed L Mon-Sat **Prices:** Fixed L £16.50, Starter £4-£8, Main £12-£17, Dessert £4.50-£4.75, Coffee £1.25, Min/Water £2.50, Group min 6 service 10% **Wine:** 20 bottles over £20, 20 bottles under £20, 4 by the glass (£3.25) **Notes:** Fixed L 3 courses, Fixed Sun L £16.50, Vegetarian menu **Seats:** 75, Pr/dining room 25 **Smoking:** No pipes, No cigars **Children:** Menu, Portions **Directions:** Adjacent to Queens University **Parking:** On street

Cayenne

Modern International

Imaginative food with global influences in innovative, buzzy surroundings

☎ 028 9033 1532 7 Ascot House, Shaftesbury Square BT2 7DB
e-mail: belinda@rankingroup.co.uk
web: www.rankingroup.co.uk

The Rankin's lively, minimalist restaurant is still the place to see and be seen, featuring a vivid colour scheme and innovative, interactive artworks by local-born artist Peter Anderson. Graphic art screened lighting with coordinated music performs alongside smartly uniformed, well-informed staff. There's a sense of theatre about the food, too, with its predominantly oriental twists (plus Pacific, Indian and Mediterranean touches) to well-sourced, quality Irish ingredients. Imaginative cooking, well presented without over embellishment. Start with salt 'n' chilli squid, followed by Chinese red roast duck with udon noodles or roast rump of Finnebrogue venison with hash brown, wild mushrooms and Guinness sauce.

Chef: Danny Millar **Owners:** Paul & Jeanne Rankin **Times:** 12-2.15/6-10.15, Closed 25-26 Dec, 12 Jul, Closed L Sat & Sun **Prices:** Fixed L £12, Fixed D £19.50, Starter £4.50-£11, Main £10.50-£20, Dessert £5.50-£5.95, Coffee £1.95, Min/Water £3.55, Service optional, Group min 6 service 10% **Wine:** 86 bottles over £20, 18 bottles under £20, 7 by the glass (£3.50-£4) **Notes:** Vegetarian available **Seats:** 130, Pr/dining room 16 **Smoking:** N/Sm area, No pipes, Air con **Children:** Portions **Directions:** Top of Great Victoria St **Parking:** Dublin Rd

Restaurant Michael Deane

BELFAST MAP 01 D5

European, Irish

Exemplary modern cooking from arguably the best restaurant in Northern Ireland

☎ 028 9033 1134 34/40 Howard St BT1 6PF
e-mail: info@michaeldeane.co.uk
web: www.michaeldeane.co.uk

Despite his celebrity status, chef-patron Michael Deane admirably takes a hands-on approach here - this despite a vibrant downstairs brasserie at this two-tier, city-centre operation, and a delicatessen and bistro just round the corner in Bedford Street. The quieter, more formal and intimate, first-floor restaurant is the flagship enterprise (an essential part of any trip to the city) and is accessed via the ground-floor brasserie, its few, crisp-white-linen dressed, candlelit tables (make booking early advisable) come laid with expensive settings. The open kitchen provides diners with the theatre of chefs-on-show, though this is a calm and disciplined brigade, while pale walls, a red-maroon ceiling, heavy drapes and plenty of darkwood lend a masculine edge, accompanied by impeccable and knowledgeable service. High-quality, precision cooking and clear flavours showcase the best of the province's produce; a modern approach of the refined, assured and confident order. Consistency is key here, there's nothing too overly faddish either, just quality through and through. Take roast turbot served with a herb gnocchi, leek and lemon fondue, langoustine provençale and a confit of fennel, or perhaps, dry-aged fillet of beef, paired with horseradish mash, tomato stuffed with a shin of beef stew, marinated foie gras and a bordelaise sauce. The carte comes sensibly compact, bolstered by an eight-course tasting option (Menu Prestige), while peripherals like bread (a variety of some eight different mini-rolls), amuse-bouche and chocolatey petits fours all hit form, too, as might an assiette of lemon dessert (tart, sorbet and crumble). An excellent wine list proves a fitting accompaniment.

Chef: Michael Deane, Derek Creagh
Owners: Michael Deane
Times: 7-9, Closed Xmas, New Year, Etr, 2 wk Jul, Sun-Tue, Closed L Wed-Thu & Sat
Prices: Fixed D £43, Service optional, Group min 6 service 10%
Wine: 150 bottles over £20
Notes: Tasting menu 9 courses £62, Vegetarian available
Seats: 30
Smoking: N/Sm in restaurant, Air con
Children: Portions
Directions: Located at rear of city hall. Howard St on left opposite Spires building
Parking: On street

BELFAST *continued* MAP 01 D5

The Crescent Townhouse

International V NEW

Townhouse brasserie with an international flavour

☎ 028 9032 3349 13 Lower Crescent BT7 1NR
e-mail: info@crescenttownhouse.com
web: www.crescenttownhouse.com

Centrally located near the Botanic Gardens and railway station, this Regency townhouse turned boutique hotel offers tasty and creative cuisine at a wallet-friendly price. Its buzzy brasserie has a globetrotting range that sets the best of traditional Irish cooking alongside more exotic Asian dishes, so you might kick off with crispy Thai chilli beef, before tucking into Finnebrogue venison with celeriac gratin, spinach, wild mushrooms and a cherry jus. A vegetarian menu is available on request, and from Monday to Saturday an early bird selection offers even better value.

Chef: Karl Taylor **Owners:** Wine Inns Ltd **Times:** 12-3/5.45-10, Closed 25-26 Dec, 1 Jan, 11-12 Jul, Closed L Sun **Prices:** Fixed D £15.50, Starter £2.95-£6.95, Main £9.50-£17.50, Dessert £2.75-£5.95, Coffee £1.50, Min/Water £3, Service optional **Wine:** 6 bottles over £20, 16 bottles under £20, 8 by the glass **Notes:** Vegetarian menu, Dress Restrictions, Smart casual **Seats:** 72, Pr/dining room 35 **Smoking:** N/Sm in restaurant, Air con **Children:** Portions **Rooms:** 17 (17 en suite) ★★★ HL **Directions:** Opposite Botanic Railway Station, on corner of Lower Crescent and Botanic Ave **Parking:** Opposite hotel

Restaurant Michael Deane

see page 651

Shu

Modern European

Chic eatery for fashion-conscious foodies

☎ 028 9038 1655 253 Lisburn Rd BT9 7EN
e-mail: eat@shu-restaurant.com
web: www.shu-restaurant.com

Located in a Georgian area of the town, Shu's classical exterior belies its cool, minimalist, contemporary interior. The restaurant is decked out in warm chocolate browns and beige, with swathes of suede and leather seating, polished, well-spaced tables and wooden floors. Smartly turned out, well-informed, confident service and a theatre-style, open kitchen give the fashionable package added edge. Shu's up-to-the-minute, modern Irish menu with French influences perfectly suits the surroundings. Serious cooking, seasonality and the use of quality local produce are keynote, delivering accurate, carefully presented, eclectic dishes to get the taste buds tingling. Menu samples include foie gras parfait with pear and ginger chutney or rump of lamb, Jerusalem artichoke purée with rosemary, garlic and balsamic.

Chef: Brian McCann **Owners:** Alan Reid **Times:** 12.30-2.30/6-10, Closed 24-26 Dec, 12-14 Jul, Sun **Prices:** Fixed D £25-£27.50, Starter £3.75-£7.25, Main £9.50-£17.50, Dessert £5, Coffee £1.55, Min/Water £3.95, Service optional, Group min 6 service 10% **Wine:** 34 bottles over £20, 19 bottles under £20, 8 by the glass (£3.75-£4) **Notes:** Vegetarian available **Seats:** 76, Pr/dining room 22 **Smoking:** N/Sm area, Air con **Children:** Portions **Directions:** From city centre take Lisburn road lower end. Restaurant in 1m **Parking:** On street

CO DOWN

BANGOR MAP 01 D5

Clandeboye Lodge Hotel

Modern International

Creative cooking in a contemporary country setting

☎ 028 9185 2500 10 Estate Rd, Clandeboye BT19 1UR
e-mail: info@clandeboyelodge.co.uk
web: www.clandeboyelodge.com

A modern build designed to be a contemporary country-house hotel, located next to the 200 acres of woodland, gardens, lawns and lake of the Clandeboye Estate. The upgraded restaurant is popular for its designer looks: spiralling chandeliers, wood panelling and marble-topped tables, as well as its courteous service from a friendly team. Inspiring menu with interesting twists and combinations - such as charred asparagus with baby leeks and soft poached egg, or rack of lamb, purple sprouting broccoli and minted peach purée.

Chef: Martin Wilson **Owners:** Pim Dalm **Times:** 12-2.30/6.30-9.30, Closed 25-26 Dec **Prices:** Fixed L £8-£18, Fixed D £15.50-£25, Starter £2.95-£5, Main £8.50-£15, Dessert £4.25-£5.50, Coffee £1.50, Min/Water £4.50, Service optional **Wine:** 9 bottles over £20, 26 bottles under £20, 13 by the glass (£3.60-£12.95) **Notes:** Fixed D 4 courses £22.50 incl1/4 bottle wine Fri-Sat, Vegetarian available, Dress Restrictions, Smart casual, Civ Wed 250 **Seats:** 60, Pr/dining room 300 **Smoking:** N/Sm in restaurant **Children:** Menu, Portions **Rooms:** 43 (43 en suite) ★★★ **Directions:** M3 follow signs for A2 (Bangor). Before Bangor turn right at junction signed to Newtownards, Clandeboye Lodge Hotel and Blackwood Golf Course **Parking:** 250

1614

Modern, Traditional

Good flavourful dining in atmospheric historic inn

☎ 028 9185 3255 Old Inn, 15 Main St, Crawfordsburn BT19 1JH
e-mail: info@theoldinn.com
web: www.theoldinn.com

The 1614 restaurant is located in Crawfordsburn's 17th-century Old Inn. Replete with original chandeliers, oak panelling and local coats of arms, the good quality soft furnishings, fixtures and fittings throughout soften the burden of history, helped along by friendly and helpful service from committed staff. Frequently changing and keenly priced menus rely on local seasonal ingredients to produce modern European-style dishes with definite local accents. Start with the seared sea scallops with cauliflower beignet and purée and basil velouté before trying a vibrant main course of baked local halibut with smoked fish risotto, basil, saffron and lobster. Finish with the 1614 rum-and-raisin trifle with honeycomb and white chocolate.

continued

Ireland

Chef: Alex Taylor **Owners:** Danny Rice **Times:** 12.30-2.30/7-9.30, Closed 25 Dec, Closed L Mon-Sat, D Sun **Prices:** Fixed D £30, Coffee £1.50, Min/Water £4, Service optional **Wine:** 8 by the glass (£2.95-£3.50) **Notes:** Sun L £22-£30, Vegetarian available, Civ Wed 85 **Seats:** 64, Pr/dining room 25 **Smoking:** N/Sm in restaurant **Children:** Menu, Portions **Rooms:** 32 (32 en suite) ★★★ HL **Directions:** Take A2 E from Belfast. 5-6m turn left at Ballyrobert lights, and 400 yds to Crawfordsburn, Inn is on left **Parking:** 100

DUNDRUM MAP 01 D5

Mourne Seafood Bar

Traditional Seafood NEW

Uncomplicated fresh fish and shellfish

☎ 028 43751377 10 Main St BT33 0LU
e-mail: bob@mourneseafood.com
web: www.mourneseafood.com

Situated in the picturesque village of Dundrum at the foot of the Mourne Mountains, this simply presented restaurant with wooden seats, wooden floors and basic table settings has a cracking atmosphere and - as the name would suggest - a preponderance of premium seafood, with most of the shellfish sourced from their own shellfish beds. Dishes are simple and effective, overwhelmingly featuring fish and seafood - try a home-made chowder followed by a hot seafood platter with oysters, langoustine, mussels and crab.

Chef: Neil Auterson **Owners:** Bob & Joanne McCoubrey **Times:** 12-9.30, Closed Mon & Tue Winter, 25 Dec **Prices:** Starter £3-£6.95, Main £6.75-£21, Dessert £4, Service included **Wine:** 6 bottles over £30, 20 bottles under £30, 4 by the glass (£2.75) **Seats:** 50, Pr/dining room 16 **Smoking:** N/Sm in restaurant **Children:** Portions **Directions:** On main road from Belfast to The Mournes, on village main st **Parking:** On street

PORTAVOGIE

The Quay's Pub & Restaurant

Modern International

Top-quality seafood dining in quayside location

☎ 028 4277 2225 81 New Harbour, Portavogie BT22 1EB
e-mail: leighgamble1969@hotmail.com
web: www.quaysrestaurant.co.uk

This modern building is right on the shore with the sea in front and Portavogie harbour behind. There's a bar, lounge and split-level restaurant specialising in seafood. Decked out in warm earthy colours with good artwork, the dining room has wooden tables and comfortable chairs adding to the relaxed atmosphere. But it's the fresh local seafood that attracts the regulars. Start with Strangford Lough rope mussels with chilli, garlic and white wine cream before a main course of pan-fried sea bass with herb parcels.

continued

Chef: David Cardwell & Aaron Hanna **Owners:** Francis & Diane Adair **Times:** 12-2.30/5-9, Closed 25 Dec, Tue **Prices:** Starter £3.50-£6, Main £6-£25, Dessert £3.95, Coffee £1.30, Min/Water £3, Service optional **Wine:** 6 bottles over £20, 23 bottles under £20, 8 by the glass **Notes:** Vegetarian available **Seats:** 96 **Smoking:** N/Sm in restaurant **Children:** Menu, Portions **Directions:** Take Portaferry road out of Newtownards and head towards Greyabbey, through Kircubbin and then Portavogie **Parking:** 100

see advert on this page

CO LONDONDERRY

LIMAVADY MAP 01 C6

The Lime Tree

Traditional, Mediterranean

Solid neighbourhood restaurant with welcoming atmosphere

☎ 028 7776 4300 60 Catherine St BT49 9DB
e-mail: info@limetreerest.com
web: www.limetreerest.com

This unassuming restaurant continues to attract regulars who enjoy the consistency of the food and the friendly atmosphere. The Mediterranean menu consists largely of classics with food cooked with skill and sensitivity, and good flavour combinations. Try pumpkin and cheddar cheese soup to start with a main of pan-fried fillets of plaice with a warm tartare cream sauce. Look out for regular theme nights that make interesting forays into international cuisine.

Chef: Stanley Matthews **Owners:** Mr & Mrs S Matthews **Times:** 6-9, Closed 25-26 Dec, Sun-Mon (ex Dec), Closed L all week **Prices:** Fixed D £13.50-£21.50, Starter £4-£8.50, Main £13.50-£18.50, Dessert £4.50-£6, Coffee £1.35, Min/Water £2.50, Service optional **Wine:** 10 bottles over £20,

continued

Ireland

LIMAVADY *continued* MAP 01 C6

30 bottles under £20, 5 by the glass (£2.95-£3.50) **Notes:** Min D price early bird menu Tue-Fri 6-7pm, Vegetarian available **Seats:** 30 **Smoking:** No pipes, No cigars **Children:** Menu, Portions **Directions:** Entering Limavady from the Derry side, the restaurant is on the right on small slip road **Parking:** 15

Radisson SAS Roe Park Resort

Modern British

Comfortable surroundings alongside a golf course

☎ 028 7772 2222 BT49 9LB
e-mail: reservations@radissonroepark.com
web: www.radissonroepark.com

This large golf resort-style hotel has a choice of dining areas. Greens Restaurant is made up of two high-ceilinged rooms and offers formal dining, while the Coach House brasserie is a more informal alternative. The modern British menu with European influences changes seasonally. Expect mains like pan-fried loin of pork with pancetta and sage mash, apple jam and pan gravy. Other options include roasted cod, rack of lamb or fillet steak all with interesting accompaniments. Some dishes can be adapted as a 'healthy option', served with steamed vegetables or mixed salad.

Chef: Adrian McDaid **Owners:** Mr Conn, Mr McKeever, Mr Wilton **Times:** 6.30-10, Closed Sun-Thu, Jan, Closed L Mon-Sat, D Mon **Prices:** Fixed L fr £10.95, Fixed D £21.95-£25.95, Starter £3.50-£6.50, Main £12.95-£16.95, Dessert £5.95, Coffee £1.50, Min/Water £3.25, Service optional **Wine:** 3 bottles over £20, 24 bottles under £20, 6 by the glass (£2.95-£3.50) **Notes:** Fixed L is carvery, Fixed D 4 courses, Vegetarian available, Dress Restrictions, Smart casual, Civ Wed 250 **Seats:** 160, Pr/dining room 50 **Smoking:** N/Sm in restaurant, Air con **Children:** Menu, Portions **Rooms:** 118 (118 en suite) ★★★★ HL **Directions:** On A6 (Londonderry-Limavady road), 0.5m from Limavady. 8m from Derry airport **Parking:** 250

LONDONDERRY MAP 01 C5

Beech Hill Hotel

Modern, Traditional

Elegant country-house serving stylish food

☎ 028 7134 9279 32 Ardmore Rd BT47 3QP
e-mail: info@beech-hill.com
web: www.beech-hill.com

An impressive 18th-century manor house standing in 32 acres of glorious woodlands and gardens. Traditionally-styled day rooms are smartly decorated and the atmosphere is relaxing. Making the most of the lovely view, the attractively extended dining room now includes a conservatory. The skilfully prepared modern Irish dishes are accurately cooked and make good use of quality ingredients. Saucing is consistent and presentation is particularly impressive - try the Donegal crab and bacon risotto, the duo of Foyle duck (confit and seared) or the Castlerock lamb with black pudding.

Chef: Raymond Moran **Owners:** Mr S Donnelly, Mrs P O'Kane **Times:** 12-2.30/6-9.45, Closed 24-25 Dec **Prices:** Fixed L £14.95, Fixed D £27.95, Starter £3.95-£7.95, Main £14.95-£19.95, Dessert fr £5.95, Coffee £1.25, Min/Water £3.50, Service optional **Wine:** 20 bottles over £20, 37 bottles under £20, 6 by the glass (£3.95) **Notes:** Fixed D 4 courses, Vegetarian available, Civ Wed 80 **Seats:** 90, Pr/dining room 80 **Smoking:** N/Sm in restaurant **Children:** Portions **Rooms:** 27 (27 en suite) ★★★ HL **Directions:** A6 Londonderry to Belfast road, turn off at Faughan Bridge. 1m further to Ardmore Chapel. Hotel entrance is opposite **Parking:** 50

Tower Hotel Derry

Modern Mediterranean

Bistro-style restaurant within the city walls

☎ 028 7137 1000 Off the Diamond, Butcher St BT48 6HL
e-mail: reservations@thd.ie
web: www.towerhotelderry.com

Right in the centre of the city, the Tower is the only hotel within the historic Derry walls, with fantastic views from the restaurant. The restaurant is a bright, relaxing space, open-plan with the Lime Tree bar, which is ideal for pre-dinner drinks. Modern dishes include roast loin of lamb with a rosemary jus, served with seasonal vegetables, or seared fillet of beef with horseradish mash, confit cherry tomatoes, Clonakilty black pudding and red wine jus.

Chef: Barry O'Brien **Owners:** Tower Hotel Group **Times:** 12.30-2.90/6-9.45, Closed Xmas, Closed L (booking required) **Prices:** Fixed L £9.95, Fixed D £13.95, Starter £3.95-£5.25, Main £8.95-£13.95, Dessert £3.95, Coffee £1.25, Service optional **Wine:** 4 bottles over £20, 14 bottles under £20, 7 by the glass (£3-£3.50) **Notes:** Vegetarian available, Civ Wed 300 **Seats:** 100, Pr/dining room 20 **Smoking:** N/Sm in restaurant, Air con **Children:** Menu, Portions **Rooms:** 93 (93 en suite) ★★★★ HL **Directions:** From Craigavon Ridge to city centre. Take 2nd exit at the end of bridge into Carlisle Rd, then to Ferryquay St **Parking:** 35

MAGHERA MAP 01 C5

Ardtara Country House

Modern International V

Modern fusion cuisine in a country-house setting

☎ 028 7964 4490 8 Gorteade Rd BT46 5SA
e-mail: valerie_ferson@ardtara.com
web: www.ardtara.com

Originally built in 1896 as the Clark Linen Factory, the building was renovated as a family home and now has all the appearances of a traditional country-house hotel. Appearances can be deceptive however and the classic décor of the dining room conceals some funky modern fusion cooking making an impact on the menu. Dishes might include a starter of cod with spicy ricotta and baby spinach millefeuille and yellow Kashmir curry sauce. A more traditional main course would be roast sirloin of McKees beef served with baked potato, Yorkshire pudding, wild mushrooms and red wine gravy.

Chef: Olivier Boudon **Owners:** Dr Alistair & Nancy Hanna **Times:** 12.3 2.30/6.30-9 **Prices:** Fixed L fr £18, Fixed D fr £28, Starter £4.50-£18, Main £14-£30, Dessert £6-£9, Service optional **Wine:** 36 bottles over £20, 47 bottles under £20, 7 by the glass **Notes:** Sun L 3 course £20, Vegetarian available, Civ Wed 120 **Seats:** 45, Pr/dining room 16 **Smoking:** N/Sm in restaurant **Children:** Portions **Rooms:** 8 (8 en suite) ★★ HL **Directions:** Take A29 to Maghera/Coleraine. Follow B75(Kilrea) to Upperlands. Past sign for W Clark & Sons, next left **Parking:** 50

Republic of Ireland

REPUBLIC OF IRELAND CO CAVAN

BALLYCONNELL MAP 01 C5

Slieve Russell Hotel Golf & Country Club

International

Enormous hotel with a solid reputation for fine dining

☎ 049 9526 444
e-mail: slieve-russell@quinn-hotels.com
web: www.quinnhotels.com

This vast, luxurious hotel is set in over 300 acres of grounds with lakes, a popular golf course and a health spa with a wide range of pampering facilities. There are two restaurants to choose from: the Setanta with a modern European bias and the Conall Cearnach for fine dining. The latter offers traditional-style cooking with an international bias and a strong emphasis on quality luxury ingredients - try a starter of fresh lobster tagliatelle in a champagne truffle-scented cream, then a main course of roast breast of Thornhill duck with duck leg confit and lavender honey-glazed peaches and lemon.

Times: 12.30-2.15/7-9.15, Closed L Mon-Sat **Rooms:** 219 (219 en suite) ★★★★ **Directions:** From Dublin take N3 towards Cavan. At rdbt before Cavan, follow Enniskillen sign to Belturbet. From Belturbet go towards Ballyconnell. Hotel approx 6m from Belturbet on left

Ireland

CAVAN MAP 01 C4

Cavan Crystal Hotel

Modern European NEW

Innovative cooking in contemporary hotel

☎ 049 436 0600 Dublin Rd
e-mail: info@cavancrystalhotel.com
web: www.cavancrystalhotel.com

Contemporary design, matched by the use of native timber, handcrafted brick and crystal chandeliers, make this a particularly distinctive new hotel. The modern dining room is on the first floor, backed by a friendly team of professionals. There's a health and beauty clinic here, and the Cavan Crystal shop and factory are on the same site. The cuisine is innovative in style, the cooking confident and using fine quality, local ingredients with integrity and some unusual twists. Accuracy, flavour balance and texture contrast all hit the right note in dishes such as cannon of lamb on creamed cabbage with shallots and bacon.

Chef: Dave Fitzgibbon **Owners:** McKenna & Quinn Partnership **Times:** 12.30-3.30/6-10, Closed 24-25 Dec **Prices:** Fixed L €21-€25, Fixed D €25-€35, Starter €4.95-€12.50, Main €18-€25, Dessert €7-€9, Coffee €1.50, Min/Water €3, Service optional **Wine:** 16 bottles over €30, 14 bottles under €30, 4 by the glass (€4.80-€5.50) **Notes:** Sun D €35 **Seats:** 95 **Smoking:** N/Sm in restaurant, Air con **Children:** Menu, Portions **Rooms:** 85 (85 en suite) ★★★★ **Directions:** Approach Cavan on N3, straight over rdbt, hotel immediately on left **Parking:** 192

VIRGINIA MAP 01 C4

The Park Hotel

European, International

Fresh produce in former hunting lodge

☎ 049 8546100 Virginia Park
e-mail: virginiapark@eircom.net
web: www.parkhotelvirginia.com

This imposing 18th-century hunting lodge was the country estate and sporting lodge of the Marquis of Headfort (1750-1939). It enjoys a superb location in 100 acres with mature gardens and woodland. The architecturally renowned restaurants are named the Marquis and Marchionness dining rooms and here you can sample some classic cuisine. The chef makes excellent use of local produce and fruit, vegetables and herbs from the estate's organic gardens. Try a main course like braised shank of Cavan lamb with roast root vegetables and rosemary jus.

Times: 12.30-3.30/6.30-9.30, Closed 25-26 Dec, Closed L Mon-Sat **Rooms:** 26 (26 en suite) ★★ **Directions:** Follow the N3 to Virginia and when in village take first left. Hotel entrance 500 yds on left

CO CLARE

BALLYVAUGHAN MAP 01 B3

Gregans Castle

Modern French, Irish

Country-house hotel dining with splendid views of The Burren

☎ 065 7077005
e-mail: res@gregans.ie
web: www.gregans.ie

With magnificent mountain views over the unique landscape of The Burren towards Galway Bay, the appropriately austere exterior of this family-run 18th-century country house belies the comfort and style to be found within. Elegant public rooms are furnished with beautiful antiques, and window tables in the restaurant make the most of the view across the bay. Skilful cooking shows enthusiasm and good use of high-quality local and organic produce, notably lamb from the village butcher. A typical meal may feature filo parcel of confit duck, coriander and ginger, followed by loin of lamb with courgette chutney and Madeira jus, and green leaf tea crème brûlée. Staff are renowned for their personal service.

Times: 7-8.30, Closed 15 Oct-5 Apr 07, Closed L all week **Rooms:** 21 (21 en suite) ★★★ **Directions:** On N67, 3.5m S of Ballyvaughan

ENNIS MAP 01 B3

Temple Gate

International

Modern dining in a Gothic-style building

☎ 065 682 3300 The Square
e-mail: info@templegatehotel.com
web: www.templegatehotel.com

Developed from a 19th-century convent, the hotel retains much of its original Gothic style but in a contemporary context. JM's Bistro provides a relaxed, elegant setting for a lengthy choice of dishes with international influences. Starters include Shanghai duck roll, West Coast tempura and Clare goat's cheese under a walnut crumble; while mains take in bistro sirloin (prime Irish steak), and medallions of monkfish, with shrimp and saffron rice timbale, wholegrain mustard and honey velouté. The Great Hall, once the convent's church, makes a fabulous setting for weddings and banquets.

Chef: Paul Shortt **Owners:** John Madden **Times:** 12.45-2.30/7-9.45, Closed 25-27 Dec, Good Fri, Closed L Request only Mon-Sat **Prices:** Fixed L €16.50-€18.50, Fixed D €25-€30, Starter €6-€10, Main €16-€26, Dessert €6-€8, Coffee €2.95, Service optional, Group min 10 **Wine:** 4 bottles over €30, 16 bottles under €30, 2 by the glass (€4.80-€5) **Notes:** Sun L €19.50-€21.50, Vegetarian available, Civ Wed 150 **Seats:** 90, Pr/dining room 150 **Smoking:** N/Sm in restaurant **Children:** Menu, Portions **Rooms:** 70 (70 en suite) ★★★ **Directions:** Follow signs for the Tourist Office, hotel is in same square **Parking:** 100

LISDOONVARNA

Sheedy's Country House Hotel

Modern Irish

Pleasant country-house cooking of the classic variety

☎ 065 707 4026
e-mail: info@sheedys.com
web: www.sheedys.com

Owned by the Sheedy family since the 18th century, this former farmhouse has an immaculate location on the edge of the Burren and oozes character. Close to Lahinch golf course, Doolin and the Cliffs of Moher, it's an ideal base for touring the region. The food is strong on classic dishes with some modern influences and if dishes don't feature home-grown vegetables and herbs, you can be sure the produce was sourced locally. You could start with a tart of St Tola goat's cheese with caramelised onions and a lemon dressing and continue happily on to slow-roast crispy duck with potato stuffing and a herb gravy.

Chef: John Sheedy **Owners:** John & Martina Sheedy **Times:** 6.45-8.30, Closed mid Oct-mid Mar **Prices:** Starter €5-€13.50, Main €19-€27, Dessert €7.50-€8.50, Coffee €2.50, Min/Water €4.50, Service optional **Wine:** 4 by the glass (€3.90-€6.50) **Notes:** Vegetarian available **Seats:** 28 **Smoking:** N/Sm in restaurant, Air con **Children:** Min 8 yrs **Rooms:** 11 (11 en suite) ★★★ **Directions:** 20m from Ennis on N87 **Parking:** 25

NEWMARKET-ON-FERGUS MAP 01 B3

Dromoland Castle

Traditional European, International V

Elegant dining in historic castle

☎ 061 368144
e-mail: sales@dromoland.ie
web: www.dromoland.ie

An imposing castle turned luxury hotel, this Renaissance building set in a 375-acre estate is steeped in history and dates back to the 16th century. The magnificent public rooms are warmed by log fires, while the atmosphere in the elegant, fine-dining Earl of Thornbury Restaurant - with its Venetian silk wall hangings, portraits, crystal chandeliers and Irish linen - is enhanced by the soothing cords of the resident harpist. Service is professional and very attentive, while the skilful kitchen's dinner menus deliver interesting combinations from classical roots, using fresh fish and game from the estate in season. Typically loin of Irish venison with pearl barley and celeriac risotto, venison sausage and cassis sauce is the style.

Chef: David McCann **Owners:** Earl of Thomond **Times:** 12.30-1.30/7-10, Closed 25-26 Dec, Closed L Mon-Sat **Prices:** Fixed L €40, Fixed D €65, Starter €16-€25, Main €31-€38, Dessert €9-€11.50, Coffee €3.50, Min/Water €6, Service added but optional 15% **Wine:** 30 bottles under €30, 8 by the glass (€7.50) **Notes:** Fixed L 3 courses, Fixed D 5 courses, Tasting menu €90, Vegetarian menu, Dress Restrictions, Jacket **Seats:** 80, Pr/dining room 40 **Smoking:** N/Sm in restaurant **Children:** Menu, Portions **Rooms:** 100 (100 en suite) ★★★★★ **Directions:** From Ennis take N18, follow signs for Shannon/Limerick. 7m follow Quin. Newmarket-on-Fergus sign. Hotel 0.5m. From Shannon take N18 towards Ennis **Parking:** 140

CO CORK

BALLYCOTTON MAP 01 C2

Bay View

French

Accomplished cuisine in comfortable country house with dramatic views

☎ 021 464 6746
e-mail: res@thebayviewhotel.com
web: www.thebayviewhotel.com

The name of this country-house hotel doesn't do justice to its breathtaking coastline views, perched on a hillside near the fishing village of Ballycotton. The garden and bay views prove an irresistible dining-room drawcard, and, given the location, it's unsurprising that local seafood is a speciality here, though it doesn't monopolise the

continued

Ireland

BALLYCOTTON *continued* MAP 01 C2

repertoire. The kitchen's modern Irish approach - underpinned by a classic French theme - also makes fine use of local meats and produce, with all suppliers admirably listed on the menu. High technical skill, creativity, clear flavours and dramatic presentation parade on balanced, well-executed dishes; think seared Castletownbere scallops with saffron mash, baby vegetables, slow-roast vine tomatoes and a smoky bacon dressing, or a 'chocolate trilogy' finish.

Chef: Ciaran Scully **Owners:** John & Carmel O'Brian **Times:** 1-2/7-9, Closed Nov-Apr, Closed L Mon-Sat **Prices:** Fixed L €28, Fixed D €47, Starter €7-€12, Main €22-€28, Dessert €7-€9, Coffee €2, Min/Water €3.50, Service optional **Wine:** 25 bottles over €30, 25 bottles under €30, 4 by the glass (€5-€7) **Notes:** Fixed L 3 courses, Fixed D 4 courses, Vegetarian available, Dress Restrictions, Smart casual **Seats:** 65, Pr/dining room 30 **Smoking:** N/Sm in restaurant **Children:** Portions **Rooms:** 35 (35 en suite) ★★★ **Directions:** At Castlemartyr on N25 (Cork-Waterford road) turn onto R632 to Garryvoe, then follow signs for Shanagarry & Ballycotton **Parking:** 40

Ireland

BALLYLICKEY MAP 01 B2

Sea View House

Traditional

Traditional Irish cooking in a delightful country house

☎ 027 50073 & 50462
e-mail: info@seaviewhousehotel.com
web: www.seaviewhousehotel.com

Secluded in colourful gardens close to Ballylickey Bridge, with views of Bantry Bay and the mountains beyond, this friendly, immaculately maintained hotel has earned a reputation for consistently high standards over many years. Several rooms, decorated in warm tones of green, and a delightful octagonal conservatory make up the dining area, which is elegantly furnished with antiques and fresh flowers. Cooking is country-house style and shows skill, enthusiasm and sound use of top-quality local produce, with fresh fish a feature on the daily fixed-price dinner menu. Examples include Bantry Bay mussels and scallops, and meatier options such as supreme of guinea fowl with red wine jus.

Chef: Eleanor O'Donavon **Owners:** Kathleen O'Sullivan **Times:** 12.30-1.45/7-9.30, Closed Nov-Mar, Closed L Mon-Sat **Prices:** Fixed L €25, Fixed D €40-€45, Starter €5.50-€10.50, Main €20-€30, Dessert fr €5.50, Min/Water €2.50, Service included, Group min 10 service 10% **Wine:** 30 bottles over €30, 10 bottles under €30, 10 by the glass (€4.50-€5.50) **Notes:** Coffee incl, Fixed L 3 courses, Vegetarian available, Dress Restrictions, Smart casual **Seats:** 50 **Smoking:** N/Sm in restaurant **Children:** Menu, Portions **Rooms:** 25 (25 en suite) ★★★ **Directions:** 3m N of Bantry towards Glengarriff, 70 yds off main road

BALTIMORE MAP 01 B1

Baltimore Harbour Hotel

Classic

Harbourside hotel offering enjoyable food

☎ 028 20361
e-mail: info@bhrhotel.ie

This quaint, very traditional seaside hotel in a pretty fishing village has been a fixture in the area for many years. The views across Baltimore harbour and the coastal islands are magnificent and there can be few better places to have a window table at sunset in the Clipper Restaurant - the adjoining Chartroom Bar is a good for a music session too. The menu features good quality West Cork produce and locally-landed seafood: hearty, moreish food to satisfy all comers - crab claw with citrus dressing to start for example, then a main course of baked cod with pesto crust and a smoked salmon sauce.

Times: 6.30-9.30, Closed Xmas. Weekdays Nov-Mar. **Rooms:** 64 (64 en suite) ★★★

Casey's of Baltimore

Irish, Seafood

Enjoy fresh fish and a warm welcome

☎ 028 20197
e-mail: info@caseysofbaltimore.com
web: www.caseysbaltimore.com

A simply styled inn on the outskirts of town where the restaurant overlooks the beautiful bay. A promising setting for the freshest of fish caught by the owner, including mussels from his own mussel beds. In addition to this fantastic sea harvest, fresh local produce includes locally sourced vegetables and steaks. The menu in Casey's Bar offers a selection of fresh seafood and steaks while the restaurant menu is a seafood lover's delight, with the likes of Roaring Bay mussels and crab claws, and hot and cold platters, leaving diners spoilt for choice.

Chef: Victoria Gilshenan **Owners:** Ann & Michael Casey **Times:** 12.30-2.30/6.30-9, Closed 21-26 Dec **Prices:** Fixed L fr €28, Fixed D €35-€50, Starter €6.50-€14, Main €15-€45, Dessert fr €6, Coffee €1.60, Min/Water €4, Service optional **Wine:** 5 bottles over €30, 20 bottles under €30, 2 by the glass (€4) **Notes:** Fixed L 3 courses, Sun L menu available, Vegetarian available **Seats:** 100 **Smoking:** N/Sm in restaurant, Air con **Children:** Menu, Portions **Rooms:** 14 (14 en suite) ★★★ **Directions:** From Cork take N71 to Skibbereen, then take R595. Hotel is at entrance to village on right **Parking:** 50

CLONAKILTY

Inchydoney Island Lodge & Spa

French, Mediterranean V

Fresh West Cork food in a glorious coastal setting

☎ 023 33143
e-mail: reservations@inchydoneyisland.com
web: www.inchydoneyisland.com

Set astride two beautiful blue-flag beaches, the building enjoys panoramic views of the Atlantic Ocean from every window. There's designer furniture in reception, a plethora of paintings for sale, and a restaurant with a contemporary look and stunning sea views. French and Mediterranean influences are evident in the menu, with fresh seafood and local organic produce used where possible, in dishes of

continued

roast rabbit loin wrapped in Parma ham with buttered linguini and vermouth cream, and pan-fried fillet of turbot on parsnip mash with orange and star anise cream. Vegetarian and various healthy options are also available: spinach and feta cheese parcel with oriental vegetables, basil oil and balsamic essence.

Chef: Mark Kirby **Owners:** Des O'Dowd **Times:** 12-9/6.30-9.45, Closed 24-26 Dec, Closed L Mon-Sat **Prices:** Fixed D €49, Starter €12, Main €30, Dessert €10, Coffee €6, Min/Water €4.95, Service added 10% **Wine:** 47 bottles over €30, 4 bottles under €30, 3 by the glass (€6.95) **Notes:** Fixed D 5 courses, Vegetarian available, Dress Restrictions, Smart casual **Seats:** 90, Pr/dining room 250 **Smoking:** N/Sm in restaurant, Air con **Children:** Menu, Portions **Rooms:** 67 (67 en suite) ★★★★ **Directions:** From Cork take N71 following 'West Cork' signs. Through Innishannon, Bandon & Clonakilty, then follow signs for Inchydoney Island **Parking:** 250

CORK MAP 01 B2

Hayfield Manor

Modern French

Simple modern cuisine in chic surroundings

☎ 021 484 5900 Perrott Av, College Rd
e-mail: reservations@hayfieldmanor.ie
web: www.hayfieldmanor.ie

Once home to the Musgrave family of Cork, the house was architect-designed with classically styled rooms. Period features like the original fireplaces, pillars, high ceilings and cornicing remain, along with contemporary additions. There are two dining options, the contemporary Perrotts restaurant serving an informal menu and the more formal Orchids restaurant. Here you will find French and European dishes with a cosmopolitan feel in a room overlooking a classical garden. Simple, stylish food makes the best of Irish produce with traditional techniques. Try a starter of warm organic goat's cheese with roast fig and honey. Follow this with a main course like organic duck breast with rösti potato, creamed Savoy cabbage and bacon.

Chef: Alan Hickey **Owners:** Mr J Scally **Times:** 12.30-2/7-10, Closed L Sat **Prices:** Fixed L €28, Fixed D €55, Starter €14-€16, Main €26-€32, Dessert €12-€14, Coffee €4.50, Min/Water €6.10, Group min 8 service 10% **Wine:** 90 bottles over €30, 6 bottles under €30, 14 by the glass (€6.35-€10) **Notes:** Tasting menu 7 courses €90, Vegetarian available **Seats:** 80, Pr/dining room 32 **Smoking:** N/Sm in restaurant, Air con **Children:** Menu, Portions **Rooms:** 88 (88 en suite) ★★★★ **Directions:** From Cork take N22 to Killarney. On Western Rd at University gates turn left into Donovan's Rd, then right into College Rd and immediately left into Perrott Ave **Parking:** 100

Maryborough Hotel & Spa

Modern International V

Wide-ranging menu in a popular hotel restaurant

☎ 021 436 5555 Maryborough Hill
e-mail: info@maryborough.ie

Just outside Cork, this 18th-century country house hotel has been extended with its modern wing housing rooms and a spa. The split-level dining room has its own walk-in wine cellar. Friendly staff serve modern dishes which display wide-ranging influences. Simpler dishes tend to be most effective like a starter of timbale of crab and avocado with lime crème fraîche and gazpacho or the main course of seared rack of Kerry lamb with herb and tomato crust and port jus. Finish with a classic pear Belle Hélène or passionfruit-infused crème brulée.

continued

Chef: Gerry Allen **Owners:** Dan O'Sullivan **Times:** 12.30-2.30/6.30-10, Closed 24-26 Dec **Prices:** Fixed L €20-€25, Fixed D €40-€45, Starter €6.90-€13.90, Main €21-€29.50, Dessert €7.50, Coffee €2.50, Min/Water €4.50, Service included, Group min 10 service 10% **Wine:** 41 bottles over €30, 32 bottles under €30, 4 by the glass (€5.20) **Notes:** Vegetarian menu, Civ Wed 100 **Seats:** 120, Pr/dining room 60 **Smoking:** N/Sm in restaurant, Air con **Children:** Min 10 yrs D, Menu, Portions **Rooms:** 79 (79 en suite) ★★★★ **Directions:** Telephone for directions **Parking:** 300

Café Paradiso

☎ 021 427 7939 16 Lancaster Quay, Western Rd
Lively vegetarian with seasonal cooking.

Jacobs

☎ 021 425 1530 30a South Mall
Skill, creativity and top-notch ingredients in an easygoing setting.

Jacques

☎ 021 427 7387 Phoenix St
Mediterranean style décor and food, with friendly service.

GARRYVOE MAP 01 C2

Garryvoe Hotel

Modern, Traditional

Sea views and simply prepared fresh local food

☎ 021 464 6718 Ballyrotton Bay, Castlemartyr
e-mail: res@garryvoehotel.com
web: www.garryvoehotel.com

Recently redeveloped hotel standing in a seaside location overlooking Ballycotton Bay and a beautiful beach. The modern restaurant has a classic look and offers a choice of menus including a bar food option, a fixed-priced dinner, an à la carte selection and daily specials. Fresh local produce is used to good effect in traditional-style dishes with seafood as a speciality. A typical choice might be prawns in garlic butter, golden fried goujons of monkfish with tartare sauce, and millefeuille of shortbread, fresh cream and strawberries.

Chef: Phillip Villiard **Owners:** Carmel & John O'Brian **Times:** 1-2.30/6.45-8.45, Closed 24-25 Dec, Closed D 24 Dec **Prices:** Fixed L €26, Fixed D €42, Coffee €2.80, Min/Water €3.50, Service optional **Wine:** 25 bottles over €30, 25 bottles under €30, 4 by the glass (€5-€7) **Notes:** Fixed L 3 courses, Fixed D 4 courses, Vegetarian available **Seats:** 80, Pr/dining room 40 **Smoking:** N/Sm in restaurant **Children:** Menu, Portions **Rooms:** 48 (48 en suite) ★★★ **Directions:** From N25 at Castlemartyr (Cork-Rosslare road) take R632 to Garryvoe **Parking:** 80

Ireland

KINSALE MAP 01 B2

Actons Hotel

European

Georgian townhouse hotel on the waterfront

☎ 021 4772135 Pier Rd
e-mail: info@actonshotelkinsale.com
web: www.actonshotelskinsale.com

Occupying several Georgian townhouses on the waterfront, this established modern hotel overlooks Kinsale's bustling harbour. Drinks and light meals are served in the bar and adjacent garden in fine weather, while more formal fare is available in the Captain's Table restaurant - a bright, contemporary, nautically-themed room with polished tables and crisp linen. A lengthy European and modern Irish menu offers plenty of choice, including steaks as well as more elaborate dishes. Unsurprisingly, seafood is a speciality.

Times: 12.30-3/7-9.30, Closed Xmas & Jan, Closed L Mon-Sat **Rooms:** 76 (76 en suite) ★★★

Trident Hotel

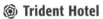

Modern, Traditional European

Waterfront hotel with harbour views

☎ 021 477 9300 Worlds End
e-mail: info@tridenthotel.com
web: www.tridenthotel.com

The hotel has a wonderful location on the waterfront in historic Kinsale. The Wharf Tavern is a lively bar, popular for its daily carvery lunch and evening bistro-style menu, an alternative to the award-winning Savannah restaurant. Here you can expect to find European-style cooking, with a modern twist on traditional dishes. Starters like Parma ham served with melon and tropical fruits might be followed by a main course of grilled Dover sole on the bone, with lemon butter. Desserts are worth waiting for, try warm sticky toffee pudding and home-made ice cream.

Chef: Gerry O'Connor **Owners:** David Good **Times:** 1-2.30/7-9.30, Closed 24-26 Dec, Closed L Mon-Sat **Prices:** Fixed L fr €24, Fixed D €25-€35, Starter €4.95-€9.50, Main €13.50-€29.50, Dessert €6.25, Coffee €2, Min/Water €6.50, Service optional **Wine:** 15 bottles over €30, 46 bottles under €30 **Notes:** Fixed L 3 courses, Fixed D 4 courses, Vegetarian available **Seats:** 90, Pr/dining room 200 **Smoking:** N/Sm in restaurant **Children:** Menu, Portions **Rooms:** 75 (75 en suite) ★★★ **Directions:** From Cork take R600 to Kinsale. Hotel at end of Pier Rd **Parking:** 60

MACROOM MAP 01 B2

Castle Hotel

European

Family-run hotel with a loyal local following

☎ 026 41074 Main St
e-mail: castlehotel@eircom.net
web: www.castlehotel.ie

There's three dining options at this popular, long-established hotel - a traditional-style Irish bar (with a good value carvery lunch every day), a continental café, and 'B's Restaurant' which serves up bistro-style food

continued

Longueville House

MALLOW MAP 01 B2

Traditional French

Classical cooking in splendid Georgian manor house

☎ 022 47156 & 47306
e-mail: info@longuevillehouse.ie
web: www.longuevillehouse.ie

This Georgian manor house oozes period charm, set in its 500-acre estate of woodlands, gardens and farm in the Blackwater Valley. Dining is country-house style in the timeless elegance of the Presidents' Restaurant, aptly lined with portraits of former Irish presidents, and in the renovated Victorian Turner Conservatory with its romantic white drapes and candlelight; both laid out with crisp white linen and quality silver and crystal.

Chef-proprietor William O'Callaghan overseas the kitchen, his menu reflecting the top-quality produce supplied almost entirely by the estate; seasonal vegetables, fruit and herbs from the walled garden, free-range eggs from their own hens and ducks, fresh river salmon, lamb and pork from the farm. The cooking comes suitably underpinned by classical French themes, with dishes displaying high skill, enthusiasm, balance and flavour. There might be a trio of Longueville lamb with celeriac mousse and thyme jus, roast woodcock with rösti potato and mushroom sauce, or more modish monkfish with mango, ginger and coriander salsa. Finish with a classic vanilla crème brûlée, or chocolate and orange fondant with caramel ice cream. Peripherals like canapés, bread and petits fours hold style through to the end.

Chef: William O'Callaghan **Owners:** O'Callaghan Family **Times:** 12.30-5/6.30-9, Closed 8 Jan-17 Mar **Prices:** Fixed D €55-€65, Starter €14-€17, Main €29.50-€31, Dessert €13-€16, Service optional, Group min 8 service 10% **Notes:** Fixed D 4 courses,Tasting menu 7 courses €75, Vegetarian available, Dress Restrictions, Smart casual **Seats:** 100, Pr/dining room 18 **Smoking:** N/Sm in restaurant **Children:** Menu, Portions **Rooms:** 20 (20 en suite) ★★★ **Directions:** 3m W of Mallow via N72 to Killarney, right at Ballyclough junct, hotel 200 yds on left **Parking:** 35

with a contemporary twist. The split-level main dining room has something of an art deco feel with high-backed chairs, and grey, black and deep red tones. Local produce is high on the agenda in dishes such as warm salad of Clonakilty pudding, grilled John Dory or home-made desserts like butterscotch cream cheesecake, which may take their toll on the waistline but they certainly won't disappoint the taste buds!

Chef: Pat Ryan **Owners:** The Buckley Family **Times:** 12-3/6-9.30, Closed 25 Dec **Prices:** Fixed L €25-€30, Fixed D €35-€45, Starter €5.50-€10, Main €19-€28.50, Dessert €5.50-€6.50, Coffee €2.50, Min/Water €2.50, Service included **Wine:** 2 bottles over €30, 10 bottles under €30 **Notes:** Fixed L 3 courses, Vegetarian available **Seats:** 50, Pr/dining room 150 **Smoking:** N/Sm in restaurant, Air con **Children:** Menu, Portions **Rooms:** 60 (60 en suite) ★★★ **Directions:** On N22, midway between Cork and Killarney **Parking:** 30

MALLOW MAP 01 B2

Longueville House

see opposite

CO DONEGAL

DONEGAL MAP 01 B5

Harvey's Point Country Hotel

European

Accomplished cooking in a tranquil setting

☎ 074 972 2208 Lough Eske
e-mail: info@harveyspoint.com
web: www.harveyspoint.com

he wooded lakeside setting for this country hotel is truly idyllic. amily-owned and run, the hotel and restaurant are well established. ervice is personal as well as professional. The restaurant's European rte changes seasonally offering a good choice including vegetarian

continued

options. Starters might include the likes of seared scallops in a puff pastry basket with white asparagus, while expect mains like loin of lamb with dauphinoise potatoes or perhaps roast veal on crispy polenta with morel sauce. Ingredients are top quality and the cooking shows flair with strong influences from the Swiss owners and chef. The Sunday lunch buffet is very popular.

Chef: Paul Montgomery **Owners:** Marc Gysling, Deirdre McGlone **Times:** 12.30-2.30/6.30-9.30, Closed Mon-Tue (Nov-Easter), Closed D Sun **Prices:** Fixed L €25.50-€32, Fixed D €50-€60, Starter €12-€15, Main €30-€35, Dessert €10-€15, Coffee €2.50, Min/Water €3.90, Service included **Wine:** 55 bottles over €30, 40 bottles under €30, 4 by the glass (€3.90-€5) **Notes:** Sun carvery €26, Dress Restrictions, Smart casual **Seats:** 100, Pr/dining room 100 **Smoking:** N/Sm in restaurant, Air con **Children:** Min 12 yrs **Rooms:** 20 (20 en suite) ★★★★ **Directions:** From Donegal 2m towards Lifford, turn left at Harveys Point sign, continue to follow signs, taking three right turns to Harveys Point gates **Parking:** 200

RATHMULLAN MAP 01 C6

Fort Royal Hotel

Modern Irish, Seafood NEW

Country house in mature gardens sloping down to the sea

☎ 074 915 8100 Fort Royal
e-mail: fortroyal@eircom.net
web: www.fortroyal.com

Family-run hotel on the western shores of Lough Swilly, with 18 acres of grounds including a 9-hole golf course. Public rooms include restful lounges, an inviting bar and a fine-dining restaurant overlooking the gardens. Genuine country house-style cooking offers fresh fish as a speciality, alongside local lamb and beef. Vegetables, fruit and herbs are supplied by the walled garden. Enjoyable dishes include crisp goat's cheese and semi sun-dried tomato tart, perfectly cooked turbot fillet with a well-judged lime butter sauce, and a luscious pannacotta with mixed berry compôte.

Prices: Food prices not confirmed for 2007. Please telephone for details **Rooms:** 15 (15 en suite) ★★★ **Directions:** Telephone for directions

CO DUBLIN

DUBLIN MAP 01 D4

Clarion Hotel Dublin IFSC

Italian

Sophisticated corporate hotel with Italian cuisine

☎ 01 433 8800 I.F.S.C
e-mail: sinergie@clarionhotelifsc.com
web: www.clarionhotelifsc.com

This well-designed, modern hotel is located in the heart of the financial service centre. The restaurant offers modern Italian dishes with some innovative ideas like 'make your own bruschetta'. Starters include carpaccio bresaola with rocket salad or one of a good selection of pasta or rice dishes. Main courses include the signature dish of home-made agnolotti with spinach and fresh ricotta, vine ripe tomatoes and basil sauce, chicken saltimbocca alla Romana or sea bass cartoccio baked in a parcel with cherry tomatoes, olives and white wine. Desserts like pannacotta or tiramisù bring proceedings to a satisfying close. The attentive staff provide a professional service.

continued

DUBLIN *continued* MAP 01 D4

Chef: Tony O'Donnell **Owners:** Giacomo Ltd **Times:** 12-2.30/6-9.45, Closed 24-26 Dec, BHs, Closed L Sat & Sun **Prices:** Fixed L €14.95, Fixed D €24.95, Starter €5.50-€9.50, Main €12-€24, Coffee €2.50, Min/Water €4.60, Service optional **Wine:** 16 bottles over €30, 19 bottles under €30, 14 by the glass (€4.75-€8) **Notes:** Vegetarian available, Dress Restrictions, Smart casual preferred **Seats:** 80, Pr/dining room 80 **Smoking:** N/Sm in restaurant, Air con **Children:** Menu, Portions **Rooms:** 147 (147 en suite) ★★★★ **Directions:** Financial Services Centre **Parking:** 40

❁ Crowne Plaza Dublin Airport

American, Asian NEW

Popular hotel restaurant with an international feel

☎ 01 8628888 Northwood Park, Santry Demesne, Santry
e-mail: info@crowneplazadublin.ie.
web: www.cpdublin-airport.com

This bright, contemporary dining room in a modern hotel enjoys a quiet setting overlooking 70 acres of wooded demesne. Touzai means 'east meets west' and it's a style that's reflected in both the décor and the menu, which fuses the techniques and flavours of Asia with those of the Pacific Rim. You might expect such temptations as wok-fried beef with lemongrass and ginger (from the Asian Delights section) or lemon sole in crisp couscous and a tomato and fennel broth (from the East and West section).

Chef: Logan Inwin **Owners:** Tifco Ltd **Times:** 12.30-2.30/6-10.30, Closed 25 Dec, Closed L Sat **Prices:** Fixed L €16.50, Fixed D €24.95, Starter €5-€9.50, Main €17.95-€26.50, Dessert €5.95, Coffee €2.95, Min/Water €5, Service optional **Wine:** 30 bottles over €30, 31 bottles under €30, 16 by the glass (€5-€9) **Notes:** Vegetarian available, Dress Restrictions, Smart dress **Seats:** 156 **Smoking:** N/Sm in restaurant, Air con **Children:** Menu, Portions **Rooms:** 204 (204 en suite) ★★★★ **Directions:** Telephone for directions **Parking:** 200

❁ Finnstown Country House

Traditional French

Crowd-pleasing country-house cooking

☎ 01 601 0700 Newcastle Rd
e-mail: manager@finnstown-hotel.ie
web: www.finnstown-hotel.ie

Just a short drive from central Dublin, this magnificent country house nestles in 45 acres of mature grounds and has a loyal local following. The period detail is impeccable throughout - particularly the dining room, which positively glows with Georgian-style opulence. With its foundation in simple, straightforward cooking, the menu adds influences from around the world with good seasonal awareness. Try a starter of grilled Toulouse sausage with red pepper and onion confit, and a main of roast crisp Silverhill duckling with stir-fried vegetables. Booking is essential at this popular, busy restaurant.

Chef: Steve McPhillips **Owners:** Eoin & Nora Hickey **Times:** 12.30-2.30/7.30-9.30, Closed Sun (buffet only 1-5pm) **Prices:** Fixed L €28.95-€29.95, Fixed D fr €42, Starter €5.25-€11.50, Main €17.50-€27.95, Dessert €7.50, Service optional **Notes:** Coffee incl, Fixed L 3 courses, Civ Wed 200 **Seats:** 80, Pr/dining room 30 **Smoking:** N/Sm in restaurant **Children:** Menu, Portions **Rooms:** 53 (53 en suite) ★★★ **Directions:** From M1 take 1st exit onto M50 southbound. 1st exit after Toll Bridge. At rdbt take 3rd left (N4 W). Left at lights. Over next 2 rbts, hotel on right **Parking:** 150

❁❁ The Herbert Park

Modern International

Contemporary cuisine overlooking the park

☎ 01 667 2200 Ballsbridge
e-mail: reservations@herbertparkhotel.ie
web: www.herbertparkhotel.ie

Set in an upmarket area of Dublin, this chic hotel offers leafy views of a delightful park. Enjoy a cocktail in the bar, a light meal in the lounge or lobby, or some accomplished cuisine in the airy Pavilion Restaurant. Local produce forms the base of a contemporary menu, which draws on Asian and South African cooking for inspiration. You might start with beetroot and vodka cured salmon with buckwheat blinis, and then sample mains such as Thai-spiced monkfish with a mussel and lemongrass broth, or lime-crusted lamb with new potato and asparagus salad and port wine jus. Jazz buffet lunch on Sundays.

Chef: Henry Jonkers **Owners:** Herbert Park Hotel Ltd **Times:** 12.30-2.30/5.30-9.30, Closed 25-26 Dec, Closed D Sun-Mon & BHs **Prices:** Food prices not confirmed for 2007. Please telephone for details **Wine:** 20 bottles over €30, 29 bottles under €30 **Notes:** Sun Jazz Buffet L €35 **Seats:** 120 **Smoking:** N/Sm in restaurant, Air con **Children:** Menu, Portions **Rooms:** 153 (153 en suite) ★★★★ **Directions:** 5 mins from city centre. S over canal into Northumberland Rd to Ballsbridge. Turn right cross bridge in Ballsbridge, 1st right down Anglesea Rd **Parking:** 80

❁❁❁❁ Restaurant Patrick Guilbaud

see opposite

❁ Stillorgan Park Hotel

Modern European

Modern hotel with contemporary menus

☎ 01 288 1621 Stillorgan Rd
e-mail: sales@stillorganpark.com
web: www.stillorganpark.com

Attractive décor and striking design are hallmarks of this modern, stylish hotel. So relax in the inviting bar over canapés before taking your table in the upbeat, split-level, contemporary-styled restaurant. The modern, well-balanced menu showcases accomplished culinary skill that features fine saucing and presentation. Expect grilled fillet of brill served with a shrimp and chilli basmati risotto, or perhaps medallions of beef with a pine nut and rosemary mash, red onion jam and port jus, while an apple and cinnamon tart with crème anglaise might head up desserts.

Chef: Enda Dunne **Times:** 12.30-3/5.45-10.15, Closed 25 Dec, Closed L Sat, D Sun **Prices:** Fixed L €18, Fixed D fr €36.50, Starter €6-€8.50, Main €18.50-€25.50, Dessert €6, Coffee €2.50, Min/Water €4, Service included **Wine:** 25% bottles over €30, 75% bottles under €30 **Notes:** Early bird menu, 5.45-7.45pm, €28, Vegetarian available **Seats:** 100, Pr/dining room 60 **Smoking:** N/Sm in restaurant, Air con **Children:** Menu, Portions **Rooms:** 165 (165 en suite) ★★★★ **Directions:** Telephone for directions **Parking:** 300

Restaurant Patrick Guilbaud

DUBLIN MAP 01 D4

Modern French

Ireland's finest restaurant

☎ 01 676 4192 Merrion Hotel, 21 Upper Merrion St 2
e-mail: restaurantpatrickguilbaud@eircom.net
web: www.restaurantpatrickguilbaud.ie

Chef: Guillaume Lebrun
Owners: Patrick Guilbaud
Times: 12.30-2.15/7.30-10.15, Closed 25 Dec, 1st wk Jan, Sun-Mon
Prices: Fixed L €33, Coffee €8, Min/Water €6, Service optional
Wine: 9000 bottles over €30
Notes: Tasting menu 7 courses €180, Vegetarian available, Dress Restrictions, Smart casual
Seats: 80, Pr/dining room 25
Smoking: N/Sm in restaurant, Air con
Children: Portions
Rooms: 143 (143 en suite) ★★★★★
Directions: Opposite Government Buildings
Parking: Parking in Square

This generous-sized, contemporary-styled dining room is light, airy and elegantly furnished, a suitably grand setting for the city's eponymous temple of gastronomy. A high-domed ceiling and glass wall along one side - overlooking an inner-courtyard garden - give a real sense of space and light, while the room is brought to life by an impressive collection of modern Irish art and a profusion of green, leafy fronds. Immaculate napery graces well-spaced tables, while service - from a veritable brigade of waiting staff - is impeccable with a friendly touch. Before descending the steps to the dining room, there's also a small, but equally stylish, bar-lounge for aperitifs. While the restaurant's location in the opulent Georgian splendour of the Merrion Hotel is equally fitting, it does have its own street entrance as well as access through the hotel lobby itself.

Patrick Guilbaud's modern-focused, classic French cuisine more than lives up to the billing, and focuses on the very best seasonal Irish produce to grace his intricate cooking, delivered via an impressive array of menu options that includes a good-value fixed-price lunch, extensive and enticing carte (including a vegetarian option) as well as a tasting offering. Expect plenty of sophisticated flair and innovation, silky technical skills and luxury. Think lobster ravioli, followed by baked zander teamed with braised leeks and potato, black trompettes, bay leaf and juniper-berry nage, and to finish, perhaps an assiette of chocolate (five hot and cold dark chocolate desserts with a bayul sauce). Ancillaries, like canapés, amuse-bouche, breads, pre-desserts and petits fours also impress and add to the high-end experience factor. Reservations are essential though, as it attracts the rich and famous and the highflying business crowd.

DUBLIN *continued* MAP 01 D4

Thorntons Restaurant at The Fitzwilliam Hotel

French V NEW

Smart hotel restaurant with an extensive menu of complex dishes

☎ 01 4787008 128 St Stephen's Green
e-mail: thorntonsrestaurant@eircom.net
web: www.thortonsrestaurant.com

Centrally located on St Stephen's Green, The Fitzwilliam is a contemporary hotel with a first-floor restaurant designed by Sir Terence Conran. The décor is cool with a deep burgundy carpet, cream walls and gold curtains, and the walls are hung with oil paintings alongside food prints by Kevin Thornton. Formal service is provided to well-spaced tables with comfortable seating. Cooking is highly seasonal using the best available local and international produce. French influences are evident in dishes of sautéed foie gras with scallops and cep sauce, braised suckling pig with trotter, Maxim potato, glazed turnip and light poitin sauce, and orange soufflé with mandarin sorbet and raspberry sauce.

Chef: Kevin Thornton **Owners:** Kevin & Muriel Thornton **Times:** 12.30-2.30/7-10.30, Closed Good Fri, 17 Mar, 25 Dec-6 Jan, Sun & Mon, Closed L Tue-Thur **Prices:** Fixed L fr €30, Starter €27-€37, Main €45, Dessert €19, Coffee €7, Min/Water €6, Service optional **Wine:** 247 bottles over €30, 6 bottles under €30, 10 by the glass (€7-€9) **Notes:** 8 course surprise menu €125, Vegetarian menu, Dress Restrictions, Smart casual, no shorts at D **Seats:** 80, Pr/dining room 30 **Smoking:** N/Sm in restaurant, Air con **Children:** Portions **Rooms:** 140 (140 en suite) ★★★★ **Directions:** Overlooking St Stephen's Green **Parking:** 80

Chapter One

☎ 01 873 2266 18/19 Parnell Square
Modern twists to consistently excellent classic French cooking.

l'Ecrivain

☎ 01 661 1919 109a Lower Baggot St
Fine French cuisine and an admirable wine list.

Les Frères Jacques

☎ 01 679 4555 74 Dame St
French classic cooking with an emphasis on seafood.

Jacob's Ladder

☎ 01 670 3865 4 Nassau St
Punchy modern food with an emphasis on healthy eating.

Mermaid Café

☎ 01 670 8236 69-70 Dame St
Californian style with lovely food at this bustling venue.

O'Connell's

☎ 01 647 3304 Bewleys Hotel, Merrion Rd
Carefully sourced contemporary cooking making the most of local produce.

One Pico

☎ 01 676 0300 5-6 Molesworth Place, School House Ln
Sophisticated and ambitious cuisine in stylish surrounds.

Roly's Bistro

☎ 01 668 2611 7 Ballsbridge Ter
Buzzing bistro with robust retro cooking.

PORTMARNOCK MAP 01 D4

Portmarnock Hotel

Modern Mediterranean

Fresh cooking in superb location

☎ 01 8460611 Strand Rd
e-mail: sales@portmarnock.com
web: www.portmarnock.com

This 19th-century former home of the Jameson Whiskey family is now a well-run and smartly presented hotel. Overlooking the sea and the PGA Championship Golf Links, it enjoys a superb location. The Osborne Restaurant makes the most of views of the garden, golf course and mountains beyond. Light, modern European cooking is the highlight here with fine use of prime local ingredients like mountain lamb and fresh fish and seafood from Howth. Typical main courses might be herb-crusted rack of spring lamb or lobster and scallop risotto with lemon confit.

Chef: Mark Doe **Owners:** Natworth Ltd **Times:** 7-10, Closed D Sun, Mon **Prices:** Fixed D €44, Starter €8.50-€17.50, Main €18.50-€29.95, Dessert €8.50-€12.50, Coffee €4.95, Min/Water €5, Service included **Wine:** 67 bottles over €30, 15 bottles under €30, 4 by the glass (€4.95) **Notes:** 7 course tasting menu, Vegetarian available, Dress Restrictions, Smart casual **Seats:** 80, Pr/dining room 24 **Smoking:** N/Sm in restaurant, Air con **Children:** Portions **Rooms:** 98 (98 en suite) ★★★★ **Directions:** Follow N1 towards Drogheda. At junct with R601 turn to Malahide. 2m turn left at T-junct, through Malahide & 2.2m hotel on left. Off M1 take Malahide junct, then onto Portmarnock **Parking:** 200

SKERRIES

Redbank House & Restaurant

Progressive Irish

Reliable cooking in a picturesque fishing village

☎ 01 8491005 8490439 5-7 Church St
e-mail: info@redbank.ie
web: www.redbank.ie

Located in a pretty fishing village 18 miles north of Dublin, this restaurant of long-standing is located in a former bank with the old bank vault now converted into a well-stocked wine cellar. The service here is faultless with a warm welcome guaranteed from friendly, accommodating staff. The food has locally-landed fish and shellfish as its central theme in a range of dishes which take inspiration from French classical, Mediterranean flavours and a dash of Asian culinary style - start with Chinese-style squid with ginger and garlic then try a main of sea trout Annagassan - sea trout fillets with a herby fish mousse, baked in a foil bag with white wine.

Chef: Terry McCoy **Owners:** Terry McCoy **Times:** 12.30-4/6-10, Closed 24-26 Dec, Closed L Mon-Sat, D Sun **Prices:** Food prices not confirmed for 2007. Please telephone for details **Wine:** 50 bottles over €30, 20 bottles under €30, 6 by the glass (€5) **Notes:** Fixed L 4 courses £19.75, Vegetarian available, Dress Restrictions, Smart casual **Seats:** 60, Pr/dining room 10 **Smoking:** N/Sm in restaurant **Rooms:** 12 (12 en suite) **Directions:** From Dublin, M1 N to Lissenhall interchange, take exit to Skerries **Parking:** On street

CO GALWAY

CASHEL MAP 01 A4

Cashel House

Irish, European

Food without fuss and a wealth of seafood in a heavenly location

☎ 095 31001
e-mail: info@cashel-house-hotel.com
web: www.cashel-house-hotel.com

This mid-19th century country-house hotel sits at the head of Cashel Bay, surrounded by 50 acres of beautiful, award-winning gardens and woodland walks. Run by the McEvilly family since 1968, it has a thoroughly established feel with assured and friendly service and an all-pervading sense of comfort. The famous Connemara lamb and an abundance of locally-landed seafood grace this extensive, largely traditional menu with a French bias - Cleggan mussels with tomato and basil, for example, or fish soup with rouille to start, and then sea bass en papillote with lemon and tarragon or simply poached lobster (plucked from their tank). Fantastic breakfasts are also worthy of note.

Chef: Arturo Amit **Owners:** Dermot & Kay McEvilly & Family **Times:** 12.30-2.30/7-8.30, Closed 6 Jan-6 Feb **Prices:** Fixed D €45, Starter €5.95-€12.50, Main €12.95-€25, Dessert fr €5.95, Coffee €3.20, Min/Water €5.95, Service added 12.5% **Wine:** 87 bottles over €30, 27 bottles under €30, 3 by the glass (€5.60) **Notes:** Vegetarian available, Smart casual **Seats:** 70, Pr/dining room 10 **Smoking:** N/Sm in restaurant **Children:** Menu, Portions **Rooms:** 32 (32 en suite) ★★★ **Directions:** S of N59. 1m W of Recess **Parking:** 30

Zetland Country House

French, European

Sea views and modern European food in refined setting

☎ 095 31111 Cashel Bay
e-mail: zetland@iol.ie
web: www.zetland.com

Built as a sporting lodge in the early 19th century, this peaceful country-house hotel is a cultivated haven on the rugged shores of Cashel Bay. Turf fires smoulder in the cosy lounges, while comfortable bedrooms have wonderful sea views. The elegant dining room retains a refined air and is the setting for sampling some excellent local produce, including herbs and vegetables from the hotel garden. The kitchen delivers modern, yet simple and earthy cooking, resulting in full-flavoured dishes. The monthly-changing fixed-price menu reflects the seasons and may offer a risotto of smoked chicken, steamed fillet of cod with saffron and mussel cream, and warm chocolate fondant with vanilla bean ice cream. Service is relaxed and personal.

continued

Chef: Samuel Lecam **Owners:** Ruaidhri Prendergast **Times:** 12-2.30/7-8.30, Closed D Sun (winter) **Prices:** Fixed L €30-€60, Service included **Wine:** 30 bottles over €30, 6 bottles under €30, 4 by the glass (€5) **Notes:** 5 course D €56 **Seats:** 75, Pr/dining room 20 **Smoking:** N/Sm in restaurant **Children:** Portions **Rooms:** 19 (19 en suite) ★★★ **Directions:** N59 from Galway towards Clifden, turn right after Recess onto R340, after approx 4m turn left onto R341, hotel 1m on right **Parking:** 40

CLIFDEN MAP 01 A4

Abbeyglen Castle Hotel

French, International

Elegant restaurant in a fine country-house hotel

☎ 095 21201 Sky Rd
e-mail: info@abbeyglen.ie
web: www.abbeyglen.ie

Hospitality is a key strength of this 19th-century country-house hotel, with all staff creating a warm presence. In this welcoming, relaxed atmosphere, the elegant first-floor restaurant has a clubby feel with background piano music playing each evening. Seafood is emphasised on the daily-changing French and international menu, including lobster and crab from a seawater tank. Connemara meat and game are there too, perhaps in the form of fillet of beef Wellington or pan-fried breast of guinea fowl with port and raisin sauce. Canapés, sorbets, home-made breads and petits fours all make a positive contribution to a meal.

Chef: Kevin Conroy **Owners:** Mr P Hughes **Times:** 7.15-9, Closed 6 Jan-1 Feb, Closed L Mon-Sun **Prices:** Fixed D €41, Starter €6.50-€10.50, Main €19-€35, Dessert €6.50, Coffee €2.20, Min/Water €5.50, Service added 12.5% **Wine:** 40 bottles over €30, 4 bottles under €30, 4 by the glass (€5-€5.50) **Notes:** Vegetarian available **Seats:** 75 **Smoking:** N/Sm in restaurant **Children:** Min 12 yrs **Rooms:** 45 (45 en suite) ★★★★ **Directions:** From Galway take N59 to Clifden. Hotel 1km on the Sky Road **Parking:** 40

Ardagh Hotel

Traditional Mediterranean

Modern cooking of local produce in a stunning setting

☎ 095 21384 Ballyconneely Rd
e-mail: ardaghhotel@eircom.net
web: www.ardaghhotel.com

Quiet family-run hotel on the shores of Ardbear Bay in scenic Connemara. While modern in appearance from the road, the interior is full of traditional charm with turf fires and comfy couches. The first-floor restaurant makes the most of the stunning views and has a bright Mediterranean feel. There is a strong emphasis on carefully cooked seafood and other excellent local produce, with lobsters, oysters and mussels from a sea tank in the foyer. Some combinations have more than a hint of Oriental influence - Ardbear mussels with lemon grass and coconut milk - while melt-in-the-mouth rack of new season lamb on roast celeriac mash is cooked a perfect pink.

Chef: C Curran, M Bauvet **Owners:** S & M Bauvet **Times:** 7.15-9.30, Closed end Nov-end Mar, Closed L all week **Prices:** Fixed D €52, Starter €12.50-€15.50, Main €26.50-€36.50, Dessert €7.50, Coffee €2.50, Min/Water €4.95, Service optional, Group min 6 service 12.5% **Wine:** 40 bottles over €30, 30 bottles under €30, 2 by the glass (€5.50) **Notes:** Fixed D 4 courses, Vegetarian available, Dress Restrictions, Smart casual, no shorts or trainers **Seats:** 50 **Smoking:** N/Sm in restaurant **Children:** Menu, Portions **Rooms:** 19 (19 en suite) ★★★ **Directions:** Galway to Clifden on N59. Signed in Clifden, 2m on Ballyconneely road **Parking:** 40

CLIFDEN MAP 01 A4

Brown's

Modern European, Irish

Welcoming hotel with a fine reputation for seafood

☎ 095 21206 & 21086 Alcock & Brown Hotel
e-mail: alcockandbrown@eircom.net
web: www.alcockandbrown-hotel.com

Brown's restaurant is a part of the very friendly, renovated hotel at the top of the town, known as the Alcock & Brown. The restaurant has fresh modern décor, transformed at night by dimmed lights and candles. There's a wide-ranging carte plus daily specials offering fairly straightforward cooking of prime ingredients, starring locally landed seafood (pan-fried scallops served with garlic butter and bacon) and excellent Connemara lamb. All desserts are made in-house and are based on traditional recipes, including a generous portion of rhubarb crumble - pure comfort food.

Chef: Paddy Conroy, Eddie Devane **Owners:** Deirdre Keogh **Times:** 12.30-2/6-9.30, Closed 22-26 Dec **Prices:** Fixed D €25, Starter €4.60-€9.95, Main €14.95-€25.50, Dessert €4.95-€6.50, Coffee €1.70, Service optional **Wine:** 4 bottles over €30, 2 bottles under €30, 5 by the glass (€5) **Notes:** Fixed D 4 courses **Seats:** 100 **Smoking:** N/Sm in restaurant, Air con **Children:** Menu, Portions **Rooms:** 19 (19 en suite) ★★★ **Directions:** From Galway city take N59 to Clifden. Follow one-way system to centre. Hotel in town square **Parking:** Street Parking

---

GALWAY MAP 01 B3/4

Ardilaun House Hotel & Leisure Club

Traditional, French

Popular hotel with a wide-ranging menu

☎ 091 521433 Taylor's Hill
e-mail: info@ardilaunhousehotel.ie
web: www.ardilaunhousehotel.ie

Newly renovated, this 19th-century townhouse is set in landscaped grounds on the edge of Galway city and boasts a number of lounges and extensive leisure facilities. Its elegant Camilaun Restaurant overlooks the garden and is a consistent performer, creating French-influenced cuisine from high-quality local ingredients. The lengthy selection of mains is designed to suit most tastes and stretches from simple dishes - pan-fried sea bass fillet with a chive butter sauce - to heavier fare such as rack of lamb with a rosemary and shallot jus. Carvery on Sundays.

Chef: Nigel Murray **Owners:** John Ryan **Times:** 1-2.15/7-9.15, Closed 23-27 Dec, Closed L Sat **Prices:** Fixed L €16.25, Fixed D €34, Starter €3.90-€8.50, Main €16.50-€26, Dessert €6.50, Coffee €2, Min/Water €2.50, Service added 10% **Wine:** 21 bottles over €30, 29 bottles under €30, 2 by the glass (€3.80) **Notes:** Vegetarian available **Seats:** 180, Pr/dining room 380 **Smoking:** N/Sm in restaurant, Air con **Children:** Menu, Portions **Rooms:** 89 (89 en suite) ★★★★ **Directions:** 1m from Galway city centre, towards Salthill on the west side of the city, near Galway Bay **Parking:** 250

Galway Bay Hotel

Modern European

Light airy restaurant with sea views and inviting cuisine

☎ 091 520520 The Promenade, Salthill
e-mail: info@galwaybayhotel.net
web: www.galwaybayhotel.net

The Lobster Pot restaurant enjoys magnificent triple-aspect views of Galway Bay. The cuisine style is modern Irish with European influences with a strong emphasis on fresh Irish produce in creating the menus. There is particular focus on fresh fish and seafood, including lobster from a tank. The carte is divided into starters, soups like Galway Bay seafood chowder, meat dishes such as garlic and pepper-crusted rack of lamb on thyme-infused gnocchi, fish dishes and desserts or a cheese board. There is a wide selection with something for everyone, from vegetarians to fish fans.

Chef: Robert Bell **Owners:** John O'Sullivan **Times:** 12.30-2.30/6.30-9.15, Closed 25 Dec (residents only) **Prices:** Fixed L €19-€28, Fixed D €36-€40, Starter €6.50-€9.50, Main €16.50-€37, Dessert €6.50-€7.50, Coffee €2.50, Min/Water €5, Service included **Wine:** 20 bottles over €30, 26 bottles under €30, 10 by the glass (€4.60-€5.75) **Notes:** Fixed D 5 courses, Vegetarian available **Seats:** 220, Pr/dining room **Smoking:** N/Sm in restaurant **Children:** Menu, Portions **Rooms:** 153 (153 en suite) ★★★★ **Directions:** 2m from Galway city centre **Parking:** 350

Glenlo Abbey Hotel

Modern Irish, International NEW

Modern cuisine in an 18th-century country residence

☎ 091 526666 Bushypark
e-mail: info@glenloabbey.ie
web: www.glenlo.com

This cut-stone abbey was built in 1740 - though today it sits in a 138-acre lakeside golf estate - and has been lovingly restored to its original glory, featuring sculptured cornices and fine antique furniture. The River Room Restaurant is an oval affair on two levels, with high ceilings, well-spaced tables and professional but relaxed service. The modern Irish cuisine displays flair and imagination, with the skilful cooking based on quality local produce, particularly seafood. Maybe pan-fried turbot, herbed mash and tarragon lobster cream would fit the bill.

Chef: Richard Hart **Owners:** Bourke Family **Times:** 12.45-3/7-9.30, Closed 24-27 Dec **Prices:** Fixed L €15-€35, Fixed D €25-€46, Starter €8.95-€18, Main €18.50-€39.50, Dessert €6.95-€9.95, Coffee €2.75, Min/Water €5 **Wine:** 50 bottles over €30, 12 bottles under €30, 3 by the glass (€6-€10) **Notes:** Vegetarian available, Dress Restrictions, Smart casual **Seats:** 70, Pr/dining room 30 **Smoking:** N/Sm in restaurant, Air con **Children:** Portions **Rooms:** 46 (46 en suite) ★★★★ **Directions:** Approx 2.5m from centre of Galway on main Clifden road **Parking:** 150

Park House Hotel & Park Room Restaurant

Traditional, International

International menu in bustling city-centre hotel

☎ 091 564924 Forster St, Eyre Square
e-mail: parkhousehotel@eircom.net
web: www.parkhousehotel.ie

A popular city-centre hotel built around a three-storey former grain store with its impressive, 19th-century stone façade. Paintings of old

continued

Galway line the walls of the celebrated Park Restaurant, which bustles with locals at lunchtime and becomes more intimate in the evening with soft lighting and elegant, linen-clothed tables. Eclectic menus trawl the globe for inspiration, offering a wide choice of soundly cooked dishes that make good use of fresh ingredients, notably local seafood. Typical choices may include rack of Irish lamb with redcurrant jus and monkfish with shrimp and basil sauce.

Chef: Robert O'Keefe, Martin Keane **Owners:** Eamon Doyle, Kitty Carr **Times:** 12-3/6-10, Closed 24-26 Dec **Prices:** Fixed D €42.50-€47.50, Starter €5.60-€11.95, Main €14.95-€29.95, Dessert €6.25, Coffee €2, Min/Water €3.50, Service optional **Wine:** 44 bottles over €30, 49 bottles under €30, 4 by the glass **Notes:** Fixed D 4 courses, ALC L avail, Vegetarian available **Seats:** 145, Pr/dining room 45 **Smoking:** N/Sm in restaurant, Air con **Children:** Menu, Portions **Rooms:** 84 (84 en suite) ★★★★ **Directions:** In city centre, off Eyre Sq **Parking:** 40

Radisson SAS Hotel & Spa Galway

International, European

Waterfront hotel with a menu to suit most tastes

☎ 091 538300 Lough Atalia Rd
e-mail: sales.galway@radissonsas.com
web: www.radissonhotelgalway.com

The décor of this waterside hotel eatery is inspired by the light and colours of nearby Lough Atalia, and teams darkwood with deep blue upholstery and panoramic views. It caters to a well-heeled business market and is often busy, with non-residents advised to book ahead. Modern Irish dishes predominate on the lengthy menu, which makes good use of local seafood and includes a number of healthy eating options. Kick off with Caesar salad or moules marinière, and then dither over the likes of pan-fried fillet of sea bass with saffron mash, or peppered rack of lamb with Puy lentil ragout and balsamic sauce.

Chef: Roy Atindra **Owners:** Marinas Restaurant **Times:** 12.30-3/6-10.30, Closed L Mon-Sat **Prices:** Fixed L €28, Fixed D €32, Starter €6.50-€18.50, Main €19.50-€26.50, Dessert €7-€8, Coffee €3.20, Min/Water €6.80, Service optional **Wine:** 38 bottles over €30, 10 bottles under €30, 11 by the glass (€6.50-€9.50) **Notes:** Fixed D 4 courses, Sun L 4 courses €28, Vegetarian available **Seats:** 220, Pr/dining room 80 **Smoking:** N/Sm in restaurant, Air con **Children:** Menu, Portions **Rooms:** 217 (217 en suite) ★★★★ **Directions:** Telephone for directions **Parking:** 260

RECESS (SRAITH SALACH) MAP 01 A4

Ballynahinch Castle

French, European

Fine dining in elegant country house

☎ 095 31006 31086
e-mail: bhinch@iol.ie
web: www.ballynahinch-castle.com

Standing in 350 acres of woodland and lakes and overlooking a bend in the Ballynahinch river, this crenallated 16th-century mansion enjoys one of the best locations in Connemara. Log fires, stunning views, personal service and an air of casual elegance are just some of the delights of staying at this peaceful castle retreat. Crisp linen, gleaming silver and glassware and relaxing river views are features of the inviting Owenmore restaurant. The fixed-price dinner offers French-Irish cooking based on impeccable local and seasonal produce, including wild salmon from the river and locally-sourced seafood. Expect risotto of Cleggan crab, roast turbot with mustard seed cream, and Amaretto parfait with plum compôte.

Times: 6.30-9, Closed 2 wks Xmas, Feb, Closed L all **Rooms:** 40 (40 en suite) ★★★★ **Directions:** Take N59 from Galway. Turn right after Recess towards Roundstone (R331) for 2m

Lough Inagh Lodge

French, Irish

Irish country dining with lovely mountain views

☎ 095 34706 & 34694 Inagh Valley
e-mail: inagh@iol.ie
web: www.loughinaghlodehotel.ie

Former 19th-century fishing lodge on the shores of Lough Inagh in deepest Connemara surrounded by the most spectacular mountain scenery. An atmosphere of old-world gentility pervades the comfortable lounges and library with their log fires, the cosy oak-panelled bar, and the intimate dining room, which enjoys stunning views. Genuine Irish country-house cooking based around excellent seafood and wild game, draws an appreciative crowd. From the fixed-price dinner menu order local lobster, wild salmon, or gratinated fillet of beef with blue cheese topping and rosemary sauce, then round off with apple sponge pudding.

Times: 7-8.45, Closed mid Dec-mid Mar **Rooms:** 12 (12 en suite) ★★★ **Directions:** From Galway take N344. After 3.5m hotel on right

RENVYLE MAP 01 A4

Renvyle House

Contemporary

Country house dining with a romantic setting and literary connections

☎ 095 43511
e-mail: info@renvyle.com
web: www.renvyle.com

Destroyed and rebuilt over several centuries, this attractive country house is located between the Connemara mountains and the wild Atlantic coast. Yeats honeymooned here and it was once the home of Buck Mulligan from James Joyce's *Ulysses*. Dinner is an atmospheric occasion with turf fires and soft lighting. The menu draws on great local produce and cooking is vibrant, with dishes such as galette of organic Irish goat's cheese with balsamic roast tomatoes and pesto dressing; and pan-roast Renvyle scallops with butternut squash risotto, mango and spring onion salsa.

Times: 7-9, Closed 4 Jan-14 Feb **Rooms:** 68 (68 en suite) ★★★ **Directions:** N59 west of Galway towards Clifden, through Oughterard & Maam Cross. At Recess turn right, Keymore turn left, Letterfrack turn right, hotel 5m

continued

ROUNDSTONE MAP 01 A4

Roundstone House Hotel

Modern Irish NEW

Great sea views and cracking seafood

☎ 095 35864

This delightful, family-run hotel in its terraced-village setting enjoys magnificent sea views to the backdrop of the rugged Connemara Mountains. There are cosy, well-appointed, linen-dressed tables in Vaughan's Restaurant, where service is suitably informal and friendly. The extensive carte comes brimful of quality produce from the abundant local larder, particularly seafood. Expect dishes such as plump mussels steamed in white wine, pan-seared scallops, mushrooms and smoked bacon or rack of Connemara lamb with parsnip and potato mash. Emphasis here is strictly on freshness, simplicity and clarity of flavour, allowing the main ingredients to shine.

Owners: Maureen Vaughan **Times:** 7-9, Closed Nov-Feb **Prices:** Food prices not confirmed for 2007. Please telephone for details **Rooms:** 12 (12 en suite) ★★ **Directions:** Telephone for directions

Ireland

CO KERRY

CAHERDANIEL (CATHAIR D"NALL)
MAP 01 A2

Derrynane Hotel

Irish, European

Enjoyable dining with spectacular Atlantic backdrop

☎ 066 947 5136
e-mail: info@derrynane.com
web: www.derrynane.com

Perched on a spectacular clifftop location on the Ring of Kerry, this friendly family-run hotel offers guests stunning ocean views of Kenmare Bay while eating in the bright, spacious dining room. The small dedicated kitchen team produces modern Irish dishes with European influences, using quality and fresh produce. A bar menu is also available and includes pannini and ciabatta alongside home-made soup, and scones.

Times: 7-9, Closed Oct-mid Apr **Rooms:** 73 (73 en suite) ★★★

Sheen Falls Lodge

KENMARE MAP 01 B2

Traditional European

Romantic waterfall setting for excellent cuisine

☎ 064 41600
e-mail: info@sheenfallslodge.ie
web: www.sheenfallslodge.ie

Once the summer residence of the Marquis of Lansdowne, today this former fishing and hunting lodge on the banks of the Sheen River has been developed into a luxury hotel. Inside it displays great opulence and style, though with a warm, cosseting and unstuffy atmosphere, while the views of the cascading falls from the vast windows of the elegant, fine-dining La Cascade restaurant (well, what else could they have called it) are quite breathtaking and a real drawcard, especially romantic at night when they're floodlit. The décor is modern and understated, the room split-level, with well-spaced tables, top-quality napery and service of the highest standard.

The kitchen draws plaudits, too, the modern approach - underpinned by a classical theme - focuses on fresh, top-quality produce from the abundant Irish larder. Sophisticated and accomplished, the cooking's intelligently not too fussy or over complex, delivering clean, clear-flavoured dishes with balanced combinations and textures. For mains you might try roast breast of duck served with butternut squash, roast chestnuts and a plum sauce, or perhaps pan-fried fillet of turbot teamed with a fricassée of ceps, leaf spinach and a garlic velouté, while an orange- and rosemary-scented millefeuille with sweet balsamic reduction and honey ice cream might catch the eye for dessert.

Chef: Philip Brazil **Owners:** Sheen Falls Estate Ltd **Times:** 7-9.30, Closed mid week before Xmas, 2 Jan-1 Feb, Closed L all week **Prices:** Fixed D €65, Starter €17.50-€22.50, Main €35-€38, Dessert €17-€19.50, Coffee €4, Min/Water €5, Service optional **Wine:** 850 bottles over €30, 25 bottles under €30, 6 by the glass (€8.50) **Notes:** Tasting menu 7 courses €90, Fixed D 4 courses, Vegetarian available, Dress Restrictions, Smart casual **Seats:** 120, Pr/dining room 20 **Smoking:** N/Sm in restaurant **Children:** Menu, Portions **Rooms:** 66 (66 en suite) ★★★★ **Directions:** From Kenmare take N71 to Glengarriff. Take 1st left after suspension bridge. 1m from Kenmare **Parking:** 75

Lime Tree

☎ 064 41225 Sheburne St

Pretty stone building housing a bustling, seasonally-inspired restaurant.

Packie's

☎ 064 41508 Henry St

Good local ingredients treated with care and intelligence.

KILLARNEY MAP 01 B2

Aghadoe Heights Hotel

Modern European

Chic hotel dining with stunning views

☎ 064 31766
e-mail: info@aghadoeheights.com
web: www.aghadoeheights.com

Frederick's restaurant occupies a bright modern space on the third floor of the hotel, with spectacular views of Killarney's lakes, mountains and golf course. You can enjoy a relaxing pre-dinner drink downstairs in the piano bar. The modern European menu features dishes like quail breast and egg pâté with Oxford sauce as a starter. Main courses might include the likes of confit of belly pork and milk-fed veal with a peach sauce, while interesting desserts include fudge and pecan parfait with macerated berries and chocolate truffle.

Chef: Robin Suter, Gavin Gleeson **Owners:** Pat & Marie Chawke **Times:** 12.30-2/6.30-9.30, Closed 25 Dec (residents only), Jan-March, Closed L Mon-Sat **Prices:** Fixed L €20-€35, Fixed D €55-€80, Starter €16-€30, Main €30-€40, Dessert €10-€18, Coffee €5, Min/Water €6.50, Service optional, Group min 10 service 12.5% **Wine:** 140 bottles over €30, 16 by the glass (€8-€25) **Notes:** Champagne Sun L, Vegetarian available, Dress Restrictions, Jacket preferred, no jeans and trainers **Seats:** 150, Pr/dining room 80 **Smoking:** N/Sm in restaurant, Air con **Children:** Menu, Portions **Rooms:** 73 (73 en suite) ★★★★★ **Directions:** 2.5m from Killarney, off N22. 11m from Kerry International Airport **Parking:** 120

Arbutus Hotel

Irish

Traditional Irish hospitality

☎ 064 31037 College St
e-mail: stay@arbutuskillarney.com
web: www.arbutuskillarney.com

Family-run since 1926, the Arbutus is a smart and friendly hotel in the centre of Killarney. Norrie Buckley's restaurant comprises three interconnecting dining rooms and provides locals and residents with traditional Irish cooking from the best Celtic produce available. Fish landed at Dingle and Kerry mountain lamb feature on the menu, the latter as a rack with a wild berry jus. Alternatives include chicken liver pâté with Cumberland sauce, salmon with lemon butter, and Baileys cheesecake with chocolate sauce. A bistro menu is served all day in the bar.

Times: 6.30-9.00, Closed 7 Dec-12 Mar, Sun, Mon **Rooms:** 35 (35 en suite) ★★★ **Directions:** At the rdbt on College St & Lewis Road. Killarney town centre

Cahernane House Hotel

French, International

Lakeside manor house dining

☎ 064 31895 Muckross Rd
e-mail: cahernane@eircom.net
web: www.cahernane.com

Formerly the residence of the Earls of Pembroke, this beautifully situated hotel is set in parkland on the edge of the Killarney National Park, with wonderful views of lakes and mountains. Elegant period furniture blends well with more modern pieces throughout comfortable public rooms to create a relaxed and warm feel. Excellent raw ingredients are used to great effect by a technically proficient and consistent kitchen, resulting in successful combinations and good natural flavours in well cooked and presented dishes. Dishes are simply described on the classic carte, for example seared scallops, smoked haddock and leek purée with onion cream, and chargrilled beef medallions, peppered duck foie gras, potato rösti and natural jus.

Chef: Patrick Kearney **Owners:** Mr & Mrs J Browne **Times:** 12-2.30/7-9.30, Closed Dec-Jan, Closed L all week ex by arrangement **Prices:** Fixed L €25-€35, Fixed D €45, Starter €8-€13, Main €26-€35, Dessert €7-€10, Coffee €2.50, Min/Water €5, Service optional **Wine:** 98 bottles over €30, 22 bottles under €30, 20 by the glass (€6.80-€14) **Notes:** Tasting menu available, Vegetarian available, Dress Restrictions, Smart casual, no shorts **Seats:** 50, Pr/dining room 18 **Smoking:** N/Sm in restaurant **Children:** Menu, Portions **Rooms:** 38 (38 en suite) ★★★★ **Directions:** From Killarney follow signs for Kenmare, then from Muckross Rd over bridge and hotel signed on right. Hotel 1m from town centre **Parking:** 50

Killarney Park

European

Fine cuisine in elegant hotel restaurant

☎ 064 35555 Kenmare Place
e-mail: info@killarneyparkhotel.ie
web: www.killarneyparkhotel.ie

This upmarket modern hotel on the edge of town offers country-house comfort and a warm atmosphere, with its roaring fires, deep sofas and friendly Irish welcome. The elegant, classical Park Restaurant continues the theme, with well-spaced, smartly laid tables and a pianist who plays each evening. The kitchen rises to the occasion, making fine use of local seasonal produce from land and sea, its modern dishes - underpinned by classical roots - displaying skill and interesting combinations. Take pan-fried fillet of home-smoked Kerry beef served with sweet potato fondant, seared foie gras and sauce béarnaise, or a blackberry and white chocolate mousse with a quenelle of berry compôte and white chocolate biscotti.

Chef: Odran Lucey **Owners:** Padraig & Janet Treacy **Times:** 7-9.30, Closed 24-26 Dec, Closed L all week **Prices:** Fixed D €60-€62, Starter €11.50-€15.95, Main €28-€32, Dessert €8.95-€9.50, Coffee €3, Min/Water €6.65, Service included **Wine:** 95 bottles over €30, 6 bottles under €30, 14 by the glass (€6.75-€10) **Notes:** Vegetarian available, Dress Restrictions, Neat clothing required **Seats:** 90, Pr/dining room 40 **Smoking:** N/Sm in restaurant, Air con **Children:** Menu, Portions **Rooms:** 72 (72 en suite) ★★★★ **Directions:** From Cork take R22 to Killarney. Take 1st exit for town centre, then at 2nd rdbt take 2nd exit. At 3rd rdbt, take 1st exit. Hotel 2nd entrance on left **Parking:** 75

PARKNASILLA MAP 01 A2

Great Southern

Traditional

Formal dining in a dramatic location

☎ 064 45122
e-mail: res@parknasilla.gsh.ie
web: www.gshotels.com

A Victorian property in an extraordinary location, with stunning Atlantic, woodland and mountain views. A sweeping staircase, stained glass windows and log fires are among the period features, and the Pygmalion Restaurant is suitably grand and elegant. The set-price dinner menu might offer salad of brill scaloppini, and spiced chicken breast with vegetable couscous. Alternatively there's a short carte of classic dishes: foie gras on toasted brioche, and fillet steak of Irish Angus beef. Cocktails are served in the clubby Doolittle Bar. (George Bernard Shaw was a frequent visitor.)

Times: 7-9, Closed Jan-11 Feb, Closed L all week **Rooms:** 83 (83 en suite) ★★★★ **Directions:** From Killarney take N71 to Kenmare. On entering town pass golf club. Hotel entrance on left at top of town

CO KILDARE

LEIXLIP MAP 01 D4

Leixlip House

Modern Irish

Fine dining in charming hotel

☎ 01 6242268 Captains Hill
e-mail: info@leixliphouse.com
web: www.leixliphouse.com

Dating from 1772, this charming hotel retains its period style with Georgian furnishings and décor. The Bradaun Restaurant is a bright airy room where diners are served by friendly, professional staff. The menu makes excellent use of the finest ingredients and harmonious combinations of flavours. Some dishes have a slightly oriental twist with the likes of Thai glass noodle and prawn salad tossed with sweet chilli sauce, other classic dishes include fillet of cod with baby fennel and beetroot dressing. Booking is essential, especially at weekends.

Times: 12.30-4/6.30-9.45, Closed 25-26 Dec, Mon, Closed L Tue-Sat **Rooms:** 19 (19 en suite) ★★★

NAAS MAP 01 D4

Killashee House Hotel & Villa Spa

Modern French, European

Elegant dining in magnificent surroundings

☎ 045 879277
e-mail: sales@killasheehouse.com
web: www.killasheehouse.com

Luxuriously appointed Victorian manor house, once a convent and also preparatory school for boys, set amid 80 acres of beautifully kept grounds. Turners Restaurant is a magnificent room on a grand scale with pillars, chandeliers, intricate plasterwork and gold and scarlet soft

continued

furnishings. A harpist plays on Friday and Saturday nights, adding to the sense of occasion. Excellent raw ingredients are used in the preparation of dishes such as seared herb-crusted tuna with white bean cassoulet and tarragon cream, and prime Irish fillet of beef with chorizo mash, slow-roasted tomato and rosemary sauce.

Chef: David Cuddihy **Owners:** Mr & Mrs Tierney **Times:** 1-2.45/7-9.45, Closed 24-25 Dec, Closed L Sat **Prices:** Fixed L €34.50-€40, Fixed D €50-€55, Coffee €2.50, Min/Water €4.25, Service optional **Wine:** 40 bottles over €30, 12 bottles under €30, 10 by the glass (€6.50-€10) **Notes:** Fixed L 3 courses, Fixed D 4 courses, Vegetarian available, Dress Restrictions, Smart casual, no jeans **Seats:** 120, Pr/dining room 650 **Smoking:** N/Sm in restaurant, Air con **Children:** Menu, Portions **Rooms:** 142 (146 en suite) ★★★★ **Directions:** 1m from Naas on old Kilcullen road. On left past Garda (police station) **Parking:** 600

NEWBRIDGE MAP 01 C3

Keadeen Hotel

International

Stylish dining in family-run hotel

☎ 045 431666
e-mail: info@keadeenhotel.ie
web: www.keadeenhotel.ie

Kildare's longest established family-owned and run four-star hotel has been welcoming guests for over 35 years. First opened in 1970, it's grown to meet the ever-changing needs and expectations of guests, whilst maintaining its tradition of superior quality and service. The Derby restaurant is a stylish venue for sophisticated country-house style dining. Service is formal but unobtrusive, befitting the elegant décor and fine table settings. The menu makes use of the very best of local produce. Expect the likes of wild mushroom risotto with grilled brie wrapped in Parma ham, followed by pan-seared John Dory on seafood colcannon with a Noilly Prat and chive sauce. The Club Bar is an alternative eating option, and offers a relaxing place to enjoy a drink or meal.

Chef: Michael Casey **Owners:** Rose O'Loughlin **Times:** 12.30-2.30/6-9.30 **Prices:** Food prices not confirmed for 2007 **Notes:** Dress Restrictions, Smart casual **Smoking:** N/Sm in restaurant, Air con **Children:** Menu, Portions **Rooms:** 75 (75 en suite) ★★★★ **Directions:** N7 from Dublin to Newbridge. Hotel 1m from Curragh racecourse & 0.5m from Newbridge town centre **Parking:** 100

STRAFFAN MAP 01 C/D4

Barberstown Castle

Irish, French

Fine dining in 13th-century castle in attractive grounds

☎ 01 628 8157
e-mail: barberstowncastle@ireland.com
web: www.barberstowncastle.ie

This one-time castle now country-house hotel features Victorian and Elizabethan dining rooms replete with period furniture overlooking the gardens. Dinner is an atmospheric, candlelit affair, while aperitifs can be taken in the elegant drawing room and informal lunch in the airy conservatory Tea Room. Service is appropriately professional, while the kitchen's modern approach is underpinned by a classical French theme, the accomplished cooking making the best of quality produce Take Irish beef fillet with a creamy potato purée, ceps and red wine sauce, or perhaps truffled pig's trotters with braised ham hock,

continued on page 67

The K Club

STRAFFAN MAP 01 C/D4

Modern Irish

Luxurious golfing hotel with impressive restaurant

☎ 01 601 7200
e-mail: hotel@kclub.ie
web: www.kclub.ie

Set in 550 acres of manicured grounds and parkland by the River Liffey, this luxurious hotel sits at the heart of a resort that includes two championship golf courses and a spa, and played host to the 2006 Ryder Cup. The golf pavilion houses two informal eateries - Legends and Monza - but it's the fine-dining option, the gracious Byerley Turk restaurant that's the real drawcard. Dominated by a painting of the thoroughbred racehorse after which it's named, Byerley Turk boasts high ceilings, ornate chandeliers, lofty windows with lavish drapes, rich brocade wall coverings, marble columns, elegantly dressed tables and views over the gardens. Dress code is formal (strictly jacket and tie), while the silver-and-cloche service is a polished affair, yet friendly to match the tone.
The contemporary Irish cuisine - underpinned by a classical French theme - is delivered via an appealing dinner carte and tasting option, built around tip-top, fresh seasonal produce from the abundant Irish larder. Clear flavours, technical proficiency and luxury abound in highly accomplished dishes like fillet of Irish beef served with seared foie gras and a Périgueux sauce. Desserts might be headed-up by a warm tarte Tatin of fig with five spices, while there's a separate soufflé menu to seduce, too.

Chef: Finbarr Higgins
Owners: Michael Smurfit
Times: 7-9.45
Prices: Starter €22.50-€29, Main €40-€48, Dessert €16.50, Coffee €6.50, Min/Water €6.75, Service included
Wine: 600 bottles over €30, 2 bottles under €30, 8 by the glass (€6-€18)
Notes: Vegetarian available, Dress Restrictions, Jacket & tie
Seats: 100, Pr/dining room 16
Smoking: N/Sm in restaurant, Air con
Children: Min 3 yrs, Portions
Rooms: 79 (79 en suite) ★★★★★
Directions: 30 minutes from Dublin. From Dublin Airport follow M4 to Maynooth, turn for Straffan, just after village on right
Parking: 100

STRAFFAN *continued* MAP 01 C/D4

buttered curly kale and Madeira sauce. Think pineapple tarte Tatin with coconut sorbet and passionfruit salsa to finish.

Chef: Bertrand Malabat **Owners:** Kenneth Healy **Times:** 12.30-2.30/7-9.30, Closed 24-28 Dec, Jan, Mon-Tue, Closed L Wed-Sat **Prices:** Starter €10.50-€14.50, Main €26-€32, Dessert €8.50, Service optional **Wine:** 105 bottles over €30, 15 bottles under €30, 2 by the glass **Notes:** Tasting menu 6 courses €65, Sun L 4 courses €35, Dress Restrictions, Smart dress **Seats:** 100, Pr/dining room 32 **Smoking:** N/Sm in restaurant **Rooms:** 59 (59 en suite) **Directions:** From Dublin take M50, exit for M4 at rdbt and follow signs for castle **Parking:** 100

The K Club

see page 671

Ireland

CO KILKENNY

KILKENNY MAP 01 C3

Kilkenny River Court

Modern Irish, European

Dining on a grand scale

☎ 056 7723388 The Bridge, John St
e-mail: reservations@kilrivercourt.com
web: www.kilrivercourt.com

This comfortable riverside hotel boasts an impressive restaurant, designed to reflect the classical beauty of Kilkenny Castle and the surrounding area. Wonderful views of the river are framed in large picture windows and no expense has been spared with the décor, using marble flooring and crystal chandeliers. An extensive menu features local produce like hand-made farmhouse cheese. Typical main courses feature charred sirloin of veal with wilted spinach leaves, buffalo mozzarella and lemon oil.

Times: 12.30-2.30/6-9.30, Closed 25-26 Jan, Closed L Mon-Sat **Rooms:** 90 (90 en suite) ★★★★ **Directions:** Telephone for directions

Lacken House & Restaurant

Modern Irish, European V NEW

Seasonal and local produce cooked with flair

☎ 056 7761085 Dublin Rd
e-mail: info@lackenhouse.ie
web: www.lackenhouse.ie

This fine Victorian house, now refurbished, is just a ten-minute walk from the centre of the city. Friendly service and high standards are evident in the dedicated team lead by the proprietors. Dinner in the intimate restaurant is available Tuesday to Saturday from the carte or fixed price menus, or a separate vegetarian menu. Particularly good presentation on slate, glass and trenchers, and good combinations using excellent seasonal and local ingredients are evident in dishes like grilled hake on red pepper escabèche or Kilkenny lamb on fondant potatoes. The restaurant is popular so booking is essential.

Times: 12-2.30/6-9.30, Closed Mon, Closed L Tue-Sat, D Sun
Notes: Vegetarian menu **Rooms:** 10 (10 en suite)

THOMASTOWN MAP 01 C3

The Lady Helen Restaurant

Modern French

Impressive country mansion offering superb fine dining

☎ 056 777 3000 Mount Juliet Conrad Hotel
e-mail: info@mountjuliet.ie
web: www.mountjuliet.com

Set in 1,500 acres of parkland, this elegant 18th-century Georgian mansion has its own golf course. The formal dining restaurant is decorated in grand country-house style. Likewise, the cooking is classical with European influences and modern interpretations, for example foie gras au torchon comes with black grape and truffle tarte Tatin and white grape and vanilla chutney. Main courses focus on game and seafood with wild boar and venison on offer alongside roasted sole or monkfish. Vegetarians are in for a treat with the crottin tortellini accompanied by celeriac dauphinoise demonstrating some serious culinary techniques. There is good use of local ingredients and fresh vegetables and herbs come from the kitchen gardens.

Chef: Paul Quinn **Owners:** Conrad Hotels **Times:** 7-9.45, Closed L all week **Prices:** Fixed D €53-€72, Starter €8-€20, Main €28-€38, Dessert €8-€12, Coffee €2.50, Min/Water €5, Service optional **Wine:** 125 bottles over €30, 18 bottles under €30, 8 by the glass (€6.50-€12) **Notes:** Fixed D 4 courses, Vegetarian available, Dress Restrictions, No Jeans or T-shirts **Seats:** 60, Pr/dining room 70 **Smoking:** N/Sm in restaurant **Children:** Min 16 yrs, Menu, Portions **Rooms:** 59 (59 en suite) ★★★★ **Directions:** Just outside Thomastown heading S on N9 **Parking:** 200

CO LIMERICK

ADARE MAP 01 B3

Dunraven Arms

Irish, Mediterranean

Fine local produce in an elegant setting

☎ 061 396633
e-mail: reservations@dunravenhotel.com
web: www.dunravenhotel.com

Behind the rustic façade of this hotel you will find the kind of sophisticated comfort that has entertained royalty. The interior is smartly decorated and warmed by lovely open fires. Large windows look out on the thatched cottages of one of Ireland's prettiest villages. The modern Irish cooking here has some Mediterranean influences. Extensive use is made of local fresh produce with good combinations of flavours and textures in dishes like pan-fried fillet of Victoria perch with plum tomato risotto and basil oil. Prime Irish roast rib beef is carved from the trolley in traditional style. A bar food menu is also available throughout the day and an informal restaurant option, 'The Inn Between' is located across the street.

Times: 12.30-2.30/7-9.30, Closed L Mon-Sat **Rooms:** 75 (75 en suite) ★★★★ **Directions:** Telephone for directions

LIMERICK MAP 01 B3

McLaughlin's

Modern International

International dining in pretty Limerick

☎ 061 335566 Castletroy Park Hotel, Dublin Rd
e-mail: sales@castletroy-park.ie
web: www.castletroy-park.ie

This modern hotel on the outskirts of Limerick boasts a range of different eating options, including a conservatory for snacks and afternoon tea, and a bar for bistro fare. The formal restaurant does a brisk trade with locals and residents alike, conjuring a comprehensive modern menu from quality local ingredients. Dishes are flavourful creations that draw inspiration from around the world: rack of lamb with a timbale of sweet potato and ratatouille perhaps, or pork in Parma ham, with gnocchi, wild mushroom and asparagus. Lunch is by appointment only.

Chef: Tom Flavin **Owners:** Fordmount Developments **Times:** 12.30-2.30/5.30-10, Closed 25-26 Dec, Closed L Mon-Sat **Prices:** Fixed L fr €24, Fixed D fr €35, Starter €6-€12, Main €18-€28, Dessert €7-€8, Coffee €2.90, Service optional **Wine:** 25 bottles over €30, 16 bottles under €30, 8 by the glass (€6-€7.50) **Notes:** Earlybird menu 5.30-7pm, Vegetarian available, Dress Restrictions, Smart dress **Seats:** 78, Pr/dining room 14 **Smoking:** N/Sm in restaurant, Air con **Children:** Menu, Portions **Rooms:** 107 (107 en suite) ★★★★ **Directions:** 5 mins from Limerick on Dublin road, follow signs for University of Limerick, hotel opposite **Parking:** 150

CO MAYO

BALLINA MAP 01 B4

Teach Iorrais Hotel

Modern European

Great dining in this wild corner of County Mayo

☎ 097 86888 Geesala
e-mail: teachlor@iol.ie
web: www.teachiorrais.com

A formal, yet country-style restaurant with a mix of warm colours, decorative lighting, an open fire and views of the mountains. Modern European dishes are cooked in classical French style, using fresh produce. The service is relaxed, friendly and professional, making diners feel at ease with the menu and wine list. Typical dishes might include a starter of black and white pudding terrine with bacon and orange salad, followed by fillet of beef with black pudding mash and smoked bacon jus. Classic desserts include the likes of sticky toffee pudding with caramel sauce and vanilla ice cream.

continued

Chef: Daniel Willimont **Owners:** Tom Gaughan **Times:** 12-3/6-10 **Prices:** Fixed D €25, Starter €4.50-€8.90, Main €17.90-€24.90, Service included **Wine:** 8 bottles over €30, 4 by the glass **Seats:** 70, Pr/dining room 60 **Smoking:** N/Sm in restaurant, Air con **Children:** Menu, Portions **Rooms:** 31 (31 en suite) ★★★ **Directions:** Please telephone for directions **Parking:** 300

FOXFORD MAP 01 B4

Healys Restaurant & Country House Hotel

Traditional British

Comfort cooking in a waterside setting

☎ 094 925 6443 Pontoon
e-mail: info@healyspontoon.com
web: www.healyspontoon.com

Perched on the edge of Lough Cullen, this 19th-century shooting lodge offers pretty views from its restaurant, a friendly venue with well-spaced tables and a simple blue and white décor. Old favourites make up the bulk of the menu: starters include prawn cocktail, Caesar salad, and deep-fried brie, while mains range from steaks and lobster to classier fare such as wild Dromoland pheasant with game chips and port wine sauce. The nostalgia trip continues into the final course with the arrival of comfort puds including trifle and crème brûlée. Bar meals also available.

Chef: Ray Barrett **Owners:** John Dever **Times:** 12.30-6.30/6-10, Closed 25 Dec **Prices:** Fixed D €39, Starter €3-€11, Main €12-€32, Dessert €4.95, Coffee €2, Min/Water €2, Service optional **Wine:** 27 bottles over €30, 70 bottles under €30, 16 by the glass (€4.45-€9.45) **Notes:** Vegetarian available **Seats:** 70 **Smoking:** N/Sm in restaurant, Air con **Children:** Portions **Rooms:** 14 (14 en suite) ★★ **Directions:** N26 to Castlebar turn onto R310 signed Pontoon, follow road for 5.6m **Parking:** 150

Ireland

Ireland

WESTPORT MAP 01 B4

Carlton Atlantic Coast Hotel

International

West Coast dining with impressive views

☎ 098 29000 The Quay
e-mail: info@atlanticcoasthotel.com
web: www.atlanticcoasthotel.com

This harbourside hotel's aptly named Blue Wave rooftop restaurant (fourth-floor) is bright and modern with wonderful views over Clew Bay. Friendly and attentive service is the style, while relaxing ground-floor lounge areas and a lively bar complete the package at this distinctive property converted from a former wool mill. The international cooking is as modern as the setting, with interesting combinations but no undue complication. There's good use of local ingredients, especially seafood. Menu samples include baked darne of salmon with wilted spinach and cucumber sambal or pan-roasted five spice duck with noodles.

Chef: Frank Walsh **Owners:** Carlton Hotel Group **Times:** 6.30-9.15, Closed 20-27 Dec, Closed L all week **Prices:** Fixed D fr €36, Min/Water €3, Service added but optional 12.5% **Wine:** 12 bottles over €30, 14 bottles under €30, 1 by the glass (€4.70) **Notes:** Coffee incl, Fixed D 4 courses €36, Vegetarian available **Seats:** 85, Pr/dining room 140 **Smoking:** N/Sm in restaurant, Air con **Children:** Menu, Portions **Rooms:** 85 (88 en suite) ★★★ **Directions:** From Westport take coast road towards Louisburgh for 1m. Hotel on harbour on left **Parking:** 80

Knockranny House Hotel

Modern International NEW

Stunning views from an elegant restaurant

☎ 098 28600
e-mail: info@khh.ie
web: www.khh.ie

This smart modern hotel on the outskirts of Westport enjoys wonderful views over the town, Clew Bay and Croach Patrick. La Fougere, the hotel's fine dining restaurant, serves up modern Irish cuisine showcasing fresh local produce (including ingredients from their own smokery) in an array of internationally inspired dishes - though as the restaurant name might suggest, the food is never too far away from French classical roots. Starters might include a delightfully fresh tian of crabmeat on a bed of cucumber jelly with horseradish cream, while a typical main would be roast loin of monkfish with a fricassée of cabbage and ceps.

Chef: John Shanagher **Owners:** Adrian & Geraldine Noonan **Times:** 1-2.30/6.30-9.30, Closed Xmas **Prices:** Fixed L €24.95, Fixed D €45, Min/Water €5, Service optional **Wine:** 20 bottles under €30, 8 by the glass (€4.50-€8) **Notes:** Fixed L 3 courses, Fixed D 4 courses, Dress Restrictions, Smart casual **Seats:** 85, Pr/dining room **Smoking:** N/Sm in restaurant **Children:** Menu, Portions **Rooms:** 54 (54 en suite) ★★★★ **Directions:** On N5 (Dublin to Castlebar road), on the left before entering Westport **Parking:** 100

CO MEATH

KILMESSAN MAP 01 D5

The Station House Hotel

French, Mediterranean NEW

Cosy, popular restaurant in converted railway station

☎ 046 9025239
e-mail: info@thestationhousehotel.com
web: www.thestationhousehotel.com

The pretty conversion of this former railway station - which saw its last train in 1967 - into a friendly, family-run hotel with a lovely homely feel, draws a loyal local following, and has a great reputation for family celebrations. The cosy restaurant delivers straightforward, uncomplicated, country-house cooking with a touch of French flair. Top-notch ingredients - think braised veal chop on a bed of spinach, or sea bass served with asparagus sauce - are skilfully treated with respect. And a popular jazz lunch is served in the banqueting suite on Sundays.

Times: 12.30-3/4.30-10.30 **Rooms:** 20 (20 en suite) ★★★

CO MONAGHAN

CARRICKMACROSS MAP 01 C4

Nuremore Hotel

see opposite

CO TIPPERARY

CASHEL MAP 01 C3

Cashel Palace Hotel

Traditional European

Country-house cuisine set in former papal kitchens

☎ 062 62707
e-mail: reception@cashel-palace.ie
web: www.cashel-palace.ie

continued

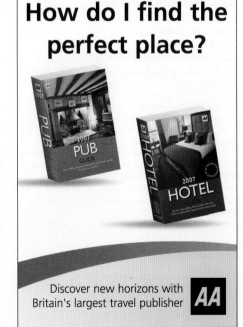

Nuremore Hotel

CARRICKMACROSS MAP 01 C4

Modern European V

Innovative cuisine with bold combinations at country-house hotel

☎ 042 966 1438
e-mail: info@nuremore.com
web: www.nuremore.com

An oasis of calm and tranquillity is a phrase that sums up the restaurant at this stylish Victorian country-house hotel overlooking parkland and a championship golf course. The elegant, split-level dining room is set with comfortable, well-spaced tables and enjoys views over gardens and lake. The recent addition of a glass-walled wine cave makes a wonderful talking point. The imaginative menu more than befits the setting, aptly demonstrating the flair and accomplished technical skill of chef Raymond McArdle's well-motivated brigade and pleasant, attentive front-of-house staff. His modern approach, underpinned by a classical French theme, utilises tip-top local produce, enhanced by contemporary styling of presentation and ingredient combination. Menu descriptions don't really do justice to the intricate work that graces dishes. Nonetheless, to show the style take an accomplished menu of millefeuille of duck foie gras with grilled pain d'épice and apricot purée, followed by sauté cannon of local black pig with crispy belly, braised ham hock and parsley, apple chutney, choucroute and a Calvados sauce, with pineapple ravioli of Asian fruits and hibiscus sorbet to finish. Peripherals like bread, amuse-bouche, pre-dessert and petits fours also hold top form through to the end.

Chef: Raymond McArdle **Owners:** Gilhooly family **Times:** 12.30-2.30/6.30-9.45, Closed L Sat **Prices:** Fixed L €20-€25, Fixed D €50-€55, Coffee €3.50, Min/Water €6, Service included **Wine:** 300 bottles over €30, 5 bottles under €30, 10 by the glass (€7.50-€9.50) **Notes:** Tasting menu €85, Sun L €38, Vegetarian menu **Seats:** 120, Pr/dining room 50 **Smoking:** N/Sm in restaurant, Air con **Children:** Menu, Portions **Rooms:** 72 (72 en suite) ★★★★ **Directions:** 11m from M1at Ardee turning (N33) **Parking:** 200

Ireland

The Bishop's Buttery restaurant delivers fine dining to the flagstoned basement of this elegantly furnished, one-time Archbishop's Palace - a Queen Anne house in the centre of town. Vaulted ceilings, open fireplace, crisp white linen and friendly, professional service all fit the bill. The cooking leans toward classic French and makes sound use of the best of Irish produce, with game in season and fish from the Waterford coast its specialities. Otherwise, expect the likes of medallions of Angus fillet, perhaps layered between a wild mushroom and foie gras duxelle and served with an Irish whiskey sauce.

Chef: George McQuinn **Owners:** Patrick & Susan Murphy **Times:** 12-2.30/6-9.30, Closed 24-26 Dec **Prices:** Fixed L €21-€25, Fixed D €35-€38, Starter €7-€12, Main €21-€32, Dessert €8-€10, Coffee €3.50, Min/Water €5, Service optional **Notes:** Dress Restrictions, Smart casual **Seats:** 60, Pr/dining room 20 **Smoking:** N/Sm in restaurant **Children:** Menu, Portions **Rooms:** 23 (23 en suite) ★★★★ **Directions:** On main street in Cashel town centre **Parking:** 60

Chez Hans

☎ 062 61177 Moor Ln
Former Wesleyan chapel offering familiar dishes.

CO WATERFORD

WATERFORD MAP 01 C2

Athenaeum House Hotel

Modern European NEW

Innovative fare in a luxury boutique hotel

☎ 051 833 999 Christendon, Ferrybank
e-mail: info@athenaeumhousehotel.com
web: www.athenaeumhousehotel.com

Well-proportioned 18th-century house on the approach to the city, now operating as a smart boutique hotel. The building, set in 10 acres of parkland on the banks of the River Suir, has been sympathetically restored in a contemporary style, and Zak's is the bright and airy restaurant where innovative food is served. The cooking has a strong classical basis, with excellent ingredients used in interesting combinations to create the likes of sea bass fillet filled with saffron fish mousse on vegetable spaghetti, or Barbary duck breast on sweetcorn, potato and chilli chervil fritter. The menu, with some non-meat options, is changed regularly.

Chef: Patrick Power **Owners:** Stan & Mailo Power **Times:** 12.30-3.30/7-9.30 **Prices:** Starter €6.50-€9.50, Main €18-€28, Dessert €8-€9, Coffee €2, Min/Water €5, Service optional **Wine:** 17 bottles over €30, 18 bottles under €30, 10 by the glass (€5-€7.60) **Notes:** Sun L €21, Vegetarian available **Seats:** 100, Pr/dining room 30 **Smoking:** N/Sm in restaurant, Air con **Children:** Menu, Portions **Rooms:** 29 (29 en suite) ★★★ **Directions:** From station on N25 towards Rosslare, through lights, then right and next right **Parking:** 40

Waterford Castle

Mediterranean, European

Formal dining in a romantic island castle

☎ 051 878203 The Island
e-mail: info@waterfordcastle.com
web: www.waterfordcastle.com

The hotel is set on its own enchanting island accessible by chain link ferry from the mainland. The castle is an impressive 16th-century building and the 310-acre island includes an 18-hole championship golf course. There are views across the surrounding deer park from the Munster Room, the oak-panelled restaurant with ornate ceilings, where a resident pianist plays most evenings. The seasonal set menu draws on excellent seafood caught at nearby Dunmore East, well-kept local cheeses and organic vegetables where possible. Spot-on cooking of a prime cut of fish is evident in cod, saffron and crab risotto, with creamy rice and clear flavours. Private dining is available in the Leinster Room.

Times: 7-9, Closed Xmas, early Jan **Rooms:** 19 (19 en suite) ★★★★ **Directions:** Telephone for directions

CO WESTMEATH

ATHLONE MAP 01 C4

Hodson Bay

European, International

Smart lakeside hotel with a fine restaurant

☎ 090 6442000 Hodson Bay
e-mail: info@hodsonbayhotel.com
web: www.hodsonbayhotel.com

With stunning views of Lough Ree and a location in the heart of some of Ireland's most beautiful countryside, this is a rural idyll that offers an exquisite taster of renowned Irish hospitality amid some fantastic scenery. L'Escale restaurant is the showcase for the hotel's fine dining and offers a menu which combines modern Irish cooking with international influences. Fresh seafood is a speciality, delivered fresh every day, with a lobster tank on the premises. A typical starter might be Atlantic lobster terrine with tomato salsa, while mains might include poached fillet of beef in Shiraz.

Times: 12.30-2.15/7-9.30 **Rooms:** 133 (133 en suite) ★★★★ **Directions:** From Athlone follow signs for Roscommon. Approx 2.5m on entering Hodson Bay follow signs for the hotel on right

Wineport Lodge

Modern, Classical

Wholesome cooking in spectacular setting

☎ 090 643 9010 Glasson
e-mail: lodge@wineport.ie
web: www.wineport.ie

A truly impressive location on the shores of the inner lakes of Lough Ree on the Shannon. Customers can arrive by road or water and dine on the deck or in the attractive dining room. Spectacular views and friendly service reflect the highest standards of Irish hospitality. Wholesome local produce is served up in generous portions. Try a starter like grilled Lissadell Bay mussels with garlic butter herb crust. Main courses might feature roast fillet of cod with honey, curry and grain mustard and red onion coriander fritters. Great children's menu and set lunch value menu. Wines are a special feature with regular wine dinners hosted by visiting wine growers.

Times: 3-10/6-10, Closed 24-26 Dec, Closed L Mon-Sat **Rooms:** 10 (10 en suite)

CO WEXFORD

GOREY MAP 01 D3

Ashdown Park Hotel

European, International

Enjoyable dining in modern hotel spa

☎ 053 948 0500 The Coach Rd
e-mail: info@ashdownparkhotel.com
web: www.ashdownparkhotel.com

The first-floor, Anderida Restaurant is part of this modern hotel spa on the outskirts of town. The contemporary and stylish restaurant interior takes on an intimate atmosphere in the evening with low lighting. Service is friendly and efficient. Good use of local, seasonal

continued

ingredients means that the simpler dishes are often the most enjoyable. Try the starter of cod brochette with cucumber and mango salad or main courses like the oven-baked stuffed chicken with champ and mustard sauce. Save space for a dessert of stewed apple-filled crêpes with cinnamon ice cream.

Chef: David Crossoir **Owners:** Pat & Tom Redmond **Times:** 12.30-2.30/6-9.30, Closed 24-25 Dec, Closed L Mon-Sat **Prices:** Fixed L €24, Fixed D €39, Starter €7.50-€13, Main €18-€30, Dessert €6.50-€8, Coffee €2.50, Min/Water €5, Service optional **Wine:** 30 bottles over €30, 30 bottles under €30, 12 by the glass (€5-€6.50) **Notes:** Vegetarian available, Dress Restrictions, Neat dress **Seats:** 110, Pr/dining room 90 **Smoking:** N/Sm in restaurant, Air con **Children:** Menu, Portions **Rooms:** 80 (80 en suite) ★★★★ **Directions:** On approach to Gorey Town take the N11 from Dublin. Take left signed for Courtown. Hotel on left **Parking:** 150

Marlfield House

Classic

Elegant restaurant in a country-house setting

☎ 055 21124
e-mail: info@marlfieldhouse.ie
web: www.marlfield.com

A family-operated country-house hotel with an air of luxury, from the opulent decorations and furnishings to the gracefully professional service. In the three rooms of the restaurant the elegantly appointed tables have irresistible views over beautiful gardens. Vegetables and herbs from the kitchen garden bring fresh flavours to top notch, mainly local ingredients including excellent beef and lamb, and the accurate cooking is reflected in succinct four-course menus. Impressive dishes might include terrine of ham hock and foie gras with a caramelised fig, and rib-eye of beef with wild mushroom ragout, red chard and port wine sauce. A velvety smooth tiramisù parfait shows a confident touch.

Times: 12.30-2/7-9, Closed 24-27 Dec, 3-30 Jan, Closed L Mon-Sat **Rooms:** 20 (20 en suite) ★★★ **Directions:** 1m from Gorey on R742 (Courtown road)

ROSSLARE MAP 01 D2

Kelly's Resort

European

Classic cuisine in famous Victorian hotel

☎ 053 32114
e-mail: kellyhot@iol.ie
web: www.kellys.ie

Founded in 1895 by William Kelly, this well-established hotel has been in the family ever since and is currently in its fourth generation of Kellys. Situated next to a five-mile stretch of sandy beach in Rosslare, it's a seaside resort par excellence where traditional service elements are still a high priority. The food has been presided over by chef Jim Aherne for over thirty years and continues to maintain high standards of quality and consistency with a steadfastly classic approach to food, based on a solid bedrock of fine French cuisine. Local produce - especially seafood and fish - are well represented. Try foie gras of duck maison with Sauterne jelly and buttered toast, followed by poached wild Wexford salmon with hollandaise, and a dessert of passionfruit bavarois with summer berries.

AA Hotel of the Year for Republic of Ireland

Times: 1-2/7.30-9, Closed mid Dec-mid Feb **Rooms:** 118 (118 en suite) ★★★★

WEXFORD MAP 01 D3

Ferrycarrig Hotel

International

Smart split-level restaurant overlooking the estuary

☎ 053 9120999 Ferrycarrig Bridge
e-mail: ferrycarrig@ferrycarrighotel.com
web: www.ferrycarrighotel.ie

The two eating outlets at this smart modern hotel have been combined into one stylish split-level restaurant overlooking the Slaney River estuary. The new, spacious room boasts bright, airy proportions, and has been elegantly refurbished. The friendly, professional staff are particularly welcoming of families. The menus have been upgraded to match the new dining room, and draw on the freshest meats and seafood from nearby Duncannon, with many suppliers credited. Salsas, dressings and quality sauces are used to good effect. If you fancy the likes of seared scallops with tomato and onion relish, and pan-fried breasts of wild mallard with confit legs and red wine jus, look no further.

Chef: Tony Carty **Owners:** Mr Griffin **Times:** 12.30-2.15/6.00-9.45 **Prices:** Food prices not confirmed for 2007. Please telephone for details **Wine:** 17 bottles over €30, 55 bottles under €30, 10 by the glass (€5-€7.25) **Notes:** Mineral water is complimentary, Vegetarian available, Civ Wed 250 **Seats:** 140, Pr/dining room 40 **Smoking:** N/Sm in restaurant, Air con **Children:** Menu, Portions **Rooms:** 102 (102 en suite) ★★★★ **Directions:** On N11 by Slaney Estuary, beside Ferrycarrig Castle **Parking:** 200

Newbay Country House & Restaurant

Modern Irish

Popular hotel with excellent, simply prepared dishes

☎ 053 42779 Newbay, Carrick
e-mail: newbay@newbayhouse.com
web: www.newbayhouse.com

Newbay's star is on the rise since a change in ownership, and booking is essential, particularly at weekends. This elegant house sits in mature gardens just a short drive from Wexford city and boasts an informal bistro in addition to its comfortable fine dining restaurant. First-rate ingredients are handled with confident simplicity allowing clear flavours to shine through, creating a lengthy range of dishes, with fish from the hotel's own trawler a speciality. Your choice might include grilled Dover sole with lemon and thyme butter or baked lobster with rocket and potato salad, and parmesan shavings.

Chef: Domonick Power **Owners:** Alec Scallan **Times:** 12-3/6-9.30 **Prices:** Fixed L €22.95, Starter €3.95-€10.95, Main €19.95-€29.95, Dessert €6.90, Coffee €2, Min/Water €2.80, Service optional **Wine:** 15 bottles over €30, 17 bottles under €30, 8 by the glass (€5-€8) **Seats:** 75 **Smoking:** N/Sm in restaurant **Children:** Menu, Portions **Rooms:** 12 (12 en suite) RR **Directions:** Take Cork Rd from Wexford, left after Citroen Garage, at x-rds turn right, restaurant on right **Parking:** 70

WEXFORD *continued* MAP 01 D3

Whitford House Hotel Health & Leisure Spa

European

A good variety of dishes in a friendly hotel setting

☎ 053 9143444 New Line Rd
e-mail: info@whitford.ie
web: www.whitford.ie

A long established family-run hotel with a strong local following, the Whitford is located a couple of kilometres from Wexford town. Dinner is served in the spacious surroundings of Footprints Restaurant, to the accompaniment of live classical music at the weekend. The European menu draws on the best of Wexford produce in dishes such as prawns and bell peppers on citrus risotto with tabouleh salsa; and seared lamb cutlets served on sun-dried tomato and goat's cheese mash. To finish, try seasonal fruit kebab with Malibu sabayon and raspberry ice.

Chef: Siobhan Devereux **Owners:** The Whitty Family **Times:** 12.30-3/7-9, Closed 23-28 Dec, Closed L Mon-Sat **Prices:** Fixed L €19.95-€21.95, Fixed D €39.95-€42, Starter €8-€10, Main €20-€28, Dessert €6.95, Coffee €2.20, Min/Water €3.95, Service optional **Wine:** 40% bottles over €30, 60% bottles under €30, 10 by the glass (€4.95-€6.95) **Notes:** Fixed D 4 courses, Vegetarian available **Seats:** 100 **Smoking:** N/Sm in restaurant, Air con **Children:** Menu, Portions **Rooms:** 36 (36 en suite) ★★★ **Directions:** From Rosslare ferry port follow N25. At Duncannon Road rdbt, turn right onto R733, hotel immediately on left. 1.5m from Wexford Town **Parking:** 150

CO WICKLOW

MACREDDIN MAP 01 D3

The Strawberry Tree Restaurant

Organic

Country-house hotel specialising in organic and wild food

☎ 0402 36444 Brooklodge Hotel & Wells Spa
e-mail: brooklodge@macreddin.ie
web: www.brooklodge.com

This luxurious country-house hotel, situated in the village, comprises a pub, café, organic bakery and smokehouse, equestrian centre and spa. However, its Strawberry Tree Restaurant provides the main event; a romantic affair replete with dark blue décor, mirror-style ceiling, mahogany furniture, chandeliers and candlelight. Serious in its attitude to organically-produced ingredients, the kitchen works closely with specialist suppliers; its menu appropriately strong on seasonality, balanced combinations and the assured provenance of organic and wild ingredients. Guests can expect dishes such as wild pheasant with Parma ham, lentil stew and balsamic jus, or perhaps steamed wild hake with leek ragout, that can be wash down with one of 20 or so globally-produced organic wines.

Chef: Norman Luedke/Evan Doyle **Owners:** The Doyle Family **Times:** 1.30-3.30/7-9.30, Closed L Mon-Sat **Prices:** Fixed D €60, Min/Water €2.40, Service optional **Wine:** 60 bottles over €30, 30 bottles under €30, 30 by the glass (€7.20) **Notes:** Fixed D 5 courses, Dress Restrictions, Smart casual **Seats:** 130, Pr/dining room 50 **Smoking:** N/Sm in restaurant, Air con **Children:** Portions **Rooms:** 54 (54 en suite) ★★★★ **Directions:** From Dublin take N11, turn off at Rathnew for Rathdrum, then through Aughrim to Macreddin (2m) **Parking:** 400

RATHNEW MAP 01 D3

Hunter's Hotel

Irish

Beautiful views and 150 years of history

☎ 0404 40106
e-mail: reception@hunters.ie
web: www.hunters.ie

Full of character and old-fashioned charm stemming from five generations of family ownership, this delightful country house is one of Ireland's oldest coaching inns and stands in beautiful gardens bordering the River Varty. The restaurant has a good reputation for classic country-house cooking. Carefully prepared dishes utilise first-class local and seasonal produce, including home-grown fruit and vegetables. Go for mussel and tomato gratin, crispy roast duckling with a well-flavoured berry jus, and almond and pear tartlet with home-made vanilla bean ice cream. Afternoon tea in the garden is a delight.

Times: 12.45-3/7.30-9, Closed 3 days Xmas **Rooms:** 16 (16 en suite) ★★★ **Directions:** 1.5km from village, off N11

WOODENBRIDGE MAP 01 D3

Woodenbridge Hotel

European

Beautiful location and fine cuisine

☎ 0402 35146
e-mail: wbhotel@iol.ie
web: www.woodenbridgehotel.com

A smart family-run hotel in the Vale of Avoca, beside the Woodenbridge Golf Club. You can enjoy a pre-dinner drink in the cosy bar while you choose where to dine. The informal eating option is the Il Ruscello Mediterranean restaurant, while fine dining is found in the grand Redmond restaurant. Here diners can enjoy a range of exciting dishes with lots of fish to choose from, as well as duck, lamb, veal and beef. An impressive wine cellar stores a good collection of wines from around the globe.

Times: 12.30-3/7-9, Closed 25 Dec, Closed L Mon-Sat **Rooms:** 23 (23 en suite) ★★★ **Directions:** 7km from Arklow

Three Rosettes

Outstanding restaurants that demand recognition well beyond their local area. Timing, seasoning and the judgement of flavour combinations will be consistently excellent, supported by other elements such as intelligent service and well-chosen wine list.

Ireland

Late entries

The following restaurants were appointed to the scheme too late for us to include in the main body of the Guide (some of them had yet to be inspected at the time of going to press). For up-to-date reports and details of any changes affecting these, and all restaurants in the Guide, please see our website www.theAA.com

England

BUCKINGHAMSHIRE

Milton Keynes

@@ Macdonald Parkside Hotel

0870 194 2128 Newport Road,
Woughton on the Green MK6 3LR

Daily-changing menus offering classic and contemporary combinations are served by attentive staff in a stylish hotel dining room in the rural outskirts of the town.

CORNWALL

Portwrinkle

@ Whitsand Bay Hotel & Golf Club

01503 230276 Portwrinkle PL11 3BU

This imposing Victorian hotel overlooks a dramatic stretch of Cornish coastline. Featuring locally sourced produce, The Bay Restaurant's classical menu includes excellent fish, delivered fresh from the day boats at nearby Looe, served in an elegant dining room with painted wood panelling and high-backed leather chairs.

St Mary's

@ St Mary's Hall Hotel

01720 422316 Church Street, Hugh Town, St Mary's, Isles of Scilly TR21 0JR

Named after the Tuscan count who built this elegant townhouse, the Café de Ferrari Restaurant combines contemporary and traditional, with bold paintings, leather, glass, natural woods and polished granite all adding to the feel. The international menu has oriental influences, featuring the likes of sushi, shellfish and steak, and in fine weather can be enjoyed on the decked terrace overlooking a Mediterranean-style garden.

Truro

@@ Tabb's Restaurant

01872 262110 85 Kenwyn Street TR1 3 BZ

Tabb's has relocated to this newly converted pub building with a contemporary cream, black and lilac décor, leather high-backed chairs and slate floors. The style of cooking is upbeat and the weekly-changing menus reflect the best of seasonal and local produce. Provençale fish soup, Cornish duck, and pan-fried local scallops show the style.

DEVON

Dartmouth

@ The Dart Marina Hotel

01803 832580 Sandquay TQ6 9PH

With its elegant décor and superb view across the river, the Riverside Restaurant provides the perfect setting for a fine-dining experience, with a few tables outside. Chef Mark Streeter's enthusiasm for local seafood, fish and poultry is evident from the modern British menu.

Late entries

Honiton

Home Farm Restaurant & Hotel

01404 831278 Wilmington EX14 9JR

Originally a 16th-century thatched farmhouse, Home Farm is now an intimate hotel and fine-dining restaurant with a cobbled courtyard and well-tended gardens. New owners have lifted the style of cooking to reflect quality rather than quantity. Typical dishes include oven-baked rack of local lamb, home-smoked beef and home-made bread rolls.

Saunton

The Saunton Sands Hotel

01271 890212 Saunton EX33 1LQ

Stunning sea views and direct access to 5 miles of sandy beach are just two of the features of this popular hotel. The restaurant serves the likes of sautéed and braised lamb layered with rösti potatoes and smoked aubergine salsa, and there's also a less formal café/bar.

GLOUCESTERSHIRE

Cheltenham

Macdonald Queen's Hotel

0870 4008107 The Promenade GL50 1NN

An elegant and imposing hotel in the busy town with high standards of hospitality. The new Napier Restaurant & Conservatory offers traditional and contemporary British cuisine and is a stylish venue for the newly awarded one Rosette cooking.

KENT

Dartford

Thistle Brands Hatch

0870 3339128 Brands Hatch DA3 8PE

Uniquely located in the 500-acre parkland of the Brands Hatch race track, this purpose-built hotel has a large open-plan restaurant serving favourites such as goat's cheese tart and grilled rack of lamb.

LANCASHIRE

Barton

Barton Grange Hotel

01772 862551 Garstang Road, Preston PR3 5AA

Close to the M6, Barton Grange is a smart, modern hotel with two restaurants: Healeys, with a funky but refined feel, open for dinner only, and the all-day dining Walled Garden restaurant, where the cooking style is British/European.

LONDON EC1

Rudland & Stubbs

020 7253 0148 35-37 Green Hill Rants, Cowcross Street EC1M 6BN

A traditional fish and seafood restaurant, with marble-topped tables and tiled walls. The style of cooking is classical yet contemporary, as in tempura of salt and pepper calamari with mango pink pepper relish. The menu includes a couple of choices for meat-lovers.

LONDON EC3

Apex City of London

0845 365 0000 No 1 Seething Lane EC3N 4AX

A striking hotel offering great hospitality and efficient service, including table service in the bar area, and dinner that is sure to prove a highlight of a stay here.

LONDON SE1

London Marriott Hotel

020 7928 5200 Westminster Bridge Road, County Hall SE1 7PB

Within County Hall, this high-ceilinged, oak-panelled restaurant looks across the river to Westminster. A good choice if you're looking for traditional, good quality food like chargrilled asparagus spears with hollandaise, and fillet of Mey Estate beef with stilton crust.

LONDON SW1

The Quilon

01871 3328563 41 Buckingham Gate SW1 6AF

Popular with locals, The Quilon captures the colour, smell and flavour of the southern Indian state of Kerala, with its modern décor, deep-yellow seating, and dishes such as fish in banana leaf.

GREATER LONDON

Hayes

The Sheraton Skyline Hotel and Conference Centre

020 8759 2535 Bath Road UB3 5BP

The hotel's Al Dente restaurant is spacious, open and decorated in rich autumn colours. The food is modern, innovative Italian; try the seared blue fin tuna with saffron risotto and rucola salad.

OXFORDSHIRE

Henley-on-Thames

Hotel du Vin & Bistro

01491 848400 New Street RG9 2BP

Located 50 yards from the waterfront, the Hotel du Vin has converted the Georgian brewery in its familiar chic style. Smart/casual dining is enjoyed in a bistro atmosphere with a strong emphasis on wine, and food is in the European style of other Hotels du Vin.

SHROPSHIRE

Oswestry

Sebastian's Hotel & Restaurant

01691 655444 45 Willow Street SY11 1AQ

Located in a 16th-century building this delightful restaurant has bags of character. The style of cooking is European/British, as in poached fillets of lemon sole with tiger prawns, and good home-made breads.

SOMERSET

Bath

The Cliffe Hotel

01225 723226 Cliffe Drive, Crowe Hill, Limpley Stoke BA2 7FY

An attractive country house set in 3 acres of gardens, with amazing views overlooking the River Avon Valley. The Four Seasons restaurant offers imaginative dishes and a selection of West Country cheeses.

Bath

Dukes Hotel

01225 787960 Great Pulteney Street BA2 4DN

An elegant Georgian building close to Pulteney Bridge houses the Cavendish restaurant. This light and airy garden room with simply presented white-clothed tables serves classical dishes prepared by a creative chef, with an emphasis on organic produce. Best end of Cornish lamb served with moussaka ravioli and fondant potato shows the style.

Late entries

Martock

Ash House Country Hotel

01935 822036 41 Main Street, Ash TA12 6PB

Modern British food such as baked crab and gruyère cheese tartlet is served in a formal dining room, complete with white-clothed tables and high-backed leather chairs. For less formal dining there's a conservatory looking out onto the well-tended gardens.

EAST SUSSEX

Brighton

Pintxo People

01273 732323 95–99 Western Road BN1 2LB

Pintxo is Basque for 'bite size'– a clue to the variety of tapas to share, as well as fine Catalan dishes in this contemporary, wooden-floored bar and restaurant at the Brighton end of Western Road, a 5-minute walk from the seafront. Leave room for dessert.

WEST SUSSEX

Chichester

West Stoke House

01243 575226 Downs Road, West Stoke PO18 9BN

Rabbit terrine, roasted loin of veal, baked chocolate in a sponge shell – simply presented but with a wow-factor – are just some of the dishes you can expect in this Georgian house on the edge of the Sussex Downs.

Horsham

Stan's Way House Restaurant

01403 255688 3 Stan's Way, East Street RH12 1HU

A relaxed restaurant with smart interior in a 14th-century, town-centre building, run by a husband-and-wife team. A typical dish might be roasted sea bass with tempura vegetables and lemon and tarragon mayonnaise.

CHANNEL ISLANDS

Herm

White House Hotel

01481 722159 Herm GY1 3HR

You can expect fresh ingredients and good flavours in dishes served in the Table d'Hôte Restaurant of this family-owned, country house-style island hotel. Typical dishes may include oriental monkfish salad and roasted fillet of pork with mustard and brandy cream.

SCOTLAND

SOUTH AYRSHIRE

Ayr

The Western House Hotel

01292 619357 2 Whitletts Road KA8 0JE

In the hotel's light and airy restaurant, with views across the Ayr racecourse and the distant sound of announcements adding to the atmosphere, you will find good, straightforward dishes like magret duck with black olives or fresh pasta.

EAST LOTHIAN

North Berwick

Macdonald Marine Hotel

0870 400 8129 Cromwell Road EH39 4LZ

Close to a golf course and the sea, the hotel's oak-panelled restaurant with its deep plum-coloured walls and high ceilings sets the scene for nicely flavoured meals, such as twice-baked tomato and basil soufflé and loin of Ballencrieff pork.

HIGHLAND

Contin

Coul House Hotel

01997 421487 Contin, by Strathpeffer IV14 9ES

An imposing 1820s country house and former hunting lodge standing in 8 acres of mature woodland and grounds, where the cuisine is a mix of modern European and classical French dishes as well as contemporary Scottish dishes, such as baked salmon topped with red pesto and Scottish brie.

WALES

CARMARTHENSHIRE

Nantgaredig

Y Polyn Bar & Restaurant

01267 290000 Capel Dewi SA32 7LH

Expect simple, gutsy dishes and great local ingredients at this pretty white-painted roadside pub. Try the superb Y Polyn fish pie, and finish with warm plum and frangipane tart.

CONWY

Llandudno

St George's Hotel

01492 877544 The Promenade LL30 2LG

A choice of two restaurants with the same menu, one overlooking the sea. Cooking is refreshingly uncomplicated and British, using Welsh lamb, beef and laverbread.

DENBIGHSHIRE

St Asaph

Oriel House Hotel

01745 582716 Upper Denbigh Road LL17 0LW

Amongst other imaginative dishes using local produce, the pot-roast pheasant with shallots and caramelised apples is definitely recommended when you visit this North Wales country-house hotel which dates back to 1780.

POWYS

Machynlleth

Wynnstay Hotel

01654 702941 Maengwyn Street SY20 8AE

Pant-Ys-Gawn goat's cheese, rump of Welsh lamb, and Llaeth-y-Llan yogurt pannacotta are just some of the dishes that reflect the true Welsh flavour of the menu available in the restaurant of this renovated 1780s coaching inn on the southern edge of Snowdonia.

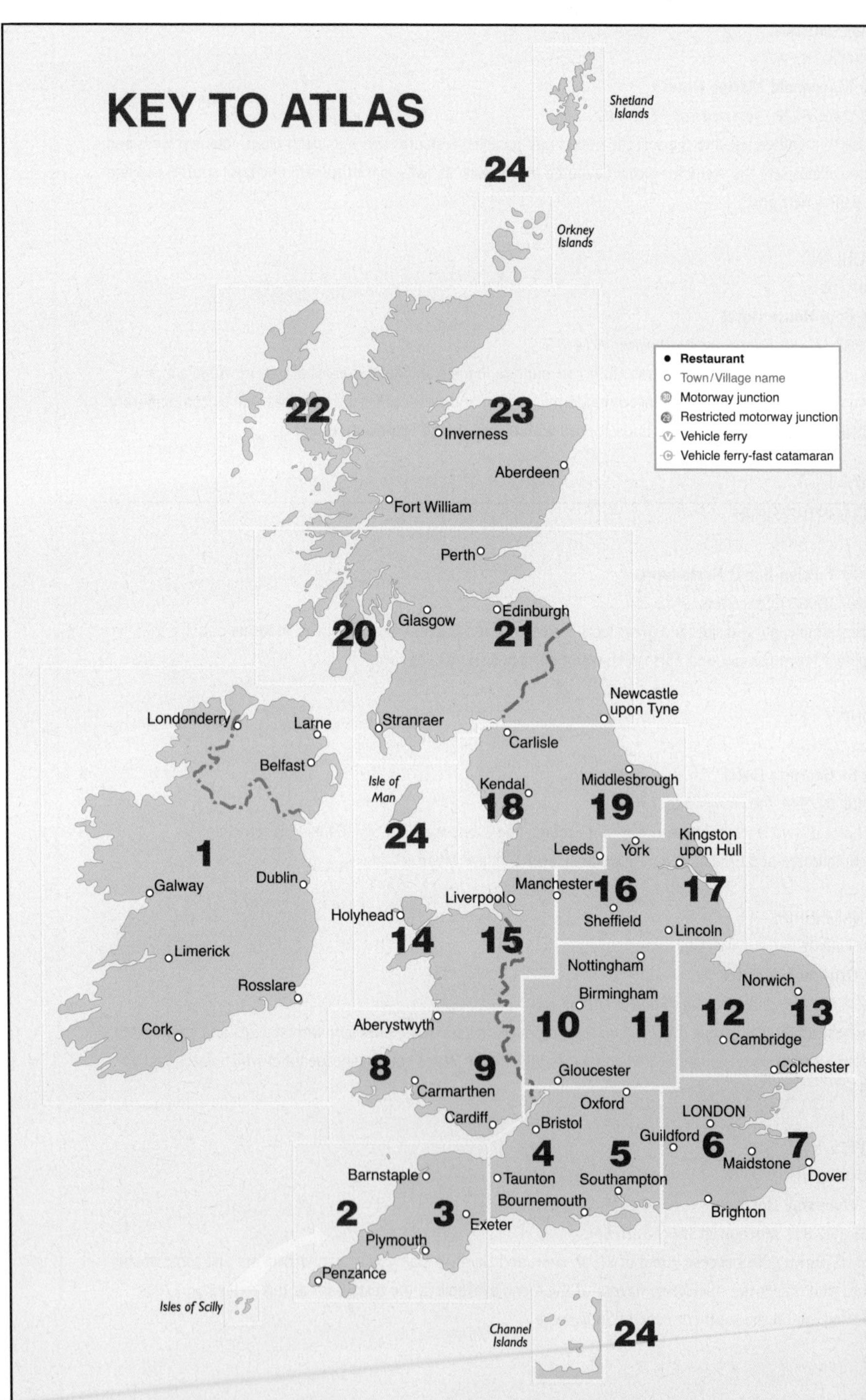
KEY TO ATLAS
Shetland Islands
24
Orkney Islands
Restaurant
Town/Village name
Motorway junction
Restricted motorway junction
Vehicle ferry
Vehicle ferry-fast catamaran
22
23
Inverness
Aberdeen
Fort William
Perth
Glasgow
Edinburgh
20
21
Newcastle upon Tyne
Londonderry
Larne
Stranraer
Carlisle
Belfast
Isle of Man
Kendal
Middlesbrough
18
19
24
1
Leeds
York
Kingston upon Hull
Galway
Dublin
Manchester
16
17
Liverpool
Holyhead
Sheffield
14
15
Lincoln
Limerick
Nottingham
Norwich
Rosslare
Birmingham
12
13
Cork
10
11
Aberystwyth
Cambridge
8
9
Gloucester
Colchester
Carmarthen
Oxford
Cardiff
LONDON
Bristol
Guildford
4
5
6
7
Maidstone
Dover
Barnstaple
Taunton
Southampton
Bournemouth
Brighton
2
3
Exeter
Plymouth
Penzance
Isles of Scilly
Channel Islands
24

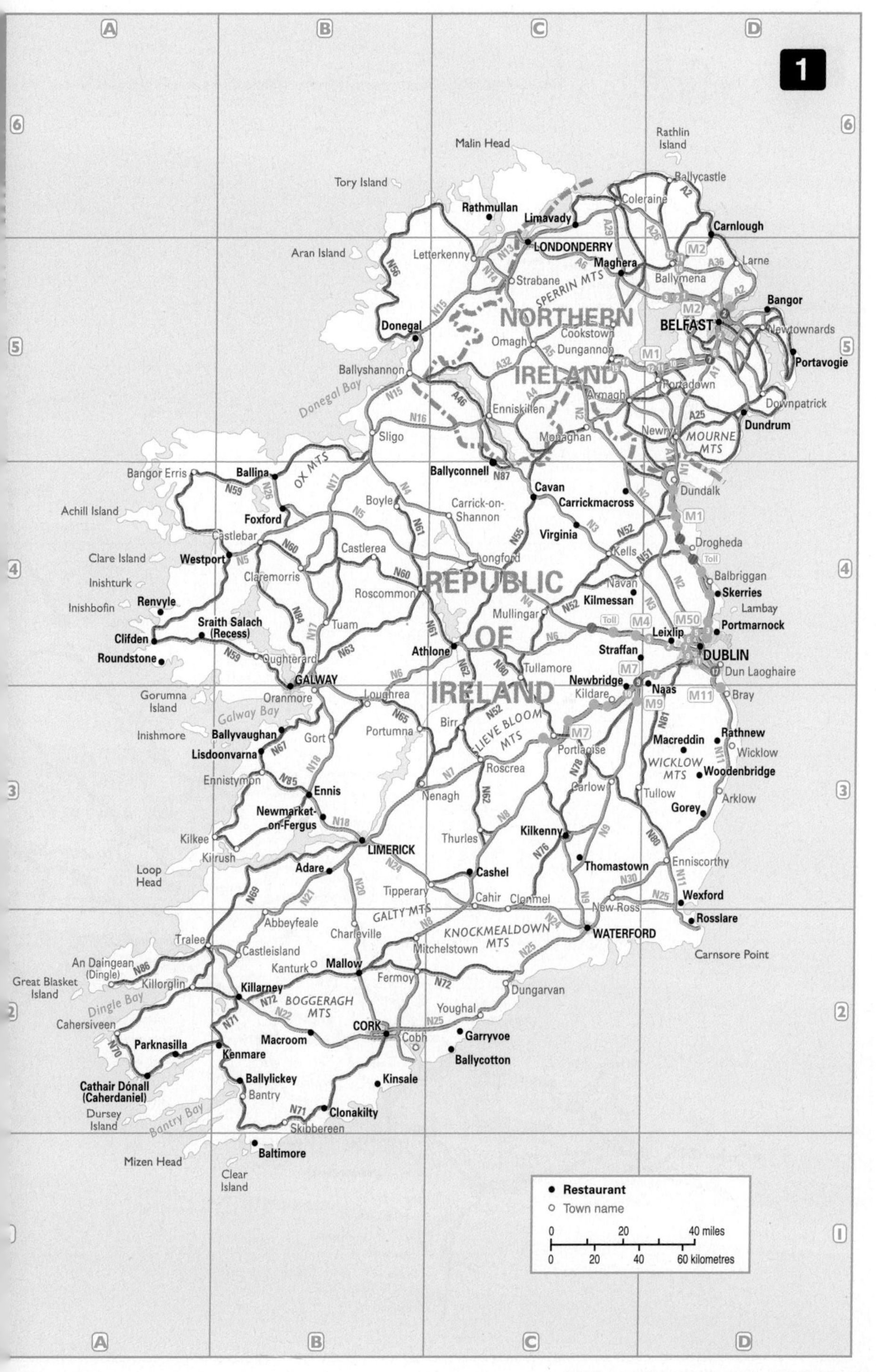

A
B
C
D
1
6
5
4
3
2
Malin Head
Rathlin Island
Tory Island
Ballycastle
Coleraine
Rathmullan
Limavady
Carnlough
Aran Island
Letterkenny
LONDONDERRY
Maghera
Larne
Strabane
Ballymena
SPERRIN MTS
Bangor
NORTHERN IRELAND
Donegal
BELFAST
Newtownards
Cookstown
Omagh
Dungannon
Portavogie
Ballyshannon
Portadown
Donegal Bay
Armagh
Enniskillen
Downpatrick
Dundrum
Sligo
Monaghan
Newry
MOURNE MTS
Bangor Erris
Ballina
OX MTS
Ballyconnell
Dundalk
Cavan
Achill Island
Boyle
Carrick-on-Shannon
Carrickmacross
Foxford
Virginia
Castlebar
Drogheda
Toll
Clare Island
Westport
Castlerea
Longford
Claremorris
Kells
Balbriggan
Inishturk
REPUBLIC OF IRELAND
Navan
Roscommon
Skerries
Inishbofin
Renvyle
Kilmessan
Mullingar
Lambay
Sraith Salach (Recess)
Tuam
Portmarnock
Clifden
Leixlip
Roundstone
Athlone
Straffan
DUBLIN
Oughterard
Tullamore
Dun Laoghaire
GALWAY
Newbridge
Naas
Gorumna Island
Oranmore
Loughrea
Kildare
Bray
Galway Bay
Birr
SLIEVE BLOOM MTS
Inishmore
Ballyvaughan
Gort
Portumna
Rathnew
Lisdoonvarna
Macreddin
Wicklow
Portlaoise
WICKLOW MTS
Roscrea
Woodenbridge
Ennistymon
Carlow
Ennis
Nenagh
Tullow
Arklow
Newmarket-on-Fergus
Gorey
Kilkee
Thurles
Kilkenny
Kilrush
LIMERICK
Enniscorthy
Loop Head
Adare
Thomastown
Cashel
Tipperary
Wexford
Cahir
Clonmel
GALTY MTS
New Ross
Abbeyfeale
Charleville
Rosslare
KNOCKMEALDOWN MTS
WATERFORD
Tralee
Castleisland
Mitchelstown
Carnsore Point
An Daingean (Dingle)
Kanturk
Mallow
Great Blasket Island
Killorglin
Fermoy
Dungarvan
Dingle Bay
Killarney
BOGGERAGH MTS
Youghal
Cahersiveen
CORK
Cobh
Garryvoe
Parknasilla
Macroom
Kenmare
Ballycotton
Kinsale
Cathair Dónall (Caherdaniel)
Ballylickey
Bantry
Dursey Island
Bantry Bay
Clonakilty
Skibbereen
Baltimore
Mizen Head
Clear Island
Restaurant
Town name
0 20 40 miles
0 20 40 60 kilometres

2

For continuation pages refer to numbered arrows

3
9
4
SUPER-MARE
Bridgwater Bay
Burnham-on-Sea
Lynton
Lynmouth
Ilfracombe
Combe Martin
Martinhoe
Brendon
Porlock Weir
Porlock
Minehead
Mortehoe
Lee
Parracombe
Wootton Courtenay
Dunster
Blue Anchor
Watchet
Kilve
Stogursey
West Huntspill
Woolacombe
EXMOOR FOREST
Challacombe
Carhampton
Holford
Cannington
Georgeham
Sampford Brett
Williton
Nether Stowey
Croyde
Bratton Fleming
Simonsbath
Exford
Wheddon Cross
QUANTOCK HILLS
Bridgwater
Saunton
Muddiford
Withypool
Crowcombe
Braunton
Brayford
Elworthy
Goathurst
Barnstaple
Winsford
Brompton Regis
North Petherton
Appledore
Instow
Westward Ho!
Northam
North Molton
Dulverton
Wiveliscombe
Fitzhead
Bishops Lydeard
Bideford
South Molton
Milverton
North Curry
Horns Cross
SS
ST
Exebridge
Petton
Taunton
Umberleigh
Knowstone
Parkham
Monkleigh
Bampton
Wellington
Sampford Arundel
Hatch Beauchamp
Great Torrington
Chittlehamholt
Corfe
Little Torrington
Burrington
Rackenford
Staple Fitzpaine
Stibb Cross
Beaford
Chulmleigh
Witheridge
Culmstock
Horton
Merton
Dolton
Chawleigh
Tiverton
Halberton
Hemyock
Milton Damerel
Eggesford
Uffculme
Willand
Shebbear
Meeth
Lapford
Cheriton Fitzpaine
Cullompton
Upottery
Black Torrington
Sheepwash
Winkleigh
Morchard Bishop
Bickleigh
Yarcombe
Broadhembury
Highampton
Hatherleigh
Copplestone
Silverton
Tytherleigh
Halwill Junction
Crediton
Stoke Canon
Fenny Bridges
Honiton
Wilmington
Beaworthy
D E V O N
Newton St Cyres
Broadclyst
Whimple
Shute
Axminster
Ashwater
Okehampton
Tedburn St Mary
EXETER
Rockbeare
Ottery St Mary
Colyton
Uplyme
Bratton Clovelly
South Zeal
Whiddon Down
Crockernwell
Newton Poppleford
Colyford
Rousdon
Seaton
Axmouth
Sourton
Dunsford
Clyst St Mary
Topsham
Branscombe
Beer
Bridestowe
Chagford
Exminster
Woodbury
Sidmouth
Lewdown
Kennford
Lifton
Lydford
Moretonhampstead
Otterton
DARTMOOR FOREST
Kenton
Budleigh Salterton
Milton Abbot
Bovey Tracey
Chudleigh
Exmouth
Postbridge
Lamerton
Mary Tavy
Widecombe in the Moor
Haytor Vale
Ideford
Dawlish
Two Bridges
Ilsington
Chudleigh Knighton
Tavistock
Bishopsteignton
Princetown
Kingsteignton
Teignmouth
Gunnislake
Gulworthy
Hexworthy
Ashburton
Newton Abbot
Callington
Horrabridge
Dousland
Holne
Kingskerswell
Maidencombe
Bere Alston
Yelverton
Buckfastleigh
Ipplepen
SY
Bere Ferrers
Shaugh Prior
Dartington
TORQUAY
South Brent
Totnes
Paignton
Saltash
Cornwood
Wrangaton
Stoke Gabriel
Tor Bay
Churston Ferrers
Plympton
Ivybridge
Harbertonford
Dittisham
Brixham
Torpoint
PLYMOUTH
Ugborough
Halwell
Millbrook
Heybrook Bay
Brixton
Yealmpton
Modbury
Kingswear
Cawsand
Holbeton
Aveton Gifford
Dartmouth
Wembury
Newton Ferrers
Stoke Fleming
SX
Bigbury-on-Sea
Kingsbridge
Slapton
Strete
Bigbury Bay
Chillington
Start Bay
Thurlestone
Hope
Torcross
Salcombe
Malborough
Hallsands
Start Point
East Prawle
Restaurant
Town/Village name
0
10 miles
0
10
20 kilometres

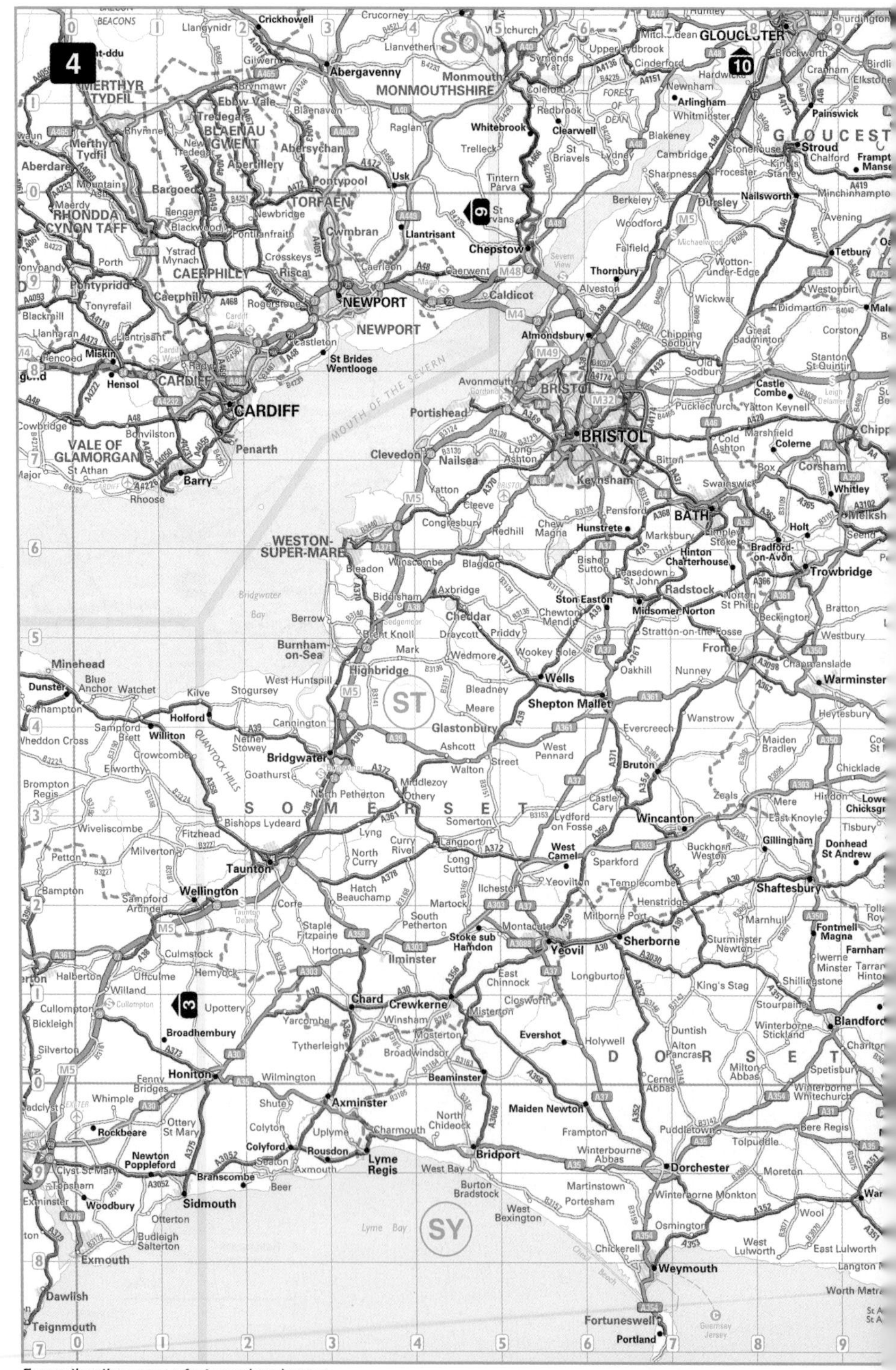

For continuation pages refer to numbered arrows

5
OXFORDSHIRE
BERKSHIRE
HAMPSHIRE
SURREY
WEST SUSSEX
ISLE OF WIGHT
NEW FOREST
SOUTH DOWNS
LAMBOURN DOWNS
SP
SU
SZ
OXFORD
Woodstock
Charlbury
Kidlington
Witney
Burford
Northleach
Faringdon
Abingdon
Didcot
Wantage
Wallingford
Thame
Aylesbury
Tring
Wendover
Berkhamsted
Chesham
Amersham
HIGH WYCOMBE
Beaconsfield
Marlow
Henley-on-Thames
Maidenhead
SLOUGH
Windsor
Egham
BRACKNELL
Wokingham
READING
Newbury
Hungerford
Marlborough
SWINDON
Lambourn
Chieveley
Yattendon
Highclere
BASINGSTOKE
Andover
Whitchurch
Stockbridge
Salisbury
Winchester
Alton
Farnham
Fleet
Aldershot
CAMBERLEY
GUILDFORD
Godalming
Haslemere
Liphook
Petersfield
Midhurst
Romsey
EASTLEIGH
SOUTHAMPTON
Brook
Cadnam
Fordingbridge
Ringwood
Burley
Brockenhurst
Lymington
New Milton
Barton-on-Sea
Christchurch
BOURNEMOUTH
Beaulieu
Bucklers Hard
Wickham
FAREHAM
WATERLOOVILLE
HAVANT
PORTSMOUTH
GOSPORT
Emsworth
Bosham
Chichester
BOGNOR REGIS
Burpham
Climping
Cowes
Ryde
Seaview
Newport
Yarmouth
Freshwater
Sandown
Shanklin
Ventnor
The Needles
Restaurant
Town/Village name
0
10 miles
0
10
20 kilometres

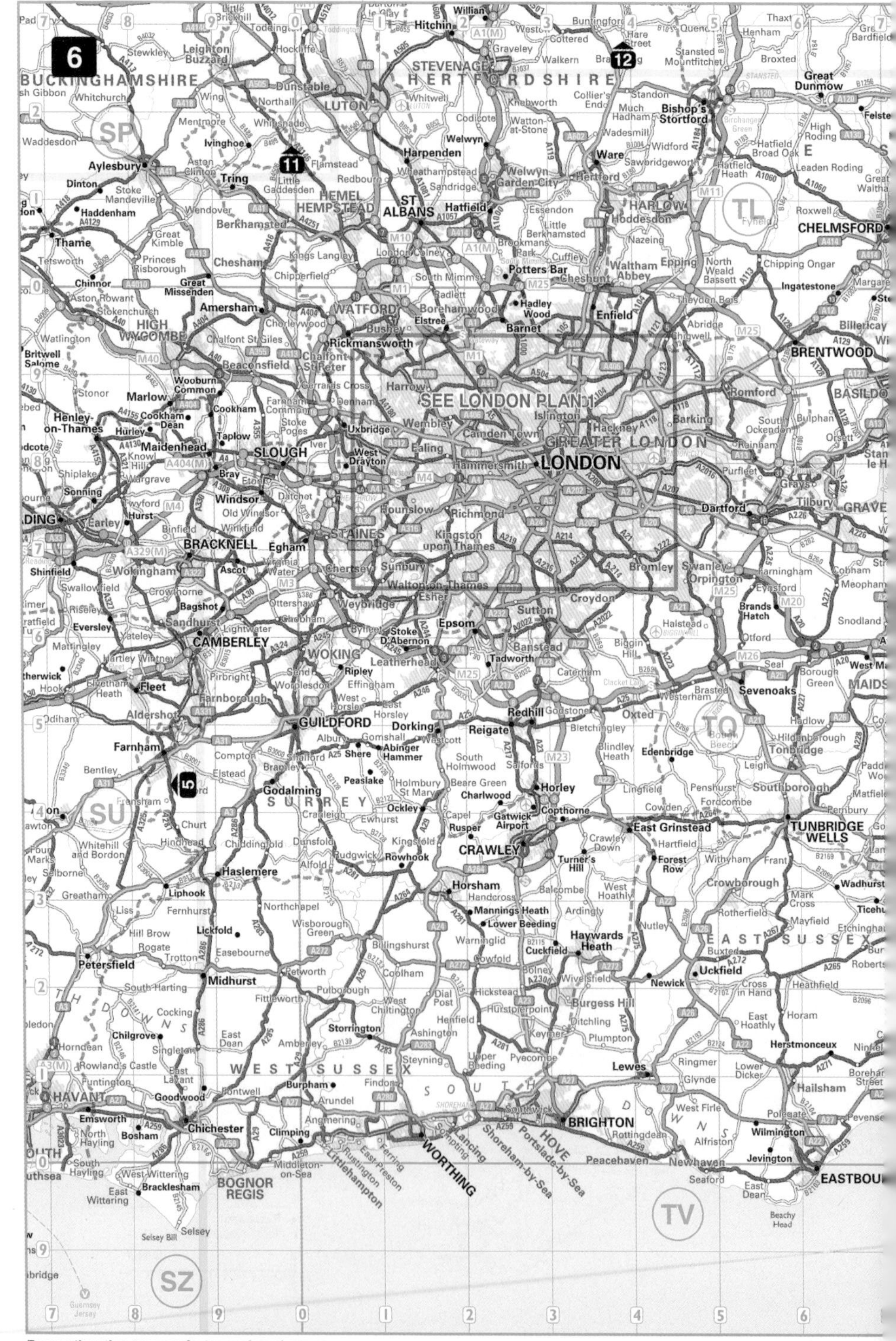

For continuation pages refer to numbered arrows

7
TM
TR
Harwich
COLCHESTER
Ardleigh
Wix
Earls Colne
Aldham
Marks Tey
Coggeshall
Copford Green
Wivenhoe
Elmstead Market
Thorpe-le-Soken
Walton on the Naze
Silver End
Kelvedon
Thorrington
Little Clacton
Frinton-on-Sea
Tiptree
Brightlingsea
St Osyth
CLACTON-ON-SEA
Witham
Tolleshunt Knights
Tolleshunt D'Arcy
West Mersea
Goldhanger
Tollesbury
River Blackwater
Bradwell-on-Sea
Maldon
Steeple
Cold Norton
Latchingdon
Southminster
South Woodham Ferrers
Burnham-on-Crouch
Hockley
Rayleigh
Rochford
Great Wakering
SOUTHEND-ON-SEA
Canvey Island
Grain
Sheerness
Minster
Hoo St Werburgh
Eastchurch
Leysdown-on-Sea
Isle of Sheppey
Iwade
MARGATE
Broadstairs
Ramsgate
Reculver
Herne Bay
Whitstable
Sarre
Upstreet
Minster
Sittingbourne
Teynham
Faversham
Ospringe
Bredhurst
Sturry
Hersden
Blean
Fordwich
Ash
Sandwich
Boughton Street
Canterbury
Wingham
Doddington
Hollingbourne
Chilham
Chartham
Bridge
Eastry
Lenham
Challock
Charing
Aylesham
Deal
Kingsdown
Sutton Valence
K E N T
Wye
Wingmore
Pluckley
Elham
St Margaret's at Cliffe
Headcorn
Smarden
Alkham
DOVER
Ashford
Bethersden
Densole
Lyminge
CHANNEL TUNNEL TERMINAL
Hawkinge
Sellindge
High Halden
Kingsnorth
Channel Tunnel (Rail)
Woodchurch
Lympne
Hythe
FOLKESTONE
Benenden
Tenterden
Hamstreet
Rolvenden
Dymchurch
Wittersham
Appledore
St Mary's Bay
Brookland
Brenzett
Northiam
New Romney
Peasmarsh
Rye
Lydd
Camber
Brede
Winchelsea
Dungeness
STRAIT OF DOVER
Guestling Green
Fairlight
HASTINGS
• Restaurant
○ Town/Village name
0
10 miles
0
10
20 kilometres

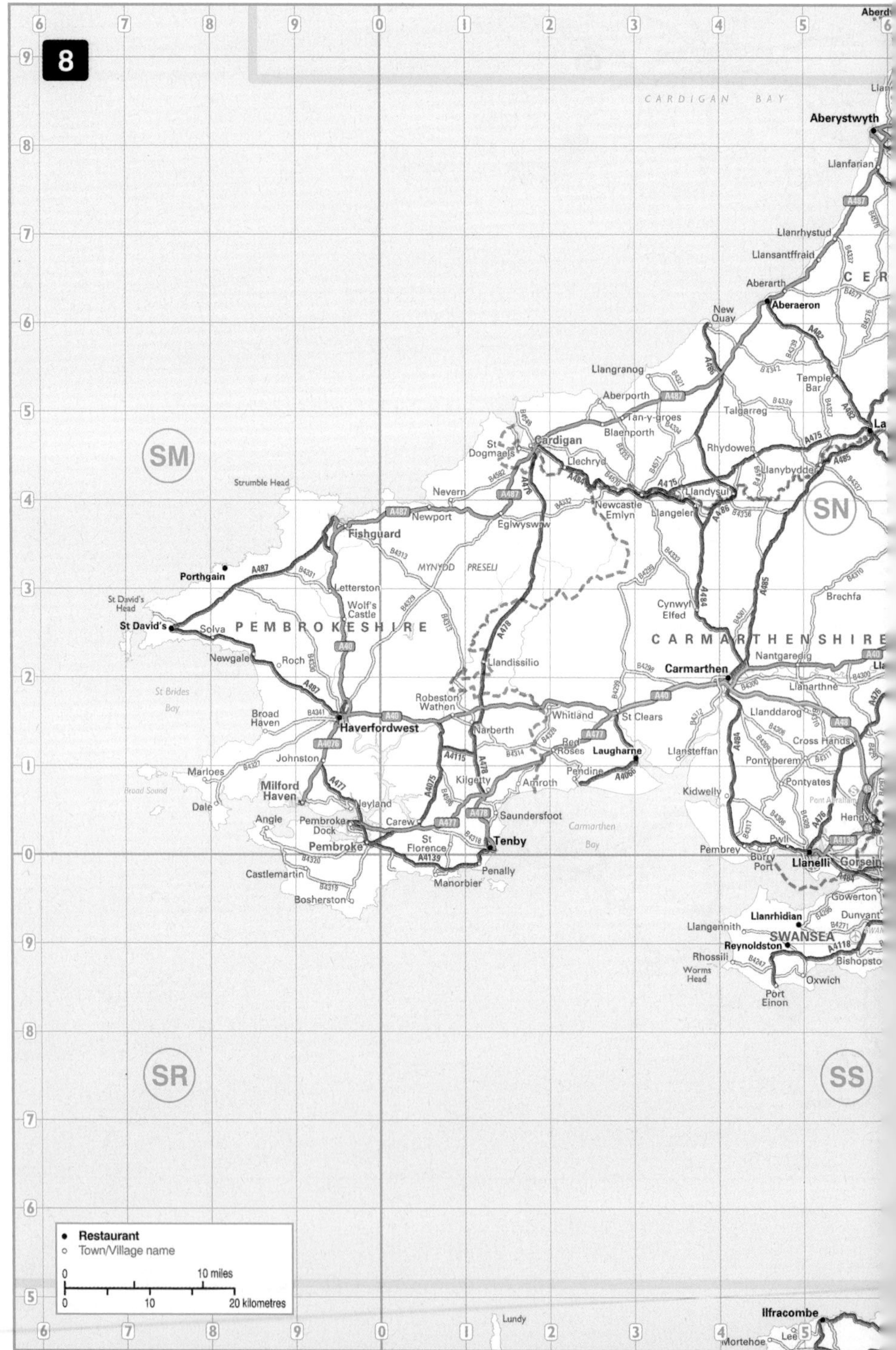

For continuation pages refer to numbered arrows

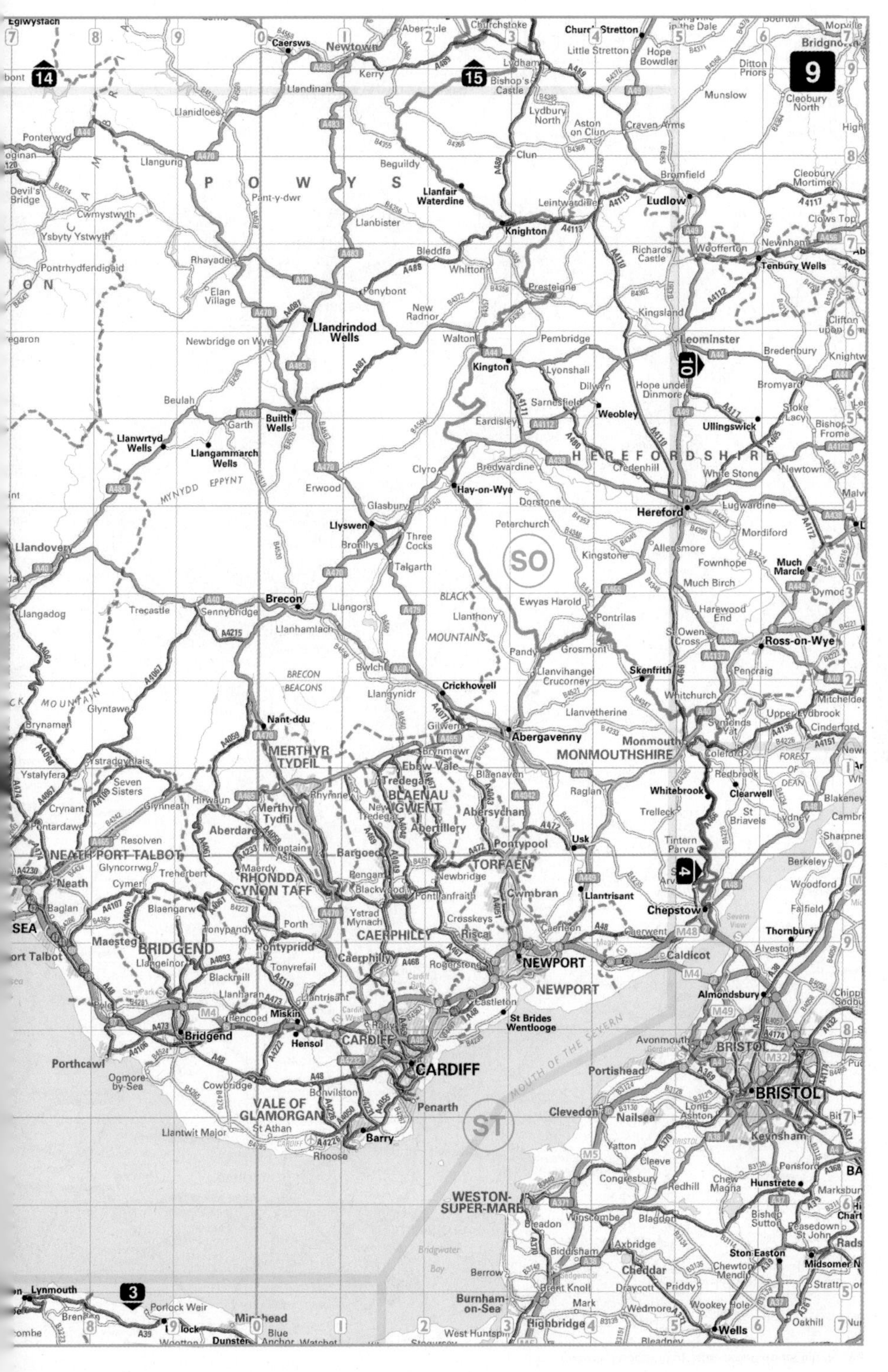

9
14
15
10
4
3
Egwyswfach
Caersws
Newtown
Abermule
Churchstoke
Church Stretton
Little Stretton
Hope Bowdler
Ditton Priors
Bridgnorth
Kerry
Lydham
Bishop's Castle
Llandinam
Llanidloes
Munslow
Cleobury North
Lydbury North
Aston on Clun
Craven Arms
Ponterwyd
Llangurig
Clun
Beguildy
Bromfield
Cleobury Mortimer
Devil's Bridge
P O W Y S
Pant-y-dwr
Llanfair Waterdine
Leintwardine
Ludlow
Cwmystwyth
Ysbyty Ystwyth
Llanbister
Knighton
Clows Top
Rhayader
Bleddfa
Whitton
Richards Castle
Woofferton
Newnham
Tenbury Wells
Pontrhydfendigaid
Elan Village
Penybont
Presteigne
New Radnor
Kingsland
Llandrindod Wells
Walton
Pembridge
Leominster
Bredenbury
Newbridge on Wye
Kington
Lyonshall
Dilwyn
Hope under Dinmore
Bromyard
Beulah
Sarnesfield
Weobley
Stoke Lacy
Builth Wells
Garth
Eardisley
Ullingswick
Bishop's Frome
Llanwrtyd Wells
Llangammarch Wells
H E R E F O R D S H I R E
Credenhill
White Stone
Newtown
Clyro
Bredwardine
MYNYDD EPPYNT
Erwood
Hay-on-Wye
Dorstone
Hereford
Lugwardine
Glasbury
Peterchurch
Mordiford
Llyswen
Three Cocks
Bronllys
Llandovery
SO
Kingstone
Allensmore
Fownhope
Much Marcle
Talgarth
Much Birch
BLACK
Ewyas Harold
Brecon
Llangadog
Trecastle
Sennybridge
Llangors
Llanthony
Pontrilas
Harewood End
Llanhamlach
St Owens Cross
Ross-on-Wye
MOUNTAINS
Pandy
Grosmont
Bwlch
Skenfrith
Pencraig
BRECON BEACONS
Crickhowell
Llanvihangel Crucorney
Llangynidr
Whitchurch
MOUNTAIN
Glyntawe
Llanvetherine
Upper Lydbrook
Brynaman
Nant-ddu
Gilwern
Abergavenny
Symonds Yat
Monmouth
Cinderford
MERTHYR TYDFIL
Brynmawr
MONMOUTHSHIRE
Coleford
FOREST OF DEAN
Ystradgynlais
Ebbw Vale
Blaenavon
Redbrook
Ystalyfera
Seven Sisters
Tredegar
Raglan
Whitebrook
Clearwell
Blakeney
Hirwaun
BLAENAU GWENT
Crynant
Glynneath
Merthyr Tydfil
Rhymney
New Tredegar
Abersychan
Trelleck
St Briavels
Lydney
Pontardawe
Aberdare
Abertillery
Resolven
Mountain Ash
Usk
Tintern Parva
Sharpness
NEATH PORT TALBOT
Bargoed
Pontypool
Berkeley
Glyncorrwg
Treherbert
Maerdy
TORFAEN
Neath
Cymer
RHONDDA CYNON TAFF
Pengam
Newbridge
Blackwood
Woodford
Pontllanfraith
Cwmbran
Llantrisant
Chepstow
Baglan
Blaengarw
Ystrad Mynach
Falfield
Porth
Crosskeys
SEA
Tonypandy
CAERPHILLY
Risca
Caerleon
Caerwent
Thornbury
Maesteg
BRIDGEND
Pontypridd
Caerphilly
Rogerstone
NEWPORT
Caldicot
Alveston
Port Talbot
Llangeinor
Tonyrefail
Blackmill
Llanharan
Llantrisant
NEWPORT
Almondsbury
Pyle
Castleton
Miskin
Pencoed
St Brides Wentlooge
Bridgend
Hensol
CARDIFF
Avonmouth
BRISTOL
Porthcawl
CARDIFF
Ogmore-by-Sea
MOUTH OF THE SEVERN
Portishead
Cowbridge
Bonvilston
BRISTOL
VALE OF GLAMORGAN
Penarth
Clevedon
Nailsea
Long Ashton
ST
Llantwit Major
St Athan
Barry
Keynsham
Rhoose
Yatton
Cleeve
Pensford
Congresbury
Redhill
Chew Magna
Hunstrete
WESTON-SUPER-MARE
Winscombe
Blagdon
Bishop Sutton
Bleadon
Axbridge
Biddisham
Bridgwater Bay
Ston Easton
Midsomer Norton
Cheddar
Berrow
Chewton Mendip
Lynmouth
Brent Knoll
Draycott
Priddy
Porlock Weir
Burnham-on-Sea
Mark
Wookey Hole
Minehead
Wedmore
Highbridge
Oakhill
Blue Anchor
Watchet
West Huntspill
Wells
Dunster

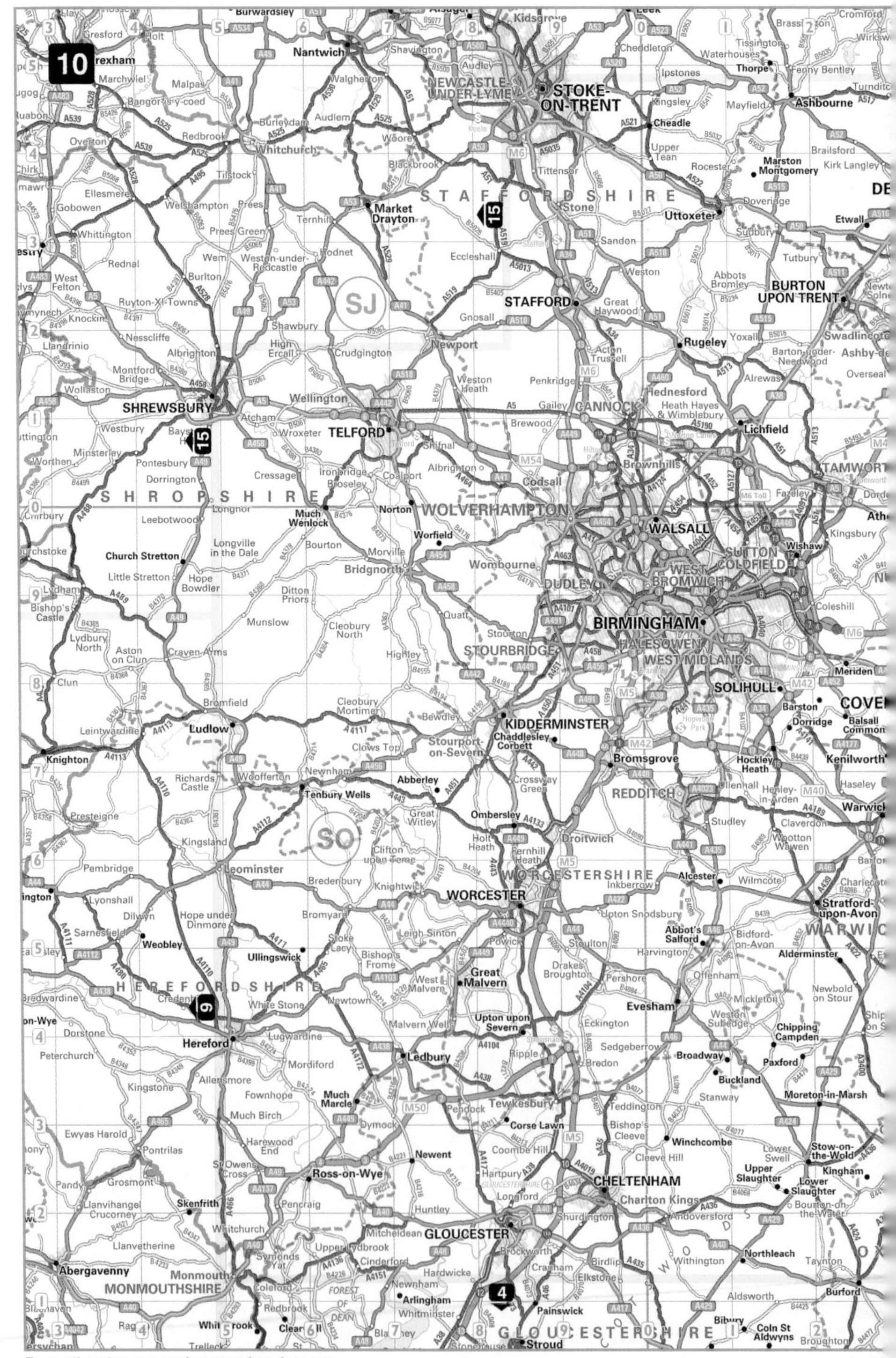

For continuation pages refer to numbered arrows

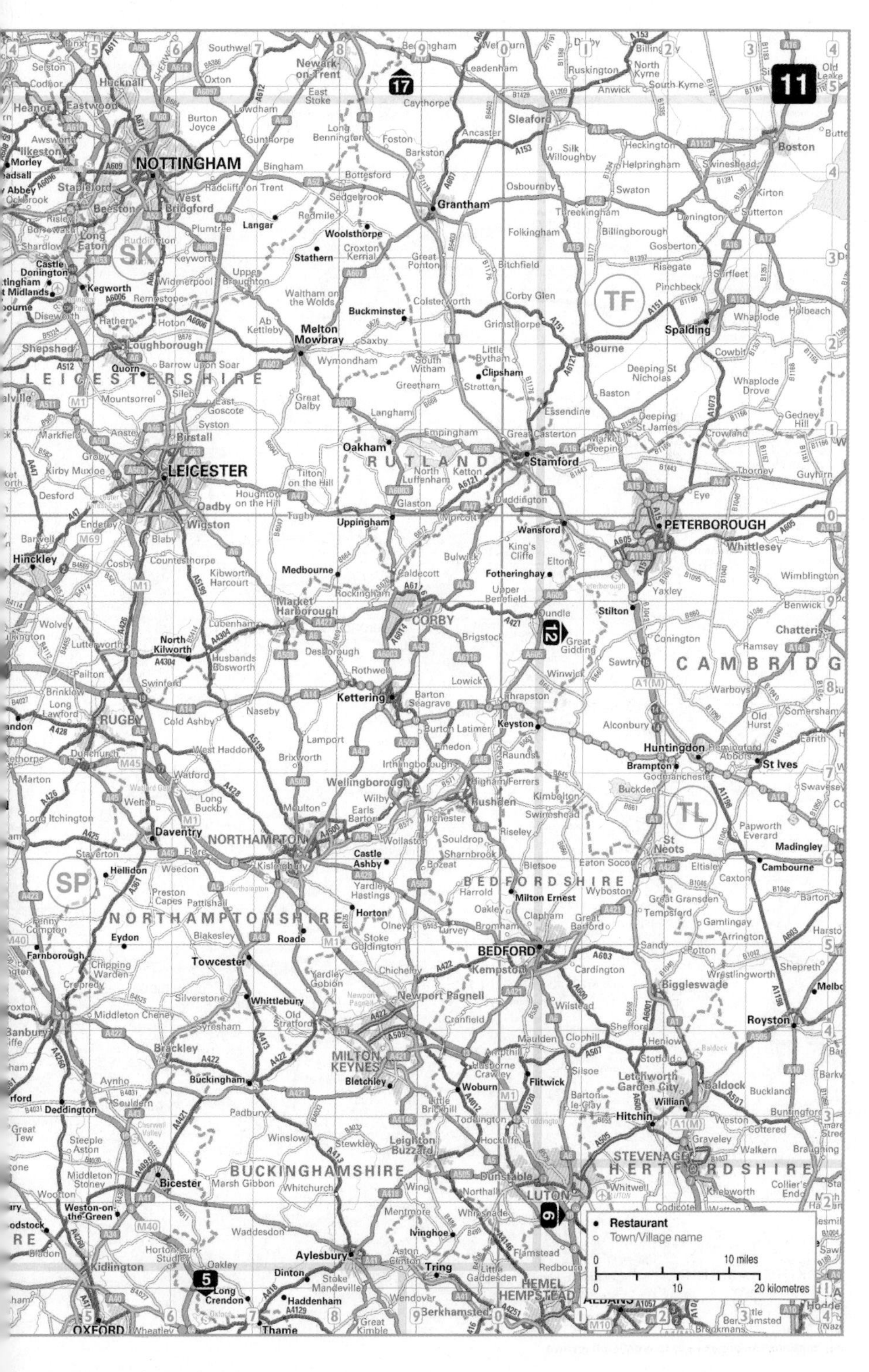

11
17
12
6
5
NOTTINGHAM
LEICESTER
PETERBOROUGH
NORTHAMPTON
BEDFORD
MILTON KEYNES
LUTON
OXFORD
LEICESTERSHIRE
RUTLAND
NORTHAMPTONSHIRE
BEDFORDSHIRE
BUCKINGHAMSHIRE
HERTFORDSHIRE
CAMBRIDG
SK
TF
SP
TL
Newark-on-Trent
Grantham
Sleaford
Boston
Spalding
Stamford
Oakham
Uppingham
Melton Mowbray
Loughborough
Hinckley
Rugby
Daventry
Kettering
Corby
Wellingborough
Rushden
Huntingdon
St Ives
St Neots
Biggleswade
Royston
Baldock
Letchworth Garden City
Hitchin
Stevenage
Dunstable
Leighton Buzzard
Aylesbury
Tring
Bicester
Buckingham
Brackley
Banbury
Towcester
Newport Pagnell
Bletchley
Woburn
Flitwick
Kidlington
Thame
Hemel Hempstead
Berkhamsted
Bourne
Market Harborough
Oundle
Langar
Woolsthorpe
Stathern
Buckminster
Clipsham
Medbourne
Fotheringhay
Stilton
North Kilworth
Keyston
Brampton
Hellidon
Castle Ashby
Horton
Milton Ernest
Eydon
Roade
Whittlebury
Deddington
Weston-on-the-Green
Long Crendon
Haddenham
Dinton
Ivinghoe
Madingley
Cambourne
Melbourn
Quorn
Kegworth
Restaurant
Town/Village name
0
10 miles
10
20 kilometres

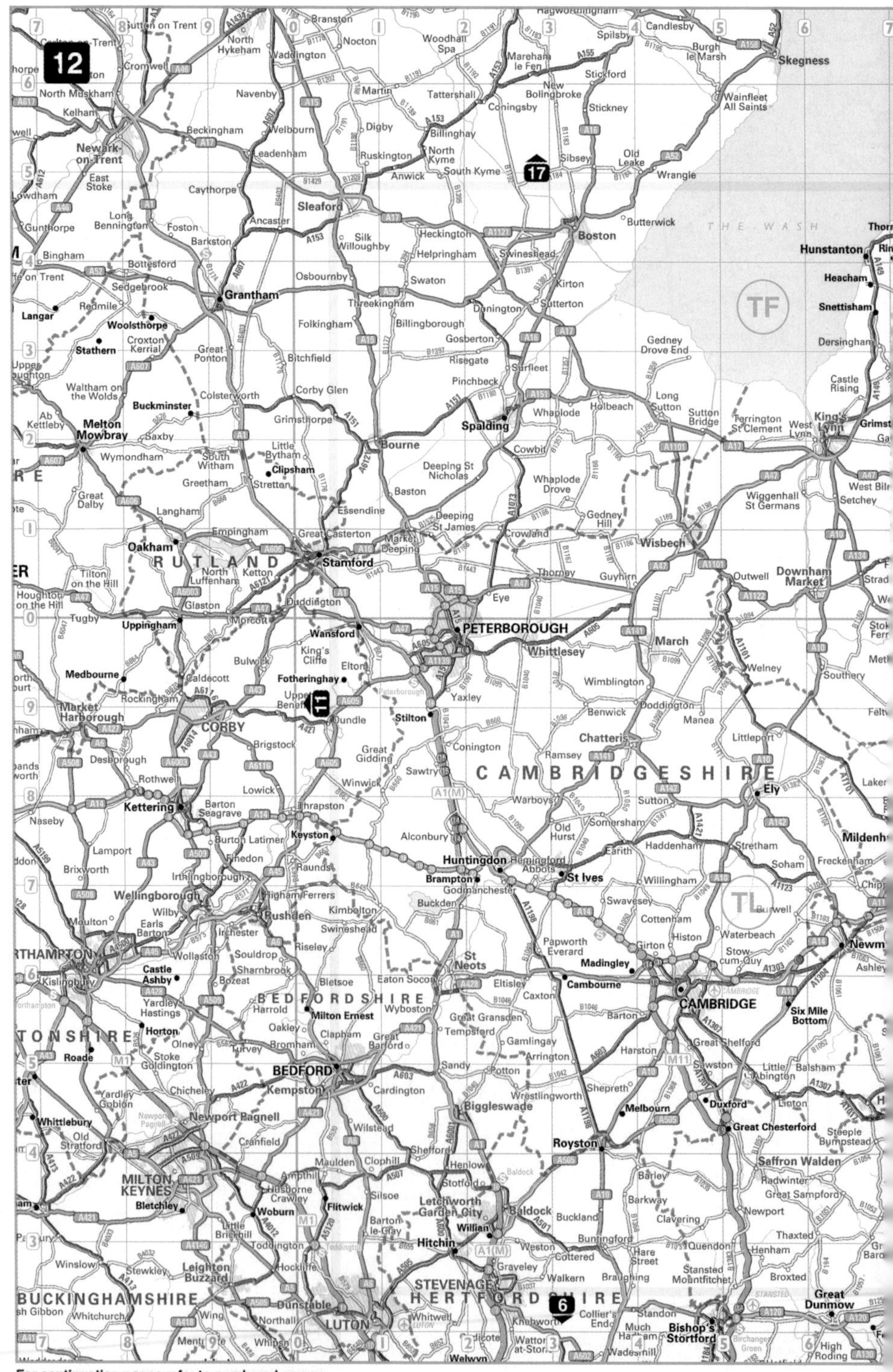

For continuation pages refer to numbered arrows

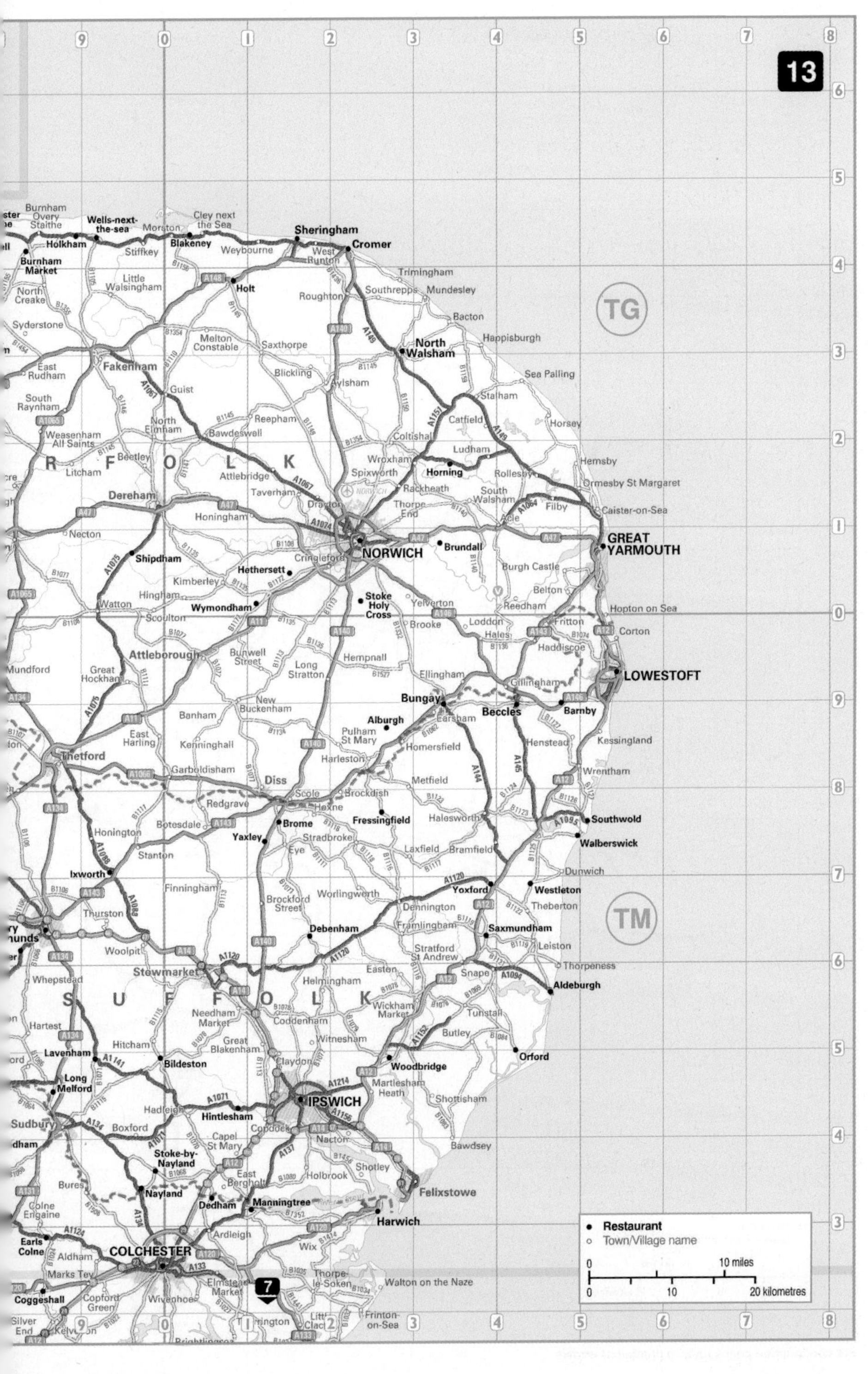

13
TG
TM
Burnham Overy Staithe
Wells-next-the-sea
Holkham
Morston
Cley next the Sea
Blakeney
Sheringham
Cromer
Burnham Market
Stiffkey
Weybourne
West Runton
Little Walsingham
North Creake
Holt
Trimingham
Roughton
Southrepps
Mundesley
Syderstone
Bacton
Melton Constable
Saxthorpe
North Walsham
Happisburgh
East Rudham
Fakenham
Blickling
Sea Palling
Guist
Aylsham
South Raynham
Stalham
Weasenham All Saints
North Elmham
Reepham
Catfield
Horsey
Bawdeswell
Coltishall
Ludham
Hemsby
Beetley
Litcham
Attlebridge
Wroxham
Horning
Rollesby
Ormesby St Margaret
Dereham
Spixworth
Taverham
Rackheath
South Walsham
Drayton
Thorpe End
Filby
Acle
Caister-on-Sea
Honingham
Necton
GREAT YARMOUTH
NORWICH
Brundall
Shipdham
Cringleford
Hethersett
Burgh Castle
Kimberley
Belton
Hingham
Stoke Holy Cross
Yelverton
Reedham
Watton
Wymondham
Hopton on Sea
Scoulton
Brooke
Loddon
Fritton
Hales
Corton
Haddiscoe
Attleborough
Bunwell Street
Hempnall
Mundford
Great Hockham
Long Stratton
LOWESTOFT
Ellingham
Gillingham
Bungay
New Buckenham
Beccles
Barnby
Banham
Alburgh
Earsham
East Harling
Pulham St Mary
Kessingland
Kenninghall
Homersfield
Henstead
Thetford
Harleston
Garboldisham
Wrentham
Diss
Metfield
Scole
Brockdish
Redgrave
Hoxne
Southwold
Botesdale
Brome
Fressingfield
Halesworth
Honington
Yaxley
Stradbroke
Walberswick
Eye
Laxfield
Bramfield
Stanton
Dunwich
Ixworth
Yoxford
Westleton
Finningham
Worlingworth
Theberton
Thurston
Brockford Street
Dennington
Framlingham
Saxmundham
Debenham
Woolpit
Stratford St Andrew
Leiston
Thorpeness
Stowmarket
Easton
Snape
Aldeburgh
Whepstead
Helmingham
S U F F O L K
Needham Market
Wickham Market
Tunstall
Hartest
Coddenham
Witnesham
Butley
Hitcham
Great Blakenham
Orford
Lavenham
Bildeston
Claydon
Woodbridge
Long Melford
Martlesham Heath
IPSWICH
Hadleigh
Shottisham
Hintlesham
Sudbury
Boxford
Copdock
Nacton
Capel St Mary
Bawdsey
Stoke-by-Nayland
Shotley
East Bergholt
Holbrook
Bures
Felixstowe
Nayland
Dedham
Manningtree
Colne Engaine
Harwich
Ardleigh
Earls Colne
Aldham
COLCHESTER
Wix
Marks Tey
Thorpe-le-Soken
Walton on the Naze
Elmstead Market
Coggeshall
Copford Green
Wivenhoe
Frinton-on-Sea
Silver End
Kelvedon
7
Restaurant
Town/Village name
0
10 miles
0
10
20 kilometres

For continuation pages refer to numbered arrows

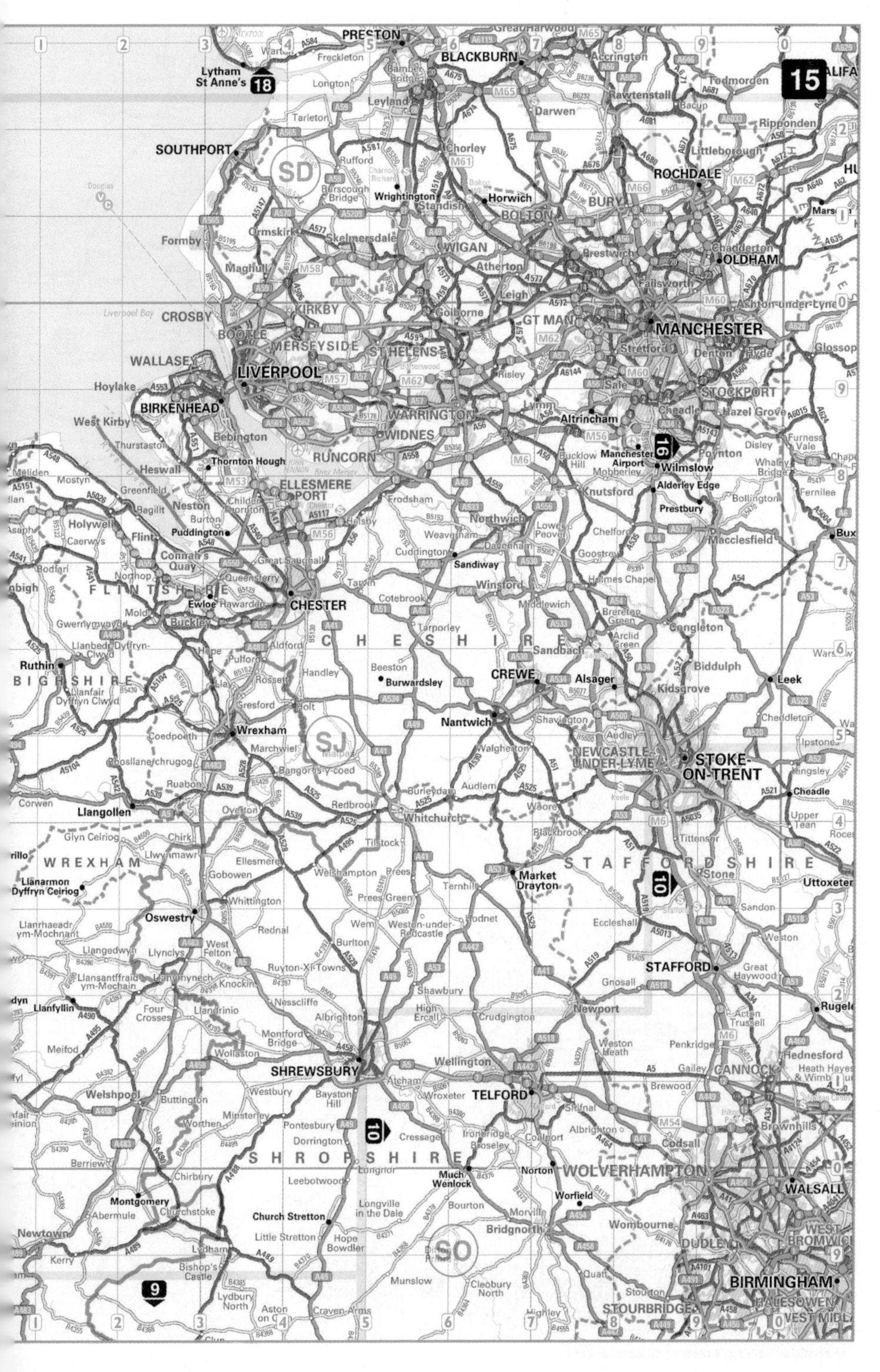

15
PRESTON
BLACKBURN
Freckleton
Accrington
Lytham
St Anne's
18
Longton
Todmorden
Leyland
Rawtenstall
Bacup
Darwen
Ripponden
Tarleton
SOUTHPORT
Chorley
Littleborough
Rufford
ROCHDALE
SD
Burscough Bridge
Wrightington
Standish
Horwich
BURY
BOLTON
Formby
Ormskirk
Skelmersdale
WIGAN
Prestwich
Chadderton
OLDHAM
Maghull
Atherton
Leigh
Failsworth
Liverpool Bay
CROSBY
KIRKBY
Golborne
GT MAN
Ashton-under-Lyne
MANCHESTER
BOOTLE
MERSEYSIDE
ST HELENS
Stretford
Denton
Hyde
Glossop
WALLASEY
LIVERPOOL
Risley
Sale
Hoylake
STOCKPORT
BIRKENHEAD
WARRINGTON
Lymm
Altrincham
Cheadle
Hazel Grove
West Kirby
Bebington
WIDNES
Manchester Airport
16
Disley
Thurstaston
Poynton
Furness Vale
Thornton Hough
RUNCORN
Bucklow Hill
Wilmslow
Mobberley
Whaley Bridge
Heswall
Mostyn
ELLESMERE PORT
Alderley Edge
Greenfield
Neston
Frodsham
Knutsford
Bollington
Bagillt
Burton
Prestbury
Holywell
Flint
Puddington
Helsby
Northwich
Weaverham
Chelford
Macclesfield
Buxton
Caerwys
Connah's Quay
Cuddington
Davenham
Lower Peover
Goostrey
Bodfari
Northop
Queensferry
Great Saughall
Sandiway
Tarvin
Winsford
Holmes Chapel
FLINTSHIRE
Ewloe
Hawarden
CHESTER
Cotebrook
Middlewich
Mold
Buckley
Brereton Green
Gwernymynydd
Tarporley
Congleton
Arclid Green
CHESHIRE
Sandbach
Llanbedr Dyffryn-Clwyd
Hope
Aldford
Pulford
Ruthin
DENBIGHSHIRE
Beeston
Burwardsley
Biddulph
Rossett
Handley
CREWE
Alsager
Leek
Llanfair Dyffryn Clwyd
Kidsgrove
Gresford
Holt
Nantwich
Shavington
Cheddleton
Coedpoeth
Wrexham
SJ
Audley
Marchwiel
Malpas
Walgherton
NEWCASTLE-UNDER-LYME
STOKE-ON-TRENT
Ipstones
Rhosllanerchrugog
Bangor-is-y-coed
Kingsley
Ruabon
Audlem
Cheadle
Burleydam
Keele
Corwen
Llangollen
Redbrook
Woore
Overton
Whitchurch
Upper Tean
Glyn Ceiriog
Chirk
Tilstock
Blackbrook
Tittensor
Llwynmawr
Ellesmere
WREXHAM
STAFFORDSHIRE
Market Drayton
Stone
Llanarmon Dyffryn Ceiriog
Gobowen
Welshampton
Prees
Uttoxeter
Ternhill
Whittington
Prees Green
10
Sandon
Llanrhaeadr-ym-Mochnant
Oswestry
Wem
Hodnet
Weston-under-Redcastle
Eccleshall
Rednal
Weston
West Felton
Burlton
Llangedwyn
Llynclys
Ruyton-XI-Towns
Stafford
Great Haywood
Llansantffraid-ym-Mechain
Llanymynech
Knockin
Gnosall
Shawbury
Llanfyllin
Four Crosses
Nesscliffe
Llandrinio
High Ercall
Crudgington
Newport
Acton Trussell
Rugeley
Albrighton
Montford Bridge
Meifod
Weston Heath
Penkridge
Wollaston
Hednesford
Wellington
SHREWSBURY
Gailey
CANNOCK
Heath Hayes & Wimblebury
Atcham
Brewood
Welshpool
Westbury
Bayston Hill
Wroxeter
TELFORD
Shifnal
Buttington
Minsterley
Albrighton
Brownhills
Worthen
Pontesbury
10
Cressage
Ironbridge
Broseley
Coalport
Codsall
Dorrington
SHROPSHIRE
Berriew
Longnor
Much Wenlock
Norton
WOLVERHAMPTON
Chirbury
Leebotwood
WALSALL
Montgomery
Longville in the Dale
Worfield
Abermule
Churchstoke
Church Stretton
Bourton
Morville
Wombourne
Newtown
Little Stretton
Hope Bowdler
Bridgnorth
WEST BROMWICH
Lydham
DUDLEY
Kerry
Bishop's Castle
SO
9
Munslow
Cleobury North
BIRMINGHAM
Lydbury North
Quatt
HALESOWEN
Aston on Clun
Craven Arms
Stourton
Highley
STOURBRIDGE
WEST MIDLANDS

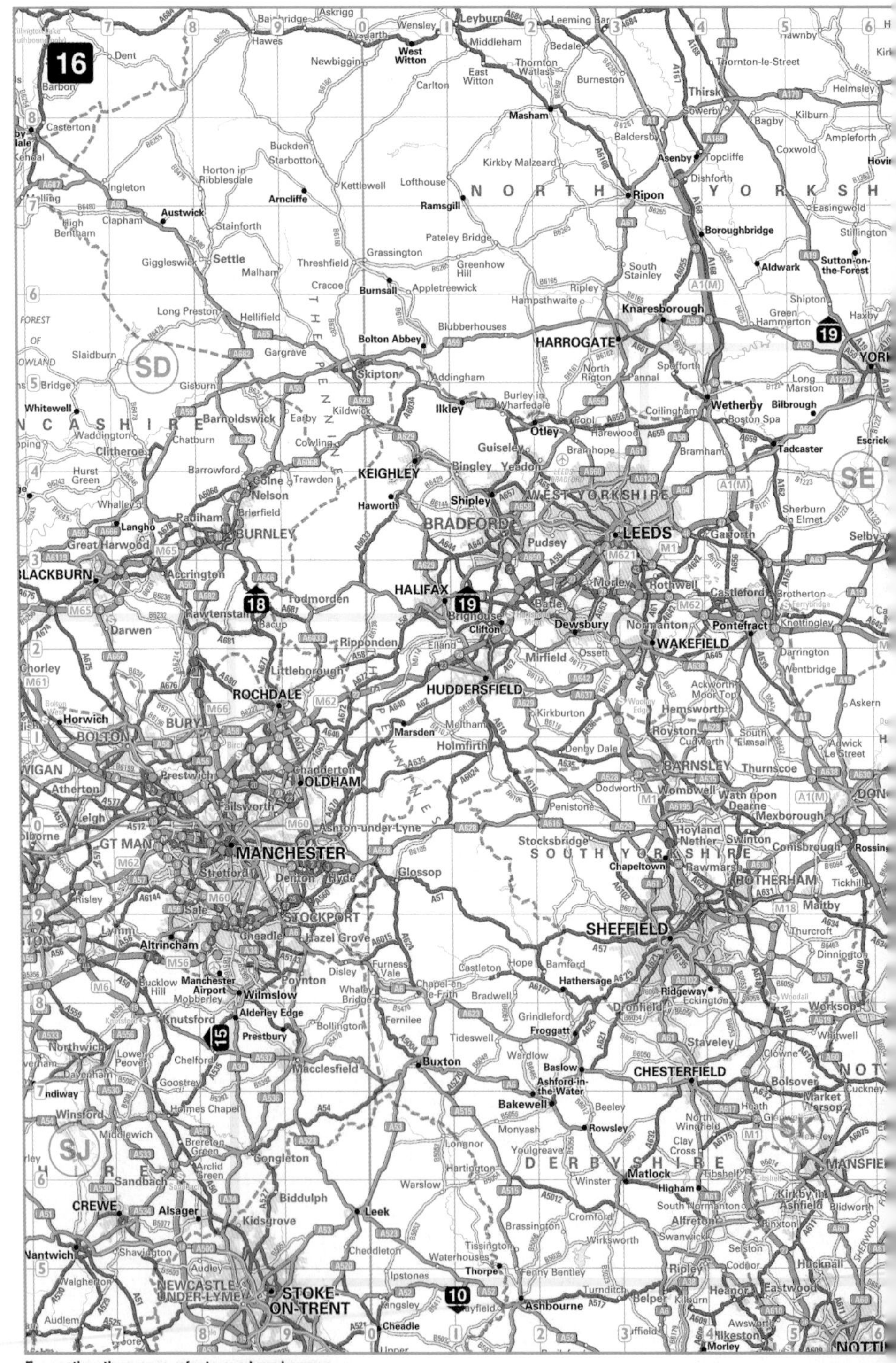

For continuation pages refer to numbered arrows

17
Restaurant
Town/Village name
10 miles
20 kilometres
Scarborough
Hackness
Lastingham
Cropton
Lockton
Wrelton
Pickering
Marton
Thornton le Dale
East Ayton
Seamer
Cayton
Snainton
Brompton
Filey
Flixton
Kirby Misperton
Staxton
Sherburn
Hunmanby
Reighton
Bempton
Flamborough Head
Flamborough
Rillington
Malton
Norton
North Grimston
Burton Fleming
Rudston
Carnaby
Bridlington
Kirkham
Sledmere
Langtoft
Kilham
Burton Agnes
Fridaythorpe
Wetwang
Driffield
Barmston
Skipsea
Stamford Bridge
North Dalton
Bainton
North Frodingham
Beeford
Atwick
Wilberfoss
EAST RIDING OF YORKSHIRE
Middleton on the Wolds
Brandesburton
Hornsea
Barmby Moor
Pocklington
Leven
TA
Shiptonthorpe
Market Weighton
Holme upon Spalding Moor
Beverley
Aldbrough
Walkington
North Cave
Sproatley
South Cave
Cottingham
Willerby
Withernsea
Elloughton
Hessle
KINGSTON UPON HULL
Hedon
Goole
Melton
North Ferriby
Winteringham
Patrington
New Holland
Barton upon Humber
Goxhill
Burton upon Stather
Winterton
Easington
River Humber
Immingham Dock
Wootton
Ulceby
Immingham
Crowle
Gunness
SCUNTHORPE
Keelby
GRIMSBY
Spurn Head
Broughton
Wrawby
Cleethorpes
Althorpe
Belton
Barnetby le Wold
Brigg
Humberston
Laceby
Waltham
Scawby
Epworth
Messingham
Swallow
Holton le Clay
Hibaldstow
Caistor
Tetney
North Cotes
Scotter
Haxey
Kirton in Lindsey
Grainthorpe
Ludborough
North Somercotes
Blyton
Saltfleet
Binbrook
Gainsborough
Middle Rasen
Glentham
Market Rasen
Louth
Saundby
Legbourne
Mablethorpe
Ingham
Faldingworth
Lissington
Sutton on Sea
Withern
East Barkwith
Torksey
Sturton by Stow
Wragby
Scamblesby
Alford
Saxilby
Newton on Trent
Huttoft
Bilsby
Langworth
Tetford
Chapel St Leonards
Baumber
Skellingthorpe
LINCOLN
LINCOLNSHIRE
Hogsthorpe
Tuxford
Edlington
Washingborough
Bardney
Horncastle
Ingoldmells
Hagworthingham
Branston
Candlesby
Sutton on Trent
Spilsby
North Hykeham
Nocton
Woodhall Spa
Burgh le Marsh
Skegness
Waddington
Mareham le Fen
Cromwell
Stickford
TF
New Bolingbroke
Navenby
Martin
Tattershall
Coningsby
Wainfleet All Saints
Stickney
Beckingham
Welbourn
Digby
Billinghay
Newark-on-Trent
Leadenham
Ruskington
North Kyme
Sibsey
Old Leake
Wrangle
South Kyme
Anwick
East Stoke
Caythorpe
Sleaford
11
12
Long Bennington
Ancaster
Butterwick
THE WASH
Thornham
Foston
Silk Willoughby
Hecking
Boston
Hunstanton
Ringstead
Swineshead
Helpringham
A165
A170
A64
A169
A1039
A614
A166
A1079
A1034
A163
A1035
A1174
A164
A63
M62
A1033
A161
A1077
A15
A160
A180
M181
M180
A18
A1173
A46
A1084
A159
A631
A157
A1031
A16
A153
A1104
A52
A1111
A156
A1500
A57
A158
A1028
A1133
A1434
A607
A155
A17
A1121
A153
A1
A19

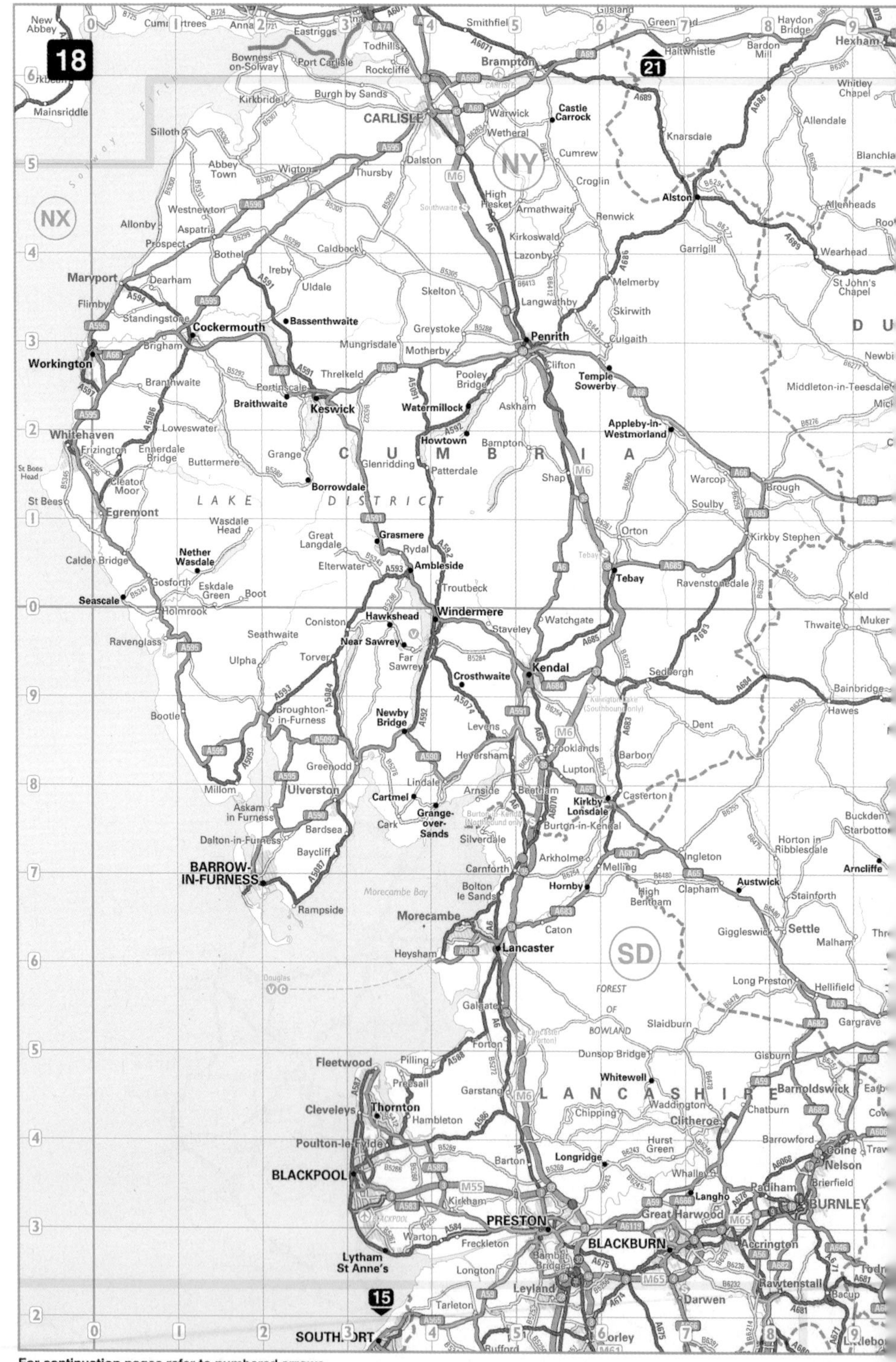

For continuation pages refer to numbered arrows

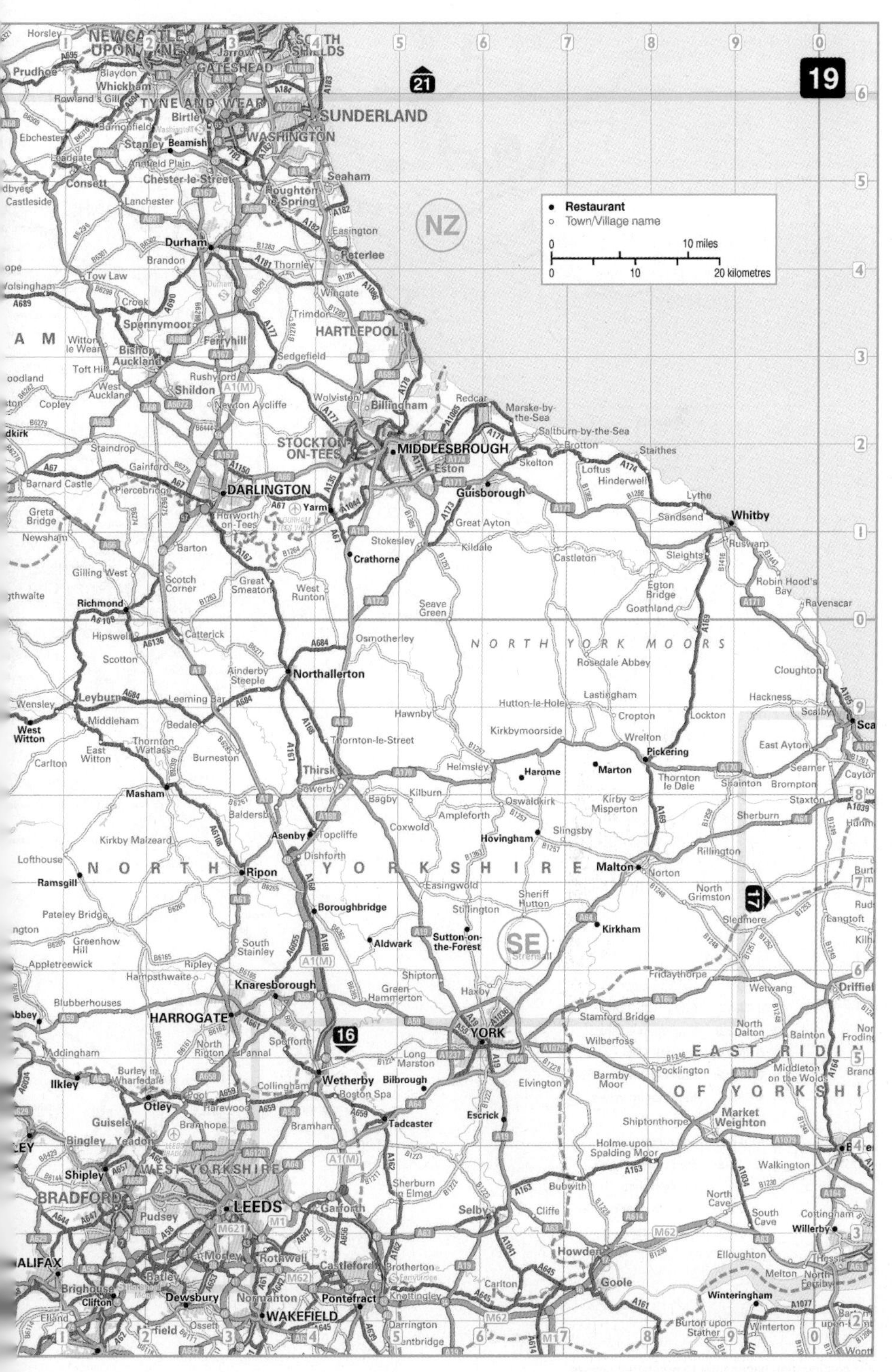
19
21
16
17
NZ
SE
Restaurant
Town/Village name
0
10 miles
0
10
20 kilometres
NEWCASTLE UPON TYNE
GATESHEAD
SOUTH SHIELDS
TYNE AND WEAR
SUNDERLAND
WASHINGTON
Horsley
Prudhoe
Blaydon
Whickham
Rowland's Gill
Birtley
Ebchester
Burnopfield
Stanley
Beamish
Leadgate
Annfield Plain
Consett
Chester-le-Street
Seaham
Houghton-le-Spring
Castleside
Lanchester
Easington
Durham
Peterlee
Brandon
Thornley
Tow Law
Wolsingham
Wingate
Crook
Trimdon
Spennymoor
HARTLEPOOL
Ferryhill
Witton le Wear
Bishop Auckland
Sedgefield
Toft Hill
West Auckland
Rushyford
Shildon
Newton Aycliffe
Copley
Wolviston
Billingham
Redcar
Marske-by-the-Sea
Saltburn-by-the-Sea
Brotton
Staithes
Staindrop
STOCKTON-ON-TEES
MIDDLESBROUGH
Skelton
Loftus
Hinderwell
Gainford
Eston
Barnard Castle
Piercebridge
DARLINGTON
Guisborough
Lythe
Yarm
Sandsend
Whitby
Greta Bridge
Hurworth-on-Tees
Great Ayton
Newsham
Stokesley
Kildale
Ruswarp
Barton
Crathorne
Castleton
Sleights
Gilling West
Scotch Corner
Great Smeaton
West Rounton
Egton Bridge
Robin Hood's Bay
Richmond
Seave Green
Goathland
Ravenscar
Hipswell
Catterick
Osmotherley
NORTH YORK MOORS
Scotton
Ainderby Steeple
Northallerton
Rosedale Abbey
Cloughton
Wensley
Leyburn
Leeming Bar
Lastingham
Hackness
Hutton-le-Hole
Scalby
West Witton
Middleham
Bedale
Hawnby
Cropton
Lockton
Kirkbymoorside
Wrelton
Thornton Watlass
Thornton-le-Street
Pickering
East Ayton
East Witton
Carlton
Burneston
Thirsk
Helmsley
Harome
Marton
Seamer
Cayton
Thornton le Dale
Snainton
Brompton
Masham
Sowerby
Kilburn
Bagby
Oswaldkirk
Kirby Misperton
Staxton
Baldersby
Ampleforth
Sherburn
Coxwold
Asenby
Topcliffe
Hovingham
Slingsby
Kirkby Malzeard
Rillington
Dishforth
Lofthouse
NORTH YORKSHIRE
Ripon
Malton
Norton
Ramsgill
Easingwold
Sheriff Hutton
North Grimston
Pateley Bridge
Boroughbridge
Stillington
Sledmere
Langtoft
Kirkham
Greenhow Hill
South Stainley
Aldwark
Sutton-on-the-Forest
Strensall
Appletreewick
Ripley
Shipton
Fridaythorpe
Driffield
Hampsthwaite
Knaresborough
Green Hammerton
Haxby
Wetwang
Blubberhouses
HARROGATE
Stamford Bridge
North Dalton
Bainton
YORK
Addingham
North Rigton
Pannal
Spofforth
Long Marston
Wilberfoss
EAST RIDING OF YORKSHIRE
Ilkley
Burley in Wharfedale
Collingham
Wetherby
Bilbrough
Elvington
Pocklington
Barmby Moor
Middleton on the Wolds
Otley
Pool
Harewood
Boston Spa
Escrick
Market Weighton
Guiseley
Bramhope
Bramham
Tadcaster
Shiptonthorpe
Bingley
Yeadon
Holme upon Spalding Moor
Shipley
WEST YORKSHIRE
Walkington
BRADFORD
Sherburn in Elmet
Bubwith
LEEDS
Garforth
North Cave
Cottingham
Pudsey
Selby
Cliffe
South Cave
Willerby
HALIFAX
Morley
Rothwell
Howden
Ellougton
Batley
Castleford
Brotherton
Carlton
Goole
Melton
North Ferriby
Brighouse
Dewsbury
Normanton
Pontefract
Knottingley
Winteringham
Clifton
Elland
Ossett
WAKEFIELD
Darrington
Burton upon Stather
Winterton
Wentbridge
A1(M)
A19
A1
A64
A59
A170
A169
A171
A174
A66
A167
A61
A168
A62
M1
M62
M621

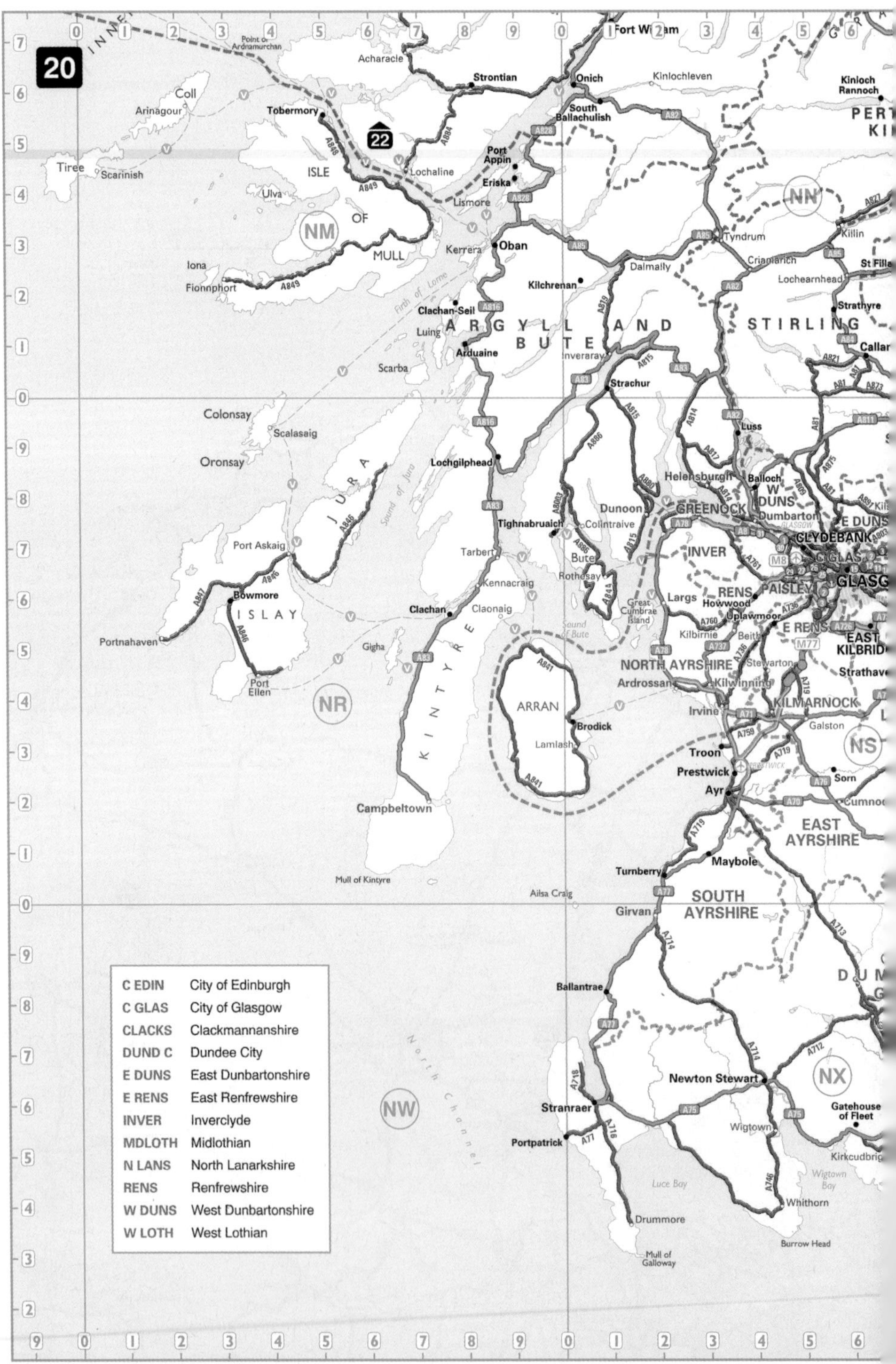

For continuation pages refer to numbered arrows

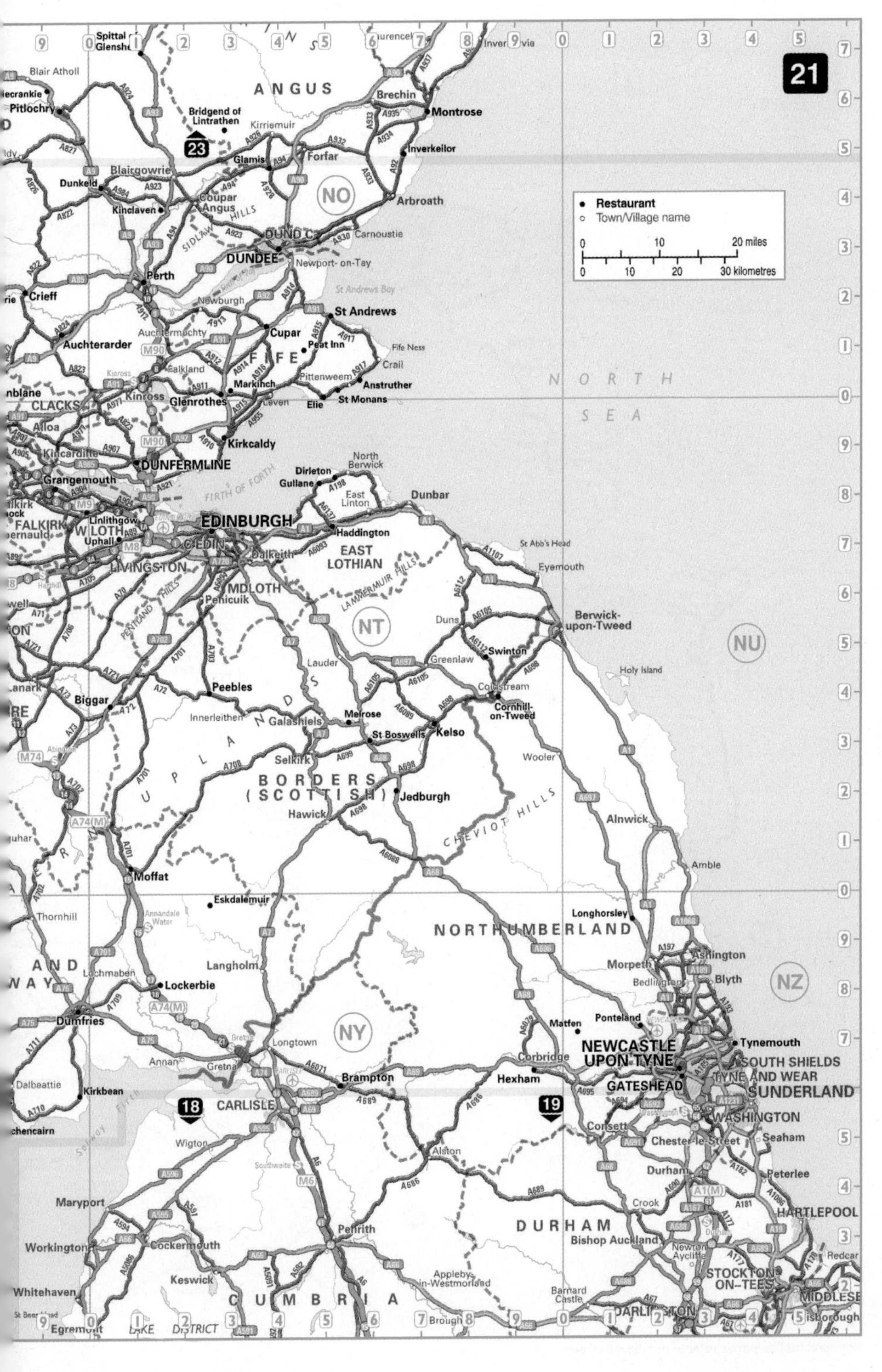
Restaurant
Town/Village name
0 10 20 miles
0 10 20 30 kilometres
ANGUS
Blair Atholl
Pitlochry
Bridgend of Lintrathen
Kirriemuir
Brechin
Montrose
Inverkeilor
Glamis
Forfar
Blairgowrie
Dunkeld
Coupar Angus
Kinclaven
Arbroath
SIDLAW HILLS
Carnoustie
DUNDEE
Newport-on-Tay
Perth
Crieff
St Andrews Bay
Newburgh
St Andrews
Auchtermuchty
Cupar
Peat Inn
Fife Ness
Auchterarder
FIFE
Crail
Falkland
Kinross
Pittenweem
Anstruther
Markinch
Glenrothes
Leven
Elie
St Monans
CLACKS
Alloa
Kincardine
Kirkcaldy
DUNFERMLINE
NORTH SEA
North Berwick
Dirleton
Gullane
FIRTH OF FORTH
East Linton
Dunbar
Grangemouth
FALKIRK
Linlithgow
W LOTH
EDINBURGH
Haddington
Uphall
Dalkeith
EAST LOTHIAN
St Abb's Head
Eyemouth
LIVINGSTON
MDLOTH
Penicuik
LAMMERMUIR HILLS
PENTLAND HILLS
Berwick-upon-Tweed
Duns
Swinton
NT
NU
NO
Lauder
Greenlaw
Holy Island
Coldstream
Peebles
Cornhill-on-Tweed
Biggar
Innerleithen
Galashiels
Melrose
Kelso
St Boswells
UPLANDS
Selkirk
Wooler
BORDERS (SCOTTISH)
Jedburgh
Hawick
CHEVIOT HILLS
Alnwick
Amble
Moffat
Eskdalemuir
Thornhill
Longhorsley
NORTHUMBERLAND
Annandale Water
Langholm
Morpeth
Ashington
Lochmaben
Bedlington
Blyth
Lockerbie
NZ
Dumfries
Matfen
Ponteland
NY
Longtown
Tynemouth
NEWCASTLE UPON TYNE
Annan
Gretna
Corbridge
SOUTH SHIELDS
Brampton
Hexham
TYNE AND WEAR
Dalbeattie
GATESHEAD
SUNDERLAND
Kirkbean
CARLISLE
WASHINGTON
Solway Firth
Consett
Wigton
Chester-le-Street
Seaham
Alston
Southwaite
Durham
Peterlee
Maryport
Crook
HARTLEPOOL
DURHAM
Workington
Cockermouth
Penrith
Bishop Auckland
Newton Aycliffe
Redcar
Keswick
Appleby-in-Westmorland
STOCKTON-ON-TEES
Whitehaven
Barnard Castle
CUMBRIA
DARLINGTON
St Bees Head
Egremont
LAKE DISTRICT
Brough
18
19
23

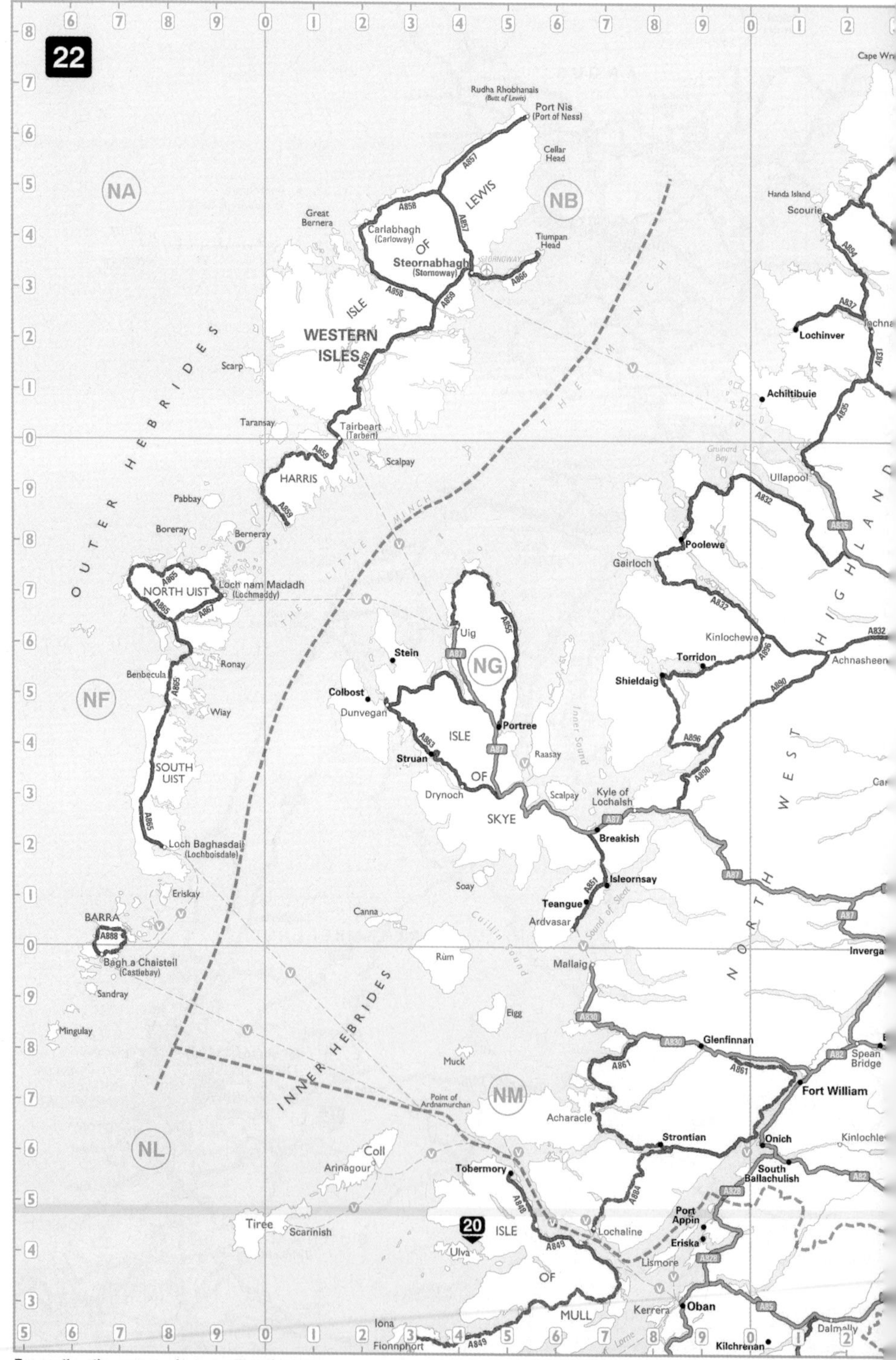

For continuation pages refer to numbered arrows

Restaurant
Town/Village name
0 10 20 miles
0 10 20 30 kilometres
Dunnet Head
Scrabster
Thurso
Gills
John o' Groats
Duncansby Head
Strathy Point
Melvich
Bettyhill
Tongue
Wick
Lybster
Dunbeath
Helmsdale
Brora
Golspie
Lairg
Altnaharra
Bonar Bridge
Dornoch
Tain
HIGHLAND
Alness
Invergordon
Cromarty
MORAY FIRTH
Dingwall
Fortrose
Nairn
Forres
Lossiemouth
Elgin
Buckie
Cullen
Portsoy
Banff
Fraserburgh
Peterhead
MORAY
Rothes
Archiestown
Craigellachie
Aberlour
Dufftown
Keith
Aberchirder
Turriff
Huntly
Muir of Ord
INVERNESS
Grantown-on-Spey
Carrbridge
Nethy Bridge
Boat of Garten
Tomintoul
Aviemore
Monadhliath Mountains
Kingussie
Newtonmore
CAIRNGORM MOUNTAINS
Oldmeldrum
Ellon
Inverurie
Kintore
Dyce
Alford
ABERDEEN CITY
ABERDEEN
ABERDEENSHIRE
Ballater
Aboyne
Banchory
Braemar
Stonehaven
GRAMPIAN MOUNTAINS
Spittal of Glenshee
Laurencekirk
Inverbervie
Blair Atholl
Killiecrankie
Kinloch Rannoch
Pitlochry
ANGUS
Brechin
Montrose
Bridgend of Lintrathen
Kirriemuir
PERTH AND KINROSS
Aberfeldy
Glamis
Forfar
Inverkeilor
Arbroath
Dunkeld
Blairgowrie
Coupar Angus
Kinclaven
SIDLAW HILLS
Killin
Carnoustie
DUNDEE
Newport-on-Tay
St Fillans
Comrie
Crieff
Perth
St Andrews Bay
NC
ND
NH
NJ
NK
NN
NO
21

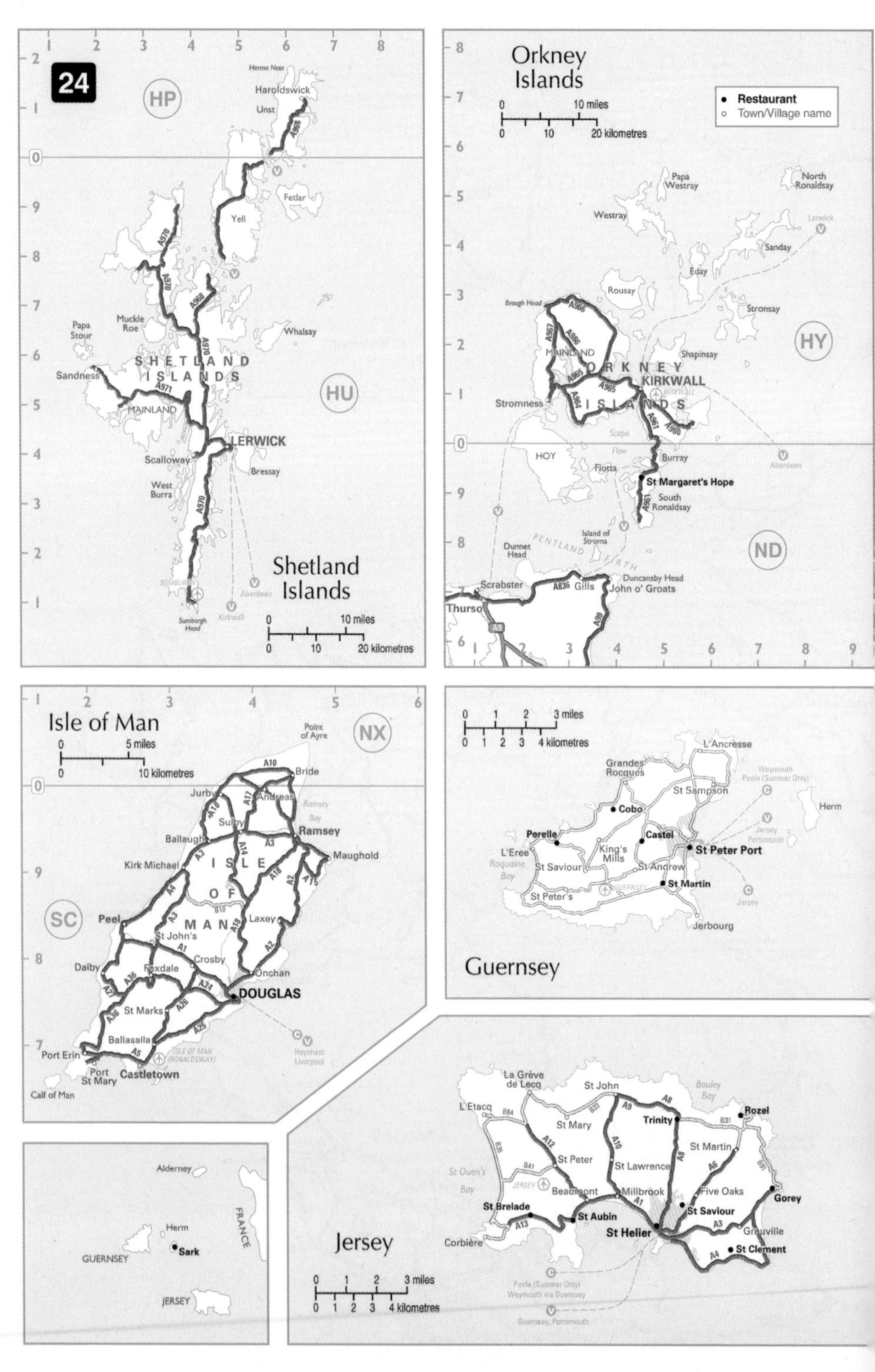

24
Shetland Islands
0 10 miles
0 10 20 kilometres
HP
HU
Herma Ness
Haroldswick
Unst
Fetlar
Yell
Whalsay
Papa Stour
Muckle Roe
SHETLAND ISLANDS
Sandness
MAINLAND
LERWICK
Scalloway
Bressay
West Burra
SUMBURGH
Sumburgh Head
Kirkwall
Aberdeen
A968
A970
A971
Orkney Islands
0 10 miles
0 10 20 kilometres
Restaurant
Town/Village name
Papa Westray
North Ronaldsay
Westray
Lerwick
Sanday
Eday
Rousay
Stronsay
Brough Head
HY
MAINLAND
ORKNEY ISLANDS
Shapinsay
KIRKWALL
Stromness
Scapa Flow
HOY
Flotta
Burray
St Margaret's Hope
South Ronaldsay
Aberdeen
Island of Stroma
PENTLAND FIRTH
Dunnet Head
ND
Duncansby Head
Scrabster
Gills
John o' Groats
Thurso
A966
A967
A986
A965
A964
A961
A960
A836
A99
A9
Isle of Man
0 5 miles
0 10 kilometres
Point of Ayre
NX
Bride
Jurby
Andreas
Ramsey Bay
Sulby
Ballaugh
Ramsey
Maughold
Kirk Michael
ISLE OF MAN
SC
Peel
Laxey
St John's
Crosby
Dalby
Foxdale
Onchan
DOUGLAS
St Marks
Ballasalla
Port Erin
ISLE OF MAN (RONALDSWAY)
Heysham Liverpool
Port St Mary
Castletown
Calf of Man
A10
A17
A3
A14
A18
A2
A15
A4
A1
A36
A27
A24
A26
A25
A5
B10
Guernsey
0 1 2 3 miles
0 1 2 3 4 kilometres
L'Ancresse
Grandes Rocques
St Sampson
Weymouth Poole (Summer Only)
Herm
Cobo
Jersey Portsmouth
Perelle
Castel
L'Eree
King's Mills
St Peter Port
Roquaine Bay
St Saviour
St Andrew
St Martin
GUERNSEY
St Peter's
Jersey
Jerbourg
Alderney
FRANCE
Herm
Sark
GUERNSEY
JERSEY
Jersey
0 1 2 3 miles
0 1 2 3 4 kilometres
La Grève de Lecq
St John
Bouley Bay
L'Etacq
Rozel
Trinity
St Mary
St Martin
St Peter
St Ouen's Bay
St Lawrence
JERSEY
Beaumont
Millbrook
Five Oaks
St Brelade
St Aubin
St Saviour
Gorey
St Helier
Grouville
Corbière
St Clement
Poole (Summer Only) Weymouth via Guernsey
Guernsey, Portsmouth
A8
A9
A10
A12
A6
A1
A3
A4
A13
B31
B33
B35
B41
B64

Index of Restaurants

0-9

1 Lombard Street - Fine Dining Restaurant, LONDON EC3 **259**
1 Up, NORWICH **374**
152 Aldeburgh, ALDEBURGH **425**
1492 Latin Fusion, LONDON SW6 **297**
1614, BANGOR **652**
2 Quail Restaurant & Rooms, DORNOCH **579**
22 Chesterton Road, CAMBRIDGE **53**
22 Mill Street, CHAGFORD **114**
3 Monkeys Restaurant, LONDON SE24 **273**
36 on the Quay, EMSWORTH **187**
5 North Street, WINCHCOMBE **172**
60 Hope Street Restaurant, BIRKENHEAD **365**
63 Tay Street, PERTH **598**
947AD at the Royalist, STOW-ON-THE-WOLD **168**

A

A Touch of Novelli at the White Horse, HARPENDEN **202**
Abbey Restaurant, The, PENZANCE **72**
Abbeyglen Castle Hotel, CLIFDEN **665**
Abode Hotel Glasgow, GLASGOW **571**
Absolute End, The, ST PETER PORT **521**
Acanthus Restaurant, PERTH **597**
Acorn Inn, The, EVERSHOT **140**
Actons Hotel, KINSALE **660**
Adlard's Restaurant, NORWICH **371**
Admiralty Restaurant, The, LONDON WC2 **349**
Agaric, ASHBURTON **110**
Aghadoe Heights Hotel, KILLARNEY **669**
Agni, LONDON W6 **339**
Ah-So Japanese Restaurant, NORWICH **372**
Airds Hotel, PORT APPIN **540**
Al Duca, LONDON SW1 **273**
Alastair Little Restaurant, LONDON W1 **306**
Alba Restaurant, ST IVES **75**
Alba Restaurant, The, BREAKISH **605**
Alba, LONDON EC1 **255**
Albannach, LONDON WC2 **349**
Albannach, The, LOCHINVER **583**
Albright Hussey Manor Hotel & Restaurant, SHREWSBURY **406**
Alchemy Restaurant, DUNDEE **550**
Aldens, BELFAST **650**
Alderley Edge Hotel, ALDERLEY EDGE **58**
Aldwark Manor, ALDWARK **490**
Alexander House Hotel & Utopia Spa, TURNERS HILL **460**
Alexandra Hotel, LYME REGIS **142**
Alias Hotel Barcelona, EXETER **116**
Alias Hotel Rossetti, MANCHESTER **172**
Alloro, LONDON W1 **306**
Almeida Restaurant, LONDON N1 **261**
Alton Grange Hotel, ALTON **180**
Alverton Manor, TRURO **80**
Amaya, LONDON SW1 **274**
Amerdale House Hotel, ARNCLIFFE **490**
Ana Bela, CARDIFF **617**
Anatolies, CAMBRIDGE **53**
Anchor & Hope, The, LONDON SE1 **267**
Anchor Inn, The, ELY **55**
Anchor, The, WALBERSWICK **435**
Anchorage, The, TOBERMORY **605**
Andrew Fairlie @ Gleneagles, AUCHTERARDER **594**
Andrews on the Weir, PORLOCK **415**
Angel & Royal Hotel, GRANTHAM **226**
Angel Hotel - Abbeygate & Vaults Restaurants, BURY ST EDMUNDS **428**
Angel Hotel, ABERGAVENNY **632**
Angel Hotel, LAVENHAM **431**
Angel Inn, The, DEBENHAM **429**
Angel Inn, The, STOKE-BY-NAYLAND **435**
Angel Restaurant, The, LONG CRENDON **47**
Angel Salem, The, LLANDEILO **618**
Angela Hartnett at The Connaught, LONDON W1 **307**
Anglesea Arms, LONDON W6 **339**
Annesley House Hotel, NORWICH **372**
Annie Bailey's, GREAT MISSENDEN **46**
Anokaa, SALISBURY **483**
Anthony's Restaurant, LEEDS **515**
Apicius, CRANBROOK **209**
Apollo Hotel, BASINGSTOKE **181**
Appleby Manor Country House Hotel, APPLEBY-IN-WESTMORLAND **83**
Appletree Country Inn, The, MARTON **499**
Arbutus Hotel, KILLARNEY **669**
Archiestown Hotel, ARCHIESTOWN **592**
Archipelago, LONDON W1 **307**
Arcoona at the Beardmore, CLYDEBANK **549**
Ardagh Hotel, CLIFDEN **665**
Ardanaiseig Hotel, The, KILCHRENAN **537**
Ardencote Manor Hotel, WARWICK **467**
Ardilaun House Hotel & Leisure Club, GALWAY **666**
Ardington Hotel, WORTHING **460**
Ardtara Country House, MAGHERA **654**
Ark, The, LONDON W8 **341**
Arkle, The, CHESTER **60**
Arlington Grill & Brasserie, NORWICH **372**
Arno's Manor Hotel, BRISTOL **41**
Artichoke, The, AMERSHAM **44**
Artigiano, LONDON NW3 **267**
Artillery Tower Restaurant, PLYMOUTH **126**
Artisan, SHEFFIELD **509**
Arundell Arms, LIFTON **123**
Ashdown Park Hotel, FOREST ROW **447**
Ashdown Park Hotel, GOREY **676**
Asia de Cuba, LONDON WC2 **349**
Assaggi, LONDON W2 **336**
Associes, Les, LONDON N8 **264**
Athenaeum Hotel, Bullochs at 116, LONDON W1 **307**
Athenaeum House Hotel, CARRICKMACROSS **676**
Atlantique Hotel, PERELLE **520**
Atrium, EDINBURGH **550**
Auberge du Lac, WELWYN **206**
Aubergine, LONDON SW10 **301**
Auchrannie Country House Hotel, BRODICK **604**
Augustine's Restaurant, CANTERBURY **208**
Aura Kitchen and Bar, LONDON SW1 **287**
Aurora at Great Eastern Hotel, LONDON EC2 **256**
Austwick Traddock, The, AUSTWICK **491**
Automat, LONDON W1 **308**
Avenue, The, LONDON SW1 **274**
Avonmouth, The, CHRISTCHURCH **137**
Awana, LONDON SW3 **288**
Aynsome Manor Hotel, BRAMPTON **86**
Ayudhya Thai Restaurant, KINGSTON UPON THAMES **358**
Azou, LONDON W6 **341**
Aztec Hotel, ALMONDSBURY **157**

B

Babur, LONDON SE23 **273**
Babylon, LONDON W8 **341**
Bachler's Conservatory, OBAN **539**
Bae Abermaw, BARMOUTH **630**
Bailiffscourt Hotel & Health Spa, CLIMPING **454**
Balbirnie House, MARKINCH **565**
Balcary Bay Hotel, AUCHENCAIRN **545**
Balinakill Country House Hotel, CLACHAN **536**
Ballachulish House, SOUTH BALLACHULISH **577**
Ballathie House Hotel, KINCLAVEN **596**
Ballynahinch Castle, RECESS (SRAITH SALACH) **667**
Balmer Lawn Hotel, BROCKENHURST **182**
Baltic, LONDON SE1 **268**
Baltimore Harbour Hotel, BALTIMORE **658**
Bam-Bou, LONDON W1 **308**
Bank Aldwych Restaurant, LONDON WC2 **349**
Bank Restaurant & Bar, BIRMINGHAM **469**
Bank Restaurant, The, CRIEFF **595**
Barbarie Hotel, La, ST MARTIN **520**
Barberstown Castle, STRAFFAN **670**
Barn Again Bistro, NEWCASTLE UPON TYNE **463**
Barnard's Restaurant, DENMEAD **185**
Barnsdale Lodge Hotel, OAKHAM **398**
Barratt's at Ty'N Rhyl, RHYL **627**
Bartley Lodge, CADNAM **185**
Barton Cross Hotel, EXETER **116**
Bath Priory Hotel and Restaurant, The, BATH **409**
Baumann's Brasserie, COGGESHALL **151**
Bay Restaurant, The, PENZANCE **72**
Bay Tree Brasserie at Pound Green Hotel, SHIPDHAM **376**
Bay Tree Hotel, The, BURFORD **387**
Bay Tree, The, MELBOURNE **108**
Bay View, BALLYCOTTON **657**
Beamish Park Hotel, BEAMISH **149**
Bean Tree, The, HARPENDEN **202**
Bear Hotel, CRICKHOWELL **640**

Bear of Rodborough, The, STROUD **168**
Bear Restaurant & Bar, STOCK **156**
Beatrice Kennedy, BELFAST **650**
Beauberry House, LONDON SE21 **272**
Beaulieu Hotel, BEAULIEU **182**
Bedford Lodge Hotel, NEWMARKET **434**
Bedruthan Steps Hotel, MAWGAN PORTH **68**
Beech Hill Hotel, LONDONDERRY **654**
Beech Hill Hotel, WINDERMERE **95**
Beeches Hotel & Victorian Gardens, NORWICH **372**
Beeches Hotel, GRIMSBY **226**
Beechwood Hotel, NORTH WALSHAM **371**
Beiderbecke's Hotel, SCARBOROUGH **502**
Belgo, LONDON NW1 **266**
Belgo, LONDON WC2 **355**
Bell at Skenfrith, The, SKENFRITH **634**
Bell Hotel, The, CHARLBURY **388**
Bell Inn Hotel, STILTON **58**
Bell Inn, BROOK **184**
Bellamy's, LONDON W1 **308**
Bellini - Edinburgh, EDINBURGH **560**
Bellplot House Hotel & Thomas's Restaurant, CHARD **412**
Bells Diner, BRISTOL **41**
Belmont House Hotel, LEICESTER **223**
Belvedere, LONDON W8 **342**
Ben Loyal Hotel, TONGUE **589**
Benares, LONDON W1 **308**
Bentley Kempinski Hotel, The, LONDON SW7 **299**
Bentley's Oyster Bar & Grill, LONDON W1 **309**
Bentley's Restaurant, WANSFORD **58**
Berkeley Square, The, LONDON W1 **309**
Bertie's, ROMSEY **192**
Best Beech Inn, The, WADHURST **451**
Best Western Bruntsfield Hotel, EDINBURGH **551**
Best Western Lee Wood Hotel, BUXTON **105**
Best Western Links Hotel, MONTROSE **536**
Best Western Mount Pleasant Hotel, ROSSINGTON **509**
Best Western Orton Hall Hotel, PETERBOROUGH **57**
Best Western Priory Hotel, BURY ST EDMUNDS **428**
Best Western Valley Hotel & Chez Maws, TELFORD **407**
Best Western Yew Lodge Hotel, NOTTINGHAM EAST MIDLANDS AIRPORT **225**
Bibendum, LONDON SW3 **288**
Bibis, LEEDS **516**
Bibury Court, BIBURY **157**
Big Blue, The, GLASGOW **577**
Bignell Park Hotel, BICESTER **386**
Bildeston Crown, The, BILDESTON **427**
Billesley Manor Hotel, STRATFORD-UPON-AVON **466**
Bindon Country House Hotel & Restaurant, WELLINGTON **418**
Bingham Hotel, Restaurant & Bar, RICHMOND (UPON THAMES) **360**
Birmingham Marriott, BIRMINGHAM **469**
Bishop's Table Hotel, FARNHAM **440**
Bishopsgate House Hotel, BEAUMARIS **612**
Bishopstrow House Hotel, WARMINSTER **484**
Bistro 21, DURHAM **149**
Bistro on the Beach, BOURNEMOUTH **135**
Black Boys Inn, HURLEY **33**
Black Horse Inn, The, CLIFTON **511**
Black Lion Hotel, The, LONG MELFORD **432**
Black Pepper, LONDON SW11 **303**
Blackfriars Restaurant, NEWCASTLE UPON TYNE **461**
Blackwell Ox Inn, The, SUTTON-ON-THE-FOREST **502**
Blagdon Manor, ASHWATER **111**
Blakeney Hotel, The, BLAKENEY **366**
Blanc Brasserie, OXFORD **393**
Blandford Street, LONDON W1 **309**
Bleeding Heart, The, LONDON EC1 **253**
Blenheim House, The, ETWALL **106**
Blue Bicycle, YORK **506**
Blue Elephant, LONDON SW6 **296**
Blue, EDINBURGH **551**
Bluebird Dining Rooms, LONDON SW3 **289**
Bluefish Restaurant, The, PORTLAND **145**
Boar's Head Hotel, The, HARROGATE **496**
Boar's Head, The, ARDINGTON **386**
Boars Head, The, BRISTOL **44**
Boat Hotel - The Capercaille, BOAT OF GARTEN **578**
Boath House, The, NAIRN **586**
Bodysgallen Hall and Spa, LLANDUDNO **624**
Bohemia, ST HELIER **527**
Boisdale of Belgravia, LONDON SW1 **274**
Boisdale of Bishopsgate, LONDON EC2 **256**
Bombay Brasserie, The, LONDON SW7 **298**
Bonars Restaurant, HADDINGTON **591**
Bonds, LONDON EC2 **256**
Borgie Lodge Hotel, TONGUE **589**
Borrowdale Gates Country House Hotel, BORROWDALE **84**
Bosville Hotel, PORTREE **606**
Botleigh Grange, SOUTHAMPTON **193**
Bottreaux Restaurant, The, BOSCASTLE **63**
Bouviers Restaurant & Hotel, Les, WIMBORNE MINSTER **148**
Bouzy Rouge, GLASGOW **577**
Bowfield Hotel & Country Club, HOWWOOD **599**
Box Tree, ILKLEY **513**
Boxwood Café, LONDON SW1 **274**
Brackenbury, The, LONDON W6 **340**
Bradford Arms Hotel, The, OSWESTRY **405**
Braidwoods, DALRY **541**
Bramhall's, ASHBOURNE **101**
Brandshatch Place Hotel, BRANDS HATCH **208**
Branston Hall Hotel, LINCOLN **226**
Brasserie at the Chester Grosvenor & Spa, La, CHESTER **61**
Brasserie Forty 4, LEEDS **514**
Brasserie Ma Cuisine Bourgeoise, La, TWICKENHAM **362**
Brasserie Ninety Nine, WAKEFIELD **518**
Brasserie Roux, LONDON SW1 **275**
Brasserie St Nicholas, SEVENOAKS **212**
Brasserie St Quentin, LONDON SW3 **295**
Brasserie, La, CARDIFF **617**
Brasserie, The, WATERGATE BAY **81**
Bratz, LICHFIELD **423**
Brazz, CARDIFF **613**
Brian Maule at Chardon d'Or, GLASGOW **571**
Brian Turner Mayfair, LONDON W1 **310**
Bridge House Hotel, BEAMINSTER **135**
Bridge House, The, ROSS-ON-WYE **199**
Bridgewood Manor, CHATHAM **209**
Brockencote Hall, CHADDESLEY CORBETT **486**
Bromsgrove Hotel, The, BROMSGROVE **485**
Bron Eifion Country House Hotel, CRICCIETH **630**
Brontë Restaurant, LEEDS **514**
Brookes Restaurant & Private Dining Room, LLANTRISANT **634**
Brooklands Grange Hotel, COVENTRY **472**
Brookleys, BROCKENHURST **182**
Brown's Restaurant, WORCESTER **489**
Brown's, CLIFDEN **666**
Brudenell, The, ALDEBURGH **425**
Brula, TWICKENHAM **363**
Brummells Seafood Restaurant, NORWICH **373**
Brunello, LONDON SW7 **297**
Bruton House Restaurant, BRUTON **411**
Bryce's Seafood Restaurant, OCKLEY **441**
Buckland Manor, BUCKLAND **158**
Buckland-Tout-Saints, KINGSBRIDGE **122**
Bucklemaker, The, BIRMINGHAM **472**
Budock Vean - The Hotel on the River, MAWNAN SMITH **68**
Bull Auberge, The, YAXLEY **436**
Bull Pub & Dining Room, The, LONDON N6 **263**
Bunchrew House Hotel, INVERNESS **581**
Burleigh Court Hotel, STROUD **169**
Burn How Garden House Hotel, WINDERMERE **95**
Burt's Hotel, MELROSE **601**
Burythorpe House Hotel, MALTON **499**
Bush Hall, HATFIELD **202**
Butler's, LONDON W1 **310**
Butlers Wharf Chop House, LONDON SE1 **268**
Butley Orford Oysterage, The, ORFORD **434**
Buttery, The, GLASGOW **571**
Buvette, La, RICHMOND (UPON THAMES) **360**
Buxted Park, UCKFIELD **450**
By Appointment, NORWICH **373**
Bybrook Restaurant at Manor House, The, CASTLE COMBE **478**

C

Cabinet at Reed, The, ROYSTON **204**
Cadmore Lodge, TENBURY WELLS **489**
Café 1, INVERNESS **583**
Café 21 Newcastle, NEWCASTLE UPON TYNE **461**
Café de Paris, GUILDFORD **440**
Café du Jardin, LONDON WC2 **355**
Café du Marché, Le, LONDON EC1 **253**
Café Gandolfi, GLASGOW **577**
Café Lazeez, LONDON SW7 **297**
Café Lowrey, PONTELAND **382**
Café Naz, LONDON E1 **250**
Café Paradiso at Alias Hotel Kandinsky, CHELTENHAM **159**
Café Paradiso, CORK **659**
Café Royale, GLASGOW **571**
Café Spice Namasté, LONDON E1 **249**
Café St Honore, Le, EDINBURGH **551**
Cahernane House Hotel, KILLARNEY **669**
Cairn Lodge, AUCHTERARDER **593**
Cairnbaan, LOCHGILPHEAD **538**
Calcot Manor, TETBURY **169**
Callow Hall, ASHBOURNE **102**
Cally Palace Hotel, GATEHOUSE OF FLEET **546**
Cambio De Tercio, LONDON SW5 **296**
Cambridge Belfry, The, CAMBOURNE **52**
Cambridge Quy Mill Hotel, CAMBRIDGE **52**
Camellia Restaurant at South Lodge Hotel, The, LOWER BEEDING **458**
Camerino, LONDON W1 **310**
Canal 125, LONDON N1 **263**
Canteen, LONDON E1 **249**
Cantina del Ponte, LONDON SE1 **268**
Cantina Vinopolis, LONDON SE1 **268**
Capital, The, LONDON SW3 **290**
Caprice Restaurant, Le, LONDON SW1 **275**
Caraffini, LONDON SW1 **275**
Carbis Bay Hotel, ST IVES **76**
Cardoon, DUNFERMLINE **563**
Carey's Manor Hotel, BROCKENHURST **183**
Carlo's, CASTLE DOUGLAS **545**
Carlton Atlantic Coast Hotel, WESTPORT **674**
Carlton House, LLANWRTYD WELLS **644**
Carluccio's Caffè, KINGSTON UPON THAMES **359**
Carluccio's Caffè, LONDON **252, 255, 335, 339**
Carluccio's Caffè, RICKMANSWORTH **205**
Carlyon Bay Hotel, ST AUSTELL **75**
Carringtons Restaurant, GLOUCESTER **164**
Carved Angel, EXETER **117**
Casablanca, WYMONDHAM **378**
Casey's of Baltimore, BALTIMORE **658**
Cashel House, CASHEL **665**
Cashel Palace Hotel, CASHEL **674**
Castell Deudraeth, PORTMEIRION **631**
Castle Brasserie, HURST **34**
Castle Green Hotel in Kendal, The, KENDAL **91**
Castle Hotel, MACROOM **660**
Castle Hotel, The, CONWY **621**
Castle House, HEREFORD **198**
Castle House, LEDBURY **198**
Castle Venlaw Hotel, PEEBLES **601**
Castleman Hotel, BLANDFORD FORUM **135**
Castleton House Hotel, GLAMIS **535**
Catch, SHEFFIELD **510**
Cavan Crystal Hotel, CAVAN **656**
Cavendish Hotel, BASLOW **103**
Cavens, KIRKBEAN **546**
Cayenne, BELFAST **650**
Cecconi's, LONDON W1 **310**
Cellar Restaurant, ANSTRUTHER **564**
Cercle, Le, LONDON SW1 **276**
Chair, LONDON W2 **337**
Chalk Lane Hotel, EPSOM **439**
Chamberlains Restaurant, LONDON EC3 **258**
Champany Inn, LINLITHGOW **592**
Champignon Sauvage, Le, CHELTENHAM **160**
Champor Champor, LONDON SE1 **268**
Chancellors at Shieldhill Castle, BIGGAR **589**
Chancery, The, LONDON EC4 **260**
Chandlers, LICHFIELD **423**
Chandlery, The, NEWPORT **635**
Channings Restaurant, EDINBURGH **551**
Chapel House Hotel, ATHERSTONE **464**
Chapter One, BROMLEY **357**
Chapter One, DUBLIN **664**
Chapter Two, LONDON SE3 **271**
Charingworth Manor, CHARINGWORTH **159**
Charlotte's Place, LONDON W5 **339**
Charlton House, SHEPTON MALLET **416**
Château La Chaire, ROZEL **524**
Cheese Society, The, LINCOLN **228**
Cheneston's Restaurant, LONDON W8 **342**
Chequers Inn, The, FROGGATT **106**
Chequers Inn, The, WOOLSTHORPE **230**
Chequers Inn, WOOBURN COMMON **52**
Cherry Tree Inn, The, HENLEY-ON-THAMES **392**
Cherwell Boathouse Restaurant, OXFORD **394**
Chesil Rectory, The, WINCHESTER **195**
Chevin Country Park Hotel, OTLEY **517**
Chewton Glen Hotel, NEW MILTON **191**
Chez Bruce, LONDON SW17 **305**
Chez Hans, CASHEL **675**
Chez Kristof, LONDON W6 **340**
Chez Lindsay, RICHMOND (UPON THAMES) **361**
Chez Manny, LONDON SW11 **303**
Chicory, LYTHAM ST ANNES **218**
Chilgrove White Horse, The, CHILGROVE **453**
Chilston Park Hotel, LENHAM **212**
China Tang, LONDON W1 **311**
Chine Hotel, BOURNEMOUTH **136**
Choice Bar & Restaurant, WINCHCOMBE **173**
Chor Bizarre, LONDON W1 **335**
Chouette, La, DINTON **46**
Christophers, LONDON WC2 **350**
Chung Ying Garden, BIRMINGHAM **469**
Churchill Arms, PAXFORD **167**
Chutney Mary Restaurant, LONDON SW10 **300**
Ciao Baby Cucina, BASINGSTOKE **181**
Cibo, LONDON W14 **347**
Cicada, LONDON EC1 **255**
Cigala, LONDON WC1 **348**
Cinnamon Club, The, LONDON SW1 **276**
Cipriani, LONDON W1 **311**
Circa, LEWES **448**
Circus Café, EDINBURGH **560**
City Café, BRISTOL **42**
Clandeboye Lodge Hotel, BANGOR **652**
Clare House, GRANGE-OVER-SANDS **88**
Clarence House Country Hotel & Restaurant, BARROW-IN-FURNESS **83**
Clarice House, BURY ST EDMUNDS **429**
Clarion Hotel & Suites Foxfields, BLACKBURN **216**
Clarion Hotel Dublin IFSC, DUBLIN **661**
Clarke's, LONDON W8 **342**
Clerkenwell Dining Room, LONDON EC1 **254**
Cley Hall Hotel, SPALDING **228**
Cliffords Cottage Restaurant, BRACKLESHAM **452**
Clive Restaurant with Rooms, The, LUDLOW **400**
Clocktower, HARROGATE **496**
Club Gascon, LONDON EC1 **253**
Cobo Bay Hotel, COBO **519**
Coconut Lagoon, LONDON EC1 **255**
Cocoon, LONDON W1 **311**
Collection, The, LONDON SW3 **289**
Colombier, Le, LONDON SW3 **289**
Colquhoun's, LUSS **538**
Combe Grove Manor Hotel & Country Club, BATH **408**
Combe House Hotel and Restaurant, Gittisham, HONITON **120**
Combe House Hotel, HOLFORD **414**
Comme Ça, CHICHESTER **452**
Compasses Inn, LOWER CHICKSGROVE **478**
Comptoir Gascon, LONDON EC1 **254**
Congham Hall, GRIMSTON **369**
Conrad at Jamesons, BRISTOL **42**
Conrah Hotel, ABERYSTWYTH **620**
Conservatory Restaurant, The, STOW-ON-THE-WOLD **167**
Contented Vine, The, LONDON SW1 **287**
Cook's Room, The, GLASGOW **577**
Coppid Beech, BRACKNELL **29**
Copthorne Hotel Aberdeen, ABERDEEN **532**
Copthorne Hotel Cardiff-Caerdydd, CARDIFF **613**
Copthorne Hotel Manchester, WINCHCOMBE **173**
Corbyn Head Hotel & Orchid Restaurant, TORQUAY **131**
Corisande Manor Hotel, NEWQUAY **69**
Corner House Hotel, TAUNTON **417**
Corney & Barrow, LONDON **252, 258, 259, 260, 261**
Cornish Range Restaurant with Rooms, The, MOUSEHOLE **69**
Cors Restaurant, The, LAUGHARNE **617**
Corse Lawn House Hotel, CORSE LAWN **163**

Corsewall Lighthouse Hotel, STRANRAER 548
Corus Hotel Elstree, ELSTREE 202
Cosmo, EDINBURGH 560
Cotswold House, CHIPPING CAMPDEN 162
Cotswold Lodge Hotel, OXFORD 393
Cottage in the Wood and Restaurant, MALVERN 487
Cottage in the Wood, The, BRAITHWAITE 85
Cottage Restaurant at Ternhill Farm House, The, MARKET DRAYTON 404
Courtyard, The, HARROGATE 496
Coventry Arms, The, CORFE MULLEN 139
Crab & Winkle Seafood Restaurant, WHITSTABLE 214
Crab and Lobster Restaurant, ASENBY 491
Crab at Chieveley, The, CHIEVELEY 31
Craggan Mill, GRANTOWN-ON-SPEY 581
Craigellachie Hotel, CRAIGELLACHIE 593
Crathorne Hall Hotel, CRATHORNE 494
Crazy Bear, The, STADHAMPTON 395
Creagan House, STRATHYRE 602
Creel Restaurant, ST MARGARET'S HOPE 605
Creggans Inn, STRACHUR 540
Crescent Restaurant at The Montcalm Nikko London, LONDON W1 311
Crescent Townhouse, The, BELFAST 652
Crewe Hall, CREWE 61
Cringletie House, PEEBLES 601
Cromlix House Hotel, DUNBLANE 602
Crooked Barn, The, LOWESTOFT 433
Crooked Billet, The, BLETCHLEY 44
Cross at Kingussie, The, KINGUSSIE 584
Cross Keys, LONDON SW3 295
Cross Lanes Hotel, WREXHAM 648
Crossways, WILMINGTON 451
Croucher's Country Hotel & Restaurant, CHICHESTER 452
Crown & Castle, The, ORFORD 434
Crown at Whitebrook, WHITEBROOK 635
Crown Hotel, EXFORD 413
Crown Hotel, The, WELLS-NEXT-THE-SEA 377
Crown House, The, GREAT CHESTERFORD 154
Crown Inn, The, CHURCH ENSTONE 389
Crown Inn, The, FONTMELL MAGNA 141
Crown Inn, The, MARSTON MONTGOMERY 107
Crown, The, SOUTHWOLD 434
Crowne Plaza Dublin Airport, DUBLIN 662
Cru, LONDON N1 263
Cucina at The Vale Hotel, La, HENSOL 647
Cuillin Hills Hotel, PORTREE 607
Culdearn House, GRANTOWN-ON-SPEY 580
Culinaria, BRISTOL 42
Culloden House Hotel, INVERNESS 581
Cumberland - Rhodes, The, LONDON W1 312
Cumbrian Lodge, SEASCALE 94
Cutting Edge, CARDIFF 613

D

D.C.H, YORK 506
Da Nello, ST PETER PORT 521
da Venditto, CARDIFF 613
Dale Head Hall Lakeside Hotel, KESWICK 91
Dale Hill Hotel & Golf Club, TICEHURST 450
Dales Country House Hotel, SHERINGHAM 375
Dalhousie Castle and Aqueous Spa, EDINBURGH 552
Dalmunzie House Hotel, ST FILLANS 599
Danesfield House Hotel & Spa, MARLOW 48
Daniel's Restaurant, EDINBURGH 561
Darleys Restaurant, DARLEY ABBEY 105
Darroch Learg Hotel, BALLATER 533
Dartmoor Inn, LYDFORD 124
Dartmoor Union Inn, The, HOLBETON 120
David Bann, EDINBURGH 561
de Vere Arms, EARLS COLNE 153
De Vere Belfry, The, WISHAW 468
De Vere Cameron House, BALLOCH 549
De Vere Dunston Hall, NORWICH 373
De Vere Grand Harbour Hotel, SOUTHAMPTON 194
De Vere Slaley Hall, HEXHAM 382
De Vere St David's Park, EWLOE 628
De Vere Whites, HORWICH 172
Deans @ Let's Eat, PERTH 597
Decks Restaurant, INSTOW 122
Deddington Arms, DEDDINGTON 389
Deep, LONDON SW6 296
Delhi Brasserie, The, LONDON SW7 299
Delhi Brasserie, The, LONDON W1 335
Depot Waterfront Brasserie, The, LONDON SW14 303
Derrynane Hotel, CAHERDANIEL (CATHAIR DNALL) 668
Designs, CASTLE DOUGLAS 545
Deux Garçons, Les, HORSHAM 457
Devonshire Arms Country House Hotel & Spa, The, BOLTON ABBEY 493
Dew Pond Restaurant, The, OLD BURGHCLERE 189
Deya at Mostyn Hotel, LONDON W1 312
Dinham Hall Hotel, LUDLOW 401
Dining Room, ASHBOURNE 102
Dining Room, The, BOROUGHBRIDGE 494
Dining Room, The, MOFFAT 547
Dining Room, The, REIGATE 442
Ditto, LONDON SW18 306
Dolserau Hall, DOLGELLAU 630
Don, The, LONDON EC4 261
Donavourd House, PITLOCHRY 598
Donnington Valley Hotel, NEWBURY 36
Dormy House Hotel, BROADWAY 485
Dornoch Castle Hotel, DORNOCH 578
Dorset Square Hotel, LONDON NW1 265
Dove Inn, The, CANTERBURY 208
Dove Restaurant with Rooms, The, ALBURGH 366
Dower House Hotel, ROUSDON 127
Dragon Hotel, MONTGOMERY 644
Drake's Restaurant, RIPLEY 443
Drakes on the Pond, ABINGER HAMMER 437
Drapers Arms, The, LONDON N1 261
Drawing Room, The, BUILTH WELLS 639
Drewe Arms, BROADHEMBURY 112
Driftwood, PORTSCATHO 74
Driftwood, ROCK 74
Dromoland Castle, NEWMARKET-ON-FERGUS 657
Drones of Pont Street, LONDON SW1 277
Drumossie Hotel, The, INVERNESS 582
Drunken Duck Inn, AMBLESIDE 82
Dryburgh Abbey Hotel, ST BOSWELLS 601
Dryfesdale Hotel, LOCKERBIE 547
Duck's at Le Marche Noir, EDINBURGH 552
Due South, BRIGHTON 444
Duke of Cornwall Hotel, PLYMOUTH 126
Dunalastair Hotel, KINLOCH RANNOCH 597
Dunkerleys Hotel, DEAL 210
Dunnikier House Hotel, KIRKCALDY 565
Dunraven Arms, ADARE 672
Dunsley Hall, WHITBY 504
Duxford Lodge Hotel, DUXFORD 53
Dylan's, BARNET 355

E

E & O, LONDON W11 345
Earsham Street Café, BUNGAY 428
East Lodge Hotel, ROWSLEY 108
Eastbury Hotel, SHERBORNE 146
Eastwell Manor, ASHFORD 206
Eat & Two Veg, LONDON W1 336
Ebury, LONDON SW1 277
Ecrivain, l', DUBLIN 664
Edamame, OXFORD 394
Edenhall Country Hotel, PENRITH 93
Edera, LONDON W11 345
Eeusk, OBAN 539
Effings, TOTNES 133
Egerton Grey Country House Hotel, BARRY 647
Egypt Mill Hotel, NAILSWORTH 165
Eight Over Eight, LONDON SW3 289
Elderton Lodge Hotel & Langtry Restaurant, CROMER 368
Elena's L'Etoile, LONDON W1 336
Elephant Bar & Restaurant, The, TORQUAY 132
Eleven Abingdon Road, LONDON W8 343
Elms Hotel & Restaurant, The, ABBERLEY 484
Elms, Passion of India, The, STOKE-ON-TRENT 424
Embassy London, LONDON W1 312
Emiles, LONDON SW15 305
Empire Hotel, LLANDUDNO 622
Enclume, L', CARTMEL 87
Enoteca Turi, LONDON SW15 304
Entropy, LEICESTER 223
Epic Bar Brasserie, BROMSGROVE 485
Equal, LONDON SE23 273
Escargot, L', The Ground Floor Restaurant, LONDON W1 313
Escargot, L', The Picasso Room, LONDON W1 314
Eslington Villa Hotel, GATESHEAD 460

Esseborne Manor, ANDOVER **181**
Essenza, LONDON W11 **347**
Establishment, The, WINCHCOMBE **173**
Estbek House, WHITBY **504**
étain, GLASGOW **572**
Etranger, L', LONDON SW7 **298**
Etrop Grange Hotel, MANCHESTER AIRPORT **179**
Ettington Park Hotel, ALDERMINSTER **464**
Evesham Hotel, The, EVESHAM **486**
Eyre Brothers, LONDON EC2 **257**

F

Fairfield House Hotel, AYR **542**
Fairlawns at Aldridge, The, WALSALL **474**
Fairwater Head Country House Hotel, AXMINSTER **111**
Fairyhill Bar & Brasserie, LLANELLI **618**
Fairyhill, REYNOLDSTON **646**
Falcon Hotel, CARMARTHEN **617**
Falcon Hotel, CASTLE ASHBY **378**
Falcon Inn, The, FOTHERINGHAY **378**
Falcondale Mansion, LAMPETER **620**
Farlam Hall Hotel, BRAMPTON **85**
Farm, The, LONDON SW6 **297**
Farringford, FRESHWATER **474**
Farthings Hotel & Restaurant, TAUNTON **417**
Fat Duck, The, BRAY **30**
Fat Olives, EMSWORTH **186**
Fawsley Hall Hotel, DAVENTRY **379**
Fayrer Garden Hotel, WINDERMERE **96**
Feathers Hotel, LEDBURY **197**
Feathers Hotel, The, LUDLOW **401**
Feathers Hotel, WOODSTOCK **397**
Felin Fach Griffin, The, BRECON **638**
Fernhill Hotel, PORTPATRICK **547**
Ferrari's Trattoria, QUORN **225**
Ferrycarrig Hotel, WEXFORD **677**
Fifteen, LONDON N1 **262**
Fifth Floor Restaurant, The, LONDON SW1 **277**
Fifty Five, BIGGAR **590**
Finn's, NEWQUAY **70**
Finnstown Country House, DUBLIN **662**
Fino, LONDON W1 **313**
Fire House Rotisserie, BATH **411**
Fire Station, LONDON SE1 **269**
FireHouse, LONDON SW7 **299**
First Coast, EDINBURGH **561**
Fischer's Baslow Hall, BASLOW **104**
Fish Shop on St John Street, LONDON EC1 **255**
Fisherman's Lodge, NEWCASTLE UPON TYNE **461**
Fishers Bistro, EDINBURGH **561**
Fishers in the City, EDINBURGH **561**
Fishers Seafood Restaurant, OXFORD **395**
Fishes Restaurant, BURNHAM MARKET **368**
Fishmarket, LONDON EC2 **257**
Fishworks, BATH **411**
Five Lakes Resort, TOLLESHUNT KNIGHTS **156**
Fleur de Lys Restaurant with Rooms, La, SHAFTESBURY **145**
Fleur de Provence, SOUTHEND-ON-SEA **156**
Flying Fish Restaurant, The, FALMOUTH **64**
Foley Arms Hotel, MALVERN **488**
Food for Thought, FOWEY **66**
Food Room, The, LONDON SW8 **300**
Footstool, The, LONDON SW1 **288**
Forburys Restaurant, READING **37**
Forest Hotel, DORRIDGE **472**
Forest Pines Hotel, SCUNTHORPE **228**
Forester Inn, DONHEAD ST ANDREW **477**
Fort Royal Hotel, RATHMULLAN **661**
Fosse at Cranborne, La, CRANBORNE **139**
Fosse Manor, STOW-ON-THE-WOLD **167**
Four Seasons Hotel Canary Wharf, LONDON E14 **251**
Four Seasons Hotel London, LONDON W1 **313**
Four Seasons Hotel, The, ST FILLANS **599**
Four Seasons Restaurant, The, LICHFIELD **423**
Fouters, AYR **542**
Fowey Hotel, FOWEY **66**
Fox & Goose Inn, FRESSINGFIELD **430**
Fox & Hounds Country Inn, PICKERING **500**
Fox and Goose, STRATFORD-UPON-AVON **466**
Fox Dining Room, The, LONDON EC2 **258**
Fox, The, WILLIAN **206**
Foxhunter, The, ABERGAVENNY **633**
Fraiche, BIRKENHEAD **364**
Franco's Restaurant, LONDON SW1 **278**
Frankie's at Criterion Grill, LONDON W1 **315**
Frankie's Italian Bar & Grill, LONDON SW3 **289**
Franklins, LONDON SE22 **272**
Fratelli's, STAMFORD **228**
Frederick's Restaurant, LONDON N1 **262**
Fredrick's Hotel, Restaurant & Spa, MAIDENHEAD **35**
Frégate, La, ST PETER PORT **521**
French Horn, The, SONNING **40**
French Table, The, SURBITON **362**
Frenchgate Hotel, RICHMOND **500**
Frère Jacques, KINGSTON UPON THAMES **359**
Frères Jacques, Les, DUBLIN **664**
Friends Restaurant, PINNER **360**
Friends, LONDON SW10 **302**
Fringe, BRIGHTON **446**

G

Gabriel Court Hotel, STOKE GABRIEL **130**
Gallery, The, LONDON NW4 **267**
Gallery Restaurant & Bar, The, EDINBURGH **561**
Galley Fish & Seafood Restaurant with Rooms, EXETER **117**
Gallois-Y-Cymro, Le, CARDIFF **614**
Galvin - Bistrot de Luxe, LONDON W1 **315**
Galvin at Windows, LONDON W1 **315**
Galway Bay Hotel, GALWAY **666**
Gamba, GLASGOW **572**
Garrack Hotel & Restaurant, ST IVES **76**
Garrigue, La, EDINBURGH **552**
Garryvoe Hotel, GARRYVOE **659**
Gaston Café Bar & Restaurant, PETERBOROUGH **57**
Gate, The, LONDON W6 **340**
Gavroche Restaurant, Le, LONDON W1 **316**
Gay Hussar, The, LONDON W1 **336**
Gee's Restaurant, OXFORD **393**
Gemini, TADWORTH **443**
General Tarleton Inn, KNARESBOROUGH **498**
George & Dragon, BURPHAM **452**
George & Dragon, ROWDE **482**
George at Hathersage, The, HATHERSAGE **106**
George Hotel - Monty's Seafood, CHELTENHAM **159**
George Hotel, YARMOUTH **476**
George Hotel, DORCHESTER (ON THAMES) **389**
George Hotel, The, CRANBROOK **209**
George of Stamford Hotel, STAMFORD **228**
Georgetown, LEEDS **516**
Georgetown, LONDON SE1 **271**
Georgian House Hotel, The, NORWICH **373**
Georgian Lodge Restaurant, The, BRADFORD-ON-AVON **476**
Ghyll Manor, RUSPER **459**
Gidleigh Park, CHAGFORD **113**
Gilby's Restaurant, CARDIFF **614**
Gilpin Lodge Country House Hotel & Restaurant, WINDERMERE **97**
Gin Trap Inn, The, RINGSTEAD **375**
Gingerman Restaurant, The, BRIGHTON **444**
Glas, LONDON SE1 **269**
Glass Boat Restaurant, BRISTOL **42**
Glass House Restaurant, The, GRANTOWN-ON-SPEY **580**
Glasshouse, The, KEW **359**
Glasshouse, The, KINGSTON UPON THAMES **359**
Glazebrook House Hotel & Restaurant, SOUTH BRENT **129**
Glen Lui, BALLATER **534**
Glenapp Castle, BALLANTRAE **543**
Glenburn Hotel, WEYMOUTH **147**
Glengarry Castle, INVERGARRY **581**
Glenlo Abbey Hotel, GALWAY **666**
Glenmorangie Highland Home at Cadboll, TAIN **588**
Glenmoriston Arms Hotel & Restaurant, INVERMORISTON **581**
Glenmoriston Town House Hotel, INVERNESS **582**
Glenskirlie House Restaurant, BANKNOCK **562**
Glenspean Lodge Hotel, ROY BRIDGE **587**
Glewstone Court, ROSS-ON-WYE **200**
Gliffaes Hotel Ltd, CRICKHOWELL **640**
Goldsmiths, BIRMINGHAM **469**
Goldstone Hall, MARKET DRAYTON **404**
Goodfellows, WELLS **418**
Goose, The, BRITWELL SALOME **387**
Gordon Ramsay at Claridge's, LONDON W1 **316**
Gordon's, INVERKEILOR **535**

Goring Hotel, LONDON SW1 **278**
Gourmet Burger Kitchen, LONDON NW6 **267**
Gourmet Burger Kitchen, LONDON SW11 **303**
Gourmet Burger Kitchen, LONDON SW15 **305**
Governor's, ST PETER PORT **522**
Graffiti at Hotel Felix, CAMBRIDGE **53**
Grafton Manor Restaurant, BROMSGROVE **486**
Granary Hotel & Restaurant, The, KIDDERMINSTER **487**
Grand Hotel (Mirabelle), EASTBOURNE **446**
Grand Hotel, The, SWANSEA **646**
Grand Hotel, TORQUAY **132**
Grange & Links Hotel, SUTTON ON SEA **228**
Grange Hotel, The, BRAMPTON **52**
Grange Hotel, The, YORK **506**
Grange Manor, The, GRANGEMOUTH **562**
Grasmere Hotel, GRASMERE **88**
Gravetye Manor Hotel, EAST GRINSTEAD **455**
Gravy, LONDON W4 **339**
Great Eastern Dining Room, LONDON EC2 **257**
Great House Restaurant, LAVENHAM **432**
Great House, The, BRIDGEND **612**
Great Southern, PARKNASILLA **670**
Green Dragon, HADDENHAM **46**
Green Island Restaurant, ST CLEMENT **525**
Green Park Hotel, PITLOCHRY **598**
Green, The, SHERBORNE **146**
Greenhead House, CHAPELTOWN **509**
Greenhouse, The, LONDON W1 **317**
Greens Bistro, LYTHAM ST ANNES **219**
Greens Restaurant and Oyster Bar, LONDON SW1 **288**
Greens, MANCHESTER **175**
Greenway, The, CHELTENHAM **161**
Gregans Castle, BALLYVAUGHAN **656**
Greggs Restaurant, SEVENOAKS **212**
Greyhound at Battersea, The, LONDON SW11 **302**
Greyhound, The, STOCKBRIDGE **194**
Greywalls Hotel, GULLANE **591**
Grill Room (Dorchester Hotel), The, LONDON W1 **318**
Grill, The, LONDON W1 **315**
Groes Inn, The, CONWY **622**
Grove, The, RICKMANSWORTH **204**
Gun, The, LONDON E14 **251**
Gurkha Square, The, FLEET **188**

H

Haandi 8, LONDON SW3 **295**
Hadley Park House, TELFORD **408**
Hadrians, The Balmoral Hotel, EDINBURGH **553**
Haigs Hotel, BALSALL COMMON **468**
Hakkasan, LONDON W1 **317**
Haldanes, EDINBURGH **553**
Haley's Hotel & Restaurant, LEEDS **514**
Hall Garth Hotel, DARLINGTON **149**
Hallidays, CHICHESTER **453**
Halmpstone Manor, BARNSTAPLE **111**
Hambleton Hall Hotel, OAKHAM **399**
Hambrough Hotel, VENTNOR **475**
Hanburys, TORQUAY **133**
Hand & Flowers, The, MARLOW **47**
Hanoi Cafe, LONDON E2 **251**
Harbour Heights Hotel, POOLE **143**
Harbour Inn, The, BOWMORE **604**
Harbourmaster Hotel, ABERAERON **618**
Harbourside Restaurant, FALMOUTH **65**
Hare & Hounds, CIRENCESTER **163**
Hare Restaurant @ The Hare & Hounds, The, LAMBOURN **34**
Harlequin Restaurant, The, KEIGHLEY **514**
Harris's Restaurant, PENZANCE **73**
Harrogate Brasserie with Rooms, HARROGATE **497**
Harrow at Little Bedwyn, The, LITTLE BEDWYN **480**
Harry Ramsdens, INVERNESS **583**
Harry's Place, GRANTHAM **227**
Harry's, ABERYSTWYTH **620**
Harry's, ROSS-ON-WYE **200**
Hart Manor, ESKDALEMUIR **546**
Hart's Restaurant, NOTTINGHAM **383**
Hartwell House Hotel Restaurant & Spa, AYLESBURY **45**
Harvard Bar & Grill, LONDON SW1 **288**
Harvey Nichols 2nd Floor Restaurant, MANCHESTER **175**
Harvey's Point Country Hotel, DONEGAL **661**
Haven Hotel, POOLE **144**
Hawtrey's Restaurant at the Barn Hotel, RUISLIP **362**
Haxted Mill & Riverside Brasserie, EDENBRIDGE **210**
Haydon House Hotel, STOKE-ON-TRENT **424**
Hayfield Manor, CORK **659**
Hazel Bank Country House, BORROWDALE **85**
Headlam Hall, DARLINGTON **149**
Headland Hotel, NEWQUAY **70**
Healds Hall Hotel, DEWSBURY **511**
Healys Restaurant & Country House Hotel, FOXFORD **673**
Hell Bay, SCILLY, ISLES OF, BRYHER **78**
Hellenic, LONDON NW3 **267**
Hellidon Lakes, HELLIDON **380**
Helyar Arms, YEOVIL **420**
Henderson's Salad Table, EDINBURGH **561**
Hengist Restaurant, AYLESFORD **207**
Henry's Cantonese Restaurant, BIRMINGHAM **472**
Herbert Park, The, DUBLIN **662**
Hey Green Country House Hotel, MARSDEN **517**
Hibiscus, LUDLOW **402**
Highfield Hotel & Restaurant, KESWICK **91**
Highfield Hotel, The, MIDDLESBROUGH **500**
Highland Cottage, TOBERMORY **605**
Hinds Head Hotel, BRAY **31**
Hintlesham Hall, HINTLESHAM **430**
Ho Wong Restaurant, GLASGOW **572**
Hodson Bay, ATHLONE **676**
Holbeck Ghyll Country House Hotel, WINDERMERE **98**
Holbrook House Hotel, WINCANTON **419**
Holdfast Cottage Hotel, MALVERN **488**
Holdsworth House Hotel, HALIFAX **511**
Holne Chase Hotel, ASHBURTON **110**
Homewood Park, HINTON CHARTERHOUSE **413**
Hoops Inn & Country Hotel, The, HORNS CROSS **121**
Horn of Plenty, GULWORTHY **119**
Horse & Trumpet, The, MEDBOURNE **224**
Horsted Place, UCKFIELD **451**
Hoste Arms Hotel, BURNHAM MARKET **368**
Hotel du Vin & Bistro, BRISTOL **43**
Hotel du Vin & Bistro, HARROGATE **497**
Hotel du Vin & Bistro, TUNBRIDGE WELLS (ROYAL) **213**
Hotel du Vin & Bistro, WINCHESTER **195**
Hotel du Vin Brighton, BRIGHTON **444**
Hotel Du Vin, BIRMINGHAM **470**
Hotel Eilean Iarmain, ISLEORNSAY **606**
Hotel Endsleigh, TAVISTOCK **130**
Hotel Hougue du Pommier, CASTEL **519**
Hotel Jerbourg, ST MARTIN **520**
Hotel L'Horizon, The Grill, ST BRELADE **525**
Hotel La Place, ST BRELADE **525**
Hotel La Tour, ST AUBIN **524**
Hotel Maes y Neuadd, TALSARNAU **632**
Hotel Metropole, LLANDRINDOD WELLS **642**
Hotel Petit Champ, SARK **529**
Hotel Portmeirion, PORTMEIRION **632**
Hotel Tresanton, ST MAWES **77**
Hour Glass, FORDINGBRIDGE **188**
House, The, LONDON N1 **262**
Howard Hotel, The, EDINBURGH **553**
Howards Restaurant, BRISTOL **44**
Howies Restaurant - Alva Street, EDINBURGH **561**
Howies Restaurant - Chapel Street, ABERDEEN **533**
Howies Restaurant - Victoria Street, EDINBURGH **561**
Howies Restaurant - Waterloo Place, EDINBURGH **561**
Hundred House Hotel, NORTON **405**
Hungry Monk Restaurant, JEVINGTON **448**
Hunstrete House Hotel, HUNSTRETE **414**
Hunter's Hotel, RATHNEW **678**
Hunters Lodge Hotel, CREWE **62**
Huntingtower Hotel, PERTH **598**
Hurtwood Inn Hotel, PEASLAKE **441**
Hythe Imperial Hotel, The, HYTHE **211**

I

Ibbetson's Restaurant, BISHOP'S STORTFORD **201**
Ickworth Hotel, The, HORRINGER **430**
Idle Rocks Hotel, ST MAWES **77**
Iggs, EDINBURGH **553**
Il Convivio, LONDON SW1 **276**
Il Punto, IPSWICH **431**
Ilsington Country House Hotel, The, ILSINGTON **121**

Imperial China, LONDON WC2 **350**
Imperial Hotel, GREAT YARMOUTH **369**
Imperial Hotel, LLANDUDNO **623**
Imran's Balti, BIRMINGHAM **472**
Incanto, HARROW ON THE HILL **358**
Inchydoney Island Lodge & Spa, CLONAKILTY **658**
Incognico, LONDON WC2 **350**
Inn at Farnborough, The, FARNBOROUGH **464**
Inn at Lathones, ST ANDREWS **566**
Inn at the Elm Tree, The, ST BRIDES WENTLOOGE **636**
Inn at Whitewell, The, WHITEWELL **222**
Inn at Woburn, The, WOBURN **28**
Inn on The Green, The, COOKHAM DEAN **33**
Inn the Park, LONDON SW1 278
Inver Lodge, LOCHINVER **583**
Inverlochy Castle Hotel, FORT WILLIAM **579**
Island Hotel, SCILLY, ISLES OF, TRESCO **78**
Island Restaurant & Bar, LONDON W2 **337**
Isle of Eriska, ERISKA **537**
Isola del Sole, LONDON SW15 **305**
Ivy, The, LONDON WC2 **350**
Izaak Walton Hotel, THORPE **110**
Iznik, LONDON N5 **263**

J

J. Sheekey, LONDON WC2 **351**
Jaan Restaurant, LONDON WC2 **351**
Jack In The Green, The, ROCKBEARE **127**
Jacob's Ladder, DUBLIN **664**
Jacobs, CORK **659**
Jacques, CORK **659**
Jali Bar & Restaurant @ The Chatsworth Hotel, HASTINGS & ST LEONARDS **447**
Jambo, WINDERMERE **96**
Jedforest Hotel, JEDBURGH **600**
Jeremy's at Borde Hill, HAYWARDS HEATH **456**
Jerichos, WINDERMERE **96**
Jersey Pottery, The Garden Restaurant, GOREY **523**
Jesmond Dene House, NEWCASTLE UPON TYNE **462**
Jessica's, BIRMINGHAM **470**
Jonathan's at the Angel, BURFORD **387**
JSW, PETERSFIELD **192**
Juboraj, CARDIFF **617**
Judges Country House Hotel, YARM **505**
Juniper, ALTRINCHAM **174**
Jurys Great Russell Street, LONDON WC1 **347**
Just Gladwins, LONDON EC3 **260**
Just St James, LONDON SW1 **278**

K

K Club, The, STRAFFAN **671**
Kai Mayfair, LONDON W1 **318**
Kare Kare, LONDON SW5 **296**
Karslake House, WINSFORD **420**
Kastoori, LONDON SW17 **306**
Kasturi, LONDON EC3 **260**
Keadeen Hotel, NEWBRIDGE **670**
Kelly's Resort, ROSSLARE **677**
Kemps Hotel, WAREHAM **147**
Kempsters Restaurant, CREWKERNE **412**
Ken Lo's Memories of China, LONDON SW1 **279**
Kensington Place, LONDON W8 **343**
Kettering Park Hotel, KETTERING **380**
Kilcamb Lodge Hotel, STRONTIAN **588**
Kilkenny River Court, KILKENNY **672**
Killarney Park, KILLARNEY **669**
Killashee House Hotel & Villa Spa, NAAS **670**
Killermont Polo Club, GLASGOW **573**
Killiecrankie House Hotel, KILLIECRANKIE **596**
Kilmichael Hotel, BRODICK **604**
Kilo, LONDON W1 **318**
Kilworth House Hotel, NORTH KILWORTH **224**
King Sitric, LONDON NW2 **266**
King's Head, The, IVINGHOE **46**
Kinghams, SHERE **442**
Kings Arms, The, STOW-ON-THE-WOLD **168**
Kings Court Hotel, ALCESTER **463**
Kings Head Hotel, The, GREAT BIRCHAM **368**
Kings Head Inn, WOODSTOCK **397**
Kings, The, CHIPPING CAMPDEN **162**
Kingsway Hotel, CLEETHORPES **226**
Kinnaird, DUNKELD **596**
Kirroughtree House, NEWTON STEWART **547**
Knife & Cleaver, BEDFORD **28**
Knockinaam Lodge, PORTPATRICK **548**
Knockranny House Hotel, WESTPORT **674**
Kwizeen, BLACKPOOL **218**

L

Label, MANCHESTER **177**
Lacken House & Restaurant, KILKENNY **672**
Lady Helen Restaurant, The, THOMASTOWN **672**
Ladyburn, MAYBOLE **542**
Laguna Kitchen & Bar, The, CARDIFF **615**
Laicram Thai Restaurant, LONDON SE3 **271**
Lainston House Hotel, WINCHESTER **196**
Lake Country House Hotel & Spa, LLANGAMMARCH WELLS **643**
Lake Isle Restaurant & Town House Hotel, UPPINGHAM **400**
Lake View Restaurant at Armathwaite Hall, BARROW-IN-FURNESS **84**
Lake Vyrnwy Hotel, LLANWDDYN **643**
Lakes Restaurant, SITTINGBOURNE **213**
Lakeside Hotel, NEWBY BRIDGE **93**
Lakeside Restaurant, WALLINGFORD **396**
Lamb at Buckland, The, FARINGDON **390**
Lamb Inn, The, BURFORD **387**
Lambs of Sheep Street, STRATFORD-UPON-AVON **467**
Lancaster House Hotel, LANCASTER **218**
Landgate Bistro, RYE **450**
Lanes Restaurant & Bar, LONDON E1 **249**
Lanes, YEOVIL **420**
Lanesborough, The, LONDON SW1 **279**
Langar Hall, LANGAR **383**
Langdale Chase Hotel, WINDERMERE **96**
Langdon Court Hotel, PLYMOUTH **126**
Langley Wood Restaurant, REDLYNCH **482**
Langmans Restaurant, CALLINGTON **64**
Langrish House, PETERSFIELD **192**
Langs Hotel, GLASGOW **573**
Langshott Manor, GATWICK AIRPORT (LONDON) **455**
Langton Arms, The, TARRANT MONKTON **147**
Langtry Restaurant, BOURNEMOUTH **136**
Lasswade Country House Hotel, LLANWRTYD WELLS **643**
Latium, LONDON W1 **318**
Launceston Place Restaurant, LONDON W8 **343**
Lavender House, The, BRUNDALL **367**
Leaping Hare Restaurant & Country Store, The, BURY ST EDMUNDS **429**
Leatherne Bottel, The, GORING **390**
Leathes Head Hotel, BORROWDALE **85**
Ledbury, The, LONDON W11 **346**
Leixlip House, LEIXLIP **670**
Lemon Tree, The, OXFORD **394**
Leonardo Restaurant, BRIGHTON **446**
Levant, LONDON W1 **318**
Levantine, LONDON W2 **337**
Lewtrenchard Manor, LEWDOWN **123**
Lickfold Inn, The, LICKFOLD **457**
Lifeboat Inn, THORNHAM **376**
Light House Restaurant, The, LONDON SW19 **306**
Lilly's, LONDON E1 **250**
Lime House, The, YORK **509**
Lime Tree, KENMARE **669**
Lime Tree, The, LIMAVADY **653**
Lindeth Fell Country House Hotel, WINDERMERE **99**
Lindeth Howe Country House Hotel, WINDERMERE **99**
Lindsay House Restaurant, LONDON W1 **321**
Linen Room, The, DUMFRIES **545**
Linnet, The, TROWBRIDGE **483**
Linthwaite House Hotel, WINDERMERE **99**
Little Barwick House Ltd, YEOVIL **421**
Living Room, The, GLASGOW **573**
Livingston's Restaurant, LINLITHGOW **592**
Llangoed Hall, LLYSWEN **644**
Llansantffraed Court Hotel, ABERGAVENNY **633**
Llanwenarth Hotel & Riverside Restaurant, ABERGAVENNY **633**
Lobster Pot, The, LONDON SE11 **272**
Lobster Pot, The, NOTTINGHAM **384**
Locanda Locatelli, LONDON W1 **322**
Loch Bay Seafood Restaurant, STEIN **588**
Loch Fyne Restaurant & Oyster Bar, CAMBRIDGE **53**
Loch Fyne Restaurant & Oyster Bar, HENLEY-ON-THAMES **392**
Loch Fyne Restaurant & Oyster Bar, NOTTINGHAM **386**
Loch Fyne Restaurant & Oyster Bar, PETERBOROUGH **57**

Loch Fyne Restaurant & Oyster Bar, TWICKENHAM **363**
Loch Fyne Restaurant & Oyster Bar, WINCHESTER **197**
Loch Fyne Restaurant, BATH **411**
Loch Fyne Restaurant, Covent Garden, LONDON WC2 **355**
Loch Fyne Restaurant, NORWICH **375**
Loch Fyne Restaurant, OXFORD **395**
Loch Melfort Hotel, ARDUAINE **536**
Loch Torridon Country House Hotel, TORRIDON **589**
Lochgreen House, TROON **544**
Lochside Lodge & Roundhouse Restaurant, BRIDGEND OF LINTRATHEN **535**
Lock Dining Bar, The, LONDON N17 **264**
Lodge on the Loch Hotel, ONICH **585**
Loft, The, LONDON SE1 **271**
London Marriott West India Quay, LONDON E14 **251**
Londonderry Arms Hotel, CARNLOUGH **650**
Longridge Restaurant, The, LONGRIDGE **220**
Longueville House, MALLOW **660**
Longueville Manor, ST SAVIOUR **528**
Lonsdale, LONDON W11 **347**
Lord Bute Hotel & Restaurant, The, CHRISTCHURCH **138**
Lord Haldon Hotel, EXETER **117**
Lords of the Manor, UPPER SLAUGHTER **171**
Los Molinos, LONDON W6 **341**
Lough Inagh Lodge, RECESS (SRAITH SALACH) **667**
Lough Pool Inn, The, ROSS-ON-WYE **200**
Louhannah, LONDON SW15 **305**
Lovelady Shield House, ALSTON **82**
Low Wood Hall Hotel, NETHER WASDALE **93**
Lower Place, The, BIRKENHEAD **365**
Lower Slaughter Manor, LOWER SLAUGHTER **164**
Lowry Hotel, The River Restaurant, MANCHESTER **175**
LSQ2 Bar and Brasserie, READING **37**
Luciano, LONDON SW1 **279**
Lucknam Park, COLERNE **479**
Lumière, CHELTENHAM **161**
Luna, La, GODALMING **440**
Luttrell Arms Hotel, The, DUNSTER **413**
Lux, GLASGOW **573**
Lygon Arms, The, BROADWAY **485**
Lynton Cottage Hotel, LYNTON **125**
Lythe Hill Hotel, HASLEMERE **441**
Lyzzick Hall Country House Hotel, KESWICK **91**

M

Ma Cuisine Le Petit Bistrot, RICHMOND (UPON THAMES) **361**
Ma Cuisine Le Petit Bistrot, TWICKENHAM **363**
MacCallums of Troon, TROON **544**
Macdonald Alveston Manor, STRATFORD-UPON-AVON **466**
Macdonald Bath Spa Hotel, Vellore Restaurant, BATH **408**
Macdonald Bear Hotel, WOODSTOCK **397**
Macdonald Berystede Hotel & Spa, ASCOT **29**
Macdonald Brandon Hall Hotel & Spa, BRANDON **464**
Macdonald Burford Bridge Hotel, DORKING **437**
Macdonald Castle Hotel, WINDSOR **40**
Macdonald Compleat Angler, MARLOW **49**
Macdonald Craxton Wood, PUDDINGTON **62**
Macdonald Crutherland House, EAST KILBRIDE **590**
Macdonald Frimley Hall Hotel & Spa, CAMBERLEY **437**
Macdonald Gisborough Hall, GUISBOROUGH **495**
Macdonald Holland House, CARDIFF **615**
Macdonald Holyrood Hotel, EDINBURGH **554**
Macdonald Houstoun House, UPHALL **592**
Macdonald Leeming House, WATERMILLOCK **94**
Macdonald Linden Hall, LONGHORSLEY **382**
Macdonald Randolph, OXFORD **394**
Macdonald Rusacks Hotel, ST ANDREWS **566**
Macdonald Shakespeare, STRATFORD-UPON-AVON **466**
Mad Hatters Restaurant, The, NAILSWORTH **166**
Maggiore's, LONDON WC2 **351**
Magpie Café, WHITBY **505**
Maharaja, BIRMINGHAM **472**
Maison Bleue, BURY ST EDMUNDS **429**
Malik's, COOKHAM **33**
Malin Court, TURNBERRY **544**
Mallory Court Hotel, LEAMINGTON SPA **465**
Malmaison Birmingham, BIRMINGHAM **470**
Malmaison Charterhouse Square, LONDON EC1 **254**
Malmaison Hotel & Brasserie, EDINBURGH **554**
Malmaison Hotel, LEEDS **515**
Malmaison Hotel, NEWCASTLE UPON TYNE **462**
Malmaison, GLASGOW **574**
Malt Shovel at Barston, The, BARSTON **468**
Mandarin Oriental Hyde Park, LONDON SW1 **281**
Manicomio, LONDON SW3 **291**
Manna, LONDON NW3 **266**
Mannings Heath Golf Club, MANNINGS HEATH **457**
Manoir aux Quat' Saisons, Le, GREAT MILTON **391**
Manor Hotel, CRICKHOWELL **640**
Manor Hotel, MERIDEN **473**
Manor House Hotel, ALSAGER **59**
Manor House Hotel, OBAN **539**
Manor House, The, BEVERLEY **489**
Manor Parc Country Hotel, CARDIFF **615**
Mansion House Hotel, ELGIN **593**
Mansion House Hotel, POOLE **144**
Marcliffe Hotel and Spa, ABERDEEN **532**
Marco Pierre White's Yew Tree Inn, HIGHCLERE **188**
Margot's, PADSTOW **70**
Marina Hotel, FOWEY **66**
Mariner Hotel, The, ABERDEEN **532**
Mariners Hotel, LYME REGIS **143**
Market Restaurant, MANCHESTER **178**
Marlfield House, GOREY **677**
Marque Central, EDINBURGH **561**
Marriott Breadsall Priory, BREADSALL **105**
Marriott Dalmahoy, EDINBURGH **554**
Marriott Goodwood Park Hotel / Richmond Room, GOODWOOD **456**
Marriott Hanbury Manor Hotel, WARE **206**
Marriott Hollins Hall Hotel & Country Club, SHIPLEY **518**
Marriott Sprowston Manor Hotel, NORWICH **374**
Marsala Zones, LONDON W1 **336**
Maryborough Hotel & Spa, CORK **659**
Maryculter House Hotel, ABERDEEN **532**
Marygreen Manor, BRENTWOOD **151**
Marynka, LINLITHGOW **592**
Masala, UXBRIDGE **363**
Masala Zones, LONDON N1 **263**
Mason's Arms Inn, The, KNOWSTONE **122**
Mason's Arms, The, SWERFORD **395**
Masons Arms, The, BRANSCOMBE **112**
Master Builders House Hotel, BUCKLERS HARD **185**
Matfen Hall, MATFEN **382**
Matilda, LONDON SW11 **303**
Matsuri High Holborn, LONDON WC1 **348**
Mayflower, CHELTENHAM **161**
Maze, LONDON W1 **321**
Mc Laughlin's, LIMERICK **673**
Mehek, LONDON EC2 **257**
Mela, LONDON WC2 **352**
Meldrum House Hotel Golf & Country Club, OLDMELDRUM **534**
Mello, BECKENHAM **355**
Melton's, YORK **507**
Melville Castle Hotel, EDINBURGH **554**
Memories - The Langham Hotel, LONDON W1 **320**
Merchants Restaurant & Bar, NOTTINGHAM **384**
Mermaid Café, DUBLIN **664**
Mermaid Inn, RYE **449**
Metro Bar and Grill, BIRMINGHAM **472**
Metro Brasserie, BELFAST **652**
Metropole, The, PADSTOW **70**
Meudon Hotel, MAWNAN SMITH **68**
Meynell and Deer Park Restaurant, BURTON UPON TRENT **422**
Michael Caines at Abode Exeter, EXETER **117**
Michael Caines at The Bristol Marriott Royal, BRISTOL **43**
Michael Moore Restaurant, LONDON W1 **336**
Middlethorpe Hall & Spa, YORK **508**
Midland Hotel, MANCHESTER **175**
Midsummer House, CAMBRIDGE **54**
Milebrook House, KNIGHTON **642**

Mill End, CHAGFORD **114**
Mill House Hotel, KINGHAM **392**
Millennium Hotel Glasgow, GLASGOW **574**
Millennium Madejski Hotel Reading, READING **37**
Miller Howe Hotel, WINDERMERE **100**
Millstone at Mellor, The, BLACKBURN **216**
Millstream Hotel, BOSHAM **452**
milsoms, DEDHAM **153**
Milton Restaurant, BANCHORY **534**
Mint Leaf, LONDON SW1 **279**
Mirabelle, LONDON W1 **320**
Miskin Manor Country Hotel, MISKIN **645**
Mistley Thorn, The, MANNINGTREE **156**
Mitsukoshi, LONDON SW1 **280**
Mju at Millennium Knightsbridge, LONDON SW1 **282**
Moat House, STAFFORD **424**
Mollington Hotel & Spa Chester, CHESTER **61**
Momo, LONDON W5 **339**
Mon Plaisir, LONDON WC2 **352**
Monde Fish Bar & Grill, Le, CARDIFF **617**
Monkey Island Hotel, BRAY **31**
Mont @ Urbis, Le, MANCHESTER **176**
Montagu Arms Hotel, BEAULIEU **182**
Montague on the Gardens, The, LONDON WC1 **348**
Montmartre, Le, LONDON N1 **263**
Moody Goose at The Old Priory, The, MIDSOMER NORTON **414**
Moonfleet Manor, WEYMOUTH **147**
Moores Restaurant & Rooms, NEWTON POPPLEFORD **125**
Moorhill House, BURLEY **185**
Moorings Hotel, FORT WILLIAM **579**
Moorings, The, BLAKENEY **367**
Moorland Links Hotel, YELVERTON **134**
Morel Restaurant, LONDON SW4 **295**
Morgan M, LONDON N7 **263**
Morgan's, ST DAVID'S **637**
Morley Hayes Hotel - Dovecote Restaurant, The, MORLEY **108**
Moro, LONDON EC1 **254**
Morrel's, KESWICK **92**
Morston Hall, BLAKENEY **366**
Mortons House Hotel, CORFE CASTLE **139**
Mosaico, LONDON W1 **323**
Moss Nook, MANCHESTER **176**
Mother India, GLASGOW **577**
Mount Haven Hotel, MARAZION **67**
Mount Somerset Hotel, TAUNTON **418**
Mourne Seafood Bar, DUNDRUM **653**
Mozarella e Pomodoro, LONDON SE5 **272**
Mr Underhills, LUDLOW **403**
Muckrach Lodge Hotel, GRANTOWN-ON-SPEY **580**
Mulberry Restaurant, MORETON-IN-MARSH **165**
Mulberry Tree, The, WRIGHTINGTON **222**
Mulberry, The, CONWY **622**
Murrayshall Country House Hotel, PERTH **598**
Museum Inn, The, FARNHAM **141**
MVH, LONDON SW13 **303**
Mytton & Mermaid Hotel, SHREWSBURY **406**

N

Nahm, LONDON SW1 **283**
Nailcote Hall, BALSALL COMMON **468**
Nant Ddu Lodge Hotel, NANT-DDU **645**
Nantyffin Cider Mill Inn, CRICKHOWELL **641**
Nare Hotel, VERYAN **81**
Nathalie, LONDON SW3 **291**
Nautique Restaurant, Le, ST PETER PORT **522**
Navy Inn, The, PENZANCE **73**
Navy Oak Restaurant & Bar, The, BURFORD **388**
Neal Street Restaurant, The, LONDON WC2 **352**
Neals Restaurant at The Chequers Inn, ROWHOOK **459**
Neigwl Hotel, ABERSOCH **628**
Neptune Inn & Restaurant, The, HUNSTANTON **370**
New Angel, The, DARTMOUTH **115**
New French Partridge, The, HORTON **380**
New House Hotel, CARDIFF **615**
New Inn At Coln, The, COLN ST ALDWYNS **163**
New Inn, SCILLY, ISLES OF, TRESCO **78**
New Mill, EVERSLEY **186**
New Park Manor Hotel & Spa, BROCKENHURST **183**
New Street Brasserie, CHELMSFORD **151**
New World Chinese Restaurant, LONDON W1 **336**
New Yard Restaurant, HELSTON **66**
Newbay Country House & Restaurant, WEXFORD **677**
Newbridge, The, USK **634**
Newcastle Marriott Hotel, Gosforth Park, NEWCASTLE UPON TYNE **462**
Newick Park Hotel & Country Estate, NEWICK **449**
Nicole's, LONDON W1 **323**
Nipa Thai Restaurant, LONDON W2 **337**
Nippon-Kan, LIPHOOK **189**
No 3 Restaurant, EDINBURGH **561**
No 5 Bistro, BATH **411**
No 5 Restaurant, GLASGOW **574**
No 6 Restaurant, LONDON W1 **324**
No 7 Fish Bistro, TORQUAY **133**
Nobu, Berkeley Street, LONDON W1 **324**
Nobu, LONDON W1 **323**
North Pole Piano Restaurant, LONDON SE10 **272**
North West Castle Hotel, PORTPATRICK **549**
Northcote Manor, BURRINGTON **112**
Northcote Manor, LANGHO **217**
Norton House Hotel, EDINBURGH **555**
Norwood Hall, ABERDEEN **533**
Notting Grill, LONDON W11 **347**
Notting Hill Brasserie, LONDON W11 **346**
Novotel London Euston, LONDON NW1 **265**
Nozomi, LONDON SW3 **291**
Number 28 at the White Hart, HENLEY-ON-THAMES **392**
Number 64, LEEK **422**
Number One, The Balmoral Hotel, EDINBURGH **555**
Number Twenty Four Restaurant, WYMONDHAM **377**
Nunsmere Hall Country House Hotel, SANDIWAY **63**
Nuremore Hotel, CARRICKMACROSS **675**
Nutfield Priory - Cloisters Restaurant, REDHILL **442**
Nuthurst Grange Country House Hotel, HOCKLEY HEATH **473**
Nutters, ROCHDALE **179**

O

O'Connell's, DUBLIN **664**
Oak Room at Great Fosters, The, EGHAM **439**
Oaks Hotel, The, PORLOCK **416**
Ocean Restaurant at the Atlantic Hotel, ST BRELADE **526**
Ockenden Manor, CUCKFIELD **454**
Odette's, LONDON NW1 **265**
Off the Wall Restaurant, EDINBURGH **556**
Old Bell Hotel, MALMESBURY **478**
Old Black Lion Inn, HAY-ON-WYE **641**
Old Bore at Rishworth, The, HALIFAX **512**
Old Bridge Hotel, HUNTINGDON **55**
Old Coastguard Hotel, MOUSEHOLE **69**
Old Deanery, The, RIPON **502**
Old Forge, STORRINGTON **459**
Old House Hotel & Restaurant, WICKHAM **195**
Old House Restaurant, The, GATWICK AIRPORT (LONDON) **456**
Old Passage Inn, The, ARLINGHAM **157**
Old Pines Hotel, SPEAN BRIDGE **587**
Old Post Office, The, CARDIFF **616**
Old Post Restaurant, CHESTERFIELD **105**
Old Quay House Hotel, The, FOWEY **66**
Old Rectory Country House, The, CONWY **623**
Old Rectory, NORWICH **374**
Old Rectory, The, MARTINHOE **125**
Old Vicarage Hotel and Restaurant, WORFIELD **407**
Old Vicarage, The, RIDGEWAY **109**
Olive Branch Bistro, The, EDINBURGH **561**
Olive Branch, MARSDEN **517**
Olive Branch, The, CLIPSHAM **398**
Olive Tree at the Queensberry Hotel, The, BATH **410**
Olivers Lodge Hotel, ST IVES **57**
One 19 The Mount, YORK **507**
One Aldwych - Axis, LONDON WC2 **352**
One Aldwych - Indigo, LONDON WC2 **353**
One Blossom Street, LONDON E1 **250**
One Paston Place, BRIGHTON **445**
One Pico, DUBLIN **664**
One-O-One, LONDON SW1 **283**
Onich Hotel, ONICH **585**
Onshore, ST IVES **77**
Open Arms Hotel, The, DIRLETON **590**
Opposition, The, STRATFORD-UPON-AVON **467**
Opus Restaurant, BIRMINGHAM **470**
Orange Tree, The, THORNHAM **377**

Oranger, L', LONDON SW1 **280**
Ord House Hotel, MUIR OF ORD **585**
Orestone Manor Hotel & Restaurant, TORQUAY **133**
Origin, LONDON WC2 **353**
Orrery, LONDON W1 **324**
Orso Restaurant, LONDON WC2 **354**
Ortolan, L', SHINFIELD **39**
Osborne House, LLANDUDNO **623**
'Oscars' at the De Vere Royal Bath Hotel, BOURNEMOUTH **136**
Osteria Antica Bologna, LONDON SW11 **303**
Osteria dell'Arancio, LONDON SW10 **300**
Ostlers Close Restaurant, CUPAR **563**
Overton Grange Country House & Restaurant, LUDLOW **403**
Owens at the Celtic Manor Resort, NEWPORT **636**
Oxo Tower Restaurant, The, LONDON SE1 **269**
Ozer, LONDON W1 **325**
Ozu, LONDON SE1 **270**

P

Packie's, KENMARE **669**
Pagoda Palace, SWINDON **483**
Painswick Hotel, PAINSWICK **167**
Painted Heron, The, LONDON SW10 **300**
Palé Hall, BALA **629**
Palmerston, The, LONDON SE22 **272**
Palmiro, MANCHESTER **176**
Panorama Hotel, TENBY **638**
Papingo Restaurant, GLASGOW **574**
Paris House Restaurant, WOBURN **29**
Park Farm Hotel, HETHERSETT **370**
Park Hotel, The, VIRGINIA **656**
Park House Hotel & Park Room Restaurant, GALWAY **666**
Park Restaurant Hotel, The, PRESTON **219**
Parkers, CHELTENHAM **161**
Parsee, The, LONDON N19 **264**
Parsonage Country House Hotel, The, ESCRICK **495**
Passione, LONDON W1 **325**
Patara, LONDON W1 **336**
Patterson's, LONDON W1 **325**
Peacock Hotel, ROWSLEY **110**
Pear Tree at Purton, The, PURTON **482**
Pear Tree Inn, The, WHITLEY **484**
Pearl Restaurant & Bar, LONDON WC1 **348**
Peasant, The, LONDON EC1 **255**
Peat Inn, The, PEAT INN **566**
Pebble Beach, BARTON-ON-SEA **181**
Penally Abbey Hotel, TENBY **638**
Pendley Manor, TRING **205**
Penhaven Country Hotel, PARKHAM **126**
Penhelig Arms Hotel, ABERDYFI **628**
Penmaenuchaf Hall Hotel, DOLGELLAU **631**
Pennyhill Park Hotel & The Spa, BAGSHOT **438**
Pen-y-Dyffryn Country Hotel, OSWESTRY **406**
Pepe Sale, READING **37**
Perry's Restaurant, WEYMOUTH **148**
Peterstone Court Hotel, BRECON **638**
Petit Blanc, Le, MANCHESTER **176**
Petit Canard, Le, MAIDEN NEWTON **143**
Petite Pomme, La, ST HELIER **528**
Pétrus, LONDON SW1 **284**
Pheasant Inn, KEYSTON **55**
Pheasant Inn, The, BURWARDSLEY **59**
Pheasant, The, BASSENTHWAITE **84**
Philpotts Mezzaluna 8, LONDON NW2 **266**
Pied à Terre, LONDON W1 **326**
Pier at Harwich, The, HARWICH **155**
Pig's Ear, The, LONDON SW3 **295**
Pinchinthorpe Hall, GUISBOROUGH **495**
Pine Trees Hotel, PITLOCHRY **599**
Pines Hotel, PRESTON **221**
Pinewood Hotel, The, SLOUGH **40**
Pink Geranium, MELBOURN **56**
Pistachio Restaurant, SAXMUNDHAM **434**
Plas Bodegroes, PWLLHELI **632**
Plateau, LONDON E14 **251**
Plough Inn, The, HATHERSAGE **106**
Plough, The, AMERSHAM **44**
Plum Pudding Brasserie, The, RUGELEY **423**
Plumed Horse Restaurant, CASTLE DOUGLAS **545**
Pond Café, The, VENTNOR **475**
Ponsbourne Park Hotel, POTTERS BAR **203**
Pont de la Tour, Le, LONDON SE1 **270**
Pool House Hotel, POOLEWE **587**
Porte des Indes, La, LONDON W1 **336**
Porth Tocyn Hotel, ABERSOCH **629**
Porthminster Beach Restaurant, ST IVES **76**
Portmarnock Hotel, PORTMARNOCK **664**
Portrait Restaurant, The, LONDON WC2 **354**
Potinière, La, GULLANE **591**
Poussin at Whitley Ridge Country House Hotel, Le, BROCKENHURST **183**
Powder Mills Hotel, BATTLE **444**
Priest House on the River, The, NOTTINGHAM EAST MIDLANDS AIRPORT **225**
Prince Hall Hotel, TWO BRIDGES **133**
Prince's House, The, GLENFINNAN **580**
Priory Bay Hotel, SEAVIEW **474**
Priory House Restaurant, The, STOKE SUB HAMDON **416**
Prism Restaurant and Bar, LONDON EC3 **259**
Probus Lamplighter Restaurant, TALLAND BAY **81**
Prospect, The, BAKEWELL **103**
Providores, The, LONDON W1 **325**
Puesdown Inn, The, NORTHLEACH **166**
Puffing Billy, The, EXETER **118**
Punchbowl Inn at Crosthwaite, The, CROSTHWAITE **88**

Q

Quaglino's, LONDON SW1 **282**
Quantro, **516**
Quantro, HARROGATE **497**
Quay, The, ILFRACOMBE **121**
Quay's Pub & Restaurant, The, PORTAVOGIE **653**
Queen's Head Hotel, HAWKSHEAD **90**
Quilon, LONDON SW1 **288**
Quince & Medlar, COCKERMOUTH **86**
Quirinale, LONDON SW1 **282**
Quo Vadis, LONDON W1 **327**
Quod Restaurant & Bar, OXFORD **394**
Quorn Country Hotel, QUORN **225**

R

Racine, LONDON SW3 **291**
Radcliffe Dining Rooms, The, TITCHFIELD **194**
Radisson SAS Hotel & Spa Galway, GALWAY **667**
Radisson SAS Hotel Liverpool - Filini, LIVERPOOL **363**
Radisson SAS Hotel Manchester Airport, MANCHESTER AIRPORT **179**
Radisson SAS Roe Park Resort, LIMAVADY **654**
Raemoir House Hotel, BANCHORY **534**
Raffles, KENILWORTH **465**
Rafters Restaurant, SHEFFIELD **510**
Raglan Arms, USK **635**
Rampsbeck Country House Hotel, WATERMILLOCK **95**
Randolph, The, SOUTHWOLD **435**
Rankins, SISSINGHURST **212**
Ransome's Dock, LONDON SW11 **302**
Rasa Samudra, LONDON W1 **327**
Rasa W1, LONDON W1 **327**
Rasa, LONDON N16 **264**
Rasoi Restaurant, LONDON SW3 **292**
Raven Hotel, MUCH WENLOCK **405**
Ravenwood Hall Hotel, BURY ST EDMUNDS **429**
Read's Restaurant, FAVERSHAM **211**
Real Greek, The, LONDON N1 **262**
Rectory Hotel, The, MALMESBURY **481**
Red Fort, The, LONDON W1 **327**
Red House Inn, WHITCHURCH **194**
Red House, MARSH BENHAM **36**
Red Lion Hotel, BURNSALL **494**
Red Lion Hotel, SALISBURY **483**
Red Lion Inn, STATHERN **225**
Red Onion, GLASGOW **577**
Redbank House & Restaurant, SKERRIES **664**
Redcoats Farmhouse Hotel, HITCHIN **203**
Redmond's, LONDON SW14 **304**
Reeves Restaurant, FELSTED **154**
Refettorio, LONDON EC4 **260**
Regatta Restaurant, ALDEBURGH **426**
Regency Park Hotel, NEWBURY **36**
Regency Restaurant, BRIGHTON **446**
Regent Hotel, AMBLESIDE **83**
Reivers Restaurant, DUMFRIES **546**
Renaissance Restaurant, BAKEWELL **103**
Renvyle House, RENVYLE **667**
Rescobie House Hotel & Restaurant, GLENROTHES **565**
Restaurant 1881, GATWICK AIRPORT (LONDON) **456**
Restaurant 1933, PRESTWICK **543**
Restaurant 42, SALCOMBE **128**
Restaurant 48, KNARESBOROUGH **498**
Restaurant 698, SWANSEA **646**
Restaurant Anise, TADCASTER **503**
Restaurant at the Bonham, The, EDINBURGH **556**

Restaurant at The Mountview Hotel, The, NETHY BRIDGE **585**
Restaurant at The Petersham, RICHMOND (UPON THAMES) **361**
Restaurant Bar and Grill, MANCHESTER **178**
Restaurant Gilmore at Strine's Farm, UTTOXETER **425**
Restaurant Gordon Ramsay, LONDON SW3 **293**
Restaurant in the Jew's House, The, LINCOLN **227**
Restaurant Martin Wishart, EDINBURGH **557**
Restaurant Michael Deane, BELFAST **651**
Restaurant Patrick Guilbaud, DUBLIN **663**
Restaurant Sat Bains with Rooms, NOTTINGHAM **385**
Restaurant Sauterelle, LONDON EC3 **259**
Restaurant, ROMALDKIRK **150**
Restaurant, The, SWANSEA **646**
Revival, ST AUSTELL **75**
Rhinefield House, BROCKENHURST **184**
Rhodes Twenty Four, LONDON EC2 **257**
Rhubarb - the restaurant at Prestonfield, EDINBURGH **556**
Rib Room & Oyster Bar, The, LONDON SW1 **285**
Riber Hall, MATLOCK **107**
Riccardos, LONDON SW3 **295**
Ricci's on the Green, WOODCOTE **397**
Richmond Gate Hotel, RICHMOND (UPON THAMES) **361**
Richmond Restaurant, The, FAREHAM **187**
Rick Stein's Café, PADSTOW **72**
Ridge Restaurant, The, SWINDON **483**
Right on the Green, TUNBRIDGE WELLS (ROYAL) **213**
Ripley's, ST MERRYN **78**
Rising Sun Hotel, LYNMOUTH **124**
Rising Sun Hotel, ST MAWES **78**
Rissons at Springvale, STRATHAVEN **590**
Ritz, The, LONDON W1 **328**
River Café, The, LONDON W8 **341**
Riverhouse, INVERNESS **582**
Riverside Brasserie, The, BRAY **31**
Riverside Hotel, EVESHAM **487**
Riverside Hotel, MILDENHALL **433**
Riverside House Hotel, ASHFORD-IN-THE-WATER **102**
Riverside Restaurant & Bar - Baltic Mill, GATESHEAD **461**
Riverside Restaurant, BRIDPORT **137**
riverstation, BRISTOL **43**
Riviera Hotel, SIDMOUTH **128**
Rivington Bar & Grill, LONDON EC2 **258**
Road Hole Grill, The, ST ANDREWS **567**
Roade House Restaurant, ROADE **381**
Roast, LONDON SE1 **270**
Robbie's Restaurant, WARWICK **467**
Rock Inn, HAYTOR VALE **120**
Rococo, GLASGOW **575**
Rocpool, INVERNESS **582**
Roebuck Inn Restaurant, The, LUDLOW **404**
Roka, LONDON W1 **328**
Roly's Bistro, DUBLIN **664**
Roman Camp Country House Hotel, CALLANDER **603**
Rombalds Hotel & Restaurant, ILKLEY **513**
Rookery Hall, NANTWICH **62**
Room, GLASGOW **575**
Rose & Crown Hotel, ROMALDKIRK **150**
Rose & Crown Hotel, The, COLCHESTER **152**
Rose & Crown, SUTTON-ON-THE-FOREST **502**
Rose & Crown, The, SNETTISHAM **376**
Rose & Crown, YEALMPTON **134**
Rosedale Hotel, PORTREE **607**
Rosehill Manor, MARKET DRAYTON **404**
Rosevine Hotel - Didiers Restaurant, PORTSCATHO **74**
Rothay Garden Hotel & Restaurant, GRASMERE **89**
Rothay Manor, AMBLESIDE **83**
Rouille Restaurant, MILFORD ON SEA **189**
Roundstone House Hotel, ROUNDSTONE **668**
Roussillon, LONDON SW1 **285**
Rowhill Grange, DARTFORD **210**
Rowton Castle Hotel, SHREWSBURY **407**
Rowton Hall Country House Hotel, CHESTER **61**
Roxburghe Hotel, The, KELSO **600**
Royal at Tighnabruaich, The, TIGHNABRUAICH **541**
Royal Chace Hotel, ENFIELD **356**
Royal Chase Hotel, SHAFTESBURY **146**
Royal China, LONDON E14 **252**
Royal China, LONDON W2 **337**
Royal Crescent Hotel - Pimpernels, BATH **410**
Royal Garden Hotel, Tenth Floor Restaurant, LONDON W8 **344**
Royal Hotel, COMRIE **595**
Royal Hotel, The, VENTNOR **475**
Royal Marine Hotel, BRORA **578**
Royal Naz, MANCHESTER **178**
Royal Oak @ Eydon, The, EYDON **378**
Royal Oak Hotel, The, BETWS-Y-COED **620**
Royal Oak Hotel, YATTENDON **41**
Royal Oak Inn, CHICHESTER **453**
Royal Oak, The, MAIDENHEAD **34**
Royal Orchid Thai Restaurant, MANCHESTER **178**
RSJ, The Restaurant on the South Bank, LONDON SE1 **270**
Rubens at the Palace, The, LONDON SW1 **285**
Rufflets Country House, ST ANDREWS **567**
Rumours, LYME REGIS **143**
Running Horse, The, WINCHESTER **197**
Rushmore's, HEACHAM **369**
Ruskin's, LONDON EC3 **260**
Russell Hotel, ST ANDREWS **568**
Russell's, BROADWAY **485**
Russells, CHELMSFORD **151**
Russets, ST IVES **77**
Ruthin Castle, RUTHIN **627**
Rutland Arms Hotel, BAKEWELL **103**

S

Sablonnerie, La, SARK **529**
Sabras Restaurant, LONDON NW10 **267**
Sagar, LONDON W6 **340**
Saint Jude's, GLASGOW **575**
St Andrews Bay Golf Resort & Spa, ST ANDREWS **568**
St Andrews Golf Hotel, ST ANDREWS **568**
St Benedicts Restaurant, NORWICH **374**
St David's Hotel & Spa, The, CARDIFF **616**
St Enodoc Hotel Restaurant, The, ROCK **74**
St Ervan Manor, PADSTOW **71**
St John Bread & Wine, LONDON E1 **249**
St John, LONDON EC1 **255**
St Martin's on the Isle, SCILLY, ISLES OF, ST MARTIN'S **79**
St Michael's Manor, ST ALBANS **204**
St Olaves Hotel & The Treasury Restaurant, EXETER **118**
St Petroc's Bistro, PADSTOW **71**
St Pierre Park Hotel, ST PETER PORT **522**
St Tudno Hotel and Restaurant, LLANDUDNO **625**
Sakura Restaurant, BATH **410**
Salford Hall Hotel, ABBOT'S SALFORD **463**
Salloos Restaurant, LONDON SW1 **285**
Salt Yard, LONDON W1 **328**
Salthouse Harbour Hotel, IPSWICH **431**
Saltwater, ST PETER PORT **523**
Salty Monk, The, SIDMOUTH **129**
Salutation Inn, The, WEOBLEY **201**
Sam's Brasserie & Bar, LONDON W4 **338**
Samling, The, WINDERMERE **100**
Sampsons Hotel & Restaurant, NEWTON ABBOT **125**
Samsi, MANCHESTER **178**
San Carlo, BIRMINGHAM **472**
San Carlo, LEICESTER **224**
San Lorenzo, LONDON SW19 **306**
San Marco, LONDON SW4 **295**
Sandbanks Hotel, POOLE **145**
Sands Restaurant, ST ANDREWS **568**
Sangsters, ELIE **563**
Santini, EDINBURGH **558**
Santini, LONDON SW1 **286**
Santo's Higham Farm Hotel, HIGHAM **107**
Saran Rom, LONDON SW6 **296**
Sardo Canale, LONDON NW1 **265**
Sardo, LONDON W1 **336**
Sartoria, LONDON W1 **328**
Satis House Hotel, YOXFORD **436**
Savoy Grill, The, LONDON WC2 **354**
Sawrey House Country Hotel, NEAR SAWREY **92**
Scallops, CARDIFF **616**
Scarista House, SCARISTA **604**
Scotsman, The, EDINBURGH **558**
Scrumpy House Restaurant & Bar, The, MUCH MARCLE **199**
Scutchers Restaurant, LONG MELFORD **432**
Sea View House, BALLYLICKEY **658**
Seafield Hotel, The, CULLEN **593**
Seafood Restaurant, The, PADSTOW **72**

Seafood Restaurant, The, ST ANDREWS **569**
Seafood Restaurant, The, ST MONANS **571**
Seafood Restaurant, The, YEALMPTON **134**
Seasons Restaurant at Colwall Park Hotel, MALVERN **488**
Seaview Hotel & Restaurant, SEAVIEW **475**
Seckford Hall Hotel, WOODBRIDGE **436**
Seeds, LLANFYLLIN **642**
Sefton Hotel, DOUGLAS **529**
Seiont Manor, CAERNARFON **630**
Seven Ledbury, LEDBURY **197**
Sevendials, BRIGHTON **445**
Shakespeare's Globe Restaurant, LONDON SE1 **271**
Shanghai, LONDON E8 **251**
Sharrow Bay Country House Hotel, HOWTOWN **90**
Shed, The, PORTHGAIN **637**
Sheedy's Country House Hotel, LISDOONVARNA **657**
Sheen Falls Lodge, KENMARE **668**
Sheene Mill, MELBOURN **56**
Shelleys, The, LEWES **448**
Sheraton Grand Hotel & Spa, The, EDINBURGH **558**
Shere Khan, MANCHESTER **178**
Sherlock Holmes Hotel, LONDON W1 **329**
Shibden Mill, HALIFAX **512**
Shikara, LONDON SW3 **295**
Shiki, NORWICH **375**
Shimla Pinks Manchester, MANCHESTER **178**
Ship in Distress, The, CHRISTCHURCH **139**
Shish Mahal, GLASGOW **576**
Shogun, Millennium Hotel Mayfair, LONDON W1 **329**
Shu, BELFAST **652**
Sidney's Restaurant, TYNEMOUTH **463**
Sienna, DORCHESTER **140**
Signor Zilli, LONDON W1 **336**
Silver Darling, The, ABERDEEN **533**
Simply Heathcotes Leeds, LEEDS **516**
Simply Heathcotes Wrightington, WIGAN **180**
Simply Heathcotes, LIVERPOOL **364**
Simply Heathcotes, MANCHESTER **177**
Simply Nico, HEATHROW AIRPORT **358**
Simply Poussin, BROCKENHURST **184**
Simply Simpsons, KENILWORTH **465**
Simpsons, BIRMINGHAM **471**
Singapore Garden Restaurant, LONDON NW6 **267**
Sir Charles Napier, CHINNOR **388**
Sir Christopher Wren's House Hotel & Spa, WINDSOR **40**
Sketch (Lecture Room & Library), LONDON W1 **330**
Sketchley Grange Hotel, HINCKLEY **222**
Slieve Russell Hotel Golf & Country Club, BALLYCONNELL **656**
Smiddy House, SPEAN BRIDGE **588**
Smiths of Smithfield, LONDON EC1 **255**
Snailmakers at Brome Grange, The, BROME **427**
Snows-on-the-Green Restaurant, LONDON W6 **340**
Soar Mill Cove Hotel, SALCOMBE **128**
Sofra - Exmouth Market, LONDON EC1 **255**
Sofra - St John's Wood, LONDON NW8 **267**
Solent Hotel, FAREHAM **187**
Solo, LEAMINGTON SPA (ROYAL) **466**
Somerville Hotel, ST AUBIN **524**
Sonny's Restaurant, LONDON SW13 **303**
Sonny's, NOTTINGHAM **384**
Sopwell House, RICKMANSWORTH **205**
Sorn Inn, The, SORN **541**
Soufflé Restaurant, BEARSTED **207**
Soufflé, InterContinental London, Le, LONDON W1 **329**
Spa Hotel, The, TUNBRIDGE WELLS (ROYAL) **214**
Spencer Arms, LONDON SW15 **304**
Spencers Restaurant & Brasserie, EMSWORTH **186**
Spice of Hampstead, LONDON NW2 **266**
Spiga Chelsea, LONDON SW3 **295**
Spiga, LONDON W1 **329**
Splinters Restaurant, CHRISTCHURCH **138**
Spoon at Sanderson, LONDON W1 **331**
Sportsman, The, WHITSTABLE **216**
Spread Eagle, The, LONDON SE10 **272**
Spread Eagle Hotel and Health Spa, MIDHURST **459**
Spread Eagle Hotel, THAME **396**
Square, The, LONDON W1 **331**
Stac Polly, EDINBURGH **558**
Stac Polly, EDINBURGH **559**
Stafford Hotel, The, LONDON SW1 **286**
Stagg Inn and Restaurant, The, KINGTON **197**
Staindrop Lodge Hotel, SHEFFIELD **510**
Stanneylands Hotel, WILMSLOW **63**
Stanwell House, LYMINGTON **189**
Stapleford Park, MELTON MOWBRAY **224**
Star at Tytherley, The, EAST TYTHERLEY **186**
Star Inn, NEWMARKET **434**
Star Inn, The, HAROME **495**
Starr Restaurant, GREAT DUNMOW **154**
Station House Hotel, The, KILMESSAN **674**
Stein's Fish & Chip Shop, PADSTOW **72**
Stillorgan Park Hotel, DUBLIN **662**
Stock, MANCHESTER **178**
Stock Hill Country House Hotel & Restaurant, GILLINGHAM **142**
Stockbridge Restaurant, The, EDINBURGH **562**
Ston Easton Park, STON EASTON **417**
Stone Trough Inn, KIRKHAM **498**
Stonefield Castle Hotel, TARBERT LOCH FYNE **541**
Stones, LEICESTER **224**
Storrs Hall Hotel, WINDERMERE **101**
Stower Grange, NORWICH **375**
Strada, London **255, 263, 295, 296, 297, 303, 306, 336, 355, 359**
Strada, RICHMOND (UPON THAMES) **361**
Stratford Manor, STRATFORD-UPON-AVON **467**
Stratford Victoria, STRATFORD-UPON-AVON **467**
Strathearn at Gleneagles, AUCHTERARDER **595**
Stravaigin, GLASGOW **576**
Strawberry Tree Restaurant, The, MACREDDIN **678**
Strawberry Tree, The, MILTON ERNEST **28**
Stretton Hall Hotel, CHURCH STRETTON **400**
Studio, The, CHURCH STRETTON **400**
Sukiyaki, RICKMANSWORTH **205**
Sultan Balti House, BRACKNELL **29**
Suma's, GOREY **523**
Summer Isles Hotel, The, ACHILTIBUIE **577**
Summer Lodge Country House Hotel, EVERSHOT **141**
Summerhouse, The, PENZANCE **73**
Sumosan Restaurant, LONDON W1 **331**
Sundial Restaurant, HERSTMONCEUX **447**
Swag and Tails, LONDON SW7 **298**
Swallows Eaves, COLYFORD **114**
Swan at Streatley, The, STREATLEY **40**
Swan at Tetsworth, The, THAME **396**
Swan Hotel, NEWBY BRIDGE **93**
Swan Hotel, SOUTHWOLD **435**
Swan Hotel, The, LAVENHAM **432**
Swan Hotel, The, STAFFORD **424**
Swan Hotel, WELLS **419**
Swan House, BECCLES **427**
Swan Inn, The, BARNBY **426**
Swan, The, WEST MALLING **214**
Sweet Olive, The, CHOLSEY **389**
Swinside Lodge, KESWICK **92**
Swinton Park, MASHAM **499**
Swynford Paddocks, SIX MILE BOTTOM **57**

T

Ta Tu, BELFAST **652**
Tai Pan, MANCHESTER **177**
Talad Thai, LONDON SW15 **304**
Talbooth Restaurant, Le, DEDHAM **152**
Talkhouse, The, CAERSWS **640**
Taman Gang, LONDON W1 **332**
Tamarind, LONDON W1 **332**
Tamasha, BROMLEY **356**
Tanners Restaurant, PLYMOUTH **127**
Tan-y-Foel Country House, BETWS-Y-COED **621**
Taplow House Hotel, TAPLOW **50**
Taps, HORNING **370**
Tarr Farm Inn, DULVERTON **412**
Tatlers, NORWICH **375**
Tatsuso Restaurant, LONDON EC2 **258**
Taychreggan Hotel, KILCHRENAN **538**
Teach Iorrais Hotel, BALLINA **673**
Teaninich Castle, ALNESS **577**
Teca, LONDON W1 **332**
Tedfords Restaurant, BELFAST **652**
Temple Gate, ENNIS **657**
Temple Sowerby House Hotel & Restaurant, TEMPLE SOWERBY **94**
Tendido Cero, LONDON SW5 **296**

Terrace, The, LONDON WC2 **355**
Terrace Dining Room, Cliveden, The, TAPLOW **50**
Terrace Restaurant at Talland Bay Hotel, TALLAND BAY **80**
Terrace Restaurant, The, FALMOUTH **65**
Terre à Terre, BRIGHTON **446**
Thackeray's, TUNBRIDGE WELLS (ROYAL) **215**
Thackeray's, WHITSTABLE **215**
Thai Edge, BIRMINGHAM **472**
Thai Edge Restaurant, BIRMINGHAM **471**
Thai Garden, The, LONDON E2 **250**
Thai Thai, STADHAMPTON **395**
Theobalds Restaurant, IXWORTH **431**
Thornbury Castle, THORNBURY **170**
Thornbury Hall Rasoi, CHEADLE **422**
Thornton Hall Hotel, THORNTON HOUGH **365**
Thorntons Restaurant at The Fitzwilliam Hotel, DUBLIN **664**
Thorpe Park Hotel & Spa, LEEDS **516**
Three Chimneys, The, COLBOST **608**
Three Choirs Vineyards, NEWENT **166**
Three Crowns Inn, ULLINGSWICK **201**
Three Hares Country Inn, The, BILBROUGH **491**
Three Horseshoes Inn, LEEK **422**
Three Horseshoes Restaurant, MADINGLEY **56**
Three Salmons Hotel, USK **635**
Three Tuns, The, PETERSFIELD **193**
Three Ways House, CHIPPING CAMPDEN **162**
Thurlestone Hotel, THURLESTONE **130**
Tickton Grange Hotel, BEVERLEY **490**
Tides Reach Hotel, SALCOMBE **128**
Tigh an Eilean Hotel, SHIELDAIG **587**
Tilleys Bistro, BATH **411**
Tillmouth Park Hotel, CORNHILL-ON-TWEED **381**
Timo, LONDON W8 **343**
Tinhay Mill Guest House and Restaurant, LIFTON **124**
Titchwell Manor Hotel, TITCHWELL **377**
Tobermory Hotel, TOBERMORY **605**
Tolbooth, STONEHAVEN **534**
Tollemache Arms, The, BUCKMINSTER **222**
Tollgate Inn, The, BRADFORD-ON-AVON **476**
Tom Aikens, LONDON SW3 **294**
Toque d'Or, La, BIRMINGHAM **472**
Toravaig House, ISLE OF ORNSAY **606**
Tors Hotel, LYNMOUTH **125**
Toto's, LONDON SW3 **292**
Tower Hotel Derry, LONDONDERRY **654**
Tower Restaurant & Terrace, EDINBURGH **559**
Town House Restaurant & Bar, The, SOLIHULL **473**
Treacle Moon, NEWCASTLE UPON TYNE **462**
Treglos Hotel, CONSTANTINE BAY **64**
Trehellas House Hotel & Restaurant, BODMIN **63**
Trelawne Hotel, MAWNAN SMITH **68**
Trenython Manor, TYWARDREATH **81**
Trident Hotel, KINSALE **660**
Trois Garçons, Les, LONDON E1 **250**
Trompette, La, LONDON W4 **338**
Trouble House, The, TETBURY **169**
Trout Hotel, The, COCKERMOUTH **86**
Trouvaille, La, LONDON W1 **332**
Truffles, BRUTON **412**
Tsunami, LONDON SW4 **295**
Tudor Farmhouse Hotel, CLEARWELL **163**
Tugga, LONDON SW3 **292**
Tuttons Brasserie, LONDON WC2 **355**
Twelve Restaurant, THORNTON **221**
Two Fat Ladies, GLASGOW **576**
Two Seven Two, NEWICK **449**
Two To Four, DORKING **439**
Ty Croeso Hotel, CRICKHOWELL **641**
Tyddyn Llan, LLANDRILLO **625**
Tylney Hall, ROTHERWICK **193**

U

Ubiquitous Chip, GLASGOW **576**
Ubon by Nobu, LONDON E14 **252**
Ullinish Lodge Hotel, STRUAN **609**
Umu, LONDON W1 **333**
Underscar Manor, KESWICK **92**
Uplawmoor Hotel, UPLAWMOOR **600**
Usk Inn, The, BRECON **639**

V

Vacherin, Le, LONDON W4 **338**
Vama, LONDON SW10 **302**
Vanilla Pod, The, MARLOW **50**
Vasco & Piero's Pavilion Restaurant, LONDON W1 **333**
Veeraswamy Restaurant, LONDON W1 **333**
Venture In Restaurant, The, OMBERSLEY **488**
Venue, The, CAMBRIDGE **53**
Vermont Hotel, NEWCASTLE UPON TYNE **463**
Verzon Bar, Brasserie & Hotel, The, LEDBURY **199**
Victoria at Holkham, The, HOLKHAM **370**
Victoria Hotel, SIDMOUTH **129**
Victoria, The, LONDON SW14 **304**
Villa D'Este, MARLOW **50**
Villa Rosa, BEDFORD **28**
Village Bistro, The, GOREY **523**
Village Pub, The, BARNSLEY **157**
Villandry, LONDON W1 **334**
Villiers Hotel Restaurant & Bar, BUCKINGHAM **45**
VinCaffe, EDINBURGH **562**
Vine House Restaurant, TOWCESTER **381**
Viners Bar & Restaurant, SUMMERCOURT **80**
Vineyard at Stockcross, The NEWBURY **38**
Vintners Rooms, The, EDINBURGH **559**
Vivat Bacchus, LONDON EC4 **261**
Volt, LONDON SW1 **286**

W

W'Sens by La Compagnie des Comptoirs, LONDON SW1 **287**
Wagamama, KINGSTON UPON THAMES **359**
Wagamama, LONDON **258, 263, 266, 288, 336, 345, 348, 349, 355**
Wagamama, MANCHESTER **178**
Wagamama, NOTTINGHAM **386**
Wagamama, RICKMANSWORTH **205**
Waldo's Restaurant, Cliveden, TAPLOW **51**
Wallett's Court, DOVER **210**
Walnut Tree Hotel, BRIDGWATER **411**
Walnut Tree Hotel, The, WEST CAMEL **419**
Walnut Tree Inn, ABERGAVENNY **633**
Wapping Food, LONDON E1 **250**
Warehouse Brasserie, SOUTHPORT **365**
Warpool Court Hotel, ST DAVID'S **637**
Washbourne Court Hotel, LOWER SLAUGHTER **165**
Washington Central Hotel, WORKINGTON **101**
Water's Edge Hotel, TRINITY **528**
Waterdine, The, LLANFAIR WATERDINE **400**
Waterford Castle, WATERFORD **676**
Waterford Lodge Hotel, CHRISTCHURCH **138**
Waterfront Wine Bar and Bistro, EDINBURGH **562**
Waters Reach, MANCHESTER **177**
Waterside Bistro, HADDINGTON **591**
Waterside Inn, BRAY **32**
Watersmeet Hotel, WOOLACOMBE **134**
Waterton Park Hotel, WAKEFIELD **519**
Waterway, The, LONDON W9 **345**
Watsons Restaurant & Bar, LEICESTER **223**
Wave Restaurant, The, ST IVES **76**
Wayfarers Restaurant, SHAFTESBURY **146**
Weary at Castle Carrock, The, CASTLE CARROCK **86**
Weavers Restaurant with Rooms, HAWORTH **512**
Weavers Shed Restaurant with Rooms, The, HUDDERSFIELD **512**
Webbes at The Fish Café, RYE **450**
Welcome to Town, The, LLANRHIDIAN **645**
Well House Hotel, LISKEARD **67**
Wellington Hotel, The, BOSCASTLE **64**
Wells Tavern, The, LONDON NW3 **266**
Wensleydale Heifer, The, WEST WITTON **503**
Wentbridge House Hotel, PONTEFRACT **518**
Wentworth Hotel, ALDEBURGH **426**
Wesley House, WINCHCOMBE **170**
West Arms Hotel, LLANARMON DYFFRYN CEIRIOG **647**
West Beach Restaurant, The, LYTHAM ST ANNES **219**
West Beach, BOURNEMOUTH **137**
West House, The, BIDDENDEN **208**
West Lodge Park Hotel, The Cedar Restaurant, HADLEY WOOD **356**
West Vale Country House, HAWKSHEAD **90**
Westbury Hotel, LONDON W1 **334**
Westin Turnberry Resort Hotel, The, TURNBERRY **544**
Westleton Crown, The, WESTLETON **436**
Westmorland Hotel & Bretherdale Restaurant, TEBAY **94**

Weston Manor Hotel, WESTON-ON-THE-GREEN 397
Westover Hall, MILFORD ON SEA 190
Whatley Manor, MALMESBURY 481
Wheatsheaf at Swinton, The, SWINTON 602
Wheatsheaf Inn, The, OAKSEY 482
Wheelers of St James's at The Highwayman, CHECKENDON 388
White Hart Hotel, DORCHESTER (ON THAMES) 390
White Hart Inn, OLDHAM 179
White Hart Inn, The, NAYLAND 433
White Hart, GREAT YELDHAM 155
White Horse & Griffin, The, WHITBY 504
White Horse Inn, The, CANTERBURY 208
White Horse, FRAMPTON MANSELL 164
White Horse, The, BRANCASTER STAITHE 367
White House Hotel, WILLITON 419
White House Restaurant, PRESTBURY 62
White Lion Hotel, ALDEBURGH 426
White Lion Hotel, UPTON UPON SEVERN 489
White Moss House, GRASMERE 89
White Star Tavern & Dining Rooms, SOUTHAMPTON 194
White Swan Inn, The, PICKERING 500
White Swan Pub & Dining Room, The, LONDON EC4 261
White Swan, The, BRECON 639
Whitford House Hotel Health & Leisure Spa, WEXFORD 678
Whittlebury Hall Hotel & Spa, WHITTLEBURY 381
Whoop Hall, The, KIRKBY LONSDALE 92
Widbrook Grange, YARMOUTH 477
Wife of Bath Restaurant, WYE 216
Wig & Mitre, LINCOLN 227
Wild Mushroom Restaurant, The, WESTFIELD 451
Wild Pheasant Hotel & Restaurant, The, LLANGOLLEN 627
Wildebeest Arms, The, STOKE HOLY CROSS 376
Willerby Manor Hotel, WILLERBY 490
Willow Tree Restaurant, The, TAUNTON 418
Willowburn Hotel, CLACHAN-SEIL 537
Wilton Court Hotel, ROSS-ON-WYE 201
Wiltons Since 1742, LONDON SW1 286
Winckley Square Chop House and Bar, PRESTON 221
Windsor Lodge Hotel & Restaurant, SWANSEA 646
Wineport Lodge, ATHLONE 676
Winter Garden, The, LONDON NW1 265
Winteringham Fields, WINTERINGHAM 229
Witchery by the Castle, The, EDINBURGH 560
Wizzy, LONDON SW6 297
Wolfscastle Country Hotel, HAVERFORDWEST 636
Wolseley, The, LONDON W1 334
Wood Hall Hotel, WETHERBY 519
Woodbury Park Hotel & Golf Country Club, WOODBURY 134
Woodenbridge Hotel, WOODENBRIDGE 678
Woodlands Hall Hotel, RUTHIN 627
Woodlands Lodge Hotel, SOUTHAMPTON 194
Woodlands Park Hotel, STOKE D'ABERNON 443
Woods Bar & Dining Room, DULVERTON 412
Woods Brasserie, CARDIFF 616
Woods Restaurant, BATH 411
Woolley Grange, YARMOUTH 477
Woolpack, The, INGATESTONE 155
Wordsworth Hotel, GRASMERE 89
World Service, NOTTINGHAM 384
Worsley Arms Hotel, HOVINGHAM 497
Wyck Hill House Hotel, STOW-ON-THE-WOLD 168
Wye Knot Restaurant, CHEPSTOW 634
Wynnstay Arms, The, RUTHIN 628
Wynnstay Hotel, OSWESTRY 406

Y

Y Bistro, LLANBERIS 631
Yalbury Cottage, DORCHESTER 140
Yang Sing Restaurant, MANCHESTER 177
Yauatcha, LONDON W1 335
Ye Olde Bulls Head Inn, BEAUMARIS 612
Yeoldon Country House Hotel, BIDEFORD 112
Yeovil Court Hotel Limited, YEOVIL 421
Yetman's, HOLT 370
Yi-Ban, LONDON E16 253
Yi-Ban Chelsea, LONDON SW6 297
YMing, LONDON W1 335
Ynyshir Hall, EGLWYSFACH 619
Yo! Sushi, LONDON EC1 255
Yo! Sushi, LONDON NW3 267
Yo! Sushi, LONDON SE1 271
Yo! Sushi, LONDON SW1 288
Yo! Sushi, LONDON W1 336
Yo! Sushi, LONDON W1 336
Yo! Sushi, LONDON W2 337
Yo! Sushi, LONDON W2 337
Yo! Sushi, LONDON WC1 349
York Pavilion Hotel, YORK 507
Yorke Arms, RAMSGILL 501
Yumi Restaurant, LONDON W1 335

Z

Zafferano, LONDON SW1 287
Zaika, LONDON W8 345
Zetland Country House, CASHEL 665
Zigni House, LONDON N1 263
Zilli Fish, LONDON W1 336
Zinc Bar and Grill, MANCHESTER 178
Zinc, EDINBURGH 562
Zuma, LONDON SW7 298

The Automobile Association wishes to thank the following picture libraries for their assistance in the preparation of this book.

Front cover: L'Enclume Restaurant, Cumbria; 1 Photodisc; 3tr AA World Travel Library/C Sawyer; 3bl Photodisc; 3bc AA World Travel Library/C Sawyer; 3br Photodisc; 4tl AA World Travel Library/M Langford; 4tr AA World Travel Library/S McBride; 4c AA World Travel Library/J Tims; 5tr Imagestate; 6tl Photodisc; 6tr AA World Travel Library/J Holmes; 7tr AA World Travel Library/C Sawyer; 8tl Imagestate; 9tl Imagestate; 9tr AA World Travel Library/C Sawyer; 11tr Imagestate; 14tl AA World Travel Library; 14tr AA World Travel Library/C Sawyer; 15tr Photodisc; 16tl Photodisc; 17tl AA World Travel Library/J Holmes; 17tr Photodisc; 20tl AA World Travel Library/C Sawyer; 21tr Imagestate; 22tl Imagestate; 23tr AA World Travel Library/P Bennett; 24tl Photodisc; 25tr Stockbyte; 26/7 ImageState; 231 ImageState; 530/1 ImageState; 610/1 ImageState; 649 ImageState; 655 ImageState.

Every effort has been made to trace the copyright holders, and we apologise in advance for any accidental errors. We would be happy to apply the corrections in the following edition of this publication.

Please send this form to:
Editor, The Restaurant Guide,
Lifestyle Guides,
The Automobile Association,
14th Floor, Fanum House,
Basingstoke RG21 4EA

or fax: 01256 491647
or e-mail: lifestyleguides@theAA.com

Please use this form to tell us about any restaurant you have visited, whether it is in the guide or not currently listed. Feedback from readers helps us to keep our guide accurate and up to date. Please note, however, that if you have a complaint to make during a visit, we strongly recommend that you discuss the matter with the restaurant management there and then, so that they have a chance to put things right before your visit is spoilt. The AA does not undertake to arbitrate between you and the restaurant management, or to obtain compensation or engage in correspondence.

Date:

Your name (block capitals)

Your address (block capitals)

....

....

....

e-mail address: ....

Restaurant name and address: (If you are recommending a new restaurant please enclose a menu or note the dishes that you ate.)

....

....

....

Comments:...

....

....

(please attach a separate sheet if necessary) **PTO**

We may use information we hold about you to write, e-mail or telephone you about other products and services offered by us and our carefully selected partners, but we can assure you that we will not disclose it to third parties.

Please tick here if you DO NOT wish to receive details of other products or services from the AA. ☐

Readers' Report Form

	YES	NO
Have you bought this guide before?	☐	☐

Please list any other similar guides that you use regularly..................................

....

....

What do you find most useful about The AA Restaurant Guide?

....

....

....

....

Please answer these questions to help us make improvements to the guide:

What are your main reasons for visiting restaurants (circle all that apply)

business entertaining | business travel | trying famous restaurants

family celebrations | leisure travel | trying new food

enjoying not having to cook yourself | to eat food you couldn't cook yourself

other .... | because I enjoy eating out regularly

How often do you visit a restaurant for lunch or dinner? (circle one choice)

once a week | once a fortnight | once a month | less than once a month

Do you use the location atlas?...

Do you generally agree with the Rosette ratings at the restaurants you visit in the guide? (if not please give examples)..

....

Who is your favourite chef? ....

Which is your favourite restaurant? ....

Which type of cuisine is your first choice e.g. French ....

Which of these factors are most important when choosing a restaurant?

Price | Service | Location | Type of food | Awards/ratings

Décor/surroundings | Other (please state):..

Which elements of the guide do you find most useful when choosing a restaurant?

Description | Photo | Rosette rating | Price | Other..........................

FOOD LOVERS

Find it with theAA.com

Click on to the AA website, **theAA.com**, to find AA listed guest houses, hotels, pubs and restaurants – some 12,000 establishments – the **AA Route Planner and Map Finder will help you find the way**.

Search for a Hotel/B&B or a Pub/Restaurant by location or establishment name and then scroll down the list of establishments for the interactive map and local routes.

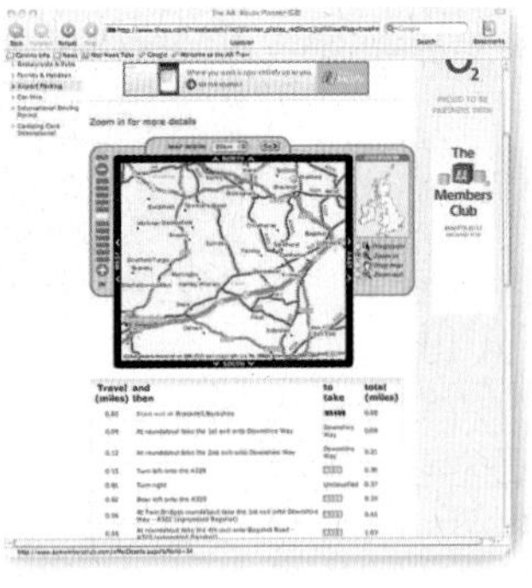

To use the **Route Planner** on the Home page, simply enter your postcode and the establishment postcode given in this guide and click **Get route**. Check your details and then you are on your way.

Discover new horizons with Britain's largest travel publisher

AA